RUSSIA

KAZAKSTAN

MONGOLIA

UZBEKISTAN
KYRGYZSTAN
TURKMENISTAN
TAJIKISTAN

CHINA

NORTH
KOREA
SOUTH
KOREA

JAPAN

IRAN
AFGHANISTAN

KUWAIT
BAHRAIN
QATAR

PAKISTAN

NEPAL

BHUTAN

TAIWAN
HONG KONG (U.K.)

OCEAN

Tropic of Cancer

20°N

SAUDI
ARABIA

EGYPT

BYA

BANGLADESH

MACAO
(Port.)

NORTHERN
MARIANA
IS. (U.S.)

UNITED ARAB
EMIRATES

OMAN

INDIA

MYANMAR

LAOS

GUAM (U.S.)

MARSHALL
ISLANDS

A

CHAD

YEMEN

THAILAND

VIET
NAM

PHILIPPINES

ERITREA

DJIBOUTI

CAMBODIA

SUDAN

ETHIOPIA

SRI
LANKA

BRUNEI

FEDERATED STATES OF
MICRONESIA

KIRIBATI

CENTRAL
AFRICAN
REPUBLIC

MALDIVES

PALAU

0°

SOMALIA

MALAYSIA

UGANDA
KENYA

SINGAPORE

NAURU

UNGO
RWANDA
BURUNDI

ZAIRE

TANZANIA

SEYCHELLES

INDONESIA

PAPUA
NEW
GUINEA

SOLOMON
ISLANDS

TUVALU

INDIAN

COMOROS

OCEAN

MAYOTTE (Fr.)

ANGOLA
MALAWI

ZAMBIA

MOZAMBIQUE

VANUATU

FIJI

NEW
CALEDONIA
(Fr.)

20°S

AMIBIA
ZIMBABWE

MADAGASCAR

MAURITIUS

BOTSWANA

REUNION
(Fr.)

Tropic of Capricorn

AUSTRALIA

SWAZILAND

SOUTH
AFRICA

LESOTHO

0        1,000        2,000 Miles

0      1,000    2,000 Kilometers

NEW
ZEALAND

Antarctic Circle

ANTARCTICA

**EUROPE INSET**

SWEDEN

FINLAND

10°W        0°

NORWAY

60°N

North
Sea

DENMARK

Baltic Sea

ESTONIA

LATVIA

(Russia)

LITHUANIA

RUSSIA

0      200      400 Miles

0     200    400 Kilometers

IRELAND

UNITED
KINGDOM

NETHERLANDS

GERMANY

POLAND

BELARUS

CZECH
REPUBLIC

SLOVAK
REPUBLIC

UKRAINE

50°N

BELGIUM

LUXEMBOURG

LIECH.

AUSTRIA

HUNGARY

MOLDOVA

CHANNEL
IS. (U.K.)

SWITZERLAND

SLOVENIA

ROMANIA

Bay of
Biscay

FRANCE

SAN
MARINO

CROATIA

YUGO-
SLAVIA

ANDORRA

ITALY

BOSNIA
AND
HERZ.

BULGARIA

Black    Sea

GEORGIA

MONACO

MACEDONIA

ARMENIA

ALBANIA

SPAIN

GREECE

TURKEY

AZERBAIJAN

40°N

IRAN

PORTUGAL

SYRIA

MALTA

CYPRUS

LEBANON

WEST
BANK

IRAQ

MOROCCO

ALGERIA

TUNISIA

Mediterranean Sea

ISRAEL

JORDAN

SAUDI
ARABIA

LIBYA

EGYPT

# MARKETING
## An Introduction

FOURTH EDITION

# Marketing
## An Introduction

Philip Kotler / Gary Armstrong
*Northwestern University* / *University of North Carolina*

Prentice Hall, Upper Saddle River, New Jersey 07458

*Acquisitions Editor:* David Borkowsky
*Assistant Editor:* John Larkin
*Editorial Assistant:* Theresa Festa
*Editor-in-Chief:* James Boyd
*Director of Development:* Steve Deitmer
*Senior Project Manager/Liaison:* Linda M. DeLorenzo
*Production Editor:* Heather Stratton, GTS Graphics
*Production Coordinator:* David Cotugno
*Managing Editor:* Valerie Q. Lentz
*Manufacturing Supervisor:* Arnold Vila
*Manufacturing Manager:* Vincent Scelta
*Design Director:* Patricia Wosczyk
*Senior Designer:* Ann France
*Interior Design:* Rosemarie Votta
*Cover Design:* Wendy Helft
*Illustrator (Interior):* GTS Graphics
*Composition and Prepress:* GTS Graphics
*Cover Art/Photo:* Sharmen Liao, Inc.

Credits and acknowledgments for materials borrowed from other sources and reproduced, with permission, in this textbook appear on page AI1.

Copyright © 1997, 1993, 1990, 1987 by Prentice-Hall, Inc.
A Simon & Schuster Company
Upper Saddle River, New Jersey 07458

**Library of Congress Cataloging-in-Publication Data**
Kotler, Philip.
    Marketing: an introduction / Philip Kotler, Gary Armstrong.—4th ed.
      p.   cm.
   Includes bibliographical references and index.
   **ISBN 0-13-252710-3**
   1. Marketing.    I. Armstrong, Gary.    II. Title.
HF5415.K625   1996
658.8—dc20
                                         96-19557
                                         CIP

Prentice-Hall International (UK) Limited, London
Prentice-Hall of Australia Pty. Limited, Sydney
Prentice-Hall Canada, Inc., Toronto
Prentice-Hall Hispanoamericana, S.A., Mexico
Prentice-Hall of India Private Limited, New Delhi
Prentice-Hall of Japan, Inc., Tokyo
Simon & Schuster Asia Pte. Ltd., Singapore
Editora Prentice-Hall do Brasil, Ltda., Rio de Janeiro

Printed in the United States of America

10 9 8 7 6 5 4 3 2 1

*To Kathy, K.C., and Mandy;*
*Nancy, Amy, Melissa, and Jessica*

# *About the Authors*

As a team, Philip Kotler and Gary Armstrong provide a blend of skills uniquely suited to writing an introductory marketing text. Professor Kotler is one of the world's leading authorities on marketing. Professor Armstrong is an award-winning teacher of undergraduate business students. Together they make the complex world of marketing practical, approachable, and enjoyable.

**Philip Kotler** is S. C. Johnson & Son Distinguished Professor of International Marketing at the Kellogg Graduate School of Management, Northwestern University. He received his master's degree at the University of Chicago and his Ph.D. at M.I.T., both in economics. Dr. Kotler is author of *Marketing Management: Analysis, Planning, Implementation, and Control* (Prentice-Hall), now in its ninth edition and the most widely used marketing textbook in graduate schools of business. He has authored several other successful books and he has written over ninety articles for leading journals. He is the only three-time winner of the coveted Alpha Kappa Psi award for the best annual article in the *Journal of Marketing*. Dr. Kotler's numerous major honors include the Paul D. Converse Award given by the American Marketing Association to honor "outstanding contributions to science in marketing" and the Stuart Henderson Britt Award as Marketer of the Year. He was named the first recipient of two major awards: the Distinguished Marketing Educator of the Year Award given by the American Marketing Association and the Philip Kotler Award for Excellence in Health Care Marketing presented by the Academy for Health Care Services Marketing. He has also received the Charles Coolidge Parlin Award, which each year honors an outstanding leader in the field of marketing. Dr. Kotler has served as chairman of the College on Marketing of the Institute of Management Sciences (TIMS) and a director of the American Marketing Association. He has consulted with many major U.S. and foreign companies on marketing strategy.

**Gary Armstrong** is Professor and Chair of Marketing in the Kenan-Flagler Business School at the University of North Carolina at Chapel Hill. He holds undergraduate and master's degrees in business from Wayne State University in Detroit, and he received his Ph.D. in marketing from Northwestern University. Dr. Armstrong has contributed numerous articles to leading business journals. As a consultant and researcher, he has worked with many companies on marketing research, sales management, and marketing strategy. But Professor Armstrong's first love is teaching. He has been very active in the teaching and administration of Kenan-Flagler's undergraduate program. His recent administrative posts include Associate Director of the Undergraduate Business Program, Director of the Business Honors Program, and others. He works closely with business student groups and has received several campuswide and Business School teaching awards. He is the only repeat recipient of the school's highly regarded Award for Excellence in Undergraduate Teaching, which he won for the third time in 1993.

# Brief Table of Contents

# Contents

## ▶ PART 2
## ANALYZING MARKETING OPPORTUNITIES

▶ **PART 3**
**DEVELOPING MARKETING STRATEGY AND THE MARKETING MIX**

## ▶ PART 4
## EXTENDING MARKETING

# *Preface*

Marketing is the business function that identifies customer needs and wants, determines which target markets the organization can serve best, and designs appropriate products, services, and programs to serve these markets. However, marketing is much more than just an isolated business function—it is a philosophy that guides the entire organization. The goal of marketing is to create customer satisfaction profitably by building value-laden relationships with important customers. The marketing department cannot accomplish this goal by itself. It must team up closely with other departments in the company, and partner with other organizations throughout its entire value-delivery system, to provide superior value to customers. Thus, marketing calls upon everyone in the organization to "think customer" and to do all they can to help create and deliver superior customer value and satisfaction.

Marketing is all around us, and we all need to know something about it. Marketing is used not only by manufacturing companies, wholesalers, and retailers, but by all kinds of individuals and organizations. Lawyers, accountants, and doctors use marketing to manage demand for their services. So do hospitals, museums, and performing arts groups. No politician can get the needed votes, and no resort the needed tourists, without developing and carrying out marketing plans.

People throughout these organizations need to know how to define and segment a market and how to position themselves strongly by developing need-satisfying products and services for chosen target segments. They must know how to price their offerings to make them attractive and affordable, and how to choose and manage intermediaries to make their products available to customers. And they need to know how to advertise and promote products so that customers will know about and want them. Clearly, marketers need a broad range of skills in order to sense, serve, and satisfy consumer needs.

Students also need to know marketing in their roles as consumers and citizens. Someone is always trying to sell us something, so we need to recognize the methods they use to do so. And when students enter the job market, they must do "marketing research" to find the best opportunities and the best ways to "market themselves" to prospective employers. Many will start their careers with marketing jobs in sales forces, in retailing, in advertising, in research, or in one of a dozen other marketing areas.

## ▶ APPROACH AND OBJECTIVES

*Marketing: An Introduction* is designed to help students learn about the basic concepts and practices of modern marketing in an enjoyable and practical way. Several factors guided the development of this text. Most students who are learning marketing want a broad picture of its basics, but they don't want to drown in a sea of details. They want to know about important marketing principles and concepts, but also how these concepts are applied in actual marketing management practice. And they want a text that presents the complex and fascinating world of marketing in an easy-to-grasp, lively, and enjoyable way.

*Marketing: An Introduction* serves all of these important needs for beginning marketing students. The book is complete, covering all of the main topics that the marketer and consumer need to know. Yet its moderate length makes it manageable for beginning marketing students to cover in a given quarter or semester.

*Marketing: An Introduction* covers important principles and concepts that are supported by research and evidence from economics, the behavioral sciences, and modern management theory. Yet it takes a practical, marketing-management approach. Concepts are applied through countless examples of situations in which well-known and little-known companies assess and solve their marketing problems. Color illustrations, "Marketing at Work" exhibits, company cases, and video cases present further applications.

Finally, *Marketing: An Introduction* makes learning marketing easy and enjoyable. Its writing style and level are well suited to the beginning marketing student. The book tells the stories that reveal the drama of modern marketing: Home Depot's enthusiasm for taking care of customers; Ritz-Carlton's penchant for taking care of those who take care of customers; Levi Strauss & Co.'s startling success in finding new ways to grow, both in the United States and abroad; Church & Dwight's climb to become "king of the (mole)hill" with Arm & Hammer baking soda products; how Dow Plastics achieved leadership in its business-to-business markets by selling "customer success"; Motorola's quest for customer-driven, "six-sigma" quality; P&G's struggle to bring sanity back to food prices; Black & Decker's new-product success through listening to the customer; how Coca-Cola abandoned Madison Avenue and "went Hollywood" to create its breakthrough "Always Cool, Always Coca-Cola" advertising campaign; how Revlon sells not just products, but hopes and dreams; how Hallmark uses integrated marketing communications to build relationships with its preferred customers; Gerber's difficult social responsibility decisions following a product-tampering scare. These and dozens of other examples and illustrations throughout each chapter reinforce key concepts and bring marketing to life for the student.

*Marketing: An Introduction* gives the beginning marketing student a complete yet manageable, conceptual yet applied and managerial introduction to the basics of marketing. Its style, level, and extensive use of examples and illustrations make the book easy to grasp and enjoyable to read.

# ▶CHANGES IN THE FOURTH EDITION

The fourth edition of *Marketing: An Introduction* offers important improvements in organization, content, and style. The revisions emphasize a number of major new marketing themes, including:

◆ *Delivering superior customer value, satisfaction, and quality*—a market-centered strategy and "taking care of the customer."

◆ *Relationship marketing—keeping* customers and capturing *customer lifetime value* by building value-laden customer relationships.

◆ *Total marketing quality—the* importance of customer-driven, total quality as a means of delivering total customer satisfaction.

◆ *Value-delivery systems—cross-functional* teamwork within companies and cross-company supply-chain partnerships to create effective customer value-delivery systems.

◆ *Global marketing—chapter-by-chapter,* integrated coverage plus a full chapter focusing on international marketing considerations.

◆ *Marketing ethics, environmentalism, and social responsibility—chapter-by-chapter* integrated coverage plus a full chapter on marketing ethics and social responsibility.

Carefully revised Chapters 1 and 2 introduce and integrate the above topics to set the stage at the beginning of the course. Then, each revised chapter reflects the current marketing emphasis on delivering customer value and satisfaction, and on building customer relationships.

Other major additions to the fourth edition include:

◆ *Marketing communications—major* and important new material in Chapter 13 on the *new marketing communications environment, direct marketing,* and *integrated marketing communications.* Chapter 14 presents new coverage of *media-creative cooperation* and *creating advertising messages.*

◆ *Sales Management—in* Chapter 15, new sections on *salesforce strategy and structure, team selling,* and *relationship marketing.*

◆ *Marketing logistics—completely* revised coverage of physical distribution to include important new issues in *integrated marketing logistics* and *supply-chain management.* This edition also includes a new section on *hybrid channels.*

◆ *Product and brand strategy—significant* new material on brand quality and brand strategy, including *co-branding, multibranding, packaging and the environment,* and the *service-profit chain.*

The fourth edition of *Marketing: An Introduction* contains many other important changes. Despite the addition of major new coverage, it contains *two fewer chapters.* The previous chapter on "Marketing Services, Organizations, Persons, Places, and Ideas" has been integrated with the previous "Designing Products" chapter to create the new Chapter 8, "Product and Service Strategies." The previous two pricing chapters have been combined, without significant loss of coverage, into a single Chapter 10, "Pricing Considerations and Strategies."

Many new chapter-opening examples and "Marketing at Work" exhibits illustrate important new concepts with actual business applications. Dozens of new examples have been added within the running text. All tables, figures, examples, and references throughout the text have been thoroughly updated. The fourth edition of *Marketing: An Introduction* contains dozens of new photos and advertisements that illustrate key points and make the text more effective and appealing. All of the real-life company cases in the fourth edition are new or revised, and the text comes with an exciting new collection of company video cases. These cases, and the quality videos that accompany them, help to bring the real world directly into the classroom.

# ▶LEARNING AIDS

Many aids are provided within this book to help students learn about marketing. The main ones are:

◆ *Chapter-opening objectives.* Each chapter begins with a set of learning objectives that preview the flow of concepts in the chapter.

◆ *Chapter-opening examples.* Each chapter starts with a dramatic marketing story that introduces the chapter material and arouses student interest.

◆ *Full-color figures, photographs, advertisements, and illustrations.* Throughout each chapter, key concepts and applications are illustrated with strong, full-color visual materials.

◆ *"Marketing at Work" exhibits.* Additional examples and important information are highlighted in "Marketing at Work" exhibits throughout the text.

◆ *Chapter-ending summaries.* At the end of each chapter, a summary wraps up the main points and concepts.

◆ *Review questions and exercises.* Each chapter contains a set of discussion questions covering the main chapter points, and "applying the concepts" exercises that build individual and group process and leadership skills.

◆ *Key terms.* Key terms are highlighted within the text and clearly defined in the margins on the pages on which they appear.

◆ *Company case studies.* Company cases for class or written discussion are provided in a section at the end of the text. These cases challenge students to apply marketing principles to real companies in real situations.

◆ *Video cases.* Ten written video cases are provided in a section at the end of the text, supported by exciting new and original case videos. The videos and cases help to bring key marketing concepts and issues to life in the classroom.

◆ *Appendixes.* Two appendixes, "Marketing Arithmetic" and "Careers in Marketing," provide additional, practical information for students.

◆ *Indexes.* Subject, company, and author indexes reference all information, key terms, and examples in the book.

# ▶SUPPLEMENTS

A successful marketing course requires more than a well-written book. Today's classroom requires a dedicated teacher and a fully integrated teaching system. The following aids support *Marketing: An Introduction:*

## FOR THE INSTRUCTOR

### *Instructor's Resource Manual and Video Guide.*
Prepared by John R. Brooks of Houston Baptist University, this teaching resource includes an overview of the text and suggested syllabi. For every chapter there is a chapter overview, annotated lecture outlines, transparency lecture notes, answers to end-of-chapter discussion and concept questions, and applied learning exercises. For each company and video case in *Marketing: An Introduction,* 4e, the manual provides a synopsis of the case, teaching notes that outline how to use the case in class, and discussion questions that focus students on issues in the case.

## Test Item File

After extensive research and review, the fourth edition Test Item File has been prepared by Gail Kirby of Santa Clara University. The testing program includes approximately 125 page-referenced items per chapter, with multiple-choice, true–false, and essay questions included.

## Computerized Test Item File

Prentice Hall Custom Test
DOS Version; Windows Version; Mac Version
Based on the number one best-selling, state-of-the-art generation software program developed by Engineering Software Associates (ESA), Prentice Hall Custom Test is not only suitable for your course, but customizable to your personal needs. With Prentice Hall Custom Test's user-friendly test creation and powerful algorithmic generation, you can originate tailor-made tests quickly, easily and error-free. Whether on the Macintosh, Windows or DOS, you can create an exam, administer it traditionally or online, evaluate and track students' results, and analyze the success of the exam—all with a simple click of the mouse.

## Full Color Transparencies

Nearly 150 color images taken from the book and outside material are available upon adoption of the fourth edition, including several EFFIE award-winning print advertisements. Every figure has been redrawn for the best presentation value and detailed lecture notes for each image appear in the instructor's resource manual.

## On Location! Custom Case Videos for Marketing

(Contact your local Prentice Hall representative for details)
Broadcast television and marketing education have joined forces for the first time to create the most exciting and valuable series of videos ever produced for business education.

As directed by reviewer feedback, each one of the six-to-eight-minute issue-oriented clips grabs and holds the students' attention by coherently linking video to major conceptual elements covered in the text, as well as expanding upon the written cases found in the instructor's manual. Facilities, advertisements, product shots, and text illustrations are integrated with marketing manager and customer interviews for maximum effect. With On Location! you can take your class on the following marketing field trips without ever having to leave the classroom:

> Patagonia: Aiming for No Growth
> The M/A/R/C Group: Talking to Customers
> Rollerblade: The Asphalt Is Calling
> Mountain Travel Sobek: All Over the World
> Mall of America: The Ultimate Destination for Fun
> Terra Chips: Eat Your Veggies!
> DHL: Worldwide Express
> MTV: Think Globally, Act Locally
> Ritz-Carlton: Simply the Best
> Lands' End: Enticing Customers "Out Our Way"

*Prentice Hall Presents*
*Multimedia Presentations for Marketing and Advertising*
A new CD-ROM that organizes hundreds of media objects into simple-to-use presentations is available to adopting instructors. The CD includes:

◆ Approximately 300 illustrations taken from the text and other sources.
◆ Many EFFIE award-winning television and print advertisements.
◆ Key concept video taken from the On Location! custom case video series.
◆ Lecture notes tying the media to each chapter in the book.

The media resources are built into Presentation Manager 2.0, a "point and click" lecture-management software program that allows the instructor to create superb state-of-the-art presentations on their own, or use pre-made presentations with notes tied to the book.

### *New York Times/Prentice Hall Themes of the Times Program*

Instructors and students will receive a complimentary newspaper supplement containing recent articles pertinent to the field. These articles, featuring the best in reporting and journalistic integrity associated with *The New York Times,* update the text material and contribute real-world applications to the topics and companies covered in the course.

## FOR THE STUDENT

### *Study Guide*

Prepared by Thomas J. Paczkowski of Cayuga Community College, this comprehensive student guide includes for each chapter: a chapter overview, chapter objectives, a chapter outline, a concept review, mini-cases with questions for analysis, and multiple-choice and true–false questions.

### *Career Paths in Marketing Version 2.0*

This multimedia CD-ROM lets students have fun while they explore the world of marketing careers. The CD, which won the 1995 *New Media Magazine* Gold Invision Award for best new educational software program, assesses students' career desires and aptitudes, and provides tips for résumé writing and interviewing, background information on many different career paths, and interactive video interviews with the actual marketing managers who appear in the On Location! video series available with the book. Available in 1997, the software provides further value by acting as a computerized study guide directly linked to the book.

# *Acknowledgments*

No book is the work only of its authors. We owe much to the pioneers of marketing who first identified its major issues and developed its concepts and techniques. Our thanks also go to our colleagues at the J. L. Kellogg Graduate School of Management, Northwestern University, and at the Kenan-Flagler Business School, University of North Carolina at Chapel Hill, for ideas and suggestions. We owe special thanks to Lew Brown and Martha McEnally, both of the University of North Carolina, Greensboro, and to Judy Block, for their valuable work in preparing high-quality company cases and video cases. We thank John R. Brooks, Jr., of Houston Baptist University, Gail Kirby of Santa Clara University, Judy Block of JRB Communications, Inc., and Tom Paczkowski of Cayuga Community College for their work in preparing the *Instructor's Resource Manual, Test Item File*, and *Color Transparencies Package*; chapter objective summaries, discussion questions, and exercises; and the *Student Learning Guide*, respectively. Finally, we thank Betsey Christian for her able editing assistance.

Many reviewers at other colleges provided valuable comments and suggestions. We are indebted to the following colleagues:

Gemmy Allen
Mountain View College

Abi Almeer
Nova University

Arvid Anderson
University of North Carolina, Wilmington

Arnold Bornfriend
Worcester State College

Donald Boyer
Jefferson College

Alejandro Camacho
University of Georgia

William J. Carner
University of Texas at Austin

Gerald Cavallo
Fairfield University

Lucette Comer
Florida International University

Ron Cooley
South Suburban College

June Cotte
University of Connecticut

Ronald Coulter
Southwest Missouri State University

John de Young
Cumberland County College

Lee Dickson
Florida International University

Mike Dotson
Appalachian State University

Peter Doukas
Westchester Community College

David Forlani
University of North Florida

Jack Forrest
Middle Tennessee State University

John Gauthier
Gateway Technical Institute

Eugene Gilbert
California State University, Sacramento

Diana Grewal
University of Miami

Esther Headley
The Wichita State University

Sandra Heusinkveld
Normandale Community College

James Jeck
North Carolina State University

**xxvii**

James Kennedy
Navarro College

Eric Kulp
Middlesex County College

Ed Laube
Macomb Community College

Gregory Lincoln
Westchester Community College

John Lloyd
Monroe Community College

Dorothy Maass
Delaware County Community College

Ajay Manrai
University of Delaware

Lalita Manrai
University of Delaware

James McAlexander
Oregon State University

Donald McBane
Clemson University

Debbora Meflin-Bullock
California State Polytechnic University

Randall Mertz
Mesa Community College

Veronica Miller
Lect., Mt. St. Mary's College

Joan Mizis
St. Louis Community College

Melissa Moore
University of Connecticut

Robert Moore
University of Connecticut

William Morgenroth
University of South Carolina, Columbia

Linda Moroble
Dallas County Community College

Sandra Moulton
Technical College of Alamance

Jim Muncy
Valdosta State

Lee Neumann
Bucks County Community College

Dave Olsen
North Hennepin Community College

Thomas Paczkowski
Cayuga Community College

George Palz
Erie Community College

Tammy Pappas
Eastern Michigan University

Alison Pittman
Brevard Community College

Lana Podolak
Community College of Beaver County

Joel Porrish
Springfield College

Robert L. Powell
Gloucester County College

Eric Pratt
New Mexico State University

Robert Ross
The Wichita State University

Andre San Augustine
The University of Arizona

Dwight Scherban
Central Connecticut State College

Eberhard Scheuing
St. John's University

Pamela Schindler
Wittenberg University

Raymond Schwartz
Montclair State College

Raj Sethuraman
University of Iowa

Reshma H. Shah
University of Pittsburgh

Jack Sheeks
Broward Community College

Dee Smith
Lansing Community College

Ira Teich
Long Island University

Donna Tillman
California State Polytechnic University

Andrea Weeks
Fashion Institute of Design & Merchandising

Sumner White
Massachusetts Bay Community College

Steve Winter
Orange County Community College

Burl Worley
Allan Hancock College

We also owe a great deal to the people at Prentice Hall who helped develop this book. Senior Acquisitions Editor for Marketing David Borkowsky supplied many good ideas and substantial support and encouragement (sometimes even prodding). John Larkin developed and published the many elements of the supplements package. John Chillingworth created and implemented the marketing communications campaign for the book. Theresa Festa patiently and expertly assisted the entire process. We also owe much thanks to Linda DeLorenzo and Heather Stratton who helped shepherd the project smoothly through production. Additional thanks go to Sue Howard.

Finally, we owe many thanks to our families—Kathy, KC, and Mandy Armstrong, and Nancy, Amy, Melissa, and Jessica Kotler—for their constant support and encouragement. To them, we dedicate this book.

Philip Kotler
Gary Armstrong

# Chapter 1

# Marketing in a Changing World: Creating Customer Value and Satisfaction

Home Depot, the giant do-it-yourself home improvement chain, is an outstanding marketing company. The reason: Home Depot is more than just customer-driven—it's customer-*obsessed*. In the words of cofounder and chief executive Bernie Marcus, "All of our people understand what the Holy Grail is. It's not the bottom line. It's an almost blind, passionate commitment to taking care of customers."

At first glance, a cavernous Home Depot store doesn't look like much. With its cement floors and drafty warehouselike interior, the store offers all the atmosphere of an airplane hangar. But the chances are good that you'll find exactly what you're looking for, priced to make it a real value. Home Depot carries a huge assortment of more than 35,000 items—anything and everything related to home improvement. And its prices run 20 to 30 percent below those of local hardware stores.

Home Depot provides more than the right products at the right prices, however. Perhaps the best part of shopping at Home Depot is the high quality of its customer service. Bernie Marcus and his partner, Arthur Blank, founded Home Depot with the simple mission of helping customers solve their home improvement problems. Their goal: "To take ham-handed homeowners who lack the confidence to do more than screw in a light bulb and transform them into Mr. and Ms. Fixits." Accomplishing this mission takes more than simply peddling the store's products and taking the customers' money. It means building lasting customer relationships.

Bernie and Arthur understand the importance of customer satisfaction. They calculate that a satisfied customer is worth more than $25,000 in customer lifetime value ($38 per store visit, times 30 visits per year, times about 22 years of patronage). Customer satisfaction, in turn, results from interactions with well-trained, highly motivated employees who consistently provide good value and high-quality service. "The most important part of our formula," says Arthur, "is the quality of caring that takes place in our stores between the employee and the customer." Thus, at Home Depot, taking care of customers begins with taking care of employees.

Home Depot attracts the best salespeople by paying above-average salaries; then it trains them thoroughly. All employees take regular "product knowledge" classes to gain hands-on experience with problems that customers will face. When it comes to creating customer value and satisfaction, Home Depot treats its employees as partners. All full-time employees receive at least 7 percent of their annual salary in company stock. As a result, Home Depot employees take ownership in the business of serving customers. Each employee wears a bright orange apron that says, "Hello, I'm _____, a Home Depot stockholder. Let me help you."

Bernie and Arthur have become energetic crusaders in the cause of customer service. For example, four Sundays a year at 6:30 A.M., the two don their own orange aprons and air *Breakfast with Bernie and Art*—a good old-fashioned revival broadcast—live over closed-circuit TV to the company's 70,000 employees nationwide. According to one account, "Bernie regularly rouses his disciples with the following: 'Where do you go if you want a job?' They yell back: 'Sears . . . Lowe's . . . Builders Square.' 'Where do you go if you want a *career*?' 'HOME DEPOT!' they roar. At times, when the excitement becomes feverish, Marcus has been known to grab a resisting Blank, plant a noisy kiss on his cheek, and exclaim, 'Arthur, I love you!' "

Home Depot avoids the high-pressure sales techniques used by some retailers. Instead, it encourages salespeople to build long-term relationships with customers—to spend whatever time it takes, visit after visit, to solve customer problems. Home Depot pays employees a straight salary so that they can spend as much time as necessary with customers without worrying about making the sale. Bernie Marcus declares, "The day I'm dead with an apple in my mouth is the day we'll pay commissions." In fact, rather than pushing customers to *overspend*, employees are trained to help customers spend *less* than they expected. "I love it when shoppers tell me they were prepared to spend $150 and our people showed them how to do the job for four or five bucks," says Bernie.

Taking care of customers has made Home Depot one of today's most successful retailers. Founded in 1978, it has grown explosively in less than 20 years to become the nation's largest do-it-yourself chain. Home Depot sales have increased at a compound annual rate of 40 percent during the past decade, and earnings have grown at a 46 percent pace. In 1996, *Fortune* magazine named Home Depot as America's most-admired retailer. In fact, a current concern in some stores is too many customers: Some outlets are generating an astounding $600 of sales per square foot (compared with Wal-Mart at $250 and Kmart at $150). This has created problems with clogged aisles, stockouts, too few salespeople, and long checkout lines. Although many retailers would welcome this kind of problem, it bothers Bernie and Arthur greatly, and they've quickly taken corrective action. Continued success, they know, depends on the passionate pursuit of customer satisfaction. Bernie will tell you, "Every customer has to be treated like your mother, your father, your sister, or your brother." And you certainly wouldn't want to keep your mother waiting in line.[1]   ■

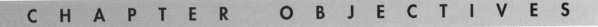

# CHAPTER OBJECTIVES

## After reading this chapter, you should be able to:

**1** Define *marketing* and discuss its core concepts.

**2** Explain the relationships between customer value, satisfaction, and quality.

**3** Discuss how marketing managers go about developing profitable customer relationships.

**4** Compare the five marketing management philosophies.

**5** Analyze the major forces that are now changing the world marketing landscape and challenging marketing strategy.

Many factors contribute to making a business successful. However, today's successful companies at all levels have one thing in common—they are strongly customer focused and heavily committed to marketing. These companies share an absolute dedication to understanding and satisfying the needs of customers in well-defined target markets. They motivate everyone in the organization to produce superior value for their customers, leading to high levels of customer satisfaction. As Bernie Marcus of Home Depot asserts in our opening story, "All of our people understand what the Holy Grail is. It's not the bottom line. It's an almost blind, passionate commitment to taking care of customers."

Marketing, more than any other business function, deals with customers. Creating customer value and satisfaction are at the very heart of modern marketing thinking and practice. Although we will explore more detailed definitions of marketing later in this chapter, perhaps the simplest definition is this one: Marketing is the delivery of customer satisfaction at a profit. The goal of marketing is to attract new customers by promising superior value and to keep current customers by delivering satisfaction.

Wal-Mart has become the world's largest retailer by delivering on its promise "We sell for less—always." Federal Express dominates the U.S. small-package freight industry by consistently making good on its promise of fast, reliable small-package delivery. Ritz-Carlton promises—and delivers—truly "memorable experiences" for its hotel guests. And Coca-Cola, long the world's leading soft drink, delivers on the simple but enduring promise, "Always Coca-Cola"—always thirst-quenching, always good with food, always cool, always a part of your life. These and other highly successful companies know that if they take care of their customers, market share and profits will follow.

Some people think that only large business organizations operating in highly developed economies use marketing, but sound marketing is critical to the success of every organization—whether large or small, for-profit or nonprofit, domestic or global. Large for-profit firms such as McDonald's, Sony, Federal Express, Wal-Mart, and Marriott use marketing. But so do nonprofit organizations such as colleges, hospitals, museums, symphonies, and even churches. Moreover, marketing is practiced not only in the United States but all around the world. Most countries in North and South America, Western Europe, and Asia have well-developed marketing systems. Even in Eastern Europe and the former Soviet republics, where marketing has long had a bad name, dramatic political and social changes have created new opportunities for marketing. Business and government leaders in most of these nations are eager to learn everything they can about modern marketing practices.

You already know a lot about marketing—it's all around you. You see the results of marketing in the abundance of products that line the store shelves in your nearby shopping mall. You see marketing in the advertisements that fill your TV screen, magazines, and mailbox. At home, at school, where you work, where you play—you are exposed to marketing in almost everything you do. Yet, there is much more to marketing than meets the consumer's casual eye. Behind it all is a massive network of people and activities competing for your attention and purchasing dollars.

The remaining pages of this book will give you a more complete and formal introduction to the basic concepts and practices of today's marketing. In this chapter, we begin by defining marketing and its core concepts, describing the major philosophies of marketing thinking and practice, and discussing some of the major new challenges that marketers now face.

# ▶ WHAT IS MARKETING?

What does the term *marketing* mean? Many people think of marketing only as selling and advertising. And no wonder: every day we are bombarded with television commercials, newspaper ads, direct mail campaigns, and sales calls. However, selling and advertising are only the tip of the marketing iceberg. Although they are important, they are only two of many marketing functions, and are often not the most important ones.

Today, marketing must be understood not in the old sense of making a sale—"telling and selling"—but in the new sense of *satisfying customer needs*. If the marketer does a good job of understanding consumer needs, develops products that provide superior value, and prices, distributes, and promotes them effectively, these products will sell very easily. Thus, selling and advertising are only part of a larger "marketing mix"—a set of marketing tools that work together to affect the marketplace.

**Marketing**
A social and managerial process by which individuals and groups obtain what they need and want through creating and exchanging products and value with others.

We define **marketing** as a social and managerial process by which individuals and groups obtain what they need and want through creating and exchanging products and value with others. To explain this definition, we examine the following important terms: *needs, wants, and demands; products; value, satisfaction, and quality; exchange, transactions, and relationships;* and *markets.* Figure 1-1 shows that these core marketing concepts are linked, with each concept building on the one before it.

## NEEDS, WANTS, AND DEMANDS

**Needs**
States of felt deprivation.

The most basic concept underlying marketing is that of human needs. Human needs are states of felt deprivation. They include basic *physical* needs for food, clothing, shelter, and safety, *social* needs for belonging and affection, and *individual* needs for knowledge and self-expression. These needs are not invented by marketers; they are a basic part of the human makeup.

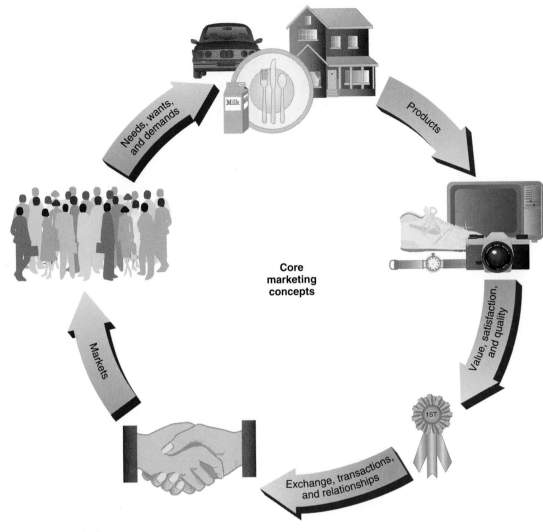

**FIGURE 1-1**
*Core marketing concepts*

**Wants**
The form taken by
human needs as they
are shaped by culture
and individual
personality.

**Demands**
Human wants that are
backed by buying
power.

**Wants** are the form taken by human needs as they are shaped by culture and individual personality. A hungry person in the United States may want a hamburger, french fries, and a Coke. A hungry person in Bali may want mangoes, suckling pig, and beans. Wants are described in terms of objects that will satisfy needs.

People have almost unlimited wants, but have limited resources. Thus, they want to choose products that provide the most value and satisfaction for their money. When backed by buying power, wants become **demands.** Consumers view products as bundles of benefits and choose products that give them the best bundle for their money. Thus, a Honda Civic means basic transportation, low price, and fuel economy. A Mercedes means comfort, luxury, and status. Given their wants and resources, people demand products with the benefits that add up to the most satisfaction.

*Outstanding marketing companies like Marriott stay close to customers. Chairman Bill Marriott personally reads guest comment cards and letters, then talks to customers through ads like this one.*

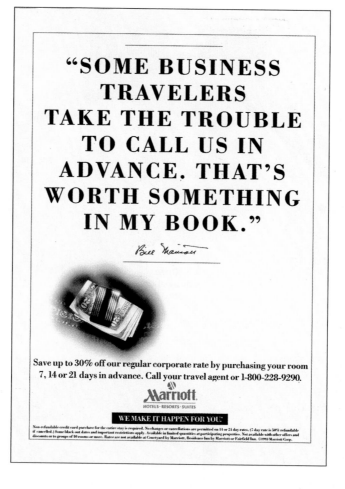

"SOME BUSINESS TRAVELERS TAKE THE TROUBLE TO CALL US IN ADVANCE. THAT'S WORTH SOMETHING IN MY BOOK."

*Bill Marriott*

Save up to 30% off our regular corporate rate by purchasing your room 7, 14 or 21 days in advance. Call your travel agent or 1-800-228-9290.

**Marriott**
HOTELS·RESORTS·SUITES

WE MAKE IT HAPPEN FOR YOU.

Non-refundable credit card purchase for the entire stay is required. No changes or cancellations are permitted on 14 or 21 day rates. (7 day rate is 50% refundable if cancelled.) Some black out dates and important restrictions apply. Available in limited quantities at participating properties. Not available with other offers and discounts or to groups of 10 rooms or more. Rates are not available at Courtyard by Marriott, Residence Inn by Marriott or Fairfield Inn. ©1993 Marriott Corp.

Outstanding marketing companies go to great lengths to learn about and understand their customers' needs, wants, and demands. They conduct consumer research about consumer likes and dislikes. They analyze customer inquiry, warranty, and service data. They observe customers using their own and competing products and train salespeople to be on the lookout for unfulfilled customer needs.

In these outstanding companies, people at all levels—including top management—stay close to customers. For example, top executives from Wal-Mart spend two days each week visiting stores and mingling with customers. At Disney World, at least once in his or her career, each manager spends a day touring the park in a Mickey, Minnie, Goofy, or other character costume. Moreover, all Disney World managers spend a week each year on the front line—taking tickets, selling popcorn, or loading and unloading rides. At Motorola, top executives routinely visit corporate customers at their offices to gain better insights into their needs. And at Marriott, to stay in touch with customers, Chairman of the Board and President Bill Marriott personally reads some 10 percent of the 8,000 letters and 2 percent of the 750,000 guest comment cards submitted by customers each year. Understanding customer needs, wants, and demands in detail provides important input for designing marketing strategies.

*Products do not have to be physical objects. In this ad, the "product" is tennis. "Imagine six hours of classes, one after another, interrupted only by a couple of fish sticks . . . Introduce your kids to tennis."*

YOU'RE
NOT THE ONLY ONE
SITTING BEHIND
A DESK ALL DAY.

*Imagine six hours of classes, one after another, interrupted only by a couple of fish sticks, some applesauce and ten minutes of kickball. That's a typical day in the life of your kids. Fortunately, there is something you can do about it. Introduce your kids to tennis. Join the USTA/Northern California by calling 510-748-7373.*

UNITED STATES TENNIS ASSOCIATION
NORTHERN CALIFORNIA
*Helping kids get a grip.*

## PRODUCTS

**Product**
Anything that can be offered to a market for attention, acquisition, use, or consumption that might satisfy a want or need. It includes physical objects, services, persons, places, organizations, and ideas.

People satisfy their needs and wants with products. A **product** is anything that can be offered to a market to satisfy a need or want. The concept of *product* is not limited to physical objects—anything capable of satisfying a need can be called a product. In addition to goods and services, products include *persons, places, organizations, activities,* and *ideas.* Consumers decide which entertainers to watch on television, which places to visit on vacation, which organizations to support through contributions, and which ideas to adopt. To the consumer, these are all products. If at times the term *product* does not seem to fit, we could substitute other terms such as *satisfier, resource,* or *offer.*

Many sellers make the mistake of paying more attention to the specific products that they offer than to the benefits produced by these products. They see themselves as selling a product rather than providing a solution to a need. A manufacturer of drill bits may think that the customer needs a drill bit, but what the customer *really* needs is a hole. These sellers may suffer from "marketing myopia."[2] They are so taken with their products that they focus only on existing wants and lose sight of underlying customer needs. They forget that a product is only a tool to solve a consumer problem. These sellers will have trouble if a new product comes along that serves the customer's need better or less expensively. The customer with the same *need* will *want* the new product.

## VALUE, SATISFACTION, AND QUALITY

Consumers usually face a broad array of products and services that might satisfy a given need. How do they choose among these many products and services? Consumers make buying choices based on their perceptions of the value that various products and services deliver.

## Customer Value

**Customer value**
The consumer's assessment of the product's overall capacity to satisfy his or her needs. The difference between total customer value and total customer cost of a marketing offer— "profit" to the customer.

**Customer value** is the difference between the values that the customer gains from owning and using a product and the costs of obtaining the product. For example, Federal Express customers gain a number of benefits. The most obvious are fast and reliable package delivery. However, when using Federal Express, customers also may receive some status and image values. Using Federal Express usually makes both the package sender and the receiver feel more important. When deciding whether to send a package via Federal Express, customers will weigh these and other values against the money, effort, and psychic costs of using the service. Moreover, they will compare the value of using Federal Express against the value of using other shippers—UPS, Airborne, the U.S. Postal Service—and select the one that gives them the greatest delivered value.

Customers often do not judge product values and costs accurately or objectively. They act on *perceived* value. For example, does Federal Express really provide faster, more reliable delivery? If so, is this better service worth the higher prices that FedEx charges? The Postal Service argues that its express service is comparable and its prices are much lower. However, judging by market share, most consumers perceive otherwise. Federal Express dominates with more than a 45 percent share of the U.S. express-delivery market, compared with the Postal Service's 8 percent.[3] The Postal Service's challenge is to change these customer value perceptions.

## Customer Satisfaction

**Customer satisfaction**
The extent to which a product's perceived performance matches a buyer's expectations. If the product's performance falls short of expectations, the buyer is dissatisfied. If performance matches or exceeds expectations, the buyer is satisfied or delighted.

**Customer satisfaction** depends on a product's perceived performance in delivering value relative to a buyer's expectations. If the product's performance falls short of the customer's expectations, the buyer is dissatisfied. If performance matches expectations, the buyer is satisfied. If performance exceeds expectations, the buyer is delighted. Smart companies aim to *delight* customers by promising only what they can deliver, then delivering *more* than they promise.

Customer expectations are based on past buying experiences, the opinions of friends, and marketer and competitor information and promises. Marketers must be careful to set the right level of expectations. If they set expectations too low, they may satisfy those who buy but fail to attract enough buyers. If they raise expectations too high, buyers will be disappointed.

Still, most of today's most successful companies are raising expectations— and delivering performance to match. These companies aim high because they know that customers who are *merely* satisfied will find it easy to switch suppliers when a better offer comes along. For example, a study by AT&T showed that 70 percent of customers who say that they are satisfied with a product or service would still be willing to switch to a competitor. In contrast, customers who are *highly* satisfied are much less ready to switch. One study showed that 75 percent of Toyota buyers were highly satisfied, and about 75 percent said they intended to buy a Toyota again.[4] Thus, customer *delight* creates an emotional tie to a product or service, not just a rational preference, and this creates high customer loyalty. Highly satisfied customers make repeat purchases, are less price sensitive, remain customers longer, and talk favorably to others about the company and its products.

Although the customer-centered firm seeks to deliver high customer satisfaction relative to competitors, it does not try to *maximize* customer satisfaction. A company can always increase customer satisfaction by lowering its price or increasing its services, but this may result in lower profits. The purpose of marketing is to generate customer value profitably. This requires a very delicate balance: The marketer must continue to generate more customer value and satisfaction but not "give away the house."[5]

## *Quality*

Quality has a direct impact on product or service performance. Thus, it is closely linked to customer value and satisfaction. In the narrowest sense, quality can be defined as "freedom from defects." But most customer-centered companies go beyond this narrow definition of quality. Instead, they define quality in terms of customer satisfaction. For example, the vice president of quality at Motorola, a company that pioneered total quality efforts in the United States, says that "Quality has to do something for the customer. . . . Our definition of a defect is 'if the customer doesn't like it, it's a defect.' "[6] Similarly, the American Society for Quality Control defines quality as the totality of features and characteristics of a product or service that bear on its ability to *satisfy customer needs*.

These customer-focused definitions suggest that quality begins with customer needs and ends with customer satisfaction. The fundamental aim of today's *total quality* movement has become *total customer satisfaction*.

**Total quality management** (TQM) is an approach in which all the company's people are involved in constantly improving the quality of products, services, and business processes. TQM swept the corporate boardrooms of the 1980s. Companies ranging from giants such as AT&T, Xerox, and Federal Express to smaller businesses such as the Granite Rock Company of Watsonville, California, have credited TQM with greatly improving their market shares and profits.

However, many companies adopted the language of TQM but not the substance, or viewed TQM as a cure-all for all the company's problems. Still others became obsessed with narrowly defined TQM principles and lost sight of broader concerns for customer value and satisfaction. As a result, many TQM programs begun in the 1980s failed, causing a backlash against TQM.

When applied in the context of creating customer satisfaction, however, total quality principles remain a requirement for success. Although many firms don't use the TQM label anymore, for most top companies, customer-driven quality has become a way of doing business. Most customers will no longer tolerate poor or average quality. Companies today have no choice but to adopt quality concepts if they want to stay in the race, let alone be profitable. Thus, the task of improving product and service quality should be a company's top priority. However, quality programs must be designed to produce measurable results. Many companies now apply the notion of "return on quality (ROQ)." They make certain that the quality they offer is the quality that customers want. This quality, in turn, yields returns in the form of improved sales and profits.[7]

Marketers have two major responsibilities in a quality-centered company. First, they must participate in forming strategies that will help the company win through total quality excellence. They must be the customer's watchdog or guardian, complaining loudly for the customer when the product or the service is not right. Second, marketers must deliver marketing quality as well as production quality. They must perform each marketing activity—marketing research, sales training, advertising, customer service, and others—to high standards. Marketing at Work 1-1 presents some important conclusions about total marketing quality strategy.

---

**Total quality management (TQM)** Programs designed to constantly improve the quality of products, services, and marketing processes.

## MARKETING AT WORK 1-1

# PURSUING A TOTAL QUALITY MARKETING STRATEGY

The Japanese have long taken to heart lessons about winning through *total quality management* (TQM). Their quest for quality paid off handsomely. Consumers around the world flocked to buy high-quality Japanese products, leaving many American and European firms playing catch-up. Japan was the first country to award a national quality prize, the Deming prize, named after the American statistician who taught the importance of quality to postwar Japan.

In recent years, however, Western firms have closed the quality gap. Many have started their own quality programs in an effort to compete both globally and domestically with the Japanese. In the mid-1980s, the United States established the Malcolm Baldrige National Quality Award, which encourages U.S. firms to implement quality practices. Not wanting to be left out of the qual-

ity race, Europe developed the European Quality Award in 1993. It also initiated an exacting set of quality standards called ISO 9000. Whereas the Baldrige and other quality awards measure less tangible aspects of quality,

---

*Ford recognizes that quality requires a total employee commitment.*

such as customer satisfaction and continuous improvement, ISO 9000 is a set of generally accepted accounting principles for documenting quality. As of 1994, 74 countries had officially recognized ISO 9000 as an international standard for quality systems. Many customers in these countries are now demanding ISO certification as a prerequisite for doing business with a seller. To earn ISO 9000 certification, sellers must undergo a quality audit every six months by a registered ISO (International Standards Organization) assessor.

Thus, total quality has become a truly global concern. Total quality stems from the following premises about quality improvement:

**1.** *Quality is in the eyes of the customer.* Quality must begin with customer needs and end with customer perceptions. As Motorola's vice president of quality suggests, "Beauty is in the eye of the beholder. If [a product] does not work the way

---

# EXCHANGE, TRANSACTIONS, AND RELATIONSHIPS

**Exchange**
The act of obtaining a desired object from someone by offering something in return.

Marketing occurs when people decide to satisfy needs and wants through exchange. **Exchange** is the act of obtaining a desired object from someone by offering something in return. Exchange is only one of many ways that people can obtain a desired object. For example, hungry people could find food by hunting, fishing, or gathering fruit. They could beg for food or take food from someone else. Or they could offer money, another good, or a service in return for food.

As a means of satisfying needs, exchange has much in its favor. People do not have to prey on others or depend on donations. Nor must they possess the skills to produce every necessity for themselves. They can concentrate on making things that they are good at making and trade them for needed items made by others. Thus, exchange allows a society to produce much more than it would with any alternative system.

that the user needs it to work, the defect is as big to the user as if it doesn't work the way the designer planned it." Thus, the fundamental aim of today's quality movement has become "total customer satisfaction."

**2.** *Quality must be reflected not just in the company's products, but in every company activity.* Leonard A. Morgan of General Electric says: "We are not just concerned with the quality of the product, but with the quality of our advertising, service, product literature, delivery, and after-sales support."

**3.** *Quality requires total employee commitment.* Quality can be delivered only by companies in which all employees are committed to quality and motivated and trained to deliver it. Successful companies remove the barriers between departments. Their employees work as teams to carry out core business processes and to create desired outcomes. Employees work to satisfy their internal customers as well as external customers.

**4.** *Quality requires high-quality partners.* Quality can be delivered only by companies whose marketing-system partners also deliver quality. Therefore, a quality-driven company must find and align itself with high-quality suppliers and distributors.

**5.** *A quality program cannot save a poor product.* The Pontiac Fiero launched a quality program, but because the car didn't have a performance engine to support its performance image, the quality program did not save the car. A quality drive cannot compensate for product deficiencies.

**6.** *Quality can always be improved.* The best companies believe in "continuous improvement of everything by everyone." The best way to improve quality is to benchmark the company's performance against the "best-of-class" competitors or the best performers in other industries, striving to equal or surpass them.

**7.** *Quality improvement sometimes requires quantum leaps.* Although the company should strive for continuous quality improvement, it must at times seek a quantum quality improvement. Companies sometimes can obtain small improvements by working harder. But large improvements call for fresh solutions and for working smarter. For example, John Young of Hewlett-Packard did not ask for a 10 percent reduction in defects, he asked for a *tenfold* reduction and got it.

**8.** *Quality does not cost more.* Managers once argued that achieving more quality would cost more and slow down production. But im-

proving quality involves learning ways to "do things right the first time." Quality is not *inspected* in; it must be *designed* in. Doing things right the first time reduces the costs of salvage, repair, and redesign, not to mention losses in customer goodwill. Motorola claims that its quality drive has saved $3 billion in manufacturing costs during the last six years.

**9.** *Quality is necessary but may not be sufficient.* Improving a company's quality is absolutely necessary to meet the needs of increasingly demanding buyers. At the same time, higher quality may not ensure a winning advantage, especially as all competitors increase their quality to more or less the same extent. For example, Singapore Airlines enjoyed a reputation as the world's best airline. However, competing airlines have attracted larger shares of passengers recently by narrowing the perceived gap between their service quality and Singapore's service quality.

*Sources:* Quotes from Lois Therrien, "Motorola and NEC: Going for Glory," *Business Week,* special issue on quality, 1991, pp. 60–61. Also see David A. Garvin, "Competing on Eight Dimensions of Quality," *Harvard Business Review,* November–December 1987, p. 109; Ronald Henkoff, "The Hot New Seal of Quality," *Fortune,* June 18, 1993, pp. 116–20; Cyndee Miller, "TQM Out; 'Continuous Process Improvement' In," *Marketing News,* May 9, 1994, pp. 5, 10; Amy Zukerman, "One Size Doesn't Fit All," *Industry Week,* January 9, 1995, pp. 37–40; and Jack Russell and Julie Ralston, "Five Years That Shook the World: Remaking Japanese Quality," *Advertising Age,* July 31, 1995, p. 18.

---

**Transaction**
A trade between two parties that involves at least two things of value, agreed-upon conditions, a time of agreement, and a place of agreement.

Whereas exchange is the core concept of marketing, a transaction, in turn, is marketing's unit of measurement. A **transaction** consists of a trade of values between two parties. In a transaction, we must be able to say that one party gives X to another party and gets Y in return. For example, you pay Sears $350 for a television set. This is a classic *monetary transaction,* but not all transactions involve money. In a *barter transaction,* you might trade your old refrigerator in return for a neighbor's secondhand television set.

In the broadest sense, the marketer tries to bring about a response to some offer. The response may be more than simply "buying" or "trading" goods and services. A political candidate, for instance, wants a response called "votes," a church wants "membership," and a social-action group wants "idea acceptance." Marketing consists of actions taken to obtain a desired response from a target audience toward some product, service, idea, or other object.

**Relationship Marketing**
The process of creating, maintaining, and enhancing strong, value-laden relationships with customers and other stakeholders.

Transaction marketing is part of the larger idea of **relationship marketing**. Beyond creating short-term transactions, marketers need to build long-term relationships with valued customers, distributors, dealers, and suppliers. They want to build strong economic and social ties by promising and consistently delivering high-quality products, good service, and fair prices. Increasingly, marketing is shifting from trying to maximize the profit on each individual transaction to building mutually beneficial relationships with consumers and other parties. The operating assumption is: Build good relationships and profitable transactions will follow.

Relationship marketing is oriented more toward the long term. The goal is to deliver long-term value to customers, and the measures of success are long-term customer satisfaction and retention. Beyond offering consistently high value and satisfaction, marketers can use a number of specific marketing tools to develop stronger bonds with consumers. First, a company might build value and satisfaction by adding *financial benefits* to the customer relationship. For example, airlines offer frequent-flyer programs, hotels give room upgrades to their frequent guests, and supermarkets give patronage refunds.

A second approach is to add *social benefits* as well as financial benefits. Here, the company works to increase its social bonds with customers by learning individual customers' needs and wants and then personalizing its products and services. For example, Ritz-Carlton Hotels employees treat customers as individuals, not as nameless, faceless members of a mass market. Whenever possible, they refer to guests by name and give each guest a warm welcome every day. They record specific guest preferences in the company's customer database, which holds more

*Relationship marketing: Increasingly, companies are moving away from a focus on individual transactions and toward a focus on building value-laden relationships with customers. Here PaineWebber declares, "We invest in relationships."*

"...and I couldn't understand why this PaineWebber broker was throwing these questions at us. I wanted to talk stocks. But he kept asking me about my kids.

He asked what our hopes were for them. Would there be college? What kind? Things like that.

I wondered why. I mean, our oldest was only in second grade.

Well, we ended up realizing we should start planning for the girls' education right then. Bought my first zero coupon bond. It's a great feeling—to know when Jenny starts college, the money's going to be there each year.

I just never expected a big company like PaineWebber to think about our little girls. But this broker, he really figured out what we needed...because he asked."

**PaineWebber**
We invest in relationships.

than 400,000 individual customer preferences, accessible by all hotels in the world-wide Ritz chain. A guest who requests a foam pillow at the Ritz in Montreal will be delighted to find one waiting in the room when he or she checks into the Atlanta Ritz months later.[8]

To build better relationships with its customers, during the summer of 1994, Saturn invited all of its almost 700,000 owners to a "Saturn Homecoming" at its manufacturing facility in Spring Hill, Tennessee. The two-day affair included family events, plant tours, and physical challenge activities designed to build trust and a team spirit. Says Saturn's manager of corporate communications, "The Homecoming party is another way of building . . . relationships, and it shows that we treat our customers differently than any other car company." More than 40,000 guests attended, coming from as far as Alaska and Taiwan.[9]

A third approach to building customer relationships is to add *structural ties* as well as financial and social benefits. For example, a business marketer might supply customers with special equipment or computer linkages that help them manage their orders, payroll, or inventory. Federal Express, for instance, offers its FedEx Ship program to thousands of its best corporate and individual customers to keep them from defecting to competitors like UPS. The program provides free computer software that allows customers to link with Federal Express's computers. Customers can use the software to arrange shipments and to check the status of their Federal Express packages.

Relationship marketing means that marketers must focus on managing their customers as well as their products. At the same time, they don't want relationships with every customer. In fact, there are undesirable customers for every company. The objective is to determine which customers the company can serve most effectively relative to competitors. Ultimately, marketing is the art of attracting and keeping *profitable customers*.

## MARKETS

**Market**
The set of all actual and potential buyers of a product or service.

The concepts of exchange and relationships lead to the concept of a market. A market is the set of actual and potential buyers of a product. These buyers share a particular need or want that can be satisfied through exchanges and relationships. Thus, the size of a market depends on the number of people who exhibit the need, have resources to engage in exchange, and are willing to offer these resources in exchange for what they want.

Originally the term *market* stood for the place where buyers and sellers gathered to exchange their goods, such as a village square. Economists use the term *market* to refer to a collection of buyers and sellers who transact in a particular product class, as in the housing market or the grain market. Marketers, however, see the sellers as constituting an industry and the buyers as constituting a market.

Modern economies operate on the principle of division of labor, where each person specializes in producing something, receives payment, and buys needed things with this money. Thus, modern economies abound in markets. Producers go to resource markets (raw-material markets, labor markets, money markets), buy resources, turn them into goods and services, and sell them to intermediaries, who sell them to consumers. The consumers sell their labor, for which they receive income to pay for the goods and services that they buy. The government is another market that plays several roles. It buys goods from resource, producer, and intermediaries markets; it pays them; it taxes these markets (including consumer markets); and it returns needed public services. Thus, each nation's economy and the whole world economy consist of complex interacting sets of markets that are linked through exchange processes.

Marketers are keenly interested in markets. Their goal is to understand the needs and wants of specific markets and to select the markets that they can serve best. In turn, they can develop products and services that will create value and satisfaction for customers in these markets, resulting in sales and profits for the company.

## MARKETING

The concept of markets finally brings us full circle to the concept of marketing. Marketing means managing markets to bring about exchanges and relationships for the purpose of creating value and satisfying needs and wants. Thus, we return to our definition of marketing as a process by which individuals and groups obtain what they need and want by creating and exchanging products and value with others.

Exchange processes involve work. Sellers must search for buyers, identify their needs, design good products and services, set reasonable prices for them, promote them effectively, and store and deliver them efficiently. Activities such as product development, research, communication, distribution, pricing, and service are core marketing activities. Although we normally think of marketing as being carried on by sellers, buyers also carry on marketing activities. Consumers do "marketing" when they search for the goods they need at prices they can afford. Company purchasing agents do "marketing" when they track down sellers and bargain for good terms.

Figure 1-2 shows the main elements in a modern marketing system. In the usual situation, marketing involves serving a market of end users in the face of competitors. The company and the competitors send their respective products and messages to consumers either directly or through marketing intermediaries. All of the actors in the system are affected by major environmental forces (demographic, economic, physical, technological, political/legal, social/cultural).

**FIGURE 1-2**
*Main actors and forces in a modern marketing system*

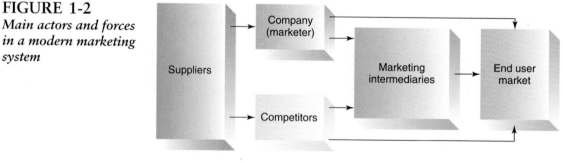

Suppliers

Company (marketer)

Competitors

Marketing intermediaries

End user market

**Environment**

Each party in the system adds value for the next level. Thus, a company's success depends not only on its own actions, but also on how well the entire system serves the needs of final consumers. Wal-Mart cannot fulfill its promise of low prices unless its suppliers provide merchandise at low costs. And Ford cannot deliver high quality to car buyers unless its dealers provide outstanding service.

# ▶MARKETING MANAGEMENT

We define **marketing management** as the analysis, planning, implementation, and control of programs designed to create, build, and maintain beneficial exchanges with target buyers for the purpose of achieving organizational objectives. Thus, marketing management involves managing demand, which in turn involves managing customer relationships.

**Marketing management**
The analysis, planning, implementation, and control of programs designed to create, build, and maintain beneficial exchanges with target buyers for the purpose of achieving organizational objectives.

## DEMAND MANAGEMENT

Some people think of marketing management as finding enough customers for the company's current output, but this is too limited a view. The organization has a desired level of demand for its products. At any point in time, there may be no demand, adequate demand, irregular demand, or too much demand, and marketing management must find ways to deal with these different demand states. Marketing management is concerned not only with finding and increasing demand, but also with changing or even reducing it.

For example, Golden Gate Bridge sometimes carries an unsafe level of traffic, and Yosemite National Park is badly overcrowded in the summertime. Power companies sometimes have trouble meeting demand during peak usage periods. In these and other cases of excess demand, the needed marketing task, called **demarketing,** is to reduce demand temporarily or permanently. The aim of demarketing is not to destroy demand, but only to reduce or shift it.[10] Thus, marketing management seeks to affect the level, timing, and nature of demand in a way that helps the organization achieve its objectives. Simply put, marketing management is *demand management*.

**Demarketing**
Marketing to reduce demand temporarily or permanently; the aim is not to destroy demand, but only to reduce or shift it.

## BUILDING PROFITABLE CUSTOMER RELATIONSHIPS

Managing demand means managing customers. A company's demand comes from two groups: new customers and repeat customers. Traditional marketing theory and practice have focused on attracting new customers and making the sale. Today, however, the emphasis is shifting. Beyond designing strategies to *attract* new customers and create *transactions* with them, companies now are going all out to *retain* current customers and build lasting customer *relationships*.

Why the new emphasis on keeping customers? In the past, companies facing an expanding economy and rapidly growing markets could practice the "leaky-bucket" approach to marketing. Growing markets meant a plentiful supply of new customers. Companies could keep filling the marketing bucket with new customers

## MARKETING AT WORK 1-2

# CUSTOMER RELATIONSHIPS: KEEPING CUSTOMERS SATISFIED

Some companies go to extremes to coddle their customers. Consider the following examples:

• An L. L. Bean customer says he lost all his fishing equipment—and nearly his life—when a raft he bought from the company leaked and forced him to swim to shore. He recovered the raft and sent it to the company along with a letter asking for a new raft and $700 to cover the fishing equipment he says he lost. He gets both.

• An American Express cardholder fails to pay more than $5,000 of his September bill. He explains that during the summer he'd purchased expensive rugs in Turkey. When he got home, appraisals showed that the rugs were worth half of what he'd paid. Rather than asking suspicious questions or demanding payment, the American Express representative notes the dispute, asks for a letter summarizing the appraisers' estimates, and offers to help solve the problem. And until the conflict is resolved, American Express doesn't ask for payment.

• Under the sultry summer sun, a Southwest Airlines flight attendant pulls shut the door and the Boeing 737 pushes away. Meanwhile, a

ticket holder, sweat streaming from her face, races down the jetway, only to find that she's arrived too late. However, the Southwest pilot spies the anguished passenger and returns to the gate to pick her up. Says Southwest's executive vice president for customers, "It broke every rule in the book, but we congratulated the pilot on a job well done."

• A frustrated homeowner faces a difficult and potentially costly home plumbing repair. He visits the nearby Home Depot store, prowls the aisles, and picks up an armful of parts and supplies—$67 worth in all—that he thinks he'll need to do the job. However, before he gets to the checkout counter, a Home Depot salesperson heads him off. After some coaxing, the salesperson finally convinces the do-it-yourselfer that there's a simpler solution to his repair problem. The cost: $5.99 and a lot less trouble.

From a dollars-and-cents point of view, these examples sound like a crazy way to do business. How can you make money by giving away your products, providing free extra services, talking your customers into paying less, or letting customers get away without paying their bills

on time? Yet studies show that going to such extremes to keep customers happy—although costly—goes hand in hand with good financial performance. Satisfied customers come back again and again. Thus, in today's highly competitive marketplace, companies can well afford to lose money on one transaction if it helps to cement a profitable long-term customer relationship.

Keeping customers satisfied involves more than simply opening a complaint department, smiling a lot, and being nice. Companies that do the best job of taking care of customers set high customer-service standards and often make seemingly outlandish efforts to achieve them. At these companies, exceptional value and service are more than a set of policies or actions—they are a company-wide attitude, an important part of the overall company culture. Concern for the consumer becomes a matter of pride for everyone in the company. American Express loves to

without worrying about losing old customers through holes in the bottom of the bucket. However, companies today are facing some new marketing realities. Changing demographics, a slow-growth economy, more sophisticated competitors, and overcapacity in many industries—all of these factors mean that there are fewer new customers to go around. Many companies are now fighting for shares of flat or fading markets. Thus, the costs of attracting new customers are rising. In fact, it costs five times as much to attract a new customer as it does to keep a current customer satisfied.[11]

Companies are also realizing that losing a customer means more than losing a single sale: It means losing the entire stream of purchases that the customer would make over a lifetime of patronage. For example, the *customer*

tell stories about how its people have rescued customers from disasters ranging from civil wars to earthquakes, no matter what the cost. The company gives cash rewards of up to $1,000 to "Great Performers" such as Barbara Weber, who moved mountains of State Department and Treasury Department bureaucratic red tape to refund $980 in stolen traveler's checks to a customer stranded in Cuba. Four Seasons Hotels, long known for outstanding service, tells its employees the story of Ron Dyment, a doorman in Toronto, who forgot to load a departing guest's briefcase into his taxi. The doorman called the guest, a lawyer in Washington, DC, and learned that he desperately needed the briefcase for a meeting the following morning. Without first asking for approval from management, Dyment hopped on a plane and returned the briefcase. The company named Dyment Employee of the Year. Similarly, the Nordstrom department store chain thrives on stories about its service heroics, such as employees dropping off orders at customers' homes or warming up customers' cars while they spend a little more time shopping. There's even a story about a customer who got a refund on a tire—Nordstrom doesn't carry tires, but it prides itself on a no-questions-asked return policy!

There's no simple formula for taking care of customers, but neither is it a mystery. According to the president of L. L. Bean, "A lot of people have fancy things to say about customer service . . . but it's just a day-in, day-out, ongoing, never-ending, unremitting, persevering, compassionate type of activity." For the companies that do it well, it's also very rewarding.

*Satisfied customers come back again and again. The customer lifetime value of a Taco Bell customer exceeds $12,000.*

*Sources*: Bill Kelley, "Five Companies That Do It Right—and Make It Pay," *Sales & Marketing Management*, April 1988, pp. 57–64; Patricia Sellers, "Companies That Serve You Best," *Fortune*, May 31, 1993, pp. 74-88; and Rahul Jacob, "Why Some Customers Are More Equal than Others," *Fortune*, September 19, 1994, pp. 215–224.

*lifetime value* of a Taco Bell customer exceeds $12,000.[12] For General Motors or Ford, a customer's lifetime value might well exceed $340,000. Thus, working to retain customers makes good economic sense. A company can lose money on a specific transaction, but still benefit greatly from a long-term relationship.

Attracting new customers remains an important marketing management task. However, today's companies must also focus on retaining current customers and building profitable, long-term relationships with them. The key to customer retention is superior customer value and satisfaction. With this in mind, many companies are going to extremes to keep their customers satisfied. (See Marketing at Work 1-2.)

# ▶ MARKETING MANAGEMENT PHILOSOPHIES

We describe marketing management as carrying out tasks to achieve desired exchanges with target markets. What *philosophy* should guide these marketing efforts? What weight should be given to the interests of the organization, customers, and society? Very often, these interests conflict.

There are five alternative concepts under which organizations conduct their marketing activities: the *production, product, selling, marketing,* and *societal marketing* concepts.

## THE PRODUCTION CONCEPT

**Production concept**
The philosophy that consumers will favor products that are available and highly affordable and that management should therefore focus on improving production and distribution efficiency.

The **production concept** holds that consumers will favor products that are available and highly affordable. Therefore, management should focus on improving production and distribution efficiency. This concept is one of the oldest philosophies that guides sellers.

The production concept is still a useful philosophy in two types of situations. The first occurs when the demand for a product exceeds the supply. Here, management should look for ways to increase production. The second situation occurs when the product's cost is too high and improved productivity is needed to bring it down. For example, Henry Ford's whole philosophy was to perfect the production of the Model T so that its cost could be reduced and more people could afford it. He joked about offering people a car of any color as long as it was black.

For many years, Texas Instruments (TI) followed a philosophy of increased production and lower costs in order to bring down prices. It won a major share of the American handheld calculator market using this approach. However, companies operating under a production philosophy run a major risk of focusing too narrowly on their own operations. For example, when TI used this strategy in the digital watch market, it failed. Although TI's watches were priced low, customers did not find them very attractive. In its drive to bring down prices, TI lost sight of something else that its customers wanted—namely, affordable, *attractive* digital watches.

## THE PRODUCT CONCEPT

**Product concept**
The idea that consumers will favor products that offer the most quality, performance, and features and that the organization should therefore devote its energy to making continuous product improvements. A detailed version of the new-product idea stated in meaningful consumer terms.

Another major concept guiding sellers, the **product concept,** holds that consumers will favor products that offer the most quality, performance, and innovative features. Thus, an organization should devote energy to making continuous product improvements. Some manufacturers believe that if they can build a better mousetrap, the world will beat a path to their door.[13] But they are often rudely shocked. Buyers may well be looking for a better solution to a mouse problem, but not necessarily for a better mousetrap. The solution might be a chemical spray, an exterminating service, or something else that works better than a mousetrap. Furthermore, a better mousetrap will not sell unless the manufacturer designs, packages, and prices it attractively; places it in convenient distribution channels; brings it to the attention of people who need it; and convinces buyers that it is a better product than those of competitors.

The product concept also can lead to "marketing myopia." For instance, railroad management once thought that users wanted *trains* rather than *transportation* and overlooked the growing challenge of airlines, buses, trucks, and automobiles. Many colleges have assumed that high school graduates want a liberal arts education and have thus overlooked the increasing challenge of vocational schools.

## THE SELLING CONCEPT

**Selling concept**
The idea that consumers will not buy enough of the organization's product unless the organization undertakes a large-scale selling and promotion effort.

Many organizations follow the **selling concept,** which holds that consumers will not buy enough of the organization's products unless it undertakes a large-scale selling and promotion effort. The concept is typically practiced with unsought goods—those that consumers do not normally think of buying, such as encyclopedias or insurance. These industries must be good at tracking down prospective buyers and selling them on product benefits.

Most firms practice the selling concept when they have overcapacity. Their aim is to sell what they make rather than make what the market wants. Such marketing carries high risks. It focuses on creating sales transactions rather than on building long-term, profitable relationships with customers. It assumes that customers who are coaxed into buying the product will like it. Or, if they don't like it, they will possibly forget their disappointment and buy it again later. These are usually poor assumptions to make about buyers. Most studies show that dissatisfied customers do not buy again. Worse yet, while the average satisfied customer tells three others about good buying experiences, the average dissatisfied customer tells ten others about his or her bad experiences.[14]

## THE MARKETING CONCEPT ~CUSTOMER DRIVEN

**Marketing concept**
The marketing management philosophy that holds that achieving organizational goals depends on determining the needs and wants of target markets and delivering the desired satisfactions more effectively and efficiently than competitors do.

The **marketing concept** holds that achieving organizational goals depends on determining the needs and wants of target markets and delivering the desired satisfactions more effectively and efficiently than competitors do. The marketing concept has been stated in a variety of colorful ways, such as "We make it happen for you" (Marriott); "To fly, to serve" (British Airways); and "We're not satisfied until you are" (General Electric). JCPenney's motto also summarizes the marketing concept: "To do all in our power to pack the customer's dollar full of value, quality, and satisfaction."

The selling concept and the marketing concept are sometimes confused. Figure 1-3 compares the two concepts. The selling concept takes an *inside-out*

**FIGURE 1-3**
*The selling and marketing concepts contrasted*

| Starting point | Focus | Means | Ends |
|---|---|---|---|
| Factory | Existing products | Selling and promoting | Profits through sales volume |

THE SELLING CONCEPT

| Market | Customer needs | Integrated marketing | Profits through customer satisfaction |
|---|---|---|---|

THE MARKETING CONCEPT

## MARKETING AT WORK 1-3

# McDonald's Applies the Marketing Concept

McDonald's Corporation, the fast-food hamburger retailer, is a master marketer. With 14,000 outlets in 79 countries and more than $23 billion in annual systemwide sales, McDonald's doubles the sales of its nearest rival, Burger King, and triples those of third-place Wendy's. Nineteen million customers pass through the famous golden arches each day, and an astounding 96 percent of all Americans eat at McDonald's each year. McDonald's now serves 145 hamburgers per sec-

ond. Credit for this performance belongs to a strong marketing orientation: McDonald's knows how to serve people and adapt to changing consumer wants.

McDonald's marketing philosophy is captured in its motto of "Q.S.C. & V.," which stands for quality, service, cleanliness, and value. Customers enter a spotlessly clean restaurant, walk up to a friendly counterperson, quickly receive a good-tasting meal, and eat it there or take it out. There are no jukeboxes or telephones to

create a teenage hangout. Nor are there any cigarette machines or newspaper racks—McDonald's is a family affair, appealing strongly to children.

McDonald's has mastered the art of serving consumers, and it carefully teaches the basics to its employees and franchisees. All franchisees take training courses at McDonald's Hamburger University in Elk Grove Village, Illinois. They emerge with a degree in Hamburgerology and a minor in

*McDonald's delivers "quality, service, cleanliness, and value" to customers around the world, here in the world's largest McDonald's in Beijing.*

perspective. It starts with the factory, focuses on the company's existing products, and calls for heavy selling and promotion to obtain profitable sales. It focuses heavily on customer conquest—getting short-term sales with little concern about who buys or why. In contrast, the marketing concept takes an *outside-in* perspective. It starts with a well-defined market, focuses on customer needs, coordinates all the marketing activities affecting customers, and makes profits by creat-

french fries. McDonald's monitors product and service quality through continuous customer surveys and puts great energy into improving hamburger production methods in order to simplify operations, bring down costs, speed up service, and bring greater value to customers. Beyond these efforts, each McDonald's restaurant works to become a part of its neighborhood through community involvement and service projects.

In its 4,700 restaurants outside of the United States, McDonald's carefully customizes its menu and service to local tastes and customs. It serves corn soup and teriyaki burgers in Japan, pasta salads in Rome, and wine and live piano music with its McNuggets in Paris. In India, where cows are considered sacred, McDonald's sells veggie burgers instead of beef. Analysts predict that, by the end of the decade, 60 percent of the company's revenues will come from foreign sales.

When McDonald's opened its first restaurant in Moscow, it quickly won the hearts of Russian consumers. However, the company had to overcome some monstrous hurdles in order to meet its high standards for consumer satisfaction in this new market. It had to educate suppliers, employees, and even consumers about the time-tested McDonald's way of doing things. Technical experts were brought in from Canada to teach Russian farmers how to grow russet Burbank potatoes for french fries, and the company built its own pasteurizing plant to ensure a plentiful supply of fresh milk. It trained Russian managers at Hamburger University and subjected each of 630 new employees (most of whom didn't know a Chicken McNugget from an Egg McMuffin) to 16 to 20 hours of training on such essentials as cooking meat patties, assembling Filet-O-Fish sandwiches, and giving service with a smile.

McDonald's even had to train consumers—most Muscovites had never seen a fast-food restaurant. Customers waiting in line were shown videos telling them everything from how to order and pay at the counter to how to handle a Big Mac. And in its usual way, McDonald's began immediately to build community involvement. On opening day, it held a kick-off party for 700 Muscovite orphans, and it donated all opening-day proceeds to the Moscow Children's Fund. As a result, the new Moscow restaurant got off to a very successful start. About 50,000 customers swarmed through the restaurant during its first day of business.

Riding on its success in Moscow, McDonald's continues to pursue opportunities to serve new customers around the globe. It soon opened its largest restaurant anywhere, in Beijing, China. The 28,000-square-foot restaurant has 29 cash registers and seats 700 people. Through this huge Beijing outlet, McDonald's treats more than ten thousand customers each day to its special brand of customer care.

Thus, McDonald's focus on consumers has made it the world's largest food-service organization. It now captures about 20 percent of America's fast-food business and is rapidly expanding its worldwide presence. McDonald's has been the nation's most profitable retailer over the past 10 years. Its huge success has been reflected in the increased value of its stock over the years: 250 shares of McDonald's stock purchased for less that $6,000 in 1965 would be worth well over a million dollars today!

*Sources*: Gail McKnight, "Here Comes Bolshoi Mac," *USA Today Weekend*, January 26–28, 1990, pp. 4–5; Rosemarie Boyle, "McDonald's Gives Soviets Something Worth Waiting For," *Advertising Age*, March 19, 1990, p. 61; "Food Draws Raves, Prices Don't at Beijing McDonald's Opening," *Durham Herald-Sun*, April 12, 1992, p. B12; Andrew E. Serwer, "McDonald's Conquers the World," *Fortune*, October 17, 1994, pp. 103–16; and Greg Burns, "All the World's a McStage," *Business Week*, May 8, 1995, p. 8.

ing long-term customer relationships based on customer value and satisfaction. Under the marketing concept, companies produce what consumers want, thereby satisfying consumers and making profits.[15]

Many successful and well-known companies have adopted the marketing concept. Procter & Gamble, Disney, Wal-Mart, Marriott, Nordstrom, and McDonald's follow it faithfully (see Marketing at Work 1-3). L. L. Bean, the highly successful catalog retailer of clothing and outdoor sporting equipment, was founded on the marketing concept. In 1912, in his first circulars, L. L. Bean included the following notice: "I do not consider a sale complete until goods are worn out and the customer still is satisfied. We will thank anyone to return goods that are not perfectly satisfactory . . . . Above all things we wish to avoid having a dissatisfied customer."

Today, L. L. Bean dedicates itself to giving "perfect satisfaction in every way." To inspire its employees to practice the marketing concept, L. L. Bean has for decades displayed posters around its offices that proclaim the following:

> What is a customer? A customer is the most important person ever in this company—in person or by mail. A customer is not dependent on us, we are dependent on him. A customer is not an interruption of our work, he is the purpose of it. We are not doing a favor by serving him, he is doing us a favor by giving us the opportunity to do so. A customer is not someone to argue or match wits with—nobody ever won an argument with a customer. A customer is a person who brings us his wants—it is our job to handle them profitably to him and to ourselves.

In contrast, many companies claim to practice the marketing concept, but do not. They have the *forms* of marketing, such as a marketing vice president, product managers, marketing plans, and marketing research, but this does not mean that they are *market-focused* and *customer-driven* companies. The question is whether they are finely tuned to changing customer needs and competitor strategies. Formerly great companies—General Motors, IBM, Sears, Zenith—all lost substantial market share because they failed to adjust their marketing strategies to the changing marketplace.

Several years of hard work are needed to turn a sales-oriented company into a marketing-oriented company. The goal is to build customer satisfaction into the very fabric of the firm. Customer satisfaction is no longer a fad. As one marketing analyst notes: "It's becoming a way of life in corporate America . . . as embedded into corporate cultures as information technology and strategic planning."[16]

# THE SOCIETAL MARKETING CONCEPT

**Societal marketing concept**
The idea that the organization should determine the needs, wants, and interests of target markets and deliver the desired satisfactions more effectively and efficiently than competitors in a way that maintains or improves the consumer's and society's well-being.

The **societal marketing concept** holds that the organization should determine the needs, wants, and interests of target markets. It should then deliver superior value to customers in a way that maintains or improves the consumer's *and the society's* well-being. The societal marketing concept is the newest of the five marketing management philosophies.

The societal marketing concept questions whether the pure marketing concept is adequate in an age of environmental problems, resource shortages, rapid population growth, worldwide economic stress, and neglected social services. Firms that sense, serve, and satisfy individual wants may not always do what's best for consumers and society in the long run. According to the societal marketing concept, the pure marketing concept overlooks possible conflicts between consumer *short-run wants* and consumer *long-run welfare*.

Consider the fast-food industry. Most people see today's giant fast-food chains as offering tasty and convenient food at reasonable prices. Yet many consumer and environmental groups have voiced concerns. Critics point out that hamburgers, fried chicken, french fries, and most other foods sold by fast-food restaurants are high in fat and salt, which may have long-term health hazards. These products are wrapped in convenient packaging, but this leads to waste and pollution. Thus, in satisfying consumer wants, the highly successful fast-food chains may be harming consumer health and causing environmental problems.

Such concerns and conflicts led to the societal marketing concept. As Figure 1-4 shows, the societal marketing concept calls upon marketers to balance three considerations in setting their marketing policies: company profits, consumer wants, and society's interests. Originally, most companies based their marketing decisions largely on short-run company profit. Eventually, they began to recognize the long-run importance of satisfying consumer wants, and the marketing concept emerged. Now many companies are beginning to consider society's interests when making their marketing decisions.

One such company is Johnson & Johnson, rated recently in a *Fortune* magazine poll as America's most admired company for community and environmental responsibility. J&J's concern for societal interests is summarized in a company document called "Our Credo," which stresses honesty, integrity, and putting people before profits. Under this credo, Johnson & Johnson would rather take a big loss than ship a bad batch of one of its products. And the company supports many community and employee programs that benefit its consumers and workers, as well as the environment. J&J's chief executive puts it this way: "If we keep trying to do what's right, at the end of the day we believe the marketplace will reward us."[17]

The company backs these words with actions. Consider the tragic tampering case in which eight people died from swallowing cyanide-laced capsules of Tylenol, a Johnson & Johnson brand. Although J&J believed that the pills had been altered in only a few stores, not in the factory, it quickly recalled all of its product. The recall cost the company $240 million in earnings. In the long run, however, the company's swift recall of Tylenol strengthened consumer confidence and loyalty, and Tylenol remains the nation's leading brand of pain reliever. In this and other cases, J&J management has found that doing what's right benefits both consumers and the company. Says the chief executive: "The Credo should not be viewed as some kind of social welfare program . . . it's just plain good business."[18] Thus, over the years, Johnson & Johnson's dedication to consumers and community service has made it one of America's most admired companies *and* one of the most profitable.

## FIGURE 1-4
*Three considerations underlying the societal marketing concept*

# ▶ MARKETING CHALLENGES INTO THE NEXT CENTURY

Marketing operates within a dynamic global environment. Every decade calls upon marketing managers to think freshly about their marketing objectives and practices. Rapid changes can quickly make yesterday's winning strategies obsolete. As management expert Peter Drucker once observed, a company's winning formula for the last decade will probably be its undoing in the next decade.

What are the marketing challenges as we head into the twenty-first century? Today's companies are wrestling with changing customer values and orientations, economic stagnation, environmental decline, increased global competition, and a host of other economic, political, and social problems. However, these problems also provide marketing opportunities. We now look more deeply into several key trends and forces that are changing the marketing landscape and challenging marketing strategy: growth of nonprofit marketing, the information technology boom, rapid globalization, the changing world economy, and the call for more socially responsible actions.

## GROWTH OF NONPROFIT MARKETING

In the past, marketing has been most widely applied in the business sector. In recent years, however, marketing also has become a major component in the strategies of many nonprofit organizations, such as colleges, hospitals, museums, symphony orchestras, and even churches. Consider the following examples:

> As hospital costs and room rates soar, many hospitals face underutilization, especially in their maternity and pediatrics sections. Many have taken steps toward marketing. A Philadelphia hospital, competing for maternity patients, offered a steak and champagne dinner with candlelight for new parents. St. Mary's Medical Center in Evanston, Indiana, uses innovative billboards to promote its emergency care service. Other hospitals, in an effort to attract physicians, have installed services such as saunas, chauffeurs, and private tennis courts.[19]

> Before even opening its doors, one new church hired a research firm to find out what its customers would want. The research showed that the "unchurched"—people with no current church connection— found church boring and church services irrelevant to their everyday lives. They complained churches were always hitting them up for money. So the church added contemporary music and skits, loosened its dress codes, and presented sermons on topics such as money management and parenting. Its direct mail piece read: "Given up on the church? We don't blame you. Lots of people have. They're fed up with boring sermons, ritual that doesn't mean anything . . . music that nobody likes . . . [and] preachers who seem to be more interested in your wallet than you. . . . Church can be different. Give us a shot." The results have been impressive. Since opening its doors a little more than a year ago, the church has attracted nearly 400 members, 80 percent of whom were not previously attending church.[20]

*Nonprofit marketing: The Arthritis Foundation boosts its budget by licensing its name and symbol to a line of pain relievers marketed by McNeil Consumer Products.*

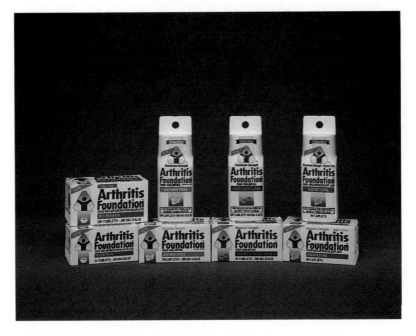

Many nonprofit organizations are now licensing their names and symbols to what they deem appropriate products and making royalties off sales. Two recent examples include the Arthritis Foundation Pain Reliever, marketed by McNeil Consumer Products, and VFW Coffee, marketed by Tetley. The VFW name may soon be associated with a product marketed by Adolph Coors. Royalties from such products can provide a significant boost to the budgets of nonprofits previously dependent on donations for survival.[21]

Similarly, many private colleges, facing declining enrollments and rising costs, are using marketing to compete for students and funds. They are defining target markets, improving their communication and promotion, and responding better to student needs and wants. Many of America's 300,000 churches, which are having trouble keeping members and attracting financial support, are conducting marketing research to gain a better understanding of member needs and are redesigning their "service offerings" accordingly. Many performing arts groups—even the Lyric Opera Company of Chicago, which has seasonal sellouts—face huge operating deficits that they must cover by more aggressive donor marketing. Finally, many longstanding nonprofit organizations—the YMCA, the Salvation Army, the Girl Scouts—have lost members and are now modernizing their missions and "products" to attract more members and donors.[22]

Even government agencies have shown an increased interest in marketing. For example, the U.S. Army has a marketing plan to attract recruits, and various government agencies are now designing *social marketing campaigns* to encourage energy conservation and concern for the environment or to discourage smoking, excessive drinking, and drug use. The once-stodgy U.S. Postal Service has developed innovative marketing plans. For example, in one nationwide campaign, the postal service worked to gain support for the U.S. Olympic team:

An official Olympic sponsor, the postal service launched a promotion designed to shower Olympic athletes with cards and to raise money for the team. It sponsored Olympic Spirit Week at 28,000 post offices around the nation, where it invited customers to sign a piece of the "world's largest postcard," a 348 foot by 523 foot giant that said "America Salutes Team USA." Customers who donated a dollar received two regular-size copies of the card. They were encouraged to send one copy to an Olympic athlete and keep the other as a souvenir. The postal service planned to spend about $100 million on Olympic sponsorship but expected a net profit of about $50 million through increased sales of postal products.[23]

The continued growth of nonprofit and public sector marketing presents new and exciting challenges for marketing managers.

# THE INFORMATION TECHNOLOGY BOOM

The boom in computer, telephone, and television technology, as well as the merging of these technologies, has had a major impact on the way businesses produce and market their products. Through videoconferencing, marketing executives in Sydney, Tokyo, Paris, and New York meet in "real time" without ever stepping onto a plane. Direct marketers can know everything from what type of car you drive to what you read to what flavor of ice cream you prefer, all with a few clicks of a mouse button. And a small business in Ann Arbor, Michigan, can advertise its products to a world-wide audience of millions, 24 hours a day, for less than the cost of an ad in a neighborhood newspaper. John Naisbitt, the author of *Megatrends* and *The Global Paradox*, says, "Telecommunications is the driving force that is simultaneously creating the huge global economy and making its parts smaller and more powerful."[24]

At the heart of this phenomenon is the Information Superhighway and its backbone, the Internet (or "net," as it's called by users). The Internet, which has no ownership or central management, is a web of more than 2.2 million computers linked by telephone on more than 32,400 connected computer networks. Accessible in 135 countries and territories, its membership is growing at the rate of 10 to 15 percent a month. Created little more than a decade ago as a link among a sprinkling of government agencies and academic communities, the Internet is fast being embraced by businesses. Companies are using the net to link employees in remote offices, stay in touch with customers and suppliers, and distribute sales information more quickly. As new technologies make the Internet more accessible and user-friendly, companies will gain access to millions of new customers at a fraction of the cost of print and television advertising.

# RAPID GLOBALIZATION

The world economy has undergone radical change during the past two decades. Geographical and cultural distances have shrunk with the advent of jet planes, fax machines, global computer and telephone hookups, world television satellite broadcasts, and other technical advances. This has allowed companies to greatly expand their geographical market coverage, purchasing, and manufacturing. The result is a vastly more complex marketing environment, for both companies and consumers.

Today, almost every company, large or small, is touched in some way by global competition—from the neighborhood florist that buys its flowers from Mexican nurseries, to the small New York clothing retailer that imports its merchandise from Asia, to the U.S. electronics manufacturer that competes in its home markets with giant Japanese rivals, to the large American consumer goods producer that introduces new products into emerging markets abroad.

American firms have been challenged at home by the skillful marketing of European and Asian multinationals. Companies like Toyota, Siemens, Nestlé, Sony, and Samsung often have outperformed their U.S. competitors in American markets. Similarly, U.S. companies in a wide range of industries have found new opportunities abroad. General Motors, Exxon, IBM, General Electric, Du Pont, Motorola, Coca-Cola, and dozens of other American companies have developed truly global operations, making and selling their products worldwide. Marketing at Work 1-4 provides just a few of countless examples of U.S. companies taking advantage of international marketing opportunities.

Today, companies are not only trying to sell more of their locally produced goods in international markets, they also are buying more components and supplies abroad. For example, Bill Blass, one of America's top fashion designers, may choose cloth woven from Australian wool with printed designs from Italy. He will design a dress and fax the drawing to a Hong Kong agent who will place the order with a China factory. Finished dresses will be airfreighted to New York, where they will be redistributed to department and specialty stores around the country.

Many domestically purchased goods and services are "hybrids," with design, materials purchases, manufacturing, and marketing taking place in several countries. Americans who decide to "buy American" might understandably decide to avoid Hondas and purchase Dodge Colts. Imagine their surprise when they learn that the Colt actually was made in Japan, whereas the Honda was primarily assembled in the United States from American-made parts.

Thus, managers in countries around the world are asking: Just what is global marketing? How does it differ from domestic marketing? How do global competitors and forces affect our business? To what extent should we "go global"? Many companies are forming strategic alliances with foreign companies, even competitors, who serve as suppliers or marketing partners. The past few years have produced some surprising alliances between competitors such as Ford and Mazda, General Electric and Matsushita, and AT&T and Olivetti. Successful companies in the next century may well be those that have built the best global networks.

# THE CHANGING WORLD ECONOMY

A large part of the world has grown poorer during the past few decades. A sluggish world economy has resulted in more difficult times for both consumers and marketers. Around the world, people's needs are greater than ever, but in many areas, people lack the means to pay for needed goods. Markets, after all, consist of people with needs *and* purchasing power. In many cases, the latter is currently lacking. In the United States, although wages have risen, real buying power has declined, especially for the less skilled members of the work force. Many U.S. households have managed to maintain their buying power only because both spouses work. However, many workers have lost their jobs as manufacturers have downsized to cut costs.

## MARKETING AT WORK 1-4

# TAKING ADVANTAGE OF GLOBAL OPPORTUNITIES

Many U.S. companies are moving aggressively to take advantage of global marketing opportunities. Here are just three examples.

### COCA-COLA

Coca-Cola has recently watched the domestic cola market go flat. Although Coca-Cola Classic captures 20 percent of the U.S. soft-drink market, the U.S. cola market has shrunk from 64 percent of all soft-drink sales in 1984 to only 59 percent now. To counter slow growth at home, Coca-Cola has expanded its international operations at a furious pace. For example, in the first six months of 1994 alone, the company opened plants or reentered markets in seven countries, including Russia, Poland, India, South Africa, and Vietnam.

Coca-Cola is revving up every aspect of its global marketing—cutting-edge advertising, new packaging, product sampling, and event sponsorships. It has treated the entire world to its innovative "Always Coca-Cola" advertising campaign, featuring everything from star-gazing polar bears to punk rockers. The company successfully resurrected the classic contour Coke bottle—the world's best-known package. Coke also revived another classic marketing practice—consumer sampling. This summer, it gave away thousands of gallons of free Coke to German consumers. As a result of these and other actions, Coke's third-quarter worldwide sales grew at the eye-popping rate of 12 percent, more than twice the growth rate of domestic sales. In international markets, Coke outsells its leading competitor, Pepsi, at a rate of three to one.

*Companies like Coca-Cola are moving aggressively to take advantage of global growth opportunities.*

Current economic conditions create both problems and opportunities for marketers. Some companies are facing declining demand and see few opportunities for growth. Others, however, are developing new solutions to changing consumer problems. Many are finding ways to offer consumers more for less. Wal-Mart rose to market leadership on two principles, emblazoned on every Wal-Mart store: "Satisfaction Guaranteed" and "We Sell for Less—Always." Consumers enter a Wal-Mart store, are welcomed by a friendly greeter, and find a huge assortment of good-quality merchandise at everyday low prices. The same principle explains the explosive growth of factory outlet malls and discount chains—these days, customers want value. This even applies to luxury products: Toyota introduced its successful Lexus luxury automobile with the headline "Perhaps the First Time in History that Trading a $72,000 Car for a $36,000 Car Could Be Considered Trading Up."

### Toys 'R' Us

Toys 'R' Us spent several years slogging through the swamps of Japanese bureaucracy before it was allowed to open the very first large U.S. discount store in Japan, the world's No. 2 toy market behind the United States. The entry of this foreign giant has Japanese toymakers and retailers edgy. The typical small Japanese toy store stocks only 1,000 to 2,000 items, whereas Toys 'R' Us stores carry as many as 15,000. And the discounter will likely offer toys at prices that are 10 to 15 percent below those of competitors.

The opening of the first Japanese store was "astonishing," attracting more than 60,000 visitors in the first three days. After just two years, Toys 'R' Us now has 24 Japanese stores, each drawing huge crowds and grabbing a 4 percent share of the market. Within another year, it plans to have 35 stores and a 10 percent market share. The U.S. retailer appears to be benefiting from profound social change in Japan. According to one source, "Japan's absentee, workaholic salaryman father is increasingly becoming a relic, and his successor is taking life easier, spending more time with his family. Japanese families now spend more time together. . . . On Sunday they . . . go out to lunch and then browse at a big store like Toys 'R' Us . . . Toys 'R' Us has made shopping a form of leisure in Japan."

If the company succeeds in Japan as well as it has in Europe, Japanese retailers will have their hands full. Toys 'R' Us began with just five Western European stores in 1985 but now has 181 and plans to open more. European sales are growing at triple the rate of total company sales.

### MTV

After ten years of relentless growth in America, Music Television's (MTV) home market has become saturated. However, the U.S. music video network is exploding abroad. For example, it's a monster hit in Europe. Established in 1990, MTV Europe now reaches 27 countries and 59 million homes, almost a million more than U.S. MTV.

The network is aggressively pan-European: Its programming and advertising are the same throughout Europe, and they are all in English. It has almost single-handedly created a Eurolanguage of simplified English. MTV meets the common concerns of teens worldwide, broadcasting news and socially conscious programming such as features on the plight of European immigrants and notes on global warming. MTV Europe has convinced advertisers that a true Euroconsumer exists. It delivers advertising from companies such as Levi Strauss, Procter & Gamble, Apple Computer, and Pepsi-Cola to a huge international audience. The company also operates MTV Asia, MTV Latino, and MTV Japan. In all, MTV reaches more than 240 million homes in 63 territories around the world.

*Sources:* Quote from Gale Eisenstodt, "Bull in the Japan Shop," *Forbes,* January 31, 1994, pp. 41–42. Also see Patricia Sellers, "Pepsi Opens Second Front," *Fortune,* August 8, 1994, pp. 70–76; Maria Mallory, "Behemoth on a Tear," *Business Week,* October 3, 1994, pp. 54–55; Havis Dawson, "Show Time! Pepsi-Cola International Plans Global Expansion," *Beverage World,* April 1995, p. 26; Kevin Cote, "Toys 'R' Us Grows in Europe," *Advertising Age,* April 27, 1992, pp. 1–16; Mark Evans, "From Toronto to Taiwan, TRU Broadens Reach," *Discount Store News,* February 6, 1995, p. 28; "MTV: Rock On," *The Economist,* August 3, 1991, p. 66; and Shawn Tully, "Teens: The Most Global Market of All," *Fortune,* May 16, 1994, pp. 90–97.

# THE CALL FOR MORE ETHICS AND SOCIAL RESPONSIBILITY

A third factor in today's marketing environment is the increased call for companies to take responsibility for the social and environmental impact of their actions. Corporate ethics has become a hot topic in almost every business arena, from the corporate boardroom to the business school classroom. And few companies can ignore the renewed demands of the environmental movement.

The ethics and environmental movements will place even stricter demands on companies in the future. Consider recent environmental developments. After the fall of communism, the West was shocked to find out about the massive environmental negligence of the former Eastern Bloc governments. In many

*Today's forward-thinking companies are responding strongly to the ethics and environmental movements. Here, ITT states "All of our companies share a common goal: To improve the quality of life. Because it's not just how you make a living that's important, it's how you live."*

Eastern European countries, the air is fouled, the water is polluted, and the soil is poisoned by chemical dumping. In June 1992, representatives from more than one hundred countries attended the Earth Summit in Rio de Janeiro to consider how to handle such problems as the destruction of rain forests, global warming, endangered species, and other environmental threats. Clearly, in the future, companies will be held to an increasingly higher standard of environmental responsibility in their marketing and manufacturing activities.

## THE NEW MARKETING LANDSCAPE

The past decade taught business firms everywhere a humbling lesson. Domestic companies learned that they can no longer ignore global markets and competitors. Successful firms in mature industries learned that they cannot overlook emerging markets, technologies, and management approaches. Companies of every sort learned that they cannot remain inwardly focused, ignoring the needs of customers and their environment.

The most powerful U.S. companies of the 1970s included companies such as General Motors (GM) and Sears. But both of these giant companies failed at marketing, and today both are struggling. Each failed to understand its changing marketplace, its customers, and the need to provide value. Today, GM is still trying to figure out why so many consumers around the world switched to Japanese and European cars. Mighty Sears has lost its way, losing market share both to fashionable department and specialty stores on the one hand and to discount mass merchandisers on the other.

As we move into the next century, companies will have to become customer oriented and market driven in all that they do. It's not enough to be product or technology driven—too many companies still design their products without customer input, only to find them rejected in the marketplace. It is not enough to be good at winning new customers—too many companies forget about customers after the sale, only to lose their future business. Not surprisingly, we are now seeing a flood of books with titles such as *The Customer Driven Company, Customers for Life, The Only Thing that Matters: Bringing the Customer into the Center of Your Business, Turning Lost Customers into Gold, Customer Bonding,* and *Sustaining Knock Your Socks Off Service.*[25] These publications emphasize that the key to success on the rapidly changing marketing landscape will be a strong focus on the marketplace and a total marketing commitment to providing value to customers.

## SUMMARY

Today's successful companies share a strong customer focus and a serious commitment to marketing. Modern marketing seeks to attract new customers by promising superior value and to keep current customers by delivering satisfaction. Sound marketing is critical to the success of all organizations, whether large or small, for-profit or nonprofit, domestic or global.

Many people think of marketing as only selling or advertising. But, in fact, marketing occurs both before and after the selling event. Marketing combines many activities—marketing research, product development, distribution, pricing, advertising, personal selling, and others—designed to sense, serve, and satisfy consumer needs while meeting the organization's goals.

*Marketing* is a process by which individuals and groups obtain what they need and want through creating and exchanging products and value with others. The core concepts of marketing are *needs, wants, and demands; products; value, satisfaction, and quality; exchange, transactions, and relationships;* and *markets.*

*Marketing management* is the analysis, planning, implementation, and control of programs designed to create, build, and maintain beneficial exchanges with target markets in order to achieve organizational objectives. Marketers must be good at managing the level, timing, and composition of demand. Managing demand means managing relationships with customers. This involves both *attracting* new customers and *retaining* current customers. Recently, marketing managers have been shifting their emphasis to building profit-

able, long-term relationships with important customers.

Marketing management can be guided by five different philosophies. The *production concept* holds that consumers favor products that are available at low cost and that management's task is to improve production efficiency and bring down prices. The *product concept* holds that consumers favor quality products, and that if products are good enough, little promotional effort is required. The *selling concept* holds that consumers will not buy enough of the company's products unless stimulated by heavy selling and promotion. The *marketing concept* holds that a company gains competitive advantage by understanding the needs and wants of a well-defined target market and doing a superior job of delivering the desired satisfactions. The *societal marketing concept* holds that the company should generate customer satisfaction *and* long-run societal well-being as the keys to achieving both its goals and its responsibilities.

Marketing operates within a dynamic global environment. Rapid changes can quickly make yesterday's winning strategies obsolete. Marketers will face many new challenges and opportunities in the next century. Today's companies are wrestling with the growth of nonprofit marketing, increased global competition, a sluggish world economy, a call for greater social responsibility, and a host of other economic, political, and social challenges. However, these challenges also offer marketing opportunities. To be successful in the twenty-first century, companies will have to be strongly market focused.

## KEY TERMS

| | | |
|---|---|---|
| Customer value | Marketing concept | Selling concept |
| Customer satisfaction | Marketing management | Societal marketing concept |
| Demands | Needs | Total quality management |
| Demarketing | Product | Transaction |
| Exchange | Product concept | Wants |
| Market | Production concept | |
| Marketing | Relationship marketing | |

## QUESTIONS FOR DISCUSSION

1. Why should *you* study marketing?

2. Historian Arnold Toynbee and economist John Kenneth Galbraith have argued that the desires stimulated by marketing efforts are not genuine: "A man who is hungry need never be told of his need for food." Is this a valid criticism of marketing? Why or why not?

3. Describe how the notions of products, exchanges, and transactions apply when you buy a soft drink from a vending machine. Do they also apply when you vote for a political candidate?

4. The layout of Stew Leonard's Dairy Store in Norwalk, Connecticut, forces every food shopper to walk a single path, in the same direction, past every item in the store. This causes severe traffic jams in the store and its parking lots during peak shopping periods. Shopping cart colli-sions and frayed nerves are common. Should management try to discourage shoppers from coming to the store during peak periods, and, if so, what demarketing techniques would you suggest? What are the risks in this strategy?

5. What is the single biggest difference between the marketing concept and the production, product, and selling concepts? Which concepts are easiest to apply in the short run? Which concept can offer the best long-term success?

6. According to economist Milton Friedman, "Few trends could so thoroughly undermine the very foundations of our free society as the acceptance by corporate officials of a social responsibility other than to make as much money for their stockholders as possible." Do you agree or disagree with Friedman's statement? What are some drawbacks of the societal marketing concept?

## APPLYING THE CONCEPTS

1. Go to McDonald's and order a sandwich. Note the questions that you are asked by the cashier, and observe how special orders are handled. Next, go to Wendy's, Burger King, or a local pizza restaurant and order a sandwich or a pizza. Note the questions that you are asked here, and observe whether special orders are handled in the same way they are handled at McDonald's.

   ◆ Do you observe any significant differences in how orders are handled?

   ◆ Consider the differences that you saw. Do you think the restaurants have different marketing management philosophies? Which is closest to the marketing concept? Is one closer to the selling or production concept?

   ◆ What are the advantages of closely following the marketing concept? Are there any disadvantages?

2. Take a trip to your local mall. Find the directory sign. List five major categories of stores, such as department stores, shoe, book, and women's clothing shops, and restaurants. List the competing stores in each category, and take

a walk past them and quickly observe their merchandise and style. Take a look at the public spaces of the mall, and note how they are decorated. Watch the shoppers in the mall.

◆ Are the competing stores really unique, or might consumers perceive one as interchangeable for another?

◆ Did the shoppers buy items efficiently from a shopping list, as in a grocery store, or were they taking a different approach?

◆ Do the different stores attempt to maximize customer value and satisfaction? What role does product or service quality play in this effort?

# REFERENCES

1. Quotes in this Home Depot tale are from Patricia Sellers, "Companies That Serve You Best," *Fortune,* May 31, 1993, pp. 74–88. Also see Graham Button, "The Man Who Almost Walked Out on Ross Perot," *Forbes,* November 22, 1993, pp. 68–76; Ronald Henkoff, "Why Every Red-Blooded Consumer Owns a Truck," *Fortune,* May 29, 1995, pp. 86–100; and Patricia Sellers, "Can Home Depot Fix Its Sagging Stock?" *Fortune,* March 4, 1996, pp. 139–146.

2. See Theodore Levitt's classic article, "Marketing Myopia," *Harvard Business Review,* July–August 1960, pp. 45–56.

3. See "Pass the Parcel," *The Economist,* March 21, 1992, pp. 73–74; "ATW Awards 20 Years of Excellence in Cargo Service: Federal Express," *Air Transport World,* February 1994, pp. 48–52; and David Greising, "Watch Out for Flying Packages," *Business Week,* November 14, 1994, p. 40.

4. Richard Whitely, "Do Selling and Quality Mix?" *Sales & Marketing Management,* October 1993, p. 70. Also see Robert E. Hall, "The Dirty Half Dozen," *Sales & Marketing Management,* February, 1995, p. 76.

5. Thomas E. Caruso, "Got a Marketing Topic? Kotler Has an Opinion," *Marketing News,* June 8, 1992, p. 21.

6. Lois Therrien, "Motorola and NEC: Going for Glory," *Business Week,* special issue on quality, 1991, pp. 60–61.

7. See David Greising, "Quality: How to Make It Pay," *Business Week,* August 8, 1994, pp. 54–59; Roland T. Rust, Anthony J. Zahorik, and Timothy L. Keiningham, "Return on Quality (ROQ): Making Service Quality Financially Accountable," *Journal of Marketing,* April 1995, pp. 58–70; and Martha T. Moore, "Is TQM Dead?" *USA Today,* October 17, 1995, pp. B1, B2.

8. Edwin McDowell, "Ritz-Carlton's Keys to Good Service," *New York Times,* March 31, 1993, p. 1; and Don Peppers, "Digitizing Desire," *Forbes,* April 10, 1995, p. 76.

9. Andy Cohen, "It's Party Time for Saturn," *Sales & Marketing Management,* June 1994, p. 19; and T. L. Stanley, Betsy Spethman, Terry Lefton, and Karen Benezra, "Brand Builders," *Brandweek,* March 20, 1995, p. 20.

10. For more discussion on demand states, see Philip Kotler, *Marketing Management: Analysis, Planning, Implementation, and Control,* 9th ed. (Englewood Cliffs, NJ: Prentice Hall, 1997), Chapter 1.

11. See Joan C. Szabo, "Service=Survival," *Nation's Business,* March 1989, pp. 16–24; Kevin J. Clancy and Robert S. Shulman, "Breaking the Mold," *Sales & Marketing Management,* January 1994, pp. 82–84; James R. Rosenfield, "Plugging the Leaky Bucket," *Sales & Marketing Management,* October 1994, pp. 34–36; Thomas O. Jones and W. Earl Sasser, Jr., "Why Satisfied Customers Defect," *Harvard Business Review,* November–December 1995, pp. 88–99; and Frederick F. Reichheld, "Learning from Customer Defections," *Harvard Business Review,* March–April 1996, pp. 56–69.

12. Sellers, "Companies That Serve You Best," pp. 74–88.

13. Ralph Waldo Emerson offered this advice: "If a man . . . makes a better mousetrap . . . the world will beat a path to his door." Several companies, however, have built better mousetraps, yet failed. One was a laser mousetrap costing $1,500. Contrary to popular assumptions, people do not automatically learn about new products, believe product claims, or willingly pay higher prices.

14. Barry Farber and Joyce Wycoff, "Customer Service: Evolution and Revolution," *Sales & Marketing Management,* May 1991, p. 47. Also see Jaclyn Fierman, "Americans Can't Get No Satisfaction," *Fortune,* December 11, 1995, pp. 186–94.

15. See Don E. Schultz, "Traditional Marketers Have Become Obsolete," *Marketing News,* June 6, 1994, p. 11.

16. Howard Schlossberg, "Customer Satisfaction: Not a Fad, but a Way of Life," *Marketing News,* June 10, 1991, p. 18. Also see Bernard J. Jaworski and Ajay K. Kohli, "Market Orientation: Antecedents and Consequences," *Journal of Marketing,* July 1993, pp. 53–70.

17. See "Leaders of the Most Admired," *Fortune,* January 29, 1990, pp. 40–54.

18. Ibid., p. 54.

19. For other examples, and for a good review of nonprofit marketing, see Philip Kotler and Alan R. Andreasen, *Strategic Marketing for Nonprofit Organizations,* 5th ed. (Englewood Cliffs, NJ: Prentice Hall, 1996).

20. See Cyndee Miller, "Churches Turn to Research for Help in Saving New Souls," *Marketing News,* April 11, 1994, pp. 1, 2; and Marc Spiegler, "Scouting for Souls," *American Demographics,* March 1996, pp. 42–50.

21. Jeff Smyth, "Non-Profits Get Market-Savvy," *Advertising Age,* May 29, 1995, pp. 1, 7.

22. For more examples, see Philip Kotler and Karen Fox, *Strategic Marketing for Educational Institutions* (Englewood Cliffs, NJ: Prentice Hall, 1985); Bradley G. Morrison and Julie Gordon Dalgleish, *Waiting in the Wings: A Larger Audience for the Arts and How to Develop It* (New York: ACA Books, 1987); Norman Shawchuck, Philip Kotler, Bruce Wren, and Gustave Rath, *Marketing*

for Congregations: Choosing to Serve People More Effectively (Nashville, TN: Abingdon Press, 1993); and Kim Cleland, "Ad, Promo Strategies Make New Converts," Advertising Age, April 10, 1995.

23. Christy Fisher, "Postal Service Plans First-Class Promotion," Advertising Age, April 6, 1992, p. 26. Also see Cyndee Miller, "U.S. Postal Service Discovers the Merits of Marketing," Marketing News, February 1, 1993, pp. 9, 18.

24. John Naisbitt, The Global Paradox (New York: William Morrow and Company, 1994), pp. 59–60.

25. Richard C. Whitely, The Customer-Driven Company (Reading, MA: Addison-Wesley, 1991); Charles Sewell; Customers for Life: How to Turn the One-Time Buyer into a Lifetime Customer (New York: Pocket Books, 1990); Karl Albrecht, The Only Thing That Matters: Bringing the Customer into the Center of Your Business (New York: Harper Business, 1992); Joan K. Cannie, Turning Lost Customers into Gold: And the Art of Achieving Zero Defections (New York: Amacom, 1993); Ron Zemke and Thomas K. Connellan, Sustaining Knock Your Socks Off Service (New York: Amacom, 1993); and Richard Cross and Janet Smith, Customer Bonding: The Five-Point System for Maximizing Customer Loyalty (Chicago: NTC Business Books, 1994).

# Strategic Planning and the Marketing Process

I nvented in 1853 by Levi Strauss, a Bavarian immigrant who sold canvas pants to California gold seekers, jeans have long been an institution in American life. And Levi Strauss & Co. has long dominated the jeans industry. From the 1950s through the 1970s, as the baby boom caused an explosion in the number of young people, selling jeans was easy. Levi Strauss & Co. concentrated on simply trying to make enough jeans to satisfy a seemingly insatiable market. However, by the early 1980s, the baby boomers were aging and their tastes were changing with their waistlines—they bought fewer jeans and wore them longer. Meanwhile, the 18–24-year-old segment of the population, the group traditionally most likely to buy jeans, was shrinking. Thus, Levi Strauss & Co. found itself fighting for its share in a fading jeans market.

Dale color a tu vida con **Levi's** 517 COLLECTION BOOT CUT

At first, despite the declining market, Levi Strauss & Co. stuck closely to its basic jeans business. It sought growth by substantially increasing its advertising and selling through national retailers like Sears and JCPenney. When these tactics failed, Levi Strauss & Co. tried diversification into faster-growing fashion and specialty apparel businesses. It hastily added a broad range of new lines, including high fashions, sportswear, and athletic wear. By 1984, Levi Strauss & Co. had diversified into a muddled array of businesses ranging from blue jeans to men's hats, skiwear, running suits, and even women's polyester pants and denim maternity wear. The results were disastrous: Profits plunged by 79 percent in just one year.

In 1984, in an effort to turn around an ailing Levi Strauss & Co., new management implemented a bold new strategic plan. It sold most of the ill-fated fashion and specialty apparel businesses and took the company back to what it had always done best—making and selling jeans. For starters, Levi Strauss & Co. rejuvenated its flagship product, the basic button-fly, shrink-to-fit 501 jeans. It invested $38 million in the now-classic "501 blues" advertising campaign, a series of hip, documentary-style "reality ads." Never before had a company spent so much on a single item of clothing. At the time, many analysts questioned this strategy. As one put it, "That's just too much to spend on one lousy pair of jeans." However, the 501 blues campaign reminded consumers of Levi Strauss & Co.'s strong tradition and refocused the company on its basic blue jeans heritage. During the next four years, the campaign more than doubled its sales of 501s.

Building on this solid-blue base, Levi Strauss & Co. began to add new products. For example, it successfully added prewashed, stonewashed, and brightly colored jeans to its basic line. In late 1986, Levi Strauss & Co. introduced Dockers products, casual and comfortable cotton pants targeted toward the aging male baby boomers. A natural extension of the jeans business, the new line had even broader appeal than anticipated. Not only did adults buy Dockers products, so did their children. It seems that every American adolescent boy needed at least one pair of casual cotton pants dressy enough to wear when meeting his girlfriend's parents. In the decade since its introduction, the Dockers line has become a one billion-dollar-a-year success. Levi Strauss & Co. has continued to develop new products for the aging boomers, such as loose-fitting jeans for men who've outgrown the company's slimmer-cut 501s.

In addition to introducing new products, Levi Strauss & Co. also stepped up its efforts to develop new markets. In 1991, for example, it developed a jeans advertising campaign designed especially for women and launched an innovative three-year, $12 million "jeans for women" advertising campaign featuring renderings of the female form in blue jeans by female artists. It also aired a national Spanish-language TV advertising campaign aimed at increasing its appeal to the young, fast-growing, and brand-loyal Hispanic market.

But Levi Strauss & Co.'s most dramatic turnaround has been in its international markets. Levi Strauss & Co. now has become the only truly global U.S. apparel maker. Its strategy is to "think globally, act locally." It operates a closely coordinated worldwide marketing, manufacturing, and distribution system. Twice each year, Levi Strauss & Co. brings together managers from around the world to share product and advertising ideas and to search for those that have global appeal. For example, the Dockers line originated in Argentina, but has now become a worldwide bestseller. However, within its global strategy, Levi Strauss & Co. encourages local units to tailor products and programs to their home markets. For example, in Brazil, it developed the Feminina line of curvaceously cut jeans that provide the ultratight fit that Brazilian women favor.

In most markets abroad, Levi Strauss & Co. boldly plays up its deep American roots. For example, James Dean is a central figure in almost all Levi's advertising in Japan. Indonesian ads show Levi-clad teenagers driving around Dubuque, Iowa, in 1960s convertibles. And almost all foreign ads feature English-language music. However, whereas Americans usually think of their Levi's products as basic knock-around wear, most European and Asian consumers view them as upscale fashion statements. The prices match the snob appeal—a pair of Levi's 501 jeans selling for $44 in the United States goes for about $63 in Tokyo and $88 in Paris.

Levi Strauss & Co.'s aggressive and innovative global marketing efforts have produced stunning results. As the domestic market continues to shrink, foreign sales have accounted for most of Levi Strauss & Co.'s growth. Overseas markets now yield

34 percent of the company's total sales and 46 percent of its profit before corporate expenses and interest. Perhaps more impressive, its foreign business is growing at five times the growth rate of its domestic business. Levi Strauss & Co. continues to look for new international market opportunities. For example, the first Rumanian shop to officially sell Levi's jeans recently opened to large crowds, and Levi Strauss & Co. is now selling to jeans-starved consumers in India, Eastern Europe, and Russia.

Dramatic strategic and marketing planning actions have transformed Levi Strauss & Co. into a vigorous and profitable company, one better matched to its changing market opportunities. By building a strong base in its core jeans business, coupled with well-planned product and market development, Levi Strauss & Co. has found ways to grow profitably despite the decline in the domestic jeans market. As one company observer suggests, Levi Strauss & Co. has learned that "with the right mix of persistence and smarts, [planning new products and] cracking new markets can seem as effortless as breaking in a new pair of Levi's stone-washed jeans."[1] ■

# CHAPTER OBJECTIVES

## After reading this chapter, you should be able to:

**1** Explain company-wide strategic planning and its four steps.

**2** Discuss how to design business portfolios and growth strategies.

**3** Assess marketing's role in strategic planning.

**4** Describe the marketing process and the forces that influence it.

**5** Discuss the marketing management functions, including the elements of a marketing plan.

All companies must look ahead and develop long-term strategies to meet the changing conditions in their industries. Each company must find the game plan that makes the most sense given its specific situation, opportunities, objectives, and resources. The hard task of selecting an overall company strategy for long-run survival and growth is called *strategic planning*.

In this chapter, we look first at the organization's overall strategic planning. Next, we discuss marketing's role in the organization as it is defined by the overall strategic plan. Finally, we explain the marketing management process—the process that marketers undertake to carry out their role in the organization.

# ▶ STRATEGIC PLANNING

Many companies operate without formal plans. In new companies, managers are sometimes so busy that they have no time for planning. In small companies, managers sometimes think that only large corporations need formal planning. In mature companies, many managers argue that they have done well without formal planning and that therefore it cannot be too important. They may resist taking the time to prepare a written plan. They may argue that the marketplace changes too quickly for a plan to be useful—that it would end up collecting dust.

Yet formal planning can yield many benefits for all types of companies, large and small, new and mature. It encourages management to think ahead systematically. It forces the company to sharpen its objectives and policies, leads to better coordination of company efforts, and provides clearer performance standards for control. The argument that planning is less useful in a fast-changing environment makes little sense. In fact, the opposite is true: Sound planning helps the company to anticipate and respond quickly to environmental changes and to better prepare for sudden developments.

Companies usually prepare annual plans, long-range plans, and strategic plans. The annual and long-range plans deal with the company's current businesses and how to keep them going. In contrast, the strategic plan involves adapting the firm to take advantage of opportunities in its constantly changing environment. We define **strategic planning** as the process of developing and maintaining a strategic fit between the organization's goals and capabilities and its changing marketing opportunities.

Strategic planning sets the stage for the rest of the planning in the firm. It consists of defining a clear company mission, setting supporting company objectives, designing a sound business portfolio, and coordinating functional strategies (see Figure 2-1). At the corporate level, the company first defines its overall purpose and mission. This mission then is turned into detailed supporting objectives that guide the whole company. Next, headquarters decides what portfolio of businesses and products is best for the company and how much support to give each one. In turn, each business and product unit must develop detailed marketing and other departmental plans that support the company-wide plan. Thus, marketing planning occurs at the business-unit, product, and market levels. It supports company strategic planning with more detailed planning for specific marketing opportunities.[2]

## DEFINING THE COMPANY MISSION

An organization exists to accomplish something. At first, it has a clear purpose or mission, but over time its mission may become unclear as the organization grows, adds new products and markets, or faces new conditions in the environment. When management senses that the organization is drifting, it must renew its search for purpose. It is time to ask: What is our business? Who is the customer? What do consumers value? What should our business be? These simple-sounding questions are among the most difficult that the company will ever have to answer. Successful companies continuously raise these questions and answer them carefully and completely.

Many organizations develop formal mission statements that answer these questions. A **mission statement** is a statement of the organization's purpose—what it wants to accomplish in the larger environment. A clear mission statement acts as an "invisible hand" that guides people in the organization.

**Strategic planning**
The process of developing and maintaining a strategic fit between the organization's goals and capabilities and its changing marketing opportunities. It consists of developing a clear company mission, supporting objectives, a sound business portfolio, and coordinated functional strategies.

**Mission statement**
A statement of the organization's purpose—what it wants to accomplish in the larger environment.

**FIGURE 2-1**
*Steps in strategic planning*

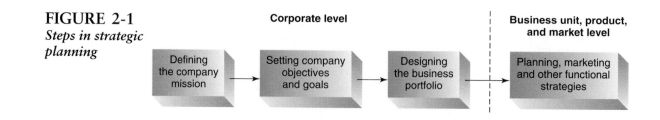

*Company mission: Xerox does more than simply make copiers. Its mission is to make businesses more productive by helping them manage documents at home or anywhere in the world. Xerox is "The Document Company."*

Traditionally, companies have defined their businesses in product terms ("We manufacture furniture") or in technological terms ("We are a chemical-processing firm"). But mission statements should be *market oriented*. Market definitions of a business are better than product or technological definitions. Products and technologies eventually become outdated, but basic market needs may last forever. A market-oriented mission statement defines the business in terms of satisfying basic customer needs. Thus, AT&T is in the communications business, not the telephone business. Citibank Visa defines its business not as issuing credit cards, but as allowing customers to exchange value—assets such as cash on deposit or equity in a home for virtually anything, anywhere in the world. And 3M does more than just make adhesives, scientific equipment, and health-care products. It solves people's problems by putting innovation to work for them. Table 2-1 provides several other examples of product-oriented versus market-oriented business definitions.

**TABLE 2-1** *Market-Oriented Business Definitions*

| Company | Product-Oriented Definition | Market-Oriented Definition |
|---|---|---|
| Revlon | We make cosmetics. | We sell lifestyle and self-expression; success and status; memories, hopes, and dreams. |
| Disney | We run theme parks. | We provide fantasies and entertainment—a place where America still works the way it's supposed to. |
| Wal-Mart | We run discount stores. | We offer products and services that deliver value to Middle Americans. |
| Xerox | We make copying, fax, and other office machines. | We make businesses more productive by helping them scan, store, retrieve, revise, distribute, print, and publish documents. |
| O. M. Scott | We sell grass seed and fertilizer. | We deliver green, healthy-looking yards. |
| Home Depot | We sell tools and home repair/improvement items. | We provide advice and solutions that transform ham-handed homeowners into Mr. and Ms. Fixits. |

Management should avoid making its mission too narrow or too broad. A pencil manufacturer that says it is in the communication equipment business is stating its mission too broadly. Missions should be *realistic*—Singapore Airlines would be deluding itself if its mission was to become the world's largest airline. Missions should also be *specific*. Many mission statements are written for public relations purposes and lack specific, workable guidelines. The statement "We want to become the leading company in this industry by producing the highest-quality products with the best service at the lowest prices" sounds good, but it is full of generalities and contradictions. It will not help the company make tough decisions. Missions should fit the *market environment*. The Girl Scouts of America would not recruit successfully in today's environment with their former mission: "to prepare young girls for motherhood and wifely duties." The organization should base its mission on its *distinctive competencies*. McDonald's could probably get into the solar energy business, but that would not take advantage of its core competence—providing low-cost food and fast service to large groups of customers.

Finally, mission statements should be *motivating*. A company's mission should not be stated as making more sales or profits—profits are only a reward for undertaking a useful activity. A company's employees need to feel that their work is significant and that it contributes to people's lives. Contrast the missions of IBM and Microsoft, the huge computer software company. When IBM sales were $50 billion, president John Akers said that IBM's goal was to become a $100 billion company by the end of the century. Meanwhile, Microsoft's long-term goal has been IAYF—"information at your fingertips"—to put information at the fingertips of every person. Microsoft's mission is much more motivating than IBM's.[3]

One recent study found that "visionary" companies set a purpose beyond making money. For example, Walt Disney Company's aim is "making people happy." But even though profits may not be part of these companies' mission statements, they are the inevitable result. The study showed that 18 visionary companies outperformed other companies in the stock market by more than six to one over the period from 1926 to 1990.[4]

## SETTING COMPANY OBJECTIVES AND GOALS

The company's mission needs to be turned into detailed supporting objectives for each level of management. Each manager should have objectives and be responsible for reaching them. For example, International Minerals and Chemical Corporation is in many businesses, including the fertilizer business. The fertilizer division does not say that its mission is to produce fertilizer. Instead, it says that its mission is to "increase agricultural productivity." This mission leads to a hierarchy of objectives, including business objectives and marketing objectives. The mission of increasing agricultural productivity leads to the company's business objective of researching new fertilizers that promise higher yields. But research is expensive and requires improved profits to support it. So improving profits becomes another major business objective. Profits can be improved by increasing sales or reducing costs. Sales can be increased by improving the company's share of the U.S. market, by entering new foreign markets, or both. These goals then become the company's current marketing objectives.

Marketing strategies must be developed to support these marketing objectives. To increase its U.S. market share, the company may increase its product's availability and promotion. To enter new foreign markets, the company may cut prices and target large farms abroad. These are its broad marketing strategies. Each broad marketing strategy must then be defined in greater detail. For example, increasing the product's promotion may require more salespeople and more advertising; if so, both requirements will have to be spelled out. In this way, the firm's mission is translated into a set of objectives for the current period. The objectives should be as specific as possible. The objective to "increase our market share" is not as useful as the objective to "increase our market share to 15 percent by the end of the second year."

# ▶DESIGNING THE BUSINESS PORTFOLIO

**Business portfolio**
The collection of businesses and products that make up the company.

Guided by the company's mission statement and objectives, management now must plan its **business portfolio**—the collection of businesses and products that make up the company. The best business portfolio is the one that best fits the company's strengths and weaknesses to opportunities in the environment. The company must (1) analyze its *current* business portfolio and decide which businesses should receive more, less, or no investment, and (2) develop growth strategies for adding *new* products or businesses to the portfolio.

## ANALYZING THE CURRENT BUSINESS PORTFOLIO

**Portfolio analysis**
A tool by which management identifies and evaluates the various businesses that make up the company.

The major activity in strategic planning is business **portfolio analysis,** whereby management evaluates the businesses making up the company. The company will want to put strong resources into its more profitable businesses and phase down or drop its weaker ones. For example, in recent years, Dial Corp has strengthened its portfolio by selling off its less attractive businesses: bus line (Greyhound), knitting supplies, meatpacking, and computer leasing businesses. At the same time, it invested more heavily in its consumer products (Dial soap, Armour Star meats, Purex laundry products, and others) and services (Premier Cruise Lines, Dobbs airport services).

**Strategic business unit (SBU)**
A unit of the company that has a separate mission and objectives and that can be planned for independently from other company businesses. An SBU can be a company division, a product line within a division, or sometimes a single product or brand.

Management's first step is to identify the key businesses making up the company. These can be called the strategic business units. A **strategic business unit (SBU)** is a unit of the company that has a separate mission and objectives and that can be planned for independently of other company businesses. An SBU can be a company division, a product line within a division, or sometimes a single product or brand.

The next step in business portfolio analysis calls for management to assess the attractiveness of its various SBUs and decide how much support each deserves. In some companies, this is done informally. Management looks at the company's collection of businesses or products and uses judgment to decide how much each SBU should contribute and receive. Other companies use formal portfolio-planning methods.

The purpose of strategic planning is to find ways in which the company can best use its strengths to take advantage of attractive opportunities in the business environment. So most standard portfolio-analysis methods evaluate SBUs on two important dimensions—the attractiveness of the SBU's market or industry and the strength of the SBU's position in that market or industry. The best-known portfolio-planning method was developed by the Boston Consulting Group, a leading management consulting firm.

**FIGURE 2-2**
*The BCG growth–share matrix*

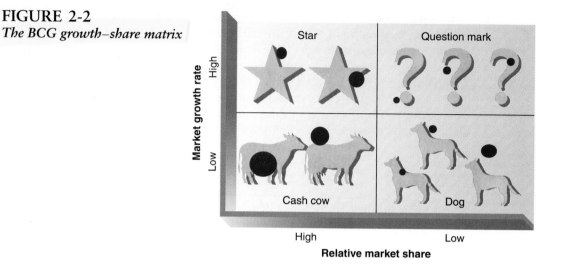

## The Boston Consulting Group Approach

Using the Boston Consulting Group (BCG) approach, a company classifies all its SBUs according to the **growth–share matrix** shown in Figure 2-2. On the vertical axis, *market growth rate* provides a measure of market attractiveness. On the horizontal axis, *relative market share* serves as a measure of company strength in the market. By dividing the growth–share matrix as indicated, four types of SBUs can be distinguished:

**Growth–share matrix**
A portfolio-planning method that evaluates a company's strategic business units in terms of their market growth rate and relative market share. SBUs are classified as stars, cash cows, question marks, or dogs.

◆ *Stars.* Stars are high-growth, high-share businesses or products. They often need heavy investment to finance their rapid growth. Eventually, their growth will slow down, and they will turn into cash cows.

◆ *Cash cows.* Cash cows are low-growth, high-share businesses or products. These established and successful SBUs need less investment to hold their market share. Thus, they produce a lot of cash that the company uses to pay its bills and to support other SBUs that need investment.

◆ *Question marks.* Question marks are low-share business units in high-growth markets. They require a lot of cash to hold their share, let alone increase it. Management has to think hard about which question marks it should try to build into stars and which should be phased out.

◆ *Dogs.* Dogs are low-growth, low-share businesses and products. They may generate enough cash to maintain themselves, but do not promise to be large sources of cash.

The ten circles in the growth–share matrix represent a company's ten current SBUs. The company has two stars, two cash cows, three question marks, and three dogs. The areas of the circles are proportional to the SBU's dollar sales. This company is in fair shape, although not in good shape. It wants to invest in the more promising question marks to make them stars and to maintain the stars so that they will become cash cows as their markets mature. Fortunately, it has two good-sized cash cows whose income helps finance the company's question marks, stars, and dogs. The company should take some decisive action concerning its dogs and its question marks. The picture would be worse if the company had no stars, too many dogs, or only one weak cash cow.

Once it has classified its SBUs, the company must determine what role each will play in the future. One of four strategies can be pursued for each SBU. The company can invest more in the business unit in order to *build* its share. Or it can invest just enough to *hold* the SBU's share at the current level. It can *harvest* the SBU, milking its short-term cash flow regardless of the long-term effect. Finally, the company can *divest* the SBU by selling it or phasing it out and using the resources elsewhere.

As time passes, SBUs change their positions in the growth-share matrix. Each SBU has a life cycle. Many SBUs start out as question marks and move into the star category if they succeed. They later become cash cows as market growth falls, then finally die off or turn into dogs toward the end of their life cycle. The company needs to add new products and units continuously so that some of them will become stars and, eventually, cash cows that will help finance other SBUs.

### Problems with Matrix Approaches

The BCG and other formal methods revolutionized strategic planning. However, such approaches have limitations. They can be difficult, time consuming, and costly to implement. Management may find it difficult to define SBUs and measure market share and growth. In addition, these approaches focus on classifying *current* businesses but provide little advice for *future* planning. Management must still rely on its own judgment to set the business objectives for each SBU, to determine what resources each will be given, and to figure out which new businesses should be added.

Formal planning approaches also can lead the company to place too much emphasis on market-share growth or growth through entry into attractive new markets. Using these approaches, many companies have plunged into unrelated and new high-growth businesses that they did not know how to manage—with very bad results. At the same time, these companies often were too quick to abandon, sell, or milk to death their healthy mature businesses. As a result, many companies that diversified too broadly in the past are now narrowing their focus and getting back to the basics of serving one or a few industries that they know best.

Despite these and other problems, and although many companies have dropped formal matrix methods in favor of more customized approaches that are better suited to their situations, most companies remain firmly committed to strategic planning. Roughly 75 percent of the Fortune 500 companies practice some form of portfolio planning.[5]

Such analysis is no cure-all for finding the best strategy. But it can help management to understand the company's overall situation, to see how each business or product contributes, to assign resources to its businesses, and to orient the company for future success. When used properly, strategic planning is just one important aspect of overall strategic management, a way of thinking about how to manage a business.

**Product/market expansion grid**
A portfolio-planning tool for identifying company growth opportunities through market penetration, market development, product development, or diversification.

## DEVELOPING GROWTH STRATEGIES

Beyond evaluating current businesses, designing the business portfolio involves finding businesses and products that the company should consider in the future. One useful device for identifying growth opportunities is the **product/market expansion grid**,[6] shown in Figure 2-3. We will apply it here to Levi Strauss & Company.

**FIGURE 2-3**
*Market opportunity identification through the product-market expansion grid*

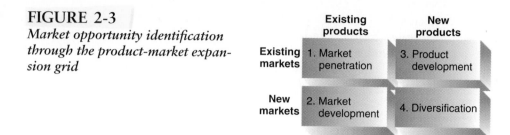

|  | Existing products | New products |
|---|---|---|
| Existing markets | 1. Market penetration | 3. Product development |
| New markets | 2. Market development | 4. Diversification |

**Market penetration**
A strategy for company growth by increasing sales of current products to current market segments without changing the product in any way.

**Market development**
A strategy for company growth that identifies and develops new market segments for current company products.

**Product development**
A strategy for company growth that offers modified or new products to current market segments. The product concept is developed into a physical product in order to assure that the product idea can be turned into a workable product.

**Diversification**
A strategy for company growth that starts or acquires businesses outside the company's current products and markets.

First, Levi Strauss management might consider whether the company's major brands can achieve deeper **market penetration**—making more sales to present customers without changing products in any way. For example, to increase its jeans sales, Levi might cut prices, increase advertising, get its products into more stores, or obtain better store displays and point-of-purchase merchandising from its retailers. Basically, Levi management would like to increase usage by current customers and attract customers of other clothing brands to Levi's.

Second, Levi Strauss management might consider possibilities for **market development**—identifying and developing new markets for its current products. For instance, managers could review new *demographic markets*—children, senior consumers, women, ethnic groups—to see if any new groups could be encouraged to buy Levi products for the first time or to buy more of them. For example, Levi recently launched new advertising campaigns to boost its jeans sales in female and Hispanic markets. Managers also could review new *geographical markets*. During the past few years, Levi has substantially increased its marketing efforts and sales to Western Europe, Asia, and Latin America. It is now targeting newly opened markets in Eastern Europe, Russia, India, and China.

Third, management could consider **product development**—offering modified or new products to current markets. Current Levi products could be offered in new styles, sizes, and colors. Or Levi could offer new lines and launch new brands of casual clothing to appeal to different users or to obtain more business from current customers. This occurred when Levi introduced its Dockers line, which now accounts for more than $1 billion in annual sales.

Fourth, Levi Strauss might consider **diversification.** It could start up or buy businesses outside of its current products and markets. For example, the company could move into industries such as men's fashions, recreational and exercise apparel, or other related businesses. Some companies try to identify the most attractive emerging industries. They feel that half the secret of success is to enter attractive industries instead of trying to be efficient in unattractive ones. However, a company that diversifies too broadly into unfamiliar products or industries can lose its market focus. For example, as discussed in the chapter opening example, prior to 1984, Levi diversified hastily into a jumbled array of businesses, including skiwear, men's suits and hats, and other specialty apparel. In 1985, however, new management sold these unrelated businesses, refocused the company on its core business of denim jeans, and designed a solid growth strategy featuring closely related new products and bolder efforts to develop international markets. These actions resulted in a dramatic turnaround in the company's sales and profits.

*Market penetration: Clorox increases market penetration by suggesting new household uses for its bleach.*

## PLANNING FUNCTIONAL STRATEGIES

The company's strategic plan establishes what kinds of businesses the company will be in and its objectives for each. Then, within each business unit, more detailed planning must take place. The major functional departments in each unit—marketing, finance, accounting, purchasing, manufacturing, information systems, human resources, and others—must work together to accomplish strategic objectives.

### Marketing's Role in Strategic Planning

There is much overlap between overall company strategy and marketing strategy. Marketing looks at consumer needs and the company's ability to satisfy them; these same factors guide the company's overall mission and objectives.

Marketing plays a key role in the company's strategic planning in several ways. First, marketing provides a guiding *philosophy*—the marketing concept—that suggests company strategy should revolve around serving the needs of important consumer groups. Second, marketing provides *inputs* to strategic planners by helping to identify attractive market opportunities and by assessing the firm's potential to take advantage of them. Finally, within individual business units, marketing designs *strategies* for reaching the unit's objectives. Once the unit's objectives are set, marketing's task is to carry them out profitably.

### Marketing and the Other Business Functions

**Value chain**
A major tool for identifying ways to create more customer value.

Customer value and satisfaction are important ingredients in the marketer's formula for success. But marketing alone cannot produce superior value for customers. *All* company departments must work together in this important task. Each department can be thought of as a link in the company's **value chain**.[7] That is, each department carries out value-creating activities to design, produce, market, deliver, and support the firm's products.

For example, Wal-Mart's goal is to create customer value and satisfaction by providing shoppers with the products that they want at the lowest possible prices. Marketers at Wal-Mart play an important role. They learn what customers need and want and stock the store's shelves with the desired products at unbeatable low prices. They prepare advertising and merchandising programs and assist shoppers with customer service. Through these and other activities, Wal-Mart's marketers help deliver value to customers. However, the marketing department needs help from the company's other departments. For example, Wal-Mart's ability to offer the right products at low prices depends on the purchasing department's skill in tracking down the needed suppliers and buying from them at low cost. Similarly, Wal-Mart's information systems department must provide fast and accurate information about which products are selling in each store. And its operations people must provide effective, low-cost merchandise handling.

A company's value chain is only as strong as its weakest link. Thus, success depends on how well each department performs its work of adding value for customers and on how well the activities of various departments are coordinated. At Wal-Mart, if purchasing can't wring the lowest prices from suppliers, or if operations can't distribute merchandise at the lowest costs, then marketing can't deliver on its promise of lowest prices.

Ideally, then, a company's different functions should work in harmony to produce value for consumers. But in practice, departmental relations are full of conflicts and misunderstandings. The marketing department takes the consumer's point of view. But when marketing tries to develop customer satisfaction, it can cause other departments to do a poorer job *in their terms*. Marketing department actions can increase purchasing costs, disrupt production schedules, increase inventories, and create budget headaches. Thus, the other departments may resist the marketing department's efforts.

Yet marketers must find ways to get all departments to "think consumer" and to develop a smoothly functioning value chain.

> Creating value for buyers is much more than a "marketing function"; rather, [it's] analogous to a symphony orchestra in which the contribution of each subgroup is tailored and integrated by a conductor— with a synergistic effect. [Creating superior value for buyers] is the proper focus of the entire business and not merely of a single department in it.[8]

Marketing managers can best gain support for their goal of consumer value and satisfaction by working to understand other company departments. They must work closely with managers of other functions to prepare integrated functional plans under which the different departments can jointly accomplish the company's overall strategic objectives.

## Marketing and Its Partners in the Marketing System

**Value delivery system** All of the organizations in the company's supply chain that work together to deliver value to the customer.

In its search for competitive advantage, the firm needs to look beyond its own value chain and into the value chains of its suppliers, distributors, and ultimately customers. More companies today are "partnering" with the other members of the marketing system to improve the performance of the entire customer **value delivery system**. For example, Campbell Soup operates a qualified supplier pro-

*Customer value delivery system: Campbell operates a qualified supplier program in which it chooses only the few suppliers who can meet its demanding quality requirements. Campbell's experts then work with suppliers to constantly improve their joint performance.*

gram in which it sets high standards for suppliers and chooses only the few who are willing to meet its demanding requirements for quality, on-time delivery, and continuous improvement. Campbell then assigns its own experts to work with suppliers to constantly improve their joint performance.

Similarly, Honda has designed a program for working closely with its suppliers to help them reduce their costs and improve quality. For example, when Honda chose Donnelly Corporation to supply all of the mirrors for its U.S.-made cars, it sent engineers swarming over Donnelly's plants, looking for ways to improve its products and operations. This helped Donnelly reduce its costs by 2 percent in the first year. As a result of its improved performance, Donnelly's sales to Honda have grown from $5 million annually to more than $60 million in less than 10 years. In turn, Honda has gained an efficient, low-cost supplier of quality components. And as a result of its partnerships with Donnelly and other suppliers, Honda can offer greater value to customers in the form of lower-cost, higher-quality cars.[9]

Today, companies are selecting partners carefully and working out mutually profitable strategies. In today's marketplace, competition no longer takes place between individual competitors. Rather, it takes place between the entire value delivery systems created by these competitors. Thus, if Honda has built a more potent value delivery system than Ford or another competitor, it will win more market share and profit.

# ▶ STRATEGIC PLANNING AND SMALL BUSINESSES

Many discussions of strategic planning focus on large corporations with many divisions and products. However, small businesses can also benefit greatly from sound strategic planning. Whereas most small ventures start out with extensive business and marketing plans used to attract potential investors, strategic planning often falls by the wayside once the business gets going. Entrepreneurs and

## MARKETING AT WORK 2-1

# FOR SMALL BUSINESSES: STRATEGIC PLANNING IN A NUTSHELL

King's Medical Company, of Hudson, Ohio, owns and manages magnetic-resonance-imaging (MRI) equipment—million-dollar-plus machines that produce X-ray-type pictures. With 20 sites in 11 states, King's Medical took on $27 million in debt while growing almost 40 percent from 1987 to 1992. Still, the company managed to hold its own and capture 12 to 20 percent profit margins. William Patton, the company's chief executive and "planning guru," points to King's Medical's planning systems —specifically the decision-making discipline and follow-through they promote—as the keys to the company's success. Patton claims, "A lot of literature says there are three critical issues to a small company: cash flow, cash flow, cash flow. I agree those issues are critical, but so are three more: planning, planning, planning."

The following steps summarize the process by which King's Medical creates its overall strategic plan, from which a number of department and individual employee plans follow. The process hinges on an assessment of the company, its place in the market, and its goals.

**1.** Identify the major elements of the business environment in which this organization has operated over the previous few years.

**2.** Describe the mission of the organization in terms of its nature and function for the next two years.

**3.** Explain the internal and external forces that will impact the mission of the organization.

**4.** Identify the basic driving force that will direct the organization in the future.

**5.** Develop a set of long-term objectives that will identify what the organization will become in the future.

**6.** Outline a general plan of action that defines the logistical, financial, and personnel factors needed to integrate the long-term objectives into the total organization.

*Source:* Leslie Brokaw, "The Secrets of Great Planning," *Inc.,* October 1992, p. 152; and Philip Kotler, *Marketing Management: Analysis, Planning, Implementation, and Control* (Englewood Cliffs, NJ: Prentice Hall, 1997), Chapter 3.

presidents of small companies are more likely to spend their time "putting out fires" than planning. But what does a small firm do when it finds that it has taken on too much debt, when its growth is exceeding production capacity, or when it's losing market share to a competitor with lower prices? Strategic planning can help small business managers to anticipate such situations and determine how to prevent or handle them. Marketing at Work 2-1 provides an example of how one small company uses very simple strategic planning tools to chart its course every three years.

Clearly, strategic planning is crucial to a small company's future. Thom Wellington, president of Wellington Environmental Consulting and Construction, Inc., says that it's important to do strategic planning at a site away from the office. An off-site location offers psychologically neutral ground where employees can be "much more candid," and it takes entrepreneurs away from the scene of the fires they spend so much time stamping out.[10]

## ▶THE MARKETING PROCESS

The strategic plan defines the company's overall mission and objectives. Within each business unit, marketing plays a role in helping to accomplish the overall strategic objectives. Marketing's role and activities in the organization are shown

**FIGURE 2-4**
*Factors influencing company marketing strategy*

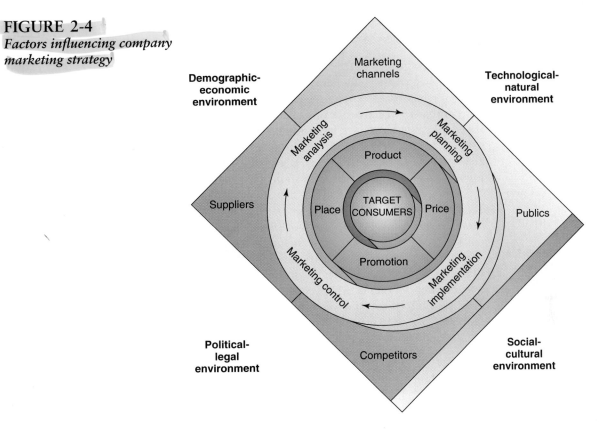

in Figure 2-4, which summarizes the entire **marketing process** and the forces influencing company marketing strategy.

Target consumers stand in the center. The company identifies the total market, divides it into smaller segments, selects the most promising segments, and focuses on serving and satisfying these segments. It designs a marketing mix made up of factors under its control—product, price, place, and promotion. To find the best marketing mix and put it into action, the company engages in marketing analysis, planning, implementation, and control. Through these activities, the company watches and adapts to the marketing environment. We will now look briefly at each element in the marketing process. In later chapters, we will discuss each element in more depth.

**Marketing process**
The process of
(1) analyzing marketing opportunities;
(2) selecting target markets; (3) developing the marketing mix; and
(4) managing the marketing effort.

# TARGET CONSUMERS

To succeed in today's competitive marketplace, companies must be customer centered, winning customers from competitors and keeping them by delivering greater value. But before it can satisfy consumers, a company must first understand their needs and wants. Thus, sound marketing requires a careful analysis of consumers. Companies know that they cannot satisfy all consumers in a given market—at least, they cannot satisfy all consumers in the same way. There are too many different kinds of consumers with too many different kinds of needs. And some companies are in a better position to serve certain segments of the market. Thus, each company must divide up the total market, choose the best segments, and design strategies for profitably serving chosen segments better than its competitors do. This process involves three steps: *market segmentation*, *market targeting*, and *market positioning*.

## Market Segmentation

The market consists of many types of customers, products, and needs, and the marketer has to determine which segments offer the best opportunity for achieving company objectives. Consumers can be grouped and served in various ways based on geographic, demographic, psychographic, and behavioral factors. The process of dividing a market into distinct groups of buyers with different needs, characteristics, or behavior who might require separate products or marketing mixes is called **market segmentation.**

Every market has market segments, but not all ways of segmenting a market are equally useful. For example, Tylenol would gain little by distinguishing between male and female users of pain relievers if both respond the same way to marketing efforts. A **market segment** consists of consumers who respond in a similar way to a given set of marketing efforts. In the car market, for example, consumers who choose the biggest, most comfortable car regardless of price make up one market segment. Another market segment would be customers who care mainly about price and operating economy. It would be difficult to make one model of car that was the first choice of every consumer. Companies are wise to focus their efforts on meeting the distinct needs of one or more market segments.

## Market Targeting

After a company has defined market segments, it can enter one or many segments of a given market. **Market targeting** involves evaluating each market segment's attractiveness and selecting one or more segments to enter. A company should target segments in which it can generate the greatest customer value and sustain it over time. A company with limited resources might decide to serve only one or a few special segments. This strategy limits sales, but can be very profitable (see Marketing at Work 2-2). Or a company might choose to serve several related segments—perhaps those with different kinds of customers but with the same basic wants. Or a large company might decide to offer a complete range of products to serve all market segments.

Most companies enter a new market by serving a single segment, and if this proves successful, they add other segments. Large companies eventually seek full market coverage. They want to be the General Motors of their industry. GM says that it makes a car for every "person, purse, and personality." The leading company normally has different products designed to meet the special needs of each segment.

## Market Positioning

After a company has decided which market segments to enter, it must decide what positions it wants to occupy in those segments. A product's *position* is the place that the product occupies relative to competitors in consumers' minds. If a product is perceived to be exactly like another product on the market, consumers would have no reason to buy it.

**Market positioning** is arranging for a product to occupy a clear, distinctive, and desirable place in the minds of target consumers relative to competing products. Thus, marketers plan positions that distinguish their products from competing brands and give them the greatest strategic advantage in their target markets. For example, at Ford "quality is job 1," and Buick is "the new symbol for qual-

---

**Market segmentation** Dividing a market into distinct groups of buyers with different needs, characteristics, or behavior who might require separate products or marketing mixes.

**Market segment** A group of consumers who respond in a similar way to a given set of marketing stimuli.

**Market targeting** The process of evaluating each market segment's attractiveness and selecting one or more segments to enter.

**Market positioning** Arranging for a product to occupy a clear, distinctive, and desirable place relative to competing products in the minds of target consumers. Formulating competitive positioning for a product and a detailed marketing mix.

*Market positioning: Red Roof Inns positions on value—it doesn't "add frills that only add to your bill." In contrast, Four Seasons Hotels positions on luxury. For those who can afford it, Four Seasons offers endless amenities—such as a seamstress, a valet, and a "tireless individual who collects your shoes each night and returns them at dawn, polished to perfection."*

ity in America." Saturn is "a different kind of company, different kind of car." Mazda "just feels right," and Toyota consumers say "I love what you do for me." Jaguar is positioned as "a blending of art and machine," whereas Mercedes is "engineered like no other car in the world." The luxurious Bentley is "the closest a car can come to having wings." Such deceptively simple statements form the backbone of a product's marketing strategy.

In positioning its product, the company first identifies possible competitive advantages upon which to build the position. To gain competitive advantage, the company must offer greater value to chosen target segments, either by charging lower prices than competitors do or by offering more benefits to justify higher prices. But if the company positions the product as *offering* greater value, it must then *deliver* that greater value. Thus, effective positioning begins with actually *differentiating* the company's marketing offer so that it gives consumers more value than they are offered by the competition. Once the company has chosen a desired position, it must take strong steps to deliver and communicate that position to target consumers. The company's entire marketing program should support the chosen positioning strategy.

## DEVELOPING THE MARKETING MIX

**Marketing mix**
The set of controllable tactical marketing tools—product, price, place, and promotion—that the firm blends to produce the response it wants in the target market.

Once the company has decided on its overall competitive marketing strategy, it is ready to begin planning the details of the marketing mix. The marketing mix is one of the major concepts in modern marketing. We define **marketing mix** as the set of controllable tactical marketing tools that the firm blends to produce the response that

# MARKETING AT WORK 2-2

## VERNOR'S THRIVES IN THE SHADOWS OF THE GIANTS

You've probably never heard of Vernor's Ginger Ale. And if you tried it, you might not even think it tastes like ginger ale. Vernor's is "aged in oak," the company boasts, and "deliciously different." The caramel-colored soft drink is sweeter and smoother than other ginger ales you've tasted. But to many people in Detroit who grew up with Vernor's, there's nothing quite like it. They drink it cold and hot; morning, noon, and night; summer and winter; from the bottle and at the soda fountain counter. They like the way the bubbles tickle their noses. And they'll say you haven't lived until you've tasted a Vernor's ice-cream float. To many, Vernor's even has some minor medicinal qualities—they use warm Vernor's to settle a child's upset stomach or to soothe a sore throat. To most Detroit adults, the familiar green-and-yellow packaging brings back many pleasant childhood memories.

The soft-drink industry is headed by two giants—Coca-Cola leads with a 42 percent market share and Pepsi challenges strongly with about 32 percent. Coke and Pepsi are the main combatants in the "soft-drink wars." They wage constant and pitched battles for retail shelf space. Their weapons include a steady stream of new products, heavy price discounts, an army of distributor salespeople, and huge advertising and promotion budgets.

A few "second-tier" brands—such as Dr Pepper, 7-Up, and Royal Crown—capture a combined 20 percent or so of the market. They challenge Coke and Pepsi in the smaller cola and noncola segments. When Coke and Pepsi battle for shelf space, these second-tier brands often get squeezed. Coke and Pepsi set the ground rules, and if the smaller brands don't follow along, they risk being pushed out or gobbled up.

At the same time, a group of specialty producers who concentrate on small but loyal market segments fights for what's left of the market. Although large in number, each of these small firms holds a tiny market share—usually less than 1 percent. Vernor's falls into this "all others" group, along with A&W root beer, Shasta sodas, Squirt, Faygo, Soho Natural Soda, Yoo-Hoo, Dr Brown's Cream Soda, A.J. Canfield's Diet Chocolate Fudge Soda, and a dozen others. While Dr Pepper and 7-Up merely get squeezed in the soft-drink wars, these small fry risk being crushed.

it wants in the target market. The marketing mix consists of everything that the firm can do to influence the demand for its product. The many possibilities can be collected into four groups of variables known as the four Ps: *product, price, place,* and *promotion.*[11] Figure 2-5 shows the particular marketing tools under each P.

*Product* means the "goods-and-service" combination the company offers to the target market. Thus, a Ford Taurus "product" consists of nuts and bolts, spark plugs, pistons, headlights, and thousands of other parts. Ford offers several Taurus styles and dozens of optional features. The car comes fully serviced and with a comprehensive warranty that is as much a part of the product as the tailpipe.

*Price* is the amount of money that customers have to pay to obtain the product. Ford calculates suggested retail prices that its dealers might charge for each Taurus. But Ford dealers rarely charge the full sticker price. Instead, they negotiate the price with each customer, offering discounts, trade-in allowances, and credit terms to adjust for the current competitive situation and to bring the price into line with the buyer's perception of the car's value.

When you compare Vernor's to Coca-Cola, for example, you wonder how Vernor's survives. Coca-Cola spends almost $350 million a year advertising its soft drinks; Vernor's spends less than $1 million. Coke offers a long list of brands and brand versions—Coke Classic, Coke II, Cherry Coke, Diet Coke, Caffeine-Free Coke, Diet Cherry Coke, Caffeine-Free Diet Coke, Sprite, Tab, Mellow Yellow, Minute Maid soda, and others; Vernor's sells only two versions—original and diet. Coke's large distributor sales force sways retailers with huge discounts and promotion allowances; Vernor's has only a small marketing budget and carries little clout with retailers. When you are lucky enough to find Vernor's at your local supermarket, it's usually tucked away on the bottom shelf with other specialty beverages. Even in Detroit, the company's strong

*Through smart market niching, Vernor's prospers in the shadows of the soft-drink giants.*

hold, stores usually give Vernor's only a few shelf facings, compared with 50 or 100 facings for the many Coca-Cola brands.

Yet Vernor's does more than survive—it thrives! How? Instead of going head to head with the

bigger companies in the major soft-drink segments, Vernor's "niches" in the market. It concentrates on serving the special needs of loyal Vernor's drinkers. Vernor's knows that it could never seriously challenge Coca-Cola for a large share of the soft-drink market. But it also knows that Coca-Cola could never create another Vernor's ginger ale—at least not in the minds of Vernor's drinkers. As long as Vernor's keeps these special customers happy, it can capture a small but profitable share of the market. And "small" in this market is nothing to sneeze at—a 1 percent market share equals $500 million in retail sales! Thus, through smart market niching, Vernor's prospers in the shadows of the soft-drink giants.

*Sources*: See Betsy Bauer, "Giants Loom Larger Over Pint-Sized Soft-Drink Firms," *USA Today*, May 27, 1986, p. 5B; Paul B. Brown, "Guerrilla Pop," *Financial World*, October 13, 1992, p. 76; and Chad Rubel, "Dr Pepper–7Up Join Pepsi, Coke in Soda Wars," *Marketing News*, April 10, 1995, p. 8.

*Place* includes company activities that make the product available to target consumers. Ford maintains a large body of independently owned dealerships that sell the company's many different models. Ford selects its dealers carefully and supports them strongly. The dealers keep an inventory of Ford automobiles, demonstrate them to potential buyers, negotiate prices, close sales, and service the cars after the sale.

*Promotion* means activities that communicate the merits of the product and persuade target customers to buy it. Ford spends more than $600 million each year on advertising to tell consumers about the company and its products. Dealership salespeople assist potential buyers and persuade them that Ford is the best car for them. Ford and its dealers offer special promotions—sales, cash rebates, low financing rates—as added purchase incentives.

An effective marketing program blends all of the marketing mix elements into a coordinated program designed to achieve the company's marketing objectives by delivering value to consumers. The marketing mix constitutes the company's tactical tool kit for establishing strong positioning in target markets.

**FIGURE 2-5**
*The four Ps of the marketing mix*

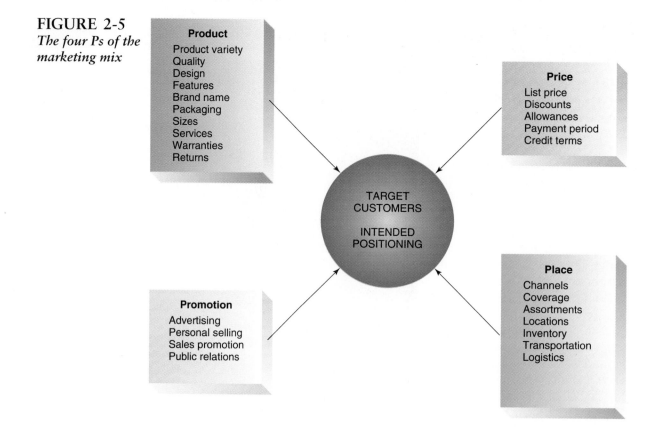

**Product**
Product variety
Quality
Design
Features
Brand name
Packaging
Sizes
Services
Warranties
Returns

**Price**
List price
Discounts
Allowances
Payment period
Credit terms

TARGET
CUSTOMERS

INTENDED
POSITIONING

**Promotion**
Advertising
Personal selling
Sales promotion
Public relations

**Place**
Channels
Coverage
Assortments
Locations
Inventory
Transportation
Logistics

# ▶MANAGING THE MARKETING EFFORT

The company wants to design and put into action the marketing mix that will best achieve its objectives in its target markets. This involves four marketing management functions: *analysis, planning, implementation,* and *control.* Figure 2-6 shows the relationship between these marketing activities. The company first develops overall strategic plans. These companywide strategic plans are then translated into marketing and other plans for each division, product, and brand.

Through implementation, the company turns the strategic and marketing plans into actions that will achieve the company's strategic objectives. Marketing plans are implemented by people in the marketing organization who work with others both inside and outside the company. Control consists of measuring and evaluating the results of marketing plans and activities and taking corrective action to make sure objectives are being reached. Marketing analysis provides information and evaluations needed for all of the other marketing activities.

## MARKETING ANALYSIS

Managing the marketing function begins with a complete analysis of the company's situation. The company must analyze its markets and marketing environment to find attractive opportunities and to avoid environmental threats. It must

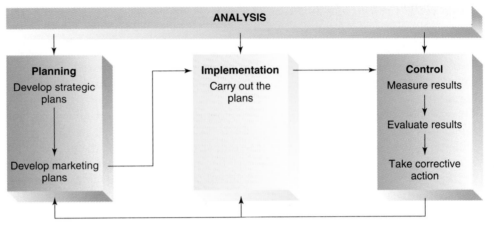

analyze company strengths and weaknesses, as well as current and possible marketing actions, to determine which opportunities it can best pursue. Marketing analysis feeds information and other inputs to each of the other marketing management functions. Marketing analysis is discussed more fully in Chapter 4.

## MARKETING PLANNING

Through strategic planning, the company decides what it wants to do with each business unit. Marketing planning involves deciding on marketing strategies that will help the company attain its overall strategic objectives. A detailed marketing plan is needed for each business, product, or brand. What does a marketing plan look like? Our discussion focuses on product or brand plans. A product or brand plan should contain the following sections: *executive summary, current marketing situation, threats and opportunities, objectives and issues, marketing strategies, action programs, budgets,* and *controls* (see Table 2-2).

### Executive Summary

The marketing plan should open with a short *executive summary* of the main goals and recommendations to be presented in the plan. It presents a brief overview of the plan for quick management review. The executive summary helps top management to find the plan's major points quickly. A table of contents should follow the executive summary.

### Current Marketing Situation

The first major section of the plan describes the target market and the company's position in it. In the current marketing situation section, the planner provides information about the market, product performance, competition, and distribution. It includes a *market description* that defines the market, including major market segments. The planner shows market size, in total and by segment, for the past several years, then reviews customer needs and factors in the marketing environment that may affect customer purchasing. Next, the *product review* shows sales, prices, and gross margins of the major products in the product line. A section on *competition* identifies major competitors and discusses each of their strategies for

**TABLE 2-2** *Contents of a Marketing Plan*

| Section | Purpose |
| --- | --- |
| Executive summary | Presents a brief overview of the proposed plan for quick management review. |
| Current marketing situation | Presents relevant background data on the market, product, competition, and distribution. |
| Threats and opportunity analysis | Identifies the main threats and opportunities that might impact the product. |
| Objectives and issues | Defines the company's objectives for the product in the areas of sales, market share, and profit, and the issues that will affect these objectives. |
| Marketing strategy | Presents the broad marketing approach that will be used to achieve the plan's objectives. |
| Action programs | Specifies *what* will be done, *who* will do it, *when* it will be done, and *how much* it will cost. |
| Budgets | A projected profit and loss statement that forecasts the expected financial outcomes from the plan. |
| Controls | Indicates how the progress of the plan will be monitored. |

product quality, pricing, distribution, and promotion. It also shows the market shares held by the company and each competitor. Finally, a section on *distribution* describes recent sales trends and developments in the major distribution channels.

## Threats and Opportunities

This section requires the manager to look ahead for major threats and opportunities that the product might face. Its purpose is to make the manager anticipate important developments that can have an impact on the firm. Managers should list as many threats and opportunities as they can imagine. Suppose Ralston-Purina's pet food division comes up with the following list:

◆ A large competitor has just announced that it will introduce a new premium pet food line, backed by a huge advertising and sales promotion blitz.

◆ Industry analysts predict that supermarket chain buyers will face more than 10,000 new grocery product introductions next year. The buyers are expected to accept only 38 percent of these new products and give each one only five months to prove itself.

◆ Because of improving economic conditions, pet ownership is expected to increase in almost all segments of the U.S. population.

◆ A recent marketing research study has found that many of today's pet food buyers are almost as concerned about their pets' health as about their own.

◆ Pet ownership and concern about proper pet care are increasing rapidly in foreign markets, especially in developing nations.

The first two items are *threats*. Not all threats call for the same attention or concern. Purina managers should assess the potential damage that each could cause and prepare plans in advance to meet them. The last three items are marketing opportunities upon which Purina might act. However, the development of opportunities usually involves risk. Managers should assess each opportunity according to its potential attractiveness and the company's probability of success and then decide whether the expected returns justify the risks.

### Objectives and Issues

Having studied the product's threats and opportunities, the manager can now set objectives and consider issues that will affect them. The objectives should be stated as goals that the company would like to attain during the plan's term. For example, the manager might want to achieve a 15 percent market share, a 20 percent pretax profit on sales, and a 25 percent pretax profit on investment. Suppose the current market share is only 10 percent. This poses a key issue: How can market share be increased? The manager should consider the major issues involved in trying to increase market share.

### Marketing Strategies

Marketing strategy
The marketing logic by which the business unit is supposed to achieve its marketing objectives.

In this section of the marketing plan, the manager outlines the broad marketing strategy or "game plan" for attaining the objectives. **Marketing strategy** is the marketing logic by which the business unit hopes to achieve its marketing objectives. It consists of specific strategies for target markets, positioning, the marketing mix, and marketing expenditure levels. Marketing strategy should pinpoint which market segments the company will target. These segments differ in needs and wants, responses to marketing, and profitability. The company would be smart to put its effort and energy into those market segments it can serve best from a competitive point of view, and then develop a marketing strategy for each targeted segment.

The manager should also outline specific strategies for such marketing mix elements as new products, personal selling, advertising, sales promotion, prices, and distribution. The manager should explain how each strategy responds to the threats, opportunities, and critical issues spelled out earlier in the plan.

### Action Programs

Marketing strategies should be turned into specific action programs that answer the following questions: *What* will be done? *When* will it be done? *Who* is responsible for doing it? And *how much* will it cost? For example, the manager may want to increase sales promotion as a key strategy for winning market share. A sales promotion action plan should be drawn up to outline special offers and their dates, trade shows entered, new point-of-purchase displays, and other promotions. The action plan shows when activities will be started, reviewed, and completed.

### Budgets

Action plans allow the manager to make a supporting *marketing budget* that is essentially a projected profit-and-loss statement. For revenues, it shows the forecasted number of units that would be sold and the average net price. On the expense side, it shows the cost of production, distribution, and marketing. The difference is the projected profit. Higher management will review the budget and either approve or modify it. Once approved, the budget is the basis for materials buying, production scheduling, personnel planning, and marketing operations. Budgeting can be very difficult, and budgeting methods range from simple "rules of thumb" to complex computer models.

*Marketers must continually plan their analysis, implementation, and control activities.*

### Controls

The last section of the plan outlines the controls that will be used to monitor progress. Typically, goals and budgets are spelled out for each month or quarter. This practice allows higher management to review the results each period and to spot businesses or products that are not meeting their goals. The managers of these businesses and products have to explain these problems and the corrective actions they will take.

## MARKETING IMPLEMENTATION

**Marketing implementation**
The process that turns marketing strategies and plans into marketing actions in order to accomplish strategic marketing objectives.

Planning good strategies is only a start toward successful marketing. A brilliant marketing strategy counts for little if the company fails to implement it properly. **Marketing implementation** is the process that turns marketing *plans* into marketing *actions* in order to accomplish strategic marketing objectives. Implementation involves day-to-day, month-to-month activities that effectively put the marketing plan to work. Whereas marketing planning addresses the *what* and *why* of marketing activities, implementation addresses the *who, where, when,* and *how.*

Many managers think that "doing things right" (implementation) is as important, or even more important, than "doing the right things" (strategy). The fact is that both are critical to success. However, companies can gain competitive advantages through effective implementation. One firm can have essentially the same strategy as another, yet win in the marketplace through faster or better execution. Still, implementation is difficult; it is often easier to think up good marketing strategies than it is to carry them out.

People at all levels of the marketing system must work together to implement marketing plans and strategies. At Procter & Gamble, for example, marketing implementation requires day-to-day decisions and actions by thousands of people both inside and outside the organization. Marketing managers make decisions about target segments, branding, packaging, pricing, promoting, and distributing. They work with people elsewhere in the company to get support for their products and programs. They talk with engineering staff about product design, with manufacturing people about production and inventory levels, and with the finance department about funding and cash flows. They also work with outside people, such as advertising agencies, to plan ad campaigns and with the media to obtain publicity support. The sales force urges retailers to advertise P&G products, provide ample shelf space, and use company displays.

Successful marketing implementation depends on how well the company blends five elements—its action programs, organization structure, decision and reward systems, human resources, and company culture—into a cohesive program that supports its strategies. First, successful implementation requires a detailed *action program* that pulls all of the people and activities together. Second, the company's formal *organization structure* plays an important role in implementing marketing strategy. One important study found that successful firms tend to have simple, flexible structures that allow them to adapt quickly to changing conditions.[12] (See Marketing at Work 2-3.)

The company's *decision and reward systems*—operating procedures that guide planning, budgeting, compensation, and other activities—also affect implementation. For example, if a company compensates managers for short-run profit results, they will have little incentive to work toward long-run market-building objectives. Effective implementation also requires careful *human resources* planning. At all levels, the company must be staffed by people who have the needed skills, motivation, and personal characteristics.

Finally, to be successfully implemented, the firm's marketing strategies must fit with its company culture. *Company culture* is a system of values and beliefs shared by people in an organization—the company's collective identity and meaning. A recent study of America's most successful companies found that these companies have almost cultlike cultures built around strong, market-oriented missions. At companies such as Wal-Mart, Microsoft, Nordstrom, Citicorp, Procter & Gamble, Walt Disney, and Hewlett-Packard, "employees share such a strong vision that they know in their hearts what's right for their company."[13]

# Marketing Department Organization

The company must design a marketing department that can carry out marketing strategies and plans. If the company is very small, one person might do all of the marketing work—research, selling, advertising, customer service, and other activities. As the company expands, a marketing department organization emerges to plan and carry out marketing activities. In large companies, this department contains many specialists. Thus, Kraft has product managers, sales managers and salespeople, market researchers, advertising experts, and other specialists.

Modern marketing departments can be arranged in several ways. The most common form of marketing organization is the *functional organization* in which

## MARKETING AT WORK 2-3

# HEWLETT-PACKARD'S STRUCTURE EVOLVES

In 1939, two engineers, Bill Hewlett and David Packard, started Hewlett-Packard in a Palo Alto garage to build test equipment. At the start, Bill and Dave did everything themselves, from designing and building their equipment to marketing it. As the firm outgrew the garage and began to offer more types of test equipment, Hewlett and Packard hired func-

tional managers to run various company activities. By the mid-1970s, Hewlett-Packard's 42 divisions employed more than 30,000 people. The company's structure evolved to support its heavy emphasis on innovation and autonomy. Each division operated as an independent unit and was responsible for its own strategic planning and marketing programs.

In 1982, in their book *In Search of Excellence*, Peters and Waterman cited H-P's structure as a major reason for the company's continued excellence. They praised H-P's unrestrictive structure and high degree of informal communication (its MBWA style—management by wandering around) that fostered autonomy by decentralizing responsibility and

*Hewlett-Packard began in this garage in 1939. It now operates globally through a sophisticated complex of facilities and communications networks. Its structure and culture have changed with growth.*

different marketing activities are headed by a functional specialist—a sales manager, advertising manager, marketing research manager, customer service manager, or new-product manager. A company that sells across the country or internationally often uses a *geographic organization* in which its sales and marketing people are assigned to specific countries, regions, and districts. Geographic organization allows salespeople to settle into a territory, get to know their customers, and work with a minimum of travel time and cost.

Companies with many, very different products or brands often create a *product management organization*. Using this approach, a product manager develops

authority. The approach became known as the "H-P way," a structure that encouraged innovation by abolishing rigid chains of command and putting managers and employees on a first-name basis.

But by the mid-1980s, although still profitable, Hewlett-Packard had begun to encounter problems in the fast-changing personal computer and minicomputer markets. In a new climate that required its fiercely autonomous divisions to work together in product development and marketing, H-P's famed innovative culture, with its heavy emphasis on autonomy and entrepreneurship, became a hindrance. Thus, Hewlett-Packard moved to bring its structure and culture in line with its changing situation. It established a system of committees to promote communication and coordinate activities within and across its many divisions.

The new structure seemed to work well—for a while. However, the move toward centralization soon got out of hand. The committees kept multiplying, and soon every decision was made by committee. By the late 1980s, the "H-P way" was completely bogged down by unwieldy bureaucracy. Entering the 1990s, H-P had no

fewer than 38 in-house committees that made decisions on everything from technical specifications for new products to the best cities for staging product launches. Instead of enhancing communication, this suffocating structure pushed up costs and increased H-P's decision-making and market-reaction time. For example, in one case, it took almost 100 people over seven weeks just to come up with a name for the company's New Wave Computing software.

In the fast-paced workstation and personal computer markets, H-P's sluggish decision making put it at a serious disadvantage against such nimble competitors as Compaq Computer Corporation and Sun Microsystems. When one of H-P's most important projects, a series of high-speed workstations, slipped a year behind schedule as a result of seemingly endless committee meetings, top management finally took action. It removed the project's 200 engineers from the formal management structure so that they could continue work on the project free of the usual committee red tape. The workstation crisis convinced H-P management that it must make similar changes throughout

the company. The result was a sweeping reorganization that wiped out H-P's committee structure and flattened the organization. A typical top executive who once dealt with 38 committees now deals with only three. Global, cross-functional teams now run individual H-P businesses. Despite the company's huge size— 98,400 employees and $25 billion in annual sales—its small, nimble, autonomous units can react quickly to the market.

Thus, in less than a decade, Hewlett-Packard's structure has evolved from the highly decentralized and informal "H-P way" to a highly centralized committee system and back again to a point in between. H-P is not likely to find a single best structure that will satisfy all of its future needs. Rather, it must continue adapting its structure to suit the requirements of its ever-changing environment.

*Sources*: See Thomas J. Peters and Robert H. Waterman, *In Search of Excellence: Lessons from America's Best-Run Companies* (New York: Harper & Row, 1982); "Who's Excellent Now?" *Business Week,* November 5, 1984, pp. 76–78; Barbara Buell, Robert D. Hof, and Gary McWilliams, "Hewlett-Packard Rethinks Itself," *Business Week,* April 1, 1991, pp. 76–79; Alan Deutschman, "How H-P Continues to Grow and Grow," *Fortune,* May 2, 1994, pp. 90–100; Daniel S. Levine, "Justice Served," *Sales & Marketing Management,* May 1995, pp. 53–61; and Stratford Sherman, "Secrets of HP's 'Muddled' Team," *Fortune,* March 18, 1996, pp. 116–20.

and implements a complete strategy and marketing program for a specific product or brand. Product management first appeared at Procter & Gamble in 1929. A new company soap, Camay, was not doing well, and a young P&G executive was assigned to give his exclusive attention to developing and promoting this product. He was successful, and the company soon added other product managers.[14] Since then, many firms, especially consumer products companies, have set up product management organizations. However, recent dramatic changes in the marketing environment have caused many companies to rethink the role of the product manager (see Marketing at Work 2-4).

## MARKETING AT WORK 2-4

# RETHINKING BRAND MANAGEMENT

Brand management has become a fixture in most consumer packaged goods companies. Brand managers plan long-term brand strategy and watch over their brand's profits. Working closely with advertising agencies, they create national advertising campaigns to build market share and long-term consumer brand loyalty. The brand management system made sense in its earlier days, when the food companies were all-powerful, consumers were brand loyal, and national media could reach mass markets effectively. Recently, however, many companies have begun to question whether this system fits well with today's radically different marketing realities.

Two major environmental forces are causing companies to rethink brand management. First, consumers, markets, and marketing strategies have changed dramatically. Today's consumers face an ever-growing set of acceptable brands and are exposed to never-ending price promotions. As a result, they are becoming less brand loyal. Also, whereas brand managers have

*Rethinking the role of the product manager: Campbell set up "brand sales managers."*

traditionally focused on long-term, national brand-building strategies targeting mass audiences, today's marketplace realities demand shorter-term, sales-building strategies designed for local markets.

A second major force affecting brand management is the growing power of retailers. Larger, more powerful, and better-informed retailers are now

demanding more trade promotions in exchange for scarce shelf space. The increase in trade promotion spending leaves fewer dollars for national advertising, the brand manager's primary marketing tool. Retailers also want more customized "multibrand" promotions that span many of the producer's brands and help retailers to compete better. Such promotions are beyond the scope of any single brand manager and must be designed at higher levels of the company.

These and other changes have significantly changed the way that companies market their products, causing marketers to rethink the brand management system that has served them so well for many years. Although it is unlikely that brand managers will soon be extinct, many companies are now groping for alternative ways to manage their brands.

One alternative is to change the nature of the brand manager's job. For example, some companies are asking their brand managers to spend more time in the field working with salespeople, learning what is happening in

---

For companies that sell one product line to many different types of markets that have different needs and preferences, a *market management organization* might be best. A market management organization is similar to the product management organization. Market managers are responsible for developing marketing strategies and plans for their specific markets. This system's main advantage is that the company is organized around the needs of specific customer segments.

stores, and getting closer to the customer. Campbell Soup created "brand sales managers," combination product managers and salespeople charged with handling brands in the field, working with the trade, and designing more localized brand strategies.

As another alternative, Procter & Gamble, Colgate-Palmolive, Kraft, RJR-Nabisco, and other companies have adopted *category management* systems. Under this system, brand managers report to a category manager who has total responsibility for an entire product line. For example, at Procter & Gamble, the brand manager for Dawn liquid dishwashing detergent reports to a manager who is responsible for Dawn, Ivory, Joy, and all other liquid detergents. The liquids manager, in turn, reports to a manager who is responsible for all of P&G's packaged soaps and detergents, including dishwashing detergents and liquid and dry laundry detergents.

Category management offers many advantages. First, rather than focusing on specific brands, category managers shape the company's entire category offering. This results in a more complete and coordinated

category offer. Perhaps the most important benefit of category management is that it links up better with new retailer "category buying" systems, in which retailers have begun making their individual buyers responsible for working with all suppliers of a specific product category.

Some companies are combining category management with another concept: *brand teams* or *category teams*. For example, instead of having several cookie brand managers, Nabisco has three cookie category management teams—one each for adult rich cookies, nutritional cookies, and children's cookies. Headed by a category manager, each category team includes several marketing people—brand managers, a sales planning manager, and a marketing information specialist—who handle brand strategy, advertising, and sales promotion. Each team also includes specialists from finance, research and development, manufacturing, engineering, and distribution. Thus, category managers act as small businesspeople, with complete responsibility for an entire category and with a full complement of people to help them plan and implement cate-

gory marketing strategies.

Thus, brand managers' jobs are changing, and these changes are much needed. The brand management system is product driven, not customer driven. Brand managers focus on pushing their brands out to anyone and everyone, and they often concentrate so heavily on a single brand that they lose sight of the marketplace. Even category management focuses on products, for example, "cookies" as opposed to "Oreos." But today, more than ever, companies must start not with brands, but with the needs of the consumers and retailers that these brands serve. Colgate recently took a step in this direction. It moved from *brand management* (Colgate brand toothpaste) to *category management* (all Colgate-Palmolive toothpaste brands) to a new stage, *customer need management* (customers' oral health needs). This last stage finally gets the organization to focus on customer needs.

*Sources*: See Robert Dewar and Don Schultz, "The Product Manager: An Idea Whose Time Has Gone," *Marketing Communications*, May 1989, pp. 28–35; "Death of the Brand Manager," *The Economist*, April 9, 1994, pp. 67–68; George S. Low and Ronald A. Fullerton, "Brands, Brand Management, and the Brand Manager System: A Critical-Historical Evaluation," *Journal of Marketing Research*, May 1994, pp. 173–90; and Rance Crain, "Brand Management's Decline May Haunt GM," *Advertising Age*, November 6, 1995, p. 16.

Large companies that produce many different products flowing into many different geographic and customer markets usually employ some *combination* of the functional, geographic, product, and market organization forms. This assures that each function, product, and market receives its share of management attention. However, it can also add costly layers of management and reduce organizational flexibility. Still, the benefits of organizational specialization usually outweigh the drawbacks.[15]

## MARKETING CONTROL

**Marketing control**

The process of measuring and evaluating the results of marketing strategies and plans and taking corrective action to ensure that marketing objectives are attained.

Because many surprises occur during the implementation of marketing plans, the marketing department must practice constant marketing control. **Marketing control** involves evaluating the results of marketing strategies and plans and taking corrective action to ensure that objectives are attained. Figure 2-7 shows that implementation involves four steps. Management first sets specific marketing goals. It then measures its performance in the marketplace and evaluates the causes of any differences between expected and actual performance. Finally, management takes corrective action to close the gaps between its goals and its performance. This may require changing the action programs or even changing the goals.

*Operating control* involves checking ongoing performance against the annual plan and taking corrective action when necessary. Its purpose is to ensure that the company achieves the sales, profits, and other goals set out in its annual plan. It also involves determining the profitability of different products, territories, markets, and channels.

*Strategic control* involves looking at whether the company's basic strategies are well matched to its opportunities. Marketing strategies and programs can quickly become outdated, and each company should periodically reassess its overall approach to the marketplace. A major tool for such strategic control is a **marketing audit.** The marketing audit is a comprehensive, systematic, independent, and periodic examination of a company's environment, objectives, strategies, and activities to determine problem areas and opportunities. The audit provides good input for a plan of action to improve the company's marketing performance.[16]

**Marketing audit**

A comprehensive, systematic, independent, and periodic examination of a company's environment, objectives, strategies, and activities to determine problem areas and opportunities and to recommend a plan of action to improve the company's marketing performance.

The marketing audit covers *all* major marketing areas of a business, not just a few trouble spots. It assesses the marketing environment, marketing strategy, the marketing organization, marketing systems, the marketing mix, and marketing productivity and profitability. The audit is normally conducted by an objective and experienced outside party who is independent of the marketing department. The findings may come as a surprise—and sometimes as a shock—to management. Management then decides which actions make sense and how and when to implement them.

## THE MARKETING ENVIRONMENT

Managing the marketing function would be hard enough if the marketer had to deal only with the controllable marketing-mix variables. But the company operates in a complex marketing environment, consisting of uncontrollable forces to which the company must adapt. The environment produces both threats and

FIGURE 2-7
*The control process*

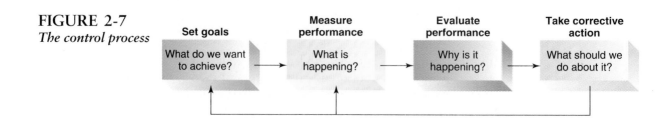

opportunities. The company must carefully analyze its environment so that it can avoid the threats and take advantage of the opportunities.

The company's marketing environment includes forces close to the company that affect its ability to serve consumers, such as other company departments, channel members, suppliers, competitors, and publics. It also includes broader demographic and economic forces, political and legal forces, technological and ecological forces, and social and cultural forces. The company needs to consider all of these forces when developing and positioning its offer to the target market. The marketing environment is discussed more fully in Chapter 3.

# SUMMARY

*Strategic planning* involves developing a strategy for long-run survival and growth. Marketing helps in strategic planning, and the overall strategic plan defines marketing's role in the company. Not all companies use formal planning or use it well, yet formal planning offers several benefits. Companies develop three kinds of plans: *annual plans, long-range plans,* and *strategic plans.*

Strategic planning sets the stage for the rest of company planning. The strategic planning process consists of developing the company's mission, objectives and goals, business portfolio, and functional plans. Developing a sound *mission statement* is a challenging undertaking. The mission statement should be market oriented, feasible, motivating, and specific if it is to direct the firm to its best opportunities. The mission statement then leads to supporting objectives and goals.

From here, strategic planning calls for analyzing the company's *business portfolio* and deciding which businesses should receive more or fewer resources. The company might use a formal portfolio-planning method like the *BCG growth–share matrix* or the General Electric strategic business grid. But most companies are now designing more customized portfolio-planning approaches that better suit their unique situations. Beyond evaluating current *strategic business units,* management must plan for growth into new businesses and products. The *product/market expansion grid* shows four avenues for growth: market penetration, market development, product development, and diversification.

Each of the company's *functional departments* provides inputs for strategic planning. Once strategic objectives have been defined, management within each business must prepare a set of *functional plans*

that coordinates the activities of the marketing, finance, manufacturing, and other departments. Each department serves as a link in the company's *value chain.* A company's success depends on how well each department performs its customer-value-adding activities and on how well the departments work together to serve the customer. Each department has a different idea about which objectives and activities are most important. The marketing department stresses the consumer's point of view. Marketing managers must understand the points of view of the company's other functions and work with other functional managers to develop a system of plans that will best accomplish the firm's overall strategic objectives. Moreover, the company needs to work closely with its partners in the marketing system to form an effective overall *value delivery system.*

To fulfill their role in the organization, marketers engage in the *marketing process.* Consumers are at the center of the marketing process. The company divides the total market into smaller segments and selects the segments that it can best serve. It then designs its *marketing mix* to differentiate its marketing offer and position this offer in selected target segments. To find the best mix and put it into action, the company engages in marketing analysis, marketing planning, marketing implementation, and marketing control.

Each business must prepare marketing plans for its products, brands, and markets. The main components of a *marketing plan* are the executive summary, current marketing situation, threats and opportunities, objectives and issues, marketing strategies, action programs, budgets, and controls. Planning good strategies is often easier than carrying them out. To be successful, companies must implement the strategies effectively. *Implementation* is the process that turns marketing strategies into marketing actions. The process consists of five key elements. The *action program* identifies crucial tasks and decisions needed to implement the marketing plan, assigns them to specific people, and establishes a timetable. The *organization structure* defines tasks and assignments and coordinates the efforts of the company's people and units. The company's *decision and reward systems* guide activities like planning, information, budgeting, training, control, and personnel evaluation and rewards. Well-designed action programs, organization structures, and decision and reward systems can encourage good implementation.

Successful implementation also requires careful *human resources planning*. The company must recruit, allocate, develop, and maintain good people. The firm's company culture can also make or break implementation. *Company culture* guides people in the company's intentions and interests; good implementation relies on strong, clearly defined cultures that fit the chosen strategy.

Most of the responsibility for implementation goes to the company's marketing department. Modern marketing departments are organized in a number of ways. The most common form is the *functional marketing organization,* in which marketing

functions are directed by separate managers who report to the marketing vice president. The company might also use a *geographic organization* in which its sales force or other functions specialize by geographic area. The company may also use the *product management organization,* in which products are assigned to product managers who work with functional specialists to develop and achieve their plans. Another form is the *market management organization,* in which major markets are assigned to market managers who work with functional specialists.

Marketing organizations carry out marketing control. *Operating control* involves monitoring current marketing results to make sure that the annual sales and profit goals are achieved. It also determines the profitability of the firm's products, territories, market segments, and channels. *Strategic control* makes sure that the company's marketing objectives, strategies, and systems fit with the current and forecasted marketing environment. It uses the *marketing audit* to determine marketing opportunities and problems and to recommend short-run and long-run actions to improve overall marketing performance. Through these activities, the company watches and adapts to the marketing environment.

## KEY TERMS

| | | |
|---|---|---|
| Business portfolio | Market targeting | Portfolio analysis |
| Diversification | Marketing audit | Product development |
| Growth–share matrix | Marketing control | Product/market expansion grid |
| Market development | Marketing implementation | Strategic business unit (SBU) |
| Market penetration | Marketing process | Strategic planning |
| Market positioning | Marketing mix | Value chain |
| Market segment | Marketing strategy | Value delivery system |
| Market segmentation | Mission statement | |

## QUESTIONS FOR DISCUSSION

1. In a series of job interviews, you ask three recruiters to describe the missions of their companies. One says, "To make profits." Another says, "To create customers." The third says, "To fight world hunger." What do these mission statements tell you about the companies?

2. An electronics manufacturer obtains the semiconductors that it uses in production from a company-owned subsidiary that also sells to other manufacturers. The subsidiary is smaller and less profitable than are competing producers, and its growth rate has been below the

industry average during the past five years. Into what cell of the BCG growth–share matrix does this strategic business unit fall? What should the parent company do with this SBU?

3. "Just-in-time" (JIT) inventory management makes suppliers responsible for delivering parts in exact quantities at precisely the right time. Companies that succeed with JIT find that benefits often go beyond inventory cost savings, and that many quality improvements come from the process of working very closely with suppliers. Assess whether the ideas of a value chain are used in JIT management. Can JIT succeed *without* using the concepts in the value chain?

4. Assume that you are considering starting a business after graduation. What is the opportunity in your town for a new music store selling tapes and compact discs? Briefly describe the target market(s) that you would pursue and the marketing mix you would develop for such a store.

5. Toyota's marketing position is summed up by its advertising slogan, "I love what you do for me." For years, the company lived up to this reputation by offering luxurious cars at a better price than those of American automakers. However, consumers noticed a marked change with the introduction in 1995 of a remodeled version of the Corolla, Toyota's best-selling car. Worried that the Corolla's sticker price had grown too steep, Toyota brought a stripped-down version of the car into the American market. Considering Toyota's marketing position, how do you think American consumers responded to these changes?

6. Overall, which is the most important part of the marketing management process: planning, implementation, or control? Discuss whether a company that "does things right" is more or less likely to succeed than a company that "does the right things."

## APPLYING THE CONCEPTS

1. Sit down with an AM/FM radio and pencil and paper. Make a simple chart with four columns titled: Frequency, Call Letters (optional but helpful), Format, and Notes. Tune across the AM and FM bands from beginning to end, and make brief notes for each station with adequate reception. In the Format column, note the type of programming, such as student-run, public, classic, rock, hip-hop, talk, religious, and so forth. Under the Notes column, write down any station slogans that you hear (such as "Your Concert Connection"), events that the station is sponsoring, and the types of advertising broadcast.

   ◆ Total the number of stations you received, and add up how many stations share each format.

   How many different market segments do these stations appear to target?

   ◆ Are any of these stations positioned in an unusually clear and distinctive way? How?

   ◆ Do advertisers choose different types of stations for different types of products? Does their market segmentation make sense? Give examples.

2. Think about the shopping area near your campus. Assume that you wish to start a business here, and are looking for a promising opportunity for a restaurant, a clothing store, or a music store.

   ◆ Is there an opportunity to open a distinctive and promising business? Describe your target market, and how you would serve it differently than current businesses do.

   ◆ What sort of marketing mix would you use for your business?

## REFERENCES

1. See "Levi's: The Jeans Giant Slipped as the Market Shifted," *Business Week,* November 5, 1984, pp. 79–80; Joshua Hyatt, "Levi Strauss Learns a Fitting Lesson," *Inc.,* August 1985, p. 17; Maria Shao, "For Levi's, A Flattering Fit Overseas," *Business Week,* November 5, 1990, pp. 76–77; "A Comfortable Fit," *The Economist,* June 22, 1991, pp. 67–68; Nina Monk, "The Levi Straddle," *Forbes,* January 17, 1994,

pp. 44–45; and Alice Z. Cuneo, "Levi's Dons New Men's Wear Appeal," *Advertising Age,* April 24, 1995, p. 12.

2. For a more detailed discussion of corporate and business-level strategic planning as they apply to marketing, see Philip Kotler, *Marketing Management: Analysis, Planning, Implementation, and Control,* 9th ed. (Englewood Cliffs, NJ: Prentice Hall, 1997), Chapters 3 and 4.

3. See Bradley Johnson, "Bill Gates' Vision of Microsoft in Every Home," *Advertising Age,* December 19, 1994, pp. 14–15. For more on mission statements, see David A. Aaker, *Strategic Market Management,* 2nd ed. (New York: Wiley, 1988), Chapter 3; Laura Nash, "Mission Statements—Mirrors and Windows," *Harvard Business Review,* March–April 1988, pp. 155–56; and David L. Calfee, "Get Your Mission Statement Working!" *Management Review,* January 1993, pp. 54–57.

4. Gilbert Fuchsberg, " 'Visioning' Mission Becomes Its Own Mission," *The Wall Street Journal,* January 7, 1994, B1, 3.

5. Richard G. Hamermesh, "Making Planning Strategic," *Harvard Business Review,* July–August 1986, pp. 115–20. Also see Gael McDonald and Christopher Roberts, "What You Always Wanted to Know About Marketing Strategy But Were Too Confused to Ask," *Management Decision,* Vol. 30, No. 7, 1992, pp. 54–60; and Henry Mintzberg, "The Rise and Fall of Strategic Planning," *Harvard Business Review,* January–February 1994, pp. 107–14.

6. H. Igor Ansoff, "Strategies for Diversification," *Harvard Business Review,* September–October 1957, pp. 113–24.

7. Michael E. Porter, *Competitive Advantage: Creating and Sustaining Superior Performance* (New York: Free Press, 1985). For more discussion on value chains and strategies for creating value, see Richard Normann and Rafael Ramirez, "From Value Chain to Value Constellation: Designing Interactive Strategy," *Harvard Business Review,* July–August, 1993, pp. 65–77; and "Strategy and the Art of Reinventing Value," *Harvard Business Review,* September–October, 1993, pp. 39–51.

8. John C. Narver and Stanley F. Slater, "The Effect of a Market Orientation on Business Profitability," *Journal of Marketing,* October 1990, pp. 20–35.

9. Myron Magnet, "The New Golden Rule of Business," *Fortune,* February 21, 1994, pp. 60–63.

10. Bradford McKee, "Think Ahead, Set Goals, and Get Out of the Office," *Nation's Business,* May 1993, p. 10.

11. The four *P* classifications were first suggested by E. Jerome McCarthy, *Basic Marketing: A Managerial Approach* (Homewood, IL: Irwin, 1960). For more discussion of this classification scheme, see Walter van Waterschoot and Christophe Van den Bulte, "The 4P Classification of the Marketing Mix Revisited," *Journal of Marketing,* October 1992, pp. 83–93.

12. See Thomas J. Peters and Robert H. Waterman, *In Search of Excellence: Lessons from America's Best-Run Companies* (New York: Harper & Row, 1982). For an excellent summary of the study's findings on structure, see Aaker, *Strategic Market Management,* pp. 154–57.

13. Brian Dumaine, "Why Great Companies Last," *Business Week,* January 16, 1995, p. 129. See James C. Collins and Jerry I. Porras, *Built to Last: Successful Habits of Visionary Companies* (New York: HarperBusiness, 1995); and Geoffrey Brewer, "Firing Line: What Separates Visionary Companies from All the Rest?" *Performance,* June 1995, pp. 12–17.

14. Joseph Winski, "One Brand, One Manager," *Advertising Age,* August 20, 1987, p. 86.

15. For more complete discussions of marketing organization approaches and issues, see Robert W. Ruekert, Orville C. Walker, Jr., and Kenneth J. Roering, "The Organization of Marketing Activities: A Contingency Theory of Structure and Performance," *Journal of Marketing,* Winter 1985, pp. 13–25; and Ravi S. Achrol, "Evolution of the Marketing Organization: New Forms for Turbulent Environments," *Journal of Marketing,* October 1991, pp. 77–93.

16. For details, see Kotler, *Marketing Management: Analysis, Planning, Implementation, and Control,* 9th ed., Chapter 24.

# The Marketing Environment

**H**ouston Effler & Partners Inc., the white-hot Boston-based advertising agency, earns its fees by helping clients like Converse and Sun Apparel communicate effectively with their changing and sometimes hard-to-understand customers. As head of the youth marketing department at Houston Effler, 25-year-old Jane Rinzler is one of the first card-carrying Generation Xers to be hired to explain her postboomer generation to puzzled clients. "Just explain to me," one client blurted recently, "why they pierce their eyebrows."

As part of her job, Rinzler prowls nightclubs and conducts focus groups, schmoozes with mainstream GenXers in malls and hip-hoppers on swank Newbury Street in Boston, and generally takes the pulse of her nearly 40 million fellow Americans who are in their 20s. Then, she puts on a business suit and feeds her intelligence reports to her bosses and to Houston Effler clients hoping to tap into this lucrative new demographic market.

On a recent afternoon, Rinzler briefed a group of executives from Converse. The agency's largest account, the footwear company markets heavily to GenXers and teens. Rinzler talked about Converse All-Stars, reporting what she has heard on the streets of Los Angeles, New York, Dallas, and Seattle about the 77-year-old sneakers. Bottom line? She announced that the shoes' longevity is well appreciated among the Generation Xers, former latchkey kids who grew up surrounded by divorce, economic instability, and disappearing jobs. "Stay true to the fact you have a classic," she advises the group. "Anything that's trusted will do well with these kids."

Rinzler likes to think of herself as a translator. "The needs and wants of this generation are so different," she says, "and . . . some people are confounded by it." Houston Effler's CEO, Doug Houston, himself a classic baby boomer, considers the GenXers a breed apart. To illustrate both his point and the influence of

Rinzler, he slides two recent magazine ads across his desk. Both are for jeans made by Sun Apparel. One of the ads, in color, is aimed primarily at teenagers. It is splashy and direct. The other, in black and white, is targeted at Generation X. Subdued and subtle, it is more image than message. "Two years ago, we wouldn't have known enough to separate the two groups," Houston says.

As another example, Rinzler shows a magazine ad for Converse's Jack Purcell sneakers. The black-and-white ad shows a young, casually dressed twentysomething woman wearing Jack Purcells without socks while leafing through what appears to be a Victoria's Secret catalog. "Oh yeah," the woman is shown to be thinking, "I stand around the gazebo in my underwear all the time." That's *it*, except for a logo in the lower corner. Not only is the sell as soft as silk, but the ad makes low-key fun of a favorite Generation X target: advertising itself.

The GenXers are a skeptical bunch who can see through the hype and glitz. Rinzler comments, "It works because it doesn't put the product in your face. It shows a lifestyle that twentysomethings can see themselves part of. The woman isn't Cindy Crawford. And mocking advertising works because twentysomethings are tired of being manipulated. But you have to do it subtly."

Rinzler is intense, dresses out at the Gap and Banana Republic (the other women in the agency favor the Ann Taylor look), has an indefatigably chirpy voice, and is never far from a Diet Coke or her Coach appointment book. But not everyone in his or her 20s lives on Diet Coke and shops the Gap. So Rinzler might do Newbury Street with someone like 21-year-old Tony Bertone, who describes himself as "kind of like a consultant for a computer company." Rinzler sees Bertone as a fashion trendsetter, the kind of guy who wears what mainstreamers like herself will be donning somewhere down the road. She'll spend a few hours with him, talking a little and listening a lot: He's one of *her* translators. She'll also pay him $200 courtesy of Converse and likely lay some footwear on him.

"The lounge look is coming back, you know what I'm saying?" Bertone announced recently as he and Rinzler eased through Allston Beat, a cutting-edge clothing store on Newbury. "Like bowling shirts and three-button polos."

"That was last year, don't you think?" Rinzler commented politely. She was wearing a navy blue jersey, white jeans and, fittingly, white Jack Purcells. Her cellular phone was tucked into her brown suede backpack. She was carrying a legal-size pad on which she occasionally made notes about what, according to Bertone, is particularly out front these days. The list included the Internet, OK Soda commercials, and videos by Nine Inch Nails.

"The scumbag look!" Bertone countered. "The Indiana trailer trash look! Thin people! Thin mustaches! Tailored pants! Black shoes! People really looking greasy! . . . Everyone looks trashy. Trashy is fresh. You know what I'm saying?" Rinzler nodded and wrote eagerly on her pad. GenXers might understand all of this, but it would be gibberish to most of the boomer generation. For this reason, the lounge look, bowling shirts, and the Internet would all turn up on her list of currently hot items when she later made her presentation to Converse.

Houston Effler's success depends on its ability to help clients like Converse navigate the complex and changing marketing environment, helping them to understand better the forces that impact their customers. Changing demographics—the aging of the baby boomers, the rise of GenXers, and others—constitute one of today's most important environmental forces. For the better part of their lives, the Generation Xers weren't even considered a target market, let alone a generation. Now, however, they've been *discovered*. For this reason, Rinzler may be the first of a new breed that will work its way into corporate America. It doesn't hurt Houston Effler to be able to tell prospective clients that it claims firsthand knowledge of the generation that often bamboozles most over-30s.[1] ∎

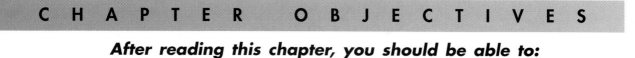

## CHAPTER OBJECTIVES

*After reading this chapter, you should be able to:*

 **1** Describe the environmental forces that affect the company's ability to serve its customers.

**2** Explain how changes in the demographic and economic environments affect marketing decisions.

 **3** Identify the major trends in the firm's natural and technological environments.

**4** Explain the key changes that occur in the political and cultural environments.

 **5** Discuss how companies can react proactively rather than reactively to the marketing environment.

---

**Marketing environment**
The actors and forces outside marketing that affect marketing management's ability to develop and maintain successful transactions with its target customers.

**Microenvironment**
The forces close to the company that affect its ability to serve its customers—the company itself, suppliers, market channel firms, customer markets, competitors, and publics.

A company's **marketing environment** consists of the actors and forces outside marketing that affect marketing management's ability to develop and maintain successful relationships with its target customers. The marketing environment offers both opportunities and threats. Successful companies know the vital importance of constantly watching and adapting to the changing environment.

A company's marketers take the major responsibility for identifying significant changes in the environment. More than any other group in the company, marketers must be the trend trackers and opportunity seekers. Although every manager in an organization needs to observe the outside environment, marketers have two special aptitudes. They have disciplined methods—marketing intelligence and marketing research—for collecting information about the marketing environment. They also normally spend more time in the customer and competitor environment. By conducting systematic environmental scanning, marketers are able to revise and adapt their marketing strategies to meet new challenges and opportunities in the marketplace.

The marketing environment is made up of a *microenvironment* and a *macroenvironment*. The **microenvironment** consists of the forces close to the company that affect its ability to serve its customers—the company, suppliers, marketing channel firms, customer markets, competitors, and publics. The **macroenvironment** consists of the larger societal forces that affect the whole microenvironment—demographic, economic, natural, technological, political, and cultural forces. We look first at the company's microenvironment.

## THE COMPANY'S MICROENVIRONMENT

Marketing management's job is to attract and build relationships with customers by creating customer value and satisfaction. However, marketing managers cannot accomplish this task alone. Their success depends on other actors in the company's

**Macroenvironment**
The larger societal forces that affect the whole microenvironment—demographic, economic, natural, technological, political, and cultural forces.

microenvironment—other company departments, suppliers, marketing intermediaries, customers, competitors, and various publics, which combine to make up the company's value delivery system.

# THE COMPANY

In designing marketing plans, marketing management takes other company groups into account—groups such as top management, finance, research and development (R&D), purchasing, manufacturing, and accounting. All these interrelated groups form the internal environment (see Figure 3-1). Top management sets the company's mission, objectives, broad strategies, and policies. Marketing managers make decisions within the plans made by top management, and marketing plans must be approved by top management before they can be implemented.

Marketing managers also must work closely with other company departments. Finance is concerned with finding and using funds to carry out the marketing plan. The R&D department focuses on the problems of designing safe and attractive products. Purchasing worries about getting supplies and materials, whereas manufacturing is responsible for producing the desired quality and quantity of products. Accounting has to measure revenues and costs to help marketing management know how well it is achieving its objectives. Together, all of these departments have an impact on the marketing department's plans and actions. Under the marketing concept, all of these functions must "think consumer," and they should work in harmony to provide superior customer value and satisfaction.

# SUPPLIERS

Suppliers are an important link in the company's overall customer "value delivery system." They provide the resources needed by the company to produce its goods and services. Supplier developments can seriously affect marketing. Marketing managers must watch supply availability—supply shortages or delays, labor strikes, and other events can cost sales in the short run and damage customer satisfaction in the long run. Marketing managers also monitor the price trends of their key inputs. Rising supply costs may force price increases that can harm the company's sales volume.

## FIGURE 3-1
*The company's internal environment*

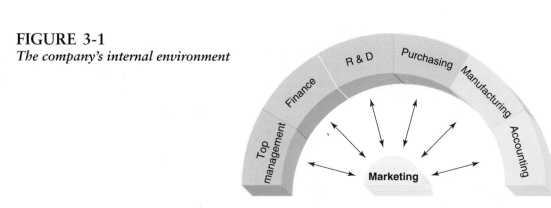

# MARKETING INTERMEDIARIES

**Marketing intermediaries** help the company to promote, sell, and distribute its goods to final buyers. They include *resellers, physical distribution firms, marketing services agencies,* and *financial intermediaries.* Resellers are distribution channel firms that help the company find customers or make sales to them. These include wholesalers and retailers who buy and resell merchandise. Selecting and working with resellers is not easy. Manufacturers no longer have many small, independent resellers from which to choose. They now face large and growing reseller organizations. These organizations frequently have enough power to dictate terms or even shut the manufacturer out of large markets.

*Physical distribution firms* help the company to stock and move goods from their points of origin to their destinations. Working with warehouse and transportation firms, a company must determine the best ways to store and ship goods, balancing such factors as cost, delivery, speed, and safety.

*Marketing services agencies* are the marketing research firms, advertising agencies, media firms, and marketing consulting firms that help the company target and promote its products to the right markets. When the company decides to use one of these agencies, it must choose carefully because these firms vary in creativity, quality, service, and price.

*Financial intermediaries* include banks, credit companies, insurance companies, and other businesses that help finance transactions or insure against the risks

**Marketing intermediaries**
Firms that help the company to promote, sell, and distribute its goods to final buyers; they include resellers, physical distribution firms, marketing services agencies, and financial intermediaries.

*Financial intermediaries: Firms like Credit Suisse offer a wide range of international financial services, from Atlanta and Abu Dhabi to Barcelona and Beijing.*

associated with the buying and selling of goods. Most firms and customers depend on financial intermediaries to finance their transactions.

Like suppliers, marketing intermediaries form an important component of the company's overall value delivery system. In its quest to create satisfying customer relationships, the company must do more than just optimize its own performance. It must form effective partnerships with suppliers and marketing intermediaries to optimize the performance of the entire system.

## CUSTOMERS

The company needs to study its customer markets closely. Figure 3-2 shows five types of customer markets. *Consumer markets* consist of individuals and households that buy goods and services for personal consumption. *Business markets* buy goods and services for further processing or for use in their production process, whereas *reseller markets* buy goods and services to resell at a profit. *Government markets* are made up of government agencies that buy goods and services in order to produce public services or transfer the goods and services to others who need them. Finally, *international markets* consist of these buyers in other countries, including consumers, producers, resellers, and governments. Each market type has special characteristics that call for careful study by the seller.

## COMPETITORS

The marketing concept states that, to be successful, a company must provide greater customer value and satisfaction than its competitors do. Thus, marketers must do more than simply adapt to the needs of target consumers. They also must gain strategic advantage by positioning their offerings strongly against competitors' offerings in the minds of consumers.

No single competitive marketing strategy is best for all companies. Each firm should consider its own size and industry position compared with those of its competitors. Large firms with dominant positions in an industry can use certain strategies that smaller firms cannot afford. But being large is not enough. There are winning strategies for large firms, but there are also losing ones. And small firms can develop strategies that give them better rates of return than large firms enjoy.

**FIGURE 3-2**
*Types of customer markets*

**FIGURE 3-3**
*Types of publics*

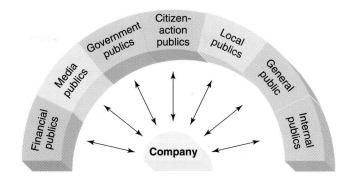

## PUBLICS

**Public**

Any group that has an actual or potential interest in or impact on an organization's ability to achieve its objectives.

The company's marketing environment also includes various publics. A **public** is any group that has an actual or potential interest in or impact on an organization's ability to achieve its objectives. Figure 3-3 shows seven types of publics.

◆ *Financial publics.* Financial publics influence the company's ability to obtain funds. Banks, investment houses, and stockholders are the major financial publics.

◆ *Media publics.* Media publics are those that carry news, features, and editorial opinion. They include newspapers, magazines, and radio and television stations.

◆ *Government publics.* Management must take government developments into account. Marketers must often consult the company's lawyers on issues of product safety, truth in advertising, and other matters.

◆ *Citizen-action publics.* A company's marketing decisions may be questioned by consumer organizations, environmental groups, minority groups, and others. Its public relations department can help it stay in touch with consumer and citizen groups.

◆ *Local publics.* Every company has local publics, such as neighborhood residents and community organizations. Large companies usually appoint a community-relations officer to deal with the community, attend meetings, answer questions, and contribute to worthwhile causes.

*Companies market to internal publics as well as to customers: Wal-Mart includes employees as models in its advertising, making them feel good about working for the company.*

◆ *General public.* A company needs to be concerned about the general public's attitude toward its products and activities. The public's image of the company affects its buying.

◆ *Internal publics.* A company's internal publics include its workers, managers, volunteers, and the board of directors. Large companies use newsletters and other means to inform and motivate their internal publics. When employees feel good about their company, this positive attitude spills over to external publics.

A company can prepare marketing plans for these major publics as well as for its customer markets. Suppose the company wants a specific response from a particular public, such as goodwill, favorable word of mouth, or donations of time or money. The company would have to design an offer to this public that is attractive enough to produce the desired response.

# ▶THE COMPANY'S MACROENVIRONMENT

The company and all of the other actors operate in a larger macroenvironment of forces that shape opportunities and pose threats to the company. Figure 3-4 shows the six major forces in the company's macroenvironment. In the remaining sections of this chapter, we examine these forces and show how they affect marketing plans.

## DEMOGRAPHIC ENVIRONMENT

Demography
The study of human populations in terms of size, density, location, age, gender, race, occupation, and other statistics.

**Demography** is the study of human populations in terms of size, density, location, age, gender, race, occupation, and other statistics. The demographic environment is of major interest to marketers because it involves people, and people make up markets.

The world population is growing at an explosive rate. It now totals more that 5.4 billion and will reach 6.2 billion by the year 2000.[2] This population explosion has been of major concern to governments and various groups throughout the world for two reasons. First, the earth's finite resources can support only so many people, particularly at the living standards to which many countries aspire. The concern is that unchecked population growth and consumption may eventually result in insufficient food supply, depletion of key minerals, overcrowding, pollution, and an overall deterioration in the quality of life.

The second cause for concern is that the greatest population growth occurs in countries and communities that can least afford it. The less-developed regions of the world currently account for 76 percent of the world population and are growing at 2 percent per year. In contrast, the population in the more-developed regions is grow-

**FIGURE 3-4**
*Major forces in the company's macro-environment*

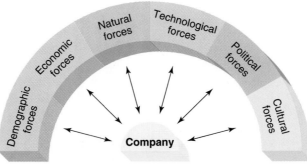

ing at only 0.6 percent per year. Less-developed countries often find it difficult to feed, clothe, and educate their growing populations. Moreover, the poorer families in these countries often have the most children, and this reinforces the cycle of poverty.

The explosive world population growth has major implications for business. A growing population means growing human needs to satisfy. Depending on purchasing power, it may also mean growing market opportunities. For example, to curb its skyrocketing population, the Chinese government has passed regulations limiting families to one child each. As a result, Chinese children are spoiled and fussed over as never before. Known in China as "little emperors," Chinese children are being showered with everything from candy to computers as a result of what's known as the "six-pocket syndrome": As many as six adults—including parents, grandparents, great-grandparents, and aunts and uncles—may be indulging the whims of each child. This trend has encouraged toy companies such as Japan's Bandai Company (known for its Mighty Morphin Power Rangers), Denmark's Lego Group, and Mattel to enter the Chinese market.[3]

Thus, marketers keep close track of demographic trends and developments in their markets, both at home and abroad. They track changing age and family structures, geographic population shifts, educational characteristics, and population diversity. Here, we discuss the most important demographic trends in the United States.

### Changing Age Structure of the U.S. Population

The U.S. population stood at more than 260 million in 1995 and may reach 300 million by the year 2020.[4] The single most important demographic trend in the United States is the changing age structure of the population. The U.S. population is getting *older* for two reasons. First, there is a long-term slowdown in the birthrate, so there are fewer young people to pull the population's average age down. Second, life expectancy is increasing, so there are more older people to pull the average age up.

**Baby boom**
The major increase in the annual birthrate following World War II and lasting until the early 1960s. The "baby boomers," now moving into middle age, are a prime target for marketers.

During the **baby boom** that followed World War II and lasted until the early 1960s, the annual birthrate reached an all-time high. The baby boom created a huge "bulge" in the U.S. age distribution—the 75 million baby boomers now account for almost one-third of the nation's population. And as the baby-boom generation ages, the nation's average age climbs with it. Because of its sheer size, many major demographic and socioeconomic changes in the United States are tied to the baby-boom generation (see Marketing at Work 3-1 on page 80).

The baby boom was followed by a "birth dearth," and by the mid-1970s the birthrate had fallen sharply. This decrease was caused by smaller family sizes resulting from Americans' desire to improve their personal living standards, from the increasing number of women working outside the home, and improved birth control. Although family sizes are expected to remain smaller, the birthrate has climbed again as the baby-boom generation moves through the childbearing years and creates a second, but smaller, "baby boomlet." However, following this boomlet, the birthrate will again decline as we move into the twenty-first century.[5]

Table 3-1 shows the changing age distribution of the U.S. population through 2050. The differing growth rates for various age groups will strongly affect marketers' targeting strategies. For example, the baby boomlet has created a large and growing "kid market." Children under 17 years of age influence an estimated $295 billion worth of purchases each year. After years of "bust," markets for children's toys and games, clothes, furniture, and food are enjoying a "boom." For instance, Sony and other electronics firms are now offering products designed for children. Many retailers are opening separate children's clothing chains, such as GapKids and Kids 'R' Us.

**TABLE 3-1**   *Percent Distribution of the U.S. Population by Age*

| Age Group | 1995 | 2000 | 2005 | 2010 | 2030 | 2040 | 2050 |
|-----------|------|------|------|------|------|------|------|
| Under 5 | 7.6 | 7.4 | 6.9 | 6.6 | 6.4 | 6.4 | 6.4 |
| 5 to 13 | 12.8 | 13.1 | 13.1 | 12.5 | 11.7 | 11.5 | 11.6 |
| 14 to 17 | 5.3 | 5.6 | 5.7 | 5.9 | 5.3 | 5.3 | 5.2 |
| 18 to 24 | 10.8 | 9.5 | 9.5 | 9.8 | 9.1 | 9.2 | 9.0 |
| 25 to 34 | 17.3 | 15.5 | 13.6 | 12.7 | 12.4 | 12.4 | 12.5 |
| 35 to 44 | 15.1 | 16.2 | 16.3 | 14.8 | 12.9 | 12.9 | 12.2 |
| 45 to 64 | 18.6 | 19.9 | 22.2 | 24.9 | 22.1 | 22.1 | 22.5 |
| 65 & older | 12.5 | 12.8 | 12.7 | 12.7 | 20.2 | 20.2 | 20.6 |

*Source:* U.S. Census Bureau, Current Population Reports, as reported in Melissa Campanelli, "Selling to Seniors: A Waiting Game," *Sales & Marketing Management,* June 1994, p. 69.

Such markets will continue to grow through the remainder of the century before decreasing again as the baby boomers move out of their childbearing years.[6]

At the other end of the spectrum, the 65-and-over group now makes up fewer than 13 percent of all Americans. By 2030, however, it will make up more than 20 percent of the population; there will be about as many people 65 and older as there are people 18 and younger. As this group grows, so will the demand for retirement communities, quieter forms of recreation, single-portion food packaging, life-care and health-care services, and leisure travel.[7]

### The Changing American Family

The American ideal of the two-children, two-car suburban family has lately been losing some of its luster. People are marrying later and having fewer children. Despite the recent "baby boomlet," the number of married couples with children will continue to decline through the end of the century. In fact, couples with children under 18 now make up only about 29 percent of all families.[8]

Also, the number of working women has increased dramatically. Currently, in the United States, 58 percent of all women 16 and older are working or looking for a job. It is expected that 65 percent of women will be in the labor force by 2005.[9] Marketers of tires, automobiles, insurance, travel, and financial services are increasingly directing their advertising to working women. As a result of the shift in the traditional roles and values of husbands and wives, with husbands

*To serve the large and growing "kid market," many retailers are opening separate children's chains. For example, Toys 'R' Us opened Kids 'R' Us.*

*Folgers and other brands are targeting smaller households with single-serve portions.*

assuming more domestic functions such as shopping and child care, more food and household appliance marketers are targeting husbands.

Finally, the number of nonfamily households is increasing. Many young adults leave home and move into apartments for a number of years before marrying. Other adults choose to remain single. Still others are divorced or widowed people living alone. By the year 2000, 47 percent of all households will be nonfamily or single-parent households—the fastest-growing categories of households. These groups have their own special needs. For example, they need smaller apartments; inexpensive and smaller appliances, furniture, and furnishings; and food that is packaged in smaller servings.

### Geographic Shifts in Population

Americans are a mobile people, with about 18 percent of the population, or 43 million people, moving each year.[10] Such population shifts interest marketers because people in different regions buy differently. Over the past two decades, the U.S. population has shifted toward the Sun Belt states. The West and South have grown, while the Midwest and Northeast states lost population. Also, for more than a century, Americans have been moving from rural to metropolitan areas. And in the 1950s, there was a massive exodus from the cities to the suburbs. Today, the migration to the suburbs continues, and the suburbs are now spilling over into rural areas. The U.S. Census Bureau calls sprawling urban areas *MSAs* (metropolitan statistical areas). Companies use MSAs in researching the best geographical segments for their products and deciding where to buy advertising time. MSA research shows, for example, that people in Seattle buy more toothbrushes per capita than people in any other U.S. city, Salt Lake City residents eat more candy bars, folks from New Orleans use more ketchup, and those in Miami drink more prune juice.[11]

### A Better-Educated and More White-Collar Population

The U.S. population is becoming better educated. For example, in 1995, 46 percent of the U.S. population over age 25 had attended some college. The rising number of educated people will increase the demand for quality products, books, magazines, and travel opportunities. This trend implies a decline in television

## MARKETING AT WORK 3-1

# THE BABY BOOMERS AND THE GENERATION XERS

Demographics involve people, and people make up markets. Thus, marketers track demographic trends and groups carefully. Two of today's most important demographic groups are the so-called *baby boomers* and the *Generation Xers*.

### THE BABY BOOMERS

The postwar baby boom, which began in 1946 and ran through 1964, produced 75 million babies. Since then, the baby boomers have become one of the biggest forces shaping the marketing environment. The boomers have presented a moving target, creating new markets as they grew through infancy to preadolescent, teenage, young-adult, and now middle-age years.

The baby boomers account for a third of the population but make up 40 percent of the workforce and earn over half of all personal income. Today, the aging boomers are moving to the suburbs, settling into home ownership, and raising families. They are also reaching their peak earning and spending years. Thus, they constitute a lucrative market for housing, furniture and appliances, children's products, low-calorie foods and beverages,

*Converse targets Generation Xers with this black and white ad for Jack Purcell sneakers. The ad is "soft sell," and makes fun of a favorite GenXer target—advertising itself.*

physical fitness products, high-priced cars, convenience products, and financial services.

Baby boomers cut across all walks of life. But marketers typically have paid the most attention to the small upper crust of the boomer generation—its more educated, mobile, and wealthy segments. These segments have gone by many names. In the

1980s, they were called "yuppies" (young urban professionals); "bumpies" (black upwardly mobile professionals); "yummies" (young upwardly mobile mommies), and "DINKs" (dual-income, no-kids couples). In the 1990s, however, yuppies and DINKs have given way to a new breed, with names such as "DEWKs" (dual earners with kids); "MOBYs" (mother older, baby younger); "WOOFs" (well-off older folks); or just plain "GRUMPIES" (just what the name suggests).

The older boomers are now in their fifties; the youngest are in their thirties. Thus, the boomers are evolving from the "youthquake generation" to the "backache generation." They're slowing up and settling down. They're raising families, experiencing the pangs of midlife, and rethinking the purpose and value of their work, responsibilities, and relationships. The maturing boomers are approaching life with a new stability and sensibility in the way they live, think, eat, and spend. The boomers have shifted their focus from the outside world to the inside world. Community and family values have become more important,

viewing because college-educated consumers are known to watch less TV than does the population at large. The workforce is also becoming more white collar. Between 1950 and 1985, the proportion of white-collar workers rose from 41 percent to 54 percent, that of blue-collar workers declined from 47 percent to 33 percent, and that of service workers increased from 12 percent to 14 percent. These trends have continued through the 1990s.[12]

and staying home with the family has become their favorite way to spend an evening. The upscale boomers still exert their affluence, but they indulge themselves in more subtle and restrained ways.

### The Generation Xers

Some marketers think that focusing on the boomers has caused companies to overlook other important segments, especially younger consumers. As noted in the chapter-opening example, focus has shifted in recent years to a new group, those born between 1965 and 1976. Author Douglas Coupland calls them "Generation X" because they are in the shadow of the boomers and lack obvious distinguishing characteristics. Others call them baby busters, the shadow generation, twentysomethings, or Yiffies (young, individualistic, freedom-minded, and few).

Unlike the boomers, the Xers did not share dramatic and wrenching experiences, such as the Kennedy and King assassinations, Vietnam War, and Watergate, that might have unified their subculture and lifestyle. However, they did share a different set of influences. Increasing divorce rates and higher employment rates among young mothers have made them the first genera-tion of latchkey kids. Whereas the boomers created a sexual revolution, the Xers reached sexual maturity in the high-risk age of AIDS. Having grown up during times of recession and corporate downsizing, Xers have developed a pessimistic economic outlook. This outlook is aggravated by problems in finding good jobs—the management ranks already are well stocked with boomers who won't retire for another 20 years or more.

As a result, Xers are a more skeptical bunch, cynical about frivolous marketing pitches that promise easy success. They know better. Xers buy lots of products, such as sweaters, boots, cosmetics, electronics, cars, fast food, beer, computers, and mountain bikes. However, their cynicism makes them more savvy and wary shoppers. Because they often did much of the family shopping when growing up, they are experienced con-sumers. Their financial pressures make them value conscious, and they like lower prices and a more functional look. The Generation Xers respond to honesty in ad-vertising, as exemplified by Nike ads that focus on fitness and a healthy lifestyle instead of hyping shoes. They like irreverent, sassy ads that mock the traditional advertising approach.

Generation Xers share new cultural concerns. They care about the environment and re-spond favorably to companies that have proven records of envi-ronmentally and socially respon-sible actions. Although they seek success, Xers are less material-istic than boomers are. They are cautious romantics who want better quality of life and are more interested in job satisfaction than in sacrificing personal happiness and growth for promotion. They prize experience, not acquisition.

The Generation Xers will have a big impact on the work-place and marketplace of the future. There are now 40 million of them poised to displace the lifestyles, culture, and materialis-tic values of the baby boomers. By the year 2010, they will have overtaken the baby boomers as a primary market for almost every product category.

*Sources*: Faye Rice, "Making Generational Marketing Come of Age," *Fortune*, June 26, 1995, pp. 110–14; Cheryl Russell, "The Baby Boom Turns 50," *American Demographics*, December 1995, pp. 22–33; Cyndee Miller, "Xers Know They're a Target Market, and They Hate That," *Marketing News*, December 6, 1993, pp. 2, 15; Karen Cooperman, "Marketing to Generation X," *Advertising Age*, February 6, 1995, p. 27; Nicholas Zill and John Robinson, "The Genera-tion X Difference," *American Demographics*, April 1995, pp. 24–33; Michele Marchetti, "Talkin' 'bout My Generation," *Sales & Marketing Management*, December 1995, pp. 65–67; and Roger Rosenblatt, "Come Together," *Modern Maturity*, January–February 1996, pp. 32–49.

## *Increasing Ethnic and Racial Diversity*

Countries vary in their ethnic and racial makeup. At one extreme is Japan, where almost everyone is Japanese. At the other extreme is the United States, with peo-ple from virtually all nations. The United States has often been called a "melting pot" in which diverse groups from many nations and cultures have melted into a single, more homogeneous whole. But there are increasing signs that such melting

*To match the growing ethnic diversity of the U.S. market, companies are creating more and more products for specific ethnic markets. Here, Sears targets the fast-growing Hispanic market.*

did not occur. Rather, the United States seems to have become more of a "salad bowl" in which various groups have mixed together but have maintained their diversity by retaining and valuing important ethnic and cultural differences.

The U.S. population is 74 percent white, with African Americans making up another 12 percent. The Hispanic population has grown rapidly and now stands at over 26 million people, almost 10 percent of the U.S. population. The U.S. Asian population also has grown rapidly in recent years and now totals more than 9 million people.[13] Many marketers of food, clothing, furniture, and other products have targeted specially designed products and promotions to one or more of these groups (see Chapter 5).

## ECONOMIC ENVIRONMENT

**Economic environment**
Factors that affect consumer buying power and spending patterns.

Markets require buying power as well as people. The **economic environment** consists of factors that affect consumer purchasing power and spending patterns. Nations vary greatly in their levels and distribution of income. Some countries have *subsistence economies*—they consume most of their own agricultural and industrial output. These countries offer few market opportunities. At the other extreme are *industrial economies,* which constitute rich markets for many different kinds of goods. Marketers must pay close attention to major trends and consumer spending patterns, both across and within world markets. Following are some of the major economic trends in the United States.

### Changes in Income

In the early 1980s, the U.S. economy entered its longest peacetime boom. During the "roaring eighties," American consumers fell into a consumption frenzy, fueled by income growth, federal tax reductions, rapid increases in housing values, and a boom in borrowing. They bought and bought, seemingly without caution, amassing record levels of debt. "It was fashionable to describe yourself as 'born to shop.' When the going gets tough, it was said, the tough go shopping."[14]

In the 1990s, baby-boomers have moved into their prime wage-earning years, and the number of small families headed by dual-career couples continues to increase. Thus, many consumers continue to demand quality products and better service, and they are able to pay for them. They are spending more on time-saving products and services, travel and entertainment, physical fitness products, cultural activities, and continuing education.

However, the free spending and high expectations of the 1980s were dashed by the recession in the early 1990s. In fact, the 1990s has become the decade of the "squeezed consumer." Along with rising incomes in some segments have come increased financial burdens—repaying debts acquired during the spending splurges of the 1980s, facing declining home values and increased taxes, and saving ahead for college tuition payments and retirement. These financially squeezed consumers have sobered up, pulled back, and adjusted to leaner times. They are spending more carefully than in the previous decade and are seeking greater value in the products and services they buy.

*Value marketing* has become the watchword for many marketers during this economic downturn. Rather than offering high quality at a high price or lesser quality at a very low price, marketers are looking for ways to offer today's more financially cautious buyers greater value—just the right combination of product quality and good service at a fair price.

Marketers should pay attention to *income distribution* as well as average income. Income distribution in the United States is still very skewed. At the top are *upper-class* consumers, whose spending patterns are not affected by current economic events and who are a major market for luxury goods. There is a comfortable *middle class* that is somewhat careful about its spending but can still afford the good life some of the time. The *working class* must stick close to the basics of food, clothing, and shelter and must try hard to save. Finally, the *underclass* (persons on welfare and many retirees) must count their pennies when making even the most basic purchases.

### Changing Consumer Spending Patterns

Table 3-2 shows the proportion of total expenditures made by U.S. households at different income levels for major categories of goods and services. Food, housing, and transportation claim most household income. However, consumers at different income levels have different spending patterns. Some of these differences were noted over a century ago by Ernst Engel, who studied how people shifted their spending as their income rose. He found that, as family income rises, the percentage spent on food declines, the percentage spent on housing remains constant (except for such utilities as gas, electricity, and public services, which decrease), and both the percentage spent on other categories and that devoted to savings increase. **Engel's laws** generally have been supported by later studies.

Changes in major economic variables such as income, cost of living, interest rates, and savings and borrowing patterns have a large impact on the marketplace. Companies watch these variables by using economic forecasting. Businesses do not have to be wiped out by an economic downturn or caught short in a boom. With adequate warning, they can take advantage of changes in the economic environment.

# NATURAL ENVIRONMENT

The **natural environment** involves the natural resources that are needed as inputs by marketers or that are affected by marketing activities. Environmental concerns

**Engel's laws**
Differences noted over a century ago by Ernst Engel regarding how people shift their spending across food, housing, transportation, health care, and other goods and services categories as family income rises.

**Natural environment**
Natural resources that are needed as inputs by marketers or that are affected by marketing activities.

**TABLE 3-2**  *Consumer spending at different income levels*

| Expenditure | % of Spending at Different Income Levels | | |
|---|---|---|---|
| | $10,000–15,000 | $20,000–30,000 | $50,000 and Over |
| Food | 17.7 | 15.8 | 12.6 |
| Housing | 24.8 | 23.0 | 24.9 |
| Utilities | 8.6 | 7.1 | 4.7 |
| Clothing | 5.4 | 5.8 | 5.8 |
| Transportation | 17.4 | 19.1 | 17.6 |
| Health care | 7.8 | 5.5 | 3.7 |
| Entertainment | 3.7 | 4.7 | 6.1 |
| Tobacco | 1.5 | 1.2 | 0.5 |
| Contributions | 2.2 | 2.9 | 4.3 |
| Insurance and pensions | 4.5 | 8.2 | 13.2 |
| Other | 6.3 | 6.7 | 6.6 |

*Source: Consumer Expenditure Survey*, U.S. Department of Labor, Bureau of Labor Statistics, Bulletin 2383, August 1991, pp. 15–17. Also see Paula Mergenhagan, "What Can Minimum Wage Buy?" *American Demographics*, January 1996, pp. 32–35.

have grown steadily during the past two decades. Some trend analysts have labeled the 1990s as the "Earth decade," claiming that the natural environment is the major worldwide issue facing business and the public. In many cities around the world, air and water pollution have reached dangerous levels. There is mounting world concern about the depletion of the earth's ozone layer and the resulting "greenhouse effect," a dangerous warming of the earth. And many environmentalists fear that we soon will be buried in our own trash. Marketers should be aware of the following four trends in the natural environment.

### Shortages of Raw Materials

Air and water may seem to be infinite resources, but some groups see long-run dangers. They warn of the potential dangers that propellants used in aerosol cans pose to the ozone layer. Water shortage is already a big problem in some parts of the United States and the world. Renewable resources, such as forests and food, also have to be used wisely. Companies in the forestry business are required to reforest timberlands in order to protect the soil and to ensure enough wood supplies to meet future demand. Food supply may be threatened because more and more of the world's limited farmable land is being developed for urban areas.

Nonrenewable resources, such as oil, coal, and various minerals, pose a serious problem. Firms making products that require these increasingly scarce resources face large cost increases, even if the materials do remain available. They may not find it easy to pass these costs on to the consumer. However, firms engaged in research and development and in exploration can help by developing new sources and materials.

### Increased Cost of Energy

Demands on one nonrenewable resource, oil, have created the most serious concern for future economic growth. The major industrial economies of the world depend heavily on oil, and until economical energy substitutes can be developed,

*Many companies are responding to consumer demands for more environmentally responsible products. Here, Chrysler notes "we are years ahead of government guidelines."*

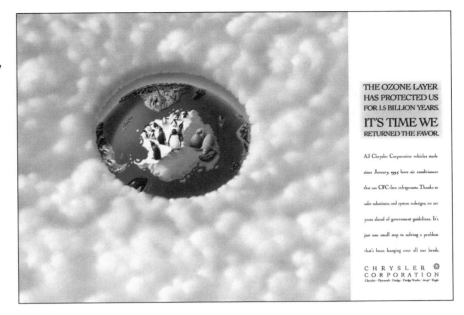

oil will continue to dominate the world political and economic picture. Large increases in the price of oil during the 1970s, and dramatic events like the 1991 Persian Gulf War that affect oil availability, have spurred the search for alternative forms of energy. Coal is again popular; and many companies are searching for practical ways to harness solar, nuclear, wind, and other forms of energy. In fact, hundreds of firms already are offering products that use solar energy for heating homes and other uses.

### Increased Pollution

Industry almost always will damage the quality of the natural environment. Consider the haphazard disposal of chemical and nuclear wastes, the dangerous mercury levels in the ocean, the quantity of chemical pollutants in the soil and food supply, and the vast numbers of nonbiodegradable bottles, plastics, and other packaging materials littering our environment.

Public concern creates a marketing opportunity for alert companies. Such concern creates a large market for pollution control solutions such as scrubbers, recycling centers, and landfill systems. It leads to a search for new ways to produce and package goods that do not cause environmental damage. Concern for the natural environment has spawned the so-called green movement. Increasing numbers of consumers have begun doing more business with ecologically responsible companies and avoiding those whose actions harm the environment. They buy "environmentally friendly" products, even if these products cost more.

Many companies are responding to such consumer demands with ecologically safer products, recyclable or biodegradable packaging, better pollution controls, and more energy-efficient operations. 3M runs a Pollution Prevention Pays program that has led to a substantial reduction in pollution and associated costs. Dow built a new ethylene plant in Alberta that uses 40 percent less energy and releases 97 percent less wastewater. AT&T uses a special software package to choose the least harmful materials, cut hazardous waste, reduce energy use, and improve product recycling in its operations. And McDonald's has eliminated polystyrene cartons and now uses recyclable paper wrappings and napkins.[15]

### Government Intervention in Natural Resource Management

The governments of different countries vary in their commitment to promoting a clean environment. For example, the German government vigorously pursues environmental quality, partly because of the strong public green movement and partly because of the ecological devastation in former East Germany. Holland has successfully implemented its National Environmental Policy Plan, which sets tight targets for pollution reduction. In contrast, many poor nations do little about pollution, largely because they lack the needed funds or political will. It is in the interests of richer nations to subsidize poorer countries' efforts to control pollution, but today even the richer nations lack the vast funds and political accord required to mount a worldwide environmental effort. The best hope is that companies around the world will voluntarily accept more social responsibility and that technology for controlling and reducing pollution will decrease in cost.

In the United States, the Environmental Protection Agency (EPA) was created in 1970 to set and enforce pollution standards and to conduct research on the causes and effects of pollution. In the future, companies doing business in the United States can expect strong controls from government and environmental lobby groups. Instead of opposing regulation, marketers should help develop solutions to the material and energy problems facing the world.

# TECHNOLOGICAL ENVIRONMENT

**Technological environment**
Forces that create new technologies, creating new product and market opportunities.

The **technological environment** is perhaps the most dramatic force now shaping our destiny. Technology has created such wonders as antibiotics, organ transplants, and notebook computers. It has also unleashed such horrors as nuclear warheads, nerve gas, and semiautomatic weapons. It has fostered such mixed blessings as the automobile, television, and credit cards. Our attitude toward technology depends on whether we are more impressed with its wonders or its blunders.

Every new technology replaces an older technology. Transistors hurt the vacuum-tube industry, xerography hurt the carbon-paper business, the auto hurt the railroads, and compact discs hurt phonograph records. When old industries have fought or ignored new technologies, their businesses have declined.

New technologies create new markets and opportunities. The marketer should watch the following trends in technology.

### Fast Pace of Technological Change

Many of today's common products were not available even a hundred years ago. Abraham Lincoln did not know about automobiles, airplanes, phonographs, radios, or the electric light. Woodrow Wilson did not know about television, aerosol cans, home freezers, automatic dishwashers, room air conditioners, antibiotics, or computers. Franklin Delano Roosevelt did not know about xerography, synthetic detergents, tape recorders, birth control pills, or earth satellites. And John F. Kennedy did not know about personal computers, compact disc players, digital watches, VCRs, or fax machines. Companies that do not keep up with technological change soon find their products outdated, and they miss new product and market opportunities.

*Technological environment: Technology is perhaps the most dramatic force shaping the marketing environment. Here, a Samburu warrior in northern Kenya makes a call on a cellular telephone.*

Scientists today are working on a wide range of new technologies that will revolutionize our products and their manufacturing processes. Exciting work is being done in biotechnology, miniature electronics, robotics, and materials science. Scientists are working on the following promising new products and services:

Practical solar energy
Cancer cures
Chemical control of mental health
Car navigation systems
Commercial space shuttle
Tiny but powerful supercomputers
Household robots that do cooking and cleaning
Nonfattening, tasty, nutritious foods
Effective superconductors
Electric cars
Electronic anesthetic for pain control
Voice- and gesture-controlled computers

Scientists also fantasize about products such as flying cars, three-dimensional televisions, space colonies, and human clones. The challenge in each case is not only technical, but also commercial—to make *practical, affordable* versions of these products.

### High R&D Budgets

The United States leads the world in research and development spending. In 1994, R&D spending exceeded $160 billion, increasing only slightly from previous years. The federal government supplied almost half of total R&D funds.[16] Government research can be a rich source of new product and service ideas. Many companies also invest heavily in their own R&D. For example, companies such as General Motors, IBM, and AT&T spend billions on R&D each year. Today's research is usually carried out by research teams rather than by lone inventors like Thomas Edison, Samuel Morse, or Alexander Graham Bell. Managing company scientists is a major challenge. They may resent too much cost control and are sometimes more interested in solving scientific problems than in creating marketable products. Companies are adding marketing people to R&D teams to try to obtain a stronger marketing orientation.

### Concentration on Minor Improvements

As a result of the high cost of developing and introducing new technologies, many companies are making minor product improvements instead of gambling on major innovations. Even basic research companies like Du Pont, Bell Laboratories, and Pfizer are being cautious. Most companies are content to put their money into copying competitors' products, making minor feature and style improvements, or offering simple extensions of current brands. Thus, much research is defensive rather than offensive.

### Increased Regulation

As products become more complex, the public needs to know that they are safe. Thus, government agencies investigate and ban potentially unsafe products. In the United States, the federal Food and Drug Administration has issued complex regulations for testing new drugs. The Consumer Product Safety Commission sets safety standards for consumer products and penalizes companies that fail to meet them. Such regulations have resulted in much higher research costs and in longer delays between new-product ideas and their implementation. Marketers should be aware of these regulations when seeking and developing new products.

Marketers need to understand the changing technological environment and the ways that new technologies can serve human needs. They need to work closely with R&D people to encourage more market-oriented research. They also must be alert to any possible negative aspects of an innovation that might harm users or arouse opposition.

## POLITICAL ENVIRONMENT

Marketing decisions are strongly affected by developments in the political environment. The **political environment** consists of laws, government agencies, and pressure groups that influence and limit various organizations and individuals in a given society.

**Political environment**
Laws, government agencies, and pressure groups that influence and limit various organizations and individuals in a given society.

### Legislation Regulating Business

Even the most liberal advocates of free-market economies agree that the system works best with at least some regulation. Well-conceived regulation can encourage competition and ensure fair markets for goods and services. Thus, governments develop *public policy* to guide commerce—sets of laws and regulations that limit business for the good of society as a whole. Almost every marketing activity is subject to a wide range of such laws and regulations.

INCREASING LEGISLATION.   Legislation affecting business around the world has increased steadily over the years. The United States has many laws on its books covering such issues as competition, fair trade practices, environmental protection, product safety, truth in advertising, packaging and labeling, pricing, and other important areas (see Table 3-3). The European Commission has been active in establishing a new framework of laws covering competitive behavior, product standards, product liability, and commercial transactions for the twelve member nations of the European Union. Several countries have gone farther than the United States in passing strong consumerism legislation. For example, Norway bans several forms of sales promotion—trading stamps, contests, premiums—as being inappropriate or unfair ways of promoting products. Thailand requires food companies selling national brands to include economy brands on the market for low-income consumers. In India, food companies must obtain special approval to launch brands that duplicate those already existing on the market, such as additional cola drinks or new brands of rice.

Understanding the public policy implications of a particular marketing activity is not a simple matter. For example, in the United States, there are many laws created at the national, state, and local levels, and these regulations often overlap. Aspirins sold in Dallas are governed both by federal labeling laws and by Texas state advertising laws. Moreover, regulations are constantly changing—what was allowed last year may now be prohibited, and vice versa. For example, with the demise of the Soviet Bloc, ex-Soviet nations are rapidly passing laws to both regulate and promote an open-market economy. Marketers must work hard to keep up with changes in regulations and their interpretations.

Business legislation has been enacted for a number of reasons. The first is to *protect companies* from each other. Although business executives may praise competition, they sometimes try to neutralize it when it threatens them. So laws are passed to define and prevent unfair competition. In the United States, such laws are enforced by the Federal Trade Commission and the Antitrust Division of the Attorney General's office.

The second purpose of government regulation is to *protect consumers* from unfair business practices. Some firms, if left to their own standards, would make shoddy products and create deceptive advertising, packaging, and pricing. Various agencies define and act against such unfair business practices.

The third purpose of government regulation is to *protect the interests of society* against unrestrained business behavior. Profitable business activity does not always create a better quality of life. Regulation arises to ensure that firms take responsibility for the social costs of their production or products.

CHANGING GOVERNMENT AGENCY ENFORCEMENT. International marketers encounter dozens, even hundreds, of agencies set up to enforce trade policies and regulations. In the United States, Congress has established federal regulatory agencies such as the Federal Trade Commission, the Food and Drug Administration, the Interstate Commerce Commission, the Federal Communications Commission, the Federal Power Commission, the Civil Aeronautics Board, the Consumer Products Safety Commission, the Environmental Protection Agency, and the Office of Consumer Affairs. Because such government agencies have some discretion in enforcing the laws, they can have a major impact on a company's marketing performance. The staffs of these agencies have sometimes appeared to be overly aggressive and unpredictable. Some agencies have been dominated by lawyers and economists who lack a practical sense of how business and marketing work. In recent years, the Federal Trade Commission has added staff marketing experts who can better understand complex business issues.

**TABLE 3-3**  *Milestone U.S. legislation affecting marketing*

*Sherman Antitrust Act (1890)*
Prohibits (1) "monopolies or attempts to monopolize"; and (2) "contracts, combinations, or conspiracies in restraint of trade" in interstate and foreign commerce.

*Federal Food and Drug Act (1906)*
Forbids the manufacture, sale, or transport of adulterated or fraudulently labeled foods and drugs in interstate commerce. Supplanted by the Food, Drug, and Cosmetic Act, 1938; amended by Food Additives Amendment in 1958 and the Kefauver-Harris Amendment in 1962. The 1962 amendment deals with pretesting of drugs for safety and effectiveness and labeling of drugs by generic name.

*Meat Inspection Act (1906)*
Provides for the enforcement of sanitary regulations in meat-packaging establishments and for federal inspection of all companies selling meats in interstate commerce.

*Federal Trade Commission Act (1914)*
Establishes the commission, a body of specialists with broad powers to investigate and to issue cease-and-desist orders to enforce Section 5, which declares that "unfair methods of competition in commerce are unlawful."

*Clayton Act (1914)*
Supplements the Sherman Act by prohibiting certain specific practices (certain types of price discrimination, tying clauses and exclusive dealing, intercorporate stockholdings, and interlocking directorates) "where the effect . . . may be to substantially lessen competition or tend to create a monopoly in any line of commerce." Provides that violating corporate officials can be held individually responsible; exempts labor and agricultural organizations from its provisions.

*Robinson-Patman Act (1936)*
Amends the Clayton Act. Adds the phrase "to injure, destroy, or prevent competition." Defines price discrimination as unlawful (subject to certain defenses) and provides the FTC with the right to establish limits on quantity discounts, to forbid brokerage allowances except to independent brokers, and to prohibit promotional allowances or the furnishing of services or facilities except where made available to all "on proportionately equal terms."

*Miller-Tydings Act (1937)*
Amends the Sherman Act to exempt interstate fair-trade (price fixing) agreements from antitrust prosecution. (The McGuire Act, 1952, reinstates the legality of the nonsigner clause.)

*Wheeler-Lea Act (1938)*
Prohibits unfair and deceptive acts and practices regardless of whether competition is injured; places advertising of foods and drugs under FTC jurisdiction.

*Lanham Trademark Act (1946)*
Requires that trademarks must be distinctive and makes it illegal to make any false representation of goods or services entering interstate commerce.

**TABLE 3-3** *(continued)*

*Antimerger Act (1950)*
Amends Section 7 of the Clayton Act by broadening the power to prevent intercorporate acquisitions where the acquisition may have a substantially adverse effect on competition.

*Automobile Information Disclosure Act (1958)*
Prohibits car dealers from inflating the factory price of new cars.

*National Traffic and Safety Act (1958)*
Provides for the creation of compulsory safety standards for automobiles and tires.

*Fair Packaging and Labeling Act (1966)*
Provides for the regulation of the packaging and labeling of consumer goods. Requires manufacturers to state what the package contains, who made it, and how much it contains. Permits industries' voluntary adoption of uniform packaging standards.

*Child Protection Act (1966)*
Bans sale of hazardous toys and articles. Amended in 1969 to include articles that pose electrical, mechanical, or thermal hazards.

*Federal Cigarette Labeling and Advertising Act (1967)*
Requires that cigarette packages contain the following statement: "Warning: The Surgeon General Has Determined That Cigarette Smoking Is Dangerous to Your Health."

*Truth-in-Lending Act (1968)*
Requires lenders to state the true costs of a credit transaction, outlaws the use of actual or threatened violence in collecting loans, and restricts the amount of garnishments. Established a National Commission on Consumer Finance.

*National Environmental Policy Act (1969)*
Establishes a national policy on the environment and provides for the establishment of the Council on Environmental Quality. The Environmental Protection Agency was established by Reorganization Plan No. 3 of 1970.

*Fair Credit Reporting Act (1970)*
Ensures that a consumer's credit report will contain only accurate, relevant, and recent information and will be confidential unless requested for an appropriate reason by a proper party.

*Consumer Product Safety Act (1972)*
Establishes the Consumer Product Safety Commission and authorizes it to set safety standards for consumer products as well as exact penalties for failure to uphold the standards.

*Consumer Goods Pricing Act (1975)*
Prohibits the use of price maintenance agreements among manufacturers and resellers in interstate commerce.

**TABLE 3-3** *(continued)*

*Magnuson-Moss Warranty/FTC Improvement Act (1975)*
Authorizes the FTC to determine rules concerning consumer warranties and provides for consumer access to means of redress, such as the "class action" suit. Also expands FTC regulatory powers over unfair or deceptive acts or practices.

*Equal Credit Opportunity Act (1975)*
Prohibits discrimination in a credit transaction because of sex, marital status, race, national origin, religion, age, or receipt of public assistance.

*Fair Debt Collection Practice Act (1978)*
Makes it illegal to abuse any person and make false statements or use unfair methods when collecting a debt.

*FTC Improvement Act (1980)*
Provides the House of Representatives and Senate jointly with veto power over FTC Trade Regulation Rules. Enacted to limit FTC's powers to regulate "unfairness" issues.

*Toy Safety Act (1984)*
Gives the government the power to recall dangerous toys quickly when they are found.

*Nutrition Labeling and Education Act (1990)*
Requires that food product labels provide detailed nutritional information.

New laws will continue to be enacted and enforced. Business executives must watch these developments when planning their products and marketing programs. Marketers need to understand the major laws affecting competition, consumers, and society at local, state, national, and international levels.[17]

### Increased Emphasis on Ethics and Socially Responsible Actions

Written regulations cannot possibly cover all potential marketing abuses, and existing laws are often difficult to enforce. However, beyond written laws and regulations, business is also governed by social codes and professional ethics. Enlightened companies encourage their managers to look beyond what the regulatory system allows and to simply "do the right thing." These socially responsible firms actively seek out ways to protect the long-run interests of their customers and the environment.

The recent rash of business scandals and increased concerns about the environment have created fresh interest in the issues of business ethics and social responsibility. Almost every aspect of marketing involves such issues. Unfortunately, because these issues usually involve conflicting interests, well-meaning people can disagree honestly about the right course of action in a particular situation. Thus, many industrial and professional trade associations have proposed codes of ethics, and many companies are now developing policies and guidelines to deal with complex social responsibility issues.

Throughout the text, we present Marketing at Work sections that summarize the main public policy and social responsibility issues surrounding major marketing decisions. These discussions involve the legal, ethical, and societal concerns that marketers face. In Chapter 18, we discuss a broad range of societal marketing topics in greater depth.

# CULTURAL ENVIRONMENT

**Cultural environment**
Institutions and other forces that affect society's basic values, perceptions, preferences, and behaviors.

The **cultural environment** is made up of institutions and other forces that affect a society's basic values, perceptions, preferences, and behaviors. People grow up in a particular society that shapes their basic beliefs and values. They absorb a world view that defines their relationships with others. The following cultural characteristics can affect marketing decision making.

## Persistence of Cultural Values

People in a given society hold many beliefs and values, which have a high degree of persistence. For example, most Americans believe in working, getting married, giving to charity, and being honest. These beliefs shape other more specific attitudes and behaviors found in everyday life. *Core* beliefs and values are passed on from parents to children and are reinforced by schools, churches, business, and government.

*Secondary* beliefs and values are more open to change. Believing in marriage is a core belief; believing that people should get married early in life is a secondary belief. Marketers may be able to influence secondary values, but have little sway over core values. For example, family-planning marketers have a far better chance of persuading Americans that people should get married later than that they should not get married at all.

## Shifts in Secondary Cultural Values

Although core values are fairly persistent, cultural swings do take place. Consider the impact of popular music groups, movie personalities, and other celebrities on young people's hair styling, clothing, and sexual behavior. Marketers try to predict cultural shifts in order to spot new opportunities or threats. Several firms offer "futures" forecasts in this connection. For example, the Yankelovich marketing research firm tracks 41 U.S. cultural values, such as "anti-bigness," "mysticism," "living for today," "away from possessions," and "sensuousness." The firm describes the percentage of the population who share the attitude as well as the percentage who go against the trend. For instance, the percentage of people who value physical fitness and well-being has risen steadily over the years. Such information helps marketers cater to trends with appropriate products and communication appeals. (See Marketing at Work 3-2 for a summary of today's cultural trends.)

The major cultural values of a society are expressed in people's views of themselves and others, as well as in their views of organizations, society, nature, and the universe.

PEOPLE'S VIEWS OF THEMSELVES.   People vary in their emphasis on serving themselves versus serving others. Some people seek personal pleasure, wanting fun, change, and escape. Others seek self-realization through religion, recreation, or the avid pursuit of careers or other life goals. People use products, brands, and services as a means of self-expression and they buy products and services that match their views of themselves.

In the 1980s, personal ambition and materialism increased dramatically, with significant marketing implications. In a "me-society," people buy their "dream

## MARKETING AT WORK 3-2

# POPCORN'S TEN CULTURAL TRENDS

Futurist Faith Popcorn runs Brain-Reserve, a marketing consulting firm that monitors cultural trends and advises companies such as AT&T, Citibank, Black & Decker, Hoffman-La Roche, Nissan, Rubbermaid, and many others on how these trends will affect their marketing and other business decisions. Using its trend predictions, BrainReserve offers several services: BrainJam generates new product ideas for clients, and BrandRenewal attempts to breathe new life into fading brands. FutureFocus develops marketing strategies and concepts that create long-term competitive advantage. Another service, TrendBank, is a database containing culture monitoring and consumer interview information. Popcorn and her associates have identified ten major cultural trends affecting U.S. consumers:

**1.** *Cashing Out.* People feel the urge to change their lives to a slower but more rewarding pace. An executive suddenly quits his or her career, escapes the hassles of big city life, and turns up in Vermont or Montana running a small newspaper, managing a bed-and-breakfast establishment, or starting a band. People cash out because they don't think the stress is worth it. They nostalgically try to return to small-town values, seeking clean air, safe schools, and plain-speaking neighbors.

**2.** *Cocooning.* Many Americans have the impulse to stay inside when the outside gets too tough and scary. More people are turning their homes into nests: redecorating their houses, watching videotapes rather than going to theatres,

---

*Down-aging: Many older people are now acting in ways not previously thought appropriate, such as signing up for adventure vacations and buying fun toys.*

cars" and take their "dream vacations." They spend more time in outdoor health activities (jogging, tennis), in thought, and on arts and crafts. The leisure industry (camping, boating, arts and crafts, and sports) faces good growth prospects in a society where people seek self-fulfillment.

ordering from catalogs rather than going to malls, and using answering machines to filter out the outside world. In reaction to increases in crime and other social problems, cocooners are burrowing in and building bunkers. Self-preservation is the underlying theme. Another breed is Wandering Cocoons, people who eat takeout food in their cars and communicate via their car phones. Socialized Cocooners form a small group of friends who frequently get together for conversation or for "salooning."

**3.** *Down-aging.* There is a tendency to act and feel younger than one's age. Today's sex symbols include Cher (over 45), Paul Newman (over 65), and Elizabeth Taylor (over 60). Older people spend more money on youthful clothes, hair coloring, and facial plastic surgery. They engage in more playful behavior and act in ways previously thought to be inappropriate for their age group. They buy adult toys, attend adult camps, and sign up for adventure vacations.

**4.** *Egonomics.* People want to develop individuality in order to be seen and treated as different from others. This is not an ego trip, but simply the wish to individualize oneself through possessions and experiences. People increasingly subscribe to narrow-interest magazines; join small groups with narrow missions; and buy customized clothing, cars, and cosmetics. Egonomics gives marketers an opportunity to succeed by offering customized goods, services, and experiences.

**5.** *Fantasy Adventure.* Many feel the need to find emotional

escapes to offset daily routines. People might seek vacations, eat exotic foods, go to Disneyland and other fantasy parks, or redecorate their homes with a faraway look. For marketers, this is an opportunity to create new fantasy products and services or to add fantasy touches to their current products and services.

**6.** *99 Lives.* Desperate people must juggle many roles and responsibilities. An example is the "Supermom" who handles a full-time career while also managing her home and children. People today feel time-poor. They attempt to relieve time pressures by using fax machines and car phones, eating at fast-food restaurants, and through other means. Marketers can meet this need by creating *cluster marketing* enterprises—all-in-one service stops, such as Video Town Launderette which, in addition to its laundry facilities, includes a tanning room, an exercise bike, copying and fax machines, and 6,000 video titles for rent.

**7.** *S.O.S. (Save Our Society).* A growing number of people want to make society more socially responsible with respect to education, ethics, and the environment. People join groups to promote more social responsibility on the part of companies and other institutions. The best response for marketers is to urge their own companies to practice more socially responsible marketing.

**8.** *Small Indulgences.* Stressed-out consumers need occasional emotional fixes. A consumer might not be able to afford a two-week trip to Europe but might spend a

weekend in New Orleans instead. He or she might eat healthily all week, then splurge with a pint of superpremium Haagen-Daz ice cream over the weekend. Marketers should be aware of the ways in which consumers feel deprived and look for opportunities to offer small indulgences that provide an emotional lift.

**9.** *Staying Alive.* People are motivated to live longer and better lives. People now know that their lifestyles can kill them—eating the wrong foods, smoking, breathing bad air, abusing drugs. They are increasingly taking responsibility for their own health and choosing better foods, exercising more regularly, and relaxing more often. Marketers can meet these needs by designing healthier products and services for consumers.

**10.** *The Vigilante Consumer.* Vigilante consumers are those who will no longer tolerate shoddy products and poor service. They want companies to be more aware and responsive. They want auto companies to take back "lemons" and fully refund their money. They subscribe to the *National Boycott News* and *Consumer Reports,* join MADD (Mothers Against Drunk Driving), buy "green products," and buy from companies that have socially responsible images, while boycotting those that don't. Marketers must serve as the consciences of their companies to bring these consumers better, more responsible products and services.

*Source*: This summary is drawn from various pages of Faith Popcorn, *The Popcorn Report* (New York: Harper Business, 1992).

PEOPLE'S VIEWS OF OTHERS. More recently, observers have noted a shift from a "me-society" to a "we-society" in which more people want to connect with and serve others. Flashy spending and self-indulgence appear to be on the way out, whereas saving, family concerns, and helping others are on the rise. This suggests a bright future for "social support" products and services that improve direct communication between people, such as health clubs, family vacations, and games. It also suggests a growing market for "social substitutes"—things like VCRs and computers that allow isolated people to feel that they are not alone.

PEOPLE'S VIEWS OF ORGANIZATIONS.    People vary in their attitudes toward corporations, government agencies, trade unions, universities, and other organizations. By and large, people are willing to work for major organizations and expect them, in turn, to carry out society's work. In recent years, there has been a decline in organizational loyalty and a growing skepticism among Americans regarding business and political organizations and institutions. People are giving a little less to organizations and are trusting them less. For example, in a recent survey of U.S. heads of households, 75 percent agreed that most big companies are out for themselves.[18]

This trend suggests that organizations need to find new ways to win consumer confidence. They need to review their advertising communications to make sure their messages are honest. They also need to make sure that their various activities enhance their image as "good corporate citizens." More companies are linking themselves to worthwhile causes, measuring their images with important publics, and using public relations to build more positive images (see Marketing at Work 3-3).[19]

PEOPLE'S VIEWS OF SOCIETY.    People vary in their attitudes toward their society, from patriots who defend it, to reformers who want to change it, to malcontents who want to leave it. People's orientation to their society influences their consumption patterns, levels of savings, and attitudes toward the marketplace.

The 1980s and 1990s have seen an increase in consumer patriotism. Many U.S. companies have responded with "made in America" themes and flag-waving promotions. For example, Black & Decker recently added a flaglike symbol to its tools. And for the past several years, the American textile industry has blitzed consumers with its "Crafted with Pride in the USA" advertising campaign, insisting that "made in the USA" matters. In 1991, many companies used patriotic appeals and promotions to express their support of American troops in the Persian Gulf War and to ride the wave of national pride and patriotism that followed.[20]

*Many companies have responded to an increase in consumer patriotism with "flag-waving" ads and programs.*

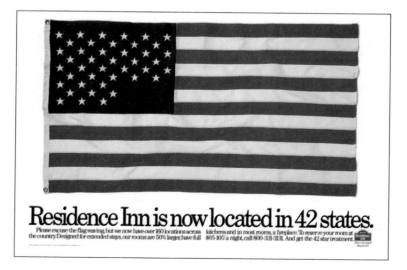

PEOPLE'S VIEWS OF NATURE.   People vary in their attitudes toward the natural world. Some feel ruled by it, others feel in harmony with it, and still others seek to master it. Growing human mastery over nature through technology and the belief that nature is bountiful have been popular attitudes in the past. More recently, however, people have recognized that nature is finite and fragile—that it can be spoiled or destroyed by human activities.

This renewed appreciation of nature is leading to more camping, hiking, boating, fishing, and other outdoor activities. Business has responded by offering more hiking gear, camping equipment, better insect repellents, and other products for nature enthusiasts. Tour operators are offering more wilderness adventures. Food producers have found growing markets for "natural" products like whole-grain cereal, naturally flavored ice cream, and health foods. Marketing communicators are using appealing natural backgrounds in advertising their products.

PEOPLE'S VIEWS OF THE UNIVERSE.   Finally, people vary in their beliefs about the origin of the universe and their place in it. Although most Americans practice religion, religious conviction and practice have been dropping off gradually through the years. As people turn away from their religious orientation, they seek goods and experiences with more immediate satisfactions. During the 1980s, people increasingly measured success in terms of career achievement, wealth, and worldly possessions. Some futurists, however, have noted an emerging renewal of interest in religion and a new spiritualism, perhaps as a part of a broader search for a new inner purpose. In the 1990s, people are moving away from materialism and dog-eat-dog ambition to seek more permanent values and a more certain grasp of right and wrong. As one trend tracker suggests: "The Nineties will see a marked change in the way society defines success, with achievements such as a happy family life and service to one's community replacing money as the measure of one's worth."[21] She continues, "The Nineties will be a far less cynical decade than the Eighties. Yes, we will still care what things cost. But we will seek to value only those things—family, community, earth, faith—that will endure."[22]

# RESPONDING TO THE MARKETING ENVIRONMENT

Many companies view the marketing environment as an "uncontrollable" element to which they must adapt. They passively accept the marketing environment and do not try to change it. They analyze the environmental forces and design strategies that will help the company avoid the threats and take advantage of the opportunities that the environment provides.

**Environmental management perspective**
A management perspective in which the firm takes aggressive actions to affect the publics and forces in its marketing environment rather than simply watching and reacting to it.

Other companies take an **environmental management perspective**.[23] Rather than simply watching and reacting, these firms take aggressive actions to affect the publics and forces in their marketing environment. Such companies hire lobbyists to influence legislation affecting their industries and stage media events to gain favorable press coverage. They run "advertorials" (ads expressing editorial points of view) to shape public opinion. They press law suits and file complaints with regulators to keep competitors in line, and they form contractual agreements to better control their distribution channels.

## MARKETING AT WORK 3-3

# CAUSE-RELATED MARKETING: DOING WELL BY DOING GOOD

These days, every product seems to be tied to some cause. Buy Purina cat food and help the American Association of Zoological Parks and Aquariums save endangered big cat species. Drink Tang and earn money for Mothers Against Drunk Driving. Drive a Dollar rental car and help support the Special Olympics. Or, if you want to help the Leukemia Society of America, buy Helping Hand trash bags or toilet paper. Pay for these purchases with the right charge card and you can support a local cultural arts group or help fight cancer or heart disease.

Cause-related marketing has become one of the hottest forms of corporate giving. It lets companies "do well by doing good" by linking purchases of the company's products or services with fundraising for worthwhile causes or charitable organizations. Cause-related marketing has grown rapidly since the early 1980s, when American Express offered to donate one cent to the restoration of the Statue of Liberty for each use of its charge card. American Express ended up having to contribute $1.7 million, but the cause-related campaign produced a 28 percent increase in card usage.

Cause-related marketing: Johnson & Johnson teams with the National Safety Council to sponsor its Safe Kids program to reduce children's injuries.

Companies now sponsor dozens of cause-related marketing campaigns each year. Many are backed by large budgets and a full complement of marketing activities. Here are some other examples:

*Johnson & Johnson teamed with the Children's Hospital Medical Center and the National Safety Council to sponsor a five-year cause-related marketing campaign to reduce preventable children's injuries, the leading killer of children. Some 43 other nonprofit groups, including the American Red Cross, National Parent Teachers Association, and the Boy and Girl Scouts of America, helped to promote the campaign. The campaign offered consumers a free safety kit for children in exchange for proofs of purchase. Consumers could also buy a child's safety video for $9.95. The video*

However, other companies find positive ways to overcome seemingly uncontrollable environmental constraints. For example, Citicorp, the U.S. banking giant, tried for years to start full-service banking in Maryland. It had only credit card and small service operations in the state. Under Maryland law, out-of-state banks

featured a game show format that made learning about safety entertaining as well as educational. To promote the campaign, J&J distributed almost 50 million advertising inserts in daily newspapers and developed a special information kit for retailers that contained posters, floor displays, and other in-store promotion materials. Safety tip sheets and emergency phone stickers were also available as free consumer handouts.

Procter & Gamble has sponsored many cause-related marketing campaigns. For example, for many years, P&G has mailed out billions of coupons on behalf of the Special Olympics for retarded children, helping make the event a household word. P&G supports its Special Olympics efforts with national advertising and public relations, and its salespeople work with local volunteers to encourage retailers to build point-of-purchase displays. In another recent cause-related marketing effort, Procter & Gamble has set up the Jif Children's Education Fund. For every pound of Jif peanut butter sold during the three-month promotion, P&G donates 10 cents to the fund, which will be distributed to parent-teacher groups at registered elementary schools in America. The program is designed to raise more than $4 million for U.S. elementary education.

Through focus group studies, Levi Strauss learned that young parents were greatly frustrated in their efforts to get their preschoolers dressed in the morning rush to work and day care. The company also learned that only 40 percent of the parents knew of its Little Levi's line of clothing for young children. So Levi paid the Bank Street College of Education to create a booklet for preschoolers called "Let's Get Dressed!" The activity booklet that uses fun games and puzzles to teach kids how to dress themselves. A companion booklet provides tips for parents on how to take the hassle out of dressing their children. Retailers offered the booklets as a gift with purchases of Little Levi's clothing and supported the campaign with in-store promotions and local ads. Readers were given an address from which they could order the booklets for 50 cents. The campaign also received substantial publicity coverage on TV talk shows and in national women's magazines. Sales of Little Levi's have tripled since the cause-related marketing campaign began.

Cause-related marketing has stirred some controversy. Critics are concerned that cause-related marketing might eventually undercut traditional "no-strings" corporate giving, as more and more companies grow to expect marketing benefits from their contributions. Critics also worry that cause-related marketing will cause a shift in corporate charitable support toward more visible, popular, and low-risk charities—those with more certain and substantial marketing appeal. For example, Master-Card's Choose to Make a Difference campaign raises money for six charities, each selected in part because of its popularity in a consumer poll. Finally, critics worry that cause-related marketing is more a strategy for selling than a strategy for giving, that "cause-related" marketing is really "cause-exploitative" marketing. Thus, companies using cause-related marketing might find themselves walking a fine line between increased sales and an improved image, and facing charges of exploitation.

However, if handled well, cause-related marketing can greatly benefit both the company and the charitable organization. The company gains an effective marketing tool while building a more positive public image. One recent study found that 66 percent of consumers will choose a product that has a relationship with a cause or charitable organization over others that don't. The charitable organization gains greater visibility and important new sources of funding, which can be substantial. In total, such campaigns now contribute some $100 million annually to the coffers of charitable organizations, and surveys show that these cause-related contributions usually add to, rather than undercut, direct company contributions. Thus, when cause marketing works, everyone benefits.

*Sources*: See Cyndee Miller, "Drug Company Begins Its Own Children's Crusade," *Marketing News*, June 6, 1988, pp. 1, 2; "School Kids Snack for Cash," *Advertising Age*, February 2, 1990, p. 36; Melanie Rigney and Julie Steenhuysen, "Conscience Raising," *Advertising Age*, August 26, 1991, p. 19; Nancy Arnott, "Marketing with a Passion," *Sales & Marketing Management*, January 1994, pp. 64–71; Geoffrey Smith, "Are Good Causes Good Marketing?" *Business Week*, March 21, 1994, pp. 64–65; and Craig Smith, "The New Corporate Philanthropy," *Harvard Business Review*, May–June 1994, pp. 105–16.

could provide only certain services and were barred from advertising, setting up branches, and other types of marketing. In March 1985, Citicorp offered to build a major credit-card center in Maryland that would create 1,000 white-collar jobs and further offered the state $1 million in cash for the property where it would locate. By imaginatively designing a proposal to benefit Maryland, Citicorp became the first out-of-state bank to provide full banking services there.[24]

Marketing management cannot always control environmental forces. In many cases, it must settle for simply watching and reacting to the environment. For example, a company would have little success trying to influence geographic population shifts, the economic environment, or major cultural values. But whenever possible, marketing managers should take a *proactive* rather than *reactive* approach to the marketing environment.

## SUMMARY

Companies must examine the *marketing environment* in order to seek opportunities and monitor threats. The marketing environment consists of all the actors and forces that affect the company's ability to transact business effectively with its target market. The company's marketing environment can be divided into the microenvironment and the macroenvironment.

The *microenvironment* consists of five components. The first is the company's *internal environment*—its several departments and management levels—which affects marketing management's decision making. The second component is *marketing channel firms* that cooperate to create value—the suppliers and marketing intermediaries (middlemen, physical distribution firms, marketing services agencies, financial intermediaries). The third component consists of the five types of *customer markets* in which the company can sell: the consumer, producer, reseller, government, and international markets. The fourth component is the *competitors* facing the company. The fifth component consists of all the *publics* that have an actual or potential interest in or impact on the organization's ability to achieve its objectives. The seven types of publics include financial, media, government, citizen action, and local, general, and internal publics.

The company's *macroenvironment* consists of major forces that shape opportunities for and pose threats to the company. These forces include demographic, economic, natural, technological, political, and cultural forces.

The *demographic environment* reveals a changing age structure, a changing family profile, geographic population shifts, a better-educated and more white-collar population, and increasing ethnic and racial diversity. The *economic environment* shows changing real income and changing consumer spending patterns. The *natural environment* exhibits future shortages of certain raw materials, increased energy costs and pollution levels, and expanding government intervention in natural resource management. The *technological environment* shows rapid technological change, unlimited innovational opportunities, high R&D budgets, concentration on minor improvements rather than major discoveries, and increased regulation of technological change. The *political environment* is characterized by increasing business regulation, strong government agency enforcement, and the growth of public interest groups. The *cultural environment* demonstrates long-run trends toward a "we-society," decreasing organizational loyalty, increasing patriotism, a renewed appreciation for nature, and a search for more meaningful and enduring values.

## KEY TERMS

Baby boom

Cultural environment

Demography

Economic environment

Engel's laws

Environmental management perspective

Macroenvironment

Marketing environment

Marketing intermediaries

Microenvironment

Natural environment

Political environment

Public

Technological environment

## QUESTIONS FOR DISCUSSION

1. What environmental trends will affect the success of Walt Disney Company throughout the 1990s? If you were in charge of marketing at Disney, what plans would you make to deal with these trends?

2. The 75 million members of the baby boom generation are aging, with the oldest members already passing their fiftieth birthdays. List some marketing opportunities and threats associated with this demographic trend.

3. In an era of megabank mergers and electronic banking, many banks are closing branches. Yet those banks that have carved out a niche with ethnic customers are opening new branches and expanding services. How would you explain this situation?

4. Americans are becoming more concerned about the natural environment. How would this trend affect a company that markets plastic sandwich bags? Discuss some effective responses such a company might make to this trend.

5. In the 1930s, President Franklin Roosevelt used his cigarette holder as a personal "trademark." Would a president be seen smoking today? How has the cultural environment changed? How might a cigarette manufacturer market its products differently to meet this new environment?

6. Some marketing goals, such as improved quality, require strong support from an internal public—a company's own employees. But surveys show that employees increasingly distrust management, and company loyalty is eroding. How can a company market internally to help meet its goals? Identify some alternative approaches.

## APPLYING THE CONCEPTS

1. Changes in the marketing environment mean that marketers must meet new consumer needs that may be quite different—even directly opposite—from those in the past. Ben & Jerry's became successful by making great-tasting ice cream with a huge butterfat content. They now offer low-fat frozen yogurt to appeal to baby boomers who are concerned about their waistlines. You can track changes in the marketing environment by looking at how companies modify their products.

    ◆ Make a list of the products that you encounter in one day that claim to be "low" or "high" in some ingredient, such as low-tar cigarettes or high-fiber cereal.

    ◆ Then write down similar products that seem to offer the opposite characteristics.

    ◆ In each case, which product do you think came first? Do you think that this is an effective response to a changing marketing environment?

2. The political environment can have a direct impact on marketers and their plans. In 1994, the election of a primarily Republican House of Representatives for the first time in decades signaled that the political environment was likely to change significantly through the middle 1990s.

    ◆ Name three industries whose marketing plans and strategies will probably be affected by these political changes in Washington.

    ◆ For each of the industries that you name, list three potential strategies to help adapt to the coming changes in the political environment.

    ◆ Although environmental changes appear likely, are they *certain*? How should companies plan for unsettled conditions?

## REFERENCES

1. Adapted from portions of Nathan Cobb, "Agent X," *The Boston Globe*, September 28, 1994, pp. 35, 40.

2. Many of the global statistical data in this chapter are drawn from the *World Almanac and Book of Facts, 1993.*

3. Sally D. Goll, "Marketing: China's (Only) Children Get the Royal Treatment," *Wall Street Journal*, February 8, 1995, pp. B1, B3.

4. Diane Crispell, "Generations to 2025," *American Demographics*, January 1995, p. 4.

5. See Joe Schwartz, "Is the Baby Boomlet Ending?" *American Demographics*, May 1992, p. 9; and Christopher Farrell, "The Baby Boomlet May Kick in a Little Growth," *Business Week*, January 10, 1994, p. 66; and Diane Crispell, "Generations to 2025," *American Demographics*, January 1995, p. 4.

6. See Christopher Power, "Getting 'Em While They're Young," *Business Week*, September 9, 1991, pp. 94–95; James U. McNeal, "Growing Up in the Market," *American Demographics*, October 1992, pp. 46–50; Horst Stipp, "New Ways to Reach Children," *American Demographics*, August 1993, pp. 50–56; T. L. Stanley, "Get Ready for Gen Y," *Brandweek*, May 15, 1995, p. 36; and Peter Zollo, "Talking to Teens," *American Demographics*, November 1995, pp. 22–27.

7. See Diane Crispell and William H. Frey, "American Maturity," *American Demographics*, March 1993, pp. 31–42; Charles F. Longino, "Myths of an Aging America," *American Demographics*, August 1994, pp. 36–43; and Melissa Campanelli, "Selling to Seniors: A Waiting Game," *Sales & Marketing Management*, June 1994, p. 69.

8. These and other statistics in this section are from "The Future of Households," *American Demographics*, December 1993, pp. 27–39; Melissa Campanelli, "It's All in the Family," *Sales & Marketing Management*, April 1994, p. 53; and Peter Francese, "America at Mid-Decade," *American Demographics*, February 1995, pp. 23–29.

9. Judith Waldrop, "What Do Working Women Want?" *American Demographics*, September 1994, pp. 36–38; and Patricia Braus, "Sorry Boys—Donna Reed Is Still Dead," *American Demographics*, September 1995, pp. 13–14.

10. See Joe Schwartz, "On the Road Again," *American Demographics*, April 1987, pp. 39–42; "Americans Keep Going West—And South," *Business Week*, May 16, 1988, p. 30; "State of Things to Come," *American Demographics*, October 1994, p. 39; and Joseph Spiers, "Where Americans Are Moving," *Fortune*, August 21, 1995, pp. 38–39.

11. See Thomas Moore, "Different Folks, Different Strokes," *Fortune*, September 16, 1985, pp. 65–68; and Sharon O'Malley, "The Rural Rebound," *American Demographics*, May 1994, pp. 24–29.

12. See Fabian Linden, "In the Rearview Mirror," *American Demographics*, April 1984, pp. 4–5; and Peter Francese, "America at Mid-Decade," *American Demographics*, February 1995, pp. 23–29.

13. See *Business Week*, December 21, 1992, pp. 29–30; Cyndee Miller, "Researcher Says U.S. Is More of a Bowl than a Melting Pot," *Marketing News*, May 10, 1993, p. 6; and Francese, "America at Mid-Decade," p. 26.

14. James W. Hughes, "Understanding the Squeezed Consumer," *American Demographics*, July 1991, pp. 44–50. Also see Patricia Sellers, "Winning Over the New Consumer," *Fortune*, July 29, 1991, pp. 113–25; and Brian O'Reilly, "Preparing for Leaner Times," *Fortune*, January 27, 1992, pp. 40–47.

15. For more discussion, see the "Environmentalism" section in Chapter 17. Also see Jacquelyn Ottman, "Environmentalism Will Be *the* Trend of the '90s," *Marketing News*, December 7, 1992, p. 13; Robert Rehak, "Green Marketing Awash in Third Wave," *Advertising Age*, November 22, 1993, p. 22; Peter Stisser, "A Deeper Shade of Green," *American Demographics*, March 1994, pp. 24–29; and Michael E. Porter and Claas van der Linde, "Green *and* Competitive: Ending the Stalemate," *Harvard Business Review*, September–October 1995, pp. 120–34.

16. John Carey, "Could America Afford the Transistor Today?" *Business Week*, March 7, 1994, pp. 80–84; and Peter Coy, "Blue-Sky Research Comes Down to Earth," *Business Week*, July 13, 1995, pp. 78–80.

17. For a summary of U.S. legal developments in marketing, see Louis W. Stern and Thomas L. Eovaldi, *Legal Aspects of Marketing Strategy: Antitrust and Consumer Protection Issues* (Englewood Cliffs, NJ: Prentice Hall, 1984); and Robert J. Posch, Jr., *The Complete Guide to Marketing and the Law* (Englewood Cliffs, NJ: Prentice Hall, 1988).

18. Adrienne Ward Fawcett, "Lifestyle Study," *Advertising Age*, April 18, 1994, pp. 12–13.

19. Also see Leah Rickard, "Spirituality, Hope on Horizon as Solace Sought," *Advertising Age*, November 7, 1994, pp. S1, S14.

20. See Kenneth Dreyfack, "Draping Old Glory Around Just About Everything," *Business Week*, October 27, 1986, pp. 66–67; Pat Sloan, "Ads Go All-American," *Advertising Age*, July 28, 1986, pp. 3, 52; "Retailers Rallying 'Round the Flag," *Advertising Age*, February 11, 1991, p. 4; and Gary Levin, "BASH, BASH, BASH: U.S. Marketers Turn Red, White, and Blue Against Japan," *Advertising Age*, February 3, 1992, pp. 1, 44.

21. Anne B. Fisher, "A Brewing Revolt Against the Rich," *Fortune*, December 17, 1990, pp. 89–94. Also see Rickard, "Spirituality, Hope on Horizon as Solace Sought," p. S-1.

22. Anne B. Fisher, "What Consumers Want in the 1990s," *Fortune*, January 21, 1990, p. 112. Also see Joseph M. Winski, "Who We Are, How We Live, What We Think," *Advertising Age*, January 20, 1992, pp. 16–18; and John Huey, "Finding New Heroes for a New Era," *Fortune*, January 25, 1993, pp. 62–69.

23. See Carl P. Zeithaml and Valerie A. Zeithaml, "Environmental Management: Revising the Marketing Perspective," *Journal of Marketing*, Spring 1984, pp. 46–53.

24. Philip Kotler, "Megamarketing," *Harvard Business Review*, March–April 1986, p. 117.

# Chapter

# 4

# *Marketing Research and Information Systems*

When Duncan Black and Alonzo Decker opened their first machine shop in 1910, portable power tools had yet to be invented. The typical industrial electric drill was a cumbersome 50-pound unit; two people were required to operate it, with a third controlling the power source. Black and Decker saw the need for a smaller, easier-to-use tool and designed a revolutionary new model—one with a smaller motor, a pistol grip, and a trigger switch. The rest is history. The original Black & Decker portable drill now resides in the Smithsonian Institution's National Museum of American History, and Black & Decker is now a leading marketer of portable power tools.

Black & Decker owes much of its success to its relentless efforts to learn all it can about customers. In 1991, market research revealed a growing but underserved power tool segment: serious do-it-yourselfers (SDIYers) who take on large, complex home improvement projects by themselves. Some 22 million strong, these serious handymen need more than the run-of-the-mill, entry-level tools used by occasional do-it-yourselfers, but less than the expensive, high-quality tools used by professionals. Black & Decker set out to develop a midrange line, Quantum, that would bridge the gap between entry level and professional tools.

The Quantum quest began with exhaustive consumer research to find out exactly what these serious do-it-yourselfers wanted in their power tools. Black & Decker first enlisted the services of 50 typical SDIYers—male homeowners, aged 25 to 54, who own more than six power tools and who undertake one or more major home improvement projects every year. For more than four months, these 50 people were subjected to intense scrutiny, serving like experimental mice in a kind of real-life laboratory. According to *Fortune* magazine: "They were questioned about the tools they use and why they had picked particular brands. B&D executives hung out with them in their homes and around their workshops. They watched how the 50 used their tools and asked why they liked or disliked certain ones, how the tools felt in their hands, and even how they cleaned up their workspace when they finished. The B&D people tagged along on shopping trips too, monitoring what the SDIYers bought and how much they spent. On occasion, executives even took an industrial psychologist with them on home visits, hoping this would tell even more about what the customer wanted." Black & Decker followed up this initial market research by interviewing hundreds of tool customers who had mailed in warranty cards, asking similar questions about tool preferences and buying behavior.

Once it understood SDIYers' needs and preferences, Black & Decker set out to create a line of tools that would give them what they wanted. It created a "fusion team"—85 Black & Decker employees from around the world, including marketers, engineers, designers, finance people, and others. Poring over the research findings, Team Quantum addressed consumers' concerns one by one. SDIYers wanted cordless tools that held their power long enough to complete long jobs— the team created a more powerful drill with a battery pack that recharged in only an hour instead of 24 hours. The handymen wanted tools that required less cleanup after the day's work was done. So the new Quantum circular saws and sanders came equipped with a bag attachment that sucked up sawdust and eliminated cleanup. Finally, although confident about their own abilities, SDIYers sometimes wanted access to expert advice on their tools and projects. To satisfy this requirement, Black & Decker set up Powersource: The Information Network for Serious Do-It-Yourselfers. This innovative program provided a toll-free hotline staffed by experienced advisers ready to answer home repair questions from 7 A.M. to 10 P.M., seven days a week. Powersource also offered customers an assortment of detailed plans for building furniture and other home improvement projects, as well as a subscription to *Shop Talk*, a newsletter containing workshop tips and project guides.

Black & Decker relied on additional consumer research to guide other important decisions. Quantum tools were colored a deep green because consumers associated this color with quality and reliability. Even the Quantum name was based on research—consumers could pronounce it easily, and they felt that the name suggested a product that was a step above others.

The new Quantum line, introduced in mid-1993 as "Serious Tools for Serious Projects," became an immediate success. Sales were brisk, and the line won a number of retailing awards, including the highly regarded Retailers' Choice Award from *Do-It-Yourself Retailing* magazine. And based on the new tool line and on its strong commitment to customer service, Black & Decker earned Vendor of the Year Awards from Wal-Mart, Builders Square, Channel Home Centers, and a number of other retailers.

Despite this early success, Black & Decker continued to listen to its customers. Within a few months of the Quantum introduction, the company held a three-day phonathon to gather the thoughts of 2,500 customers concerning their new Quantum tools. As *Fortune* reported: "Nearly 200 employees—assembly-line workers, marketing executives, and everyone in between—flew from around the world to company headquarters in Towson, Maryland, where the cafeteria had been set up with phone banks, computers, and, in the words of Quantum program manager Clifford Hall, 'lots of pizza.' Says he: 'We want everyone associated with Quantum to hear what the consumer has to say.' " All of this marketing research appears to be paying off handsomely. According to one industry analyst, "Black & Decker has become very good at taking market share away from rival companies. They just know their customer."[1]   ■

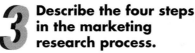

# CHAPTER OBJECTIVES

## After reading this chapter, you should be able to:

**1** Explain the importance of information to the company.

**2** Define the marketing information system and discuss its parts.

**3** Describe the four steps in the marketing research process.

**4** Identify the different kinds of information the company might use.

**5** Compare the advantages and disadvantages of various methods of collecting information.

In order to produce superior value and satisfaction for customers, companies need information at almost every turn. As the Black & Decker story highlights, good products and marketing programs begin with a thorough understanding of consumer needs and wants. Companies also need an abundance of information on competitors, resellers, and other actors and forces in the marketplace. Increasingly, marketers are viewing information not just as an input for making better decisions, but also as an important strategic asset and marketing tool.[2]

During the past century, most companies were small and knew their customers firsthand. Managers picked up marketing information by being around people, observing them, and asking questions. During this century, however, many factors have increased the need for more and better information. As companies become national or international in scope, they need more information on larger, more distant markets. As incomes increase and buyers become more selective, sellers need better information about how buyers respond to different products and appeals. As sellers use more complex marketing approaches and face more competition, they need information on the effectiveness of their marketing tools. Finally, in today's rapidly changing environments, managers need up-to-date information to make timely decisions.

Fortunately, increasing information requirements have been met by an explosion of information technologies. The past 30 years have witnessed the emergence of small computers, microfilming, cable television, fax machines, video recorders, CD-ROM drives, and a host of other devices that have revolutionized information handling. Using improved information systems, companies now can provide information in great quantities. In fact, today's managers sometimes receive too much information. For example, one study found that with all the companies offering data, and with all the information now available through supermarket scanners, a packaged-goods brand manager is bombarded with one million to one *billion* new numbers each week.[3] As one analyst points out: "Running out of information is not a problem, but drowning in it is."[4]

Yet marketers frequently complain that they lack enough information of the *right* kind or have too much of the *wrong* kind. Often, important information arrives too late to be useful, or on-time information is not accurate. Thus, marketing managers need more and better information. Companies have greater capacity to provide managers with good information, but often have not made good use of it. Many companies are now studying their managers' information needs and designing information systems to meet those needs.

# ▶THE MARKETING INFORMATION SYSTEM

**Marketing information system (MIS)**
People, equipment, and procedures to gather, sort, analyze, evaluate, and distribute needed, timely, and accurate information to marketing decision makers.

A **marketing information system (MIS)** consists of people, equipment, and procedures to gather, sort, analyze, evaluate, and distribute needed, timely, and accurate information to marketing decision makers. Figure 4-1 shows that the MIS begins and ends with marketing managers. First, it interacts with these managers to *assess information needs*. Next, it *develops needed information* from internal company records, marketing intelligence activities, marketing research, and information analysis. Finally, the MIS *distributes information* to managers in the right form at the right time to help them make better marketing decisions.

## ASSESSING INFORMATION NEEDS

A good marketing information system balances the information managers would *like* to have against what they really *need* and what is *feasible* to offer. The company begins by interviewing managers to find out what information they would like. But managers do not always need all the information they ask for, and they may not ask for all they really need. Moreover, the MIS cannot always supply all the information that managers request.

Some managers will ask for whatever information they can get without thinking carefully about what they really need. Too much information can be as harmful as too little. Other managers may omit things they ought to know, or may not know to ask for some types of information they should have. For example, managers might

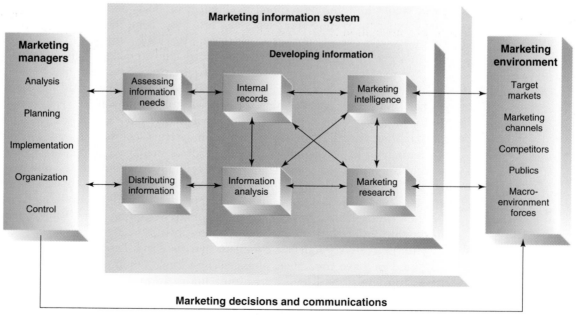

FIGURE 4-1
*The marketing information system*

need to know that a competitor plans to introduce a new product during the coming year. Because they do not know about the new product, they do not think to ask about it. The MIS must watch the marketing environment in order to provide decision makers with information they should have to make key marketing decisions.

Sometimes the company cannot provide the needed information, either because it is not available or because of MIS limitations. For example, a brand manager might want to know how competitors will change their advertising budgets next year and how these changes will affect industry market shares. The information on planned budgets probably is not available. Even if it is, the company's MIS may not be advanced enough to forecast resulting changes in market shares.

Finally, the costs of obtaining, processing, storing, and delivering information can mount quickly. The company must decide whether the benefits of having an item of information are worth the costs of providing it, and both value and cost are often hard to assess. By itself, information has no worth; its value comes from its *use*. In many cases, additional information will do little to change or improve a manager's decision, or the costs of the information may exceed the returns from the improved decision. Marketers should not assume that additional information will always be worth obtaining. Rather, they should weigh carefully the costs of obtaining additional information against the benefits resulting from its use.[5]

## DEVELOPING INFORMATION

The information needed by marketing managers can be obtained from *internal company records, marketing intelligence,* and *marketing research*. The information analysis system then processes it to make it more useful for managers.

### Internal Records

**Internal records information**
Information gathered from sources within the company to evaluate marketing performance and detect marketing problems and opportunities.

Most marketing managers use internal records and reports regularly, especially for making day-to-day planning, implementation, and control decisions. **Internal records information** consists of information gathered from sources within the company to evaluate marketing performance and to identify marketing problems and opportunities. The accounting department prepares financial statements and keeps detailed records of sales, costs, and cash flows. Manufacturing reports on production schedules, shipments, and inventories. The sales force reports on reseller reactions and competitor activities. The marketing department maintains a database of customer demographics, psychographics, and buying behavior. The customer service department provides information on customer satisfaction or service problems. Research studies done for one department may provide useful information for several others. Managers can use information gathered from these and other sources within the company to evaluate performance, detect problems, and create new marketing opportunities.

Here are examples of how companies use internal records information in making better marketing decisions:[6]

> *Spiegel.* Tucked away inside the bowels of many a computerized billing system are megabytes of data about what customers order.... Spiegel, the big direct-mail marketer, mined its database and hit gold [in the form of] *E Style,* a catalog aimed at black women. To create it, Spiegel [advertised] its regular wish book in *Ebony* and *Essence* magazines to create a mailing list. Then, using its database, Spiegel kept track of these

customers' purchasing patterns, using what they bought as a guide to putting together a catalogue with specific appeal to African American women. *E Style*, for instance, offers lots of hats because Spiegel's database shows that black women buy them. . . . *E Style* sales are running 50 percent above the company's original projections.

*Frito-Lay.* Frito-Lay uses its sophisticated internal information system to analyze daily sales performance. Each day, Frito-Lay's salespeople report their day's efforts via handheld computers to Frito-Lay headquarters in Dallas. Twenty-four hours later, Frito-Lay's marketing managers have a complete report analyzing the previous day's sales of Fritos, Doritos, and other brands. The system helps marketing managers make better decisions and makes the salespeople more effective. It greatly reduces the number of hours spent filling out reports, giving salespeople extra time for selling.

Internal records can usually be accessed more quickly and cheaply than other information sources, but they also present some problems. Because internal information was collected for other purposes, it may be incomplete or in the wrong form for making marketing decisions. For example, sales and cost data used by the accounting department for preparing financial statements must be adapted for use in evaluating product, sales force, or channel performance. In addition, a large company produces great amounts of information, and keeping track of it all is difficult. The marketing information system must gather, organize, process, and index this mountain of information so that managers can find it easily and get it quickly.

## Marketing Intelligence

**Marketing intelligence**
Everyday information about developments in the marketing environment that helps managers prepare and adjust marketing plans.

**Marketing intelligence** is everyday information about developments in the marketing environment. The marketing intelligence system determines what intelligence is needed, collects it by searching the environment, and delivers it to marketing managers.

Marketing intelligence can be gathered from many sources. Much intelligence can be collected from the company's own personnel—executives, engineers and scientists, purchasing agents, and the sales force. But company people are often busy and fail to pass on important information. The company must "sell" its people on their importance as intelligence gatherers, train them to spot new developments, and urge them to report intelligence back to the company.

The company must also persuade suppliers, resellers, and customers to pass along important intelligence. Information on competitors can be obtained from what they say about themselves in annual reports, speeches and press releases, and advertisements. The company can also learn about competitors from what others say about them in business publications and at trade shows. Or the company can watch what competitors do—buying and analyzing competitors' products, monitoring their sales, and checking for new patents (see Marketing at Work 4-1).

Companies also buy intelligence information from outside suppliers. Nielsen Marketing Research sells data on brand shares, retail prices, and percentages of stores stocking different brands. Information Resources, Inc., sells supermarket scanner purchase data from a panel of 60,000 households nationally, with measures of trial and repeat purchasing, brand loyalty, and buyer demographics.[7]

For a fee, companies can subscribe to any of more than 3,000 online databases or information search services. For example, the Adtrack online database tracks all the advertisements of a quarter page or larger from 150 major consumer and business publications. Companies can use these data to assess their own and competitors' advertising strategies and styles, shares of advertising space, media usage, and ad budgets. The Donnelly Demographics database provides demographic data from the U.S. census plus Donnelly's own demographic projections by state, city, or zip code. Companies can use it to measure markets and develop segmentation strategies. The Electronic Yellow Pages, which contains listings from nearly all the nation's 4,800 phone books, is the largest directory of American companies available. A firm such as Burger King might use this database to count McDonald's restaurants in different geographic locations. Online databases are available in most parts of the world. For example, the Eurobases and Euroscope databases provide a wealth of information on commercial, legal, and cultural aspects of European affairs.[8]

A readily available online database exists to fill almost any marketing information need. General database services such as CompuServe, Dialog, and Nexis put an incredible wealth of information at the fingertips of marketing decision makers. A company doing business in Germany can check out CompuServe's German Company Library of financial and product information on more than 48,000 German-owned firms. A U.S. auto parts manufacturer can punch up Dun & Bradstreet Financial Profiles and Company Reports to develop biographical sketches of key General Motors, Ford, and Chrysler executives. Just about any information a marketer might need—demographic data, today's Associated Press news wire reports, a list of active U.S. trademarks in the United States—is available from online databases.[9]

Some companies set up an office to collect and circulate marketing intelligence. The staff scans major publications, summarizes important news, and sends bulletins to marketing managers. It develops a file of intelligence information and helps managers evaluate new information. These services greatly improve the quality of information available to marketing managers.

## Marketing Research

Managers cannot always wait for information to arrive in bits and pieces from the marketing intelligence system. They often require formal studies of specific situations. For example, Toshiba wants to know how many and what kinds of people or companies will buy its new superfast laptop computer. Or Barat College in Lake Forest, Illinois, needs to know what percentage of its target market has heard of Barat, how they heard, what they know, and how they feel about Barat. In such situations, the marketing intelligence system will not provide the detailed information needed. Managers will need marketing research.

**Marketing research**
Information used to identify and define marketing opportunities and problems; to generate, refine, and evaluate marketing actions; to monitor marketing performance; and to improve understanding of the marketing process.

We define **marketing research** as the systematic design, collection, analysis, and reporting of data and findings relevant to a specific marketing situation facing an organization. Every marketer needs research. Marketing researchers engage in a wide variety of activities, ranging from market potential and market share studies, to assessments of customer satisfaction and purchase behavior, to studies of pricing, product, distribution, and promotion activities.

A company can conduct marketing research in its own research department or have some or all of it done outside. Whether a company uses outside firms depends on its own research skills and resources. Although most large companies have their own marketing research departments, they often use outside firms to do special research tasks or studies. A company with no research department has to buy the services of research firms.

# MARKETING AT WORK 4-1

# INTELLIGENCE GATHERING: SNOOPING ON COMPETITORS

Competitive intelligence gathering has grown dramatically as more and more companies need to know what their competitors are doing. Many well-known companies are now busily snooping on their competitors. Techniques that companies use to collect their own marketing intelligence fall into four major groups.

### GETTING INFORMATION FROM RECRUITS AND COMPETITORS' EMPLOYEES

Companies can obtain intelligence through job interviews or from conversations with competitors' employees. According to *Fortune*:

*When they interview students for jobs, some companies pay special attention to those who have worked for competitors, even temporarily. Job seekers are eager to impress and often have not been warned about divulging what is proprietary. They sometimes volunteer valuable information. . . . Companies sometimes even advertise and hold interviews for jobs that don't exist in order to entice competitors' employees to spill the beans.*

*Companies send engineers to conferences and trade shows to question competitors' technical people. Often conversations start innocently—just a few fellow technicians discussing processes and problems . . . [yet competitors'] engineers and scientists often brag about surmounting technical challenges, in the process divulging sensitive information.*

### GETTING INFORMATION FROM PEOPLE WHO DO BUSINESS WITH COMPETITORS

Key customers can keep the company informed about competitors and their products, and intelligence can be gathered by infiltrating customers' business operations:

*For example, a while back Gillette told a large Canadian account the date on which it planned to begin selling its new Good News disposable razor in the United States. The Canadian distributor promptly called Bic and told it about the impending product launch. Bic put on a crash program and was able to start selling its razor shortly after Gillette did.*

*Companies may provide their engineers free of charge to customers. . . . The close, cooperative relationship that the engineers on loan cultivate* with the customers' design staff often enables them to learn what new products competitors are pitching.

### GETTING INFORMATION FROM PUBLISHED MATERIALS AND PUBLIC DOCUMENTS

Keeping track of seemingly meaningless published information can provide intelligence about competitors. For instance, the types of people that a company seeks in help-wanted ads can indicate something about its new strategies and products. Government agencies are another good source. For example:

*Although it is often illegal for a company to photograph a competitor's plant from the air, there are legitimate ways to get the photos. . . .*

*Collecting intelligence: Porsche notes that "it's not unusual for car companies to check out each other's creations . . . A new Porsche gets an inordinate amount of attention."*

## Four other car companies have already bought one. Whatever do you suppose they want them for?

Porsche 968: The next evolution.

Reverse engineering

*Aerial photos often are on file with the U.S. Geological Survey or Environmental Protection Agency. These are public documents, available for a nominal fee.*

*Zoning and tax assessment offices often have tax information on local factories and even have blueprints of the facilities, showing square footage and types of machinery. It's all publicly available.*

## GETTING INFORMATION BY OBSERVING COMPETITORS OR ANALYZING PHYSICAL EVIDENCE

Companies can get to know competitors better by buying their products or examining other physical evidence. An increasingly important form of competitive intelligence is benchmarking, taking apart competitors' products and imitating or improving upon their best features. Popular since the early 1980s, benchmarking has helped Xerox to turn around its copying business and Ford to develop the successful Taurus.

*When Ford decided to build a better car back in the early Eighties, it compiled a list of some 400 features its customers said were the most important, then set about finding the car with the best of each. Then it tried to match or top the best of the competition. The result: the hot-selling Taurus.*

By 1993, thanks in large part to such benchmarking efforts, the Taurus had overtaken the Honda Accord as America's best-selling passenger car. When updating the 1996 Taurus, Ford benchmarked all over again.

Beyond looking at competitors' products, companies can examine many other types of physical evidence. For example, in the absence of better information on market share and shipping volumes, companies have measured the rust on rails of railroad sidings to their competitors' plants or have counted the tractor-trailers leaving loading bays. Some companies even rifle their competitors' garbage:

*Once it has left the competitors' premises, refuse is legally considered abandoned property. While some companies now shred the paper coming out of their design labs, they often neglect to do this for almost-as-revealing refuse from the marketing or public relations departments.*

In a recent example of garbage snatching, Avon admitted that it had hired private detectives to paw through the dumpster of rival Mary Kay Cosmetics. Although an outraged Mary Kay sued to get its garbage back, Avon claimed that it had done nothing illegal. The dumpster had been located in a public parking lot, and Avon had videotapes to prove it.

The growing use of marketing intelligence raises a number of ethical issues. Although most of the above techniques are legal, and some are considered to be shrewdly competitive, many involve questionable ethics. In a recent survey, senior executives rated the ethics of various marketing intelligence practices. Many practices were rated as "clearly unethical," such as planting spies in competitors' facilities, bribing competitors' employees, and conducting phony job interviews. Others—such as reverse engineering, surveying competitors' customers, and reviewing competitors' patent applications, job advertisements, and financial statements—were perceived as "clearly ethical." More problematic, however, are practices rated in the fuzzy middle category, such as obtaining intelligence information by searching competitors' trash, hiring away competitors' key executives or other employees, or posing as a potential customer or supplier.

Companies should take advantage of publicly available information, but they should avoid practices that might be considered illegal or unethical. With all the legitimate intelligence sources now available, a company does not have to break the law or accepted codes of ethics to obtain good intelligence.

*Sources*: Excerpts from Steven Flax, "How to Snoop on Your Competitors," *Fortune,* May 14, 1984, pp. 29–33; Brian Dumaine, "Corporate Spies Snoop to Conquer," *Fortune,* November 7, 1988, pp. 68–76; and Jeremy Main, "How to Steal the Best Ideas Around," *Fortune,* October 19, 1992, pp. 102–6. Copyright © 1984, 1988, and 1992, Time Inc. All rights reserved. Also see Wendy Zellner and Bruce Hager, "Dumpster Raids? That's Not Very Ladylike, Avon," *Business Week,* April 1, 1991, p. 32; Shaker A. Zahra, "Unethical Practices in Competitive Analysis: Patterns, Causes and Effects," *Journal of Business Ethics,* 13, 1994, pp. 53–62; Kathleen Kerwin, "The Shape of a New Machine," *Business Week,* July 24, 1995, pp. 60–66; and Michael Haddigan, "Competitor Intelligence Considered More Vital Now," *Marketing News,* October 9, 1995, p. 3.

### Information Analysis

Information gathered by the company's marketing intelligence and marketing research systems often requires more analysis, and managers may need help in applying the information to their marketing problems and decisions. This help may include advanced statistical analysis to learn more about both the relationships within a set of data and their statistical reliability. Such analysis allows managers to go beyond means and standard deviations in the data and to answer questions about markets, marketing activities, and outcomes.

Information analysis might also involve a collection of mathematical models that will help marketers make better decisions. Each model represents some real system, process, or outcome. These models can help answer the questions of "what if" and "which is best." During the past 20 years, marketing scientists have developed numerous models to help marketing managers make better marketing-mix decisions, design sales territories and sales-call plans, select sites for retail outlets, develop optimal advertising mixes, and forecast new-product sales.[10]

# DISTRIBUTING INFORMATION

Marketing information has no value until managers use it to make better marketing decisions. The information gathered through marketing intelligence and marketing research must be distributed to the right marketing managers at the right time. Most companies have centralized marketing information systems that provide managers with regular performance reports, intelligence updates, and reports on the results of studies. Managers need these routine reports for making regular planning, implementation, and control decisions. But marketing managers also may need nonroutine information for special situations and on-the-spot decisions. For example, a sales manager having trouble with a large customer may want a summary of the account's sales and profitability over the past year. Or a retail store manager who has run out of a best-selling product may want to know the current inventory levels in the chain's other stores. In companies with only centralized information systems, these managers must request the information from the MIS staff and wait. Often, the information arrives too late to be useful.

Developments in information technology have caused a revolution in information distribution. With recent advances in computers, software, and telecommunication, most companies have decentralized their marketing information systems. In many companies, marketing managers have direct access to the information network through personal computers and other means. From any location, they can obtain information from internal records or outside information services, analyze the information using statistical packages and models, prepare reports on a word processor or desktop publishing system, and communicate with others in the network through electronic communications.

Such systems offer exciting prospects. They allow managers to get the information they need directly and quickly and to tailor it to their own needs. As more managers develop the skills needed to use such systems, and as technological improvements make them more economical, more and more marketing companies will use decentralized marketing information systems.

# ►THE MARKETING RESEARCH PROCESS

The marketing research process (see Figure 4-2) consists of four steps: *defining the problem and research objectives, developing the research plan, implementing the research plan,* and *interpreting and reporting the findings.*

## DEFINING THE PROBLEM AND RESEARCH OBJECTIVES

The marketing manager and the researcher must work closely together to define the problem carefully, and they must agree on the research objectives. The manager best understands the decision for which information is needed; the researcher best understands marketing research and how to obtain the information.

Managers should know enough about marketing research to help in the planning and the interpretation of research results. If they know little about marketing research, they may obtain the wrong information, accept wrong conclusions, or ask for information that costs too much. Experienced marketing researchers who understand the manager's problem should also be involved at this stage. The researcher must be able to help the manager define the problem and suggest ways that research can help the manager make better decisions.

Defining the problem and the research objectives is often the hardest step in the research process. The manager may know that something is wrong, without knowing the specific causes. For example, managers of a large discount store chain hastily decided that falling sales were caused by poor advertising, and they ordered research to test the company's advertising. When this research showed that current advertising was reaching the right people with the right message, the managers were puzzled. It turned out that the real problem was that the chain was not delivering the prices, products, and service promised in the advertising. Careful problem definition would have avoided the cost and delay of doing advertising research. In the classic New Coke case, the Coca-Cola Company defined its research problem too narrowly, with disastrous results (see Marketing at Work 4-2).

After the problem has been defined carefully, the manager and researcher must set the research objectives. A marketing research project might have one of three types of objectives. The objective of **exploratory research** is to gather preliminary information that will help define the problem and suggest hypotheses. The objective of **descriptive research** is to describe things such as the market potential for a product or the demographics and attitudes of consumers who buy the product. The objective of **causal research** is to test hypotheses about cause-and-effect relationships. For example, would a 10 percent decrease in tuition at a private college result in an enrollment increase sufficient to offset the reduced tuition?

**Exploratory research** Marketing research to gather preliminary information that will help to better define problems and suggest hypotheses for their solutions.

**Descriptive research** Marketing research to better describe marketing problems, situations, or markets, such as the market potential for a product or the demographics and attitudes of potential consumers.

**Causal research** Marketing research to test hypotheses about cause-and-effect relationships.

**FIGURE 4-2**
*The marketing research process*

| Defining the problem and research objectives | Developing the research plan for collecting information | Implementing the research plan— collecting and analyzing the data | Interpreting and reporting the findings |

Managers often start with exploratory research and later follow with descriptive or causal research.

The statement of the problem and the research objectives guides the entire research process. The manager and researcher should put the statement in writing to be certain that they agree on the purpose and expected results of the research.

## DEVELOPING THE RESEARCH PLAN

The second step of the marketing research process calls for determining the information needed, developing a plan for gathering it efficiently, and presenting the

---

## MARKETING AT WORK 4-2

# THE RISE AND FALL OF NEW COKE: WHAT'S THE PROBLEM?

In 1985, the Coca-Cola Company made a classic marketing blunder. After 99 successful years, it set aside its long-standing rule—"don't mess with Mother Coke"—and dropped its original-formula Coke! In its place came *New* Coke with a sweeter, smoother taste.

At first, amid the introductory flurry of advertising and publicity, New Coke sold well. But sales soon went flat, as a stunned public reacted. Coke began receiving sacks of mail and more than 1,500 phone calls each day from angry consumers. A group called Old Cola Drinkers staged protests, handed out T-shirts, and threatened a class-action suit unless Coca-Cola brought back the old formula. Most marketing experts predicted that New Coke would be the "Edsel of the Eighties." After only three months, the Coca-Cola Company brought old Coke back. Now called "Coke Classic," it sold

*When Coca-Cola introduced New Coke, consumers reacted angrily —they staged protests, handed out T-shirts, and threatened class action suits to get the old formula back.*

side-by-side with New Coke on supermarket shelves. The company said that New Coke would remain its "flagship" brand, but consumers had a different idea. By the end of 1985, Classic was outselling New Coke in supermarkets by two to one.

Quick reaction saved the company from potential disaster. It stepped up efforts for Coke Classic and slotted New Coke into a supporting role. Coke Classic again became the company's main brand—and the country's leading soft drink. New Coke became the company's "attack brand"—its Pepsi stopper—and ads boldly compared New Coke's taste with Pepsi's. Still, New Coke managed only a 2 percent market share. In the spring of 1990, the company repackaged New Coke and relaunched it as a brand extension with a new name— Coke II. Today, Coke Classic captures more than 20 percent of the U.S. soft drink market; Coke II holds a miniscule 0.1 percent.

Why was New Coke introduced in the first place? What went wrong? Many analysts blame the blunder on poor marketing research.

In the early 1980s, although Coke was still the leading soft

plan to marketing management. The plan outlines sources of existing data and spells out the specific research approaches, contact methods, sampling plans, and instruments that researchers will use to gather new data.

## Determining Specific Information Needs

Research objectives must be translated into specific information needs. For example, suppose Campbell decides to conduct research on how consumers would react to the company replacing its familiar red-and-white soup cans with new bowl-shaped plastic containers that it has used successfully for a number of its other products. The containers would cost more, but would allow consumers to heat

drink, it was slowly losing market share to Pepsi. For years, Pepsi had successfully mounted the "Pepsi Challenge," a series of televised taste tests showing that consumers preferred the sweeter taste of Pepsi. By early 1985, although Coke led in the overall market, Pepsi led in share of supermarket sales by 2 percent. (That doesn't sound like much, but 2 percent of the huge soft-drink market amounts to $1 billion in retail sales!) Coca-Cola had to do something to stop the loss of its market share, and the solution appeared to be a change in Coke's taste.

Coca-Cola began the largest new product research project in the company's history. It spent more than two years and $4 million on research before settling on a new formula. It conducted some 200,000 taste tests—30,000 on the final formula alone. In blind tests, 60 percent of consumers chose the new Coke over the old, and 52 percent chose it over Pepsi. Research showed that New Coke would be a winner, and the company introduced it with confidence. So what happened?

Looking back, we can see that Coke defined its marketing research problem too narrowly. The research looked only at taste; it did not explore consumers' feelings about dropping the old Coke and replacing it with a new version. It took no account of the *intangibles*— Coke's name, history, packaging, cultural heritage, and image. However, to many people, Coke stands alongside baseball, hot dogs, and apple pie as an American institution; it represents the very fabric of America. Coke's symbolic meaning turned out to be more important to many consumers than its taste. Research addressing a broader set of issues would have detected these strong emotions.

Coke's managers may also have used poor judgment in interpreting the research and planning strategies around it. For example, they took the finding that 60 percent of consumers preferred New Coke's taste to mean that the new product would win in the marketplace, as when a political candidate wins

with 60 percent of the vote. But the results also meant that 40 percent still liked the original formula. By dropping the old Coke, the company trampled the taste buds of a large core of loyal Coke drinkers who didn't want a change. The company might have been wiser to leave the old Coke alone and introduce New Coke as a brand extension, as it later did successfully with Cherry Coke.

The Coca-Cola Company has one of the largest, best-managed, and most advanced marketing research operations in America. Good marketing research has kept the company atop the rough-and-tumble soft-drink market for decades. But marketing research is far from an exact science. Consumers are full of surprises and figuring them out can be awfully tough. If Coca-Cola can make a large marketing research mistake, any company can.

*Sources:* See "Coke 'Family' Sales Fly as New Coke Stumbles," *Advertising Age,* January 17, 1986, p. 1; Jack Honomichl, "Missing Ingredients in 'New' Coke's Research," *Advertising Age,* July 22, 1985, p. 1; Andrew Wallenstein, "Coca-Cola's Glory Days," *Advertising Age,* April 17, 1995, p. 4; and Leah Rickard, "Remembering New Coke," *Advertising Age,* April 17, 1995, p. 6.

the soup in a microwave oven and eat it without using dishes. This research might call for the following specific information:

◆ The demographic, economic, and lifestyle characteristics of current soup users. Busy working couples might find the convenience of the new packaging worth the price; families with children might want to pay less and wash the pan and bowls.

◆ Consumer-usage patterns for soup: how much soup they eat, where, and when. The new packaging might be ideal for adults eating lunch on the go, but less convenient for parents feeding lunch to several children.

◆ Retailer reactions to the new packaging. Failure to get retailer support could hurt sales of the new package.

◆ The number of microwave ovens in consumer kitchens and business lunchrooms. (The number of microwaves will limit usage of the new containers.)

◆ Consumer attitudes toward the new packaging. The red-and-white Campbell can has become an American institution—will consumers accept the new packaging?

◆ Forecasts of sales of both new and current packages. Will the new packaging increase Campbell's profits?

Campbell managers will need these and many other types of information to decide whether to introduce the new packaging.

### Gathering Secondary Information

To meet the manager's information needs, the researcher can gather secondary data, primary data, or both. **Secondary data** consist of information that already exists somewhere, having been collected for another purpose. **Primary data** consist of information collected for the specific purpose at hand.

Researchers usually start by gathering secondary data. Table 4-1 shows the many secondary data sources, including *internal* and *external* sources. Secondary data usually can be obtained more quickly and at a lower cost than primary data.

---

**Secondary data**
Information that already exists somewhere, having been collected for another purpose.

**Primary data**
Information collected for the specific purpose at hand.

---

*Secondary data sources: In this ad, Information Resources, Inc. (IRI) tells customers that its information "makes the difference in decision making." With secondary data provided by IRI, companies can be better informed and more responsive.*

IN A DOG EAT DOG WORLD, IT'S BETTER NOT TO BE A DOG.

information resources

| TABLE 4-1 | Sources of Secondary Data |
|---|---|

**Internal sources**

Internal sources include company profit-and-loss statements, balance sheets, sales figures, sales-call reports, invoices, inventory records, and prior research reports.

**Government publications**

*Statistical Abstract of the U.S.,* updated annually, provides summary data on demographic, economic, social, and other aspects of the American economy and society.

*U.S. Industrial Outlook* provides projections of industrial activity by industry and includes data on production, sales, shipments, employment, etc.

*Marketing Information Guide* provides a monthly annotated bibliography of marketing information.

Other government publications include the *Annual Survey of Manufacturers; Business Statistics; Census of Manufacturers; Census of Population; Census of Retail Trade, Wholesale Trade, and Selected Service Industries; Federal Reserve Bulletin; and Survey of Current Business.*

**Periodicals and books**

*Standard & Poor's Industry Surveys* provide updated statistics and analyses of industries.

*Moody's Manuals* provide financial data and names of executives in major companies.

Marketing journals include the *Journal of Marketing, Journal of Marketing Research,* and *Journal of Consumer Research.*

Useful trade magazines include *Advertising Age, Chain Store Age, Progressive Grocer, Sales & Marketing Management,* and *Stores.*

Useful general business magazines include *Business Week, Fortune, Forbes,* and *Harvard Business Review.*

**Commercial Data**

Here are just a few of the dozens of commercial research houses selling data to subscribers:

*Nielsen Marketing Research* (a division of D&B Marketing Information Services) provides supermarket scanner data on sales, market share, and retail prices (ScanTrack), data on household purchasing (ScanTrack National Electronic Household Panel), data on television audiences (Nielsen National Television Index), and others.

*Information Resources, Inc.* provides supermarket scanner data for tracking grocery product movement (InfoScan) and single-source data collection (BehaviorScan).

*The Arbitron Company* provides local market radio audience and advertising expenditure information, along with a wealth of other media and ad spending data.

*MMRI (Simmons Market Research Bureau)* provides annual reports covering television markets, sporting goods, and proprietary drugs, giving lifestyle and geodemographic data by sex, income, age, and brand preferences (selective markets and media reaching them).

**International Data**

Here are only a few of the many sources providing international information:

*United Nations* publications include the *Statistical Yearbook,* a comprehensive source of international data for socioeconomic indicators; *Demographic Yearbook,* a collection of demographics data and vital statistics for 220 countries; and the *International Trade Statistics Yearbook,* which provides information on foreign trade for specific countries and commodities.

*Europa Yearbook* provides surveys on history, politics, population, economy, and natural resources for most countries of the world, along with information on major international organizations.

Other sources include *Political Risk Yearbook, Country Studies, OECD Economic Surveys, Economic Survey of Europe, Asian Economic Handbook,* and *International Financial Statistics.*

For example, a visit to the library might provide all the information Campbell needs on microwave oven usage, at almost no cost. A study to collect primary information might take weeks or months and cost thousands of dollars. Also, secondary sources can sometimes provide data that an individual company cannot collect on its own—information that either is not directly available or would be too expensive to collect. For example, it would be too expensive for Campbell to conduct a continuing retail store audit to find out about the market shares, prices, and displays of competitors' brands. But it can buy the InfoScan service from Information Resources, Inc., which provides this information from 2,700 scanner-equipped supermarkets in 64 U.S. markets.

Secondary data can also present problems. The needed information may not exist; researchers can rarely obtain all the data that they need from secondary sources. For example, Campbell will not find existing information about consumer reactions to new packaging that it has not yet placed on the market. Even when data can be found, they might not be very usable. The researcher must evaluate secondary information carefully to make certain that it is *relevant* (fits research project needs), *accurate* (reliably collected and reported), *current* (up-to-date enough for current decisions), and *impartial* (objectively collected and reported).

Secondary data provide a good starting point for research and often help to define problems and research objectives. In most cases, however, the company must also collect primary data.

### Planning Primary Data Collection

Good decisions require good data. Just as researchers must carefully evaluate the quality of secondary information, they also must take great care when collecting primary data to assure that it will be relevant, accurate, current, and unbiased. Table 4-2 shows that designing a plan for primary data collection calls for a number of decisions on *research approaches, contact methods, sampling plan,* and *research instruments.*

**Observational research**
The gathering of primary data by observing relevant people, actions, and situations.

**RESEARCH APPROACHES.** Observational research is the gathering of primary data by observing relevant people, actions, and situations. For example, a maker of personal care products might pretest its ads by showing them to people and measuring eye movements, pulse rates, and other physical reactions. Or a bank might evaluate possible new branch locations by checking traffic patterns, neighborhood conditions, and the location of competing branches. Steelcase used observation to help design new office furniture for use by work teams.

To learn firsthand how teams actually operate, it set up video cameras at various companies and studied the tapes, looking for motions and behavior patterns that customers themselves might not even notice. It found that teams work best when they can do some work together and some

**TABLE 4-2** *Planning Primary Data Collection*

| Research Approaches | Contact Methods | Sampling Plan | Research Instruments |
|---|---|---|---|
| Observation | Mail | Sampling unit | Questionnaire |
| Survey | Telephone | Sample size | Mechanical instruments |
| Experiment | Personal computer | Sampling procedure | |

privately. So Steelcase designed highly successful modular office units called Personal Harbor. These units are "rather like telephone booths in size and shape." They can be arranged around a common space where a team works, letting people work together but also alone when necessary. Says a Steelcase executive, "Market data wouldn't necessarily have pointed us that way. It was more important to know how people actually work."[11]

Urban Outfitters, the fast-growing specialty clothing chain, prefers observation to other types of market research. "We're not after people's statements," notes the chain's president, "we're after their actions." The company develops customer profiles by videotaping and taking photographs of customers in its stores. This helps managers determine what people are actually wearing and allows them to make quick decisions on merchandise.[12]

Several companies sell information collected through *mechanical* observation. For example, Nielsen Media Research attaches *people meters* to television sets in selected homes to record who watches which programs. It then rates the size and demographic makeup of audiences for different television programs. The television networks use these ratings to judge program popularity and to set charges for advertising time. Advertisers use the ratings when selecting programs for their commercials. *Checkout scanners* in retail stores record consumer purchases in detail. Consumer products companies and retailers use scanner information to assess and improve product sales and store performance. Some marketing research firms now offer **single-source data systems** that electronically monitor both consumers' purchases and consumers' exposure to various marketing activities in an effort to better evaluate the link between the two (see Marketing at Work 4-3).

Observational research can be used to obtain information that people are unwilling or unable to provide. In some cases, observation may be the only way to obtain the needed information. In contrast, some things simply cannot be observed, such as feelings, attitudes and motives, or private behavior. Long-term or infrequent behavior is also difficult to observe. Because of these limitations, researchers often use observation along with other data collection methods.

**Survey research** is the approach best suited for gathering *descriptive* information. A company that wants to know about people's knowledge, attitudes, preferences, or buying behavior can often find out by asking individuals directly.

Survey research is the most widely used method for primary data collection, and it is often the only method used in a research study. More than 72 million Americans are interviewed each year in surveys.[13] The major advantage of survey research is its flexibility. It can be used to obtain many different kinds of information in many different situations. Depending on the survey design, it may also provide information more quickly and at lower cost than observational or experimental research.

However, survey research also presents some problems. Sometimes people are unable to answer survey questions because they cannot remember or have never thought about what they do and why. Or people may be unwilling to respond to unknown interviewers or about things they consider private. Respondents may answer survey questions even when they do not know the answer in order to appear smarter or more informed. Or they may try to help the interviewer by giving pleasing answers. Finally, busy people may not take the time for a survey, or they may resent the intrusion into their privacy.

**Single-source data systems**
Electronic monitoring systems that link consumers' exposure to television advertising and promotion (measured using television meters) with what they buy in stores (measured using store checkout scanners).

**Survey research**
The gathering of primary data by asking people questions about their knowledge, attitudes, preferences, and buying behavior.

## MARKETING AT WORK 4-3

# SINGLE-SOURCE DATA SYSTEMS: A POWERFUL WAY TO MEASURE MARKETING IMPACT

Information Resources, Inc., knows all there is to know about the members of its panel households—what they eat for lunch, what they put in their coffee, and what they use to wash their hair, quench their thirsts, or make up their faces. The research company electronically monitors the television programs these people watch and tracks the brands they buy, the coupons they use, where they shop, and what newspapers and magazines they read. These households are a part of IRI's BehaviorScan service, a *single-source data system* that links consumers' exposure to television advertising, sales promotion, and other marketing efforts with their store purchases. BehaviorScan and other single-source data sys-

*Single-source data systems link marketing efforts directly with consumer buying behavior. Here, a BehaviorScan panel member makes a purchase.*

tems have revolutionized the way that consumer products companies measure the impact of their marketing activities.

The basics of single-source research are straightforward, and the IRI BehaviorScan system provides a good example. IRI maintains a panel of 60,000 households in 27 markets. The company meters each home's television set to track who watches what and when, and it quizzes family members to find out what they read. It carefully records important facts about each household, such as family income, number and ages of children, lifestyle, and product and store buying history.

IRI also employs a panel of retail stores in each of its markets. For a fee, these stores agree to carry the new products that IRI wishes to test, and they allow IRI to control such factors as shelf location, stocking,

**Experimental research** The gathering or primary data by selecting matched groups of subjects, giving them different treatments, controlling related factors, and checking for differences in group responses.

Whereas observation is best suited for exploratory research and surveys for descriptive research, **experimental research** is best suited for gathering *causal* information. Experiments involve selecting matched groups of subjects, giving them different treatments, controlling unrelated factors, and checking for differences in group responses. Thus, experimental research tries to explain cause-and-effect relationships. Observation and surveys may be used to collect information in experimental research.

Before adding a new sandwich to the menu, researchers at McDonald's might use experiments to answer questions such as the following:

- How much will the new sandwich increase McDonald's sales?
- How will the new sandwich affect the sales of other menu items?
- Which advertising approach would have the greatest effect on sales of the sandwich?
- How would different prices affect the sales of the product?
- Should the new item be targeted toward adults, children, or both?

To test the effects of two different prices, McDonald's could set up the following simple experiment. It could introduce the new sandwich at one price in its

point-of-purchase displays, and pricing for these products.

Each BehaviorScan household receives an identification number. When household members shop for groceries in IRI panel stores, they give their identification number to the store checkout clerk. All the information about the family's purchases—brands bought, package sizes, prices paid—is recorded by the store's electronic scanner and immediately entered by computer into the family's purchase file. The system also records any other in-store factors that might affect purchase decisions, such as special competitor price promotions or shelf displays.

Thus, IRI builds a complete record of each household's demographic and psychographic makeup, purchasing behavior, media habits, and the conditions surrounding purchase. But IRI takes the process a step farther.

Through cable television, IRI controls the advertisements being sent to each household. It can beam different ads and promotions to different panel households and then use the purchasing information obtained from scanners to assess which ads had more or less impact and how various promotions affected different kinds of consumers. In short, from a single source, companies can obtain information that links their marketing efforts directly with consumer buying behavior.

BehaviorScan and other single-source systems have their drawbacks, and some researchers are skeptical. One hitch is that such systems produce truckloads of data, more than most companies can handle. Another problem is cost: Single-source data can cost marketers hundreds of thousands of dollars a year per brand. Also, because such systems are set

up in only a few market areas, usually small cities, the marketer often finds it difficult to generalize from the measures and results. Finally, although single-source systems provide important information for assessing the impact of promotion and advertising, they shed little light on the effects of other key marketing actions.

Despite these drawbacks, more and more companies are relying on single-source data systems to test new products and new marketing strategies. When properly used, such systems can provide marketers with fast and detailed information about how their products are selling, who is buying them, and what factors affect purchase.

*Sources*: See Joanne Lipman, "Single-Source Ad Research Heralds Detailed Look at Household Habits," *Wall Street Journal,* February 16, 1988, p. 39; Magid H. Abraham and Leonard M. Lodish, "Getting the Most Out of Advertising and Promotion," *Harvard Business Review,* May–June 1990, pp. 50–60; and Jack Honomichl, "The Honomichl Top 50," *Marketing News,* June 5, 1995, p. H6.

restaurants in one city and at another price in restaurants in another city. If the cities are similar, and if all other marketing efforts for the sandwich are the same, then differences in sales in the two cities could be related to the price charged. More complex experiments could be designed to include other variables and other locations.

CONTACT METHODS. Information can be collected by mail, telephone, personal interview, or computer. Table 4-3 shows the strengths and weaknesses of each of these contact methods.

*Mail questionnaires* can be used to collect large amounts of information at a low cost per respondent. Respondents may give more honest answers to more personal questions on a mail questionnaire than to an unknown interviewer in person or over the phone. Also, no interviewer is involved to bias the respondent's answers. However, mail questionnaires are not very flexible; all respondents answer the same questions in a fixed order, and the researcher cannot adapt the questionnaire based on earlier answers. Mail surveys usually take longer to complete, and the response rate—the number of people returning completed questionnaires—is often very low. Finally, the researcher often has little control over the

**TABLE 4-3** *Strengths and Weaknesses of Contact Methods*

|  | Mail | Telephone | Personal | Computer |
|---|---|---|---|---|
| Flexibility | Poor | Good | Excellent | Good |
| Quantity of data that can be collected | Good | Fair | Excellent | Good |
| Control of interviewer effects | Excellent | Fair | Poor | Excellent |
| Control of sample | Fair | Excellent | Fair | Fair |
| Speed of data collection | Poor | Excellent | Good | Good |
| Response rate | Fair | Good | Good | Fair |
| Cost | Good | Fair | Poor | Fair |

*Source:* Adapted with permission of Macmillan Publishing Company from *Marketing Research: Measurement and Method,* 7th ed., by Donald S. Tull and Del I. Hawkins. Copyright 1993 by Macmillan Publishing Company.

mail questionnaire sample. Even with a good mailing list, it is hard to control *who* at the mailing address fills out the questionnaire.

*Telephone interviewing* is the best method for gathering information quickly, and it provides greater flexibility than mail questionnaires. Interviewers can explain difficult questions, and they can skip some questions or probe on others, depending on the answers they receive. Response rates tend to be higher than with mail questionnaires, and telephone interviewing also allows greater sample control. Interviewers can ask to speak to respondents with the desired characteristics, or even by name.

However, with telephone interviewing, the cost per respondent is higher than with mail questionnaires. Also, people may not want to discuss personal questions with an interviewer. Using an interviewer also introduces interviewer bias—the way interviewers talk, how they ask questions, and other differences may affect respondents' answers. Finally, different interviewers may interpret and record responses differently, and under time pressures some interviewers might even cheat by recording answers without asking questions.

*Personal interviewing* takes two forms—individual and group interviewing. *Individual interviewing* involves talking with people in their homes or offices, on the street, or in shopping malls. Such interviewing is flexible. Trained interviewers can hold a respondent's attention for a long time and can explain difficult questions. They can guide interviews, explore issues, and probe as the situation requires. They can show subjects actual products, advertisements, or packages and observe reactions and behavior. In most cases, personal interviews can be conducted fairly quickly. However, individual personal interviews may cost three to four times as much as telephone interviews.

*Group interviewing* consists of inviting six to ten people to gather for a few hours with a trained moderator to talk about a product, service, or organization. The participants normally are paid a small sum for attending. The meeting is held in a pleasant place and refreshments are served to foster an informal setting. The moderator encourages free and easy discussion, hoping that group interactions will bring out actual feelings and thoughts. At the same time, the moderator "focuses" the discussion—hence the name **focus-group interviewing.** The comments are recorded through written notes or on videotapes that are studied later.

Today, modern communications technology is changing the way that focus groups are conducted:

**Focus-group interviewing**
Personal interviewing that consists of inviting six to ten people to gather for a few hours with a trained interviewer to talk about a product, service, or organization. The interviewer "focuses" the group discussion on important issues.

In the old days, advertisers and agencies flew their staff to Atlanta or Little Rock to watch focus groups from behind one-way mirrors. The staff usually spent more time in hotels and taxis than they did doing research. Today, they are staying home. Video-conferencing links, television monitors, remote-control cameras, and digital transmission are boosting the amount of focus group research done over long-distance lines. [In a typical video-conferencing system], two cameras focused on the group are controlled by clients who hold a remote keypad. Executives in a far-off boardroom can zoom in on faces and pan the focus group at will. . . . A two-way sound system connects remote viewers to the backroom, focus group room, and directly to the monitor's earpiece. [Recently], while testing new product names in one focus group, the [client's] creative director. . . had an idea and contacted the moderator, who tested the new name on the spot.[14]

Focus-group interviewing has become one of the major marketing research tools for gaining insight into consumer thoughts and feelings. However, focus-group studies usually employ small sample sizes to keep time and costs down, and it may be hard to generalize from the results. Because interviewers have more freedom in personal interviews, the problem of interviewer bias is greater.

Selecting the best contact method depends on what information the researcher wants as well as the number and types of respondents to be contacted. Advances in computers and communications have had a large impact on methods of obtaining information. For example, most research firms now do Computer-Assisted Telephone Interviewing (CATI). Professional interviewers call respondents around the country, often using phone numbers drawn at random. When the

*Marketing researchers observe a focus group session.*

*Computer-assisted telephone interviewing: The interviewer reads questions from the screen and types the respondent's answers directly into the computer, reducing errors and saving time.*

respondent answers, the interviewer reads a set of questions from a video screen and types the respondent's answers directly into the computer.

Other firms use *computer interviewing* in which respondents sit down at a computer, read questions from a screen, and type their own answers into the computer. The computers might be located at a research center, trade show, shopping mall, or retail location. For example, Boston Market uses touch-screen computers in its restaurants to obtain instant feedback from customers. Some researchers are even using Completely Automated Telephone Surveys (CATS), which employ voice response technology to conduct interviews. The recorded voice of an interviewer asks the questions, and respondents answer by pressing numbers on their push-button phones.[15]

For example, in 1993, PepsiCo used automated telephone interviews to obtain market information from Diet Coke drinkers. It sent direct-mail pieces to a million Diet Coke drinkers inviting them to call an interactive toll-free number, "talk" to Ray Charles, and possibly win a prize. But first they had to use their push-button phone to answer a series of market research questions designed to help Pepsi understand Diet Coke users. More than half a million people called and were greeted by Ray and the Uh-Huh Girls. Between questions, to break the monotony that can plague interactive calls, callers heard musical sound-bites and lots of "Uh-Huhs." At the end of the 3½ minute survey, Ray and the girls returned to award instant prizes, including a one-year supply of Diet Pepsi or a miniature Diet Pepsi vending machine. But PepsiCo was the real winner—the company received vital information on brand preferences, consumption rates, and lifestyle activities of more than 500,000 of its major competitor's customers.[16]

**SAMPLING PLANS.** Marketing researchers usually draw conclusions about large groups of consumers by studying a small sample of the total consumer popula-

**Sample**

A segment of the population selected for marketing research to represent the population as a whole.

tion. A **sample** is a segment of the population selected to represent the population as a whole. Ideally, the sample should be representative so that the researcher can make accurate estimates of the thoughts and behaviors of the larger population.

Designing the sample requires three decisions. First, *who* is to be surveyed (what *sampling unit*)? The answer to this question is not always obvious. For example, to study the decision-making process for a family automobile purchase, should the researcher interview the husband, wife, other family members, dealership salespeople, or all of these? The researcher must determine what information is needed and who is most likely to have it.

Second, *how many* people should be surveyed (what *sample size*)? Large samples give more reliable results than small samples. It is not necessary to sample the entire target market or even a large portion to get reliable results, however. If well chosen, samples of less than 1 percent of a population can often give good reliability.

Third, *how* should the people in the sample be *chosen* (what *sampling procedure*)? Table 4-4 describes different kinds of samples. Using *probability samples,* each population member has a known chance of being included in the sample, and researchers can calculate confidence limits for sampling error. But when probability sampling costs too much or takes too much time, marketing researchers often take *nonprobability samples,* even though their sampling error cannot be measured. These varied ways of drawing samples have different costs and time limitations, as well as different accuracy and statistical properties. Selecting the best method depends on the needs of the research project.

**RESEARCH INSTRUMENTS.**   In collecting primary data, marketing researchers have a choice of two main research instruments: the *questionnaire* and *mechanical devices*. The *questionnaire,* by far the most common instrument, is very flexible—there are many ways to ask questions. Questionnaires must be developed carefully and tested before they can be used on a large scale. A carelessly prepared questionnaire usually contains several errors (see Table 4-5).

In preparing a questionnaire, the marketing researcher must first decide what questions to ask. Questionnaires frequently leave out questions that should be answered and include questions that cannot be answered, will not be answered, or need not be answered. Each question should be checked to see that it contributes to the research objectives.

**TABLE 4-4**   *Types of Samples*

| *Probability sample* | |
| --- | --- |
| Sample random sample | Every member of the population has a known and equal chance of selection. |
| Stratified random sample | The population is divided into mutually exclusive groups (such as age groups), and random samples are drawn from each group. |
| Cluster (area) sample | The population is divided into mutually exclusive groups (such as blocks), and the researcher draws a sample of the groups to interview. |
| *Nonprobability sample* | |
| Convenience sample | The researcher selects the easiest population members from which to obtain information. |
| Judgment sample | The researcher uses his or her judgment to select population members who are good prospects for accurate information. |
| Quota sample | The researcher finds and interviews a prescribed number of people in each of several categories. |

**TABLE 4-5** *A "Questionable Questionnaire"*

Suppose that a summer camp director had prepared the following questionnaire to use in interviewing the parents of prospective campers. How would you assess each question?

1. What is your income to the nearest hundred dollars?
   *People don't usually know their income to the nearest hundred dollars nor do they want to reveal their income that closely. Moreover, a researcher should never open a questionnaire with such a personal question.*
2. Are you a strong or weak supporter of overnight summer camping for your children?
   *What do "strong" and "weak" mean?*
3. Do your children behave themselves well at a summer camp? Yes ( )  No ( )
   *"Behave" is a relative term. Furthermore, are "yes" and "no" the best response options for this question? Besides, will people answer this honestly and objectively? Why ask the question in the first place?*
4. How many camps mailed literature to you last year? This year?
   *Who can remember this?*
5. What are the most salient and determinant attributes in your evaluation of summer camps?
   *What are "salient" and "determinant" attributes? Don't use big words on me!*
6. Do you think it is right to deprive your child of the opportunity to grow into a mature person through the experience of summer camping?
   *A loaded question. Given the bias, how can any parent answer "yes"?*

The *form* of each question can influence the response. Marketing researchers distinguish between closed-end questions and open-end questions. *Closed-end questions* include all the possible answers, and subjects make choices among them. Examples include multiple-choice questions and scale questions. *Open-end questions* allow respondents to answer in their own words. In a survey of airline users, Delta might simply ask, "What is your opinion of Delta Airlines?" Or it might ask people to complete a sentence: "When I choose an airline, the most important consideration is. . . ." These and other kinds of open-end questions often reveal more than closed-end questions because respondents are not limited in their answers. Open-end questions are especially useful in exploratory research, when the researcher is trying to find out *what* people think but not measuring *how many* people think in a certain way. Closed-end questions, on the other hand, provide answers that are easier to interpret and tabulate.

Researchers should also use care in the *wording* and *ordering* of questions. They should use simple, direct, unbiased wording. Questions should be arranged in a logical order. The first question should create interest if possible, and difficult or personal questions should be asked last so that respondents do not become defensive.

Although questionnaires are the most common research instrument, *mechanical instruments* also are used. We discussed two mechanical instruments—people meters and supermarket scanners—earlier in the chapter. Another group of mechanical devices measures subjects' physical responses. For example, a galvanometer measures the strength of interest or emotions aroused by a subject's exposure to different stimuli, such as an ad or picture. The galvanometer detects the minute degree of sweating that accompanies emotional arousal. The tachisto-

*Mechanical research instruments: Eye cameras determine where eyes land and how long they linger on a given item.*

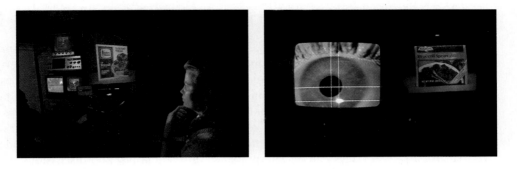

scope flashes an ad to a subject at an exposure that ranges from less than one-hundredth of a second to several seconds. After each exposure, respondents describe everything they recall. Eye cameras are used to study respondents' eye movements to determine at what points their eyes focus first and how long they linger on a given item.[17]

### Presenting the Research Plan

At this stage, the marketing researcher should summarize the plan in a *written proposal*. A written proposal is especially important when the research project is large and complex or when an outside firm carries it out. The proposal should cover the management problems addressed and the research objectives, the information to be obtained, the sources of secondary information or methods for collecting primary data, and the way that the results will help management decision making. The proposal should also include research costs. A written research plan or proposal assures that the marketing manager and researchers have considered all the important aspects of the research, and that they agree on why and how the research will be done.

## IMPLEMENTING THE RESEARCH PLAN

The researcher next puts the marketing research plan into action. This involves collecting, processing, and analyzing the information. Data collection can be carried out by the company's marketing research staff or by outside firms. The company retains more control over the collection process and data quality by using its own staff. However, outside firms that specialize in data collection can often do the job more quickly and at lower cost.

The data collection phase of the marketing research process is generally the most expensive and the most subject to error. The researcher should watch field-work closely to make sure that the plan is implemented correctly and to guard against problems with contacting respondents, with respondents who refuse to cooperate or who give biased or dishonest answers, and with interviewers who make mistakes or take shortcuts.

Researchers must process and analyze the collected data to isolate important information and findings. They need to check data from questionnaires for accuracy and completeness and code it for computer analysis. The researchers then tabulate the results and compute averages and other statistical measures.

## INTERPRETING AND REPORTING THE FINDINGS

The researcher must now interpret the findings, draw conclusions, and report them to management. The researcher should not try to overwhelm managers with numbers and fancy statistical techniques. Rather, the researcher should present important findings that are useful in the major decisions faced by management.

However, interpretation should not be left only to the researchers. They are often experts in research design and statistics, but the marketing manager knows more about the problem and the decisions that must be made. In many cases, findings can be interpreted in different ways, and discussions between researchers and managers will help point to the best interpretations. The manager will also want to check that the research project was carried out properly and that all the necessary analysis was completed. Or, after seeing the findings, the manager may have additional questions that can be answered through further sifting of the data. Finally, the manager is the one who ultimately must decide what action the research suggests. The researchers may even make the data directly available to marketing managers so that they can perform new analyses and test new relationships on their own.

Interpretation is an important phase of the marketing process. The best research is meaningless if the manager blindly accepts wrong interpretations from the researcher. Similarly, managers may have biased interpretations—they tend to accept research results that show what they expected and to reject those that they did not expect or want. Thus, managers and researchers must work together closely when interpreting research results, and both must share responsibility for the research process and resulting decisions.[18]

## ▶ OTHER MARKETING RESEARCH CONSIDERATIONS

This section discusses marketing research in two special contexts: marketing research by small businesses and nonprofit organizations, and international marketing research. Finally, we look at public policy and ethics issues in marketing research.

## MARKETING RESEARCH IN SMALL BUSINESSES AND NONPROFIT ORGANIZATIONS

Managers of small businesses and nonprofit organizations often think that marketing research can be done only by experts in large companies with big research budgets. But many of the marketing research techniques discussed in this chapter also can be used by smaller organizations in a less formal manner and at little or no expense.

Managers of small businesses and nonprofit organizations can obtain good marketing information simply by *observing* things around them. For example, retailers can evaluate new locations by observing vehicle and pedestrian traffic. They can visit competing stores to check on facilities and prices. They can evaluate their customer mix by recording how many and what kinds of customers shop in the store at different times. Competitor advertising can be monitored by collecting advertisements from local media.

Managers can conduct informal *surveys* using small convenience samples. The director of an art museum can learn what patrons think about new exhibits by conducting informal "focus groups"—inviting small groups to lunch and having discussions on topics of interest. Retail salespeople can talk with customers visiting the store; hospital officials can interview patients. Restaurant managers might make random phone calls during slack hours to interview consumers about where they eat out and what they think of various restaurants in the area.

Managers also can conduct their own simple *experiments*. For example, by changing the themes in regular fund-raising mailings and watching the results, a nonprofit manager can find out much about which marketing strategies work best. By varying newspaper advertisements, a store manager can learn the effects of things such as ad size and position, price coupons, and media used.

Small organizations can obtain most of the secondary data available to large businesses. In addition, many associations, local media, chambers of commerce, and government agencies provide special help to small organizations. The U.S. Small Business Administration offers dozens of free publications that give advice on topics ranging from planning advertising to ordering business signs. Local newspapers often provide information on local shoppers and their buying patterns.

In summary, secondary data collection, observation, surveys, and experiments can all be used effectively by small organizations with small budgets. Although these informal research methods are less complex and less costly, they still must be conducted carefully. Managers must think carefully about the objectives of the research, formulate questions in advance, recognize the biases that are introduced by smaller samples and less skilled researchers, and conduct the research systematically.

# INTERNATIONAL MARKETING RESEARCH

International marketing researchers follow the same steps as domestic researchers, from defining the research problem and developing a research plan to interpreting and reporting the results. However, these researchers often face more and different problems. Whereas domestic researchers deal with fairly homogeneous markets within a single country, international researchers deal with differing markets in many different countries. These markets often vary greatly in their economic development levels, cultures and customs, and buying patterns.

In many foreign markets, the international researcher has a difficult time finding good *secondary data*. Whereas U.S. marketing researchers can obtain reliable secondary data from any of dozens of domestic research services, many countries have almost no research services at all. Some of the largest international research services operate in many countries. For example, Nielsen Marketing Research, a division of Dun & Bradstreet Information Services and the world's largest marketing research company, has offices in 70 countries outside the United States.[19] However, most research firms operate in only a relative handful of countries. Thus, even when secondary information is available, it usually has to be obtained from many different sources on a country-by-country basis, making the information difficult to combine or compare.

*Some research firms offer global services. As this ad notes, Roper Starch last year "conducted over 4 million interviews in more than 80 countries." However, most research firms operate in no more than a few countries.*

Because of the scarcity of good secondary data, international researchers must often collect their own primary data. Here, again, researchers face problems not found domestically. For example, they may find it difficult simply to develop good samples. U.S. researchers can use current telephone directories, census tract data, and any of several sources of socioeconomic data to construct samples. However, such information is largely lacking in many countries.

Once the sample is drawn, the U.S. researcher can usually reach most respondents easily by telephone, by mail, or in person. Reaching respondents is often not so easy in other parts of the world. Researchers in Mexico cannot rely on telephone and mail data collection; most data collection is door to door and concentrated in three or four of the largest cities. And most surveys in Mexico bypass the large segment of the population where native tribes speak languages other than Spanish. In some countries, few people have phones—there are only four phones per thousand people in Egypt, six per thousand in Turkey, and thirty-two per thousand in Argentina. In other countries, the postal system is notoriously unreliable. In Brazil, for instance, an estimated 30 percent of the mail is never delivered. In many developing countries, poor roads and transportation systems make certain areas hard to reach, making personal interviews difficult and expensive.[20]

Differences in cultures from country to country cause additional problems for international researchers. Language is the most obvious culprit. For example, questionnaires must be prepared in one language and then translated into the languages of each country researched. Responses must then be translated back into the original language for analysis and interpretation. This adds to research costs and increases the risks of error.

Translating a questionnaire from one language to another is anything but easy. Many idioms, phrases, and statements mean different things in different cultures. For example, a Danish executive noted: "Check this out by having a

*Customs in some countries prohibit people from talking with strangers—a researcher simply may not be allowed to speak with people about brand attitudes or buying behavior.*

different translator put back into English what you've translated from English. You'll get the shock of your life. I remember [an example in which] 'out of sight, out of mind' had become 'invisible things are insane.' "[21]

Buying roles and consumer decision processes vary greatly from country to country, further complicating international marketing research. Consumers in different countries also vary in their attitudes toward marketing research. People in one country may be very willing to respond; in other countries, nonresponse can be a major problem. For example, customs in some Islamic countries prohibit people from talking with strangers—a researcher simply may not be allowed to speak by phone with women about brand attitudes or buying behavior. In certain cultures, research questions often are considered too personal. For example, in many Latin American countries, people may feel embarrassed to talk with researchers about their choices of shampoo, deodorant, or other personal care products. Even when respondents are *willing* to respond, they may not be *able* to because of high functional illiteracy rates. And middle-class people in developing countries often make false claims in order to appear well-off. For example, in a study of tea consumption in India, over 70 percent of middle-income respondents claimed that they used one of several national brands. However, the researchers had good reason to doubt these results—more than 60 percent of the tea sold in India is unbranded generic tea.

Despite these problems, the recent growth of international marketing has resulted in a rapid increase in the use of international marketing research. Global companies have little choice but to conduct such research. Although the costs and problems associated with international research may be high, the costs of not doing it—in terms of missed opportunities and mistakes—might be even higher. Once recognized, many of the problems associated with international marketing research can be overcome or avoided.

## PUBLIC POLICY AND ETHICS IN MARKETING RESEARCH

Most marketing research benefits both the sponsoring company and its consumers. Through marketing research, companies learn more about consumers' needs, resulting in more satisfying products and services. However, the misuse of marketing research can also harm or annoy consumers. Two major public policy and ethics issues in marketing research are intrusions on consumer privacy and the misuse of research findings.

### Intrusions on Consumer Privacy

Most consumers feel positively about marketing research and believe that it serves a useful purpose. Some actually enjoy being interviewed and giving their opinions. However, others strongly resent or even mistrust marketing research. A few consumers fear that researchers might use sophisticated techniques to probe their deepest feelings and then use this knowledge to manipulate their buying. Others may have been taken in by previous "research surveys" that actually turned out to be attempts to sell them something. Still other consumers confuse legitimate marketing research studies with telemarketing or database development efforts and say "no" before the interviewer can even begin. Most, however, simply resent the intrusion. They dislike mail or telephone surveys that are too long or too personal, or that interrupt them too often or at inconvenient times.

Increasing consumer resentment has become a major problem for the research industry. This resentment has led to lower survey response rates in recent years; one study found that 38 percent of Americans now refuse to be interviewed in an average survey, up dramatically from a decade ago.[22] The research industry is considering several options for responding to this problem. One is to expand its "Your Opinion Counts" program to educate consumers about the benefits of marketing research and to distinguish it from telephone selling and database building. Another option is to provide a toll-free number that people can call to verify that a survey is legitimate. The industry also has considered adopting broad standards, perhaps based on Europe's International Code of Marketing and Social Research Practice. This code outlines researchers' responsibilities to respondents and to the general public. For example, it says that researchers should make their names and addresses available to participants, and it bans companies from representing activities like database compilation or sales and promotional pitches as research.

### Misuse of Research Findings

Research studies can be powerful persuasion tools; companies often use study results as claims in their advertising and promotion. Today, however, many research studies appear to be little more than vehicles for pitching the sponsor's products. In fact, in some cases, the research surveys appear to have been designed just to produce the intended effect. Few advertisers openly rig their research designs or blatantly misrepresent the findings; most abuses tend to be subtle "stretches." Consider the following examples:[23]

> A study by Chrysler contends that Americans overwhelmingly prefer Chrysler to Toyota after test driving both. However, the study included just 100 people in each of two tests. More importantly, none of the people surveyed owned a foreign car, so they appear to be favorably predisposed to U.S. cars.

A Black Flag survey asked: "A roach disk . . . poisons a roach slowly. The dying roach returns to the nest and after it dies is eaten by other roaches. In turn these roaches become poisoned and die. How effective do you think this type of product would be in killing roaches?" Not surprisingly, 79 percent said effective.

A poll sponsored by the disposable diaper industry asked: "It is estimated that disposable diapers account for less than 2 percent of the trash in today's landfills. In contrast, beverage containers, third-class mail, and yard waste are estimated to account for about 21 percent of the trash in landfills. Given this, in your opinion, would it be fair to ban disposable diapers?" Again, not surprisingly, 84 percent said no.

Thus, subtle manipulations of the study's sample, or the choice or wording of questions, can greatly affect the conclusions reached.

In others cases, so-called independent research studies are actually paid for by companies with an interest in the outcome. Small changes in study assumptions or in how results are interpreted can subtly affect the direction of the results. For example, at least four widely quoted studies compare the environmental effects of using disposable diapers to those of using cloth diapers. The two studies sponsored by the cloth-diaper industry conclude that cloth diapers are more environmentally friendly. Not surprisingly, the other two studies, sponsored by the paper-diaper industry, conclude just the opposite. Yet both appear to be correct *given* the underlying assumptions used.

Recognizing that surveys can be abused, several associations—including the American Marketing Association and the Council of American Survey Research Organizations—have developed codes of research ethics and standards of conduct. In the end, however, unethical or inappropriate actions cannot simply be regulated away. Each company must accept responsibility for policing the conduct and reporting of its own marketing research to protect consumers' best interests as well as its own.

## SUMMARY

In carrying out their marketing responsibilities, marketing managers need a great deal of information. Despite the growing supply of information, managers often lack enough information of the right kind or have too much of the wrong kind. In order to overcome these problems, many companies are taking steps to improve their marketing information systems.

A well-designed *marketing information system* (MIS) begins and ends with the user. The MIS first *assesses information needs* by interviewing marketing managers and surveying their decision environment to determine what information is desired, needed, and feasible to obtain.

The MIS next *develops information* and helps managers to use it more effectively. *Internal records* provide information on the company's own sales, costs, inventories, cash flows, and accounts receivable and payable. Such data can be obtained quickly and cheaply, but must often be adapted for marketing decisions. The *marketing intelligence system* supplies marketing executives with everyday information about developments in the external marketing environment. Intelligence can be collected from company employees, customers, suppliers, and resellers; or by monitoring published reports, conferences, advertisements, competitor actions, and other activities in the environment. *Marketing research* involves collecting information relevant to a specific marketing problem facing the company.

Finally, the marketing information system *distributes information* gathered from internal sources, marketing intelligence, and marketing research to the right managers at the right times. More and more companies are decentralizing their information systems through networks that allow managers to have direct access to information.

Every marketer needs marketing research, and most large companies have their own marketing research departments. Marketing research involves a four-step process. The first step consists of the manager and researcher carefully *defining the problem and setting the research objectives*. The objective may be *exploratory*, *descriptive*, or *causal*. The second step consists of developing a *research plan* for collecting data from primary and secondary sources. *Primary data collection* calls for choosing a *research approach* (observation, survey, experiment); choosing a *contact method* (mail, telephone, personal, computer); designing a *sampling plan* (whom to survey, how many to survey, and how to choose them); and developing *research instruments* (questionnaire, mechanical). The third step consists of *implementing the marketing research plan* by collecting, processing, and analyzing the information. The fourth step consists of *interpreting and reporting the findings*. Further information analysis helps marketing managers to apply the information and provides them advanced statistical procedures and models from which to develop more rigorous findings.

Some marketers face special marketing research considerations, such as conducting research in small-business, nonprofit, or international situations. Marketing research can be conducted effectively by small organizations with small budgets. International marketing researchers follow the same steps as domestic researchers but often face more and different problems. All organizations need to understand and respond responsibly to the major public policy and ethics issues surrounding marketing research.

## KEY TERMS

Causal research

Descriptive research

Experimental research

Exploratory research

Focus-group interviewing

Internal records information

Marketing information system (MIS)

Marketing intelligence

Marketing research

Observational research

Primary data

Sample

Secondary data

Single-source data systems

Survey research

## QUESTIONS FOR DISCUSSION

1. As a salesperson calling on industrial accounts, you would learn a lot that would help decision makers in your company. What kinds of information would you pass on to your company? How would you decide whether something is worth reporting?

2. Companies often test new products in plain white packages with no brand name or other marketing information. What does this "blind" testing really measure? Are there any issues in applying these results to the "real world"?

3. Relying on secondary data for marketing information can sometimes be a problem. For example, marketers in south Florida who turned to building permits and utility customer records to estimate population and household size were faced with uncertainty as a result of Hurricane Andrew's widespread destruction in 1992. Displaced families had to find alternate living arrangements, and this created unpredictable changes in household size. If you were a marketing researcher, how would you try to assess these changes? What alternate living situations would you consider? Based on this analysis, can marketing research information "go stale"?

4. You own an elegant, high-priced restaurant in North Miami Beach, Florida, and want to improve the level of service offered by your 30-person staff. How could observational research help you to accomplish this goal?

5. What type of research would be appropriate in the following situations, and why?

- Kellogg wants to investigate the impact of young children's preferences on their parents' decisions about which breakfast foods they buy.

- Your college bookstore wants to get some insights into how students feel about the store's merchandise, prices, and service.

- McDonald's is considering where to locate a new outlet in a fast-growing suburb.

- Gillette wants to determine whether a new line of deodorant for children will be profitable.

6. Focus group interviewing is both a widely used and widely criticized research technique in marketing. What are the advantages and disadvantages of focus groups? What are some kinds of questions that are appropriate for focus groups to investigate?

# APPLYING THE CONCEPTS

1. "Blind" taste tests often have surprising results. Demonstrate this by conducting a product test in your classroom.

- Purchase three comparable brands of sodas such as Coca-Cola, Pepsi, and a regional favorite or store brand. Also buy three small paper cups for each student. Remove *all* identification from the bottles including labels and caps, and use paper to cover any differences in bottle design. Label each product with neutral names such as Brand G, Brand H, and Brand I. Pour a small sample of each into cups labeled with the neutral pseudonyms and distribute them.

- Ask the following questions and tabulate the answers: (a) What brand do you usually buy? (b) Which of these samples do you prefer? (c) What brand do you think each sample is?

- Write students' preferences on the board, then reveal which brand was which sample. Are the results what you had expected? Why or why not?

2. Run a small focus group in class to learn about the pros and cons of this technique.

- Pick one class member as a moderator, and select six to eight other volunteers. Try to include at least one strong personality and one shy member. Set them up in a circle at the front of class.

- Discuss a mildly controversial issue that is of current interest to the class. Avoid issues that are very controversial or emotional. Run the group for 10 to 15 minutes.

- Discuss the focus group "results" with the class. Were the conclusions fair or biased? What did class members find useful about the technique, and what problems did they see?

# REFERENCES

1. Quotes from Susan Caminiti, "A Star Is Born," *Fortune,* special issue on "The Tough New Consumer," Autumn/Winter 1993, pp. 44–47. Also see Terry Lefton, "B&D Retools with Quantum," *Brandweek,* July 5, 1993, p. 4; Black & Decker's 1993 Annual Report, p. 9; and Norton Paley, "Back From the Dead," *Sales & Marketing Management,* July 1995, pp. 30–31.

2. Rashi Glazer, "Marketing in an Information-Intensive Environment: Strategic Implications of Knowledge as an Asset," *Journal of Marketing,* October 1991, pp. 1–19.

3. "Harnessing the Data Explosion," *Sales & Marketing Management,* January 1987, p. 31; and Joseph M. Winski, "Gentle Rain Turns Into Torrent," *Advertising Age,* June 3, 1991, p. 34.

4. John Neisbitt, *Megatrends: Ten New Directions Transforming Our Lives* (New York: Warner Books, 1984), p. 16. Also see, Rick Tetzeli, "Surviving the Information Overload," *Fortune,* July 11, 1994, pp. 60–64.

5. See Thomas A. Stewart, "What Information Costs," *Fortune,* July 10, 1995, pp. 119–21.

6. See Jeffrey Rotfeder and Jim Bartimo, "How Software Is Making Food Sales a Piece of Cake," *Business Week,* July 2, 1990, pp. 54–55; and Terence P. Paré, "How to Find Out What They Want," *Fortune,* special issue on "The Tough New Consumer," Autumn/Winter 1993, pp. 39–41.

7. For more on major marketing research organizations, see "The Honomichl 50," a special section in *Marketing News,* June 5, 1995, pp. H1–H43.

8. See Katherine S. Chaing, "How to Find Online Information," *American Demographics,* September 1993, pp. 52–55; and Diana Bentley, "Switched On About the EC," *International Management,* January/February 1993, pp. 74–76.

9. See Christel Beard and Betsy Wiesen-danger, "The Marketer's Guide to Online Databases," *Sales & Marketing Management,* January 1993, pp. 36–41.

10. For more on statistical analysis, consult a standard text, such as Donald S. Tull and Del I. Hawkins, *Marketing Research* (New York: Macmillan, 1993). For a review of marketing models, see Gary L. Lilien, Philip Kotler, and Sridhar Moorthy, *Marketing Models* (Englewood Cliffs: Prentice Hall, 1992).

11. Justin Martin, "Ignore Your Customer," *Fortune,* May 1, 1995, pp. 121–26.

12. *Ibid.,* p. 126.

13. Mark Landler, "The 'Bloodbath' in Market Research," *Business Week,* February 11, 1991, pp. 72–74.

14. Rebecca Piirto Heather, "Future Focus Groups," *American Demographics,* January 1994, p. 6. For more on focus groups, see Leslie M. Harris, "Technology, Techniques Drive Focus Group Trends," *Marketing News,* February 27, 1995, p. 8; and Norton Paley, "Getting in Focus," *Sales & Marketing Management,* March 1995, pp. 92–95.

15. Diane Crispell, "People Talk, Computers Listen," *American Demographics,* October 1989, p. 8; and Peter J. DePaulo and Rick Weitzer, "Interactive Phones Technology Delivers Survey Data Quickly," *Marketing News,* June 6, 1994, pp. 33–34.

16. Debra Aho, "Pepsi Puts Callers in Touch with Ray," *Advertising Age,* November 15, 1993, p. 20.

17. For more on mechanical measures, see Michael J. McCarthy, "Mind Probe," *The Wall Street Journal,* March 22, 1991, p. B3.

18. For a discussion of the importance of the relationship between market researchers and research users, see Christine Moorman, Gerald Zaltman, and Rohit Deshpande, "Relationships Between Providers and Users of Market Research: The Dynamics of Trust Within and Between Organizations," *Journal of Marketing Research,* August 1992, pp. 314–28; Christine Moorman, Rohit Deshpande, and Gerald Zaltman, "Factors Affecting Trust in Market Research Relationships," *Journal of Marketing,* January 1993, pp. 81–101; and Arlene Farber Sirkin, "Maximizing the Client-Researcher Partnership," *Marketing News,* September 13, 1994, p. 38.

19. Jack Honomichl, "Top 50 U.S. Marketing/Ad/Opinion Research Firms Profiled," *Marketing News,* June 5, 1995, p. H2. Also see "Directory of International Marketing Research Firms," *Marketing News,* July 31, 1995, pp. 14–20.

20. Many of the examples in this section, along with others, are found in Subhash C. Jain, *International Marketing Management,* 3rd ed. (Boston: PWS-Kent Publishing Company, 1990), pp. 334–39. Also see Vern Terpstra and Ravi Sarathy, *International Marketing* (Chicago: The Dryden Press, 1991), pp. 208–13; Jack Honomichl, "Research Cultures Are Different in Mexico, Canada," *Marketing News,* May 5, 1993, pp. 12–13; and Naghi Namakforoosh, "Data Collection Methods Hold Key to Research in Mexico," *Marketing News,* August 29, 1994, p. 28.

21. Jain, *International Marketing Management,* p. 338.

22. "MRA Study Shows Refusal Rates Are Highest at Start of Process," *Marketing News,* August 16, 1993, p. A15. Also see Judith Waldrop, "The Business of Privacy," *American Demographics,* October 1994, pp. 46–55.

23. Cynthia Crossen, "Studies Galore Support Products and Positions, But Are They Reliable?" *Wall Street Journal,* November 14, 1991, pp. A1, A9. Also see Betsy Spethmann, "Cautious Consumers Have Surveyers Wary," *Advertising Age,* June 10, 1991, p. 34.

# 5

# *Consumer Markets and Consumer Buyer Behavior*

In the early 1980s, Nike won the opening battle in what many now call the "great sneaker wars." Based on the power of its hot-selling running shoes, which were designed for fitness but used mostly for fun, Nike unseated Adidas and sprinted into the lead in the $6 billion U.S. athletic shoe market. But fashion is fickle, and Nike's lead was short-lived. In 1986, upstart Reebok caught Nike from behind with its new, soft leather aerobics shoe. It turned sweaty sneakers into fashion statements and zoomed to the front. By 1987, Reebok had captured over 30 percent of the market, while Nike's share had slumped to 18 percent.

In 1988, however, Nike retaliated. It targeted the reemerging "performance" market with the hard-hitting $20 million "Just Do It" advertising campaign featuring sports stars. The company also introduced dozens of new products aimed at narrow segments in the rapidly fragmenting athletic shoe market. By 1990, Nike was selling footwear for almost every conceivable sport: hiking, walking, cycling—even cheerleading and windsurfing. The numbers now attest to Nike's rejuvenation: Its current market share of the athletic shoe market is 37 percent, and Reebok's share has fallen to less than 20 percent. In the basketball shoe segment, Nike owns a 50 percent share, compared with only 15 percent for Reebok.

Because sneakers can be a major means of self-expression, people's choices are usually shaped by a rich mix of influences. Thus, understanding consumer behavior in this seesaw market can be extremely difficult; trying to predict behavior can be even tougher. The shoe companies introduce scores of new styles and colors every year, chasing fads that often fade at blinding speed. One day salespeople will sell all they can get of a new style; the next day, they can't discount it enough.

Mistakes can be costly. For example, consider Reebok's disastrous 1993 introduction of its Shaq Attaq model. Endorsed by basketball sensation Shaquille

O'Neal, the Shaq Attaq arrived in stores with a loud thud. The new sneakers were white with light blue trim, and they cost about $130. Unfortunately, black shoes were the hot look that year, and few customers wanted to pay more than $100 for a pair of sneakers. In the first half of 1993, Reebok's sales of basketball shoes fell 20 percent.

The fickle youth market is the biggest battleground in the sneaker wars, and the inner city is at the front. Consumers between 15 and 22 years old buy 30 percent of all sneakers and influence an additional 10 percent through word of mouth. Many trends start in the nation's inner cities and spread to suburbia and the rest of Middle America. Urban kids represent authenticity to kids in the suburbs, so trends that catch on in the inner city often spread quickly to the rest of the country. It isn't surprising, then, that sneaker makers openly court inner-city shoe store owners and their young customers. Nike and the other shoe manufacturers often give free sneakers to trend-setting teens whom the masses will copy. Reebok even rebuilds inner-city playgrounds and repaves basketball courts to woo this constituency. And companies often launch new sneakers in the inner city first to see how they catch on before going national.

These days, shoes are the first and foremost fashion statement. Gone are the days when sneakers were mostly cheap, functional, and drab, when the choices were white or black canvas, low top or high top, with maybe a variation or two for avid runners. Now, sneakers are a status symbol, part of a subculture. Sneaker prices start at around $50 a pair and run to more than $180. You can get good sneakers for less, but nobody who is anybody would be caught dead in them.

Sneaker crazes are often hard to explain. For example, the early-1990s fad of wearing sneakers with the laces untied apparently began because proud owners wanted to keep their shoes looking factory fresh. Pretty soon, everyone was doing it, and that was just the beginning. Next, some wearers untied the lace on one shoe only; then, they removed the laces completely. Soon after that, wearers switched back to tying their shoes, but with laces from a different shoe. Then, many were wearing sneakers that didn't match—say, a white Chuck Taylor Converse on one foot and a Black Cons Converse on the other—but brands couldn't be mixed. In some neighborhoods, teenage girls have reported that the first thing they look at when a boy asks them out is his choice of sneakers. Teenage romances have been thwarted by brand differences.

Now, tastes in sneakers appear to have changed once again, with Generation Xers leading the way. Losing favor are high-tech shoes that pump up, fasten with Velcro, blink, or glow in the dark. Today's sneaker buyers appear to be heading back to the basics, looking for, of all things, authenticity and sensibility in their sneakers statements. Notes one analyst: "Turn off your LED heel lights. And for heaven's sakes, stop inflating that silly pump! Generation Xers and hip boomers alike are downscaling with down-to-earth antique sneaks—Pro Keds, Converse One Stars and Dr. Js, Adidas Gazelles, and Puma Swedes. 'We're all teched-out,' explains [one industry insider. Says another,] 'Things are so complicated now. People are naturally looking back.' "

Like previous fashion swings, this return-to-the-classics craze has trickled up, not down—it comes from the streets. Today's Xers prefer the "athe-leisure" look befitting their more laid-back lifestyles. They don't work out in their sneakers, they wear them to work, and then to dance. Some are turning away from sneakers altogether, instead opting for hiking boots and other rugged footwear from fast-growing outdoor shoe makers like Timberland Company.

Nike's oldest competitor, Converse, is taking full advantage of recent trends. It's featuring its once-again fashionable Converse All-Star. First introduced in 1917, this venerable veteran of the sneaker wars has sold an estimated 520 million pairs over the past 75 years. Converse is also bringing back models from its 1970s catalogs, including the One-Star, its Pro Leather model (worn by 1970s basketball great Julius Irving), and the Jack Purcell (originally a badminton shoe, later popular with tennis players of the 1960s).

Thus, today, the sneaker wars continue to rage, and Nike is watching its flanks for new trends and new competitors. Sneaker fashions come and go rapidly, reflecting the ever-changing lives and lifestyles of the consumers who buy the shoes. Nike knows that winning the sneaker wars, or even just surviving, requires a keen understanding of consumer behavior.[1] ■

## CHAPTER OBJECTIVES

### After reading this chapter, you should be able to:

**1** Define the consumer market and construct a simple model of consumer buyer behavior.

**2** Name the four major factors that influence consumer buyer behavior.

**3** List the stages in the buyer decision process.

**4** Describe the adoption process for new products.

---

The Nike example shows that many different factors affect consumer buying behavior. Buying behavior is never simple, yet understanding it is the essential task of marketing management.

This chapter explores the dynamics of consumer behavior and the consumer market. **Consumer buying behavior** refers to the buying behavior of final consumers—individuals and households who buy goods and services for personal consumption. All of these final consumers combined make up the **consumer market.** The American consumer market consists of more than 260 million people who consume many trillions of dollars worth of goods and services each year, making it one of the most attractive consumer markets in the world. The world consumer market consists of more than 5.7 *billion* people. At present growth rates, the world population will exceed seven billion people by 2010.[2]

Consumers around the world vary tremendously in age, income, education level, and tastes. They also buy an incredible variety of goods and services. These diverse consumers make their choices among various products based on a fascinating array of factors.

**Consumer buying behavior**
The buying behavior of final consumers—individuals and households who buy goods and services for personal consumption.

**Consumer market**
All the individuals and households who buy or acquire goods and services for personal consumption.

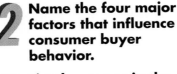

## MODEL OF CONSUMER BEHAVIOR

Consumers make many buying decisions every day. Most large companies research consumer buying decisions in great detail to answer questions about what consumers buy, where they buy, how and how much they buy, when they buy, and why they buy. Marketers can study actual consumer purchases to find out what they buy, where, and how much. But learning about the *whys* of consumer buying behavior is not so easy—the answers are often locked deep within the consumer's head.

The central question for marketers is: How do consumers respond to various marketing efforts that the company might use? The company that really understands how consumers will respond to different product features, prices, and advertising appeals has a great advantage over its competitors. The starting point is the stimulus–response model of buyer behavior shown in Figure 5-1. This figure shows that marketing and other stimuli enter the consumer's "black box" and produce certain responses. Marketers must figure out what is in the buyer's black box.[3]

Marketing stimuli consist of the four *P*s: product, price, place, and promotion. Other stimuli include major forces and events in the buyer's environment: economic, technological, political, and cultural. All these inputs enter the buyer's black box, where they are turned into a set of observable buyer responses: product choice, brand choice, dealer choice, purchase timing, and purchase amount.

The marketer wants to understand how the stimuli are changed into responses inside the consumer's black box, which has two parts. First, the buyer's characteristics influence how he or she perceives and reacts to the stimuli. Second, the buyer's decision process itself affects the buyer's behavior. This chapter looks first at buyer characteristics as they affect buying behavior, and then discusses the buyer decision process.

# CHARACTERISTICS AFFECTING CONSUMER BEHAVIOR

Consumer purchases are influenced strongly by cultural, social, personal, and psychological characteristics, as shown in Figure 5-2. For the most part, marketers cannot control such factors, but they must take them into account. We illustrate these characteristics with the case of a hypothetical consumer named Jennifer Flores. Jennifer is a married college graduate who works as a brand manager in a leading consumer packaged-goods company. She wants to find a new leisure-time activity that will provide some contrast to her working day. This need has led her to consider buying a camera and taking up photography. Many characteristics in her background will affect the way that she evaluates cameras and chooses a brand.

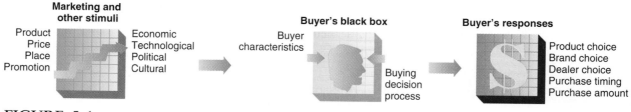

**FIGURE 5-1**
*Model of buyer behavior*

FIGURE 5-2
*Factors influencing consumer behavior*

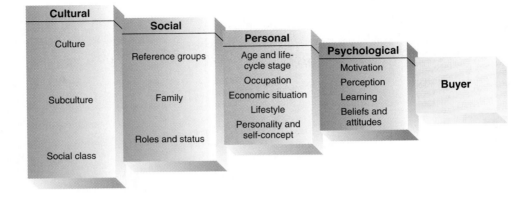

# CULTURAL FACTORS

Cultural factors exert the broadest and deepest influence on consumer behavior. The marketer needs to understand the role played by the buyer's *culture*, *subculture*, and *social class*.

## Culture

**Culture**
The set of basic values, perceptions, wants, and behaviors learned by a member of society from family and other important institutions.

**Culture** is the most basic cause of a person's wants and behavior. Human behavior is largely learned. Growing up in a society, a child learns basic values, perceptions, wants, and behaviors from the family and other important institutions. A child in the United States normally learns or is exposed to the following values: achievement and success, activity and involvement, efficiency and practicality, progress, material comfort, individualism, freedom, humanitarianism, youthfulness, and fitness and health.

Every group or society has a culture, and cultural influences on buying behavior may vary greatly from country to country. Failure to adjust to these differences can result in ineffective marketing or embarrassing mistakes. For example, business representatives of a U.S. community trying to market itself in Taiwan found this out the hard way. Seeking more foreign trade, they arrived in Taiwan bearing gifts of green baseball caps. It turned out that the trip was scheduled a month before Taiwan elections, and that green was the color of the political opposition party. Worse yet, the visitors learned after the fact that, according to Taiwan culture, a man wears green to signify that his wife has been unfaithful. The head of the community delegation later noted: "I don't know whatever happened to those green hats, but the trip gave us an understanding of the extreme differences in our cultures."[4] International marketers must understand the culture in each international market and adapt their marketing strategies accordingly.

Jennifer Flores's cultural background will affect her camera buying decision. Jennifer's desire to own a camera may result from her being raised in a modern society that has developed camera technology and a whole set of consumer learnings and values. Jennifer knows what cameras are. She knows how to read instructions, and her society has accepted the idea of women photographers.

Marketers are always trying to spot *cultural shifts* in order to discover new products that might be wanted. For example, the cultural shift toward greater concern about health and fitness has created a huge industry for exercise equipment

*McDonald's targets important sub-cultures, such as blacks and mature consumers.*

and clothing, lower-fat and more natural foods, and health and fitness services. The shift toward informality has resulted in more demand for casual clothing and simpler home furnishings. And the increased desire for leisure time has resulted in more demand for convenience products and services, such as microwave ovens, takeout meals, and fast food.

## Subculture

**Subculture**

A group of people with shared value systems based on common life experiences and situations.

Each culture contains smaller **subcultures**, or groups of people with shared value systems based on common life experiences and situations. Subcultures include nationalities, religions, racial groups, and geographic regions. Many subcultures make up important market segments, and marketers often design products and marketing programs tailored to their needs. Here are examples of four such important subculture groups.[5]

HISPANIC CONSUMERS.   The U.S. Hispanic market—Americans of Cuban, Mexican, Central American, South American, and Puerto Rican descent—consists of 26 million consumers who buy more than $200 billion of goods and services each year. Expected to number almost 40 million by the year 2010, Hispanics are easy to reach through the growing selection of Spanish-language broadcast and print media that cater to them. Hispanics have long been a target for marketers of food, beverages, and household care products. But as the segment's buying power has increased, Hispanics have emerged as an attractive market for pricier products such as computers, financial services, photography equipment, large appliances, life insurance, and automobiles. Hispanic consumers tend to buy more branded, higher-quality products—generics don't sell well to Hispanics. Perhaps more important, Hispanics are very brand loyal, and they favor companies who show special interest in them. Because of the segment's strong brand loyalty, companies that gain the first foothold have an important head start in this fast-growing market.

Sears makes a special effort to target Hispanic consumers. The retail chain has designated more than 130 of its stores with customer bases exceeding 20 percent Latino as special Hispanic stores. "We make a special effort to staff those stores with bilingual sales personnel, to use bilingual signage, and to support community programs," says a Sears spokesperson. Choosing merchandise for the Latino marketplace is primarily a color and size issue. "What we find in Hispanic communities is that people tend to be smaller than the general market, and that there is greater demand for special-occasion clothing and a preference for bright colors. In hardlines, there isn't much difference from the mainstream market."[6]

Targeting Hispanics may also provide an additional benefit. With the passage of the North American Free Trade Agreement (NAFTA)—which reduces trade barriers between the United States, Mexico, and Canada—U.S. and Mexican companies are seeking new opportunities to market "pan-American" brands. Companies on both sides of the border see the U.S. Hispanic population as a bridge for spanning U.S. and Latin American markets.[7]

AFRICAN AMERICAN CONSUMERS.   If the U.S. population of 31 million African Americans, with a total purchasing power of $218 billion annually, were a separate nation, their buying power would rank twelfth in the free world. The black population in the United States is growing in affluence and sophistication. Blacks spend relatively more than whites on clothing, personal care, home furnishings, and fragrances; and relatively less on food, transportation, and recreation. Although more price conscious, blacks are also strongly motivated by quality and selection. They place more importance than other groups on brand names, are more brand loyal, do less "shopping around," and shop more at neighborhood stores. In recent years, many large companies—Sears, McDonald's, Procter & Gamble, Coca-Cola—have stepped up their efforts to tap this lucrative market. They employ black-owned advertising agencies and place ads in black consumer magazines. Some companies develop special products, packaging, and appeals for the black consumer market. During the past few years, JCPenney has revamped about 170 stores to target African Americans, changing its merchandise and store layout, and using black models in its ads.[8]

ASIAN AMERICAN CONSUMERS.   Asian Americans, the fastest-growing and most affluent U.S. demographic segment, now number more than 9 million. Chinese constitute the largest group, followed by Filipinos, Japanese, Asian Indians, and Koreans. The segment is expected to grow to more than 12 million by the year 2000. Asian American family income exceeds the national average by 19 percent. Long-distance telephone companies and financial services marketers have long targeted Asian American consumers, but until recently, packaged-goods firms, automobile companies, retailers, and fast-food chains have lagged in pursuing this segment. Language and cultural traditions appear to be the biggest barriers. For example, 66 percent of Asian Americans are foreign-born, and 56 percent of those aged five years and older do not speak English fluently. Still, because of the segment's rapidly growing buying power, many firms are now looking seriously at this market.[9]

MATURE CONSUMERS.   As the U.S. population ages, "mature" consumers—those 65 and older—are becoming a very attractive market. Now 32 million strong, the seniors market will grow to over 40 million consumers by the year 2000. Seniors are better off financially, spending about $200 billion each year, and they average twice the disposable income of consumers in the under-35 group. Too often stereotyped as feeble-minded geezers glued to their rocking chairs, seniors have long been the target of the makers of laxatives, tonics, and denture products. But many marketers realize that most seniors are not sick, feeble, deaf, or confused. Most are healthy and active, and they have many of the same needs and wants as younger consumers. Because seniors have more time and money, they are an ideal market for exotic travel, restaurants, high-tech home entertainment products, leisure goods and services, designer furniture and fashions, financial services, and life- and health-care services. Their desire to look as young as they feel makes seniors good candidates for specially designed cosmetics and personal care products, health foods, home physical fitness products, and other items that combat the effects of aging. As the seniors segment grows in size and buying power, and as the stereotypes of seniors as doddering, creaky, impoverished shut-ins fade, more and more marketers are developing specific strategies for this important market. For example, Sears's 40,000-member "Mature Club" offers older consumers 25 percent discounts on everything from eyeglasses to lawnmowers. Southwestern Bell publishes the "Silver Pages," crammed full of ads offering discounts and coupons to 20 million seniors in 90 markets. To appeal more to mature consumers, McDonald's employs older folks as hosts and hostesses in its restaurants and casts them in its ads. GrandTravel of Chevy Chase, Maryland, sponsors barge trips through Holland, safaris to Kenya, and other exotic vacations for grandparents and their grandchildren. And Kellogg recently aired a new TV spot for All-Bran cereal in which individuals ranging in age from 53 to 81 are featured playing ice hockey, water skiing, running hurdles, and playing baseball, all to the tune of "Wild Thing."[10]

Jennifer Flores's buying behavior will be influenced by her subculture identification. These factors will affect her food preferences, clothing choices, recreation activities, and career goals. Subcultures attach different meanings to picture taking, and this could affect both Jennifer's interest in cameras and the brand she buys.

## Social Class

**Social classes**
Relatively permanent and ordered divisions in a society whose members share similar values, interests, and behaviors.

Almost every society has some form of social class structure. **Social classes are society's relatively permanent and ordered divisions whose members share similar values, interests, and behaviors.** Social scientists have identified seven American social classes (see Table 5-1).

Social class is not determined by a single factor, such as income, but is measured as a combination of occupation, income, education, wealth, and other variables. In some social systems, members of different classes are reared for certain roles and cannot change their social positions. In the United States, however, the lines between social classes are not fixed and rigid; people can move to a higher social class or drop into a lower one. Marketers are interested in social class because people within a given social class tend to exhibit similar buying behavior.

Social classes show distinct product and brand preferences in areas such as clothing, home furnishings, leisure activity, and automobiles. Jennifer Flores's social class may affect her camera decision. If she comes from a higher social class background, her family probably owned an expensive camera, and she may have dabbled in photography.

| TABLE 5-1 | *Characteristics of Seven Major American Social Classes* |
|---|---|

*Upper uppers (less than 1 percent)*
Upper uppers are the social elite who live on inherited wealth and have well-known family backgrounds. They give large sums to charity, run debutante balls, own more than one home, and send their children to the finest schools. They are a market for jewelry, antiques, homes, and vacations. They often buy and dress conservatively rather than showing off their wealth. While small in number, upper uppers serve as a reference group for others.

*Lower uppers (about 2 percent)*
Lower uppers have earned high income or wealth through exceptional ability in the professions or business. They usually begin in the middle class. They tend to be active in social and civic affairs and buy for themselves and their children the symbols of status, such as expensive homes, educations, swimming pools, and automobiles. They include the new rich who consume conspicuously to impress those below them. They want to be accepted in the upper-upper stratum, a status more likely to be achieved by their children than by themselves.

*Upper middles (12 percent)*
Upper middles possess neither family status nor unusual wealth. They are primarily concerned with "career." They have attained positions as professionals, independent businesspersons, and corporate managers. They believe in education and want their children to develop professional or administrative skills. They are joiners and highly civic-minded. They are the quality market for good homes, clothes, furniture, and appliances.

*Middle class (32 percent)*
The middle class is made up of average-pay white- and blue-collar workers who live on the "the better side of town" and try to "do the proper things." To keep up with the trends, they often buy products that are popular. Most are concerned with fashion, seeking the better brand names. Better living means owning a nice home in a nice neighborhood with good schools. They believe in spending more money on worthwhile experiences for their children and aiming them toward a college education.

*Working class (38 percent)*
The working class consists of those who lead a "working-class lifestyle," whatever their income, school background, or job. They depend heavily on relatives for economic and emotional support, for advice on purchases, and for assistance in times of trouble. The working class maintains sharper sex role divisions and stereotyping.

*Upper lowers (9 percent)*
Upper lowers are working (are not on welfare), although their living standard is just above poverty. They perform unskilled work for very poor pay although they strive toward a higher class. Often, upper lowers lack education. Although they fall near the poverty line financially, they manage to "present a picture of self-discipline" and "maintain some effort at cleanliness."

*Lower lowers (7 percent)*
Lower lowers are on welfare, visibly poverty stricken, and usually out of work or have "the dirtiest jobs." Often, they are not interested in finding a job and are permanently dependent on public aid or charity for income. Their homes, clothes, and possessions are "dirty," "raggedy," and "broken-down."

*Source:* See Richard P. Coleman, "The Continuing Significance of Social Class to Marketing," *Journal of Consumer Research,* December 1983, pp. 265–80. © Journal of Consumer Research, Inc., 1983.

# SOCIAL FACTORS

A consumer's behavior is also influenced by social factors, such as the consumer's *small groups, family,* and *social roles and status.*

## Groups

**Group**

Two or more people who interact to accomplish individual or mutual goals.

A person's behavior is influenced by many small **groups.** Groups that have a direct influence and to which a person belongs are called *membership groups.* Some are *primary groups* with whom there is regular but informal interaction—such as family, friends, neighbors, and co-workers. Some are *secondary groups,* which are more formal and have less regular interaction. These include organizations like religious groups, professional associations, and trade unions.

*Reference groups* serve as direct (face-to-face) or indirect points of comparison or reference in forming a person's attitudes or behavior. People are often influenced by reference groups to which they do not belong. For example, an *aspirational group* is one to which the individual wishes to belong, as when a teenage basketball player hopes to play someday for the Chicago Bulls. He identifies with this group, although there is no face-to-face contact between him and the team. Marketers try to identify the reference groups of their target markets. Reference groups expose a person to new behaviors and lifestyles, influence the person's attitudes and self-concept, and create pressures to conform that may affect the person's product and brand choices.

**Opinion leaders**

People within a reference group who, because of special skills, knowledge, personality traits, or other characteristics, exert influence on others.

Manufacturers of products and brands subject to strong group influence must figure out how to reach the opinion leaders in the relevant reference groups. **Opinion leaders** are people within a reference group who, because of special skills, knowledge, personality traits, or other characteristics, exert influence on others. Opinion leaders are found at all levels of society, and one person may be an opinion leader in certain product areas and an opinion follower in others. Marketers try to identify opinion leaders for their products and direct marketing efforts toward them. Chrysler used opinion leaders to launch its LH-series cars—the Concorde, Dodge Intrepid, and Eagle Vision. It lent cars on weekends to 6,000 community and business leaders in 25 cities. In surveys, 98 percent of the test-drivers said that they would recommend the models to friends. And it appears that they did—Chrysler sold out production the first year.[11]

The importance of group influence varies across products and brands. It tends to be strongest when the product is visible to others whom the buyer respects. Purchases of products that are bought and used privately are not much affected by group influences because neither the product nor the brand will be noticed by others. If Jennifer Flores buys a camera, both the product and the brand will be visible to others whom she respects, and her decision to buy the camera and her brand choice may be influenced strongly by some of her groups, such as friends who belong to a photography club.

## Family

Family members can strongly influence buyer behavior. The family is the most important consumer buying organization in society, and it has been researched extensively. Marketers are interested in the roles and influence of husbands, wives, and children on the purchase of different products and services.

Husband-wife involvement varies widely by product category and by stage in the buying process. Buying roles change with evolving consumer lifestyles. In

*Family buying decisions: Depending on the product and situation, individual family members exert different amounts of influence.*

the United States, the wife traditionally has been the main purchasing agent for the family, especially in the areas of food, household products, and clothing. But with 70 percent of women holding jobs outside the home and the willingness of husbands to do more of the family's purchasing, all this is changing. For example, women now buy about 45 percent of all cars, and men account for about 40 percent of food-shopping dollars.[12] Such roles vary widely in different countries and social classes. As always, marketers must research specific patterns in their target markets.

In the case of expensive products and services, husbands and wives more often make joint decisions. Jennifer Flores's husband may play an *influencer role* in her camera-buying decision. He may have an opinion about her buying a camera and about the kind of camera to buy. At the same time, she will be the primary decider, purchaser, and user.[13]

### Roles and Status

A person belongs to many groups—family, clubs, organizations. The person's position in each group can be defined in terms of both role and status. With her parents, Jennifer Flores plays the role of daughter; in her family, she plays the role of wife; in her company, she plays the role of brand manager. A *role* consists of the activities that people are expected to perform according to the persons around them. Each of Jennifer's roles will influence some of her buying behavior.

Each role carries a *status* reflecting the general esteem given to it by society. People often choose products that show their status in society. For example, the role of brand manager has more status in our society than the role of daughter. As a brand manager, Jennifer will buy the kind of clothing that reflects her role and status.

## PERSONAL FACTORS

A buyer's decisions are also influenced by personal characteristics such as the buyer's *age and life-cycle stage, occupation, economic situation, lifestyle,* and *personality and self-concept.*

## Age and Life-Cycle Stage

People change the goods and services that they buy over their lifetimes. Tastes in food, clothes, furniture, and recreation are often age related. Buying is also shaped by the stage of the *family life cycle*—the stages through which families might pass as they mature over time. Table 5-2 lists the stages of the family life cycle. Marketers often define their target markets in terms of life-cycle stage and develop appropriate products and marketing plans for each stage. Traditional family life-cycle stages include young singles and married couples with children. Today, however, marketers are increasingly catering to a growing number of alternative, non-traditional stages such as unmarried couples, couples marrying later in life, childless couples, single parents, extended parents (those with young adult children returning home), and others.

## Occupation

A person's occupation affects the goods and services bought. Blue-collar workers tend to buy more rugged work clothes, whereas white-collar workers buy more business suits. Marketers try to identify the occupational groups that have an above-average interest in their products and services. A company can even specialize in making products that are needed by a given occupational group. Thus, computer software companies will design different products for brand managers, accountants, engineers, lawyers, and doctors.

## Economic Situation

A person's economic situation will affect product choice. Jennifer Flores can consider buying an expensive Nikon if she has enough spendable income, savings, or borrowing power. Marketers of income-sensitive goods watch trends in personal income, savings, and interest rates. If economic indicators point to a recession, marketers can take steps to redesign, reposition, and reprice their products.

## Lifestyle

People coming from the same subculture, social class, and occupation may have quite different lifestyles. **Lifestyle** is a person's pattern of living as expressed in his or her **psychographics**. It involves measuring consumers' major *AIO dimensions—activities* (work, hobbies, shopping, sports, social events), *interests* (food, fashion, family, recreation), and *opinions* (about themselves, social issues, business, prod-

**Lifestyle**
A person's pattern of living as expressed in his or her activities, interests, and opinions.

**Psychographics**
The technique of measuring lifestyles and developing lifestyle classifications; it involves measuring the major AIO dimensions (activities, interests, opinions).

**TABLE 5-2** *Family Life-Cycle Stages*

| Young | Middle-Aged | Older |
|-------|-------------|-------|
| Single | Single | Older married |
| Married without children | Married without children | Older unmarried |
| Married with children | Married with children | |
| Divorced with children | Married without dependent children | |
| | Divorced without children | |
| | Divorced with children | |
| | Divorced without dependent children | |

*Sources:* Adapted from Patrick E. Murphy and William A. Staples, "A Modernized Family Life Cycle," *Journal of Consumer Research*, June 1979, p. 16; © Journal of Consumer Research, Inc., 1979. Also see Leon G. Schiffman and Leslie Lazar Kanuk, *Consumer Behavior* (Englewood Cliffs, NJ: Prentice Hall, 1994), pp. 361–70.

*Lifestyles: Lee Relaxed Riders fit the lifestyle of the modern woman on the go. "Nobody fits your body . . . or the way you live . . . better than Lee."*

Dig in the garden. Wash the car. Go to a movie. Walk the dog. Burp the kid.

*Lee Relaxed Rider™ jeans are designed to fit the natural curves of a woman's body. But most importantly, they're designed to fit the natural curves of a woman's life. Dress them up. Or dress them down. When you're ready to go. Or when it's time to relax. Nobody fits your body...or the way you live...better than Lee.*

R E L A X E D · R I D E R S

Lee

*The brand that fits.*

ucts). Lifestyle captures something more than the person's social class or personality. It profiles a person's whole pattern of acting and interacting in the world.

Several research firms have developed lifestyle classifications. The most widely used is the SRI *Values and Lifestyles (VALS)* typology. VALS 2 classifies people according to how they spend their time and money. It divides consumers into eight groups based on two major dimensions: self-orientation and resources. *Self-orientation* groups include *principle-oriented* consumers who buy based upon their views of the world; *status-oriented* buyers who base their purchases on the actions and opinions of others; and *action-oriented* buyers who are driven by their desire for activity, variety, and risk taking. Consumers within each orientation are further classified into those with *abundant resources* and those with *minimal resources,* depending on whether they have high or low levels of income, education, health, self-confidence, energy, and other factors. Consumers with either very high or very low levels of resources are classified without regard to their self-orientations (actualizers, strugglers).[14]

Iron City beer, a well-known brand in Pittsburgh, used VALS 2 to update its image and improve sales. Iron City was losing sales—its aging core users were drinking less beer, and younger men weren't buying the brand. According to VALS research, experiencers drink the most beer, followed by strivers. To assess Iron City's image problems, the company interviewed men in these categories. It gave the men stacks of pictures of different kinds of people and asked them first to identify Iron City brand users and then people most like themselves. The men pictured Iron City drinkers as blue-collar steelworkers stopping off at the local bar. However, they saw themselves as more modern, hard working, and fun loving. They strongly rejected the outmoded, heavy-industry image of Pittsburgh. Based on this research, Iron City created ads linking its beer to the new self-image of target consumers. The ads mingled images of the old Pittsburgh with those of the new, dynamic city and scenes of young experiencers and strivers having fun and working hard. Within just one month of the start of the campaign, Iron City sales shot up by 26 percent.[15]

Lifestyle classifications are by no means universal—they can vary significantly from country to country. McCann-Erikson London, for example, found the following British lifestyles: Avant Guardians (interested in change); Pontificators (traditionalists, very British); Chameleons (follow the crowd); and Sleepwalkers (contented underachievers). Contrast this with Survey Research Malaysia's seven lifestyle categories for its developing country: Upper Echelons (driven by status and the desire to stand out); Not Quite Theres (ambitious for self and family); Rebel Hangouts (want to stand out from the mainstream); Sleepwalkers (just want to get through the day); Inconspicuous (want to blend in); Kampung Trend-Setters (ambitious, city influenced, village dwellers); and Rural Traditionalists (abide by traditional rules).[16] Finally, advertising agency D'Arcy, Masius, Benton, & Bowles identified five categories of Russian consumers: Kuptsi (merchants), Cossacks, Students, Business Executives, and Russian Souls. Cossacks are characterized as ambitious, independent, and status seeking, Russian Souls as passive, fearful of choices, and hopeful. Thus, a typical Cossack might drive a BMW, smoke Dunhill cigarettes, and drink Remy Martin liquor, whereas a Russian Soul would drive a Lada, smoke Marlboros, and drink Smirnoff vodka.[17]

When used carefully, the lifestyle concept can help the marketer understand changing consumer values and how they affect buying behavior. Jennifer Flores, for example, can choose to live the role of a capable homemaker, a career woman, or a free spirit—or all three. She plays several roles, and the way that she blends them expresses her lifestyle. If she becomes a professional photographer, this would change her lifestyle, in turn changing what and how she buys.

## *Personality and Self-Concept*

**Personality**

A person's distinguishing psychological characteristics that lead to relatively consistent and lasting responses to his or her own environment.

Each person's distinct personality influences his or her buying behavior. **Personality** refers to the unique psychological characteristics that lead to relatively consistent and lasting responses to one's own environment. Personality is usually described in terms of traits such as self-confidence, dominance, sociability, autonomy, defensiveness, adaptability, and aggressiveness. Personality can be useful in analyzing consumer behavior for certain product or brand choices. For example, coffee makers have discovered that heavy coffee drinkers tend to be high on sociability. Thus, Maxwell House ads show people relaxing and socializing over a cup of steaming coffee.

Many marketers use a concept related to personality—a person's *self-concept* (also called *self-image*). The basic self-concept premise is that people's possessions contribute to and reflect their identities; that is, "we are what we have." Thus, in order to understand consumer behavior, the marketer must first understand the relationship between consumer self-concept and possessions. For example, the founder and chief executive of Barnes & Noble, the nation's number one bookseller, notes that people buy books to support their self-images:

> People have the mistaken notion that the thing you do with books is read them. Wrong. . . . People buy books for what the purchase says about them—their taste, their cultivation, their trendiness. Their aim . . . is to connect themselves, or those to whom they give the books as gifts, with all the other refined owners of Edgar Allen Poe collections

> or sensitive owners of Virginia Woolf collections. . . . [The result is that] you can sell books as consumer products, with seductive displays, flashy posters, an emphasis on the glamour of the book, and the fashion-ableness of the bestseller and the trendy author.18

Jennifer Flores may see herself as outgoing, creative, and active. Therefore, she will favor a camera that projects the same qualities. If the Nikon is promoted as a camera for outgoing, creative, and active people, then its brand image will match her self-image.

# PSYCHOLOGICAL FACTORS

A person's buying choices are further influenced by four major psychological factors: *motivation, perception, learning,* and *beliefs and attitudes.*

## Motivation

We know that Jennifer Flores became interested in buying a camera. Why? What is she *really* seeking? What *needs* is she trying to satisfy?

**Motive (drive)**
A need that is sufficiently pressing to direct the person to seek satisfaction of the need.

A person has many needs at any given time. Some are *biological,* arising from states of tension such as hunger, thirst, or discomfort. Others are *psychological,* arising from the need for recognition, esteem, or belonging. Most of these needs will not be strong enough to motivate the person to act at a given point in time. A need becomes a *motive* when it is aroused to a sufficient level of intensity. A **motive** (or *drive*) is a need that is sufficiently pressing to direct the person to seek satisfaction. Psychologists have developed theories of human motivation. Two of the most popular—the theories of Sigmund Freud and Abraham Maslow—have quite different meanings for consumer analysis and marketing.

### Freud's Theory of Motivation

Freud assumed that people are largely unconscious about the real psychological forces shaping their behavior. He believed that, as people grow up, they repress many urges. These urges are never eliminated or under perfect control; they emerge in dreams, in slips of the tongue, in neurotic and obsessive behavior, or ultimately in psychoses. Thus, Freud suggested that a person does not fully understand his or her motivation.

If Jennifer Flores wants to purchase an expensive camera, she may describe her motive as wanting a hobby or career. At a deeper level, she may be purchasing the camera to impress others with her creative talent. At a still deeper level, she may be buying the camera to feel young and independent again.

Motivation researchers collect in-depth information from small samples of consumers to uncover the deeper motives for their product choices. They use nondirective depth interviews and various "projective techniques" to throw the ego off guard—techniques such as word association, sentence completion, picture interpretation, and role playing. Motivation researchers have reached some interesting and sometimes odd conclusions about what may be in the buyer's mind regarding certain purchases. For example, one classic study concluded that consumers resist prunes because they are wrinkled looking and remind people of sickness and old age. Despite its sometimes unusual conclusions, motivation research remains a useful tool for marketers seeking a deeper understanding of consumer behavior (see Marketing at Work 5-1).[19]

# MARKETING AT WORK 5-1

## "Touchy-Feely" Research Into Consumer Motivations

The term *motivation research* refers to qualitative research designed to probe consumers' hidden, subconscious motivations. Because consumers often don't know or can't describe just why they act as they do, motivation researchers use a variety of nondirective and projective techniques to reveal underlying emotions and attitudes toward brands and buying situations. The techniques range from sentence completion, word association, and inkblot or cartoon interpretation tests, to having consumers describe typical brand users or form daydreams and fantasies about brands or buying situations. Some of these techniques verge on the bizarre. One writer offers the following tongue-in-cheek summary of a motivation research session:

*Good morning, ladies and gentlemen. We've called you here today for a little consumer research. Now, lie down on the couch, toss your inhibitions out the window, and let's try a little free association. First, think about brands as if they were your friends. Imagine you could talk to your TV dinner. What would he say? And what would you say to him? . . . Now, think of your shampoo as an animal. Go on, don't be shy. Would it be a panda or a lion? A snake or a*

*wooly worm? For our final exercise, let's all sit up and pull out our magic markers. Draw a picture of a typical cake-mix user. Would she wear an apron or a negligee? A business suit or a can-can dress?*

Such projective techniques seem pretty goofy. But more and more, marketers are turning to these touchy-feely approaches to probe consumer psyches and develop better marketing strategies.

Many advertising agencies employ teams of psychologists, anthropologists, and other social scientists to carry out motivation research. One agency routinely conducts one-on-one, therapy-like interviews to delve into the inner workings of consumers' minds. Another agency asks consumers to describe their favorite brands as animals or cars (say, Cadillacs versus Chevrolets) in order to assess the prestige associated with various brands. Still another agency has consumers draw figures of typical brand users:

*In one instance, the agency asked 50 interviewees to sketch likely buyers of two different brands of cake mixes. Consistently, the group portrayed Pillsbury customers as*

*Motivation research: When asked to sketch figures of typical cake-mix users, subjects portrayed Pillsbury customers as grandmotherly types and Duncan Hines buyers as svelte and contemporary.*

## Maslow's Theory of Motivation

Abraham Maslow sought to explain why people are driven by particular needs at particular times.[20] Why does one person spend much time and energy on personal safety and another on gaining the esteem of others? Maslow's answer is that human needs are arranged in a hierarchy, from the most pressing to the least pressing.

apron-clad, grandmotherly types, while they pictured Duncan Hines purchasers as svelte, contemporary women.

In a similar study, American Express had people sketch likely users of its gold card versus its green card. Respondents depicted gold card holders as active, broad-shouldered men; green card holders were perceived as "couch potatoes" lounging in front of television sets. Based on these results, the company positioned its gold card as a symbol of responsibility for people capable of controlling their lives and finances.

Some motivation research studies employ more basic techniques, such as simply mingling with or watching consumers to find out what makes them tick. In an effort to understand the teenage consumer market better, ad agency BSB Worldwide videotaped teenagers' rooms in 25 countries. It found surprising similarities across countries and cultures:

From the steamy playgrounds of Los Angeles to the stately boulevards of Singapore, kids show amazing similarities in taste, language, and attitude. . . . From the gear and posters on display, it's hard to tell whether the rooms are in Los Angeles, Mexico City, or Tokyo. Basketballs sit alongside soccer balls. Closets overflow with staples from an international, unisex uniform: baggy Levi's or Diesel jeans, NBA jackets, and rugged shoes from Timberland or Doc Martens.

Bugle Boy found that traditional focus groups fail miserably in getting the scoop on teens and GenXers. These often-cynical young people are skeptical of sales pitches and just won't speak up in a conference room with two-way mirrors. Working with Chilton Research, Bugle Boy found an innovative solution. It plucked four young men out of obscurity, handed each of them an 8-mm video camera, and told them to document their lives. The young amateurs were given only broad categories to work with: school, home, closet, and shopping. Bugle Boy then used the videos to prompt discussions of product and lifestyle issues in "free-form" focus groups held in unconventional locations, such as restaurants. Says one Bugle Boy ad manager, "I think this really helped us to get a handle on what these kids do. It let us see what their lives are all about, their awareness of the Bugle Boy brand, and how they perceive the brand."

Similarly, researchers at Sega of America's ad agency have learned a lot about video game buying behavior by hanging around with 150 kids in their bedrooms and by shopping with them in malls. Above all else, they learned, kids like to do everything fast. As a result, in Sega's most recent 15-second commercials, some images fly by so quickly that adults cannot recall seeing them, even after repeated showings. The kids, weaned on MTV, recollect them keenly.

Some marketers dismiss such motivation research as mumbo jumbo. And these approaches do present some problems: They use small samples, and researcher interpretations of results are often highly subjective, sometimes leading to rather exotic explanations of otherwise ordinary buying behavior. However, others believe strongly that these approaches can provide interesting nuggets of insight into the relationships between consumers and the brands that they buy. To marketers who use them, motivation research techniques provide a flexible and varied means of gaining insights into deeply held and often mysterious motivations behind consumer buying behavior.

Sources: Excerpts from Annetta Miller and Dody Tsiantar, "Psyching Out Consumers," Newsweek, February 27, 1989, pp. 46–47; and Shawn Tully, "Teens: The Most Global Market of All," Fortune, May 6, 1994, pp. 90–97. Also see Rebecca Piirto, "Words that Sell," American Demographics, January 1992, p. 6; "They Understand Your Kids," Fortune, Special Issue, Autumn/Winter 1993, pp. 29–30; and Cyndee Miller, "Sometimes a Researcher Has No Alternative But to Hang Out in a Bar," Marketing News, January 3, 1994, pp. 16, 26.

Maslow's hierarchy of needs is shown in Figure 5-3. In order of importance, they are *physiological* needs, *safety* needs, *social* needs, *esteem* needs, and *self-actualization* needs. A person tries to satisfy the most important need first. When that need is satisfied, it will stop being a motivator and the person will then try to satisfy the next most important need. For example, starving people (physiological

## FIGURE 5-3

*Maslow's hierarchy of needs (Source: Adapted from* Motivation and Personality, *2nd ed., by Abraham H. Maslow. Copyright © 1970 by Abraham H. Maslow. Reprinted by permission of Harper & Row, Publishers, Inc.)*

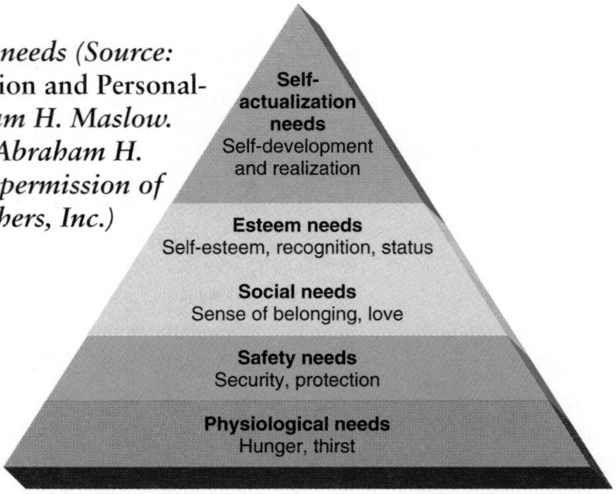

Self-actualization needs
Self-development and realization

Esteem needs
Self-esteem, recognition, status

Social needs
Sense of belonging, love

Safety needs
Security, protection

Physiological needs
Hunger, thirst

need) will not take an interest in the latest happenings in the art world (self-actualization needs), nor in how they are seen or esteemed by others (social or esteem needs), nor even in whether they are breathing clean air (safety needs). But as each important need is satisfied, the next most important need will come into play.

Maslow's hierachy is not universal for all cultures. As the heroes of Hollywood movies demonstate, Anglo-Saxon culture values self-actualization and individuality above all else. In Japan and German-speaking countries, however, people are more highly motivated by a need for personal security and conformity, while in France, Spain, Portugal, and other Latin and Asian countries, people are more motivated by the need for security and belonging.[21]

What light does Maslow's theory throw on Jennifer Flores's interest in buying a camera? We can guess that Jennifer has satisfied her physiological, safety, and social needs; they do not motivate her interest in cameras. Her camera interest might come from a strong need for more esteem from others. Or it might come from a need for self-actualization; she might want to be a creative person and express herself through photography.

### Perception

A motivated person is ready to act. A person's actions are influenced by his or her perception of the situation. Two people with the same motivation and in the same situation may act quite differently because they perceive the situation differently. Jennifer Flores might consider a fast-talking camera salesperson loud and phony, but another camera buyer might consider the same salesperson intelligent and helpful.

Why do people perceive the same situation differently? All of us learn by the flow of information through our five senses: sight, hearing, smell, touch, and taste. However, each of us receives, organizes, and interprets this sensory information in an individual way. **Perception** is the process by which people select, organize, and interpret information to form a meaningful picture of the world.

People can form different perceptions of the same stimulus because of three perceptual processes: selective attention, selective distortion, and selective retention. People are exposed to a great amount of stimuli every day. For example, the average person may be exposed to more than 1,500 ads in a single day. It is impossible for a person to pay attention to all these stimuli. *Selective attention*—the ten-

**Perception**

The process by which people select, organize, and interpret information to form a meaningful picture of the world.

dency for people to screen out most of the information to which they are exposed—forces marketers to work especially hard to attract the consumer's attention. Their message will be lost on most people who are not in the market for the product. Moreover, even people who are in the market may not notice the message unless it stands out from the surrounding sea of other ads.

Even noted stimuli do not always come across in the intended way. Each person fits incoming information into an existing mind-set. *Selective distortion* describes the tendency of people to interpret information in a way that will support what they already believe. Jennifer Flores may hear the salesperson mention some good and bad points about a competing camera brand. Because she already has a strong leaning toward Nikon, she is likely to distort those points in order to conclude that Nikon is the better camera. Selective distortion means that marketers must try to understand the mind-sets of consumers and how these will affect interpretations of advertising and sales information.

People also will forget much that they learn. They tend to retain information that supports their attitudes and beliefs. Because of *selective retention,* Jennifer is likely to remember good points made about the Nikon and to forget good points made about competing cameras.

Because of selective exposure, distortion, and retention, marketers face a difficult task in getting their messages through to customers. This fact explains why marketers use so much drama and repetition in sending messages to their market. Interestingly, although most marketers worry about whether their offers will be perceived at all, some consumers are worried that they will be affected by marketing messages without even knowing it (see Marketing at Work 5-2).

## Learning

**Learning**
Changes in an individual's behavior arising from experience.

When people act, they learn. **Learning** describes changes in an individual's behavior arising from experience. Learning theorists say that most human behavior is learned. Learning occurs through the interplay of *drives, stimuli, cues, responses,* and *reinforcement.*

We saw that Jennifer Flores has a drive for self-actualization. A *drive* is a strong internal stimulus that calls for action. Her drive becomes a motive when it is directed toward a particular *stimulus object*—in this case, a camera. Jennifer's response to the idea of buying a camera is conditioned by the surrounding cues. *Cues* are minor stimuli that determine when, where, and how the person responds. Seeing cameras in a shop window, hearing of a special sale price, and receiving her husband's support are all cues that can influence Jennifer's *response* to her interest in buying a camera.

Suppose Jennifer buys the Nikon. If the experience is rewarding, she will probably use the camera more and more. Her response to cameras will be *reinforced.* Then the next time that she shops for a camera, binoculars, or some similar product, the probability is greater that she will buy a Nikon product.

The practical significance of learning theory for marketers is that they can build up demand for a product by associating it with strong drives, using motivating cues, and providing positive reinforcement.

## Beliefs and Attitudes

**Belief**
A descriptive thought that a person holds about something.

Through doing and learning, people acquire beliefs and attitudes. These, in turn, influence their buying behavior. A **belief** is a descriptive thought that a person has about something. Jennifer Flores may believe that a Nikon camera takes great pictures, stands up well under hard use, and costs $550. These beliefs may be based

## MARKETING AT WORK 5-2

# SUBLIMINAL PERCEPTION—CAN CONSUMERS BE AFFECTED WITHOUT KNOWING IT?

In 1957, a researcher announced that he had flashed the phrases "Eat popcorn" and "Drink Coca-Cola" on a screen in a New Jersey movie theater every five seconds for 1/300th of a second. He reported that although the audience did not consciously recognize these messages, viewers absorbed them subconsciously and bought 58 percent more popcorn and 18 percent more Coke. Suddenly, advertising agencies and consumer-protection groups became intensely interested in *subliminal perception*. People voiced fears of being brainwashed, and California and Canada declared the practice illegal. Although the researcher later admitted to making up the data, and scientists failed to

replicate the original results in other studies, the issue did not die. In 1974, Wilson Bryan Key claimed in his book *Subliminal Seduction* that consumers were still being manipulated by advertisers in print ads and television commercials.

Subliminal perception has since been studied by many psychologists and consumer researchers. None of these experts has been able to show that subliminal messages have any effect on consumer behavior. It appears that subliminal advertising simply doesn't have the power attributed to it by its critics. Most advertisers scoff at the notion of an industry conspiracy to manipulate consumers through "invisible" messages. As

one advertising agency executive put it, "We have enough trouble persuading consumers using a series of up-front thirty-second ads—how could we do it in 1/300th of a second?"

Although advertisers may avoid outright subliminal advertising, some critics claim that television advertising employs techniques approaching the subliminal. With more and more viewers reaching for their remote controls to avoid ads by switching channels or fast-forwarding through VCR tapes, advertisers are using new tricks to grab viewer attention and to affect consumers in ways that they may not be aware of. Many ad agencies employ psychologists and neurophysiologists to help de-

---

on real knowledge, opinion, or faith, and may or may not carry an emotional charge. For example, Jennifer Flores's belief that a Nikon camera is heavy may or may not matter in making her decision.

Marketers are interested in the beliefs that people formulate about specific products and services, because these beliefs make up product and brand images that affect buying behavior. If some of the beliefs are wrong and prevent purchase, the marketer needs to launch a campaign to correct them.

People have attitudes regarding religion, politics, clothes, music, food, and almost everything else. An **attitude** describes a person's relatively consistent evaluations, feelings, and tendencies regarding an object or idea. Attitudes put people into a frame of mind of liking or disliking things, of moving toward or away from them. Thus, Jennifer Flores may hold such attitudes as "Buy the best," "The Japanese make the best products in the world," and "Creativity and self-expression are among the most important things in life." If so, buying the Nikon camera would fit well with Jennifer's existing attitudes.

Attitudes are difficult to change. A person's attitudes fit a pattern, and changing one attitude may require difficult adjustments in many others. Thus, a company should usually try to fit its products to existing attitudes rather than attempt

**Attitude**
A person's consistently favorable or unfavorable evaluations, feelings, and tendencies toward an object or idea.

velop subtle psychological advertising strategies.

For example, some advertisers purposely try to confuse viewers, throw them off balance, or even make them uncomfortable:

*[They use] film footage that wouldn't pass muster with a junior-high film club. You have to stare at the screen just to figure out what's going on—and that, of course, is the idea. Take the ads for Wang computers. In these hazy, washed-out spots, people walk partially in and out of the camera frame talking in computer jargon. But the confusion grabs attention. . . . Even people who don't understand a word are riveted to the screen.*

Other advertisers use the rapid-fire technique. Images flash by so quickly that you can barely register them. Pontiac used such "machine-gun editing" in recent ads—the longest shot flashed by in one and one-half seconds, the shortest in one-quarter of a second. The ads scored high in viewer recall.

Some advertisers go after our ears as well as our eyes, taking advantage of the powerful effects that some sounds have on human brain waves:

*Advertisers are using sounds to take advantage of the automatic systems built into the brain that force you to stop what you're doing and refocus on the screen. . . . You can't ignore these sounds. That's why commercials are starting off with noises ranging from a baby crying (Advil) to a car horn (Hertz) to a factory whistle (Almond Joy). In seeking the right sound . . . advertisers can be downright merciless. . . . Ads for Nuprin pain reliever kick off by assaulting viewers with the whine of a dentist's drill . . . to help the viewer recall the type of pain we've all experienced. Hey, thanks.*

A few experts are concerned that new high-tech advertising might even hypnotize consumers, whether knowingly or not. They suggest that several techniques—rapid scene changes, pulsating music and sounds, repetitive phrases, and flashing logos—might actually start to put some viewers under a spell.

Some critics think that such subtle, hard-to-resist psychological techniques are unfair to consumers—that advertisers can use these techniques to bypass consumers' defenses and affect them without their being aware of it. The advertisers who use these techniques, however, view them as innovative, creative approaches to advertising.

*Sources:* Excerpts from David H. Freedman, "Why You Watch Commercials—Whether You Mean to or Not," *TV Guide*, February 20, 1988, pp. 4–7. Also see Wilson Bryan Key, *The Age of Manipulation: The Con in Confidence, The Sin in Sincere* (New York: Holt, 1989); Timothy E. Moore, "Subliminal Advertising: What You See Is What You Get," *Journal of Marketing*, Spring 1982, pp. 38–47; Michael J. McCarthy, "Mind Probe," *The Wall Street Journal*, March 22, 1991, p. B3; and Martha Rogers and Kirk H. Smith, "Public Perceptions of Subliminal Advertising," *Journal of Advertising Research*, March/April 1993, pp. 10–17.

to change attitudes. Of course, there are exceptions in which the great cost of trying to change attitudes may pay off. For example, in the late 1950s, Honda entered the U.S. motorcycle market, facing a major decision. It could either sell its motorcycles to the small but already established motorcycle market or try to increase the size of this market by attracting new types of consumers. Increasing the size of the market would be more difficult and expensive because many people had negative attitudes toward motorcycles. They associated motorcycles with black leather jackets, switchblades, and outlaws. Despite these adverse attitudes, Honda took the second course of action. It launched a major campaign to position motorcycles as good clean fun. Its theme "You meet the nicest people on a Honda" worked well, and many people adopted a new attitude toward motorcycles. Going into the 1990s, however, Honda faced a similar problem. With the aging of the baby boomers, the market had once more shifted toward only hard-core motorcycling enthusiasts. So Honda again set out to change consumer attitudes. It unveiled a new "Come Ride With Us" campaign to reestablish the wholesomeness of motorcycling and to position it as fun and exciting for everyone.[22]

We can now appreciate the many forces acting on consumer behavior. The consumer's choice results from the complex interplay of cultural, social, personal,

*Attitudes are hard to change, but it can be done. Honda's classic "You meet the nicest people on a Honda" campaign changed people's attitudes about who rides motorcycles.*

and psychological factors. Although many of these factors cannot be influenced by the marketer, they can be useful in identifying interested buyers and in shaping products and appeals to serve consumer needs better.

# ▶ THE BUYER DECISION PROCESS

Now that we have looked at the influences that affect buyers, we are ready to look at how consumers make buying decisions. Figure 5-4 shows that the buyer decision process consists of five stages: *need recognition, information search, evaluation of alternatives, purchase decision,* and *postpurchase behavior.* Clearly, the buying process starts long before an actual purchase and continues long after. Marketers need to focus on the entire buying process rather than on just the purchase decision.

The figure implies that consumers pass through all five stages with every purchase. But in more routine purchases, consumers often skip or reverse some of these stages. A woman buying her regular brand of toothpaste would recognize the need and go right to the purchase decision, skipping information search and evaluation.

**FIGURE 5-4**
*Buyer decision process*

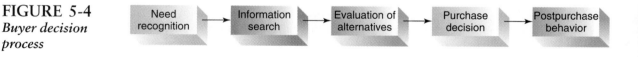

However, we use the model in Figure 5-4 because it shows all of the considerations that arise when a consumer faces a new and complex purchase situation.

To illustrate this model, we will again follow Jennifer Flores and try to understand how she became interested in buying an expensive camera, and the stages she went through to make the final choice.

## NEED RECOGNITION

**Need recognition**
The first stage of the buyer decision process in which the consumer recognizes a problem or need.

The buying process starts with **need recognition**—with the buyer recognizing a problem or need. The buyer senses a difference between his or her *actual* state and some *desired* state. The need can be triggered by *internal stimuli* when one of the person's normal needs—hunger, thirst, sex—rises to a level high enough to become a drive. A need can also be triggered by *external stimuli*. Jennifer Flores passes a bakery, and the sight of freshly baked bread stimulates her hunger; she admires a neighbor's new car; or she watches a television commercial for a Caribbean vacation. At this stage, the marketer should research consumers to find out what kinds of needs or problems arise, what caused them, and how they led the consumer to this particular product.

Jennifer Flores might answer that she felt the need for a new hobby when her busy season at work slowed down, and she thought of buying a camera after

*Need recognition can be triggered by advertising. This Pacific Bell ad alerts parents to the need for The Message Center: "Let's say your kid's always getting messages on your answering machine . . . Let's say he's real popular."*

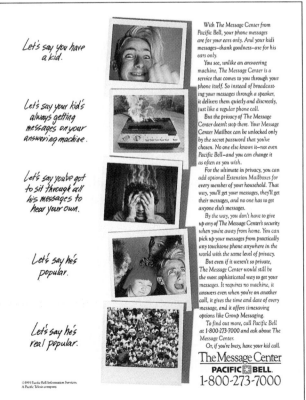

talking to a friend about photography. By gathering such information, the marketer can identify the factors that most often trigger interest in the product and can develop marketing programs that involve these factors.

# INFORMATION SEARCH

An aroused consumer may or may not search for more information. If the consumer's drive is strong and a satisfying product is near at hand, the consumer is likely to buy it then. If not, the consumer may store the need in memory or undertake an **information search** related to the need.

At one level, the consumer may simply enter *heightened attention.* Here, Jennifer Flores becomes more receptive to information about cameras. She pays attention to camera ads, cameras used by friends, and conversations about cameras. Or Jennifer may go into *active information search,* in which she looks for reading material on cameras, phones friends about their cameras, and gathers information in other ways. The amount of searching that she does will depend on the strength of her drive, the amount of information she starts with, the ease of obtaining more information, the value that she places on additional information, and the satisfaction that she gets from searching.

The consumer can obtain information from any of several sources. These include:

**Information search**
The stage of the buyer decision process in which the consumer is aroused to search for more information; the consumer may simply have heightened attention to information or may go into active information search.

- ◆ *Personal sources.* Family, friends, neighbors, acquaintances
- ◆ *Commercial sources.* Advertising, salespeople, dealers, packaging, displays
- ◆ *Public sources.* Mass media, consumer-rating organizations
- ◆ *Experiential sources.* Handling, examining, using the product

The relative influence of these information sources varies with the product and the buyer. Generally, the consumer receives the most information about a product from commercial sources—those controlled by the marketer. The most effective sources, however, tend to be personal. Personal sources appear to be even more important in influencing the purchase of services.[23] Commercial sources normally *inform* the buyer, but personal sources *legitimize* or *evaluate* products for the buyer. For example, doctors normally learn of new drugs from commercial sources, but turn to other doctors for evaluative information.

As more information is obtained, the consumer's awareness and knowledge of the available brands and features increases. In her information search, Jennifer Flores learned about the many camera brands available. The information also helped her drop certain brands from consideration. A company must design its marketing mix to make prospects aware of and knowledgeable about its brand. It should carefully identify consumers' sources of information and the importance of each source. Consumers should be asked how they first heard about the brand, what information they received, and what importance they placed on different information sources.

**Alternative evaluation**
The stage of the buyer decision process in which the consumer uses information to evaluate alternative brands in the choice set.

# EVALUATION OF ALTERNATIVES

We have seen how the consumer uses information to arrive at a set of final brand choices. How does the consumer choose among the alternative brands? The marketer needs to know about **alternative evaluation**—that is, how the consumer processes information to arrive at brand choices. Unfortunately, consumers do not use a simple, single evaluation process in all buying situations. Instead, several evaluation processes are at work.

Certain basic concepts help explain consumer evaluation processes. First, we assume that each consumer sees a product as a bundle of *product attributes*. For cameras, product attributes might include picture quality, ease of use, camera size, price, and other features. Consumers will vary as to which of these attributes they consider relevant, and they will pay the most attention to those attributes connected with their needs.

Second, the consumer will attach different *degrees of importance* to different attributes according to his or her unique needs and wants. Third, the consumer is likely to develop a set of *brand beliefs* about where each brand stands on each attribute. The set of beliefs that are held about a particular brand is known as the **brand image.** Based on his or her experience and the effects of selective perception, distortion, and retention, the consumer's beliefs may differ from true attributes.

**Brand image**
The set of beliefs that consumers hold about a particular brand.

Fourth, the consumer's expected *total product satisfaction* will vary with levels of different attributes. For example, Jennifer Flores may expect her level of satisfaction with a camera to increase with better picture quality; to peak with a medium-weight camera as opposed to a very light or very heavy one; and to be higher for a 35-mm camera than for a 110-mm camera. If we combine the attribute levels that give her the highest perceived satisfaction, they make up Jennifer's ideal camera. The camera would also be her preferred camera if it were available and affordable.

Fifth, the consumer arrives at attitudes toward the different brands through some type of *evaluation procedure*. Consumers have been found to use one or more of several evaluation procedures, depending on the consumer and the buying decision.

We will illustrate these concepts with Jennifer Flores's camera-buying situation. Suppose Jennifer has narrowed her choices to four cameras. And suppose that she is primarily interested in four attributes—picture quality, ease of use, camera size, and price. Jennifer has formed beliefs about how each brand rates on each attribute. The marketer wishes to predict which camera Jennifer will buy.

Clearly, if one camera rated best on all the attributes, we could predict that Jennifer would choose it. But the brands vary in appeal. Some buyers will base their buying decision on only one attribute, and their choices are easy to predict. If Jennifer wants picture quality above everything, she will buy the camera that she thinks has the best picture quality. But most buyers consider several attributes, each with different importance. If we knew the importance weights that Jennifer assigns to each of the four attributes, we could predict her camera choice more reliably.

How consumers go about evaluating purchase alternatives depends on the individual consumer and the specific buying situation. In some cases, consumers use careful calculations and logical thinking. At other times, the same consumers do little or no evaluating; instead, they buy on impulse and rely on intuition. Sometimes, consumers make buying decisions on their own; sometimes, they turn to friends, consumer guides, or salespeople for buying advice.

Marketers should study buyers to find out how they actually evaluate brand alternatives. If they know what evaluative processes go on, marketers can take steps to influence the buyer's decision. Suppose that Jennifer is inclined to buy a Nikon camera because she rates it high on picture quality and ease of use. What strategies might another camera maker, say Minolta, use to influence people like Jennifer?

There are several. Minolta could modify its camera so that it delivers better pictures or other features that consumers like Jennifer want. It could try to change buyers' beliefs about how its camera rates on key attributes, especially if consumers currently underestimate the camera's qualities. It could try to change buyers' beliefs about Nikon and other competitors. Finally, it could try to change the list of attributes that buyers consider, or the importance attached to these attributes. For example, it might advertise that all good cameras have about equal picture quality, and that its lighter-weight, lower-priced camera is a better buy for people like Jennifer.

## PURCHASE DECISION

**Purchase decision**
The stage of the buyer decision process in which the consumer actually buys the product.

In the evaluation stage, the consumer ranks brands and forms purchase intentions. Generally, the consumer's **purchase decision** will be to buy the most preferred brand, but two factors can come between the purchase *intention* and the purchase *decision*. The first factor is the *attitudes of others*. If Jennifer Flores's husband feels strongly that Jennifer should buy the lowest-priced camera, then the chances of Jennifer buying a more expensive camera will be reduced.

The second factor is *unexpected situational factors.* The consumer may form a purchase intention based on factors such as expected income, expected price, and expected product benefits. However, unexpected events may change the purchase intention. Jennifer Flores may lose her job, some other purchase may become more urgent, or a friend may report being disappointed in her preferred camera. Or a close competitor may drop its price. Thus, preferences and even purchase intentions do not always result in actual purchase choice.

## POSTPURCHASE BEHAVIOR

**Postpurchase behavior**
The stage of the buyer decision process in which consumers take further action after purchase, based on their satisfaction or dissatisfaction.

The marketer's job does not end when the product is bought. After purchasing the product, the consumer will be satisfied or dissatisfied and will engage in **postpurchase behavior** of interest to the marketer. What determines whether the buyer is satisfied or dissatisfied with a purchase? The answer lies in the relationship between the *consumer's expectations* and the product's *perceived performance*. If the product falls short of expectations, the consumer is disappointed; if it meets expectations, the consumer is satisfied; if it exceeds expectations, the consumer is delighted.

Consumers base their expectations on information that they receive from sellers, friends, and other sources. If the seller exaggerates the product's performance, consumer expectations will not be met, and dissatisfaction will result. The larger the gap between expectations and performance, the greater the consumer's dissatisfaction. This suggests that sellers should make product claims that faithfully represent the product's performance so that buyers are satisfied.

Some sellers might even understate performance levels to boost consumer satisfaction with the product. For example, Boeing sells aircraft worth tens of millions of dollars each, and consumer satisfaction is important for repeat purchases and the company's reputation. Boeing's salespeople tend to be conservative when they estimate their product's potential benefits. They almost always underestimate fuel efficiency—they promise a 5 percent savings that turns out to be 8 percent. Customers are delighted with better-than-expected performance; they buy again and tell other potential customers that Boeing lives up to its promises.

Cognitive dissonance
Buyer discomfort caused by postpurchase conflict.

Almost all major purchases result in **cognitive dissonance,** or discomfort caused by postpurchase conflict. After the purchase, consumers are satisfied with the benefits of the chosen brand and are glad to avoid the drawbacks of the brands not bought. However, every purchase involves compromise. Consumers feel uneasy about acquiring the drawbacks of the chosen brand and losing the benefits of the brands not purchased. Thus, consumers feel at least some postpurchase dissonance for every purchase.[24]

Why is it so important to satisfy the customer? Such satisfaction is important because a company's sales come from two basic groups: *new customers* and *retained customers*. It usually costs more to attract new customers than to retain current ones, and the best way to retain current customers is to keep them satisfied. Satisfied customers buy a product again, talk favorably to others about the product, pay less attention to competing brands and advertising, and buy other products from the company. Many marketers go beyond merely *meeting* the expectations of customers—they aim to *delight* the customer. A delighted customer is even more likely to purchase again and to talk favorably about the product and company.

A dissatisfied consumer responds differently. Whereas, on average, a satisfied customer tells three people about a good product experience, a dissatisfied customer gripes to 11 people. In fact, one study showed that 13 percent of the people who had a problem with an organization complained about the company to more than 20 people.[25] Clearly, bad word of mouth travels farther and faster than good word of mouth and can quickly damage consumer attitudes about a company and its products.

Therefore, a company would be wise to measure customer satisfaction regularly. It cannot simply rely on dissatisfied customers to volunteer their complaints when they are dissatisfied. Some 96 percent of unhappy customers never tell the company about their problem. Companies should set up systems that *encourage* customers to complain (see Marketing at Work 5-3). In this way, the company can learn how well it is doing and how it can improve. The 3M Company claims that over two-thirds of its new-product ideas come from listening to customer complaints. But listening is not enough; the company also must respond constructively to the complaints that it receives.

Beyond seeking out and responding to complaints, marketers can take additional steps to reduce consumer postpurchase dissatisfaction and to help customers feel good about their purchases. For example, Toyota writes or phones new car owners with congratulations on having selected a fine car. It places ads showing satisfied owners talking about their new cars ("I love what you do for me, Toyota!"). Toyota also obtains customer suggestions for improvements and lists the locations of available services.

# ▶ THE BUYER DECISION PROCESS FOR NEW PRODUCTS

We have looked at the stages buyers go through in trying to satisfy a need. Buyers may pass quickly or slowly through these stages, and some of the stages may even be reversed. Much depends on the nature of the buyer, the product, and the buying situation.

# MARKETING AT WORK 5-3

## POSTPURCHASE SATISFACTION: TURNING COMPANY CRITICS INTO LOYAL CUSTOMERS

What should companies do with dissatisfied customers? Everything they can! Unhappy customers not only stop buying, but also can quickly damage the company's image. Studies show that customers tell four times as many other people about bad experiences as they do about good ones. In contrast, dealing effectively with gripes can actually boost customer loyalty as well as the company's image. According to one study, 95 percent of consumers who register complaints will again do business with the company if their complaint is resolved quickly. Moreover, customers whose complaints have been satisfactorily resolved tell an average of five other people about the good treatment that they received. Thus, enlightened companies don't try to hide from dissatisfied customers. To the contrary, they go out of their way to *encourage* customers to complain, then bend over backwards to make disgruntled buyers happy again.

The first opportunity to handle gripes often comes at the point of purchase. Many retailers and other service firms teach their customer-contact people how to resolve problems and diffuse customer anger. They arm customer service representatives with liberal return and refund policies and other damage-control tools. Some companies go to extremes to see things the customer's way and to reward complaining, seemingly without regard for profit impact. For example, Hechinger, the large hardware and garden products retailer, accepts returns of items even when customers have obviously abused them. In other cases, it sends a dozen roses to purchasers who are particularly upset. Specialty retailer Neiman Marcus is equally gracious to complainers. "We're not just looking for today's sale. We want a long-term relationship with our customers," says Gwen Baum, the chain's director of customer satisfaction. "If that means taking back a piece of Baccarat crystal that isn't from one of our stores, we'll do it." This generosity appears to help profits more than harm them; both Hechinger and Neiman Marcus enjoy earnings well above industry averages. Such actions create tremendous buyer loyalty and goodwill, and, for most retailers, customers who return items that they bought elsewhere or have already used account for less than 5 percent of all returns.

Many companies have also set up toll-free 800-number systems to coax out and deal with consumer problems. Today, more

*Making buyers happy: GE's Answer Center handles customers' concerns 365 days a year, 24 hours a day.*

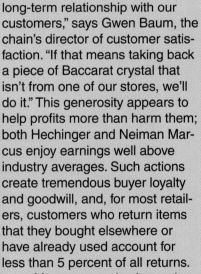

---

**New product**
A good, service, or idea that is perceived by some potential customers as new.

We now look at how buyers approach the purchase of new products. A **new product** is a good, service, or idea that is perceived by some potential customers as new. It may have been around for a while, but our interest is in how consumers learn about products for the first time and make decisions on whether

than two-thirds all U.S. manufacturers offer 800 numbers to handle complaints, inquiries, and orders. For example, Coca-Cola set up its 1-800-GET-COKE lines in late 1983 after studies showed that only one unhappy person in 50 bothers to complain. "The other 49 simply switch brands," explains the company's director of consumer affairs, "so it just makes good sense to seek them out."

Every weekday, Pillsbury handles the complaints, compliments, and questions of more than 2,000 people who call its 800 number. On the day before Thanksgiving, the busiest day, Pillsbury's customer service reps, mostly women with college degrees and training in nutrition and home economics, assist 3,000 callers with their holiday dinners. For callers who speak little or no English, Pillsbury can dial an AT&T number that hooks up interpreters for any of 140 languages in a three-way call with the customer and company.

Now in its tenth year, the Gerber Helpline (1-800-GERBER) has received more than 4 million calls. Helpline staffers, most of them mothers or grandmothers themselves, provide baby care advice to more than 2,400 callers a day, 365 days a year. In 1994, the helpline received 647,875 calls. The helpline is staffed by English, French, and Spanish-speaking operators, and interpreters are available for most other languages. Callers include new parents, day care providers, and even health professionals. One in five calls to the helpline come from a man. Callers ask a wide variety of questions, from when to feed baby specific foods to how to babyproof a home. "It used to be that mom or grandmom was right around the corner to answer your baby questions," notes the manager of Gerber helpline. "But more and more, that's not the case. For new or expectant parents, it's nice to know that they can pick up the phone any time of day and talk to someone that understands and can help."

General Electric's Answer Center may be the most extensive 800-number system in the nation. It handles more than three million calls a year, only 5 percent of them complaints. At the heart of the system is a giant database that provides the center's service reps with instant access to more than one million answers concerning 8,500 models in 120 product lines. The center receives some unusual calls, such as when a submarine off the Connecticut coast requested help fixing a motor, or when technicians on a James Bond film couldn't get their underwater lights working. Still, according to GE, its people resolve 90 percent of complaints or inquiries on the first call, and complainers often become even more loyal customers. Although the company spends an average of $3.50 per call, it reaps two to three times that much in new sales and warranty savings.

The best way to keep customers happy is to provide good products and services in the first place. Beyond that, however, a company must develop a good system for ferreting out and handling those consumer problems that inevitably occur. Such a system can be much more than a necessary evil—customer happiness usually shows up on the company's bottom line. One recent study found that dollars invested in complaint-handling and inquiry systems yield an average return of between 100 percent and 200 percent. Maryanne Rasmussen, vice president of worldwide quality at American Express, offers this formula: "Better complaint handling equals higher customer satisfaction equals higher brand loyalty equals higher performance."

*Sources:* Quotes from Patricia Sellers, "How to Handle Consumer Gripes," *Fortune,* October 24, 1988, pp. 88–100; and "On Mother's Day, Advice Goes a Long Way," *PR Newswire,* Ziff Communications, May 2, 1995. Also see Frank Rose, "Now Quality Means Service Too," *Fortune,* April 22, 1991, pp. 97–108; Roland T. Rust, Bala Subramanian, and Mark Wells, "Making Complaints a Management Tool," *Marketing Management,* Fall 1992, pp. 41–45; Carl Quintanilla and Richard Gibson, " 'Do Call Us': More Companies Install 1-800 Phone Lines," *The Wall Street Journal,* April 20, 1994, pp. B1, B4; and Weld F. Royal, "Cashing in on Complaints," *Sales & Marketing Management,* May, 1995, pp. 86–92.

**Adoption process**
The mental process through which an individual passes from first hearing about an innovation to final adoption.

to adopt them. We define the **adoption process** as "the mental process through which an individual passes from first learning about an innovation to final adoption,"[26] and *adoption* as an individual's decision to become a regular user of the product.

## STAGES IN THE ADOPTION PROCESS

Consumers go through five stages in the process of adopting a new product:

◆ *Awareness.* The consumer becomes aware of the new product, but lacks information about it.

◆ *Interest.* The consumer seeks information about the new product.

◆ Evaluation. The consumer considers whether trying the new product makes sense.

◆ *Trial.* The consumer tries the new product on a small scale to improve his or her estimate of its value.

◆ *Adoption.* The consumer decides to make full, regular use of the new product.

This model suggests that the new-product marketer should think about how to help consumers move through these stages. A manufacturer of large-screen televisions may discover that many consumers in the interest stage do not move to the trial stage because of uncertainty and the large investment. If these same consumers were willing to use a large-screen television on a trial basis for a small fee, the manufacturer should consider offering a trial-use plan with an option to buy.

## INDIVIDUAL DIFFERENCES IN INNOVATIVENESS

People differ greatly in their readiness to try new products. In each product area, there are "consumption pioneers" and early adopters. Other individuals adopt new products much later. People can be classified into the adopter categories shown in Figure 5-5. After a slow start, an increasing number of people adopt the new product. The number of adopters reaches a peak and then drops off as fewer non-adopters remain. Innovators are defined as the first 2.5 percent of the buyers to adopt a new idea (those beyond two standard deviations from mean adoption time); the early adopters are the next 13.5 percent (between one and two standard deviations); and so forth.

The five adopter groups have differing values. *Innovators* are venturesome—they try new ideas at some risk. *Early adopters* are guided by respect—they are opinion leaders in their communities and adopt new ideas early but carefully. The *early majority* are deliberate—although they are rarely leaders, they adopt new

**FIGURE 5-5**

*Adopter categorization on the basis of relative time of adoption of innovations (Source: Redrawn from Everett M. Rogers,* Diffusion of Innovations, *3rd ed. (New York: 1983), p. 247. Adapted with permission of Macmillan Publishing Company, Inc. Copyright © 1962, 1971, 1983 by The Free Press.*

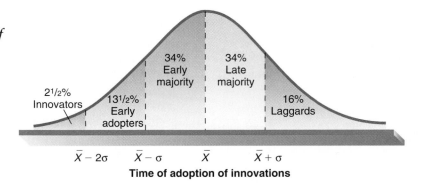

ideas before the average person does. The *late majority* are skeptical—they adopt an innovation only after a majority of people have tried it. Finally, *laggards* are tradition bound—they are suspicious of changes and adopt the innovation only when it has become something of a tradition itself.

This adopter classification suggests that an innovating firm should research the characteristics of innovators and early adopters and should direct marketing efforts toward them. In general, innovators tend to be relatively younger, better educated, and higher in income than later adopters and nonadopters. They are more receptive to unfamiliar things, rely more on their own values and judgment, and are more willing to take risks. They are less brand loyal and more likely to take advantage of special promotions such as discounts, coupons, and samples.

## INFLUENCE OF PRODUCT CHARACTERISTICS ON RATE OF ADOPTION

The characteristics of the new product affect its rate of adoption. Some products catch on almost overnight (Frisbees), whereas others take a long time to gain acceptance (personal computers). Five characteristics are especially important in influencing an innovation's rate of adoption. For example, consider the characteristics of large-screen televisions in relation to the rate of adoption:

◆ *Relative advantage.* The degree to which the innovation appears superior to existing products. The greater the perceived relative advantage of using a large-screen TV—say, in picture quality and ease of viewing—the sooner such TVs will be adopted.

◆ *Compatibility.* The degree to which the innovation fits the values and experiences of potential consumers. Large-screen TVs, for example, are highly compatible with the lifestyles found in upper-middle-class homes.

◆ *Complexity.* The degree to which the innovation is difficult to understand or use. Large-screen TVs are not very complex and will therefore take less time to penetrate the U.S. home market than more complex innovations.

◆ *Divisibility.* The degree to which the innovation may be tried on a limited basis. Large-screen TVs are expensive. To the extent that people can lease them with an option to buy, their rate of adoption will increase.

◆ *Communicability.* The degree to which the results of using the innovation can be observed or described. Because large-screen TVs lend themselves to demonstration and description, their use will spread faster among consumers.

Other characteristics influence the rate of adoption, such as initial and ongoing costs, risk and uncertainty, and social approval. The new-product marketer has to research all these factors when developing the new product and its marketing program.

## ▶ CONSUMER BEHAVIOR ACROSS INTERNATIONAL BORDERS

Understanding consumer behavior is difficult enough for companies marketing within the borders of a single country. For companies operating in many countries, however, understanding and serving the needs of consumers can be daunting. Although consumers in different countries may have some things in common, their values, attitudes, and behaviors often vary greatly. International marketers must understand such differences and adjust their products and marketing programs accordingly (see Marketing at Work 5-4).

Sometimes the differences are obvious. For example, in the United States, where most people eat cereal regularly for breakfast, Kellogg focuses its marketing on persuading consumers to select a Kellogg brand rather than a competitor's brand. In France, however, where most people prefer croissants and coffee or no breakfast at all, Kellogg advertising simply attempts to convince people that they should eat cereal for breakfast. Its packaging includes step-by-step instructions on how to prepare cereal. In India, where many consumers eat

## MARKETING AT WORK 5-4

# CONSUMER-BEHAVIOR DIFFERENCES ACROSS BORDERS: GLOBAL STANDARDIZATION OR ADAPTATION?

The marketing concept holds that marketing programs will be more effective if tailored to the unique needs of each targeted customer group. If this concept applies within a country, it should apply even more in international markets where demographic, economic, political, and cultural conditions vary widely. Consumers in different countries have varied needs and wants, spending power, product preferences, and shopping patterns. Because most marketers believe that these differences are hard to change, they adapt their products, prices, distribution channels, and promotion approaches to fit consumer desires in each country.

However, some global marketers are bothered by what they see as too much adaptation. For example, Gillette sells over 800 products in more than 200 countries. It now finds itself in a situation where it uses different brand names and formulations for the same products in different countries. For example, Gillette's Silkience shampoo is called Soyance in France, Sientel in Italy,

*Coca-Cola sells highly standardized products worldwide, but even Coke adapts its product and packaging somewhat to local tastes and conditions.*

and Silience in Germany; it uses the same formula in some cases, but varies it in others. It also varies the product's advertising messages because each Gillette country manager proposes several changes that he or she

thinks will increase local sales. These and similar adaptations for its hundreds of other products raise Gillette's costs and dilute its global brand power.

As a result, many companies have imposed more standardization on their products and marketing efforts. They have created so-called world brands that are marketed in much the same way worldwide. Whereas traditional marketers cater to differences between specific markets with highly adapted products, marketers who standardize globally sell more or less the same product the same way to all consumers. These marketers believe that advances in communication, transportation, and travel are turning the world into a common marketplace. They claim that people around the world want basically the same products and lifestyles. Everyone wants things that make life easier and that increase both free time and buying power. Despite what consumers say they want, all consumers want good products at lower prices.

heavy, fried breakfasts and 22 percent of consumers skip the meal altogether, Kellogg's advertising attempts to convince buyers to switch to a lighter, more nutritious breakfast diet.[27]

Often, differences across international markets are more subtle. They may result from physical differences in consumers and their environments. For example, Remington makes smaller electric shavers to fit the smaller hands of Japanese consumers; as well as battery-powered shavers for the British market, where few bathrooms have electrical outlets. Other differences result from varying customs. Consider the following examples:

Thus, proponents of global standardization claim that international marketers should adapt products and marketing programs only when local wants cannot be changed or avoided. Standardization results in lower production, distribution, marketing, and management costs, and thus lets the company offer consumers higher quality and more reliable products at lower prices. They would advise an auto company to make a world car, a shampoo company to make a world shampoo, and a farm-equipment company to make a world tractor. And, in fact, some companies have successfully marketed global products—for example, Coca-Cola, McDonald's hamburgers, A. T. Cross pens and pencils, Black & Decker tools, and Sony Walkmans. Yet, even in these cases, companies make some adaptations. Coca-Cola is less sweet or less carbonated in certain countries; McDonald's uses chili sauce instead of ketchup on its hamburgers in Mexico; and Cross pens and pencils have different advertising messages in some countries.

Moreover, the assertion that global standardization will lead to lower costs and prices, causing more goods to be snapped up by price-sensitive consumers, is debatable. Mattel Toys had sold its Barbie doll successfully in dozens of countries without modification. But in Japan, it did not sell well. Takara, Mattel's Japanese licensee, surveyed eighth-grade Japanese girls and their parents and found that they thought the doll's breasts were too big and that its legs were too long. Mattel, however, was reluctant to modify the doll because this would require additional production, packaging, and advertising costs. Finally, Takara won out and Mattel made a special Japanese Barbie. Within two years, Takara had sold over two million of the modified dolls. Clearly, incremental revenues far exceeded the incremental costs.

Rather than assuming that their products can be introduced without change in other countries, companies should review possible adaptations in product features, brand name, packaging, advertising themes, prices, and other elements and determine which would add more revenues than costs. One study showed that companies made adaptations in one or more areas in 80 percent of their foreign-directed products.

So which approach is best—global standardization or adaptation? Clearly, standardization is not an all-or-nothing proposition, but rather a matter of degree. Companies are justified in looking for more standardization to help keep down costs and prices and build greater global brand power. But they must remember that, although standardization saves money, competitors are always ready to offer more of what consumers in each country want, and they might pay dearly for replacing long-run marketing thinking with short-run financial thinking. Some international marketers suggest that companies should "think globally but act locally." The corporate level gives strategic direction; local units focus on the individual consumer differences. Global marketing, yes; global standardization, not necessarily.

*Sources*: See Theodore Levitt, "The Globalization of Markets," *Harvard Business Review*, May–June 1983, pp. 92–102; Kamran Kashani, "Beware the Pitfalls of Global Marketing," *Harvard Business Review*, September–October 1989, pp. 91–98; Saeed Saminee and Kendall Roth, "The Influence of Global Marketing Standardization on Performance," *Journal of Marketing*, April 1992, pp. 1–17; David M. Szymanski, Sundar G. Bharadwaj, and Rajan Varadarajan, "Standardization versus Adaptation of International Marketing Strategy: An Empirical Investigation," *Journal of Marketing*, October 1993, pp. 1–17; and Ashish Banerjee, "Global Campaigns Don't Work; Multinationals Do," *Advertising Age*, April 18, 1994, p. 23.

◆ Shaking your head from side to side means "no" in most countries but "yes" in Bulgaria and Sri Lanka.

◆ In South America, Southern Europe, and many Arab countries, touching another person is a sign of warmth and friendship. In the Orient, it is considered an invasion of privacy.

◆ In Norway or Malaysia, it's rude to leave any food on your plate after a meal; in Egypt, it's rude *not* to leave something on your plate.

◆ A door-to-door salesperson might find it tough going in Italy, where it is improper for a man to call on a woman if she is home alone.[28]

Failing to understand such differences between countries in customs and behaviors can spell disaster for a marketer's international products and programs.

Marketers must decide on the degree to which they will adapt their products and marketing programs to meet the unique cultures and needs of consumers in various markets. On the one hand, they want to standardize their offerings in order to simplify operations and take advantage of cost economies. On the other hand, adapting marketing efforts within each country results in products and programs that better satisfy the needs of local consumers. The question of whether to adapt or standardize the marketing mix across international markets has created a lively debate in recent years.

## SUMMARY

Markets have to be understood before marketing strategies can be developed. The consumer market buys goods and services for personal consumption. Consumers vary tremendously in age, income, education, tastes, and other factors. Marketers must understand how consumers transform marketing and other inputs into buying responses. *Consumer behavior* is influenced by the buyer's characteristics and by the buyer's decision process. *Buyer characteristics* include four major factors: cultural, social, personal, and psychological.

*Culture* is the most basic determinant of a person's wants and behavior. It includes the basic values, perceptions, preferences, and behaviors that a person learns from family and other key institutions. *Subcultures* are "cultures within cultures" that have distinct values and lifestyles. People with different cultural and subcultural characteristics have different product and brand preferences. Marketers may want to focus their marketing programs on the special needs of certain groups.

*Social factors* also influence a buyer's behavior. A person's *reference groups*—family, friends, social organizations, professional associations—strongly affect product and brand choices. The buyer's age, life-cycle stage, occupation, economic circumstances, lifestyle, personality, and other *personal characteristics* influence his or her buying decisions. Consumer *lifestyles*—the whole pattern of acting and interacting in the world—are also an important influence on buyers' choices. Finally, consumer buying behavior is influenced by four major *psychological factors*: motivation, perception, learning, and attitudes. Each of these factors provides a different perspective for understanding the workings of the buyer's "black box." Although many of these factors cannot be controlled by marketers, they are useful in identifying and understanding the consumers that marketers are trying to influence.

In making a purchase, the buyer goes through a decision process consisting of *need recognition, information search, evaluation of alternatives, purchase decision,* and *postpurchase behavior.* The marketer's job is to understand the buyer's behavior at each stage and the influences that are operating in the process. This allows the marketer to develop significant and effective marketing programs for the target market.

With regard to new products, consumers respond at different rates, depending on the consumer's characteristics and the product's characteristics. Manufacturers try to bring their new products to the attention of potential early adopters, particularly those with opinion leader characteristics.

Understanding consumer behavior is difficult enough for companies marketing within the borders of a single country. For companies operating internationally, however, understanding and serving the needs of consumers can be far more difficult. Consumers in different countries may vary dramatically in their values, attitudes, and behaviors. International marketers must understand such differences and adjust their products and marketing programs accordingly.

## KEY TERMS

Adoption process
Alternative evaluation
Attitude
Belief
Brand image
Cognitive dissonance
Consumer buying behavior
Consumer market

Culture
Groups
Information search
Learning
Lifestyle
Motive (or drive)
Need recognition
New product

Opinion leaders
Perception
Personality
Postpurchase behavior
Psychographics
Purchase decision
Social classes
Subculture

## QUESTIONS FOR DISCUSSION

1. What factors could you add to the model shown in Figure 5-1 to make it a more complete description of consumer behavior?

2. Just as it is a mistake for marketers to consider the U.S. population a homogeneous group with the same values and culture, it is also a mistake for marketers to assume that all Hispanic consumers fit into the same subculture or have similar buying habits. Comment on this statement.

3. Marketers at The Gap, the San Francisco-based clothing chain with nearly 900 stores nationwide, have noticed a "Gap-lash" of sorts. While baby boomers buy Gap clothing for themselves, their children—Generation Xers—want no part of the attire, which they consider "uncool." How would reference group analysis help Gap marketers better understand this marketing dilemma?

4. An advertising agency president says, "Perception is reality." What does he mean by this? How is perception important to marketers?

5. Would you buy a new American car? Why or why not? What would be needed to change your attitude?

6. Why is the postpurchase behavior stage included in the model of the buying process? What relevance does this stage have for marketers?

## APPLYING THE CONCEPTS

1. Different types of products can fulfill different functional and psychological needs.

   ◆ List five public or private luxury products that are very interesting or important to you. Some possibilities might include cars, clothing, sports equipment, music, or cosmetics. List five other necessities that you use which have little interest to you, such as pencils, laundry detergent, or gasoline.

   ◆ Make a list of words that describe how you feel about each of the products that you listed. Are there differences between the types of words you used for luxuries and necessities? What does this tell you about the different psychological needs that these products fulfill?

2. Examining our own purchases can reveal ways in which buying decisions really occur.

◆ Describe the five stages of your own buyer decision process for a major purchase such as a camera, stereo, or car.

◆ Next, describe your decision process for a minor purchase such as a candy bar or a soda.

◆ Are the decision processes the same for major and minor purchases? Which steps differ, and why?

## REFERENCES

1. Excerpts from Geoffrey Smith, "Can Reebok Regain Its Balance," *Business Week,* December 20, 1993, pp. 108–9; and Elizabeth Snead, "For Complex Times, Simple Footwear," *USA Today,* February 7, 1994, pp. D1, D2. Also see Dori Jones Yang and Michael Oneal, "Can Nike Just Do It?" *Business Week,* April 18, 1994, pp. 86–90; Smith, "Sneakers that Jump into the Past," *Business Week,* March 13, 1995, p. 71; Jeff Jensen, "Nike's Hard-Driving Methods Hit Nerve," *Advertising Age,* September 18, 1995, p. 4; and Smith, "Reebok is Tripping Over Its Own Laces," *Business Week,* February 26, 1996, pp. 62–66.

2. See Philip Cateora, *International Marketing,* 8th ed. (Homewood, IL.: Irwin, 1993), pp. 74–75.

3. Several models of the consumer buying process have been developed by marketing scholars. For a summary, see Leon G. Schiffman and Leslie Lazar Kanuk, *Consumer Behavior,* 5th ed. (Englewood Cliffs, NJ: Prentice Hall, 1994), pp. 644–56.

4. For this and other examples of the effects of culture in international marketing, see Cateora, *International Marketing,* Chapter 4.

5. For more on marketing to Hispanics, blacks, and mature consumers, see Jeffery D. Zbar, "U.S. Hispanics Gain Marketing Influence," *Advertising Age,* October 23, 1995, p. 42, Christy Fisher, "Hispanic Media See Siesta Ending," *Advertising Age,* January 24, 1994, pp. S1, S6; Leah Rickard, "Minorities Show Brand Loyalty," *Advertising Age,* May 9, 1994, p. 29; Thomas G. Exter, "The Largest Minority," *American Demographics,* February 1993, p. 59; Eugene Morris, "The Difference in Black and White," *American Demographics,* January 1993, pp. 44–49; Raymond Serafin and Riccardo A. Davis, "Detroit Moves to Woo Blacks," *Advertising Age,* April 11, 1994, p. 10; Melissa Campanelli, "The Senior Market: Rewriting the Demographics and Definitions," *Sales & Marketing Management,* February 1991, pp. 63–70; Tibbett L. Speer, "Older Consumers Follow Different Rules," *American Demographics,* February 1993, pp. 21–22; and Cyndee Miller, "Image of Seniors Improves in Ads," *Marketing News,* December 6, 1993, p. 8.

6. Jacquelyn Lynn, "Tapping the Riches of Bilingual Markets," *Management Review,* March 1995, pp. 56–61.

7. See "Special Report: Marketing to Hispanics," *Advertising Age,* January 23, 1995, pp. 29–37; Arline Neufeld and Christopher Purdy, "Here's What You Need to Know about the Hispanic Market Today," *Telemarketing,* May 1995, p. 70; and Francis J. Mulhern and Jerome D. Williams, "Understanding Hispanic Shopping Behavior," *Stores,* April 1995, p. RR3.

8. For more on the African-American market, see "Marketing to African-Americans," a special section in *Advertising Age,* July 17, 1995, pp. S1–S4.

9. See Christy Fisher, "Marketers Straddle Asian-America Curtain," *Advertising Age,* November 7, 1994; John Steere, "How Asian-Americans Make Purchasing Decisions," *Marketing News,* March 13, 1995, p. 9; and "Asian Demographics," *Media Week,* April 17, 1995, p. S1.

10. See Tibbett L. Speer, "Older Consumers Follow Different Rules," *American Demographics,* February 1993, pp. 21–22; Laurie Freeman, "Completing the Span of 'Bridge' to Boomers," *Advertising Age,* November 7, 1994, p. S8; Margaret A. Wylde, "How to Size Up the Current and Future Markets: Technologies and the Older Adult," *ASAP,* March 22, 1995, p. 15; and "What Do Mature Consumers Want?" *USA Today Magazine,* April 1995, p. 10.

11. Patricia Sellers, "The Best Way to Reach Your Buyers," *Fortune,* special issue on "The Tough New Consumer," Autumn/Winter, 1993, pp. 14–17. Also see, Chip Walker, "Word of Mouth," *American Demographics,* July 1995, pp. 38–43.

12. Debra Goldman, "Spotlight Men," *Adweek,* August 13, 1990, pp. M1–M6; Dennis Rodkin, "A Manly Sport: Building Loyalty," *Advertising Age,* April 15, 1991, pp. S1, S12; Nancy Ten Kate, "Who Buys the Pants in the Family?" *American Demographics,* January 1992, p. 12; and Laura Zinn, "Real Men Buy Paper Towels, Too," *Business Week,* November 9, 1992, pp. 75–76.

13. For more on family decision making, see Schiffman and Kanuk, *Consumer Behavior,* Chapter 12; Michael B. Menasco and David J. Curry, "Utility and Choice: An Empirical Study of Husband/Wife Decision Making," *Journal of Consumer Research,* June 1989, pp. 87–97; Kim P. Corfman, "Perceptions of Relative Influence: Formation and Measurement," *Journal of Marketing Research,* May 1991, pp. 125–36; and Robert Boutilier, "Family's Strings," *American Demographics,* August 1993, pp. 44–47. For cross-cultural comparisons, see John B. Ford, Michael S. LaTour, and Tony L. Henthorne, "Perception of Marital Roles in Purchase-Decision Processes: A Cross-Cultural Study," *Journal of the Academy of Marketing Science,* Spring 1995, pp. 120–31.

14. See Martha Farnsworth Riche, "Psychographics for the 1990s," *American Demographics,* July 1989, pp. 25–31; and Rebecca Piirto, "VALS the Second Time," *American Demographics,* July 1991, p. 6.

15. This and other examples of companies using VALS 2 can be found in Rebecca Piirto, "Measuring Minds in the 1990s," *American Demographics,* December 1990, pp. 35–39; and Piirto, "VALS the Second Time," p. 6. For a good discussion of other

lifestyle topics, see Basil G. Englis and Michael Solomon, "To Be or Not to Be: Lifestyle Imergy, Reference Groups, and the Clustering of America," *Journal of Advertising,* March 1995, p. 13.

16. See John Saunders and Veronica Wong, *Kotler & Armstrong's Principles of Marketing,* First European Edition (London: Prentice Hall, 1996), Chapter 7. For an excellent discussion of cross-cultural lifestyle systems, see their Marketing Highlight 7–2.

17. Stuart Elliot, "Sampling Tastes of a Changing Russia," *The New York Times,* April 1, 1992, pp. D1, D19.

18. Myron Magnet, "Let's Go For Growth," *Fortune,* March 7, 1994, p. 70.

19. See Annetta Miller and Dody Tsiantar, "Psyching Out Consumers," *Newsweek,* February 27, 1989, pp. 46–47; and Rebecca Piirto, "Words that Sell," *American Demographics,* January 1992, p. 6.

20. Abraham H. Maslow, *Motivation and Personality,* 2nd ed. (New York: Harper & Row, 1970), pp. 80–106. Also see Rudy Schrocer, "Maslow's Hierarchy of Needs as a Framework for Identifying Emotional Triggers," *Marketing Review,* February 1991, pp. 26, 28.

21. Geert Hofstede, *Cultural Consequences* (London: Sage, 1984).

22. See "Honda Hopes to Win New Riders by Emphasizing 'Fun' of Cycles," *Marketing News,* August 28, 1989, p. 6.

23. Keith B. Murray, "A Test of Services Marketing Theory: Consumer Information Acquisition Theory," *Journal of Marketing,* January 1991, pp. 10–25.

24. See Leon Festinger, *A Theory of Cognitive Dissonance* (Stanford, CA: Stanford University Press, 1957); and Schiffman and Kanuk, *Consumer Behavior,* pp. 274–75.

25. See Karl Albrect and Ron Zemke, *Service America!* (Homewood, IL:

Dow-Jones Irwin, 1985), pp. 6–7; Frank Rose, "Now Quality Means Service Too," *Fortune,* April 22, 1991, pp. 97–108; and Chip Walker, "Word of Mouth," *American Demographics,* July 1995, p. 40.

26. The following discussion draws heavily from Everett M. Rogers, *Diffusion of Innovations,* 3rd ed. (New York: Free Press, 1983). Also see Hubert Gatignon and Thomas S. Robertson, "A Propositional Inventory for New Diffusion Research," *Journal of Consumer Research,* March 1985, pp. 849–67.

27. Mir Maqbool Alam Khan, "Kellogg Reports Brisk Cereal Sales in India," *Advertising Age,* November 14, 1994, p. 60.

28. For these and other examples, see William J. Stanton, Michael J. Etzel, and Bruce J. Walker, *Fundamentals of Marketing* (New York: McGraw-Hill, Inc., 1991), p. 536.

# 6

# *Business Markets and Business Buyer Behavior*

Gulfstream Aerospace Corporation sells business jets with price tags as high as $28 million. Identifying potential buyers isn't a problem—worldwide, only about 4,200 customers, including 40 governments, have the wherewithal to own and operate multimillion dollar business aircraft. Customers include Disney, American Express, Coca-Cola, General Motors, IBM, and many others, including Bill Cosby and King Fahd of Saudi Arabia. Gulfstream's more difficult problems involve reaching key decision makers for jet purchases, understanding their complex motivations and decision processes, analyzing what factors will be important in their decisions, and designing marketing approaches.

Gulfstream recognizes the importance of *rational* motives and *objective* factors in buyers' decisions. Customers justify the expense of a corporate jet on utilitarian grounds, such as security, flexibility, responsiveness to customers, and efficient time use. A company buying a jet will evaluate Gulfstream aircraft on quality and performance, prices, operating costs, and service. At times, these "objective factors" may appear to be the only things that drive the buying decision. But having a superior product isn't enough to land the sale; Gulfstream also must consider the more subtle *human factors* that affect the choice of a jet.

The purchase process may be initiated by a company's chief executive officer (CEO), a board member wishing to increase efficiency or security, the company's chief pilot, or through Gulfstream efforts like advertising or a sales visit. The CEO will be central in deciding whether to buy the jet, but he or she will be heavily influenced by the company's pilot, financial officer, and members of top management. The involvement of so many people in the purchase decision creates a group dynamic that Gulfstream must factor into its sales planning. Who makes up the buying group? How will the parties interact? Who will dominate and who will submit? What priorities do the individuals have?

Each party in the buying process has subtle roles and needs. For example, the salesperson who tries to impress both the CEO with depreciation schedules and the chief pilot with minimum runway statistics will almost certainly not sell a plane if he or she overlooks the psychological and emotional components of the buying decision. The chief pilot, as an equipment expert, often has veto power over purchase decisions and may be able to stop the purchase of a certain brand of jet by simply expressing a negative opinion about, say, the plane's bad-weather capabilities. In this sense, the pilot not only influences the decision but also serves as an information "gatekeeper" by advising management on the equipment to select. The users of the jet—middle and upper management of the buying company, important customers, and others—may have at least an indirect role in choosing the equipment. Although the corporate legal staff will handle the purchase agreement and the purchasing department will acquire the jet, these parties may have little to say about whether or how the plane will be obtained and which type will be selected.

According to one salesperson, in dealing with the CEO, the biggest factor is not the plane's hefty price tag, but its image. You need all the numbers for support, but if you can't find the kid inside the CEO and excite him or her with the raw beauty of the new plane, you'll never sell the equipment. If you sell the excitement, you sell the jet.

Some buying influences may come as a big surprise. Gulfstream may never really know who is behind the purchase of a plane. Although many people inside the customer company can be influential, the most important influence may turn out to be the CEO's spouse.

In some ways, selling corporate jets to business buyers is like selling cars and kitchen appliances to families. Gulfstream asks the same questions as do consumer marketers: Who are the buyers and what are their needs? How do buyers make their buying decisions and what factors influence these decisions? What marketing program will be most effective? But the answers to these questions are usually different for the business buyer. Thus, Gulfstream faces many of the same challenges that consumer marketers do—and some additional ones.[1]  ■

# CHAPTER OBJECTIVES

## *After reading this chapter, you should be able to:*

**1** Explain how business markets differ from consumer markets.

**2** Identify the major factors that influence business buyer behavior.

**3** List and define the steps in the business buying-decision process.

**4** Explain how institutional and government buyers make their buying decisions.

In one way or another, most large companies sell to other organizations. Many companies, such as Du Pont, Xerox, Boeing, Motorola, and countless other firms, sell *most* of their products to other businesses. Even large consumer-products companies, which make products used by final consumers, must first sell their products to other businesses. For example, General Mills makes many familiar consumer products—Cheerios, Betty Crocker cake mixes, Gold Medal flour, and others. But to sell these products to consumers, General Mills must first sell them to the wholesalers and retailers that serve the consumer market. General Mills also sells products such as specialty chemicals directly to other businesses.

**Business market**
All the organizations that buy goods and services to use in the production of other products and services or for the purpose of reselling or renting them to others at a profit.

The **business market** consists of all the organizations that buy goods and services to use in the production of other products and services that are sold, rented, or supplied to others. It also includes retailing and wholesaling firms that acquire goods for the purpose of reselling or renting them to others at a profit. In the **business buying process,** business buyers determine which products and services their organizations need to purchase, and then find, evaluate, and choose from among the alternative suppliers and brands. Companies that sell to other business organizations must do their best to understand business markets and business buyer behavior.

## ▶ BUSINESS MARKETS

**Business buying process**
The decision-making process by which business buyers establish the need for purchased products and services and identify, evaluate, and choose among alternative brands and suppliers.

The business market is *huge:* In the United States alone, it consists of over 13 million organizations that buy trillions of dollars worth of goods and services each year. In fact, business markets involve far more dollars and items than do consumer markets. For example, think about the large number of business transactions involved in the production and sale of a single set of Goodyear tires. Various suppliers sell Goodyear the rubber, steel, equipment, and other goods that it needs to produce the tires. Goodyear then sells the finished tires to retailers, who in turn sell them to consumers. Thus, many sets of *business* purchases were made for only one set of *consumer* purchases. In addition, Goodyear sells tires as original equipment to manufacturers who install them on new vehicles, and as replacement tires to companies that maintain their own fleets of company cars, trucks, buses, or other vehicles.

### CHARACTERISTICS OF BUSINESS MARKETS

In some ways, business markets are similar to consumer markets. Both involve people who assume buying roles and make purchase decisions to satisfy needs. However, business markets differ in many ways from consumer markets. The main differences, shown in Table 6-1 and discussed below, are in *market structure and demand,* the *nature of the buying unit,* and the *types of decisions and the decision process* involved.

#### Market Structure and Demand
The business marketer normally deals with *far fewer but far larger buyers* than the consumer marketer does. For example, when Goodyear sells replacement tires to final consumers, its potential market includes the owners of the millions of cars currently in use in the United States. But Goodyear's fate in the business market depends on getting orders from one of only a few large auto makers. Even in large business markets, a few buyers normally account for most of the purchasing.

| **TABLE 6-1** *Characteristics of Business Markets* |
| --- |

*Marketing structure and demand*
　Business markets contain *fewer but larger buyers.*
　Business customers are more *geographically concentrated.*
　Business buyer demand is *derived* from final consumer demand.
　Demand in many business markets is *more inelastic*—not affected as much in the short run by price
　　changes.
　Demand in business market has *larger and more frequent fluctuations.*

*Nature of the buying unit*
　Business purchases involve *more buyers.*
　Business buying involves a *more professional purchasing effort.*

*Types of decisions and the decision process*
　Business buyers usually face more *complex buying decisions.*
　The business buying process is *more formalized.*
　In business buying, buyers and sellers work more closely together and build close, long-run *relationships.*

**Derived demand**
Business demand that
ultimately comes from
(derives from) the de-
mand for consumer
goods.

Business markets are also more *geographically concentrated.* More than half
the nation's business buyers are concentrated in eight states: California, New York,
Ohio, Illinois, Michigan, Texas, Pennsylvania, and New Jersey. Further, business
demand is **derived demand**—it ultimately derives from the demand for consumer
goods. General Motors buys steel because consumers buy cars. If consumer demand
for cars drops, so will the demand for steel and all the other products used to make
cars. Therefore, business marketers sometimes promote their products directly to
final consumers to increase business demand (see Marketing at Work 6-1).

Many business markets have *inelastic demand;* that is, total demand for
many business products is not affected much by price changes, especially in the
short run. A drop in the price of leather will not cause shoe manufacturers to buy
much more leather unless it results in lower shoe prices that, in turn, will increase
consumer demand for shoes.

Finally, business markets have more *fluctuating demand.* The demand for
many business goods and services tends to change more—and more quickly—than
the demand for consumer goods and services does. A small percentage increase in
consumer demand can cause large increases in business demand. Sometimes a rise
of only 10 percent in consumer demand can cause as much as a 200 percent rise
in business demand during the next period.

### Nature of the Buying Unit

Compared with consumer purchases, a business purchase usually involves *more
buyers* and a *more professional purchasing effort.* Often, business buying is done
by trained purchasing agents who spend their working lives learning how to buy
better. The more complex the purchase, the more likely that several people will
participate in the decision-making process. Buying committees made up of technical experts and top management are common in purchasing major goods. Therefore, business marketers must have well-trained salespeople to deal with well-
trained buyers.

## Types of Decisions and the Decision Process

Business buyers usually face *more complex* buying decisions than do consumer buyers. Purchases often involve large sums of money, complex technical and economic considerations, and interactions among many people at many levels of the buyer's organization. Because the purchases are more complex, business buyers may take longer to make their decisions. For example, the purchase of a large computer system might take many months or more than a year to complete and could involve millions of dollars, thousands of technical details, and dozens of people ranging from top management to lower-level users.

The business buying process tends to be *more formalized* than the consumer buying process. Large business purchases usually call for detailed product specifications, written purchase orders, careful supplier searches, and formal approval. The buying firm might even prepare policy manuals that detail the purchase process.

Finally, in the business buying process, buyer and seller are often much *more dependent* on each other. Consumer marketers are usually at a distance from their customers. In contrast, business marketers may roll up their sleeves and work closely with their customers during all stages of the buying process—from helping customers define problems, to finding solutions, to supporting after-sale operation. They often customize their offerings to individual customer needs. In the short run, sales go to suppliers who meet buyers' immediate product and service needs. However, business marketers also must build close *long-run* relationships with customers. In the long run, business marketers keep a customer's sales by meeting current needs *and* by working with customers to help them succeed with their own customers (see Marketing at Work 6-2).[2]

# A MODEL OF BUSINESS BUYER BEHAVIOR

At the most basic level, marketers want to know how business buyers will respond to various marketing stimuli. Figure 6-1 shows a model of business buyer behavior. In this model, marketing and other stimuli affect the buying organization and produce certain buyer responses. As with consumer buying, the marketing stimuli for business buying consist of the four Ps: product, price, place, and promotion. Other stimuli include major forces in the environment: economic, technological,

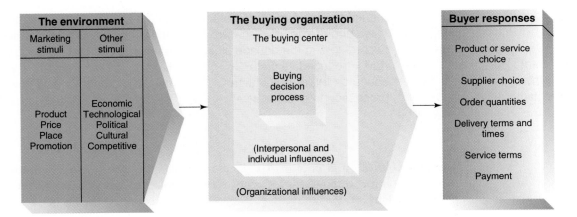

**FIGURE 6-1**
*A model of business buyer behavior*

## MARKETING AT WORK 6-1

# INTEL: YOU CAN'T SEE IT, BUT YOU'RE GOING TO LOVE IT

In mid-1991, Intel launched its "Intel Inside" advertising campaign to sell personal computer buyers on the virtues of Intel microprocessors, the tiny chips that serve as the brains of microcomputers. So what, you say? Lots of companies run big consumer ad campaigns. However, although such a campaign might be business as usual for companies like Coca-Cola, Nike, or IBM that market products directly to final consumers, it was anything but usual for Intel.

Computer buyers can't buy a microprocessor chip directly; in fact, most will never even see one. Demand for microprocessors is *derived demand:* It comes from demand for products that *contain* microprocessors. Consumers simply buy the computer and take whatever brand of chip the computer manufacturer chooses to include. Traditionally, chip companies like Intel market only to the manufacturers who buy chips directly. In contrast, the innovative "Intel Inside" campaign appeals directly to computer buyers—Intel's customers' customers. If Intel can create brand preference among buyers for *its*

Intel launched its highly successful "Intel Inside" logo advertising campaign to convince computer buyers that it really does matter what chip comes inside their computers.

chips, this in turn will make Intel chips more attractive to computer manufacturers.

Intel invented the first microprocessor in 1971 and for almost 25 years has held a near-monopoly, dominating the chip market for desktop computers. Its sales and profits have soared accordingly. In the decade since IBM introduced its first PCs based on Intel's 8088 microprocessor, Intel sales have jumped ninefold to almost $11.5 billion, and its earnings have grown even faster. Its popular i286, i386, i486, and Pentium chips power 80 percent of all PCs sold today.

However, a rush of imitators—Advanced Micro Devices (AMD), Cyrix, and others—have cracked Intel's monopoly, flooding the market with new and improved clones of Intel chips. The onslaught of clones quickly

political, cultural, and competitive. These stimuli enter the organization and are turned into buyer responses: product or service choice; supplier choice; order quantities; and delivery, service, and payment terms. In order to design good marketing-mix strategies, the marketer must understand what happens within the organization to turn stimuli into purchase responses.

escalated into a price war for Intel's earlier-generation chips, denting Intel's bottom line. And although Intel has the market for its latest-generation processors to itself for a year or two, it has the cloners constantly nipping at its heels.

Intel has responded fiercely to the growing competition, slashing prices, spending heavily to develop new chips, and advertising to differentiate its products. In 1994, Intel invested a whopping $1 billion in R&D and $2.4 billion in capital spending to get new products to the market more quickly. Its Pentium microprocessor is a veritable one-chip mainframe. It contains 3.1 million transistors and will process 100 million instructions per second (MIPS), as compared with only one-quarter million transistors and five MIPS for the old i386 chip. Intel plans to create a new chip family every two years. The new P6 processor, launched in 1995, is more than twice as fast as the Pentium processor. And the P7 processor, due in 1997, will double the speed of the P6. By the year 2000, Intel will offer a chip with an astounding 100 million transistors and two *billion* instructions per second—that's roughly equal to today's supercomputers.

Still, the clone makers are likely to continue their attacks, and advertising provides another means by which Intel can differentiate its "originals" from competitors' imitations. The "Intel Inside" program consists of two major efforts. First, in its brand-awareness ads, Intel attempts to convince microcomputer buyers that Intel microprocessors really are better. The first ad of the series contained the headline "How to spot the very best PC" nestled in a bed of colorful "Intel Inside" logos. The ad copy advised:

*Intel is the world's leader in microprocessor design and development. In fact, Intel introduced the very first microprocessor. So with the Intel Inside logo, you know you've got unquestioned compatibility and unparalleled quality. And you'll know you're getting the very best in PC technology.*

As a second major element of the "Intel Inside" program, Intel subsidizes ads by PC manufacturers that include the "Intel Inside" logo. So far, more than 100 companies have featured the logo in their ads, including IBM, NCR, Dell, Zenith Data Systems, and AST. Participating manufacturers claim that the campaign has increased their advertising effectiveness. "The 'Intel Inside'

program has been a good program for us," says the advertising manager of a large computer manufacturing firm. "It has helped add some credibility and enhancements to our messages." In the first two years of the campaign, more than $250 million worth of "Intel Inside" logo advertising appeared, with computer manufacturers picking up an estimated $150 million of the bill.

It remains to be seen whether the "Intel Inside" program can continue to convince buyers to care about what chips come in their computers. But as long as microprocessors remain anonymous little lumps hidden inside a user's computer, Intel remains at the mercy of the clone makers and other competitors. In contrast, if Intel can convince buyers that its chips are superior, it will achieve a strong advantage in its dealings with computer makers.

*Sources:* Quote from Kate Bertrand, "Advertising a Chip You'll Never See," *Business Marketing,* February 1992, p. 19. Also see Richard Brandt, "Intel: What a Tease—and What a Strategy," *Business Week,* February 22, 1993, p. 40; Nancy Arnott, "Inside Intel's Marketing Coup," *Sales & Marketing Management,* February 1994, pp. 78–81; Robert D. Hof, "Intel: Far Beyond the Pentium," *Business Week,* February 20, 1995, pp. 88–90; Robert D. Hof, "Intel Unbound," *Business Week,* October 9, 1995, pp. 148–54; and Bradley Johnson, "'Intel Inside' Program Expands Global Reach," *Advertising Age,* January 6, 1996, p. 9. Intel Inside, i286, i386, i486, and Pentium are trademarks or registered trademarks of Intel Corporation.

Within the organization, buying activity consists of two major parts: the buying center, made up of all the people involved in the buying decision, and the buying decision process. The model shows that the buying center and the buying decision process are influenced by internal organizational, interpersonal, and individual factors, as well as by external environmental factors.

# MARKETING AT WORK 6-2

## BUSINESS MARKETERS SELL CUSTOMER SUCCESS

In the late 1980s, the Dow Chemical Company realigned its dozen or so widely varied plastics businesses into a single business unit called Dow Plastics. One of the first things Dow had to do was to decide how to position its new division competitively. Initial research with Dow's and competitors' customers showed that Dow Plastics rated a distant third in customer preference behind industry leaders Du Pont and GE Plastics. The research also revealed, however, that customers were unhappy with the service, or lack thereof, that they received from all three suppliers. "Vendors peddled resins as a commodity," says the head of Dow Plastics' advertising agency. "They competed on price and delivered on time, but gave no service."

These findings led to a positioning strategy that went far beyond simply selling good products and delivering them on time. Dow Plastics set out to build deeper relationships with customers. The company was selling not just products and services, but customer success. Says the agency executive, "Whether they're using Dow's plastics to make bags for Safeway or for complex aerospace applications, we have to help them succeed in their markets." This new thinking was summed up in the position-

Dow Plastics tells customers, "We don't succeed unless you do." Building deeper customer relationships helped Dow move from number three to become a leader in its market.

ing statement: "We don't succeed unless you do."

The new positioning helped Dow Plastics to become a truly customer-oriented company. It got Dow out of selling plastics and into selling customer success. The slogan and underlying philosophy created a unifying identity for the business—one based on building relationships with customers and helping them to succeed with their own businesses. Customer problems became more than just engineering challenges. Dow's customers sell to somebody else, so the com-

pany now faced new challenges of marketing to and helping satisfy customers' customers.

As a result of its new customer-relationship orientation, Dow Plastics has become a leader in the plastics industry. The customer-success philosophy permeates everything that the business does. Whenever company people encounter a new product or market, the first question they always ask is, "How does this fit with 'We don't succeed unless you do'?"

*Source:* Portions adapted from Nancy Arnott, "Getting the Picture: The Grand Design—We Don't Succeed Unless You Do," *Sales & Marketing Management,* June 1994, pp. 74–76.

# ►BUSINESS BUYER BEHAVIOR

The model in Figure 6-1 suggests four questions about business buyer behavior: What buying decisions do business buyers make? Who participates in the buying process? What are the major influences on buyers? How do business buyers make their buying decisions?

## MAJOR TYPES OF BUYING SITUATIONS

There are three major types of buying situations.[3] At one extreme is the *straight rebuy*, which is a fairly routine decision. At the other extreme is the *new task*, which may call for thorough research. In the middle is the *modified rebuy*, which requires some research.

**Straight rebuy**
A business buying situation in which the buyer routinely reorders something without any modifications.

In a **straight rebuy,** the buyer reorders something without any modifications. It is usually handled on a routine basis by the purchasing department. Based on past buying satisfaction, the buyer simply chooses from the various suppliers on its list. "In" suppliers try to maintain product and service quality. They often propose automatic reordering systems so that the purchasing agent will save reordering time. The "out" suppliers try to offer something new or exploit dissatisfaction so that the buyer will consider them. They try to get their foot in the door with a small order and then enlarge their purchase share over time.

**Modified rebuy**
A business buying situation in which the buyer wants to modify product specifications, prices, terms, or suppliers.

In a **modified rebuy,** the buyer wants to modify product specifications, prices, terms, or suppliers. The modified rebuy usually involves more decision participants than the straight rebuy. The "in" suppliers may become nervous and feel pressured to put their best foot forward to protect an account. "Out" suppliers may see the modified rebuy situation as an opportunity to make a better offer and gain new business.

**New task**
A business buying situation in which the buyer purchases a product or service for the first time.

A company buying a product or service for the first time faces a **new-task** situation. In such cases, the greater the cost or risk, the larger the number of decision participants and the greater their efforts to collect information will be. The new-task situation is the marketer's greatest opportunity and challenge. The marketer not only tries to reach as many key buying influences as possible, but also provides help and information.

The buyer makes the fewest decisions in the straight rebuy and the most in the new-task decision. In the new-task situation, the buyer must decide on product specifications, suppliers, price limits, payment terms, order quantities, delivery times, and service terms. The order of these decisions varies with each situation, and different decision participants influence each choice.

**Systems buying**
Buying a packaged solution to a problem, without all the separate decisions involved.

Many business buyers prefer to buy a packaged solution to a problem from a single seller. Called **systems buying,** this practice began with government buying of major weapons and communication systems. Instead of buying and putting all the components together, the government asked for bids from suppliers who would supply the components *and* assemble the package or system.

Sellers increasingly have recognized that buyers like this method and have adopted systems selling as a marketing tool.[4] Systems selling is a two-step process. First, the supplier sells a group of interlocking products. For example, the supplier sells not only glue, but also applicators and dryers. Second, the supplier sells a system of production, inventory control, distribution, and other services to meet the buyer's need for a smooth-running operation.

Systems selling is a key business marketing strategy for winning and holding accounts. The contract often goes to the firm that provides the most complete system meeting the customer's needs. For example, the Indonesian government requested bids to build a cement factory near Jakarta. An American firm's proposal included choosing the site, designing the cement factory, hiring the construction crews, assembling the materials and equipment, and turning the finished factory over to the Indonesian government. A Japanese firm's proposal included all of these services, plus hiring and training workers to run the factory, exporting the cement through their trading companies, and using the cement to build some needed roads and new office buildings in Jakarta. Although the Japanese firm's proposal cost more, it won the contract. Clearly, the Japanese viewed the problem not as just building a cement factory (the narrow view of systems selling) but of running it in a way that would contribute to the country's economy. They took the broadest view of the customer's needs. This is true systems selling.

## PARTICIPANTS IN THE BUSINESS BUYING PROCESS

Who does the buying of the trillions of dollars worth of goods and services needed by business organizations? The decision-making unit of a buying organization is called its **buying center,** defined as all the individuals and units that participate in the business decision-making process.

**Buying center**
All the individuals and units that participate in the business buying-decision process.

The buying center includes all members of the organization who play a role in the purchase decision process. This group includes the actual users of the product or service, those who make the buying decision, those who influence the buying decision, those who do the actual buying (purchasing agents), and those who control buying information.

The buying center is not a fixed and formally identified unit within the buying organization. It is a set of buying roles assumed by different people for different purchases. Within the organization, the size and makeup of the buying center will vary for different products and for different buying situations. For some routine purchases, one person—say a purchasing agent—may assume all the buying center roles and serve as the only person involved in the buying decision. For more complex purchases, the buying center may include 20 or 30 people from different levels and departments in the organization. According to one survey, the average number of people involved in a buying decision ranges from about three (for services and items used in day-to-day operations) to almost five (for such high-ticket purchases as construction work and machinery). Another survey detected a trend toward team-based buying; 87 percent of surveyed purchasing executives at Fortune 1000 companies expect teams of people from different functions to be making buying decisions in the year 2000.[5]

Business marketers working in global markets may face even greater levels of buying center influence. A recent study comparing the buying decision processes in the United States, Sweden, France, and Southeast Asia found that U.S. buyers may be lone eagles compared with their counterparts in some other countries. Sweden had the highest team buying effort while the United States had the lowest, even though the U.S. and Swedish firms had very similar demographics. In mak-

*This ad recognizes the secretary as a key buying influence.*

ing purchasing decisions, Swedish firms depended on technical staff, both their own and suppliers', much more than the firms in other countries.[6]

The buying center concept presents a major marketing challenge. The business marketer must learn who participates in the decision, each participant's relative influence, and what evaluation criteria each decision participant uses. For example, Baxter International, the large health-care products and services company, sells disposable surgical gowns to hospitals. It identifies the hospital personnel involved in this buying decision as the vice president of purchasing, the operating room administrator, and the surgeons. Each participant plays a different role. The vice president of purchasing analyzes whether the hospital should buy disposable gowns or reusable gowns. If analysis favors disposable gowns, then the operating room administrator compares competing products and prices and makes a choice. This administrator considers the gown's absorbency, antiseptic quality, design, and cost, and normally buys the brand that meets requirements at the lowest cost. Finally, surgeons affect the decision later by reporting their satisfaction or dissatisfaction with the brand.

The buying center usually includes some obvious participants who are involved formally in the buying decision. For example, the decision to buy a corporate jet will probably involve the company's CEO, chief pilot, a purchasing agent, some legal staff, a member of top management, and others formally charged with the buying decision. It may also involve less obvious, informal participants, some of whom may actually make or strongly affect the buying decision. Sometimes, even the people in the buying center are not aware of all the buying participants. As the Gulfstream example showed, the decision about which corporate jet to buy may actually be made by a corporate board member who has an interest in flying and who knows a lot about airplanes. This board member may work behind the scenes to sway the decision. Many business buying decisions result from the complex interactions of ever-changing buying center participants.

# MAJOR INFLUENCES ON BUSINESS BUYERS

Business buyers are subject to many influences when they make their buying decisions. Some marketers assume that the major influences are economic. They think buyers will favor the supplier who offers the lowest price, or the best product, or the most service. They concentrate on offering strong economic benefits to buyers. However, business buyers actually respond to both economic and personal factors. Far from being cold, calculating, and impersonal, business buyers are human and social as well. They react to both reason and emotion.

When suppliers' offers are very similar, business buyers have little basis for strictly rational choice. Because they can meet organizational goals with any supplier, buyers can allow personal factors to play a larger role in their decisions. However, when competing products differ greatly, business buyers are more accountable for their choice and tend to pay more attention to economic factors.

Figure 6-2 lists various groups of influences on business buyers—environmental, organizational, interpersonal, and individual.[7]

## Environmental Factors

Business buyers are influenced heavily by factors in the current and expected *economic environment,* such as the level of primary demand, the economic outlook, and the cost of money. As economic uncertainty rises, business buyers cut back on new investments and attempt to reduce their inventories.

An increasingly important environmental factor is shortages in key materials. Many companies now are more willing to buy and hold larger inventories of scarce materials to ensure adequate supply. Business buyers also are affected by technological, political, and competitive developments in the environment. Culture and customs can strongly influence business buyer reactions to the marketer's

*Industrial buyers respond to more than just economic factors. In this ad, the words stress performance but the illustration suggests a smooth, comfortable ride.*

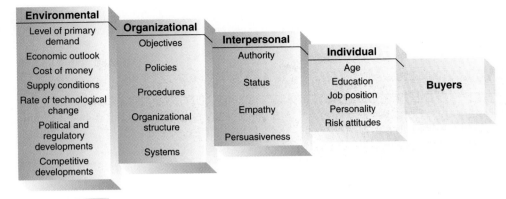

## FIGURE 6-2
*Major influences on business buyer behavior*

behavior and strategies, especially in the international marketing environment (see Marketing at Work 6-3). The business marketer must observe these many factors, determine how they will affect the buyer, and try to turn these challenges into opportunities.

### Organizational Factors

Each buying organization has its own objectives, policies, procedures, structure, and systems. The business marketer must know these *organizational factors* as thoroughly as possible. Questions such as these arise: How many people are involved in the buying decision? Who are they? What are their evaluative criteria? What are the company's policies and limits on its buyers?

### Interpersonal Factors

The buying center usually includes many participants who influence each other. The business marketer often finds it difficult to determine what kinds of *interpersonal factors* and group dynamics enter into the buying process. As one writer notes: "Managers do not wear tags that say 'decision maker' or 'unimportant person.' The powerful are often invisible, at least to vendor representatives."[8] Nor does the buying center participant with the highest rank always have the most influence. Participants may have influence in the buying decision because they control rewards and punishments, are well liked, have special expertise, or have a special relationship with other important participants. Interpersonal factors are often very subtle. Whenever possible, business marketers must try to understand these factors and design strategies that take them into account.

### Individual Factors

Each participant in the business buying decision process brings in personal motives, perceptions, and preferences. These individual factors are affected by personal characteristics such as age, income, education, professional identification, personality, and attitudes toward risk. Also, buyers have different buying styles. Some may be technical types who make in-depth analyses of competitive proposals before choosing a supplier. Other buyers may be intuitive negotiators who are adept at pitting the sellers against one another for the best deal.

# MARKETING AT WORK 6–3

## INTERNATIONAL MARKETING MANNERS: WHEN IN ROME, DO AS THE ROMANS DO

Picture this: Consolidated Amalgamation, Inc., thinks it's time that the rest of the world enjoyed the same fine products that it has offered American consumers for two generations. It dispatches vice president Harry E. Slicksmile to Europe to explore the territory. Mr. Slicksmile stops first in London, where he makes short work of some bankers—he rings them up on the phone. He handles Parisians with similar ease: After securing a table at La Tour d'Argent, he greets his luncheon guest, the director of an industrial engineering firm, with the words, "Just call me Harry, Jacques."

In Germany, Mr. Slicksmile is a powerhouse. Whisking through a lavish, state-of-the-art marketing presentation, complete with the flip charts and audiovisuals, he shows 'em that this Georgia boy *knows* how to make a buck. Heading on to Milan, Harry strikes up a conversation with the Japanese businessman sitting next to him on the plane. He flips his card onto the guy's tray and, when the two say goodbye, shakes hands warmly and clasps the man's right arm. Later, for his appointment with the owner of an Italian packaging-design firm, our hero wears his comfy corduroy sport coat, khaki pants, and deck shoes. Everybody knows Italians are zany and laid back, right?

Wrong. Six months later, Consolidated Amalgamation has nothing to show for the trip but a pile of bills. In Europe, they weren't wild about Harry.

This hypothetical case has been exaggerated for emphasis. Americans are seldom such dolts. But experts say success in international business has a lot to do with knowing the territory and its people. By learning English and extending themselves in other ways, the world's business leaders have met Americans more than halfway. In contrast, Americans too often do little except assume that others will march to their music. "We want things to be 'American' when we travel. Fast. Convenient. Easy. So we become 'ugly Americans' by demanding that others change," says one American world trade expert. "I think more business would be done if we tried harder."

Poor Harry tried, all right, but in all the wrong ways. The British do not, as a rule, make deals over the phone as much as Americans do. It's not so much a "cultural" difference as a difference in approach. A proper Frenchman neither likes instant familiarity—questions about family, church, or alma mater—nor refers to strangers by their first names. "That poor fellow, Jacques, probably wouldn't show anything, but he'd recoil. He'd *not*

*In order to succeed in global markets, American companies must help their managers to understand the needs, customs, and cultures of international business buyers.*

be pleased," explains an expert on French business practices. "It's considered poor taste," he continues. "Even after months of business dealings, I'd wait for him or her to make the invitation [to use first names] . . . You are always right, in Europe, to say 'Mister.'"

Harry's flashy presentation would likely have been a flop with the Germans, who dislike overstatement and ostentatiousness. According to one German expert, however, German businessmen have become accustomed to dealing with Americans. Although differences in body language and customs remain, the past 20 years have softened them. "I hugged an American woman at a business meeting last night," he said. "That would be normal in France, but [older] Germans still have difficulty [with the custom]." He says that calling secretaries by their first names would still be considered rude: "They have a right to be called by the surname. You'd certainly ask—and get—permission first." In Germany, people address each other formally and correctly: Someone with two doctorates (which is fairly common) must be referred to as "Herr Doktor Doktor."

When Harry Slicksmile grabbed his new Japanese acquaintance by the arm, the executive probably considered him disrespectful and presumptuous. Japan, like many Asian countries, is a "no-contact culture" where even shaking hands is an unusual experience. Harry made

matters worse by tossing his business card. Japanese people revere the business card as an extension of self and as an indicator of rank. They do not *hand* it to people, they *present* it—with both hands. In addition, the Japanese are sticklers about rank. Unlike Americans, they don't heap praise on subordinates in a room; they will praise only the highest-ranking official present.

Hapless Harry's last gaffe was assuming that Italians are like Hollywood's stereotypes of them. The flair for design and style that has characterized Italian culture for centuries is embodied in the businesspeople of Milan and Rome. They dress beautifully and admire flair, but they blanch at garishness or impropriety in others' attire.

In order to compete successfully in global markets, or even to deal effectively with international firms in their home markets, companies must help their managers to understand the needs, customs, and cultures of international business buyers. Here are additional examples of a few rules of social and business etiquette that managers should understand when doing business in another country.

- *France.* Dress conservatively, except in the south where more casual clothes are worn. Do not refer to people by their first names—the French are formal with strangers.
- *Germany.* Be especially punctual. An American businessman invited to someone's home should present

flowers, preferably unwrapped, to the hostess. During introductions, greet women first and wait until they extend their hands before extending yours.

- *Indonesia.* Learn how to sing at least one song. At the end of formal gatherings, people often take turns singing unaccompanied.
- *Italy.* Whether you dress conservatively or go native in a Giorgio Armani suit, keep in mind that Italian businesspeople are style conscious. Make appointments well in advance. Prepare for and be patient with Italian bureaucracies.
- *Japan.* Don't imitate Japanese bowing customs unless you understand them thoroughly—who bows to whom, how many times, and when. It's a complicated ritual. Presenting business cards is another ritual. Carry many cards, present them with both hands so your name can be easily read, and hand them to others in order of descending rank. Expect Japanese business executives to take time making decisions and to work through all of the details before making a commitment.
- *Saudi Arabia.* Although men will kiss each other in greeting, they will never kiss a woman in public. An American woman should wait for a man to extend his hand before offering hers. If a Saudi offers refreshment, accept—it is an insult to decline it.
- *United Kingdom.* Toasts are often given at formal dinners. If the host honors you with a toast, be prepared to reciprocate. Business entertaining is done more often at lunch than at dinner.

*Sources:* Adapted from Susan Harte, "When in Rome, You Should Learn to Do What the Romans Do," *The Atlanta Journal-Constitution,* January 22, 1990, pp. D1, D6. Also see Lufthansa's *Business Travel Guide/Europe;* Sergey Frank, "Global Negotiating," *Sales & Marketing Management,* May 1992, pp. 64–69; and Andrea L. Simpson, "Doing Business in Asia Pacific Requires New Skills," *Marketing News,* August 4, 1995, p. 4.

# THE BUSINESS BUYING PROCESS

Table 6-2 lists the eight stages of the business buying process.[9] Buyers who face a new-task buying situation usually go through all stages of the buying process. Buyers making modified or straight rebuys may skip some of the stages. We will examine these steps for the typical new-task buying situation.

## Problem Recognition

The buying process begins when someone in the company recognizes a problem or need that can be met by acquiring a specific product or service. **Problem recognition** can result from internal or external stimuli. Internally, the company may decide to launch a new product that requires new production equipment and materials. Or a machine may break down and need new parts. Perhaps a purchasing manager is unhappy with a current supplier's product quality, service, or prices. Externally, the buyer may get some new ideas at a trade show, see an ad, or receive a call from a salesperson who offers a better product or a lower price. In fact, in their advertising, business marketers often alert customers to potential problems and then show them how their products provide solutions.

## General Need Description

Having recognized a need, the buyer next prepares a **general need description** that lists the desired characteristics and quantity of the needed item. For standard items, this process presents few problems. For complex items, however, the buyer may have to work with others—engineers, users, consultants—to define the item. The team may want to rank the importance of reliability, durability, price, and other attributes desired in the item. In this phase, the alert business marketer can help the buyers define their needs and provide information about the value of different product characteristics.

## Product Specification

The buying organization next develops the item's technical **product specifications,** often with the help of a value analysis engineering team. **Value analysis** is an approach to cost reduction in which components are studied carefully to determine if they can be redesigned, standardized, or made by less costly methods of production. The team decides on the best product characteristics and specifies them accordingly. Sellers, too, can use value analysis as a tool to help secure a new account. By showing buyers a better way to make an object, outside sellers can turn straight rebuy situations into new-task situations that give them a chance to obtain new business.

## Supplier Search

The buyer now conducts a **supplier search** to find the best vendors. The buyer can compile a small list of qualified suppliers by reviewing trade directories, doing a computer search, or phoning other companies for recommendations. The newer the buying task, and the more complex and costly the item, the greater the amount of time the buyer will spend searching for suppliers. The supplier's task is to get listed in major directories and build a good reputation in the marketplace. Salespeople should watch for companies in the process of searching for suppliers and make certain that their firm is considered.

---

**Problem recognition**
The first stage of the business buying process in which someone in the company recognizes a problem or need that can be met by acquiring a product or a service.

**General need description**
The stage in the business buying process in which the company describes the general characteristics and quantity of a needed item.

**Product specification**
The stage of the business buying process in which the buying organization decides on and specifies the best technical product characteristics for a needed item.

**Value analysis**
An approach to cost reduction in which components are studied carefully to determine if they can be redesigned, standardized, or made by less costly methods of production.

**Supplier search**
The stage of the business buying process in which the buyer tries to find the best vendors.

**TABLE 6-2**   *Major Stages of the Business Buying Process in Relation to Major Buying Situations*

| Stages of the Buying Process | Buying Situations | | |
|---|---|---|---|
| | New Task | Modified Rebuy | Straight Rebuy |
| Problem recognition | Yes | Maybe | No |
| General need description | Yes | Maybe | No |
| Product specification | Yes | Yes | Yes |
| Supplier search | Yes | Maybe | No |
| Proposal solicitation | Yes | Maybe | No |
| Supplier selection | Yes | Maybe | No |
| Order routine specification | Yes | Maybe | No |
| Performance review | Yes | Yes | Yes |

*Source:* Adapted from Patrick J. Robinson, Charles W. Faris, and Yoram Wind, *Industrial Buying and Creative Marketing* (Boston: Allyn & Bacon, 1967), p. 14.

Many business buyers go to extremes in searching for and qualifying suppliers. Consider the hurdles that the Campbell Soup Company and Xerox have set up in qualifying suppliers:

The Campbell Qualified Supplier Program requires would-be suppliers to pass through three stages: qualified supplier, approved supplier, and select supplier. To become qualified, the supplier has to demonstrate technical capabilities, financial health, cost effectiveness, high quality standards, and innovativeness. A supplier that satisfies these criteria then applies for approval, which is granted only after the supplier has attended a Campbell Vendor Seminar, accepted an implementation team visit, and agreed to make certain changes and commitments. Once approved, the supplier becomes a select supplier only when it demonstrates high product uniformity, continuous quality improvement, and just-in-time delivery capabilities.

Xerox qualifies only suppliers who meet ISO 9000 international quality standards (see Chapter 2). But to win the company's top award—certification status—a supplier must first complete the Xerox Multinational Supplier Quality Survey. The survey requires the supplier to issue a quality assurance manual, adhere to continuous improvement principles, and demonstrate effective systems implementation. Once a supplier has been qualified, it must participate in Xerox's Continuous Supplier Involvement process, in which the two companies work together to create specifications for quality, cost, delivery times, and process capability. The final step toward certification requires a supplier to undergo additional quality training and an evaluation based on the same criteria as the Malcolm Baldrige National Quality Award. Not surprisingly, only 176 suppliers worldwide have achieved the 95 percent rating required for certification as a Xerox supplier.[10]

## Proposal Solicitation

**Proposal solicitation**
The stage of the business buying process in which the buyer invites qualified suppliers to submit proposals.

In the **proposal solicitation** stage of the business buying process, the buyer invites qualified suppliers to submit proposals. In response, some suppliers will send only a catalog or a salesperson. However, when the item is complex or expensive, the buyer will usually require detailed written proposals or formal presentations from each potential supplier.

Business marketers must be skilled in researching, writing, and presenting proposals in response to buyer proposal solicitations. Proposals should be marketing documents, not just technical documents. Presentations should inspire confidence and should make the marketer's company stand out from the competition.

## Supplier Selection

**Supplier selection**
The stage of the business buying process in which the buyer reviews proposals and selects a supplier or suppliers.

The members of the buying center now review the proposals and select a supplier or suppliers. During **supplier selection,** the buying center often will draw up a list of the desired supplier attributes and their relative importance. In one survey, purchasing executives listed the following attributes as most important in influencing the relationship between supplier and customer: quality products and services, on-time delivery, ethical corporate behavior, honest communication, and competitive prices.[11] Other important factors include repair and servicing capabilities, technical aid and advice, geographic location, performance history, and reputation. The members of the buying center will rate suppliers against these attributes and identify the best suppliers.

Buyers may attempt to negotiate with preferred suppliers for better prices and terms before making the final selections. In the end, they may select a single supplier or a few suppliers. Many buyers prefer multiple sources of supplies to avoid being totally dependent on one supplier and to allow comparisons of prices and performance of several suppliers over time.

## Order-Routine Specification

**Order-routine specifications**
The stage of the business buying process in which the buyer writes the final order with the chosen supplier(s), listing the technical specifications, quantity needed, expected time of delivery, return policies, and warranties.

The buyer now prepares an **order-routine specification.** It includes the final order with the chosen supplier or suppliers and lists items such as technical specifications, quantity needed, expected time of delivery, return policies, and warranties. In the case of maintenance, repair, and operating items, buyers may use *blanket contracts* rather than periodic purchase orders. A blanket contract creates a long-term relationship in which the supplier promises to resupply the buyer as needed at agreed prices for a set time period. The seller holds the stock, and the buyer's computer automatically prints out an order to the seller when stock is needed. A blanket order eliminates the expensive process of renegotiating a purchase each time that stock is required. It also allows buyers to write more, but smaller, purchase orders, resulting in lower inventory levels and carrying costs.

Blanket contracting leads to more single-source buying and to buying more items from that source. This practice locks the supplier in tighter with the buyer and makes it difficult for other suppliers to break in unless the buyer becomes dissatisfied with prices or service.

## Performance Review

**Performance review**
The stage of the business buying process in which the buyer rates its satisfaction with suppliers, deciding whether to continue, modify, or cancel them.

In this stage, the buyer reviews supplier performance. The buyer may contact users and ask them to rate their satisfaction. The **performance review** may lead the buyer to continue, modify, or cancel the arrangement. The seller's job is to monitor the same factors used by the buyer to make sure that the seller is giving the expected satisfaction.

We have described the stages that typically would occur in a new-task buying situation. The eight-stage model provides a simple view of the business buying decision process. The actual process is usually much more complex. In the modified rebuy or straight rebuy situation, some of these stages would be compressed or bypassed. Each organization buys in its own way, and each buying situation has unique requirements. Different buying center participants may be involved at different stages of the process. Although certain buying-process steps usually do occur, buyers do not always follow them in the same order, and they may add other steps. Often, buyers will repeat certain stages of the process.

# ▶INSTITUTIONAL AND GOVERNMENT MARKETS

So far, our discussion of organizational buying has focused largely on the buying behavior of business buyers. Much of this discussion also applies to the buying practices of institutional and government organizations. However, these two non-business markets have additional characteristics and needs. Thus, in this final section, we will address the special features of institutional and government markets.

## INSTITUTIONAL MARKETS

**Institutional market**
Schools, hospitals, nursing homes, prisons, and other institutions that provide goods and services to people in their care.

The **institutional market** consists of schools, hospitals, nursing homes, prisons, and other institutions that provide goods and services to people in their care. Institutions differ from one another in their sponsors and in their objectives. For example, Humana hospitals are run for profit, whereas a nonprofit Sisters of Charity Hospital provides health care to the poor, and a government-run hospital might provide special services to veterans.

Many institutional markets are characterized by low budgets and captive patrons. For example, hospital patients have little choice but to eat whatever food the hospital supplies. A hospital purchasing agent has to decide on the quality of food to buy for patients. Because the food is provided as a part of a total service package, the buying objective is not profit. Nor is strict cost minimization the goal; patients receiving poor-quality food will complain to others and damage the hospital's reputation. Thus, the hospital purchasing agent must search for institutional food vendors whose quality meets or exceeds a certain minimum standard and whose prices are low.

Many marketers set up separate divisions to meet the special characteristics and needs of institutional buyers. For example, Heinz produces, packages, and prices its ketchup and other products differently to better serve the requirements of hospitals, colleges, and other institutional markets.

## GOVERNMENT MARKETS

**Government market**
Governmental units—federal, state, and local—that purchase or rent goods and services for carrying out the main functions of government.

The **government market** offers large opportunities for many companies, both big and small. In most countries, government organizations are major buyers of goods and services. In the United States alone, federal, state, and local governments contain more than 82,000 buying units. Government buying and business buying are similar in many ways. But there are also differences that must be understood by companies that wish to sell products and services to governments. To succeed in the government market, sellers must locate key decision makers, identify the factors that affect buyer behavior, and understand the buying decision process.

Government organizations typically require suppliers to submit bids, and normally they award the contract to the lowest bidder. In some cases, the government unit makes allowance for the supplier's superior quality or reputation for completing contracts on time. Governments also buy on a negotiated contract basis, primarily in the case of complex projects involving major R&D costs and risks, and in cases where there is little competition.

Government organizations tend to favor domestic suppliers over foreign suppliers. A major complaint of multinationals operating in Europe is that each country shows favoritism toward its nationals in spite of superior offers that are made by foreign firms. The European Economic Commission is gradually removing this bias.

Like consumer and business buyers, government buyers are affected by environmental, organizational, interpersonal, and individual factors. One unique thing about government buying is that it is carefully watched by outside publics, ranging from Congress to a variety of private groups interested in how the government spends taxpayers' money. Because their spending decisions are subject to public review, government organizations require considerable paperwork from suppliers, who often complain about excessive paperwork, bureaucracy, regulations, decision-making delays, and frequent shifts in procurement personnel.

Most governments provide would-be suppliers with detailed guides describing how to sell to the government. For example, the U.S. Small Business Administration prints a booklet entitled *U.S. Government Purchasing, Specifications, and Sales Directory,* which lists thousands of items most frequently purchased by the government and the specific agencies most frequently buying them. The Government Printing Office issues the *Commerce Business Daily,* which lists major current and planned purchases and recent contract awards, both of which can provide leads to subcontracting markets. The Commerce Department publishes *Business America,* which provides interpretations of government policies and programs and gives concise information on potential worldwide trade opportunities. In several major cities, the General Services Administration operates *Business Service Centers* with staffs to provide a complete education on the way that government agencies buy, the steps that suppliers should follow, and the procurement opportunities available. Various trade magazines and associations provide information on how to reach schools, hospitals, highway departments, and other government agencies.

Still, suppliers have to master the system and find ways to cut through the red tape. For example, the U.S. government has always been ADI Technology Corporations's most important client—federal contracts account for about 90 percent of its nearly $6 million in annual revenues. Yet managers at this small professional services company often shake their heads at all the work that goes into winning the coveted government contracts. A comprehensive bid proposal runs from 500 to 700 pages because of federal paperwork requirements. And the company's president estimates that the firm has spent as much as $20,000, mostly in worker hours, to prepare a single bid proposal. Fortunately, government buying reforms are being put in place that will simplify contracting procedures and make bidding more attractive, particularly to smaller vendors. These reforms include more emphasis on buying commercial off-the-shelf items instead of items built to the government's specs, using on-line communication with vendors to eliminate the massive paperwork, and holding a "debriefing" by the appropriate government agency explaining to vendors why they lost a bid, enabling them to increase their chances of winning the next time around.[12]

Noneconomic criteria also play a growing role in government buying. Government buyers are asked to favor depressed business firms and areas; small business firms; minority-owned firms; and business firms that avoid race, sex, or age discrimination. Sellers need to keep these factors in mind when deciding to seek government business.

Many companies that sell to the government have not been marketing oriented for a number of reasons. Total government spending is determined by elected officials rather than by any business effort to develop this market. Government buying has emphasized price, making suppliers invest their effort in technology to bring costs down. When the product's characteristics are specified carefully, product differentiation is not a marketing factor. Nor do advertising or personal selling matter much in winning bids on an open-bid basis.

Several companies, however, have established separate government marketing departments. Rockwell, Kodak, and Goodyear are examples. These companies anticipate government needs and projects, participate in the product specification phase, gather competitive intelligence, prepare bids carefully, and produce stronger communications to describe and enhance their companies' reputations.[13]

## SUMMARY

The business market is vast. In many ways, business markets are like consumer markets, but business markets usually have fewer, larger buyers who are more geographically concentrated. Business demand is *derived*, largely *inelastic*, and more *fluctuating*. More buyers usually are involved in the business buying decision, and business buyers are better trained and more professional than are consumer buyers. In general, business purchasing decisions are more complex, and the buying process is more formal than consumer buying.

The *business market* includes firms that buy goods and services in order to produce products and services to sell to others. It also includes retailing and wholesaling firms that buy goods in order to resell them at a profit. Business buyers make decisions that vary with the three types of buying situations: *straight rebuys, modified rebuys,* and *new tasks.* The decision-making unit of a buying organization—the *buying center*—may consist of many

persons playing many roles. The business marketer needs to know the following: Who are the major participants? In what decisions do they exercise influence? What is their relative degree of influence? What evaluation criteria does each decision participant use? The business marketer also needs to understand the major environmental, interpersonal, and individual influences on the buying process. The business buying decision process itself consists of eight stages: *problem recognition, general need description, product specification, supplier search, proposal solicitation, supplier selection, order-routine specification,* and *performance review.* As business buyers become more sophisticated, business marketers must keep in step by upgrading their marketing accordingly.

The *institutional market* consists of schools, hospitals, prisons, and other institutions that provide goods and services to people in their care. These markets are characterized by low budgets and captive patrons. The *government market* is also vast. Government buyers purchase products and services for defense, education, public welfare, and other public needs. Government buying practices are highly specialized and specified, with open bidding or negotiated contracts characterizing most of the buying. Government buyers operate under the watchful eye of Congress and many private watchdog groups. Hence, they tend to require more forms and signatures and to respond more slowly in placing orders.

## KEY TERMS

Business market

Business buying process

Buying center

Derived demand

General need description

Government market

Institutional market

Modified rebuy

New task

Order-routine specification

Performance review

Problem recognition

Product specification

Proposal solicitation

Straight rebuy

Supplier search

Supplier selection

Systems buying

Value analysis

## QUESTIONS FOR DISCUSSION

1. In what ways can your school be considered an industrial marketer? What are its products and who are its customers?

2. Which of the major types of buying situations are represented by the following?

   ◆ Chrysler's purchase of computers that go in cars and adjust engine performance to changing driving conditions.

   ◆ Volkswagen's purchase of spark plugs for its line of vans.

   ◆ Honda's purchase of light bulbs for a new Acura model.

3. How could a marketer of office equipment identify the buying center for a law firm's purchase of dictation equipment for each of its partners?

4. Assume that you are selling a fleet of cars to be used by a company's sales force. The salespeople need larger cars, which are more profitable for you, but the fleet buyer wants to buy smaller cars. Who might be in the buying center? How might you meet the varying needs of these participants?

5. What are the advantages and disadvantages of buying from single suppliers versus multiple suppliers?

6. Do you agree or disagree with the following statement: Government red tape puts an unfair burden on small businesses involved in selling goods and services to the government.

## APPLYING THE CONCEPTS

1. Many companies that were formerly vertically integrated, producing their own raw materials or parts, are now using outside suppliers to produce them instead. The extreme examples of this practice, such as Dell Computer, own no production facilities and have suppliers make everything to order. This type of company has been nicknamed a "virtual corporation."

   ◆ Determine whether you think that buyers and suppliers are likely to be closer or more adversarial in this type of corporate structure.

   ◆ Name the advantages and disadvantages of this sort of supplier relationship for (a) the buyer and (b) the supplier.

2. American corporations are working to improve quality, and many are using techniques such as

continuous quality improvement (CQI). A major element of CQI is *feedback;* when defects are discovered, the cause of the problem is identified, and changes are made to prevent problems in the future.

◆ List some of the ways using CQI might affect the relationship and information flow between buyers and suppliers.

◆ Using CQI also means that purchasing agents become responsible for quality as well as costs. How does this change the role of the purchasing department within the firm?

## REFERENCES

1. Portions adapted from Thomas V. Bonoma, "Major Sales: Who Really Does the Buying," *Harvard Business Review,* May–June 1982. Copyright © 1982 by the President and Fellows of Harvard College; all rights reserved. Quote from John Huey, "The Absolute Best Way to Fly," *Fortune,* May 30, 1994, pp. 121–28. Also see William C. Symonds and David Greisling, "A Dogfight Over 950 Customers," *Business Week,* February 6, 1995.

2. See James C. Anderson and James A. Narus, "Value-Based Segmentation, Targeting, and Relationship-Building in Business Markets," ISBM Report #12-1989, The Institute for the Study of Business Markets, Pennsylvania State University, University Park, PA, 1989; Lawrence A. Crosby, Kenneth R. Evans, and Deborah Cowles, "Relationship Quality and Services Selling: An Interpersonal Influence Perspective," *Journal of Marketing,* July 1990, pp. 68–81; Minda Zetlin, "It's All the Same to Me," *Sales & Marketing Management,* February 1994, pp. 71–75; and Rahul Jacob, "Why Some Customers Are More Equal than Others," *Fortune,* September 19, 1994, pp. 215–24.

3. Patrick J. Robinson, Charles W. Faris, and Yoram Wind, *Industrial Buying Behavior and Creative Marketing* (Boston: Allyn & Bacon, 1967). Also see Erin Anderson, Weyien Chu, and Barton Weitz, "Industrial Purchasing: An Empirical Exploration of the Buyclass Framework," *Journal of Marketing,* July 1987, pp. 71–86.

4. For more on systems selling, see Robert R. Reeder, Edward G. Brierty, and Betty H. Reeder, *Industrial Marketing: Analysis, Planning, and Control* (Englewood Cliffs, NJ: Prentice Hall, 1991), pp. 264–67.

5. For results of both surveys, see "I Think You Have a Great Product, But It's Not My Decision," *American Salesman,* April 1994, pp. 11–13. For more on influence strategies within buying centers, see R. Venkatesh, Ajay K. Kohli, and Gerald Zaltman, "Influence Strategies in Buying Centers," *Journal of Marketing,* October 1995, pp. 71–82.

6. Melvin R. Matson and Esmail Salshi-Sangari, "Decision Making in Purchases of Equipment and Materials: A Four-Country Comparison," *International Journal of Physical Distribution & Logistics Management,* Vol. 23, No. 8, 1993, pp. 16–30.

7. Frederick E. Webster, Jr., and Yoram Wind, *Organizational Buying Behavior* (Englewood Cliffs, NJ: Prentice Hall, 1972), pp. 33–37.

8. Bonoma, "Major Sales," p. 114. Also see Ajay Kohli, "Determinants of Influence in Organizational Buying: A Contingency Approach," *Journal of Marketing,* July 1989, pp. 50–65.

9. Robinson, Faris, and Wind, *Industrial Buying Behavior,* p. 14.

10. See "Xerox Multinational Supplier Quality Survey," *Purchasing,* January 1995, p. 112.

11. See "What Buyers Really Want," *Sales & Marketing Management,* October 1989, p. 30; and M. Bixby Cooper, Cornelia Droge, and Patricia J. Daugherty, "How Buyers and Operations Personnel Evaluate Service," *Industrial Marketing Management,* 20, no. 1, 1991, pp. 81–90.

12. Laura M. Litvan, "Selling to Uncle Sam: New, Easier Rules," *Nation's Business,* March 1995, pp. 46–48.

13. For more on U.S. government buying, see Don Hill, "Who Says Uncle Sam's a Tough Sell?" *Sales & Marketing Management,* July 1988, pp. 56–60; Daniel Gottlieb, "Procurement Reform Finally Passes," *Purchasing,* October 6, 1994, p. 19; and Richard J. Wall and Carolyn M. Jones, "Navigating the Rugged Terrain of Government Contracts," *Internal Auditor,* April 1995, p. 32.

# *Market Segmentation, Targeting, and Positioning for Competitive Advantage*

**P**rocter & Gamble makes eleven brands of laundry detergent (Tide, Cheer, Bold, Gain, Era, Dash, Oxydol, Solo, Dreft, Ivory Snow, and Ariel). It also sells eight brands of hand soap (Zest, Coast, Ivory, Safeguard, Camay, Oil of Olay, Kirk's, and Lava); six shampoos (Prell, Head & Shoulders, Ivory, Pert, Pantene, and Vidal Sassoon); four brands each of liquid dishwashing detergents (Joy, Ivory, Dawn, and Liquid Cascade), toothpaste (Crest, Gleam, Complete, and Denquel), and cof-

fee (Folger's, High Point, Butternut, and Maryland Club); three brands each of floor cleaner (Spic & Span, Top Job, and Mr. Clean) and toilet tissue (Charmin, Banner, and Summit); and two brands each of deodorant (Secret and Sure), cooking oil (Crisco and Puritan), fabric softener (Downy and Bounce), and disposable diapers (Pampers and Luvs). Moreover, many of the brands are offered in several sizes and formulations (for example, you can buy large or small packages of powdered or liquid Tide in any of three forms—regular, unscented, or with bleach).

These P&G brands compete with one another on the same supermarket shelves. But why would P&G introduce several brands in one category instead of concentrating its resources on a single leading brand? The answer lies in the fact that different people want different *mixes of benefits* from the products they buy. Take laundry detergents as an example. People use laundry detergents to get their clothes clean. But they also want other things from their detergents, such as economy, bleaching power, fabric softening, fresh smell, strength or mildness, and lots of suds. We all want *some* of every one of these benefits from our detergent, but we may have different *priorities* for each benefit. To some people, cleaning and bleaching power are most important; to others, fabric softening matters most; still others want a mild, fresh-scented detergent. Thus, there are groups—or segments—of laundry detergent buyers, and each segment seeks a special combination of benefits.

Procter & Gamble has identified at least eleven important laundry detergent segments, along with numerous subsegments, and has developed a different brand designed to meet the special needs of each. The eleven P&G brands are positioned for different segments as follows:

- *Tide* is "so powerful, it cleans down to the fiber." It's the all-purpose family detergent for extra-tough laundry jobs. "Tide's in, dirt's out." *Tide with Bleach* is "so powerful, it whitens down to the fiber."

- *Cheer with Color Guard* gives "outstanding cleaning *and* color protection. So your family's clothes look clean, bright, and more like new." Cheer is also specially formulated for use in hot, warm, or cold water—it's "all tempera-Cheer." *Cheer Free* is "dermatologist tested . . . contains no irritating perfume or dye."

- *Bold* is the detergent with fabric softener. It "cleans, softens, and controls static." *Bold Liquid* adds "the fresh fabric softener scent."

- *Gain,* originally P&G's "enzyme" detergent, was repositioned as the detergent that gives you clean, fresh-smelling clothes—it "freshens like sunshine."

- *Era* has "built-in stain removers." It "gets tough stains out and does a great job on your whole wash too."

- *Dash* is P&G's value entry. It "attacks tough dirt," but "Dash does it for a great low price."

- *Oxydol* contains bleach. It "makes your white clothes really white and your colored clothes really bright. So don't reach for the bleach—grab a box of Ox!"

- *Solo* contains detergent and fabric softener in liquid form. It's targeted heavily toward the Northeast, a strong liquid detergent market.

- *Dreft* is also formulated for baby's diapers and clothes. It contains borax, "nature's natural sweetener" for "a clean you can trust."

- *Ivory Snow* is "Ninety-nine and forty-four one hundredths percent pure." It's the "mild, gentle soap for diapers and baby clothes."

- *Ariel* is a tough cleaner targeted to the Hispanic market. It's also the number one brand in Mexico and P&G's major brand in Europe.

By segmenting the market and having several detergent brands, P&G has an attractive offering for consumers in all important preference groups. All its brands combined capture more than a 53 percent share of the $3.2 billion U.S. laundry detergent market—much more than any single brand could obtain by itself. ■

# C H A P T E R   O B J E C T I V E S

## *After reading this chapter, you should be able to:*

**1** Define *market segmentation, market targeting,* and *market positioning.*

**2** List and discuss the major bases for segmenting consumer and business markets.

 **3** Explain how companies identify attractive market segments and choose a market-coverage strategy.

 **4** Explain how companies can position their products for maximum competitive advantage in the marketplace.

# ▶MARKETS

The term *market* has acquired many meanings over the years. In its original meaning, a market is a physical place where buyers and sellers gather to exchange goods and services. Medieval towns had market squares where sellers brought their goods and buyers shopped for goods. In today's cities, buying and selling occur in shopping areas rather than markets. To an economist, a market describes all the buyers and sellers who transact over some good or service. Thus, the soft-drink market consists of sellers such as Coca-Cola and PepsiCo, and of all the consumers who buy soft drinks. To a marketer, a **market** is the set of all actual and potential buyers of a product or service.

**Market**
The set of all actual and potential buyers of a product or service.

Organizations that sell to consumer and business markets recognize that they cannot appeal to all buyers in those markets, or at least not to all buyers in the same way. Buyers are too numerous, too widely scattered, and too varied in their needs and buying practices. And different companies vary widely in their abilities to serve different segments of the market. Rather than trying to compete in an entire market, sometimes against superior competitors, each company must identify the parts of the market that it can serve best.

Sellers have not always practiced this philosophy. Their thinking has passed through three stages:

◆ *Mass marketing.* In mass marketing, the seller mass produces, mass distributes, and mass promotes one product to all buyers. At one time, Coca-Cola produced only one drink for the whole market, hoping that it would appeal to everyone. The argument for mass marketing is that it should lead to the lowest costs and prices and create the largest potential market.

◆ *Product-variety marketing.* Here, the seller produces two or more products that have different features, styles, quality, sizes, and so on. Later, Coca-Cola produced several soft drinks packaged in different sizes and containers that were designed to offer variety to buyers rather than to appeal to different market segments. The argument for product-variety marketing is that consumers have different tastes that change over time. Consumers seek variety and change.

◆ *Target marketing.* Here, the seller identifies market segments, selects one or more of them, and develops products and marketing mixes tailored to each. For example, Coca-Cola now produces soft drinks for the sugared-cola segment (Coca-Cola Classic and Cherry Coke), the diet segment (Diet Coke and Tab), the no-caffeine segment (Caffeine-Free Coke), and the noncola segment (Minute Maid sodas).

Today's companies are moving away from mass marketing and product-variety marketing and toward target marketing. Target marketing can better help sellers find their marketing opportunities. Sellers can develop the right product for each target market and adjust their prices, distribution channels, and advertising to reach the target market efficiently. Instead of scattering their marketing efforts (the "shotgun" approach), they can focus on the buyers who have greater purchase interest (the "rifle" approach).

**Micromarketing**
A form of target marketing in which companies tailor their marketing programs to the needs and wants of narrowly defined geographic, demographic, psychographic, or behavioral segments.

As a result of the increasing fragmentation of American mass markets into hundreds of micromarkets, each with different needs and lifestyles, target marketing is increasingly taking the form of **micromarketing**. Using micromarketing, companies tailor their marketing programs to the needs and wants of narrowly

**Market segmentation**
Dividing a market into distinct groups of buyers with different needs, characteristics, or behavior who might require separate products or marketing mixes.

**Market targeting**
The process of evaluating each market segment's attractiveness and selecting one or more segments to enter.

defined geographic, demographic, psychographic, or behavioral segments. The ultimate form of target marketing is *customized marketing* in which the company adapts its product and marketing program to the needs of a specific customer or buying organization (see Marketing at Work 7-1). Smart companies are moving rapidly into micromarketing, often called niche marketing. As an advertising agency executive observed: "There will be no market for products that everybody likes a little, only for products that somebody likes a lot."[1] Other experts assert that companies will have to "niche or be niched."[2]

Figure 7-1 shows the three major steps in target marketing. The first is **market segmentation**—dividing a market into distinct groups of buyers with different needs, characteristics, or behaviors who might require separate products or marketing mixes. The company identifies different ways to segment the market and develops profiles of the resulting market segments. The second step is **market targeting**—evaluating each market segment's attractiveness and selecting one or more of the market segments to enter. The third step is **market positioning**—setting the competitive positioning for the product and creating a detailed marketing mix.

# ▶MARKET SEGMENTATION

**Market positioning**
Formulating competitive positioning for a product and creating a detailed marketing mix.

Markets consist of buyers, and buyers differ in one or more ways. They may differ in their wants, resources, locations, buying attitudes, and buying practices. Because buyers have unique needs and wants, each buyer is potentially a separate market. Ideally, then, a seller might design a separate marketing program for each buyer. For example, Boeing manufactures airplanes for only a few major buyers and customizes its products and marketing program to satisfy each specific customer.

However, most sellers face larger numbers of smaller buyers and do not find complete segmentation worthwhile. Instead, they look for broad *classes* of buyers who differ in their product needs or buying responses. For example, General Motors has found that high- and low-income groups differ in their car-buying needs and wants. It also knows that young consumers' needs and wants differ

**FIGURE 7-1**
*Steps in market segmentation, targeting, and positioning*

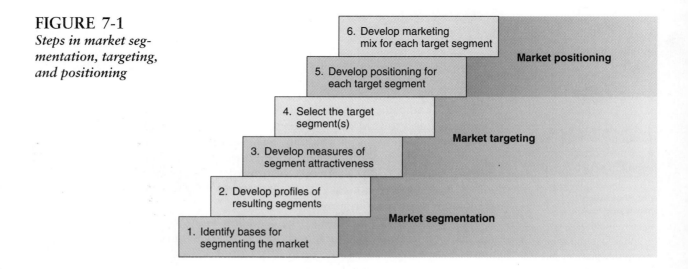

from those of older consumers. Thus, GM has designed specific models for different income and age groups. In fact, it sells models for segments with varied *combinations* of age and income. For instance, GM designed its Buick Park Avenue for older, higher-income consumers. Age and income are only two of many bases that companies use for segmenting their markets.

## BASES FOR SEGMENTING CONSUMER MARKETS

There is no single way to segment a market. A marketer has to try different segmentation variables, alone and in combination, to find the best way to view the market structure. Table 7-1 outlines the major variables that might be used in segmenting consumer markets. Here we look at the major *geographic, demographic, psychographic,* and *behavioral variables.*

### Geographic Segmentation

**Geograpic segmentation**
Dividing a market into different geographical units such as nations, states, regions, counties, cities, or neighborhoods.

**Geographic segmentation** calls for dividing the market into different geographical units such as nations, regions, states, counties, cities, or neighborhoods. A company may decide to operate in one or a few geographical areas, or to operate in all areas but pay attention to geographical differences in needs and wants.

Many companies today are localizing their products, advertising, promotion, and sales efforts to fit the needs of individual regions, cities, and even neighborhoods. For example, Campbell sells Cajun gumbo soup in Louisiana and Mississippi, and makes its nacho cheese soup spicier in Texas and California. P&G sells Ariel laundry detergent primarily in Los Angeles, San Diego, San Francisco, Miami, and south Texas, areas with larger concentrations of Hispanic consumers.[3]

*Geographic segmentation: Fleeing the fiercely competitive major cities, Hampton Inn is setting up smaller units in small-town America. This Hampton Inn has 54 rooms instead of the usual 135.*

## MARKETING AT WORK 7-1

# MICROMARKETING: A NEW MARKETING ERA

For most of this century, major consumer-products companies have held fast to mass marketing principles, marketing the same set of products in about the same way to all consumers. But many are now using a new approach—*micromarketing*. Instead of using standardized marketing, they are tailoring their products and programs to suit the tastes of specific geographic, demographic, psychographic, and behavioral segments.

Several factors have fueled the move toward micromarketing. First, the world's mass markets have slowly broken down into a profusion of smaller micromarkets—the baby boomer segment here, the Generation Xers there; here the Hispanic market, there the African American market; here working women, there single parents; here the Sun Belt, there the Rust Belt. Today, marketers find it very hard to create a single product or program that appeals to all of these diverse groups.

Second, improved information and marketing research technologies have also spurred micromarketing. For example, retail store scanners now allow instant tracking of product sales from store to store, helping companies pinpoint exactly which specific segments are buying what.

Third, scanners give retailers mountains of market information, and this information gives

them more power over manufacturers. Retailers generally prefer localized promotions targeted toward the characteristics of consumers in their own cities and neighborhoods. Thus, to keep retailers happy, and to get precious retail shelf space for their products, manufacturers must now do more micromarketing.

One of the most common forms of micromarketing is *regionalization*—tailoring brands and promotions to suit individual geographic regions, cities, and even neighborhoods or specific stores. Campbell Soup, a pioneer in regionalization, has created many successful regional brands.

For example, it sells spicy Ranchero beans, Brunswick stew, and spicy hot chili in the Southwest, Cajun gumbo soup in the South, and red bean soup in Hispanic areas. Wal-Mart also adjusts its supercenter merchandise offerings to match the needs and preferences of consumers in different locations. For example, in Canton, Texas, which is surrounded by numerous recreational lakes, Wal-Mart's supercenter allots vastly more space to fishing supplies and boating equipment. In Panama City Beach, Florida, Wal-Mart offers a larger selection of live plants and trees.

*Mass customization: With its new Personal Pair jeans program, Levi Strauss & Co. uses in-store computers to create jeans cut to the customer's measurements.*

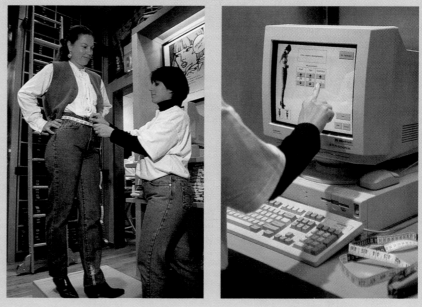

Beyond regionalization, companies are also targeting specific demographic, psychographic, and behavioral micromarkets. For example, for its Crest toothpaste, Procter & Gamble employs six separate advertising campaigns targeting different age and ethnic segments including children, African Americans, and Hispanics. To reach these and other micromarkets, Procter & Gamble uses highly focused media, such as cable television, direct mail, event sponsorships, electronic point-of-purchase media, and advertising display boards in such varied locations as doctors' and dentists' waiting rooms or elementary and high school cafeterias.

In the extreme, micromarketing becomes *mass customization*—serving large numbers of customers, but giving each exactly what he or she wants. Marketers now are experimenting with new systems for providing customized products and services that range from hotel stays and furniture to clothing and bicycles. For example, Ritz-Carlton makes a computerized record of individual guest preferences available to every one of its 28 hotels. If a guest asked for a foam pillow the last time that she stayed at the Ritz in Montreal, there will be one waiting for her months or even years later when she checks into the Ritz in Atlanta.

Software Sportswear, of Greenwich, Connecticut, makes customized swimsuits using a video monitor and special computer software. A computer, linked to a camera, calculates the customer's measurements and prints out a custom-fitted pattern for a bathing suit. The video screen shows the bedazzled and delighted buyer how the new suit will look on her from the front, side, and rear. The buyer chooses the fabric from about 150 samples, the custom-made design is sent to the producer's tailors, and the suit is stitched up in about a week. Levi Strauss & Co. recently launched a similar program, its Personal Pair jeans program for women, in which in-store computers create jeans that are cut to a specific customer's measurements.

Another example is the National Industrial Bicycle Company in Japan (the Panasonic brand in the United States) that uses flexible manufacturing to turn out large numbers of bikes specially fitted to the needs of individual buyers. Customers visit their local bike shop where the shopkeeper measures them on a special frame and faxes the specifications to the factory. At the factory, the measurements are punched into a computer, which creates blueprints in three minutes that would take a draftsman 60 times that long. The computer then guides robots and workers through the production process. The factory is ready to produce any of 18 million variations on 18 bicycle models in 199 color patterns and about as many sizes as there are people. The price is steep—between $545 and $3,200—but within two weeks the buyer is riding a custom-made, one-of-a-kind machine.

Business-to-business marketers are also finding new ways to customize their offerings. For example, Motorola salespeople now use a hand-held computer to custom-design pagers following customer wishes. The design data are transmitted to the Motorola factory, and production starts within 17 minutes. The customized pagers are ready for shipment within two hours.

Although micromarketing offers much promise, it also presents some problems. Trying to serve dozens or even hundreds of diverse micromarkets is vastly more complex than mass marketing. And offering many different products and promotion programs results in higher manufacturing and marketing costs. Despite these problems, most marketers agree that micromarketing signals the start of a whole new marketing era. Gone are the days, they say, when a company can effectively market one product to masses of consumers using a single promotion program.

*Sources:* See B. Joseph Pine, *Mass Customization* (Boston: Harvard Business School Press, 1993); Roberta Maynard, "Tailoring Products for a Niche of One," *Nation's Business,* November 1993, p. 42; Alice Z. Cuneo, "Levi Strauss Sizes the Retail Scene," *Advertising Age,* January 22, 1995, p. 4; B. Joseph Pine, Don Peppers, and Martha Rogers, "Do You Want to Keep Your Customers Forever?" *Harvard Business Review,* March–April 1995, pp. 103–14; Don Peppers, "Digitizing Desire, Part Two," *Forbes,* April 10, 1995, p. 76.

**TABLE 7-1** *Major Segmentation Variables for Consumer Markets*

*Geographic*

| | |
|---|---|
| World region or country | North America, Western Europe, Middle East, Pacific Rim, China, India, Canada, Mexico |
| Country region | Pacific, Mountain, West North Central, West South Central, East North Central, East South Central, South Atlantic, Middle Atlantic, New England |
| City or metro size | Under 5,000; 5,000–20,000; 20,000–50,000; 50,000–100,000; 100,000–250,000; 250,000–500,000; 500,000–1,000,000; 1,000,000–4,000,000; 4,000,000 or over |
| Density | Urban, suburban, rural |
| Climate | Northern, southern |

*Demographic*

| | |
|---|---|
| Age | Under 6, 6–11, 12–19, 20–34, 35–49, 50–64, 65+ |
| Gender | Male, female |
| Family size | 1–2, 3–4, 5+ |
| Family life cycle | Young, single; young, married, no children; young, married with children; older, married with children; older, married, no children under 18; older, single; other |
| Income | Under $10,000; $10,000–$20,000; $20,000–$30,000; $30,000–$50,000; $50,000–$100,000; $100,000 and over |
| Occupation | Professional and technical; managers, officials, and proprietors; clerical, sales; craftspeople; foremen; operatives; farmers; retired; students; homemakers; unemployed |
| Education | Grade school or less; some high school; high school graduate; some college; college graduate |
| Religion | Catholic, Protestant, Jewish, Muslim, Hindu, other |
| Race | White, African American, Asian, Hispanic |
| Nationality | North American, South American, British, French, German, Italian, Japanese |

*Psychographic*

| | |
|---|---|
| Social class | Lower lowers, upper lowers, working class, middle class, upper middles, lower uppers, upper uppers |
| Lifestyle | Achievers, strivers, strugglers |
| Personality | Compulsive, gregarious, authoritarian, ambitious |

*Behavioral*

| | |
|---|---|
| Occasions | Regular occasion, special occasion |
| Benefits | Quality, service, economy, convenience, speed |
| User status | Nonuser, ex-user, potential user, first-time user, regular user |
| Usage rate | Light user, medium user, heavy user |
| Loyalty status | None, medium, strong, absolute |
| Readiness stage | Unaware, aware, informed, interested, desirous, intending to buy |
| Attitude toward product | Enthusiastic, positive, indifferent, negative, hostile |

Other companies are seeking to cultivate as-yet untapped territory. For example, many large companies are fleeing the fiercely competitive major cities and suburbs to set up shop in small-town America. Hampton Inns has opened a chain of smaller-format motels in towns too small for its standard-sized units. For example, Townsend, Tennessee, with a population of only 329, is small even by small-town standards. But looks can be deceiving. Situated on a heavily traveled and picturesque route between Knoxville and the Smoky Mountains, the village serves both business and vacation travelers. Hampton Inns opened a unit in Townsend and plans to open 100 more in small towns. It costs less to operate in these towns, and the company builds smaller units to match lower volume. The Townsend Hampton Inn, for example, has 54 rooms instead of the usual 135.[4]

## Demographic Segmentation

**Demographic segmentation** consists of dividing the market into groups based on variables such as age, gender, family size, family life cycle, income, occupation, education, religion, race, and nationality. Demographic factors are the most popular bases for segmenting customer groups. One reason is that consumer needs, wants, and usage rates often vary closely with demographic variables. Another is that demographic variables are easier to measure than most other types of variables. Even when market segments are first defined using other bases, such as personality or behavior, their demographic characteristics must be known in order to assess the size of the target market and to reach it efficiently.

### AGE AND LIFE-CYCLE STAGE

Consumer needs and wants change with age. Some companies use **age and life-cycle segmentation,** offering different products or using different marketing

**Demographic segmentation**
Dividing the market into groups based on demographic variables such as age, sex, family size, family life cycle, income, occupation, education, religion, race, and nationality.

**Age and life-cycle segmentation**
Dividing a market into different age and life-cycle groups.

*Demographic segmentation: Johnson & Johnson targets children with Band-Aid Sesame Street Bandages; Big Bird and Cookie Monster "help turn little people's tears into great big smiles." Toyota is marketing to women who "aren't only working hard, they're playing hard."*

approaches for different age and life-cycle groups. For example, many companies now use different products and appeals to target teens, Generation Xers, baby boomers, or mature consumers. Mazda targets its 929 model at baby boomers, using conservative advertising cues—women in pearls, classical music—and themes of luxury and safety. In contrast, Mazda aims its MX-3 at Generation Xers, using bright colors, loud music, and the pitch that it has taken the "plain old apple pie car and replaced it with a jalapeño."[5] McDonald's targets children, teens, adults, and seniors with different ads and media. Its ads to teens feature dance-beat music, adventure, and fast-paced cutting from scene to scene; ads to seniors are softer and more sentimental.

However, marketers must be careful to guard against stereotypes when using age and life-cycle segmentation. Although you might find some 70-year-olds in wheelchairs, you will find others on tennis courts. Similarly, whereas some 40-year-old couples are sending their children off to college, others are just beginning new families. Thus, age is often a poor predictor of a person's life cycle, health, work or family status, needs, and buying power.

**Gender segmentation**
Dividing a market into different groups based on sex.

**GENDER.** **Gender segmentation** has long been used in clothing, cosmetics, and magazines. Recently, other marketers have noticed opportunities for gender segmentation. For example, although early deodorants were used by both sexes, many producers are now featuring brands for a single sex. Procter & Gamble was among the first with Secret, a brand specially formulated for a woman's chemistry, packaged and advertised to reinforce the female image.

The automobile industry also uses gender segmentation extensively. Women buy half of all new cars sold in the United States and influence 80 percent of all new-car purchasing decisions. By the year 2000, women will purchase an estimated 60 percent of all new cars. Thus, women have become a valued target market for the auto companies. "Selling to women should be no different than selling to men," notes one analyst. "But there are subtleties that make a difference."[6] Women have different frames, less upper-body strength, and greater safety concerns. To address these issues, automakers are designing cars with hoods and trunks that are easier to open, seats that are easier to adjust, and seat belts that fit women better. They've also intensified their safety focus, emphasizing features such as air bags and remote door locks.

In advertising, more and more car manufacturers are targeting women directly. In contrast to the car advertising of past decades, these ads portray women as competent and knowledgeable consumers who are interested in what a car is all about, not just the color. For example, in one Pontiac ad, a savvy young woman brings her brother to a dealership to help her pick a color for her new car. In another, "a woman daydreams about a romantic ride with an attractive male, wending along a coastal highway that brings them to an elegant restaurant. She's driving."[7]

**Income segmentation**
Dividing a market into different income groups.

**INCOME.** **Income segmentation** has long been used by the marketers of products and services such as automobiles, boats, clothing, cosmetics, financial services, and travel. Many companies target affluent consumers with luxury goods and convenience services. Stores like Neiman Marcus pitch everything from expensive jewelry and fine fashions to glazed Australian apricots priced at $20 a pound.[8] American Express offers not only green cards but gold cards, corporate cards, and even platinum cards aimed at different customer income and spending groups. Ramada Inns offers a wide variety of lodgings: Ramada Limited for economy travelers, Ramada Inn for those seeking a mid-priced, full-service hotel, and Ramada Plaza offering upper-mid-priced lodgings. For those willing to pay more and seeking even higher levels of service, Ramada Hotels offer three-star service and Ramada Renaissance hotels offer four-star accommodations.

However, not all companies that use income segmentation target the affluent. About 40 percent of U.S. households have incomes of $25,000 or less. Despite their lower spending power, the nation's 40 million lower-income households offer an attractive market to many marketers. Many companies, such as Family Dollar stores, profitably target lower-income consumers. When Family Dollar real estate experts scout locations for new stores, they look for lower-middle-class neighborhoods where people wear less expensive shoes and drive old cars that drip a lot of oil. The income of a typical Family Dollar customer rarely exceeds $17,000 a year, and the average customer spends only about $6 per trip to the store. Yet the store's low-income strategy has made it one of the most profitable discount chains in the country. Chase Manhattan Bank is even opening up accounts for and issuing credit cards to homeless war veterans who live in New York. Some 350 vets have opened accounts with a combined balance of more than $2 million (largely because of lump-sum benefits they receive for injuries).[9]

### Psychographic Segmentation

**Psychographic segmentation** divides buyers into different groups based on social class, lifestyle, or personality characteristics. People in the same demographic group can have very different psychographic makeups.

**Psychographic segmentation**
Dividing a market into different groups based on social class, lifestyle, or personality characteristics.

*Lifestyle segmentation: Duck Head targets a casual student lifestyle, claiming, "You can't get them old until you get them new."*

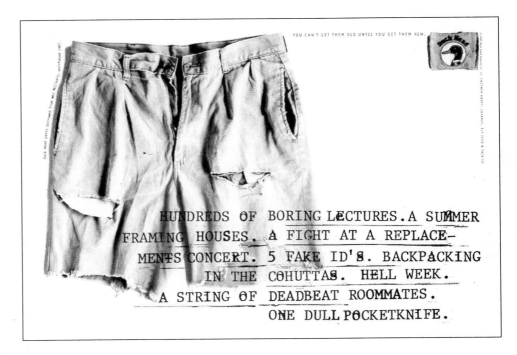

YOU CAN'T GET THEM OLD UNTIL YOU GET THEM NEW.

HUNDREDS OF BORING LECTURES. A SUMMER FRAMING HOUSES. A FIGHT AT A REPLACEMENTS CONCERT. 5 FAKE ID'S. BACKPACKING IN THE COHUTTAS. HELL WEEK. A STRING OF DEADBEAT ROOMMATES. ONE DULL POCKETKNIFE.

In Chapter 5, we described American *social classes* and showed that social class has a strong effect on preferences in cars, clothes, home furnishings, leisure activities, reading habits, and retailers. Many companies design products or services for specific social classes, building in features that appeal to these classes.

In Chapter 5, we also discussed how the products that people buy reflect their *lifestyles*. Marketers are increasingly segmenting their markets by consumer lifestyles. For example, Duck Head apparel targets a casual student lifestyle, claiming "You can't get them old until you get them new." *Redbook* magazine targets a lifestyle segment it calls "*Redbook* Jugglers," defined as 25- to 44-year-old women who must juggle husband, family, home, and job. According to a recent *Redbook* ad, "She's a product of the 'me generation,' the thirty-something woman who balances home, family, and career—more than any generation before her, she refuses to put her own pleasures aside. She's old enough to know what she wants. And young enough to go after it." According to *Redbook,* this consumer makes an ideal target for marketers of health food and fitness products. She wears out more exercise shoes, swallows more vitamins, drinks more diet soda, and works out more often than do other consumer groups.

Marketers also have used *personality* variables to segment markets, giving their products personalities that correspond to consumer personalities. Successful market segmentation strategies based on personality have been used for products such as cosmetics, cigarettes, insurance, and liquor.[10]

Honda's marketing campaign for its motor scooters provides a good example of personality segmentation. Honda *appears* to target its Spree, Elite, and Aero motor scooters at hip and trendy 14- to 22-year-olds. But it *actually* designs ads geared to a much broader personality group. One ad, for example, shows a delighted child bouncing up and down on his bed while the announcer says, "You've been trying to get there all your life." The ad reminds viewers of the euphoric feelings they got when they broke away from authority and did things their parents told them not to do. It suggests that they can feel that way again by riding a Honda scooter. So even though Honda seems to be targeting young consumers, the ads appeal to trendsetters and independent personalities in all age groups. In fact, more than half of Honda's scooter sales are to young professionals and older buyers—15 percent are purchased by the over-50 group. Honda is appealing to the rebellious, independent kid in all of us.[11]

## Behavioral Segmentation

**Behavioral segmentation** divides buyers into groups based on their knowledge, attitudes, uses, or responses to a product. Many marketers believe that behavior variables are the best starting point for building market segments.

**Behavioral segmentation**
Dividing a market into groups based on consumer knowledge, attitude, use, or response to a product.

**Occasion segmentation**
Dividing a market into groups according to occasions when buyers get the idea to buy, actually make their purchase, or use the purchased item.

OCCASIONS. Buyers can be grouped according to occasions when they get the idea to buy, actually make their purchase, or use the purchased item. **Occasion segmentation** can help firms build up product usage. For example, orange juice is most often consumed at breakfast, but orange growers have promoted drinking orange juice as a cool and refreshing drink at other times of the day. In contrast, Coca-Cola's "Coke in the Morning" advertising campaign attempts to increase Coke consumption by promoting the beverage as an early morning pick-me-up. Some holidays, such as Mother's Day and Father's Day, were originally promoted partly to increase the sale of candy, flowers, cards, and other gifts.

*Occasion segmentation: Kodak has developed special versions of its single-use camera for just about any picture-taking occasion, from underwater photography to taking baby pictures.*

Kodak uses occasion segmentation in designing and marketing its single-use cameras. The customer simply shoots the roll of pictures and returns the film, camera and all, to be processed. By mixing lenses, film speeds, and accessories, Kodak has developed special versions of the camera for just about any picture-taking occasion, from underwater photography to baby pictures:

> Standing on the edge of the Grand Canyon? [Single-use cameras] can take panoramic, wide-angle shots. Snorkeling? Focus on that flounder with a [different single-use camera]. Sports fans are another target: Kodak now markets a telephoto version with ultrafast . . . film for the stadium set. . . . Planners are looking at a model equipped with a short focal-length lens and fast film requiring less light. . . . They figure parents would like . . . to take snapshots of their babies without the disturbing flash. . . . In one Japanese catalog aimed at young women, Kodak sells a package of five pastel-colored cameras . . . including a version with a fish-eye lens to create a rosy, romantic glow.12

**BENEFITS SOUGHT.** A powerful form of segmentation is to group buyers according to the different *benefits* that they seek from the product. **Benefit segmentation** requires finding the major benefits that people look for in the product class, the kinds of people who look for each benefit, and the major brands that deliver each benefit. One of the best examples of benefit segmentation was conducted in the toothpaste market (see Table 7-2). Research found four benefit segments: economic, medicinal, cosmetic, and taste. Each benefit group had special demographic, behavioral, and psychographic characteristics. For example, the people seeking to prevent decay tended to have large families, were heavy toothpaste users, and were conservative. Each segment also favored certain brands. Most current brands

**Benefit segmentation**
Dividing a market into groups according to the different benefits that consumers seek from the product.

**TABLE 7-2** *Benefit Segmentation of the Toothpaste Market*

| Benefit Segments | Demographics | Behavior | Psychographics | Favored Brands |
|---|---|---|---|---|
| Economy (low price) | Men | Heavy users | High autonomy, value oriented | Brands on sale |
| Medicinal (decay prevention) | Large families | Heavy users | Hypochondriac, conservative | Crest |
| Cosmetic (bright teeth) | Teens, young adults | Smokers | High sociability, active | Aqua-Fresh, Ultra Brite |
| Taste (good tasting) | Children | Spearmint lovers | High self-involvement, hedonistic | Colgate, Aim |

*Source:* Adapted from Russell I. Haley, "Benefit Segmentation: A Decision Oriented Research Tool," *Journal of Marketing*, July 1963, pp. 30–35. See also Russell I. Haley, "Benefit Segmentation: Backwards and Forwards," *Journal of Advertising Research*, February–March 1984, pp. 19–25.

appeal to one of these segments. For example, Crest toothpaste stresses protection and appeals to the family segment, whereas Aim looks and tastes good and appeals to children.

Companies can use benefit segmentation to clarify the benefit segment to which they are appealing, its characteristics, and the major competing brands. They can also search for new benefits and launch brands that deliver them.

USER STATUS. Markets can be segmented into groups of nonusers, ex-users, potential users, first-time users, and regular users of a product. Potential users and regular users may require different kinds of marketing appeals. For example, one study found that blood donors are low in self-esteem, low risk takers, and more highly concerned about their health; nondonors tend to be the opposite on all three dimensions. This suggests that social agencies should use different marketing approaches for keeping current donors and attracting new ones. A company's market position also influences its focus. Market share leaders focus on attracting potential users, whereas smaller firms focus on attracting current users away from the market leader.

USAGE RATE. Markets also can be segmented into light-, medium-, and heavy-user groups. Heavy users are often a small percentage of the market, but account for a high percentage of total buying. Figure 7-2 shows usage rates for some popular consumer products. Product users were divided into two halves, a light-user half and a heavy-user half, according to their buying rates for the specific products. Using beer as an example, the figure shows that 41 percent of the households studied buy beer. However, the heavy-user half accounted for 87 percent of the beer consumed—almost seven times as much as the light-user half. Clearly, a beer company would prefer to attract one heavy user to its brand rather than several light users. Thus, most beer companies target the heavy beer drinker, using appeals such as Schaefer's "one beer to have when you're having more than one," or Miller Lite's "tastes great, less filling."

LOYALTY STATUS. A market can also be segmented by consumer loyalty. Consumers can be loyal to brands (Tide), stores (Wal-Mart), and companies (Ford). Buyers can be divided into groups according to their degree of loyalty. Some con-

**FIGURE 7-2**

*Heavy and light users of common consumer products (Source: See Victor J. Cook and William Mindak, "A Search for Constants: The 'Heavy Users' Revisited!" Journal of Consumer Marketing, Vol. 1, No. 4 [Spring 1984], p. 80.)*

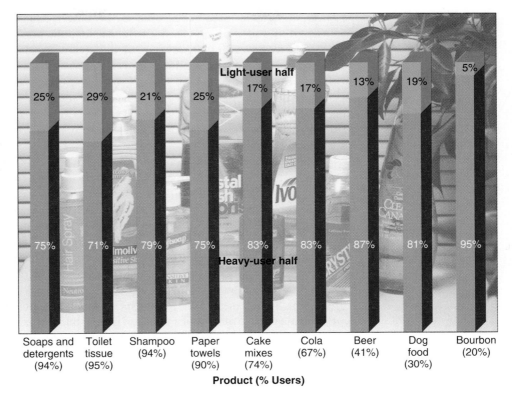

sumers are completely loyal: They buy one brand all the time. Others are somewhat loyal: They are loyal to two or three brands of a given product or favor one brand, while sometimes buying others. Still other buyers show no loyalty to any brand: They either want something different each time they buy or they buy whatever's on sale.

A company can learn a lot by analyzing loyalty patterns in its market. It should start by studying its own loyal customers. Colgate finds that its loyal buyers are more middle class, have larger families, and are more health conscious. These characteristics pinpoint the target market for Colgate. By studying its less loyal buyers, the company can detect which brands are most competitive with its own. If many Colgate buyers also buy Crest, Colgate can attempt to improve its positioning against Crest, possibly by using direct-comparison advertising. By looking at customers who are shifting away from its brand, the company can learn about its marketing weaknesses. As for nonloyal buyers, the company may attract them by putting its brand on sale.

## *Targeting Multiple Segments*

Very often, companies may begin their marketing with one targeted segment, then expand into other segments. Consider the experiences of Paging Network, Inc. (PageNet), a small developer of paging systems. PageNet couldn't differentiate itself from such major competitors as Southwestern Bell and Pacific Telesis by boasting unique technology. Moreover, the company was already competing on price, setting its prices about 20 percent below those of competitors. Thus, PageNet used smart segmentation to boost its competitive advantage.

First, PageNet used geographic segmentation, targeting easily accessible markets in Ohio and its home state of Texas. In both areas, local competitors were vulnerable to PageNet's aggressive pricing. Once these markets were secure, the company introduced its products into 13 more geographically dispersed market segments that represented the most growth potential. But PageNet's segmenting strategy didn't end with geography. The small company next developed profiles of major users of paging services and targeted the most promising user groups. Among the primary user groups targeted were salespeople, messengers, and service people.

Flush with success, PageNet set out to capture the largest possible percentage of the total market for pagers. To reach its objective of 75 percent market penetration, PageNet used lifestyle segmentation to target additional consumer groups, such as parents who leave their babies with sitters and elderly people living alone whose families want to keep an eye on them. Looking to broaden its segments even further by reaching larger audiences, PageNet began to distribute its products through the electronics departments of Kmart, Wal-Mart, and Home Depot. It gave these outlets very attractive discounts in return for the right to keep the revenue from the monthly service charges on any pagers sold. With a sales forecast of 80,000 new users, PageNet's managers calculated that the enormous potential revenue from service charges would more than make up for the smaller up-front profits from the discounted products. The results of this multiple segmentation strategy: PageNet is continuing to add new customers at the rate of 50 percent per year.[13]

## SEGMENTING BUSINESS MARKETS

Consumer and business marketers use many of the same variables to segment their markets. Business buyers can be segmented geographically or by benefits sought, user status, usage rate, and loyalty status. Yet, business marketers also use some additional variables, such as business customer demographics (industry, company size); operating characteristics; purchasing approaches; situational factors; and personal characteristics.

By going after segments instead of the whole market, companies have a much better chance to deliver value to consumers and to receive maximum rewards for close attention to consumer needs. Thus, Hewlett Packard's Computer Systems Division targets specific industries that promise the best growth prospects, such as telecommunications and financial services. Its "red team" sales force specializes in developing and serving major customers in these targeted industries.[14]

Within the chosen industry, a company can further segment by *customer size* or *geographic location*. For example, Hewlett Packard's "blue team" telemarkets to smaller accounts and to those that don't fit neatly into the strategically targeted industries on which H-P focuses. A company might set up separate systems for dealing with larger or multiple-location customers. For example, Steelcase, a major producer of office furniture, first segments customers into ten industries, including banking, insurance, and electronics. Next, company salespeople work with independent Steelcase dealers to handle smaller, local, or regional Steelcase customers in each segment. But many national, multiple-location customers, such as Exxon or IBM, have special needs that may reach beyond the scope of individual dealers. So Steelcase uses national accounts managers to help its dealer networks handle its national accounts.

Within a given target industry and customer size, the company can segment by purchase approaches and criteria. As in consumer segmentation, many marketers believe that *buying behavior* and *benefits* provide the best basis for segmenting business markets. For example, a recent study of the customers of Signode Corporation's industrial packaging division revealed four segments, each seeking a different mix of price and service benefits:

◆ *Programmed buyers.* These buyers view Signode's products as not very important to their operations. They buy the products as a routine purchase, usually pay full price, and accept below-average service. Clearly, this is a highly profitable segment for Signode.

◆ *Relationship buyers.* These buyers regard Signode's packaging products as moderately important and are knowledgeable about competitors' offerings. They prefer to buy from Signode as long as its price is reasonably competitive. They receive a small discount and a modest amount of service. This segment is Signode's second most profitable.

◆ *Transaction buyers.* These buyers see Signode's products as very important to their operations. They are price and service sensitive. They receive about a 10 percent discount and above-average service. They are knowledgeable about competitors' offerings and are ready to switch for a better price, even if it means losing some service.

◆ *Bargain hunters.* These buyers see Signode's products as very important and demand the deepest discount and the highest service. They know the alternative suppliers, bargain hard, and are ready to switch at the slightest sense of dissatisfaction. Signode needs these buyers for volume purposes, but they are not very profitable.[15]

This segmentation scheme has helped Signode to do a better job of designing marketing strategies that take into account each segment's unique reactions to varying levels of price and service.[16]

## SEGMENTING INTERNATIONAL MARKETS

Few companies have either the resources or the will to operate in all, or even most, of the countries that dot the globe. Although some large companies, such as Coca-Cola or Sony, sell products in more than 150 countries, most international firms focus on a smaller set. Operating in many countries presents new challenges. The different countries of the world, even those that are close together, can vary dramatically in their economic, cultural, and political makeup. Thus, just as they do within their domestic markets, international firms need to group their world markets into segments with distinct buying needs and behaviors.

Companies can segment international markets using one or a combination of several variables. They can segment by *geographic location,* grouping countries by regions such as Western Europe, the Pacific Rim, the Middle East, or Africa. In fact, countries in many regions already have organized geographically into market groups or "free trade zones," such as the European Union, the European Free Trade Association, and the North American Free Trade Association. These associations reduce trade barriers between member countries, creating larger and more homogeneous markets.

Geographic segmentation assumes that nations close to one another will have many common traits and behaviors. Although this is often the case, there are many exceptions. For example, although the United States and Canada have much in common, both differ culturally and economically from neighboring Mexico. Even within a region, consumers can differ widely. For example, many U.S. marketers think that all Central and South American countries are the same, including their 400 million inhabitants. However, the Dominican Republic is no more like Brazil than Italy is like Sweden. Many Latin Americans don't speak Spanish, including 140 million Portuguese-speaking Brazilians and the millions in other countries who speak a variety of native dialects.[17]

World markets can be segmented on the basis of *economic factors*. For example, countries might be grouped by population income levels or by their overall level of economic development. Some countries, such as the so-called Group of Seven—the United States, Britain, France, Germany, Japan, Canada, and Italy—have established, highly industrialized economies. Other countries have newly industrialized or developing economies (Singapore, Taiwan, Korea, Brazil, Mexico). Still others are less developed (China, India). A company's economic structure shapes its population's product and service needs and, therefore, the marketing opportunities that it offers.

Countries can be segmented by *political and legal factors* such as the type and stability of government, receptivity to foreign firms, monetary regulations, and the amount of bureaucracy. Such factors can play a crucial role in a company's choice of which countries to enter and how. *Cultural factors* also can be used, grouping markets according to common languages, religions, values and attitudes, customs, and behavioral patterns.

*Intermarket separation: Teens show surprising similarity no matter where in the world they live. For instance, this young woman could live almost anywhere. Thus, many companies target teenagers with worldwide marketing campaigns.*

Segmenting international markets on the basis of geographic, economic, political, cultural, and other factors assumes that segments should consist of clusters of countries. However, many companies use a different approach, called **intermarket segmentation.** Using this approach, they form segments of consumers who have similar needs and buying behavior even though they are located in different countries. For example, Mercedes-Benz targets the world's well-to-do, regardless of their country. And Pepsi uses ads filled with kids, sports, and rock music to target the world's teenagers. A recent study of more than 6,500 teenagers from 26 countries showed that teens around the world live surprisingly parallel lives. As one expert notes, "From Rio to Rochester, teens can be found enmeshed in much the same regimen: watching '90210,' drinking Coke, moshing to Green Day, dining on Big Macs, surfin' the Net on their Macintosh computers . . . And then there's the international teen uniform: baggy Levi's or Diesel jeans, T-shirt, Nikes or Doc Martens, and leather jacket."[18] Many companies are targeting teens with globally standardized products and advertisements. For example, Pepsi recently introduced sugar-free Pepsi Max in 16 countries, including Britain, Australia, and Japan, with a single set of ads aimed at teens who like to live on the wild side.[19]

**Intermarket segmentation**
Forming segments of consumers who have similar needs and buying behavior even though they are located in different countries.

## REQUIREMENTS FOR EFFECTIVE SEGMENTATION

Clearly, there are many ways to segment a market, but not all segmentations are effective. For example, buyers of table salt could be divided into blond and brunette customers. But hair color obviously does not affect the purchase of salt. Furthermore, if all salt buyers bought the same amount of salt each month, believed that all salt is the same, and wanted to pay the same price, the company would not benefit from segmenting this market.

To be useful, market segments must have the following characteristics:

◆ *Measurability.* The size, purchasing power, and profiles of the segments can be measured. Certain segmentation variables are difficult to measure. For example, there are 24 million left-handed people in the United States—almost equaling the entire population of Canada. Yet few products are targeted toward this left-handed segment. The major problem may be that the segment is hard to identify and measure. There are no data on the demographics of lefties, and the Census Bureau does not keep track of left-handedness in its surveys. Private data companies keep reams of statistics on other demographic segments, but not on left-handers.[20]

◆ *Accessibility.* The market segments can be effectively reached and served. Suppose that a fragrance company finds that heavy users of its brand are single men and women who stay out late and socialize a lot. Unless this group lives or shops at certain places and is exposed to certain media, its members will be difficult to reach.

◆ *Substantiality.* The market segments are large or profitable enough to serve. A segment should be the largest possible homogeneous group worth pursuing with a tailored marketing program. It would not pay, for example, for an automobile manufacturer to develop cars for persons whose height is less than four feet.

◆ *Actionability.* Effective programs can be designed for attracting and serving the segments. For example, although one small airline identified seven market segments, its staff was too small to develop separate marketing programs for each segment.

# ►MARKET TARGETING

Marketing segmentation reveals the firm's market-segment opportunities. The firm now has to evaluate the various segments and decide how many and which ones to target. We now look at how companies evaluate and select target segments.

## EVALUATING MARKET SEGMENTS

In evaluating different market segments, a firm must look at three factors: segment size and growth, segment structural attractiveness, and company objectives and resources.

### Segment Size and Growth

The company must first collect and analyze data on current segment sales, growth rates, and expected profitability for various segments. It will be interested in segments that have the right size and growth characteristics. But "right size and growth" is a relative matter. Some companies want to target segments with large current sales, a high growth rate, and a high profit margin. However, the largest, fastest-growing segments are not always the most attractive ones for every company. Smaller companies may find that they lack the skills and resources needed to serve the larger segments, or that these segments are too competitive. Such companies may select segments that are smaller and less attractive, in an absolute sense, but that are potentially more profitable for them.

### Segment Structural Attractiveness

A segment might have desirable size and growth and still not offer attractive profits. The company must examine several major structural factors that affect long-run segment attractiveness.[21] For example, a segment is less attractive if it already contains many strong and aggressive *competitors*. The existence of many actual or potential *substitute products* may limit prices and the profits that can be earned in a segment. The relative *power of buyers* also affects segment attractiveness. If the buyers in a segment possess strong bargaining power relative to sellers, they will try to force prices down, demand more quality or services, and set competitors against one another, all at the expense of seller profitability. Finally, a segment may be less attractive if it contains *powerful suppliers* who can control prices or reduce the quality or quantity of ordered goods and services. Suppliers tend to be powerful when they are large and concentrated, when few substitutes exist, or when the supplied product is an important input.

### Company Objectives and Resources

Even if a segment has the right size and growth and is structurally attractive, the company must consider its own objectives and resources in relation to that segment. Some attractive segments could be dismissed quickly because they do not mesh with the company's long-run objectives. Although such segments might be tempting in themselves, they might divert the company's attention and energies away from its main goals. Or they might be a poor choice from an environmental, political, or social-responsibility viewpoint. For example, in recent years, several companies and industries have been criticized for unfairly targeting vulnerable segments—children, the aged, low-income minorities, and others—with questionable products or tactics (see Marketing at Work 7-2).

If a segment fits the company's objectives, the company then must decide whether it possesses the skills and resources needed to succeed in that segment. If the company lacks the strengths needed to compete successfully in a segment and cannot readily obtain them, it should not enter the segment. Even if the company possesses the *required* strengths, it needs to employ skills and resources *superior* to those of the competition in order to really win in a market segment. The company should enter segments only where it can offer superior value and gain advantages over competitors.

## SELECTING MARKET SEGMENTS

**Target market**
A set of buyers sharing common needs or characteristics that the company decides to serve.

After evaluating different segments, the company must decide which and how many segments to serve. This is the problem of *target-market selection*. A **target market** consists of a set of buyers who share common needs or characteristics that the company decides to serve. Figure 7-3 shows that the firm can adopt one of three market-coverage strategies: *undifferentiated marketing, differentiated marketing,* and *concentrated marketing.*

**FIGURE 7-3**
*Three alternative market-coverage strategies.*

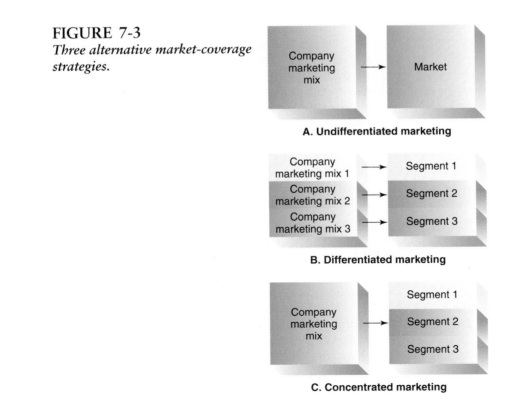

A. Undifferentiated marketing

B. Differentiated marketing

C. Concentrated marketing

## MARKETING AT WORK 7-2

# SOCIALLY RESPONSIBLE MARKET TARGETING

Market segmentation and targeting form the core of modern marketing strategy. Smart targeting helps companies to be more efficient and effective by focusing on the segments that they can satisfy best. Targeting also benefits consumers: Companies reach specific groups of consumers with offers carefully tailored to satisfy their needs. However, market targeting sometimes generates controversy and concern. Issues usually involve the targeting of vulnerable or disadvantaged consumers with controversial or potentially harmful products.

For example, over the years, the cereal industry has been heavily criticized for its marketing efforts that are directed toward children. Critics worry that sophisticated advertising, in which high-powered appeals are presented through the mouths of lovable animated characters will overwhelm children's defenses.

They claim that toys and other premiums offered with cereals distract children and make them want a particular cereal for the wrong reasons. All of this, critics fear, will entice children to gobble too much sugared cereal or to eat poorly balanced breakfasts. The marketers of toys and other children's products have been similarly battered, often with good justification. Some critics have even called for a complete ban on advertising to children. Children cannot understand the selling intent of the advertiser, critics reason, so any advertising targeted toward children is inherently unfair. To encourage responsible advertising to children, the Children's Advertising Review Unit, the advertising industry's self-regulatory agency, has published extensive children's advertising guidelines that recognize the special needs of child audiences.

Cigarette, beer, and fast-food marketers have also generated much controversy in recent years with their attempts to target inner-city minority consumers. For example, McDonald's and other chains have drawn criticism for pitching their high-fat, salt-laden fare to low-income, inner-city residents who are much more likely than suburbanites to be heavy consumers. R. J. Reynolds took heavy flak in 1990 when it announced plans to market Uptown, a menthol cigarette targeted toward low-income blacks. It quickly dropped the brand in the face of a loud public outcry and heavy pressure from black leaders. G. Heileman Brewing made a similar mistake with PowerMaster, a potent malt liquor targeted toward the black community. Although the brand seemed to make sense initially, it was ill-fated from the start:

**Undifferentiated marketing**
A market-coverage strategy in which a firm decides to ignore market segment differences and go after the whole market with one offer.

### Undifferentiated Marketing

Using an **undifferentiated marketing** strategy, a firm might decide to ignore market segment differences and go after the whole market with one offer. The offer focuses on what is *common* in the needs of consumers rather than on what is *different*. The company designs a product and a marketing program that appeal to the largest number of buyers. It relies on mass distribution and mass advertising, and it aims to give the product a superior image in people's minds. An example of undifferentiated marketing is the Hershey Company's marketing some years ago of only one chocolate candy bar for everyone.

Undifferentiated marketing provides cost economies. The narrow product line keeps down production, inventory, and transportation costs. The undifferen-

*Sales of ordinary beer (3.5 percent alcohol) have slowly been going pffffft for years now, while sales of some higher-proof beers have risen 25 to 30 percent annually. So the decision by G. Heileman Brewing to extend its Colt 45 malt liquor line with PowerMaster, a new high-test malt (5.9 percent alcohol), wasn't [at first glance] dumb. But malt liquor is consumed primarily by blacks. And targeting blacks with anything less wholesome than farina has become risky. . . . Heileman nonetheless rushed in where a smarter company might reasonably have hesitated. . . . PowerMaster became "a magnet of controversy from the moment it raised its alcohol-enhanced head. Federal officials, industry leaders, black activists, and media types weighed in with protests that Power-Master . . . was an example of a bad product, bad marketing, and, essentially, a bad idea." . . . [Only] weeks after its planned debut, [PowerMaster] was just a malty memory.*

Even some industry insiders objected to the Heileman's targeting tactics. For example, when the PowerMaster controversy erupted, the president of Anheuser-Busch wrote to Heileman's chairman, suggesting that the planned product might indicate "that we put profits before the consideration of the communities we serve."

Not all attempts to target children, minorities, or other special segments draw such criticism. In fact, most provide benefits to targeted consumers. For example, Colgate-Palmolive's Colgate Junior toothpaste has special features designed to get children to brush longer and more often: It's less foamy, has a milder taste, and contains sparkles, and it exits the tube in a star-shaped column. Golden Ribbon Playthings has developed a highly acclaimed and very successful black character doll named "Huggy Bean" targeted toward minority consumers. Huggy comes with books and toys that connect her with her African heritage. Many cosmetics companies have responded to the special needs of minority segments by adding products specifically designed for black, Hispanic, or Asian women. For example, Maybelline introduced a highly successful line called Shades of You targeted to black women, and other companies have followed with their own lines of multicultural products.

Thus, in market targeting, the issue is not really *who* is targeted but rather *how* and for *what*. Controversies arise when marketers attempt to profit at the expense of targeted segments — when they unfairly target vulnerable segments or target them with questionable products or tactics. Socially responsible marketing calls for segmentation and targeting that serve not just the interests of the company, but also the interests of those who are targeted.

*Sources:* Excerpts from "PowerMaster," *Fortune,* January 13, 1992, p. 82. Also see "Selling Sin to Blacks," *Fortune,* October 21, 1991, p. 100; Dorothy J. Gaiter, "Black-Owned Firms Are Catching an Afrocentric Wave," *The Wall Street Journal,* January 8, 1992, p. B2; Maria Mallory, "Waking Up to a Major Market," *Business Week,* March 23, 1992, pp. 70–73; Cyndee Miller, "Cosmetics Firms Finally Discover the Ethnic Market," *Marketing News,* August 30, 1993, p. 2; Michael Wilke, "Toy Companies Take Up Diversity Banner," *Advertising Age,* February 27, 1995, pp. 1, 8; and D. Kirk Davidson, "Targeting Is Innocent until It Exploits the Vulnerable," *Marketing News,* September 11, 1995, p. 10.

tiated advertising program keeps down promotion costs. The absence of segment marketing research and planning lowers the costs of marketing research and product management.

Most modern marketers, however, have strong doubts about this strategy. Difficulties arise in developing a product or brand that satisfies all consumers. Firms using undifferentiated marketing typically develop an offer aimed at the largest segments in the market. When several firms do this, heavy competition develops in the largest segments, and less satisfaction results in the smaller ones. The final result is that the larger segments may be less profitable because they attract heavy competition. Recognition of this problem has led firms to be more interested in smaller market segments.

## Differentiated Marketing

Using a **differentiated marketing** strategy, a firm decides to target several market segments and designs separate offers for each. General Motors tries to produce a car for every "purse, purpose, and personality." Nike offers athletic shoes for a dozen or more different sports, from running, fencing, and aerobics to bicycling and baseball. And Wal-Mart appeals to the needs of different shopper segments with Wal-Mart discount stores, Wal-Mart Supercenters, and Sam's Warehouse stores. By offering product and marketing variations, these companies hope for higher sales and a stronger position within each market segment. They hope that a stronger position in several segments will strengthen consumers' overall identification of the company with the product category. They also hope for more loyal purchasing, because the firm's offerings better match each segment's desires.

A growing number of firms have adopted differentiated marketing. Differentiated marketing typically creates more total sales than does undifferentiated marketing. Procter & Gamble gets a higher total market share with eleven brands of laundry detergent than it could with only one. But differentiated marketing also increases the costs of doing business. Modifying a product to meet different market-segment needs usually involves extra research and development, engineering, or special tooling costs. A firm usually finds it more expensive to produce, say, ten units of ten different products than one hundred units of one product. Developing separate marketing plans for the separate segments requires extra marketing research, forecasting, sales analysis, promotion planning, and channel management. And trying to reach different market segments with different advertising increases promotion costs. Thus, the company must weigh increased sales against increased costs when deciding on a differentiated marketing strategy.

## Concentrated Marketing

A third market-coverage strategy, **concentrated marketing,** is especially appealing when company resources are limited. Instead of going after a small share of a large market, the firm goes after a large share of one or a few submarkets. For example, Oshkosh Truck is the world's largest producer of airport rescue trucks and front-loading concrete mixers. Recycled Paper Products concentrates on the market for alternative greeting cards. And Soho Natural Sodas concentrates on a narrow segment of the soft-drink market. Here's another example of a highly successful market nicher:

> During the Persian Gulf war, when the mighty U.S. Fleet edged its way up the Gulf to Desert Storm, it was led by five little plastic boats. The little British Royal Navy Hunt Class MCMVs (Mine Counter-Measure Vehicles) were in a league of their own at the dangerous job of clearing a path for the main fleet. They were made by Vosper Thornycraft, a small British company that has mastered the art of concentrated marketing around the world. It now dominates the niche for glass reinforced plastic mine hunters and patrol craft—just the ships a small navy wants. Vosper has strengthened its position by offering maritime training and support services along with its vessels. For example, many of the company's clients come from the Middle East and travel with their families, so Vosper has built an Arabic school for 70 pupils next to its maritime training center. As a result of its successful niching strategy, the company's value has increased more than twelve-fold during the past ten years.[22]

Concentrated marketing provides an excellent way for small new businesses to get a foothold in the climb against larger, more resourceful competitors. Through concentrated marketing, the firm achieves a strong market position in the segments (or niches) that it serves because of its greater knowledge of the segments' needs and the special reputation it acquires (see Marketing at Work 7-3). The firm also enjoys many operating economies because of specialization in production, distribution, and promotion. If the segment is well chosen, the firm can earn a high rate of return on its investment.

At the same time, concentrated marketing involves higher-than-normal risks. The particular market segment can turn sour. Or larger competitors may decide to enter the same segment. For example, California Cooler's success in the wine cooler segment attracted many large competitors, causing the original owners to sell to a larger company that had more marketing resources. For these reasons, many companies prefer to diversify in several market segments.

Rapid advances in computer and communications technology are allowing many large mass marketers to act more like concentrated marketers. Using detailed customer databases, these marketers segment their mass markets into small groups of like-minded buyers. For example, using home-delivery information, Pizza Hut has developed a database containing electronic profiles of the pizza-eating habits of some nine million customers across the country. It uses this database to develop carefully targeted promotions. In a recent summer promotion, "lovers of Neapolitan-style pizza got offers for those, not for thin-crust pizza. Consumers who had been willing to try new foods got a mailing for Bigfoot, a giant-pizza innovation. Customers who had not ordered in a while got deeper discounts than others. [These targeted promotions were] very precise—and very successful."[23]

### Choosing a Market-Coverage Strategy

Many factors need to be considered when choosing a market-coverage strategy. Which strategy is best depends on *company resources*. When the firm's resources are limited, concentrated marketing makes the most sense. The best strategy also depends on the degree of *product variability*. Undifferentiated marketing is more suited for uniform products such as grapefruit or steel. Products that can vary in design, such as cameras and automobiles, are more suited to differentiation or concentration. The *product's stage in the life cycle* also must be considered. When a firm introduces a new product, it is practical to launch only one version, and undifferentiated marketing or concentrated marketing makes the most sense. In the mature stage of the product life cycle, however, differentiated marketing begins to make more sense. Another factor is *market variability*. If most buyers have the same tastes, buy the same amounts, and react the same way to marketing efforts, undifferentiated marketing is appropriate. Finally, *competitors' marketing strategies* are important. When competitors use segmentation, undifferentiated marketing can be suicidal. Conversely, when competitors use undifferentiated marketing, a firm can gain an advantage by using differentiated or concentrated marketing.

**Product position**
The way that the product is defined by consumers on important attributes—the place that the product occupies in consumers' minds relative to competing products.

# ▶POSITIONING FOR COMPETITIVE ADVANTAGE

Once a company has decided which segments of the market it will enter, it must decide what "positions" it wants to occupy in those segments. A **product's position** is the way that the product is *defined by consumers* on important attributes—

## MARKETING AT WORK 7-3

# MARKET NICHING: KING OF THE (MOLE)HILL

Ask almost anyone you know to name a brand of baking soda, and they'll answer without hesitating: Arm & Hammer. In fact, they'll find it hard to name any other brand. Arm & Hammer baking soda, in its familiar little yellow box, has dominated the U.S. market for more than 115 years. But ask that same person to name the company that *makes* Arm & Hammer baking soda, and they'll probably draw a blank. The company is Church & Dwight. And although you won't find the firm listed among the Fortune 500, Church & Dwight is a giant in its baking soda niche. Founded in 1846, Church & Dwight is the world's leading producer of sodium bicarbonate—good ol' NaHCO$_3$.

Until the late 1960s, Church & Dwight was pretty much a one-product company, marketing sodium bicarbonate to consumers as Arm & Hammer baking soda or selling it in bulk to other companies for a variety of uses, from cake mixes to fire extinguishers. During the past two decades, however, as the con-sumer market for pure baking soda has matured, Church & Dwight has expanded its niche dramatically by finding endless uses for its versatile white powder. In 1970, the company began its push into new consumer markets with a line of laundry products that capitalized both on the powerful Arm & Hammer brand name and on consumer concerns about the environment. It introduced phosphate-free—but sodium-bicarbonate-rich—Arm & Hammer detergent, which has since become the company's best-selling product, accounting for about a third of total sales. During the 1980s, Church & Dwight followed with a number of well-known consumer products, ranging from baking soda tooth-paste to carpet deodorizers and air fresheners.

Although baking-soda-based consumer products make up the bulk of Church & Dwight's current sales, the usefulness of sodium bicarbonate extends well beyond household cooking and cleaning. Church & Dwight also does a brisk and growing indus-trial business, which now con-tributes about 25 percent of annual sales. Business applications range from baking soda as a leavening agent in bakery products to use in oil well drilling muds. It's even used in animal nutrition products. For example, Church & Dwight markets an Arm & Hammer product called Megalac, a high-energy feed additive that helps dairy cows neutralize digestive acids and supplements the sodium bicarbonate produced naturally, resulting in better feed efficiency and increased milk production.

*Well-focused Church & Dwight has built a commanding position by concentrating on small, highly specialized niches.*

the place the product occupies in consumers' minds relative to competing products. Thus, Tide is positioned as a powerful, all-purpose family detergent; Solo is positioned as a liquid detergent with fabric softener; Cheer is positioned as the detergent for all temperatures of water. In the automobile market, Toyota Tercel and Suburu are positioned on economy, Mercedes and Cadillac on luxury, and Porsche and BMW on performance. Volvo positions powerfully on safety.

Consumers are overloaded with information about products and services. They cannot reevaluate products every time that they make a buying decision. To

Business markets may provide some of Church & Dwight's best opportunities for growth. As the world looks for new, more environmentally friendly solutions to nagging problems, the company has responded with a smorgasbord of new uses and products. For example, it recently introduced Armex, a blasting material made of baking soda and other ingredients. Armex has many advantages over current silicon-based sandblasting media, which can contribute to silicosis, a lung disease. Armex not only eliminates health and environmental hazards, it also has a more delicate touch: The sharp edges of its baking soda crystals wear down faster, stripping paint and grime without damaging underlying surfaces. Armex was originally developed to help strip tar and paint from the inside of the Statue of Liberty. Among the company's other new products is Armakleen, an industrial cleanser for printed circuit boards. It provides an environmentally safe alternative to current cleaners that contain chlorofluorocarbons (CFCs), thought to damage the earth's ozone layer.

In addition to developing new baking-soda-based products for its business markets, Church & Dwight has created a torrent of new commercial uses for plain old baking soda. For example, it has recently begun selling the stuff as an additive to municipal drinking water. Experiments have shown that baking soda neutralizes acids in the water supply, helping to inhibit corrosion and preventing lead and other toxic metals from leaching out of the plumbing. Church & Dwight is even rumored to be experimenting with baking soda as a safe and effective fungicide for plants.

Church & Dwight battles daily with much larger competitors—consumer companies like Procter & Gamble, Lever, and Colgate, and such international heavyweights as Rhône Poulenc and Solvay. At first glance, the company might appear to be fighting a losing battle. For example, in the $3.6 billion U.S. detergent market, Arm & Hammer commands only a 4 percent market share, compared to P&G's 53 percent and Colgate's 24 percent. However, in the baking soda segment of the detergent market, Arm & Hammer dominates. In fact, when it comes to *anything* that has to do with baking soda, Church & Dwight is "king of the hill"—capturing 60 percent of the world market for sodium bicarbonate. And even if the hill is more of a molehill than a mountain, Church & Dwight outperforms many of its much larger competitors. The well-focused company has built a commanding position by concentrating on small, highly specialized market niches. During the past 10 years, its annual sales have more than tripled, to $492 million, and profits have increased fourfold. Thus, Church & Dwight has proven once again what many concentrated marketers have learned—small can be beautiful.

*Sources:* James P. Meagher, "Church & Dwight: It Scores Big with the Brand-Name Pull of Arm & Hammer," *Barron's,* December 10, 1990, pp. 49–50; Peter Coombes, "Church & Dwight: On the Rise," *Chemical Week,* September 20, 1989, pp. 16–18; Peter Nulty, "Church & Dwight: No Product is Too Dull to Shine," *Fortune,* July 27, 1992, pp. 95–96; and Riccardo A. Davis, "Arm & Hammer Seeks Growth Abroad," *Advertising Age,* August 17, 1992, pp. 3, 42.

simplify the buying process, consumers organize products into categories—they "position" products, services, and companies in their minds. A product's position is the complex set of perceptions, impressions, and feelings that consumers hold for the product compared with competing products. Consumers position products with or without the help of marketers. But marketers do not want to leave their products' positions to chance. They must *plan* positions that will give their products the greatest advantage in selected target markets, and they must design marketing mixes to create these planned positions.

# POSITIONING STRATEGIES

Marketers can follow several positioning strategies. They can position their products on specific *product attributes*—Honda Civic advertises its low price; BMW promotes performance. Products can be positioned on the needs that they fill or the *benefits* that they offer—Crest reduces cavities; Aim tastes good. Or products can be positioned according to *usage occasions*—in the summer, Gatorade can be positioned as a beverage for replacing athletes' body fluids; in the winter, it can be positioned as the drink to use when the doctor recommends plenty of liquids. Another approach is to position the product for certain classes of *users*—Johnson & Johnson improved the market share for its baby shampoo from 3 percent to 14 percent by repositioning the product as one for adults who wash their hair frequently and need a gentle shampoo.

A product can also be positioned directly *against a competitor.* For example, in its ads, Citibank VISA compares itself directly with American Express, saying "You'd better take your VISA card, because they don't take American Express." In its famous "We're number two, so we try harder" campaign, Avis successfully positioned itself against the larger Hertz. A product may also be positioned *away from competitors*—for many years, 7-Up has positioned itself as the "un-cola," the fresh and thirst-quenching alternative to Coke and Pepsi. And Barbasol television ads position the company's shaving cream and other products as "great toiletries for a lot less money."

Finally, the product can be positioned for different *product classes.* For example, some margarines are positioned against butter, others against cooking oils. Camay hand soap is positioned with bath oils rather than with soap. Marketers often use a *combination* of these positioning strategies. Arm & Hammer baking soda has been positioned as a deodorizer for refrigerators and garbage disposals (product class *and* usage situation).

*Positioning: When you think of automobile safety, what brand comes to mind? Volvo has positioned itself powerfully on safety.*

# CHOOSING AND IMPLEMENTING A POSITIONING STRATEGY

Some firms find it easy to choose their positioning strategy. For example, a firm that is well known for quality in certain segments will go for this position in a new segment if there are enough buyers seeking quality. But in many cases, two or more firms will pursue the same position. Then, each will have to find other ways to set itself apart, such as promising "high quality for a lower cost" or "high quality with more technical service." Each firm must differentiate its offer by building a unique bundle of competitive advantages that appeals to a substantial group within the segment.

The positioning task consists of three steps: identifying a set of possible competitive advantages upon which to build a position, selecting the right competitive advantages, and effectively communicating and delivering the chosen position to the market.

## Identifying Possible Competitive Advantages

Consumers typically choose products and services that give them the greatest value. Thus, the key to winning and keeping customers is to understand their needs and buying processes better than competitors do and to deliver more value. To the extent that a company can position itself as providing superior value to selected target markets, either by offering lower prices than competitors do or by providing more benefits to justify higher prices, it gains **competitive advantage.** But solid positions cannot be built on empty promises. If a company positions its product as *offering* the best quality and service, it must then *deliver* the promised quality and service. Thus, positioning begins with actually *differentiating* the company's marketing offer so that it will give consumers more value than competitors' offers do.

Not every company will find many opportunities for differentiating its offer and gaining competitive advantage. Some companies find many minor advantages that are easily copied by competitors and are, therefore, highly perishable. The solution for these companies is to keep identifying new potential advantages and introducing them one by one to keep competitors off balance. These companies do not expect to gain a single major permanent advantage. Instead, they hope to gain many minor ones that can be introduced to win market share over a period of time.

In what specific ways can a company differentiate its offer from those of competitors? A company or market offer can be differentiated along the lines of *product, services, personnel,* or *image.*

**PRODUCT DIFFERENTIATION.**   A company can differentiate its physical product. At one extreme, some companies offer highly standardized products that allow little variation: chicken, steel, or aspirin for example. Yet even here, some meaningful differentiation is possible. For example, Perdue claims that its branded chickens are better—fresher and more tender—and gets a 10 percent price premium based on this differentiation.

Other companies offer products that can be highly differentiated, such as automobiles, commercial machinery, and furniture. Here, the company faces an abundance of design parameters. It can offer a variety of standard or optional *features* that are not provided by competitors. Thus, Volvo provides new and better safety features; Delta Airlines offers wider seating and free in-flight telephone use.

---

**Competitive advantage**
An advantage over competitors gained by offering consumers greater value, either through lower prices or by providing more benefits that justify higher prices.

Companies can also differentiate their products on *performance*. Whirlpool designs its dishwasher to run more quietly; Procter & Gamble formulates Liquid Tide to get clothes cleaner. *Style* and *design* can also be important differentiating factors. Thus, many car buyers pay a premium for Jaguar automobiles because of their unique look, even though Jaguar has sometimes had a poor reliability record. Similarly, companies can differentiate their products on such attributes as *consistency, durability, reliability,* or *repairability.*

**SERVICES DIFFERENTIATION.** In addition to differentiating its physical product, the firm can also differentiate the services that accompany the product. Some companies gain competitive advantage through speedy, convenient, or careful *delivery.* Deluxe, the check supply company, has built an impressive reputation for shipping out replacement checks one day after receiving an order—without being late once in 12 years. And Bank One has opened full-service branches in supermarkets to provide location convenience along with Saturday, Sunday, and weekday-evening hours.

*Installation* can also differentiate one company from another. IBM, for example, is known for its quality installation service. It delivers all pieces of purchased equipment to the site at one time rather than sending individual components to sit and wait for others to arrive. And when asked to move IBM equipment and install it in another location, IBM often moves competitors' equipment as well.

*Finding competitive advantage: Ritz-Carlton differentiates its hotels through outstanding service provided by carefully selected and well-trained personnel. "Our highly trained staff is second to none. . . ."*

Companies can further distinguish themselves through their *repair* services. Many an automobile buyer will gladly pay a little more and travel a little farther to buy a car from a dealer that provides top-notch repair service.

Some companies differentiate their offers by providing *customer training* service. Thus, General Electric not only sells and installs expensive X-ray equipment in hospitals, but also trains the hospital employees who will use this equipment. Other companies offer free or paid *consulting services*—data, information systems, and advising services that buyers need. For example, McKesson Corporation, a major drug wholesaler, consults with its 12,000 independent pharmacists to help them set up accounting, inventory, and computer ordering systems. By helping its customers compete better, McKesson gains greater customer loyalty and sales.

Companies can find many other ways to add value through differentiated services. Milliken & Company provides one of the best examples of a company that has gained competitive advantage through superior service. Milliken sells shop towels to industrial launderers who rent them to factories. These towels are physically similar to competitors' towels, yet Milliken charges a higher price and enjoys the leading market share. How can it charge more for what is essentially a commodity? The answer is that Milliken continuously "decommoditizes" this product through continuous service enhancements. Milliken trains its customers' salespeople, supplies them with prospect leads and sales promotional material, and lends its own salespeople to work on Customer Action Teams. It provides computer order entry and freight optimization systems, carries out marketing research for customers, and sponsors quality improvement workshops. Launderers are more than willing to buy Milliken shop towels and pay a price premium because the extra services improve their profitability.[24]

**PERSONNEL DIFFERENTIATION.**   Companies can gain a strong competitive advantage through hiring and training better people than their competitors do. Thus, Singapore Airlines enjoys an excellent reputation largely because of the graciousness of its flight attendants. McDonald's people are courteous, IBM people are professional and knowledgeable, and Disney people are friendly and upbeat. The sales forces of such companies as Connecticut General Life and Merck enjoy excellent reputations which set their companies apart from competitors. Wal-Mart has differentiated its superstores by employing "people greeters" who welcome shoppers, give advice on where to find items, mark merchandise brought back for returns or exchanges, and hand out small gifts to children.

Personnel differentiation requires that a company select its customer-contact people carefully and train them well. For example, guests at a Disney theme park quickly learn that every Disney employee is competent, courteous, and friendly. From the hotel check-in agents, to the monorail drivers, to the ride attendants, to the people who sweep Main Street USA, each employee understands the importance of understanding customers, communicating with them clearly and cheerfully, and responding quickly to their requests and problems. Each is carefully trained to "make a dream come true."

**IMAGE DIFFERENTIATION.**   Even when competing offers look the same, buyers may perceive a difference based on company or brand images. Thus, companies work to establish *images* that differentiate them from competitors. A company or brand image should convey the product's distinctive benefits and positioning. Developing a strong and distinctive image calls for creativity and hard work. A company cannot plant an image in the public's mind overnight using only a few advertisements. If Motorola means "quality," this image must be supported by everything the company says and does.

*Symbols* can provide strong company or brand recognition and image differentiation. Companies design signs and logos that provide instant recognition. They associate themselves with objects or characters that symbolize quality or other attributes, such as the McDonald's golden arches, the Prudential rock, or the Pillsbury doughboy. The company might build a brand around some famous person, as with perfumes such as Passion (Elizabeth Taylor) and Uninhibited (Cher). Some companies even become associated with colors, such as IBM (blue) or Campbell (red and white).

The chosen symbols must be communicated through advertising that conveys the company's or brand's personality. The ads attempt to establish a storyline, a mood, a performance level—something distinctive about the company or brand. The atmosphere of the physical space in which the organization produces or delivers its products and services can be another powerful image generator. Hyatt hotels have become known for their atrium lobbies and Victoria Station restaurants for their boxcar locations. Thus, a bank that wants to distinguish itself as the "friendly bank" must choose the right building and interior design, layout, colors, materials, and furnishings to reflect these qualities.

A company can also create an image through the types of events that it sponsors. For example, AT&T and IBM have identified themselves closely with cultural events, such as symphony performances and art exhibits. Other organizations support popular causes. For example, Heinz gives money to hospitals, and Quaker gives food to the homeless.

## Selecting the Right Competitive Advantages

Suppose that a company is fortunate enough to discover several potential competitive advantages. It now must choose the ones on which it will build its positioning strategy. It must decide *how many* differences to promote and *which ones*.

**HOW MANY DIFFERENCES TO PROMOTE?**   Many marketers think that companies should aggressively promote only one benefit to the target market. Ad man Rosser Reeves, for example, said a company should develop a *unique selling proposition* (USP) for each brand and stick to it. Companies should assign each brand an attribute and tout it as "number one" on that attribute. Buyers tend to remember "number one" well, especially in an overcommunicated society. Thus, Crest toothpaste consistently promotes its anticavity protection, and Volvo promotes safety. What are some "number one" positions that are attractive to promote? The major ones are "best quality," "best service," "lowest price," "best value," and "most advanced technology." A company that hammers away at one of these positions and consistently delivers on it will probably become best known and remembered for it.

Other marketers think that companies should position themselves on more than one differentiating factor. This may be necessary if two or more firms claim to be best on the same attribute. Steelcase, an office furniture systems company, differentiates itself from competitors on two benefits: best on-time delivery and best installation support.

Today, in a time when the mass market is fragmenting into many small segments, companies are trying to broaden their positioning strategies to appeal to more segments. For example, Lever Brothers introduced the first "3-in-1" bar soap—Lever

2000—offering cleansing, deodorizing, *and* moisturizing benefits. Clearly, many buyers want all three benefits, and the challenge is to convince them that one brand can deliver all three. Judging from Lever 2000's outstanding success, Lever Brothers easily met the challenge. However, as companies increase the number of claims for their brands, they risk disbelief and a loss of clear positioning.

In general, a company needs to avoid three major positioning errors. The first is *underpositioning*—failing to ever really position the company at all. Some companies discover that buyers have only a vague idea of what the company produces or they do not really know anything special about it. The second error is *overpositioning*—giving buyers too narrow a picture of the company. Thus, a consumer might think that the Steuben glass company makes only fine art glass costing $1,000 and up, when in fact it also makes affordable fine glass starting at around $50. Finally, companies must avoid *confused positioning*—leaving buyers with a confused image of a company. For example, Burger King has struggled without success for years to establish a profitable and consistent position. Over the past decade, it has fielded six separate advertising campaigns, with themes ranging from "Herb the nerd doesn't eat here," and "This is a Burger King town," to "The right food for the right times," to "Sometimes you've got to break the rules" and "BK Tee Vee." This barrage of positioning statements has left consumers confused and Burger King with poor sales and profits. "None of the campaigns dealt with the issue of why a consumer should go to Burger King rather than McDonalds," says one marketing expert.[25]

**WHICH DIFFERENCES TO PROMOTE?**  Not all brand differences are meaningful or worthwhile. Not every difference makes a good differentiator. Each difference has the potential to create company costs as well as customer benefits. Therefore, the company must carefully select the ways in which it will distinguish itself from competitors. A difference is worth establishing to the extent that it satisfies the following criteria: It is

- ◆ *Important*. The difference delivers a highly valued benefit to target buyers.
- ◆ *Distinctive*. Competitors do not offer the difference, or the company can offer it in a more distinctive way.
- ◆ *Superior*. The difference is superior to other ways that customers might obtain the same benefit.
- ◆ *Communicable*. The difference is communicable and visible to buyers.
- ◆ *Preemptive*. Competitors cannot easily copy the difference.
- ◆ *Affordable*. Buyers can afford to pay for the difference.
- ◆ *Profitable*. The company can introduce the difference profitably.

Many companies have introduced differentiations that failed one or more of these tests. The Westin Stamford hotel in Singapore advertises that it is the world's tallest hotel, a distinction that is not important to many tourists—in fact, it turns many off. Polaroid's Polarvision, which produced instantly developed home movies, bombed too. Although Polarvision was distinctive and even preemptive, it was inferior to another way of capturing motion on film—namely, camcorders. And when Pepsi introduced its clear Crystal Pepsi in 1993, customers were unimpressed: Although the new drink was distinctive, consumers didn't see "clarity" as an important benefit in a soft drink.[26] Thus, choosing competitive advantages upon which to position a product or service can be difficult, yet such choices may be crucial to success (see Marketing at Work 7-4).

## MARKETING AT WORK 7-4

# SCHOTT: POSITIONING FOR SUCCESS

Schott, the German manufacturer of glass for industrial and consumer products, had a problem deciding how to position its innovative product, Ceran, in the American market. The product, a glass-ceramic material made to cover the cooking surface of electric ranges, seemed to have everything going for it. It was completely nonporous (and thus stain resistant), easy to clean, and durable. Best of all, when one burner was lit, the heat didn't spread; it stayed confined to the circle directly above the burner. And after 10 years, cooktops made of Ceran still looked and performed like new.

Schott anticipated some difficulty igniting demand for Ceran in U.S. markets. First, it would have to win over American range manufacturers, who would then have to promote Ceran to middle markets—dealers, designers, architects, and builders. These middle-market customers

*Now properly positioned on their inherent beauty and design versatility, Schott's Ceran cooktops are selling very well.*

would, in turn, need to influence final consumers. Thus, Schott's U.S. subsidiary set out to sell Ceran aggressively to its target of 14 North American appliance manufacturers. The subsidiary positioned Ceran on its impressive technical and engineering attributes—showing cross-sections of stoves and using plenty of high-tech talk—then waited optimistically for the orders to roll in. The appliance companies listened politely to the rep's pitch,

## Communicating and Delivering the Chosen Position

Once it has chosen a position, the company must take strong steps to deliver and communicate the desired position to target consumers. All the company's marketing-mix efforts must support the positioning strategy. Positioning the company calls for concrete action, not just talk. If the company decides to build a position on better quality and service, it must first *deliver* that position. Designing the marketing mix—product, price, place, and promotion—essentially involves working out the tactical details of the positioning strategy. Thus, a firm that seizes on a "high-quality position" knows that it must produce high-quality products, charge a high price, distribute through high-quality dealers, and advertise in high-quality media. It must hire and train more service people, find retailers who have a good reputation for service, and develop sales and advertising messages that broadcast

ordered sample quantities—25 or so of each available color—and then . . . nothing. Absolutely nothing.

Research by Schott's advertising agency revealed two problems. First, Schott had completely failed to position Ceran among the manufacturers' customers. The material was still virtually unknown, not only among final consumers, but also among dealers, designers, architects, and builders. Second, the company was attempting to position the product on the wrong benefits. When selecting a rangetop to buy, customers seemed to care less about the sophisticated engineering that went into it and more about its appearance and cleanability. Their biggest questions were, "How does it look?" and "How easy is it to use?"

Based on these findings, Schott repositioned Ceran, shifting emphasis toward the material's inherent beauty and design versatility. And it launched an extensive promotion campaign to communicate the new position to middle-market and final buyers. Advertising to designers and remodelers revolved around lines like "Formalware for your kitchen," which presented the black rangetop as being as streamlined and elegant as a tuxedo. As a follow-up, to persuade designers and remodelers to add Ceran to their palette of materials, Schott positioned Ceran as "More than a rangetop, a means of expression." To reinforce this beauty and design positioning, ads featured visuals, including a geometric grid of a rangetop with one glowing red burner.

In addition to advertising, Schott's agency launched a massive public relations effort that resulted in substantial coverage in home design and remodeling publications. It also produced a video news release featuring Ceran that was picked up by 150 local TV stations nationwide. To reinforce a weak link in the selling chain—appliance salespeople who were poorly equipped to answer customer questions about Ceran—the agency created a video that the salespeople could show customers on the TVs in their own appliance stores.

The now properly and strongly positioned Ceran is selling well. Virtually all North American appliance makers are buying production quantities of Ceran and using it in their rangetops. All offer not one, but several smooth-top models. Schott is the major smooth-top supplier in the United States, and smooth tops now account for more than 20 percent of the electric stove market. And at a recent kitchen and bath show, 69 percent of all range models on display had smooth tops. To keep up with increasing demand, Schott has built a U.S. plant just to produce Ceran for the North American market.

*Source:* Adapted from Nancy Arnott, "Heating Up Sales: Formalware for Your Kitchen," *Sales & Marketing Management,* June 1994, pp. 77–78.

its superior service. This is the only way to build a consistent and believable high-quality, high-service position.

Companies often find it easier to come up with a good positioning strategy than to implement it. Establishing or changing a position usually takes a long time. In contrast, positions that have taken years to build can quickly be lost. Once a company has built the desired position, it must take care to maintain the position through consistent performance and communication. It must closely monitor and adapt the position over time to match changes in consumer needs and competitors' strategies. However, the company should avoid abrupt changes that might confuse consumers. Instead, a product's position should evolve gradually as it adapts to the ever-changing marketing environment.

## SUMMARY

Sellers can take three approaches to a market. *Mass marketing* is the decision to mass-produce and mass-distribute one product and attempt to attract all kinds of buyers. *Product variety marketing* is the decision to produce two or more market offers differentiated in style, features, quality, or sizes, designed to offer variety to the market and to set the seller's products apart from competitor's products. *Target marketing* is the decision to identify the different groups that make up a market and to develop products and marketing mixes for selected target markets. Sellers today are moving away from mass marketing and product differentiation toward target marketing because this approach is more helpful in spotting market opportunities and developing more effective products and marketing mixes.

The key steps in target marketing are market segmentation, market targeting, and market positioning. *Market segmentation* is the act of dividing a market into distinct groups of buyers who might merit separate products or marketing mixes. The marketer tries different variables to see which give the best segmentation opportunities. For consumer marketing, the major segmentation variables are geographic, demographic, psychographic, and behavioral. Business markets can be segmented by business consumer demographics, operating characteristics, purchasing approaches, and personal characteristics. The effectiveness of segmentation analysis depends on finding segments that are *measurable, accessible, substantial,* and *actionable.*

Next, the seller has to target the best market segments. The company first evaluates each segment's size and growth characteristics, structural attractiveness, and compatibility with company resources and objectives. It then chooses one of three market-coverage strategies. The seller can ignore segment differences (*undifferentiated marketing*), develop different market offers for several segments (*differentiated marketing*), or go after one or a few market segments (*concentrated marketing*). Much depends on company resources, product variability, product life-cycle stage, and competitive marketing strategies.

Once a company has decided what segments to enter, it must decide on its *market positioning* strategy—on which positions to occupy in its chosen segments. It can position its products on specific product attributes, according to usage occasion, for certain classes of users, or by product class. It can position either against or away from competitors. The positioning task consists of three steps: identifying a set of possible competitive advantages upon which to build a position, selecting the right competitive advantages, and effectively communicating and delivering the chosen position to the market.

## KEY TERMS

Age and life-cycle segmentation
Behavioral segmentation
Benefit segmentation
Competitive advantage
Concentrated marketing
Demographic segmentation
Differentiated marketing

Gender segmentation
Geographic segmentation
Income segmentation
Intermarket segmentation
Market
Market positioning
Market segmentation

Market targeting
Micromarketing
Occasion segmentation
Product position
Psychographic segmentation
Target market
Undifferentiated marketing

## QUESTIONS FOR DISCUSSION

1. The average Cadillac buyer is a 63-year-old white male, a fact responsible for declining sales. How can market segmentation analysis help Cadillac attract a broader customer base? Refer in your answer to issues of age, income, gender, and life-cycle and benefit segmentation.

2. Gucci, the maker of fine Italian leather goods and fashions, had fallen on hard times. Family feuding forced the sale of the company to the Bahrain-based investment bank Investcorp, which, in turn, took Gucci public. During the years of family squabbling, the Gucci name lost much of its appeal among high-income consumers. Quality was down, and distribution was too wide to maintain the aura of product exclusivity. The company faced the challenge of winning its core buyers back. Describe some of the steps you would take to woo back Gucci's core buyers?

3. What variables are used in segmenting the market for beer? Give examples.

4. Think about your classmates in this course. Can you classify them into different segments with specific names? What is your major segmentation variable? Could you effectively market products to these segments?

5. Some industrial suppliers make above-average profits by offering service, selection, and reliability, all at a premium price. How can these suppliers segment the market to find customers who are willing to pay more for these benefits?

6. Describe the roles that product attributes and perceptions of attributes play in positioning a product. Can an attribute held by several competing brands be used in a successful positioning strategy?

## APPLYING THE CONCEPTS

1. By looking at advertising, and at products themselves, we can often see how marketers are attempting to position their products, and what target market they hope to reach.

   ◆ Define the positionings of and the target markets for Coca-Cola, Pepsi Cola, Mountain Dew, Dr. Pepper, and 7-Up.

   ◆ Define the positionings of and target markets for McDonald's, Burger King, Wendy's, and a regional restaurant chain in your area such as Jack in the Box, Bojangle's, or Friendly's.

   ◆ Do you think that the soft drinks and restaurants have distinctive positionings and target markets? Are some more clearly defined than others?

2. It is possible to market people as well as products or services. When we are marketing a person, we can *position* that individual for a particular target market. Describe briefly how you would position yourself for the following target markets.

   ◆ For a potential employer.

   ◆ For a potential boyfriend or girlfriend.

   ◆ For your mother or father.

   Would you position yourself in different ways for these different target markets? How do the positionings differ? Why do they differ?

## REFERENCES

1. Laurel Cutler, quoted in "Stars of the 1980s Cast Their Light," *Fortune*, July 3, 1989, p. 76.

2. Robert E. Linneman and John L. Stanton, Jr., *Making Niche Marketing Work: How to Grow Bigger by Acting Smaller* (New York: McGraw-Hill, Inc., 1991).

3. Jennifer Lawrence, "Don't Look for P&G to Pare Detergents," *Advertising Age*, May 31, 1993, pp. 1, 3.

4. Bruce Hager, "Podunk Is Beckoning," *Business Week*, December 2, 1991, p. 76; and David Greisling, "The Boonies Are Booming," *Business Week*, October 9, 1995, pp. 104–10.

5. Cyndee Miller, "Xers Know They're a Target Market, and They Hate That," *Advertising Age*, December 6, 1993, pp. 2, 15.

6. "Automakers Learn Better Roads to Women's Market," *Marketing News*, October 12, 1992, p. 2. Also see Betsy Sharkey, "The Many Faces of Eve," *Adweek*, June 25, 1990, pp. 44–49; Tim Triplett, "Automakers Recognizing Value of Women's Market," *Marketing News*, April 11, 1994, pp. 1, 2; Julie Ralston, "Chevy Targets Women," *Advertising Age*, August 7, 1995, p. 24; and Gerry Myers, "Selling to Women," *American Demographics*, April 1996, pp. 36–42.

7. Raymond Serafin, "I Am Woman, Hear Me Roar . . . In My Car," *Advertising Age*, November 7, 1994, pp. 1, 8. Also see, Leah Rickard, "Subaru, GMC Top Push to Win Over Women," *Advertising Age*, April 3, 1995, p. S24; and Gerry Myers, "Selling to Women," *American Demographics*, April 1996, pp. 36–41.

8. See "The Wealthy," *Advertising Age*, April 3, 1995, p. S28.

9. Steve Lawrence, "The Green in Blue-Collar Retailing," *Fortune*, May 27,

1985, pp. 74–77; Brian Bremner, "Looking Downscale without Looking Down," Business Week, October 8, 1990, pp. 62–67; Jan Larsen, "Reaching Downscale Markets," American Demographics, November 1991, pp. 38–40; and Cyndee Miller, "The Have-Nots: Firms with the Right Products and Services Succeed among Low-Income Consumers," Marketing News, August 1, 1994, pp. 1, 2.

10. For a detailed discussion of personality and buyer behavior, see Leon G. Schiffman and Leslie Lazar Kanuk, Consumer Behavior, 5th ed. (Englewood Cliffs, NJ: Prentice Hall, 1994), Chapter 5.

11. See Laurie Freeman and Cleveland Horton, "Spree: Honda's Scooters Ride the Cutting Edge," Advertising Age, September 5, 1985, pp. 3, 35.

12. Mark Maremont, "The Hottest Thing Since the Flashbulb," Business Week, September 7, 1992. Also see Laura Loro, "Single-Use Cameras Snap the Photo Industry," Advertising Age, September 28, 1994, p. 28.

13. See Norton Paley, "Cut Out for Success," Sales & Marketing Management, April 1994, pp. 43–44.

14. Daniel S. Levine, "Justice Served," Sales & Marketing Management, May 1995, pp. 53–61.

15. V. Kasturi Rangan, Rowland T. Moriarty, and Gordon S. Swartz, "Segmenting Customers in Mature Industrial Markets," Journal of Marketing, October 1992, pp. 72–82. Also see "Penetrating Purchaser Personalities," Marketing Management, Spring 1995, p. 22.

16. For more on segmenting business markets, see John Berrigan and Carl Finkbeiner, Segmentation Marketing: New Methods for Capturing Business (New York: Harper Business, 1992); Rodney L. Griffith and Louis G. Pol, "Segmenting Industrial Markets," Industrial Marketing Management, No. 23, 1994, pp. 39–46; and Sally Dibb and Lyndon Simkin, "Implementation Problems in Industrial Market Segmentation," Industrial Marketing Management, No. 23, 1994, pp. 55–63.

17. Marlene L. Rossman, "Understanding Five Nations of Latin America," Marketing News, October 11, 1985, p. 10; as quoted in Subhash C. Jain, International Marketing Management, 3rd ed. (Boston: PWS-Kent Publishing Company, 1990), p. 366.

18. Cyndee Miller, "Teens Seen as the First Truly Global Consumer," Advertising Age, March 27, 1995, p. 9.

19. Shawn Tully, "Teens: The Most Global Market of All," Fortune, May 16, 1994, pp. 90–97.

20. See Joe Schwartz, "Southpaw Strategy," American Demographics, June 1988, p. 61; and "Few Companies Tailor Products for Lefties," Wall Street Journal, August 2, 1989, p. 2.

21. See Michael Porter, Competitive Advantage (New York: Free Press, 1985), pp. 4–8 and pp. 234–36.

22. See John Saunders and Veronica Wong, Kotler & Armstrong's Principles of Marketing, First European Edition (London: Prentice Hall, 1996), Chapter 8.

23. Christopher Power, "How to Get Closer to Your Customers," Business Week, special issue on economies of scale, 1993, pp. 42–45.

24. See Tom Peters, Thriving on Chaos (New York: Alfred A. Knopf, Inc., 1987), pp. 56–57.

25. "Big Flops," American Demographics, February 1995, pp. 1, 6.

26. Tim Triplett, "Consumers Show Little Taste for Clear Beverages," Marketing News, May 23, 1994, pp. 1, 11.

# 8
# Product and
# Services Strategy

Each year, Revlon sells more than $1 billion worth of cosmetics, toiletries, and fragrances to consumers around the world. Its many successful perfume products make Revlon number one in the popular-price segment of the $4 billion fragrance market. In one sense, Revlon's perfumes are no more than careful mixtures of oils and chemicals that have nice scents. But Revlon knows that when it sells perfume, it sells much more than fragrant fluids; it sells what the fragrances can do for the women who use them.

Of course, a perfume's scent contributes to its success or failure. Fragrance marketers agree: "No smell; no sell." Most new aromas are developed by elite "perfumers" at one of many select "fragrance houses." Perfume is shipped from the fragrance houses in big, ugly drums—hardly the stuff of which dreams are made! Although a $180-an-ounce perfume may cost no more than $10 to produce, to perfume consumers the product is much more than a few dollars worth of ingredients and a pleasing smell.

Many things beyond the ingredients and scent add to a perfume's allure. In fact, when Revlon designs a new perfume, the scent may be the *last* element developed. Revlon first researches women's feelings about themselves and their relationships with others. It then develops and tests new perfume concepts that match women's changing values, desires, and lifestyles. When Revlon finds a promising new concept, it creates and names a scent to fit the idea. Revlon's research in the early 1970s showed that women were feeling more competitive with men and that they were striving to find individual identities. For this new woman of the 1970s, Revlon created Charlie, the first of the "lifestyle" perfumes. Thousands of women adopted Charlie as a bold statement of independence, and it quickly became the world's best-selling perfume.

In the late 1970s, Revlon research showed a shift in women's attitudes—"women had made the equality point, which Charlie addressed. Now women were hungering for an expression of femininity." The Charlie girls had grown up; they now wanted perfumes that were subtle rather than shocking. Thus, Revlon subtly shifted Charlie's position: The perfume still made its "independent lifestyle" statement, but with an added tinge of "femininity and romance." Revlon also launched a perfume for the woman of the 1980s, Jontue, which was positioned on a theme of romance.

Revlon continues to refine Charlie's position, now targeting the woman of the 1990s who is "able to do it all, but smart enough to know what she wants to do." After almost 20 years, aided by continuous but subtle repositioning, Charlie remains a best-selling mass-market perfume.

A perfume's *name* is an important product attribute. Revlon uses such names as Charlie, Fleurs de Jontue, Ciara, Scoundrel, Guess, and Unforgettable to create images that support each perfume's positioning. Last year, it introduced Ajee, which means "the power of woman," targeted toward African Americans. Competitors offer perfumes with such names as Obsession, Passion, Uninhibited, Wildheart, Opium, Joy, Beautiful, White Linen, Youth Dew, and Eternity. These names suggest that the perfumes will do something more than just make you smell better. Oscar de la Renta's Ruffles perfume *began* as a name, one chosen because it created images of whimsy, youth, glamour, and femininity—all well suited to the target market of young, stylish women. Only later was a scent selected to go with the product's name and positioning.

Revlon must also carefully *package* its perfumes. To consumers, the bottle and package are the most real symbols of the perfume and its image. Bottles must feel comfortable and be easy to handle, and they must look impressive when displayed in stores. Most important, they must support the perfume's concept and image.

So when a woman buys perfume, she buys much, much more than simply a fragrant liquid. The perfume's image, its promises, its scent, its name and package, the company that makes it, the stores that sell it—all become a part of the total perfume product. When Revlon sells perfume, it sells more than just the tangible product. It sells lifestyle, self-expression, and exclusivity; achievement, success, and status; femininity, romance, passion, and fantasy; memories, hopes, and dreams.[1] ■

# CHAPTER OBJECTIVES

## After reading this chapter, you should be able to:

**1** Define *product* and the major classifications of consumer and industrial products.

**2** Describe the roles of product branding, packaging, and labeling.

**3** Explain the decisions that companies make when developing product lines and mixes.

**4** Identify the four characteristics that affect the marketing of a service.

**5** Explain how organizations, persons, places, and ideas are marketed.

Clearly, perfume is more than just perfume when Revlon sells it. This chapter begins with a deceptively simple question: *What is a product?* After answering this question, we look at ways to classify products in consumer and business markets. Then we discuss the important decisions that marketers make regarding individual products, product lines, and product mixes. Finally, we examine the special characteristics and marketing requirements of services.

# ▶ WHAT IS A PRODUCT?

**Product**
Anything that can be offered to a market for attention, acquisition, use, or consumption that might satisfy a want or need.

A Sony CD player, a Supercuts haircut, a Billy Joel concert, a Hawaiian vacation, a GMC truck, H&R Block tax preparation services, and advice from an attorney are all products. We define a **product** as anything that can be offered to a market for attention, acquisition, use, or consumption and that might satisfy a want or need. Products include more than just tangible goods. Broadly defined, products include physical objects, services, persons, places, organizations, ideas, or mixes of these entities. Services are products that consist of activities, benefits, or satisfactions that are offered for sale, such as banking, hotel, tax preparation, and home repair services. Services are essentially intangible and do not result in the ownership of anything. Because of the importance of services in the world economy, we will look at them more closely in a section at the end of this chapter.

Product planners need to think about products and services on three levels. The most basic level is the *core product*, which addresses the question: *What is the buyer really buying?* As Figure 8-1 illustrates, the core product stands at the center of the total product. It consists of the core, problem-solving benefits that consumers seek when they buy a product or service. A woman buying lipstick buys more than lip color. Charles Revson of Revlon saw this early: "In the factory, we make cosmetics; in the store, we sell hope." And Ritz-Carlton Hotels knows that it offers its guests more than simply rooms for rent—it provides "memorable travel experiences." Thus, when designing products, marketers must first define the core of *benefits* that the product will provide to consumers.

The product planner must next build an *actual product* around the core product. Actual products may have as many as five characteristics: a *quality level*,

*Core, actual, and augmented product: consumers perceive this Sony camcorder as a complex bundle of tangible and intangible features and services that deliver a core benefit—a convenient, high-quality way to capture important moments.*

*features, design,* a *brand name,* and *packaging.* For example, a Sony camcorder is an actual product. Its name, parts, styling, features, packaging, and other attributes have all been combined carefully to deliver the core benefit—a convenient, high-quality way to capture important moments.

Finally, the product planner must build an *augmented product* around the core and actual products by offering additional consumer services and benefits. Sony must offer more than just a camcorder. It must provide consumers with a complete solution to their picture-taking problems. Thus, when consumers buy a Sony camcorder, Sony and its dealers also might give buyers a warranty on parts and workmanship, free lessons on how to use the camcorder, quick repair services when needed, and a toll-free telephone number to call if they have problems or questions.

**FIGURE 8-1**
*Three levels of product*

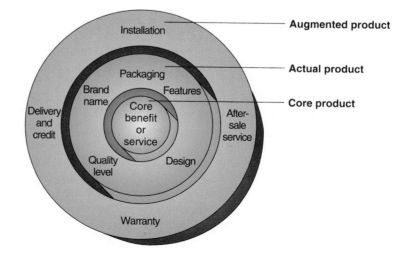

Therefore, a product is more than a simple set of tangible features. Consumers tend to see products as complex bundles of benefits that satisfy their needs. When developing products, marketers first must identify the *core* consumer needs that the product will satisfy. They must then design the *actual* product and find ways to *augment* it in order to create the bundle of benefits that will best satisfy consumers.

# ▶ PRODUCT CLASSIFICATIONS

In developing marketing strategies for their products and services, marketers have developed several product-classification schemes. First, marketers divide products and services into two broad classes based on the types of consumer that use them—*consumer products* and *industrial products*.

## CONSUMER PRODUCTS

**Consumer products**
Products bought by final consumers for personal consumption.

**Consumer products** are those bought by final consumers for personal consumption. Marketers usually classify these goods further based on *how consumers go about buying them*. Consumer products include *convenience products, shopping products, specialty products*, and *unsought products*. These products differ in the ways that consumers buy them, and therefore in how they are marketed (see Table 8-1).

**TABLE 8-1**   *Marketing Considerations for Consumer Products*

| Marketing Considerations | Type of Consumer Product | | | |
|---|---|---|---|---|
| | Convenience | Shopping | Specialty | Unsought |
| Customer buying behavior | Frequent purchase, little planning, little comparison or shopping effort, low customer involvement | Less frequent purchase, much planning and shopping effort, comparison of brands on price, quality, style | Strong brand preference and loyalty, special purchase effort, little comparison of brands, low price sensitivity | Little product awareness, knowledge, or, if aware, little interest (or negative interest) |
| Price | Low price | Higher price | High price | Varies |
| Distribution | Widespread distribution, convenient locations | Selective distribution in fewer outlets | Exclusive distribution in only one or a few outlets per market area | Varies |
| Promotion | Mass advertising and sales promotion by the producer | Advertising and personal selling by producer and resellers | More carefully targeted promotion by producer and resellers | Aggressive advertising and personal selling by producer and resellers |
| Examples | Toothpaste, magazines, laundry detergent | Major appliances, televisions, furniture, clothing | Luxury goods, such as Rolex watches or fine crystal | Life insurance, Red Cross blood donations |

**Convenience products**
Consumer products that the customer usually buys frequently, immediately, and with a minimum of comparison and buying effort.

**Shopping products**
Consumer products that the customer, in the process of selection and puchase, characteristically compares on such bases as suitability, quality, price, and style.

**Specialty products**
Consumer products with unique characteristics or brand identification for which a significant group of buyers is willing to make a special purchase effort.

**Unsought products**
Consumer products that the consumer either does not know about or knows about but does not normally think of buying.

**Industrial products**
Products bought by individuals and organizations for further processing or for use in conducting a business.

**Convenience products** are consumer products and services that the customer usually buys frequently, immediately, and with a minimum of comparison and buying effort. Examples include soap, candy, and newspapers. They are usually low priced, and marketers place them in many outlets to make them readily available when customers need them.

**Shopping products** are less frequently purchased consumer products that customers compare carefully on suitability, quality, price, and style. When buying shopping products, consumers spend much time and effort in gathering information and making comparisons. Examples include furniture, clothing, used cars, and major appliances. Shopping products marketers usually distribute their products through fewer outlets but provide deeper sales support to help customers in their comparison efforts.

**Specialty products** are consumer products with unique characteristics or brand identification for which a significant group of buyers is willing to make a special purchase effort. Examples include specific brands and types of cars, high-priced photographic equipment, and custom-made men's suits. A Rolls-Royce, for example, is a specialty product because buyers are usually willing to travel great distances to buy one. Buyers normally do not compare specialty products. They invest only the time needed to reach dealers carrying the wanted products.

**Unsought products** are consumer products that the consumer either does not know about or knows about but does not normally think of buying. Most major new innovations are unsought until the consumer becomes aware of them through advertising. Classic examples of known but unsought products are life insurance and blood donations to the Red Cross. By their very nature, unsought products require a lot of advertising, personal selling, and other marketing efforts.

# INDUSTRIAL PRODUCTS

**Industrial products** are those purchased for further processing or for use in conducting a business. Thus, the distinction between a consumer product and an industrial product is based on the *purpose* for which the product is bought. If a consumer buys a lawn mower for use around the yard, the lawn mower is a consumer product. If the same consumer buys the same lawn mower for use in a landscaping business, the lawn mower is an industrial product.

The three groups of industrial products include materials and parts, capital items, and supplies and services. *Materials and parts* include raw materials and manufactured materials and parts. Raw materials consist of farm products (wheat, cotton, livestock, fruits, vegetables) and natural products (fish, lumber, crude petroleum, iron ore). Manufactured materials and parts consist of component materials (iron, yarn, cement, wires) and component parts (small motors, tires, castings). Most manufactured materials and parts are sold directly to industrial users. Price and service are the major marketing factors; branding and advertising tend to be less important.

*Capital items* are industrial products that aid in the buyer's production or operations, including installations and accessory equipment. Installations consist of major purchases such as buildings (factories, offices) and fixed equipment (generators, drill presses, large computer systems, elevators). Accessory equipment includes portable factory equipment and tools (hand tools, lift trucks) and office equipment (fax machines, desks). They have a shorter life than installations and simply aid in the production process.

The final group of business products is *supplies and services.* Supplies include operating supplies (lubricants, coal, paper, pencils) and repair and maintenance items (paint, nails, brooms). Supplies are the convenience products of the industrial field because they are usually purchased with a minimum of effort or comparison. Business services include maintenance and repair services (window cleaning, computer repair) and business advisory services (legal, management consulting, advertising). Such services are usually supplied under contract.

# ▶ INDIVIDUAL PRODUCT DECISIONS

Figure 8-2 shows the important decisions in the development and marketing of individual products and services. We will focus on decisions about *product attributes, branding, packaging, labeling,* and *product-support services.*

## PRODUCT ATTRIBUTES

Developing a product or service involves defining the benefits that it will offer. These benefits are communicated and delivered by product attributes such as *quality, features,* and *design.*

### Product Quality

**Product quality**
The ability of a product to perform its functions; it includes the product's overall durability, reliability, precision, ease of operation and repair, and other valued attributes.

Quality is one of the marketer's major positioning tools. **Product quality** has two dimensions—level and consistency. In developing a product, the marketer must first choose a *quality level* that will support the product's position in the target market. Here, product quality means *performance quality*—the ability of a product to perform its functions. It includes the product's overall durability, reliability, precision, ease of operation and repair, and other valued attributes. For example, a Rolls-Royce provides higher performance quality than does a Chevrolet: It has a smoother ride, handles better, and lasts longer. It is more expensive and sells to a market with more means and requirements. Companies rarely try to offer the highest possible performance quality level—few customers want or can afford the high levels of quality offered in products such as a Rolls-Royce automobile, a Sub Zero refrigerator, or a Rolex watch. Instead, companies choose a quality level that matches target market needs and the quality levels of competing products.

Beyond quality level, high quality also can mean high levels of quality *consistency.* Here, product quality means *conformance quality*—freedom from defects and *consistency* in delivering a targeted level of performance. All companies should strive for high levels of conformance quality. In this sense, a Chevrolet can have just as much quality as a Rolls-Royce. Although a Chevy doesn't perform as well as a Rolls, it can as consistently deliver the quality that customers pay for and expect.

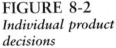

**FIGURE 8-2**
*Individual product decisions*

During the past two decades, a renewed emphasis on quality has spawned a global quality movement. Most firms now practice "Total Quality Management" (TQM), an effort to constantly improve product and process quality in every phase of their operations. Beyond simply reducing product defects, the ultimate goal of total quality is to improve customer value. For example, when Motorola first began its total quality program in the early 1980s, its goal was to drastically reduce manufacturing defects. In recent years, however, Motorola's quality concept has evolved into one of "customer-defined quality" and "total customer satisfaction." (See Marketing at Work 8-1.)

Recently, the total quality management movement has drawn criticism. Many companies have viewed TQM as a magic cure-all and have created token total

## MARKETING AT WORK 8-1

# MOTOROLA'S CUSTOMER-DRIVEN "SIX-SIGMA" QUALITY

Founded in 1928, Motorola introduced the first commercially successful car radio—hence the name Motorola, suggesting "sound in motion." During World War II, it developed the first two-way radios ("walkie-talkies"), and by the 1950s, Motorola had become a household name in consumer electronics products. In the 1970s, however, facing intense competition mostly from Japanese firms, Motorola abandoned the radios and televisions that had made it famous. Instead, it focused on advanced telecommunications and electronics products—two-way radios, pagers, cellular telephones, semiconductors, and related gear. Despite that effort, by the early 1980s, Japanese competitors were still beating Motorola to the market with higher-quality products at lower prices.

During the past decade, however, Motorola has come roaring back. It now leads all competitors in the global two-way mobile radio market and ranks number one in cellular tele-

phones, with a 45 percent worldwide market share. Motorola is the world's fifth-largest semiconductor producer, behind only Intel, NEC, Toshiba, and Fujitsu. Once in danger of being forced

*"Quality means the world to us," claims Motorola. An obsession with customer-driven quality has helped the company to achieve worldwide leadership in many product markets.*

out of the pager business altogether, Motorola now dominates that market with an astonishing 85 percent global market share. And rather than suffering at the hands of Japanese competitors, Motorola's sales in Japan now exceed $2 billion, accounting for about 8 percent of total company sales.

How has Motorola achieved such remarkable leadership? The answer is deceptively simple: an obsessive dedication to *quality.* In the early 1980s, Motorola launched an aggressive crusade to improve product quality, first by tenfold, then by a hundredfold. It set the unheard-of goal of "six-sigma" quality. Six sigma is a statistical term that means "six standard deviations from a statistical performance average." In plain English, the six-sigma standard means that Motorola set out to slash product defects to fewer than 3.4 per million for every process—99.9997 percent defect free. "Six sigma" became Motorola's rallying cry. In 1988, it received one of the first annual

quality programs that applied quality principles only superficially. As a result, recent surveys show that two-thirds or more of American managers think that TQM has failed in their companies. However, despite the recent backlash against TQM, basic quality principles appear sound:

> It's true that obsessively focusing on quality alone can take your eye off other critical variables—such as what your customers might want. Yes, many TQM programs have been badly executed, particularly those imposed from above in cookie cutter fashion. And, yes, TQM is, as the refrain goes, no panacea. But make no mistake, total quality's principles still represent a sound way to do business.... Many companies that

Malcolm Baldrige National Quality Awards recognizing "preeminent quality leadership."

Motorola's initial efforts focused on manufacturing improvements. The goal was to prevent defects by *designing* products for quality and making things right the *first* time and *every* time. Meeting the six-sigma standard meant that everyone in the organization had to strive for quality improvement. Thus, total quality has become an important part of Motorola's basic corporate culture. Motorola spends $160 million annually to educate employees about quality, among other things, and then rewards people when they make things right. The company also forces its suppliers to meet exacting quality standards. Some suppliers grumble, but those that survive benefit greatly from their own quality improvements. As an executive from one of Motorola's suppliers puts it, "If we can supply Motorola, we can supply God."

More recently, as Motorola has developed a deeper understanding of the meaning of quality, its initial focus on preventing manufacturing defects has

evolved into an emphasis on *customer-driven quality* and customer value. "Quality," notes Motorola's vice president of quality, "has to do something for the customer. If [a product] does not work the way the user needs it to work, the defect is as big to the user as if it doesn't work the way the designer planned it. Our definition of a defect is 'if the customer doesn't like it, it's a defect.'"

Thus, since the late 1980s, the fundamental aim of Motorola's quality movement has been total customer satisfaction. Instead of focusing just on manufacturing defects, Motorola surveys customers about their quality needs, analyzes customer complaints, and studies service records in a constant quest to improve value to the customer. Motorola's executives routinely visit customers to gain better insights into their needs. As a result, Motorola's total quality management has done more than reduce product defects; it has helped the company to shift from an inwardly focused, engineering orientation to a market-driven, customer-focused one. The company has now expanded

its quality program to all of its departments and processes, from manufacturing and product development to market research, finance, and even advertising.

Some skeptics are concerned that Motorola's obsession might be too expensive. Not so, claims Motorola. In fact, the reverse is true—superior quality is the lowest-cost way to do things. The costs of monitoring and fixing mistakes can far exceed the costs of getting things right in the first place. Motorola estimates that its quality efforts have resulted in cumulative savings of more than $9 billion during the past eight years.

And so Motorola's quest for quality continues. By the year 2001, Motorola is shooting for near-perfection—a mind-boggling rate of just *one* defect per *billion.*

*Sources:* Quotes from "Future Perfect," *The Economist,* January 4, 1992, p. 61; Lois Therrien, "Motorola and NEC: Going for Glory," *Business Week,* Special issue on quality, 1991, pp. 60–61; and B. G. Yovovich, "Motorola's Quest for Quality," *Business Marketing,* September 1991, pp. 14–16. Also see Ronald Henkoff, "Keeping Motorola on a Roll," *Fortune,* April 18, 1994, pp. 67–78; and J. Ward Best, "The Making of Motorola," *Durham Herald-Sun,* February 12, 1995, pp. A1, A11.

have successfully adopted TQM don't even use the phrase "total quality" anymore; it has simply become a way of doing business.[2]

More and more, companies are taking a "return on quality" approach, viewing quality as an investment and holding quality efforts accountable for bottom-line results.[3]

Thus, many companies today have turned quality into a potent strategic weapon. They gain an edge over competitors by consistently and profitably meeting customers' needs and preferences for quality. In fact, quality has now become a competitive necessity—in the 1990s and beyond, only companies with the best quality will thrive.

## Product Features

A product can be offered with varying features. A "stripped-down" model, one without any extras, is the starting point. The company can create higher-level models by adding more features. Features are a competitive tool for differentiating the company's product from competitors' products. Being the first producer to introduce a needed and valued new feature is one of the most effective ways to compete.

How can a company identify new features and decide which ones to add to its product? The company should periodically survey buyers who have used the product and ask these questions: How do you like the product? Which specific features of the product do you like most? Which features could we add to improve the product? How much would you pay for each feature? The answers provide the company with a rich list of feature ideas. The company then can assess each feature's *value* to customers versus its *cost* to the company. Features that customers value little in relation to costs should be dropped; those that customers value highly in relation to costs should be added.

## Product Design

Another way to add customer value is through distinctive *product design*. Some companies have reputations for outstanding design, such as Black & Decker in cordless appliances and tools, Steelcase in office furniture and systems, Bose in audio equipment, and Ciba Corning in medical equipment. Many companies, however, lack a "design touch." Their product designs function poorly or are dull or common looking. Yet design can be one of the most powerful competitive weapons in a company's marketing arsenal.

Design is a larger concept than style. *Style* simply describes the appearance of a product. Styles can be eye-catching or yawn-inspiring. A sensational style may grab attention, but it does not necessarily make the product *perform* better. In some cases, it might even result in worse performance. For example, a chair may look great yet be very uncomfortable. Unlike style, *design* is more than skin deep—it goes to the very heart of a product. Good design contributes to a product's usefulness as well as to its looks.

Design offers one of the most potent tools for differentiating and positioning a company's products and services. Good design can attract attention, improve product performance, cut production costs, and give the product a strong competitive advantage in the target market. For example, the radical design of the first Ford Taurus, with its sleek styling, passenger comforts, engineering advances, and efficient manufacturing, made it America's best-selling car. Braun, a German division of Gillette which has elevated design to a high art, has had outstanding success with its coffee makers, food processors, hair dryers, electric razors, and other small appliances. And Black & Decker has learned that innovative design can be very profitable:

> What could be handier than a flashlight that you don't have to hold while you're probing under the sink for the cause of a leaky faucet? Black & Decker's flexible snakelight looks just like its namesake and attaches itself to almost anything, leaving your hands free. It can also stand up like an illuminated cobra to light your work space. The design won Black & Decker a gold medal in the Industrial Design Excellence Awards competition. More importantly, in a market where the average price is just $6, consumers are paying $30 for this flexible flashlight.

# BRANDING

**Brand**
A name, term, sign, symbol, or design, or a combination of these intended to identify the goods or services of one seller or group of sellers and to differentiate them from those of competitors.

A **brand** is a name, term, sign, symbol, or design, or a combination of these that identifies the maker or seller of a product. It is a seller's promise to deliver consistently a specific set of features, benefits, and services to buyers. Consumers view a brand as an important part of a product, and branding can add value to a product. For example, most consumers would perceive a bottle of White Linen perfume as a high-quality, expensive product. But the same perfume in an unmarked bottle would likely be viewed as lower in quality, even if the fragrance were identical.

Branding has become so strong that today hardly anything goes unbranded. Salt is packaged in branded containers, common nuts and bolts are packaged with a distributor's label, and automobile parts—spark plugs, tires, filters—bear brand names that differ from those of the auto makers. Even fruits and vegetables are branded—Sunkist oranges, Dole pineapples, and Chiquita bananas.

Branding helps buyers in many ways. Brand names help consumers identify products that might benefit them. The brand name becomes the basis on which a whole story can be built about a product's special qualities. Brands also tell the buyer something about product quality. Buyers who always buy the same brand know that they will get the same quality each time they buy.

Branding also gives the seller several advantages. The brand name makes it easier for the seller to process orders and track down problems. Thus, Anheuser-Busch receives an order for a hundred cases of Michelob beer instead of an order for "some of your better beer." The seller's brand name and trademark provide legal protection for unique product features that otherwise might be copied by competitors. Branding lets the seller attract a loyal and profitable set of customers. Branding helps the seller to segment markets. For example, General Mills can offer Cheerios, Wheaties, Total, Lucky Charms, and many other cereal brands, not just one general product for all consumers.

**Brand equity**
The value of a brand, based on the extent to which it has high brand loyalty, name awareness, perceived quality, strong brand associations, and other assets such as patents, trademarks, and channel relationships.

## Brand Equity

Powerful brand names command strong consumer preference. Companies around the world invest heavily to create strong national or even global recognition and preference for their brand names. Perhaps the most distinctive skill of professional marketers is their ability to create, maintain, protect, and enhance brands.

Brands vary in the amount of power and value that they have in the marketplace. A powerful brand has high **brand equity.** Brands have higher brand equity to the extent that they have higher brand loyalty, name awareness, perceived quality, strong brand associations, and other assets such as patents, trademarks, and channel relationships. A brand with strong brand equity is a very valuable asset.

Measuring the actual equity of a brand name is difficult. Because it is so hard to measure, companies usually do not list brand equity on their balance sheets. However, according to one estimate, the brand equity of Coca-Cola is $39 billion, Marlboro $39 billion, IBM $17 billion, and Kodak $12 billion.[5] The world's top brands include such superpowers as Coca-Cola, Campbell, Disney, Kodak, Sony, Mercedes-Benz, and McDonald's (see Marketing at Work 8-2).

High brand equity provides a company with many competitive advantages. A powerful brand enjoys a high level of consumer brand awareness and loyalty. Because consumers expect stores to carry the brand, the company has more leverage in bargaining with resellers. Because the brand name carries high credibility, the company can more easily launch brand extensions. Above all, a powerful brand offers the company some defense against fierce price competition. Some analysts see brands as *the* major enduring asset of a company, outlasting the company's specific products and facilities.

Branding poses challenging decisions to the marketer. Figure 8-3 shows the key branding decisions.

## Brand Name Selection

A good name can add greatly to a product's success. However, finding the best brand name is a difficult task. It begins with a careful review of the product and its benefits, the target market, and proposed marketing strategies.

Among desirable qualities for a brand name: (1) It should suggest something about the product's benefits and qualities. Examples: Diehard, Easy-Off, Craftsman, Sunkist, Spic and Span, Snuggles. (2) It should be easy to pronounce, recognize, and remember. Short names help. Examples: Tide, Aim, Puffs. But longer ones are sometimes effective. Examples: "Love My Carpet" carpet cleaner, "I Can't Believe It's Not Butter" margarine, Better Business Bureau. (3) The brand name should be distinctive. Examples: Taurus, Kodak, Exxon. (4) The name should translate easily into foreign languages. Before spending $100 million to change its name to Exxon, Standard Oil of New Jersey tested several names in 54 languages in more than 150 foreign markets. It found that the name Enco referred to a stalled engine when pronounced in Japanese. (5) It should be capable of registration and legal protection. A brand name cannot be registered if it infringes on existing brand names.

Once chosen, the brand name must be protected. Many firms try to build a brand name that will eventually become identified with the product category.

**FIGURE 8-3**
*Major branding decisions*

## MARKETING AT WORK 8-2

# THE WORLD'S MOST POWERFUL BRAND NAMES

Coca-Cola, McDonald's, AT&T, Campbell, Disney, Kodak, Kellogg, Hershey—such familiar brand names are household words to most Americans. Companies around the world invest billions of dollars each year to create preference for these and hundreds of other major brands. For example, AT&T, the nation's most heavily advertised brand name, is backed by almost $700 million in advertising each year. Powerful brand names provide strong competitive advantage in the marketplace.

What are the world's most powerful brands? A study by Landor Associates, an image consulting firm, surveyed 9,000 consumers in the United States, Western Europe, and Japan about their familiarity with and esteem for more than 6,000 brands. From the results, it developed brand "image-power" rankings. Listed below are the top 10 brands for each part of the world.

The Landor study suggests that few brands have yet achieved true global status. Although some 20 brands were internationally known, and another 45 were poised for global prominence, no product made it onto the top 10 lists of all three markets. Only two brands—Coca-Cola and Sony—appeared in each market's top 40. And only six other brands made the top 100 in each market: Disney, Nestlé, Toyota, McDonald's, Panasonic, and Kleenex. The study also shows that Americans like American products. The list of top 10 American brands reads like a page out of the corporate American history book. And of the top 100 ranked brands in the United States, 97 claim American roots.

The rankings also suggest strong cultural differences among consumers in the United States, Europe, and Japan. For example, Americans appear food oriented—six of the top 10 brands are food related. In the other regions, cars and high-tech brands are more revered. Based on the top 10 list, American consumers appear satisfied with simple pleasures like a Big Mac, chocolates, and, as a real self-indulgent treat, luxury ice creams. European and Japanese consumers seem to have more expensive tastes. Thus, the Landor study suggests that a global marketer may face many cultural hurdles in its attempts to create worldwide brands.

Some critics question the value of asking consumers to rate brands on such subjective factors as "esteem." People will probably hold a Mercedes in higher esteem than a brand of laundry detergent. Thus, noticeably absent from the list are top brands from some of the world's most powerful marketers, including such giant consumer goods companies as Procter & Gamble, Unilever, and Philip Morris. Further, people often don't buy the brands that they regard most highly; many people who hold a Mercedes in high esteem can't afford one. But no matter how you measure brand power, few marketers doubt the value of a powerful brand. As one brand consultant observes, regardless of where you go in the world, "When you mention Kodak, I'm pretty sure everyone sees that yellow box."

### The World's Most Powerful Brand Names

| United States | Europe | Japan |
|---|---|---|
| Coca-Cola | Coca-Cola | Sony |
| Campbell | Sony | National |
| Disney | Mercedes-Benz | Mercedes-Benz |
| Pepsi-Cola | BMW | Toyota |
| Kodak | Philips | Takashimaya (department store) |
| NBC | Volkswagen | Rolls-Royce |
| Black & Decker | Adidas | Seiko |
| Kellogg | Kodak | Matsushita |
| McDonald's | Nivea | Hitachi |
| Hershey | Porsche | Suntory |

*Sources:* Portions adapted from Cathy Taylor, "Consumers Know Native Brands Best," *Adweek,* September 17, 1990, p. 31. Also see Interbrand, *World's Greatest Brands* (New York: John Wiley & Son, 1992); Diane Crispell and Kathleen Brandenburg, "What's in a Brand?" *American Demographics,* May 1993, pp. 26–32; T. L. Stanley, "How They Rate," *Brandweek,* April 3, 1995, pp. 45–48; Kevin Brown, "The Top 200 Mega-Brands," *Advertising Age,* May 1, 1995, p. 34; and Betsy Morris, "The Brand's the Thing," *Fortune,* March 4, 1996, pp. 72–84.

Brand names such as Kleenex, Levi's, Jell-O, Scotch Tape, and Formica have succeeded in this way. However, their very success may threaten the company's rights to the name. Many originally protected brand names, such as cellophane, aspirin, nylon, kerosene, linoleum, yo-yo, trampoline, escalator, thermos, and shredded wheat, are now generic names that any seller can use.[6]

## Brand Sponsor

**Manufacturer's brand (national brand)**
A brand created and owned by the producer of a product or service.

**Private brand (or middleman, distributor, or store brand)**
A brand created and owned by a reseller of a product or service.

A manufacturer has four sponsorship options. The product may be launched as a **manufacturer's brand** (or national brand), as when Kellogg and IBM sell their output under their own manufacturer's brand names. Or the manufacturer may sell to resellers who give it a **private brand** (also called a *store brand* or *distributor brand*). For example, BASF Wyandotte, the world's second-largest antifreeze maker, sells its Alugard antifreeze through middlemen who market the product under about 80 private brands, including Kmart, True Value, Pathmark, and Rite Aid. Although most manufacturers create their own brand names, others market *licensed brands*. For example, Rose Art Industries sells its children's art sets under the Kodak brand name licensed from Eastman Kodak Company. Finally, two companies can *co-brand* a product, as when General Mills and Hershey Foods combined brands to create Reese's Peanut Butter Puffs cereal.

**MANUFACTURERS' BRANDS VERSUS PRIVATE BRANDS.**   Manufacturers' brands have long dominated the retail scene. In recent times, however, an increasing number of retailers and wholesalers have created their own brands. For example, Sears has created several names—Diehard batteries, Craftsman tools, Kenmore appliances, Weatherbeater paints—that buyers look for and demand. Wal-Mart offers its own Sam's American Choice and Great Value brands of beverages and food products to compete against major national brands. Wal-Mart claims that its own brands offer better value—"great taste at Wal-Mart's always low prices."

Private brands can be hard to establish and costly to stock and promote. However, they also yield higher profit margins for the middleman, and they give middlemen exclusive products that cannot be bought from competitors, resulting in greater store traffic and loyalty. For example, if Sears promotes General Electric appliances, other stores that sell GE products will also benefit. Further, if Sears drops the GE brand, it loses the benefit of its previous promotion for GE. But when Sears promotes its private brand of Kenmore appliances, Sears alone benefits from the promotion, and consumer loyalty to the Kenmore brand becomes loyalty to Sears.

**Slotting fees**
Payments demanded by retailers from producers before they will accept new products and find "slots" for them on the shelves.

The competition between manufacturers' and private brands is called the *battle of the brands*. In this battle, middlemen have many advantages. They control what products they stock, where they go on the shelf, and which ones they will feature in local circulars. They charge manufacturers **slotting fees**—payments demanded by retailers before they will accept new products and find "slots" for them on the shelves. Retailers price their store brands lower than comparable manufacturers' brands, thereby appealing to budget-conscious shoppers, especially in difficult economic times. And most shoppers know that store brands are often made by one of the larger manufacturers anyway.

As store brands improve in quality and as consumers gain confidence in their store chains, store brands are posing a strong challenge to manufacturers' brands. Consider the case of Loblaw, the Canadian supermarket chain. Its President's

Choice Decadent Chocolate Chip Cookie is now the leading cookie brand in Canada. Loblaw's private label President's Choice cola racks up 50 percent of Loblaw's canned cola sales. Loblaw even sells its brand through other retailers. For example, President's Choice Decadent Chocolate Chip Cookies are now sold by Jewel Food Stores in Chicago, where they are the number one seller, beating out even Nabisco's Chips Ahoy brand.[7]

In U.S. supermarkets, taken as a single brand, private-label products are the number one, two, or three brand in over 40 percent of all grocery product categories. Private labels are even more prominent in Europe, accounting for as much as 36 percent of supermarket sales in Britain and 24 percent in France. French retail giant Carrefour sells more than 3,000 in-house brands, ranging from cooking oil to car batteries.[8] To fend off private brands, leading brand marketers will have to invest in R&D to bring out new brands, new features, and continuous quality improvements. They must design strong advertising programs to maintain high customer awareness and preference. And they must find ways to "partner" with major distributors in a search for distribution economies and improved joint performance.[9]

**LICENSING.** Most manufacturers take years and spend millions to create their own brand names. However, some companies license names or symbols previously created by other manufacturers, as well as names of well-known celebrities and characters from popular movies and books—for a fee, any of these can provide an instant and proven brand name. Apparel and accessories sellers pay large royalties to adorn their products—from blouses to ties, and linens to luggage—with the names or initials of such fashion innovators as Bill Blass, Calvin Klein, Pierre Cardin, Gucci, and Halston. Sellers of children's products attach an almost endless list of character names to clothing, toys, school supplies, linens, dolls, lunch boxes, cereals, and other items.

*Warner Brothers has mastered the art of licensing. Its merchandise emblazoned with Looney Tunes characters generates more than $1 billion in annual retail sales for more that 225 licensees.*

The character names range from such classics as Disney, Peanuts, Barbie, and Flintstones characters, to the Muppets, Garfield, Batman, and the Simpsons.

Name and character licensing has become a big business in recent years. Annual sales of licensed products total more than $13 billion in the United States and $102 billion worldwide.[10] Many companies have mastered the art of peddling their established brands and characters. For example, through savvy marketing, Warner Bros. has turned Bugs Bunny, Daffy Duck, Foghorn Leghorn, and more than 100 other Looney Tunes characters into the world's favorite cartoon brand. The Looney Tunes license, arguably the most sought-after nonsports license in the industry, generates $1 billion in annual retail sales by more than 225 licensees. And Warner Bros. has yet to tap the full potential of many of its secondary characters. The Tasmanian Devil, for example, initially appeared in only *five* cartoons. But through cross-licensing agreements with organizations like Harley-Davidson and the NFL, Taz has become something of a pop icon. He has now reappeared in cartoons, and consumers can expect to see more of him in commercials. Warner Bros. sees similar potential for characters like Michigan J. Frog, and Speedy Gonzales for the Hispanic market.[11]

**Co-branding**
The practice of using the established brand names of two different companies on the same product.

CO-BRANDING.   Although companies have been **co-branding** products for many years, there has been a recent resurgence in co-branded products. Co-branding occurs when two established brand names of different companies are used on the same product. For example, Pillsbury joined Nabisco to create Pillsbury Oreo Bars Baking Mix. Ford and Eddie Bauer co-branded a sport utility vehicle—the Ford Explorer, Eddie Bauer edition. Apple Computer teamed up with Citibank to offer VISA and MasterCard credit cards to Apple enthusiasts. And Kellogg joined forces with ConAgra to co-brand Healthy Choice from Kellogg's cereals. In most co-branding situations, one company licenses another company's well-known brand to use in combination with its own.

Co-branding offers many advantages. Because each brand dominates in a different category, the combined brands create broader consumer appeal and greater brand equity. Co-branding also allows a company to expand its existing brand into a category that it might otherwise have difficulty entering alone. For example, by licensing its Healthy Choice brand to Kellogg, ConAgra entered the breakfast segment with a solid product. In return, Kellogg could leverage the broad awareness of the Healthy Choice name in the cereal category.

Co-branding also has limitations. Such relationships usually involve complex legal contracts and licenses. Co-branding partners must carefully coordinate advertising, sales promotion, and other marketing efforts. Finally, when co-branding, each partner must trust that the other will take good care of its brand. As one Nabisco manager puts it, "Giving away your brand is a lot like giving away your child—you want to make sure everything is perfect."[12]

## Brand Strategy

A company has four choices when it comes to brand strategy (see Figure 8-4). It can introduce *line extensions* (existing brand names extended to new forms, sizes, and flavors of an existing product category), *brand extensions* (existing brand names extended to new product categories), *multibrands* (new brand names introduced in the same product category), or *new brands* (new brand names in new product categories).

**FIGURE 8-4**
*Four brand strategies*

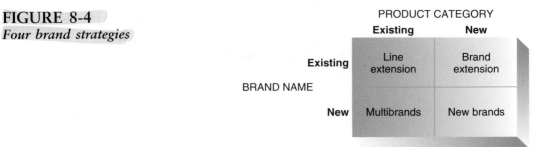

LINE EXTENSIONS.   **Line extensions** occur when a company introduces additional items in a given product category under the same brand name, such as new flavors, forms, colors, ingredients, or package sizes. Thus, Dannon recently introduced several line extensions, including seven new yogurt flavors, a fat-free yogurt, and a large economy-size yogurt. The vast majority of new product activity consists of line extensions.

A company might introduce line extensions as a low-cost, low-risk way of introducing new products in order to meet consumer desires for variety, of utilizing excess manufacturing capacity, or simply commanding more shelf space from resellers. However, line extensions involve some risks. An overextended brand name might lose its specific meaning. In the past, when consumers asked for a Coke, they received a 6-ounce bottle of the classic beverage. Today, the vendor has to ask: Classic or Cherry Coke? Regular or diet? Caffeine or caffeine-free? Bottle or can? What size? Another risk is that sales of an extension may come at the expense of other items in the line. A line extension works best when it takes sales away from competing brands, not when it "cannibalizes" the company's other items.[13]

BRAND EXTENSIONS.   A **brand extension** involves the use of a successful brand name to launch new or modified products in a new category. Procter & Gamble put its Ivory name on dishwashing detergent, liquid hand soap, and shampoo with excellent results. Fruit of the Loom took advantage of its very high name recognition to launch new lines of socks, men's fashion underwear, women's underwear, athletic apparel, and even baby clothes. Honda uses its company name to cover such different products as its automobiles, motorcycles, snowblowers, lawn mowers, marine engines, and snowmobiles. This allows Honda to advertise that it can fit "six Hondas in a two-car garage."

Several specialty clothing retailers, such as The Gap and Ann Taylor, are extending their brands into the bath- and body-products arena. Gap stores throughout the United States now feature soap, lotion, shampoo, conditioner, shower gel, bath salts, and perfume spray. And because specialty retailers are already drawing large crowds of shoppers, they can launch personal-care lines with little or no advertising. For example, Ann Taylor's brand equity is so strong among its core consumers that women bought its new fragrance, Destination, out of the company's catalog without any idea what it smelled like.[14]

A brand extension strategy offers many advantages. A well-regarded brand name helps the company enter new product categories more easily and gives a new product instant recognition and faster acceptance. Sony puts its name on most of its new electronic products, creating an instant perception of high quality for each

**Line extension**
Using a successful brand name to introduce additonal items in a given product category under the same brand name, such as new flavors, forms, colors, added ingredients, or package sizes.

**Brand extension**
Using a successful brand name to launch a new or modified product in a new category.

*Brand extensions: Fruit of the Loom has leveraged its well-known name to launch new lines of socks, women's underwear, men's fashion underwear, and even baby clothes.*

Cute things now come in small packages.

At Fruit of the Loom, we've designed a trio of new playwear items that are as sweet and unique as your baby. Well, almost.

**Fruit of the Loom. Clothes that make you feel good.**

Available at your favorite mass merchandise stores.

new product. Brand extensions also save the high advertising cost usually required to familiarize consumers with a new brand name.

At the same time, a brand extension strategy involves some risk. Brand extensions such as Bic pantyhose, Heinz pet food, Life Savers gum, and Clorox laundry detergent met early deaths. If an extension brand fails, it may harm consumer attitudes toward the other products carrying the same brand name. Further, a brand name may not be appropriate to a particular new product, even if it is well made and satisfying—would you consider buying Texaco milk or Alpo chili? And a brand name may lose its special positioning in the consumer's mind through overuse. Companies that are tempted to transfer a brand name must research how well the brand's associations fit the new product.[15]

**MULTIBRANDS.** Companies often introduce additional brands in the same category. **Multibranding** offers a way to establish different features and appeal to different buying motives. Thus, P&G markets nine different brands of laundry detergent. Multibranding also allows a company to lock up more reseller shelf space. Or the company may want to protect its major brand by setting up *flanker* or *fighter brands*. For example, Seiko uses different brand names for its higher-priced watches (Seiko Lasalle) and lower-priced watches (Pulsar) to protect the flanks of its mainstream Seiko brand. Sometimes a company inherits different brand names

**Multibranding**
A strategy under which a seller develops two or more brands in the same product category.

in the process of acquiring a competitor, and each brand name has a loyal following. Thus, Electrolux, the Swedish multinational, owns a stable of acquired brand names for its appliance lines—Frigidaire, Kelvinator, Westinghouse, Zanussi, White, and Gibson. Finally, companies may develop separate brand names for different regions or countries, perhaps to suit different cultures or languages. For example, Procter & Gamble dominates the U.S. laundry detergent market with Tide, which in all its forms captures more than a 31 percent market share. In Europe, however, P&G leads with its Ariel detergent brand, whose annual sales of $1.5 billion make it Europe's number two packaged-goods brand behind Coca-Cola. In the United States, P&G targets Ariel to Hispanic markets.

A major drawback of multibranding is that each brand might obtain only a small market share, and none may be very profitable. The company may end up spreading its resources over many brands instead of building a few brands to a highly profitable level. These companies should reduce the number of brands they sell in a given category and set up tighter screening procedures for new brands.

NEW BRANDS.    A company may create a new brand name when it enters a new product category for which none of the company's current brand names are appropriate. For example, Sears establishes separate family names for different product categories (Kenmore for appliances, Craftsman for tools, and Homart for major home installations). Japan's Matsushita uses separate names for its different families of products: Technics, Panasonic, National, and Quasar. Or, the company might believe that the power of its existing brand name is waning and a new brand name is needed. Finally, the company may obtain new brands in new categories through acquisitions. For example, S. C. Johnson & Son, marketer of Pledge furniture polish, Glade air freshener, Raid insect spray, Edge shaving gel, and many other well-known brands, added several new powerhouse brands through its acquisition of Drackett Company, including Windex, Drano, and Vanish toilet bowl cleaner.

As with multibranding, offering too many new brands can result in a company spreading its resources too thin. And in some industries, such as consumer packaged goods, consumers and retailers have become concerned that there are already too many brands, with too few differences between them. Thus, Procter & Gamble, Frito-Lay, and other large consumer product marketers are now pursuing *megabrand* strategies—weeding out weaker brands and focusing their marketing dollars only on brands that can achieve the number one or two market-share positions in their categories.

# PACKAGING

**Packaging**
The activities of designing and producing the container or wrapper for a product.

Many products offered to the market have to be packaged. **Packaging** includes the activities of designing and producing the container or wrapper for a product. The package may include the product's primary container (the tube holding Colgate toothpaste); a secondary package that is thrown away when the product is about to be used (the cardboard box containing the tube of Colgate); and the shipping package necessary to store, identify, and ship the product (a corrugated box carrying six dozen tubes of Colgate toothpaste). Labeling is also part of packaging and consists of printed information appearing on or with the package.

Traditionally, packaging decisions were based primarily on cost and production factors. The primary function of the package was to contain and protect the product. In recent times, however, numerous factors have made packaging an important marketing tool. Increased competition and clutter on retail store shelves means that packages now must perform many sales tasks—from attracting attention, to describing the product, to making the sale. Companies are realizing the power of good packaging to create instant consumer recognition of the company or brand. For example, in an average supermarket, which stocks 15,000 to 17,000 items, the typical shopper passes by some 300 items per minute, and 53 percent of all purchases are made on impulse. In this highly competitive environment, the package may be the seller's last chance to influence buyers. It becomes a "five-second commercial." The Campbell Soup Company estimates that the average shopper sees its familiar red and white can 76 times a year, creating the equivalent of $26 million worth of advertising.[16]

Innovative packaging can give a company an advantage over competitors. Liquid Tide quickly attained a 10 percent share of the heavy-duty detergent market, partly because of the popularity of its container's innovative drip-proof spout and cap. In contrast, poorly designed packages can cause headaches for consumers and lost sales for the company.

Developing a good package for a new product requires making many decisions. The first task is to establish the packaging concept. The *packaging concept* states what the package should *be* or *do* for the product. Should the main functions of the package be to offer product protection, introduce a new dispensing method, suggest certain qualities about the product or the company, or something else? Decisions then must be made on specific elements of the package, such as size, shape, materials, color, text, and brand mark. These various elements must work together to support the product's position and marketing strategy. The package must be consistent with the product's advertising, pricing, and distribution.[17]

In recent years, product safety has also become a major packaging concern. We have all learned to deal with hard-to-open "childproof" packages. And after the rash of product tampering scares during the 1980s, most drug producers and food makers are now putting their products in tamper-resistant packages. In making packaging decisions, the company also must heed growing environmental concerns and make decisions that serve society's interests as well as immediate customer and company objectives. Increasingly, companies will be asked to take responsibility for the environmental costs of their products and packaging (see Marketing at Work 8-3).

## LABELING

Labels may range from simple tags attached to products to complex graphics that are part of the package. They perform several functions, and the seller has to decide which ones to use. At the very least, the label *identifies* the product or brand, such as the name Sunkist stamped on oranges. The label might also *grade* the product—canned peaches are grade-labeled A, B, and C. The label might *describe* several things about the product—who made it, where it was made, when it was made, its contents, how it is to be used, and how to use it safely. Finally, the label might *promote* the product through attractive graphics.

There has been a long history of legal concerns about packaging and labels. The Federal Trade Commission Act of 1914 held that false, misleading, or deceptive labels or packages constitute unfair competition. Labels can mislead customers, fail to describe important ingredients, or fail to include important safety warnings. As a result, several federal and state laws regulate labeling. The most prominent is the Fair Packaging and Labeling Act of 1966, which set mandatory labeling requirements, encouraged voluntary industry packaging standards, and allowed federal agencies to set packaging regulations in specific industries.

Labeling has been affected in recent times by *unit pricing* (stating the price per unit of standard measure), *open dating* (stating the expected shelf life of the product), and *nutritional labeling* (stating the nutritional values in the product). The Nutritional Labeling and Educational Act of 1990 requires sellers to provide detailed nutritional information on food products, and recent sweeping actions by the Food and Drug Administration regulate the use of health-related terms such as *low-fat, lite,* and *high-fiber*.[18] Sellers must ensure that their labels contain all the required information.

## PRODUCT-SUPPORT SERVICES

Customer service is another element of product strategy. A company's offer to the marketplace usually includes some services, which can be a minor or a major part of the total offer. Later in the chapter, we will discuss services as products in themselves. Here, we discuss *product-support services*—services that augment actual products. More and more companies are using product-support services as a major tool in gaining competitive advantage.

A company should design its product and support services to meet the needs of target customers profitably. Determining customer service needs and the value customers assign to different services involves more than simply monitoring complaints that come in over toll-free telephone lines or on comment cards. The company should periodically survey its customers to assess the value of current services and to obtain ideas for new ones. For example, Cadillac holds regular focus-group interviews with owners and carefully watches complaints that come into its dealerships. From this close monitoring, Cadillac has learned that buyers are very upset by repairs that are not done correctly the first time. As a result, the company has set up a system directly linking each dealership with a group of 10 engineers who can help walk mechanics through difficult repairs. Such actions helped Cadillac jump, in one year, from fourteenth to seventh in independent rankings of service.[19]

Once the company has assessed the value of various support services to customers, it must assess the costs of providing them. It can then develop a package of services that will both delight customers and yield profits to the company.

Given the importance of customer service as a marketing tool, many companies have set up strong customer service operations to handle complaints and adjustments, credit service, maintenance service, technical service, and consumer information. For example, Whirlpool, Procter & Gamble, and many other companies have set up 1-800 telephone hotlines. By keeping records on the types of requests and complaints, the customer service group can press for needed changes in product design, quality control, and marketing efforts. An active customer service operation coordinates all of the company's services, creates consumer satisfaction and loyalty, and helps the company find ways to distinguish itself from competitors.[20]

## MARKETING AT WORK 8-3

# THE GERMAN PACKAGING ORDINANCE: MAKING THE POLLUTER PAY

The principle of "the polluter pays" once seemed far-fetched, a pipe dream of radical environmentalists. But as the rest of the world watches, the notion that sellers should be responsible for the environmental costs of their products is being put to the test in Germany. The Packaging Ordinance (Verpackungsordnung), enacted in June 1991, made private industry responsible for the collecting, sorting, and ultimate recycling of packaging waste.

The new German legislation deals separately with three different kinds of packaging: *primary packaging*—the container that holds the product, like a perfume bottle; *secondary packaging*— outer material whose main function is point-of-purchase display and protection during shipping, like the box around the perfume bottle; and *transport packaging*— the carton or crate used to ship the perfume in bulk to stores. The ordinance decreed that all three types of packaging must be taken back by retailers and returned to manufacturers—a daunting prospect for both parties. How-

*In Germany, sellers are now responsible for the environmental costs of their products. This widely used "green dot" emblem indicates that a package is acceptable for industry collection systems.*

ever, it allowed that, if the industry could come up with an alternative, then retailers would not have to take back the first and by far the largest category of waste, primary sales packaging.

The industry's solution was the Dual System (DSD), a non-

profit company set up by German businesses that collects waste directly from consumers in addition to the country's municipal collection systems. DSD is funded by licensing fees for the now widely used *green dot*: a green arrow emblem indicating

## PRODUCT DECISIONS AND SOCIAL RESPONSIBILITY

Product decisions have attracted much public attention. When making such decisions, marketers should consider carefully a number of public policy issues and regulations involving acquiring or dropping products, patent protection, product quality and safety, and product warranties.

Regarding the addition of new products, the government may prevent companies from adding products through acquisitions if the effect threatens to lessen competition. Companies dropping products must be aware that they have legal

that a package is collectible by DSD. Now, rather than tossing their packaging out with the municipal trash, for which they must pay a fee, consumers can take it to a nearby yellow DSD bin to be collected for free.

Under the DSD system, although they must still collect secondary and transport packaging, stores are no longer required to take back huge mounds of primary sales packaging. However, there's a catch: To be eligible as DSD trash, a sales package must have the green dot. So, not surprisingly, retailers are reluctant to carry products without the green dot. Further, there is a growing preference among German consumers for recyclable packaging materials and for less packaging in general. Thus, the Packaging Ordinance will strongly affect how companies package their products for the German market.

The ordinance puts the "polluter pays" principle to work by creating incentives rather than through direct regulation. Unlike other European Union (EU) countries, Germany has no ban on specific packaging materials. Instead, green dot license prices are based, in part, on the difficulty of recycling a particular material. This sets market mechanisms in motion. If a given packaging material is costly to recycle, the price of using it will rise and companies will switch to something else. Thus, the ordinance is stimulating companies to find imaginative ways to market goods with less packaging. Colgate, for example, designed a toothpaste tube that stands on its head on store shelves without a box. Hewlett-Packard redesigned the chassis for its workstations and personal computers, reducing transport packaging by 30 percent.

The major problem with the landmark German recycling program is the lack of a market for recycled material. Notes one packaging expert: "There seems to be widespread belief in the trash fairy, who comes overnight and turns garbage into gold for free. . . . [But] when you're talking trash, it's difficult to believe that anyone will pay for it." In fact, it's no secret that much of the packaging collected in DSD bins is not being recycled, but rather is piling up in warehouses or being exported. When German plastics turned up in French dumps and incinerators last year, it caused a Europe-wide scandal.

Still, the ordinance serves as a wake-up call to both businesses and consumers, in Germany and around the world. It says, "Hey folks, we've got a problem, and something must be done about it." And despite its flaws, the ordinance does seem to be moving the country, however timidly, toward its goal of waste reduction. Producers and retailers are now working together to help solve environmental problems.

France and Austria have passed similar legislation, and France has begun using the green dot, although with a different collection system. In Germany, new ordinances are on the horizon, including ones for mandating producer take-back of cars and electronic equipment. And the European Union is now working on a directive that would set minimum standards for recycling in all of its member states. "It may take another year or two, but the train is running," assures one German ministry official. "The idea of product responsibility is spreading around the world."

*Source:* Adapted from Marilyn Stern, "Is This the Ultimate in Recycling?" *Across the Board,* May 1993, pp. 28-31. Also see Peter Sibbald, "Manufacturing for Reuse," *Fortune,* February 6, 1995, pp. 102-12.

obligations, written or implied, to their suppliers, dealers, and customers who have a stake in the discontinued product. Companies also must obey U.S. patent laws when developing new products. A company cannot make its product "illegally similar" to another company's established product.

Manufacturers must comply with specific laws regarding product quality and safety. The Federal Food, Drug, and Cosmetic Act protects consumers from unsafe and adulterated food, drugs, and cosmetics. Various acts provide for the inspection of sanitary conditions in the meat- and poultry-processing industries. Safety legislation has been passed to regulate fabrics, chemical substances, automobiles, toys, and drugs and poisons. The Consumer Product Safety Act of 1972 established a Consumer Product Safety Commission, which has the authority to ban or seize potentially harmful products and set severe penalties for violation of the law.

If consumers have been injured by a product that has been designed defectively, they can sue manufacturers or dealers. Product liability suits are now occurring in federal and state courts at the rate of almost 110,000 per year, with individual awards often running in the millions of dollars.[21] This phenomenon has resulted in huge increases in product-liability insurance premiums, causing big problems in some industries. Some companies pass these higher rates along to consumers by raising prices. Others are forced to discontinue high-risk product lines.

Many manufacturers offer written product warranties to convince customers of their products' quality. To protect consumers, Congress passed the Magnuson-Moss Warranty Act in 1975. The act requires that full warranties meet certain minimum standards, including repair "within a reasonable time and without charge" or a replacement or full refund if the product does not work "after a reasonable number of attempts" at repair. Otherwise, the company must make it clear that it is offering only a limited warranty. The law has led several manufacturers to switch from full to limited warranties and others to drop warranties altogether as a marketing tool.

# ▶ PRODUCT LINE DECISIONS

We have looked at product strategy decisions such as branding, packaging, labeling, and support services for individual products and services. But product strategy also calls for building a product line. A **product line** is a group of products that are closely related because they function in a similar manner, are sold to the same customer groups, are marketed through the same types of outlets, or fall within given price ranges. For example, Nike produces several lines of athletic shoes, Motorola produces several lines of telecommunications products, and AT&T offers several lines of long-distance telephone services. In developing product line strategies, marketers face a number of tough decisions.

**Product line**
A group of products that are closely related because they function in a similar manner, are sold to the same customer groups, are marketed through the same types of outlets, or fall within given price ranges.

The major product line decision involves *product line length*—the number of items in the product line. The line is too short if the manager can increase profits by adding items; the line is too long if the manager can increase profits by dropping items. Product line length is influenced by company objectives. Companies that want to be positioned as full-line companies or that are seeking high market share and growth usually carry longer lines. Companies that are keen on high short-term profitability generally carry shorter lines of selected items.

Product lines tend to lengthen over time. The product line manager may feel pressure to add new products to use up excess manufacturing capacity. The sales force and distributors may pressure the manager for a more complete product line to satisfy their customers. Or, the product line manager may want to add items to the product line to increase sales and profits.

However, as the manager adds items, several costs rise: design and engineering costs, inventory costs, manufacturing changeover costs, order processing costs, transportation costs, and promotional costs to introduce new items. Eventually, someone calls a halt to the mushrooming product line. Top management may freeze things because of insufficient funds or manufacturing capacity. Or the controller may question the line's profitability and call for a study. The study will probably show a number of money-losing items, and they will be pruned from the line in a major effort to increase profitability. This pattern of uncontrolled product line growth followed by heavy pruning is typical and may repeat itself many times.[22]

The company must manage its product lines carefully. It can systematically increase the length of its product line in two ways: by *stretching* its line and by *filling* its line. *Product line stretching* occurs when a company lengthens its product line beyond its current range. The company can stretch its line downward, upward, or both ways.

Many companies initially locate at the upper end of the market and later stretch their lines *downward.* A company may stretch downward because it finds faster growth taking place at the low end. It may add a low-end product to plug a market hole that otherwise would attract a new competitor, or to respond to a competitor's attack on the upper end. Xerox expanded into the small copier segment for all of these reasons. Although Xerox has long dominated the medium and large copier segments, by the late 1980s, the small copier segment was growing at a much faster rate. Canon, Sharp, and other Japanese competitors had entered the low-end segment, where they quickly dominated. Moreover, these competitors used their success at the low end as a base for competing with Xerox in the mid-size copier segment. Thus, to meet shifts in the market demand and to blunt competitor thrusts, Xerox introduced a line of small copiers.

*Product line stretching: Marriott stretched its hotel product line to include serveral branded hotels aimed at a different target market. Residence Inn, for example, provides a "home away from home" for people who travel for a living, who are relocating, or who are on assignment and need inexpensive temporary lodging.*

Companies at the lower end of the market may want to stretch their product lines *upward.* They may be attracted by a faster growth rate or higher margins at the higher end, or they may simply want to position themselves as full-line manufacturers. Sometimes, companies stretch upward in order to add prestige to their current products. General Electric accomplished all of these goals when it added its Monogram line of high-quality built-in kitchen appliances targeted at the select few households earning more than $100,000 a year and living in homes valued at over $400,000.

Companies in the middle range of the market may decide to stretch their lines in *both directions.* Marriott did this with its hotel product line. Along with regular Marriott hotels, it added the Marriott Marquis line to serve the upper end of the market, and the Courtyard and Fairfield Inn lines to serve the lower end. Each branded hotel line is aimed at a different target market. Marriott Marquis aims to attract and please top executives; Marriotts, middle managers; Courtyards, salespeople; and Fairfield Inns, vacationers and others on a tight travel budget. The major risk with this strategy is that some travelers will trade down after finding that the lower-price hotels in the Marriott chain give them pretty much everything they want. However, Marriott would rather capture its customers who move downward than lose them to competitors.

An alternative to product line stretching is *product line filling*—adding more items within the present range of the line. There are several reasons for product line filling: reaching for extra profits, trying to satisfy dealers, use excess capacity, be the leading full-line company, and plug holes to keep out competitors. Thus, Sony filled its Walkman line by adding solar-powered and waterproof Walkmans, and an ultralight model that attaches to a sweatband for joggers, bicyclers, tennis players, and other exercisers. However, line filling is overdone if it results in cannibalization and customer confusion. The company should ensure that new items are noticeably different from existing ones.

# ▶ PRODUCT MIX DECISIONS

**Product mix (or product assortment)**
The set of all product lines and items that a particular seller offers for sale to buyers.

An organization with several product lines has a product mix. A **product mix** (or **product assortment**) consists of all the product lines and items that a particular seller offers for sale. Avon's product mix consists of four major product lines: cosmetics, jewelry, fashions, and household items. Each product line consists of several sublines. For example, cosmetics breaks down into lipstick, eyeliner, powder, and so on. Each line and subline has many individual items. Altogether, Avon's product mix includes 1,300 items. In contrast, a typical Kmart stocks 15,000 items, 3M markets more than 60,000 products, and General Electric manufactures as many as 250,000 items.

A company's product mix has four important dimensions: width, length, depth, and consistency. Table 8-2 illustrates these concepts with selected Procter & Gamble consumer products.

The *width* of P&G's product mix refers to the number of different product lines the company carries. Table 8-2 shows a product mix width of six lines. (In fact, P&G produces many more lines, including mouthwashes, paper towels, disposable diapers, pain relievers, and cosmetics.)

The *length* of P&G's product mix refers to the total number of items that the company carries. In Table 8-2, the total number of items is 42. We can also

| TABLE 8-2 | *Product Mix Width and Product Mix Length Shown for Selected Procter & Gamble Products* |

| | Detergents | Toothpaste | Bar Soap | Deodorants | Fruit Juices | Lotions |
|---|---|---|---|---|---|---|
| | Ivory Snow | Gleem | Ivory | Secret | Citrus Hill | Wondra |
| | Dreft | Crest | Camay | Sure | Sunny Delight | Noxema |
| | Tide | Complete | Lava | | Winter Hill | Oil of Olay |
| | Joy | Denquel | Kirk's | | Texsun | Camay |
| Product | Cheer | | Zest | | Lincoln | Raintree |
| Mix | Oxydol | | Safeguard | | Speas Farm | Tropic Tan |
| Length | Dash | | Coast | | | Bain de Soleil |
| | Cascade | | Oil of Olay | | | |
| | Ivory Liquid | | | | | |
| | Gain | | | | | |
| | Dawn | | | | | |
| | Ariel | | | | | |
| | Era | | | | | |
| | Bold 3 | | | | | |
| | Liquid Tide | | | | | |

*Product Mix Width* (arrow across top) and *Product Mix Length* (arrow down left side)

compute the average length of a line at P&G by dividing the total length (here, 42) by the number of lines (here, 6). In Table 8-2, the average P&G product line consists of seven brands.

The *depth* of P&G's product mix refers to the number of versions offered of each product in the line. Thus, if Crest comes in three sizes and two formulations (paste and gel), Crest has a depth of six. By counting the number of versions within each brand, we can calculate the average depth of P&G's product mix.

The *consistency* of the product mix refers to how closely related the various product lines are in end use, production requirements, distribution channels, or in some other way. P&G's product lines are consistent insofar as they are consumer products that go through the same distribution channels. The lines are less consistent insofar as they perform different functions for buyers.

These product mix dimensions provide the handles for defining the company's product strategy. The company can increase its business in four ways. It can add new product lines, thus widening its product mix. In this way, its new lines build on the company's reputation in its other lines. The company can lengthen its existing product lines to become a more full-line company. Or it can add more versions of each product and thus deepen its product mix. Finally, the company can pursue more product line consistency—or less—depending on whether it wants to have a strong reputation in a single field or in several fields.

# ▶SERVICES MARKETING

One of the major world trends in recent years has been the dramatic growth of services. As a result of rising affluence, more leisure time, and the growing complexity of products that require servicing, the United States has become the world's first service economy. Services now generate 74 percent of U.S. gross domestic product. Whereas service jobs accounted for 55 percent of all U.S. jobs in 1970,

*The convenience industry: Services that save you time— for a price.*

by 1993, they accounted for 79 percent of total employment. Services are expected to be responsible for *all* net job growth through the year 2005.[23]

Services are growing even faster in the world economy, making up a quarter of the value of all international trade. Business services account for almost 30 percent of all U.S. exports, resulting in a substantial trade surplus for services, versus a large deficit for goods. More and more, the global economy is dominated by services. In fact, a variety of service industries—from banking, insurance, and communications to transportation, travel, and entertainment—now accounts for well over 60 percent of the economy in developed countries worldwide. The global growth rate for services almost doubles the growth rate for manufacturing.

Service industries vary greatly. *Governments* offer services through courts, employment services, hospitals, loan agencies, military services, police and fire departments, postal service, regulatory agencies, and schools. *Private nonprofit organizations* offer services through museums, charities, churches, colleges, foundations, and hospitals. A large number of *business organizations* offer services— airlines, banks, hotels, insurance companies, consulting firms, medical and law practices, entertainment companies, real estate firms, advertising and research agencies, and retailers.

Not only are there traditional service industries, but new types keep popping up all the time:

> Want someone to fetch a meal from a local restaurant? In Austin, Texas, you can call EatOutIn. Plants need to be watered? In New York, you can call the Busy Body's Helper. Too busy to wrap and mail your packages? Stop by any one of the 72 outlets of Tender Sender, headquartered in Portland, Oregon. "We'll find it, we'll do it, we'll wait for it," chirps Lois Barnett, the founder of Personalized Services in Chicago. She and her crew of six will walk the dog, shuttle the kids to Little League, or wait in line for your theater tickets. Meet the convenience peddlers. They want to save you time. For a price, they'll do just about anything that's legal.[24]

Some service businesses are very large, with total sales and assets in the trillions of dollars. There are also tens of thousands of smaller service providers. Selling services presents some special problems calling for special marketing solutions.

# NATURE AND CHARACTERISTICS OF A SERVICE

**Service**
Any activity or benefit that one party can offer to another that is essentially intangible and does not result in the ownership of anything.

A **service** is any activity or benefit that one party can offer to another that is essentially intangible and does not result in the ownership of anything. Its production may or may not be tied to a physical product. Activities such as renting a hotel room, depositing money in a bank, traveling on an airplane, getting a haircut, having a car repaired, watching a professional sport, seeing a movie, and getting advice from a lawyer all involve buying a service.

A company must consider four special service characteristics when designing marketing programs: *intangibility, inseparability, variability,* and *perishability.* These characteristics are summarized in Figure 8-5 and discussed in the following sections.

**Service intangibility**
Services cannot be seen, tasted, felt, heard, or smelled before they are bought.

**Service intangibility** means that services cannot be seen, tasted, felt, heard, or smelled before they are bought. For example, people undergoing cosmetic surgery cannot see the result before the purchase, and airline passengers have nothing but a ticket and the promise of safe delivery to their destinations.

To reduce uncertainty, buyers look for "signals" of service quality. They draw conclusions about quality from the place, people, price, equipment, and communications that they can see. Therefore, the service provider's task is to make the service tangible in one or more ways. Whereas product marketers try to add intangibles to their tangible offers, service marketers try to add tangibles to their intangible offers.

**Service inseparability**
Services are produced and consumed at the same time and cannot be separated from their providers, whether the providers are people or machines.

Physical goods are produced, then stored, later sold, and still later consumed. In contrast, services are first sold, then produced and consumed at the same time. **Service inseparability** means that services cannot be separated from their providers, whether the providers are people or machines. If a service employee provides the service, then the employee is a part of the service. Because the customer is also present as the service is produced, *provider-customer interaction* is a special feature of services marketing. Both the provider and the customer affect the service outcome.

**Service variability**
The quality of services may vary greatly, depending on who provides them and when, where, and how.

**Service variability** means that the quality of services depends on who provides them, as well as when, where, and how they are provided. For example, some hotels—say, Marriott—have reputations for providing better service than others. Still, within a given Marriott hotel, one registration-desk employee may be cheerful and efficient, whereas another standing just a few feet away may be

**FIGURE 8-5**
*Four service characteristics*

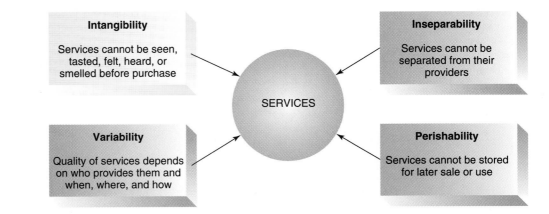

unpleasant and slower. Even the quality of a single Marriott employee's service varies according to his or her energy and frame of mind at the time of each customer encounter.

**Service perishability**
Services cannot be stored for later sale or use.

**Service perishability** means that services cannot be stored for later sale or use. Some doctors charge patients for missed appointments because the service value existed only at that point and disappeared when the patient did not show up. The perishability of services is not a problem when demand is steady. However, when demand fluctuates, service firms often have difficult problems. For example, because of rush-hour demand, public transportation companies have to own much more equipment than they would if demand were even throughout the day. Thus, service firms often design strategies for producing a better match between demand and supply. For instance, hotels and resorts charge lower prices in the off-season to attract more guests. And restaurants hire part-time employees to serve during peak periods.

# MARKETING STRATEGIES FOR SERVICE FIRMS

Just like manufacturing businesses, good service firms use marketing to position themselves strongly in chosen target markets. Southwest Airlines positions itself as "Just Plane Smart" for commuter flyers—a no-frills, short-haul airline charging very low fares. The Ritz-Carlton Hotel positions itself as offering a memorable experience that "enlivens the senses, instills well-being, and fulfills even the unexpressed wishes and needs of our guests." These and other service firms establish their positions through traditional marketing mix activities.

However, because services differ from tangible products, they often require additional marketing approaches. In a product business, products are fairly standardized and can sit on shelves waiting for customers. But in a service business, the customer and front-line service employee *interact* to create the service. Thus, service providers must interact effectively with customers to create superior value during service encounters. Effective interaction, in turn, depends on the skills of front-line service employees and on the service production and support processes backing these employees.

## *The Service-Profit Chain*

**Service-profit chain**
The chain that links service firm profits with employee and customer satisfaction.

Successful service companies focus their attention on *both* their customers and their employees. They understand the **service-profit chain,** which links service firm profits with employee and customer satisfaction. This chain consists of five links:[25]

◆ *Internal service quality*—superior employee selection and training, a quality work environment, and strong support for those dealing with customers, which results in . . .

◆ *Satisfied and productive service employees*—more satisfied, loyal, and hardworking employees, which results in . . .

◆ *Greater service value*—more effective and efficient customer value creation and service delivery, which results in . . .

◆ *Satisfied and loyal customers*—satisfied customers who remain loyal, repeat purchase, and refer other customers, which results in . . .

◆ *Healthy service profits and growth*—superior service firm performance.

**FIGURE 8-6**
*Three types of service marketing*

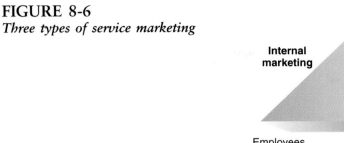

Therefore, reaching service profits and growth goals begins with taking care of those who take care of customers (see Marketing at Work 8-4).

All of this suggests that service marketing requires more than just traditional external marketing using the four *P*s. Figure 8-6 shows that service marketing also requires *internal marketing* and *interactive marketing*. **Internal marketing** means that the service firm must effectively train and motivate its customer-contact employees and all the supporting service people to work as a *team* to provide customer satisfaction. For the firm to deliver consistently high service quality, marketers must get everyone in the organization to practice a customer orientation. In fact, internal marketing must *precede* external marketing.[26]

**Interactive marketing** means that service quality depends heavily on the quality of the buyer-seller interaction during the service encounter. In product marketing, product quality rarely depends on how the product is obtained. But in services marketing, service quality depends on both the service deliverer and the quality of the delivery. Thus, service marketers cannot assume that they will satisfy the customer simply by providing good technical service. They have to master interactive marketing skills as well.

Today, as competition and costs increase, and as productivity and quality decrease, more service marketing sophistication is needed. Service companies face three major marketing tasks: They want to increase their *competitive differentiation, service quality,* and *productivity.*

### Managing Service Differentiation

In these days of intense price competition, service marketers often complain about the difficulty of differentiating their services from those of competitors. If customers view the services of different providers as similar, they care less about the provider than the price.

The solution to price competition is to develop a differentiated offer, delivery, and image. The *offer* can include innovative features that set one company's offer apart from competitors' offers. For example, airlines have introduced such innovations as in-flight movies, advance seating, air-to-ground telephone service, and frequent-flyer award programs to differentiate their offers. British Airways even offers international travelers a sleeping compartment, hot showers, and cooked-to-order breakfasts.

Service companies can differentiate their service *delivery* by having more able and reliable customer-contact people, by developing a superior physical environment

**Internal marketing**
Marketing by a service firm to train and effectively motivate its customer-contact employees and all the supporting service people to work as a team to provide customer satisfaction.

**Interactive marketing**
Marketing by a service firm that recognizes that perceived service quality depends heavily on the quality of buyer-seller interaction.

## MARKETING AT WORK 8-4

# RITZ-CARLTON: TAKING CARE OF THOSE WHO TAKE CARE OF CUSTOMERS

Ritz-Carlton, a chain of 28 luxury hotels renowned for outstanding service, caters to the top 5 percent of corporate and leisure travelers. The company's credo sets lofty customer-service goals: "The Ritz-Carlton Hotel is a place where the genuine care and comfort of our guests is our highest mission. We pledge to provide the finest personal service and facilities for our guests who will always enjoy a warm, relaxed, yet refined ambience. The Ritz-Carlton experience enlivens the senses, instills well-being, and fulfills even the unexpressed wishes and needs of our guests."

The credo is more than just words on paper—Ritz-Carlton delivers on its promises. In surveys of departing guests, some 95 percent report that they've had a truly memorable experience. In fact, at Ritz-Carlton, exceptional service encounters have become almost commonplace. Take the experiences of Nancy and Harvey Heffner of Manhattan, who stayed at the Ritz-Carlton in Naples, Florida. As reported in the *New York Times:*

*"The hotel is elegant and beautiful,"* Mrs. Heffner said, *"but more important is the beauty expressed by the staff. They can't do enough to please you."* When the couple's son became sick last year in Naples, the hotel staff brought him hot tea with honey at all hours of the night, she said. When Mr. Heffner had to fly home on business for a day and his return flight was delayed, a driver for the hotel waited in the lobby most of the night.

Such personal, high-quality service has also made the Ritz-Carlton a favorite among conventioneers. Comments one convention planner, "They not only treat us like kings when we hold our top-level meetings in their hotels, but we just never get any complaints."

In 1991, Ritz-Carlton received 121 quality-related awards, along with industry-best rankings by all three hotel-rating organizations. In 1992, it became the first hotel company to win the Malcolm Baldrige National Quality Award. More importantly, service quality has resulted in high customer retention: More than 90 percent of Ritz-Carlton customers return. And despite its hefty $150 average room rate, the chain enjoys a 70 percent occupancy rate, almost nine points above the industry average.

Most of the responsibility for

*Ritz-Carlton understands that outstanding service begins with taking care of those who take care of customers.*

keeping guests satisfied falls to Ritz-Carlton's customer-contact employees. Thus, the hotel chain takes great care in selecting its personnel. "We want only people who care about people," notes Patrick Mene, the company's vice president of quality. Once selected, employees are given intensive training in the art of coddling customers. New employees attend a two-day orientation, in which top management drums into them the "20 Ritz-Carlton Basics." Basic number one: "The Credo will be known, owned, and energized by all employees."

Employees are taught to do everything they can to never lose a guest. "There's no negotiating at Ritz-Carlton when it comes to solving customer problems," says Mene. Staff learn that *anyone* who receives a customer complaint *owns* that complaint until it's resolved. They are trained to drop whatever they're doing to help a customer—no matter what they're doing or what their department. Ritz-Carlton employees are empowered to handle problems on the spot, without consulting higher-ups. Each employee can spend up to $2,000 to redress a guest grievance, and each is allowed to break from his or her routine for as long as needed to make a guest happy. "We master customer satisfaction at the individual level," adds Mene. "This is our most sensitive listening post

. . . our early warning system." Thus, while competitors are still reading guest comment cards to learn about customer problems, Ritz-Carlton has already resolved them.

Ritz-Carlton instills a sense of pride in its employees. "You serve," they are told, "but you are not servants." The company motto states, "We are ladies and gentlemen serving ladies and gentlemen." Employees understand their role in Ritz-Carlton's success. "We might not be able to afford a hotel like this," says employee Tammy Patton, "but we can make it so people who can afford it will want to keep coming here."

And so they do. When it comes to customer satisfaction, no detail is too small. Customer-contact people are taught to greet guests warmly and sincerely, using guests' names when possible. They learn to use the proper language when speaking to guests—words like "Good morning," "Certainly," "I'll be happy to," and "My pleasure," never "Hi" or "How's it going?" The Ritz-Carlton Basics urge employees to escort guests to another area of the hotel rather than pointing out directions, to answer the phone within three rings and with a "smile," and to take pride and care in their personal appearance.

Ritz-Carlton recognizes and rewards employees who perform

feats of outstanding service. Under its 5-Star Awards program, outstanding performers are nominated by peers and managers, and winners receive plaques at dinners celebrating their achievements. For on-the-spot recognition, managers award Gold Standard Coupons, redeemable for items in the gift shop and free weekend stays at the hotel. Ritz-Carlton further rewards and motivates its employees with events such as Super Sports Day, an employee talent show, luncheons celebrating employee anniversaries, a family picnic, and special themes in employee dining rooms. As a result, Ritz-Carlton's employees appear to be just as satisfied as its customers. Employee turnover is less than 30 percent a year, compared with 45 percent at other luxury hotels.

Ritz-Carlton's success is based on a simple philosophy: To take care of customers, you must first take care of those who take care of customers. Satisfied employees deliver high service value, which then creates satisfied customers. Satisfied customers, in turn, create sales and profits for the company.

*Sources:* Quotes from Edwin McDowell, "Ritz-Carlton's Keys to Good Service," *New York Times,* March 31, 1993, p. D1; and Howard Schlossberg, "Measuring Customer Satisfaction Is Easy to Do—Until You Try," *Marketing News,* April 26, 1993, pp. 5, 8. Also see Rahul Jacob, "Why Some Customers Are More Equal than Others," *Fortune,* September 19, 1994, pp. 215–24; and Don Peppers, "Digitizing Desire," *Forbes,* April 10, 1995, p. 76.

in which the service product is delivered, or by designing a superior delivery process. For example, a bank might offer its customers electronic home banking as a better way to deliver banking services than having to drive, park, and wait in line.

Finally, service companies also can work on differentiating their *images* through symbols and branding. For example, the Harris Bank of Chicago adopted the lion as a symbol on its stationery and advertising and even offered stuffed animals to new depositors. The well-known "Harris lion" confers an image of strength on the bank. Other well-known service symbols include The Travelers' red umbrella, Merrill Lynch's bull, and Allstate's "good hands."

### *Managing Service Quality*

One of the major ways that a service firm can differentiate itself is by delivering consistently higher quality than its competitors do. Like manufacturers before them, many service industries have now joined the total quality movement.[27] Customer retention is perhaps the best measure of quality—a service firm's ability to hang onto its customers depends on how consistently it delivers value to them.

Like product marketers, service providers need to identify the expectations of target customers concerning service quality. Unfortunately, service quality is

*To differentiate its service, British Airways offers international travelers such features as sleeping compartments and hot showers. As the comments in this ad show, customers really appreciate such services.*

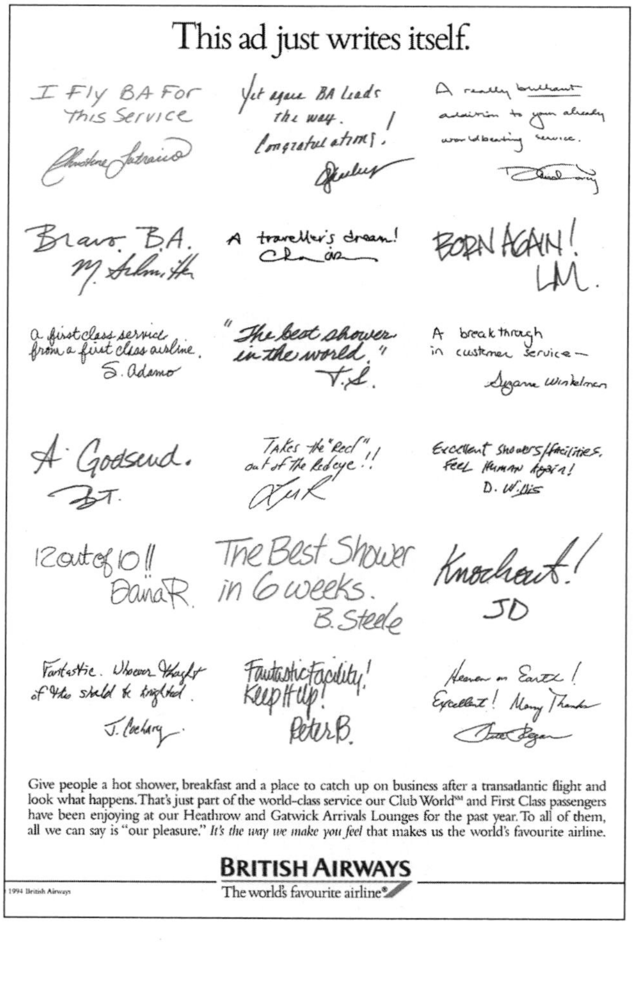

harder to define and judge than product quality. For instance, it is harder to get agreement on the quality of a haircut than on the quality of a hair dryer. Moreover, although greater service quality results in greater customer satisfaction, it also results in higher costs. Still, investments in service usually pay off through increased customer retention and sales.

Many service companies have invested heavily to develop streamlined and efficient service-delivery systems. They want to ensure that customers will receive consistently high-quality service in every service encounter. However, unlike product manufacturers who can adjust their machinery and inputs until everything is perfect, service quality will always vary, depending on the interactions between employees and customers. Problems will inevitably occur. As hard as they try, even the best companies occasionally have a late delivery, burned steak, or grumpy employee. However, although a company cannot always prevent service problems, it can learn to recover from them. And good *service recovery* can turn angry customers into loyal ones. In fact, good recovery can win more customer purchasing and loyalty than if things had gone well in the first place.[28] Therefore, companies should take steps not only to provide good service every time, but also to recover from service mistakes when they do occur.

The first step is to *empower* front-line service employees—to give them the authority, responsibility, and incentives that they need to recognize, care about, and tend to customer needs. At Marriott, for example, well-trained employees are given the authority to do whatever it takes, on the spot, to keep guests happy. They are also expected to help management ferret out the cause of guests' problems and to inform managers of ways to improve overall hotel service and guests' comfort.[29]

Studies of well-managed service companies show that they share a number of common virtues regarding service quality. First, top service companies are "*customer obsessed.*" They have a distinctive strategy for satisfying customer needs that wins enduring customer loyalty. Second, they have a *top management commitment* to quality. Management at companies such as Ritz-Carlton, Disney, Home Depot, Federal Express, and McDonald's looks not only at financial performance but also at service performance. Third, the best service providers set *high service quality standards.* Top service companies do not settle merely for "good" service, they aim for 100 percent defect-free service. A 98 percent performance standard may sound good, but, using this standard, 64,000 Federal Express packages would be lost each day, 10 words would be misspelled on each printed page, 400,000 prescriptions would be misfilled daily, and drinking water would be unsafe eight days a year.[30]

Fourth, the top service firms *watch service performance closely*—both their own and that of competitors. They use methods such as comparison shopping, customer surveys, and suggestion and complaint forms. For example, General Electric sends out 700,000 response cards each year to households who rate their service people's performance. Citibank takes regular measures of "ART"—accuracy, responsiveness, and timeliness—and sends out employees who act as customers to check on service quality.

Good service companies also communicate their concerns about service quality to employees and provide performance feedback. At Federal Express, quality measurements are everywhere. When employees walk in the door in the morning, they see the previous week's on-time percentages. Then, the company's in-house television station gives them detailed breakdowns of what happened yesterday and any potential problems for the day ahead.[31]

### Managing Service Productivity

With their costs rising rapidly, service firms are under great pressure to increase service productivity. They can do so in several ways. The service providers can train current employees better, or they can hire new ones who will work harder or more skillfully for the same pay. Or the service providers can increase the quantity of their service by giving up some quality. Doctors working for health maintenance organizations (HMOs) have moved toward handling more patients and devoting less time to each. The provider can "industrialize the service" by adding equipment and standardizing production, as in McDonald's assembly-line approach to fast-food retailing. Commercial dishwashing, jumbo jets, and multiple-unit movie theaters all represent technological expansions of service.

Finally, the service provider can harness the power of technology. While we often think of technology's power to save time and money for manufacturing companies, it also has great—and often untapped—potential to make service workers more productive. Consider these examples:[32]

> Respiratory therapists at the University of California at San Diego Medical Center now carry miniature computers in their lab pockets. In the past, therapists had to wait at the nurses' station for patients' records. Today, therapists call up the information on hand-held computers, which pluck the data from a central computer. As a result, they can spend more time working directly with patients.
>
> Using a help-desk computerized system called Apriori, Storage Dimensions can answer customer-service questions on the spot. When a customer calls Storage Dimensions with a problem, the operator inputs key words. If the customer's question has been asked and answered before, as so many have, a solution document "bubbles up" to the top of the PC screen and the customer's problems get solved on the spot. Since installing Apriori, SD has reduced problem resolution time from an average of two hours to 20 minutes. As an added bonus, the company has also used information gleaned during the "help" conversations to generate sales leads and product-development ideas.

However, companies must avoid pushing productivity so hard that quality is reduced. Some productivity steps help standardize quality, increasing customer satisfaction. But others lead to overstandardization and can diminish customized service. Attempts to industrialize a service or cut costs can make a company more efficient in the short run but reduce its longer-run ability to innovate, maintain service quality, or respond to consumer needs. In some cases, service providers accept reduced productivity to create more service differentiation or quality.

# ▶ MARKETING ORGANIZATIONS, PERSONS, PLACES, AND IDEAS

Marketing has broadened in recent years to cover "marketable" entities other than products and services—namely, organizations, persons, places, and ideas.

Organizations often carry out activities to "sell" the organization itself.

**Organization marketing**
Activities undertaken to create, maintain, or change attitudes and behavior of target audiences toward an organization.

**Organization marketing** consists of activities undertaken to create, maintain, or change the attitudes and behavior of target consumers toward an organization. Both profit and nonprofit organizations practice organization marketing. Business firms sponsor public relations or corporate advertising campaigns to polish their images. Nonprofit organizations, such as churches, colleges, charities, museums, and performing arts groups, market their organizations in order to raise funds and attract members or patrons. *Corporate image advertising* is a major tool that companies use to market themselves to various publics. Companies can use corporate advertising to build up or maintain a favorable image over many years. Or they can use it to counter events that might hurt their image.

**Person marketing**
Activities undertaken to create, maintain, or change attitudes or behavior toward particular persons.

**Person marketing** consists of activities undertaken to create, maintain, or change attitudes or behavior toward particular people. All kinds of people and organizations practice person marketing. Politicians market themselves to get votes and program support. Entertainers and sports figures use marketing to promote their careers and improve their incomes. Professionals such as doctors, lawyers, accountants, and architects market themselves in order to build their reputations and increase business. Business leaders use person marketing as a strategic tool to develop their companies' fortunes as well as their own. Businesses, charities, sports teams, fine arts groups, religious groups, and other organizations also use person marketing. Associating with well-known personalities often helps these organizations achieve their goals.

**Place marketing**
Activities undertaken to create, maintain, or change attitudes or behavior toward particular places.

**Place marketing** involves activities undertaken to create, maintain, or change attitudes or behavior toward particular places. Examples include business site marketing and tourism marketing. *Business site marketing* involves developing, selling, or renting business sites for factories, stores, offices, warehouses, and conventions. Large developers research companies' land needs and respond with real estate solutions, such as industrial parks, shopping centers, and new office buildings. Most

*Corporate image advertising is a major tool companies use to market themselves: Norfolk Southern, the "thoroughbred of transportation," stands on solid footing.*

states operate industrial development offices that try to sell companies on the advantages of locating new plants in their states. They spend large sums on advertising and offer to fly prospects to the site at no cost. Even entire nations such as Canada, Ireland, Greece, Mexico, and Turkey have marketed themselves as good locations for business investment.

*Tourism marketing* involves attracting vacationers to spas, resorts, cities, states, and even entire nations. The effort is carried out by travel agents, airlines, motor clubs, oil companies, hotels, motels, and governmental agencies. Today, almost every city, state, and country markets its tourist attractions. Texas has advertised "It's Like a Whole Other Country," Michigan has touted "YES M!CH!GAN," and Missouri advises "Wake Up to Missouri." Philadelphia invites you to "Get To Know Us!" and Palm Beach, Florida, advertises "The Best of Everything" at low off-season prices.

**Idea marketing**
Also called social marketing—the marketing of social ideas, such as public health campaigns, environmental campaigns, and other campaigns such as family planning, human rights, and racial equality.

**Social marketing**
The design, implementation, and control of programs seeking to increase the acceptability of a social idea, cause, or practice among a target group.

*Ideas* also can be marketed. In one sense, all marketing is **idea marketing,** whether it involves marketing the general idea of brushing your teeth or the specific idea that Crest provides the most effective decay prevention. Here, however, we narrow our focus to the marketing of *social ideas,* such as public health campaigns to reduce smoking, alcoholism, drug abuse, and overeating; environmental campaigns to promote wilderness protection, clean air, and conservation; and other campaigns such as family planning, human rights, and racial equality. This area has been called **social marketing,** and it includes the creation and implementation of programs seeking to increase the acceptability of a social idea, cause, or practice within targeted groups. Social marketing has been applied mainly to family planning, environmental protection, energy conservation, improved health and nutrition, auto driver safety, and public transportation—and there have been some encouraging successes.

The Advertising Council of America has developed dozens of social advertising campaigns, including "Smokey the Bear," "Keep America Beautiful," "Join the Peace Corps," "Buy Bonds," "Go to College," "Stop the Violence," and "Say No to Drugs." But social marketing involves much more than just advertising. Many public marketing campaigns fail because they assign advertising the primary role and fail to develop and use all the marketing-mix tools.

# ▶ INTERNATIONAL PRODUCT AND SERVICES MARKETING

International product and service marketers face special challenges. First, they must figure out what products and services to introduce and in which countries. Then, they must decide how much to standardize or adapt their products and services for world markets. On the one hand, companies would like to standardize their offerings. Standardization helps a company to develop a consistent worldwide image. It also results in lower manufacturing costs and eliminates duplication of research and development, advertising, and product design efforts. On the other hand, consumers around the world differ in their cultures, attitudes, and buying behaviors. And markets vary in their economic conditions, competition, legal requirements, and physical environments. Companies must respond to these differences by adapting their product offerings. Something as simple as an electrical outlet can create big product problems:

Those who have traveled across Europe know the frustration of electrical plugs, different voltages, and other annoyances of international travel. . . . Philips, the electrical appliance manufacturer, has to produce 12 kinds of irons to serve just its European market. The problem is that Europe does not have a universal [electrical] standard. The ends of irons bristle with different plugs for different countries. Some have three prongs, others two; prongs protrude straight or angled, round or rectangular, fat, thin, and sometimes sheathed. There are circular plug faces, squares, pentagons, and hexagons. Some are perforated and some are notched. One French plug has a niche like a keyhole; British plugs carry fuses.[33]

Packaging also presents new challenges for international marketers. Packaging issues can be subtle. For example, names, labels, and colors may not translate easily from one country to another. A firm using yellow flowers in its logo might fare well in the United States, but meet with disaster in Mexico, where a yellow flower symbolizes death or disrespect. Similarly, although "Nature's Gift" might be an appealing name for gourmet mushrooms in America, it would be deadly in Germany, where "gift" means "poison." Packaging may also have to be tailored to meet the physical characteristics of consumers in various parts of the world. For instance, soft drinks are sold in smaller cans in Japan to better fit the smaller hands of Japanese customers. Thus, although product and package standardization can produce benefits, companies usually must adapt their offerings to the unique needs of specific international markets.

Service marketers also face special challenges when going global. Some service industries have a long history of international operations. For example, the commercial banking industry was one of the first to grow internationally. Banks had to provide global services in order to meet the foreign exchange and credit needs of their home-country clients wanting to sell overseas. In recent years, many banks have become truly global operations. Germany's Deutsche Bank, for example, has branches in 41 countries. Thus, for its clients around the world who wish to take advantage of growth opportunities created by German reunification, Deutsche Bank can raise money not just in Frankfurt, but also in Zurich, London, Paris, and Tokyo.

The travel industry has also become international. American hotel and airline companies grew quickly in Europe and Asia during the economic expansion that followed World War II. Credit card companies soon followed—the early worldwide presence of American Express has now been matched by VISA and MasterCard. Business travelers and vacationers like the convenience, and they have now come to expect that their credit cards will be honored wherever they go.

Professional and business services industries such as accounting, management consulting, and advertising have only recently become global. The international growth of these firms followed the globalization of the manufacturing companies they serve. For example, as their client companies began to employ worldwide marketing and advertising strategies, advertising agencies and other marketing services firms responded by globalizing their own operations. For instance, the ten largest U.S. advertising agencies now make over 50 percent of their billings abroad.[34]

Retailers are among the latest service businesses to go international. As their home markets become saturated with stores, American retailers such as Wal-Mart, Kmart, Toys 'R' Us, Office Depot, Saks Fifth Avenue, and Disney are expanding into faster-growing markets abroad. Japanese retailer, Yaohan, now operates the largest shopping center in Asia, the 21-story Nextage Shanghai Tower in China, and Carrefour of France is the leading retailer in Brazil and Argentina. Asian shoppers now buy American products in Dutch-owned Makro stores, now Southeast Asia's biggest store group with regional sales of more than $2 billion.[35]

Service companies wanting to operate in other countries are not always welcomed with open arms. Whereas manufacturers usually face straightforward tariff, quota, or currency restrictions when attempting to sell their products in another country, service providers are likely to face more subtle barriers. In some cases, rules and regulations affecting international service firms reflect the host country's traditions. In others, they appear to protect the country's own fledgling service industries from large global competitors with greater resources. In still other cases, however, the restrictions seem to have little purpose other than to make entry difficult for foreign service firms.

A new Turkish law, for example, forbids international accounting firms from bringing capital into the country to set up offices and requires them to use the names of local partners in their marketing rather than their own internationally known company names. To audit the books of a multinational company's branch in Buenos Aires, an accountant must have the equivalent of a high school education in Argentinean geography and history. In New Delhi, India, international insurance companies are not allowed to sell property and casualty policies to the country's fast-growing business community or life insurance to its huge middle class.[36]

Despite such difficulties, the trend toward growth of global service companies will continue, especially in banking, airlines, telecommunications, and professional services. Today, service firms are no longer simply following their manufacturing customers. Instead, they are taking the lead in international expansion.[37]

*Retailers are among the latest service businesses to go global. Here, Asian shoppers buy American products in a Dutch-owned Makro store in Kuala Lumpur.*

## SUMMARY

*Product* is a complex concept that must be defined carefully. Each product or service offered to customers can be viewed on three levels. The *core product* is the essential benefit that the customer is really buying. The *actual product* includes the features, styling, quality, brand name, and packaging. The *augmented product* is the actual product plus the various services offered with it, such as warranty, installation, maintenance, and free delivery.

All products can be classified into two groups according to the purpose for which they are purchased. *Consumer products* are usually classified according to consumer shopping habits (convenience products, shopping products, specialty products, and unsought products). *Industrial products* are classified according to their cost and the way they enter the production process (materials and parts, capital items, and supplies and services).

Companies have to develop strategies for the items in their product lines. They must decide on product attributes, branding, packaging, labeling, and product-support services. *Product attribute decisions* involve the product quality, features, and design that the company will offer. Regarding *brands*, the company must decide on brand name selection, brand sponsorship, and brand strategy.

Products require *packaging decisions* to create benefits such as protection, economy, convenience, and promotion. Products also require *labeling* for identification and possible grading, description, and promotion of the product. Companies must also develop *product-support services* that are desired by customers and are also effective against competitors. *Customer service* should be used as a marketing tool to create customer satisfaction and competitive advantage.

Most companies produce a product line rather than a single product. A *product line* is a group of products that are related in function, customer-purchase needs, or distribution channels. Each product line requires a product strategy. *Line stretching* involves extending a line downward, upward, or in both directions. *Line filling* involves adding items within the present range of the line.

*Product mix* describes the set of product lines and items offered to customers by a particular seller. The product mix can be described by four dimensions: width, length, depth, and consistency. These dimensions are the tools for developing the company's product strategy.

As we move increasingly toward a *world service economy,* marketers need to know more about marketing services. *Services* are *intangible, inseparable, variable,* and *perishable.* Each characteristic poses problems and marketing requirements. Marketers have to find ways to make the service more tangible; to increase the productivity of providers who are inseparable from their products; to standardize quality in the face of variability; and to improve demand movements and supply capacities in the face of service perishability.

Good service companies focus attention on *both* customers and employees. They understand the *service-profit chain,* which links service firm profits with employee and customer satisfaction. Services marketing strategy calls not only for external marketing but also for *internal marketing* to motivate employees and *interactive marketing* to create service delivery skills among service providers. To succeed, service marketers must create *competitive differentiation,* offer high *service quality,* and find ways to increase *service productivity.*

Organizations, persons, places, and ideas are also marketed. *Organization marketing* is undertaken to create, maintain, or change the attitudes or behavior of target audiences toward an organization. *Person marketing* consists of activities undertaken to create, maintain, or change attitudes or behavior toward particular persons. *Place marketing* involves activities undertaken to create, maintain, or change attitudes or behavior toward particular places. *Idea marketing* involves efforts to market ideas. In the case of social ideas, it is called *social marketing* and consists of the design, implementation, and control of programs seeking to increase the acceptability of a social idea, cause, or practice among a target group.

## KEY TERMS

Brand
Brand equity
Brand extension
Co-branding
Consumer products
Convenience products
Idea marketing
Industrial products
Interactive marketing
Internal marketing
Line extension
Manufacturer's brand (or national brand)

Multibranding
Organization marketing
Packaging
Person marketing
Place marketing
Private brand (or store brand)
Product
Product line
Product mix (or product assortment)
Product quality
Service intangibility
Service inseparability

Service perishability
Service variability
Service-profit chain
Services
Shopping products
Slotting fees
Social marketing
Specialty products
Unsought products

## QUESTIONS FOR DISCUSSION

1. List and explain the core, actual, and augmented products of the educational experience that universities offer.

2. Explain why many people are willing to pay more for branded products than for unbranded products. What does this tell you about the value of branding?

3. ITT Sheraton recently began to change the name of its 88 Sheraton Inns located throughout the country. The new chain will be known as Four Points Hotels. What are the possible risks and rewards of this strategy? Link your answer to brand strategy.

4. A "hot" concept in fast-food marketing is home delivery of everything from pizza to hamburgers to fried chicken. Why do you think that demand for this service is growing? How can marketers gain a competitive advantage by satisfying the growing demand for increased services?

5. Illustrate how a theater can deal with the intangibility, inseparability, variability, and perishability of the service that it provides. Give specific examples.

6. Many people feel that too much time and money are spent marketing political candidates. They also complain that modern political campaigns overemphasize the politician's image at the expense of issues. Discuss your opinion of political-candidate marketing. Would some other approach to campaigning help consumers to make better voting decisions?

## APPLYING THE CONCEPTS

1. Go to an area nearby that has a number of fast-food outlets. Compare the product mix of McDonald's to Kentucky Fried Chicken. Are there differences in width or depth? How could they stretch their lines upward or downward?

2. Perishability is very important in the airline industry: Unsold seats are gone forever, and too many unsold seats mean large losses. With computerized ticketing, airlines can easily use pricing to deal with perishability and variations in demand.

◆ Call a travel agent or use an online service such as EasySabre to check airline fares. Get prices on the same route for 60 days in advance, two weeks, one week, and today. Is there a clear pattern to the fares?

◆ When a store is overstocked on ripe fruit, it may lower the price to sell out quickly. What are airlines doing to their prices as the seats get close to "perishing"? Why? What would you recommend as a pricing strategy to increase total revenues?

## REFERENCES

1. See "What Lies Behind the Sweet Smell of Success," *Business Week,* February 27, 1984, pp. 139–43; S. J. Diamond, "Perfume Equals Part Mystery, Part Marketing," *Los Angeles Times,* April 22, 1988, Section 4, p. 1; "Charlie Relaunch Spearheads Busy Time for Revlon," *Cosmetics International,* May 10, 1993, p. 2; "Leaders Follow Scent to Growth in Fragrances," *Advertising Age,* September 28, 1994, pp. 20, 30; and Pat Sloan, "Lauder Senses It's Time to Change with Pleasures," *Advertising Age,* May 22, 1995, p. 16.

2. Rahul Jacob, "More Than a Dying Fad?" *Fortune,* October 18, 1993, pp. 66–72. Also see Cyndee Miller, "TQM Out; 'Continuous Process Improvement' In," *Marketing News,* May 9, 1994, pp. 5, 10; and David Greising, "Quality: How to Make It Pay," *Business Week,* August 8, 1994, pp. 54–59.

3. See Roland T. Rust, Anthony J. Zahorik, and Timothy L. Keiningham, "Return on Quality (ROQ): Making Service Quality Financially Accountable," *Journal of Marketing,* April 1995, pp. 58–70.

4. Joseph Weber, "A Better Grip on Hawking Tools," *Business Week,* June 5, 1995, p. 99. For more on product design, see Peter H. Bloch, "Seeking the Ideal Form: Product Design and Consumer Response," *Journal of Marketing,* July 1995, pp. 16–29.

5. Kurt Badenhausen, "Brands: The Management Factor," *Financial World,* August 1, 1995, pp. 50–69. Also see David A. Aaker, *Managing Brand Equity* (New York: The Free Press, 1991); Peter H. Farquhar, Julia Y. Han, and Yuji Ijiri, "Brands on the Balance Sheet," *Marketing Management,* Winter 1992, pp. 16–22; Kevin Lane Keller, "Conceptualizing, Measuring, and Managing Customer-Based Brand Equity," *Journal of Marketing,* January 1993, pp. 1–22; and T. L. Stanley, "How They Rate," *Brandweek,* April 3, 1995, pp. 45–48.

6. See Tim Triplett, "Generic Fear to Xerox Is Brand Equity to FedEx," *Advertising Age,* August 15, 1994, pp. 12, 13. For an interesting discussion of good brand names, see Al Ries, "What's In a Name?" *Sales & Marketing Management,* October 1995, pp. 36–38.

7. Emily DeNitto, "They Aren't Private Labels Anymore—They're Brands," *Advertising Age,* September 13, 1993, p. 8.

8. See Chip Walker, "What's in a Brand?" *American Demographics,* February 1991, pp. 54–56; Emily DeNitto, "No End to Private Label March," *Advertising Age,* November 1, 1993, p. S6; Patrick Oster, "The Eurosion of Brand Loyalty," *Business Week,* July 19, 1993, p. 22; and Marcia Mogelonsky, "When Stores Become Brands," *American Demographics,* February 1995, pp. 32–38.

9. See Peter Kim, "Restore Brand Equity!" *Directors & Boards,* Summer 1993, pp. 21–29; Pat Sloan, "Brands Are Back," *Advertising Age,* May 8, 1995, pp. 1, 40; Cyndee Miller, "Big Brands Fight Back Against Private Labels," *Marketing News,* January 16, 1995, p. 1; and John A. Quelch and David Harding, "Brands versus Private Labels: Fighting to Win," *Harvard Business Review,* January–February 1996, pp. 99–109.

10. Martin Lieberman, "Corporations Latch Onto Licensing," *Advertising Age,* August 14, 1995, p. 28; and Kate Fitzgerald, "License to Sell," *Advertising Age,* January 12, 1996, pp. S1, S10.

11. Terry Lefton, "Warner Brothers' Not Very Looney Path To Licensing Gold," *Brandweek,* February 14, 1994, pp. 36–37.

12. Kim Cleland, "Multimarketer Melange an Increasingly Tasty Option on the Store Shelf," *Advertising Age,* May 2, 1994, p. S10; Phil Carpenter, "Some Cobranding Caveats to Obey," *Marketing News,* November 7, 1994, p. 4; and Allyson L. Stewart, "Cobranding Just Starting in Europe," *Marketing News,* February 13, 1995, p. 5.

13. For more on line extensions, see Kevin Lane Keller and David A. Aaker, "The Effects of Sequential Introduction of Line Extensions," *Journal of Marketing Research,* February 1992, pp. 35–50; Srinivas K. Reddy, Susan L. Holak, and Subodh Bhat, "To Extend or Not to Extend: Success Determinants of Line Extensions," *Journal of Marketing Research,* May 1994, pp. 243–62; and Bruce G. S. Hardle, Leonard M. Lodish, James V. Kilmer, David R. Beatty, et al., "The Logic of Product-Line Extensions," *Harvard Business Review,* November–December 1994, pp. 53–62.

14. Pam Weitz, "Trying to Move from the Wardrobe to the Bathroom," *Brandweek,* April 24, 1995, pp. 36, 38.

15. For more on the use of brand extensions and consumer attitudes toward them, see David A. Aaker and Kevin L. Keller, "Consumer Evaluations of Brand Extensions," *Journal of Marketing,* January 1990, pp. 27–41; and Susan M. Broniarczyk and Joseph W. Alba, "The Importance of Brand in Brand Extension," *Journal of Marketing Research,* May 1994, pp. 214–28.

16. See Bill Abrams, "Marketing," *Wall Street Journal,* May 20, 1982, p. 33; and Bernice Kanner, "Package Deals," *New York,* August 22, 1988, pp. 267–68.

17. See Pam Weitz, "Repackaging," *Brandweek,* February 27, 1995, pp. 25–27.

18. Cyndee Miller, "Food Industry Faces Sweeping Label Requirements," *Marketing News,* June 6, 1994, pp. 5, 12; and J. Howard Beale, Regulatory

Consistency and Common Sense: FTC Policy Toward Food Advertising Under Revised Labeling Regulations," *Journal of Public Policy and Marketing,* Spring 1995, p. 154.

19. Bro Uttal, "Companies That Serve You Best," *Fortune,* December 7, 1987, p. 116.

20. For an excellent discussion of support services, see James C. Anderson and James A. Narus, "Capturing the Value of Supplementary Services," *Harvard Business Review,* January–February 1995, pp. 75–83.

21. See Paula Mergenbagen, "Product Liability: Who Sues?" *American Demographics,* June 1995, p. 48.

22. For a discussion of product line expansion issues, see John A. Quelch and David Kenny, "Extend Profits, Not Product Lines," *Harvard Business Review,* September–October 1994, pp. 153–60.

23. See Ronald Henkoff, "Service Is Everybody's Business," *Fortune,* June 27, 1994, pp. 48–60; and Adrian Palmer and Catherine Cole, *Services Marketing: Principles and Practice* (Englewood Cliffs, NJ: Prentice Hall, 1995), pp. 56–60.

24. "Presto! The Convenience Industry: Making Life a Little Simpler," *Business Week,* April 27, 1987, p. 86; also see Ronald Henkoff, "Piety, Profits, and Productivity," *Fortune,* June 1992, pp. 84–85.

25. See James L. Heskett, Thomas O. Jones, Gary W. Loveman, W. Earl Sasser, Jr., and Leonard A. Schlesinger, "Putting the Service-Profit Chain to Work," *Harvard Business Review,* March–April, 1994, pp. 164–74.

26. See Walter E. Green, Gary D. Wells, and Larry J. Schrest, "Internal Marketing: The Key to External Marketing," *Journal of Services Marketing,* Vol. 8, No. 4, 1994, pp. 5–13.

27. For excellent discussions on service quality, see A. Parasuraman, Valerie A. Zeithaml, and Leonard L. Berry, "A Conceptual Model of Service Quality and Its Implications for Future Research," *Journal of Marketing,* Fall 1985, pp. 41–50; Zeithaml, Parasuraman, and Berry, *Delivering Service Quality: Balancing Customer Perceptions and Expectations* (New York: The Free Press, 1990); J. Joseph Cronin, Jr. and Steven A. Taylor, "Measuring Service Quality: A Reexamination and Extension," *Journal of Marketing,* July 1992, pp. 55–68; and Parasuraman, Zeithaml, and Berry, "Reassessment of Expectations as a Comparison Standard in Measuring Service Quality: Implications for Further Research," *Journal of Marketing,* January 1994, pp. 111–24.

28. Christopher W. L. Hart, James L. Heskett, and W. Earl Sasser, Jr., "The Profitable Art of Service Recovery," *Harvard Business Review,* July–August 1990, pp. 148–56. For a discussion of service firm behaviors that cause lost customers, see Susan M. Keveney, "Customer Switching Behavior in Service Industries: An Exploratory Study," *Journal of Marketing,* April 1995, pp. 71–82.

29. Ronald Henkoff, "Finding and Keeping the Best Service Workers," *Fortune,* October 3, 1994, pp. 110–22.

30. See James L. Heskett, W. Earl Sasser, Jr., and Christopher W. L. Hart, *Service Breakthroughs* (New York: Free Press, 1990).

31. Barry Farber and Joyce Wycoff, "Customer Service: Evolution and Revolution," *Sales & Marketing Management,* May 1991, pp. 44–51.

32. Nilly Landau, "Are You Being Served?" *International Business,* March 1995, pp. 38–40.

33. Philip Cateora, *International Marketing,* 8th ed. (Homewood, IL: Irwin, 1993), p. 270.

34. Michael R. Czinkota and Ilkka A. Ronkainen, *International Marketing,* 2nd ed. (Chicago: Dryden, 1990), p. 679.

35. Carla Rapoport, "Retailers Go Global," *Fortune,* February 20, 1995, pp. 102–8.

36. Lee Smith, "What's at Stake in the Trade Talks," *Fortune,* August 27, 1990, pp. 76–77.

37. See Tom Hayes, "Services Go International," *Marketing News,* March 14, 1994, pp. 14–15.

# 9

# New-Product Development and Product Life-Cycle Strategies

3M markets more than 60,000 products. These products range from sandpaper and adhesives to contact lenses, heart-lung machines, and futuristic synthetic ligaments; and from reflecting road signs to never-rust wool soap pads and hundreds of sticky tapes—Scotch Tape, masking tape, superbonding tape, and even refastening disposable diaper tape. 3M views *innovation* as its path to growth, and new products as its lifeblood. The company's goal is to derive an astonishing 30 percent of each year's sales from products introduced within the previous four years (recently stepped up from its longstanding goal of 25 percent in five years).

More astonishing, it usually succeeds! Each year, 3M launches more than 200 new products. Its legendary emphasis on innovation has consistently made 3M one of America's most admired companies.

New products don't just happen. 3M works hard to create an environment that supports innovation. It regularly invests about 7 percent of its annual sales, in research and development—twice as much as the average company.

3M encourages everyone to look for new products. The company's renowned "15 percent rule" allows all technical employees to spend up to 15 percent of their time "bootlegging"—working on projects of personal interest whether those projects directly benefit the company or not. When a promising idea comes along, 3M forms a venture team made up of the researcher who developed the idea and volunteers from manufacturing, sales, marketing, and legal. The team nurtures the product and protects it from rigorous company scrutiny. Team members stay with the product until it succeeds or fails and then return to their previous jobs or remain with the new. Some teams have tried three or four times before finally making a success of an idea. Each year, 3M hands out Golden Step Awards to venture teams whose new products earned more than $2 million in U.S. sales, or $4 million in worldwide sales, within three years of introduction.

In its obsessive quest for new products, 3M stays close to its customers. Customer preferences are constantly reassessed at each stage of a new product's development. Marketing people work closely with scientists in developing new products, and R&D people are closely involved in developing overall marketing strategy.

3M knows that it must try thousands of new-product ideas to hit one big jackpot. It accepts blunders and dead ends as a normal part of creativity and innovation. In fact, its philosophy seems to be "if you aren't making mistakes, you probably aren't doing anything." But as it turns out, "blunders" have turned into some of 3M's most successful products. Old-timers at 3M love to tell the story about the chemist who accidentally spilled a new chemical compound on her tennis shoes. Some days later, she noticed that the spots hit by the chemical had not gotten dirty. Eureka! The chemical compound eventually became Scotchgard fabric protector.

And then there's the one about 3M scientist Spencer Silver. Silver started out to develop a superstrong adhesive; instead, he came up with one that didn't stick very well at all. He sent the apparently useless substance on to other 3M researchers to see whether they could find something to do with it. Nothing happened for several years. Then Arthur Fry, another 3M scientist, had a problem—and an idea. As a choir member in a local church, Dr. Fry was having trouble marking places in his hymnal—the little scraps of paper he used kept falling out. He tried dabbing some of Dr. Silver's weak glue on one of the scraps. It stuck nicely and later peeled off without damaging the hymnal. Thus were born 3M's Post-it Notes, a product that is now one of the top-selling office supply products in the world![1] ■

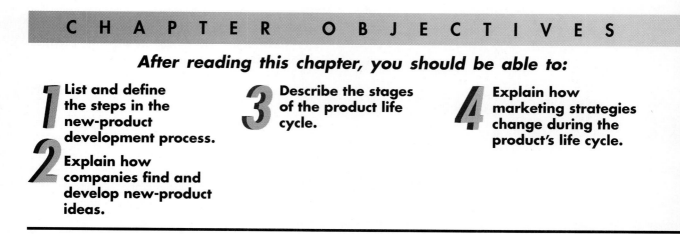

# CHAPTER OBJECTIVES

## After reading this chapter, you should be able to:

**1** List and define the steps in the new-product development process.

**2** Explain how companies find and develop new-product ideas.

**3** Describe the stages of the product life cycle.

**4** Explain how marketing strategies change during the product's life cycle.

A company has to be good at developing new products. It also must manage them in the face of changing tastes, technologies, and competition. Every product seems to go through a life cycle—it is born, goes through several phases, and eventually dies as newer products come along that better serve consumer needs.

This product life cycle presents two major challenges. First, because all products eventually decline, the firm must find new products to replace aging ones (the problem of *new-product development*). Second, the firm must understand how its products age and adapt its marketing strategies as products pass through life-cycle stages (the problem of *product life-cycle strategies*). We first look at the problem of finding and developing new products and then at the problem of managing them successfully over their life cycles.

# ▶NEW-PRODUCT DEVELOPMENT STRATEGY

**New-product development**
The development of original products, product improvements, product modifications, and new brands through the firm's own R&D efforts.

Given the rapid changes in consumer tastes, technology, and competition, companies must develop a steady stream of new products and services. A firm can obtain new products in two ways. One is through *acquisition*—by buying a whole company, a patent, or a license to produce someone else's product. The other is through **new-product development** in the company's own research and development department. As the costs of developing and introducing major new products have climbed, many large companies have acquired existing brands rather than creating new ones. Other firms have saved money by copying competitors' brands or by reviving old brands.

By *new products* we mean original products, product improvements, product modifications, and new brands that the firm develops through its own research and development efforts. In this chapter, we concentrate on new-product development.

Innovation can be very risky. Ford lost $350 million on its Edsel automobile; RCA lost $580 million on its SelectaVision video disk player; and Texas Instruments lost a staggering $660 million before withdrawing from the home computer business. Other costly product failures from sophisticated companies include New Coke (Coca-Cola Company), LA low-alcohol beer (Anheuser-Busch), Zap Mail electronic mail (Federal Express), Polarvision instant movies (Polaroid), Premier "smokeless" cigarettes (R. J. Reynolds), and Clorox detergent (Clorox Company).

New products continue to fail at a disturbing rate. One study estimated that new consumer packaged goods (consisting mostly of line extensions) fail at a rate of 80 percent. Another study found that about 33 percent of new industrial products fail at launch.[2] According to one marketing expert, "if companies can improve their effectiveness at launching new products, they could double their bottom line. It's one of the areas left with the greatest potential for improvement."[3]

Why do so many new products fail? There are several reasons. Although an idea may be good, the market size may have been overestimated. Perhaps the actual product was not designed as well as it should have been. Or maybe it was incorrectly positioned in the market, priced too high, or advertised poorly. A high-level executive might push a favorite idea despite poor marketing research findings. Sometimes the costs of product development are higher than expected, and sometimes competitors fight back harder than expected.

Because so many new products fail, companies are anxious to learn how to improve their odds of new product success. One way is to identify successful new products and find out what they have in common. One study examined 200 moderate- to high-technology new-product launches, looking for factors that are shared by successful products but not by failed products. It found that the number one success factor is a *unique superior product,* one with higher quality, new features, and higher value in use. Specifically, products with a high product advantage succeed 98 percent of the time, compared with products with a moderate advantage

(58 percent success) or minimal advantage (18 percent success). Another key success factor is a *well-defined product concept* prior to development, in which the company carefully defines and assesses the target market, the product requirements, and the benefits before proceeding.[4] In all, to create successful new products, a company must understand its consumers, markets, and competitors and develop products that deliver superior value to customers.

So companies face a problem—they must develop new products, but the odds weigh heavily against success. The solution lies in strong new-product planning and in setting up a systematic *new-product development process* for finding and developing new products. Figure 9-1 shows the eight major steps in this process.

# IDEA GENERATION

New-product development starts with **idea generation**—the systematic search for new-product ideas. A company typically has to generate many ideas in order to find a few good ones. A recent survey of product managers found that, of 100 proposed new product ideas, 39 begin the product development process, 17 survive the development process, eight actually reach the marketplace, and only one eventually reaches its business objectives.[5] The search for new-product ideas should be systematic rather than haphazard. Otherwise, although the company may find many ideas, most will not be good ones for its type of business. Top management can avoid this error by carefully defining its new-product development strategy. Major sources of new-product ideas include internal sources, customers, competitors, distributors and suppliers, and others.

Many new-product ideas come from *internal sources* within the company. The company can find new ideas through formal research and development. It can pick the brains of its scientists, engineers, and manufacturing people. Or company executives can brainstorm new-product ideas. The company's salespeople are another good source because they are in daily contact with customers. Toyota claims that its employees submit two million ideas annually—about 35 suggestions per employee—and that more than 85 percent of them are implemented.

## FIGURE 9-1

*Major stages in new-product development*

*New-product ideas from customers: United States Surgical Corporation became the innovative leader in laparoscopic surgery by watching and listening to surgeons, even gowning up and joining them in the operating room.*

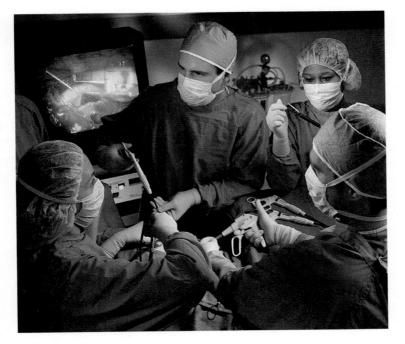

Good new-product ideas also come from watching and listening to *customers*. The company can conduct surveys or focus groups to learn about consumer needs and wants. It can analyze customer questions and complaints to find new products that better solve consumer problems. Or company engineers or salespeople can meet with customers to get suggestions. General Electric's Video Products Division design engineers talk with final consumers to get ideas for new home electronics products.

Companies can learn a great deal from observing and listening to customers. United States Surgical Corporation (USSC) has developed most of its surgical instruments by working closely with surgeons. The company was quick to pick up on early experiments in laparoscopy—surgery performed by inserting a tiny TV camera into the body along with slim, long-handled instruments. In recent years, USSC's focus has changed from marketing individual surgical instruments to offering a total package of products and services aimed at helping hospitals achieve cost-effective surgery. Now, the company pays close attention to the "Total Customer," which includes not only surgeons but also representatives of materials management, purchasing, finance, and other areas of the hospital. USSC now captures about 58 percent of the single-use laparoscopy market.[6]

Finally, consumers often create new products and uses on their own, and companies can benefit by finding these products and putting them on the market. Customers can also be a good source of ideas for new uses for existing products that can expand their market and extend their life. For example, the WD-40 Company, maker of the multipurpose household lubricant and solvent, sponsors an annual contest to elicit ideas for new uses from customers (see Marketing at Work 9-1). Similarly, Avon capitalized on new uses discovered by consumers for its Skin-So-Soft bath oil and moisturizer. For years, customers have been spreading the word that Skin-So-Soft bath oil is also a terrific bug repellent. Whereas some consumers were content simply to perfume their bath water with the fragrant oil,

## MARKETING AT WORK 9-1

# WD-40: Slick Ways to Create New Uses

Along with duct tape and the trusty hammer, WD-40 has become one of the truly essential survival items in most American homes. Originally developed in 1953 to prevent rust and corrosion on Atlas missiles, it takes its name from the 40th and final attempt at creating a *water displacement* formula. Over the past 40 years, WD-40 has achieved a kind of "cult" status—it's now found in more than 80 percent of American households.

The WD-40 Company has shown a real knack for extending the life of WD-40 and for expanding the market by finding new uses for its popular substance. Many fresh concepts come from current users, who enter one of the company's annual contests for new use ideas. Winners of last year's "Invent Your Own Use" contest received cash prizes, and many had their ideas featured in the company's "There's Always Another Use" ad campaign.

Some entrants suggest simple and practical uses. This year's winning entry came from a teacher who used WD-40 to clean old chalkboards in her

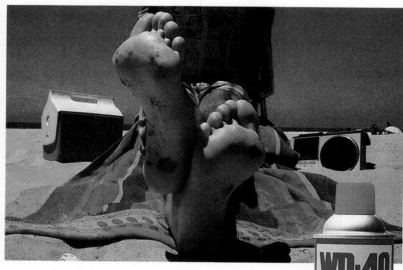

# USE #993

What in tarnation to do. *Holly Sherlock Rose of Coral Springs, Florida takes more than sunscreen and a blanket to the beach. According to Holly, for getting tar off there's nothing like WD-40®. It's also great for removing adhesive labels from glass and other non-porous surfaces. Just spray, wait and wipe.*

WD-40. THERE'S ALWAYS ANOTHER USE.

*The WD-40 Company has shown a real knack for extending the life of WD-40 and for expanding the market by finding new uses for its popular substance.*

others carried it in their backpacks to mosquito-infested campsites or kept a bottle on the deck of their beach houses. Now, Avon is offering Skin-So-Soft Moisturizing Suncare Plus, a triple-action product that provides an insect repellent and waterproof SPF 15 sunscreen as well as moisturizers.[7]

*Competitors* are another good source of new-product ideas. Companies watch competitors' ads and other communications to get clues about their new products. They buy competing new products, take them apart to see how they work, analyze their sales, and decide whether their companies should bring out a new product of their own. For example, when designing its highly successful Tau-

classroom. "Amazingly, the boards started coming to life again," she reports. "Not only were they restored, but years of masking and scotch tape residue came off as well." Others entrants report some pretty unusual uses. First place last year went to a California woman whose parakeet, "Cookie," fell off her shoulder and landed on sticky mouse-trap paper. When she tried to free the bird, she got both her hands stuck. The vet used good old WD-40 to free both victims. Still other reported uses seem highly improbable—one entrant claims that after spraying his Frisbee with WD-40, it flew out of sight, never to be seen again.

By now, almost everyone has discovered that WD-40 comes in handy for lubricating machinery, protecting tools from rust, loosening nuts and bolts, quieting squeaky hinges, and freeing stuck doors, drawers, windows, and zippers. And many fans know that you can use WD-40 to remove sticky labels from glassware, plastic, and metal items; bubble gum from hair and carpets; scuff marks from vinyl floors; and crayon marks from just about anywhere.

Whether it be crayon on walls or bubble gum in hair, WD-40 is a lifesaver for the parents of precocious mess-makers. For example, when one user's two-year-old daughter took crayons in hand to create a colorful rainbow on the living room wall, a few squirts of WD-40 took care of the problem.

Such common uses make good sense, but did you hear about the nude burglary suspect who had wedged himself in a vent at a cafe in Denver? The fire department extracted him with a large dose of WD-40. Or how about the Mississippi naval officer who used WD-40 to repel an angry bear? Then there's the college student who wrote to say that a friend's nightly amorous activities on a noisy old bed in the next room were causing everyone in his dorm to lose sleep—he solved the problem by treating the squeaky bedsprings with WD-40.

Others report using WD-40 to clean paint brushes, renew old printer and typewriter ribbons, keep snow from sticking to snow shovels, and clean hard-water stains and soap scum off shower doors and bathroom tiles. One

inventive cemetery grounds-keeper even uses WD-40 to clean and polish headstones. Many a fishermen reports that spraying a little WD-40 on bait helps attract more fish. Some recreational users claim that spraying their golf clubs, golf balls, or bowling balls has greatly improved their game.

WD-40 has been used to unstick just about everything, including a repairman's finger from a toilet fitting, a little boy's head from his potty-training seat, and a cow's head from a fence. Reports the farmer, "We just sprayed a little WD-40 on his head, and he slipped right out." Ranchers and race horse trainers say they use WD-40 to untangle manes and tails and to repel mud from hooves. And then there's the Florida man who found an entirely different way to use the product. When modern-day pirates boarded his boat, he hit one of the would-be hijackers over the head with a can of WD-40, which knocked him off the boat and saved the day.

*Source:* Numerous WD-40 Company press releases created by Phillips-Ramsey Advertising & Public Relations, San Diego, California. Also see John Hahn, "A Little Squirt Comes to the Rescue," *The Seattle Post-Intelligencer,* September 2, 1994, p. C2.

rus, Ford tore down more than 50 competing models, layer by layer, looking for things to copy or improve upon. It copied the Audi's accelerator-pedal "feel," the Toyota Supra fuel gauge, the BMW 528e tire and jack storage system, and 400 other such outstanding features. Ford did this again when it redesigned the Taurus in 1992.[8]

Finally, *distributors and suppliers* contribute many good new-product ideas. Resellers are close to the market and can pass along information about consumer problems that need solutions and new-product possibilities. Suppliers can tell the company about new concepts, techniques, and materials that can be used to develop new products. Other idea sources include trade magazines, shows, and seminars; government agencies; new-product consultants; advertising agencies; marketing research firms; university and commercial laboratories; and inventors.

# IDEA SCREENING

**Idea screening**
Screening new-product ideas in order to spot good ideas and drop poor ones as soon as possible.

The purpose of idea generation is to create a large number of ideas. The purpose of the succeeding stages is to *reduce* that number. The first idea-reducing stage is **idea screening.** The purpose of screening is to spot good ideas and drop poor ones as soon as possible. Product-development costs rise dramatically in later stages, so companies must proceed only with product ideas that will turn into profitable products.

Most companies require their executives to write up new-product ideas on a standard form that can be reviewed by a new-product committee. The write-up describes the product, the target market, and the competition. It makes some rough estimates of market size, product price, development time and costs, manufacturing costs, and rate of return. The committee then evaluates the idea against a set of general criteria. For example, at Kao Company, the large Japanese consumer products company, the committee asks such questions as: Is the product truly useful to consumers and society? Is it good for our particular company? Does it mesh well with the company's objectives and strategies? Do we have the people, skills, and resources to make it succeed? Does it deliver more value to customers than competing products? Is it easy to advertise and distribute? Many companies have well-designed systems for rating and screening net-product ideas.

# CONCEPT DEVELOPMENT AND TESTING

**Product concept**
A detailed version of the new-product idea stated in meaningful consumer terms.

An attractive idea must be developed into a **product concept.** It is important to distinguish between a product idea, a product concept, and a product image. A *product idea* is an idea for a possible product that the company can see itself offering to the market. A *product concept* is a detailed version of the idea stated in meaningful consumer terms. A *product image* is the way that consumers perceive an actual or potential product.

## Concept Development

Suppose that General Motors wants to commercialize its experimental electric car. This car can go as fast as 80 miles per hour and as far as 90 miles before needing to be recharged. GM estimates that the electric car's operating costs are about half those of a regular car.[9]

GM's task is to develop this new product into alternative product concepts, find out how attractive each concept is to customers, and choose the best one. It might create the following product concepts for the electric car:

◆ *Concept 1:* an inexpensive subcompact designed as a second family car to be used around town. The car is ideal for running errands and visiting friends.
◆ *Concept 2:* a medium-cost, medium-size car designed as an all-purpose family car.
◆ *Concept 3:* a medium-cost sporty compact appealing to young people.
◆ *Concept 4:* an inexpensive subcompact appealing to conscientious people who want basic transportation, low fuel cost, and low pollution.

### Concept Testing

**Concept testing**
Testing new-product concepts with a group of target consumers to determine if the concepts have strong consumer appeal.

**Concept testing** involves testing new-product concepts with groups of target consumers. The concepts may be presented to consumers symbolically or physically. Here, in words, is Concept 1:

> An efficient, fun-to-drive, electric-powered subcompact car that seats four. Great for shopping trips and visits to friends. Costs half as much to operate as similar gasoline-driven cars. Goes up to 80 miles per hour and does not need to be recharged for 90 miles. Priced, fully equipped, at $18,000.

For some concept tests, a word or picture description might be sufficient. However, a more concrete and physical presentation of the concept increases the reliability of the concept test. Today, marketers are finding innovative ways to make product concepts more real to concept-test subjects (see Marketing at Work 9-2).

After being exposed to the concept, consumers then may be asked to react to it by answering the questions in Table 9-1. The answers will help the company decide which concept has the strongest appeal. For example, the last question asks about the consumer's intention to buy. Suppose 10 percent of the consumers said they "definitely" would buy and another 5 percent said "probably." The company could project these figures to the full population in this target group to estimate sales volume. Even then, the estimate is uncertain because people do not always carry out their stated intentions.

Many firms routinely test new product concepts with consumers before attempting to turn them into actual new products. For example, each month Richard Saunders Inc.'s Acu-POLL research system tests 35 new product concepts in-person on 100 nationally representative grocery store shoppers. The poll rates participants' interest in buying a given new product, their perceptions of how new and different the product idea is, and their judgment of the product's value compared with its price. In a recent poll, Nabisco's Oreo Chocolate Cones concept received a rare A+ rating, meaning that consumers think it is an outstanding concept that they would try. Other product concepts didn't fare so well. Nubrush Anti-Bacterial Toothbrush Spray disinfectant, from Applied Microdontics,

---

| **TABLE 9-1** | *Questions for Electric Car Concept Test* |
|---|---|

1. Do you understand the concept of an electric car?
2. Do you believe the claims about the electric car's performance?
3. What are the major benefits of the electric car compared with a conventional car?
4. What improvements in the car's features would you suggest?
5. For what uses would you prefer an electric car to a conventional car?
6. What would be a reasonable price to charge for the electric car?
7. Who would be involved in your decision to buy such a car? Who would drive it?
8. Would you buy such a car? (Definitely, probably, probably not, definitely not)

## MARKETING AT WORK 9-2

# THE NEW WORLD OF CONCEPT TESTING: STEREOLITHOGRAPHY AND VIRTUAL REALITY

In product concept testing, the more the presentation of the concept resembles the final product or experience, the more dependable the results. Today, many firms are developing interesting new methods for product concept testing.

For example, 3D Systems, Inc., uses a technique known as 3-D printing—or "stereolithography"—to create three-dimensional models of physical products, such as small appliances and toys. The process begins with a computer-generated, three-dimensional image of the prototype. A computer first simulates a three-dimensional design and then electronically "slices" the image into wafer-thin segments. The digital information that designs each of these segments is then used to guide a robotically controlled laser beam, which focuses

*Using sterolithography, Logitech was able to design, build, and assemble a fully-functional prototype of this computer mouse in less than two weeks.*

on a soup of liquid plastic formulated to turn solid when exposed to light. The laser builds the object as it creates layer upon microthin layer of hardened plastic. Within a few hours, the process

turns out plastic prototypes that would otherwise take weeks to create. Researchers can show these models to consumers to elicit their comments and reactions.

Stereolithography has produced some amazing success stories. Logitech, a company that produces computer mice and other peripherals, used stereolithography to win a highly-sought contract from a major computer maker. Logitech was delighted when the computer maker requested a bid to manufacture a specific mouse. The only hitch—the bid had to be submitted within only two weeks. Using stereolithography, Logitech designed, built, and assembled a fully functional, superior-quality prototype within the allotted time. The amazed customer awarded the contract to Logitech on the spot.

received an F rating. Consumers found Nubrush to be overpriced, and most don't think that they have a problem with their current toothbrushes being "infected."[10]

## MARKETING STRATEGY DEVELOPMENT

**Marketing strategy development**
Designing an initial marketing strategy for a new product based on the product concept.

Suppose that GM finds that Concept 1 for the electric car tests best. The next step is **marketing strategy development,** designing an initial marketing strategy for introducing this car to the market.

The *marketing strategy statement* consists of three parts. The first part describes the target market; the planned product positioning; and the sales, market share, and profit goals for the first few years. Thus:

Beyond making prototypes, 3-D printing (also called "desktop manufacturing") offers exciting prospects for manufacturing custom-made products at the push of a button. In the future, 3-D "factories" may churn out custom-designed parts. Companies may be able to store their entire inventories electronically in computer memory banks and possibly even fax solid objects to distant locations.

When a large physical product such as an automobile is involved, it can be tested using virtual reality. Researchers use a software package to design a car on a computer. Subjects can then manipulate the simulated car on the computer as if it were a real object. By operating certain controls, a respondent can approach the simulated car, open the door, sit in the car, start the engine, hear the sound, drive away, and experience the ride—all on the computer. The entire experience can be enhanced by placing the simulated car in a simulated showroom and having a simulated salesperson approach the customer with a certain manner and words. After completing this experience, respondents are asked questions about what they liked and disliked, as well as the likelihood of their buying such a car. Researchers can vary car features and salesroom encounters to see which have the greatest appeal. Although this approach may be expensive, researchers learn a great deal about designing the right car before investing millions of dollars to build the real product.

Atlanta-based MarketWare Corp. has created virtual reality software called Visionary Shopper, which runs on PCs and allows consumers to stroll through store aisles on a computer screen and examine packages as though the shelf were really in front of them. Consumers can even rotate the package, seemingly by hand. The marketer can measure reactions to changes in pricing, promotions, shelf layouts, and other variables. The VR system is more appealing to consumers who are tired of market research phone calls and mailings. In addition, it might prove more accurate than market surveys. For example, consumers might not think twice about "removing" two six-packs of beer from the virtual reality shelves yet underreport the amount of beer they consume on a traditional survey, for fear of being seen as a heavy drinker. What's more, consumers who provide companies with data by strolling through virtual stores may be honing skills that will come in quite handy in the future. Notes a MarketWare executive, "This *is* how people will shop someday."

*Sources:* Quotes from "The Ultimate Widget: 3-D 'Printing' May Revolutionize Product Design and Manufacturing," *U.S. News & World Report*, July 20, 1992, p. 55; and John Saunders and Veronica Wong, *Kotler & Armstrong's Principles of Marketing*, First European Edition (London: Prentice Hall, 1996), Chapter 6. Also see Benjamin Wooley, *Virtual Worlds* (London: Blackwell, 1992); "The World Leader in Senseware Orchestrates a Sales Tour de Force Using Solid Imaging," *The Edge*, 3D Systems, Inc., Spring 1993, pp. 4–5; and Joseph Ogando, "Stereolithography + Cast Ceramic = Tooling in Record Time," *Plastics Technology*, May 1995, p. 96.

The target market is households that need a second car for going shopping, running errands, and visiting friends. The car will be positioned as more economical to buy and operate, and more fun to drive, than cars now available to this market. The company will aim to sell 200,000 cars in the first year, at a loss of not more than $30 million. In the second year, the company will aim for sales of 220,000 cars and a profit of $50 million.

The second part of the marketing strategy statement outlines the product's planned price, distribution, and marketing budget for the first year:

The electric car will be offered in three colors and will have optional air-conditioning and power-drive features. It will sell at a retail price of

$18,000—with 15 percent off the list price to dealers. Dealers who sell more than 10 cars per month will get an additional discount of 5 percent on each car sold that month. An advertising budget of $20 million will be split fifty-fifty between national and local advertising. Advertising will emphasize the car's economy and fun. During the first year, $100,000 will be spent on marketing research to find out who is buying the car and to determine their satisfaction levels.

The third part of the marketing strategy statement describes the planned long-run sales, profit goals, and marketing mix strategy:

GM intends to capture a 3 percent long-run share of the total auto market and realize an after-tax return on investment of 15 percent. To achieve this, product quality will start high and be improved over time. Price will be raised in the second and third years if competition permits. The total advertising budget will be raised each year by about 10 percent. Marketing research will be reduced to $60,000 per year after the first year.

## BUSINESS ANALYSIS

**Business analysis**
A review of the sales, costs, and profit projections for a new product to determine whether these factors satisfy the company's objectives.

Once management has decided on its product concept and marketing strategy, it can evaluate the business attractiveness of the proposal. **Business analysis** involves a review of the sales, costs, and profit projections for a new product to find out whether they satisfy the company's objectives. If they do, the product can move to the product-development stage.

To estimate sales, the company should look at the sales history of similar products and should survey market opinion. It should estimate minimum and maximum sales to assess the range of risk. After preparing the sales forecast, management can estimate the expected costs and profits for the product, including marketing, R&D, manufacturing, accounting, and finance costs. The company then uses the sales and costs figures to analyze the new product's financial attractiveness.

## PRODUCT DEVELOPMENT

**Product development**
The product concept is developed into a physical product in order to assure that the product idea can be turned into a workable product.

So far, for many new-product concepts, the product may have existed only as a verbal description, a drawing, or perhaps a crude mock-up. If the product concept passes the business test, it moves into the **product development** stage. Here, R&D or engineering develops the product concept into a physical product. The product-development step, however, now calls for a large jump in investment. It will reveal whether the product idea can be turned into a workable product.

The R&D department develops and tests one or more physical versions of the product concept. R&D hopes to design a prototype that will satisfy and excite consumers and that can be produced quickly and at budgeted costs. Developing a successful prototype can take days, weeks, months, or even years. Often, products undergo rigorous functional tests to make sure that they perform safely and effectively. Here are some examples of such functional tests:

A scuba-diving Barbie doll must swim and kick for 15 straight hours to satisfy Mattel that she will last at least one year. But because Barbie may find her feet in small owners' mouths rather than in the bathtub, Mattel has devised another, more tortuous test: Barbie's feet are clamped by two steel jaws to make sure that her skin doesn't crack—and choke—potential owners.

At Shaw Industries, temps are paid $5 an hour to pace up and down five long rows of sample carpets for up to eight hours a day, logging an average of 14 miles each. One regular reads three mysteries a week while pacing and shed 40 pounds in two years. Shaw Industries counts walkers' steps and figures that 20,000 steps equal several years of average carpet wear.

At Gillette, 200 volunteers from various departments come to work unshaven each day, troop to the second floor of the company's South Boston manufacturing and research plant, and enter small booths with a sink and mirror. There they take instructions from technicians on the other side of a small window as to which razor, shaving cream, or aftershave to use, and then they fill out questionnaires. "We bleed so you'll get a good shave at home," says one Gillette employee.[11]

The prototype must have the required functional features and also convey the intended psychological characteristics. The electric car, for example, should impress consumers as being well built and safe. Management must learn what makes consumers decide that a car is well built. Some consumers slam the door to hear the sound. If the car does not have "solid-sounding" doors, consumers may assume that it is poorly built.

When the prototypes are ready, they must be tested. Functional tests are then conducted under laboratory and field conditions to make sure that the product performs safely and effectively. The new car must start easily; it must be comfortable; it must be able to withstand heavy impact in crash tests. Consumer tests are conducted, in which consumers test drive the car and rate its attributes.

# TEST MARKETING

**Test marketing**
The stage of new-product development where the product and marketing program are tested in more realistic market settings.

If the product passes functional and consumer tests, the next step is **test marketing,** the stage at which the product and marketing program are introduced into more realistic market settings. Test marketing gives the marketer experience with marketing the product before going to the great expense of full introduction. It allows the company to test the product and its entire marketing program—positioning strategy, advertising, distribution, pricing, branding and packaging, and budget levels.

The amount of test marketing needed varies with each new product. Test marketing costs can be enormous, and test marketing takes time that may allow competitors to gain advantages. When the costs of developing and introducing the product are low, or when management is already confident about a new product, the company may do little or no test marketing. Companies often do not test market simple line extensions or copies of successful competitor products. For example, Procter & Gamble introduced its Folger's decaffeinated coffee crystals without test marketing, and Pillsbury rolled out Chewy granola bars and chocolate-covered Granola Dipps with no standard test market. However, when introducing a new product requires a big investment, or when management is not sure of the product or marketing program, a company may do a lot of test marketing. For instance, Lever USA spent two years testing its highly successful Lever 2000 bar soap in Atlanta before introducing it internationally.

The costs of test marketing can be high, but they are often small when compared with the costs of making a major mistake. For example, London-based Unilever learned a costly lesson when it decided to skip formal test marketing for its new European laundry detergent, Power. It was so excited about Power's patented manganese-based catalyst, the Accelerator, that it skipped testing and forged ahead with a $300 million European introduction. It introduced the product despite a warning from its archrival Procter & Gamble that the new stain-annihilating detergent also annihilated customers' clothing. Unilever ignored P&G's warning, and the new Power brand was a disaster. Of course, P&G was not motivated by altruism but by its own hidden agenda: It was secretly preparing to relaunch its flagship European brand Ariel as Ariel Future, a stain-fighting concentrated detergent. P&G ended up bombarding journalists across Europe with color photos of tattered rags washed in Power, next to pristine garments laundered with its own Ariel.[12]

## COMMERCIALIZATION

**Commercialization**
Introducing a new product into the market.

Test marketing gives management the information needed to make a final decision about whether to launch the new product. If the company goes ahead with **commercialization**—introducing the new product into the market—it will face high costs. The company will have to build or rent a manufacturing facility. And it may have to spend, in the case of a new consumer packaged good, between $10 million and $100 million for advertising and sales promotion in the first year. For example, McDonald's spent more than $5 million *per week* on the introductory advertising campaign for its McDLT sandwich.

The company launching a new product must first decide on introduction *timing*. If the electric car will eat into the sales of the company's other cars, its introduction may be delayed. If the electric car can be improved further, or if the economy is down, the company may wait until the following year to launch it.

Next, the company must decide *where* to launch the new product—in a single location, a region, the national market, or the international market. Few companies have the confidence, capital, and capacity to launch new products into full national or international distribution. They develop a planned *market rollout* over time. In particular, small companies may enter attractive cities or regions one at a time. Larger companies, however, may quickly introduce new models into several regions or into the full national market.

Companies with international distribution systems may introduce new products through global rollouts. Colgate-Palmolive uses a "lead-country" strategy. For example, it launched its Palmolive Optims shampoo and conditioner first in Australia, the Philippines, Hong Kong, and Mexico, then rapidly rolled it out into Europe, Asia, Latin America, and Africa. International companies are increasingly introducing their new products in swift global assaults. Procter & Gamble did this with its Pampers Phases line of disposable diapers. In the past, P&G typically introduced a new product in the U.S. market. If it was successful, overseas competitors would copy the product in their home markets before P&G could expand distribution globally. With Pampers Phases, however, the company introduced the

*Colgate-Palmolive introduces its new products internationally using a "lead-country" strategy, launching the product first in a few important regions, followed by a swift global rollout.*

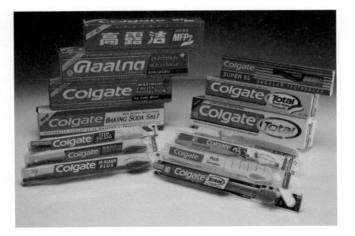

**Sequential product development**
A new-product development approach in which one company department works individually to complete its stage of the process before passing the new product along to the next department and stage.

**Simultaneous product development**
An approach to developing new products in which various company departments work closely together, overlapping the steps in the product-development process to save time and increase effectiveness.

new product into global markets within one month of introducing it in the United States. It planned to have the product on the shelf in 90 countries within just 12 months of introduction. Such rapid worldwide expansion solidified the brand's market position before foreign competitors could react. P&G has since mounted worldwide introductions of several other new products.[13]

## SPEEDING UP NEW-PRODUCT DEVELOPMENT

Many companies organize their new-product development process into an orderly sequence of steps, starting with idea generation and ending with commercialization. Under this **sequential product development** approach, one company department works individually to complete its stage of the process before passing the new product along to the next department and stage. This orderly, step-by-step process can help bring control to complex and risky projects. But it also can be dangerously slow. In fast-changing, highly competitive markets, such slow-but-sure product development can cost the company potential sales and profits to the benefit of more nimble competitors.

Today, in order to get their new products to market more quickly, many companies are dropping the *sequential product development* method in favor of the faster, more flexible **simultaneous product development** approach. Under the new approach, various company departments work closely together, overlapping the steps in the product development process to save time and increase effectiveness (see Marketing at Work 9-3).[14]

## ▶PRODUCT LIFE-CYCLE STRATEGIES

After launching a new product, management wants it to enjoy a long and happy life. Although it does not expect the product to sell forever, the company wants to earn a decent profit to cover all the effort and risk that went into launching it. Management is aware that each product's life cycle has an uncertain length and character.

# MARKETING AT WORK 9-3

## SPEEDING NEW PRODUCTS TO MARKET

Philips, the giant Dutch consumer electronics company, marketed the first practical video cassette recorder (VCR) in 1972, gaining a three-year lead on its Japanese competitors. But in the seven years that it took Philips to develop its second VCR generation, Japanese manufacturers had launched at least three generations of new products. A victim of its own creaky product-development process, Philips never recovered from the Japanese onslaught. This story is typical. In today's fast-changing, fiercely competitive world, turning out new products too slowly can result in product failures, lost sales and profits, and crumbling market positions. "Speed to market" and reducing new-product development "cycle time" have become pressing concerns to companies in all industries.

Large companies have typically used a sequential product-development approach in which they develop new products in an orderly series of steps. In a kind of relay race, each company department completes its phase of the development process before passing the new product on. This sequential process has merits—it helps to bring order to risky and complex new-product development projects. But the approach can also be fatally slow.

To speed up their product-development cycles, many companies have adopted a faster, team-oriented approach called simultaneous product development. Instead of passing the new product from department to department, the company assembles a team of people from various departments that stays with the new product from start to finish. Such teams usually include people from the marketing, finance, design, manufacturing, and legal departments, and even supplier and customer companies. Simultaneous development is more like a rugby match than a relay race—team members pass the new product back and forth as they move downfield toward the common goal of a speedy new-product launch.

Top management gives the product development team general strategic direction, but no clear-cut product idea or work plan. It challenges the team with stiff and seemingly contradictory goals—"turn out carefully planned and superior new products, but do it quickly"—and then gives the team whatever freedom and resources it needs to meet the challenge. In the sequential

*A Black & Decker "fusion team" developed the highly acclaimed Quantum tool line in only 12 months. The team included 85 marketers, engineers, designers, finance people, and others from the United States, Britain, Germany, Italy, and Switzerland.*

process, a bottleneck at one phase can seriously slow the entire project. In the simultaneous approach, if one functional area hits snags, it works to resolve them while the team moves on.

The Allen-Bradley Company, a maker of industrial controls, realized tremendous benefits by using simultaneous development. Under its old sequential approach, the company's marketing department handed off a new product idea to designers. The designers, working in isolation, prepared concepts and passed them along to product engineers. The engineers, also working by themselves, developed expensive prototypes and handed them off to manufacturing, which tried to find a way to build the new product. Finally, after many years and dozens of costly design compromises and delays, marketing was asked to sell the new product, which it often found to be too high priced or sadly out of date. Now, all of Allen-Bradley's departments work together to develop new products. The results have been astonishing. For example, the company recently developed a new electrical control in just two years; under the old system, it would have taken six years.

Black & Decker used the simultaneous approach—which it calls concurrent engineering—to develop its Quantum line of tools targeted toward serious do-it-yourselfers. B&D assigned a "fusion team" called Team Quantum, which consisted of 85 Black & Decker employees from around the world, to get the right product line to customers as quickly as possible. The team included engineers, finance people, marketers, designers, and others from the United States, Britain, Germany, Italy, and Switzerland. From idea to launch, including three months of consumer research, the team developed the highly acclaimed Quantum line in only 12 months.

The auto industry has also discovered the benefits of simultaneous product development. The approach is called simultaneous engineering at GM, the team concept at Ford, and process-driven design at Chrysler. The first American cars built using this process, the Ford Taurus and Mercury Sable, have been major marketing successes. Using simultaneous product development, Ford slashed development time from 60 months to less than 40. It squeezed 14 weeks from its cycle by simply getting the engineering and finance departments to review designs at the same time instead of sequentially. Ford also used the team approach in developing the dramatically redesigned 1996 Taurus. Its international Team Taurus consisted of engineers, designers, marketers, accountants, suppliers, factory-floor workers, and others who worked together to design and test the vehicle and bring it quickly to market. It claims that such actions have helped cut average engineering costs for a project by 35 percent. In an industry that has typically taken five or six years to turn out a new model, Mazda now brags about two- to three-year product-development cycles—a feat that would be impossible without simultaneous development.

However, the simultaneous approach does have its limitations. Superfast product development can be riskier and more costly than the slower, more orderly sequential approach. And it often creates increased organizational tension and confusion. But in rapidly changing industries facing increasingly shorter product life cycles, the rewards of fast and flexible product development far exceed the risks. Companies that get new and improved products to the market faster than their competitors gain a dramatic competitive edge. They can respond more quickly to emerging consumer tastes and charge higher prices for more advanced designs. As one auto industry executive states, "What we want to do is get the new car approved, built, and in the consumer's hands in the shortest time possible. . . . Whoever gets there first gets all the marbles."

*Sources:* Hirotaka Takeuchi and Ikujiro Nonaka, "The New New-Product Development Game," *Harvard Business Review*, January–February 1986, pp. 137–46; Homer F. Hagedorn, "High Performance in Product Development: An Agenda for Senior Management," in Arthur D. Little Company, *PRISM*, First Quarter, 1992, pp. 47–58; Susan Caminiti, "A Star Is Born," *Fortune*, November 29, 1993, pp. 45–47; Shona L. Brown and Kathleen M. Eisenhardt, "Product Development: Past Research, Present Findings, and Future Directions," *Academy of Management Review*, April 1995, p. 343; Louis S. Richman, "Managing Through a Downturn," *Fortune*, August 7, 1995, pp. 59–64; and Kathleen Kerwin, "The Shape of a New Machine," *Business Week*, July 24, 1995, pp. 60–66.

**FIGURE 9-2**
*Sales and profits over the product's life from inception to demise*

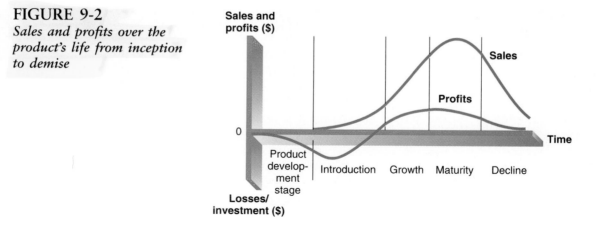

Figure 9-2 shows a typical **product life cycle** (PLC)—the course that a product's sales and profits take over its lifetime. The product life cycle has five distinct stages:

**Product life-cycle (PLC)**
The course of a product's sales and profits over its lifetime. It involves five distinct stages: product development, introduction, growth, maturity, and decline.

1. *Product development* begins when the company finds and develops a new-product idea. During product development, sales are zero and the company's investment costs mount.
2. *Introduction* is a period of slow sales growth as the product enters in the market. Profits are nonexistent in this stage because of the heavy expenses of product introduction.
3. *Growth* is a period of rapid market acceptance and increasing profits.
4. *Maturity* is a period of slowdown in sales growth because the product has achieved acceptance by most potential buyers. Profits level off or decline because of increased marketing outlays to defend the product against competition.
5. *Decline* is the period when sales fall off and profits drop.

Not all products follow this S-shaped product life cycle. Some products are introduced and die quickly; others stay in the mature stage for a long, long time. Some enter the decline stage and are then cycled back into the growth stage through strong promotion or repositioning.

The PLC concept can describe a *product class* (gasoline-powered automobiles), a *product form* (minivans), or a *brand* (the Ford Taurus). The PLC concept applies differently in each case. Product classes have the longest life cycles—the sales of many product classes stay in the mature stage for a long time. Product forms, in contrast, tend to have the standard PLC shape. Product forms such as cream deodorants, the dial telephone, and phonograph records passed through a regular history of introduction, rapid growth, maturity, and decline. A specific brand's life cycle can change quickly because of changing competitive attacks and responses. For example, although teeth-cleaning products (product class) and toothpastes (product form) have enjoyed fairly long life cycles, the life cycles of specific brands have tended to be much shorter.

The PLC concept can also be applied to what are known as styles, fashions, and fads. Their special life cycles are shown in Figure 9-3. A **style** is a basic and

**Style**
A basic and distinctive mode of expression.

**FIGURE 9-3**
*Styles, fashions, and fads*

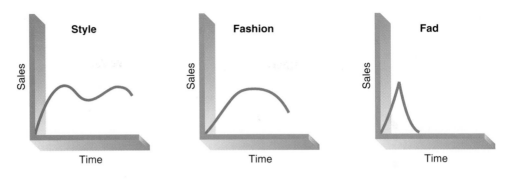

distinctive mode of expression. For example, styles appear in homes (colonial, ranch); clothing (formal, business, casual); and art (realistic, surrealistic, abstract). Once a style is invented, it may last for generations, coming in and out of vogue. A style has a cycle showing several periods of renewed interest. A **fashion** is a currently accepted or popular style in a given field. For example, the conservative "preppie look" in the clothing of the late 1970s gave way to the "loose and layered look" of the 1980s, which in turn yielded to the more tailored look of the 1990s. Fashions tend to grow slowly, remain popular for a while, then decline slowly.

**Fashion**
A currently accepted or popular style in a given field.

**Fads**
Fashions that enter the market quickly, are adopted with great zeal, peak early, and decline very fast.

**Fads** are fashions that enter quickly, are adopted with great zeal, peak early, and decline very fast. They last only a short time and tend to attract only a limited following. "Pet rocks" have become the classic example of a fad. Upon hearing his friends complain about how expensive it was to care for their dogs, advertising copywriter Gary Dahl joked about his pet rock and was soon writing a spoof of a dog-training manual for it. Soon Dahl was selling some 1.5 million ordinary beach pebbles at $4 a pop. Yet the fad, which broke in October 1975, had sunk like a stone by the next February. Dahl's advice to those who want to succeed with a fad: "Enjoy it while it lasts." Other examples of fads include Rubik's Cubes, Cabbage Patch dolls, and yo-yos. Fads do not survive for long because they normally do not satisfy a strong need or satisfy it well. For example, Rubik's Cube sales reached more than 30 million in only a few years, then plummeted.[15]

The PLC concept can be applied by marketers as a useful framework for describing how products and markets work. But using the PLC concept for forecasting product performance or for developing marketing strategies presents some practical problems.[16] For example, managers may have trouble identifying which stage of the PLC the product is in, pinpointing when the product moves into the next stage, and determining the factors that affect the product's movement through the stages. In practice, it is difficult to forecast the sales level at each PLC stage, the length of each stage, and the shape of the PLC curve.

Using the PLC concept to develop marketing strategy can also be difficult because strategy is both a cause and a result of the product's life cycle. The product's current PLC position suggests the best marketing strategies, and the resulting marketing strategies affect product performance in later life-cycle stages. Yet, when used carefully, the PLC concept can help in developing good marketing strategies for different stages of the product life cycle.

We looked at the product-development stage of the product life cycle in the first part of the chapter. We now look at strategies for each of the other life-cycle stages.

# INTRODUCTION STAGE

**Introduction stage**
The product life-cycle stage when the new product is first distributed and made available for purchase.

The **introduction stage** starts when the new product is first launched. Introduction takes time, and sales growth is apt to be slow. Well-known products such as instant coffee, frozen orange juice concentrate, and powdered coffee creamers lingered for many years before they entered a stage of rapid growth.

In this stage, as compared with other stages, profits are negative or low because of the low sales and high distribution and promotion expenses. Much money is needed to attract distributors and build their inventories. Promotion spending is relatively high to inform consumers of the new product and get them to try it. Because the market is not generally ready for product refinements at this stage, the company and its few competitors produce basic versions of the product. These firms focus their selling on those buyers who are the readiest to buy.

A company, especially the *market pioneer,* must choose a launch strategy that is consistent with its intended product positioning. It should realize that the initial strategy is just the first step in a larger, more complex marketing plan for the product's entire life cycle. If the pioneer chooses its launch strategy to make a "killing," it will be sacrificing long-run revenue for the sake of short-run gain. As the pioneer moves through later stages of the product's life cycle, it will have to continuously formulate new pricing, promotion, and other marketing strategies. It has the best chance of building and retaining market leadership if it plays its cards correctly from the start.

# GROWTH STAGE

**Growth stage**
The product life-cycle stage at which a product's sales start climbing quickly.

If the new product satisfies the market, it will enter a **growth stage,** in which sales will start climbing quickly. Early adopters will continue to buy, and later buyers will start following their lead, especially if they hear favorable word of mouth. Attracted by the opportunities for profit, new competitors will enter the market. They will introduce new product features, and the market will expand. The increase in competitors leads to an increase in the number of distribution outlets, and sales jump just to build reseller inventories. Prices remain where they are or fall only slightly. Companies keep their promotion spending at the same or a slightly higher level. Educating the market remains a goal, but now the company also must meet the competition.

Profits increase during the growth stage, as promotion costs are spread over a large volume and as unit-manufacturing costs fall. The firm uses several strategies to sustain rapid market growth as long as possible. It improves product quality and adds new product features and models. It enters new market segments and new distribution channels. It shifts some advertising from building product awareness to building product conviction and purchase, and it lowers prices at the right time to attract more buyers.

In the growth stage, the firm faces a trade-off between high market share and high current profit. By spending a lot of money on product improvement, promotion, and distribution, the company can capture a dominant position. In doing so, however, it gives up maximum current profit, which it hopes to make up in the next stage.

## MATURITY STAGE

**Maturity stage**
The stage in the product life cycle where sales growth slows or levels off.

At some point, a product's sales growth will slow down, and the product will enter a **maturity stage.** This maturity stage normally lasts longer than the previous stages, and it poses strong challenges to marketing management. Most products are in the maturity stage of the life cycle, and therefore most of marketing management deals with mature products.

The slowdown in sales growth results in many producers with many products to sell. In turn, this overcapacity leads to greater competition. Competitors begin marking down prices, increasing their advertising and sales promotions, and upping their R&D budgets to find better versions of the product. These steps lead to a decrease in profit. Some of the weaker competitors start dropping out, and the industry eventually contains only well-established competitors.

Although many products in the mature stage appear to remain unchanged for long periods, most successful ones are actually evolving to meet changing consumer needs (see Marketing at Work 9-4). Product managers should do more than simply continue with or defend their mature products—a good offense is the best defense. They should consider modifying the market, product, and marketing mix.

In *modifying the market,* the company tries to increase the consumption of the current product. It looks for new users and market segments, as when Johnson & Johnson targeted the adult market with its baby powder and shampoo. Managers also look for ways to increase usage among present customers. Campbell has done this by offering recipes and convincing consumers that "soup is good food." Or the company may want to reposition the brand to appeal to a larger or faster-growing segment, as Arrow did when it introduced its new line of casual shirts and announced, "We're loosening our collars."

The company might also try *modifying the product*—changing characteristics such as quality, features, or style to attract new users and to inspire more usage. It might improve the product's quality and performance—its durability, reliability, speed, taste. Or it might add new features that expand the product's usefulness, safety, or convenience. For example, Sony keeps adding new styles and features to its Walkman and Discman lines, and Volvo adds new safety features to its cars. Finally, the company can improve the product's styling and attractiveness. Thus, car manufacturers restyle their cars to attract buyers who want a new look. The makers of consumer food and household products introduce new flavors, colors, ingredients, or packages to revitalize consumer buying.

Finally, the company can try *modifying the marketing mix*—improving sales by changing one or more marketing-mix elements. They can cut prices to attract new users and competitors' customers. They can launch a better advertising campaign or use aggressive sales promotions—trade deals, cents-off promotions, premiums, and contests. The company can also move into larger market channels, using mass merchandisers, if these channels are growing. Finally, the company can offer new or improved services to buyers.

## MARKETING AT WORK 9-4

# CRAYOLA CRAYONS: A LONG AND COLORFUL LIFE CYCLE

Binney & Smith Company began making crayons down by Bushkill Creek near Easton, Pennsylvania, in 1903. Partner Edwin Binney's wife, Alice, named them Crayola crayons—after the French *craie,* meaning "stick of color," and *ola,* meaning "oil." In the 90-odd years since, Crayola crayons have become a household staple, not just in the United States, but in more than 60 countries around the world, with boxes printed in 11 languages. If you placed all the Crayola crayons made in a single year end to end, they would circle the earth four and a half times.

Few people can forget their first pack of "64s"—64 beauties neatly arranged by shade in the familiar green and yellow flip-top box with a sharpener on the back. The aroma of a freshly opened Crayola box still drives kids into a frenzy and takes members of the older generation back to fond childhood memories. Binney & Smith, now a subsidiary of Hallmark, dominates the crayon market. Sixty-five percent of all American children between the ages of two and seven pick up a crayon at least once a day and color for an aver-

age of 28 minutes. Nearly eighty percent of the time, they pick up a Crayola crayon.

In some ways, Crayola crayons haven't changed much since 1903, when they were sold in an eight-pack for a nickel. Crayola has always been the number one brand, and the crayons are still made by hand in much the same way as they were originally. But a closer look reveals that Binney & Smith has

made many adjustments in order to keep the Crayola brand in the mature stage and out of decline. Over the years, the company has added a steady stream of new colors, shapes, sizes, and packages. It increased the number of colors from the original eight in 1903 (red, yellow, blue, green, orange, black, brown, and white) to 48 in 1949, and to 64 in 1958. In 1972, it added eight fluorescent colors with hot names like

*Crayola's colorful lifecycle: Over the years, Binney & Smith has added a steady stream of new colors, shapes, sizes, and packages.*

## DECLINE STAGE

**Decline stage**
The product life-cycle stage at which a product's sales decline.

The sales of most product forms and brands eventually dip. The decline may be slow, as in the case of oatmeal cereal; or rapid, as in the case of phonograph records. Sales may plunge to zero, or they may drop to a low level where they continue for many years. This is the **decline stage.**

Laser Lemon, Screamin' Green, and Atomic Tangerine; and in 1993, it introduced an additional 16 new colors, including Macaroni & Cheese and Purple Mountains Majesty. It also created a new line of glow-in-the-dark colors and crayons that change colors. Most recently, Crayola introduced 16 new crayons filled with miniature scent capsules including grape, lime, pine, chocolate, licorice, bananas, and bubble gum that burst when rubbed on paper. (Scents considered, but not selected, included leather, hamburger, mildew, and skunk!) In all, Crayola crayons now come in 96 colors and a variety of packages, including a 96-crayon attache-like case.

Over the years, the Crayola line has grown to include many new sizes and shapes. In addition to the standard 3⅝-inch crayon, it now includes flat, jumbo, and "So Big" crayons. Crayola Washable Crayons were added in 1991. Binney & Smith also extended the Crayola brand to new markets when it developed Crayola Markers and innovative related products such as Overwriters and Changeables that offer many color possibilities.

Finally, the company has added several programs and services to help strengthen its relationships with Crayola customers. For example, in 1984 it began its Dream Makers art education program, a national elementary school art program designed to help students capture their dreams on paper and to support art education in schools. In 1986, it set up a toll-free 1-800-CRAYOLA hotline to provide better customer service. And in 1994, it launched Crayola Kids magazine, aimed at three- to eight-year-olds, which offers features such as illustrated stories, crafts to make, games, puzzles, and a parents' guide with expert advice on helping to develop reading skills and creativity.

Not all of Binney & Smith's life-cycle adjustments have been greeted with open arms by consumers. For example, facing flat sales throughout the 1980s, the company conducted market research that showed that children were ready to break with tradition in favor of some exciting new colors. They were seeing and wearing brighter colors and wanted to be able to color with them as well. So, in 1990, Binney & Smith retired eight colors from the time-honored box of 64— Raw Umber, Lemon Yellow, Maize, Blue Grey, Orange Yellow, Orange Red, Green Blue, and Violet Blue—into the Crayola Hall of Fame. In their place, it introduced eight more-modern shades: Cerulean, Vivid Tangerine, Jungle Green, Fuchsia, Dandelion, Teal Blue, Royal Purple, and Wild Strawberry. The move unleashed a groundswell of protest from loyal Crayola users, who formed such organizations as the Raw Umber and Maize Preservation Society (RUMPS) and the National Committee to Save Lemon Yellow. Binney & Smith received an average of 334 calls a month from concerned customers. Company executives were flabbergasted. "We were aware of the loyalty and nostalgia surrounding Crayola crayons," a spokesperson says, "but we didn't know we [would] hit such a nerve." Still, fans of the new colors outnumbered the protestors, and the new colors are here to stay. However, the company reissued the old standards in a special collector's tin—it sold all of the 2.5 million tins made. Thus, the Crayola brand continues through its long and colorful life cycle.

*Sources:* Quote from "Hue and Cry Over Crayola May Revive Old Colors," *Wall Street Journal,* June 14, 1991, p. B1. Also see Margaret O. Kirk, "Coloring Our Children's World Since '03," *Chicago Tribune,* October 29, 1986, Sec. 5, p. 1; Mike Christiansen, "Waxing Nostalgic: Crayola Retires a Colorful Octet," *Atlanta Constitution,* August 8, 1990, pp. B1, B4; Judith D. Schwartz, "Back to School with Binney & Smith's Crayola," *Brandweek,* September 1993, pp. 26, 28.; "These Crayons Smell," *Advertising Age,* August 15, 1994, p. 1; and "Crayolas Move Out of the Box," *Publishers Weekly,* August 1, 1994, p. 24.

Sales decline for many reasons, including technological advances, shifts in consumer tastes, and increased competition. As sales and profits decline, some firms withdraw from the market. Those remaining may prune their product offerings. They may drop smaller market segments and marginal trade channels, or they may cut the promotion budget and reduce their prices further.

**TABLE 9-2** *Summary of Product Life-Cycle Characteristics, Objectives, and Strategies*

|  | Introduction | Growth | Maturity | Decline |
|---|---|---|---|---|
| *Characteristics* |  |  |  |  |
| Sales | Low sales | Rapidly rising sales | Peak sales | Declining sales |
| Costs | High cost per customer | Average cost per customer | Low cost per customer | Low cost per customer |
| Profits | Negative | Rising profits | High profits | Declining profits |
| Customers | Innovators | Early adopters | Middle majority | Laggards |
| Competitors | Few | Growing number | Stable number beginning to decline | Declining number |
| *Marketing Objectives* | Create product and trial | Maximize market share | Maximize profit while defending market share | Reduce expenditure and milk the brand |
| *Strategies* |  |  |  |  |
| Product | Offer a basic product | Offer product extensions, service, warranty | Diversify brand and models | Phase out weak items |
| Price | Use cost-plus formula | Price to penetrate market | Price to match or best competitors | Cut price |
| Distribution | Build selective distribution | Build intensive distribution | Build more intensive distribution | Go selective: phase out unprofitable outlets |
| Advertising | Build product awareness among early adopters and dealers | Build awareness and interest in the mass market | Stress brand differences and benefits | Reduce to level needed to retain hard-core loyals |
| Sales promotion | Use heavy sales promotion to entice trial | Reduce to take advantage of heavy consumer demand | Increase to encourage brand switching | Reduce to minimal level |

*Source:* Philip Kotler, *Marketing Management: Analysis, Planning, Implementation, and Control,* 9th ed. (Englewood Cliffs, NJ: Prentice Hall, 1997), Chapter 12.

Carrying a weak product can be very costly to a firm, and not just in profit terms. There are many hidden costs. A weak product may take up too much of management's time. It often requires frequent price and inventory adjustments. It requires advertising and sales force attention that might be better used to make successful products more profitable. A product's failing reputation can cause customer concerns about the company and its other products. The biggest cost may well lie in the future. Keeping weak products delays the search for replacements, creates a lopsided product mix, hurts current profits, and weakens the company's foothold on the future.

For these reasons, companies need to pay more attention to their aging products. The firm's first task is to identify those products that are in the decline stage by regularly reviewing sales, market shares, costs, and profit trends. Then, management must decide whether to maintain, harvest, or drop each of these declining products.

Management may decide to *maintain* its brand without change in the hope that competitors will leave the industry. For example, Procter & Gamble made good profits by remaining in the declining liquid-soap business as others withdrew. Or management may decide to reposition the brand in hopes of moving it back into the growth stage of the product life cycle. For instance, after watching sales of its Tostitos tortilla chips plunge 50 percent from their mid-1980s high, Frito-Lay reformulated the chips by doubling their size, changing their shape from round to triangular, and using white corn flour instead of yellow. The new Tostitos Restaurant Style Tortilla Chips have ridden the crest of the recent Tex-Mex food craze's record revenues.

Management may decide to *harvest* the product, which means reducing various costs (plant and equipment, maintenance, R&D, advertising, sales force) and hoping that sales hold up. If successful, harvesting will increase the company's profits in the short run. Or management may decide to *drop* the product from the line. It can sell it to another firm or simply liquidate it at salvage value. If the company plans to find a buyer, it will not want to run down the product through harvesting.

Table 9-2 summarizes the key characteristics of each stage of the product life cycle. The table also lists the marketing objectives and strategies for each stage.[17]

## SUMMARY

Organizations must develop new products and services. Their current products face limited life spans and must be replaced by newer products. But new products can fail—the risks of innovation are as great as the rewards. The key to successful innovation lies in a total-company effort, strong planning, and a systematic *new-product development process*.

The new-product development process consists of eight stages: *idea generation, idea screening, concept development and testing, marketing strategy development, business analysis, product development, test marketing,* and *commercialization*. At each stage, a decision must be made on whether the idea should be further developed or dropped. The company wants to minimize the chances of poor ideas moving forward or good ideas being rejected.

Each product has a *life cycle* marked by a changing set of problems and opportunities. The sales of the typical product follow an S-shaped curve made up of five stages. The cycle begins with

the *product-development stage* when the company finds and develops a new-product idea. The *introduction stage* is marked by slow growth and low profits as the product enters into distribution to the market. If successful, the product enters a *growth stage* marked by rapid sales growth and increasing profits. During this stage, the company tries to improve the product, enter new market segments and distribution channels, and reduce its prices slightly. Then comes a *maturity stage* in which sales growth slows down and profits stabilize. The company seeks strategies to renew sales growth, including market, product, and marketing-mix modification. Finally, the product enters a *decline stage* in which sales and profits dwindle. The company's task during this stage is to identify the declining product and decide whether it should be maintained, harvested, or dropped. If dropped, the product can be sold to another firm or liquidated for salvage value.

## KEY TERMS

Business analysis

Commercialization

Concept testing

Decline stage

Fads

Fashion

Growth stage

Idea generation

Idea screening

Introduction stage

Marketing strategy development

Maturity stage

New-product development

Product concept

Product development

Product life cycle (PLC)

Sequential product development

Simultaneous product development

Style

Test marketing

## QUESTIONS FOR DISCUSSION

1. Before videotape cameras were available for home use, Polaroid introduced Polavision, a system for making home movies that did not require laboratory processing. Like most other home movie systems, Polavision film cassettes lasted only a few minutes and did not record sound. Despite the advantage of "instant developing" and heavy promotional expenditures by Polaroid, Polavision never gained wide acceptance. Discuss why you think Polavision flopped, given Polaroid's previous record of new-product successes.

2. Many companies have formal new-product development systems and committees. Yet one recent study found that most successful new products were those that had been developed outside the formal system. Suggest reasons why this might be true.

3. Less then one-third of new product ideas come from the customer. Does this low percentage conflict with the marketing concept's philosophy of "find a need and fill it"? Why or why not?

4. Test market results for a new product are usually better than the business results that the same brand achieves after it is launched. Name some reasons for this.

5. In 1985, the Coca-Cola Company introduced New Coke in order to halt the company's loss of market share in its sugared cola segment. Just 77 days later, the Coca-Cola Company pulled New Coke off the market as a result of consumer outrage and brought back old Coke (now called Classic Coke). In 1995, ten years after this marketing debacle, Coca-Cola's CEO Roberto C. Goizueta acknowledged that the company had been "rocked to the heels" by the experience, but that it had also "learned crucial lessons." Relate the introduction of New Coke to flawed product life-cycle analysis. What kind of lessons do you think that Coca-Cola learned from the decision to replace a 99-year-old formula?

6. How can a company tell products with long life cycles apart from current fads and fashions? What products now on the market do you think are fads or fashions that will soon disappear?

## APPLYING THE CONCEPTS

1. List at least ten new product ideas for your favorite fast-food chain. Out of all these ideas, which ones (if any) do you think would have a good chance of succeeding? What percentage of your ideas did you rate as having a good chance of success? (Divide the number of potentially successful ideas by the total number of ideas that you listed, and multiply the result by 100 to get a percentage.) Can you explain why the potentially successful ideas seem stronger?

2. Go to the grocery store and make a list of 15 items that appear to be new products. Rate each product for its level of innovation, with a 10 being extremely novel and highly innovative, and a 1 being a very minor change such as an improved package or fragrance. How truly new and innovative are these products overall? Do you think that companies tend to be risk averse because "pioneers are the ones who get shot"?

## REFERENCES

1. See Russell Mitchell, "Masters of Innovation: How 3M Keeps Its New Products Coming," *Business Week,* April 10, 1989, pp. 58–64; Gregory E. David, "Product Development: Minnesota Mining & Manufacturing," *Financial World,* September 28, 1993, p. 58; Kevin Kelly, "The Drought Is Over at 3M," *Business Week,* November 7, 1994, pp. 140–41; "The Mass Production of Ideas," *The Economist,* March 18, 1995, p. 72; Tim Stevens, "Tool Kit for Innovators," *Industry Week,* June 5, 1995, p. 28; and Thomas A. Stewart, "3M Fights Back," *Fortune,* February 5, 1996, pp. 94–99.

2. Kevin J. Clancy and Robert S. Shulman, *The Marketing Revolution: A Radical Manifesto for Dominating the Marketplace* (New York: Harper Business, 1991), p. 6; and Robert G. Cooper, "New Product Success in Industrial Firms," *Industrial Marketing Management,* 1992, pp. 215–23. Also see Gary Strauss, "Building on Brand Names: Companies Freshen Old Product Lines," *USA Today,* March 20, 1992, pp. B1, B2; and Betsy Spethmann, "Test Market USA," *Brandweek,* May 8, 1995, p. 40.

3. See Christopher Power, "Flops," *Business Week,* August 16, 1993, pp. 76–82, here p. 77.

4. Robert G. Cooper and Elko J. Kleinschmidt, *New Product: The Key Factors in Success* (Chicago: American Marketing Association, 1990).

5. Jon Berry and Edward F. Ogiba, "It's Your Boss: Why New Products Fail," *Brandweek,* October 19, 1992, p. 16.

6. For this and other examples, see Jennifer Reese, "Getting Hot Ideas from Customers," *Fortune,* May 18, 1992, pp. 86–87.

7. Pam Weisz, "Avon's Skin-So-Soft Bugs Out," *Brandweek,* June 6, 1994, p. 4.

8. Russell Mitchell, "How Ford Hit the Bullseye with Taurus," *Business Week,* June 30, 1986, pp. 69–70; "Copycat Stuff? Hardly!" *Business Week,* September 14, 1987, p. 112; and Jeremy Main, "How to Steal the Best Ideas Around," *Fortune,* October 19, 1992, pp. 102–6.

9. See David Woodruff, "Electric Cars," *Business Week,* May 30, 1994, pp. 104–14; and Noel Perrin, "All Charged Up," *The Boston Globe Magazine,* November 6, 1994, pp. 16–18.

10. Adrienne Ward Fawcett, "Oreo Cones Make Top Grade in Poll," *Advertising Age,* June 14, 1993, p. 30.

11. See Lawrence Ingrassia, "Keeping Sharp: Gillette Holds Its Edge by Endlessly Searching for a Better Shave," *Wall Street Journal,* December 10, 1992, A1, A6; and Faye Rice, "Secrets of Product Testing," *Fortune,* November 28, 1994, pp. 172–74.

12. Laurel Wentz, "Unilever's Power Failure a Wasteful Use of Haste," *Advertising Age,* March 6, 1995, p. 42.

13. Jennifer Lawrence, "P&G Rushes on Global Diaper Rollout," *Advertising Age,* October 14, 1991, p. 6; and Bill Saporito, "Behind the Tumult at P&G," *Fortune,* March 7, 1994, pp. 75–82.

14. For a good review of research on new product development, see Shona L. Brown and Kathleen M. Eisenhardt, "Product Development: Past Research, Present Findings, and Future Directions," *Academy of Management Review,* April 1995, p. 343.

15. See Martin G. Letscher, "How To Tell Fads from Trends," *American Demographics,* December 1994, pp. 38–45; and John Grossmann, "A Follow-Up on Four Fabled Frenzies," *Inc.,* October 1994, pp. 66–67.

16. See George S. Day, "The Product Life Cycle: Analysis and Applications Issues," *Journal of Marketing,* Fall 1981, pp. 60–67; John E. Swan and David R. Rink, "Fitting Marketing Strategy to Varying Life Cycles," *Business Horizons,* January–February 1982, pp. 72–76; and Sak Onkvisit and John J. Shaw, "Competition and Product Management: Can the Product Life Cycle Help?" *Business Horizons,* July–August 1986, pp. 51–62.

17. For a more comprehensive discussion of marketing strategies over the course of the product life cycle, see Philip Kotler, *Marketing Management,* 8th ed. (Englewood Cliffs, NJ: Prentice Hall, 1994), Chapter 14.

# Pricing Products: Pricing Considerations and Strategies

Entering the 1992 summer season, American Airlines and its competitors were looking for ways to kick-start the stalled travel industry. Coming off two years of record billion-dollar-plus losses, the troubled U.S. airline industry faced many problems—an ailing economy, rising costs, industry overcapacity, and severe price competition.

One major factor contributing to the industry's woes was its convoluted pricing structure. For years, the airlines had offered a bewildering array of fares, including deep promotional discounts designed to stimulate air travel. But such promotional pricing often erupted into costly price wars that sapped long-term industry profits. Perhaps worse, the complex fare structure and never-ending promotions resulted in customer confusion and frustration. Both business and leisure travelers were flying less, and both persisted in their long-held beliefs that the airlines were gouging them on price. As the feeble economy dragged on, even people traveling at the lowest rates were complaining about the high cost of airline travel.

In mid-April 1992, American Airlines stepped forward with a bold new fare plan that it hoped would simplify the industry's fare structure, put an end to constant price squabbling, and restore its own and the industry's profitability. The leading U.S. carrier ran four-page ads in major newspapers across the country, announcing "The Next Page in the History of Air Fares." Gone were super-low promotional fares and special discounts for children, senior citizens, the military, bereaved families, and large corporate users. In their place was a slimmed-down structure with just four fares: *anytime coach fares* (now an average of 38 percent lower than previous full coach fares); lower-price *first class fares* (20 percent to 50 percent lower than before); *21-day advance-purchase fares* (at about half the price of full coach fares); and *7-day advance-purchase fares* (running $20 to $60 more than 21-day fares).

The new plan was good for everyone, American claimed. Although some of the cheapest fares rose slightly, consumers benefitted from the overall 38 percent cut in top fares. At the same time, it helped the airlines: Eliminating deep discounts meant that average fares would rise. For the plan to work, however, American would need help from two key groups: customers and competitors. The plan wouldn't restore industry profits unless it stimulated increased travel. And American couldn't go it alone—competitors would have to charge similar fares. Unfortunately, American got little help from either group.

Although the lower fares resulted in favorable consumer reactions, they didn't cause the hoped-for stampede to the ticket counter. During the high-flying 1980s, the airlines had schooled travelers to wait for special discounts and promotions. When American eliminated them in the recessionary 1990s, consumers balked. They waited to see if the new fares would stick. On the other side of the ticket counter, most major competing carriers followed American's lead—for a while. However, weaker airlines such as Trans World Airlines (TWA), America West, and Continental—all operating under bankruptcy—began to undercut American's new prices as soon as they were announced. TWA responded immediately with fares 10 to 20 percent below American's. America West undercut fares on transcontinental trips and promoted cheaper off-peak fares. No-frills Southwest Airlines announced a kids-fly-free program for the summer. US Air discounted fares from major Northeast cities to Florida, and Continental quickly followed.

Still hoping to succeed with its simplified fare plan, powerful American Airlines responded to these breaches with remarkable restraint. It cut its fares only as necessary in markets where it competed with TWA, America West, Southwest, US Air, and the other renegade airlines. However, once the discounting started, it soon snowballed. In late April, Northwest Airlines broke ranks. To attract family travelers for the summer season, it launched an adults-fly-free promotion, which gave a free ticket to any adult traveling with a child. Northwest ran its first ads announcing the promotion on Tuesday evening, May 26. Before the night had ended, the carrier's reservations had risen 53 percent; by midday Wednesday, they'd jumped an incredible 176 percent. American responded with a vengeance to Northwest's defection, slashing all of its advance-purchase fares in half. The other airlines jumped in, setting off a brutal 10-day price war.

The incredibly low fares created a tidal wave of demand. Consumers swamped travel agents and airline ticket counters, greedily buying up two, three, or more tickets for summer trips. On Sunday, May 31, at the height of the buying frenzy, reservations at Northwest were up 563 percent compared with sales a week earlier. On Tuesday, June 2, Delta received a mind-boggling 2.5 million calls, compared with 300,000 on a typical day. The industry sold a summer's worth of travel in a little over a week.

Although those days in May and early June marked a happy time for air travelers, they spelled disaster for the airlines. As one analyst notes, "For most of the stronger airlines . . . it wiped out chances for a profitable summer. For the weaker ones, the low fares may have been the kiss of death." When the air cleared, the industry had lost more than $3 billion dollars in 1992.

Travel agents also lost out, working harder for lower commissions. They had to reissue previously purchased tickets at the new lower prices. And although the major airlines eventually allowed the agents to keep the commissions that they'd earned on the earlier purchases, prices of new tickets were often so low that the agents couldn't make enough in commissions to cover the costs of writing them. Many travel agents blamed American; some even vowed to steer future business to other carriers when possible. To make matters worse, Continental sued American, claiming that it had engaged in predatory pricing—setting fares that could not be profitable in order to drive out weaker competitors. American responded that it was only trying to establish an industry pricing discipline that would let it and other airlines earn a profit. The charges were later found to be groundless, and American won the suit.

By fall, on many American Airlines routes, travelers were once again confronted with a complex array of fares. American's revolutionary fare plan never really had a chance to get off the ground. Instead, its attempts to bring sanity to the industry's pricing practices created even greater losses, in terms of both dollars and credibility with consumers. ■

# C H A P T E R   O B J E C T I V E S

## *After reading this chapter, you should be able to:*

**1** Explain the internal and external factors affecting a firm's pricing decisions.

**2** Compare the three general approaches to setting prices.

**3** Describe the major strategies for pricing new products.

**4** Explain how companies find a set of prices that maximizes the profits from the total product mix.

**5** Explain how companies adjust their prices to take into account different types of customers and situations.

**6** Tell why companies decide to change their prices and how they might react to competitors' price changes.

All profit organizations and many nonprofit organizations must set prices on their products or services. *Price* goes by many names:

> Price is all around us. You pay *rent* for your apartment, *tuition* for your education, and a *fee* to your physician or dentist. The airline, railway, taxi, and bus companies charge you a *fare;* the local utilities call their price a *rate;* and the local bank charges you *interest* for the money you borrow. The price for driving your car on Florida's Sunshine Parkway is a *toll,* and the company that insures your car charges you a *premium.* The guest lecturer charges an *honorarium* to tell you about a government official who took a *bribe* to help a shady character steal *dues* collected by a trade association. Clubs or societies to which you belong may make a special *assessment* to pay unusual expenses. Your regular lawyer may ask for a *retainer* to cover her services. The "price" of an

executive is a *salary*, the price of a salesperson may be a *commission*, and the price of a worker is a *wage*. Finally, although economists would disagree, many of us feel that *income taxes* are the price we pay for the privilege of making money.[2]

**Price**
The amount of money charged for a product or service, or the sum of the values that consumers exchange for the benefits of having or using the product or service.

In the narrowest sense, **price** is the amount of money charged for a product or service. More broadly, price is the sum of all the values that consumers exchange for the benefits of having or using the product or service. Historically, price has been the major factor affecting buyer choice. This is still true in poorer nations, among poorer groups, and with commodity products. However, in recent decades, nonprice factors have become increasingly important in buyer-choice behavior.

Price is the only element in the marketing mix that produces revenue; all other elements represent costs. Price is also one of the most flexible elements of the marketing mix. Unlike product features and channel commitments, price can be changed quickly. At the same time, pricing and price competition is the number one problem facing many marketing executives. Yet, many companies do not handle pricing well. The most common mistakes are: pricing that is too cost oriented; prices that are not revised often enough to reflect market changes; pricing that does not take the rest of the marketing mix into account; and prices that are not varied enough for different products, market segments, and purchase occasions.

In this chapter, we focus on the problem of setting prices. We look first at the factors that marketers must consider when setting prices and at general pricing approaches. Then we examine pricing strategies for new-product pricing, product-mix pricing, price changes, and price adjustments for buyer and situational factors.

# FACTORS TO CONSIDER WHEN SETTING PRICES

A company's pricing decisions are affected both by internal company factors and external environmental factors (see Figure 10-1).[3]

## INTERNAL FACTORS AFFECTING PRICING DECISIONS

Internal factors that affect pricing decisions include the company's marketing objectives, marketing-mix strategy, costs, and organization.

**FIGURE 10-1**
*Factors affecting price decisions*

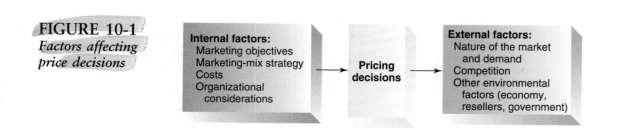

Internal factors:
  Marketing objectives
  Marketing-mix strategy
  Costs
  Organizational
    considerations

Pricing decisions

External factors:
  Nature of the market
    and demand
  Competition
  Other environmental
    factors (economy,
    resellers, government)

## Marketing Objectives

Before setting a price, the company must decide on its overall strategy for the product. If the company has selected its target market and positioning carefully, then its marketing-mix strategy, including price, will be fairly straightforward. For example, if General Motors decides to produce a new sports car to compete with European sports cars in the high-income segment, this suggests charging a high price. Motel 6, Econo Lodge, and Red Roof Inn have positioned themselves as motels that provide economical rooms for budget-minded travelers; this position requires charging a low price. Thus, pricing strategy is largely determined by decisions on market positioning.

At the same time, the company may seek additional objectives. The clearer a firm is about its objectives, the easier it is to set price. Examples of common objectives are *survival, current profit maximization, market-share leadership,* and *product-quality leadership.*

Companies set *survival* as their major objective if they are troubled by too much capacity, heavy competition, or changing consumer wants. To keep a plant going, a company may set a low price, hoping to increase demand. In this case, profits are less important than survival. As long as their prices cover variable costs and some fixed costs, they can stay in business. However, survival is only a short-term objective. In the long run, the firm must learn how to add value or face extinction.

Many companies use *current profit maximization* as their pricing goal. They estimate what demand and costs will be at different prices and choose the price that will produce the maximum current profit, cash flow, or return on investment. In all cases, the company wants current financial results rather than long-run performance. Other companies want to obtain *market-share leadership*. They believe that the company with the largest market share will enjoy the lowest costs and highest long-run profit. To become the market-share leader, these firms set prices as low as possible.

A company might decide that it wants to achieve *product-quality leadership.* This normally calls for charging a high price to cover higher performance quality and the high cost of R&D. For example, Hewlett-Packard focuses on the high-quality, high-price end of the hand-calculator market. Similarly, Pitney Bowes pursues a product-quality leadership strategy for its fax equipment. While Sharp, Canon, and other competitors fight over the low-price fax machine market with machines selling at around $500, Pitney Bowes targets large corporations with machines selling at about $5,000. As a result, it captures some 45 percent of the large-corporation fax niche.[4]

A company might also use price to attain other more specific objectives. It can set prices low to prevent competition from entering the market or set prices at competitors' levels to stabilize the market. Prices can be set to keep the loyalty and support of resellers or to avoid government intervention. Prices can be reduced temporarily to create excitement for a product or to draw more customers into a retail store. One product may be priced to help the sales of other products in the company's line. Thus, pricing may play an important role in helping to accomplish the company's objectives at many levels.

## Marketing-Mix Strategy

Price is only one of the marketing-mix tools that a company uses to achieve its marketing objectives. Price decisions must be coordinated with product design, distribution, and promotion decisions to form a consistent and effective marketing program.

*Target costing: In creating its highly successful, lower-priced Prolinea line, Compaq started with a target price set by marketing and profit-margin goals from management. Then the design team determined what costs had to be in order to charge the target price.*

**Target costing**
Setting a product's price by starting with target cost and working back.

Decisions made for other marketing-mix variables may affect pricing decisions. For example, producers using many resellers who are expected to support and promote their products may have to build larger reseller margins into their prices.

Companies often make their pricing decisions first and then base other marketing-mix decisions on the prices that they want to charge. Here, price is a crucial product positioning factor that defines the product's market, competition, and design. Many firms support such price-positioning strategies with a technique called **target costing,** a potent strategic weapon. Target costing reverses the usual process of first designing a new product, determining its cost, and then asking "Can we sell it for that?" Instead, it starts with a target cost and works back.

Compaq Computer Corporation calls this process "design to price." After being battered for years by lower-priced rivals, Compaq used this approach to create its highly successful, lower-priced Prolinea personal computer line. Starting with a price target set by marketing, and with profit-margin goals from management, the Prolinea design team determined what costs *had* to be in order to charge the target price. From this crucial calculation, all else followed. To achieve target costs, the design team negotiated doggedly with all the company departments responsible for different aspects of the new product, and with outside suppliers of needed parts and materials. Compaq engineers designed a machine with fewer and simpler parts, manufacturing overhauled its factories to reduce production costs, and suppliers found ways to provide quality components at needed prices. By meeting its target *costs,* Compaq was able to set its target *price* and establish the desired price position. As a result, Prolinea sales and profits soared.[5]

Other companies deemphasize price and use other marketing-mix tools to create *nonprice* positions. Often, the best strategy is not to charge the lowest price, but rather to differentiate the marketing offer to make it worth a higher price. For example, for years, Johnson Controls, a producer of climate control systems for office buildings, used initial price as its primary competitive tool. However, research showed that customers were more concerned about the total cost of installing and maintaining a system than about its initial price. Repairing broken systems was expensive, time-consuming, and risky. Customers had to shut down the heat or air conditioning in the whole building, disconnect a lot of wires, and face the dangers of electrocution. Johnson decided to change its strategy. It designed an entirely new system called Metasys. To repair the new system, customers need only pull out an old plastic module and slip in a new one—no tools required. Metasys costs more to make than the old system, and customers pay a higher initial price, but it costs less to install and maintain. Despite its higher asking price, the new Metasys system brought in $500 million in revenues in its first year.[6]

Thus, the marketer must consider the total marketing mix when setting prices. If the product is positioned on nonprice factors, then decisions about quality, promotion, and distribution will strongly affect price. If price is a crucial positioning factor, then price will strongly affect decisions made about the other marketing-mix elements. However, even when featuring price, marketers need to remember that customers rarely buy on price alone. Instead, they seek products that give them the best value in terms of benefits received for the price paid (see Marketing at Work 10-1).

## Costs

Costs set the floor for the price that the company can charge for its product. The company wants to charge a price that both covers all its costs for producing, distributing, and selling the product and delivers a fair rate of return for its effort and risk. Many companies work to become the low-cost producers in their industries. Companies with lower costs can set lower prices that result in greater sales and profits.

A company's costs take two forms: fixed and variable. *Fixed costs* (also known as overhead) are those that do not vary with production or sales level. For example, a company must pay each month's bills for rent, heat, interest, and executive salaries, whatever the company's output. *Variable costs* vary directly with the level of production. Each personal computer produced by Compaq involves a cost of computer chips, wires, plastic, packaging, and other inputs. These costs tend to be the same for each unit produced. They are called variable because their total varies with the number of units produced. *Total costs* are the sum of the fixed and variable costs for any given level of production. Management wants to charge a price that will at least cover the total production costs at a given level of production.

The company must watch its costs carefully. If it spends more than competitors to produce and sell its product, the company will have to charge a higher price or make less profit, putting it at a competitive disadvantage.

## Organizational Considerations

Management must decide who within the organization should set prices. Companies handle pricing in a variety of ways. In small companies, prices are often set by top management rather than by the marketing or sales departments. In large companies, pricing typically is handled by divisional or product line managers. In industrial markets, salespeople may be allowed to negotiate with customers within certain price ranges. Even so, top management sets the pricing objectives and policies, and it often approves the prices proposed by lower-level management or salespeople. In industries in which pricing is a key factor (aerospace, railroads, oil companies), companies often have a pricing department to set the best prices or help others in setting them. This department reports to the marketing department or

## MARKETING AT WORK 10-1

# CarMax: Good Prices and a Whole Lot More

Would you buy a used car from this . . . er, retail store? Circuit City, the nation's leading consumer electronics and appliance retailer, thinks that you will. Its new CarMax Auto Superstores are a far cry from the usual, sometimes less than reputable, used car lot. The first CarMax, in Richmond, Virginia, is located on a sprawling 12-acre site filled with 500 used, but still gleaming, cars, trucks, and minivans. As you might expect, given Circuit City's low-price guarantees, price figures prominently into CarMax's positioning—it promises "no-haggle, below-book prices." However, unlike Circuit City stores, CarMax does not claim to charge the *lowest* prices. Instead, price is only a part—and perhaps not even the most important part—of a broader mix of values that CarMax delivers to its customers.

More than a dozen years ago, when Circuit City first opened, the highly fragmented consumer electronics industry evoked images of sleazy salespeople, bait-and-switch promotions, and high-pressure selling. Although chains like Mad Man Muntz and Crazy Eddie sold at low prices, they left many cus-

*At CarMax, price is only part of the formula. Delighted used-car buyers receive a wide mix of values, including selection, convenience, and peace of mind.*

tomers uneasy. Had they gotten the best value? Would the store stand behind its products? With its large and modern stores, wide selection of goods, knowledgeable salespeople, liberal returns policies, and affordable financing, Circuit City brought new respectability to consumer electronics and appliance retailing.

Now, CarMax faces a similar situation with used cars—a highly fragmented industry prone

to strong consumer concerns about reliability. Research shows that, when buying a used car, 40 percent of consumers question the reputation of the dealer. Circuit City wants to bring the same respectability to used-car retailing that it brought to consumer electronics. It wants customers to be able to buy used cars from CarMax with the same ease and peace of mind that they purchase television sets, personal comput-

top management. Others who influence pricing include sales managers, production managers, finance managers, and accountants.

## EXTERNAL FACTORS AFFECTING PRICING DECISIONS

External factors that affect pricing decisions include the nature of the market and demand, competition, and other environmental elements.

ers, camcorders, and refrigerators from Circuit City superstores.

Buying a used car from CarMax is a dramatically different experience. CarMax offers a large selection of cars, without a clunker in the bunch—most are less than five years old and sell for $8,000 to $15,000. Customers walk into a brightly lit showroom, where they are greeted by "sales associates" dressed in polo shirts, khakis, and sneakers. They use computer touch-screens to search the CarMax inventory for cars that meet their specifications and budgets. The computer screen shows color pictures of various choices, and the customer can print out any car's specifications, features, mileage, and price, along with a report of repairs on the car to get it ready for sale. The printout even contains a photo of the car and a map showing its location on the lot.

When ready, customers are driven in golf carts to see cars on the lot, while their children enjoy the latest toys and games in the supervised KidCare Center. If the customer decides to purchase a car, financing can be arranged in less than 15 minutes through Circuit City's finance company.

Moreover, CarMax will buy the customer's old car for a set price, whether or not he or she buys a new one. The entire car-buying process, from rumbling in with the old clunker to purring out with a shiny new model, can take less than an hour.

In addition to being quick and convenient, almost everything about CarMax inspires customer confidence. CarMax gives each car a 110-point quality inspection and backs it with a 30-day comprehensive warranty. It even offers a money-back guarantee—a customer who is not 100 percent satisfied can bring the car back within five days for a full refund. CarMax allows no high-pressure selling. Salespeople are carefully selected and trained to help people find the car that's just right for them. They receive commissions based on how many cars they sell, but not on prices. This prevents commission-hungry salespeople from steering customers to more expensive cars.

Finally, at CarMax, a price is a price. Prices are marked right on the car, and no haggling is allowed. CarMax prices aren't the lowest around, but they are usually competitive—right around book value. However,

these slightly higher prices don't appear to bother customers. Recent studies have shown that many customers willingly pay more to avoid the hassle of negotiating for better deals and to ensure that they get a good car, at a fair price, backed by a reliable seller.

As one industry expert notes, the used car industry has typically "ranked from shady to illegal. The public perception [is] horrible, just horrible. People have no confidence." CarMax is setting out to change that perception. At CarMax, "You don't feel like you're going to a used-car den where you're about to be taken—you get an above-board, airy feeling." Many customers actually enjoy the used car-buying process at CarMax. "You don't have the high pressure," says one customer. "You get a quality selection, and it's no hassle." Thus, at CarMax, price is important, but so are selection and convenience. And it's hard to put a price on peace of mind.

*Sources:* Quotes from Michael Janofsky, "Circuit City Takes a Spin at Used Car Marketing," *The New York Times,* October 25, 1993, p. D1. Also see Bloomberg Business News, "Executive Update," *Investor's Business Daily,* October 8, 1993, p. 3; Douglas Lavin, "Cars Are Sold Like Stereos by Circuit City," *Wall Street Journal,* June 8, 1994, p. B1; Gabrella Stern, "'Nearly New' Autos for Sales: Dealers Buff Up Their Marketing of Used Cars," *Wall Street Journal,* February 19, 1995, p. B1; and Raymond Serafin, "National Marketers Test Drive Used Cars," *Advertising Age,* December 4, 1995, pp. 1, 34.

## *The Market and Demand*

Whereas costs set the lower limit of prices, the market and demand set the upper limit. Both consumer and industrial buyers balance the price of a product or service against the benefits of owning it. Thus, before setting prices, the marketer must understand the relationship between price and demand for its product.

In this section, we explain how the price–demand relationship varies for different types of markets and how buyer perceptions of price affect the pricing decision. We then discuss methods for measuring the price–demand relationship.

PRICING IN DIFFERENT TYPES OF MARKETS.   The seller's pricing freedom varies with different types of markets. Economists recognize four types of markets, each presenting a different pricing challenge.

Under *pure competition*, the market consists of many buyers and sellers trading in a uniform commodity such as wheat, copper, or financial securities. No single buyer or seller has much effect on the going market price. A seller cannot charge more than the going price because buyers can obtain as much as they need at the going price. Nor would sellers charge less than the market price because they can sell all they want at this price. In a purely competitive market, marketing research, product development, pricing, advertising, and sales promotion play little or no role. Thus, sellers in these markets do not spend much time on marketing strategy.

Under *monopolistic competition*, the market consists of many buyers and sellers who trade over a range of prices rather than a single market price. A range of prices occurs because buyers see differences in sellers' products and are willing to pay different prices for them. Sellers try to develop differentiated offers for different customer segments and, in addition to price, freely use branding, advertising, and personal selling to set their offers apart. For example, H.J. Heinz, Vlasic, and several other national brands of pickles compete with dozens of regional and local brands, all differentiated by price and nonprice factors. Because there are many competitors, each firm is less affected by competitors' marketing strategies than in oligopolistic markets.

Under *oligopolistic competition*, the market consists of a few sellers who are highly sensitive to each other's pricing and marketing strategies. The product can be uniform (steel, aluminum) or nonuniform (cars, computers). There are few sellers because it is difficult for new sellers to enter the market. Each seller is alert to competitors' strategies and moves. If a steel company slashes its price by 10 percent, buyers will quickly switch to this supplier. The other steelmakers must respond by lowering their prices or increasing their services. An oligopolist is never sure that it will gain anything permanent through a price cut. In contrast, if an oligopolist raises its price, its competitors might not follow this lead. The oligopolist would then have to retract its price increase or risk losing customers to competitors.

*Monopolistic competition: Canadian pickle marketer Bick's sets its pickles apart from dozens of other brands using both price and nonprice factors.*

In a *pure monopoly*, the market consists of one seller. The seller may be a government monopoly (the U.S. Postal Service), a private regulated monopoly (a power company), or a private nonregulated monopoly (Du Pont when it introduced nylon). Pricing is handled differently in each case. A government monopoly can pursue a variety of pricing objectives. It might set a price below cost because the product is important to buyers who cannot afford to pay full cost. Or the price might be set either to cover costs or to produce good revenue. It can even be set quite high to slow down consumption. In a regulated monopoly, the government permits the company to set rates that will yield a "fair return" and allow the company to maintain and expand its operations as needed. Nonregulated monopolies are free to set a price at what the market will bear. However, they do not always charge the full price for a number of reasons: a desire not to attract competition, a desire to penetrate the market faster with a low price, or a fear of government regulation.

**CONSUMER PERCEPTIONS OF PRICE AND VALUE.** In the end, the consumer decides whether a product's price is right. Pricing decisions, like other marketing-mix decisions, must be buyer oriented. When consumers buy a product, they exchange something of value (the price) to get something of value (the benefits of having or using the product). Effective buyer-oriented pricing involves understanding how much value consumers place on the benefits that they receive from the product and setting a price that fits this value.

A company often finds it hard to measure the values that customers will attach to its product. For example, calculating the cost of ingredients in a meal at a fancy restaurant is relatively easy. But assigning a value to other satisfactions such as taste, environment, relaxation, conversation, and status is elusive. And these values vary both for different consumers and different situations. Still, consumers use these values to evaluate a product's price. If customers perceive that the price is greater than the product's value, they will not buy the product. If consumers perceive that the price is below the product's value, they will buy it, but the seller loses profit opportunities.

**Demand curve**
A curve that shows the number of units that the market will buy in a given time period, at different prices that might be charged.

**ANALYZING THE PRICE–DEMAND RELATIONSHIP.** Each price that the company might charge will lead to a different level of demand. The relation between the price charged and the resulting demand level is shown in the **demand curve** in Figure 10-2A. The demand curve shows the number of units that the market will buy

**FIGURE 10-2**
*Demand curves*

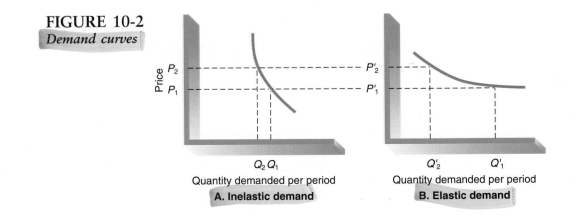

A. Inelastic demand

B. Elastic demand

in a given time period at different prices that might be charged. In the normal case, demand and price are inversely related: That is, the higher the price, the lower the demand. Thus, the company would sell less if it raised its price from $P_1$ to $P_2$. In short, consumers with limited budgets probably will buy less of something if its price is too high.

In the case of prestige goods, the demand curve sometimes slopes upward, as shown in Figure 10-2B. For example, one perfume company found that, by raising its price, it sold more perfume rather than less. Consumers thought that the higher price meant a better or more desirable perfume. However, if the company charges too high a price, the level of demand will be lower.

Most companies try to measure their demand curves by estimating demand at different prices. The type of market makes a difference. In a monopoly, the demand curve shows the total market demand resulting from different prices. If the company faces competition, its demand at different prices will depend on whether competitors' prices stay constant or change with the company's own prices.

In measuring the price–demand relationship, the market researcher must not allow other factors affecting demand to vary. For example, if Sony increased its advertising at the same time that it lowered its television prices, we would not know how much of the increased demand was due to the lower prices and how much was due to the increased advertising. The same problem arises if a holiday weekend occurs when the lower price is set; increased gift giving over the holidays causes people to buy more televisions. Economists show the impact of nonprice factors on demand through shifts in the demand curve rather than movements along it.

**Price elasticity**
A measure of the sensitivity of demand to changes in price.

**PRICE ELASTICITY OF DEMAND.**   Marketers also need to know **price elasticity**—how responsive demand will be to a change in price. If demand hardly changes with a small change in price, we say that the demand is *inelastic*. If demand changes greatly, we say that the demand is *elastic*.

What determines the price elasticity of demand? Buyers are less price sensitive when the product they are buying is unique or when it is high in quality, prestige, or exclusiveness. They are also less price sensitive when substitute products are hard to find or when they cannot easily compare the quality of substitutes. Finally, buyers are less price sensitive when the total expenditure for a product is low relative to their income or when the cost is shared by another party.[7]

If demand is elastic rather than inelastic, sellers will consider lowering their price. A lower price produces more total revenue. This practice makes sense as long as the extra costs of producing and selling more do not exceed the extra revenue.

## Competitors' Costs, Prices, and Offers

Another external factor affecting the company's pricing decisions is competitors' costs and prices and possible competitor reactions to the company's own pricing moves. A consumer who is considering the purchase of a Canon camera will evaluate Canon's price and value against the prices and values of comparable products made by Nikon, Minolta, Pentax, and others. In addition, the company's pricing strategy may affect the nature of the competition that it faces. If Canon follows a high-price, high-margin strategy, it may attract competition. A low-price, low-margin strategy, however, may stop competitors or drive them out of the market.

Canon needs to benchmark its costs against its competitors' costs to learn whether it is operating at a cost advantage or disadvantage. It also needs to learn the price and quality of each competitor's offer. Once Canon is aware of competitors' prices and offers, it can use them as a starting point for its own pricing. If Canon's cameras are similar to Nikon's, it will have to price close to Nikon or lose sales. If Canon's cameras are not as good as Nikon's, the firm will not be able to charge as much. If Canon's products are better than Nikon's, it can charge more. Basically, Canon will use price to position its offer relative to the competition.

### Other External Factors

When setting prices, the company also must consider other factors in its external environment. *Economic conditions* can have a strong impact on the firm's pricing strategies. Economic factors such as boom or recession, inflation, and interest rates affect pricing decisions because they affect both the costs of producing a product and consumer perceptions of the product's price and value. The company also must consider what impact its prices will have on other parties in its environment. How will *resellers* react to various prices? The company should set prices that give resellers a fair profit, encourage their support, and help them to sell the product effectively. The *government* is another important external influence on pricing decisions. Marketers need to know the laws affecting price and make sure that their pricing policies are defensible. Finally, *social concerns* may have to be taken into account. In setting prices, a company's short-term sales, market share, and profit goals may have to be tempered by broader societal considerations (see Marketing at Work 10-2).

## ▶ GENERAL PRICING APPROACHES

The price that the company charges will be somewhere between one that is too low to produce a profit and one that is too high to produce any demand. Figure 10-3 summarizes the major considerations in setting price. Product costs set a floor to the price; consumer perceptions of the product's value set the ceiling. The company must consider competitors' prices and other external and internal factors to find the best price between these two extremes.

Companies set prices by selecting a general pricing approach that includes one or more of these three sets of factors. We will examine the following approaches: the *cost-based approach* (cost-plus pricing, break-even analysis, and target profit pricing); the *buyer-based approach* (value-based pricing); and the *competition-based approach* (going-rate and sealed-bid pricing).

**FIGURE 10-3**
*Major considerations in setting price*

| LOW PRICE | | | | | HIGH PRICE |
|---|---|---|---|---|---|
| **No possible profit at this price** | Product costs | Competitors' prices and other external and internal factors | Consumer perceptions of value | | **No possible demand at this price** |

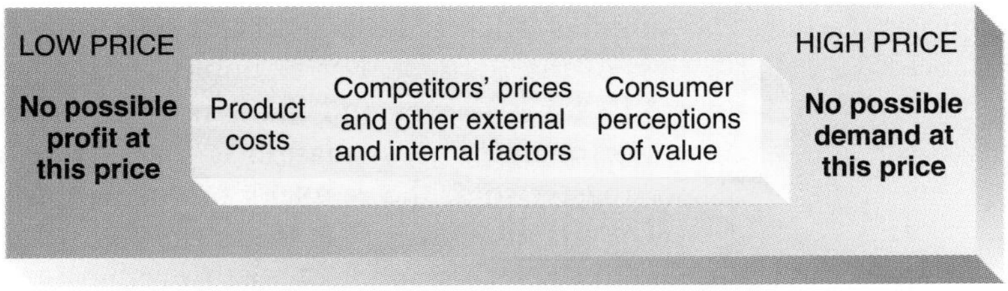

# MARKETING AT WORK 10-2

## PRICING PHARMACEUTICAL PRODUCTS: MORE THAN SALES AND PROFITS

The U.S. pharmaceutical industry historically has been the nation's most profitable industry. However, critics claim that this success has come at the expense of consumers. It is possible only because competitive forces do not operate well in the pharmaceutical market. Consumers don't usually shop around for the best deal on medicines—they simply take what the doctor orders. Because physicians who write the prescriptions don't pay for the medicines they recommend, they have little incentive to be price conscious. Moreover, third-party payers—insurance companies, health plans, and government programs—often pay all or part of the bill. Finally, in the pharmaceutical industry, the huge investment and time needed to develop and test a new drug discourages competitors from challenging the market leader and forcing lower prices.

These market factors sometimes leave pharmaceutical companies free to practice monopoly pricing, resulting in seemingly outlandish cases of price gouging. One such case involves the drug levamisole. Thirty years ago, Johnson & Johnson introduced levamisole as a drug used to deworm sheep. When farmers using the drug noticed that dewormed sheep also suffered fewer cases of shipping fever, researchers began investigating the drug for human use. Under the sponsorship of the National Cancer Institute, and with free pills provided by Johnson & Johnson, Dr. Charles Moertel of the Mayo Comprehensive Cancer Center tested levamisole in combination with another drug as a treatment for cancer. The combination proved effective for patients with advanced colon cancer. It reduced recurrence of the disease by 40 percent and cut deaths by a third.

The FDA quickly approved levamisole for human use. In 1990, the Janssen division of Johnson & Johnson introduced the drug under the brand name Ergamisol. All went well until an Illinois farm woman noticed that her cancer pills contained the same active ingredient as the medicine she used to deworm her sheep. It wasn't the fact that both humans and sheep were using the drug that disturbed her. What really rankled her was that the sheep medicine sells for pennies a pill, whereas the human medicine sells for $5 to $6 per tablet. In a year's time, humans may spend from $1,250 to $3,000 for Ergamisol; the cost for treating sheep may be as low as $14.95.

The price discrepancy has caused quite a stir. Doctors at the MacNeal Hospital Cancer Center in Chicago surveyed local pharmacies and found that patients paid an average of $1,200 per year for levamisole. At the annual meetings of the American Society for Clinical Oncology in May 1992, Dr. Moertel blasted Johnson & Johnson for its unconscionable pricing of the drug. His salvo marked the first time that marketplace issues had taken center stage at that scholarly forum, and it had great impact. And as if publicity from Dr. Moer-

## COST-BASED PRICING

**Cost-plus pricing** Adding a standard markup to the cost of the product.

The simplest pricing method is **cost-plus pricing**—adding a standard markup to the cost of the product. For example, an appliance retailer might pay a manufacturer $20 for a toaster and mark it up to sell at $30—a 50 percent markup on cost. The retailer's gross margin is $10. If the store's operating costs amount to $8 per toaster sold, the retailer's profit margin will be $2.

The manufacturer that made the toaster probably used cost-plus pricing. If the manufacturer's standard cost of producing the toaster was $16, it might have added a 25 percent markup, setting the price to the retailers at $20. Similarly, contel's comments were not enough, in August 1992, Chicago consumer Frank Glickman filed suit against Janssen. He claimed that he was forced to pay "an outrageous, unconscionable, and extortionate price for a life-saving drug" that is sold at a fraction of the cost for treating sheep.

Janssen replied that the cost of Ergamisol is reasonable when compared with other life-saving drugs such as AZT, which can cost $6,000 to $8,000 a year. The company also claimed that the price reflects decades of costly research and testing conducted to determine if levamisole could be used to treat humans. The company said it had conducted over 1,400 studies with 40,000 subjects. Dr. Moertel disagreed. He claimed that the Cancer Institute, funded by the American taxpayer, sponsored the levamisole studies. Further, he asserted, FDA approval was obtained on the basis of his research, which cost Janssen only pennies. He also pointed out that Janssen had 25 years to recoup its investment before it ever sold the drug to humans.

The levamisole example highlights many important drug pricing issues. Most consumers appreciate the steady stream of beneficial drugs produced by the U.S. pharmaceutical industry. However, there is increasing concern that the industry may be taking advantage of its monopoly pricing power; the United States remains the only country in the world that has no governmental review of pharmaceutical prices. Unlike purchases of other consumer products, drug purchases cannot be postponed. Nor can consumers shop around to save money. Because of patents and FDA approvals, few competing brands exist, and they don't go on sale. Perhaps the most serious concern is that high drug prices may have life-and-death consequences. Without levamisole, many of the 22,000 patients diagnosed with advanced colon cancer each year would die. Thus, some critics claim that drug company profits may come at the expense of human life.

As a result, the industry is facing ever-greater pressure from the federal government, insurance companies, and consumer advocates to exercise restraint in setting prices. Legislation has been passed to curb drug pricing, and more is pending. Rather than waiting for tougher legislation on prices, some forward-thinking drug companies are taking action on their own. For example, Merck and Glaxo have agreed to keep their average price hikes at or below inflation. Bristol-Meyers Squibb has voluntarily provided discounts to agencies such as the U.S. Public Health Service and to federally funded drug- and alcohol-treatment centers. Glaxo and other companies make free drugs available to people who cannot afford them. These companies recognize that, in setting prices, their short-term sales, market share, and profit goals must be tempered by broader societal considerations. They know that, in the long run, socially responsible pricing will benefit both the consumer and the company.

*Sources:* Quote from Marilyn Chase, "Doctor Assails J&J Price Tag on Cancer Drug," *Wall Street Journal,* May 20, 1992, p. B1. Also see "Cancer Patient Sues Johnson & Johnson over Drug Pricing," *The Wall Street Journal,* August 13, 1992, p. B6; Mike King, "Colon Cancer Drug: 5 Cents for an Animal, $5 for Humans," *Atlanta Constitution,* March 11, 1991, p. E1; Patricia Winters, "Drugmakers Portrayed as Villains, Worry about Image," *Advertising Age,* February 22, 1993, pp. 1, 42; Shawn Tully, "The Plot to Keep Drug Prices High," *Fortune,* December 27, 1993, pp. 120–24; and Joseph Weber, "Drug Prices: So Much for Restraint," *Business Week,* March 4, 1996, p. 40.

struction companies submit job bids by estimating the total project cost and adding a standard markup for profit. Lawyers, accountants, and other professionals typically price by adding a standard markup to their costs. Some sellers tell their customers that they will charge cost plus a specified markup; for example, aerospace companies price this way to the government.

Does using standard markups to set prices make sense? Generally, no. Any pricing method that ignores demand and competitor prices is not likely to lead to the best price. Although some companies use cost-plus pricing successfully, others encounter difficulties. Steel manufacturer Nucor Corporation has had great success with cost-plus pricing. Notes the company's general manager, "We base the price on what it costs to run the mill to capacity twenty-four hours a day."[8] The strategy works because Nucor's very low costs allow it to charge very low prices relative to competitors. In contrast, the retail graveyard is full of merchants who insisted on using standard markups after their competitors had gone to discount pricing.

Still, markup pricing remains popular for many reasons. First, sellers are more certain about costs than about demand. By tying the price to cost, sellers simplify pricing—they do not have to make frequent adjustments as demand changes. Second, when all firms in the industry use this pricing method, prices tend to be similar and price competition is thus minimized. Third, many people feel that cost-plus pricing is fairer to both buyers and sellers. Sellers earn a fair return on their investment but do not take advantage of buyers when buyers' demand becomes great.

Another cost-oriented pricing approach is **break-even pricing,** or a variation called **target profit pricing.** The firm tries to determine the price at which it will break even or make the target profit that it is seeking. Target pricing is used by General Motors, which prices its automobiles to achieve a 15 to 20 percent profit on its investment. This pricing method is also used by public utilities, which are constrained to make a fair return on their investment.

Target pricing uses the concept of a *break-even chart,* which shows the total cost and total revenue expected at different sales volume levels. Figure 10-4 shows a hypothetical break-even chart. Here, fixed costs are $6 million regardless of sales volume, and variable costs are $5 per unit. Variable costs are added to fixed costs to form total costs, which rise with each unit sold. The slope of the total revenue curve reflects the price. Here, the price is $15 (for example, the company's revenue is $12 million on 800,000 units, or $15 per unit).

At the $15 price, the company must sell at least 600,000 units to *break even;* that is, at this level, total revenues will equal total costs of $9 million. If the company wants a target profit of $2 million, it must sell at least 800,000 units to obtain the $12 million of total revenue needed to cover the costs of $10 million plus the $2 million of target profits. In contrast, if the company charges a higher

> **Break-even pricing** (target profit pricing) Setting price to break even on the costs of making and marketing a product, or setting price to make a target profit.

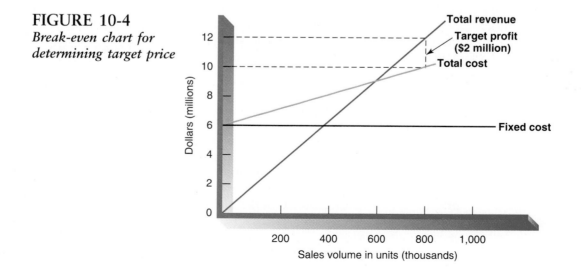

**FIGURE 10-4**
*Break-even chart for determining target price*

price, say $20 million, it will not need to sell as many units to break even or to achieve its target profit. In fact, the higher the price, the lower the company's break-even point will be.

However, as the *price* increases, *demand* decreases, and the market may not buy even the lower volume needed to break even at the higher price. Much depends on the relationship between price and demand. For example, suppose the company calculates that given its current fixed and variable costs, it must charge a price of $30 for the product in order to earn its desired target profit. But marketing research shows that few consumers will pay more than $25. In this case, the company will have to trim its costs in order to lower the break-even point so that it can charge the lower price that consumers expect.

Thus, although break-even analysis and target profit pricing can help the company to determine minimum prices needed to cover expected costs and profits, they do not take the price–demand relationship into account. When using this method, the company must also consider the impact of price on sales volume needed to realize target profits and the likelihood that the needed volume will be achieved at each possible price.

## VALUE-BASED PRICING

**Value-based pricing**
Setting price based on buyers' perceptions of value rather than on the seller's cost.

An increasing number of companies are basing their prices on the product's perceived value. **Value-based pricing** uses buyers' perceptions of value, not the seller's cost, as the key to pricing. Value-based pricing means that the marketer cannot design a product and marketing program and then set the price. Price is considered along with the other marketing-mix variables *before* the marketing program is set.

Figure 10-5 compares cost-based pricing with value-based pricing. Cost-based pricing is product driven. The company designs what it considers to be a good product, totals the costs of making the product, and sets a price that covers costs plus a target profit. Marketing must then convince buyers that the product's value at that price justifies its purchase. If the price turns out to be too high, the company must settle for lower markups or lower sales, both resulting in disappointing profits.

**FIGURE 10-5**
*Cost-based versus value-based pricing*

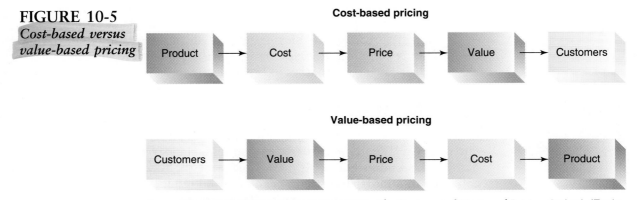

*Source:* Thomas T. Nagle and Reed K. Holden, *The Strategy and Tactics of Pricing*, 2nd ed. (Englewood Cliffs, NJ: Prentice Hall, 1995), p. 5.

*Perceived value: A less expensive pen might write as well, but some consumers will pay much more for the intangibles. This Parker model runs $185. Others are priced as high as $3,500.*

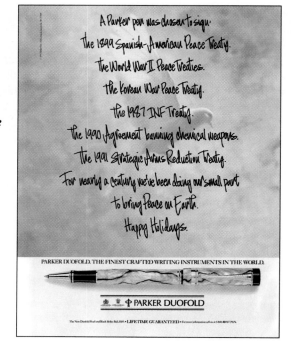

A Parker pen was chosen to sign:

The 1899 Spanish-American Peace Treaty.

The World War II Peace Treaties.

The Korean War Peace Treaty.

The 1987 INF Treaty.

The 1990 Agreement banning chemical weapons.

The 1991 Strategic Arms Reduction Treaty.

For nearly a century we've been doing our small part to bring Peace on Earth.

Happy Holidays.

PARKER DUOFOLD. THE FINEST CRAFTED WRITING INSTRUMENTS IN THE WORLD.

♦ PARKER DUOFOLD

The New Duofold Pearl and Black Roller Ball, $195. • LIFETIME GUARANTEED • For more information call us at 1-800-BEST PEN.

Value-based pricing reverses this process. The company sets its target price based on customer perceptions of the product value. The targeted value and price then drive decisions about product design and what costs can be incurred. As a result, pricing begins with analyzing consumer needs and value perceptions, and price is set to match consumers' perceived value.

A company using value-based pricing must find out what value buyers assign to different competitive offers. However, measuring perceived value can be difficult. Sometimes consumers are asked how much they would pay for a basic product and for each benefit added to the offer. Or a company might conduct experiments to test the perceived value of different product offers. If the seller charges more than the buyers' perceived value, the company's sales will suffer. Many companies overprice their products, and their products sell poorly. Other companies underprice; underpriced products sell very well, but they produce less revenue than they would if price were raised to the perceived-value level.

During the recessionary, slow-growth 1990s, marketers have noted a fundamental shift in consumer attitudes toward price and quality. Many companies have changed their pricing approaches to bring them into line with these new economic conditions and consumer price perceptions. More and more, marketers have adopted **value pricing** strategies—offering just the right combination of quality and good service at a fair price. In many cases, this has involved the introduction of less expensive versions of established, brand-name products. Campbell introduced its Great Starts budget frozen-food line, Holiday Inn opened several Holiday Express budget hotels, Revlon's Charles of the Ritz offered the Express Bar collection of affordable cosmetics, and fast-food restaurants such as Taco Bell and McDonald's offered "value menus." In other cases, value pricing has involved

Value pricing
Offering just the right combination of quality and good service at a fair price.

redesigning existing brands in order to offer more quality for a given price or the same quality for less (see Marketing at Work 10-3).

An important type of value pricing at the retail level is *everyday low pricing (EDLP)*. EDLP involves charging a constant, everyday low price with few or no temporary price discounts. In contrast, *high–low pricing* involves charging higher prices on an everyday basis, but running frequent promotions to temporarily lower prices on selected items below the EDLP level.[9]

In recent years, high–low pricing has given way to EDLP in retail settings ranging from General Motors car dealerships to upscale department stores such as Nordstrom. Retailers adopt EDLP for many reasons, the most important of which is that constant sales and promotions are costly and have eroded consumer confidence in the credibility of everyday shelf prices. Consumers also have less time and patience for such time-honored traditions as watching for supermarket specials and clipping coupons.

The king of EDLP is Wal-Mart, which practically defined the concept. Except for a few sale items every month, Wal-Mart promises everyday low prices on everything that it sells. In contrast, Sears's attempts at EDLP in 1989 failed. To offer everyday low prices, a company must first *have* everyday low costs. Wal-Mart's EDLP strategy works well because its expenses are only 15 percent of sales. Sears, however, spends 29 percent of sales to cover administrative and other overhead costs. As a result, Sears now offers what the industry calls everyday *fair* pricing, a policy similar to Bloomingdale's, under which it tries to offer customers differentiated products at a consistent, fair price with fewer markdowns.[10]

## COMPETITION-BASED PRICING

Consumers will base their judgments of a product's value on the prices that competitors charge for similar products. One form of **competition-based pricing** is *going-rate pricing*, in which a firm bases its price largely on competitors' prices, with less attention paid to its own costs or to demand. The firm might charge the same, more, or less than its major competitors. In oligopolistic industries that sell a commodity such as steel, paper, or fertilizer, firms normally charge the same price. The smaller firms follow the leader: They change their prices when the market leader's prices change, rather than when their own demand or costs change. Some firms may charge a bit more or less, but they hold the amount of difference constant. Thus, minor gasoline retailers usually charge a few cents less than the major oil companies, without letting the difference increase or decrease.

Going-rate pricing is quite popular. When demand elasticity is hard to measure, firms feel that the going price represents the collective wisdom of the industry concerning the price that will yield a fair return. They also feel that holding to the going price will prevent harmful price wars.

Competition-based pricing is also used when firms *bid* for jobs. Using *sealed-bid pricing*, a firm bases its price on how it thinks that competitors will price rather than on its own costs or on the demand. The firm wants to win a contract, and winning the contract requires pricing less than other firms.

Yet the firm cannot set its price below a certain level. It cannot price below cost without harming its position. In contrast, the higher the company sets its price above its costs, the lower its chance of getting the contract.

## MARKETING AT WORK 10-3

# VALUE PRICING: OFFERING MORE FOR LESS

Marketers have a new buzzword for the 1990s, and it's spelled V-A-L-U-E. Throughout the 1980s, marketers pitched luxury, prestige, extravagance—even expensiveness—for everything from ice cream to autos. But after the recession began, they started redesigning, repackaging, repositioning, and remarketing products to emphasize value. Now, value pricing—offering more for a lot less by underscoring a product's quality, while at the same time featuring its price—has gone from a groundswell to a tidal wave.

Value pricing can mean many things to marketers. To some, it means price cutting. To others, it means special deals, such as providing more of a product at the same price. And to still others, it means a new image—one that convinces consumers they're receiving a good deal. No matter how it's defined, however, value pricing has become a prime strategy for wooing consumers.

Marketers are finding that the flat economy and changing consumer demographics have created a new class of sophisticated, bargain-hunting shoppers who are careful of what, where,

*Value pricing: Taco Bell pioneered value pricing with its incredibly successful value meals. To support value prices, it redesigned its restaurants to reduce costs and improve customer service.*

and how they shop. Whereas it used to be fashionable to flaunt affluence and spend conspicuously, now it's fashionable to say you got a good deal. To convince consumers that they're getting more for their money, companies from fast-food chains to stock brokerages and car makers have revamped their marketing pitches:

• Mobil's Hefty division slashed prices as much as 20 percent and added 20 percent more plastic

bags per box. Hefty also trashed its two-decade-old marketing effort centering on bag strength. The new motto: "Our strength is value." Says one Mobil manager: "People are looking for value in the 1990s, even in trash bags."

• PepsiCo's Taco Bell chain introduced an incredibly successful "value menu" offering 59-cent tacos and 15 other items for either 59 cents, 79 cents, or 99 cents. McDonald's followed suit with its Extra-Value Meals, underscored by the ad theme, "Good food. Good value." Soon, Wendy's,

## ▶ NEW-PRODUCT PRICING STRATEGIES

Pricing involves complex dynamics. And as the American Airlines example demonstrates forcefully, pricing decisions are subject to an incredibly complex array of environmental and competitive forces. A company sets not a single price, but rather a *pricing structure* that covers different items in its line. This pricing struc-

Burger King, and other competitors entered the fray with their own value-pricing schemes.

• Stock brokerage Shearson-Lehman Hutton is searching for a new ad campaign to help it counter the low-price claims of discount stockbrokers. "People are asking, 'Am I getting what I paid for, and is there value in it?'" notes a Shearson marketing executive. "Companies are being challenged to [define] the value they offer versus the price they charge." The new campaign will focus on services such as investment advice and financial planning that make Shearson's full-service offering a better value, even at the higher prices that it charges.

• In a recent world tour, General Electric Chairman Jack Welch noted that customers around the globe are now more interested in price than technology. "The value decade is upon us," he states. "If you can't sell a top-quality product at the world's lowest price, you're going to be out of the game." As a result, in products ranging from refrigerators to CAT scanners and jet engines, GE is working to offer basic, dependable units at unbeatable prices.

• Buick is pitching its top-of-the-line, full-size Park Avenue as "America's best car value" at a suggested list price of $25,800. Buick's boast is backed by findings from IntelliChoice, an independent research firm that ranked the Park Avenue number one on factors such as maintenance costs, fuel economy, and depreciation. "We're saying that you don't have to buy [an economy car] to get value for your dollar," says Buick's national advertising manager. "You don't have to give up luxury, performance, or size to get great value."

Value pricing involves more than just cutting prices. It means finding the delicate balance between quality and price that gives target consumers the value that they seek. To consumers, "value" is not the same as "cheap." Value pricing requires price cutting coupled with finding ways to maintain or even improve quality while still making a profit. Consumers who enjoyed high-quality brand-name products during the 1980s now want the same high quality, but at much lower prices. Thus, value pricing often involves redesigning products and production processes to lower costs and preserve profit margins at lower prices. For example, before launching its value menu, Taco Bell redesigned its restaurants to increase customer traffic and reduce costs. It shrank its kitchens, expanded seating space, and introduced new menu items specifically designed for easy preparation in the new, smaller kitchens.

Although the trend toward value pricing began with the recession, its roots run much deeper. The trend reflects marketers' reactions to a fundamental change in consumer attitudes, resulting from the aging of the baby boomers and their increased financial pressures. Today's "squeezed consumers"—saddled with debt acquired during the free-spending 1980s and facing increased expenses for child rearing, home buying, and the pending costs of caring for aging parents and their own health care and retirement—will continue to demand more value long after the economy improves. Even before the economy soured, buyers were beginning to rethink the price–quality equation. Thus, value pricing will likely remain a crucial strategy throughout the 1990s and beyond. Winning over tomorrow's increasingly shrewd consumers will require finding ever-new ways to offer them more for less.

*Sources:* Portions adapted from Gary Strauss, "Marketers Plea: Let's Make a Deal," *USA Today,* September 29, 1992, pp. B1–B2; Stratford Sherman, "How to Prosper in the Value Decade," *Fortune,* November 30, 1992, pp. 90–104. Also see Joseph B. White, "'Value Pricing' Is Hot As Shrewd Consumers Seek Low-Cost Quality," *Wall Street Journal,* March 12, 1991, pp. A1, A9; Faye Rice, "What Intelligent Consumers Want," *Fortune,* December 28, 1992, pp. 56–60; Bill Kelley, "The New Consumer Revealed," *Sales & Marketing Management,* May 1993, pp. 46–52; and Bradford W. Morgan, "It's the Myth of the 'Value Consumer,'" *Brandweek,* February 28, 1994, p. 17.

ture changes over time as products move through their life cycles. The company adjusts product prices to reflect changes in costs and demand and to account for variations in buyers and situations. As the competitive environment changes, the company considers when to initiate price changes and when to respond to them.

We will now examine the major dynamic pricing strategies available to management. In this section, we look at *new-product pricing strategies* for products in the introductory stage of the product life cycle. In the sections that follow, we will examine *product-mix pricing strategies* for related products in the product mix, *price-adjustment strategies* that account for customer differences and changing situations, and strategies for initiating and responding to *price changes*.

Pricing strategies usually change as the product passes through its life cycle. The introductory stage is especially challenging. We can distinguish between pricing a product that imitates existing products and pricing an innovative product that is patent protected.

A company that plans to develop an imitative new product faces a product-positioning problem. It must decide where to position the product versus competing products in terms of quality and price. Figure 10-6 shows four possible positioning strategies. First, the company might decide to use a *premium pricing* strategy—producing a high-quality product and charging the highest price. At the other extreme, it might decide on an *economy pricing* strategy—producing a lower-quality product but charging a low price. These strategies can coexist in the same market as long as the market consists of at least two groups of buyers: those who seek quality and those who seek price. Thus, Rolex offers very high-quality watches at very high prices, and Timex offers good quality watches at more affordable prices.

The *good-value* strategy represents a way to attack the premium pricer. It says, "We have high quality, but at a lower price." If this really is true, and quality-sensitive buyers believe the good-value pricer, they will sensibly buy the product and save money—unless the premium product offers more status or snob appeal. Using an *overcharging* strategy, the company overprices the product in relation to its quality. In the long run, however, customers will likely feel cheated. They will stop buying the product and will complain to others about it. Thus, this strategy should be avoided.

Companies bringing out an innovative, patent-protected product face the challenge of setting prices for the first time. They can choose between two strategies: *market-skimming pricing* and *market-penetration pricing*.

**Market-skimming pricing**
Setting a high price for a new product to skim maximum revenues layer by layer from the segments that are willing to pay the high price; the company makes fewer, but more profitable, sales.

## MARKET-SKIMMING PRICING

Many companies that invent new products initially set high prices to skim revenues layer by layer from the market. Intel is a prime user of this strategy, called **market-skimming pricing**. When Intel first introduces a new computer chip, it charges the highest price that it can, given the benefits of the new chip over competing chips. It sets a price that makes it *just* worthwhile for some segments of

**FIGURE 10-6**
*Price–quality strategies*

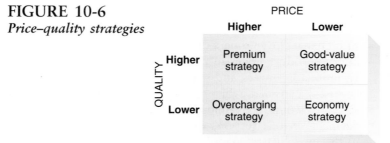

| | | PRICE | |
|---|---|---|---|
| | | Higher | Lower |
| QUALITY | Higher | Premium strategy | Good-value strategy |
| | Lower | Overcharging strategy | Economy strategy |

*Rolex pursues a premium pricing strategy, selling very high quality watches at a high price. In contrast, Timex uses a value-pricing strategy, offering good quality watches at more affordable prices.*

the market to adopt computers containing the chip. As initial sales slow down, and as competitors threaten to introduce similar chips, Intel lowers the price to draw in a new price-sensitive layer of customers.

For example, when Intel first brought out its Pentium chips, it priced them at about $1,000 each. As a result, computer producers priced their first Pentium PCs at $3,500 or more, attracting as customers only serious computer users and business buyers. However, after introduction, Intel cut Pentium prices by 30 percent per year, eventually allowing the price of Pentium PCs to drop into the typical price range of home buyers. In this way, Intel skimmed a maximum amount of revenue from the various segments of the market.[11]

Market skimming makes sense only under certain conditions. First, the product's quality and image must support its higher price, and enough buyers must want the product at that price. Second, the costs of producing a smaller volume cannot be so high that they cancel the advantage of charging more. Finally, competitors must not be able to enter the market easily and undercut the high price.

## MARKET-PENETRATION PRICING

Market-penetration pricing

Setting a low price for a new product in order to attract a large number of buyers and a large market share.

Rather than setting a high initial price to *skim* off small but profitable market segments, some companies use **market-penetration pricing.** They set a low initial price in order to *penetrate* the market quickly and deeply—to attract a large number of buyers quickly and win a large market share. The high sales volume results in falling costs, allowing the company to cut its price even further. For example, Dell and Gateway used penetration pricing to sell high-quality computer products through lower-cost mail-order channels. Their sales soared when IBM, Compaq, Apple, and other competitors selling through retail stores could not match their prices. Wal-Mart, Home Depot, and other discount retailers also use penetration pricing. They charge low prices to attract high volume. The high volume results in lower costs which, in turn, let the discounters keep prices low.

Several conditions favor setting a low price. First, the market must be highly price sensitive so that a low price produces more market growth. Second, production and distribution costs must fall as sales volume increases. Finally, the low price must help keep out the competition—otherwise, the price advantage may be only temporary. For example, Dell and Gateway faced difficult times when IBM and Compaq established their own direct distribution channels.

# ▶ PRODUCT-MIX PRICING STRATEGIES

The strategy for setting a product's price often has to be changed when the product is part of a product mix. In this case, the firm looks for a set of prices that maximizes the profits on the total product mix. Pricing is difficult because the various products have related demand and costs and face different degrees of competition. We will now take a closer look at five product-mix pricing situations: *product-line pricing, optional-product pricing, captive-product pricing, by-product pricing,* and *product-bundle pricing.*

## PRODUCT LINE PRICING

Companies usually develop product lines rather than single products. For example, Snapper makes many different lawn mowers, ranging from simple walk-behind versions priced at $259.95, $299.95, and $399.95, to elaborate riding mowers

*Product-line pricing: Infinity offers a line of home stereo speakers at prices ranging from $275 to $50,000 per pair.*

priced at $1,000 or more. Each successive lawn mower in the line offers more features. Similarly, Kodak offers not just one type of film, but an assortment, including regular Kodak film, higher-priced Kodak Royal Gold film for special occasions, and a lower-priced seasonal film called Funtime that competes with store brands. It offers each brand in a variety of exposures and film speeds. In **product-line pricing,** management must decide on the price steps to set between the various products in a line.

> **Product-line pricing**
> Setting the price steps between various products in a line, based on cost differences between products, customer evaluations of different features, and competitors' prices.

The price steps should take into account cost differences between the products in the line, customer evaluations of their different features, and competitors' prices. In many industries, sellers use well-established *price points* for the products in their line. Thus, men's clothing stores might carry men's suits at three price levels: $185, $325, and $495. The customer probably will associate low-, average-, and high-quality suits with the three price points. Even if the three prices are raised a little, men will normally buy suits at their own preferred price points. The seller's task is to establish perceived quality differences that support the price differences.

## OPTIONAL-PRODUCT PRICING

> **Optional-product pricing**
> Pricing optional or accessory products that are being sold along with a main product.

Many companies use **optional-product pricing**—offering to sell optional or accessory products along with their main product. For example, a car buyer may choose to order power windows, cruise control, and a radio with a CD player. Pricing these options is a sticky problem. Automobile companies have to decide which items to include in the base price and which to offer as options. For many years, U.S. auto companies' normal pricing strategy was to offer a stripped-down model at a low price to pull people into the showrooms, and then to devote most of the showroom space to feature-loaded cars at higher prices. The economy model was stripped of so many comforts and features that most buyers rejected it. Now, U.S. automakers have taken a cue from Japanese carmakers by including many popular options in the sticker price. At General Motors and Ford, a value-priced or special-edition car comes with a fixed set of popular options such as air conditioning, power windows and door locks, and a rear window defroster, offered at a package price.

## CAPTIVE-PRODUCT PRICING

> **Captive-product pricing**
> Setting a price for products that must be used along with a main product, such as razor blades, camera film, and computer software.

Companies that make products that must be used in conjunction with a main product are practicing **captive-product pricing.** Examples of captive products are razor blades, camera film, and computer software. Producers of the main products (razors, cameras, and computers) often price them low and set high markups on the supplies. Thus, Polaroid prices its cameras low because it makes its profits on the film that it sells. And Gillette sells low-priced razors but makes money on the replacement blades. Camera makers who do not sell supplies have to price their main products higher in order to make the same overall profit.

In the case of services, this strategy is called *two-part pricing*. The price of the service is broken into a *fixed fee* plus a *variable usage rate*. Thus, a telephone company charges a monthly rate (the fixed fee) plus charges for calls beyond some minimum number (the variable usage rate). Amusement parks charge admission plus fees for food, midway attractions, and rides over a minimum number. The service firm must decide how much to charge for the basic service and how much for the variable usage. The fixed amount should be low enough to induce usage of the service; profit can be made on the variable fees.

## BY-PRODUCT PRICING

**By-product pricing**
Setting a price for by-products in order to make the main product's price more competitive.

In producing processed meats, petroleum products, chemicals, and other products, there are often by-products. If the by-products have no value and if getting rid of them is costly, this affects the pricing of the main product. Using **by-product pricing,** the manufacturer seeks a market for these by-products and accepts any price that covers more than the cost of storing and delivering them. This practice allows the seller to reduce the main product's price in order to make it more competitive. By-products can even be profitable. For example, many lumber mills have begun to sell bark chips and sawdust profitably as decorative mulch for home and commercial landscaping.

Sometimes companies don't realize how valuable their by-products are. For example, most zoos don't realize that one of their by-products—their occupants' manure—can be an excellent source of additional revenue. But the Zoo-Doo Compost Company has helped many zoos understand the costs and opportunities involved with these by-products. Zoo-Doo licenses its name to zoos and receives royalties on manure sales. "Many zoos don't even know how much manure they are producing or the cost of disposing of it," explains president and founder Pierce Ledbetter.[12] Zoos are often so pleased with any savings that they can find on disposal that they don't think to move into active by-product sales. However, sales of the aromatic by-product can be substantial. So far, novelty sales have been the largest, with tiny containers of Zoo Doo (and even "Love, Love Me Doo" valentines) available in 160 zoo stores and 700 additional retail outlets. For the long-term market, Zoo-Doo looks to organic gardeners who buy 15 to 70 pounds of manure at a time. Zoo Doo is already planning a "Dung of the Month" club to reach this lucrative by-products market.

## PRODUCT-BUNDLE PRICING

**Product-bundle pricing**
Combining several products and offering the bundle at a reduced price.

Using **product-bundle pricing,** sellers often combine several of their products and offer the bundle at a reduced price. Thus, theaters and sports teams sell season tickets at less cost per game than single tickets; hotels sell specially priced packages that include room, meals, and entertainment; computer makers include attractive software packages with their personal computers. Price bundling can promote the sales of products that consumers might not otherwise buy, but the combined price must be low enough to get them to buy the bundle.[13]

## ▶PRICE-ADJUSTMENT STRATEGIES

Companies usually adjust their basic prices to account for various customer differences and changing situations. Here we examine six price-adjustment strategies: *discount and allowance pricing, segmented pricing, psychological pricing, promotional pricing, geographical pricing,* and *international pricing.*

## DISCOUNT AND ALLOWANCE PRICING

**Discount**
A straight reduction in price on purchases during a stated period of time.

Most companies adjust their basic price to reward customers for certain responses, such as early payment of bills, volume purchases, and off-season buying. These price adjustments—called *discounts* and *allowances*—can take many forms.

A **discount** is a straight reduction in price on purchases during a stated period of time. Sellers use discounts to adjust prices for different buyers and purchase situations. A *cash discount* is a price reduction to buyers who pay their bills promptly. A typical example is "2/10, net 30," which means that although payment is due within 30 days, the buyer can deduct 2 percent if the bill is paid within 10 days. The discount must be granted to all buyers meeting these terms. Such discounts are customary in many industries and help to improve the sellers' cash situation and reduce bad debts and credit-collection costs.

A *quantity discount* is a price reduction to buyers who purchase in large volume. A typical example might be "$10 per unit for less than 100 units, $9 per unit for 100 or more units." By law, quantity discounts must be offered equally to all customers and must not exceed the seller's cost savings associated with selling large quantities. These savings include lower selling, inventory, and transportation expenses. Discounts provide an incentive to the customer to buy more from one given seller, rather than from many different sources.

A *functional discount* (also called a *trade discount*) is offered by the seller to trade channel members who perform certain functions, such as selling, storing, and record keeping. Manufacturers may offer different functional discounts to different trade channels because of the varying services that they perform, but manufacturers must offer the same functional discounts within each trade channel.

A *seasonal discount* is a price reduction to buyers who purchase merchandise or services out of season. For example, lawn and garden equipment manufacturers offer seasonal discounts to retailers during the fall and winter to encourage early ordering in anticipation of the heavy spring and summer selling seasons. Hotels, motels, and airlines offer seasonal discounts in their slower selling periods. Seasonal discounts allow the seller to keep production steady during an entire year.

**Allowance**
Promotional money paid by manufacturers to retailers who agree to feature the manufacturer's products in some way.

**Allowances** are another type of reduction from the list price. For example, *trade-in allowances* are price reductions given for turning in an old item when buying a new one. Trade-in allowances are most common in the automobile industry, but are also given for other durable goods. *Promotional allowances* are payments or price reductions to reward dealers for participating in advertising and sales-support programs.

## SEGMENTED PRICING

**Segmented pricing**
Selling products or services at two or more prices, even though the difference in prices is not based on differences in costs.

Companies often adjust their basic prices to allow for differences in customers, products, and locations. In **segmented pricing,** the company sells a product or service at two or more prices, even though the difference in prices is not based on differences in costs.

Segmented pricing takes several forms. Under customer-segment pricing, different customers pay different prices for the same product or service. Museums, for example, will charge a lower admission for students and senior citizens. Under *product-form pricing,* different versions of the product are priced differently, but not according to differences in their costs. For instance, Black & Decker sells its most expensive iron for $54.98, which is $12 more than the price of its next most expensive iron. The top model has a self-cleaning feature, yet this extra feature costs only a few more dollars to make. Using *location pricing,* a company charges different prices for different locations, even though the cost of offering each location is the same. For instance, theaters vary their seat prices because of audience preferences for certain locations, and state universities charge higher tuition for out-of-state students. Finally, using *time pricing,* a firm varies its price by the season, the month, the day, and even the hour. Public utilities vary the prices that they charge commercial users by time of day and weekend versus weekday. The telephone company offers lower "off-peak" charges, and resorts give seasonal discounts.

For segmented pricing to be an effective strategy, certain conditions must exist. The market must be segmentable, and the segments must show different degrees of demand. Members of the segment paying the lower price should not be able to turn around and resell the product to the segment paying the higher price. Competitors should not be able to undersell the firm in the segment being charged the higher price. Nor should the costs of segmenting and watching the market exceed the extra revenue obtained from the price difference. The practice should not lead to customer resentment and ill will. Finally, the segmented pricing must be legal.

## PSYCHOLOGICAL PRICING

Price says something about the product. For example, many consumers use price to judge quality. A $100 bottle of perfume may contain only $3 worth of scent, but some people are willing to pay the $100 because this price indicates something special.

**Psychological pricing**
A pricing approach that considers the psychology of prices and not simply the economics; the price is used to say something about the product.

In using **psychological pricing,** sellers consider the psychology of prices and not simply the economics. For example, one study of the relationship between price and quality on perceptions of cars found that consumers assume that higher-priced cars have higher quality.[14] By the same token, higher-quality cars are judged by consumers to be even higher priced than they actually are. When consumers can determine the quality of a product by examining it or by calling on past experience with it, they rely less on price as an indication of quality. When consumers cannot judge quality because they lack the information or skill, price becomes an important quality signal.

For example, Heublein effectively used price to signal quality for its Smirnoff vodka, America's leading brand. Some years ago, Smirnoff was attacked by another brand, Wolfschmidt, priced at one dollar less per bottle. Instead of lowering the price of Smirnoff by a dollar, Heublein raised the price by a dollar and put the increased revenue into advertising. At the same time, the company introduced a new brand, Relska, to compete with Wolfschmidt and still another brand, Popov, priced even lower than Wolfschmidt. This product-line pricing strategy positioned Smirnoff as the elite brand and Wolfschmidt as an ordinary brand. Heublein's clever tactics produced a large increase in its overall profits. Using price as a signal, Heublein now sells roughly the same product at three different quality positions.

**Reference prices**
Prices that buyers carry in their minds and refer to when looking at a given product.

Another aspect of psychological pricing is **reference prices**—prices that buyers carry in their minds and refer to when looking at a given product. The reference price might be formed by noting current prices, remembering past prices, or assessing the buying situation. Sellers can influence or use these consumers' reference prices when setting price. For example, a company could display its product next to more expensive ones in order to imply that it belongs in the same class. Department stores often sell women's clothing in separate departments differentiated by price; clothing found in the more expensive department is assumed to be of better quality. Companies also influence consumers' reference prices by stating high manufacturer's suggested prices, by indicating that the product was originally priced much higher, or by pointing to a competitor's higher price.

Even small differences in price can suggest product differences. Consider a stereo priced at $300 compared with one priced at $299.95. The actual price difference is only five cents, but the psychological difference can be much greater. For example, some consumers will see the $299.95 as a price in the $200 range rather than the $300 range. Whereas the $299.95 will more likely be seen as a bargain price, the $300 price suggests more quality. Some psychologists even argue that each digit has symbolic and visual qualities that should be considered in pricing. Thus, 8 is round and even and creates a soothing effect, whereas 7 is angular and creates a jarring effect.[15]

## PROMOTIONAL PRICING

**Promotional pricing**
Temporarily pricing products below list price, and sometimes even below cost, to increase short-run sales.

With **promotional pricing**, companies temporarily price their products below list price and sometimes even below cost. Promotional pricing takes several forms. Supermarkets and department stores will price a few products as *loss leaders* to attract customers to the store in the hope that they will buy other items at normal markups. Sellers will also use *special-event pricing* in certain seasons to draw more customers. Thus, linens are promotionally priced every January to attract weary Christmas shoppers back into stores. Manufacturers will sometimes offer *cash rebates* to consumers who buy the product from dealers within a specified time; the manufacturer sends the rebate directly to the customer. Rebates have recently been popular with auto makers and producers of durable goods and small

*Promotional pricing: Companies often reduce their prices temporarily to attract customers and boost sales.*

nm presents
the spring clearance

**33% to 50% off**
women's leisure sportswear,
dresses and suits,
candy, and epicure items.

**40% off**
women's career sportswear,
fashion accessories, and jewelry.

**33% off**
women's hosiery and
intimate apparel.

**25% to 33% off**
children's merchandise.

Sale runs April 8–14;
shop early for the best selection.

Savings off original prices. Interim markdowns
may have been taken. Selected merchandise only.

appliances. Some manufacturers offer *low-interest financing, longer warranties,* or *free maintenance* to reduce the consumer's "price." This practice has recently become a favorite of the auto industry. Or, the seller may simply offer *discounts* from normal prices to increase sales and reduce inventories.

# GEOGRAPHIC PRICING

**Geographic pricing**
Deciding how to price products for customers located in different parts of the country or world.

A company also must decide on its **geographic pricing** policy—how to price its products to customers located in different parts of the country or world. Should the company risk losing the business of more distant customers by charging them higher prices to cover the higher shipping costs? Or should the company charge all customers the same prices regardless of location? We will look at five geographic pricing strategies for the following hypothetical situation:

> The Peerless Paper Company is located in Atlanta, Georgia, and sells paper products to customers all over the United States. The cost of freight is high and affects the companies from whom customers buy their paper. Peerless wants to establish a geographic pricing policy. It is trying to determine how to price a $100 order to three specific customers: Customer A (Atlanta); Customer B (Bloomington, Indiana), and Customer C (Compton, California).

One option is for Peerless to ask each customer to pay the shipping cost from the Atlanta factory to the customer's location. All three customers would pay the same factory price of $100, with Customer A paying, say, $10 for shipping; Customer B, $15; and Customer C, $25. Called *FOB-origin pricing*, this practice means that the goods are placed *free on board* a carrier. At that point, the title and responsibility pass to the customer, who pays the freight from the factory to the destination. Because each customer picks up its own cost, supporters of FOB pricing feel that this is the fairest way to assess freight charges. The disadvantage, however, is that Peerless will be a high-cost firm to distant customers.

*Uniform delivered pricing* is the exact opposite of FOB pricing. Here, the company charges the same price plus freight to all customers, regardless of their location. The freight charge is set at the average freight cost. Suppose this is $15. Uniform delivered pricing therefore results in a higher charge to the Atlanta customer (who pays $15 freight instead of $10) and a lower charge to the Compton customer (who pays $15 instead of $25). On the one hand, the Atlanta customer would rather buy paper from another local paper company that uses FOB-origin pricing. On the other hand, Peerless has a better chance of winning over the California customer. Other advantages of uniform delivered pricing are that it is fairly easy to administer and it lets the firm advertise its price nationally.

*Zone pricing* falls between FOB-origin pricing and uniform delivered pricing. The company sets up two or more zones. All customers within a given zone pay a single total price; the more distant the zone, the higher the price. For example, Peerless might set up an east zone and charge $10 freight to all customers in this zone, a midwest zone in which it charges $15, and a west zone in which it charges $25. In this way, the customers within a given price zone receive no price advantage from the company. For example, customers in Atlanta and Boston pay the same total price to Peerless. The complaint, however, is that the Atlanta customer is paying part of the Boston customer's freight cost.

Using *basing-point pricing*, the seller selects a given city as a "basing point" and charges all customers the freight cost from that city to the customer location, regardless of the city from which the goods are actually shipped. For example, Peerless might set Chicago as the basing point and charge all customers $100 plus the freight from Chicago to their locations. This means that an Atlanta customer pays the freight cost from Chicago to Atlanta, even though the goods may be shipped from Atlanta. If all sellers used the same basing-point city, delivered prices would be the same for all customers, and price competition would be eliminated. Industries such as sugar, cement, steel, and automobiles used basing-point pricing for years, but this method has become less popular today. Some companies set up multiple basing points to create more flexibility; they quote freight charges from the basing-point city nearest to the customer.

Finally, the seller who is anxious to do business with a certain customer or geographical area might use *freight-absorption pricing*. Using this strategy, the seller absorbs all or part of the actual freight charges in order to get the desired business. The seller might reason that if it can get more business, its average costs will fall and more than compensate for its extra freight cost. Freight-absorption pricing is used for market penetration and to hold on to increasingly competitive markets.

## INTERNATIONAL PRICING

Companies that market their products internationally must decide what prices to charge in the different countries in which they operate. In some cases, a company can set a uniform worldwide price. For example, Boeing sells its jetliners at about the same price everywhere, whether in the United States, Europe, or a Third World country. However, most companies adjust their prices to reflect local market conditions and cost considerations.

The price that a company should charge in a specific country depends on many factors, including economic conditions, competitive situations, laws and regulations, and development of the wholesaling and retailing system. Consumer perceptions and preferences may also vary from country to country, calling for different prices. Or the company may have different marketing objectives in various world markets, which require changes in pricing strategy. For example, Sony might introduce a new product into mature markets in highly developed countries with the goal of quickly gaining mass-market share, which would call for a penetration pricing strategy. In contrast, it might enter a less developed market by targeting smaller, less price-sensitive segments. In this case, market-skimming pricing makes sense.

Costs play an important role in setting international prices. Travelers abroad are often surprised to find that goods that are relatively inexpensive at home may carry outrageously higher price tags in other countries. A pair of Levis selling for $30 in the United States goes for about $63 in Tokyo and $88 in Paris. A McDonald's Big Mac selling for a modest $2.25 here costs $5.75 in Moscow. And an Oral-B toothbrush selling for 19 cents at home costs 90 cents in China. Conversely, a Gucci handbag going for only $60 in Milan, Italy, fetches $240 in the United States. In some cases, such *price escalation* may result from differences in selling strategies or market conditions. In most instances, however, it is simply a result of the higher costs of selling in foreign markets—the additional costs of modifying the product, higher shipping and insurance costs, import tariffs and taxes, costs associated with exchange-rate fluctuations, and higher channel and physical distribution costs.

*International price escalation: A pair of Levi's selling for $44 in the United States goes for over $60 in a Levi's boutique in Korea and other Pacific Rim countries.*

For example, Campbell found that its distribution costs in the United Kingdom were 30 percent higher than in the United States. U.S. retailers typically purchase soup in large quantities—48-can cases of a single soup by the dozens, hundreds, or carloads. In contrast, English grocers purchase soup in small quantities—typically in 24-can cases of *assorted* soups. Each case must be hand-packed for shipment. To handle these small orders, Campbell had to add a costly extra wholesale level to its European channel. The smaller orders also mean that English retailers order two or three times as often as their U.S. counterparts, bumping up billing and order costs. These and other factors caused Campbell to charge much higher prices for its soups in the United Kingdom.[16]

Thus, international pricing presents some special problems and complexities. We discuss international pricing issues in more detail in Chapter 16.

## ▶PRICE CHANGES

After developing their pricing structures and strategies, companies often face situations in which they must initiate price changes or respond to price changes by competitors.

### INITIATING PRICE CHANGES

In some cases, the company may find it desirable to initiate either a price cut or a price increase. In both cases, it must anticipate possible buyer and competitor reactions.

## Initiating Price Cuts

Several situations may lead a firm to consider cutting its price. One such circumstance is excess capacity. In this case, the firm needs more business and cannot get it through increased sales effort, product improvement, or other measures. It may drop its "follow-the-leader" pricing—charging about the same price as their leading competitor—and aggressively cut prices to boost sales. But as the airline, construction equipment, and other industries have learned in recent years, cutting prices in an industry loaded with excess capacity may lead to price wars as competitors try to hold on to market share.

Another situation leading to price changes is falling market share in the face of strong price competition. Several American industries—automobiles, consumer electronics, cameras, watches, and steel, for example—lost market share to Japanese competitors whose high-quality products carried lower prices than did their American counterparts. In response, American companies resorted to more aggressive pricing action. General Motors, for example, cut its subcompact car prices by 10 percent on the West Coast, where Japanese competition was strongest.[17]

A company may also cut prices in a drive to dominate the market through lower costs. Either the company starts with lower costs than its competitors or it cuts prices in the hope of gaining market share that will further cut costs through larger volume. Bausch & Lomb used an aggressive low-cost, low-price strategy to become an early leader in the competitive soft contact lens market.

## Initiating Price Increases

In contrast, many companies have had to *raise* prices in recent years. They do this knowing that the price increases may be resented by customers, dealers, and even their own sales force. Yet a successful price increase can greatly increase profits. For example, if the company's profit margin is 3 percent of sales, a 1 percent price increase will increase profits by 33 percent if sales volume is unaffected.

A major factor in price increases is cost inflation. Rising costs squeeze profit margins and lead companies to regular rounds of price increases. Companies often raise their prices by more than the cost increase in anticipation of further inflation. Another factor leading to price increases is overdemand: When a company cannot supply all its customers' needs, it can raise its prices, ration products to customers, or both.

Companies can increase their prices in a number of ways to keep up with rising costs. Prices can be raised almost invisibly by dropping discounts and adding higher-priced units to the line. Or prices can be pushed up openly. In passing price increases on to customers, the company should avoid the image of price gouging. The price increases should be supported with a company communication program telling customers why prices are being increased. The company sales force should help customers find ways to economize.

Where possible, the company should consider ways to meet higher costs or demand without raising prices. For example, it can shrink the product instead of raising the price, as candy bar manufacturers often do. Or it can substitute less expensive ingredients, or remove certain product features, packaging, or services. Or it can "unbundle" its products and services, removing and separately pricing elements that were formerly part of the offer. IBM, for example, now offers computer systems training and consulting as a separately priced service.

*Buyer reactions to price changes? What would you think if the price of Joy was suddenly cut in half?*

## Buyer Reactions to Price Changes

Whether the price is raised or lowered, the action affects buyers, competitors, distributors, and suppliers and may interest government as well. Customers do not always interpret prices in a straightforward way. They may view a price *cut* in several ways. For example, what would you think if Sony were suddenly to cut its VCR prices in half? You might think that these VCRs are about to be replaced by newer models or that they have some fault and are not selling well. You might think that Sony is abandoning the VCR business and may not stay in this business long enough to supply future parts. You might believe that quality has been reduced. Or you might think that the price will come down even further and that it will pay to wait and see.

Similarly, a price *increase*, which normally would lower sales, may have some positive meanings for buyers. What would you think if Sony *raised* the price of its latest VCR model? On the one hand, you might think that the item is very "hot" and may be unobtainable unless you buy it soon. Or you might think that the recorder is an unusually good value. On the other hand, you might think that Sony is greedy and charging what the traffic will bear.

## Competitor Reactions to Price Changes

A firm considering a price change has to worry about the reactions of its competitors as well as its customers. Competitors are most likely to react when the number of firms involved is small, the product is uniform, and the buyers are well informed.

How can the firm figure out the likely reactions of its competitors? If the firm faces one large competitor, and if the competitor tends to react in a set way to price changes, that reaction can be easily anticipated. But if the competitor treats each price change as a fresh challenge and reacts according to its self-interest, the company will have to figure out just what makes up the competitor's self-interest at the time.

The problem is complex because, like the customer, the competitor can interpret a company price cut in many ways. It might think that the company is trying to grab a larger market share, that the company is doing poorly and trying to boost its sales, or that the company wants the whole industry to cut prices to increase total demand.

When there are several competitors, the company must guess each competitor's likely reaction. If all competitors behave alike, this amounts to analyzing only a typical competitor. In contrast, if the competitors do not behave alike—perhaps because of differences in size, market shares, or policies—then separate analyses are necessary. However, if some competitors will match the price change, there is good reason to expect that the rest will also match it.

## RESPONDING TO PRICE CHANGES

Here we reverse the question and ask how a firm should respond to a price change by a competitor. The firm needs to consider several issues: Why did the competitor change the price? Was it to take more market share, to use excess capacity, to meet changing cost conditions, or to lead an industrywide price change? Is the price change temporary or permanent? What will happen to the company's market share and profits if it does not respond? Are other companies going to respond? And what are the competitor's and other firms' responses to each possible reaction likely to be?

Besides these issues, the company must make a broader analysis. It has to consider its own product's stage in the life cycle, the product's importance in the company's product mix, the intentions and resources of the competitor, and the possible consumer reactions to price changes. The company cannot always make an extended analysis of its alternatives at the time of a price change, however. The competitor may have spent much time making this decision, but the company may have to react within hours or days. About the only way to cut reaction time is to plan ahead both for possible competitor price changes and for possible responses.

Figure 10-7 shows the ways that a company might assess and respond to a competitor's price cut. Once the company has determined that the competitor has cut its price and that this price reduction is likely to harm company sales and profits, it might decide simply to hold its current price and profit margin. The company might believe that it will not lose too much market share, or that it would lose too much profit if it reduced its own price. It might decide that it should wait and respond when it has more information on the effects of the competitor's price change. For now, it might be willing to hold on to good customers, while giving up the poorer ones to the competitor. The argument against this holding strategy, however, is that the competitor may get stronger and more confident as its sales increase, and that the company may end up waiting too long to act.

If the company decides that effective action can and should be taken, it might make any of four responses. First, it could *reduce its price* to match the competitor's price. It may decide that the market is price sensitive, and that it would lose too much market share to the lower-priced competition. Or it might worry that recapturing lost market share later would be too hard. Cutting price will reduce the company's profits in the short run. Some companies might also reduce their product quality, services, and marketing communications to retain profit margins,

**FIGURE 10-7**
*Assessing and responding to competitor price changes*

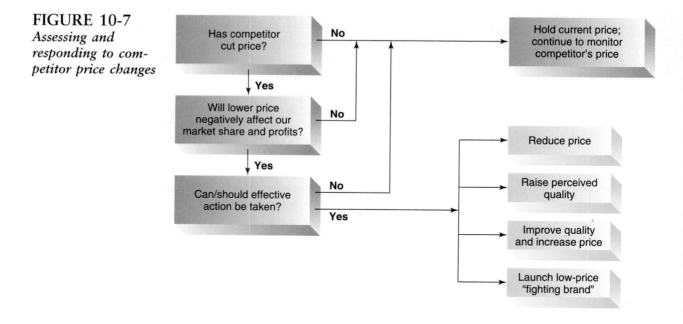

but this ultimately will hurt long-run market share. The company should try to maintain its quality as it cuts prices.

Alternatively, the company might maintain its price but *raise the perceived quality* of its offer. It could improve its communications, stressing the relative quality of its product over that of the lower-price competitor. The firm may find it cheaper to maintain price and spend money to improve its perceived value than to cut price and operate at a lower margin.

Or, the company might *improve quality and increase price,* moving its brand into a higher price position. The higher quality justifies the higher price, which in turn preserves the company's higher margins. Or the company can hold price on the current product and introduce a new brand at a higher price position.

Finally, the company might *launch a low-price "fighting brand."* Often, one of the best responses is to add lower-price items to the line or to create a separate lower-price brand. This is necessary if the particular market segment being lost is price sensitive and will not respond to arguments of higher quality. Thus, when attacked on price by Fuji, Kodak introduced low-priced Funtime film. When challenged on price by store brands and other low-priced entrants, Procter & Gamble turned a number of its brands into fighting brands, including Luvs disposable diapers, Joy dishwashing detergent, and Camay beauty soap. In response to price pressures, Miller cut the price of its High Life brand by 20 percent in most markets, and sales jumped 9 percent in less than a year.[18]

Pricing strategies and tactics form an important element of a company's marketing mix. In setting prices, companies must carefully consider a great many internal and external factors before choosing a price that will give them the greatest competitive advantage in selected target markets. However, companies are not usually free to charge whatever prices they wish. Several laws restrict pricing practices, and a number of ethical considerations affect pricing decisions. Marketing at Work 10-4 discusses the many public policy issues surrounding pricing.

## MARKETING AT WORK 10-4

# PUBLIC POLICY AND PRICING

When Russia lifted controls on bread prices as part of its dramatic move toward a free-market economy, Moscow bakers phoned around each morning to agree on regular rounds of price increases. This caused the *Wall Street Journal* to comment: "They still don't get it!" Those who have grown up under a well-regulated, free-market economy understand that such price fixing is clearly against the rules of fair competition. Setting prices is an important element of a competitive marketplace, and many federal and state laws govern the rules of fair play in pricing.

The most important pieces of legislation affecting pricing are the Sherman, Clayton, and Robinson-Patman Acts, initially adopted to curb the formation of monopolies and to regulate business practices that might unfairly restrain trade. Because these federal statutes can be applied only to interstate commerce, some states have adopted similar provisions for companies that operate locally. Public policy on pricing centers on three potentially damaging pricing practices: price fixing, price discrimination, and deceptive pricing.

### PRICE FIXING

Federal legislation on price fixing states that sellers must set prices without talking to competitors. Otherwise, price collusion is suspected. Price fixing is illegal per se; that is, the government does not accept any excuses for price fixing. Even a simple conversation between competitors can have serious consequences. For example, during the early 1980s, American Airlines and Braniff were immersed in a price war in the Texas market. Each carrier undercut the other until both were offering absurdly low fares and each was losing money on many flights. In the heat of the battle, American's CEO, Robert Crandall, called the president of Braniff and said: "Raise your . . . fares 20 percent. I'll raise mine the next morning." Fortunately for Crandall, the Braniff president warned him off, saying, "We can't talk about pricing!" As it turns out, the phone conversation had been recorded, and the U.S. Justice Department began action against Crandall and American for price fixing. The charges were eventually dropped. The courts ruled that because Braniff had rejected Crandall's proposal, no actual collusion had occurred, and that a proposal to fix prices was not an actual violation of the law. This case and others like it have made most executives very reluctant to discuss prices in any way with competitors. In obtaining information on competitors' pricing, they rely only on openly published materials, such as trade association surveys and competitors' catalogs.

### PRICE DISCRIMINATION

The Robinson-Patman Act seeks to ensure that sellers offer the same price terms to a given level of trade. For example, every retailer is entitled to the same price terms whether the retailer is Sears or the local bicycle shop. However, price discrimination is allowed if the seller can prove that its costs are different when selling to different retailers—for example, that it costs less per unit to sell a large volume of bicycles to Sears than to sell a few bicycles to a local dealer. Or the seller can discriminate in its pricing if the seller manufactures different qualities of the same product for different retailers. The seller has to prove that these differences are proportional. Price differentials may also be used to "match competition" in "good faith," provided that the firm is trying to meet competitors at its own level of competition and that the price discrimination is temporary, localized, and defensive rather than offensive.

### DECEPTIVE PRICING

Deceptive pricing occurs when a seller states prices or price savings that are not actually available to consumers. Some such deceptions are difficult for consumers to discern, as when an airline advertises a low one-way fare that is available only with the purchase of a round-trip ticket, or when a retailer sets artificially high "regular" prices, then announces "sale" prices close to its previous everyday prices. Many federal and state statutes regulate against deceptive pricing practices. For

*(continued)*

example, the Automobile Information Disclosure Act requires automakers to attach a statement to new-car windows stating the manufacturer's suggested retail price, the prices of optional equipment, and the dealer's transportation charges. The FTC issues its *Guides Against Deceptive Pricing,* warning sellers not to advertise a price reduction unless it is a saving from the usual retail price, not to advertise "factory" or "wholesale" prices unless such prices are what they are claimed to be, and not to advertise comparable value prices on imperfect goods. Many states have developed retail advertising guidelines to ensure that locally advertised prices are accurately stated and clearly understood by consumers.

## OTHER REGULATED PRICING PRACTICES

Sellers also are prohibited from using *predatory pricing*—selling below cost with the intention of destroying competition. Wholesalers and retailers in over half the states face laws requiring a minimum percentage markup over their cost of merchandise plus transportation. These laws attempt to protect small sellers from larger ones who might sell items below cost to attract customers. *Resale price maintenance* is also prohibited: A manufacturer cannot require dealers to charge a specified retail price for its product. Although the seller can propose a manufacturer's *suggested* retail price to dealers, it cannot refuse to sell to a dealer who takes independent pricing action, nor can it punish the dealer by shipping late or denying advertising allowances.

*Sources:* For more on public policy and pricing, see Louis W. Stern and Thomas L. Eovaldi, *Legal Aspects of Marketing Strategy* (Englewood Cliffs, NJ: Prentice Hall, 1984), Chapter 5; Robert J. Posch, *The Complete Guide to Marketing and the Law* (Englewood Cliffs, NJ: Prentice Hall, 1988), Chapter 28; and Thomas T. Nagle and Reed K. Holden, *The Strategy and Tactics of Pricing* (Englewood Cliffs, NJ: Prentice Hall, 1995), Chapter 14.

## SUMMARY

Despite the increased role of nonprice factors in the modern marketing process, *price* remains an important element in the marketing mix. Many internal and external factors influence the company's pricing decisions. *Internal factors* include the firm's *marketing objectives, marketing-mix strategy, costs,* and *organization for pricing.*

The pricing strategy is largely determined by the company's *target market and positioning objectives.* Common pricing objectives include survival, current profit maximization, market-share leadership, and product-quality leadership. However, price is only one of the *marketing-mix tools* that the company uses to accomplish its objectives, and pricing decisions affect and are affected by product design, distribution, and promotion decisions. *Costs* set the floor for the company's price: The price must cover all the costs of making and selling the product, plus a fair rate of return. Finally, management must decide who within the *organization* is responsible for setting price.

*External factors* that influence pricing decisions include the nature of the market and demand; competitors' prices and offers; and factors such as the economy, reseller needs, and government actions. The seller's pricing freedom varies with different types of markets. Pricing is especially challenging in markets characterized by monopolistic competition or oligopoly. In the end, however, the consumer decides whether the company has set the right price. The consumer weighs the price against the perceived values of using the product: If the price exceeds the sum of the values, consumers will not buy the product.

Consumers differ in the values that they assign to different product features, and marketers often vary their pricing strategies for different price segments. When assessing the market and demand, the company estimates the demand curve, which shows the probable quantity purchased per period at alternative price levels. The more *inelastic* the demand, the higher the company can set its price. *Demand* and *consumer value perceptions* set the ceiling for prices.

Consumers compare a product's price to the prices of *competitors'* products. A company must learn the price and quality of competitors' offers and use them as a starting point for its own pricing.

The company can select one or a combination of three general pricing approaches: the *cost-based approach* (cost-plus pricing, break-even analysis, and target profit pricing); the *value-based approach* (value-based pricing); and the *competition-based approach* (going-rate or sealed-bid pricing).

Pricing is a dynamic process. Companies design a *pricing structure* that covers all their products. They change this structure over time and adjust it to account for different customers and situations. Pricing strategies usually change as a product passes through its life cycle. The company can decide on one of several price–quality strategies for introducing an imitative product. In pricing innovative new products, it can follow a *skimming policy* by initially setting high prices to "skim" the maximum amount of revenue from various segments of the market. Or it can use *penetration pricing* by setting a low initial price to win a large market share.

When the product is part of a product mix, the firm searches for a set of prices that will maximize the profits from the total mix. The company decides on *price steps* for items in its product line and on the pricing of *optional products*, *captive products*, *by-products*, and *product bundles*.

Companies apply a variety of *price-adjustment strategies* to account for differences in consumer segments and situations. One is *discount and allowance pricing*, in which the company establishes cash discounts, quantity discounts, functional discounts, seasonal discounts, and allowances. A second is *segmented pricing*, in which the company sets different prices for different customers, product forms, places, or times. A third is *psychological pricing*, in which the company adjusts the price to better communicate a product's intended position. A fourth is *promotional pricing*, in which the company decides on loss-leader pricing, special-event pricing, and psychological discounting. A fifth is *geographic pricing*, in which the company decides how to price to distant customers, choosing from such alternatives as FOB pricing, uniform delivered pricing, zone pricing, basing-point pricing, and freight-absorption pricing. A sixth is *international pricing*, in which the company adjusts its price to meet different conditions and expectations in different world markets.

When a firm considers initiating a *price change*, it must consider customers' and competitors' reactions. Customers' reactions are influenced by the meaning that customers perceive in the price change. Competitors' reactions flow from a set reaction policy or a fresh analysis of each situation. The firm that faces a price change initiated by a competitor must try to understand the competitor's intent as well as the likely duration and impact of the change. If a swift reaction is desirable, the firm should preplan its reactions to different possible price actions by competitors. When facing a competitor's price change, the company might sit tight, reduce its own price, raise perceived quality, improve quality and raise price, or launch a fighting brand.

## KEY TERMS

Allowances

Break-even pricing (target profit pricing)

By-product pricing

Captive-product pricing

Competition-base pricing

Cost-plus pricing

Demand curve

Discount

Geographic pricing

Market-penetration pricing

Market-skimming pricing

Optional-product pricing

Price

Price elasticity

Product-bundle pricing

Product-line pricing

Promotional pricing

Psychological pricing

Reference prices

Segmented pricing

Target costing

Value-based pricing

Value pricing

## QUESTIONS FOR DISCUSSION

1. When Singapore Airlines announced that it was awarding Rolls-Royce PLC a $1.8 billion contract to build engines for the 61 new Boeing 777 jet airliners that it was adding to its fleet, the victory was both good news and bad news for Rolls-Royce. As the biggest sale in company history, the Singapore Airlines deal would allow Rolls-Royce to remain competitive with its chief rivals, General Electric and Pratt & Whitney. However, operating in a sluggish market where supply exceeded demand, Rolls-Royce was forced to sell the engines for less than it cost to produce them. Analyze Rolls-Royce's pricing decision in terms of the various internal and external environmental factors discussed in this chapter.

2. Detergent A is priced at $2.19 for 32 ounces, and detergent B is priced at $1.99 for 26 ounces. Which brand appears most attractive? Which is actually the better value, assuming equal quality? Is there a psychological reason to price in this way?

3. Sales of Fleischmann's gin *increased* when prices were raised 22 percent over a two-year period. Explain what this tells you about the demand curve and the elasticity of demand for Fleischmann's gin. What does this suggest about using perceived-value pricing in marketing alcoholic beverages?

4. Describe which strategy—market skimming or market penetration—these companies use in pricing their products:
   ◆ McDonald's.
   ◆ Curtis Mathes (television and other home electronics).
   ◆ Bic Corporation (pens, lighters, shavers, and related products).
   ◆ IBM.
   Are these the right strategies for these companies? Why or why not?

5. The formula for chlorine bleach is virtually identical for all brands. Clorox charges a premium price for this same product, yet remains the unchallenged market leader. What does this imply about the value of a brand name? Analyze the ethical issues involved in this type of pricing.

6. A clothing store sells men's suits at three price levels: $180, $250, and $340. If shoppers use these price points as references in comparing different suits, appraise the effect of adding a new line of suits at a cost of $280. Would you expect sales of the $250 suits to increase, decrease, or stay the same?

## APPLYING THE CONCEPTS

1. Do a pricing survey of several gasoline stations in different locations in your area. If possible, check prices at: stations at an exit ramp on a major highway, stations at a local strip of businesses, convenience stores, and a smaller station that is not near any other stations. Write down the brand of gasoline, prices of regular and premium grades, type of location, distance to the nearest competitor, and the competitor's prices. Is there a pattern to the pricing of gasoline at various outlets? Do you think that these stations are using cost-based, buyer-based, or going-rate pricing?

2. Go to your local supermarket and observe sizes and prices within product categories. Determine if the package sizes (the weight or number of units contained) are comparable across brands. Find at least two instances where a manufacturer seems to have made a smaller package in order to achieve a lower retail price. Does this appear effective? If your market has unit pricing labels, see whether the unit price is higher, lower, or the same as this brand's competitors. Does unit pricing information change your opinion about the effectiveness of this strategy?

3. Go to your local supermarket and observe sizes and prices within product categories. Determine if the package sizes (the weight of number of units contained) are comparable across brands. Find at least two instances where a manufacturer seems to have made a smaller package in order to achieve a lower retail price.

Does this appear effective? If your market has unit pricing labels, see whether the unit price is higher, lower, or the same as this brand's competitors. Does unit pricing information change your opinion about the effectiveness of this strategy?

## REFERENCES

1. Quotes from Andrea Rothman, "The Superlosers in the Supersaver War," *Business Week*, June 15, 1992, p. 44. Also see Bridget O'Brian and James S. Hirsch, "Flying Low: Simplifying Their Fares Proves More Difficult than Airlines Expected," *Wall Street Journal*, June 4, 1992, pp. A1, A5; Wendy Zellner, "The Airlines Are Killing Each Other Again," *Business Week*, June 8, 1992, p. 32; Holt Hackney, "AMR: Starting Its Descent?" *Financial World*, December 7, 1993, p. 20; and Dan Blake, "Airline Industry Finds New Ways to Lose Money," *Durham Herald-Sun*, December 12, 1994, pp. B1, B11.

2. See David J. Schwartz, *Marketing Today: A Basic Approach*, 3rd ed. (New York: Harcourt Brace Jovanovich, 1981), pp. 270–73.

3. For an excellent discussion of factors affecting pricing decisions, see Thomas T. Nagle and Reed K. Holden, *The Strategy and Tactics of Pricing*, 2nd ed. (Englewood Cliffs, NJ: Prentice Hall, Inc., 1995), Chapter 1. Also see Robert J. Dolan, "How Do You Know When the Price Is Right?" *Harvard Business Review*, September–October 1995, pp. 174–83.

4. Norton Paley, "Fancy Footwork," *Sales & Marketing Management*, July 1994, pp. 41–42.

5. Christopher Farrell, "Stuck! How Companies Cope When They Can't Raise Prices," *Business Week*, November 15, 1993, pp. 146–55. Also see John Y. Lee, "Use Target Costing to Improve Your Bottom Line," *The CPA Journal*, January 1994, pp. 68–71; and Andrew E. Serwer, "How to Escape a Price War," *Fortune*, June 13, 1994, pp. 82–90.

6. Brian Dumaine, "Closing the Innovation Gap," *Fortune*, December 2, 1991, pp. 56–62.

7. See Nagle and Holden, *The Strategy and Tactics of Pricing*, Chapter 4. For examples of price elasticity marketing studies, see "Elastic Brands: Marketing in Britain," *The Economist*, November 9, 1994, p. 75; and Stephen J. Hoch, Byung-Do Kim, Alan L. Montgomery, and Peter E. Rossi, "Determinants of Store-Level Price Elasticity," *Journal of Marketing Research*, February 1995, pp. 17–29.

8. Melissa Campanelli, "The Price to Pay," *Sales & Marketing Management*, September 1994, pp. 96–102.

9. See Stephen J. Hoch, Xavier Drèze, and Mary E. Purk, "EDLP, Hi-Lo, and Margin Arithmetic," *Journal of Marketing*, October 1994, pp. 16–27.

10. See Adam Bryant, "Many Companies Try to Simplify Pricing," *New York Times*, October 18, 1992, pp. 4, 6; Stephanie Strom, "Retailers' Latest Tactic: If It Says $15, It Means $15," *New York Times*, September 29, 1992, p. D1.

11. See David Kirkpatrick, "Intel Goes for Broke," *Fortune*, May 16, 1994, pp. 62–68; and Neal Boudette, "Intel Forcing Buyers into Faster Migration from 486 to Pentium," *PC Week*, April 24, 1995, p. 1.

12. Susan Krafft, "Love, Love Me Doo," *American Demographics*, June 1994, pp. 15–16.

13. See Nagle, *The Strategy and Tactics of Pricing*, pp. 225–28; and Manjit S. Yadav and Kent B. Monroe, "How Buyers Perceive Savings in a Bundle Price: An Examination of a Bundle's Transaction Value," *Journal of Marketing Research*, August 1993, pp. 350–58.

14. Gary M. Erickson and Johnny K. Johansson, "The Role of Price in Multi-Attribute Product Evaluations," *Journal of Consumer Research*, September 1985, pp. 195–99.

15. For more reading on reference prices and psychological pricing, see Nagle and Holden, *The Strategy and Tactics of Pricing*, Chapter 12; and K. N. Rajendran and Gerard J. Tellis, "Contextual and Temporal Components of Reference Price," *Journal of Marketing*, January 1994, pp. 22–34.

16. Philip R. Cateora, *International Marketing*, 7th ed. (Homewood, IL: Irwin, 1990), p. 540.

17. For more on price cutting and its consequences, see Kathleen Madigan, "The Latest Mad Plunge of the Price Slashers," *Business Week*, May 11, 1992, p. 36; and Bill Saporito, "Why the Price Wars Never End," *Fortune*, March 23, 1992, pp. 68–78.

18. Jonathon Berry and Zachary Schiller, "Attack of the Fighting Brands," *Business Week*, May 2, 1994, p. 125.

# 11

# Distribution Channels and Logistics Management

For more than 60 years, Goodyear Tire & Rubber Company sold replacement tires exclusively through its powerful network of independent Goodyear dealers. Both Goodyear and its 2,500 dealers profited from this partnership. Goodyear received the undivided loyalty of its single-brand dealers, and the dealers gained the exclusive right to sell the highly respected Goodyear tire line. In mid-1992, however, Goodyear shattered tradition and jolted its dealers by announcing that it would now sell Goodyear-brand tires through Sears auto centers, placing Goodyear dealers in direct competition with the giant retailer. This departure from the previously sacred dealer network left many dealers shaken and angry. Said one Goodyear dealer: "You feel like after 35 years of marriage, your [spouse] is stepping out on you." Said another, "I feel like they just stabbed me in the back."

Several factors forced the change in Goodyear's distribution system. During the late 1980s, massive international consolidation reshaped the tire industry, leaving only five competitors. Japan's Bridgestone acquired Firestone, Germany's Continental bought General Tire, Italy's Pirelli snapped up Armstrong, and France's Michelin acquired Uniroyal Goodrich. After six decades as the world's largest tire maker, Goodyear slipped to second behind Michelin. As the only remaining U.S.-owned tire company, instead of having its way with smaller domestic rivals, Goodyear now found itself battling for U.S. market share against large and newly strengthened international competitors.

To add to Goodyear's woes, consumers were changing how and where they bought tires. Tires have become more of an impulse item, and value-minded tire buyers were increasingly buying from cheaper, multibrand discount outlets, department stores, and warehouse clubs. The market share of these outlets had grown 30 percent in the previous five years, while that of tire dealers had fallen 4 percent. By selling exclusively through its dealer network, Goodyear simply wasn't putting its tires where many consumers were buying them. The shifts in consumer buying were also causing problems for dealers. Although Goodyear offered an ample variety of premium lines, it provided its dealers with none of the lower-priced lines that many consumers were demanding.

Entering the 1990s, Goodyear was foundering. Although it remained number one in the United States, its share of the U.S. replacement-tire market had fallen 3 percent in only five years. Battling a prolonged recession and vicious price competition from Michelin and Bridgestone, Goodyear had its first money-losing year since the Great Depression. Drastic measures were needed.

Enter new management, headed by Stanley Gault, the miracle-working manager who had transformed Rubbermaid from a sleepy Ohio rubber company into one of America's most admired market leaders. Gault took the helm in mid-1991 and moved quickly to streamline Goodyear, reducing its heavy debt, cutting costs, and selling off noncore businesses. But the biggest changes came in marketing. Under Gault, Goodyear speeded up new-product development and boosted ad spending. For example, in late 1991, it introduced four new tires simultaneously: the innovative, nonhydroplaning Aquatred, the Wrangler line for pickup trucks and vans, a fuel-efficient "green" tire, and a new high-performance Eagle model. In 1992, Goodyear brought out 12 more new tires—three times the usual number.

Gault also wasted little time in shaking up Goodyear's stodgy distribution system. In addition to selling its tires through Sears, the company began selling the Goodyear brand at Wal-Mart. Marketing research showed that one out of four Wal-Mart customers is a potential Goodyear buyer, and that these buyers come from a segment unlikely to be reached by independent Goodyear dealers. The company also began drumming up new private-label business. Its Kelly-Springfield unit soon inked a deal to sell private-label tires through Wal-Mart, and agreements with Kmart, Montgomery Ward, and even the warehouse clubs also seem likely. Goodyear has since begun exploring other new distribution options as well. For example, it is now testing a no-frills, quick-serve discount store concept—Just Tires—designed to fend off low-priced competitors. In another test, it recently began selling Goodyear-brand tires to multibrand retailers in selected U.S. cities.

The marketing, distribution, and other changes have Goodyear rolling again. In its first year under Gault, Goodyear's sales and earnings soared, its market share increased 1 percent, and its stock price quadrupled. In 1993 and 1994, Goodyear made more profit than its nine direct competitors combined. The expanded distribution system appears to be a significant plus, at least in the short run. For example, by itself, Sears controls 10 percent of the U.S. replacement-tire market. Even a 20 percent share of Sears's business for Goodyear means three million additional tires per year, enough to erase more than half of the company's previous market-share losses.

In the long run, however, developing new channels risks eroding the loyalty and effectiveness of Goodyear's prized exclusive dealer network, one of the company's major competitive assets. To be fully effective, Goodyear and its dealers must work together in harmony for their mutual benefit. But Goodyear's agreements with Sears and other retailers have created hard feelings on the dealers' part. Some disgruntled dealers are striking back by taking on and aggressively promoting cheaper, private-label brands that offer higher margins to dealers and more appeal to some value-conscious consumers. Such dealer actions may eventually weaken the Goodyear name and the premium price that it can command.

Goodyear has taken steps to bolster anxious dealers. For example, it is now supplying dealers with a much-needed line of lower-priced Goodyear-brand tires. Goodyear sincerely believes that expanded distribution will help its dealers more than harm them. In the end, selling through Sears means better visibility for the Goodyear name, Gault contends, and the resulting expansion of business will mean more money for dealer support. However, many dealers remain skeptical. In the long run, dealer defections could lessen Goodyear's market power and offset sales gains from new channels. For example, shortly after the Sears announcement, one large Goodyear dealership in Florida adopted several lower-priced private brands, reducing its sales of Goodyear tires by 20 percent, but increasing its profit margins. The defiant dealer notes: "We [now] sell what we think will give the customer the best value, and that's not necessarily Goodyear." Thus, although Goodyear may be rolling again, the ride's not over. There are still many bumps in the road ahead.[1] ■

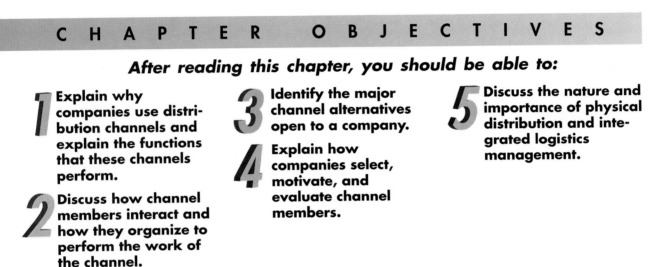

# C H A P T E R   O B J E C T I V E S

## After reading this chapter, you should be able to:

**1** Explain why companies use distribution channels and explain the functions that these channels perform.

**2** Discuss how channel members interact and how they organize to perform the work of the channel.

**3** Identify the major channel alternatives open to a company.

**4** Explain how companies select, motivate, and evaluate channel members.

**5** Discuss the nature and importance of physical distribution and integrated logistics management.

Marketing channel decisions are among the most important decisions that management faces. A company's channel decisions directly affect every other marketing decision. The company's pricing depends on whether it uses mass merchandisers or high-quality specialty stores. The firm's sales force and advertising decisions depend on how much persuasion, training, and motivation the dealers need. Whether a company develops or acquires certain new products may depend on how well those products fit the abilities of its channel members.

Companies often pay too little attention to their distribution channels, however, sometimes with damaging results. For example, automobile manufacturers have lost large shares of their parts and service business to companies like NAPA, Midas, Goodyear, and others because they have resisted making needed changes in their dealer franchise networks. In contrast, many companies have used imaginative distribution systems to *gain* a competitive advantage. Federal Express's creative and imposing distribution system made it the leader in the small-package delivery industry. And General Electric gained a strong advantage in selling its major appliances by supporting its dealers with a sophisticated computerized order processing and delivery system.

Distribution channel decisions often involve long-term commitments to other firms. For example, companies like Ford, IBM, or Pizza Hut can easily change their advertising, pricing, or promotion programs. They can scrap old products and introduce new ones as market tastes demand. But when they set up distribution channels through contracts with franchisees, independent dealers, or large retailers, they cannot readily replace these channels with company-owned stores if conditions change. Therefore, management must design its channels carefully, with an eye on tomorrow's likely selling environment as well as today's.

This chapter examines four major questions concerning distribution channels: *What is the nature of distribution channels? How do channel firms interact and organize to do the work of the channel? What problems do companies face in designing and managing their channels? What role does physical distribution play in attracting and satisfying customers?* In Chapter 13, we will look at distribution channel issues from the viewpoint of retailers and wholesalers.

# ▶ THE NATURE OF DISTRIBUTION CHANNELS

**Distribution channel (marketing channel)**
A set of interdependent organizations involved in the process of making a product or service available for use or consumption by the consumer or business user.

Most producers use intermediaries to bring their products to market. They try to forge a **distribution channel**—a set of interdependent organizations involved in the process of making a product or service available for use or consumption by the consumer or business user.[2]

## WHY ARE MARKETING INTERMEDIARIES USED?

Why do producers give some of the selling job to intermediaries? After all, doing so means giving up some control over how and to whom the products are sold. The use of intermediaries results from their greater efficiency in making goods available to target markets. Through their contacts, experience, specialization, and scale of operation, intermediaries usually offer the firm more than it can achieve on its own.

Figure 11-1 shows how using intermediaries can provide economies. Part A shows three manufacturers, each using direct marketing to reach three customers. This system requires nine different contacts. Part B shows the three manufacturers working through one distributor, who contacts the three customers. This system requires only six contacts. In this way, intermediaries reduce the amount of work that must be done by both producers and consumers.

From the economic system's point of view, the role of marketing intermediaries is to transform the assortments of products made by producers into the assortments wanted by consumers. Producers make narrow assortments of products in large quantities, but consumers want broad assortments of products in small quantities. In the distribution channels, intermediaries buy the large quantities of many producers and break them down into the smaller quantities and broader assortments wanted by consumers. Thus, intermediaries play an important role in matching supply and demand.

## DISTRIBUTION CHANNEL FUNCTIONS

A distribution channel moves goods from producers to consumers. It overcomes the major time, place, and possession gaps that separate goods and services from those who would use them. Members of the marketing channel perform many key functions. Some help to complete transactions.

FIGURE 11-1
*How a distributor reduces the number of channel transactions*

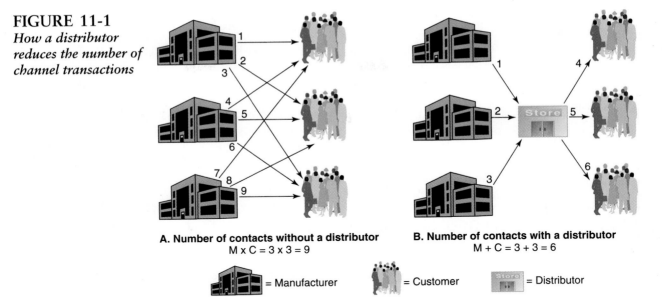

**A. Number of contacts without a distributor**
M x C = 3 x 3 = 9

**B. Number of contacts with a distributor**
M + C = 3 + 3 = 6

= Manufacturer        = Customer        = Distributor

◆ *Information:* gathering and distributing marketing research and intelligence information about actors and forces in the marketing environment that are needed for planning and aiding exchange.

◆ *Promotion:* developing and spreading persuasive communications about an offer.

◆ *Contact:* finding and communicating with prospective buyers.

◆ *Matching:* shaping and fitting the offer to the buyer's needs, including such activities as manufacturing, grading, assembling, and packaging.

◆ *Negotiation:* reaching an agreement on price and other terms of the offer so that ownership or possession can be transferred.

Others help to fulfill the completed transactions.

◆ *Physical distribution:* transporting and storing goods.

◆ *Financing:* acquiring and using funds to cover the costs of the channel work.

◆ *Risk taking:* assuming the risks of carrying out the channel work.

The question is not *whether* these functions need to be performed—they must be—but rather *who* is to perform them. All of the functions have three things in common: They use up scarce resources, they can often be performed better through specialization, and they can be shifted among channel members. To the extent that the manufacturer performs these functions, its costs go up and its prices must increase. At the same time, when some of these functions are shifted to intermediaries, the producer's costs and prices may be lower, but the intermediaries must charge more to cover the costs of their work. In dividing the work of the channel, the various functions should be assigned to the channel members who can perform them most efficiently and effectively to provide satisfactory assortments of goods to target consumers.

# NUMBER OF CHANNEL LEVELS

**Channel level**
A layer of middlemen that performs some work in bringing the product and its ownership closer to the final buyer.

**Direct marketing channel**
A marketing channel that has no intermediary levels.

**Indirect marketing channels**
Channels containing one or more intermediary levels.

Distribution channels can be described by the number of channel levels involved. Each layer of marketing intermediaries that performs some work in bringing the product and its ownership closer to the final buyer is a **channel level.** Because the producer and the final consumer both perform some work, they are part of every channel. We use the *number of intermediary levels* to indicate the *length* of a channel. Figure 11-2A shows several consumer distribution channels of different lengths.

Channel 1, called a **direct marketing channel,** has no intermediary levels. It consists of a company selling directly to consumers. For example, Avon, Amway, and Tupperware sell their products door to door or through home and office sales parties; Land's End sells clothing direct through mail order and by telephone; and Singer sells its sewing machines through its own stores. The remaining channels in Figure 11-2A are **indirect marketing channels.** Channel 2 contains one intermediary level. In consumer markets, this level is typically a retailer. For example, the makers of televisions, cameras, tires, furniture, major appliances, and many other products sell their goods directly to large retailers such as Wal-Mart and

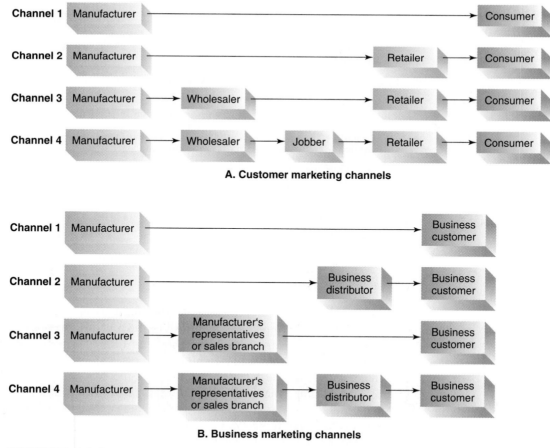

**FIGURE 11-2**
*Consumer and business marketing channels*

*Direct marketing channels: Lands' End sells direct through mail order and by telephone.*

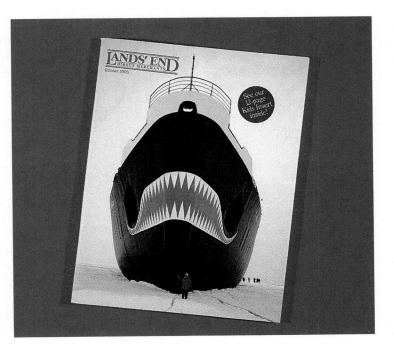

Sears, which then sell the goods to final consumers. Channel 3 contains two intermediary levels: a wholesaler and a retailer. This channel is often used by small manufacturers of food, drugs, hardware, and other products. Channel 4 contains three intermediary levels. In the meatpacking industry, for example, jobbers usually come between wholesalers and retailers. The jobber buys from wholesalers and sells to smaller retailers who generally are not served by larger wholesalers. Distribution channels with even more levels are sometimes found, but less often. From the producer's point of view, a greater number of levels means less control and greater channel complexity.

Figure 11-2B shows some common business distribution channels. The business marketer can use its own sales force to sell directly to business customers. It can also sell to industrial distributors, who in turn sell to business customers. It can sell through manufacturer's representatives or its own sales branches to business customers, or it can use these representatives and branches to sell through industrial distributors. Thus, business markets commonly include multilevel distribution channels.

All of the institutions in the channel are connected by several types of *flows*. These include the *physical flow* of products, the *flow of ownership*, the *payment flow*, the *information flow*, and the *promotion flow*. These flows can make even channels with only one or a few levels very complex.

## ►CHANNEL BEHAVIOR AND ORGANIZATION

Distribution channels are more than simple collections of firms tied together by various flows. They are complex behavioral systems in which people and companies interact to accomplish individual, company, and channel goals. Some channel systems consist only of informal interactions among loosely organized firms; others consist of formal interactions guided by strong organizational structures. Moreover, channel systems do not stand still: New types of intermediaries surface, and whole new channel systems evolve. Here we look at channel behavior and at how members organize to do the work of the channel.

# CHANNEL BEHAVIOR

A distribution channel consists of firms that have banded together for their common good. Each channel member is dependent on the others. For example, a Ford dealer depends on the Ford Motor Company to design cars that meet consumer needs. In turn, Ford depends on the dealer to attract consumers, persuade them to buy Ford cars, and service cars after the sale. The Ford dealer also depends on other dealers to provide good sales and service that will uphold the reputation of Ford and its dealer body. In fact, the success of individual Ford dealers depends on how well the entire Ford distribution channel competes with the channels of other auto manufacturers.

Each channel member plays a role in the channel and specializes in performing one or more functions. For example, IBM's role is to produce personal computers that consumers will like and to create demand through national advertising. Computerland's role is to display these IBM computers in convenient locations, to answer buyers' questions, to close sales, and to provide service. The channel will be most effective when each member is assigned the tasks that it can do best.

Ideally, because the success of individual channel members depends on overall channel success, all channel firms should work together smoothly. They should understand and accept their roles, coordinate their goals and activities, and cooperate to attain overall channel goals. By cooperating, they can more effectively sense, serve, and satisfy the needs of the target market.

However, individual channel members rarely take such a broad view. They are usually more concerned with their own short-run goals and their dealings with those firms that are closest to them in the channel. Cooperating to achieve overall channel goals sometimes means giving up individual company goals. Although channel members are dependent on one another, they often act alone in their own short-run best interests. They often disagree on the roles each should play—on who should do what and for what rewards. Such disagreements over goals and roles generate **channel conflict** (see Marketing at Work 11-1).

*Horizontal conflict* occurs among firms at the same level of the channel. For instance, some Ford dealers in Chicago complained about other dealers in the city who stole sales from them by being too aggressive in their pricing and advertising or by selling outside their assigned territories. Some Pizza Inn franchisees complained about other Pizza Inn franchisees cheating on ingredients and giving poor service, thereby hurting the overall Pizza Inn image.

*Vertical conflict* is even more common and refers to conflicts between different levels of the same channel. For example, General Motors came into conflict with its dealers some years ago by trying to enforce service, pricing, and advertising policies. Coca-Cola came into conflict with some of its bottlers who agreed to bottle competitor Dr Pepper. McCulloch caused conflict when it decided to bypass its wholesale distributors and sell its chain saw directly to large retailers such as JCPenney and Kmart, which then competed directly with its smaller deal-

**Channel conflict**
Disagreement among marketing channel members on goals and roles—who should do what and for what rewards.

ers. And Goodyear caused conflict with its dealer network when it decided to sell tires through mass merchandisers.

Some conflict in the channel takes the form of healthy competition. Such competition can be good for the channel—without it, the channel could become passive and noninnovative. But sometimes conflict can damage the channel. For the channel to perform well as a whole, each channel member's role must be specified, and channel conflict must be managed. Cooperation, role assignment, and conflict management in the channel are attained through strong channel leadership. The channel will perform better if it includes a firm, agency, or mechanism that has the power to assign roles and manage conflict.

In a large company, the formal organization structure assigns roles and provides needed leadership. But in a distribution channel made up of independent firms, leadership and power are not formally set. Traditionally, distribution channels have lacked the leadership needed to assign roles and manage conflict. In recent years, however, new types of channel organizations have appeared that provide stronger leadership and improved performance.

## VERTICAL MARKETING SYSTEMS

**Conventional distribution channel**
A channel consisting of one or more independent producers, wholesalers, and retailers, each a separate business seeking to maximize its own profits even at the expense of profits for the system as a whole.

Historically, distribution channels have been loose collections of independent companies, each showing little concern for overall channel performance. These *conventional distribution channels* have lacked strong leadership and have been troubled by damaging conflict and poor performance. One of the biggest recent channel developments has been the *vertical marketing systems* that have emerged to challenge conventional marketing channels. Figure 11-3 contrasts the two types of channel arrangements.

A **conventional distribution channel** consists of one or more independent producers, wholesalers, and retailers. Each is a separate business seeking to

**FIGURE 11-3**
*Comparison of conventional distribution channel with vertical marketing system*

**Vertical marketing system (VMS)**
A distribution channel structure in which producers, wholesalers, and retailers act as a unified system.

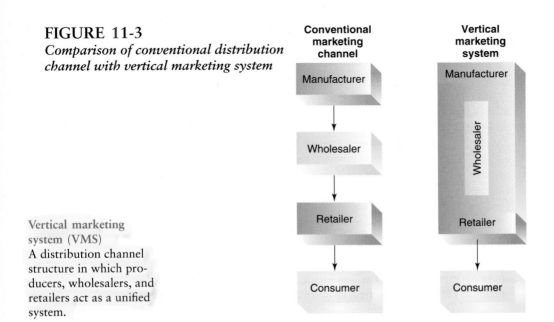

## MARKETING AT WORK 11-1

# CHANNEL CONFLICT: PROCTER & GAMBLE WRESTLES WITH RESELLERS

Procter & Gamble, the huge consumer packaged-goods producer, is part of a complex food-industry distribution channel consisting of producers, wholesale food distributors, and grocery retailers. Despite the immense popularity of its brands with consumers, P&G has never gotten along all that well with retailers and wholesalers. Instead, over the years, the company has acquired a reputation for wielding its market power in a somewhat high-handed fashion, without enough regard for reseller wishes. In early 1992, P&G's relations with many of these resellers took a decided turn for the worse. "We think that [P&G] will end up where most dictators end up—in trouble," fumed the chairman of Stop & Shop, a chain of 119 groceries in the Northeast. Hundreds of miles away, the assistant manager of Paulbeck's Super Valu in International Falls, Minnesota, shared these harsh feelings: "We should drop their top dogs—like half the sizes of Tide—and say 'Now see who put you on the shelf and who'll take you off of it.'"

The cause of the uproar was P&G's new "value pricing" policy. Under this sweeping new plan, the company began phasing out most of the large promotional discounts that it had offered resellers in the past. At the same time, it lowered its everyday wholesale list prices for these products by 10 to 25 percent. P&G insists that price fluctuations and promotions had gotten out of hand. During the previous decade, average trade discounts had more than tripled. Some 44 percent of all marketing dollars spent by manufacturers went to trade promotions, up from 24 percent only a decade earlier.

Manufacturers have come to rely on price-oriented trade promotions to differentiate their brands and boost short-term sales. In turn, wholesalers and retail chains have been conditioned to wait for manufacturers' "deals." Many have perfected "forward buying"—stocking up during manufacturer's price promotions on far more merchandise than they can sell, then reselling it to consumers at higher prices once the promotion is over. Such forward buying creates costly production and distribution inefficiencies. P&G's

factories had to gear up to meet the resulting huge demand swings. Meanwhile, supermarkets needed more buyers to find the best prices and extra warehouses to store and handle merchandise bought "on deal." P&G claims that only 30 percent of trade promotion money was actually reaching consumers in the form of lower prices, while 35 percent was lost to inefficiencies, and another 35 percent wound up in retailers' pockets. The industry's "promotion sickness" has also infected consumers. Wildly fluctuating retail prices have eroded brand loyalty by teaching consumers to shop for what's on sale, rather than to assess the merits of each brand.

Through value pricing, P&G sought to restore the price integrity of its brands and to begin weaning the industry and consumers from discount pricing. But the strategy created substantial conflict in P&G's distribution channels. Discounts are the bread and butter of many retailers and wholesalers, who had used products purchased from P&G at special low prices for weekly sales to lure value-minded consumers into super-

maximize its own profits, even at the expense of profits for the system as a whole. No channel member has much control over the other members, and no formal means exists for assigning roles and resolving channel conflict. In contrast, a **vertical marketing system (VMS)** consists of producers, wholesalers, and retailers acting as a unified system. One channel member owns the others, has

markets or stores. In other cases, retailers and wholesalers relied on the discounts to pad their profits through forward buying. And although the average costs of products to resellers remained unchanged, resellers lost promotional dollars that they—not P&G—controlled. Thus, the new system gave P&G greater control over how its products are marketed, but reduced retailer and wholesaler pricing flexibility.

P&G's new strategy was risky. It alienated some of the very businesses that sell its wares to the public, and it gave competitors an opportunity to take advantage of the ban on promotions by highlighting their own specials. P&G counted on its enormous market clout; retailers could ill afford, the company hoped, to eliminate heavily advertised powerhouse brands such as Tide detergent, Crest toothpaste, Folger's coffee, Pert shampoo, and Ivory soap. But even P&G's size and power were sorely tested. Some large chains such as A&P, Safeway, and Rite Aid drugstores began pruning out selected P&G sizes or dropping marginal brands such as Prell and Gleem. Certified Grocers, a Midwestern wholesaler, dropped about 50 of the 300 P&G varieties that it stocked. And numerous other chains considered moving P&G brands from prime, eye-level space to less visible shelves, meanwhile stocking more profitable private-label brands and competitors' products in P&G's place. SuperValu, the nation's largest wholesaler, which also runs retail stores, added surcharges to some P&G products and pared back orders to make up for profits it says that it's lost.

Despite these strong reactions, P&G has stayed the course with its bold new pricing approach. The company believes that value pricing will benefit all parties—manufacturers, resellers, and consumers—through lower and more stable costs and prices. Many resellers and even competitors are quietly cheering P&G's actions from the sidelines, hoping that order will be restored to prices and promotions. P&G says that many of its largest retailers—especially mass merchandisers like Wal-Mart, which already employ everyday low pricing strategies—love the new system and in fact inspired it.

P&G's struggle to reshape the industry's distorted pricing system demonstrates the dynamic forces of cooperation, power, and conflict found in distribution channels. Clearly, for the good of all parties, P&G and its resellers should work as partners to market food products profitably to consumers. But often, channels don't operate that smoothly; conflicts and power struggles sometimes flare up. In recent years, as more and more products have competed for limited supermarket shelf space, and as scanners have given retailers ever-greater leverage through market information, the balance of channel power has shifted—perhaps too far—toward grocery retailers. With its new pricing policy, P&G appears to be trying to wrestle back some of its lost marketplace control. The stakes are high: The new program stands to either empower P&G and overhaul the way that most wholesalers and retailers do business, or to damage P&G's market share and force it to retreat. In the short run, the conflict will produce some bruises for all parties. In the long run, however, the struggle will probably be healthy for the channel, helping it to adapt and grow.

*Sources:* Portions adapted from Valerie Reitman, "Retail Resistance: Eliminated Discounts on P&G Goods Annoy Many Who Sell Them," *Wall Street Journal,* August 11, 1992, pp. A1, A3. Also see Jennifer Lawrence and Judann Dagnoli, "P&G's Low-Price Strategy Cuts Trade Fees, Irks Retailers," *Advertising Age,* December 23, 1991, p. 3; Zachary Schiller, "Not Everyone Loves a Supermarket Special," *Business Week,* February 17, 1992, pp. 64–68; "P&G Plays Pied Piper on Pricing," *Advertising Age,* March 9, 1992, p. 6; Zachary Schiller, "Ed Artzt's Elbow Grease Has P&G Shining," *Business Week,* October 10, 1994, pp. 84–86; and Jack Neff, "Diaper Battle Puts EDLP on Injured List," *Advertising Age,* August 14, 1995, p. 3.

contracts with them, or wields so much power that they all cooperate. The VMS can be dominated by the producer, wholesaler, or retailer. Vertical marketing systems evolved to control channel behavior and manage channel conflict. They achieve economies through size, bargaining power, and elimination of duplicated services.

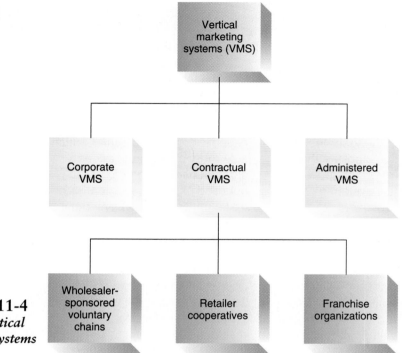

**FIGURE 11-4**
*Types of vertical marketing systems*

We look now at the three major types of VMSs shown in Figure 11-4. Each type uses a different means for setting up leadership and power in the channel. In a *corporate VMS,* coordination and conflict management are attained through common ownership at different levels of the channel. In a *contractual VMS,* they are attained through contractual agreements among channel members. In an *administered VMS,* leadership is assumed by one or a few dominant channel members. We now take a closer look at each type of VMS.

### Corporate VMS

**Corporate VMS**
A vertical marketing system that combines successive stages of production and distribution under single ownership.

A **corporate VMS** combines successive stages of production and distribution under single ownership. In such corporate systems, cooperation and conflict management are handled through regular organizational channels. For example, Sears obtains more than 50 percent of its goods from companies that it partly or wholly owns. AT&T markets telephones and related equipment through its own chain of Phone Centers. Giant Food Stores operates an ice-making facility, a soft-drink bottling operation, an ice-cream-making plant, and a bakery that supplies Giant stores with everything from bagels to birthday cakes.

Gallo, the world's largest winemaker, does much more than simply turn grapes into wine. It owns Fairbanks Trucking Company, one of California's biggest intrastate trucking firms. Fairbanks trucks continuously haul wine out of Gallo wineries and raw materials back in. The raw materials include lime from Gallo's quarry near Sacramento. Gallo also makes its own bottles—more than two million a day—and its Midcal Aluminum Co. turns out bottle caps as fast as the bottles are filled. Whereas most wineries concentrate on production while neglecting

*Corporate vertical marketing systems: AT&T markets telephones and related equipment through its own chain of Phone Centers.*

**Contractual VMS**
A vertical marketing system in which independent firms at different levels of production and distribution join together through contracts to obtain more economies or sales impact than they could achieve alone.

**Wholesaler-sponsored voluntary chains**
Contractual vertical marketing systems in which wholesalers organize voluntary chains of independent retailers to help them compete with large corporate chain organizations.

**Retailer cooperatives**
Contractual vertical marketing systems in which retailers organize a new, jointly owned business to carry on wholesaling and possibly production.

**Franchise organization**
A contractual vertical marketing system in which a channel member, called a franchiser, links several stages in the production-distribution process.

marketing, Gallo participates in every aspect of selling "short of whispering in the ear of each imbiber." Gallo owns its distributors in several markets and would probably buy many more if the laws in most states did not forbid it.[3]

## Contractual VMS

A **contractual VMS** consists of independent firms at different levels of production and distribution who join together through contracts to obtain more economies or sales impact than each could achieve alone. Contractual VMSs have expanded rapidly in recent years. There are three types of contractual VMSs: wholesaler-sponsored voluntary chains, retailer cooperatives, and franchise organizations.

**Wholesaler-sponsored voluntary chains** are systems in which wholesalers organize voluntary chains of independent retailers to help them compete with large chain organizations. The wholesaler develops a program in which independent retailers standardize their selling practices and achieve buying economies that let the group compete effectively with chain organizations. Examples include the Independent Grocers Alliance (IGA), Western Auto, and Sentry Hardwares.

**Retailer cooperatives** are systems in which retailers organize a new, jointly owned business to carry on wholesaling and possibly production. Members buy most of their goods through the retailer co-op and plan their advertising jointly. Profits are passed back to members in proportion to their purchases. Nonmember retailers also may buy through the co-op but do not share in the profits. Examples include Certified Grocers, Associated Grocers, and True Value Hardware.

In **franchise organizations,** a channel member called a *franchiser* links several stages in the production-distribution process. Franchising has been the fastest-growing retailing form in recent years. The more than 500,000 franchise operations in the United States now account for about one-third of all retail sales and may account for one-half by the year 2000.[4] Almost every kind of business has been franchised—from motels and fast-food restaurants to dental centers and dating services, from wedding consultants and maid services to funeral homes and fitness centers. Although the basic idea is an old one, some forms of franchising are quite new.

There are three forms of franchises. The first is the *manufacturer-sponsored retailer franchise system,* as found in the automobile industry. Ford, for example, licenses dealers to sell its cars; the dealers are independent businesspeople who agree to meet various conditions of sales and service. The second type of franchise is the *manufacturer-sponsored wholesaler franchise system,* as found in the soft-drink industry. Coca-Cola, for example, licenses bottlers (wholesalers) in various markets who buy Coca-Cola syrup concentrate and then carbonate, bottle, and sell the finished product to retailers in local markets. The third franchise form is the *service-firm-sponsored retailer franchise system,* in which a service firm licenses a system of retailers to bring its service to consumers. Examples are found in the auto-rental business (Hertz, Avis); the fast-food service business (McDonald's, Burger King); and the motel business (Holiday Inn, Ramada Inn).

The fact that most consumers cannot tell the difference between contractual and corporate VMSs shows how successfully the contractual organizations compete with corporate chains. Chapter 13 presents a fuller discussion of the various contractual VMSs.

### Administered VMS

**Administered VMS**
A vertical marketing system that coordinates successive stages of production and distribution, not through common ownership or contractual ties, but through the size and power of one of the parties.

An **administered VMS** coordinates successive stages of production and distribution—not through common ownership or contractual ties but through the size and power of one of the parties. Manufacturers of a top brand can obtain strong trade cooperation and support from resellers. For example, General Electric, Procter & Gamble, Kraft, and Campbell Soup can command unusual cooperation from resellers regarding displays, shelf space, promotions, and price policies. And large retailers like Wal-Mart and Toys 'R' Us can exert strong influence on the manufacturers that supply the products they sell (see Marketing at Work 11-2).

## HORIZONTAL MARKETING SYSTEMS

**Horizontal marketing systems**
A channel arrangement in which two or more companies at one level join together to follow a new marketing opportunity.

Another channel development is the **horizontal marketing system,** in which two or more companies at one level join together to follow a new marketing opportunity. By working together, companies can combine their capital, production capabilities, or marketing resources to accomplish more than any one company could working alone. Companies might join forces with competitors or noncompetitors. They might work with each other on a temporary or permanent basis, or they may create a separate company.

◆ The Lamar Savings Bank of Texas arranged to locate its savings offices and automated teller machines in Safeway stores. Lamar gained quicker market entry at a low cost, and Safeway was able to offer in-store banking convenience to its customers.

◆ Coca-Cola and Nestlé formed a joint venture to market ready-to-drink coffee and tea worldwide. Coke provided worldwide experience in marketing and distributing beverages and Nestlé contributed two established brand names—Nescafé and Nestea.

◆ H&R Block and Hyatt Legal Services formed a joint venture in which Hyatt houses its legal clinics in H&R Block's tax-preparation offices. Hyatt pays a fee for office space, secretarial assistance, and office equipment usage. By working out of H&R Block's nationwide office network, Hyatt gains quick market penetration. In turn, H&R Block benefits from renting its facilities, which otherwise have a highly seasonal pattern.

◆ Such channel arrangements work well globally. Because of its excellent coverage of international markets, Nestlé jointly sells General Mills's cereal brands in markets outside North America. Seiko Watch's distribution partner in Japan, K. Hattori, markets Schick's razors there, giving Schick the leading market share in Japan, despite Gillette's overall strength in other markets.[5]

The number of such horizontal marketing systems has increased dramatically in recent years, and the end is nowhere in sight.

## HYBRID MARKETING SYSTEMS

**Hybrid marketing channels**
Multichannel distribution systems in which a single firm sets up two or more marketing channels to reach one or more customer segments.

In the past, many companies used a single channel to sell to a single market or market segment. Today, with the proliferation of customer segments and channel possibilities, more and more companies have adopted *multichannel distribution systems*—often called **hybrid marketing channels.** Such multichannel marketing occurs when a single firm sets up two or more marketing channels to reach one or more customer segments. The use of hybrid channel systems has increased greatly in recent years.

Figure 11-5 shows a hybrid channel. In the figure, the producer sells directly to consumer segment 1 using direct-mail catalogs and telemarketing, and reaches consumer segment 2 through retailers. It sells indirectly to business segment 1 through distributors and dealers, and to business segment 2 through its own sales force.

IBM provides a good example of a company that uses such a hybrid channel effectively. For years, IBM sold computers only through its own sales force. However, when the market for small, low-cost computers exploded, this single

**FIGURE 11-5**
*Hybrid marketing channel*

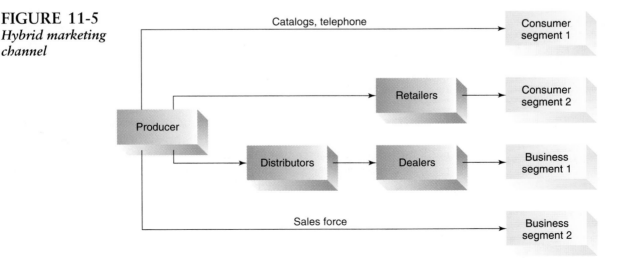

# MARKETING AT WORK 11-2

## Toys 'R' Us Administers Its Channel

Toys 'R' Us operates 619 toy supermarkets that pull in $8.7 billion in annual sales and capture about 21 percent of the huge U.S. toy market. And the giant retailer is growing rapidly, both in the United States and abroad. Because of its size and massive market power, Toys 'R' Us exerts strong influence on toy manufacturers—on their product, pricing, and promotion strategies, and on almost everything else that they do.

Critics worry that Toys 'R' Us is *too* big and influential and that it takes unfair advantage of toy producers. The reactions of Toys 'R' Us buyers can make or break a new toy. For example, Hasbro invested some $20 million to develop Nemo—a home video game system to compete

with the hugely successful Nintendo system—but then quickly canceled the project when Toys 'R' Us executives reacted negatively. Toys 'R' Us also sells its

*Administered channels: Large retailers like Toys 'R' Us can exert strong influence on other members of the marketing channel.*

toys at everyday low prices. This sometimes frustrates toy manufacturers because Toys 'R' Us is selling toys at far below recommended retail prices, forcing producers to settle for lower margins and profits. And some analysts have accused Toys 'R' Us of placing an unfair burden on smaller toy makers by requiring all of its suppliers to pay a fee if they want their toys to be included in Toys 'R' Us newspaper advertisements.

But other industry experts think that Toys 'R' Us helps the toy industry more than hurts it. For example, whereas other retailers feature toys during the Christmas season, Toys 'R' Us has created a year-round market for toys. Moreover, its low prices cause greater

channel was no longer adequate. To serve the diverse needs of the many segments in the rapidly fragmenting computer market, IBM added 18 new channels in less than 10 years.[6] For example, in addition to selling through the vaunted IBM sales force, the company now sells its complete line of computers and accessories through IBM Direct, its catalog and telemarketing operation. Consumers can also buy IBM personal computers from a network of independent IBM dealers, or from any of several large retailers, including Wal-Mart, Circuit City, and Office Depot. IBM dealers and value-added resellers sell IBM computer equipment and systems to a variety of special business segments.

Hybrid channels offer many advantages to companies facing large and complex markets. With each new channel, the company expands its sales and market coverage and gains opportunities to tailor its products and services to the specific needs of diverse customer segments. But such hybrid channel systems are harder to control, and they generate conflict as more channels compete for customers and sales. For example, when IBM began selling directly to customers at low prices through catalogs and telemarketing, many of its retail dealers cried "unfair competition" and threatened to drop the IBM line or to give it less emphasis.

In some cases, the multichannel marketer's channels are all under its own ownership and control. For example, Dayton-Hudson operates department stores, mass-merchandising stores, and specialty stores, each offering different product

overall industry sales and force producers to operate more efficiently. Finally, Toys 'R' Us shares its extensive market data with toy producers, giving them immediate feedback on which products and marketing programs are working and which are not.

Clearly, Toys 'R' Us and the toy manufacturers need each other; the toy makers need Toys 'R' Us to market their products aggressively, and the giant retailer needs a corps of healthy producers to provide a constant stream of popular new products to fill its shelves. Through the years, both sides have recognized this interdependence. For example, in the mid-1970s, when Toys 'R' Us was threatened by bankruptcy because of the financial problems of its parent company, the Toy Manufacturers Association worked directly with banks to save the troubled retailer. The banks granted credit to Toys 'R' Us largely because several major toy manufacturers were willing to grant such credit on their own. By taking such action, the Association demonstrated a clear recognition that the entire toy industry benefited by keeping Toys 'R' Us healthy.

Similarly, Toys 'R' Us has recognized its stake in seeing that toy manufacturers succeed. In recent years, as flat toy sales have plunged many large manufacturers into deep financial trouble, Toys 'R' Us has provided a strong helping hand. For example, Toys 'R' Us often helps toy manufacturers through cash shortages and other financial difficulties by granting credit and prepaying bills. Also, its savvy buyers preview new products for toy makers, making early and valuable suggestions on possible design and marketing improvements. Such advice helped Galoob Toys convert its Army Gear line—toys that change into different weapons—from a potential flop into a top-20 seller. And following the advice of Toys 'R' Us, Ohio Arts altered the advertising strategy for its Zaks plastic building toys, increasing sales by 30 percent. The president of Tyco Toys concludes, "Toys 'R' Us gets a lot of flak for being large and taking advantage of manufacturers, but I would like to have more customers who help us as much as they do."

*Sources:* Amy Dunkin, "How Toys 'R' Us Controls the Game Board," *Business Week,* December 19, 1988, pp. 58–60; Louis W. Stern and Adel I. El-Ansary, *Marketing Channels,* (Englewood Cliffs, NJ: Prentice Hall, 1992), pp. 14–15; Susan Caminiti, "After You Win the Fun Begins," *Fortune,* May 2, 1994, p. 76; and Kate Fitzgerald, "Competitors Swarm Powerful Toys 'R' Us," *Advertising Age,* February 27, 1995, p. 4.

*Hybrid channels: For years, IBM sold computers only through its sales force. However, it now serves the rapidly fragmenting market through a wide variety of channels, including its IBM Direct catalog and telemarketing operation.*

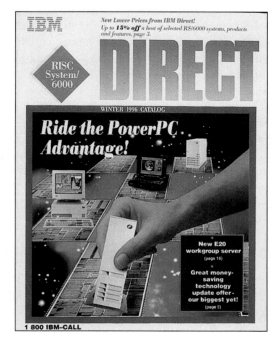

assortments to different market segments. Such arrangements eliminate conflict with outside channels, but the marketer may face internal conflict over how much financial support each channel deserves.

# ►CHANNEL DESIGN DECISIONS

We now look at several channel decisions that manufacturers are facing. In designing marketing channels, manufacturers struggle between what is ideal and what is practical. A new firm usually starts by selling in a finite market area. Because it has limited capital, it typically uses only a few existing intermediaries in each market—a few manufacturers' sales agents, a few wholesalers, some existing retailers, a few trucking companies, and a few warehouses. Deciding on the *best* channels might not be a problem: The problem might simply be how to convince one or a few good intermediaries to handle the line.

If the new firm is successful, it might branch out to new markets. Again, the manufacturer will tend to work through the existing intermediaries, although this strategy might mean using hybrid marketing channels. In smaller markets, the firm might sell directly to retailers; in larger markets, it might sell through distributors. In one part of the country, it might grant exclusive franchises because that is the way that merchants normally work; in another, it might sell through all outlets willing to handle the merchandise. In one country, it might use international sales agents; in another, it might partner with a local firm.[7]

Consider the case of Snapple, a small soft-drink manufacturer that became world-famous by carefully examining its marketing-channel opportunities. Snapple started in the early 1970s by selling almost exclusively to health-food distributors in the New York City area. Then it gradually expanded into mom-and-pop delis and convenience stores. "At the beginning," says one Snapple executive, "chain stores were looking for companies that could pay a lot of money for slotting allowances [money paid to put products on store shelves]. We were a small company and didn't have the money to give at the time." Snapple's decision to use the often-neglected convenience store channel was well rewarded. In terms of product penetration, share of shelf space, and sales volume, Snapple has surpassed every brand but Coke in this channel. By the time the company went national in 1992, it was able to leverage its strong performance in convenience stores, mom-and-pop stores, health clubs, and small grocery stores to gain shelf space in 80 percent of U.S. supermarket chains.[8]

Thus, channel systems often evolve to meet market opportunities and conditions. However, for maximum effectiveness, channel analysis and decision making should be more purposeful. Designing a channel system calls for analyzing consumer service needs, setting the channel objectives and constraints, identifying the major channel alternatives, and evaluating them.

## Analyzing Consumer Service Needs

As noted earlier, marketing channels can be thought of as *customer value delivery systems* in which each channel member adds value for the customer. Thus, designing the distribution channel begins with finding out what values consumers in various target segments want from the channel. Do consumers want to buy from nearby locations, or are they willing to travel to more distant centralized locations? Would they rather buy in person or over the phone or through the mail? Do they want immediate delivery or are they willing to wait? Do consumers value breadth of assortment or do they prefer specialization? Do consumers want many add-on services (delivery, credit, repairs, installation), or will they obtain these elsewhere? The more decentralized the channel, the faster the delivery, the greater the assortment provided, and the more add-on services supplied, the greater the channel's service level.

Consider the distribution channel service needs of business computer system buyers. The delivery of service might include such things as demonstration of the product before the sale or provision of long-term warranties and flexible financing. After the sale, there might be training programs for using the equipment and a program to install and repair it. Customers might appreciate being given "loaners" while their equipment is being repaired or receiving technical advice over a telephone hotline.

But providing the fastest delivery, greatest assortment, and most services may not be possible or practical. The company and its channel members may not have the resources or skills needed to provide all the desired services. Also, providing higher levels of service results in higher costs for the channel and higher prices for consumers. The company must balance consumer service needs against not only the feasibility and costs of meeting these needs but against customer price preferences. The success of off-price and discount retailing shows that consumers are often willing to accept lower service levels if this means lower prices.

## Setting the Channel Objectives and Constraints

Channel objectives should be stated in terms of the desired service level of target consumers. Usually, a company can identify several segments that want different levels of channel service. The company should decide which segments to serve and the best channels to use in each case. In each segment, the company wants to minimize the total channel cost of meeting customer service requirements.

The company's channel objectives are also influenced by the nature of its products, company policies, marketing intermediaries, competitors, and the environment. *Product characteristics* greatly affect channel design. For example, perishable products require more direct marketing to avoid delays and too much handling. Bulky products, such as building materials or soft drinks, require channels that minimize shipping distance and the amount of handling.

*Company characteristics* also play an important role. For example, the company's size and financial situation determine which marketing functions it can handle itself and which it must give to intermediaries. And a company marketing strategy based on speedy customer delivery affects the functions that the company wants its intermediaries to perform, the number of its outlets, and the choice of its transportation methods.

The *characteristics of intermediaries* also influence channel design. The company must find intermediaries who are willing and able to perform the needed tasks. In general, intermediaries differ in their abilities to handle promotion, customer contact, storage, and credit. For example, manufacturer's representatives who are hired by several different firms can contact customers at a low cost per customer

*Product characteristics affect channel decisions: Fresh flowers must be delivered quickly with a minimum of handling.*

because several clients share the total cost. However, the selling effort behind the product is less intense than if the company's own sales force did the selling.

When designing its channels, a company must also consider its *competitors' channels*. In some cases, a company may want to compete in or near the same outlets that carry competitors' products. Thus, food companies want their brands to be displayed next to competing brands; Burger King wants to locate near McDonald's. In other cases, producers may avoid the channels used by competitors. Avon, for example, decided not to compete with other cosmetics makers for scarce positions in retail stores and instead set up a profitable door-to-door selling operation.

Finally, *environmental factors*, such as economic conditions and legal constraints, affect channel design decisions. For example, in a depressed economy, producers want to distribute their goods in the most economical way, using shorter channels and dropping unnecessary services that add to the final price of the goods. Legal regulations prevent channel arrangements that "may tend to lessen competition substantially or tend to create a monopoly."

## IDENTIFYING MAJOR ALTERNATIVES

When the company has defined its channel objectives, it should next identify its major channel alternatives in terms of *types* of intermediaries, *number* of intermediaries, and the *responsibilities* of each channel member.

### Types of Intermediaries

A firm should identify the types of channel members that are available to carry out its channel work. For example, suppose that a manufacturer of test equipment has developed an audio device that detects poor mechanical connections in machines with moving parts. Company executives think that this product would have a market in all industries where electric, combustion, or steam engines are made or used. This market includes industries such as aviation, automobile, railroad, food canning, construction, and oil. The company's current sales force is small, and the problem is how best to reach these different industries. The following channel alternatives might emerge from management discussion:

- ◆ *Company sales force.* Expand the company's direct sales force. Assign salespeople to territories and have them contact all prospects in the area or develop separate company sales forces for different industries.
- ◆ *Manufacturer's agency.* Hire manufacturer's agents—independent firms whose sales forces handle related products from many companies—in different regions or industries to sell the new test equipment.
- ◆ *Industrial distributors.* Find distributors in the different regions or industries who will buy and carry the new line. Give them exclusive distribution, good margins, product training, and promotional support.

Sometimes a company must develop a channel other than the one that it prefers because of the difficulty or cost of using the preferred channel. Still, the decision may turn out extremely well. For example, the U.S. Time Company first tried to sell its inexpensive Timex watches through regular jewelry stores, but most jewelry stores refused to carry them. The company then managed to get its watches into mass-merchandise outlets. This turned out to be a wise decision because of the rapid growth of mass merchandising. Similarly, when Chiodo Candy Company found that it was getting clobbered in supermarkets by candy giant E. J. Brach, it began casting about for alternative distribution channels. It came up with a winner in warehouse club stores. The warehouse clubs didn't require any shelving fees and were receptive to new products. To meet these stores' demand for large packages, Chiodo developed a plastic tub that could hold up to two pounds of penny candy. Soon club buyers were ordering more than 8,000 tubs at a time.[9]

### Number of Marketing Intermediaries

Companies must also determine the number of channel members to use at each level. Three strategies are available: intensive distribution, exclusive distribution, and selective distribution.

**Intensive distribution**
Stocking the product in as many outlets as possible.

Producers of convenience products and common raw materials typically seek **intensive distribution**—a strategy in which they stock their products in as many outlets as possible. These goods must be available where and when consumers want them. For example, toothpaste, candy, and other similar items are sold in millions of outlets to provide maximum brand exposure and consumer convenience. Procter & Gamble, Campbell, Coca-Cola, and other consumer goods companies distribute their products in this way.

**Exclusive distribution**
Giving a limited number of dealers the exclusive right to distribute the company's products in their territories.

By contrast, some producers purposely limit the number of intermediaries handling their products. The extreme form of this practice is **exclusive distribution**, in which the producer gives only a limited number of dealers the exclusive right to distribute its products in their territories. Exclusive distribution is often found in the distribution of new automobiles and prestige women's clothing. For example, Rolls-Royce dealers are few and far between; even large cities may have only one or two dealers. By granting exclusive distribution, Rolls-Royce gains stronger distributor selling support and more control over dealer prices, promotion, credit, and services. Exclusive distribution also enhances the car's image and allows for higher markups.

**Selective distribution**
The use of more than one, but fewer than all, of the intermediaries who are willing to carry the company's products.

Between intensive and exclusive distribution lies **selective distribution**—the use of more than one, but fewer than all, of the intermediaries who are willing to

*Exclusive distribution: Rolls-Royce sells exclusively through a limited number of dealerships. Such limited distribution enhances the car's image and generates stronger dealer support.*

carry a company's products. Most television, furniture, and small appliance brands are distributed in this manner. For example, Maytag, Whirlpool, and General Electric sell their major appliances through dealer networks and selected large retailers. By using selective distribution, they do not have to spread their efforts over many outlets, including many marginal ones. They can develop good working relationships with selected channel members and expect a better-than-average selling effort. Selective distribution gives producers good market coverage with more control and less cost than does intensive distribution.

### Responsibilities of Channel Members

The producer and intermediaries need to agree on the terms and responsibilities of each channel member. They should agree on price policies, conditions of sale, territorial rights, and specific services to be performed by each party. The producer should establish a list price and a fair set of discounts for intermediaries. It must define each channel member's territory, and it should be careful about where it places new resellers. Mutual services and duties need to be spelled out carefully, especially in franchise and exclusive distribution channels. For example, McDonald's provides franchisees with promotional support, a record-keeping system, training, and general management assistance. In turn, franchisees must meet company standards for physical facilities, cooperate with new promotion programs, provide requested information, and buy specified food products.

## EVALUATING THE MAJOR ALTERNATIVES

Suppose that a company has identified several channel alternatives and wants to select the one that will best satisfy its long-run objectives. Each alternative should be evaluated against economic, control, and adaptive criteria.

Using *economic criteria,* a company compares the likely profitability of different channel alternatives. It estimates the sales that each channel would produce and the costs of selling different volumes through each channel. The company must also consider *control issues.* Using intermediaries usually means giving them some control over the marketing of the product, and some intermediaries take more control than others. Other things being equal, the company prefers to keep as much control as possible. Finally, the company must apply adaptive criteria. Channels often involve long-term commitments to other firms, making it hard to adapt the channel to the changing marketing environment. The company wants to keep the channel as flexible as possible. Thus, to be considered, a channel involving long-term commitment should be greatly superior on economic and control grounds.

# DESIGNING INTERNATIONAL DISTRIBUTION CHANNELS

International marketers face many additional complexities in designing their channels. Each country has its own unique distribution system that has evolved over time and changes very slowly. These channel systems can vary widely from country to country. Thus, global marketers usually have to adapt their channel strategies to the existing structures within each country. In some markets, the distribution system is complex and hard to penetrate, consisting of many layers and large numbers of intermediaries. Consider Japan.

> The Japanese distribution system stems from the early seventeenth century when cottage industries and a [quickly growing] urban population spawned a merchant class. . . . Despite Japan's economic achievements, the distribution system has remained remarkably faithful to its antique pattern. . . . [It] encompasses a wide range of wholesalers and other agents, brokers, and retailers, differing more in number than in function from their American counterparts. There are myriad tiny retail shops. An even greater number of wholesalers supplies goods to them, layered tier upon tier, many more than most U.S. executives would think necessary. For example, soap may move through three wholesalers plus a sales company after it leaves the manufacturer before it ever reaches the retail outlet. A steak goes from rancher to consumers in a process that often involves a dozen middle agents. . . . The distribution network . . . reflects the traditionally close ties among many Japanese companies . . . [and places] much greater emphasis on personal relationships with users. . . . Although [these channels appear] inefficient and cumbersome, they seem to serve the Japanese customer well. . . . Lacking much storage space in their small homes, most Japanese homemakers shop several times a week and prefer convenient [and more personal] neighborhood shops.[10]

Many Western firms have met with great difficulty in trying to break into the closely knit, tradition-bound Japanese distribution network.

At the other extreme, distribution systems in developing countries may be scattered and inefficient, or altogether lacking. For example, China and India are huge markets, each containing hundreds of millions of people. In reality, however,

*The Japanese distribution system has remained remarkably traditional. A profusion of tiny retail shops are supplied by an even greater number of small wholesalers.*

these markets are much smaller than the population numbers suggest. Because of inadequate distribution systems in both countries, most companies can profitably access only a small portion of the population located in each country's most affluent cities.[11]

Thus, international marketers face a wide range of channel alternatives. Designing efficient and effective channel systems between and within various country markets poses a difficult challenge. We discuss international distribution decisions further in Chapter 16.

# ►CHANNEL MANAGEMENT DECISIONS

Once the company has reviewed its channel alternatives and decided on the best channel design, it must implement and manage the chosen channel. Channel management calls for selecting and motivating individual channel members and evaluating their performance over time.

## SELECTING CHANNEL MEMBERS

Producers vary in their ability to attract qualified marketing intermediaries. Some producers have no trouble signing up channel members. For example, Toyota had no trouble attracting new dealers for its Lexus line. In fact, it had to turn down many would-be resellers. In some cases, the promise of exclusive or selective distribution for a desirable product will draw plenty of applicants.

At the other extreme are producers who have to work hard to line up enough qualified intermediaries. When Polaroid started, for example, it could not get photography stores to carry its new cameras, and it had to go to mass-merchandising outlets. Similarly, small food producers often have difficulty getting supermarket chains to carry their products.

When selecting intermediaries, the company should determine what characteristics distinguish the better ones. It will want to evaluate each channel member's years in business, other lines carried, growth and profit record, cooperativeness, and reputation. If the intermediaries are sales agents, the company will want to evaluate the number and character of other lines carried, and the size and quality of the sales force. If the intermediary is a retail store that wants exclusive or selective distribution, the company should evaluate the store's customers, location, and future growth potential.

## MOTIVATING CHANNEL MEMBERS

Once selected, channel members must be continuously motivated to do their best. The company must sell not only *through* the intermediaries, but *to* them. Most producers see the problem as finding ways to gain intermediary cooperation. They use the carrot-and-stick approach. At times, they offer *positive* motivators such as higher margins, special deals, premiums, cooperative advertising allowances, display allowances, and sales contests. At other times, they use *negative* motivators, such as threatening to reduce margins, slow down delivery, or end the relationship altogether. A producer using this approach usually has not done a good job of studying the needs, problems, strengths, and weaknesses of its distributors.

More advanced companies try to forge long-term partnerships with their distributors. This involves building a planned, professionally managed, vertical marketing system that meets the needs of both the manufacturer *and* the distributors.[12] Thus, Procter & Gamble and Wal-Mart work together to create superior value for final consumers. They jointly plan merchandising goals and strategies, inventory levels, and advertising and promotion plans. Similarly, General Electric works closely with its smaller independent dealers to help them be successful in selling the company's products (see Marketing at Work 11-3). In managing its channels, a company must convince distributors that they can make their money by being part of an advanced vertical marketing system.

## EVALUATING CHANNEL MEMBERS

The producer must regularly check the channel member's performance against standards such as sales quotas, average inventory levels, customer delivery time, treatment of damaged and lost goods, cooperation in company promotion and training programs, and services to the customer. The company should recognize and reward intermediaries who are performing well. Those who are performing poorly should be helped or, as a last resort, replaced.

A company may periodically "requalify" its intermediaries and prune the weaker ones. For example, when IBM first introduced its PS/2 personal computers, it reevaluated its dealers and allowed only the best ones to carry the new models. Each IBM dealer had to submit a business plan, send a sales and service employee to IBM training classes, and meet new sales quotas. Only about two-thirds of IBM's 2,200 dealers qualified to carry the PS/2 models.[13]

## MARKETING AT WORK 11-3

# GENERAL ELECTRIC ADOPTS A "VIRTUAL INVENTORY" SYSTEM TO SUPPORT ITS DEALERS

Before the late 1980s, General Electric worked at selling *through* its dealers rather than *to* them or *with* them. GE operated a traditional system of trying to load up the channel with GE appliances, on the premise that "loaded dealers are loyal dealers." Loaded dealers had less space to feature other brands and would recommend GE appliances to reduce their high inventories. To load its dealers, GE offered the lowest price when the dealer ordered a full truckload of GE appliances.

GE eventually realized that this approach created many problems, especially for smaller independent appliance dealers who could ill afford to carry a large stock. These dealers were hard-pressed to meet price competition from larger multibrand dealers. Rethinking its strategy from the point of view of creating dealer satisfaction and profitability, GE created an alternative distribution model called the Direct Connect system. Under this system, GE dealers carry only display models. They rely on a "virtual inventory" to fill orders. Dealers can access GE's order-processing system 24 hours a day, check on model availability, and place orders for next-day delivery. Using the Direct Connect system, dealers also can get GE's best price, financing from GE Credit, and no interest charges for the first 90 days.

Dealers benefit by having much lower inventory costs while still having a large virtual inventory available to satisfy their customers' needs. In exchange for this advantage, dealers must commit to selling nine major GE product categories; generating 50 percent of their sales from GE products; opening their books to GE for review; and paying GE every month through electronic funds transfer.

As a result of Direct Connect, dealer profit margins have skyrocketed. GE has also benefited. Its dealers are now more committed and dependent on GE, and the new order-entry

system has saved GE substantial clerical costs. GE now knows the actual sales of its goods at the retail level, which helps it to schedule its production more accurately. It now can produce in response to demand rather than to meet inventory replenishment rules. And GE has been able to simplify its warehouse locations so as to be able to deliver appliances to 90 percent of the United States within 24 hours. Thus, by forging a partnership, GE has helped both its dealers and itself.

Source: See Michael Treacy and Fred Wiersema, "Customer Intimacy and Other Discipline Values," Harvard Business Review, January–February 1993, pp. 84–93.

---

*Creating dealer satisfaction and profitability: Using GE's Direct Connect system, dealers can access GE's order-processing system 24 hours a day, check on model availability, and place orders for next-day delivery. They can also get GE's best price, financing from GE Credit, and no interest.*

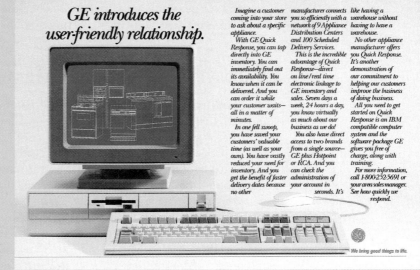

Finally, manufacturers need to be sensitive to their dealers. Those who treat their dealers lightly risk not only losing their support but also causing some legal problems. Marketing at Work 11-4 describes various rights and duties pertaining to manufacturers and their channel members.

# PHYSICAL DISTRIBUTION AND LOGISTICS MANAGEMENT

In today's global marketplace, selling a product is sometimes easier than getting it to customers. Companies must decide on the best way to store, handle, and move their products and services so that they are available to customers in the

## MARKETING AT WORK 11-4

### PUBLIC POLICY AND DISTRIBUTION DECISIONS

For the most part, companies are legally free to develop whatever channel arrangements suit them. In fact, the laws affecting channels seek to prevent the exclusionary tactics of some companies that might keep another company from using a desired channel. Of course, this means that the company must itself avoid using such exclusionary tactics. Most channel law deals with the mutual rights and duties of the channel members once they have formed a relationship.

**EXCLUSIVE DEALING**
Many producers and wholesalers like to develop exclusive channels for their products. When the seller allows only certain outlets to carry its products, this strategy is called *exclusive distribution.* When the seller requires that these dealers not handle competitors' products, its strategy is called *exclusive dealing.* Both parties benefit from exclusive arrangements: The seller obtains more loyal and dependable out-

lets, and the dealers obtain a steady source of supply and stronger seller support. But exclusive arrangements exclude other producers from selling to these dealers. This situation brings exclusive dealing contracts under the scope of the Clayton Act of 1914. They are legal as long as they do not substantially lessen competition or tend to create a monopoly and as long as both parties enter into the agreement voluntarily.

**EXCLUSIVE TERRITORIES**
Exclusive dealing often includes exclusive territorial agreements. The producer may agree not to sell to other dealers in a given area, or the buyer may agree to sell only in its own territory. The first practice is normal under franchise systems as a way to increase dealer enthusiasm and commitment. It is also perfectly legal: A seller has no legal obligation to sell through more outlets than it wishes. The second practice, whereby the producer

tries to keep a dealer from selling outside its territory, has become a major legal issue.

**TYING AGREEMENTS**
Producers of a strong brand sometimes sell it to dealers only if the dealers will take some or all of the rest of the line. This is called *full-line forcing.* Such tying agreements are not necessarily illegal, but they do violate the Clayton Act if they tend to lessen competition substantially. The practice may prevent consumers from freely choosing among competing suppliers of these other brands.

**DEALERS' RIGHTS**
Producers are free to select their dealers, but their right to terminate dealers is somewhat restricted. In general, sellers can drop dealers "for cause." But they cannot drop dealers if, for example, the dealers refuse to cooperate in a doubtful legal arrangement, such as exclusive dealing or tying agreements.

right assortments, at the right time, and in the right place. Logistics effectiveness will have a major impact on both customer satisfaction and company costs. A poor distribution system can destroy an otherwise good marketing effort. Here we consider the *nature and importance of marketing logistics, goals of the logistics system, major logistics functions,* and the necessity of *integrated logistics management.*

## NATURE AND IMPORTANCE OF PHYSICAL DISTRIBUTION AND MARKETING LOGISTICS

**Physical distribution (marketing logistics)** The tasks involved in planning, implementing, and controlling the physical flow of materials, final goods, and related information from points of origin to points of consumption to meet customer requirements at a profit.

To some managers, physical distribution means only trucks and warehouses. But modern logistics involves much more than this. **Physical distribution**—or **marketing logistics**—includes planning, implementing, and controlling the physical flow of materials, final goods, and related information from points of origin to points of consumption to meet customer requirements at a profit.

Traditional physical distribution has typically started with products at the plant and tried to find low-cost solutions to get them to customers. However, today's marketers prefer *market logistics* thinking, which starts with the marketplace and works backwards to the factory. Logistics addresses not only the problem of outbound distribution (moving products from the factory to customers), but also the problem of inbound distribution (moving products and materials from suppliers to the factory). It involves the management of entire *supply chains,* value-added flows from suppliers to final users, as shown in Figure 11-6. Thus, the logistics manager's task is to coordinate the whole-channel physical distribution system—the activities of suppliers, purchasing agents, marketers, channel members, and customers. These activities include forecasting, information systems, purchasing, production planning, order processing, inventory, warehousing, and transportation planning.

Companies today are placing greater emphasis on logistics for several reasons. First, customer service and satisfaction have become the cornerstones of marketing strategy in many businesses, and distribution is an important customer service element. More and more, effective logistics is becoming a key to winning and keeping customers. Companies are finding that they can attract more customers by giving better service or lower prices through better physical distribution. On the other hand, companies may lose customers when they fail to supply the right products on time.

Second, logistics is a major cost element for most companies. According to one study, American companies last year "spent $670 billion—a gaping 10.5 percent of Gross Domestic Product—to wrap, bundle, load, unload, sort, reload, and transport goods."[14] About 15 percent of an average product's price is accounted for by shipping and transport alone. Poor physical distribution decisions result in high costs. Even large companies sometimes make too little use of modern decision tools for coordinating inventory levels; transportation modes; and plant, warehouse, and store locations. Improvements in physical distribution efficiency can yield tremendous cost savings for both the company and its customers.

Third, the explosion in product variety has created a need for improved logistics management. For example, in 1911, the typical A&P grocery store carried only 270 items. The store manager could keep track of this inventory on about 10 pages of notebook paper stuffed in a shirt pocket. Today, the average A&P

**FIGURE 11-6**
*Marketing logistics:
managing supply chains*

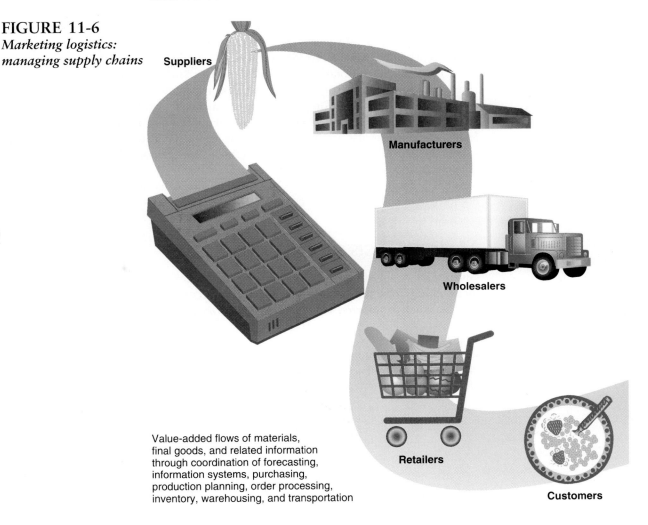

Value-added flows of materials,
final goods, and related information
through coordination of forecasting,
information systems, purchasing,
production planning, order processing,
inventory, warehousing, and transportation

carries a bewildering stock of more than 16,700 items, some 62 times more than in 1911.[15] Ordering, shipping, stocking, and controlling such a variety of products present a sizable logistics challenge.

Finally, improvements in information technology have created opportunities for major gains in distribution efficiency. The increased use of computers, point-of-sale scanners, uniform product codes, satellite tracking, electronic data interchange (EDI), and electronic funds transfer (EFT) has allowed companies to create advanced systems for order processing, inventory control and handling, and transportation routing and scheduling.

## GOALS OF THE LOGISTICS SYSTEM

Some companies state their logistics objective as providing maximum customer service at the least cost. Unfortunately, no logistics system can *both* maximize customer service *and* minimize distribution costs. Maximum customer service implies rapid delivery, large inventories, flexible assortments, liberal returns policies, and other services, all of which raise distribution costs. In contrast, minimum distribution costs imply slower delivery, smaller inventories, and larger shipping lots, which represent a lower level of overall customer service.

The goal of the marketing logistics system should be to provide a targeted level of customer service at the least cost. A company must first research the importance of various distribution services to its customers, and then set desired service levels for each segment. The company normally wants to offer at least the same level of service as its competitors. But the objective is to maximize *profits,* not sales. Therefore, the company must weigh the benefits of providing higher levels of service against the costs. Some companies offer less service than their competitors and charge a lower price. Other companies offer more service and charge higher prices to cover higher costs.

## MAJOR LOGISTICS FUNCTIONS

Given a set of logistics objectives, the company is ready to design a logistics system that will minimize the cost of attaining these objectives. The major logistics functions include *order processing, warehousing, inventory management,* and *transportation.*

### Order Processing

Orders can be submitted in many ways—by mail or telephone, through salespeople, or via computer and EDI. In some cases, the suppliers might actually generate orders for their customers:

> One Kmart quick response program calls for selected suppliers to manage the retailer's inventory replenishment for their products. Kmart transmits daily records of product sales to the vendor, who analyzes the sales information, comes up with an order, and sends it back to Kmart through EDI. Once in Kmart's system, the order is treated as though Kmart itself created it. Says a Kmart executive, "We don't modify the order, and we don't question it. . . . Our relationship with those vendors is such that we trust them to create the type of order that will best meet our inventory needs."[16]

Once received, orders must be processed quickly and accurately. The order processing system prepares invoices and sends order information to those who need it. The appropriate warehouse receives instructions to pack and ship the ordered items. Products out of stock are back-ordered. Shipped items are accompanied by shipping and billing documents, with copies going to various departments.

Both the company and its customers benefit when the order-processing steps are carried out efficiently. Ideally, salespeople send in their orders daily, often using on-line computers. The order department quickly processes these orders, and the warehouse sends the goods out on time. Bills go out as soon as possible. Most companies now use computerized order-processing systems that speed up the order-shipping-billing cycle. For example, General Electric operates a computer-based system that, upon receipt of a customer's order, checks the customer's credit standing as well as whether and where the items are in stock. The computer then issues an order to ship, bills the customer, updates the inventory records, sends a production order for new stock, and relays the message back to the salesperson that the customer's order is on its way—all in less than 15 seconds.

## Warehousing

Every company must store its goods while they wait to be sold. A storage function is needed because production and consumption cycles rarely match. For example, Snapper, Toro, and other lawn mower manufacturers must produce all year long and store up their product for the heavy spring and summer buying season. The storage function overcomes differences in needed quantities and timing.

A company must decide on *how many* and *what types* of warehouses it needs, and *where* they will be located. The more warehouses that the company uses, the more quickly goods can be delivered to customers. However, more locations mean higher warehousing costs. The company, therefore, must balance the level of customer service against distribution costs.

Some company stock is kept at or near the plant, with the rest located in warehouses around the country. The company might own private warehouses, rent space in public warehouses, or both. Companies have more control over owned warehouses, but that ties up their capital and is less flexible if desired locations change. In contrast, public warehouses charge for the rented space and provide additional services (at a cost) for inspecting goods, packaging them, shipping them, and invoicing them. By using public warehouses, companies also have a wide choice of locations and warehouse types.

**Distribution center**
A large, highly automated warehouse designed to receive goods from various plants and suppliers, take orders, fill them efficiently, and deliver goods to customers as quickly as possible.

Companies may use either *storage warehouses* or *distribution centers*. Storage warehouses store goods for moderate to long periods. **Distribution centers** are designed to move goods rather than just store them. They are large and highly automated warehouses designed to receive goods from various plants and suppliers, take orders, fill them efficiently, and deliver goods to customers as quickly as possible. For example, Wal-Mart operates huge distribution centers. One center, which serves the daily needs of 165 Wal-Mart stores, contains some 28 acres of space under a single roof. Laser scanners route as many as 190,000 cases of goods

*Automated warehouses: This sophisticated Compaq computer distribution center can ship any of 500 different types of Compaq computers and options within four hours of receiving an order.*

per day along 11 miles of conveyer belts, and the center's 1,000 workers load or unload 310 trucks daily.[17]

Warehousing facilities and equipment technology have improved greatly in recent years. Older, multistoried warehouses with slow elevators and outdated materials-handling methods are facing competition from newer, single-storied *automated warehouses* with advanced materials-handling systems under the control of a central computer. In these warehouses, only a few employees are necessary. Computers read orders and direct lift trucks, electric hoists, or robots to gather goods, move them to loading docks, and issue invoices. These warehouses have reduced worker injuries, labor costs, theft, and breakage and have improved inventory control.

### Inventory

Inventory levels also affect customer satisfaction. The major goal is to maintain the delicate balance between carrying too much inventory and carrying too little. Carrying too much inventory results in higher-than-necessary inventory-carrying costs and stock obsolesence. Carrying too little may result in stock-outs, costly emergency shipments or production, and customer dissatisfaction. In making inventory decisions, management must balance the costs of carrying larger inventories against resulting sales and profits.

Inventory decisions involve knowing both *when* to order and *how much* to order. In deciding when to order, the company balances the risks of running out of stock against the costs of carrying too much. In deciding how much to order, the company needs to balance order-processing costs against inventory-carrying costs. Larger average-order size results in fewer orders and lower order-processing costs, but it also means larger inventory-carrying costs.

During the past decade, many companies have greatly reduced their inventories and related costs through *just-in-time* logistics systems. Through such systems, producers and retailers carry only small inventories of parts or merchandise, often only enough for a few days of operations. New stock arrives exactly when needed, rather than being stored in inventory until being used. Just-in-time systems require accurate forecasting along with fast, frequent, and flexible delivery, so that new supplies will be available when needed. However, these systems result in substantial savings in inventory carrying and handling costs.

### Transportation

Marketers need to take an interest in their company's *transportation* decisions. The choice of transportation carriers affects the pricing of products, delivery performance, and condition of the goods when they arrive—all of which will affect customer satisfaction.

In shipping goods to its warehouses, dealers, and customers, the company can choose among five transportation modes: rail, water, truck, pipeline, and air. Table 11-1 summarizes the characteristics of each transportation mode.

RAIL. Although railroads lost market share until the mid-1970s, today they remain the nation's largest carrier, accounting for 37 percent of total cargo moved. Railroads are one of the most cost-effective modes for shipping large amounts of bulk products—coal, sand, minerals, farm and forest products—over long distances. In addition, railroads have recently begun to increase their customer services. They have designed new equipment to handle special categories of goods, provided flatcars for carrying truck trailers by rail (piggyback), and provided in-transit services such as the diversion of shipped goods to other destinations en

**TABLE 11-1** *Characteristics of Major Transportation Modes*

| Transportation Mode | Intercity Cargo Volume* (%) | | | Typical Products Shipped |
|---|---|---|---|---|
| | 1970 | 1980 | 1991 | |
| Rail | 771 (39.8%) | 932 (37.5%) | 1078 (37.4%) | Farm products, minerals, sand, chemicals, automobiles |
| Truck | 412 (21.3) | 555 (22.3) | 758 (26.3) | Clothing, food, books, computers, paper goods |
| Water | 319 (16.5) | 407 (16.4) | 462 (16.0) | Oil, grain, sand, gravel, metallic ores, coal |
| Pipeline | 431 (22.3) | 588 (23.6) | 578 (20.0) | Oil, coal, chemicals |
| Air | 3.3 (0.17) | 4.8 (0.19) | 10 (0.3) | Technical instruments, perishable products, documents |

*In billions of cargo ton-miles.
Source: *Statistical Abstract of the United States*, 1993.

route and the processing of goods en route. Thus, after decades of losing out to truckers, railroads appear ready for a comeback.[18]

TRUCK. Trucks have increased their share of transportation steadily and now account for 25 percent of total cargo. They account for the largest portion of transportation *within* cities as opposed to *between* cities. Each year in the United States, trucks travel more than 600 billion miles—equal to nearly 1.3 million round trips to the moon—carrying 2.5 billion tons of freight.[19] Trucks are highly flexible in their routing and time schedules. They can move goods door to door, saving shippers the need to transfer goods from truck to rail and back again at a loss of time and risk of theft or damage. Trucks are efficient for short hauls of

*Roadway and other trucking firms have added many services in recent years, such as satellite tracking of shipments and sleeper tractors that keep freight moving around the clock.*

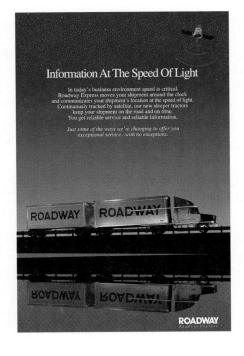

high-value merchandise. In many cases, their rates are competitive with railway rates, and trucks can usually offer faster service. Trucking firms have added many services in recent years. For example, Roadway Express now offers satellite tracking of shipments and sleeper tractors that move freight around the clock.

WATER.   A large amount of goods are moved by ships and barges on U.S. coastal and inland waterways. Mississippi River barges alone account for 15 percent of the freight shipped in the United States. On the one hand, the cost of water transportation is very low for shipping bulky, low-value, nonperishable products such as sand, coal, grain, oil, and metallic ores. On the other hand, water transportation is the slowest transportation mode and is sometimes affected by the weather.

PIPELINE.   Pipelines are a specialized means of shipping petroleum, natural gas, and chemicals from sources to markets. Pipeline shipment of petroleum products costs less than rail shipment, but more than water shipment. Most pipelines are used by their owners to ship their own products.

AIR.   Although air carriers transport less than 1 percent of the nation's goods, they are becoming more important as a transportation mode. Air-freight rates are much higher than rail or truck rates, but air freight is ideal when speed is needed or distant markets have to be reached. Among the most frequently air-freighted products are perishables (fresh fish, cut flowers) and high-value, low-bulk items (technical instruments, jewelry). Companies find that air freight also reduces inventory levels, packaging costs, and the number of warehouses needed.

Until the late 1970s, routes, rates, and service in the transportation industry were heavily regulated by the federal government. Today, most of these regulations have been eased. Deregulation has caused rapid and substantial changes. Railroads, ships and barges, trucks, airlines, and pipeline companies are now much more competitive, flexible, and responsive to the needs of their customers. These changes have resulted in better services and lower prices for shippers. But such changes also mean that marketers must do better transportation planning if they want to take full advantage of new opportunities in the changing transportation environment.

In choosing a transportation mode for a product, shippers consider as many as five criteria, as shown in Table 11-2. Thus, if a shipper needs speedy delivery, air and truck are the prime choices. If the goal is low cost, then water or pipeline might be best. Trucks appear to offer the most advantages—a fact that explains their growing share of the transportation market.

**TABLE 11-2** *Rankings of Transportation Modes (1 = Highest Rank)*

| | Speed (Door-to-Door Delivery Time) | Dependability (Meeting Schedules on Time) | Capability (Ability to Handle Various Products) | Availability (No. of Geographic Points Served) | Cost (Per Ton-Mile) |
|---|---|---|---|---|---|
| Rail | 3 | 4 | 2 | 2 | 3 |
| Water | 4 | 5 | 1 | 4 | 1 |
| Truck | 2 | 2 | 3 | 1 | 4 |
| Pipeline | 5 | 1 | 5 | 5 | 2 |
| Air | 1 | 3 | 4 | 3 | 5 |

*Source:* See Carl M. Guelzo, *Introduction to Logistics Management* (Englewood Cliffs, NJ: Prentice Hall, 1986), p. 46.

Containerization
Putting the goods in
boxes or trailers that are
easy to transfer between
two transportation
modes.

Thanks to containerization, shippers are increasingly combining two or more modes of transportation. **Containerization** consists of putting goods in boxes or trailers that are easy to transfer between two transportation modes. *Piggyback* describes the use of rail and trucks; *fishyback,* water and trucks; *trainship,* water and rail; and *airtruck,* air and trucks. Each combination offers advantages to the shipper. For example, not only is piggyback cheaper than trucking alone, but it also provides flexibility and convenience.

# INTEGRATED LOGISTICS MANAGEMENT

Integrated logistics
management
The logistics concept
that emphasizes team-
work, both inside the
company and among all
the marketing channel
organizations, to maxi-
mize the performance of
the entire distribution
system.

Today, more and more companies are adopting the concept of **integrated logistics management.** This concept recognizes that providing better customer service and trimming distribution costs requires *teamwork,* both inside the company and among all the marketing channel organizations. Inside the company, the various functional departments must work closely together to maximize the company's own logistics performance. The company must also integrate its logistics system with those of its suppliers and customers to maximize the performance of the entire distribution system.

## Cross-Functional Teamwork Inside the Company

In most companies, responsibility for various logistics activities is assigned to many different functional units—marketing, sales, finance, manufacturing, purchasing. Too often, each function tries to optimize its own logistics performance without regard for the activities of the other functions. However, transportation, inventory, warehousing, and order-processing activities interact, often in an inverse way. For example, lower inventory levels reduce inventory-carrying costs. But they may also reduce customer service and increase costs from stock-outs, back-orders, special production runs, and costly fast-freight shipments. Because distribution activities involve strong trade-offs, decisions by different functions must be coordinated to achieve superior overall logistics performance.

Thus, the goal of integrated logistics management is to harmonize all of the company's distribution decisions. Close working relationships among functions can be achieved in several ways. Some companies have created permanent logistics committees made up of managers who are responsible for different physical distribution activities. These committees meet often to set policies for improving overall logistics performance. Companies can also create management positions that link the logistics activities of functional areas. For example, Procter & Gamble has created "supply managers" who manage all of the supply chain activities for each of its product categories.[20] Many companies have a vice president of logistics with cross-functional authority. In fact, according to one logistics expert, three-fourths of all major wholesalers and retailers and a third of major manufacturing companies have senior logistics officers at the vice president or higher level.[21] The location of the logistics functions within the company is a secondary concern. The important thing is that the company coordinate its logistics and marketing activities to create high market satisfaction at a reasonable cost.

## Building Channel Partnerships

The members of a distribution channel are linked closely in delivering customer satisfaction and value. One company's distribution system is another company's supply system. The success of each channel member depends on the performance of the entire supply chain. For example, Wal-Mart can charge the lowest prices at retail only if its entire supply chain—consisting of thousands of merchandise suppliers, transport companies, warehouses, and service providers—operates at maximum efficiency.

Companies must do more than improve their own logistics. They must also work with other channel members to improve whole-channel distribution. For example, it makes little sense for Levi Strauss to ship finished jeans to its own warehouses, then from these warehouses to JCPenney warehouses, from which they are then shipped to JCPenney's stores. If the two companies can work together, Levi Strauss might be able to ship much of its merchandise directly to JCPenney's stores, saving time, inventory, and shipping costs for both. Today, smart companies are coordinating their logistics strategies and building strong partnerships with suppliers and customers to improve customer service and reduce channel costs.

These channel partnerships can take many forms. Many companies have created *cross-functional, cross-company teams.* For example, Procter & Gamble has a team of almost 100 people living in Bentonville, Arkansas, home of Wal-Mart. The P&Gers work with their counterparts at Wal-Mart to jointly find ways to squeeze costs out of their distribution system. Working together benefits not only P&G and Wal-Mart, but also their final consumers. Haggar Apparel Company has a similar system called "multiple points of contact," in which a Haggar team works with JCPenney people at corporate, divisional, and store levels. As a result of this partnership, Penney now receives Haggar merchandise within 18 days of placing an order—10 days fewer than its next-best supplier. And Haggar ships the merchandise "floor ready"—hangered and pretagged—reducing the time it takes Penney to move the stock from receiving docks to the sales floor from four days to just one.[22]

Other companies partner through *shared projects.* For example, many larger retailers are working closely with suppliers on in-store programs. Home Depot allows key suppliers to use its stores as a testing ground for new merchandising programs. The suppliers spend time at Home Depot stores watching how their product sells and how customers relate to it. They then create programs specially tailored to Home Depot and its customers. Western Publishing Group, publisher of Little Golden Books for children, formed a similar partnership with Toys 'R' Us. Western and the giant toy retailer coordinated their marketing strategies to create minibookstore sections—called Books 'R' Us—within each Toys 'R' Us store. Toys 'R' Us provides the locations, space, and customers; Western serves as distributor, consolidator, and servicer for the Books 'R' Us program.[23] Clearly, both the supplier and customer benefit from such partnerships.

Channel partnerships may also take the form of *information sharing* and *continuous inventory replenishment* systems. Companies manage their supply chains through information. Suppliers link up with customers through EDI systems to share information and coordinate their logistics decisions. Here are just two examples:

> Increasingly, high-performance retailers are sharing point-of-sale scanner data with their suppliers through electronic data interchange. Wal-Mart was one of the first companies to provide suppliers with timely sales data. With its Retail Link system, major suppliers have "earth stations"

installed by which they are directly connected to Wal-Mart's information network. Now, the same system that tells Wal-Mart what customers are buying lets suppliers know what to produce and where to ship the goods. For example, Wal-Mart sells millions of Wrangler jeans each year. Every night, Wal-Mart sends sales data collected on its scanners directly to VF Corporation (which makes Wrangler jeans), which then restocks automatically. So if a Wal-Mart customer buys a pair of Wranglers on Tuesday morning, by the evening, records of the sales arrive in VF's central computer. If VF has a replacement pair in stock, it's shipped directly to the store the next day—and by Thursday, Wal-Mart's shelf is replenished. If not, VF's computers automatically order up a replacement—and a new pair of jeans is shipped within a week.[24]

Bailey Controls, a manufacturer of control systems for big factories, from steel and paper mills to chemical and pharmaceutical plants, . . . treats some of its suppliers almost like departments of its own plants. Bailey has plugged two of its main electronics suppliers into itself. Future Electronics is hooked on through an electronic data interchange system. Every week, Bailey electronically sends Future its latest forecasts of what materials it will need for the next six months, so that Future can stock up in time. Bailey itself stocks only enough inventory for a few days of operation, as opposed to the three or four months worth it used to carry. Whenever a bin of parts falls below a designated level, a Bailey employee passes a laser scanner over the bin's bar code, instantly alerting Future to send the parts at once. Arrow Electronics . . . is plugged in even more closely: It has a warehouse in Bailey's factory, stocked according to Bailey's twice-a-month forecasts. Bailey provides the space, Arrow the warehouseman and the $500,000 of inventory.[25]

Today, as a result of such partnerships, many companies have switched from *anticipatory-based distribution systems* to *response-based distribution systems*.[26] In anticipatory distribution, the company produces the amount of goods called for by a sales forecast. It builds and holds stock at various supply points such as the plant, distribution centers, and retail outlets. Each supply point reorders automatically when its order point is reached. When sales are slower than expected, the company tries to reduce its inventories by offering discounts, rebates, and promotions. For example, the American auto industry produces cars far in advance of demand, and these cars often sit for months in inventory until the companies undertake aggressive promotion.

A response-based distribution system, in contrast, is *customer-triggered*. The producer continuously builds and replaces stock as orders arrive. It produces what is currently selling. For example, Japanese carmakers take orders for cars, then produce and ship them within four days. Some large appliance manufacturers, such as Whirlpool and GE, are moving to this system. Benetton, the Italian fashion house, uses a *quick-response system*, dyeing its sweaters in the colors that are currently selling instead of trying to guess far in advance which colors people will want. Producing for order rather than for forecast substantially cuts down inventory costs and risks.

## SUMMARY

*Distribution channel decisions* are among the most complex and challenging decisions facing the firm. Each channel system creates a different level of sales and costs. Once a distribution channel has been chosen, the firm usually has to stick with it for a long time. The chosen channel strongly affects, and is affected by, the other elements in the marketing mix.

Each firm needs to identify alternative ways to reach its market. Available means vary from direct selling to using one, two, three, or more intermediary *channel levels*. Marketing channels face continuous and sometimes dramatic change. Three of the most important trends are the growth of *vertical, horizontal,* and *hybrid marketing systems*. These trends affect channel cooperation, conflict, and competition.

*Channel design* begins with assessing customer channel-service needs and company channel objectives and constraints. The company then identifies the major channel alternatives in terms of the *types* of intermediaries, the *number* of intermediaries, and the *channel responsibilities* of each. Each channel alternative must be evaluated according to economic, control, and adaptive criteria. Channel management calls for selecting qualified intermediaries and motivating them. Individual channel members must be evaluated regularly.

Just as the marketing concept is receiving increased recognition, more business firms are paying attention to the *physical distribution,* or *marketing logistics*. Logistics is an area of potentially high cost savings and improved customer satisfaction. Marketing logistics involves coordinating the activities of the entire *supply chain* to deliver maximum value to customers. No logistics system can both maximize customer service and minimize distribution costs. Instead, the goal of logistics management is to provide a *targeted* level of service at the least cost. The major logistics functions include *order processing, warehousing, inventory management,* and *transportation.*

The *integrated logistics concept* recognizes that improved logistics requires teamwork in the form of close working relationships across functional areas inside the company and across various organizations in the supply chain. Companies can achieve logistics harmony among functions using cross-functional logistics teams, integrative supply managers, and senior-level logistics executives with cross-functional authority. Channel partnerships can be cross-company teams, shared projects, and information-sharing systems. Through such partnerships, many companies have switched from *anticipatory-based distribution systems* to customer-triggered *response-based distribution systems.*

## KEY TERMS

Administered VMS
Channel conflict
Channel level
Containerization
Contractual VMS
Conventional distribution channel
Corporate VMS
Direct marketing channel
Distribution center

Distribution channel (marketing channel)
Exclusive distribution
Franchise organization
Horizontal marketing systems
Hybrid marketing channels
Indirect marketing channel
Integrated logistics management

Intensive distribution
Physical distribution (or marketing logistics)
Retailer cooperatives
Selective distribution
Vertical marketing system (VMS)
Wholesaler-sponsored voluntary chains

## QUESTIONS FOR DISCUSSION

1. The Book-of-the-Month Club (BOMC) has been successfully marketing books by mail for over 50 years. Discuss why so few publishers sell books directly by mail. Suggest reasons for how the BOMC has survived competition from B. Dalton, Waldenbooks, Borders, and other large booksellers in recent years.

2. According to the International Franchising Association, between 30 percent and 50 percent of all new franchise applicants are people who formerly worked in large corporations and who lost their jobs as a result of corporate downsizing. How do you think these mid-level, mid-career corporate executives will adapt to life as franchise owners? How will their previous corporate experience help them? How will it hurt them?

3. Why have horizontal marketing arrangements become more common in recent years? Suggest several pairs of companies that you think could have successful horizontal marketing programs.

4. Describe the channel service needs of (a) consumers buying computers for home use, (b) retailers buying computers to resell to individual consumers, and (c) purchasing agents buying computers for company use. What channels would a computer manufacturer design to satisfy these different service needs?

5. Decide which distribution strategies—intensive, selective, or exclusive—are used for the following products, and why?

   ◆ Piaget watches.
   ◆ Acura automobiles.
   ◆ Snickers candy bars.

6. Identify several consequences of running out of stock that need to be considered when planning desired inventory levels.

## APPLYING THE CONCEPTS

1. Discount malls and so-called "factory outlet centers" are increasing in popularity. Many of their stores are operated by manufacturers who normally sell only through middlemen. If you have one of these malls nearby, visit it and study the retailers. What sort of merchandise is sold in these stores? Do any of them appear to be factory owned? If so, do these factory stores compete with the manufacturer's normal retailers? Appraise the pros and cons of operating these stores.

2. Go through a camera or computer magazine, and pay special attention to large ads for mail-order retailers. Look for ads for brand-name products that use selective distribution, such as Nikon cameras or Compaq computers. Locate an ad that is clearly from an authorized dealer, and one that appears not to be. How can you judge which channel is legitimate? Are there price differences between the legitimate and the unauthorized dealers, and if so, are they what you would expect?

## REFERENCES

1. Quotes from Dana Milbank, "Independent Tire Dealers Rebelling Against Goodyear," *Wall Street Journal*, July 8, 1992, p. B1; and Zachary Schiller, "Goodyear Is Gunning Its Marketing Engine," *Business Week*, March 16, 1992, p. 42. Also see Peter Nulty, "The Bounce Is Back at Goodyear," *Fortune*, September 7, 1992, pp. 70–72; Zachary Schiller, "And Fix That Flat Before You Go, Stanley," *Business Week*, January 16, 1995, p. 35; and Lloyd Stoyer, "Reassured and Fired Up," *Modern Tire Dealer*, March 1995, p. 52.

2. Louis Stern and Adel I. El-Ansary, *Marketing Channels*, 4th ed. (Engle-

wood Cliffs, NJ: Prentice Hall, 1992), p. 3.

3. Jaclyn Fierman, "How Gallo Crushes the Competition," *Fortune,* September 1, 1986, p. 27.

4. See Richard C. Hoffman and John F. Preble, "Franchising Into the Twenty-First Century," *Business Horizons,* November–December 1993, pp. 35–43.

5. See Allan J. Magrath, "Collaborative Marketing Comes of Age—Again," *Sales & Marketing Management,* September 1991, pp. 61–64; and Andrew E. Serwer, "What Price Loyalty?" *Fortune,* January 10, 1995, 103–4.

6. See Rowland T. Moriarity and Ursala Moran, "Managing Hybrid Marketing Systems," *Harvard Business Review,* November–December 1990, pp. 146–55; and Frank V. Cespedes and E. Raymond Corey, "Managing Multiple Channels," *Business Horizons,* July–August 1990, pp. 67–77.

7. For a technical discussion of how service-oriented firms choose to enter international markets, see M. Krishna Erramilli, "Service Firms' International Entry-Mode Approach: A Modified Transaction-Cost Analysis Approach," *Journal of Marketing,* July 1993, pp. 19–38.

8. Kent Phillips, "Brand of the Year," *Beverage World,* May 1994, p. 140; Melissa Campanelli, "Profiles in Marketing: Arnold Greenberg," *Sales & Marketing Management,* August 1993, p. 12; Tim Stephens, "What Makes Snapple Pop?" *Beverage World,* October 1994, pp. 200, 202.

9. Teri Lammers Prior, "Channel Surfers," *Inc.,* February 1995, pp. 65–68.

10. Subhash C. Jain, *International Marketing Management,* 3rd ed. (Boston, MA: PWS-Kent Publishing, 1990), pp. 489–91. Also see Emily Thronton, "Revolution in Japanese Retailing," *Fortune,* February 7, 1994, pp. 143–47.

11. See Philip Cateora, *International Marketing,* 7th ed. (Homewood, IL: Irwin, 1990), pp. 570–71.

12. See James A. Narus and James C. Anderson, "Turn Your Industrial Distributors into Partners," *Harvard Business Review,* March–April 1986, pp. 66–71; Marty Jacknis and Steve Kratz, "The Channel Empowerment Solution," *Sales & Marketing Management,* March 1993, pp. 44–49; Jan B. Heide, "Interorganizational Governance in Marketing Channels," *Journal of Marketing,* January 1994, pp. 71–85; Donald V. Fites, "Make Your Dealers Your Partners," *Harvard Business Review,* March–April, 1996, pp. 84–95.

13. See Katherine M. Hafner, "Computer Retailers: Things Have Gone from Worse to Bad," *Business Week,* June 8, 1987, p. 104.

14. Ronald Henkoff, "Delivering the Goods," *Fortune,* November 18, 1994, pp. 64–78. Also see Shlomo Maital, "The Last Frontier of Cost Reduction," *Across the Board,* February 1994, pp. 51–52.

15. Shlomo Maital, "The Last Frontier of Cost Reduction," p. 52.

16. "Linking with Vendors for Just-In-Time Service," *Chain Store Age Executive,* June 1993, pp. 22A–24A.

17. John Huey, "Wal-Mart: Will It Take Over the World?" *Fortune,* January 30, 1989, pp. 52–64.

18. Shawn Tully, "Comeback Ahead for Railroads," *Fortune,* June 17, 1991, pp. 107–13.

19. See "Trucking Deregulation: A Ten-Year Anniversary," *Fortune,* August 13, 1990, pp. 25–35.

20. "Managing Logistics in the 1990s," *Logistics Perspectives,* Anderson Consulting, Cleveland, OH, July 1990, pp. 1–6.

21. Maital, "The Last Frontier of Cost Reduction," p. 51.

22. Sandra J. Skrovan, "Partnering with Vendors: The Ties that Bind," *Chain Store Age Executive,* January 1994, pp. 6MH–9MH; and Robert D. Buzzell and Gwen Ortmeyer, "Channel Partnerships Streamline Distribution," *Sloan Management Review,* March 22, 1995, p. 85.

23. Skrovan, "Partnering with Vendors," p. 6MH; and Susan Caminiti, "After You Win, the Fun Begins," *Fortune,* May 2, 1994, p. 76.

24. See Joseph Weber, "Just Get It to the Store on Time," *Business Week,* March 6, 1995, pp. 66–67; and Gary Robbins, "Pushing the Limits of VMI (Vendor Managed Inventory)," *Stores,* March 1995, p. 42.

25. Myron Magnet, "The New Golden Rule of Business," *Fortune,* February 21, 1994, pp. 60–64.

26. Based on an address by Professor Donald J. Bowersox at Michigan State University on August 5, 1992.

# 12

# Retailing and Wholesaling

For more than 40 years, Scandinavian furniture giant IKEA (pronounced *eye-KEY-ah*) has sold its stylish, low-cost furniture worldwide. Smart targeting, careful attention to customer needs, and rock-bottom prices have made IKEA the world's largest home furnishings company.

When IKEA opened its first U.S. store in 1985, it caused quite a stir. On opening day, people flocked to the suburban Philadelphia store from as far away as Washington, DC. Traffic on the nearby turnpike backed up for six miles, and at one point the store was jammed so tightly with customers that management ordered the doors closed until the crowds thinned out. In the first week, the IKEA store packed in 150,000 people who bought over $1 million worth of furniture. When the dust had settled, the store was still averaging 50,000 customers a week. Similarly, when IKEA opened its store in Elizabeth, New Jersey, about 15 miles from Manhattan, the response bordered on a riot. On the first day of business, the New Jersey Turnpike was backed up for nine miles as 26,000 shoppers converged on the new store, generating $1 million in sales and doubling IKEA's opening-day record.

IKEA is one of a breed of retailers called "category killers." These retailers get their name from their marketing strategy: Carry a huge selection of merchandise in a single product category at such good prices that you destroy the competition. Category killers now operate in a wide range of industries, including furniture, toys, records, sporting goods, housewares, and consumer electronics.

This is a home furnishings store?

IKEA (👁️🔑-ah!)

An IKEA store is about three football fields in size. Each store stocks more than 6,000 items—all furnishings and housewares, ranging from coffee mugs to leather sofas to kitchen cabinets. IKEA sells Scandinavian-design "knock-down" furniture—each item reduces to a flat-pack kit for assembly at home. Consumers browse through the store's comfortable display area, where signs and stickers on each item note its price, details of its construction, assembly instructions, its location in the adjacent warehouse, even which other pieces complement the item. Customers wrestle desired items from warehouse stacks, haul their choices away on large trollies, and pay at giant-sized checkout counters. The store provides a reasonably priced restaurant for hungry shoppers and a supervised children's play area for weary parents. But best of all, IKEA's prices are low. The store operates on a simple philosophy: Provide a wide variety of well-designed home furnishings at prices that the majority of people can afford.

Although the first category killer, Toys 'R' Us, appeared during the late 1950s, other retailers only recently adopted the idea. Unlike warehouse clubs and other "off-price" retailers, which offer the lowest prices but few choices within any given category, category killers offer an exhaustive selection in one line. Toys 'R' Us stocks 18,000 different toy items in football-field-size stores. Huge Sportmart stores stock 100,000 sporting goods items, including 70 types of sleeping bags, 265 styles of athletic socks, 12,000 pairs of shoes, and 15,000 fishing lures. And Branden's, the housewares and home furnishings category killer, offers a choice of 30 different coffee pots, 25 irons, 100 patterns of bedsheets, and 800 kitchen gadgets. With such large assortments, category killers generate big sales that often allow them to charge prices as low as those of their discount competitors.

The category killers face a few problems, however. For example, IKEA has encountered occasional difficulty managing its huge inventory, sometimes over-promising or inconveniencing customers. The company's expansive stores also require large investments and huge markets. Some consumers find that they want more personal service than IKEA gives or that the savings aren't worth the work required to find products in the huge store, haul them out, and assemble them at home. Despite such problems, IKEA has gained worldwide prosperity beyond its founders' dreams. It now has 121 stores in 23 countries, racking up over $5 billion a year in sales. Since opening its initial U.S. store in Philadelphia, it has opened other stores in Washington, DC; Baltimore; Pittsburgh; Elizabeth, New Jersey; Long Island; Manhattan; Los Angeles; and other cities. In all, IKEA plans to open 60 stores around the country over the next 25 years.

Most retailing experts predict great success for stores like IKEA. One retailing analyst, Wallace Epperson, Jr., estimates "IKEA will win at least a 15 percent share of any market it enters and will expand the market as it does so." If Mr. Epperson is any indication, IKEA's prospects are good. Touring IKEA in his professional capacity, Mr. Epperson couldn't resist the store. "I spent $400," he said. "It's incredible."[1] ∎

# C H A P T E R   O B J E C T I V E S

## *After reading this chapter, you should be able to:*

**1** Explain the roles of retailers and wholesalers in the distribution channel.

**2** Describe the major types of retailers and give examples of each.

**3** Identify the major types of wholesalers and give examples of each.

**4** Explain the marketing decisions facing retailers and wholesalers.

In this chapter, we discuss *retailing* and *wholesaling*. In the first section, we look at the nature and importance of retailing, major types of store and nonstore retailers, the decisions that retailers make, and the future of retailing. In the second section, we discuss these same topics as they relate to wholesalers.

## ▶RETAILING

**Retailing**
All activities involved in selling goods or services directly to final consumers for their personal, nonbusiness use.

**Retailers**
Businesses whose sales come *primarily* from retailing.

What is retailing? We all know that Wal-Mart, Sears, and Kmart are retailers, but so are Avon representatives, the local Holiday Inn, and a doctor treating patients. **Retailing** includes all the activities involved in selling goods or services directly to final consumers for their personal, nonbusiness use. Many institutions—manufacturers, wholesalers, and retailers—do retailing. But most retailing is done by **retailers**: businesses whose sales come *primarily* from retailing. And although most retailing is done in retail stores, in recent years, nonstore retailing—selling by mail, telephone, door-to-door contact, vending machines, and numerous electronic means—has grown tremendously. Finally, although many retail stores are independently owned, an increasing number are now banding together under some form of corporate or contractual organization. Because store retailing accounts for most of the retail business, we will discuss it first. Next, we look at nonstore retailing and then at various forms of retailer organizations.

## ▶STORE RETAILING

Retail stores come in all shapes and sizes, and new retail types keep emerging. The most important types of retail stores are described in Table 12-1 and discussed in the following sections. They can be classified in terms of several characteristics, including the *amount of service* that they offer, the breadth and depth of their *product lines*, and the *relative prices* they charge.

### AMOUNT OF SERVICE

Different products require different amounts of service, and customer service preferences vary. Retailers may offer one of three levels of service—self-service, limited service, and full service.

*Self-service retailers* increased rapidly in the United States during the Great Depression of the 1930s. Customers were willing to perform their own "locate-compare-select" process to save money. Today, self-service is the basis of all discount operations and typically is used by sellers of convenience goods (such as supermarkets) and nationally branded, fast-moving shopping goods (such as catalog showrooms like Service Merchandise or Best Products).

*Limited-service retailers,* such as Sears or JCPenney, provide more sales assistance because they carry more shopping goods about which customers need information. Their increased operating costs result in higher prices. In *full-service retailers,* such as specialty stores and first-class department stores, salespeople assist customers in every phase of the shopping process. Full-service stores usually carry more specialty goods for which customers like to be "waited on." They provide more liberal return policies, various credit plans, free delivery, home servicing, and

**TABLE 12-1**    *Major Types of Retailers*

| Type | Description | Examples |
|---|---|---|
| Specialty stores | Carry a narrow product line with a deep assortment within that line: apparel stores, sporting-goods stores, furniture stores, florists, and bookstores. Specialty stores can be subclassified by the degree of narrowness in their product line. A clothing store would be a *single-line store;* a men's clothing store would be a *limited-line store;* and a men's custom-shirt store would be a *superspecialty store.* | Athlete's Foot (sport shoes only); Tall Men (tall-men's clothing); The Limited (women's clothing); The Body Shop (cosmetics and bath supplies) |
| Department stores | Carry several product lines—typically clothing, home furnishings, and household goods—with each line operated as a separate department managed by specialist buyers or merchandisers. | Sears, Saks Fifth Avenue, Marshall Field, May, JCPenney, Nordstrom, Macy's |
| Supermarkets | Relatively large, low-cost, low-margin, high-volume, self-service operations designed to serve the consumer's total needs for food, laundry, and household-maintenance products. | Safeway, Kroger, A&P, Winn-Dixie, Publix, Food Lion, Vons, Jewel |
| Convenience stores | Relatively small stores that are located near residential areas, are open long hours seven days a week, and carry a limited line of high-turnover convenience products. Their long hours and their use by consumers mainly for "fill-in" purchases make them relatively high-price operations. | 7-Eleven, Circle K, Stop-N-Go |
| Superstore | Larger stores that aim at meeting consumers' total needs for routinely purchased food and nonfood items. They include *supercenters,* combined supermarket and discount stores, which feature cross merchandising. They also include so-called *category killers* that carry a very deep assortment of a particular line. Another superstore variation is *hypermarkets,* huge stores that combine supermarket, discount, and warehouse retailing to sell routinely purchased goods as well as furniture, large and small appliances, clothing, and many other items. | *Supercenters:* Wal-Mart Supercenters, and Super Kmart Centers; *Category killers:* Toys 'R' Us (toys), Petsmart (pet supplies), Staples (office supplies), Home Depot (home improvement); *Hypermarkets:* Carrefour (France); Pyrca (Spain); Meijer's (Netherlands) |
| Discount stores | Sell standard merchandise at lower prices by accepting lower margins and selling higher volumes. A true discount store *regularly* sells its merchandise at lower prices, offering mostly national brands, not inferior goods. Discount retailers include both general merchandise and specialty merchandise stores. | *General discount stores:* Wal-Mart, Kmart, Target; *Specialty discount stores:* Circuit City (electronics), Crown Bookstores (books) |
| Off-price retailers | Sell a changing and unstable collection of higher-quality merchandise, often leftover goods, overruns, and irregulars obtained at reduced prices from manufacturers or other retailers. They buy at less than regular wholesale prices and charge consumers less than retail. They include three main types: | |

**TABLE 12-1**   *(continued)*

| Type | Description | Examples |
|---|---|---|
| Factory outlets | Owned and operated by manufacturers and normally carry the manufacturer's surplus, discontinued, or irregular goods. Such outlets increasingly group together in *factory outlet malls,* where dozens of outlet stores offer prices as much as 50 percent below retail on a broad range of items. | Mikasa (dinnerware), Dexter (shoes), Ralph Lauren and Liz Claiborne (upscale apparel) |
| Independent-off-price retailers | Owned and run either by entrepreneurs or by divisions of larger retail corporations. | Filene's Basement, Loehmann's, TJX COS. (Hit or Miss and T.J. maxx) |
| Warehouse clubs (or wholesale clubs) | Sell a limited selection of brand-name grocery items, appliances, clothing, and a hodgepodge of other goods at deep discounts to members who pay $25 to $50 annual membership fees. They serve small businesses and other club members out of huge, low-overhead, warehouselike facilities and offer few frills or services. | Wal-Mart owned Sam's Club, Max Clubs, Price-Costco, BJ's Wholesale Club |
| Catalog showrooms | Sell a broad selection of high-markup, fast-moving, brand-name goods at discount prices. These include jewelry, power tools, cameras, luggage, small appliances, toys, and sporting goods. Customers order the goods from a catalog in the showroom, then pick them up from a merchandise pick-up area in the store. | Service Merchandise, Best Products |

extras such as lounges and restaurants. More services result in much higher operating costs, which are passed along to customers as higher prices.

## PRODUCT LINE

**Specialty store**
A retail store that carries a narrow product line with a deep assortment within that line.

**Department store**
A retail organization that carries a wide variety of product lines—typically clothing, home furnishings, and household goods.

Retailers can also be classified by the length and breadth of their product assortments. Some retailers, such as **specialty stores,** carry narrow product lines with deep assortments within those lines. Today, specialty stores are flourishing. The increasing use of market segmentation, market targeting, and product specialization has resulted in a greater need for stores that focus on specific products and segments.

In contrast, **department stores** carry a wide variety of product lines. These stores grew rapidly through the first half of this century. However, over the past few decades, department stores have lost ground to more focused and flexible specialty stores on the one hand, and to more efficient, lower-priced discounters on the other. In response, many have added "bargain basements" to meet the discount threat. Others have set up "boutiques" and other store formats that compete with specialty stores. Still others are trying mail-order and telephone selling. Service remains the key differentiating factor. Department stores such as Nordstrom and Neiman Marcus are renewing their emphasis on service in an effort to keep old customers and win new ones.

*Today, specialty stores are flourishing: they offer high-quality products, convenient locations, good hours, and excellent service.*

**Supermarkets**
Large, low-cost, low-margin, high-volume, self-service stores that carry a wide variety of food, laundry, and household products.

**Supermarkets** are the most frequently shopped type of retail store. Today, however, they are facing slow sales growth because of decreased population growth and heightened competition from convenience stores, discount food stores, and superstores. Supermarkets have also been hit hard by the rapid growth of out-of-home eating. Thus, most supermarkets are making improvements to attract more customers. In the battle for "share of stomachs," some supermarkets have moved upscale, providing their own on-the-premises bakeries and gourmet deli counters, as well as fresh seafood departments and prepackaged takeout food. Others are cutting costs, establishing more efficient operations, and lowering prices in order to compete more effectively with food discounters.[2]

**Convenience store**
A small store located near a residential area that is open long hours seven days a week and carries a limited line of high-turnover convenience goods.

**Convenience stores** are small stores that carry a limited line of high-turnover convenience goods. In the 1990s, the convenience store industry has suffered from overcapacity as its primary market of young, blue-collar men shrunk. As a result, many chains have redesigned their stores with female customers in mind. They've upgraded colors, improved lighting, dropped video games, and priced more competitively. A number of convenience chains are also experimenting with micromarketing—tailoring each store's merchandise to the specific needs of its surrounding neighborhood. For example, a Stop-N-Go in an affluent neighborhood carries fresh produce, gourmet pasta sauces, chilled mineral water, and expensive wines. Stop-N-Go stores in Hispanic neighborhoods carry Spanish-language magazines and other goods catering to the specific needs of Hispanic consumers.[3]

**Superstore**
A store almost twice the size of a regular supermarket that carries a large assortment of routinely purchased food and nonfood items and offers many services.

**Superstores** are much larger than regular supermarkets and offer a large assortment of routinely purchased food products, nonfood items, and services. Examples include Safeway's Pak 'N Pay and Pathmark Super Centers. Almost 80 percent of the new Safeway stores that opened during the past several years have been superstores. Wal-Mart, Kmart, and other discount retailers are now opening *supercenters*, which are combination food and discount stores that emphasize cross-merchandising. For example, at a Super Kmart Center, toasters are above the fresh-baked bread, kitchen gadgets are across from produce, and infant centers carry everything from baby food to clothing. Supercenters are growing in the United States at an annual rate of 25 percent, compared with a supermarket industry growth rate of only 1 percent.[4]

*Many convenience store operators are trying micromarketing. For example, this Stop-N-Go store in a Hispanic neighborhood carries Spanish-language magazines and other items catering to the specific needs of Hispanic customers.*

**Hypermarkets**
Huge stores that combine supermarket, discount, and warehouse retailing; in addition to food, they carry furniture, appliances, clothing, and many other products.

Recent years have also seen the advent of superstores that are actually giant specialty stores, the so-called "category killers" that carry a very deep assortment of a particular line and a knowledgeable staff. Another variation, **hypermarkets,** are huge superstores, perhaps as large as *six* football fields. Although hypermarkets have been very successful in Europe and other world markets, they have met with little success in the United States. Despite their size, most hypermarkets have only limited product variety, and many people balk at the extensive walking required to shop in them.[5]

Finally, for some businesses, the "product line" is actually a service. Service retailers include hotels and motels, banks, airlines, colleges, hospitals, movie theaters, tennis clubs, bowling alleys, restaurants, repair services, hair-care shops, and dry cleaners. Service retailers in the United States are growing faster than product retailers, and each service industry has its own retailing drama. Banks look for new ways to distribute their services, including automatic teller machines, direct deposit, and telephone and on-line banking. Health organizations are changing the ways that consumers get and pay for health services. The amusement industry has spawned Disney World and other theme parks, and H&R Block has built a franchise network to help consumers pay as little as possible to Uncle Sam.

## RELATIVE PRICES

Retailers can also be classified according to the prices that they charge. Most retailers charge regular prices and offer standard-quality goods and customer service. Others offer higher-quality goods and service at higher prices. The retailers that feature low prices are discount stores, "off-price" retailers, and catalog showrooms (see Table 12-1).

### Discount Stores

**Discount store**
A retail institution that sells standard merchandise at lower prices by accepting lower margins and selling at higher volume.

A **discount store** sells standard merchandise at lower prices by accepting lower margins and selling higher volume. The early discount stores cut expenses by offering few services and by operating in warehouselike facilities in low-rent, heavily traveled districts. In recent years, facing intense competition from other discounters and department stores, many discount retailers have "traded up." They have improved decor, added new lines and services, and opened suburban branches, which have led to higher costs and prices.

### Off-Price Retailers

**Off-price retailers**
Retailers that buy at less than regular wholesale prices and sell at less than retail.

When the major discount stores traded up, a new wave of **off-price retailers** moved in to fill the low-price, high-volume gap. Ordinary discounters buy at regular wholesale prices and accept lower margins to keep prices down. In contrast, off-price retailers buy at less than regular wholesale prices and charge consumers less than retail. Off-price retailers have made the biggest inroads in clothing, accessories, and footwear. But they can be found in all areas, from no-frills banking and discount brokerages to food stores and electronics.

The three main types of off-price retailers are *independents, factory outlets,* and *warehouse clubs.* **Independent off-price retailers** are either owned and run by entrepreneurs or are divisions of larger retail corporations. Although many off-price operations are run by smaller independents, most large off-price retailer operations are owned by bigger retail chains. Examples include Loehmann's (owned by Associated Dry Goods, owner of Lord & Taylor), Filene's Basement (Federated Department Stores), and T.J. maxx (TJX Cos.).

**Independent off-price retailers**
Off-price retailers that are either owned and run by entrepreneurs or are divisions of larger retail corporations.

**Factory outlets**
Off-price retailing operations that are owned and operated by manufacturers and that normally carry the manufacturer's surplus, discontinued, or irregular goods.

**Factory outlets**—such as The Burlington Coat Factory Warehouse, Manhattan's Brand Name Fashion Outlet, and the factory outlets of Levi Strauss, Carters, and Ship 'n Shore—sometimes group together in *factory outlet malls* and *value-retail centers,* where dozens of outlet stores offer prices as low as 50 percent below retail on a wide range of items. Whereas outlet malls consist primarily of manufacturers' outlets, value-retail centers combine manufacturers' outlets with off-price retail stores and department store clearance outlets. Factory outlet malls have become one of the hottest growth areas in retailing.

*Factory outlet malls and value-retail centers have blossomed in recent years, making them one of retailing's hottest growth areas.*

The malls are now moving upscale, narrowing the gap between factory outlets and more traditional forms of retailers. As the gap narrows, the discounts offered by outlets are getting smaller. However, a growing number of factory outlets now feature brands such as Esprit and Liz Claiborne, causing department stores to protest to the manufacturers of these brands. Given their higher costs, the department stores have to charge more than the off-price outlets. Manufacturers counter that they send last year's merchandise and seconds to the factory outlet malls, not the new merchandise that they supply to the department stores. The malls are also located far from urban areas, making access to them more difficult. Still, the department stores are concerned about the growing number of shoppers who are willing to make weekend trips to stock up on branded merchandise at substantial savings.[6]

**Warehouse club (wholesale club)**
Off-price retailer that sells a limited selection of brand-name grocery items, appliances, clothing, and a hodgepodge of other goods at deep discounts to members who pay annual membership fees.

**Warehouse clubs** (or *wholesale clubs*, or *membership warehouses*), such as Sam's and Price-Costco, operate in huge, drafty warehouselike facilities and offer few frills. Customers themselves must wrestle furniture, heavy appliances, and other large items to the checkout line. Such clubs make no home deliveries and accept no credit cards, but they do offer rock-bottom prices. Warehouse clubs took the country by storm in the 1980s, but growth slowed considerably in the 1990s as a result of growing competition among warehouse store chains and effective reactions by supermarkets.[7]

In general, although off-price retailing blossomed during the 1980s, competition has stiffened as more and more off-price retailers have entered the market. The growth of off-price retailing slowed a bit recently because of effective counterstrategies by department stores and regular discounters. Still, off-price retailing remains a vital and growing force in modern retailing.

## Catalog Showrooms

**Catalog showroom**
A retail operation that sells a wide selection of high-markup, fast-moving, brand-name goods at discount prices.

A **catalog showroom** sells a wide selection of high-markup, fast-moving, brand-name goods at discount prices. These include jewelry, power tools, cameras, luggage, small appliances, toys, and sporting goods. Catalog showrooms make their money by cutting costs and margins to provide low prices that will attract a higher volume of sales. The catalog showroom industry is led by companies such as Best Products and Service Merchandise.

Emerging in the late 1960s, catalog showrooms became one of retailing's hottest new forms, but they have been struggling in recent years. For one thing, department stores and discount retailers now run regular sales that match showroom prices. In addition, off-price retailers consistently beat catalog showroom prices. As a result, many showroom chains are broadening their lines, doing more advertising, renovating their stores, and adding services in order to attract more business.

# RETAIL ORGANIZATIONS

**Chain stores**
Two or more outlets that are commonly owned and controlled, have central buying and merchandising, and sell similar lines of merchandise.

Although many retail stores are independently owned, an increasing number are banding together under some form of corporate or contractual organization. The major types of retail organizations—*corporate chains, voluntary chains and retailer cooperatives, franchise organizations, merchandising conglomerates*—are described in Table 12-2.

The corporate chain store is one of the most important retail developments of this century. **Chain stores** are two or more outlets that are commonly owned and

*TABLE 12-2* Major Types of Retail Organizations

| Type | Description | Examples |
|---|---|---|
| Corporate chain stores | Two or more outlets that are commonly owned and controlled, employ central buying and merchandising, and sell similar lines of merchandise. Corporate chains appear in all types of retailing, but they are strongest in department stores, variety stores, food stores, drugstores, shoe stores, and women's clothing stores. | Tower Records, Fayva (shoes), Pottery Barn (dinnerware and home furnishings) |
| Voluntary chains | Wholesaler-sponsored groups of independent retailers engaged in bulk buying and common merchandising. | Independent Grocers Alliance (IGA), Sentry Hardwares, Western Auto, True Value |
| Retailer cooperatives | Groups of independent retailers who set up a central buying organization and conduct joint promotion efforts. | Associated Grocers (groceries), ACE (hardware) |
| Franchise organizations | Contractual association between a *franchiser* (a manufacturer, wholesaler, or service organization) and *franchisees* (independent businesspeople who buy the right to own and operate one or more units in the franchise system). Franchise organizations are normally based on some unique product, service, or method of doing business, or on a trade name or patent, or on goodwill that the franchiser has developed. | McDonald's, Subway, Pizza Hut, Jiffy Lube, Meineke Mufflers, 7-Eleven |
| Merchandising conglomerates | A free-form corporation that combines several diversified retailing lines and forms under central ownership, along with some integration of their distribution and management functions. | Dayton-Hudson, F. W. Woolworth |

controlled. They have many advantages over independents. Their size allows them to buy in large quantities at lower prices. They can afford to hire corporate-level specialists to deal with areas such as pricing, promotion, merchandising, inventory control, and sales forecasting. And corporate chains gain promotional economies because their advertising costs are spread over many stores and over a large sales volume.

The great success of corporate chains caused many independents to band together in one of two forms of contractual associations. One is the *voluntary chain*—a wholesaler-sponsored group of independent retailers that engages in group buying and common merchandising. The other form of contractual association is the *retailer cooperative*—a group of independent retailers that bands together to set up a jointly owned central wholesale operation and conducts joint merchandising and promotion efforts. These organizations give independents the buying and promotion economies that they need to meet the prices of corporate chains.

Another form of contractual retail organization is a **franchise.** The main difference between franchise organizations and other contractual systems (voluntary chains and retail cooperatives) is that franchise systems are normally based on some unique product or service; on a method of doing business; or on the trade

**Franchise**
A contractual association between a manufacturer, wholesaler, or service organization (a franchiser) and independent businesspeople (franchisees) who buy the right to own and operate one or more units in the franchise system.

name, goodwill, or patent that the franchiser has developed. Franchising has been prominent in fast foods, video stores, health/fitness centers, hair cutting, auto rentals, motels, travel agencies, real estate, and dozens of other product and service areas. Franchising is described in detail in Marketing at Work 12-1.

Finally, *merchandising conglomerates* are corporations that combine several different retailing forms under a central ownership. Examples include Dayton-Hudson, JCPenney, and F. W. Woolworth. For example, Dayton-Hudson operates Target (discount stores), Mervyn's (lower-price clothing), B. Dalton (books), and many other chains in addition to its Dayton's, Hudson's, and other department stores. Woolworth, in addition to its variety stores, operates numerous specialty chains, including Kinney Shoe Stores, Foot Locker, Champs Sports, Herald Square Stationers, Northern Reflections, Frame Scene, Afterthoughts (costume jewelry and handbags), and Face Fantasies (budget cosmetics). Diversified retailing, which provides superior management systems and economies that benefit all the separate retail operations, is likely to increase through the close of the 1990s.

## ▶NONSTORE RETAILING

Although most goods and services are sold through stores, nonstore retailing has been growing much faster than has store retailing. Traditional store retailers are facing increasing competition from nonstore retailers who sell through catalogs, direct mail, telephone, home TV shopping shows, on-line computer shopping services, home and office parties, and other direct retailing approaches. Nonstore retailing now accounts for more than 14 percent of all consumer purchases, and it may account for a third of all sales by the end of the century. Nonstore retailing includes *direct marketing, direct selling,* and *automatic vending*.

## DIRECT MARKETING

**Direct marketing**
Marketing through various advertising media that interact directly with consumers, generally calling for the consumer to make a direct response.

**Direct marketing** uses various advertising media to interact directly with consumers, generally calling for the consumer to make a direct response. Mass advertising typically reaches an unspecified number of people, most of whom are not in the market for a product or will not buy it until some future date. Direct-advertising vehicles are used to obtain immediate orders directly from targeted consumers. Although direct marketing initially consisted mostly of direct mail and mail-order catalogs, it has taken on several additional forms in recent years, including telemarketing, direct radio and television marketing, and on-line computer shopping.

Direct marketing has boomed in recent years. All kinds of organizations use direct marketing: manufacturers, retailers, service companies, catalog merchants, and nonprofit organizations, to name a few. Its growing use in consumer marketing is largely a response to the "demassification" of mass markets, which has resulted in an ever-greater number of fragmented market segments with highly individualized needs and wants. Direct marketing allows sellers to focus efficiently on these minimarkets with offers that better match specific consumer needs.

Other trends also have fueled the growth of direct marketing. The increasing number of women entering the workforce has decreased the time that families have to shop. The higher costs of driving, traffic congestion and parking headaches, the shortage of retail sales help, limited store hours, and longer lines

## MARKETING AT WORK 12-1

# FRANCHISE FEVER

Once considered upstarts among independent businesses, franchises now command 35 percent of all retail sales in the United States. These days, it's nearly impossible to stroll down a city block or drive on a suburban street without seeing a Wendy's, a McDonald's, a Jiffy Lube, or a 7-Eleven. One of the best-known and most successful franchisers, McDonald's, now has 14,000 stores worldwide and racks up more than $23 billion in systemwide sales. Gaining fast is Subway Sandwiches and Salads, one of the fastest-growing franchises. With more than 8,500 shops in the United States, it even surpasses McDonald's 7,900 domestic units. Franchising is even moving into new areas like education. For example, LearnRight Corporation, in State College, Pennsylvania, franchises its methods for teaching students thinking skills.

How does a franchising system work? The individual franchises are a tightly knit group of enterprises whose systematic operations are planned, directed, and controlled by the operation's innovator, called a *franchiser.* Generally, franchises are distinguished by three characteristics:

1. *The franchiser owns a trade or service mark and licenses it to franchisees in return for royalty payments.*

2. *The franchisee is required to pay for the right to be part of the system.* Yet this initial fee is only a small part of the total amount that franchisees invest when they sign a franchising contract. Start-up costs include rental and lease of equipment and fixtures, and sometimes a regular license fee. McDonald's franchisees may invest as much as $600,000 in initial start-up costs. The franchisee then pays McDonald's a service fee and a rental charge that equal 11.5 percent of the franchisee's sales volume. Subway's success is partly due to its

low start-up cost of $45,000 to $70,000, which is lower than 70 percent of other franchise system start-up costs.

3. *The franchiser provides its franchisees with a marketing and operations system for doing business.* McDonald's requires franchisees to attend its "Hamburger University" in Oak Brook, Illinois, for three weeks to learn how to manage the business. Franchisees must also adhere to certain procedures in buying materials.

In the best cases, franchising is mutually beneficial to both franchiser and franchisee. Franchisers can cover a new territory in little more than the time it takes the franchisee to sign a contract. They can achieve enormous purchasing power (consider the purchase order that Holiday Inn is likely to make for bed linens, for instance). Franchisers also benefit from the franchisees' familiarity with local communities and conditions, and from the motivation

at checkout counters have all promoted in-home shopping. The concept of toll-free telephone numbers and the increased use of credit cards have helped sellers reach and transact with consumers outside of stores more easily. Finally, the growth of computer power and communication technology has allowed marketers to build better customer databases and communication channels with which to reach the best prospects for specific products.

Direct marketing has also grown rapidly in business-to-business marketing. It can help reduce the high costs of reaching business markets through the sales force. Lower-cost media, such as telemarketing and direct mail, can be used to identify the best prospects and prime them before making an expensive sales call.

Direct marketing provides many benefits to consumers as well. Instead of driving their cars through congested city streets to shop in crowded shopping malls, customers can use their telephones or computers to whiz along the *information superhighway.* Today's sophisticated communications networks carry voice, video,

and hard work of employees who are entrepreneurs rather than "hired hands." Similarly, franchisees benefit from buying into a proven business with a well-known and accepted brand name. And they receive ongoing support in areas ranging from marketing and advertising to site selection, staffing, and financing.

As a result of the franchise explosion in recent years, many types of franchisers (such as fast-food franchisers) are facing worrisome market saturation. One indication is the number of franchisee complaints filed with the Federal Trade Commission against parent companies, which has been growing by more than 50 percent annually since 1990. The most common complaint: Franchisers "encroach" on existing franchisees' territory by bringing in another store. Another complaint is higher-than-advertised failure rates. Subway, in particular, has been criticized for misleading its franchisees by telling them that it has only a 2 percent failure rate

when the reality is much different. In addition, some franchisees feel that they've been misled by exaggerated claims of support, only to feel abandoned after the contract is signed and $100,000 is invested.

There will *always* be a conflict between the franchisers, who seek systemwide growth, and the franchisees, who want to earn a good living from their individual franchises. Some new directions that may deliver both franchiser growth and franchisee earnings are:

- *Strategic alliances with major outside corporations,* such as that between film company Fuji USA and Moto Photo, a one-hour photo developer. Fuji gained instant market penetration through Moto Photo's 400 locations, and Moto Photo franchisees enjoyed Fuji's brand-name recognition and advertising reach.
- *Expansion abroad.* Fast-food franchises have become very popular throughout the world. For example, Domino's has entered Japan with master franchisee Ernest Higa, who owns 106 stores in Japan with

combined sales of $140 million. Part of Higa's success can be attributed to adapting Domino's product to the Japanese market, where food presentation is everything. Higa carefully charted the placement of pizza toppings and made cutmark perforations in the boxes for perfectly uniform slices.

- *Nontraditional site locations.* Franchises are opening in airports, sports stadiums, college campuses, hospitals, gambling casinos, theme parks, convention halls, and even riverboats.

Thus, it appears, franchise fever will not cool down soon. Experts expect that, by the turn of the century, franchises will capture almost 50 percent of all U.S. retail sales.

*Sources:* Norman D. Axelrad and Robert E. Weigand, "Franchising—A Marriage of System Members," in Sidney Levy, George Frerichs, and Howard Gordon, eds., *Marketing Managers Handbook,* 3d ed. (Chicago: Dartnell, 1994), pp. 919–34; Lawrence S. Welch, "Developments in International Franchising," *Journal of Global Marketing,* Vol. 6, Nos. 1–2, 1992, pp. 81–96; Meg Whittemore, "New Directions in Franchising," *Nation's Business,* January 1995, pp. 45–52; Andrew E. Serwer, "McDonald's Conquers the World," *Fortune,* October 17, 1994, pp. 103–16; "Trouble in Franchise Nation," *Fortune,* March 6, 1995, pp. 115–29; and Carol Steinberg, "Millionaire Franchisees," *Success,* March 1995, pp. 65–69.

and data over fiber optic telephone lines, linking buyers and sellers in convenient, exciting ways. People who buy through direct mail or by telephone say that such shopping is convenient, hassle-free, and fun. It saves them time, and it introduces them to new lifestyles and a larger selection of merchandise. Consumers can compare products and prices from their armchairs by browsing through catalogs at their leisure. They can order and receive products without having to leave their homes. Industrial customers can learn about and order products and services without tying up valuable time by meeting and listening to salespeople.

Direct marketing also provides benefits to sellers. It allows greater *selectivity.* A direct marketer can buy a mailing list containing the names of almost any group—millionaires, parents of newborn babies, left-handed people, or recent college graduates. The direct-marketing message can be *personalized* and *customized.* The marketer can search its database, select consumers with specific characteristics, and send them very individualized laser-printed letters.

With direct marketing, the seller can build a *continuous customer relationship*, tailoring a steady stream of offers to a regular customer's specific needs and interests (see Marketing at Work 12-2). Direct marketing can also be *timed* to reach prospects at just the right moment. Moreover, because it reaches more interested prospects at the best times, direct-marketing materials receive *higher readership and response*. Direct marketing also permits easy *testing* of specific messages and media. And because results are direct and immediate, direct marketing lends itself more readily to *response measurement*. Finally, direct marketing provides *privacy*—the direct marketer's offer and strategy are not visible to competitors. We will discuss the major forms of direct marketing in detail in the next chapter.

## MARKETING AT WORK 12-2

# DIRECT MARKETING: FINGERHUT BUILDS STRONG CUSTOMER RELATIONSHIPS

As Betty Holmes of Detroit, Michigan, sifts through the day's stack of mail, one item in particular catches her eye. It's only a catalog, but it's speaking directly to her. A laser-printed personal message on the catalog's cover states: "Thank you, Mrs. Holmes, for your recent purchase of women's apparel. To show our thanks, we are offering you up to 5 free gifts, plus deferred payment until July 31st." The note goes on, with amazing accuracy, to refer Betty to specific items in the catalog that will likely interest her.

The catalog is from Fingerhut, the huge direct-mail marketer. A typical Fingerhut catalog offers between 500 and 700 products, mostly domestics and household electronics, with prices ranging from $15 to $600. Fingerhut operates on a *huge* scale. Each year, it sends out some 558 million mailings—

*Fingerhut sends out over 1 million mailings per day to a portion of the 25 million households detailed in its database. Each mailing is specially tailored to the customer's interests and purchasing history.*

that's well over 1.5 million mailings per day to a portion of the 25 million households detailed in the company's database. Betty Holmes buys regularly from Fingerhut, and the company tracks her purchases carefully. Then, it sends a steady flow of direct mail offers specially tailored to her purchasing history and interests.

When new customers first respond to a direct-mail offer, Fingerhut asks them to fill out a questionnaire about the kinds of products that interest them. Using information from this questionnaire, along with information about later purchases, Fingerhut has built an impressive marketing database that allows it to target the most likely buyers with products that interest them most. Instead of sending out the same catalogs and letters to all of its customers, Fingerhut tailors its offers to what each customer is likely to buy. Moreover, promotions such as the Birthday Club

## DIRECT SELLING

**Door-to-door retailing**
Selling door to door, office to office, or at home-sales parties.

**Door-to-door retailing,** which started centuries ago with roving peddlers, has grown into a huge industry. The pioneers in door-to-door selling are the Fuller Brush Company, vacuum cleaner companies like Electrolux, and book-selling companies such as World Book and Southwestern. The image of door-to-door selling improved greatly when Avon entered the industry with its Avon representative—the homemaker's friend and beauty consultant. Tupperware and Mary Kay Cosmetics helped to popularize home sales parties, in which several friends and neighbors attend a party at a private home where products are demonstrated and sold.

provide opportunities to create special offers that sell more products. A month before a child's birthday, Birthday Club customers receive a free birthday gift for their child if they agree to try any one of the products that Fingerhut offers in an accompanying mailing. A customer who responds to these and other offers might become one of millions of "promotable" customers who receive Fingerhut mailings.

The key to Fingerhut's success is the long-term relationships that the company builds with its customers. Fingerhut carefully matches its direct-mail offers to individual customer needs, characteristics, and purchasing histories, and then makes it as easy as possible for targeted customers to buy. Fingerhut tries to establish a strong relationship that goes beyond its merchandise. Credit is an important cornerstone of that relationship. The average Fingerhut customer, typically an "empty-nester" or someone just starting a family, has a household income of

$28,000. The customer's median age is 40, and 80 percent of the customers are female. Despite selling to moderate-income consumers, Fingerhut controls its credit risks by what it offers to whom. When a new customer makes a first order, the amount of credit allowed may be limited to $50. If the customer pays promptly, the next mailing offers higher-ticket items. Good customers, who pay their bills regularly, get cards and rewards to reinforce this behavior. For example, an award envelope cheers "Congratulations! You've been selected to receive our 'exceptional customer award!'" and contains a certificate suitable for framing.

Fingerhut stays in continuous touch with its preferred customers through regular special promotions—an annual sweepstakes, free gifts, a deferred-billing promotion, and others. These special offers are all designed with one goal in mind: to create a reason for Fingerhut to be in the customer's mailbox.

Once in the mailbox, the personalized messages and targeted offers get attention.

The skillful use of database marketing and relationship building have made Fingerhut one of the nation's largest direct-mail marketers. Founded in 1948 by brothers Manny and William Fingerhut, the company now sells more than $1.9 billion worth of merchandise each year through mail order. In fact, one in every six U.S. households has *bought* something from the company. Fingerhut's success is no accident. "Most of our competitors use a full catalog; they could care less about what the individuals want," notes a Fingerhut executive. "Fingerhut finds out what each customer wants and builds an event around each promotion."

*Sources:* See Eileen Norris, "Fingerhut Gives Customers Credit," *Advertising Age,* March 6, 1986, p. 19; Brian Bremner, "Looking Downscale without Looking Down," *Business Week,* October 8, 1990, pp. 62–67; Gary Levin, "Fingerhut Points to TV Shopping," *Advertising Age,* April 4, 1994, p. 20; Leah Rickard and Julie Ralston, "Catalogers Order Changes to Beat Costs," *Advertising Age,* July 10, 1995, p. 1.

The advantages of door-to-door selling are consumer convenience and personal attention. But the high costs of hiring, training, paying, and motivating the sales force result in higher prices. Although some door-to-door companies are still thriving, door-to-door selling has a somewhat uncertain future. The increase in the number of single-person and working-couple households decreases the chances of finding a buyer at home. Home-party companies are having trouble finding nonworking women who want to sell products part time. And with recent advances in interactive direct-marketing technology, the door-to-door salesperson may well be replaced in the future by the household telephone, television, or home computer.

## AUTOMATIC VENDING

**Automatic vending**
Selling through vending machines.

**Automatic vending** is not new—in 215 B.C., Egyptians could buy sacrificial water from coin-operated dispensers. But this method of selling soared after World War II. There are now about 4.5 million vending machines in the United States—one machine for every 55 people. Today's automatic vending uses space-age and computer technology to sell a wide variety of convenience and impulse goods—cigarettes, beverages, candy, newspapers, foods and snacks, hosiery, cosmetics, paperback books, T-shirts, insurance policies, pizza, audio tapes and videocassettes, and even shoeshines and fishing worms.

Vending machines are found everywhere—in factories, offices, lobbies, retail stores, gasoline stations, airports, and train and bus terminals. Automatic teller machines provide bank customers with checking, savings, withdrawal, and funds-transfer services. Compared with store retailing, vending machines offer consumers greater convenience (available 24 hours, self-service) and fewer damaged goods. But the expensive equipment and labor required for automatic vending make it a costly channel, and prices of vended goods are often 15 to 20 percent higher than are those in retail stores. Customers also must put up with aggravating machine breakdowns, out-of-stock items, and the fact that merchandise cannot be returned.[8]

## ▶ RETAILER MARKETING DECISIONS

Retailers are searching for new marketing strategies to attract and hold customers. In the past, retailers attracted customers with unique products, more or better services than their competitors offered, or credit cards. Today, national brand manufacturers, in their drive for volume, have placed their branded goods everywhere. Thus, stores offer more similar assortments—national brands are found not only in department stores, but also in mass-merchandise and off-price discount stores. As a result, stores are looking more and more alike; they have become "commoditized." In any city, a shopper can find many stores but few assortments.

Service differentiation among retailers has also eroded. Many department stores have trimmed their services, whereas discounters have increased theirs. Customers have become smarter and more price sensitive. They see no reason to pay more for identical brands, especially when service differences are shrinking. And because bank credit cards are now accepted at most stores, consumers no longer need credit from a particular store. For all these reasons, many retailers today are rethinking their marketing strategies.

As shown in Figure 12-1, retailers face major marketing decisions about their *target markets and positioning, product assortment and services, price, promotion,* and *place.*

## TARGET MARKET AND POSITIONING DECISION

Retailers must first define their target markets and then decide how they will position themselves in these markets. Should the store focus on upscale, midscale, or downscale shoppers? Do target shoppers want variety, depth of assortment, convenience, or low prices? Until they define and profile their markets, retailers cannot make consistent decisions about product assortment, services, pricing, advertising, store decor, or any of the other decisions that must support their positions.

Too many retailers fail to define their target markets and positions clearly. They try to have "something for everyone" and end up satisfying no market well. In contrast, successful retailers define their target markets well and position themselves strongly. For example, in 1963, Leslie H. Wexner borrowed $5,000 to create The Limited, which started out as a single store targeted to young, fashion-conscious women. All aspects of the store—clothing assortment, fixtures, music, colors, personnel—were orchestrated to match the target consumer. He continued to open more stores, but a decade later, his original customers were no longer in the "young" group. To catch the new "youngs," he started the Limited Express. Over the years, he started or acquired other highly targeted store chains, including Lane Bryant, Victoria's Secret, Lerner, Express, Structure, Limited Too, and others to reach new segments. Today, The Limited, Inc. operates more than 4,000 stores in several different segments of the market, with sales of more than $7.3 billion.[9]

Even large stores such as Wal-Mart, Kmart, and Sears must define their major target markets in order to design effective marketing strategies. In fact, in recent years, thanks to strong targeting and positioning, Wal-Mart has zoomed past Sears and Kmart to become the nation's largest retailer (see Marketing at Work 12-3).[10]

## PRODUCT ASSORTMENT AND SERVICES DECISION

Retailers must decide on three major product variables: *product assortment, services mix,* and *store atmosphere.*

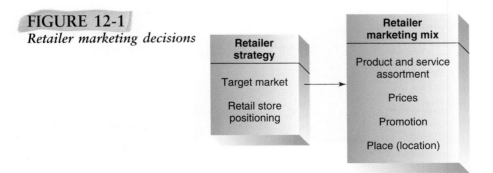

**FIGURE 12-1**
*Retailer marketing decisions*

**Retailer strategy**
Target market
Retail store positioning

**Retailer marketing mix**
Product and service assortment
Prices
Promotion
Place (location)

## MARKETING AT WORK 12-3

# WAL-MART: THE NATION'S LARGEST RETAILER

In 1962, Sam Walton and his brother opened the first Wal-Mart discount store in small-town Rogers, Arkansas. It was a big, flat, warehouse-type store that sold everything from apparel to automotive supplies to small appliances at very low prices. Experts gave the fledgling retailer little chance—conventional wisdom suggested that discount stores could succeed only in large cities. Yet, from these modest beginnings, the chain expanded rapidly, opening new stores in one small southern town after another. By the mid-1980s, Wal-Mart had exploded onto the national retailing scene. It began building stores in larger cities such as Dallas, St. Louis, and Kansas City. Incredibly, less than 30 years after opening its first store, Wal-Mart overtook long-time industry leader Sears to become the nation's largest retailer.

Wal-Mart's phenomenal growth shows few signs of slowing. The company has now built more stores in larger cities and is expanding into Mexico and Canada. Sales in 1995 approached $100 billion, and management fully expects that sales will reach more than $150 billion by the turn of the century. Over the past decade, Wal-Mart's annual return to investors has averaged more than 45 percent, rewarding investors handsomely. An investment of $1,650 in Wal-Mart stock in 1970 would be worth a whopping $3 million today!

What are the secrets behind this spectacular success? Wal-Mart listens to and takes care of its customers, treats employees as partners, and keeps a tight rein on costs.

### LISTENING TO AND TAKING CARE OF CUSTOMERS

Wal-Mart positioned itself strongly in a well-chosen target market. Initially, Sam Walton focused on value-conscious consumers in small-town America. The chain built a strong everyday low-price position long before it became fashionable in retailing. It grew rapidly by bringing the lowest possible prices to towns ignored by national discounters—towns such as Van Buren, Arkansas, and Idabel, Oklahoma.

Wal-Mart knows its customers and takes good care of them. As one analyst puts it, "The company gospel . . . is relatively simple: Be an agent for customers, find out what they want, and sell it to them for the lowest possible price." Thus, the company listens carefully—for example, each top Wal-Mart executive spends at least two days a week visiting stores, talking directly with customers and getting a firsthand look at operations. Then, Wal-Mart delivers what customers want: a broad selection of carefully selected goods at unbeatable prices.

But the right merchandise at the right price isn't the only key to Wal-Mart's success. Wal-Mart also provides the kind of service that keeps customers satisfied. A sign reading "Satisfaction Guaranteed" hangs prominently at each store's entrance. Another sign inside the store reads "At Wal-Mart, our goal is: You're always next in line!" Customers are often welcomed by "people greeters" eager to lend a helping hand or just to be friendly. And, sure enough, the store opens extra checkout counters to keep waiting lines short.

Going the extra mile for customers has paid off. A recent

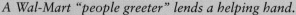

*A Wal-Mart "people greeter" lends a helping hand.*

independent survey in towns where Wal-Mart competes with Kmart and Target found that Wal-Mart's shoppers were the most satisfied; Kmart's the least. Perhaps more telling, whereas the typical Kmart store rings up average sales of about $150 per square foot per year, the typical Wal-Mart store hauls in $250.

### TREATING EMPLOYEES AS PARTNERS

Wal-Mart believes that, in the final accounting, the company's people are what really make it better. Thus, it works hard to show employees that it cares about them. Wal-Mart calls employees "associates," a practice now widely copied by competitors. The associates work as partners, become deeply involved in operations, and share rewards for good performance.

*Everyone at Wal-Mart [is] an associate—from [the CEO] . . . to a cashier named Janet at the Wal-Mart on Highway 50 in Ocoee, Florida. "We," "us," and "our" are the operative words. Wal-Mart department heads, hourly associates who look after one or more of 30-some departments ranging from sporting goods to electronics, see figures that many companies never show general managers: costs, freight charges, profit margins. The company sets a profit margin for each store, and if the store exceeds it, then the hourly associates share part of the additional profit.*

The partnership concept is deeply rooted in the Wal-Mart corporate culture. Wal- Mart's concern for its employees translates into high employee satisfac-

tion, which in turn translates into greater customer satisfaction.

### KEEPING A TIGHT REIN ON COSTS

Wal-Mart has the lowest cost structure in the industry; operating expenses amount to only 16 percent of sales, compared with 23 percent at Kmart. Thus, Wal-Mart can charge lower prices but still reap higher profits, allowing it to offer better service. This creates a "productivity loop." Wal-Mart's lower prices and better service attract more shoppers, producing more sales, making the company more efficient, and enabling it to lower prices even more.

Wal-Mart's low costs result in part from superior management and more sophisticated technology. Its Bentonville, Arkansas, headquarters contains a computer-communications system that the Defense Department would envy, giving managers around the country instant access to sales and operating information. And its huge, fully automated distribution centers employ the latest technology to supply stores efficiently. Wal-Mart also spends less than competitors on advertising—only 0.5 percent of sales, compared with 2.5 percent at Kmart and 3.8 percent at Sears. Because Wal-Mart has what customers want at the prices they'll pay, its reputation has spread rapidly by word of mouth. It has not needed more advertising.

Finally, Wal-Mart keeps costs down through good old

"tough buying." Whereas the company is known for the warm way it treats customers, it is equally well known for the cold, calculated way it wrings low prices from suppliers. The following passage describes a visit to Wal-Mart's buying offices.

*Don't expect a greeter and don't expect friendly. . . . Once you are ushered into one of the spartan little buyers' rooms, expect a steely eye across the table and be prepared to cut your price. "They are very, very focused people, and they use their buying power more forcefully than anyone else in America," says the marketing vice president of a major vendor. "All the normal mating rituals are [forbidden]. Their highest priority is making sure everyone at all times in all cases knows who's in charge, and it's Wal-Mart. They talk softly, but they have piranha hearts, and if you aren't totally prepared when you go in there, you'll have your [head] handed to you."*

Some observers wonder whether Wal-Mart can be so big and still retain its focus and positioning. They wonder if an ever-larger Wal-Mart can stay close to its customers and employees. The company's managers are betting on it. Says one top executive: "We'll be fine as long as we never lose our responsiveness to the consumer."

*Sources:* Quoted material from Bill Saporito, "Is Wal-Mart Unstoppable?" *Fortune,* May 6, 1991, pp. 50–59; and John Huey, "Wal-Mart: Will It Take Over the World?" *Fortune,* January 30, 1989, pp. 52–61. Also see Christy Fisher, "Wal-Mart's Way," *Advertising Age,* February 18, 1991, p. 3; Bill Saporito, "And the Winner Is Still . . . Wal-Mart," *Fortune,* May 2, 1994, pp. 62–70; and "David Glass Builds on Wal-Mart Legacy," *USA Today,* July 27, 1995, p. 4B.

The retailer's *product assortment* should match target shoppers' expectations. The retailer must determine both the product assortment's *width* and its *depth*. Thus, a restaurant can offer a narrow and shallow assortment (small lunch counter), a narrow and deep assortment (delicatessen), a wide and shallow assortment (cafeteria), or a wide and deep assortment (large restaurant). Another product assortment element is the *quality* of the goods: The customer is interested not only in the range of choice but also in the quality of the products available.

No matter what the store's product assortment and quality level, there always will be competitors with similar assortments and quality. Therefore, the retailer must search for other ways to differentiate itself from similar competitors. It can use any of several product-differentiation strategies. For one, it can offer merchandise that no other competitor carries—its own private brands or national brands on which it holds exclusives. For example, The Limited designs most of the clothes carried by its store, and Saks gets exclusive rights to carry a well-known designer's labels. Second, the retailer can feature blockbuster merchandising events—Bloomingdale's is known for running spectacular shows featuring goods from a certain country, such as India or China. Or the retailer can offer surprise merchandise, as when Loehmann's offers surprise assortments of seconds, overstocks, and closeouts. Finally, the retailer can differentiate itself by offering a highly targeted product assortment: Lane Bryant carries clothing for larger women; Brookstone offers an unusual assortment of gadgets in what amounts to an adult toy store.

Retailers also must decide on a *services mix* to offer customers. The old mom-and-pop grocery stores offered home delivery, credit, and conversation—services that today's supermarkets ignore. The services mix is one of the key tools of nonprice competition for setting one store apart from another.

The *store's atmosphere* is another element in its product arsenal. Every store has a physical layout that makes moving around in it either hard or easy. Every store has a "feel"; one store is cluttered, another charming, a third plush, a fourth somber. The store must have a planned atmosphere that suits the target market and moves customers to buy.

Increasingly, retailers are turning their stores into theaters that transport customers into unusual, exciting shopping environments. For example, toy seller F.A.O. Schwartz opened a three-story toy store on Chicago's upscale North Michigan Avenue that has customers lining up to get in. Once in, customers take an escalator to the third floor, then make their way down through various boutiques where crowds gather around spectacular Lego exhibits, Barbie Doll departments, giant stuffed zoo animals, and even a talking tree. Similarly, bookseller Barnes & Noble uses atmospherics to turn shopping for books into entertainment. It has found that, "to consumers, shopping is a social activity. They do it to mingle with others in a prosperous-feeling crowd, to see what's new, to enjoy the theatrical dazzle of the display, to treat themselves to something interesting or unexpected." Thus, Barnes & Noble stores are designed with "enough woody, traditional, soft-colored library to please book lovers; enough sophisticated modern architecture and graphics, sweeping vistas, and stylish displays to satisfy fans of the theater of consumption. And for everyone, plenty of space, where they can meet other people and feel at home. . . . [Customers] settle in at heavy chairs and tables to browse through piles of books; they fill the cafes [designed] to increase the festivities. . . ." As one Barnes & Noble executive notes: "The feel-good part of the store, the quality of life contribution, is a big part of the success."[11]

*Store atmospheres: Toy seller FAO Schwartz has created boutiques where crowds gather around spectacular Lego exhibits, giant stuffed zoo animals, and even a talking tree.*

Perhaps the most dramatic conversion of stores into theatre is the Mall of America near Minneapolis. Containing more than 800 specialty stores, the Mall is a veritable playground. Under a single roof, it shelters a 7-acre Knott's Berry Farm amusement park featuring 23 rides and attractions, an ice-skating rink, an Underwater World featuring hundreds of marine specimens and a dolphin show, and a two-story miniature golf course. One of the stores, Oshman Supersports USA, features a basketball court, a boxing gym, a baseball batting cage, a 50-foot archery range, and a simulated ski slope.[12]

All of this confirms that retail stores are much more than simply assortments of goods. They are environments to be experienced by the people who shop in them. Store atmospheres offer a powerful tool by which retailers can differentiate their stores from those of competitors.

## PRICE DECISION

A retailer's price policy is a crucial positioning factor and must be decided in relation to its target market, its product and service assortment, and its competition. All retailers would like to charge high markups and achieve high volume, but the two seldom go together. Most retailers seek *either* high markups on lower volume (most specialty stores) *or* low markups on higher volume (mass merchandisers and discount stores). Thus, Bijan's on Rodeo Drive in Beverly Hills prices men's suits starting at $1,000 and shoes at $400—it sells a low volume but makes a hefty profit on each sale. At the other extreme, T.J. maxx sells brand-name clothing at discount prices, settling for a lower margin on each sale but selling at a much higher volume.

Retailers also must pay attention to pricing tactics. Most retailers will put low prices on some items to serve as "traffic builders" or "loss leaders." On some occasions, they run storewide sales. On others, they plan markdowns on slower-moving merchandise. For example, shoe retailers may expect to sell 50 percent of their shoes at the normal markup, 25 percent at a 40 percent markup, and the remaining 25 percent at cost.

## PROMOTION DECISION

Retailers use the normal promotion tools—advertising, personal selling, sales promotion, and public relations—to reach consumers. They advertise in newspapers, magazines, radio, and television. Advertising may be supported by newspaper inserts and direct-mail pieces. Personal selling requires carefully training salespeople in how to greet customers, meet their needs, and handle their complaints. Sales promotions may include in-store demonstrations, displays, contests, and visiting celebrities. Public relations activities, such as press conferences and speeches, store openings, special events, newsletters, magazines, and public service activities, are always available to retailers.

## PLACE DECISION

Retailers often cite three critical factors in retailing success: *location, location,* and *location*! A retailer's location is key to its ability to attract customers. And the costs of building or leasing facilities have a major impact on the retailer's profits. Thus, site-location decisions are among the most important that the retailer makes. Small retailers may have to settle for whatever locations they can find or afford. Large retailers usually employ specialists who select locations using sophisticated methods. Two of the savviest location experts in recent years have been the off-price retailer T.J. maxx and toy-store giant Toys 'R' Us. Both put the majority of their new locations in rapidly growing areas where the population closely matches their customer base. The undisputed winner in the "place race" has been Wal-Mart, whose strategy of being the first mass merchandiser to locate in small and rural markets has been one of the key factors in its phenomenal success.

Most stores today cluster together to increase their customer pulling power and to give consumers the convenience of one-stop shopping. The main types of store clusters are the central business district and the shopping center.

*Central business districts* were the main form of retail cluster until the 1950s. Every large city and town had a central business district with department stores, specialty stores, banks, and movie theaters. When people began to move to the suburbs, however, these central business districts, with their traffic, parking, and crime problems, began to lose business. Downtown merchants opened branches in suburban shopping centers, and the decline of the central business districts continued. In recent years, many cities have joined with merchants to try to revive downtown shopping areas by building malls and providing underground parking. Some central business districts have made a comeback; others remain in a slow and possibly irreversible decline.

A **shopping center** is a group of retail businesses that are planned, developed, owned, and managed as a unit. A *regional shopping center,* the largest and most dramatic shopping center, contains from 40 to over 200 stores. It is like a mini-downtown and attracts customers from a wide area. Larger regional malls often have several department stores and a wide variety of specialty stores on several shop-

**Shopping center**
A group of retail businesses planned, developed, owned, and managed as a unit.

*Shopping centers:
The spectacular Mall
of America near Min-
neapolis contains
more than 800 stores,
45 restaurants, 7
theaters, and a 7-acre
indoor theme park. It
attracts 35 million
visitors a year.*

ping levels. A *community shopping center* contains between 15 and 40 retail stores.
It normally contains a branch of a department store or variety store, a supermarket, specialty stores, professional offices, and sometimes a bank. Most shopping centers are *neighborhood shopping centers* or *strip malls* that generally contain between
5 and 15 stores. They are close and convenient for consumers. They usually contain a supermarket, perhaps a discount store, and several service stores—dry cleaner,
self-service laundry, drugstore, video-rental outlet, barber or beauty shop, hardware
store, or other stores. Such neighborhood centers account for 87 percent of all shopping centers and 51 percent of all shopping center retail sales.[13]

Combined, all shopping centers now account for about one-third of all retail
sales, but they may have reached their saturation point. Many areas contain too
many malls, and as sales per square foot are dropping, vacancy rates are climbing. Some experts predict a shopping mall "shakeout," with as many as 20 percent of the regional shopping malls now operating in the United States closing by
the year 2000. Despite the recent development of many new megamalls, such as
the spectacular Mall of America near Minneapolis, the current trend is toward
smaller malls located in medium-size and smaller cities in fast-growing areas such
as the Southwest.[14]

# ▶THE FUTURE OF RETAILING

Several trends will affect the future of retailing. The slowdown in population and
economic growth means that retailers can no longer enjoy sales and profit growth
through natural expansion in current and new markets. Growth will have to come
from increasing shares of current markets. But greater competition and new types
of retailers make it harder to improve market shares.

The retailing industry suffers from severe overcapacity. There is too much retail space—more than 18 square feet for every man, woman, and child, more than double that of 1972. Consumer demographics, lifestyles, and shopping patterns are also changing rapidly. Thus, the 1990s have been difficult for retailers:

> Going-out-of-business signs, bankruptcy filings, and constant sales attest to tough times in the retail industry. Such mercantile stalwarts as B. Altman and Garfinkel's have disappeared. The parent company of Bloomingdale's, Burdines, and Rich's is in [bankruptcy]. Rumors abound about R. H. Macy and other potential casualties. . . . "Retailing is not an area of hope," says [one retailing executive]. "It's not fun. It's almost a war." And the casualties are almost certain to keep mounting. By the end of the '90s, . . . half of the nation's current retailers will be out of business. . . . The companies that succeed will be the ones that avoid crippling debt, focus tightly on specific customers or products, and hook into technology to hold down costs and enhance service. A tough act.[15]

To be successful, then, retailers will have to choose target segments carefully and position themselves strongly. Moreover, quickly rising costs will make more efficient operation and smarter buying essential to successful retailing. As a result, retail technologies are growing in importance as competitive tools. Progressive retailers are using computers to produce better forecasts, control inventory costs, order electronically from suppliers, communicate between stores, and even sell to consumers within stores. They are adopting checkout scanning systems, in-store television, on-line transaction processing, and electronic funds transfer.

**Wheel of retailing concept**
A concept of retailing that states that new types of retailers usually begin as low-margin, low-price, low-status operations but later evolve into higher-priced, higher-service operations, eventually becoming like the conventional retailers that they replaced.

Many retailing innovations are partially explained by the **wheel of retailing concept.**[16] According to this concept, many new types of retailing forms begin as low-margin, low-price, low-status operations. They challenge established retailers that have become "fat" by letting their costs and margins increase. The new retailers' success leads them to upgrade their facilities and offer more services. In turn, their costs increase, forcing them to increase their prices. Eventually, the new retailers become like the conventional retailers they replaced. The cycle begins again when still newer types of retailers evolve with lower costs and prices. The wheel of retailing concept seems to explain the initial success and later troubles of department stores, supermarkets, and discount stores and the recent success of off-price retailers.

New retail forms will continue to emerge to meet new consumer needs and new situations. But the life cycle of new retail forms is getting shorter. Department stores took about 100 years to reach the mature stage of the life cycle; more recent forms, such as catalog showrooms and furniture warehouse stores, reached maturity in about ten years. In such an environment, seemingly solid retail positions can crumble quickly.

Consider the Price Club, the original warehouse store chain. When Sol Price opened his first warehouse store outside San Diego in 1976, he launched a retailing revolution. Selling everything from tires and office supplies to five-pound tubs of peanut butter at superlow prices, his store chain was generating $2.6 billion a year in sales within 10 years. But Price refused to expand beyond its California base. And as the industry quickly matured, Price ran headlong into wholesale clubs run by such retail giants as Wal-Mart and Kmart. Only 17 years later, in a stunning reversal of fortune, a faltering Price sold out to competitor Costco. Price's rapid rise and fall "serves as a stark reminder to mass-market retailers that past success means little in a fiercely competitive and rapidly changing industry."[17] Of the top ten discount retailers in 1962 (the year that Wal-Mart and Kmart began), not one still exists today.[18] Thus, retailers can no longer sit back with a successful formula. To remain successful, they must keep adapting.

# ▶ WHOLESALING

**Wholesaling**
All activities involved in selling goods and services to those buying for resale or business use.

**Wholesaler**
A firm engaged primarily in wholesaling *activity*.

**Wholesaling** includes all activities involved in selling goods and services to those buying for resale or business use. A retail bakery is engaging in wholesaling when it sells pastry to the local hotel. We call **wholesalers** those firms engaged *primarily* in wholesaling activity.

Wholesalers buy mostly from producers and sell mostly to retailers, industrial consumers, and other wholesalers. But why are wholesalers used at all? For example, why would a producer use wholesalers rather than selling directly to retailers or consumers? Quite simply, wholesalers are often better at performing one or more of the following channel functions:

◆ *Selling and promoting*. Wholesalers' sales forces help manufacturers reach many small customers at a low cost. The wholesaler has more contacts and is often more trusted by the buyer than is the distant manufacturer.

◆ *Buying and assortment building*. Wholesalers can select items and build assortments needed by their customers, thereby saving the consumers much work.

◆ *Bulk-breaking*. Wholesalers save their customers money by buying in carload lots and breaking bulk (breaking large lots into small quantities).

◆ *Warehousing*. Wholesalers hold inventories, thereby reducing the inventory costs and risks of suppliers and customers.

◆ *Transportation*. Wholesalers can provide quicker delivery to buyers because they are closer than the producers.

◆ *Financing*. Wholesalers finance their customers by giving credit, and they finance their suppliers by ordering early and paying bills on time.

◆ *Risk bearing*. Wholesalers absorb risk by taking title and bearing the cost of theft, damage, spoilage, and obsolescence.

◆ *Market information*. Wholesalers give information to suppliers and customers about competitors, new products, and price developments.

◆ *Management services and advice*. Wholesalers often help retailers train their salesclerks, improve store layouts and displays, and set up accounting and inventory control systems.

# ▶ TYPES OF WHOLESALERS

**Merchant wholesalers**
Independently owned businesses that take title to the merchandise that they handle.

Wholesalers fall into three major groups (see Table 12-3): *merchant wholesalers, brokers and agents,* and *manufacturers' sales branches and offices.* **Merchant wholesalers** are the largest single group of wholesalers, accounting for roughly 50 percent of all wholesaling. Merchant wholesalers include two broad types: full-service wholesalers and limited-service wholesalers. *Full-service wholesalers* provide a full set of services, whereas the various *limited-service wholesalers* offer fewer services to their suppliers and customers. The several different types of limited-service wholesalers perform varied specialized functions in the distribution channel.

*TABLE 12-3*   *Major Types of Wholesalers*

| Type | Description |
|---|---|
| **Merchant wholesalers** | Independently owned businesses that take title to the merchandise that they handle. In different trades, they are called *jobbers, distributors,* or *mill supply houses.* Include full-service wholesalers and limited-service wholesalers. |
| Full-service wholesalers | Provide a full line of services: carrying stock, maintaining a sales force, offering credit, making deliveries, and providing management assistance. There are two types: |
| Wholesale merchants | Sell primarily to retailers and provide a full range of services. *General-merchandise wholesalers* carry several merchandise lines, while *general-line wholesalers* carry one or two lines in greater depth. *Specialty wholesalers* specialize in carrying only part of a line. (Examples: health-food wholesalers, seafood wholesalers.) |
| Industrial distributors | Sell to manufacturers rather than to retailers. Provide several services, such as carrying stock, offering credit, and providing delivery. May carry a broad range of merchandise, a general line, or a specialty line. |
| Limited-service wholesalers | Offer fewer services than full-service wholesalers. Limited-service wholesalers are of several types: |
| Cash-and-carry wholesalers | Carry a limited line of fast-moving goods and sell to small retailers for cash. Normally do not deliver. Example: A small fish store retailer may drive to a cash-and-carry fish wholesaler, buy fish for cash, and bring the merchandise back to the store. |
| Truck wholesalers (or truck jobbers) | Perform primarily a selling and delivery function. Carry a limited line of semiperishable merchandise (such as milk, bread, snack foods), which they sell for cash as they make their rounds of supermarkets, small groceries, hospitals, restaurants, factory cafeterias, and hotels. |
| Drop shippers | Do not carry inventory or handle the product. Upon receiving an order, they select a manufacturer, who ships the merchandise directly to the customer. The drop shipper assumes title and risk from the time that the order is accepted to its delivery to the customer. They operate in bulk industries, such as coal, lumber, and heavy equipment. |
| Rack jobbers | Serve grocery and drug retailers, mostly in nonfood items. They send delivery trucks to stores, where the delivery people set up toys, paperbacks, hardware items, health and beauty aids, or other items. They price the goods, keep them fresh, set up point-of-purchase displays, and keep inventory records. Rack jobbers retain title to the goods and bill the retailers only for the goods sold to consumers. |
| Producers' cooperatives | Owned by farmer members. They assemble farm produce to sell in local markets. The co-op's profits are distributed to members at the end of the year. They often attempt to improve product quality and promote a co-op brand name, such as Sun-Maid raisins, Sunkist oranges, or Diamond walnuts. |
| Mail-order wholesalers | Send catalogs to retail, industrial, and institutional customers featuring jewelry, cosmetics, specialty foods, and other small items. Maintain no outside sales force. Main customers are businesses in small outlying areas. Orders are filled and sent by mail, truck, or other transportation. |

**TABLE 12-3**   *(continued)*

| Type | Description |
|---|---|
| **Brokers and agents** | Do not take title to goods. Main function is to facilitate buying and selling, for which they earn a commission on the selling price. Generally specialize by product line or customer types. |
| Brokers | Chief function is bringing buyers and sellers together and assisting in negotiation. They are paid by the party who hired them, and do not carry inventory, get involved in financing, or assume risk. Examples: food brokers, real-estate brokers, insurance brokers, and security brokers. |
| Agents | Represent either buyers or sellers on a more permanent basis than brokers do. There are several types: |
| Manufacturers' agents | Represent two or more manufacturers of complementary lines. A formal written agreement with each manufacturer covers pricing, territories, order handling, delivery service and warranties, and commission rates. Often used in such lines as apparel, furniture, and electrical goods. Most manufacturers' agents are small businesses, with only a few skilled salespeople as employees. They are hired by small manufacturers who cannot afford their own field sales forces, and by large manufacturers who use agents to open new territories or to cover territories that cannot support full-time salespeople. |
| Selling agents | Have contractual authority to sell a manufacturer's entire output. The manufacturer either is not interested in the selling function or feels unqualified. The selling agent serves as a sales department and has significant influence over prices, terms, and conditions of sale. Found in such product areas as textiles, industrial machinery and equipment, coal and coke, chemicals, and metals. |
| Purchasing agents | Generally have a long-term relationship with buyers and make purchases for them, often receiving, inspecting, warehousing, and shipping the merchandise to the buyers. They provide helpful market information to clients and help them obtain the best goods and prices available. |
| Commission merchants | Take physical possession of products and negotiate sales. Normally, they are not employed on a long-term basis. Used most often in agricultural marketing by farmers who do not want to sell their own output and do not belong to producers' cooperatives. The commission merchant takes a truckload of commodities to a central market, sells it for the best price, deducts a commission and expenses, and remits the balance to the producer. |
| **Manufacturers' and retailers' branches and offices** | Wholesaling operations conducted by sellers or buyers themselves rather than through independent wholesalers. Separate branches and offices can be dedicated to either sales or purchasing. |
| Sales branches and offices | Set up by manufacturers to improve inventory control, selling, and promotion. *Sales branches* carry inventory and are found in such industries as lumber and automotive equipment and parts. *Sales offices* do not carry inventory and are most prominent in dry-goods and notions industries. |
| Purchasing offices | Perform a role similar to that of brokers or agents but are part of the buyer's organization. Many retailers set up purchasing offices in major market centers such as New York and Chicago. |

*Merchant wholesalers: A typical Fleming Companies, Inc. wholesale food distribution center. The average Fleming warehouse contains 500,000 square feet of floor space (with 30-foot high ceiling), carries 16,000 different food items, and serves 150 to 200 retailers within a 500-mile radius.*

**Broker**
A wholesaler who does not take title to goods and whose function is to bring buyers and sellers together and assist in negotiation.

**Agent**
A wholesaler who represents buyers or sellers on a relatively permanent basis, performs only a few functions, and does not take title to goods.

*Brokers* and *agents* differ from merchant wholesalers in two ways: They do not take title to goods, and they perform only a few functions. Like merchant wholesalers, they generally specialize by product line or customer type. A **broker** brings buyers and sellers together and assists in negotiation. **Agents** represent buyers or sellers on a more permanent basis. *Manufacturers' agents* (also called manufacturers' representatives) are the most common type of agent wholesaler. Together, brokers and agents account for 11 percent of the total wholesale volume.

The third major type of wholesaling is that done in **manufacturers' sales branches and offices** by sellers or buyers themselves rather than through independent wholesalers. Manufacturers' offices and sales branches account for about 31 percent of all wholesale volume.

## ▶WHOLESALER MARKETING DECISIONS

**Manufacturer's sales branches and offices**
Wholesaling by sellers or buyers themselves rather than through independent wholesalers.

Wholesalers have experienced mounting competitive pressures in recent years. They have faced new sources of competition, more demanding customers, new technologies, and more direct-buying programs on the part of large industrial, institutional, and retail buyers. As a result, they have had to improve their strategic decisions on target markets and positioning, and on the marketing mix—product assortments and services, price, promotion, and place (see Figure 12-2).

### TARGET MARKET AND POSITIONING DECISION

Like retailers, wholesalers must define their target markets and position themselves effectively—they cannot serve everyone. They can choose a target group by size

**FIGURE 12-2**
*Wholesaler marketing decisions*

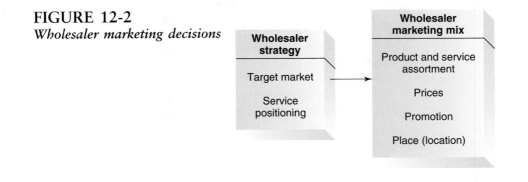

of customer (only large retailers), type of customer (convenience food stores only), need for service (customers who need credit), or other factors. Within the target group, they can identify the more profitable customers, design stronger offers, and build better relationships with them. They can propose automatic reordering systems, set up management-training and advising systems, or even sponsor a voluntary chain. They can discourage less profitable customers by requiring larger orders or adding service charges to smaller ones.

# ►MARKETING MIX DECISIONS

Like retailers, wholesalers must decide on product assortment and services, prices, promotion, and place. The wholesaler's "product" is the assortment of *products and services* that it offers. Wholesalers are under great pressure to carry a full line and to stock enough for immediate delivery. But this practice can damage profits. Wholesalers today are cutting down on the number of lines that they carry, choosing to keep only the more profitable ones. Wholesalers are also rethinking which services count most in building strong customer relationships and which should be dropped or charged for. The key is to find the mix of services most valued by their target customers.

*Price* is also an important wholesaler decision. Wholesalers usually mark up the cost of goods by a standard percentage—say, 20 percent. Expenses may run 17 percent of the gross margin, leaving a profit margin of 3 percent. In grocery wholesaling, the average profit margin is often less than 2 percent. Wholesalers are trying new pricing approaches. They may cut their margin on some lines in order to win important new customers. They may ask suppliers for special price breaks when they can turn them into an increase in the supplier's sales.

Although *promotion* can be critical to wholesaler success, most wholesalers are not promotion-minded. Their use of trade advertising, sales promotion, personal selling, and public relations is largely scattered and unplanned. Many are behind the times in personal selling; they still see selling as a single salesperson talking to a single customer instead of as a team effort to sell, build, and service major accounts. Wholesalers also need to adopt some of the nonpersonal promotion techniques used by retailers. They need to develop an overall promotion strategy and to make greater use of supplier promotion materials and programs.

Finally, *place* is important: Wholesalers must choose their locations and facilities carefully. Wholesalers typically locate in low-rent, low-tax areas and tend to invest little money in their buildings, equipment, and systems. As a result, their materials-handling and order-processing systems are often outdated. In recent years, however, large and progressive wholesalers are reacting to rising costs by investing in automated warehouses and on-line ordering systems. Orders are fed from the retailer's system directly into the wholesaler's computer, and the items are picked up by mechanical devices and automatically taken to a shipping platform where they are assembled. Most large wholesalers employ computers to carry out accounting, billing, inventory control, and forecasting. Modern wholesalers are adapting their services to the needs of target customers and finding cost-reducing methods of doing business.

# ▶ TRENDS IN WHOLESALING

Progressive wholesalers constantly watch for better ways to meet the changing needs of their suppliers and target customers. They recognize that, in the long run, their only reason for existence comes from increasing the efficiency and effectiveness of the entire marketing channel. To achieve this goal, they must constantly improve their services and reduce their costs.

McKesson, the nation's leading wholesaler of pharmaceuticals and health care products, provides an example of progressive wholesaling. To thrive, McKesson had to remain more cost effective than manufacturers' sales branches. The company automated its 36 warehouses, established direct computer links with drug manufacturers, designed a computerized accounts-receivable program for pharmacists, and provided drugstores with computer terminals for ordering inventories. Thus, McKesson has delivered better value to both manufacturers and retail customers.

One study predicts several developments in the wholesaling industry.[19] Consolidation will significantly reduce the number of wholesaling firms. The remain-

*Progressive wholesaling: To deliver better value to its customers, McKesson automated its warehouses, set up direct computer links with drug manufacturers, and provided drugstores with computer terminals for ordering inventories and maintaining medical profiles on their customers.*

ing wholesaling companies will grow larger, primarily through acquisition, merger, and geographic expansion. Geographic expansion will require that distributors learn how to compete effectively over wider and more diverse areas. The increased use of computerized and automated systems will help wholesalers. By 1990, more than three-fourths of all wholesalers were using on-line order systems.

The distinction between large retailers and large wholesalers continues to blur. Many retailers now operate formats such as wholesale clubs and hypermarkets that perform many wholesale functions. In return, many large wholesalers are setting up their own retailing operations. SuperValu and Flemming, both leading food wholesalers, now operate their own retail outlets. In fact, more than 20 percent of SuperValu's $12.6 billion in sales comes from its Cub Foods, Shop 'n Save, Save-A-Lot, Laneco, and Scott's supermarket operations.[20]

Wholesalers will continue to increase the services that they provide to retailers—retail pricing, cooperative advertising, marketing and management information reports, accounting services, and others. Rising costs on the one hand, and the demand for increased services on the other, will put the squeeze on wholesaler profits. Wholesalers who do not find efficient ways to deliver value to their customers will soon drop by the wayside.

Finally, facing slow growth in their domestic markets and such developments as the North American Free Trade Agreement, many large wholesalers are now going global. The National Association of Wholesaler-Distributors predicts that, by the year 2000, wholesalers will generate 18 percent of their sales outside the United States, twice the current share.[21] For example, in 1991, McKesson bought out its Canadian partner, Provigo. The company now receives about 13 percent of its total revenues from Canada.

## SUMMARY

Retailing and wholesaling consist of many organizations bringing goods and services from the point of production to the point of use. *Retailing* includes all activities involved in selling goods or services directly to final consumers for their personal, nonbusiness use. Retailers can be classified as store retailers and nonstore retailers. *Store retailers* can be further classified by the *amount of service* that they provide (self-service, limited service, or full service); *product line sold* (specialty stores, department stores, supermarkets, convenience stores, superstores, and service businesses); and *relative prices* (discount stores, off-price retailers, and catalog showrooms). Today, many retailers are banding together in corporate and contractual *retail organizations* (corporate chains, voluntary chains and retailer cooperatives, franchise organizations, and merchandising conglomerates).

Although most goods and services are sold through stores, nonstore retailing has been growing much faster than store retailing. *Nonstore retailers* now account for more than 14 percent of all consumer purchases, and they may account for a third of all sales by the end of the century. Nonstore retailing consists of *direct marketing, direct selling,* and *automatic vending.*

Each retailer must make decisions about its target markets, product assortment and services, price, promotion, and place. Retailers must choose target markets carefully and position themselves strongly.

*Wholesaling* includes all the activities involved in selling goods or services to those who are buying for the purpose of resale or for business use. Wholesalers perform many functions, including selling and promoting, buying and assortment building, bulk-breaking, warehousing, transporting, financing, risk bearing, supplying market information, and providing management services and advice. Wholesalers fall into three groups. First, *merchant wholesalers* take possession of the goods. They include *full-service wholesalers* (wholesale merchants, industrial distributors) and *limited-service wholesalers* (cash-and-carry wholesalers, truck wholesalers, drop shippers, rack jobbers, producers' cooperatives, and mail-order wholesalers). Second, *brokers* and *agents* do not take possession of the goods but are paid a commission for aiding buying and selling. Finally, *manufacturers' sales branches and offices* are wholesaling operations conducted by nonwholesalers to bypass the wholesalers. Wholesaling is holding its own in the economy. Progressive wholesalers are adapting their services to the needs of target customers and are seeking cost-reducing methods of doing business.

## KEY TERMS

Agent

Automatic vending

Broker

Catalog showroom

Chain stores

Convenience store

Department store

Direct marketing

Discount store

Door-to-door retailing

Factory outlets

Franchise

Independent off-price retailers

Manufacturers' sales branches and offices

Merchant wholesalers

Off-price retailers

Retailers

Retailing

Shopping center

Specialty store

Supermarkets

Superstore

Warehouse club (or wholesale club)

Wheel of retailing concept

Wholesaler

Wholesaling

## QUESTIONS FOR DISCUSSION

1. In the past, many graduate business majors have avoided careers in retailing; the last job they want is that of retail-store manager. Yet as a result of the explosive growth of such superstores as Wal-Mart, Home Depot, Target, and Computer City, there are enormous career opportunities for thousands of retail-store managers. The most successful store managers earn more than $100,000 a year by the time they are 30. Considering what you learned in this chapter, would you consider a career in retailing?

2. Warehouse clubs that are restricted to members only, such as Costco and Sam's Wholesale, are growing rapidly. They offer a very broad, but shallow, line of products, often in institutional packaging, at very low prices. Some members buy for resale, others buy to supply a business, and still others buy for personal use. Are these stores wholesalers or retailers? How can you make a distinction?

3. Off-price retailers provide tough price competition to other retailers. Do you think that large retailers' growing power in channels of distribution will affect manufacturers' willingness to sell to off-price retailers at rates that are below regular wholesale? What policy should Sony have regarding selling to off-price retailers?

4. Postal-rate hikes make it more expensive to send direct mail, catalogs, and purchased products to consumers. Identify ways that you would expect direct mail and catalog marketers to respond to an increase in postage rates.

5. A typical "country store" in a farming community sells a variety of food and nonfood items: snacks, staples, hardware, and many other types of goods. What kinds of wholesalers do the owners of such stores use to obtain the items that they sell? Are these the same suppliers that a supermarket uses?

6. Compare the fundamental differences between retailers, wholesalers, and manufacturers in the types of marketing decisions that they make. Give examples of the marketing decisions made by the three groups that show their similarities and differences.

## APPLYING THE CONCEPTS

1. Collect all the catalogs that you have received in the mail recently.

   ◆ Sort them by type of product line. Is there some pattern to the types of direct marketers that are targeting you?

   ◆ Where do you think these catalog companies got your name?

   ◆ How do you think a company that was selling your name and address to a direct marketer would describe your buying habits?

2. Watch a cable television shopping channel, or tune into a late-night television shopping show (often found on UHF stations above Channel 13).

   ◆ How are these shows attempting to target buyers? Do they mix football cleats and fine china in the same program, or are they targeting more carefully?

   ◆ How much of the merchandise shown appears to be close-outs? How can you tell?

## REFERENCES

1. The quote is from Steve Weiner, "With Big Selection and Low Prices, 'Category Killer' Stores Are a Hit," *Wall Street Journal,* June 17, 1986, p. 33. Also see Bill Saporito, "IKEA's Got 'Em Lining Up," *Fortune,* March 11, 1991, p. 72; "North America's Top 100 Furniture Stores," *Furniture Today,* May 18, 1992, p. 50; Laura Loro, "IKEA," *Advertising Age,* July 4, 1994, p. S2; and "IKEA Format," *WWD (Women's Wear Daily),* May 2, 1995, p. 23.

2. See "Supermarkets Need to Improve in Food Service, Survey Finds," *Supermarket News,* May 15, 1995, p. 14.

3. See "Stop-N-Go Micromarkets New Upscale Mix," *Chain Store Age Executive,* January 1990, p. 145; Christy Fisher, "Convenience Chains Pump for New Life," *Advertising Age,* April 23, 1990, p. 80; Doug Zapper, "Convenience Store Industry Embraces Change," *Chain Store Executive,* August 1993, pp. 27A–28A; and Joan Lang, "Convenience Stores," *ID: The Voice of Foodservice Distribution,* May 1, 1995, p. 34.

4. Leah Rickard, "Supercenters Entice Shoppers," *Advertising Age,* March 20, 1995, p. 1, 10; Chad Rubel, "Discount Stores Battle Each Other with Supercenters," *Marketing News,* January 16, 1995, pp. 1, 10; and Don Longo, "Supercenters Get Repackaged for 1990s' One-Stop Shopper," *Discount Store News,* April 3, 1995, p. F3.

5. See Laurie M. Grossman, "Hypermarkets: A Sure-Fire Hit Bombs," *The Wall Street Journal,* June 25, 1992, p. B1; Emily DeNitto, "Hypermarkets Seem to Be Big Flop in U.S.," *Advertising Age,* October 4, 1993, p. 20; and Zina Moukheiber, "Squeezing the Tomatoes," *Forbes,* February 13, 1995, p. 55.

6. See Sharon Edelson, "Once a Poor Relation, Outlets Go Legit—and Trouble Looms," *WWD (Women's Wear Daily),* April 24, 1995, p. 64; and Stephanie Forest, "I Can Get It for You Retail," *Business Week,* September 18, 1995, pp. 84–88.

7. Ronald Henkoff, "Why Every Red-Blooded Consumer Owns a Truck, and a Five-Pound Jar of Peanut Butter, . . . ," *Fortune,* May 29, 1995, pp. 86–100.

8. See J. Taylor Buckley, "Machines Start New Fast-Food Era," *USA Today,* July 19, 1991, pp. B1, B2; Laurie McLaughlin, "Vending Machines Open to New Ideas," *Advertising Age,* August 19, 1991, p. 35; and Robert Emproto, "Vends of Change," *Beverage World,* February 1995, p. 56.

9. Dyan Machan, "Knowing Your Limits," *Forbes,* June 5, 1995, p. 128.

10. See R. Craig Endicott, "Price No Longer Enough for Retailers," *Advertising Age,* September 28, 1994, p. 33.

11. Myron Magnet, "Let's Go for Growth," *Fortune,* March 7, 1994, pp. 60–72.

12. Kenneth Labich, "What Will It Take to Keep Them Hanging Out at the Mall?" *Fortune,* May 29, 1995, pp. 102–6.

13. Chip Walker, "Strip Malls: Plain but Powerful," *American Demographics,* October 1991, pp. 48–50.

14. See Kate Fitzgerald, "Mega Malls: Built for the '90s, or the '80s?" *Advertising Age,* January 27, 1992, pp. S1, S8; Gretchen Morgenson, "The Fall of the Mall," *Forbes,* May 24, 1993, pp. 106–12; Debra Hazel, "Developers, Retailers Ask: 'Is Bigger Better?'" *Chain Store Age Executive,* May 1995, p. 64; and Kelly Shermach, "Niche Malls: Innovation for an Industry in Decline," *Marketing News,* February 1996, pp. 1, 2.

15. Laura Zinn, "Retailing: Who Will Survive?" *Business Week,* November 26, 1990, p. 134. Also see Susan Caminiti, "The New Retailing Champs," *Fortune,* September 24, 1990, pp. 85–100; and Mary Kuntz, "Reinventing the Store," *Business Week,* November 27, 1995, pp. 84–96.

16. See Malcolm P. McNair and Eleanor G. May, "The Next Revolution of the Retailing Wheel," *Harvard Business Review,* September–October 1978, pp. 81–91; Stephen Brown, "The Wheel of Retailing: Past and Future," *Journal of Retailing,* Summer 1990, pp. 143–47; Stephen Brown, "Variations on a Marketing Enigma: The Wheel of Retailing Theory," *The Journal of Marketing*

*Management,* Vol. 7, No. 2, 1991, pp. 131–55; and Barry Davies, Peter Jones, and John Pal, "Spokes in the Wheel of Retailing," *International Journal of Retail & Distribution Management,* March 1992, p. 35.

17. Amy Barrett, "A Retailing Pacesetter Pulls Up Lame," *Business Week,* July 12, 1993, pp. 122–23.

18. Bill Saporito, "Is Wal-Mart Unstoppable?" *Fortune,* May 6, 1991, pp. 50–59. For more on retailing trends, see Eleanor G. May, C. William Ress, and Walter J. Salmon, *Future Trends in Retailing* (Cambridge, MA: Marketing Science Institute, February 1985); Daniel Sweeney, "Toward 2000," *Chain Store Age Executive,* January 1990, pp. 27–39; and Howard L. Green, "New Consumer Realities for Retailers," *Advertising Age,* April 25, 1994, pp. 4–5.

19. See Arthur Andersen & Co., *Facing the Forces of Change: Beyond Future Trends in Wholesale Distribution* (Washington, DC: Distribution Research and Education Foundation, 1987), p. 7. Also see Joseph Weber, "It's 'Like Somebody Had Shot the Postman,'" *Business Week,* January 13, 1992, p. 82.

20. *SuperValu Distribution and Retailing Handbook* (Minneapolis, MN: SuperValu, Inc., November 1993).

21. Joseph Weber, "On a Fast Boat to Anywhere," *Business Week,* January 11, 1993, p. 94.

# Integrated Marketing Communication Strategy

Founded 25 years ago at Love Field in Dallas, Southwest Airlines sees itself as the "love" airline. The company even uses LUV as its New York Stock Exchange symbol. Southwest showers most of this love on its passengers, in the form of shockingly low prices for highly dependable, no-frills service. In 1992, Southwest received the Department of Transportation's first-ever Triple Crown Award for best on-time service, best baggage handling, *and* best customer service. Southwest rated first in customer satisfaction among the nation's nine major airlines. It repeated this feat in 1993, 1994, and 1995.

Customers have returned Southwest's love by making it the industry's most profitable airline. In an industry plagued by huge losses, Southwest has experienced 23 straight years of profits. In 1992, when the industry lost $3 billion, Southwest *made* $91 million. All this from an airline only one-quarter the size of industry leader American Airlines.

Southwest's amazing success results from two factors: a superior marketing strategy and outstanding marketing communications. The marketing strategy is a simple one—Southwest knows its niche and stays with it. It has positioned itself firmly as *the* short-haul, no-frills, low-price airline. Its average flight time is one hour, its average one-way fare just $58. In fact, its prices are so low that when it enters a new market, it actually increases total air traffic by attracting customers who might otherwise travel by car or bus. For example, when Southwest began its Louisville–Chicago flight at a one-way rate of $49 versus competitors' $250, total air passenger traffic between the two cities increased from 8,000 people weekly to 26,000.

To these practical benefits, Southwest adds one more key positioning ingredient—lots of good fun. With its happy-go-lucky CEO, Herb Kelleher, leading the charge, Southwest refuses to take itself seriously. For example, when an aviation company recently confronted Southwest for using its slogan, "Just Plane Smart," Kelleher challenged the company's CEO to a public arm-wrestling match, with the slogan going to the winner. Kelleher was quickly pinned, but the CEO showdown became a national media event, winning Southwest lots of publicity. And Southwest was later allowed to continue using the slogan.

In another instance, Northwest Airlines ran ads claiming that it ranked number one in customer satisfaction among the nation's seven largest airlines. Southwest, which rated number one among the *nine* largest airlines, responded in classic Southwest fashion. Print ads boldly proclaimed: "After lengthy deliberation at the highest levels, and extensive consultation with our legal department, we have arrived at an official corporate response to Northwest Airlines' claim to be number one in customer satisfaction. Liar, liar. Pants on fire."

As the arm wrestling and "Liar, liar" incidents suggest, Southwest has little trouble communicating with consumers in a very memorable way. But beyond these special cases, the airline dispenses a carefully coordinated flow of marketing communications, ranging from media advertising, special events, and public relations to direct marketing and personal selling.

Entering a new city presents the greatest communications challenge. For example, when Southwest entered Baltimore in 1993, East Coast consumers knew almost nothing about the airline. The Baltimore campaign began with public relations and community affairs events. Says the president of Southwest's advertising agency, "We always start out with the public relations side. . . . Then we integrate government relations, community affairs, service announcements, special events, and advertising and promotion. By the time Southwest comes into the market, the airline already is part of the community."

Five weeks before the first flight, CEO Kelleher and Maryland's Governor William Schaefer held a news conference to announce Southwest's entry into Baltimore. The governor gave Kelleher a basket of products made in Maryland; Kelleher gave the governor a flotation device—a "lifesaver" from high airfares for the people of Baltimore. Southwest next dramatized its $49 fare between Baltimore and Cleveland by flying 49 school children to Cleveland for a day to visit the Rain Forest at Cleveland Metroparks Zoo. This event garnered substantial media coverage in both Baltimore and Cleveland.

A week later, Southwest employees took to Baltimore's streets, handing out fliers on street corners promoting Southwest's "Just Plane Smart" slogan. At about the same time, Southwest sent direct mail to frequent short-haul travelers in the Baltimore area offering a special promotion to join its Company Club frequent-flier program. The public relations and community affairs efforts set the stage. Next, the company began running "Just Plane Smart" television and print commercials, and outdoor ads shouted "Hello, Baltimore, Goodbye High Fares." The integrated communications campaign was incredibly successful. In all, 90,000 Baltimore passengers purchased tickets before the start of service—a company record for advance bookings.

When the introductory fanfare had settled down, Southwest set up a Baltimore marketing office to continue working on local advertising, promotions, and community events. And now, of course, Baltimore travelers will be treated to the unique brand of more personal communication dispensed by Southwest's cheerful employees.

> Southwest workers often go out of their way to amuse, surprise, or somehow entertain passengers. During delays at the gate, ticket agents will award prizes to the passenger with the largest hole in his or her sock. Flight attendants have been known to hide in overhead luggage bins and then pop out when passengers start filing onboard. Veteran

Southwest fliers looking for a few yuks have learned to listen up to announcements over the intercom. A recent effort: "Good morning, ladies and gentlemen. Those of you who wish to smoke will please file out to our lounge on the wing, where you can enjoy our feature film, *Gone With the Wind*." On the same flight, an attendant later announced: "Please pass all plastic cups to the center aisle so that we can wash them out and use them for the next group of passengers."

Southwest owes much of its success to its ability to deliver dependable no-frills, low-cost service to its customers. But success also depends on Southwest's skill at blending all of its promotion tools—advertising, sales promotion, public relations, and personal selling—into an integrated program that communicates the Southwest story.[1] ∎

# CHAPTER OBJECTIVES

## After reading this chapter, you should be able to:

**1** Name and define the four tools of the promotion mix.

**2** Discuss the steps in developing effective marketing communication.

**3** Explain the methods for setting the promotion budget and factors that affect the design of the promotion mix.

**4** Identify the major factors that are changing today's marketing communications environment.

**5** Explain direct marketing and its many forms.

**6** Discuss the process and advantages of integrated marketing communications.

Modern marketing calls for more than just developing a good product, pricing it attractively, and making it available to target customers. Companies also must *communicate* with their customers, and what they communicate should not be left to chance. For most companies, the question is not *whether* to communicate, but *how much to spend* and *in what ways*.

A modern company manages a complex marketing communications system (see Figure 13-1). The company communicates with its intermediaries (retailers and wholesalers), consumers, and various publics. In turn, the intermediaries communicate with their consumers and publics. Consumers have word-of-mouth communication with each other and with other publics. Meanwhile, each group provides feedback to every other group.

A company's total marketing communications program—called its **promotion mix**—consists of the specific blend of advertising, personal selling, sales promotion, and public relations tools that the company uses to pursue its advertising and marketing objectives. Definitions of the four major promotion tools follow:

**Promotion mix**
The specific mix of advertising, personal selling, sales promotion, and public relations that a company uses to pursue its advertising and marketing objectives.

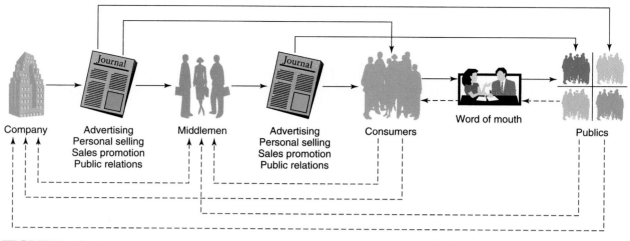

## FIGURE 13-1
*The marketing-communications system*

Advertising
Any paid form of non-personal presentation and promotion of ideas, goods, or services by an identified sponsor.

Personal selling
Personal presentation by the sales force for the purpose of making sales and building customer relationships.

Sales promotion
Short-term incentives to encourage purchase or sales of a product or service.

Public relations
Building good relations with the company's various publics by obtaining favorable publicity, building up a good "corporate image," and handling or heading off unfavorable rumors, stories, and events.

◆ **Advertising**: Any paid form of nonpersonal presentation and promotion of ideas, goods, or services by an identified sponsor.

◆ **Personal selling**: Personal presentation by the firm's sales force for the purpose of making sales and building customer relationships.

◆ **Sales promotion**: Short-term incentives to encourage the purchase or sale of a product or service.

◆ **Public relations**: Building good relations with the company's various publics by obtaining favorable publicity, building up a good "corporate image," and handling or heading off unfavorable rumors, stories, and events.[2]

Each category consists of specific tools. For example, advertising includes print, broadcast, outdoor, and other forms. Personal selling includes sales presentations, trade shows, and incentive programs. Sales promotion includes point-of-purchase displays, premiums, discounts, coupons, specialty advertising, and demonstrations. Communication goes beyond all these specific promotion tools. The product's design, its price, the shape and color of its package, and the stores that sell it—*all* communicate something to buyers. Thus, although the promotion mix is the company's primary communication activity, the entire marketing mix—promotion *and* product, price, and place—must be coordinated for greatest communication impact.

In this chapter, we begin by examining two questions: First, *what are the major steps in developing effective marketing communication?* Second, *how should the promotion budget and mix be determined?* We then look at recent dramatic changes in marketing communications that have resulted from shifting marketing strategies and advances in computers and information technologies. Next, we review the fast-growing field of *direct-marketing communications*. Finally, we summarize the legal, ethical, and social responsibility issues in marketing communications. In Chapter 14, we look at *mass-communication tools*: advertising, sales promotion, and public relations. Chapter 15 examines the *sales force* as a communication and promotion tool.

# ▶ STEPS IN DEVELOPING EFFECTIVE COMMUNICATION

Marketing communicators need to know what audiences they wish to reach and what responses they want. They must be good at developing messages that take into account how the target audience responds to them. They must deliver these messages through media that reach target audiences, and they must gather feedback so that they can assess the audience's responses to the message. In summary, the marketing communicator must do the following: Identify the target audience; determine the response sought; choose a message; choose the media through which to send the message; and collect feedback.

## IDENTIFYING THE TARGET AUDIENCE

A marketing communicator starts with a clear target audience in mind. The audience may be potential buyers or current users, those who make the buying decision or those who influence it. The audience may be individuals, groups, special publics, or the general public. The target audience heavily affects the communicator's decisions on *what* will be said, *how* it will be said, *when* it will be said, *where* it will be said, and *who* will say it.

## DETERMINING THE RESPONSE SOUGHT

Once the target audience has been defined, the marketing communicator must decide what response is sought. Of course, in most cases, the final response is *purchase*. But purchase is the result of a long process of consumer decision making. The marketing communicator needs to know where the target audience now stands and to what stage it needs to be moved. The target audience may be in any of six **buyer-readiness stages** that consumers normally pass through on their way to making a purchase. These stages include *awareness, knowledge, liking, preference, conviction,* or *purchase* (see Figure 13-2).

The marketing communicator's target market may be totally unaware of the product, know only its name, or know a thing or two about it. The communicator must first build *awareness* and *knowledge*. For example, when Nissan introduced its Infiniti automobile line, it began with an extensive "teaser" advertising campaign to create name familiarity. Initial ads for the Infiniti created curiosity

**Buyer-readiness stages** The stages that consumers normally pass through on their way to purchase, including awareness, knowledge, liking, preference, conviction, and purchase.

**FIGURE 13-2**
*Buyer-readiness stages*

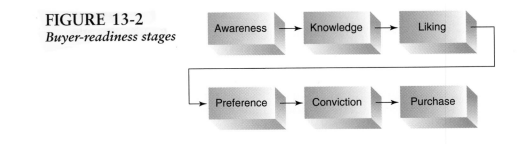

and awareness by showing the car's name but not the car. Later ads created knowledge by informing potential buyers of the car's high quality and many innovative features.

Assuming that target consumers *know* the product, how do they *feel* about it? Once potential buyers knew about the Infiniti, Nissan's marketers wanted to move them through successively stronger stages of feelings toward the car. These stages included *liking* (feeling favorable about the Infiniti), *preference* (preferring Infiniti to other car brands), and *conviction* (believing that Infiniti is the best car for them). Infiniti marketers used a combination of the promotion mix tools to create positive feelings and conviction. Advertising extolled the Infiniti's advantages over competing brands. Press releases and other public relations activities stressed the car's innovative features and performance. Dealer salespeople told buyers about options, value for the price, and after-sale service.

Finally, some members of the target market might be convinced about the product, but not quite get around to making the *purchase*. Potential Infiniti buyers might have decided to wait for more information, or for the economy to improve. The communicator must lead these consumers to take the final step. Actions might include offering special promotional prices, rebates, or premiums. Salespeople might call or write to selected customers, inviting them to visit the dealership for a special showing.

Of course, marketing communications alone cannot create positive feelings and purchases for Infiniti. The car itself must provide superior value for the customer. In fact, outstanding marketing communications can actually speed the demise of a poor product. The more quickly potential buyers learn about the poor product, the more quickly they become aware of its faults. Thus, good marketing communication calls for "good deeds followed by good words."

## CHOOSING A MESSAGE

Having defined the desired audience response, the communicator turns to developing an effective message. Ideally, the message should get *attention*, hold *interest*, arouse *desire*, and obtain *action* (a framework known as the *AIDA model*). In practice, few messages take the consumer all the way from awareness to purchase, but the AIDA framework suggests the desirable qualities of a good message.

In putting the message together, the marketing communicator must decide what to say *(message content)* and how to say it *(message structure and format)*.

### Message Content
The communicator has to figure out an appeal or theme that will produce the desired response. There are three types of appeals: rational, emotional, and moral. *Rational appeals* relate to the audience's self-interest. They show that the product will produce the desired benefits. Examples are messages showing a product's quality, economy, value, or performance. Thus, in its ads, Mercedes offers automobiles that are "engineered like no other car in the world," stressing engineering, design, performance, and safety.

*Emotional appeals* attempt to stir up either negative or positive emotions that can motivate purchase. Communicators may use positive emotional appeals such as love, humor, pride, and joy. Or, they may include fear, guilt, and shame appeals that get people to do things that they should (brush their teeth, buy new tires), or to stop doing things they shouldn't (smoke, drink too much, eat fatty

*A mild fear appeal: "When you get a cavity, there's no second chance."*

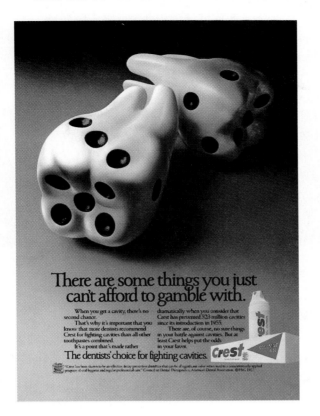

There are some things you just can't afford to gamble with.

When you get a cavity, there's no second chance.
That's why it's important that you know that more dentists recommend Crest for fighting cavities than all other toothpastes combined.
It's a point that's made rather dramatically when you consider that Crest has prevented 523 million cavities since its introduction in 1955.
There are, of course, no sure things in your battle against cavities. But at least Crest helps put the odds in your favor.

**The dentists' choice for fighting cavities.**

foods). For example, a Crest ad invokes mild fear when it claims, "There are some things you just can't afford to gamble with" (cavities). Etonic ads ask, "What would you do if you couldn't run?" They go on to note that Etonic athletic shoes are designed to avoid injuries—they're "built so you can last."

*Moral appeals* are directed to the audience's sense of what is right and proper. They are often used to urge people to support social causes such as a cleaner environment, better race relations, equal rights for women, and aid to the needy. An example of a moral appeal is the March of Dimes appeal: "God made you whole. Give to help those He didn't."

## Message Structure and Format

The marketing communicator also needs a strong *structure and format* for the message. In a print ad, the communicator has to decide on the headline, copy, illustration, and color. To attract attention, advertisers can use novelty and contrast; eye-catching pictures and headlines; distinctive formats; message size and position; and color, shape, and movement. If the message is to be carried over the radio, the communicator has to choose words, sounds, and voices. The "sound" of an announcer promoting banking services should be different from one promoting quality furniture.

If the message is to be carried on television or in person, then all these elements plus body language have to be determined. Presenters deliberately use certain facial expressions, gestures, dress, posture, and hair style. If the message is carried on the product or its package, the communicator has to select texture, scent, color, size, and shape.

*To capture attention and communicate persuasively, advertisers often use eye-catching pictures and headlines, novelty and contrast. This General Motors ad ran in* Seventeen *magazine.*

"When my date drinks, I go home with another man."

General Motors.

Compared to a date who drinks and drives, a taxi driver is a knight in shining armor. So don't be shy about calling him. Or anyone else who will get you home safely. And don't let the people you know get behind the wheel if they've been drinking. Be a real friend—take their keys and share the cab. At General Motors, we not only want you to drive safely. We want you to ride safely, too.

# CHOOSING MEDIA

The communicator now must select *channels of communication*. There are two broad types of communication channels—*personal* and *nonpersonal*.

## Personal Communication Channels

**Personal communication channels**
Channels through which two or more people communicate directly with each other.

In **personal communication channels**, two or more people communicate directly with each other. They might communicate face to face, over the telephone, or even through the mail. Personal communication channels are effective because they allow for personal addressing and feedback.

Some personal communication channels are controlled directly by the company. For example, company salespeople contact buyers in the target market. But other personal communications about the product may reach buyers through channels that are not directly controlled by the company. These might include independent experts—consumer advocates, consumer buying guides, and others—making statements to target buyers. Or they might be neighbors, friends, family members, and associates talking to target buyers. This last channel, known as **word-of-mouth influence**, has considerable effect in many product areas.

**Word-of-mouth influence**
Personal communication about a product between target buyers and neighbors, friends, family members, and associates.

Personal influence carries great weight for products that are expensive, risky, or highly visible. For example, buyers of automobiles and major appliances often go beyond mass-media sources to seek the opinions of knowledgeable people.

Companies can take steps to put personal communication channels to work for them. For example, they can create *opinion leaders*—people whose opinions are sought by others—by supplying certain people with the product on attractive terms. For instance, they can work through influential community members such as local radio personalities, high school class presidents, and heads of local organizations. And they can use influential people in their advertisements or develop advertising that has high "conversation value."

## Nonpersonal Communication Channels

**Nonpersonal communication channels**
Media that carry messages without personal contact or feedback, including major media, atmospheres, and events.

**Nonpersonal communication channels** are media that carry messages without personal contact or feedback. They include major media, atmospheres, and events. Major *media* include print media (newspapers, magazines, direct mail); broadcast media (radio, television); and display media (billboards, signs, posters). *Atmospheres* are designed environments that create or reinforce the buyer's leanings toward purchasing a product. Thus, lawyers' offices and banks are designed to communicate confidence and other qualities that might be valued by their clients. *Events* are staged occurrences that communicate messages to target audiences. For example, public relations departments arrange press conferences, grand openings, shows and exhibits, public tours, and other events.

Nonpersonal communication affects buyers directly. In addition, using mass media often affects buyers indirectly by causing more personal communication. Communications first flow from television, magazines, and other mass media to opinion leaders and then from these opinion leaders to others. Thus, opinion leaders step between the mass media and their audiences and carry messages to people who are less exposed to media. This suggests that mass communicators should aim their messages directly at opinion leaders, letting them carry the message to others.

### The Message Source

In either personal or nonpersonal communication, the message's impact on the target audience is also affected by how the audience views the communicator. Messages delivered by highly credible sources are more persuasive. For example, pharmaceutical companies want doctors to tell about their products' benefits because doctors are very credible figures. Many food companies aim promotions at doctors, dentists, and other health-care providers to motivate these professionals to recommend their products to patients (see Marketing at Work 13-1). Marketers also hire well-known actors, athletes, and even cartoon characters to deliver their messages. Basketball star Michael Jordan soars for Gatorade, McDonald's, and

*Celebrities impart some of their own likability and trustworthiness to the products they endorse. Here, Shaquille O'Neal speaks powerfully for Pepsi.*

## MARKETING AT WORK 13-1

# PROMOTING PRODUCTS THROUGH DOCTORS AND OTHER PROFESSIONALS

Food marketers are discovering that the best way to a consumer's stomach may be through a doctor's recommendation. Today's more nutrition-conscious consumers often seek advice from doctors and other health-care professionals about which products are best for them. Kellogg, Procter & Gamble, Quaker, and other large food companies are increasingly recognizing what pharmaceutical companies have known for years—professional recommendations can strongly influence consumer buying decisions. So food companies are stepping up promotion to doctors, dentists, and others, hoping to inform them about product benefits and motivate them to recommend the promoted brands to their patients.

Doctors receive the most attention from food marketers. For example, Cumberland Packing runs ads in medical journals for its Sweet 'N Low sugar substitute, saying, "It's one thing you can do to make your patient's diet a little easier to swallow." And Kellogg launched its "Project Nutrition" promotion to sell doctors on the merits of eating high-fiber cereal breakfasts. The promotion consists of cholesterol screenings of 100,000 Americans around the country, ads targeting doctors in the *Journal of the American Medical Association* and the *New England Journal of Medicine,* and a new quarterly newsletter called Health Vantage mailed to 50,000 U.S. medical professionals. Similarly, Quaker sends out to doctors nationwide a quarterly newsletter, *Fiber Report,* that includes articles, research reports, and feature stories about the importance of fiber in diets.

Procter & Gamble provides literature about several of its products that doctors can pass along to patients. And P&G actively seeks medical endorsements. Years ago, a heavily promoted American Dental Association endorsement helped make P&G's Crest the leading brand of toothpaste. The recent Crest Guarantee offer continues this tradition. In this program, a

Nike, and giant Shaquille O'Neal towers for Pepsi. Fred Flintstone teams with TV weatherman Willard Scott to pitch for Days Inns. Jerry Seinfeld stumps for American Express. In fact, *Advertising Age* magazine recently named the entire cast of the *Seinfeld* television series as its Star Presenter of the Year.[3]

## COLLECTING FEEDBACK

After sending the message, the communicator must research its effect on the target audience. This involves asking the target audience members whether they remember the message, how many times they saw it, what points they recall, how they felt about the message, and their past and present attitudes toward the product and company. The communicator also wants to measure behavior resulting from the message—how many people bought a product, talked to others about it, or visited the store.

Feedback on marketing communications may suggest changes in the promotion program or in the product offer itself. For example, when the Boston Market restaurant chain enters new market areas, it uses television advertising and newspaper coupons to inform area consumers about the restaurant and to draw them in. Suppose that feedback research shows that 80 percent of all consumers in an

Crest user first visits the dentist, who rates the patient's dental condition and returns an enrollment card to P&G. The buyer then uses Crest for six months and once again visits the dentist, who verifies the visit. If the user (or the user's parent) isn't satisfied with the results of the second visit, P&G will refund six months' worth of Crest purchases, up to $15. Clearly, this program is designed to build loyalty among both customers *and* dentists.

P&G isn't the only marketer targeting dentists. The makers of Trident gum, Equal sugar substitute, Plax mouth rinse, and dozens of other products reach dentists through colorful brochures, samples, and ads in dental journals. As part of its Wrigley Dental Programs, Wrigley advertises Extra sugar-free gum to dentists as a preventive dentistry tool for their patients.

Other professionals targeted by food companies include veterinarians, teachers, and even high school coaches. Quaker does extensive product sampling of its Gaines and Ken-L Ration pet foods through veterinarians. It also runs ads for Gatorade in magazines read by high school sports trainers and coaches, and sponsors a fleet of vans that comb the country, offering Gatorade information and samples in key markets. Thus, food companies actively court as spokespeople any professionals who provide health or nutrition advice to their customers.

Many doctors and other health-care providers welcome the promotions as good sources of information about healthy foods and nutrition that can help them give better advice to their patients. Others, however, do not feel comfortable recommending specific food brands; some even resent attempts to influence them through promotion. Although it may take a lot of time and investment to persuade these professionals to change their attitudes, the results probably will justify the effort and expense. If a company can convince key health-care providers that the product is worthy of endorsement, it will gain powerful marketing allies. As one marketer puts it, "If a doctor hands you a product to use, that recommendation carries a lot of weight."

*Source:* See Laurie Freeman and Julie Liesse Erickson, "Doctored Strategy: Food Marketers Push Products through Physicians," *Advertising Age,* March 28, 1988, p. 12; and Jennifer Lawrence, "P&G Polishes Guarantee for Crest," *Advertising Age,* September 1, 1992, pp. 1, 34.

area recall seeing Boston Market ads and are aware of what the restaurant offers. Sixty percent of these aware consumers have eaten at the restaurant, but only 20 percent of those who tried it were satisfied. These results suggest that although promotion is creating *awareness,* the restaurant isn't giving consumers the *satisfaction* that they expect. Therefore, Boston Market needs to improve its food or service while staying with the successful communication program. In contrast, suppose the research shows that only 40 percent of area consumers are aware of the restaurant, only 30 percent of those who are aware have tried it, but 80 percent of those who have tried it return. In this case, Boston Market needs to strengthen its promotion program to take advantage of the restaurant's power to create customer satisfaction.

# ▶ SETTING THE TOTAL PROMOTION BUDGET AND MIX

We have looked at the steps in planning and sending communications to a target audience. But how does the company decide on the total *promotion budget* and its division among the major promotional tools to create the *promotion mix*? We now look at these questions.

# SETTING THE TOTAL PROMOTION BUDGET

One of the hardest marketing decisions facing a company is how much to spend on promotion. John Wanamaker, the department store magnate, once said: "I know that half of my advertising is wasted, but I don't know which half. I spent $2 million for advertising, and I don't know if that is half enough or twice too much." Thus, it is not surprising that industries and companies vary widely in how much they spend on promotion. Promotion spending may be 20 to 30 percent of sales in the cosmetics industry and only 2 or 3 percent in the industrial machinery industry. Within a given industry, both low and high spenders can be found.

How does a company decide on its promotion budget? We look at four common methods used to set the total budget for advertising: the *affordable method*, the *percentage-of-sales method*, the *competitive-parity method*, and the *objective-and-task method*.[4]

## Affordable Method

Some companies use the **affordable method**: They set the promotion budget at the level that they think the company can afford. Small businesses often use this method, reasoning that the company cannot spend more on advertising than it has. They start with total revenues, deduct operating expenses and capital outlays, and then devote some portion of the remaining funds to advertising.

Unfortunately, this method of setting budgets completely ignores the effects of promotion on sales. It tends to place advertising last among spending priorities, even in situations where advertising is critical to the firm's success. It leads to an uncertain annual promotion budget, which makes long-range market planning difficult. Although the affordable method can result in overspending on advertising, it more often results in underspending.

## Percentage-of-Sales Method

Other companies use the **percentage-of-sales method**, setting their promotion budget at a certain percentage of current or forecasted sales. Or they budget a percentage of the unit sales price. The percentage-of-sales method has advantages. It is simple to use and helps management think about the relationships between promotion spending, selling price, and profit per unit.

Despite these claimed advantages, however, the percentage-of-sales method has little to justify it. It wrongly views sales as the *cause* of promotion rather than as the *result*. The budget is based on availability of funds rather than on opportunities. It may prevent the increased spending sometimes needed to turn around falling sales. Because the budget varies with year-to-year sales, long-range planning is difficult. Finally, the method does not provide any basis for choosing a *specific* percentage, except what has been done in the past or what competitors are doing.

## Competitive-Parity Method

Still other companies use the **competitive-parity method**, setting their promotion budgets to match competitors' outlays. They monitor competitors' advertising or get industry promotion-spending estimates from publications or trade associations, and then set their budgets based on the industry average.

Two arguments support this method. First, competitors' budgets represent the collective wisdom of the industry. Second, spending what competitors spend helps prevent promotion wars. Unfortunately, neither argument is valid. There are no grounds for believing that the competition has a better idea of what a company should be spending on promotion than does the company itself. Companies differ greatly, and each has its own special promotion needs. Finally, there is no evidence that budgets based on competitive parity prevent promotion wars.

### Objective-and-Task Method

The most logical budget setting method is the **objective-and-task method,** whereby the company sets its promotion budget based on what it wants to accomplish with promotion. This budgeting method entails (1) defining specific promotion objectives, (2) determining the tasks needed to achieve these objectives, and (3) estimating the costs of performing these tasks. The sum of these costs is the proposed promotion budget.

The objective-and-task method forces management to spell out its assumptions about the relationship between dollars spent and promotion results. But it is also the most difficult method to use. Often, it is hard to figure out which specific tasks will achieve specific objectives. For example, suppose Sony wants 95 percent awareness for its latest camcorder model during the six-month introductory period. What specific advertising messages and media schedules should Sony use to attain this objective? How much would these messages and media schedules cost? Sony management must consider such questions, even though they are hard to answer.

**Objective-and-task method**
A method for setting promotion budgets based on what the company wants to accomplish with promotion.

# SETTING THE PROMOTION MIX

The company now must divide the total promotion budget among the major promotion tools—advertising, personal selling, sales promotion, and public relations. It must blend the promotion tools carefully into a coordinated *promotion mix*. Companies within the same industry differ greatly in the design of their promotion mixes. For example, Avon spends most of its promotion funds on personal selling and direct marketing, whereas Revlon spends heavily on consumer advertising. Electrolux sells most of its vacuum cleaners door to door, whereas Hoover relies more on advertising and promotion to retailers. We now look at the many factors that influence the marketer's choice of promotion tools.

### The Nature of Each Promotion Tool

Each promotion tool—*advertising, personal selling, sales promotion,* and *public relations*—has unique characteristics and costs. Marketers must understand these characteristics in order to select the proper tools.

**ADVERTISING.** The many forms of advertising contribute uniquely to the overall promotion mix. Advertising can reach masses of geographically dispersed buyers at a low cost per exposure. It also enables the seller to repeat a message many times, and it lets the buyer receive and compare the messages of various competitors. Because of advertising's public nature, consumers tend to view advertised products as standard and legitimate; buyers know that purchasing advertised products will be understood and accepted publicly. Large-scale advertising says something positive about the seller's size, popularity, and success.

Advertising is also very expressive; it allows the company to dramatize its products through the artful use of visuals, print, sound, and color. On the one hand, advertising can be used to build up a long-term image for a product (such as Coca-Cola ads). On the other hand, advertising can trigger quick sales (as when Sears advertises a weekend sale).

Advertising also has some shortcomings. Although it reaches many people quickly, advertising is impersonal and cannot be as persuasive as company salespeople. For the most part, advertising can carry on only a one-way communication with the audience, and the audience does not feel that it has to pay attention or respond. In addition, advertising can be very costly. Although some advertising forms, such as newspaper and radio advertising, can be done on small budgets, other forms, such as network TV advertising, require very large budgets.

PERSONAL SELLING.   Personal selling is the most effective tool at certain stages of the buying process, particularly in building up buyers' preferences, convictions, and actions. Compared with advertising, personal selling has several unique qualities. It involves personal interaction between two or more people, so that each person can observe the other's needs and characteristics and make quick adjustments. Personal selling also allows all kinds of relationships to spring up, ranging from a matter-of-fact selling relationship to a deep personal friendship. The effective salesperson keeps the customer's interests at heart in order to build a long-term relationship. Finally, with personal selling, the buyer usually feels a greater need to listen and respond, even if the response is a polite "no thank you."

These unique qualities come at a cost, however. A sales force requires a longer-term commitment than does advertising—advertising can be turned on and off, but sales force size is harder to change. Personal selling is also the company's most expensive promotion tool, costing industrial companies an average of over $200 per sales call.[5] U.S. firms spend up to three times as much on personal selling as they do on advertising.

*With personal selling, the customer feels a greater need to listen and respond, even if the response is a polite "no, thank you."*

**SALES PROMOTION.** Sales promotion includes a wide assortment of tools—coupons, contests, cents-off deals, premiums, and others—all of which have many unique qualities. They attract consumer attention and provide information that may lead to a purchase. They offer strong incentives to purchase by providing inducements or contributions that give additional value to consumers. And sales promotions invite and reward quick response. Whereas advertising says "buy our product," sales promotion says "buy it now."

Companies use sales-promotion tools to create a stronger and quicker response. Sales promotion can be used to dramatize product offers and to boost sagging sales. Sales promotion effects are usually short-lived, however, and are not effective in building long-run brand preference.

**PUBLIC RELATIONS.** Public relations offers several unique qualities. It is very believable—news stories, features, and events seem more real and believable to readers than ads do. Public relations can also reach many prospects who avoid salespeople and advertisements—the message gets to the buyers as "news" rather than as a sales-directed communication. And, like advertising, public relations can dramatize a company or product.

Marketers tend to underuse public relations or to use it as an afterthought. Yet a well-thought-out public relations campaign, used with other promotion mix elements, can be very effective and economical.

### Promotion Mix Strategies

**Push strategy**
A promotion strategy that calls for using the sales force and trade promotion to push the product through channels.

**Pull strategy**
A promotion strategy that calls for spending a lot on advertising and consumer promotion to build up consumer demand to pull the product through the channel.

Marketers can choose from two basic promotion mix strategies—*push* promotion or *pull* promotion. Figure 13-3 contrasts the two strategies. The relative emphasis on the specific promotion tools differs for push and pull strategies. A **push strategy** involves "pushing" the product through distribution channels to final consumers. The producer directs its marketing activities (primarily personal selling and trade promotion) toward channel members to induce them to carry the product and to promote it to final consumers. Using a **pull strategy**, the producer directs

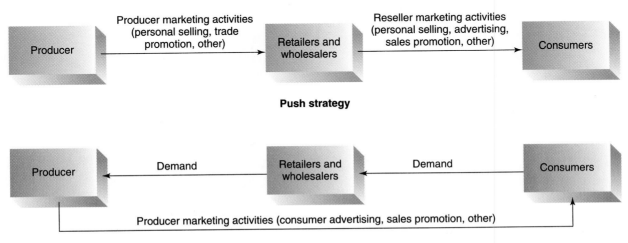

**FIGURE 13-3**
*Push versus pull promotion strategy*

its marketing activities (primarily advertising and consumer promotion) toward final consumers to induce them to buy the product. If the pull strategy is effective, consumers then will demand the product from channel members, who will in turn demand it from producers. Thus, under a pull strategy, consumer demand "pulls" the product through the channels.

Some small industrial goods companies use only push strategies; some direct-marketing companies use only pull. However, most large companies use some combination of both. For example, Frito-Lay uses mass-media advertising to pull its products, and a large sales force and trade promotions to push its products through the channels. In recent years, consumer goods companies have been decreasing the pull portions of their promotion mixes in favor of more push (see Marketing at Work 13-2).

Companies consider many factors when developing their promotion mix strategies, including type of product/market, the buyer-readiness stage, and the product life-cycle stage.

**TYPE OF PRODUCT/MARKET.** The importance of different promotion tools varies between consumer and business markets (see Figure 13-4). Consumer goods companies usually pull more, putting more of their funds into advertising, followed by sales promotion, personal selling, and then public relations. In contrast, industrial goods companies tend to push more, putting most of their funds into personal selling, followed by sales promotion, advertising, and public relations. In general, personal selling is used more heavily with expensive and risky goods and in markets with fewer and larger sellers.

Although advertising is less important than sales calls in business markets, it still plays an important role. Business-to-business advertising can build product awareness and knowledge, develop sales leads, and reassure buyers. Similarly, personal selling can add a lot to consumer goods marketing efforts. It is simply not the case that "salespeople put products on shelves and advertising takes them off." Well-trained consumer goods salespeople can sign up more dealers to carry a par-

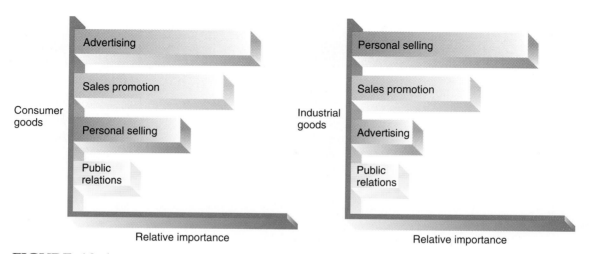

**FIGURE 13-4**
*Relative importance of promotion tools in consumer versus industrial markets*

## MARKETING AT WORK 13-2

# ARE CONSUMER GOODS COMPANIES GETTING TOO "PUSHY"?

Consumer packaged-goods companies like Kraft, Procter & Gamble, RJR/Nabisco, Campbell, and Gillette grew into giants by using mostly pull promotion strategies. They used massive doses of national advertising to differentiate their products, build market share, and maintain customer loyalty. But during the past two decades, these companies have gotten more "pushy," deemphasizing national advertising and putting more of their promotion budgets into personal selling and sales promotions. Trade promotions (trade allowances, displays, cooperative advertising) now account for about 47 percent of total marketing spending by consumer product companies; consumer promotions (coupons, cents-off deals, premiums) account for another 28 percent. That leaves only 25 percent of total marketing spending for media advertising, down from 42 percent just 15 years ago.

Why have these companies shifted so heavily toward push strategies? One reason is that mass-media campaigns have become more expensive and less effective in recent years. Network television costs have risen sharply while audiences have fallen off, making national advertising less cost effective. Companies also have increased their market segmentation efforts and are tailoring their marketing programs more narrowly, making national advertising less suitable than localized retailer promotions. And in these days of brand extensions and "me-too" products, companies sometimes have trouble finding meaningful product differences to feature in advertising. So they have differentiated their products through price reductions, premium offers, coupons, and other push techniques.

Another factor speeding the shift from pull to push has been the greater strength of retailers. Today's retailers are larger and have more access to product sales and profit information. They now have the power to demand and get what they want—and what they want is more push. Whereas national advertising bypasses them on its way to the masses, push promotion benefits them directly. Consumer promotions give retailers an immediate sales boost, and cash from trade allowances pads retailer profits. Thus, producers must often use push just to obtain good shelf space and advertising support from important retailers.

However, many marketers are concerned that the reckless use of push will lead to fierce price competition and a never-ending spiral of price slashing and deal making. This situation would mean lower margins, and companies would have less money to invest in the research and development, packaging, and advertising needed to improve products and maintain long-run consumer preference and loyalty. If used improperly, push promotion can mortgage a brand's future for short-term gains. Sales promotion buys short-run reseller support and consumer sales, but advertising builds long-run brand equity and consumer preference. By robbing the advertising budget to pay for more sales promotion, companies might win the battle for short-run earnings but lose the war for long-run consumer loyalty and market share.

Many consumer companies are now rethinking their promotion strategies and reversing the trend by shifting their promotion budgets back slightly toward advertising. Many have realized that it's not a question of sales promotion versus advertising, or of push versus pull. Success lies in finding the best mix of the two: consistent advertising to build long-run brand value and consumer preference, and sales promotion to create short-run trade support and consumer excitement. The company needs to blend both push and pull elements into an integrated promotion program that meets immediate consumer and retailer needs as well as long-run strategic needs.

*Sources:* James C. Schroer, "Ad Spending: Growing Marketing Share," *Harvard Business Review,* January–February 1990, pp. 44–48; John Philip Jones, "The Double Jeopardy of Sales Promotions," *Harvard Business Review,* September–October 1990, pp. 145–52; Zachary Schiller, "Not Everyone Loves a Supermarket Special," *Business Week,* February 17, 1992, pp. 64–68; Lois Therrien, "Brands on the Run," *Business Week,* April 19, 1993, pp. 26–29; and *16th Annual Survey of Promotional Practices,* (Oakbrook Terrace, IL: Donnelly Marketing Inc., June 1994), p. 9.

ticular brand, convince them to give the brand more shelf space, and urge them to use special displays and promotions.

**BUYER-READINESS STAGE.**   The effects of the promotional tools vary for the different buyer-readiness stages. Advertising, along with public relations, plays the major role in the awareness and knowledge stages, more important than that played by "cold calls" from salespeople. Customer liking, preference, and conviction are more affected by personal selling, which is closely followed by advertising. Finally, closing the sale is mostly done with sales calls and sales promotion. Clearly, personal selling, given its high costs, should focus on the later stages of the customer buying process.

**PRODUCT LIFE-CYCLE STAGE.**   The effects of different promotion tools also vary with stages of the product life cycle. In the introduction stage, advertising and public relations are good for producing high awareness, and sales promotion is useful in promoting early trial. Personal selling must be used to get the trade to carry the product. In the growth stage, advertising and public relations continue to be powerful influences, whereas sales promotion can be reduced because fewer incentives are needed. In the mature stage, sales promotion again becomes important relative to advertising. Buyers know the brands, and advertising is needed only to remind them of the product. In the decline stage, advertising is kept at a reminder level, public relations is dropped, and salespeople give the product only scant attention. Sales promotion, however, might continue strong.

# THE CHANGING FACE OF MARKETING COMMUNICATIONS

During the past several decades, companies around the world have perfected the art of mass marketing—selling highly standardized products to masses of customers. In the process, they have developed effective mass media advertising techniques to support their mass marketing strategies. These companies routinely invest millions of dollars in the mass media, reaching tens of millions of customers with a single ad. However, as we move toward the twenty-first century, marketing managers are facing some new marketing communications realities.

## THE CHANGING COMMUNICATIONS ENVIRONMENT

Two major factors are changing the face of today's marketing communications. First, as mass markets have fragmented, marketers are shifting away from mass marketing. More and more, they are developing focused marketing programs designed to build closer relationships with customers in more narrowly defined micromarkets. Second, vast improvements in computer and information technology are speeding the movement toward segmented marketing. Today's information technology helps marketers to keep closer track of customer needs; more information about consumers at the individual and household levels is available than ever before. New technologies also provide new communications avenues for reaching smaller customer segments with more tailored messages.

The shift from mass marketing to segmented marketing has had a dramatic impact on marketing communications. Just as mass marketing gave rise to a new generation of mass media communications, the shift toward one-on-one marketing is spawning a new generation of more specialized and highly targeted communications efforts.[6]

Given this new communications environment, marketers must rethink the roles of various media and promotion mix tools. Mass media advertising has long dominated the promotion mixes of consumer product companies. However, although television, magazines, and other mass media remain very important, their dominance is now declining. *Market* fragmentation has resulted in *media* fragmentation—an explosion of more focused media that better match today's targeting strategies. For example, in 1960, by purchasing commercial time on the three major television networks, an advertiser could reach 90 percent of the U.S. population during an average week. Today, that number has fallen to less than 60 percent, as cable television and satellite broadcasting systems now offer advertisers dozens or even hundreds of alternative channels that reach smaller, specialized audiences. Similarly, the relatively few mass magazines of the 1940s and 1950s, such as *Look, Life, Saturday Evening Post,* have been replaced by more than

*Thousands of specialized magazines match today's targeting strategies. Meredith Corporation alone publishes more than 50 magazines targeting home and family, including* Better Homes and Gardens, Ladies' Home Journal, *and* Country Home.

11,000 special-interest magazines reaching more focused audiences. Beyond these channels, advertisers are making increased use of new, highly targeted media, ranging from video screens on supermarket shopping carts to online computer services and CD-ROM catalogs.

More generally, advertising appears to be giving way to other elements of the promotion mix. In the glory days of mass marketing, consumer product companies spent a lion's share of their promotion budgets on mass-media advertising. Today, media advertising captures only about 26 percent of total promotion spending.[7] The rest goes to various sales promotion activities, which can be focused more effectively on individual consumer and trade segments. In all, companies are doing less *broadcasting* and more *narrowcasting*. They are using a richer variety of focused communication tools in an effort to reach their many diverse target markets. Some observers envision a future in which today's advertising-supported mass media will be replaced almost entirely by one-on-one, interactive marketing media such as online computer services and two-way television.

# GROWTH OF DIRECT MARKETING

**Direct marketing**
Marketing through various advertising media that interact directly with consumers, generally calling for the consumer to make a direct response.

The new face of marketing communications is most apparent in the rapidly growing field of direct marketing. Now the fastest-growing form of marketing, direct marketing reflects the trend toward targeted or one-on-one marketing communications. As discussed in the previous chapter, **direct marketing** consists of direct communications with carefully targeted consumers to obtain an immediate response. Through direct marketing, sellers can closely match their marketing offers and communications to the needs of narrowly defined segments.

All kinds of consumer and business-to-business marketers use direct marketing—producers, wholesalers, retailers, nonprofit organizations, and government agencies. Direct marketers employ a variety of communications tools. In addition to old favorites such as television, direct mail, and telephone marketing, direct marketers employ powerful new forms of telecommunications and computer-based media. These tools are often used in combinations that move the customer from initial awareness of an offer to purchase and after-sale service.

## Forms of Direct Marketing Communication

The four major forms of direct marketing are *direct-mail and catalog marketing, telemarketing, television marketing,* and *online shopping.*

**Direct-mail marketing**
Direct marketing through single mailings that include letters, ads, samples, foldouts, and other "salespeople on wings" sent to prospects on mailing lists.

**DIRECT-MAIL AND CATALOG MARKETING.**   **Direct-mail marketing** involves mailings of letters, ads, samples, foldouts, and other "salespeople on wings" sent to prospects on mailing lists. The mailing lists are developed from customer lists or obtained from mailing-list houses that provide names of people fitting almost any description—the superwealthy, mobile-home owners, veterinarians, pet owners, or just about anything else.

Direct mail is well suited to direct, one-on-one communication. Direct mail permits high target-market selectivity, can be personalized, is flexible, and allows easy measurement of results. Whereas the cost per thousand people reached is higher than with mass media such as television or magazines, the people who are reached are much better prospects. Direct mail has proved successful in promoting all kinds of products, from books, magazine subscriptions, and insurance to gift items, clothing, gourmet foods, and industrial products. Direct mail is also used heavily by charities, which raise billions of dollars each year and account for about 25 percent of all direct-mail revenues.

The direct-mail industry constantly seeks new methods and approaches. For example, videocassettes have become one of the fastest-growing direct mail media. With VCRs now in 85 percent of American homes, marketers mailed out an estimated 85 million tapes in 1995. For instance, to introduce its Donkey Kong Country video game, Nintendo of America created a 13-minute MTV-style video and sent 2 million copies to avid video-game players. This direct mail video helped Nintendo sell 6.1 million units of the game in only 45 days, making it the fastest-selling game in industry history.[8] Similarly, Soloflex uses a video brochure to help sell its $1,000 in-home exercise equipment. The 22-minute video shows an attractive couple demonstrating the exercises possible with the system. Soloflex claims that almost half of those who view the video brochure later place an order via telephone, compared with only a 10 percent response from those receiving regular direct mail.[9]

**Catalog marketing** involves selling through catalogs that are mailed to a select list of customers or made available in stores. Some very large general-merchandise retailers—such as JCPenney and Spiegel—sell a full line of merchandise through catalogs. But recently, the giants have been challenged by thousands of specialty catalogs that serve highly specialized market niches. As a result, Sears discontinued its 97-year-old annual "Big Book" catalog in 1993 after years of unprofitable operation, opting instead to put its name on dozens of smaller, more specialized catalogs.[10]

Over 14 billion copies of more than 8,500 different consumer catalogs are mailed out annually, and the average household receives some 50 catalogs a year. Consumers can buy just about anything from a catalog. Hanover House sends out 22 different catalogs selling everything from shoes to decorative lawn birds. Sharper Image sells $2,400 jet-propelled surfboards. The Banana Republic Travel and Safari Clothing Company features everything that you would need to go hiking in the Sahara or the rain forest.

**Catalog marketing**
Direct marketing through catalogs that are mailed to a select list of customers or made available in stores.

*Billions of catalogs are mailed out each year; the average housebould receives 50 catalogs annually.*

Specialty department stores, such as Neiman Marcus, Bloomingdale's, and Saks Fifth Avenue, send catalogs to cultivate upper-middle-class markets for high-priced, often exotic, merchandise. Several major corporations have also developed or acquired mail-order divisions. For example, Avon now issues ten women's fashion catalogs along with catalogs for children's and men's clothes. And Walt Disney Company mails out over 6 million catalogs each year featuring videos, stuffed animals, and other Disney items.

Most consumers enjoy receiving catalogs and sometimes are even willing to pay to get them. Many catalog marketers are now even selling their catalogs at bookstores and magazine stands. Some companies, such as Royal Silk, Neiman Marcus, Sears, and Spiegel, are also experimenting with videotape, computer diskette, and CD-ROM catalogs. Royal Silk sells a 35-minute video catalog to its customers for $5.95. The tape contains a polished presentation of Royal Silk products, tells customers how to care for silk, and provides ordering information.

Many business-to-business marketers also rely heavily on catalogs. Whether in the form of a simple brochure, three-ring binder, or book, or encoded on a videotape or computer disk, catalogs remain one of today's hardest-working sales tools. For some companies, in fact, catalogs have even taken the place of salespeople. In all, companies mail out more than 1.1 *billion* business-to-business catalogs each year, reaping more than $50 billion worth of catalog sales.[11]

**Telemarketing**
Using the telephone to sell directly to consumers.

**TELEMARKETING.** **Telemarketing**—using the telephone to sell directly to consumers—has become the major direct-marketing communication tool. Marketers use *outbound* telephone marketing to sell directly to consumers and businesses. *Inbound* toll-free 800 numbers are used to receive orders from television and radio ads, direct mail, or catalogs. The average household receives 19 telephone sales calls each year and makes 16 calls to place orders. In 1995, marketers spent an estimated $54.1 billion on outbound calls to consumers and businesses, generating an estimated $385 billion in sales. During 1990, AT&T logged more than seven billion 800-number calls. Some industry analysts boldly predict that by the turn of the century, half of all retail sales will be completed by telephone.[12]

Other marketers use 900 numbers to sell consumers information, entertainment, or the opportunity to voice an opinion. For example, for a charge, consumers can obtain weather forecasts from American Express (1-900-WEATHER—75 cents a minute); pet care information from Quaker Oats (1-900-990-PETS—95 cents a minute); advice on snoring and other sleep disorders from Somnus (1-900-USA-SLEEP—$2 for the first minute, then $1 a minute); or golf lessons from *Golf Digest* (1-900-454-3288—95 cents a minute). Altogether, the 900-number industry now generates $860 million in annual revenues.[13]

Business-to-business marketers use telemarketing extensively. In fact, more than $115 billion worth of industrial products were marketed by phone last year. For example, General Electric uses telemarketing to generate and qualify sales leads and to manage small accounts. Raleigh Bicycles uses telemarketing to reduce the amount of personal selling needed for contacting its dealers; in the first year, sales-force travel costs were reduced 50 percent, and sales in a single quarter increased 34 percent.[14]

Most consumers appreciate many of the offers that they receive by telephone. Properly designed and targeted telemarketing provides many benefits, including purchasing convenience and increased product and service information. However, the recent explosion in unsolicited telephone marketing has annoyed many consumers who object to the almost daily "junk phone calls" that pull them away from the dinner table or clog up their answering machines. Lawmakers around the country are responding with legislation ranging from banning unsolicited telemarketing calls during certain hours to letting households sign up for a national "Don't Call Me" list. Most telemarketers support some action against random and poorly targeted telemarketing. As a Direct Marketing Association official notes, "We want to target people who want to be targeted."[15]

**TELEVISION MARKETING.** **Television marketing** takes one of two major forms. The first is *direct-response advertising.* Direct marketers air television spots, often 60 or 120 seconds long, that persuasively describe a product and give customers a toll-free number for ordering. Television viewers often encounter 30-minute advertising programs, or *infomercials,* for a single product. Such direct-response advertising works well for magazines, books, small appliances, tapes and CDs, collectibles, and many other products.

Some successful direct-response ads run for years and become classics. For example, Dial Media's ads for Ginsu knives ran for seven years and sold almost three million sets of knives worth more than $40 million in sales; its Armourcote cookware ads generated more than twice that much. And the now-familiar 30-minute Psychic Friends infomercials have aired more than 12,000 times during the past two years, offering callers access to its national network of psychics and generating more than $100 million worth of business. For years, infomercials have been associated with somewhat questionable pitches for juicers, get-rich-quick schemes, and nifty ways to stay in shape without working very hard at it. Recently, however, a number of top marketing companies—GTE, Johnson & Johnson, MCA Universal, Sears, Procter & Gamble, Revlon, Apple Computer, Toyota, and others—have begun using infomercials to sell their wares over the phone, refer customers to retailers, or send out coupons and product information. In all, infomercials produced almost $1 billion in sales in 1994.[16]

*Home shopping channels,* another form of television direct marketing, are television programs or entire channels dedicated to selling goods and services. Some home shopping channels, such as the Quality Value Channel (QVC) and the Home Shopping Network (HSN), broadcast 24 hours a day. On HSN, the program's hosts offer bargain prices on products ranging from jewelry, lamps, collectible dolls, and clothing to power tools and consumer electronics that are usually obtained by the home shopping channel at closeout prices. The show is upbeat, with the hosts honking horns, blowing whistles, and praising viewers for their good taste. Viewers call an 800 number to order goods. At the other end of the operation, 400 operators handle more than 1,200 incoming lines, entering orders directly into computer terminals. Orders are shipped within 48 hours.

Sales through home shopping channels grew from $450 million in 1986 to an estimated $2 billion in 1994. More than half of all U.S. homes have access to QVC, HSN, or other home shopping channels such as Value Club of America, Home Shopping Mall, or TelShop. Sears, Kmart, JCPenney, Spiegel, and other major retailers are now looking into the home shopping industry. Many experts think that advances in two-way, interactive television will make video shopping one of the major forms of direct marketing by the end of the century.[17]

**ONLINE SHOPPING.** **Online computer shopping** is conducted through interactive online computer systems, which link consumers with sellers electronically. These

---

**Television marketing**
Direct marketing via television, using direct-response advertising or home shopping channels.

**Online computer shopping**
Shopping conducted through interactive online computer systems, which link consumers with sellers electronically.

services create computerized catalogs of products and services offered by producers, retailers, banks, travel organizations, and others. Consumers use a home computer to hook into the system through cable or telephone lines.

Three currently successful online systems in the United States are CompuServe, Prodigy, and America Online. Prodigy, developed through a partnership by IBM and Sears, offers in-home shopping services and much more. Through Prodigy, subscribers can order thousands of products and services electronically from dozens of major stores and catalogs. They can also do their banking with local banks; buy and sell investments through a discount brokerage service; book airline, hotel, and car-rental reservations; play games, quizzes, and contests; check *Consumer Reports* ratings of various products; receive the latest sports scores and statistics; obtain weather forecasts; and exchange messages with other subscribers around the country.

The latest online marketing medium is the vast and burgeoning global web of computer networks called the Internet. The Internet was created by the Defense Department during the 1960s, initially to link government labs, contractors, and military installations. Today, this huge, public computer network links computer users of all types all around the world. Anyone with a PC, a modem, and the right software can browse the Internet's World Wide Web to obtain or share information on almost any subject and to interact with other users. Currently, about three million users browse the World Wide Web weekly—mostly young, college-educated, and affluent consumers. The number is expected to grow to more than 11 million by 1998.

Although most marketers don't as yet actually sell their products on the Internet, the Web is emerging as a key new marketing medium. Many companies, small and large, are setting up "websites" that offer information about themselves and their products. For example, the makers of Ragu spaghetti sauce have a website that offers Italian phrases, recipes, and a sweepstakes. Burlington Coat Factory's website supplies product information, coupons, and a store locator. Reebok offers sports tips and athlete interviews, and Miller Genuine Draft offers a "virtual tap room" where Web surfers can obtain sports news. And McDonald's launched McFamily, which offers entertainment and parenting advice.

Although relatively few consumers now subscribe to such electronic systems, the number is expected to grow in future years. In fact, some experts predict that computers, televisions, and telephones will soon mutate into a single "smart box," which users will manipulate to receive entertainment, information, and direct access to "video shopping malls." By the turn of the century, they assert, all of us will enjoy the wonders of interactive, online shopping.[18]

### Direct Marketing Databases

**Marketing database**
An organized set of data about individual customers or prospects that can be used to generate and qualify customer leads, sell products and services, and maintain customer relationships.

Successful direct marketing begins with a good customer database. A **marketing database** is an organized set of data about individual customers or prospects, including geographic, demographic, psychographic, and buying behavior data. The database can be used to locate good potential customers, tailor products and services to the special needs of targeted consumers, and maintain long-term customer relationships. A recent survey found that almost two-thirds of all large consumer products companies are currently using or building such databases for targeting their marketing efforts.[19]

Procter & Gamble, for example, uses its database to market Pampers disposable diapers, using such tactics as "individualized" birthday cards for babies with reminders to move up to the next size. Kraft Foods has amassed a list of more than 30 million users of its products who have responded to coupons or other Kraft promotions. Based on their interests, the company sends these customers tips on such things as nutrition and exercise, as well as recipes and coupons for specific Kraft brands. Blockbuster, the massive entertainment company, uses its database of 36 million households and two million daily transactions to help its video-rental customers select movies and to steer them to other Blockbuster subsidiaries. And American Express uses its customer database to tailor offers to cardholders. In Belgium, it is testing a system that links cardholder spending patterns with postal-zone data. If a new restaurant opens, for example, the company might offer a special discount to cardholders who live within walking distance and who eat out a lot.[20]

Building a marketing database takes much time and money, but it can pay handsome dividends. For example, a General Electric customer database contains each customer's demographic and psychographic characteristics along with an appliance purchasing history. Using this database, GE marketers assess how long specific customers have owned their current appliances and which past customers might be ready to purchase again. They can determine which customers need a new GE video recorder, compact disc player, stereo receiver, or other appliance to go with other recently purchased electronics products. Or they can identify the best past GE purchasers and send them gift certificates or other promotions to apply against their next GE purchases. A rich customer database allows GE to build profitable new business by locating good prospects, anticipating customer needs, cross-selling products and services, and rewarding loyal customers.[21]

## INTEGRATED MARKETING COMMUNICATIONS

The recent shifts from mass marketing to targeted marketing, along with innovations in information technology and the rapid growth of direct marketing, have had a major impact on the nature of marketing communications. In their efforts to communicate with more fragmented and diverse target segments, marketers are employing a richer variety of more focused promotional tools. As a result, consumers are being exposed to a greater variety of marketing communications from and about the company.

However, customers don't distinguish between message sources the way that marketers do. In the consumer's mind, advertising messages from different media such as television, magazines, or online computer services blur into one. Messages delivered via different promotional approaches—such as advertising, personal selling, sales promotion, public relations, or direct marketing—all become part of a single overall message about the company. Conflicting messages from these different sources can result in confused company images and brand positions.

All too often, companies fail to integrate their various communications channels. The result is a hodgepodge of communications to consumers. Mass advertisements say one thing, a price promotion sends a different signal, a product label creates still another message, and company sales literature says something altogether different.

The problem is that these communications often come from different company sources. Advertising messages are planned and implemented by the advertising department or advertising agency. Personal selling communications are developed by sales management. Other functional specialists are responsible for public relations, sales promotion, direct marketing, and other forms of marketing communications. Moreover, members of various departments often differ in their views on how to split the promotion budget. The sales manager would rather hire a few more salespeople than spend $150,000 on a single television commercial. The public relations manager feels that he or she can do wonders with some money shifted from advertising to public relations.

In the past, no one person was responsible for thinking through the communication roles of the various promotion tools and coordinating the promotion mix. Today, however, more companies are adopting the concept of **integrated marketing communications**. Under this concept, the company carefully integrates and coordinates its many communications channels—mass media advertising, personal selling, sales promotion, public relations, direct marketing, packaging, and others—to deliver a clear, consistent, and compelling message about the organization and its products.[22] (See Marketing at Work 13-3 for examples.)

The company works out the roles that the various promotional tools will play and the extent to which each will be used. It carefully coordinates the promotional activities and the timing of when major campaigns take place. It keeps track of its promotional expenditures by product, promotional tool, product life-cycle stage, and observed effect in order to improve future use of the promotion mix tools. Finally, to help implement its integrated marketing strategy, the company appoints a marketing communications director who has overall responsibility for the company's communications efforts. To integrate its external communications effectively, the company must first integrate its internal communications activities.[23]

Integrated marketing communications produces better communications consistency and greater sales impact. It places the responsibility in someone's hands—where none existed before—to unify the company's image as it is shaped by thousands of company activities. It leads to a total marketing communication strategy aimed at showing how the company and its products can help customers solve their problems.

**Integrated marketing communications** The concept under which a company carefully integrates and coordinates its many communications channels to deliver a clear, consistent, and compelling message about the organization and its products.

# ▶ SOCIALLY RESPONSIBLE MARKETING COMMUNICATION

Whoever is in charge, people at all levels of the organization must be aware of the growing body of legal and ethical issues surrounding marketing communications. Most marketers work hard to communicate openly and honestly with consumers and resellers. Still, abuses may occur, and public policy makers have developed a substantial body of laws and regulations to govern advertising, personal selling, and direct marketing activities.

## ADVERTISING

By law, companies must avoid false or deceptive advertising. Advertisers must not make false claims, such as suggesting that a product cures something when it does not. They must avoid ads that have the capacity to deceive, even though no one may actually be deceived. An automobile cannot be advertised as getting 32 miles per gallon unless it does so under typical conditions, and a diet bread cannot be advertised as having fewer calories simply because its slices are thinner.

Sellers must avoid bait-and-switch advertising that attracts buyers under false pretenses. For example, a large retailer advertised a sewing machine at $179. However, when consumers tried to buy the advertised machine, the seller downplayed its features, placed faulty machines on showroom floors, understated the machine's performance, and took other actions in an attempt to switch buyers to a more expensive machine. Such actions are both unethical and illegal.

A company's trade promotion activities are also closely regulated. For example, under the Robinson-Patman Act, sellers cannot favor certain customers through their use of trade promotions. They must make promotional allowances and services available to all resellers on proportionately equal terms.

Beyond simply avoiding legal pitfalls, such as deceptive or bait-and-switch advertising, companies can use advertising to encourage and promote socially responsible programs and actions. For example, State Farm joined with the National Council for Social Studies, National Science Teachers Association, and other national teachers' organizations to create a Good Neighbor Award to recognize primary and secondary teachers for innovation, leadership, and involvement in their profession. State Farm promotes the award through a series of print advertisements.

*Social responsibility: State Farm encourages and promotes social responsibility with its Good Neighbor Award ads.*

## MARKETING AT WORK 13-3

# INTEGRATED MARKETING COMMUNICATIONS AT HEWLETT-PACKARD AND HALLMARK

An ever-increasing number of companies are learning that carefully integrated marketing communications can pay big dividends. Here are just two examples.

### HEWLETT-PACKARD: INTEGRATED BUSINESS-TO-BUSINESS MARKETING

Hewlett-Packard puts integrated marketing communications to work in its business-to-business markets. H-P uses a closely coordinated mix of advertising, event marketing, direct marketing, and personal selling to sell workstations to high-level corporate buyers. At the broadest level, corporate image television ads, coupled with targeted ads in trade magazines, position H-P as a supplier of high-quality solutions to customers' workstation problems. Beneath this broad advertising umbrella, H-P then uses direct marketing to polish its image, update its customer database, and generate leads for the sales force. Finally, company sales reps follow up to close sales and build customer relationships.

H-P's highly successful program of "interactive audio teleconferences" illustrates the company's mastery of integrated communications. These teleconferences are like mammoth conference calls in which H-P representatives discuss key industry issues and H-P practices with current and potential customers. To garner participation in the program, H-P employs a five-week, seven-step "registration process." First, four weeks before a teleconference, H-P mails out an introductory direct-mail package, complete with an 800 number and business reply cards. One or two days after the mail package is received, H-P telemarketers call prospects to register them for the conference, and registrations are confirmed immediately by direct mail. A week before the teleconference, H-P mails out detailed briefing packages, and three days before the event, calls are made again to confirm participation. A final confirmation call is made the day before the teleconference. Finally, one week after the event, H-P uses follow-up direct mail and telemarketing to qualify sales leads and develop account profiles for sales reps.

What is the result of this integrated marketing communications effort? A response rate of 12 percent, as compared with just 1.5 percent using a traditional mail and telemarketing approach. Moreover, 82 percent of those who say they'll participate actually take part, as compared with only 40 percent for past, nonsynchronized efforts. The program has generated qualified sales leads at 200 percent above the forecasted level, and the average workstation sale has increased 500 percent.

Not surprisingly, Hewlett-Packard is sold on integrated marketing communications. However, H-P managers warn that integrated marketing requires great dedication and practical rigor. Perhaps the toughest challenge is the intense and detailed coordination of the efforts of many company departments required for success. To achieve coordination, H-P assigns cross-functional teams made up of representatives from sales, advertising, marketing, production, and information systems to oversee its integrated communications efforts.

### HALLMARK CARDS: INTEGRATED CONSUMER MARKETING

Hallmark's general brand advertising and program sponsorship are well known. Over the years, the company has relied heavily on

## PERSONAL SELLING

A company's salespeople must follow the rules of "fair competition." Most states have enacted deceptive sales laws that spell out what is not allowed. For example, salespeople may not lie to consumers or mislead them about the advantages

mass-media television and print advertising to position Hallmark as the card to give "When you care enough to send the very best." It has also sponsored the highly regarded *Hallmark Hall of Fame* TV specials to reinforce its wholesome, family-oriented image.

Over the past five years, however, Hallmark has transformed itself from a traditional advertiser to a leader in state-of-the-art integrated marketing communications. Hallmark now uses a well-engineered combination of network TV, print advertising, newspaper-distributed coupons, in-store promotions, point-of-sale materials, and direct marketing to lure customers into its stores.

In the late 1980s, the number one greeting card marketer realized that its core customers, working women, were changing. These women had become busier than ever and therefore harder to reach through traditional mass-media advertising. Also, Hallmark's product line had expanded beyond greeting cards to include gifts, collectibles, and home entertaining and decorating products. To rebuild relationships with working women, Hallmark developed three very successful database marketing programs, tied directly into its overall advertising program. These include "The Very Best," a full-color newsletter sent six

times a year to 3.5 million customers; the Hallmark Gold Crown Card, a consumer reward program used by more than 13 million customers; and the Hallmark Gold Crown Catalogue, which focuses on in-store customers but also on mail-order purchases to 5 to 10 million customers.

"The Very Best" cultivates Hallmark's most frequent and loyal customers, who receive regular personalized mailings filled with information about new products, including coupons and incentives to pull them into Hallmark's 5,000 Gold Crown stores nationwide. "The Very Best" mailings also provide information about holiday entertaining and gift giving. Hallmark's goal is to build closer, more personal relationships with important customers. "We want our communications to be very warm and relevant," says Ira Stolzer, Hallmark's director of advertising. "We want each woman on our 'Very Best' list to feel like she's getting a mailing from her sister." According to Mr. Stolzer, the results have been "absolutely phenomenal. People really enjoy being on our mailing lists, and in focus groups we've had incredible feedback from them." In each mailing, Hallmark invites comments about the program. This has created a positive dialogue between Hallmark and its customers.

*Integrated Marketing Communications: Hallmark uses several very successful database marketing programs tied directly into its overall advertising program.*

Hallmark is careful to see that all the different parts of its marketing communications work together. The same team oversees media advertising, in-store marketing, and direct mailings. The integrated effort has put many new weapons in Hallmark's communications arsenal. "In the old days we might have said, 'Here's a marketing problem, let's solve it with some TV and print advertising,' and that was all there was to it," Mr. Stolzer says. "Today, we have . . . multiple solutions and [can be] extremely creative [in finding] effective ways to reach our target customers."

*Sources:* Portions based on Mark Suchecki, "Integrated Marketing: Making It Pay," *Direct,* October 1993, p. 43; Kate Fitzgerald, "In Line for Integrated Hall of Fame," *Advertising Age,* November 8, 1993, p. S12; and Susan Chandler, "Can Hallmark Get Well Soon?" *Business Week,* June 19, 1995, pp. 62–63.

of buying a product. To avoid bait-and-switch practices, salespeople's statements must match advertising claims.

Different rules apply to consumers who are called upon at home versus those who go to a store in search of a product. Because people called upon at home may be taken by surprise and may be especially vulnerable to high-pressure selling techniques, the Federal Trade Commission has adopted a *three-day cooling-off rule* to give special protection to customers who are not seeking products. Under this rule, customers who agree in their own homes to buy something costing more than $25 have 72 hours in which to cancel a contract or return merchandise and get their money back, no questions asked.

Much personal selling involves business-to-business trade. In selling to businesses, salespeople may not offer bribes to purchasing agents or to others who can influence a sale. They may not obtain or use technical or trade secrets of competitors through bribery or industrial espionage. Finally, salespeople must not disparage competitors or competing products by suggesting things that are not true.[24]

# DIRECT MARKETING

Direct marketers and their customers usually enjoy mutually rewarding relationships. Occasionally, however, a darker side emerges. The aggressive and sometimes shady tactics of a few direct marketers can bother or harm consumers, giving the entire industry a bad name. Abuses range from simple excesses that irritate consumers to instances of unfair practices or even outright deception and fraud. During the past few years, the direct marketing industry has also faced growing concerns about invasion of privacy issues.[25]

## Irritation, Unfairness, Deception, and Fraud

Direct marketing excesses sometimes annoy or offend consumers. Most of us dislike direct-response TV commercials that are too loud, too long, and too insistent. Especially bothersome are dinnertime or late-night phone calls. Beyond irritating consumers, some direct marketers have been accused of taking unfair advantage of impulsive or less sophisticated buyers. TV shopping shows and program-long "infomercials" seem to be the worst culprits. They feature smooth-talking hosts, elaborately staged demonstrations, claims of drastic price reductions, "while they last" time limitations, and unequaled ease of purchase to inflame buyers who have low sales resistance.

Worse yet, so-called "heat merchants" design mailers and write copy intended to mislead buyers. Political fundraisers, among the worst offenders, sometimes use gimmicks such as "look-alike" envelopes that resemble official documents, simulated newspaper clippings, and fake honors and awards. Other direct marketers pretend to be conducting research surveys when they are actually asking leading questions to screen or persuade consumers. Fraudulent schemes, such as investment scams or phony collections for charity, have also multiplied in recent years. Crooked direct marketers can be hard to catch; direct marketing customers often respond quickly, do not interact personally with the seller, and usually expect to wait for delivery. By the time that buyers realize that they have been bilked, the thieves are usually somewhere else, plotting new schemes.

## Invasion of Privacy

Invasion of privacy is perhaps the toughest public policy issue now confronting the direct marketing industry. These days, it seems that almost every time consumers order products by mail or telephone, enter a sweepstakes, apply for a credit card, or take out a magazine subscription, their names are entered into some company's already-bulging database. Using sophisticated computer technologies, direct marketers can use these databases to "microtarget" their selling efforts.

Consumers often benefit from such database marketing—they receive more offers that are closely matched to their interests. However, many critics worry that marketers may know *too* much about consumers' lives, and that they may use this knowledge to take unfair advantage of consumers. At some point, they claim, the extensive use of databases intrudes on consumer privacy. For example, they ask, should AT&T be allowed to sell marketers the names of customers who frequently call the 800 numbers of catalog companies? Is it right for credit bureaus to compile and sell lists of people who have recently applied for credit cards—people who are also considered prime direct-marketing targets because of their spending behavior? Or is it right for states to sell the names and addresses of driver's license holders, along with height, weight, and gender information, allowing apparel retailers to target tall or overweight people with special clothing offers? Such practices have spawned a quiet but determined "privacy revolt" among consumers and public policy makers.

In a recent survey of consumers, 79 percent of respondents said that they were concerned about threats to their personal privacy. In another survey, *Advertising Age* asked advertising industry executives how they felt about database marketing and the privacy issue. The responses of two executives show that even industry insiders have mixed feelings:

> There are profound ethical issues relating to the marketing of specific household data—financial information, for instance. . . . For every household in the United States, the computer can guess with amazing accuracy . . . things like credit use, net worth, and investments, the kind of information most people would never want disclosed, let alone sold to any marketer.

> It doesn't bother me that people know I live in a suburb of Columbus, Ohio, and have X number of kids. It [does] bother me that these people know the names of my wife and kids and where my kids go to school. They . . . act like they know me when the bottom line is they're attempting to sell me something. I do feel that database marketing has allowed companies to cross the fine line of privacy. . . . [And] in a lot of cases, I think they know they have crossed it.[26]

The direct marketing industry is addressing issues of ethics and public policy. Direct marketers know that, left untended, such problems will lead to increasingly negative consumer attitudes, lower response rates, and calls for more restrictive state and federal legislation. More importantly, most direct marketers want the same things that consumers want: honest and well-designed marketing offers targeted only toward consumers who will appreciate and respond to them. Direct marketing is just too expensive to waste on consumers who don't want it.

## SUMMARY

*Promotion* is one of the four major elements of the company's marketing mix. The main promotion tools—*advertising, sales promotion, public relations,* and *personal selling*—work together to achieve the company's communication objectives.

In preparing marketing communications, the communicator's first task is to identify the target audience and its characteristics. Next, the communicator has to define the response sought, whether it be *awareness, knowledge, liking, preference, conviction,* or *purchase.* Then a message should be constructed with an effective content and structure. *Media* must be selected, both for personal and non-personal communication. Finally, the communicator must collect *feedback* by watching how much of the market becomes aware, tries the product, and is satisfied in the process.

The company also has to decide how much to spend for promotion. The most popular approaches are to spend what the company can afford, to use a percentage of sales, to base promotion on competitors' spending, or to base it on an analysis and costing of the communication objectives and tasks.

The company has to divide the *promotion budget* among the major tools to create the *promotion mix.* Companies can pursue a *push* or a *pull* promotional strategy, or a combination of the two. What specific blend of promotion tools is best depends on the type of product/market, the desirability of the buyer's readiness stage, and the product life-cycle stage.

Recent shifts in marketing strategy from mass marketing to targeted or one-on-one marketing, coupled with advances in computers and information technology, have had a dramatic impact on marketing communications. Although still important, the mass media are giving way to a profusion of smaller, more focused media. Companies are doing less *broadcasting* and more *narrowcasting.*

This shift is most evident in the rapidly growing field of direct marketing, which employs direct, one-on-one communications channels to obtain an immediate buying response. Major forms of direct marketing include *direct-mail and catalog marketing, telemarketing, television marketing,* and *online shopping.* Successful direct marketing begins with a good *marketing database,* which can be used to locate potential customers, tailor products and services, and target marketing communications.

As marketing communicators adopt richer but more fragmented media and promotion mixes to reach their diverse markets, they run the danger of creating a communications hodgepodge for consumers. To prevent this, more companies are adopting the concept of *integrated marketing communications,* which calls for carefully integrating all sources of company communication to deliver a clear and consistent message to target markets.

Finally, people at all levels of the organization must be aware of the many legal and ethical issues surrounding marketing communications. Companies must work hard and proactively at communicating openly, honestly, and agreeably with their customers and resellers.

## KEY TERMS

Advertising
Affordable method
Buyer-readiness stages
Catalog marketing
Competitive-parity method
Direct marketing
Direct-mail marketing
Integrated marketing communications

Marketing database
Nonpersonal communication channels
Objective-and-task method
Online computer shopping
Percentage-of-sales method
Personal communication channels
Personal selling
Promotion mix

Public relations
Pull strategy
Push strategy
Sales promotion
Telemarketing
Television marketing
Word-of-mouth influence

## QUESTIONS FOR DISCUSSION

1. Which form of marketing communications does each of the following represent?
   - A U2 T-shirt sold at a concert.
   - A *Rolling Stone* interview with Eric Clapton, arranged by his manager.
   - A scalper auctioning tickets at a Pearl Jam concert.
   - A record store selling Boyz II Men albums for $2 off during the week that their latest music video debuts on network television.

2. In 1990, Pete Rose was banned from the game of baseball because of gambling and sentenced to prison because of tax evasion. Five years later, PepsiCo's Pizza Hut chain hired Rose as a spokesperson for its newest product, Stuffed Crust Pizza, then fired him 48 hours before the first commercial was scheduled to be shot. Among the reasons that may have contributed to PepsiCo's last-minute pullout was Rose's time in prison. How do you feel about PepsiCo's decision, and do you think that Rose would have been an effective spokesperson?

3. How can an organization get feedback on the effects of its communication efforts? Describe how (a) the March of Dimes and (b) Procter & Gamble can get feedback on the results of their communications.

4. Companies spend billions of dollars on advertising to build a quality image for their products. At the same time, they spend billions more on discount-oriented sales promotions, offering lower prices as a main reason to purchase. Discuss whether promotion is enhancing or reducing the effect of advertising. Can you find an example where they enhance one another?

5. Why do some industrial marketers advertise on national television, when their target audience is only a fraction of the actual viewers? List some nonconsumer-oriented commercials you have seen on TV, and describe what the marketers were trying to accomplish with them.

6. Most consumers consider the Internet a relatively primitive place to shop. Customers connecting online to a retailer's World Wide Web site can browse through relatively few items as compared with glossy catalogs and elaborate store displays. And, because of security problems with online credit card purchases, customers usually must place orders via phone, fax, or even regular mail. With all these problems and with only $350 million a year in online sales, why do you think that such established retailers as L.L. Bean, Sharper Image, JCPenney, and Lands' End have sites on the World Wide Web?

## APPLYING THE CONCEPTS

1. Think of a nationally advertised product or service that has been running a consistent advertising message for a number of years. Go to the library and copy several examples of print advertising for this brand from back issues of magazines.

   ◆ When you examine these ads closely, how consistent are the message content, structure, and format?

   ◆ Which response(s) do you think that this campaign is seeking: awareness, knowledge, liking, preference, conviction, or purchase?

   ◆ Do you think that the advertising campaign is successful in getting the desired response? Why or why not?

2. Consider an automobile brand with which you are familiar. List examples of how this brand uses advertising, personal selling, sales promotion, and public relations. (Public relations examples may be difficult to spot, but consider how cars are used in movies or television programs, or as celebrity vehicles for sports tournaments or parades.) Does this automaker use promotion tools in a coordinated way that builds a consistent image, or are the efforts fragmented? Explain.

## REFERENCES

1. Based on information from Charles Butler, "General Excellence: Southwest Airlines," *Sales & Marketing Management*, August 1993, p. 38; and Jennifer Lawrence, "Integrated Mix Makes Expansion Fly," *Advertising Age*, November 8, 1993, pp. S10, S12. Extract from Kenneth Labich, "Is Herb Kelleher America's Best CEO?" *Fortune*, May 2, 1994, pp. 44-52. Also see "Southwest's New Deal," *Fortune*, January 16, 1995, p. 94; and David Greising, "How High Can the Airlines Fly?" *Business Week*, August 7, 1995, pp. 25–26.

2. For these and other definitions, see Peter D. Bennett, *Dictionary of*

*Marketing Terms* (Chicago: American Marketing Association, 1988).

3. Joe Mandese, "Star Presenter of the Year," *Advertising Age,* September 25, 1995, pp. 1, 6.

4. For a more comprehensive discussion on setting promotion budgets, see J. Thomas Russell and W. Ronald Lane, *Kleppner's Advertising Procedure* (Englewood Cliffs, NJ: Prentice Hall, 1996), Chapter 6.

5. See "Median Costs Per Call by Industry," *Sales & Marketing Management,* June 28, 1993, p. 65.

6. For more discussion, see Don E. Schultz, Stanley I. Tannenbaum, and Robert F. Lauterborn, *Integrated Marketing Communication* (Chicago, IL: NTC Publishing, 1992), pp. 11, 17.

7. *17th Annual Survey of Promotional Practices,* Donnelly Marketing Inc., Oakbrook Terrace, IL, August 1995, p. 9.

8. Junu Bryan Kim, "Marketing with Video: The Cassette Is in the Mail," *Advertising Age,* May 22, 1995, p. S-1.

9. Richard L. Bencin, "Telefocus: Telemarketing Gets Synergized," *Sales & Marketing Management,* February 1992, pp. 49–53, here p. 50.

10. Kate Fitzgerald, "With 'Big Book' Buried, Rivals See Opportunity," *Advertising Age,* February 1, 1993, p. 36; Gary Levin, "J. C. Penney Tops List of Catalog Spenders," *Advertising Age,* October 10, 1995, p. S-2; and Susan Chandler, "Sears: No More 'Big Book,' But Lots of Little Books," *Business Week,* December 19, 1994, pp. 82–83.

11. Bristol Voss, "Calling All Catalogs!" *Sales & Marketing Management,* December 1990, pp. 32–37; and Thayer C. Taylor, "Catalogs Come of Age," *Sales & Marketing Management,* December 1993, pp. 39–41.

12. Robert Wasserman, "How to Evaluate the Results of Your Call Center's Efforts," *Telemarketing,* March 1995, p. 77; and "Telemarketing Cited as Chief Form of Direct Marketing," *Marketing News,* January 1, 1996, p. 9.

13. For more discussion, see Junu Bryan Kim, "800/900: King of the Road in Marketing Value, Usage," *Advertising Age,* February 17, 1992, pp. S1, S4.

14. See Bill Kelley, "Is There Anything That Can't Be Sold by Phone?" *Sales & Marketing Management,* April 1989, pp. 60–64; Rudy Oetting and Geri Gantman, "Dial M for Maximize," *Sales & Marketing Management,* June 1991, pp. 100–6; Richard L. Bencin, "Telefocus: Telemarketing Gets Synergized," *Sales & Marketing Management,* February 1992, pp. 49–57; and Martin Everett, "Selling by Telephone," *Sales & Marketing Management,* December 1993, pp. 75–79.

15. See Judith Waltrop, "The Business of Privacy," *American Demographics,* October 1994, pp. 46–55; and Ira Teinowitz, "FTC's Revised Rules Calm Telemarketers," *Advertising Age,* June 5, 1995, p. 8.

16. Jim Auchmute, "But Wait, There's More!" *Advertising Age,* October 17, 1985, p. 18; Chad Rubel, "Infomercials Evolve as Major Firms Join Successful Format," *Marketing News,* January 2, 1995, pp. 1, 36; and Jacqueline M. Graves, "The Fortune 500 Opt for Infomercials," *Fortune,* March 6, 1995, p. 20; Kim Cleland, "Infomercial Audience Crosses Over Cultures," *Advertising Age,* January 15, 1996, p. i8.

17. See Rebecca Piirto, "The TV Beast," *American Demographics,* May 1993, pp. 34–42.

18. For more on online marketing, see Debra Aho Williamson, "Building a New Industry," *Advertising Age,* March 13, 1995, pp. S-1, S-4; Mary Kuntz, "Burma Shave Signs on the I-Way," *Business Week,* April 17, 1995, pp. 102–4; David Kirkpatrick, "As the Internet Sizzles: Online Services Battle for Stakes," *Fortune,* May 1, 1995, pp. 86–96; David A. Andelman, "Betting on the Net," *Sales & Marketing Management,* June 1995, pp. 47–59; and "Vision 2000: Catching Consumers in the World Wide Web," in Philip Kotler, *Marketing Management: Analysis, Planning, Implementation, and Control,* 9th ed. (Englewood Cliffs, NJ: Prentice Hall, 1997), Chapter 1.

19. *17th Annual Survey of Promotional Practices,* Donnelly Marketing Inc., Oakbrook Terrace, IL, August 1995, p. 9.

20. See Jonathan Berry, "A Potent New Tool for Selling: Database Marketing," *Business Week,* September 4, 1994, pp. 56–62; "How to Turn Junk Mail into a Gold Mine," *The Economist,* April 1, 1995, p. 51; and

Weld F. Royal, "Do Databases Really Work?" *Sales & Marketing Management,* October 1995, pp. 66–74.

21. See Joe Schwartz, "Databases Deliver the Goods," *American Demographics,* September 1989, pp. 23–25; Gary Levin, "Database Draws Fevered Interest," *Advertising Age,* June 8, 1992, p. 31; Jonathan Berry, "A Potent New Tool for Selling: Database Marketing," *Business Week,* September 5, 1994, pp. 56–62; and Richard Cross and Janet Smith, "Customer Bonding and the Information Core," *Direct Marketing Magazine,* February, 1995, p. 28.

22. See Schultz, Tannenbaum, and Lauterborn, *Integrated Marketing Communication,* Chapters 3 and 4; Don Schultz, "It's Time to Come Up with Strategies, Not Just Tactics," *Marketing News,* August 20, 1990, p. 11; and Kim Cleland, "Few Wed Marketing, Communications," *Advertising Age,* February 27, 1995, p. 10.

23. See Don E. Schultz, "Making Mid-Decade Course Corrections," *Marketing News,* February 13, 1995, p. 10.

24. For more on the legal aspects of promotion, see Louis W. Stern and Thomas I. Eovaldi, *Legal Aspects of Marketing Policy* (Englewood Cliffs, NJ: Prentice Hall, 1984), Chapters 7 and 8; Robert J. Posch, *The Complete Guide to Marketing and the Law* (Englewood Cliffs, NJ: Prentice Hall, 1988), Chapters 15 to 17; and Kevin Kelly, "When a Rival's Trade Secret Crosses Your Desk . . ." *Business Week,* May 20, 1991, p. 48.

25. Portions of this section are based on Terrence H. Witkowski, "Self-Regulation Will Suppress Direct Marketing's Downside," *Marketing News,* April 24, 1989, p. 4. Also see Cyndee Miller, "Privacy vs. Direct Marketing," *Marketing News,* March 1, 1993, pp. 1, 14; Judith Waltrop, "The Business of Privacy," *American Demographics,* October 1994, pp. 46–55; Katie Muldoon, "The Industry Must Rebuild Its Image," *Direct,* April 1995, p. 106; and Jim Castelli, "How to Handle Personal Information," *American Demographics,* March 1996, pp. 50–57.

26. Melanie Rigney, "Too Close for Comfort, Execs Warn," *Advertising Age,* January 13, 1992, p. 31. Also see "Summary of '1992 Harris-Equifax Consumer Privacy Survey,'" *Marketing News,* August 16, 1993, p. A18.

# Advertising, Sales Promotion, and Public Relations

In 1992, fed up after years of being outadvertised by rival Pepsi, Coca-Cola did the unthinkable. It abandoned Madison Avenue and went Hollywood. Forsaking its 38-year relationship with McCann-Erickson, the huge Madison Avenue advertising agency, Coca-Cola awarded creative control over its flagship Coke brand to—of all things—a Hollywood talent agency called Creative Artists Agency (CAA). The result: a breathtaking but highly controversial new ad campaign—Always Coca-Cola.

Going into the 1990s, Coca-Cola's advertising had gone stale. Pepsi's snazzier ads consistently outranked Coke's more sedate entries in consumer awareness surveys. Coca-Cola executives worried that Coke's brand personality was becoming blurred or dated. In 1989, Coca-Cola had tapped a panel of ten unconventional marketing thinkers for their views on reaching the increasingly fractured and fickle consumer marketplace. The panel's conclusion: "A brand advertised in the normal way, with normal media, is likely to develop a normal image, and not something special." Their advice: "Don't be normal."[1] Yet, in Coke's view, the big Madison Avenue agencies were stamping out the same old cookie-cutter ad campaigns that they'd been producing for decades.

So, in a radical effort to revitalize its advertising, Coca-Cola hired Creative Artists Agency, Hollywood's premier talent agency. Why CAA? For one thing, CAA gave Coke access to many first-rate Hollywood stars, writers, and directors. But most importantly, CAA provided a pipeline into the pop culture. The talent agency knows what's hot in Hollywood—the talk, music, fashions, sports—and what's hot in Hollywood will soon be hot everywhere.

Coca-Cola initially hired Creative Artists Agency as a "creative consultant." Within months, however, CAA was competing with McCann-Erickson—Hollywood against Madison Avenue—for creative control of the 1993 Coke Classic campaign, scheduled to be one of Coke's biggest advertising efforts ever. On presentation day, McCann-Erickson proposed the usual half-dozen ads positioning Coke as the all-world, something-for-everyone soft drink. In refreshing contrast, CAA dazzled Coke executives with a whirlwind 60-minute show in which it pitched some 50 excitingly different contemporary ad ideas. When the lights came up, CAA got more than two dozens ads to produce. McCann got two.

Coca-Cola launched CAA's groundbreaking "Always Coca-Cola" ads in spring 1993. The new campaign was anything but normal, anything but Madison Avenue. For the first time, Coke dropped its longstanding "one sight, one sound, one sell" approach, in which a few standardized, broadly targeted ads celebrated Coke's universal appeal. Instead, following the global trend toward media and market fragmentation, the Always Coca-Cola campaign featured a large number of ads narrowly targeted to specific media, audiences, and seasons.

The ads themselves were wildly different from the usual Coke fare. They also varied dramatically from one ad to the next in tone and approach, with no apparent connecting theme: a Coke bottle sweating to the sounds of summer; a global Coke orchestra making music with only Coke bottles; dancers rhythmically attacking a giant block of ice and reducing it to shavings; a Harry-Met-Sally-like couple tracking Coke's role in their relationship from the 1920s through their 50th anniversary; animated polar bears massing on an ice floe, watching the northern lights and blissfully chugging Coca-Cola. Some ads were concrete, others highly abstract. Some had story lines, others had no clear theme. Some were refined, others bawdy. About all they had in common was the Always slogan and the red Coke-button icon.

In producing the trendier ads, CAA enlisted the talents of some of Hollywood's best-known producers—Rob Reiner (known for such movies as *Stand by Me, When Harry Met Sally,* and *A Few Good Men*), Francis Coppola (*Dracula, Apocalypse Now,* and *Godfather I–III*), David Lynch (*Dune, Twin Peaks,* and *Elephant Man*), and Richard Donner (*Lethal Weapon 1–3* and *Superman*).

The new Always Coca-Cola campaign clearly broke new ground; it also created much controversy. Although some industry insiders praised the CAA ads as innovative, clever, playful, and even sexy, most Madison Avenue regulars bashed the campaign as all technique and no strategy. Many experts had mixed feelings, as reflected in this assessment by advertising critic Bob Garfield:

> [CAA] delivered a substantially, sometimes maddeningly, flawed pool of two dozen commercials that nonetheless represent the best Coca-Cola advertising campaign in at least a decade. Sometimes ingenious. Sometimes surprising. Sometimes delightful. Sometimes extraordinary. Sometimes, my goodness, breathtaking. Not always, but some of the time. . . .[2]

While the new spots were intriguing and very entertaining, they appeared to lack overall strategic direction. Many observers, even Coca-Cola insiders, worried that the campaign was little more than a grab bag of contemporary and very clever but loosely connected short features.

Despite the controversy, Coke commissioned CAA to create another 30 ads for its 1994 campaign. Whereas the initial Always Coca-Cola ads drew mixed reviews, the 1994 encore drew consistently high praise. According to Garfield:

> The new pool of 30 spots is the best Coke advertising, and maybe the best soft-drink advertising, in decades. The collaboration of Coca-Cola

and CAA, having produced some startlingly good and startlingly bad results a year ago, seems to have . . . coalesced around the strongest elements of the introductory campaign. The contour bottle, . . . [the red Coke button] logo, and the irresistible jingle . . . are leveraged to the max. The wonderfully resonant Always Coca-Cola slogan, instead of being a tagline in a series of . . . unrelated ministories, is now central to nearly every spot. . . . These spots are as cohesive and integrated as the first ones were haphazard and unfocused. . . . They manage to be both contemporary and classic while addressing diverse audiences in differing language and style. . . . And around the world, people are getting thirsty.[3]

The breakthrough Always Coca-Cola campaign has left an indelible impression on the advertising industry. Perhaps the highest praise for CAA comes from a high-level McCann-Erickson executive. He says: "What I believe [CAA's Always Coca-Cola commercials] have done most effectively is shout out the news that this 107-year-old [brand] isn't about to act like a 107-year-old. Creatively, they threw away the book, risked the rancor of old creative pros and old consumers, and cranked out a whole new regimen of [ads]."[4] ∎

## CHAPTER OBJECTIVES

### After reading this chapter, you should be able to:

**1** Define the roles of advertising, sales promotion, and public relations in the promotion mix.

**2** Describe the major decisions involved in developing an advertising program.

**3** Explain how sales promotion campaigns are developed and implemented.

**4** Explain how companies use public relations to communicate with their publics.

Companies must do more than make good products—they must inform consumers about product benefits and carefully position products in consumers' minds. To do this, they must skillfully use the mass-promotion tools of *advertising, sales promotion,* and *public relations.* In this chapter, we take a closer look at each of these tools.

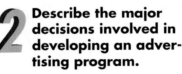

## ADVERTISING

Advertising can be traced back to the very beginnings of recorded history. Archaeologists working in the countries around the Mediterranean Sea have dug up signs announcing various events and offers. The Romans painted walls to announce gladiator fights, and the Phoenicians painted pictures promoting their wares on large rocks along parade routes. A Pompeii wall painting praised a politician and

**Advertising**
Any paid form of non-personal presentation and promotion of ideas, goods, or services by an identified sponsor.

asked for votes. During the Golden Age in Greece, town criers announced the sale of cattle, crafted items, and even cosmetics. An early "singing commercial" went as follows: "For eyes that are shining, for cheeks like the dawn / For beauty that lasts after girlhood is gone / For prices in reason, the woman who knows / Will buy her cosmetics from Aesclyptos."

Modern advertising, however, is a far cry from these early efforts. U.S. advertisers now run up an annual advertising bill of more than $150 billion. Although advertising is used mostly by business firms, it also is used by a wide range of nonprofit organizations, professionals, and social agencies that advertise their causes to various target publics. In fact, the fortieth largest advertising spender is a nonprofit organization—the U.S. government. Advertising is a good way to inform and persuade, whether the purpose is to sell Coca-Cola worldwide or to get consumers in a developing nation to drink milk or use birth control.

The top 100 national advertisers account for more than one-fourth of all advertising.[5] Table 14-1 lists the top ten advertisers in 1994. Procter & Gamble is the leader with almost $2.7 billion, or about 16.6 percent of its total U.S. sales. P&G is also the *world's* largest advertiser, spending a whopping $3.6 billion globally. The other major spenders are found in the retailing, auto, and food industries. Advertising as a percentage of sales varies greatly by industry. For example, percentage spending is low in the auto industry but high in food, drugs, toiletries, and cosmetics. The company spending the largest percentage of its sales on advertising was Warner-Lambert (28 percent).

# ▶MAJOR DECISIONS IN ADVERTISING

Marketing management must make five important decisions when developing an advertising program (see Figure 14-1).

**TABLE 14-1** *Top Ten National Advertisers*

| Rank | Company | Total U.S. Advertising (Millions) | Total U.S. Sales (Millions) | Advertising as a Percent of Sales |
|---|---|---|---|---|
| 1 | Procter & Gamble | $2,690 | $ 16,213 | 16.6 |
| 2 | Philip Morris | 2,413 | 40,878 | 5.9 |
| 3 | General Motors | 1,929 | 122,387 | 1.6 |
| 4 | Ford | 1,186 | 75,661 | 1.3 |
| 5 | Sears | 1,134 | 54,559* | |
| 6 | AT&T | 1,103 | 67,769 | 1.6 |
| 7 | PepsiCo | 1,097 | 20,246 | 5.4 |
| 8 | Chrysler | 972 | 45,655 | 2.1 |
| 9 | Walt Disney | 935 | 7,698 | 12.2 |
| 10 | Johnson & Johnson | 934 | 7,812 | 11.9 |

*Worldwide sales. U.S. sales not available. Percent of sales not calculated.
*Source:* Reprinted with permission from "100 Leading National Advertisers," *Advertising Age,* September 27, 1995.

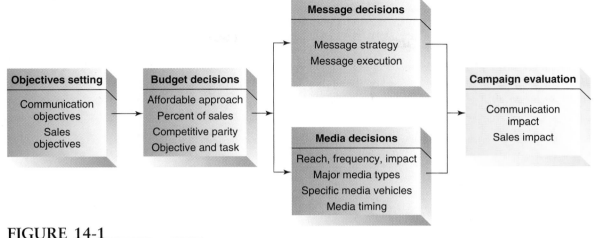

## FIGURE 14-1
*Major decisions in advertising*

## SETTING OBJECTIVES

The first step in developing an advertising program is to set *advertising objectives*. These objectives should be based on past decisions about the target market, positioning, and marketing mix, which define the job that advertising must do in the total marketing program.

An **advertising objective** is a specific communication *task* to be accomplished with a specific *target* audience during a specific period of *time*. Advertising objectives can be classified by primary purpose—whether the aim is to *inform, persuade*, or *remind*. Table 14-2 lists examples of each of these objectives.

**Advertising objective**
A specific communication *task* to be accomplished with a specific *target* audience during a specific period of *time*.

---

**TABLE 14-2**  *Possible Advertising Objectives*

| | | |
|---|---|---|
| Informative advertising | Telling the market about a new product | Describing available services |
| | Suggesting new uses for a product | Correcting false impressions |
| | Informing the market of a price change | Reducing consumer's fears |
| | Explaining how the product works | Building a company image |
| Persuasive advertising | Building brand preference | Persuading customer to purchase now |
| | Encouraging switching to your brand | Persuading customer to receive a sales call |
| | Changing customer's perception of product attributes | |
| Reminder advertising | Reminding consumer that the product may be needed in the near future | Keeping it in customer's mind during off-seasons |
| | Reminding consumer where to buy it | Maintaining its top-of-mind awareness |

*Comparison advertising: Visa compares its card directly to those of major competitors —"Of all the cards in all the wallets of all the men and women in America, there's one that towers over all the others. The Visa card."*

**Informative advertising**
Advertising used to inform consumers about a new product or feature and to build primary demand.

**Persuasive advertising**
Advertising used to build selective demand for a brand by persuading consumers that it offers the best quality for their money.

**Comparison advertising**
Advertising that compares one brand directly or indirectly with one or more other brands.

**Reminder advertising**
Advertising used to keep consumers thinking about a product.

**Informative advertising** is used heavily when introducing a new product category. In this case, the objective is to build primary demand. Thus, producers of compact-disc players first informed consumers of the sound and convenience benefits of CDs. **Persuasive advertising** becomes more important as competition increases. Here, the company's objective is to build selective demand. For example, once compact-disc players were established, Sony began trying to persuade consumers that its brand offered the best quality for their money.

Some persuasive advertising has become **comparison advertising**, in which a company directly or indirectly compares its brand with one or more other brands. For example, in its classic comparison campaign, Avis positioned itself against the market-leading Hertz by claiming, "We're number two, so we try harder." More recently, VISA advertised: "American Express is offering you a new credit card, but you don't have to accept it. Heck, 7 million merchants don't." Comparison advertising also has been used for products such as soft drinks, computers, deodorants, toothpastes, automobiles, pain relievers, and long-distance telephone service.[6]

**Reminder advertising** is important for mature products—it keeps consumers thinking about the product. Expensive Coca-Cola ads on television are designed primarily to remind people about Coca-Cola, not to inform or persuade them.

## SETTING THE ADVERTISING BUDGET

After determining its advertising objectives, the company next sets its *advertising budget* for each product. Four commonly used methods for setting promotion budgets are discussed in Chapter 13. Here we discuss some additional factors that should be considered.

Setting the advertising budget is no easy task. How does a company know if it is spending the right amount? Some critics charge that large consumer packaged-goods firms tend to spend too much on advertising, and industrial companies generally underspend on advertising. They claim that, on the one hand, the large consumer companies use lots of image advertising without really knowing its effects. They overspend as a form of "insurance" against not spending enough. On the other hand, industrial advertisers tend to rely too heavily on their sales forces to bring in orders. They underestimate the power of company and product image in preselling industrial customers. Thus, they do not spend enough on advertising to build customer awareness and knowledge.

How much impact does advertising spending really have on consumer buying and brand loyalty? A research study analyzing household purchases of frequently bought consumer products led to the following surprising conclusion:

> Advertising appears effective in increasing the volume purchased by loyal buyers but less effective in winning new buyers. For loyal buyers, high levels of exposure per week may be unproductive because of a leveling off of ad effectiveness. . . . Advertising appears unlikely to have some cumulative effect that leads to loyalty. . . . Features, displays, and especially price have a stronger impact on response than does advertising.[7]

These findings did not sit well with the advertising community, and several people attacked the study's data and methodology. They claimed that the study measured mostly short-run sales effects, and therefore favored pricing and sales-promotion activities, which tend to have more immediate impact. In contrast, most advertising takes many months, or even years, to build strong brand positions and consumer loyalty. These long-run effects are difficult to measure. A more recent study of BehaviorScan data over a ten-year period found that advertising does produce long-term sales growth, even two years after a campaign ends.[8] This debate underscores the fact that measuring the results of advertising spending remains a poorly understood subject.

## ADVERTISING STRATEGY

Advertising strategy consists of two major elements: creating advertising *messages* and selecting advertising *media*. In the past, most companies developed messages and media plans independently. Media planning was often seen as secondary to the message creation process. The creative department first created good advertisements; then the media department selected the media best for carrying these advertisements to desired target audiences. This often caused friction between creatives and media planners.

Today, however, media fragmentation, soaring media costs, and more focused target marketing strategies have promoted the importance of the media planning function. In some cases, an advertising campaign might start with a great message idea, followed by the choice of appropriate media. In other cases, however, a campaign might begin with a good media opportunity, followed by advertisements designed to take advantage of that opportunity. Increasingly, companies are realizing the benefits of planning these two important elements *jointly*. Messages and media should blend harmoniously to create an effective overall advertising campaign. This realization has resulted in greater cooperation between the creative and media functions. (See Marketing at Work 14-1.)

### Creating the Advertising Message

A large advertising budget does not guarantee a successful advertising campaign. Two advertisers can spend the same amount on advertising, yet have very different results. No matter how big the budget, advertising can succeed only if commercials gain attention and communicate well.

THE CHANGING MESSAGE ENVIRONMENT.   Good advertising messages are especially important in today's costly and cluttered advertising environment. The average consumer has 22 television stations and 11,500 magazines from which to choose. Add the countless radio stations and a continuous barrage of catalogs, direct-mail ads, and out-of-home media, and consumers are being bombarded with ads at home, at work, and at all points in between.

*Breaking through advertising clutter: How would you advertise an ordinary bathroom fixture? American Standard notes: "Designing a toilet or a sink may not be as glamorous as, say, designing a Maserati. . . . but more people will be sitting on our seats than theirs."*

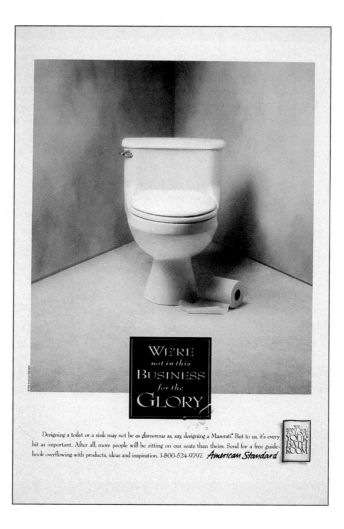

## MARKETING AT WORK 14-1

# THE MEDIUM AND THE MESSAGE: A NEW HARMONY

There's a creative revolution taking place in ad agencies today, but it isn't necessarily coming from the creatives. More and more, creative directors are turning to the media departments to make their best ideas work harder. Media planning is no longer an after-the-fact complement to a new ad campaign. Media planners are now working more closely with creatives to allow media selection to help shape the creative process, often before a single ad is written. In some cases, media people are even initiating ideas for new campaigns.

Among the more noteworthy ad campaigns based on tight media–creative partnerships is the one for Vin & Sprit AB's Absolut vodka. V&S and TBWA, its New York ad agency, meet once each year with a slew of magazines to set Absolut's media

schedule. The schedule consists of up to 100 magazines, ranging from consumer and business magazines to theater playbills. The agency's creative department is charged with creating media-specific ads.

The result is a wonderful assortment of very creative ads for Absolut, tightly targeted to audiences of the media in which they appear. For example, an "Absolut Bravo" ad in playbills has roses adorning a clear bottle, while business magazines contain an "Absolut Merger" foldout. Los Angeles-area magazines carry "Absolut LA" ads featuring an LA-style swimming pool in the shape of an Absolut bottle. In New York-area magazines, "Absolut Manhattan" ads feature a satellite photo of Manhattan, with Central Park assuming the dis-

tinctive outline of an Absolut bottle. In Chicago, the windy city, ads show an Absolut bottle with the letters on the label blown askew. In some cases, the creatives even developed ads for magazines not yet on the schedule, as was the case with a clever "Absolut Centerfold" ad for *Playboy* magazine. The ad portrayed a clear, unadorned playmate bottle ("11-inch bust, 11-inch waist, 11-inch hips").

At a time of soaring media costs and cluttered communication channels, increased creative–media harmony can pay big dividends. The Absolut experience has had a positive impact on TBWA's approach to the advertising creative process. Says the agency's CEO, "What [V&S] has done for us is to give us a more open mind and put more demand on all departments to be creative in their ideas than might be the case otherwise." And closer cooperation between creative and media people has paid off handsomely for V&S. Largely as a result of its breakthrough advertising, V&S now captures a 63 percent share of the imported vodka market. Sales rocketed from just 12,000 cases in 1980 to more than 2.9 million cases in 1994.

*Sources:* Adapted from Gary Levin, " 'Meddling' in Creative More Welcome," *Advertising Age*, April 9, 1990, pp. S4, S8. Also see William Wells, John Burnett, and Sandra Moriarty, *Advertising: Principles and Practice*, Second Edition (Englewood Cliffs, NJ: Prentice Hall, 1992), p. 266; "Absolut Vodka Sales, Share of Category Rise in Year Since Transfer of Marketing Rights," press release, David S. Wachman Associates, New York, February 15, 1995; and Junu Bryan Kim, "Strategy Regains Prominence with Planners," *Advertising Age*, July 24, 1995, p. S10.

*Media planners for Absolut Vodka work with creatives to design ads targeted to specific media audiences. "Absolut Bravo" appears in theater playbills. "Absolut Chicago" targets consumers in the Windy City.*

If all this advertising clutter bothers some consumers, it also causes big problems for advertisers. Take the situation facing network television advertisers. They regularly pay $200,000 or more for 30 seconds of advertising time during a popular prime-time TV program—even more if it's an especially popular program such as *Seinfeld* ($490,000) or *Home Improvement* ($470,000 per spot), or an event like the Super Bowl (more than $1 million!).[9] In such cases, their ads are sandwiched in with a smorgasbord of some 60 other commercials, announcements, and network promotions per hour.

Until recently, television viewers were pretty much a captive audience for advertisers. Viewers had only a few channels from which to choose. Those who found the energy to get up and change channels during boring commercial breaks usually found only more of the same on the other channels. But with the growth in cable TV, VCRs, and remote-control units, today's viewers have many more options. They can avoid ads by watching commercial-free cable channels. They can "zap" commercials by pushing the fast-forward button during taped programs. With remote control, they can instantly turn off the sound during a commercial or "zip" around the channels to see what else is on.

Thus, just to gain and hold attention, today's advertising messages must be better planned, more imaginative, more entertaining, and more rewarding to consumers. Creative strategy will therefore play an increasingly important role in advertising success.

**Message Strategy.**    The first step in creating effective advertising messages is to decide what general message will be communicated to consumers—to plan a *message strategy*. The purpose of advertising is to get consumers to think about or react to the product or company in a certain way. People will react only if they believe that they will benefit from doing so. Thus, developing an effective message strategy begins with identifying customer *benefits* that can be used as advertising appeals. In searching for benefits to feature, many creative people start by talking to consumers, dealers, experts, and competitors. Others try to imagine consumers buying or using the product to figure out which benefits they seek. Ideally, advertising message strategy follows directly from the company's broader positioning strategy.

Message strategy statements tend to be plain, straightforward outlines of benefits and positioning points that the advertiser wants to stress. The advertiser must now develop a compelling *creative concept*—or *"big idea"*—that will bring the message strategy to life in a distinctive and memorable way. At this stage, simple message ideas become great ad campaigns. Usually, a copywriter and art director team up to generate many creative concepts, hoping that one of these concepts will turn out to be the big idea. The creative concept may emerge as a visualization, a phrase, or a combination of the two.

The creative concept guides the choice of specific appeals to be used in an advertising campaign. Advertising appeals should have three characteristics. First, they should be *meaningful*, pointing out benefits that make the product more desirable or interesting to consumers. Second, appeals must be *believable*—consumers must believe that the product or service will deliver the promised benefits. However, the most meaningful and believable benefits may not be the best ones to feature. Appeals should also be *distinctive*—they should tell how the product is better than the competing brands. For example, the most meaningful benefit of owning a wristwatch is that it keeps accurate time, yet few watch ads feature this benefit. Instead, based on the distinctive benefits they offer, watch advertisers might select any of a number of advertising themes. For years, Timex has been the affordable watch that "Takes a lickin' and keeps on tickin'." In contrast, Swatch has featured style and fashion, whereas Rolex stresses luxury and status.

**MESSAGE EXECUTION.**   The impact of the message depends not only on *what* is said, but also on *how* it is said. The advertiser now has to turn the "big idea" into an actual ad execution that will capture the target market's attention and interest. The creative people must find the best style, tone, words, and format for executing the message. Any message can be presented in different *execution styles,* such as the following:

- *Slice of life.* This style shows one or more "typical" people using the product in a normal setting. For example, two mothers at a picnic discuss the nutritional benefits of Jif peanut butter.
- *Lifestyle.* This style shows how a product fits in with a particular lifestyle. For example, a National Dairy Board ad shows women exercising and talks about how milk adds to a healthy, active lifestyle.
- *Fantasy.* This style creates a fantasy around the product or its use. For instance, Revlon's first ad for Jontue perfume showed a barefoot woman wearing a chiffon dress and coming out of an old French barn, crossing a meadow, meeting a handsome young man on a white horse, and riding away with him.
- *Mood or image.* This style builds a mood or image around the product, such as beauty, love, or serenity. No claim is made about the product except through suggestion. Bermuda tourism ads create such moods.
- *Musical.* This style shows one or more people or cartoon characters singing a song about the product. Sears intones, "Come see the softer side of Sears."

*Visa uses humor to set the right tone for its student market.*

- ◆ *Personality symbol.* This style creates a character that represents the product. The character might be *animated* (the Jolly Green Giant, Cap'n Crunch, Garfield the Cat) or *real* (the Marlboro man, Betty Crocker, Morris the 9 Lives Cat).

- ◆ *Technical expertise.* This style shows the company's expertise in making the product. Thus, Maxwell House shows one of its buyers carefully selecting coffee beans, and Gallo tells about its many years of winemaking experience.

- ◆ *Scientific evidence.* This style presents survey or scientific evidence that the brand is better or better liked than one or more other brands. For years, Crest toothpaste has used scientific evidence to convince buyers that Crest is better than other brands at fighting cavities.

- ◆ *Testimonial evidence.* This style features a highly believable or likable source endorsing the product. It could be a celebrity like Bill Cosby (Jell-O Pudding or Kodak film) or ordinary people saying how much they like a given product ("My doctor said Mylanta").

The advertiser also must choose a *tone* for the ad. Procter & Gamble always uses a positive tone: Its ads say something very positive about its products. P&G also avoids humor that might take attention away from the message. In contrast, Little Caesar's "pizza, pizza" ads use humor—in the form of the comical Little Caesar character—to drive home the advertiser's "two for the price of one" message.

The advertiser must use memorable and attention-getting *words* in the ad. For example, the following themes on the left would have much less impact without the creative phrasing on the right:

| Message Theme | Creative Copy |
| --- | --- |
| 7-Up is not a cola. | "The Uncola" |
| A BMW is a well-engineered automobile. | "The Ultimate Driving Machine" |
| If you drink a lot of beer, Schaefer is a good beer to drink. | "The one beer to have when you're having more than one." |
| We don't rent as many cars, so we have to do more for our customers. | "We're number two, so we try harder." (Avis) |
| Hanes socks last longer than less expensive ones. | "Buy cheap socks and you'll pay through the toes." |
| Through the United Way, you can give to many charities with one donation. | "We're putting all our begs in one ask it." |

Finally, *format* elements make a difference on an ad's impact as well as on its cost. A small change in ad design can make a big difference on its effect. The *illustration* is the first thing the reader notices—it must be strong enough to draw attention. Next, the *headline* must effectively entice the right people to read the copy. Finally, the *copy*—the main block of text in the ad—must be simple but strong and convincing. Moreover, these three elements must effectively work *together*.

## Selecting Advertising Media

The major steps in media selection are (1) deciding on *reach, frequency,* and *impact;* (2) choosing among major *media types;* (3) selecting specific *media vehicles;* and (4) deciding on *media timing*.

DECIDING ON REACH, FREQUENCY, AND IMPACT.   To select media, the advertiser must decide what reach and frequency are needed to achieve advertising objectives. *Reach* is a measure of the *percentage* of people in the target market who are exposed to the ad campaign during a given period of time. For example, the advertiser might try to reach 70 percent of the target market during the first three months of the campaign. *Frequency* is a measure of how many *times* the average person in the target market is exposed to the message. For example, the advertiser might want an average exposure frequency of three. The advertiser also must decide on the desired *media impact*—the *qualitative value* of a message exposure through a given medium. For example, for products that need to be demonstrated, messages on television may have more impact than messages on radio because television uses sight *and* sound. The same message in one magazine (say, *Newsweek*) may be more believable than in another (say, *The National Enquirer*). In general, the more reach, frequency, and impact that the advertiser seeks, the higher the advertising budget will have to be.

CHOOSING AMONG MAJOR MEDIA TYPES.   The media planner has to know the reach, frequency, and impact of each of the major media types. As summarized in Table 14-3, the major media types are newspapers, television, direct mail, radio, magazines, and outdoor. Each medium has advantages and limitations.

Media planners consider many factors when making their media choices. The *media habits of target consumers* will affect media choice—advertisers look for media that reach target consumers effectively. So will the *nature of the product*—for example, fashions are best advertised in color magazines, and Polaroid cameras are best demonstrated on television. Different *types of messages* may require different media. A message announcing a major sale tomorrow requires radio or

| TABLE 14-3 | *Profiles of Major Media Types* |
| --- | --- |

| Medium | Advantages | Limitations |
| --- | --- | --- |
| Newspapers | Flexibility; timeliness; good local market coverage; broad acceptability; high believability | Short life; poor reproduction quality; small pass-along audience |
| Television | Good mass market coverage; low cost per exposure; combines sight, sound, and motion; appealing to the senses | High absolute costs; high clutter; fleeting exposure; less audience selectivity |
| Direct mail | High audience selectivity; flexibility; no ad competition within the same medium; allows personalization | Relatively high cost per exposure; "junk mail" image |
| Radio | Good local acceptance, high geographic and demographic selectivity; low cost | Audio only, fleeting exposure; low attention ("the half-heard" medium); fragmented audiences |
| Magazines | High geographic and demographic selectivity; credibility and prestige; high-quality reproduction; long life and good pass-along readership | Long ad purchase lead time; high cost; no guarantee of position |
| Outdoor | Flexibility; high repeat exposure; low cost; low message competition; good positional selectivity | Little audience selectivity; creative limitations |

newspapers; a message with a lot of technical data might require magazines or direct mailings. *Cost* is another major factor in media choice. Whereas television is very expensive, for example, newspaper advertising costs much less. The media planner looks at both the total cost of using a medium and at the cost per thousand exposures—the cost of reaching 1,000 people using the medium.

Media impact and cost must be reexamined regularly. For a long time, television and magazines have dominated in the media mixes of national advertisers, with other media often being neglected. Recently, however, the costs and clutter of these media have gone up, audiences have dropped, and marketers are adopting strategies beamed at narrower segments. As a result, advertisers are increasingly turning to alternative media, ranging from cable TV and outdoor advertising to parking meters and shopping carts (see Marketing at Work 14-2).

## MARKETING AT WORK 14-2

# ADVERTISERS SEEK ALTERNATIVE MEDIA

As network television costs soar and audiences shrink, many advertisers are looking for new ways to reach consumers. And the move toward micromarketing strategies, focused more narrowly on specific consumer groups, has also fueled the search for alternative media to replace or supplement network television. Advertisers are shifting larger portions of their budgets to media that cost less and target more effectively.

Two media benefiting most from the shift are outdoor advertising and cable television. Billboards have undergone a resurgence in recent years. Although outdoor advertising spending has recently leveled off, advertisers now spend more than $1.1 billion annually on outdoor media, a 25 percent increase over ten years ago. Gone are the ugly eyesores of the past; in their place, we are now seeing cleverly designed, colorful attention-grabbers. Outdoor advertising provides an excellent way to

*Marketers have discovered a dazzling array of "alternative media."*

reach important local consumer segments.

Cable television is also booming. Today, more than 95 percent of all U.S. households have cable access, and nearly 65 percent of households subscribe. Cable TV advertising revenues

have been the fastest-growing segment in the communications industry. In 1981, cable television captured less than 1 percent of total television advertising revenues. By 1994, its share had risen to 9 percent, while broadcast networks' share fell by about

**Media vehicles**
Specific media within
each general media type,
such as specific maga-
zines, television shows,
or radio programs.

SELECTING SPECIFIC MEDIA VEHICLES.  The media planner now must choose the best **media vehicles**—specific media within each general media type. For example, television vehicles include *Seinfeld*, *Friends*, *Murphy Brown*, and *ABC World News Tonight*. Magazine vehicles include *Newsweek*, *People*, and *Sports Illustrated*.

Media planners must compute the cost per thousand persons reached by a vehicle. For example, if a full-page, four-color advertisement in *Newsweek* costs $126,000 and *Newsweek*'s readership is 3.1 million people, the cost of reaching each group of 1,000 persons is about $40. The same advertisement in *Business Week* may cost only $64,400 but reach only 870,000 persons—at a cost per thousand of about $74. The media planner would rank each magazine by cost per thousand and favor those magazines with the lower cost per thousand for reaching target consumers.

the same amount. Cable systems allow narrow programming formats such as all sports, all news, nutrition programs, arts programs, and others that target select groups. Advertisers can take advantage of such "narrowcasting" to "rifle in" on special market segments rather than use the "shotgun" approach offered by network broadcasting.

Cable TV and outdoor advertising seem to make good sense. But, increasingly, ads are popping up in far less likely places. In their efforts to find less costly and more highly targeted ways to reach consumers, advertisers have discovered a dazzling collection of "alternative media." As consumers, we're used to ads on television, in magazines and newspapers, on the radio, and along the roadways. But these days, no matter where you go or what you do, you probably will run into some new form of advertising.

Small billboards attached to shopping carts and ads on shopping bags urge you to buy Jell-O Pudding Pops or Pampers disposable diapers. As you wait in line to pay for your groceries,

television screens tuned to the "Checkout Channel" treat you to the latest news interspersed with food-product ads. As you approach your car, signs atop parking meters hawk everything from Jeeps to Minolta cameras to Recipe dog food. You escape to the ballpark, only to find billboard-size video screens running Budweiser ads, while a blimp with an electronic message board circles lazily overhead.

You pay to see a movie at your local theater, but first you are subjected to a two-minute science-fiction fantasy that turns out to be an ad for General Electric portable stereo boxes. Then the movie itself is full of not-so-subtle promotional plugs for Pepsi, Domino's pizza, Alka-Seltzer, MasterCard, Fritos, or any of a dozen other products. At the airport, you're treated to the CNN Airport Network; at the local rail station, it's the Commuter Channel. Boats cruise along public beaches flashing advertising messages for Sundown sunscreen or Gatorade to sunbathers. Even church bulletins carry ads for Campbell's soup. Advertisers

seeking a really out-of-this-world alternative can pay $500,000 for 58 feet of prime advertising space on the hull of a Conestoga 1620 expendable rocket scheduled for launch by NASA.

Some of these alternative media seem a bit far-fetched, and they sometimes irritate consumers. But for many marketers, these media can save money and provide a way to reach selected consumers where they live, shop, work, and play. Of course, this may leave you wondering if there are any commercial-free havens remaining for ad-weary consumers. The back seat of a taxi, perhaps, or public elevators, or stalls in a public restroom? Forget it! Each has already been invaded by innovative marketers.

*Sources:* See Kathy Martin, "What's Next? Execs Muse Over Boundless Ad Possibilities," *Advertising Age,* August 27, 1990; John P. Cortez, "Ads Head for the Bathroom," *Advertising Age,* May 18, 1992, p. 24; Richard Szathmary, "The Great (and Not So Great) Outdoors," *Sales & Marketing Management,* March 1992, pp. 75–81; Cyndee Miller, "Outdoor Gets Makeover," *Marketing News,* April 10, 1995, p. 1; Keith J. Kelly, "Flops Fail to Derail Place-Based," *Advertising Age,* August 8, 1994, p. 12; Rebecca Piirto, "Cable TV," *American Demographics,* June 1995, pp. 40–46; and Chuck Ross, "Cable TV," *Advertising Age,* March 25, 1996, pp. 23–24.

The media planner also must consider the costs of producing ads for different media. Whereas newspaper ads may cost very little to produce, flashy television ads may cost millions. On average, advertisers must pay $222,000 to produce a single 30-second television commercial. Nike recently paid a cool $2 million to make a single ad called "The Wall."[10]

In selecting media vehicles, the media planner must balance media cost measures against several media impact factors. First, the planner should balance costs against the media vehicle's *audience quality*. For a baby lotion advertisement, for example, *New Parents* magazine would have a high-exposure value; *Gentleman's Quarterly* would have a low-exposure value. Second, the media planner should consider *audience attention*. Readers of *Vogue,* for example, typically pay more attention to ads than do *Newsweek* readers. Third, the planner should assess the vehicle's *editorial quality*—*Time* and *The Wall Street Journal* are more believable and prestigious than *The National Enquirer.*

**DECIDING ON MEDIA TIMING.**   The advertiser also must decide how to schedule advertising over the course of a year. Suppose that sales of a product peak in December and drop in March. The firm can schedule its advertising to vary with the seasonal pattern, to oppose the seasonal pattern, or to be the same all year. Most firms do some seasonal advertising. Some do *only* seasonal advertising: For example, Hallmark advertises its greeting cards only before major holidays.

Finally, the advertiser has to choose the pattern of the ads. *Continuity* means scheduling ads evenly within a given period. *Pulsing* means scheduling ads unevenly over a given time period. Thus, 52 ads could either be scheduled at one per week during the year or pulsed in several bursts. The idea is to advertise heavily for a short period to build awareness that carries over to the next advertising period. Those who favor pulsing feel that it can be used to achieve the same impact as a steady schedule, but at a much lower cost. However, some media planners believe that, although pulsing achieves minimal awareness, it sacrifices depth of advertising communications.

## ADVERTISING EVALUATION

The advertising program should evaluate both the communication effects and the sales effects of advertising regularly. Measuring the *communication effects* of an ad—*copy testing*—tells whether the ad is communicating well. Copy testing can be done either before or after an ad is printed or broadcast. Before the ad is placed, the advertiser can show it to consumers, ask them how they like it, and measure recall or attitude changes resulting from it. After the ad is run, the advertiser can measure how the ad affected consumer recall or product awareness, knowledge, and preference.

But what *sales* are caused by an ad that increases brand awareness by 20 percent and brand preference by 10 percent? The *sales effects* of advertising are often harder to measure than the communication effects. Sales are affected by many factors besides advertising—such as product features, price, and availability.

One way to measure the sales effect of advertising is to compare past sales with past advertising expenditures. Another way is through experiments. For example, to test the effects of different advertising spending levels, Pizza Hut could vary the amount that it spends on advertising in different market areas and measure the differences in the resulting sales levels. It could spend the normal amount in one market area, half the normal amount in another area, and twice the normal amount in a third area. If the three market areas are similar, and if all other marketing efforts in the area are the same, then differences in sales in the three cities could be related to advertising level. More complex experiments could be designed to include other variables, such as difference in the ads or media used.

# ORGANIZING FOR ADVERTISING

Different companies organize in different ways to handle advertising. In small companies, advertising might be handled by someone in the sales department. Large companies set up advertising departments whose job it is to set the advertising budget, work with the ad agency, and handle direct-mail advertising, dealer displays, and other advertising not done by the agency. Most large companies use outside advertising agencies because they offer several advantages.

**Advertising agency**
A marketing service organization that assists other companies in the planning, creation, and implementation of their advertising programs.

How does an **advertising agency** work? Advertising agencies were started in the mid-to-late 1800s by salespeople and brokers who worked for the media and received a commission for selling advertising space to companies. As time passed, the salespeople began to help customers prepare their ads. Eventually, they formed agencies and grew closer to the advertisers than to the media. Today's agencies employ specialists who can often perform advertising tasks better than the company's own staff. Agencies also bring an outside point of view to solving the company's problems, along with lots of experience from working with different clients and situations. Thus, today, even companies with strong advertising departments use advertising agencies.

Some ad agencies are huge—the largest U.S. agency, Leo Burnett, has annual billings (the dollar amount of advertising placed for clients) of more than $2.2 billion. In recent years, many agencies have grown by gobbling up other agencies, thus creating huge agency holding companies. The largest of these agency "megagroups," WPP Group, includes several large agencies—Ogilvy & Mather, J. Walter Thompson, Fallon McElligott, and others—with combined billings exceeding $20 billion.[11]

Most large advertising agencies have the staff and resources to handle all phases of an advertising campaign for their clients, from creating a marketing plan to developing ad campaigns and preparing, placing, and evaluating ads. Agencies usually have four departments: *creative*, which develops and produces ads; *media*, which selects media and places ads; *research*, which studies audience characteristics and wants; and *business*, which handles the agency's business activities. Each account is supervised by an account executive, and people in each department are usually assigned to work on one or more accounts.

Ad agencies traditionally have been paid through commissions and fees. In the past, the agency typically received 15 percent of the media cost as a rebate. For example, suppose the agency bought $60,000 of magazine space for a client. The magazine would bill the advertising agency for $51,000 ($60,000 less 15 percent), and the agency then billed the client for $60,000, keeping the $9,000 commission. If the client bought space directly from the magazine, it would have paid $60,000 because commissions are only paid to recognized advertising agencies.

However, both advertisers and agencies have become more and more unhappy with the commission system. Larger advertisers complain that they pay more for the same services received by smaller ones simply because they place more advertising. Advertisers also believe that the commission system drives agencies away from low-cost media and short advertising campaigns. Agencies are unhappy because they perform extra services for an account without getting any more pay. As a result, the trend is now toward paying either a straight fee or a combination commission and fee. Some large advertisers are now tying agency compensation to the performance of the agency's advertising campaigns. Today, only about 35 percent of companies still pay their agencies on a commission-only basis.[12]

Another trend is affecting the advertising agency business: Many agencies have sought growth by diversifying into related marketing services. These new diversified agencies offer a complete list of integrated marketing and promotion services under one roof, including advertising, sales promotion, public relations, direct marketing, and marketing research. Some have even added marketing consulting, television production, and sales training units in an effort to become full "marketing partners" to their clients.

However, most agencies are finding that advertisers don't want much more from them than traditional media advertising services plus direct marketing, sales promotion, and sometimes public relations. Thus, many agencies have recently dropped unrelated activities in order to focus more on traditional services. Some have even started their own "creative boutiques," smaller and more independent agencies that can develop creative campaigns for clients free of large-agency bureaucracy.

## INTERNATIONAL ADVERTISING DECISIONS

International advertisers face many complexities not encountered by domestic advertisers. The most basic issue concerns the degree to which global advertising should be adapted to the unique characteristics of various country markets. Some large advertisers have attempted to support their global brands with highly standardized worldwide advertising. Standardization produces many benefits—lower advertising costs, greater global advertising coordination, and a more consistent worldwide image. However, standardization also has drawbacks. Most importantly, it ignores the fact that country markets differ greatly in their cultures, demographics, and economic conditions. Thus, most international advertisers "think globally but act locally." They develop global advertising *strategies* that make their worldwide advertising efforts more efficient and consistent. Then they adapt their advertising *programs* to make them more responsive to consumer needs and expectations within local markets.

Companies adapt their global advertising to varying degrees. Kellogg's Frosted Flakes commercials are almost identical worldwide, with only minor adjustments for local cultural differences. For example, one campaign uses a tennis theme that has worldwide appeal and features teenage actors with generic good looks—neither too Northern European nor too Latin American. Of course, Kellogg translates the commercials into different languages. In the English version, Tony growls "They're Gr-r-reat!" whereas in the German version it's "Gr-r-rossartig!" Other adaptations are more subtle. In the American ad, after winning the match, Tony leaps over the net in celebration. In other versions, he simply "high fives" his young partner. The reason: Europeans do not jump over the net after winning at tennis.[13]

In contrast, Parker Pen Company changes its advertising substantially from country to country. In Germany, ads show a hand holding a Parker pen writing the headline "This is how you write with precision." In the United Kingdom, where Parker is the brand leader, ads emphasize the exotic processes used to make pens, such as gently polishing the gold nibs with walnut chips. In the United States, ads stress status and image, with headlines such as "Here's how you tell who's boss," and "There are times when it has to be Parker." In this way, the company creates different images that match customer motives in each market.[14]

Global advertisers face several additional problems. For instance, advertising media costs and availability differ vastly from country to country. Some countries have too few media to handle all of the advertising offered to them. Other countries are peppered with so many media that an advertiser cannot gain national coverage at a reasonable cost. Media prices often are negotiated and may vary greatly. For example, one study found that the cost of reaching 1,000 consumers in 11 different European countries ranged from $1.58 in Belgium to $5.91 in Italy. For women's magazines, the advertising cost per page ranged from $2.51 per thousand circulation in Denmark to $10.87 in Germany.[15]

Countries also differ in the extent to which they regulate advertising practices. Many countries have extensive systems of laws restricting how much a company can spend on advertising, the media used, the nature of advertising claims, and other aspects of the advertising program. Such restrictions often require that advertisers adapt their campaigns from country to country. Consider the following example:

> A 30-second Kellogg commercial produced for British TV would have to have [several] alterations to be acceptable [elsewhere] in Europe: Reference to iron and vitamins would have to be deleted in the Netherlands. A child wearing a Kellogg's T-shirt would be edited out in France where children are forbidden from endorsing products on TV. In Germany, the line "Kellogg makes cornflakes the best they've ever been" would be cut because of rules against making competitive claims. After alterations, the 30-second commercial would be [only] about five seconds long.[16]

Thus, although advertisers may develop global strategies to guide their overall advertising efforts, specific advertising programs usually must be adapted to meet local cultures and customs, media characteristics, and advertising regulations.

# SALES PROMOTION

**Sales promotion**
Short-term incentives to encourage purchase or sales of a product or service.

Advertising is joined by two other mass-promotion tools—*sales promotion* and *public relations*. **Sales promotion** consists of short-term incentives to encourage purchase or sales of a product or service. Whereas advertising offers reasons to buy a product or service, sales promotion offers reasons to buy *now*. Examples are found everywhere. A freestanding insert in the Sunday newspaper contains a coupon offering 50 cents off on Folger's coffee. The end-of-the-aisle display in the local supermarket tempts impulse buyers with a wall of Coke cartons. An executive buys a new Compaq laptop computer and gets a free carrying case, or a family buys a new Taurus and receives a rebate check for $500. A hardware store chain receives a 10 percent discount on selected Black & Decker portable power tools if it agrees to advertise them in local newspapers. Sales promotion includes a wide variety of promotion tools designed to stimulate earlier or stronger market response.

# RAPID GROWTH OF SALES PROMOTION

Sales-promotion tools are used by most organizations, including manufacturers, distributors, retailers, trade associations, and nonprofit institutions. They are targeted toward final buyers *(consumer promotions)*, business customers *(business promotions)*, retailers and wholesalers *(trade promotions)*, and members of the sales force *(sales force promotions)*. Today, in many consumer packaged-goods companies, sales promotion accounts for 75 percent or more of all marketing expenditures. Sales-promotion expenditures have been increasing by 12 percent annually, compared with advertising's increase of only 7.6 percent.[17]

Several factors have contributed to the rapid growth of sales promotion, particularly in consumer markets. First, inside the company, product managers face greater pressures to increase their current sales, and promotion is viewed as an effective short-run sales tool. Second, externally, the company faces more competition and competing brands are less differentiated. Increasingly, competitors are using sales promotion to help differentiate their offers. Third, advertising efficiency has declined because of rising costs, media clutter, and legal restraints. Finally, consumers have become more deal oriented, and retailers are demanding more deals from manufacturers.

The growing use of sales promotion has resulted in *promotion clutter*, similar to advertising clutter. Consumers are increasingly tuning out promotions, weakening their ability to trigger immediate purchase. In fact, the extent to which U.S. consumers have come to take promotions for granted was illustrated dramatically by the reactions of Eastern European consumers when Procter & Gamble recently gave out samples of a newly introduced shampoo. To P&G, the sampling campaign was just business as usual. To consumers in Poland and Czechoslovakia, however, it was little short of a miracle:

> With nothing expected in return, Warsaw shoppers were being handed free samples of Vidal Sassoon Wash & Go shampoo. Just for the privilege of trying the new product; no standing in line for a product that may not even be on the shelf. Some were so taken aback that they were moved to tears. In a small town in Czechoslovakia, the head of the local post office was so pleased to be part of the direct-mail sampling program, he sent the P&G staffer roses to express his thanks. The postmaster told the P&G'er: "This is the most exciting thing that's ever happened in this post office—it's a terrific experience to be part of this new market economy that's coming.[18]

Although no sales promotion is likely to create such excitement among promotion-prone consumers in the United States and other Western countries, manufacturers now are searching for ways to rise above the clutter, such as offering larger coupon values or creating more dramatic point-of-purchase displays.

In using sales promotion, a company must set objectives, select the right tools, develop the best program, pretest and implement it, and evaluate the results.

# SETTING SALES-PROMOTION OBJECTIVES

Sales-promotion objectives vary widely. Sellers may use *consumer promotions* to increase short-term sales or to help build long-term market share. The objective may be to entice consumers to try a new product, lure consumers away from competitors' products, get consumers to "load up" on a mature product, or hold and reward loyal customers. Objectives for *trade promotions* include getting retailers to carry new items and more inventory, getting them to advertise the product and give it more shelf space, and getting them to buy ahead. For the *sales force*, objectives include getting more sales force support for current or new products or getting salespeople to sign up new accounts. Sales promotions are usually used together with advertising or personal selling. Consumer promotions usually must be advertised and can therefore add excitement and pulling power to ads. Trade and sales-force promotions support the firm's personal selling process.

In general, sales promotions should be *consumer relationship building*. Rather than creating only short-term sales volume or temporary brand switching, they should help to reinforce the product's position and build long-term relationships with consumers. Increasingly, marketers are avoiding "quick fix," price-only promotions in favor of promotions designed to build brand equity. For example, in France, Nestlé set up roadside Relais Bébé centers, where travelers can stop to feed and change their babies. At each center, Nestlé hostesses provide free disposable diapers, the use of changing tables and high chairs, and free samples of Nestlé baby food. Each summer, 64 hostesses welcome 120,000 baby visits and dispense 6,000,000 samples of baby food. This ongoing promotion provides real value to parents and an ideal opportunity to build relationships with customers. At key mealtime moments, Nestlé hostesses are in direct contact with mothers in a unique, brand-related relationship. Nestlé also provides a toll-free phone number for free baby-nutrition counseling.[19]

Even price promotions can be designed to help build customer relationships. Examples include all of the "frequency marketing programs" and clubs that have mushroomed in recent years (see Marketing at Work 14-3). If properly designed, every sales-promotion tool has consumer relationship building potential.

# SELECTING SALES-PROMOTION TOOLS

Many tools can be used to accomplish sales-promotion objectives. Descriptions of the main consumer- and trade-promotion tools follow.

## Consumer-Promotion Tools

The main consumer-promotion tools include samples, coupons, cash refunds, price packs, premiums, advertising specialties, patronage rewards, point-of-purchase displays and demonstrations, and contests, sweepstakes, and games.

**Samples** are offers of a trial amount of a product. Some samples are free; for others, the company charges a small amount to offset its cost. The sample might be delivered door to door, sent by mail, handed out in a store, attached to another product, or featured in an ad. Sampling is the most effective—but most expensive—way to introduce a new product. Sometimes, samples are combined into sample packs, which can then be used to promote other products and services. An example is Blockbuster Video's "Bonus Box" promotion, in which customers who

**Samples**
Offers to consumers of a trial amount of a product.

## MARKETING AT WORK 14-3

# PROMOTING CUSTOMER RELATIONSHIPS: FREQUENCY MARKETING PROGRAMS AND CLUBS

Many companies have developed sales promotion programs that build long-term relationships with customers rather than creating only short-term sales volume. The most common efforts are *frequency marketing programs* and *club marketing programs,* which give select customers special privileges and awards that keep them coming back, buying more, and staying loyal.

### FREQUENCY MARKETING PROGRAMS

Frequency marketing programs (FMP) reward customers who buy frequently or in large amounts. Such programs capture more lifetime value from a company's best customers by developing long-term, interactive, value-added relationships with them.

American Airlines was one of the first companies to pioneer a frequency marketing program. In the early 1980s, it offered the AAdvantage program through which frequent flyers could accumulate credits for miles flown with American and redeem them for free airline tickets, seat upgrades,

or other benefits. Hotels soon adopted FMPs. Marriott took the lead with its Honored Guest Program, quickly followed by Hyatt (with its Gold Passport Program) and other hotel chains. Frequent

---

*Frequency marketing programs: The Sears Best Customer Program boosted customer retention by 11 percent and increased sales from the retailer's best customers by 9 percent.*

*Exclusive savings day just for you...*
*Sears Best Customer*

**ADDITIONAL**
**10% OFF ALL SALE PRICES**

*Plus 10% off all regular prices, too!*
*Feb. 1st is your bonus savings day.*
*Sale goes public Feb. 2nd, 3rd & 4th.*

SB
SEARS BEST CUSTOMER

---

guests receive room upgrades or free rooms after earning enough points. Next, car rental firms sponsored FMPs, and credit card companies began to offer points based on their cards' usage level. For example, Sears offers rebates to their Discover cardholders on charges made against the card, and Shell Oil card users can earn free gasoline.

Typically, the first company to introduce an FMP gains the most benefit. However, after competitors respond, FMPs can become a burden to all the offering companies. Soon, many customers belong to several competing FMPs, and companies may find that they are giving away many flights, rooms, and merchandise without gaining much advantage. Despite these problems, frequency marketing programs remain an important tool for building long-term relationships with customers.

### CLUB MARKETING PROGRAMS

Many companies have created club concepts around their products. Club membership may be

---

rent at least three movies receive a box containing samples of Triples and other General Mills cereals, Hawaiian Punch from Procter & Gamble, Hidden Valley dip from Clorox, and Lever 2000 soap from Lever Brothers. Blockbuster hands out more than four million of these boxes over a typical July Fourth weekend.[20]

**Coupons**
Certificates that give buyers a saving when they purchase a specified product.

**Coupons** are certificates that give buyers a saving when they purchase specified products. More than 310 billion coupons are distributed in the United States each year, nearly 10 times the number distributed 20 years ago. Consumers redeem almost eight billion of these coupons at an average face value of 59 cents per coupon, saving over $4.7 billion on their shopping bills. Coupons can be mailed, offered automatically on purchase of a product or by paying a fee. Some clubs have been very successful:

• The Valley View Center Mall in Dallas recently unveiled its Smart Shoppers Club, a program that rewards customers who tap onto their computerized interactive touch-screen kiosks. To obtain a membership and personal identification number, mallgoers fill out a short application that asks simple demographic and psychographic questions. Then, each time members visit the mall, they input their ID number into one of the mall's three touch-screen kiosks and receive daily discount retail coupons, prizes awarded randomly each week, and a calendar of events. While customers reap discounts and prizes, Valley View retailers get valuable marketing information about their customers. The shopping center is one of only about 10 of the nation's 35,000 malls to use this high-tech consumer loyalty program.

• Norwegian Cruise Lines (NCL) sponsors a loyalty program called Latitudes, a co-branding effort with VISA. The program includes a two-for-one cruise offer and a Latitudes VISA card that rewards users with points redeemable for discounts on NCL cruises.

• Waldenbooks sponsors a Preferred Reader Program which has attracted over four million members, each paying an annual fee of $10 to receive mailings about new books, a 10 per-cent discount on book purchases, a $5 rebate on every $100 spent, toll-free ordering, and many other services.

• Lladro, maker of fine porcelain figurines, sponsors a Collectors Society with an annual membership fee of $35. Members receive a free subscription to a quarterly magazine, a bisque plaque, free enrollment in the Lladro Museum of New York, and member-only tours to visit the company and Lladro family in Valencia, Spain.

• Gateway Federal, a Cincinnati thrift bank, sponsors The Stateman's Club for customers who maintain a minimum deposit of $10,000. Its 10,000 members receive over 26 benefits including free checking, money orders, and traveler's checks; social gatherings and guest lecturers; and complimentary refreshments. Members have access to IBM computers and other equipment, and they can reserve the club room for private receptions after regular hours.

• Harley-Davidson sponsors the Harley Owners Group (HOG) that now numbers 127,000 members. The first-time buyer of a Harley-Davidson motorcycle gets a free one-year membership, with annual renewal costing $35. HOG benefits include a magazine (*Hog Tales*), a touring handbook, an emergency pick-up service, a specially designed insurance program, theft recovery reward service, discount hotel rates, and a Fly & Ride program enabling members to rent Harleys while on an air-travel vacation.

Well-executed clubs and frequency marketing programs can produce significant results. For example, when Sears found that it was losing too many of its best customers to competitors, it launched its Best Customer Program. It defined its best customers as those who shop at Sears frequently and in a variety of departments, and who spend a large amount of money annually at the store. About 7.2 million Sears customers fit this definition, and the retailer estimates that each is worth about six times more to Sears than the average new customer. Best Customers receive special benefits and privileges, such as guaranteed response to a service call within 24 hours. The program has improved Sears's customer retention rate by 11 percent and increased sales from Best Customers by 9 percent.

*Sources:* See Cyndee Miller, "Rewards for the Best Customers," *Marketing News*, July 5, 1993, pp. 1, 6; Gary Levin, "Marketers Flock to Loyalty Offers," *Advertising Age*, May 24, 1993, p. 13; "Club for the Smart," *Marketing News*, May 23, 1994, p. 1; Norwegian Cruise Lines Launches Loyalty Program," *Adweek*, April 10, 1995, p. 9; and Richard G. Barlow, "Five Mistakes of Frequency Marketing," *Direct Marketing Magazine*, March 1995, p. 16.

**Cash refund offers (rebates)**
Offers to refund part of the purchase price of a product to consumers who send a proof of purchase to the manufacturer.

included with other products, or placed in ads. They can stimulate sales of a mature brand or promote early trial of a new brand. Stores now feature electronic point-of-sale coupon printers as well as "paperless coupon systems" which dispense personalized discounts to targeted buyers at the checkout counter in stores. Early tests using instant coupon machines have produced average redemption rates of 24 percent and boosted sales about 32 percent.[21]

**Cash refund offers** (or **rebates**) are like coupons except that the price reduction occurs after the purchase rather than at the retail outlet. The consumer sends a "proof of purchase" to the manufacturer, who then refunds part of the purchase

*Point-of-sale coupon-ing: Using Checkout Direct technology, marketers can dispense personalized coupons to carefully targeted buyers at the checkout counter. This avoids the waste of poorly targeted coupons delivered through FSIs (coupon pages inserted into newspapers).*

price by mail. For example, Toro ran a clever preseason promotion on some of its snowblower models, offering a rebate if the snowfall in the buyer's market area turned out to be below average. Competitors were not able to match this offer on such short notice, and the promotion was very successful.

**Price packs** (also called **cents-off deals**) offer consumers savings off the regular price of a product. The reduced prices are marked by the producer directly on the label or package. Price packs can be single packages sold at a reduced price (such as two for the price of one) or two related products banded together (such as a toothbrush and toothpaste). Price packs are very effective—even more so than coupons—in stimulating short-term sales.

**Premiums** are goods offered either free or at low cost as an incentive to buy a product. In its "Treasure Hunt" promotion, for example, Quaker Oats inserted $5 million worth of gold and silver coins in Ken-L Ration dog-food packages. In its recent premium promotion, Cutty Sark offered a brass tray with the purchase of one bottle of its scotch and a desk lamp with the purchase of two. A premium may come inside the package (in-pack) or outside the package (on-pack). If reusable, the package itself may serve as a premium—such as a decorative tin. Premiums are sometimes mailed to consumers who have sent in a proof of purchase, such as a product box top.

**Advertising specialties** are useful articles imprinted with an advertiser's name that are given as gifts to consumers. Typical items include pens, calendars, key rings, matches, shopping bags, T-shirts, caps, nail files, and coffee mugs. U.S. companies spend over $4.5 billion each year on advertising specialties. Such items can be very effective. In a recent study, 63 percent of all consumers surveyed were either carrying or wearing an ad specialty item. More than three-quarters of those

**Price packs (cents-off deals)**
Reduced prices that are marked by the producer directly on the label or package.

**Premiums**
Goods offered either free or at low cost as an incentive to buy a product.

**Advertising specialties**
Useful articles imprinted with an advertiser's name that are given as gifts to consumers.

who had an item could recall the advertiser's name or message before showing the item to the interviewer.[22]

**Patronage rewards** are cash or other awards offered for the regular use of a certain company's products or services. For example, airlines offer frequent flyer plans, awarding points for miles traveled that can be turned in for free airline trips. Marriott Hotels has adopted an "honored guest" plan that awards points to users of their hotels. Baskin-Robbins offers frequent-purchase awards—for every ten purchases, customers receive a free quart of ice cream.

**Point-of-purchase (POP) promotions** include displays and demonstrations that take place at the point of purchase or sale. An example is a five-foot-high cardboard display of Cap'n Crunch next to Cap'n Crunch cereal boxes. However, many retailers are unwilling or unable to use the hundreds of displays, signs, and posters that they receive from manufacturers each year. Manufacturers have responded by offering better POP materials, tying them in with television or print messages, and offering to set them up.

**Contests, sweepstakes,** and **games** give consumers the chance to win something, such as cash, trips, or goods, by luck or through extra effort. A *contest* calls for consumers to submit an entry—a jingle, guess, design, or suggestion—to be judged by a panel that will select the best entries. A *sweepstakes* calls for consumers to submit their names for a drawing. A *game* presents consumers with something—bingo numbers, missing letters—every time they buy, which may help them win a prize. A sales contest urges dealers or the sales force to increase their efforts, with prizes going to the top performers.

## Trade-Promotion Tools

More sales-promotion dollars are directed to retailers and wholesalers (63 percent) than to consumers (37 percent). Trade promotion can persuade retailers or wholesalers to carry a brand, give it shelf space, promote it in advertising, and push it to consumers. Shelf space is so scarce these days that manufacturers often have to offer price-offs, allowances, buy-back guarantees, or free goods to retailers and wholesalers to get products on the shelf and, once there, to stay on it.

Manufacturers use several trade-promotion tools. Many of the tools used for consumer promotions—contests, premiums, displays—can also be used as trade promotions. Or the manufacturer may offer a straight **discount** off the list price on each case purchased during a stated period of time (also called a *price-off, off-invoice,* or *off-list*). The offer encourages dealers to buy in quantity or to carry a new item. Dealers can use the discount for immediate profit, for advertising, or for price reductions to their customers.

Manufacturers also may offer an **allowance** (usually so much off per case) in return for the retailer's agreement to feature the manufacturer's products in some way. An *advertising allowance* compensates retailers for advertising the product. A *display allowance* compensates them for using special displays.

Manufacturers may offer *free goods,* which are extra cases of merchandise, to middlemen who buy a certain quantity or who feature a certain flavor or size. They may offer *push money*—cash or gifts to dealers or their sales force to "push" the manufacturer's goods. Manufacturers may give retailers free *specialty advertising items* that carry the company's name, such as pens, pencils, calendars, paperweights, matchbooks, memo pads, ashtrays, and yardsticks.

---

**Patronage rewards**
Cash or other awards for the regular use of a certain company's products or services.

**Point-of-purchase (POP) promotions**
Displays and demonstrations that take place at the point of purchase or sale.

**Contests, sweepstakes, games**
Promotional events that give consumers the chance to win something—such as cash, trips, or goods—by luck or through extra effort.

**Discount**
A straight reduction in price on purchases during a stated period of time.

**Allowance**
Promotional money paid by manufacturers to retailers who agree to feature the manufacturer's products in some way.

### Business-Promotion Tools

Companies spend billions of dollars each year on promotion to industrial customers. These business promotions are used to generate business leads, stimulate purchases, reward customers, and motivate salespeople. Business promotion includes many of the same tools used for consumer or trade promotions. Here, we focus on two major business-promotion tools—conventions and trade shows, and sales contests.

Many companies and trade associations organize *conventions and trade shows* to promote their products. Firms selling to the industry show their products at the trade show. More than 5,800 trade shows take place every year, drawing as many as 85 million people. Vendors receive many benefits, such as opportunities to find new sales leads, contact current customers, introduce new products, meet new customers, sell more to present customers, and educate customers with publications and audiovisual materials. Trade shows also help companies reach many prospects not reached through their sales forces. About 90 percent of a trade show's visitors see a company's salespeople for the first time at the show. Business marketers may spend as much as 35 percent of their annual promotion budgets on trade shows.[23]

A *sales contest* is a contest for salespeople or dealers to motivate them to increase their sales performance over a given period. Sales contests motivate and recognize good company performers, who may receive trips, cash prizes, or other gifts. Some companies award points for performance, which the receiver can turn in for any of a variety of prizes. Sales contests work best when they are tied to measurable and achievable sales objectives (such as finding new accounts, reviving old accounts, or increasing account profitability).

*More than 5,800 trade shows take place every year, giving sellers chances to introduce new products and meet new customers. At this consumer electronics trade show, 2,000 exhibitors attracted more than 91,000 professional visitors.*

# DEVELOPING THE SALES-PROMOTION PROGRAM

The marketer must make several other decisions in order to define the full sales-promotion program. First, the marketer must decide on the *size of the incentive.* A certain minimum incentive is necessary if the promotion is to succeed; a larger incentive will produce more sales response. The marketer also must set *conditions for participation.* Incentives might be offered to everyone or only to select groups.

The marketer must decide how to *promote and distribute the promotion* program itself. A 50-cents-off coupon could be given out in a package, at the store, by mail, or in an advertisement. Each distribution method involves a different level of reach and cost. Increasingly, marketers are blending several media into a total campaign concept. The *length of the promotion* is also very important. If the sales-promotion period is too short, many prospects (who may not be buying during that time) will miss it. If the promotion runs too long, the deal will lose some of its "act now" force.

*Evaluation* is also very important. Yet many companies fail to evaluate their sales-promotion programs, and others evaluate them only superficially. Manufacturers can use one of many evaluation methods. The most common method is to compare sales before, during, and after a promotion. Suppose that a company has a 6 percent market share before the promotion, which jumps to 10 percent during the promotion, falls to 5 percent right after, and rises to 7 percent later on. The promotion seems to have attracted new triers and more buying from current customers. After the promotion, sales fell as consumers used up their inventories. The long-run rise to 7 percent means that the company gained some new users. If the brand's share had returned to the old level, then the promotion would have changed only the *timing* of demand rather than the *total* demand.

Consumer research would also show the kinds of people who responded to the promotion and what they did after it ended. *Surveys* can provide information on how many consumers recall the promotion, what they thought of it, how many took advantage of it, and how it affected their buying. Sales promotions can also be evaluated through *experiments* that vary factors such as incentive value, length, and distribution method.

Clearly, sales promotion plays an important role in the total promotion mix. To use it well, the marketer must define the sales-promotion objectives, select the best tools, design the sales-promotion program, implement the program, and evaluate the results. Marketing at Work 14-4 describes some award-winning sales-promotion campaigns.

# ▶ PUBLIC RELATIONS

Another major mass-promotion tool is **public relations**—building good relations with the company's various publics by obtaining favorable publicity, building up a good "corporate image," and handling or heading off unfavorable rumors, stories, and events. Public relations departments may perform any or all of the following functions:[24]

 *Press relations or press agentry:* Creating and placing newsworthy information in the news media to attract attention to a person, product, or service

**Public relations**
Building good relations with the company's various publics by obtaining favorable publicity, building up a good "corporate image," and handling or heading off unfavorable rumors, stories, and events.

◆ *Product publicity:* Publicizing specific products
◆ *Public affairs:* Building and maintaining national or local community relations
◆ *Lobbying:* Building and maintaining relations with legislators and government officials to influence legislation and regulation
◆ *Investor relations:* Maintaining relationships with shareholders and others in the financial community
◆ *Development:* Public relations with donors or members of nonprofit organizations to gain financial or volunteer support

Public relations is used to promote products, people, places, ideas, activities, organizations, and even nations. Trade associations have used public relations to rebuild interest in declining commodities such as eggs, apples, milk, and potatoes. New York City turned its image around when its "I Love New York" campaign took root, bringing millions more tourists to the city. Johnson & Johnson's masterly use of public relations played a major role in saving Tylenol from extinction after its product-tampering scare. Nations have used public relations to attract more tourists, foreign investment, and international support.

Public relations can have a strong impact on public awareness at a much lower cost than advertising (see Marketing at Work 14-4). The company does not pay for the space or time in the media. Rather, it pays for a staff to develop and circulate information and to manage events. If the company develops an interesting story, it could be picked up by several different media, having the same effect as advertising that would cost millions of dollars. And it has more credibility than advertising. Public relations results can sometimes be spectacular.

> Georgia-Pacific developed a World's Fastest Roofer contest to give its roofing contractor target market hands-on experience with Summit, a new high-quality shingle whose key feature was its ease of installation. Contestants installed 100 square feet of shingles, and judges chose the winner based on roofing speed and job quality. First prize was an all-expenses-paid trip to Hawaii for two. The contest began with eight regional eliminations held at G-P distribution centers around the country. Months in advance, each distribution center promoted the contest to area roofers using direct-mail promotional materials furnished by the G-P public relations department. In all, more than 150 roofers competed in the local contests. The eight regional winners were flown to Atlanta to compete in the national contest, timed to coincide with National Roofing Week. Tie-ins with a home-oriented Atlanta radio station resulted in widespread on-air promotion and raised several thousand dollars for an Atlanta children's hospital. The mayor of Atlanta issued a proclamation recognizing roofers, National Roofing Week, and Georgia-Pacific. Caps, T-shirts, and posters were used to merchandise the event both locally and nationally. After the contest, G-P sent a print and video media kit to key national media and media in the hometowns of contest participants. The budget: only $50,000 to $75,000. The results: The promotion generated more than 2.5 million media impressions and increased sales in Georgia-Pacific's targeted markets by 90 percent.

Despite its potential strengths, public relations often is described as a marketing stepchild because of its limited and scattered use. The public relations

## MARKETING AT WORK 14-4

# PUBLIC RELATIONS: STRETCHING THE MARKETING BUDGET

Italian sports-carmaker Lamborghini sells less than 100 of its cars each year in the United States. Marketing Lamborghinis is no simple matter. The car is pure poetry in motion—but at a steep price. The Diablo VT's 492-horsepower engine delivers a top speed of 202 mph and goes from 0 to 60 mph in just 4.1 seconds. The price: $239,000. Just to lease a Diablo VT runs $2,999 a month, with a $52,000 down payment. Moreover, because so few Lamborghinis are sold, most people rarely see one. Thus, to gain exposure and persuade would-be buyers, the company must invest its modest $600,000 U.S. marketing budget carefully.

Lamborghini's eventual goal is to sell 1,500 to 2,000 units a year in the United States. This goal is based partly on expanding its product lineup to include a sport-utility vehicle priced in the $75,000-to-$100,000 range. To reach this ambitious sales goal, however, the carmaker will need to increase its exposure and awareness. It currently advertises in several selective business, travel, and lifestyle magazines, emphasizing the car's speed and sensual appeal. In addition, the company recently fielded a direct-mail campaign to 50,000 prospective buyers with median household incomes of $1.5 million.

When it comes to advertising, however, $600,000 doesn't go far. So Lamborghini stretches its limited marketing budget with an assortment of less expensive public relations efforts. The company actively courts the press. For example, it makes the car available to auto journalists for test drives. This resulted in a recent *New York Times* review describing the car as "kinetic sculpture, proof of affluence, and amusement park ride wrapped into one." And after a test drive, a *Fortune* journalist wrote, "On the beauty meter, the screaming lemon-yellow Diablo rates right up there with a roomful of Matisse originals. . . . Neighbors I have never met come rushing out of their homes to get a closer look." Lamborghini also sponsors tasteful public relations events. For example, it recently held a cocktail party for 200 people at a Georgio Armani store in Boston,

*The $239,000 Lamborghini Diablo VT moved one journalist to say that "on the beauty meter . . . it rates right up there with a roomful of Matisse originals. . . . Neighbors I have never met come rushing out of their homes to get a closer look."*

with an invitation list put together by the store and *The Robb Report,* a publication devoted to the lifestyles of the wealthy.

Lamborghini is constantly seeking new ways to expose the car to its affluent audience. As a result of good public relations efforts, the Lamborghini Diablo VT was designated as a pace car for the 1995 PPG Indy Car World Series. This gave Lamborghini exposure at 15 race sites and allowed local dealers to give prospective buyers a ride around the track in the days before a race. Says a Lamborghini executive, "We sold three cars by doing that last year at the Detroit Grand Prix." Also, for the first time, Lamborghini is making a demonstrator available to its 19 U.S. dealers, so that prospects can test-drive the car without the dealer worrying about mileage and insurance costs.

Lamborghini's total annual U.S. *sales* of $22 million amount to only a tiny fraction of the *advertising budgets* of the major carmakers. However, through the innovative use of public relations, the company successfully stretches its modest marketing budget to gain exposure among affluent buyers.

*Sources:* Raymond Serafin, "Even Lamborghini Must Think Marketing," *Advertising Age,* May 1, 1995, p. 4; and Faye Rice, "Lamborghini's Sales Drive," *Fortune,* June 12, 1995, p. 13.

department is usually located at corporate headquarters. Its staff is so busy dealing with various publics—stockholders, employees, legislators, city officials—that public relations programs to support product marketing objectives may be ignored. And marketing managers and public relations practitioners do not always talk the same language. Many public relations practitioners see their job as simply communicating. In contrast, marketing managers tend to be much more interested in how advertising and public relations affect sales and profits.

This situation is changing, however. Many companies now want their public relations departments to manage all of their activities with a view toward marketing the company and improving the bottom line. Some companies are setting up special units called *marketing public relations* to support corporate and product promotion and image making directly. Many companies hire marketing public relations firms to handle their PR programs or to assist the company public relations team.

## MAJOR PUBLIC RELATIONS TOOLS

Public relations professionals use several tools. One of the major tools is *news*. PR professionals find or create favorable news about the company and its products or people. Sometimes news stories occur naturally, and sometimes the PR person suggests events or activities that would create news. *Speeches* can also create product and company publicity. Increasingly, company executives must field questions from the media or give talks at trade associations or sales meetings, and these events can either build or hurt the company's image. Another common PR tool is *special events,* ranging from news conferences, press tours, grand openings, and fireworks displays to laser shows, hot-air balloon releases, multimedia presentations, and star-studded spectaculars designed to reach and interest target publics.

Public relations people also prepare *written materials* to reach and influence their target markets. These materials include annual reports, brochures, articles, and company newsletters and magazines. *Audiovisual materials,* such as films, slide-and-sound programs, and video- and audiocassettes, are being used increasingly as communication tools. *Corporate-identity materials* can also help create a corporate identity that the public immediately recognizes. Logos, stationery, brochures, signs, business forms, business cards, buildings, uniforms, and company cars and trucks all become marketing tools when they are attractive, distinctive, and memorable.

Companies can also improve public goodwill by contributing money and time to *public-service activities.* For example, Procter & Gamble and Publishers' Clearing House held a joint promotion to raise money for the Special Olympics. The Publishers' Clearing House mailing included product coupons, and Procter & Gamble donated 10 cents per redeemed coupon to the Special Olympics. In another example, B. Dalton Booksellers donated $3 million during a four-year period to the fight against illiteracy.

## MAJOR PUBLIC RELATIONS DECISIONS

In considering when and how to use product public relations, management should set PR objectives, choose the PR messages and vehicles, implement the PR plan, and evaluate the results.

*Attractive, distinctive, memorable company logos become strong marketing tools.*

## Setting Public Relations Objectives

The first task is to set *objectives* for public relations. Some years ago, the Wine Growers of California hired a public relations firm to develop a program to support two major marketing objectives: convince Americans that wine drinking is a pleasant part of good living, and improve the image and market share of California wines among all wines. The following public relations objectives were set: develop magazine stories about wine and get them placed in top magazines (such as *Time* and *House Beautiful*) and in newspapers (food columns and feature sections); develop stories about the many health values of wine and direct them to the medical profession; and develop specific publicity for the young adult market, the college market, governmental bodies, and various ethnic communities. These objectives were turned into specific goals so that final results could be evaluated.

## Choosing Public Relations Messages and Vehicles

The organization next selects its major public relations message themes and the PR tools that it will use. Message themes should be guided by the organization's overall marketing and communications strategies. Public relations is an important part of the organization's overall integrated marketing communications program. Thus, public relations messages should be carefully integrated with the organization's advertising, personal selling, direct marketing, and other communications.

In some cases, the choices of public relations messages and tools will be clear-cut. In others, the organization will have to create news rather than find it. Creating events is especially important in publicizing fund-raising drives for nonprofit organizations. Fund-raisers have developed a large set of special events such as art exhibits, auctions, benefit evenings, book sales, contests, dances, dinners, fairs, fashion shows, phonathons, rummage sales, tours, and walkathons. No sooner is one type of event created, such as a walkathon, than competitors create new versions, such as readathons, bikeathons, and jogathons.

### Implementing the Public Relations Plan

Implementing public relations requires care. Take the matter of placing stories in the media. A *great* story is easy to place, but most stories are not great and may not get past busy editors. Thus, one of the main assets that a public relations person can have is personal relationships with media editors. In fact, PR professionals are often former journalists who know many media editors and know what they want. They view media editors as a market to be satisfied so that editors will continue to use their stories.

### Evaluating Public Relations Results

Public relations results are difficult to measure because PR is used with other promotion tools, and its impact is often indirect. If PR is used before other tools come into play, its contribution is easier to evaluate.

The easiest measure of publicity effectiveness is the number of exposures in the media. Public relations people give the client a "clippings book" showing all the media that carried news about the product. Such exposure measures are not very satisfying, however. They do not tell how many people actually read or heard the message, or what they thought afterward. In addition, because of the media overlap in readership and viewership, it does not give information on the *net* audience reached.

A better measure is the change in product awareness, knowledge, and attitude resulting from the publicity campaign. Assessing the change requires measuring the before-and-after levels of these measures. The Potato Board learned, for example, that the number of people who agreed with the statement "Potatoes are rich in vitamins and minerals" went from 36 percent before its public relations campaign to 67 percent after the campaign. That change represented a large increase in product knowledge.

Sales and profit impact, if obtainable, is the best measure of public relations effort. For example, 9 Lives sales increased 43 percent at the end of a major "Morris the Cat" publicity campaign. However, advertising and sales promotion also had been stepped up, and their contribution had to be considered.

## SUMMARY

Three major tools of mass promotion are advertising, sales promotion, and public relations. They are mass-marketing tools, as opposed to personal selling, which targets specific buyers.

*Advertising*—the use of paid media by a seller to inform, persuade, and remind about its products or organization—is a strong promotion tool. American marketers spend more than $150 billion each year on advertising, and it takes many forms and has many uses. *Advertising decision making* consists of decisions about the objectives, the budget, the message, the media, and, finally, the evaluation of results. Advertisers should set clear *objectives* as to whether the advertising is supposed to inform, persuade, or remind buyers. The advertising *budget* can be based on what is affordable, on a percentage of sales, on competitors' spending, or on the objectives and tasks. The *message decision* calls for planning a message strategy and executing it effectively. The *media decision* calls for defining reach, frequency, and impact goals; choosing major media types; selecting media vehicles; and deciding on media timing. Message and media decisions must be closely coordinated for maximum campaign effectiveness. Finally, *evaluation* calls for evaluating the communication and sales effects of advertising before, during, and after the advertising is placed.

*Sales promotion* covers a wide variety of short-term incentive tools—coupons, premiums, contests, buying allowances—designed to stimulate final and business consumers, the trade, and the company's own sales force. Sales-promotion spending has been growing faster than advertising spending in recent years. Sales promotion calls for setting sales-promotion objectives; selecting tools; developing and implementing the sales-promotion program; and evaluating the results.

*Public relations*—gaining favorable publicity and creating a favorable company image—is the least used of the major promotion tools, although it has great potential for building awareness and preference. Public relations involves setting PR objectives, choosing PR messages and vehicles, implementing the PR plan, and evaluating PR results.

## KEY TERMS

Advertising
Advertising agency
Advertising objective
Advertising specialties
Allowance
Cash refund offers (rebates)
Comparison advertising

Contests, sweepstakes, games
Coupons
Discount
Informative advertising
Media vehicles
Patronage rewards
Persuasive advertising

Point-of-purchase promotions (POP)
Premiums
Price packs (cents-off deals)
Public relations
Reminder advertising
Sales promotion
Samples

## QUESTIONS FOR DISCUSSION

1. Contrast the benefits and drawbacks of comparison advertising. Which has more to gain from using comparison advertising: the leading brand in a market or a lesser brand? Why?

2. Explain what factors call for more *frequency* in an advertising media schedule, and what factors call for more *reach*. How can you increase one without sacrificing the other or increasing the advertising budget?

3. Companies often run advertising, sales promotion, and public relations efforts at the same time. Can their effects be separated? Discuss how a company might evaluate the effectiveness of each element in this mix.

4. Manufacturers distribute coupons nearly every week in some product categories, such as coffee, breakfast cereal, and snack foods. Does this affect brand loyalty? In what ways?

5. Assess why many companies are spending more on trade promotions and consumer promotions than on advertising. Is heavy spending on sale promotions a good strategy for long-term profits? Why or why not?

6. The newest public relations frontier is located on the Internet. Cyberspace travelers are posting their problems with goods and services on electronic bulletin boards and causing companies to respond to their pressure. For example, the Intel Corporation found itself in the middle of a public relations flap over its flawed Pentium chip. User dissatisfaction with the chip was first voiced on an Internet "news group" and ultimately led Intel to recall the chip. What kinds of special problems do you think that companies will face as they deal with public relations issues in cyberspace?

## APPLYING THE CONCEPTS

1. Buy a Sunday paper and look through the color advertising and coupon inserts. Find several examples that combine advertising, sales, promotion, and/or public relations. For instance, a manufacturer may run a full-page ad that also includes a coupon and information on its sponsorship of a charity event, such as Easter Seals or Special Olympics.

   ◆ Do you think that these approaches using multiple tools are more or less effective than a simple approach? Why?

   ◆ Try to find ads from two direct competitors. Are these brands using similar promotional tools in similar ways?

2. Find two current television advertisements that you think are particularly effective, and two more that you feel are ineffective.

   ◆ Describe precisely why you think the better ads are effective, and why the ineffective ads fall short.

   ◆ How would you improve the less effective ads? If you feel that they are too poor to be improved, write a rough draft of an alternate ad for each.

## REFERENCES

1. Patricia Sellers, "How CAA Bottled Coca-Cola," *Fortune,* November 15, 1993, p. 156.

2. Bob Garfield, "Coke Ads Great, but Not Always," Advertising Age, February 22, 1993, pp. 1, 60.

3. Bob Garfield, "CAA Casts Perfect Spell in Latest Coca-Cola Ads," *Advertising Age,* February 14, 1994, p. 40.

4. Larry Jabbonsky, "The Return of a Lightning Rod," *Beverage World,* August 1993, p. 6. For more on the development of the Always Coca-Cola campaign, see Melanie Wells and Marcy Magiera, "Coke Features Classic Images," *Advertising Age,* February 14, 1994, p. 5; Kevin Goldman, "Here Comes the Sun: New Icon for Coca-Cola Transcends Language," *Wall Street Journal,* April 13, 1995, p. B8; and Mark Gleason, "Coke Classic Steers In-House, via Ovitz," *Advertising Age,* November 13, 1995, pp. 3, 6.

5. Statistical information in this section on advertising's size and composition draws on "Ad Dollars Outside the U.S.," *Advertising Age,* December 14, 1992, p. S1; and the "100 Leading National Advertisers" issue of *Advertising Age,* September 27, 1995.

6. Leah Rickard, "New Ammo for Comparative Ads," *Advertising Age,* February 14, 1994, p. 26; and Gary Levin, "Marketers Get Really Nasty with In-Your-Face Advertising," *Advertising Age,* October 17, 1994, p. 2.

7. Gerard J. Tellis, "Advertising Exposure, Loyalty, and Brand Purchase: A Two-Stage Model of Choice," *Journal of Marketing Research,* May 1988, pp. 134–35. For counterpoints, see Magid M. Abraham and Leonard M. Lodish, "Getting the Most Out of Advertising and Promotion," *Harvard Business Review,* May–June 1990, pp. 50–60.

8. Gary Levin, "Tracing Ads' Impact," *Advertising Age,* November 4, 1991, p. 49.

9. Joe Mandese, "Seinfeld is NBC's $1M/Minute-Man," *Advertising Age,* September 18, 1995, pp. 1, 42; and Dottie Enrico, "Pepsi Hits the Spot with Super Bowl Ads," *USA Today,* January 29, 1996, p. 3B.

10. Joe Mandese, "Cost to Make TV Ad Nears Quarter Million," *Advertising Age,* July 4, 1994, pp. 3, 6.

11. "U.S. Agency Brand Ranked by Gross Income," *Advertising Age,* April 10, 1995, p. S8; and "World's Top 50 Advertising Organizations," *Advertising Age,* April 10, 1995, p. S18.

12. Iris Cohen Selinger, "Big Profits, Risks with Incentive Fees," *Advertising Age,* May 15, 1995, p. 3.

13. Michael Lev, "Advertisers Seek Global Messages," *New York Times,* November 18, 1991, p. D9.

14. Philip R. Cateora, *International Marketing,* 7th ed. (Homewood, IL: Irwin, 1990), p. 462.

15. *Ibid.,* p. 475.

16. Cateora, *International Marketing,* pp. 466–67. For other examples, see Dexter Roberts, "Winding Up for the Big Pitch," *Business Week,* October 23, 1995, p. 52.

17. *16th Annual Survey of Promotional Practices,* Donnelly Marketing Inc., Oakbrook Terrace, IL, June 1994, p. 9. Also see *17th Annual Survey of Promotional Practices,* Donnelly Marketing Inc., Oakbrook Terrace, IL, August 1995, pp. 9–15.

18. Jennifer Lawrence, "Free Samples Get Emotional Reception," *Advertising Age,* September 30, 1991, p. 10.

19. "Nestlé Banks on Databases," *Advertising Age,* October 25, 1993, p. 16.

20. Terry Lefton, "Blockbuster Re-Ups 'Bonus Box,'" *Brandweek,* August 9, 1994, p. 3. Also see "Free for All," *Brandweek,* March 13, 1995, p. S5.

21. Larry Armstrong, "Coupon Clippers, Save Your Scissors," *Business Week,* June 20, 1994, pp. 164–66; and "Targeted Couponing Slows Redemption Slide," *Marketing News,* February 12, 1996, p. 11.

22. See "Power to the Key Ring and T-Shirt," *Sales & Marketing Management,* December 1989, p. 14; and J. Thomas Russell and W. Ronald Lane, *Kleppner's Advertising Procedure,* 12th ed. (Englewood Cliffs, NJ: Prentice Hall, 1993), pp. 408–10.

23. See Richard Szathmary, "Trade Shows," *Sales & Marketing Management,* May 1992, pp. 83–84; and Sri-nath Gopalakrishna, Gary L. Lilien, Jerome D. Williams, and Ian Sequeira, "Do Trade Shows Pay Off?" *Journal of Marketing,* July 1995, pp. 75–83.

24. Adapted from Scott M. Cutlip, Allen H. Center, and Glen M. Brown, *Effective Public Relations,* 7th ed. (Englewood Cliffs, NJ: Prentice Hall, 1994), pp. 8–21.

# Chapter 15

# Personal Selling
# and Sales Management

In 1982, Eastman Chemical Company in Kingsport, Tennessee, began a customer-driven quality program called "Customers and Us." As a result, little more than a decade later, Eastman captured a 1993 Malcolm Baldrige National Quality Award for outstanding quality leadership. Eastman's quality program is deceptively simple—it focuses on doing everything possible to improve the quality of the company's relationships with its customers.

Not surprisingly, Eastman's 500 salespeople have played a prominent role in the company's customer-driven quality program and in its winning the Baldrige Award. Eastman knows that its salespeople have to be good at performing the basic selling tasks—finding qualified customers, presenting Eastman's products, and getting orders. And its sales managers must be good at hiring outstanding sales prospects, training them to sell effectively, and motivating them to perform at a high level. Each year, the sales force generates more than $5 billion in sales for Eastman's business units, ranging from packaging plastics and coatings to fine chemicals. However, at Eastman, salespeople do more than simply travel their territories, hawking the company's wares. What makes Eastman's sales force special is its penchant for building and maintaining long-term, mutually profitable *relationships* with the company's 7,000 customers worldwide.

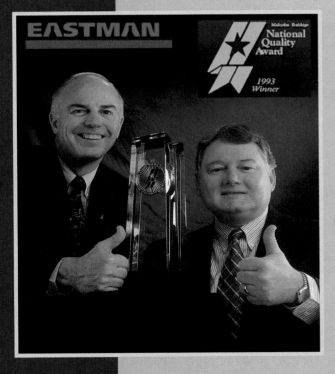

Building strong customer relationships is an important criterion for the Baldrige Award. Among other things, Baldrige examiners look at how a company uses sales contacts to manage customer relationships; how it trains salespeople to understand products, listen to customers, and deal with customer problems and complaints; how it gets information from customers; and how it manages customer's expectations. Eastman's carefully selected, extensively trained salespeople excel at keeping customers satisfied.

The sales force forms a critical link between Eastman and its customers. Given the company's deep dedication to customer satisfaction, the sales force often finds itself in the position of coordinating many of Eastman's 18,000 employees in team efforts focused on improving customer relationships. The acronym for Eastman's customer-driven, team-oriented problem-solving approach is MEPS, which stands for "Making Eastman the Preferred Supplier." The objective of the MEPS program is to improve the processes that link Eastman to its customers. When specific customer problems are found, MEPS teams are formed to solve them. MEPS projects vary widely, but they are all sales driven and customer focused.

One Eastman sales rep, for instance, initiated a MEPS project when a customer was having a persistent problem with black specks in one of its chemical products. The sales rep put together a cross-functional team to study the problem, including people from Eastman's supply and distribution, manufacturing, and product support services groups. The MEPS team solved the problem by recommending that new equipment be installed at the customer's facility. Another project arose when customers complained that they found Eastman's standard "conditions of sale," printed on the back of order sheets, somewhat offensive. The conditions made it sound as though Eastman was saying, "We know you're out to get us, and we're going to make sure you don't." The MEPS team refined and shortened the terms of sale and made them more friendly.

To resolve customer problems, Eastman must first know what they are, so the company tries to make it easy for customers to complain. It asks about complaints on frequent customer satisfaction surveys, encourages salespeople to ask about problems, and provides a 24-hour, toll-free number for receiving complaints. The sales organization is responsible for managing the customer satisfaction survey, which is printed in nine different languages and administered to customers around the world. On the survey, customers rate Eastman on 25 performance factors, including such things as product quality, pricing practices, on-time and correct delivery, and sharing market information. Salespeople take the survey seriously. Trainees are taught that "the second most important thing they have to do is get their customer satisfaction surveys out to and back from customers," says Eastman's sales training manager. "Number one, of course, is getting orders."

The customer survey provides important feedback, but it has also become one of the sales force's most powerful marketing tools. It is the sales reps' responsibility to discuss survey results with customers. It is also the reps' job to let customers know what Eastman is doing to fix problems detected by the survey. Thus, according to an Eastman sales executive, "The survey results give you something you can go back and talk about to customers over three or four visits." More importantly, customers appreciate the survey. It shows that Eastman is listening to them and working hard to satisfy their needs. As one customer notes, "The survey is just a piece of paper. . . . What I value is the professional courtesy, the fact that [Eastman] follows up continually. . . ."

Thus, Eastman's salespeople have learned that the best way to keep getting orders is to build long-term relationships with customers. The company's focus on quality and customer satisfaction has given its sales force renewed energy and a new sense of purpose. "At one time, I would have called them stodgy," says the buyer at Tectonic Industries, which does about $3 million in business with Eastman each year. "Now they're aggressive, eager to do a good job, and you don't have to chase after them."[1]  ■

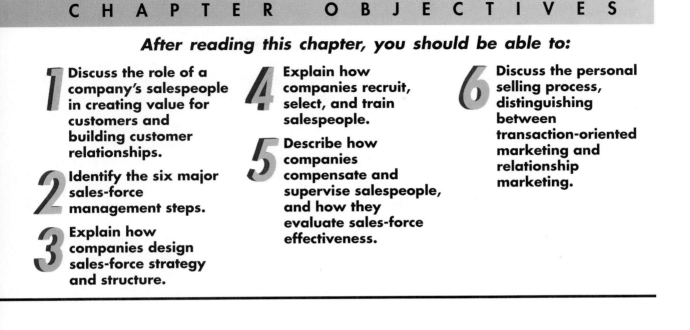

C H A P T E R   O B J E C T I V E S

## After reading this chapter, you should be able to:

**1** Discuss the role of a company's salespeople in creating value for customers and building customer relationships.

**2** Identify the six major sales-force management steps.

**3** Explain how companies design sales-force strategy and structure.

**4** Explain how companies recruit, select, and train salespeople.

**5** Describe how companies compensate and supervise salespeople, and how they evaluate sales-force effectiveness.

**6** Discuss the personal selling process, distinguishing between transaction-oriented marketing and relationship marketing.

Robert Louis Stevenson once noted that "everyone lives by selling something." We are all familiar with the sales forces employed by business organizations to sell products and services to customers around the world. But sales forces are also found in many other kinds of organizations. For example, colleges use recruiters to attract new students, and churches use membership committees to attract new members. Hospitals and museums use fundraisers to contact donors and raise money. Even governments use sales forces. The U.S. Postal Service, for instance, uses a sales force to sell Express Mail and other services to corporate customers, and the Agricultural Extension Service sends out agricultural specialists to sell farmers on new farming methods. In this chapter, we examine the role of personal selling in the organization, sales-force management decisions, and basic principles of personal selling.

## ▶THE ROLE OF PERSONAL SELLING

There are many types of personal selling jobs, and the role of personal selling can vary greatly from one company to another. Here, we look at the nature of personal selling positions and at the role that the sales force plays in modern marketing organizations.

## THE NATURE OF PERSONAL SELLING

Selling is one of the oldest professions in the world. The people who do the selling go by many names: *salespeople, sales representatives, account executives, sales consultants, sales engineers, agents, district managers,* and *marketing representatives,* to name just a few.

People hold many stereotypes of salespeople—including some unfavorable ones. "Salesman" may bring to mind the image of Arthur Miller's pitiable Willy Loman in the play *Death of a Salesman*. Or you might think of Meredith Willson's cigar-smoking, back-slapping, joke-telling Harold Hill in *The Music Man*. Both examples depict salespeople as loners, traveling their territories trying to foist their wares on unsuspecting or unwilling buyers.

However, modern salespeople are a far cry from these unfortunate stereotypes. Today, most salespeople are well-educated, well-trained professionals who work to build and maintain long-term relationships with customers. They build these relationships by listening to their customers, assessing customer needs, and organizing the company's efforts to solve customer problems. Consider Boeing, the aerospace giant that dominates the worldwide commercial aircraft market with a 55 percent market share. It takes more than a friendly smile, some patter, and a handshake to sell multimillion-dollar airplanes:

> Selling high-tech aircraft at $70 million or more a copy is complex and challenging. A single big sale can easily run into the billions of dollars. Boeing salespeople head up an extensive team of company specialists— sales and service technicians, financial analysts, planners, engineers— all dedicated to finding ways to satisfy airline customer needs. The salespeople begin by becoming experts on the airlines, much like Wall Street analysts would. They find out where each airline wants to grow, when it wants to replace planes, and details of its financial situation. The team runs Boeing and competing planes through computer systems, simulating the airline's routes, cost per seat, and other factors to show that their planes are most efficient. Then the high-level negotiations begin. The selling process is nerve-rackingly slow—it can take two or three years from the first sales presentation to the day the sale is announced. Sometimes top executives from both the airline and Boeing are brought in to close the deal. After getting the order, salespeople then must stay in almost constant touch to keep track of the account's equipment needs and to make certain the customer stays satisfied. Success depends on building solid, long-term relationships with customers, based on performance and trust. According to one analyst, Boeing's salespeople "are the vehicle by which information is collected and contacts are made so all other things can take place."[2]

**Salesperson**
An individual acting for a company by performing one or more of the following activities: prospecting, communicating, servicing, and information gathering.

The term **salesperson** covers a wide range of positions. At one extreme, a salesperson might be simply an *order taker*, such as the department store salesperson standing behind the counter. At the other extreme are *order getters*, salespeople whose positions demand the *creative selling* of products and services ranging from appliances, industrial equipment, or airplanes to insurance, advertising, or consulting services. Other salespeople engage in *missionary selling*: These salespeople are not expected or permitted to take an order, but only build goodwill or educate buyers. An example is a salesperson for a pharmaceutical company who calls on doctors to educate them about the company's drug products and to urge them to prescribe these products to their patients.[3] In this chapter, we focus on the more creative types of selling and on the process of building and managing an effective sales force.

*The term "salesper-son" covers a wide range of positions, from the clerk selling in a retail store to the engineering salesper-son who consults with client companies.*

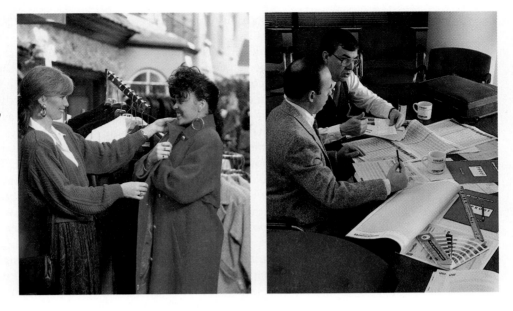

# THE ROLE OF THE SALES FORCE

Personal selling is the interpersonal arm of the promotion mix. Advertising consists of one-way, nonpersonal communication with target consumer groups. In contrast, personal selling involves two-way, personal communication between salespeople and individual customers—whether face-to-face, by telephone, through video conferences, or by other means. This means that personal selling can be more effective than advertising in more complex selling situations. Salespeople can probe customers to learn more about their problems. They can adjust the marketing offer to fit the special needs of each customer and can negotiate terms of sale. They can build long-term personal relationships with key decision makers.

The role of personal selling varies from company to company. Some firms have no salespeople at all—for example, companies that sell only through mail-order catalogs, or companies that sell through manufacturer's reps, sales agents, or brokers. In most firms, however, the sales force plays a major role. In companies that sell business products, such as Xerox or Du Pont, the company's salespeople work directly with customers. In fact, to many customers, salespeople may be the only contact. To these customers, the sales force *is* the company. In consumer product companies such as Procter & Gamble or Wilson Sporting Goods that sell through intermediaries, final consumers rarely meet salespeople or even know about them. Still, the sales force plays an important behind-the-scenes role. It works with wholesalers and retailers to gain their support and to help them be more effective in selling the company's products.

The sales force serves as a critical link between a company and its customers. In many cases, salespeople serve both masters—the seller and the buyer. First, they *represent the company to customers.* They find and develop new customers and communicate information about the company's products and services. They sell products by approaching customers, presenting their products, answering objections, negotiating prices and terms, and closing sales. In addition, salespeople provide services to customers, carry out market research and intelligence work, and fill out sales call reports.

At the same time, salespeople *represent customers to the company,* acting inside the firm as "champions" of customers' interests. Salespeople relay customer concerns about company products and actions back to those who can handle them. They learn about customer needs, and work with others in the company to develop greater customer value. Thus, the salesperson often acts as an account manager who manages the relationship between the seller and buyer.

As companies move toward a stronger market orientation, their sales forces are becoming more market focused and customer oriented. The old view was that salespeople should be concerned with sales and the company should be concerned with profit. However, the current view holds that salespeople should be concerned with more than just producing *sales*—they must also know how to produce *customer satisfaction* and *company profit.* They should be able to look at sales data, measure market potential, gather market intelligence, and develop marketing strategies and plans. They should know how to orchestrate the firm's efforts toward delivering customer value and satisfaction. A market-oriented rather than a sales-oriented sales force will be more effective in the long run. Beyond winning new customers and making sales, it will help the company to create long-term, profitable relationships with customers.

## ▶ MANAGING THE SALES FORCE

**Sales-force management**
The analysis, planning, implementation, and control of sales-force activities.

We define **sales-force management** as the analysis, planning, implementation, and control of sales-force activities. It includes designing sales-force strategy and structure, and recruiting, selecting, training, compensating, supervising, and evaluating the firm's salespeople. These major sales-force management decisions are shown in Figure 15-1 and are discussed in the following sections.

### DESIGNING SALES-FORCE STRATEGY AND STRUCTURE

Marketing managers face several sales-force strategy and design questions. How should salespeople and their tasks be structured? How big should the sales force be? Should salespeople sell alone or work in teams with other people in the company? Should they sell in the field or by telephone? We address these issues below.

**FIGURE 15-1**
*Major sales-force management decisions*

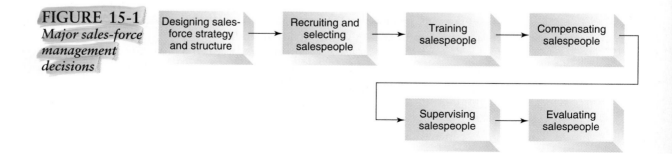

## Sales-Force Structure

A company can divide up sales responsibilities along any of several lines. The decision is simple if the company sells only one product line to one industry with customers in many locations. In that case, the company would use a *territorial sales-force structure*. However, if the company sells many products to many types of customers, it might need either a *product sales-force structure,* a *customer sales-force structure,* or a combination of the two.

**TERRITORIAL SALES-FORCE STRUCTURE.** In the **territorial sales-force structure,** each salesperson is assigned to an exclusive geographic area and sells the company's full line of products or services to all customers in that territory. This sales organization has many advantages. It clearly defines the salesperson's job, and because only one salesperson works the territory, he or she gets all the credit or blame for territory sales. The territorial structure also increases the salesperson's desire to build local business relationships that, in turn, improve selling effectiveness. Finally, because each salesperson travels within a limited geographic area, travel expenses are relatively small.

A territorial sales organization is often supported by many levels of sales management positions. For example, Campbell Soup uses a territorial structure in which each salesperson is responsible for selling all Campbell Soup products. Starting at the bottom of the organization, *sales merchandisers* report to *sales representatives,* who report to *retail supervisors,* who report to *directors of retail sales operations,* who report to one of twenty-two *regional sales managers.* Regional sales managers, in turn, report to one of four *general sales managers* (West, Central, South, and East), who report to a *vice president and general sales manager.*

**PRODUCT SALES-FORCE STRUCTURE.** Salespeople must know their products—especially when the products are numerous and complex. This need, together with the growth of product management, has led many companies to adopt a **product sales-force structure,** in which the sales force sells along product lines. For example, Kodak uses different sales forces for its film products than for its industrial products. The film-products sales force deals with simple products that are distributed intensively, whereas the industrial-products sales force deals with complex products that require technical understanding.

The product structure can lead to problems, however, if a single large customer buys many different company products. For example, Baxter International, a hospital supply company, has several product divisions, each with a separate sales force. Several Baxter salespeople might end up calling on the same hospital on the same day. This means that they travel over the same routes and wait to see the same customer's purchasing agents. These extra costs must be compared with the benefits of better product knowledge and attention to individual products.

**CUSTOMER SALES-FORCE STRUCTURE.** More and more companies are now using a **customer sales-force structure,** in which they organize the sales force along customer or industry lines. Separate sales forces may be set up for different industries, for serving current customers versus finding new ones, and for major accounts versus regular accounts.

Organizing the sales force around customers can help a company to become more customer focused and build closer relationships with important customers. For example, giant ABB, the $29-billion-a-year Swiss-based industrial equipment maker, recently changed from a product-based to a customer-based sales force. The

**Territorial sales-force structure**
A sales-force organization that assigns each salesperson to an exclusive geographic territory in which that salesperson carries the company's full line.

**Product sales-force structure**
A sales-force organization under which salespeople specialize in selling only a portion of the company's products or lines.

**Customer sales-force structure**
A sales-force organization under which salespeople specialize in selling only to certain customers or industries.

new structure resulted in a stronger customer orientation and improved service to clients:

> Until four months ago, David Donaldson sold boilers for ABB. . . . After 30 years, Donaldson sure knew boilers, but he didn't know much about the broad range of other products offered by ABB's U.S. Power Plant division. Customers were frustrated because as many as a dozen ABB salespeople called on them at different times to peddle their products. ABB's bosses decided that this was a poor way to run a salesforce. So [recently], David Donaldson and 27 other power plant salespeople began new jobs. [Donaldson] now also sells turbines, generators, and three other product lines. He handles six major accounts . . . instead of a [mixed batch] of 35. His charge: Know the customer intimately and sell him the products that help him operate productively. Says Donaldson: "My job is to make it easy for my customer to do business with us. . . . I show him where to go in ABB whenever he has a problem." The president of ABB's power plant businesses [adds]: "If you want to be a customer-driven company, you have to design the sales organization around individual buyers rather than around your products."[4]

**COMPLEX SALES-FORCE STRUCTURES.** When a company sells a wide variety of products to many types of customers over a broad geographical area, it often combines several types of sales-force structures. Salespeople can be specialized by customer and territory, by product and territory, by product and customer, or by territory, product, and customer. No single structure is best for all companies and situations. Each company should select a sales-force structure that best serves the needs of its customers and fits its overall marketing strategy.

## Sales-Force Size

Once the company has set its structure, it is ready to consider *sales-force size*. Salespeople constitute one of the company's most productive—and most expensive—assets. Therefore, increasing their number will increase both sales and costs.

Many companies use some form of **workload approach** to set sales-force size. Using this approach, a company first groups accounts into different classes according to size, account status, or other factors related to the amount of effort required to maintain them. It then determines the number of salespeople needed to call on each class of accounts the desired number of times. The company might think as follows: Suppose that we have 1,000 Type-A accounts and 2,000 Type-B accounts. Type-A accounts require 36 calls a year, and Type-B accounts require 12 calls a year. In this case, the sales force's *workload*—the number of calls it must make per year—is 60,000 calls [(1,000 × 36) + (2,000 × 12) = 36,000 + 24,000 = 60,000]. Suppose that our average salesperson makes 1,000 calls a year. Thus, the company needs 60 salespeople (60,000 ÷ 1,000).

## Other Sales-Force Strategy and Structure Issues

Sales management must also decide who will be involved in the selling effort and how various sales and sales-support people will work together.

**OUTSIDE AND INSIDE SALES FORCES.** The company may have an **outside sales force** (or *field sales force*), an **inside sales force**, or both. Outside salespeople travel to call on customers. Inside salespeople conduct business from their offices via telephone or visits from prospective buyers.

---

**Workload approach**
An approach to setting sales-force size in which the company groups accounts into different classes and then determines how many salespeople are needed to call on them the desired number of times.

**Outside sales force (or field sales force)**
Outside salespeople who travel to call on customers.

**Inside sales force**
Salespeople who conduct business from their offices via telephone or visits from prospective buyers.

To reduce time demands on their outside sales forces, many companies have increased the size of their inside sales forces. Inside salespeople include technical support people, sales assistants, and telemarketers. *Technical support people* provide technical information and answers to customers' questions. *Sales assistants* provide clerical backup for outside salespeople. They call ahead and confirm appointments, conduct credit checks, follow up on deliveries, and answer customers' questions when outside salespeople cannot be reached. *Telemarketers* use the phone to find new leads and qualify prospects for the field sales force, or to sell and service accounts directly.

The inside sales force frees outside salespeople to spend more time selling to major accounts and finding major new prospects. Depending on the complexity of the product and customer, a telemarketer makes from 20 to 33 decision-maker contacts a day, compared with the average of four that an outside salesperson makes. And for many types of products and selling situations, **telemarketing** can be as effective as a personal call but much less expensive. For example, whereas a typical personal sales call can cost well over $200, a routine industrial telemarketing call costs only about $5 and a complex call about $20.[5] Telemarketing can be used successfully by both large and small companies:

> Du Pont uses experienced former field salespeople as telesales reps to help sell the company's complex chemical and specialty products. Housed in Du Pont's state-of-the-art Customer Telecontact Center, telemarketers handle technical questions from customers, smooth out product and distribution problems, and alert field sales reps to hot prospects. Notes one Du Pont telemarketer: "I'm more effective on the phone. [When you're in the field], if some guy's not in his office, you lose an hour. On the phone, you lose 15 seconds. Through my phone calls, I'm

**Telemarketing**
Using the telephone to sell directly to consumers.

*Experienced telemarketers sell complex business-to-business products by phone at Du Pont's Corporate Telemarketing Center. Says one: "I'm more effective on the phone . . . and you don't have to outrun the dogs."*

in the field as much as the rep is, and I can cover a considerably larger territory."[6]

Climax Portable Machine Tools has proven that a small company can use telemarketing to save money and still lavish attention on buyers. Under the old system, Climax sales engineers spent one-third of their time on the road, training distributor salespeople and accompanying them on calls. They could make about four contacts a day. Now, each of five sales engineers on Climax's telemarketing team calls about 30 prospects a day, following up on leads generated by ads and direct mail. Because it takes about five calls to close a sale, the sales engineers update a prospect's computer file after each contact, noting the degree of commitment, requirements, next call date, and personal comments. "If anyone mentions he's going on a fishing trip, our sales engineer enters that in the computer and uses it to personalize the next phone call," says Climax's president, noting that's just one way to build good relations. Another is that the first mailing to a prospect includes the sales engineer's business card with his picture on it. Of course, it takes more than friendliness to sell $15,000 machine tools over the phone (special orders may run $200,000), but the telemarketing approach is working well. When Climax customers were asked, "Do you see the sales engineer often enough?" the response was overwhelmingly positive. Obviously, many people didn't realize that the only contact they'd had with Climax had been on the phone.[7]

**TEAM SELLING.** The days when a single salesperson handled a large and important customer are vanishing rapidly. Today, as products become more complex, and as customers grow larger and more demanding, one person simply cannot handle all of a large customer's needs anymore. Instead, most companies now are using **team selling** to service large, complex accounts. Sales teams might include personnel from sales, marketing, engineering, finance, technical support, and even upper management. For example, Procter & Gamble assigns teams consisting of salespeople, marketing managers, technical service people, and logistics and information-systems specialists to work closely with large retail customers such as Wal-Mart, Kmart, and Target. In such team-selling situations, salespeople become "orchestrators" who help coordinate a whole-company effort to build profitable relationships with important customers (see Marketing at Work 15-1).[8]

Yet companies recognize that simply asking their employees for teamwork does not produce it. They must revise their compensation and recognition systems to give credit for work on shared accounts, and they must set up better goals and measures for sales-force performance. They must emphasize the importance of teamwork in their training programs, while at the same time honoring the importance of individual initiative.

**Team selling**
Using teams of people from sales, marketing, engineering, finance, technical support, and even upper management to service large, complex accounts.

# RECRUITING AND SELECTING SALESPEOPLE

At the heart of any successful sales-force operation is the recruitment and selection of good salespeople. The performance difference between an average salesperson and a top salesperson can be substantial. According to one study, sales superstars sell an average of 1.5 to 2 times more than the average salesperson.[9] In a typical sales force, the top 30 percent of the salespeople might bring in 60 percent of the sales. Thus, careful salesperson selection can greatly increase over-all sales-force performance.

Beyond the differences in sales performance, poor selection results in costly turnover. One study found an average annual sales-force turnover rate of 27 per-cent for all industries. The costs of high turnover can be great. When a salesper-son quits, the costs of finding and training a new salesperson—plus the costs of lost sales—can run as high as $50,000 to $75,000. And a sales force with many new people is less productive.[10]

### What Makes a Good Salesperson?

Selecting salespeople would not be a problem if the company knew what traits to look for. If it knew that good salespeople were outgoing, aggressive, and energetic, for example, it could simply check applicants for these characteristics. But many successful salespeople are bashful, soft-spoken, and laid back.

Still, the search continues for the magic list of traits that spells sure-fire sales success. One survey suggests that good salespeople have a lot of enthusiasm, per-sistence, initiative, self-confidence, and job commitment. They are committed to sales as a way of life and have a strong customer orientation. Another study sug-gests that good salespeople are independent and self-motivated, and are excellent listeners. Still another study advises that salespeople should be a friend to the cus-tomer as well as persistent, enthusiastic, attentive, and—above all—honest. They must be internally motivated, disciplined, hard-working, and able to build strong relationships with customers.[11]

How can a company find out what traits salespeople in its industry should have? Job *duties* suggest some of the traits a company should look for. Are a lot of planning and paperwork required? Does the job call for much travel? Will the salesperson face a lot of rejections? Will the salesperson be working with high-level buyers? The successful salesperson should be suited to these duties. The com-pany should also look at the characteristics of its most successful salespeople for clues to needed traits.

### Recruiting Procedures

After management has decided on needed traits, it must *recruit* salespeople. The human resources department looks for applicants by getting recommendations from current salespeople, using employment agencies, placing classified ads, and contacting college students. Until recently, companies sometimes found it hard to sell college students on selling. Many thought that selling was a job and not a profession, that salespeople had to be deceitful to be effective, and that selling involved too much insecurity and travel. In addition, some women believed that selling was a man's career. To counter such objections, recruiters now offer high starting salaries and income growth and tout the fact that more than one-fourth of the presidents of large U.S. corporations started out in marketing and sales. They point out that more than 23 percent of all salespeople in the United States are women. Women account for a much higher percentage of the sales force in some industries, such as lodging (63 percent), banking and financial services (53 percent), and health services (52 percent).[12] (See Marketing at Work 15-2.)

## MARKETING AT WORK 15-1

# TEAM SELLING: FROM "SOLOISTS" TO "ORCHESTRATORS"

For years, the customer has been solely in the hands of the salesperson. The salesperson identified the prospect, arranged the call, explored the customer's needs, created and proposed a solution, closed the deal, and turned cheerleader as others delivered what he or she promised. For selling relatively simple products, this approach can work well. But if the products are more complex and the service requirements greater, the salesperson simply can't go it alone. Consider the following example:

*This was Michael Quintano's big chance. The 23-year-old, up-and-coming MCI sales rep had only called on customers billing less than $2,000 a month. Then, from out of the blue, he hit upon Nat Schwartz and Company (NS&C), a china and crystal retail-telemarketer with monthly telephone billings exceeding $7,000. In over his head, he offered MCI veteran Al Rodriguez a split on the commission in return for some help. When the pair visited NS&C headquarters, they found a store*

*filled with nothing but china and crystal. "No way does this store bill $7,000. We'll close this deal in one or two calls," Quintano thought. However, when they were led to a bustling back room filled with telemarketers working the phones, their visions of a quick close were swiftly put on hold. Quintano and Rodriguez realized they would have to expand their sales team. They called on sales manager Stephen Smith and MCI Telecommunications consultant Tom Mantone, who during two meetings with NS&C cleared up questions about technical details such as phone line installations. That smoothed the way for Quintano and Rodriguez to close the deal. Thus, by relying on team selling, Michael Quintano landed the largest account of his career.*

More and more, companies are finding that sales teams can unearth problems, solutions, and sales opportunities that no individual salesperson could. Such teams might include experts from any area or level of the selling firm—sales, marketing, technical and support services, R&D, engineering, operations, finance, and

others. In team selling situations, the salesperson shifts from "soloist" to "orchestrator." One such salesperson puts it in sports terms. "It's my job to be the quarterback. [Taking care of a large customer] gets farmed out to different areas of the company, and different questions have to be answered by different people. We set up a game plan and then go in and make the call."

Some companies, like IBM and Xerox, have used teams for a long time. Others have only recently reorganized to adopt the team concept. John Hancock, for example, recently set up sales-and-service teams in six territories. Each team is led by a director of sales who acts as a mini-CEO, managing all aspects of customer contact: sales, service, and technical support. The result is an informed, dedicated team that is closer to the customer.

When a customer's business becomes so complex that a

## Selecting Salespeople

Recruiting will attract many applicants, from whom the company must select the best. The selection procedure can vary from a single informal interview to lengthy testing and interviewing. Many companies give formal tests to sales applicants. Tests typically measure sales aptitude, analytical and organizational skills, personality traits, and other characteristics. Test results count heavily in such companies as IBM, Prudential, Procter & Gamble, and Gillette. Gillette claims that tests have reduced turnover by 42 percent and that test scores have correlated well with the later performance of new salespeople. But test scores provide only one piece of information in a set that includes personal characteristics, references, past employment history, and interviewer reactions.[13]

single company's sales organization can't provide a complete solution, firms might even create multicompany sales teams. For example, teams from MCI, IBM, and Rolm recently joined forces in an effort to provide solutions to a large customer that was setting up a complex data-application network. MCI's team provided information on data communication, IBM's on computer hardware and software, and Rolm's on switching equipment. "The meeting provided the customer with one point of contact to solve a variety of needs," said an MCI sales executive.

Some companies have even opened special sites for team sales meetings, called *executive briefing centers*. Xerox runs six of these centers. Xerox sales teams invite key people from important accounts to one of the centers, where center staff conduct briefings, arrange video conferences with experts in other parts of the country, and provide other services that help the team build business and improve customer service.

Team selling does have some pitfalls. For example, selling teams can confuse or overwhelm customers who are used to working with only one salesperson. Salespeople who are used to having customers all to themselves may have trouble learning to work with and trust others on a team. Finally, difficulties in evaluating individual contributions to the team selling effort can create some sticky compensation issues.

Still, team selling can produce dramatic results. For example, Dun & Bradstreet, the world's largest marketer of business information and related services, recently established sales teams made up of representatives from its credit, collection, and marketing business units, which up to then had worked separately. Their mission was to work as a team to call on executives in customer organizations, learn about customer needs, and offer solutions. The teams concentrated on D&B's top 50 customers. When one of the D&B sales teams asked to

meet with the chief financial officer of a major telecommunications company, the executive responded, "I'm delighted you asked, but why talk?" He found out after a one-hour meeting. The D&B team listened as he discussed problems facing his organization, and by the end of the information-seeking session, the team had come up with several solutions for the executive, and had identified $1.5 million in D&B sales opportunities from what had been a $700,000 customer. More teams met with more clients, creating more opportunities. About a year after the program started, D&B's marketing department had targeted $200 million in sales opportunities, about half of which would not have been found under the old system. Now these teams are getting together with D&B's top 200 customers.

*Sources:* Portions adapted from Joseph Conlin, "Teaming Up," *Sales & Marketing Management*, October 1993, pp. 98–104; and Richard C. Whiteley, "Orchestrating Service," *Sales & Marketing Management*, April 1994, pp. 29–30. Also see Christopher Meyer, "How the Right Measures Help Teams Excel," *Harvard Business Review*, May–June 1994, pp. 95–103.

## TRAINING SALESPEOPLE

Many companies used to send their new salespeople into the field almost immediately after hiring them. They would be given samples, order books, and general instructions ("sell west of the Mississippi"). Training programs were luxuries. To many companies, a training program translated into much expense for instructors, materials, space, and salary for a person who was not yet selling, and a loss of sales opportunities because the person was not in the field.

Today's new salespeople, however, may spend anywhere from a few weeks or months to a year or more in training. The average training period is four months. Norton Company, the industrial abrasives manufacturer, puts its new salespeople through a 12-month training program. The first six months are spent at company

## MARKETING AT WORK 15-2

# On the Job with Two Successful Saleswomen

The word *salesman* now has an archaic ring. The entry of women into what was once the male bastion of professional selling has been swift and dramatic. More than 28 percent of people selling industrial products are women, compared with just 7 percent in 1975. In some industries, this percentage reaches as high as 60 percent. Here are two examples of highly successful technical saleswomen.

### CATHERINE HOGAN, ACCOUNT MANAGER, BELL ATLANTIC NETWORK SERVICES

As an undergraduate student, Catherine Hogan had few thoughts about a career in sales, especially *technical* sales. "I was a warm, fuzzy person," she says, "artsy-craftsy." Now, just six years later, she's in the thick of it, successfully handling a complex line of technical products in what was once a male-dominated world.

Why the change? "I needed to get out there and feel the heat—take risks, handle customers, and be responsible for their complaints," says Hogan. Still far from being a technical person, she has quickly acquired a working knowledge of modern communications services and the ways they can be delivered to businesses through Bell Atlantic's phone network.

So rapidly is the company diversifying that, artsy-craftsy or not, Hogan finds herself studying up on new hardware, software, and leasing programs so she can explain them both to business customers and to Bell's own account executives, who have ongoing responsibilities for those customers. The account executives can handle their customers' local applications by themselves,

*Successful saleswomen Catherine Hogan and Joyce Nardone—the word "salesman" now has an archaic ring.*

headquarters, with the remaining time spent out in the field. The initial period focuses on selling skills, product knowledge, the company, and the distributors that sell Norton products. Salespeople even spend two weeks with a Norton distributor. Among other things, they learn that distributors have dozens of salespeople calling on them all the time. After initial training, every year Norton brings back about a third of its 200 salespeople to company headquarters to undergo follow-up training.[14]

Training programs have several goals. Salespeople need to know and identify with the company, so most training programs begin by describing the company's history and objectives, its organization, its financial structure and facilities, and its chief products and markets. Salespeople also need to know the company's products, so sales trainees are shown how products are produced and how they work. They also need to know customers' and competitors' characteristics, so the training program teaches them about competitors' strategies and about different types of customers and their needs, buying motives, and buying habits. Because

but they work with Hogan when customers want long-distance voice or data services. This sort of team selling requires empathy and skill. On joint calls, Hogan is careful not to interfere when the account executive is negotiating with a customer.

On a more personal level, Hogan has worked through the pros and cons of being something of a novelty in an industry that is undergoing wrenching change. "People are used to seeing middle-age, white males with a technical background in this industry," she says. "It's challenging being young, female, and ethnic." Her advice to others in similar situations? "Go beyond what the world prescribes for you. Be strong enough to lance the dragon but soft enough to wear silk."

**JOYCE NARDONE, SALES MANAGER, FACSIMILE DIVISION, AMFAX AMERICA**
For a vivid picture of what it takes to succeed in sales, listen to

Joyce Nardone exclaim about the terrors and triumphs of selling to strangers who've never heard your name before you walk in the door. "I'm good at cold-calling, but it takes a long time to learn to take rejection," she says. "Sometimes just getting out of the car is a feat in itself."

So resilient is the 24-year-old Joyce, however, that prior to her recent promotion to management, she compiled an impressive record of knocking on doors for Amfax America, an office equipment dealer whose main line is Sharp facsimile machines and copiers. "You have to be friendly and upbeat," she says. "If you look like a winner, they'll buy from you."

As good as she is at cold-calling, Nardone adds a special ingredient in a business that traditionally has been built around the one-time sale: She keeps up with her customers and makes sure they're satisfied with the product. "I have over 100 clients, and I consider them my

friends," she says. "Most people don't bother to go back, but I'll bring them a free roll of paper or fax them a Hanukkah or Christmas card." As a result, customers often refer other companies to Nardone, so she has a steady stream of new business.

Fortunately, management recognizes her talents, too. Nardone is now in charge of the sales force for Amfax's Facsimile Division. As manager, she is responsible for training, motivation, and overall performance of eight direct salespeople. She also coordinates advertising and trade show exhibits. Her advice to new salespeople? "To discover customers' needs, *listen* to them!"

*Sources:* Adapted from portions of Martin Everett, "Selling's New Breed: Smart and Feisty," *Sales & Marketing Management,* October 1989, pp. 52–64. Also see Bill Kelley, "Selling in a Man's World," *Sales & Marketing Management,* January 1991, pp. 28–35; "What's Selling? Sales Jobs," *Sales & Marketing Management,* September 1993, p. 11; and Nancy Arnott, "It's a Woman's World," *Sales & Marketing Management,* March 1995, pp. 55–59.

salespeople must know how to make effective presentations, they are trained in the principles of selling. Finally, salespeople need to understand field procedures and responsibilities. They learn how to divide time between active and potential accounts and how to use an expense account, prepare reports, and route communications effectively.

## COMPENSATING SALESPEOPLE

To attract salespeople, a company must have an appealing compensation plan. These plans vary greatly both by industry and by companies within the same industry. The level of compensation must be close to the "going rate" for the type of sales job and needed skills. For example, the average earnings of an experienced, middle-level industrial salesperson amount to about $47,000.[15] To pay less than the going rate would attract too few quality salespeople; to pay more would be an unnecessary expense for the company.

Compensation is made up of several elements—a fixed amount, a variable amount, expenses, and fringe benefits. The fixed amount, usually a salary, gives the salesperson some stable income. The variable amount, which might be commissions or bonuses based on sales performance, rewards the salesperson for greater effort. Expense allowances, which repay salespeople for job-related expenses, let salespeople undertake needed and desirable selling efforts. Fringe benefits, such as paid vacations, sickness or accident benefits, pensions, and life insurance, provide job security and satisfaction.

Management must decide what *mix* of these compensation elements makes the most sense for each sales job. Different combinations of fixed and variable compensation give rise to four basic types of compensation plans—straight salary, straight commission, salary plus bonus, and salary plus commission. A study of sales-force compensation plans showed that about 14 percent of companies paid straight salary, 19 percent paid straight commission, 26 percent paid salary plus bonus, 37 percent paid salary plus commission, and 10 percent paid salary plus commission plus bonus.[16]

The sales-force compensation plan can both motivate salespeople and direct their work. For example, if sales management wants salespeople to emphasize new account development, it might pay a bonus for opening new accounts. Thus, the compensation plan should direct the sales force toward achieving goals that are consistent with overall marketing objectives. Table 15-1 illustrates how a company's compensation plan should reflect its overall marketing strategy. For example, if the overall strategy is to grow rapidly and gain market share, the compensation plan should reward high sales performance and encourage salespeople to capture new accounts. This might translate into a larger commission component coupled with new account bonuses. In contrast, if the marketing goal is to max-

**TABLE 15-1**    *The Relationship between Overall Marketing Strategy and Sales-Force Compensation*

| | Strategic Goal | | |
| --- | --- | --- | --- |
| | **To Rapidly Gain Market Share** | **To Solidify Market Leadership** | **To Maximize Profitability** |
| Ideal Salesperson | • An independent self-starter | • A competitive problem solver | • A team player<br>• A relationship manager |
| Sales Focus | • Deal making<br>• Sustained high effort | • Consultative selling | • Account penetration |
| Compensation Role | • To capture accounts<br>• To reward high performance | • To reward new and existing sales | • To manage the product mix<br>• To encourage team selling<br>• To reward account management |

*Source:* Adapted from Sam T. Johnson, "Sales Compensation: In Search of a Better Solution," *Compensation & Benefits Review,* November–December 1993, pp. 53–60.

imize profitability of current accounts, the compensation plan might contain a larger base salary component, with additional incentives based on current account sales or customer satisfaction.[17]

# SUPERVISING SALESPEOPLE

New salespeople need more than a territory, compensation, and training—they need *supervision*. Through supervision, the company *directs* and *motivates* the sales force to do a better job.

## Directing Salespeople

How much should sales management be involved in helping salespeople manage their territories? It depends on everything from the company's size to the experience of its sales force. Thus, companies vary widely in how closely they supervise their salespeople.

Many companies help their salespeople in identifying customer targets and setting call norms. They classify customers based on sales volume, profit, and growth potential, and then they set call norms accordingly. Companies may also specify how much time their sales forces should spend prospecting for new accounts. If left alone, many salespeople spend most of their time with current customers, who are better-known quantities. Moreover, whereas a prospect may never deliver any business, salespeople can depend on current accounts for some business.

Companies also direct salespeople in how to use their time efficiently. One tool is the *annual call plan* that shows for any given month which customers and prospects to call on and which activities to carry out. Activities include taking part in trade shows, attending sales meetings, and carrying out marketing research. Another tool is *time-and-duty analysis*. In addition to time spent selling, the salesperson spends time traveling, waiting, eating, taking breaks, and doing administrative chores.

Figure 15-2 shows how salespeople spend their time. On average, actual face-to-face selling time accounts for only 30 percent of total working time! If selling time could be raised from 30 percent to 40 percent, this would be a 33 percent increase in the time spent selling. Companies are always on the hunt for ways to save time—using phones instead of traveling, simplifying record-keeping forms, finding better call and routing plans, and supplying more and better customer information.

Many firms have adopted *sales-force automation systems,* computerized sales-force operations for more efficient order-entry transactions, improved customer service, and better salesperson decision-making support. A recent study of 100 large companies found that 48 percent are "actively pursuing" sales-force automation; another 34 percent are planning or considering it.[18] Salespeople use computers to profile customers and prospects, analyze and forecast sales, manage accounts, schedule sales calls, enter orders, check inventories and order status, prepare sales and expense reports, process correspondence, and carry out many other activities. Sales-force automation not only lowers sales-force costs and improves productivity, it also improves the quality of sales management decisions. Here is an example of successful sales-force automation:

> Owens-Corning recently put its salesforce on line with FAST—its newly-developed Field Automation Sales Team system. FAST gives

**FIGURE 15-2**
*How salespeople
spend their time*
Source: Dartnell Corporation; 27th Survey of Sales Force Compensation.
© 1992 Dartnell Corporation.

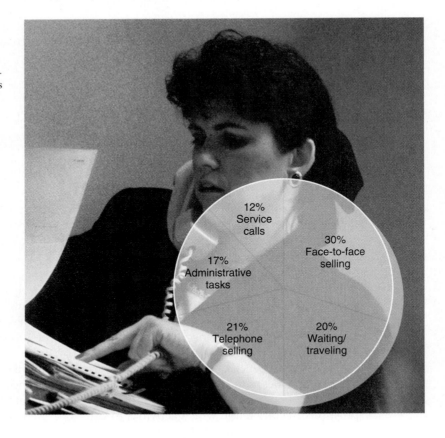

Owens-Corning salespeople a constant supply of information about their company and the people they're dealing with. Using laptop computers, each salesperson can access three types of programs. First, FAST gives them a set of *generic tools,* everything from word processing to fax transmission to creating presentations on-line. Second, it provides *product information*—tech bulletins, customer specifications, pricing information, and other data that can help close a sale. Finally, it offers up a wealth of *customer information*—buying history, types of products ordered, and preferred payment terms. Reps previously stored such information in loose-leaf books, calendars, and account cards. FAST makes working directly with customers easier than ever. Salespeople can prime themselves on backgrounds of clients; call up prewritten sales letters; transmit orders and resolve customer-service issues on the spot during customer calls; and have samples, pamphlets, brochures, and other materials sent to clients with a few keystrokes.[19]

## Motivating Salespeople

Some salespeople will do their best without any special urging from management. To them, selling may be the most fascinating job in the world. But selling can also be frustrating. Salespeople often work alone, and they must sometimes travel away from home. They may face aggressive, competing salespeople and difficult customers. They sometimes lack the authority to do what is needed to win a sale and

*Sales-force auto-mation: Owens-Corning's FAST sales-force automation system makes working directly with customers easier than ever.*

may thus lose large orders that they have worked hard to obtain. Therefore, sales-people often need special encouragement to do their best.

Management can boost sales-force morale and performance through its organizational climate, sales quotas, and positive incentives. *Organizational climate* describes the feeling that salespeople have about their opportunities, value, and rewards for a good performance within the company. Some companies treat sales-people as if they are not very important. Other companies treat their salespeople as their prime movers and allow virtually unlimited opportunity for income and promotion. Not surprisingly, in companies that hold their salespeople in low esteem, there is high turnover and poor performance. Where salespeople are held in high esteem, there is less turnover and higher performance.

**Sales quotas**
Standards set for sales-people, stating the amount they should sell and how sales should be divided among the company's products.

Many companies motivate their salespeople by setting **sales quotas**—standards stating the amount that they should sell and how sales should be divided among the company's products. Compensation is often related to how well sales-people meet their quotas. Sales quotas are set at the time that the annual marketing plan is developed. The company first decides on a sales forecast that is reasonably achievable. Based on this forecast, management plans production, workforce size, and financial needs. It then sets sales quotas for its regions and territories. Generally, sales quotas are set higher than the sales forecast to encourage sales managers and salespeople to give their best effort. If they fail to make their quotas, the company may still make its sales forecast.

Companies also use various *positive incentives* to increase sales-force effort. *Sales meetings* provide social occasions, breaks from routine, chances to meet and talk with "company brass," and opportunities to air feelings and to identify with a larger group. Companies also sponsor *sales contests* to spur the sales force to make a selling effort above what would normally be expected. Other incentives include honors, merchandise and cash awards, trips, and profit-sharing plans.

*Sales-force incentives: Many companies award cash, merchandise, trips, or other gifts as incentives for outstanding sales performance. Here, Sony offers to help companies design their sales-force incentive programs.*

Motivate your sales force by showing them there's gold at the end of the rainbow.

All salespeople are motivated by money. But that's not necessarily the best way to reward them for a job well done. After all, once they put that cash in their wallets, it will probably be spent on everyday bills and groceries.

That's why there's no better way to reward a sales force than with the American Express® Gift Cheque. It's every bit as flexible as cash. But it's more valuable, because it encourages people to go out and get something they truly want. And that makes it a more memorable incentive.

American Express Gift Cheques are also

easy to order and administer. They can be purchased in bulk at special corporate rates and delivered right to you. Or we can help you design a direct fulfillment program, custom-tailored to fit your company's needs.

So when it's time for a sales push, let your sales force know it's also a golden opportunity for them. With the American Express Gift Cheque.

For more information about American Express Gift Cheques and how to get them, call 1-800-777-7332.

**Gift Cheques**

© 1989 American Express Travel Related Services Company, Inc.

# EVALUATING SALESPEOPLE

We have thus far described how management communicates its expectations to salespeople and how it motivates them to fulfill those expectations. This process requires good feedback. And good feedback means getting regular information from salespeople to evaluate their performance.

Management gets information about its salespeople in several ways. The most important source is the *sales report*. Additional information comes from personal observation, customers' letters and complaints, customer surveys, and conversations with other salespeople.

Sales reports are divided into plans for future activities and write-ups of completed activities. The best example of the first is the *work plan* that salespeople submit a week or month in advance. The work plan describes intended calls and routing. From this report, the sales force plans and schedules activities. It also informs management of the salespeople's whereabouts and provides a basis for comparing plans and performance. Salespeople can then be evaluated on their ability to "plan their work and work their plan." Sometimes, managers contact individual salespeople to suggest improvements in work plans.

Companies may also require their salespeople to draft *annual territory marketing plans* in which they outline their plans for building new accounts and increasing sales from existing accounts. Such reports cast salespeople as territory marketing managers. Sales managers study these territory plans, make suggestions, and use the plans to develop sales quotas.

Salespeople write up their completed activities on *call reports*. Call reports keep sales management informed of the salesperson's activities, show what is happening with each customer's account, and provide information that might be useful in later calls. Salespeople also turn in *expense reports* for which they are partly or wholly repaid. Some companies also ask for reports on new business, lost business, and local business and economic conditions. These reports supply the raw data from which sales management can evaluate sales-force performance. Are salespeople making too few calls per day? Are they spending too much time per call? Are they spending too much money on entertainment? Are they closing enough orders per hundred calls? Are they finding enough new customers and holding onto enough old customers?

Sales management may also evaluate salespeople *qualitatively*. It looks at a salesperson's knowledge of the company, products, customers, competitors, territory, and tasks. The sales manager may also review personal traits—manner, appearance, speech, and temperament—as well as any problems in motivation or compliance. Each company must decide on its own criteria.

Using sales-force reports and other information, sales management formally evaluates members of the sales force. Formal evaluation forces management to develop and communicate clear standards for judging performance. It also provides salespeople with constructive feedback and motivates them to perform well.

# ▶PRINCIPLES OF PERSONAL SELLING

We now turn from designing and managing a sales force to the actual personal selling process. Personal selling is an ancient art that has spawned a large body of literature and many principles. Effective salespeople operate on more than just instinct—they are highly trained in methods of territory analysis and customer management.

## THE PERSONAL SELLING PROCESS

Companies spend hundreds of millions of dollars on seminars, books, cassettes, and other materials to teach salespeople the "art" of selling. Millions of books on selling are purchased every year, with tantalizing titles such as *How to Sell Anything to Anybody, How I Raised Myself from Failure to Success in Selling, The Four-Minute Sell, The Best Seller, The Power of Enthusiastic Selling, Where Do You Go from No. 1?,* and *Winning through Intimidation.* One of the most enduring books on selling is Dale Carnegie's *How to Win Friends and Influence People.*

Most companies take a *customer-oriented approach* to personal selling. They train salespeople to identify customer needs and to find solutions. This approach assumes that customer needs provide sales opportunities, that customers appreciate good suggestions, and that customers will be loyal to salespeople who have their long-term interests at heart. One recent survey found that purchasing agents appreciate salespeople who understand their needs and meet them. As one purchasing agent states:

> My *expectation* of salespeople is that they've done their homework, uncovered some of our needs, probed to uncover other needs, and presented convincing arguments of mutual benefits for both organizations. . . . [The problem is that] I don't always see that.[20]

The problem-solver salesperson fits better with the marketing concept than does a hard-sell salesperson. The qualities that purchasing agents *dislike most* in salespeople include being pushy, late, and unprepared or disorganized. The qualities that they *value most* include honesty, dependability, thoroughness, and follow-through.

## STEPS IN THE SELLING PROCESS

**Selling process**
The steps that the salesperson follows when selling, which include prospecting and qualifying, preapproach, approach, presentation and demonstration, handling objections, closing, and follow-up.

Most training programs view the **selling process** as consisting of several steps that the salesperson must master (see Figure 15-3). These steps focus on the goal of getting new customers and obtaining orders from them. However, most salespeople spend much of their time maintaining existing accounts and building long-term customer *relationships*. We discuss the relationship aspect of the personal selling process in the final section of the chapter.

### Prospecting and Qualifying

**Prospecting**
The step in the selling process in which the salesperson identifies qualified potential customers.

The first step in the selling process is **prospecting**—identifying qualified potential customers. The salesperson often has to approach many prospects in order to get just a few sales. Although the company supplies some leads, salespeople need skill in finding their own. They can ask current customers for the names of prospects. They can build referral sources, such as suppliers, dealers, noncompeting salespeople, and bankers. They can join organizations to which prospects belong or can engage in speaking and writing activities that will draw attention. They can search for names in newspapers or directories and use the telephone and mail to track down leads. Or they can drop in unannounced on various offices (a practice known as "cold calling").

Salespeople need to know how to *qualify* leads—that is, how to identify the good ones and screen out the poor ones. Prospects can be qualified by looking at their financial ability, volume of business, special needs, location, and possibilities for growth.[21]

### Preapproach

**Preapproach**
The step in the selling process in which the salesperson learns as much as possible about a prospective customer before making a sales call.

Before calling on a prospect, the salesperson should learn as much as possible about the organization (what it needs, who is involved in the buying) and its buyers (their characteristics and buying styles). This step is known as the **preapproach**. The salesperson can consult standard sources *(Moody's, Standard & Poor's, Dun & Bradstreet)*, acquaintances, and others to learn about the company. The salesperson should set *call objectives*, which may be to qualify the prospect, to gather information, or to make an immediate sale. Another task is to decide on the best approach, which might be a personal visit, a phone call, or a letter. Timing should

**FIGURE 15-3**
*Major steps in effective selling*

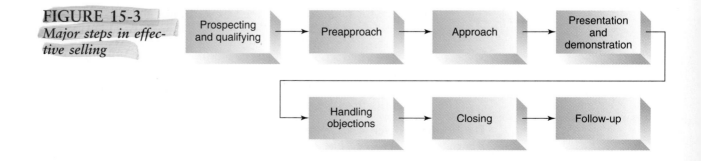

be considered carefully because many prospects are busiest at certain times. Finally, the salesperson should give thought to an overall sales strategy for the account.

### Approach

**Approach**
The step in the selling process in which the salesperson meets and greets the buyer to get the relationship off to a good start.

During the **approach** step, the salesperson should know how to meet and greet the buyer and get the relationship off to a good start. This step involves the salesperson's appearance, opening lines, and the follow-up remarks. The opening lines should be positive, such as "Mr. Johnson, I am Chris Bennett from the Alltech Company. My company and I appreciate your willingness to see me. I will do my best to make this visit profitable and worthwhile for you and your company." This opening might be followed by some key questions to learn more about the customer's needs or by showing a display or sample to attract the buyer's attention and curiosity.

### Presentation and Demonstration

**Presentation**
The step in the selling process in which the salesperson tells the product "story" to the buyer, showing how the product will make or save money for the buyer.

During the **presentation** step of the selling process, the salesperson tells the product "story" to the buyer, showing how the product will make or save money. The salesperson describes the product features but concentrates on presenting customer benefits. Using a *need-satisfaction approach,* the salesperson investigates the customer's needs by getting the customer to do most of the talking. This approach calls for good listening and problem-solving skills. One marketing director describes the approach this way:

> [High-performing salespeople] make it a point to understand customer needs and goals before they pull anything out of their product bag. . . . Such salespeople spend the time needed to get an in-depth knowledge of the customer's business, asking questions that will lead to solutions our systems can address.[22]

Sales presentations can be improved with demonstration aids, such as booklets, flip charts, slides, videotapes or videodiscs, and product samples. If buyers can see or handle the product, they will better remember its features and benefits.

*In the sales presentation, the salesperson tells the product story to the buyers.*

## Handling Objections

Customers almost always have objections during the presentation or when placing an order. The problem can be either logical or psychological, and objections are often unspoken. In **handling objections**, the salesperson should use a positive approach, seek out hidden objections, ask the buyer to clarify any objections, use objections as opportunities to provide more information, and turn the objections into reasons for buying. Every salesperson needs training in the skills of handling objections.

## Closing

After handling the prospect's objections, the salesperson now tries to close the sale. Some salespeople do not get around to **closing** or do not handle it well. They may lack confidence, feel guilty about asking for the order, or fail to recognize the right moment to close the sale. Salespeople should know how to recognize closing signals from the buyer, including physical actions, comments, and questions. For example, the customer might sit forward and nod approvingly or ask about prices and credit terms. Salespeople can use one of several closing techniques. They can ask for the order, review points of agreement, offer to help write up the order, ask whether the buyer wants this model or that one, or note that the buyer will lose out if the order is not placed now. The salesperson may offer the buyer special reasons to close, such as a lower price or an extra quantity at no charge.

## Follow-up

The last step in the selling process—**follow-up**—is necessary if the salesperson wants to ensure customer satisfaction and repeat business. Right after closing, the salesperson should complete any details on delivery time, purchase terms, and other matters. The salesperson should then schedule a follow-up call when the initial order is received to make sure that there is proper installation, instruction, and servicing. This visit should reveal any problems, assure the buyer of the salesperson's interest, and reduce any buyer concerns that might have arisen since the sale.

# RELATIONSHIP MARKETING

The principles of personal selling as just described are *transaction oriented;* their aim is to help salespeople close a specific sale with a customer. But in many cases, the company is not seeking simply a sale; it has targeted a major customer that it would like to win and keep. The company would like to show the customer that it has the capabilities to serve the customer over the long haul, in a mutually profitable *relationship*.

Most companies today are moving away from transaction marketing, with its emphasis on making a sale. Instead, they are practicing **relationship marketing**, which emphasizes maintaining profitable long-term relationships with customers by creating superior customer value and satisfaction. They are realizing that, when operating in maturing markets and facing stiffer competition, it costs a lot more to wrest new customers from competitors than to keep current customers.

Today's customers are large and often global. They prefer suppliers who can sell and deliver a coordinated set of products and services to many locations. They favor suppliers who can quickly solve problems that arise in different parts of the nation or world, and who can work closely with customer teams to improve products and processes. For these customers, the sale is only the beginning of the relationship.

**Handling objections**
The step in the selling process in which the salesperson seeks out, clarifies, and overcomes customer objections to buying.

**Closing**
The step in the selling process in which the salesperson asks the customer for an order.

**Follow-up**
The last step in the selling process in which the salesperson follows up after the sale to ensure customer satisfaction and repeat business.

**Relationship marketing**
The process of creating, maintaining, and enhancing strong, value-laden relationships with customers and other stakeholders.

Unfortunately, some companies are not set up for these developments. They often sell their products through separate sales forces, each working independently to close sales. Their technical people may not be willing to lend time to educate a customer. Their engineering, design, and manufacturing people may have the attitude that "it's our job to make good products and the salesperson's to sell them to customers." However, other companies are recognizing that winning and keeping accounts requires more than making good products and directing the sales force to close lots of sales. It requires a carefully coordinated, whole-company effort to create value-laden, satisfying relationships with important customers.

Relationship marketing is based on the premise that important accounts need focused and continuous attention. Studies have shown that the best salespeople are those who are highly motivated and good closers, but more than this, they are customer-problem solvers and relationship builders (see Marketing at Work 15-3).

## MARKETING AT WORK 15-3

# GREAT SALESPEOPLE—DRIVE, DISCIPLINE, AND RELATIONSHIP BUILDING SKILLS

What sets great salespeople apart from all the rest? What separates the masterful from the merely mediocre? In an effort to profile top sales performers, Gallup Management Consulting, a division of the well-known Gallup polling organization, has interviewed as many as a half million salespeople. Its research suggests that the best salespeople possess four key talents: intrinsic motivation, disciplined work style, the ability to close a sale, and perhaps most importantly, the ability to build relationships with customers.

### INTRINSIC MOTIVATION
"Different things drive different people—pride, happiness, money, you name it," says one expert. "But all great salespeople have one thing in common: an unrelenting drive to excel." This strong, internal drive can be shaped and molded, but it can't be taught. The source of the mo-

tivation varies—some are driven by money, some by hunger for recognition, some by a yearning to build relationships. The Gallup research revealed four general personality types, all high performers, but all with different sources of motivation. *Competitors* are people who not only want to win, but crave the satisfaction of beating specific rivals—other companies *and* their fellow salespeople. They'll come right out and say to a colleague, "With all due respect, I know you're salesperson of the year, but I'm going after your title." The *ego-driven* are salespeople who just want to experience the glory of winning. They want to be recognized as being the best, regardless of the competition. *Achievers* are a rare breed who are almost completely self-motivated. They like accomplishment, and routinely set goals that are higher than what is expected of them. They often

make the best sales managers because they don't mind seeing other people succeed, as long as the organization's goals are met. Finally, *service-oriented* salespeople are those whose strength lies in their ability to build and cultivate relationships. They are generous, caring, and empathetic. "These people are golden," says the national training manager of Minolta Corporation's business equipment division. "We need salespeople who will take the time to follow up on the ten questions a customer might have, salespeople who love to stay in touch."

No one is purely a competitor, an achiever, ego-driven, or service-driven. There's at least some of each in most top performers. "A *competitor* with a strong sense of *service* will probably bring in a lot of business, while doing a great job of taking care of customers," observes the *(continued)* managing director of the Gallup Management Consulting Group. "Who could ask for anything more?"

**DISCIPLINED WORK STYLE**
Whatever their motivation, if salespeople aren't organized and focused, and if they don't work hard, they can't meet the ever-increasing demands that customers are making these days. Great salespeople are tenacious about laying out detailed, organized plans, then following through in a timely, disciplined way. There's no magic here, just solid organization and hard work. "Our best sales reps never let loose ends dangle," says the president of a small business equipment firm. "If they say they're going to make a follow-up call on a customer in six months, you can be sure that they'll be on the doorstep in six months." Top sellers rely on hard work, not luck or gimmicks. "Some people say it's all technique or luck," notes one sales trainer. "But luck happens to the best salespeople when they get up early, work late,

stay up till two in the morning working on a proposal, or keep making calls when everyone is leaving at the end of the day."

**THE ABILITY TO CLOSE THE SALE**
Other skills mean little if a seller can't ask for the sale. No close, no sale. Period. So what makes for a great closer? For one thing, an unyielding persistence, say managers and sales consultants. Claims one, "Great closers are like great athletes. They're not afraid to fail, and they don't give up until they close." Part of what makes the failure rate tolerable for top performers is their deep-seated belief in themselves and what they are selling. Great closers have a high level of self-confidence and believe that they are doing the right thing. And they've got a burning need to make the sale happen—to do whatever it takes within legal and ethical parameters to get the business.

**THE ABILITY TO BUILD RELATIONSHIPS**
Perhaps most important in to-day's relationship-marketing envi-

ronment, top salespeople are customer-problem solvers and relationship builders. They have an instinctive understanding of their customers' needs. Talk to sales executives and they'll describe top performers in these terms: Empathetic. Patient. Caring. Responsive. Good listeners. Even *honest.* Top sellers can put themselves on the buyer's side of the desk and see the world through their customers' eyes. Today, customers are looking for business partners, not golf partners. "At the root of it all," says a Dallas sales consultant, "is an integrity of intent. High performers don't just want to be liked, they want to add value." High-performing salespeople, he adds, are "always thinking about the big picture, where the customer's organization is going, and how they can help them get there."

*Source:* Adapted from Geoffrey Brewer, "Mind Reading: What Drives Top Salespeople to Greatness?" *Sales & Marketing Management,* May 1994, pp. 82–88. Also see Barry J. Farber, "Success Stories for Salespeople," *Sales & Marketing Management,* May 1995, pp. 30–31.

Good salespeople working with key customers do much more than simply call when they think a customer might be ready to place an order. They also study the account and understand its problems. They call or visit customers frequently, work with customers to help solve problems and improve business, and take an interest in customers as people.

## SUMMARY

Most companies use salespeople, and many companies assign them a key role in the marketing mix. The high cost of the sales force calls for an effective *sales management process* consisting of six steps:

*designing sales-force strategy and structure; recruiting and selecting; training; compensating; supervising;* and *evaluating* salespeople.

As an element of the marketing mix, the sales

force is very effective in achieving certain marketing objectives and carrying out such activities as prospecting, communicating, selling and servicing, and information gathering. A market-oriented sales force needs skills in marketing analysis and planning, in addition to the traditional selling skills.

In designing a sales force, sales management must address issues such as what type of sales-force structure will work best (territorial, product, or customer structured); how large the sales force should be; who will be involved in the selling effort; and how its various sales and sales-support people will work together (inside or outside sales forces and team selling).

To hold down the high costs of hiring the wrong people, salespeople must be *recruited* and *selected* carefully. *Training* programs familiarize new salespeople not only with the art of selling, but with the company's history, its products and policies, and the characteristics of its market and competitors.

The sales-force *compensation* system helps to reward, motivate, and direct salespeople. All salespeople need *supervision*, and many need continuous encouragement because they face many frustrations and must make many decisions. Periodically, the company must *evaluate* their performance to help them do a better job.

The art of selling involves a seven-step *selling process: prospecting and qualifying, preapproach, approach, presentation and demonstration, handling objections, closing,* and *follow-up.* These steps help marketers to close a specific sale. However, a seller's dealings with customers should be guided by the larger concept of *relationship marketing.* The company's sales force should help to orchestrate a whole-company effort to develop profitable long-term relationships with key customers based on superior customer value and satisfaction.

## KEY TERMS

Approach

Closing

Customer sales-force structure

Follow-up

Handling objections

Inside sales force

Outside sales force

Preapproach

Presentation

Product sales-force structure

Prospecting

Relationship marketing

Sales-force management

Salesperson

Sales quotas

Selling process

Team selling

Telemarketing

Territorial sales-force structure

Workload approach

## QUESTIONS FOR DISCUSSION

1. Grocery stores require their suppliers' salespeople to not only sell but also serve as aisle clerks. These salespeople must arrange and restock shelves, build special displays, and set up point-of-purchase material. Is it important for a manufacturer to meet these demands? Are there creative ways to free the salesperson's time for more productive uses?

2. Explain why so many sales-force compensation plans combine salary with bonus or commission. What are the advantages and disadvantages of using bonuses as incentives, rather than using commissions?

3. Many people feel that they do not have the ability to be successful salespeople. What role

does training play in helping someone to develop selling ability?

4. Some companies have installed computerized inventory tracking that automatically sends reorders to the supplier's computer as needed. Predict whether this process is likely to expand. Discuss the effects that this could have on the role of the salesperson.

5. Good salespeople are familiar with their competitors' products as well as their own. What would you do if your company expected you to sell a product that you thought was inferior to the competition's? Why?

6. Salespeople present an image of themselves— and their company—to potential customers. As

company representatives, they try to communicate credibility, and they accomplish this, in part, by the way they dress. Many corporations, including IBM, have relaxed their dress codes for internal office attire, but have not necessarily extended these new standards to sales visits. How are customers likely to respond to salespeople who are casually dressed?

## APPLYING THE CONCEPTS

1. In order to experience a sales pitch, go to a retailer where the salespeople are likely to be working on commission, such as a car dealership, an appliance and electronics dealer, or a clothing store.

   ◆ Rate your salesperson. Were his or her approach, presentation, and demonstration effective?

   ◆ Consider your emotional response to the sales pitch. Did you enjoy the experience, or find it hard to endure? Why did you react this way?

2. Visit a retailer that specializes in complex products such as computers and software, stereo, or video equipment. Ask a salesperson to explain a product to you, and pose specific questions.

   ◆ Was the salesperson knowledgeable and able to answer your questions in a helpful and believable way?

   ◆ Did you feel that the salesperson's expertise added value to the product, or not?

   ◆ Would you rather buy this product from the salesperson you spoke with, or purchase it by mail order for a slightly lower price?

## REFERENCES

1. Based on William Keenan, Jr., "What's Sales Got to Do With It?" Also see, Melissa Campanelli, "Eastman Chemical: A Formula for Quality," *Sales & Marketing Management,* October 1994, p. 88; and Keenan, "Plugging into Your Customers' Needs," *Sales & Marketing Management,* January 1996, pp. 62–66.

2. See Bill Kelley, "How to Sell Airplanes, Boeing-Style," *Sales & Marketing Management,* December 9, 1985, pp. 32–34. Also see Dori Jones Yang and Andrea Rothman, "Boeing Cuts Its Altitude as the Clouds Roll In," *Business Week,* February 8, 1993, p. 25.

3. For a comparison of several classifications, see William C. Moncrief III, "Selling Activity and Sales Position Taxonomies for Industrial Salesforces," *Journal of Marketing Research,* August 1986, pp. 261–70.

4. Patricia Sellers, "How to Remake Your Salesforce," *Fortune,* May 4, 1992, pp. 96–103, here p. 96. Also see Melissa Campanelli, "Reshuffling the Deck," *Sales & Marketing Management,* June 1994, pp. 83–89.

5. See Rudy Oetting and Geri Gantman, "Dial 'M' for Maximize," *Sales & Marketing Management,* June 1991, pp. 100–106; and "Median Costs per Call by Industry," *Sales & Marketing Management,* June 28, 1993, p. 65.

6. See Martin Everett, "Selling by Telephone," *Sales & Marketing Management,* December 1993, pp. 75–79.

7. See "A Phone Is Better Than a Face," *Sales & Marketing Management,* October 1987, p. 29. Also see Aimee L. Stern, "Telemarketing Polishes Its Image," *Sales & Marketing Management,* June 1991, pp. 107–10; and Richard L. Bencin, "Telefocus: Telemarketing Gets Synergized," *Sales & Marketing Management,* February 1992, pp. 49–57.

8. See Frank V. Cespedes, Stephen X. Doyle, and Robert J. Freedman, "Teamwork for Today's Selling," *Harvard Business Review,* March–April 1989, pp. 44–54, 58; Joseph Conlin, "Teaming Up," *Sales & Marketing Management,* October 1993, pp. 98–104; and Richard C. Whiteley, "Orchestrating Service," *Sales & Marketing Management,* April 1994, pp. 29–30.

9. See Perri Capel, "Are Good Salespeople Born or Made?" *American Demographics,* July 1993, pp. 12–13.

10. See George H. Lucas, Jr., A. Parasuraman, Robert A. Davis, and Ben M. Enis, "An Empirical Study of Sales-force Turnover," *Journal of Marketing,* July 1987, pp. 34–59; Lynn G. Coleman, "Sales Force Turnover Has Managers Wondering Why," *Marketing News,* December 4, 1989, p. 6; and Thomas R. Wotruba and Pradeep K. Tyagi, "Met Expectations and Turnover in Direct Selling," *Journal of Marketing,* July 1991, pp. 24–35.

11. See Geoffrey Brewer, "Mind Reading: What Drives Top Salespeople to Greatness?" *Sales & Marketing Management,* May 1994, pp. 82–88; and Barry J. Farber, "Success Stories for Salespeople," *Sales & Marketing Management,* May 1995, pp. 30–31.

12. "23 Percent of U.S. Salespeople Are Women," *American Salesman,* April 1995, p. 8.

13. See "To Test or Not to Test," *Sales & Marketing Management,* May 1994, p. 86.

14. See Matthew Goodfellow, "Hiring and Training: A Call for Action," *Sales & Marketing Management,* May 1992, pp. 87–88; Bill Kelley, "Training: 'Just Plain Lousy' or 'Too Important to Ignore'?" *Sales & Marketing Management,* March 1993, pp. 66–70; and Rick Mendosa, "Is There a Payoff?" *Sales & Marketing Management,* June 1995, pp. 64–71.

15. See *1993 Sales Manager's Budget Planner, Sales & Marketing Management,* June 28, 1993, p. 72.

16. The percentages add to more than 100 percent because some companies use more than one type of plan. See "1989 Survey of Selling Costs," *Sales & Marketing Management,* February 20, 1989, p. 26.

17. For a good discussion of sales-force compensation, see Sam T. Johnson, "Sales Compensation: In Search of a Better Solution," *Compensation & Benefits Review,* November–December 1993, pp. 53–60; and Andy Cohen, "Right on Target," *Sales & Marketing Management,* December 1994, pp. 59–63.

18. Thayer C. Taylor, "SFA: The Newest Orthodoxy," *Sales & Marketing Management,* February 1993, pp. 26–28. Also see Rowland T. Moriarty and Gordon S. Swartz, "Automation to Boost Sales and Marketing," *Harvard Business Review,* January–February 1989, pp. 100–8; "Road Warrior: A Special Focus on Sales Automation," *Sales & Marketing Management,* June 1994, Part 2; and Andy Cohen, "Smooth Sailing," *Sales & Marketing Management,* May 1995, Part 2, pp. 10–16.

19. Tony Seideman, "Who Needs Managers?" *Sales & Marketing Management,* Part 2, June 1994, pp. 15–17.

20. Derrick C. Schnebelt, "Turning the Tables," *Sales & Marketing Management,* January 1993, pp. 22–23. Also see Jaclyn Fierman, "The Death and Rebirth of the Salesman," *Fortune,* July 25, 1994, pp. 80–91.

21. See Robyn Griggs, "Taking the Leads," *Sales & Marketing Management,* September 1995, pp. 46–47.

22. Thayer C. Taylor, "Anatomy of a Star Salesperson," *Sales & Marketing Management,* May 1986, p. 50. Also see Stephen B. Castleberry and C. David Shepherd, "Effective Interpersonal Listening and Personal Selling," *Journal of Personal Selling and Sales Management,* Winter 1993, pp. 35–49.

# Chapter 16

# *The Global Marketplace*

In the late 1970s, Apple Computer invaded Japan. The $7 billion Japanese personal computer market, second only to the huge U.S. market, offered very attractive growth opportunities. If Apple had made the right moves then, it might well have sewn up Japan before the competition could establish itself. However, more than a decade later, Apple had achieved little more than novelty sales and a tiny 1.4 percent market share.

Looking back, far from making all the right moves in Japan, Apple did just about everything wrong. Its mostly American managers never really took the time to understand the Japanese market. Instead, they treated Japan largely as an extension of Apple's U.S. market. For example, repeated requests from Japanese dealers

to tailor the Macintosh computer for Japanese use fell on deaf ears. Even though the Mac's powerful graphics capabilities made it ideal for handling Kanji, the complex Chinese characters used in written Japanese, Apple insisted on selling its American version in Japan pretty much as is. To make matters worse, the first Macs arrived in Japan with shoddy packaging and keyboards that didn't work. Apple didn't even provide a Japanese-language operating manual.

Japanese buyers were also put off by the Mac's high prices—almost double those of comparable Japanese machines. Moreover, Apple's machines were distributed poorly, and the company seldom advertised its products in Japan or displayed them at trade shows. Finally, when Apple entered Japan, it quickly acquired a reputation among local software houses for "Yankee arrogance." Rather than pay software developers to convert their packages to run on Macs, a common practice in Japan, Apple *charged* them for technical information. It also refused to join any Japanese trade associations or even to loan Macs to the software developers. In contrast, when NEC entered the personal computer market in the early 1980s, it did all it could to court software houses. As a result, by the late 1980s, only 15 Japanese software packages existed for the Mac, compared with more than 5,000 for NEC computers, helping NEC to corner a staggering 60 percent market share.

By 1988, Apple Computer Japan had become an embarrassment. Mac sales were paltry, and Japan's hard-line America-bashers were pointing to Apple Computer Japan as a classic example of "ugly American" incompetence. Apple finally saw the light. With newfound insight, it set out to reverse its fortunes in Japan. As a first step, Apple recruited an all-Japanese executive team—a new president from Toshiba, an engineering manager from Sony, and a support services manager from NCR Japan. The new team moved quickly to slash prices, broaden distribution, and repair its reputation with Japanese software developers, dealers, and consumers.

Apple introduced three lower-priced Macs. The least expensive of these, a machine selling for less than $1,500, would later grow to account for more than half of Apple's unit sales in Japan. The company also prepared to offer a family of Japanese-language products, including a new Japanese-character version of its highly acclaimed Postscript laser printer and KanjiTalk, a Japanese-language operating system. To strengthen distribution, Apple recruited several major blue-chip Japanese companies to sell Macs, including business equipment giant Brother Industries, stationery leader Kokuyo, Mitsubishi, Sharp, and Minolta. And it began to open Apple Centers, outlets that sell only Apple products targeted at the corporate market.

Perhaps most importantly, Apple Computer Japan set out to patch up relations with Japanese software houses. It joined the Japan Personal Computer Software Association (JPSA) and began to aggressively recruit software developers. It even brought in engineers from top U.S. software firms to work as partners with the Japanese firms in developing Japanese versions of proven American packages. The software houses responded. By 1992, 200 Mac-compatible software programs were available, and the number was increasing daily. Some of Japan's largest software developers now endorse and distribute Macs. And a recent JPSA survey shows that Macs are the number-two choice behind NEC among Japanese software writers as the machine they hope to buy next.

To complete the makeover and repair its tarnished image, Apple launched a full-scale promotion campaign, including heavy TV and print advertising that portrayed the Mac as a creative, easy-to-use tool. Apple also sponsored several high-profile events, such as the first Japanese Ladies' Professional Golf Association tournament and a Janet Jackson concert in Tokyo. The concert drew 60,000 fans, each of whom found a bag of Apple literature on his or her chair. To further enhance its new image, Apple marketed the "Apple Collection" of T-shirts, coffee mugs, key chains, hats, and other merchandise emblazoned with the colorful Apple logo through Tokyo retailers.

Apple's overhaul produced amazing results—Macs now have sprouted up everywhere in Japan. Apple dominates in the desktop publishing and graphics design segments and is grabbing share from Japanese competitors in several other important areas. More and more, Macs are popping up in college classrooms, as well as in primary and secondary schools, where Apple has earned a reputation as easy to use. Whereas Apple is struggling in the United States, Japan has now become its fastest-growing market, with sales exceeding $1.2 billion. Its market share has grown to 16 percent, making it second only to the still dominant NEC (53.4 percent). Apple's outstanding success in Japan may provide the model for the ailing company's worldwide revival.

Its experiences in Japan have taught Apple that international marketing involves more than simply taking what's successful at home and exporting it abroad. Rather, entering a foreign market requires a strong commitment and a keen understanding of sometimes very different cultures and marketing environments. It usually means adapting the company's products, programs, and approaches to the special needs and circumstances of each new global market. For an ever-growing number of Japanese, Apple's new, more fitting approach has transformed the old "rotten Apple" to a new "Apple of their eye."[1]  ■

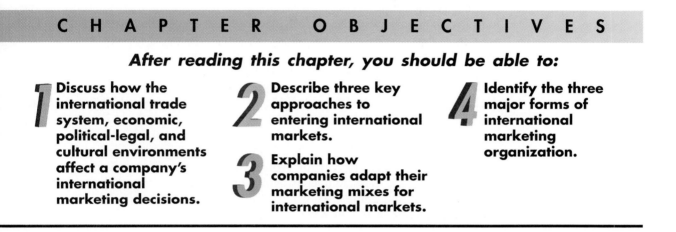

## CHAPTER OBJECTIVES

### After reading this chapter, you should be able to:

**1** Discuss how the international trade system, economic, political-legal, and cultural environments affect a company's international marketing decisions.

**2** Describe three key approaches to entering international markets.

**3** Explain how companies adapt their marketing mixes for international markets.

**4** Identify the three major forms of international marketing organization.

In the past, U.S. companies paid little attention to international trade. If they could pick up some extra sales through exporting, that was fine. But the big market was at home, and it teemed with opportunities. The home market was also much safer and easier. Managers did not need to learn other languages, deal with strange and changing currencies, face political and legal uncertainties, or adapt their products to different customer needs and expectations. Today, however, the situation is much different.

## GLOBAL MARKETING INTO THE TWENTY-FIRST CENTURY

The 1990s mark the first decade in which companies around the world must start thinking globally. Time and distance are shrinking rapidly with the advent of faster communication, transportation, and financial flows. Products developed in one country are finding enthusiastic acceptance in other countries.

True, many companies have been carrying on international activities for decades. Coca-Cola, IBM, Kodak, Nestlé, Bayer, Sony, and other companies are familiar to most consumers around the world. But today, global competition is intensifying. Foreign firms are expanding aggressively into new international markets, and home markets are no longer as rich in opportunity. Domestic companies that never thought about foreign competitors suddenly find these competitors in their own backyards. The firm that stays at home to play it safe might not only lose its chance to enter other markets but also risks losing its home market.

In the United States, names such as Sony, Toyota, Nestlé, Norelco, Mercedes, and Panasonic have become household words. Other products and services that appear to be American are really produced or owned by foreign companies: Bantam books, Baskin-Robbins ice cream, GE and RCA televisions, Firestone tires, Carnation milk, Pillsbury food products, Universal Studios, and Motel 6, to name just a few. The United States has also attracted huge foreign investments in basic industries such as steel, petroleum, tires, and chemicals, and in tourist and real estate ventures. Few U.S. industries are now safe from foreign competition.

Although some companies would like to stem the tide of foreign imports through protectionism, this response would be only a temporary solution. In the long run, it would raise the cost of living and protect inefficient U.S. firms. The answer is that more U.S. firms must learn how to enter foreign markets and increase their global competitiveness. Many U.S. companies have been successful at international marketing: Colgate, IBM, Xerox, Corning, Coca-Cola, McDonald's, General Electric, Caterpillar, Ford, Kodak, 3M, Boeing, Motorola, and dozens of other American firms have made the world their market. But there are too few like them. In fact, just five U.S. companies account for 12 percent of all exports; 1,000 manufacturers (out of 300,000) account for 60 percent.[2]

The longer that companies delay taking steps toward internationalizing, the more they risk being shut out of growing markets in Western Europe, Eastern Europe, the Pacific Rim, and elsewhere. Domestic businesses that thought they were safe now find companies from neighboring countries invading their home markets. All companies will have to answer some basic questions: What market position should we try to establish in our country, in our economic region, and globally? Who will our global competitors be, and what are their strategies and resources? Where should we produce or source our products? What strategic alliances should we form with other firms around the world?

Ironically, although the need for companies to go abroad is greater today than in the past, so are the risks. Companies that go global confront several major

*Many American companies have made the world their market.*

problems. High debt, inflation, and unemployment in many countries have resulted in highly unstable governments and currencies, which limit trade and expose U.S. firms to many risks. Governments are placing more regulations on foreign firms, such as requiring joint ownership with domestic partners, mandating the hiring of nationals, and limiting profits that can be taken from the country. Moreover, foreign governments often impose high tariffs or trade barriers in order to protect their own industries. Finally, corruption is an increasing problem—officials in several countries often award business not to the best bidder, but to the highest briber.

Still, companies selling in global industries have no choice but to internationalize their operations. A *global industry* is one in which the competitive positions of firms in given local or national markets are affected by their global positions. A **global firm** is one that, by operating in more than one country, gains marketing, production, R&D, and financial advantages that are not available to purely domestic competitors. The global company sees the world as one market. It minimizes the importance of national boundaries and raises capital, obtains materials and components, and manufactures and markets its goods wherever it can do the best job. For example, Ford's "world truck" sports a cab made in Europe and a chassis built in North America. It is assembled in Brazil and imported to the United States for sale. Thus, global firms gain advantages by planning, operating, and coordinating their activities on a worldwide basis.

Because firms around the world are globalizing at a rapid rate, domestic firms in global industries must act quickly before the window closes on them. This does not mean that small and medium-size firms must operate in a dozen countries to succeed. These firms can practice global nichemanship. But the world is becoming smaller, and every company operating in a global industry—whether large or small—must assess and establish its place in world markets.

As shown in Figure 16-1, a company faces six major decisions in international marketing. Each decision will be discussed in detail in this chapter.

**Global firm**
A firm that, by operating in more than one country, gains R&D, production, marketing, and financial advantages in its costs and reputation that are not available to purely domestic competitors.

# ▶ LOOKING AT THE GLOBAL MARKETING ENVIRONMENT

Before deciding whether to operate internationally, a company must thoroughly understand the international marketing environment. That environment has changed a great deal in the last two decades, creating both new opportunities and new problems. The world economy has globalized. World trade and investment have grown rapidly, with many attractive markets opening up in Western and

**FIGURE 16-1**
*Major international marketing decisions*

Eastern Europe, China and the Pacific Rim, Russia, and elsewhere. There has been a growth of global brands in automobiles, food, clothing, electronics, and many other categories. The number of global companies has grown dramatically. Meanwhile, the United States's dominant position has declined. Other countries, such as Japan and Germany, have increased their economic power in world markets. The international financial system has become more complex and fragile, and U.S. companies face increasing trade barriers erected to protect domestic markets from outside competition.

# THE INTERNATIONAL TRADE SYSTEM

The U.S. company looking abroad must start by understanding the international *trade system*. When selling to another country, the U.S. firm faces various trade restrictions. The most common is the **tariff**, which is a tax levied by a foreign government against certain imported products. The tariff may be designed either to raise revenue or to protect domestic firms. The exporter may also face a **quota**, which sets limits on the amount of goods that the importing country will accept in certain product categories. The purpose of the quota is to conserve on foreign exchange and to protect local industry and employment. An **embargo**, or boycott, is the strongest form of quota, which totally bans some kinds of imports.

American firms may face **exchange controls** that limit the amount of foreign exchange and the exchange rate against other currencies. The company may also face **nontariff trade barriers**, such as biases against U.S. company bids or restrictive product standards that discriminate against American product features:

> One of the cleverest ways the Japanese have found to keep foreign manufacturers out of their domestic market is to plead "uniqueness." Japanese skin is different, the government argues, so foreign cosmetics companies must test their products in Japan before selling there. The Japanese say their stomachs are small and have room for only the *mikan*, the local tangerine, so imports of U.S. oranges are limited. Now the Japanese have come up with what may be the flakiest argument yet: Their snow is different, so ski equipment should be too."[3]

At the same time, certain forces *help* trade between nations. Examples are the General Agreement on Tariffs and Trade and various regional free trade agreements.

## The General Agreement on Tariffs and Trade

The General Agreement on Tariffs and Trade (GATT) is a 45-year-old treaty designed to promote world trade by reducing tariffs and other international trade barriers. Since the treaty's inception in 1948, member nations (currently numbering 117) have met in eight rounds of GATT negotiations to reassess trade barriers and set new rules for international trade. The first seven rounds of negotiations reduced the average worldwide tariffs on manufactured goods from 45 percent to just 5 percent.

The most recent GATT negotiations, dubbed the Uruguay Round, dragged on for seven long years before concluding in 1993. Although the benefits of the Uruguay Round won't be felt for many years, the new accord should promote robust long-term global trade growth. It reduces the world's remaining merchandise tariffs by 30 percent, which could boost global merchandise trade by up to

**Tariff**
A tax levied by a government against certain imported products.

**Quota**
A limit on the amount of goods that an importing country will accept in certain product categories.

**Embargo**
A ban on the import of a certain product.

**Exchange controls**
A government's limits on the amount of its foreign exchange with other countries and on its exchange rate against other currencies.

**Nontariff trade barriers**
Nonmonetary barriers to foreign products, such as biases against a foreign company's bids or restrictive product standards.

10 percent, or $270 billion in current dollars, by the year 2002. The new agreement also extends GATT to cover trade in agriculture and a wide range of services, and it toughens international protection of copyrights, patents, trademarks, and other intellectual property.[4] Beyond reducing trade barriers and setting standards for trade, GATT also provides a forum for resolving international trade disputes. When member nations fail to resolve trade disputes among themselves, special GATT panels can be set up to recommend action.

### Regional Free Trade Zones

**Economic community**
A group of nations organized to work toward common goals in the regulation of international trade.

Certain countries have formed *free trade zones* or **economic communities**—groups of nations organized to work toward common goals in the regulation of international trade. One such community is the *European Union (EU)*. The EU's members are the major Western European nations, with a combined population exceeding 320 million people. The EU works to create a single European market by reducing physical, financial, and technical barriers to trade among member nations. Founded in 1957, the European Union has yet to achieve the true "common market" originally envisioned. In 1985, however, member countries renewed their commitment to economic integration (see Marketing at Work 16-1).

In North America, the United States and Canada phased out trade barriers in 1989. In January 1994, the *North American Free Trade Agreement (NAFTA)* established a free trade zone with the United States, Mexico, and Canada. The agreement created a single market of 360 million people who produce and consume $6.7 trillion worth of goods and services. As it is implemented over a 15-year period, NAFTA will eliminate all trade barriers and investment restrictions between the three countries. Prior to NAFTA, tariffs on American products entering Mexico averaged 13 percent, while U.S. tariffs on Mexican goods averaged 6 percent.

*Wal-Mart and other companies are expanding rapidly in Mexico and Canada to take advantage of the many opportunities presented by NAFTA. The trade agreement establishes a single market of 360 million people in Mexico, Canada, and the United States.*

## MARKETING AT WORK 16-1

# RESHAPING THE EUROPEAN UNION

Formed in 1957, the European Union (EU)—or Common Market—set out to create a single European market by reducing trade barriers among its member nations and by developing European policies on trade with non-member nations. However, the dream of a true "common market" was quickly buried under heaps of regulations and nationalistic squabbling. Despite early common market initiatives, Europe remained a fragmented maze of isolated and protected national markets, making it a difficult and confusing place to do business. In 1985, however, the European Union countries renewed their efforts toward a common market. They jointly enacted the Single European Act, which called for sweeping deregulation to eliminate barriers to the free flow of products, services, finances, and labor among member countries.

The European Union represents one of the world's single largest markets. It contains 340 million consumers and accounts for 20 percent of the world's ex-ports, compared with 14 percent for the United States and 12 percent for Japan. By the year 2000, the EU could contain as many as 450 million people in 25 countries, as more European nations seek admission to the free trade area. Thus, European economic unification promises tremendous opportunities for U.S. firms—as trade barriers drop, lower costs will result in greater operating efficiency and productivity. European markets will grow and become more accessible. As a result, most U.S. companies have drafted new strategies for cultivating the invigorated European market.

Yet, many U.S. managers have mixed reactions: Just as European unification has created many opportunities, it also poses threats. As a result of increased unification, European companies will grow bigger and more competitive. Thus, many companies from the United States, Japan, and other non-European countries are bracing for an onslaught of new European competition, both in Western Europe and in other world markets. Perhaps an even bigger concern, however, is that lower barriers *inside* Europe will only create thicker *outside* walls. Some observers envision a "Fortress Europe" that heaps favors on firms from EU countries but hinders outsiders by imposing obstacles such as stiffer import quotas, local content requirements, and other nontariff barriers. Companies that already operate in Europe are shielded from such protectionist moves. Thus, companies that sell to Europe but are not now operating there have been rushing to become insiders before unification threatens to close them out. They are building their own operations in Europe, acquiring existing businesses there, or forming strategic alliances with established European firms.

Renewed unification efforts have created much excitement within the European Union, but they also have drawn criticism. There is still confusion and disagreement among Europeans as to the scope and nature of the desired changes. Thus, progress

Other free trade areas are forming in Latin America and South America. For example, MERCOSUL now links Brazil, Colombia, and Mexico, and Chile and Mexico have formed a successful free trade zone. Venezuela, Colombia, and Mexico—the "Group of Three"—are negotiating a free trade area as well. It is likely that NAFTA will eventually merge with this and other arrangements to form an all-Americas free trade zone.[5]

Although the recent trend toward free trade zones has caused great excitement and new market opportunities, this trend also raises some concerns. For example, groups of countries that trade freely among themselves may tend to

toward unification has been slow—many doubt that complete unification will ever be achieved. By mid-1993, of 219 EU laws called for in the original blueprint for a single market, only 106 had been implemented with the needed legislation in all 12 EU countries. The most difficult issues—those involving the free flow of money, people, and goods—are still unresolved. For example, in December 1991, European Union leaders approved the Maastricht Treaty, an amendment to the original EU charter, which calls for establishing a single European currency and central bank by 1999. Before the treaty can become law, however, all 12 member states must approve it by legislative vote or by referendum. So far, the treaty is off to a rocky start—in 1992, Danish voters rejected the treaty, and the French passed it by only a narrow margin. Thus, although the creation of a common currency would greatly ease trade, such a measure is unlikely to be a reality for at least another decade, if at all.

Beyond these currency issues, actions such as standardizing taxes, abolishing border checks, and forging other European efforts will require changing the entire economic makeup of Europe. Individual countries will have to give up some of their independence for the common good, pushing aside the nationalism that has ruled European history for centuries. For these reasons, the odds are low that Europe will ever realize the full unification vision.

Even if the European Union does manage to standardize its general trade regulations, creating an economic community will not create a homogeneous market. With nine different languages and distinctive national customs, Europe will be anything but a "common market." Although economic and political boundaries may fall, social and cultural differences will remain. And although the unification effort may create common general standards, companies marketing in Europe will still face a daunting mass of local rules. Take advertising, for example. One large advertising agency has prepared a 52-page book containing dense statistics on country-by-country restrictions. Ireland, for example, forbids ads for liquor but allows them for beer and wine—as long as they run after 7 P.M.; Spain allows ads only for drinks with less than 23 percent alcohol, and they can run only after 9:30 P.M. In Holland, ads for sweets have to show a toothbrush in the corner of the television screen. European unification will have little effect on such local rules.

Thus, the European market will always be far more diverse than either the U.S. or Japanese markets. It is unlikely that the European Union will ever become the "United States of Europe." Nonetheless, great changes are occurring in Europe. Even if only partly successful, European unification will make a more efficient and competitive Europe a global force to be reckoned with. The best-prepared companies will benefit most. Thus, whether they cheer it or fear it, all companies must prepare now for the New Europe or risk being shut out later.

*Sources:* See Cyndee Miller, "Marketers Optimistic About EC Despite Monetary Muddle," *Marketing News,* October 26, 1992, p. 2; Andrew Hilton, "Mythology, Markets, and the Emerging Europe," *Harvard Business Review,* November–December 1992, pp. 50–54; several articles in a special section of *The Economist,* July 3, 1993, pp. SS12–SS17; and Bill Javetski, "The Single Market Itself Is in Question," *Business Week,* November 1, 1993, p. 52.

increase barriers to outsiders (for example, creating a "Fortress Europe"). In the United States, unions fear that NAFTA will lead to the further exodus of manufacturing jobs to Mexico where wage rates are much lower. And environmentalists worry that companies that are unwilling to play by the strict rules of the U.S. Environmental Protection Agency will relocate in Mexico where pollution regulation has been lax.

Each nation has unique features that must be understood. A nation's readiness for different products and services and its attractiveness as a market to foreign firms depend on its economic, political–legal, and cultural environments.

# ECONOMIC ENVIRONMENT

The international marketer must study each country's economy. Two economic factors reflect the country's attractiveness as a market: the country's industrial structure and its income distribution.

The country's *industrial structure* shapes its product and service needs, income levels, and employment levels. The four types of industrial structures are as follows:

◆ *Subsistence economies.* In a subsistence economy, the vast majority of people engage in simple agriculture. They consume most of their output and barter the rest for simple goods and services. They offer few market opportunities.

◆ *Raw-material-exporting economies.* These economies are rich in one or more natural resources but poor in other ways. Much of their revenue comes from exporting these resources. Examples are Chile (tin and copper), Zaire (copper, cobalt, and coffee), and Saudi Arabia (oil). These countries are good markets for large equipment, tools and supplies, and trucks. If there are many foreign residents and a wealthy upper class, they are also a market for luxury goods.

◆ *Industrializing economies.* In an industrializing economy, manufacturing accounts for 10 to 20 percent of the country's economy. Examples include Egypt, the Philippines, India, and Brazil. As manufacturing increases, the country needs more imports of raw textile materials, steel, and heavy machinery, and fewer imports of finished textiles, paper products, and automobiles. Industrialization typically creates a new rich class and a small but growing middle class, both demanding new types of imported goods.

◆ *Industrial economies.* Industrial economies are major exporters of manufactured goods and investment funds. They trade goods among themselves and also export them to other types of economies for raw materials and semifinished goods. The varied manufacturing activities of these industrial nations and their large middle class make them rich markets for all sorts of goods.

The second economic factor is the country's *income distribution*. Countries with subsistence economies may consist mostly of households with very low family incomes. In contrast, industrialized nations may have low-, medium-, and high-income households. Still other countries may have only households with either very low or very high incomes. However, even people in low-income countries may find ways to buy products that are important to them, or sheer population numbers can counter low average incomes. Also, in many cases, poorer countries may have small segments of wealthy consumers:

Recall that in the U.S. the first satellite dishes sprang up in the poorest parts of Appalachia. . . . The poorest slums of Calcutta are home to 70,000 VCRs. In Mexico, homes with color televisions out-number those with running water. Remember also that low average-income figures may conceal a lively luxury market. In Warsaw (average annual income: $2,500) well-dressed shoppers flock to elegant boutiques stocked with Christian Dior perfume and Valentino shoes. . . . In China, where per capita income is less than $600, the Swiss company Rado is selling thousands of its $1,000 watches.[6]

Thus, international marketers face many challenges in understanding how the economic environment will affect decisions about which global markets to enter and how.

*Income distribution: Even poorer countries may have small but wealthy segments. Although citizens of Budapest, Hungary have relatively low annual incomes, well-dressed shoppers flock to elegant stores like this one, stocked with luxury goods.*

# POLITICAL–LEGAL ENVIRONMENT

Nations vary greatly in their political–legal environments. At least four political–legal factors should be considered in deciding whether to do business in a given country: attitudes toward international buying, government bureaucracy, political stability, and monetary regulations.

In their *attitudes toward international buying,* some nations are quite receptive to foreign firms, and others are quite hostile. For example, Mexico has been attracting foreign businesses for many years by offering investment incentives and site-location services. In contrast, India has frustrated foreign businesses with import quotas, currency restrictions, and limits on the percentage of the management team that can be nonnationals. As a result of these hassles, many U.S. companies left India.

A second factor is *government bureaucracy*—the extent to which the host government runs an efficient system for helping foreign companies, including efficient customs handling, good market information, and other factors that aid in doing business. Americans are often shocked by how quickly barriers to trade disappear in some countries if a suitable payment (bribe) is made to some official.

*Political stability* is another issue. Governments change hands, sometimes violently. Even without a change, a government may decide to respond to new popular feelings. The foreign company's property may be taken, its currency holdings may be blocked, or import quotas or new duties may be set. International marketers may find it profitable to do business in an unstable country, but the unstable situation will affect how they handle business and financial matters.

Finally, companies must also consider a country's *monetary regulations.* Sellers want to take their profits in a currency of value to them. Ideally, the buyer can pay in the seller's currency or in other world currencies. Short of this, sellers might accept a blocked currency—one whose removal from the country is restricted by the buyer's government—if they can buy other goods in that country that they need themselves or can sell elsewhere for a needed currency. Besides currency limits, a changing exchange rate also creates high risks for the seller.

**Countertrade**
International trade
involving the direct or
indirect exchange of
goods for other goods
instead of cash.

Most international trade involves cash transactions. Yet many nations have too little hard currency to pay for their purchases from other countries. They may want to pay with other items instead of cash, which has led to a growing practice called **countertrade**. Countertrade may account for more than one-half of all international trade by the year 2000. It takes several forms. *Barter* involves the direct exchange of goods or services, as when the Germans built a steel plant in Indonesia in exchange for oil. Another form is *compensation* (or *buyback*), whereby the seller sells a plant, equipment, or technology to another country and agrees to take payment in the resulting products. Thus, Goodyear provided China with materials and training for a printing plant in exchange for finished labels. Another form is *counterpurchase,* in which the seller receives full payment in cash but agrees to spend some portion of the money in the other country within a stated time period. For example, Pepsi sells its cola syrup to Russia for rubles and agrees to buy Russian-made Stolichnaya vodka for sale in the United States.

Countertrade deals can be very complex. For example, Daimler-Benz recently agreed to sell 30 trucks to Romania in exchange for 150 Romanian jeeps, which it then sold to Ecuador for bananas, which were in turn sold to a German supermarket chain for German currency. Through this roundabout process, Daimler-Benz finally obtained payment in German money. In another case, when Occidental Petroleum Company wanted to sell oil to Yugoslavia, it hired a trading firm, SGD International, to arrange a countertrade. SGD arranged for a New York City automobile dealer-distributor, Global Motors Inc., to import more than $400 million worth of Yugoslavian Yugo automobiles, paid for by Occidental oil. Global then paid Occidental in cash. SGD, however, was paid in Yugos, which it peddled piecemeal by trading them for everything from cash to Caribbean resort hotel rooms, which it in turn sold to tour packagers and travel agencies for cash.[7]

## CULTURAL ENVIRONMENT

Each country has its own folkways, norms, and taboos. The seller must examine the ways that consumers in different countries think about and use certain products before planning a marketing program. There are often surprises. For example, the average French man uses almost twice as many cosmetics and beauty aids as his wife. The Germans and the French eat more packaged, branded spaghetti than do Italians. Italian children like to eat chocolate bars between slices of bread as a snack. And women in Tanzania will not give their children eggs for fear of making them bald or impotent.

Business norms and behavior also vary from country to country. American business executives need to be briefed on these factors before conducting business in another country. Here are some examples of the variety of different global business behaviors:[8]

◆ South Americans like to sit or stand very close to each other when they talk business—in fact, almost nose-to-nose. The American business executive tends to keep backing away as the South American moves closer. Both may end up being offended.

◆ Fast and tough bargaining, which works well in some parts of the world, is often inappropriate in Japan and other Asian countries. Moreover, in face-to-face communications, Japanese business executives rarely say no. Thus, Americans tend to become impatient with having to spend time in polite conversation about the weather or other such topics before getting down to business. And they become frustrated when they don't know where they stand. How-

*Adapting to the cultural environment: Compared with the European version of this ad (left), Guy Laroche tones down the sensuality in the Arab version (right); the man is clothed and the woman barely touches him.*

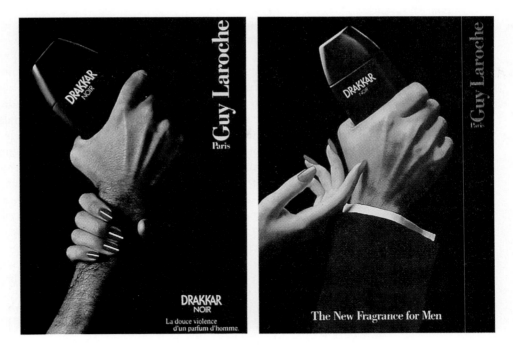

ever, when Americans come to the point quickly, Japanese business executives may find this behavior offensive.

◆ In France, wholesalers don't want to promote a product. They ask their retailers what they want and deliver it. If an American company builds its strategy around the French wholesaler's cooperation in promotions, it is likely to fail.

◆ When American executives exchange business cards, each usually gives the other's card a cursory glance and stuffs it in a pocket for later reference. In Japan, however, executives dutifully study each other's cards during a greeting, carefully noting company affiliation and rank. They hand their card to the most important person first.

Thus, each country and region has cultural traditions, preferences, and behaviors that the marketer must study.

# ▶DECIDING WHETHER TO GO INTERNATIONAL

Not all companies need to venture into international markets to survive. For example, many companies are local businesses that need to market well only in the local marketplace. However, companies that operate in global industries, where their strategic positions in specific markets are affected strongly by their overall global positions, must compete on a worldwide basis if they are to succeed.

Any of several factors might draw a company into the international arena. Global competitors might attack the company's domestic market by offering better products or lower prices. The company might want to counterattack these competitors in their home markets to tie up their resources. Or the company might discover foreign markets that present higher profit opportunities than the domestic market does. The company's domestic market might be shrinking, or the company might need an enlarged customer base in order to achieve economies of scale. Or it might want to reduce its dependence on any one market so as to reduce its risk. Finally, the company's customers might be expanding abroad and require international servicing.

Before going abroad, the company must weigh several risks and answer many questions about its ability to operate globally. Can the company learn to understand the preferences and buyer behavior of consumers in other countries? Can it offer competitively attractive products? Will it be able to adapt to other countries' business cultures and deal effectively with foreign nationals? Do the company's managers have the necessary international experience? Has management considered the impact of regulations and the political environments of other countries?

Because of the risks and difficulties of entering international markets, most companies do not act until some situation or event thrusts them into the global arena. Someone—a domestic exporter, a foreign importer, a foreign government—may ask the company to sell abroad. Or the company may be saddled with overcapacity and need to find additional markets for its goods.

# ▶ DECIDING WHICH MARKETS TO ENTER

Before going abroad, the company should try to define its international *marketing objectives and policies*. It should decide what *volume* of foreign sales it wants. Most companies start small when they go abroad. Some plan to stay small, seeing international sales as a small part of their business. Other companies have bigger plans, seeing international business as equal to or even more important than their domestic business.

The company must also choose *how many* countries it wants to market in. For example, the Bulova Watch Company decided to operate in many international markets and expanded into more than 100 countries. As a result, it spread itself too thin, made profits in only two countries, and lost around $40 million. Generally, it makes better sense to operate in fewer countries with deeper penetration in each.

Next, the company needs to decide on the *types* of countries to enter. A country's attractiveness depends on the product, geographical factors, income and population, political climate, and other factors. The seller may prefer certain country groups or parts of the world. In recent years, many major new markets have emerged, offering both substantial opportunities and daunting challenges (see Marketing at Work 16-2).

After listing possible international markets, the company must screen and rank each one. Consider the following example:

> Many mass marketers dream of selling to China's more than 1 billion people. Some think of the market less elegantly as more than 2 billion armpits. To PepsiCo, though, the market is mouths, and the People's Republic is especially enticing: it is the most populous country in the world, and Coca-Cola does not yet dominate it.[9]

PepsiCo's decision to enter the Chinese market seems fairly simple and straightforward: China is a huge market without established competition. In addition to selling Pepsi soft drinks, the company hopes to build many of its Pizza Hut restaurants in China. Yet we can still question whether market size *alone* is reason enough for selecting China. PepsiCo also must consider other factors: Will the Chinese government remain stable and supportive? Does China have the pro-

| TABLE 16-1 | *Indicators of Market Potential* |
|---|---|
| Demographic characteristics | Size of population<br>Rate of population growth<br>Degree of urbanization<br>Population density<br>Age structure and composition of the population |
| Geographic characteristics | Physical size of a country<br>Topographical characteristics<br>Climate conditions |
| Economic factors | GNP per capita<br>Income distribution<br>Rate of growth of GNP<br>Ratio of investment to GNP |
| Technological factors | Level of technological skill<br>Existing production technology<br>Existing consumption technology<br>Education levels |
| Sociocultural factors | Dominant values<br>Lifestyle patterns<br>Ethnic groups<br>Linguistic fragmentation |
| National goals and plans | Industry priorities<br>Infrastructure investment plans |

*Source:* Susan P. Douglas, C. Samuel Craig, and Warren Keegan, "Approaches to Assessing International Marketing Opportunities for Small and Medium-Sized Business," *Columbia Journal of World Business*, Fall 1982, pp. 26–32.

duction and distribution technologies needed to produce and market Pepsi products profitably? Will Pepsi and pizza fit Chinese tastes, means, and lifestyles?

Possible global markets should be ranked on several factors, including market size, market growth, cost of doing business, competitive advantage, and risk level. The goal is to determine the potential of each market, using indicators such as those shown in Table 16-1. Then the marketer must decide which markets offer the greatest long-run return on investment.

# ▶DECIDING HOW TO ENTER THE MARKET

**Exporting**
Entering a foreign market by sending and selling products through international marketing middlemen (indirect exporting) or the company's own department, branch, or sales representatives or agents (direct exporting).

Once a company has decided to sell in a foreign country, it must determine the best mode of entry. Its choices are *exporting, joint venturing,* and *direct investment.* Figure 16-2 shows three market entry strategies, along with the options that each one offers. As the figure shows, each succeeding strategy involves more commitment and risk, but also more control and potential profits.[10]

## EXPORTING

The simplest way to enter a foreign market is through **exporting.** The company may passively export its surpluses from time to time, or it may make an active

## MARKETING AT WORK 16-2

# THE LAST MARKETING FRONTIERS: CHINA, VIETNAM, AND CUBA

As communist and formerly communist countries reform their markets, and as the United States continues to dismantle its trade barriers, U.S. companies are eagerly anticipating the profits that await them. Here are "snapshots" of the opportunities and challenges that marketers face in three of the world's global marketing frontiers.

### CHINA: 1.2 BILLION CONSUMERS

In Guangdong province, Chinese "yuppies" walk department store aisles to buy $95 Nike or Reebok sneakers and think nothing of spending $4 on a jar of Skippy peanut butter at the supermarket. Although consumers here might make as little as $130 a month, they still have plenty of spending money because of subsidized housing and health care, and lots of savings under the mattress. In Shenzen, Guangdong's second-largest city, consumers have the highest disposable income in all of China—$3,900 annually. With purchasing power like this, a population of 1.2 billion, and the fastest-growing economy in the world, China is encouraging companies from around the planet to set up shop there. Instead of the communist propaganda of yore, modern Chinese

billboards exclaim, "Give China a chance."

Yet for all the market potential, there are many hurdles to jump in establishing businesses in China and marketing to the Chinese. For one, China is not one market, but many, and regional governments may discriminate against certain goods. Distribution channels are undeveloped, consisting of thousands of tiny mom-and-pop stores that can afford to stock only a few bottles or packages at a time. And

China's dismal infrastructure can turn a rail shipment traveling from Guanzhou to Beijing into a month-long odyssey. Smart firms, such as Allied Signal, try to jump these hurdles by partnering with Chinese government bodies; in some regions, doing so is a must for establishing a business. Others acquire Chinese business partners who can help them penetrate distribution channels and hire experienced personnel.

A major concern to some U.S. businesses has been China's

*With 72 million customers, Vietnam seems like a marketer's dream. However, the country's communication and transportation systems rank among the world's worst.*

commitment to expand exports to a particular market. In either case, the company produces all its goods in its home country. It may or may not modify them for the export market. Exporting involves the least change in the company's product lines, organization, investments, or mission.

distressing human-rights record. Levi Strauss has turned its back on China's vast market for blue jeans because of such concerns. But other U.S. firms counter that industry can be part of the solution. "Supporting the business sector will result in economic and political freedoms for the Chinese people," says a 3M spokesman.

#### VIETNAM: AN UNTAPPED MARKET

Vietnam seems like a marketer's dream: 72 million consumers, 80 percent of whom are younger than 40; loads of natural resources, including oil, gold, gas, and timber; and a coastline of pristine beaches that could turn out to be the hot new tourist spot. With the ending of the U.S. trade embargo against Vietnam, this dream has become a reality for many U.S. companies. While European and Asian companies have been taking advantage of the Vietnamese market reforms that began in 1986, their foothold doesn't faze many U.S. marketers, who are banking on the popularity of American brands.

Amid all the excitement, however, there are some notes of caution. The per capita income of most Vietnamese is only $200 a year, and like China, Vietnam's transportation and communication systems rank among the world's worst. While the country and its markets develop, marketers are spending their money

cautiously. Because most consumers are seeing foreign products for the first time ever, companies are investing most of their marketing dollars in very simple advertising campaigns. For this reason, radio and billboards are fruitful venues for advertising. One billboard in Ho Chi Minh City boasts a single word: Sony.

#### CUBA: WATCHING AND WAITING

While the United States is tightening the screws on Havana by extending its Cuban trade embargo, other countries are tightening their grip on the Cuban market. U.S. policy makers hope that the embargo will pressure Fidel Castro to liberalize his repressive regime. The drawback, however, is that other nations have refused to participate in the embargo. For example, at Havana In-Bond, a quasi-free trade zone on the capital's outskirts, warehouses are packed with Mexican goods entering Cuba. Cuba is one of the lushest Caribbean islands, so the biggest influx has been the boom in hotels built or managed by Spanish, Canadian, and Mexican operators. Tourist revenues totaled about $900 million in 1994, overtaking sugar exports as Cuba's top hard-currency earner.

While U.S. companies are currently losing out on a potentially lucrative market, many are preparing for Castro's imminent

fall and the subsequent lifting of the embargo. "Here we have a consumer market of 11 million that is a 32-minute flight away with 30 years of pent-up demand. Is that not exciting?" says Ana Maria Fernandez Haar, a Cuban-American who is president of the IAC Advertising Group. Procter & Gamble, United Airlines, American Airlines, and Sprint are just a few of the marketers interested in serving a free Cuban market. For now, though, foreign companies will continue to make inroads in Cuba, and U.S. marketers must simply watch and wait.

As with the emerging markets of China and Vietnam, Cuba's infrastructure needs years of rebuilding. Some areas have no running water, gasoline, sewer systems, or energy sources. "They'll have to take care of the basic concept of survival before they can think about pizza and Pepsi," says Joe Zubizarreta, a Cuban-born advertising executive.

*Sources:* Marlene Piturro, "Capitalist China?" *Brandweek,* May 16, 1994, pp. 22–27; Bryan Batson, "Chinese Fortunes," *Sales & Marketing Management,* March 1994, pp. 93–98; Valerie Reitman, "Enticed by Visions of Enormous Numbers, More Western Marketers Move into China," *Wall Street Journal,* July 12, 1993, pp. B1, B3; Cyndee Miller, "U.S. Firms Rush to Claim Share of Newly Opened Vietnam Market," *Marketing News,* March 14, 1994, p. 11; Geoffrey Brewer, "American Businesses Bank On," *Sales & Marketing Management,* April 1994, p. 15; Christy Fisher, "U.S. Marketers Wait for Opening in Cuba," *Advertising Age,* August 29, 1994, pp. 1, 6.

Companies typically start with *indirect exporting,* working through independent international marketing intermediaries. Indirect exporting involves less investment because the firm does not require an overseas sales force or set of contacts. It also involves less risk. International marketing intermediaries—domestic-

**FIGURE 16-2**
*Market-entry strategies*

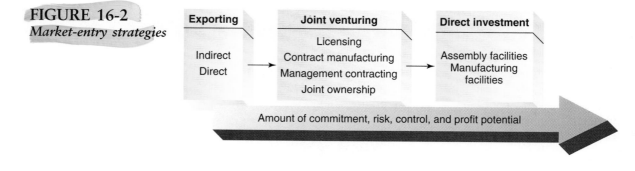

based export merchants or agents, cooperative organizations, and export-management companies—bring know-how and services to the relationship, so the seller normally makes fewer mistakes.

Sellers may eventually move into *direct exporting*, whereby they handle their own exports. The investment and risk are somewhat greater in this strategy, but so is the potential return. A company can conduct direct exporting in several ways. It can set up a domestic export department that carries out export activities. It can set up an overseas sales branch that handles sales, distribution, and perhaps promotion. The sales branch gives the seller more presence and program control in the foreign market and often serves as a display center and customer service center. The company can also send home-based salespeople abroad at certain times in order to find business opportunities. Finally, the company can do its exporting either through foreign-based distributors who buy and own the goods or through foreign-based agents who sell the goods on behalf of the company.

## JOINT VENTURING

**Joint venturing**
Entering foreign markets by joining with foreign companies to produce or market a product or service.

A second method of entering a foreign market is **joint venturing**—joining with foreign companies to produce or market products or services. Joint venturing differs from exporting in that the company joins with a partner to sell or market abroad. It differs from direct investment in that an association is formed with someone in the foreign country. There are four types of joint ventures: licensing, contract manufacturing, management contracting, and joint ownership.

### Licensing

**Licensing**
A method of entering a foreign market in which the company contracts with a licensee in the foreign market, offering the right to use a manufacturing process, trademark, patent, trade secret, or other item of value for a fee or royalty.

**Licensing** is a simple way for a manufacturer to enter international marketing. The company enters into an agreement with a licensee in the foreign market. For a fee or royalty, the licensee buys the right to use the company's manufacturing process, trademark, patent, trade secret, or other item of value. The company thus gains entry into the market at little risk; the licensee gains production expertise or a well-known product or name without having to start from scratch.

Coca-Cola markets internationally by licensing bottlers around the world and supplying them with the syrup needed to produce the product. In Japan, Budweiser beer flows from Kirin breweries, Lady Borden ice cream is churned out at Meiji Milk Products dairies, and Marlboro cigarettes roll off production lines at Japan Tobacco, Inc. Tokyo Disneyland is owned and operated by Oriental Land Company under license from the Walt Disney Company. The 45-year license gives Disney licensing fees plus 10 percent of admissions and 5 percent of food and mer-

*Licensing: Tokyo Disneyland is owned and operated by the Oriental Land Co., Ltd. (a Japanese development company), under license from Walt Disney Company.*

夜がきれい、君もきれい、スターライト★デート。

chandise sales. In Mexico, Wal-Mart is joining with Cifra, the country's top retailer, to open Wal-Mart Supercenters and Sam's Clubs.[11]

Licensing has potential disadvantages, however. The firm has less control over the licensee than it would over its own production facilities. Furthermore, if the licensee is very successful, the firm has given up these profits, and if and when the contract ends, it may find that it has created a competitor.

## Contract Manufacturing

**Contract manufacturing**
A joint venture in which a company contracts with manufacturers in a foreign market to produce a product.

Another option is **contract manufacturing**—the company contracts with manufacturers in the foreign market to produce its product or provide its service. Sears used this method in opening up department stores in Mexico and Spain, where it found qualified local manufacturers to produce many of the products that it sells. The drawbacks of contract manufacturing are the decreased control over the manufacturing process and the loss of potential profits on manufacturing. The benefits are the chance to start faster, with less risk, and the eventual opportunity either to form a partnership with or to buy out the local manufacturer.

## Management Contracting

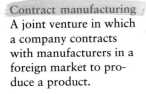

**Management contracting**
A joint venture in which the domestic firm supplies the management know-how to a foreign company that supplies the capital.

Under **management contracting,** the domestic firm supplies management know-how to a foreign company that supplies the capital. The domestic firm exports management services rather than products. Hilton uses this arrangement in managing hotels around the world.

Management contracting is a low-risk method of getting into a foreign market, and it yields income from the beginning. The arrangement is even more attractive if the contracting firm has an eventual option to buy some share in the managed company. The arrangement is not sensible, however, if the company can put its scarce management talent to better uses or if it can make greater profits by undertaking the whole venture. Management contracting also prevents the company from setting up its own operations for a period of time.

### Joint Ownership

**Joint ownership** ventures consist of one company joining forces with foreign investors to create a local business in which they share joint ownership and control. A company may buy an interest in a local firm, or the two parties may form a new business venture. Joint ownership may be needed for economic or political reasons. The firm may lack the financial, physical, or managerial resources to undertake the venture alone. Or a foreign government may require joint ownership as a condition for entry.

Joint ownership has certain drawbacks. The partners may disagree over investment, marketing, or other policies. Whereas many U.S. firms prefer to reinvest earnings for growth, local firms often prefer to take out these earnings. Furthermore, whereas U.S. firms emphasize the role of marketing, local investors may rely on selling.

## DIRECT INVESTMENT

The biggest involvement in a foreign market comes through **direct investment**— the development of foreign-based assembly or manufacturing facilities. If a company has gained experience in exporting and if the foreign market is large enough, foreign production facilities offer many advantages. The firm may have lower costs in the form of cheaper labor or raw materials, foreign government investment incentives, and freight savings. The firm may improve its image in the host country because it creates jobs. Generally, a firm develops a deeper relationship with government, customers, local suppliers, and distributors, allowing it to better adapt its products to the local market. Finally, the firm keeps full control over the investment and therefore can develop manufacturing and marketing policies that serve its long-term international objectives.

The main disadvantage of direct investment is that the firm faces many risks, such as restricted or devalued currencies, falling markets, or government takeovers. In some cases, a firm has no choice but to accept these risks if it wants to operate in the host country.

## ▶ DECIDING ON THE GLOBAL MARKETING PROGRAM

Companies that operate in one or more foreign markets must decide how much, if at all, to adapt their marketing mixes to local conditions. At one extreme are global companies that use a **standardized marketing mix** worldwide. Proponents of global standardization claim that it results in lower production, distribution, marketing, and management costs, allowing companies to offer consumers higher quality and more reliable products at lower prices. This is the thinking behind Coca-Cola's decision that Coke should taste about the same around the world and Ford's production of a "world car" that suits the needs of most consumers in most countries.

**Adapted marketing mix**
An international marketing strategy for adjusting the marketing-mix elements to each international target market, bearing more costs but hoping for a larger market share and return.

At the other extreme is an **adapted marketing mix.** In this case, the producer adjusts the marketing mix elements to each target market, bearing more costs but hoping for a larger market share and return. Nestlé, for example, varies its product line and its advertising in different countries. Proponents argue that consumers in different countries vary greatly in their geographic, demographic, economic, and cultural characteristics, resulting in different needs and wants, spending power, product preferences, and shopping patterns. Therefore, companies should adapt their marketing strategies and programs to fit unique consumer needs in each country.

The question of whether to adapt or standardize the marketing mix has been much debated in recent years. However, global standardization is not an all-or-nothing proposition, but rather a matter of degree. Companies should look for more standardization to help keep down costs and prices and to build greater global brand power. But they must not replace long-run marketing thinking with short-run financial thinking. Although standardization saves money, marketers must make certain that they offer what consumers in each country want.[12]

Many possibilities exist between the extremes of standardization and complete adaptation. For example, Coca-Cola sells virtually the same Coke beverage worldwide, and it pulls advertisements for specific markets from a common pool of ads designed to have cross-cultural appeal. However, the company sells a variety of other beverages created specifically for the taste buds of local markets. Similarly, McDonald's uses the same basic operating formula in its restaurants around the world, but adapts its menu to local tastes. For example, in India, where cows are considered sacred, McDonald's serves chicken, fish, and vegetable burgers instead of hamburgers. And although Whirlpool ovens, refrigerators, clothes washers, and other major appliances share the same interiors worldwide, their outer styling and features are designed to meet the preferences of consumers in different countries.[13]

## PRODUCT

Five strategies allow for adapting product and promotion to a foreign market (see Figure 16-3).[14] We first discuss the three product strategies and then turn to the two promotion strategies.

**Straight product extension**
Marketing a product in a foreign market without any change.

**Straight product extension** means marketing a product in a foreign market without any change. Top management tells its marketing people: "Take the product as is and find customers for it." The first step, however, should be to find out whether foreign consumers use that product and what form they prefer.

**FIGURE 16-3**
*Five international product and promotion strategies*

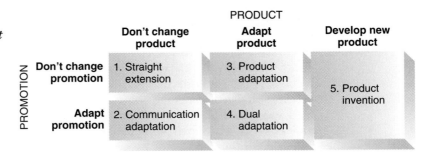

| | PRODUCT | | |
|---|---|---|---|
| PROMOTION | **Don't change product** | **Adapt product** | **Develop new product** |
| **Don't change promotion** | 1. Straight extension | 3. Product adaptation | |
| | | | 5. Product invention |
| **Adapt promotion** | 2. Communication adaptation | 4. Dual adaptation | |

Straight extension has been successful in some cases and disastrous in others. Coca-Cola, Kellogg cereals, Heineken beer, and Black & Decker tools are all sold successfully in about the same form around the world. But General Foods introduced its standard powdered Jell-O in the British market only to find that British consumers prefer a solid-wafer or cake form. Likewise, Philips began to make a profit in Japan only after it reduced the size of its coffee makers to fit into smaller Japanese kitchens and its shavers to fit smaller Japanese hands. Straight extension is tempting because it involves no additional product-development costs, manufacturing changes, or new promotion. But it can be costly in the long run if products fail to satisfy foreign consumers.

**Product adaptation**
Adapting a product to meet local conditions, wants, or needs in foreign markets.

**Product adaptation** involves changing the product to meet local conditions, needs, or wants. For example, McDonald's serves beer in Germany and coconut, mango, and tropic mint shakes in Hong Kong. General Foods blends different coffees for the British (who drink their coffee with milk), the French (who drink their coffee black), and Latin Americans (who prefer a chicory taste). In Japan, Mister Donut serves coffee in smaller and lighter cups that better fit the fingers of the average Japanese consumer; even the doughnuts are a little smaller. In Brazil, Levi's developed its Femina jeans featuring curvaceous cuts that provide the ultratight fit traditionally favored by Brazilian women. Campbell sells soups that match unique tastes of consumers in different countries. For example, it sells duck-gizzard soup in the Guangdong Province of China; in Poland, it features *flaki,* a peppery tripe soup. And IBM adapts its worldwide product line to meet local needs. For example, IBM must make dozens of different keyboards—20 for Europe alone—to match different languages.[15]

**Product invention**
Creating new products or services for foreign markets.

**Product invention** consists of creating something new for the foreign market. This strategy can take two forms. It might mean reintroducing earlier product forms that happen to be well adapted to the needs of a given country. For example, the National Cash Register Company reintroduced its crank-operated cash register at half the price of a modern cash register and sold large numbers in the Orient, Latin America, and Spain. Or a company might create a new product to meet a need in another country. For example, an enormous need exists for low-cost, high-protein foods in less developed countries. Companies such as Quaker Oats, Swift, Monsanto, and Archer Daniels Midland are researching the nutrition needs of these countries, creating new foods, and developing advertising campaigns to gain product trial and acceptance. Product invention can be costly, but the payoffs are worthwhile.

## PROMOTION

Companies can either adopt the same promotion strategy that they used in the home market or change it for each local market. Consider advertising messages. Some global companies use a standardized advertising theme around the world. Exxon used "Put a tiger in your tank," which gained international recognition. Of course, the copy may be varied in minor ways to adjust for language differences. In Japan, for instance, where consumers have trouble pronouncing "snap, crackle, pop," the little Rice Krispies critters say "patchy, pitchy, putchy." Colors are also changed sometimes to avoid taboos in other countries. Purple is associated with death in most of Latin America; white is a mourning color in Japan; and green is associated with jungle sickness in Malaysia. Even names must be changed. In Sweden, Helene Curtis changed the name of its Every Night Shampoo to Every Day because Swedes usually wash their hair in the morning. Kellogg also had to rename Bran Buds cereal in Sweden, where the name roughly translates as "burned farmer." (See Marketing at Work 16-3 for more on language blunders in international marketing.)

## MARKETING AT WORK 16-3

# WATCH YOUR LANGUAGE!

Many U.S. multinationals have had difficulty crossing the language barrier, with results ranging from mild embarrassment to outright failure. Seemingly innocuous brand names and advertising phrases can take on unintended meanings that are offensive or ridiculous when translated into other languages. Careless translations can make a marketer look downright foolish to foreign consumers. We've all run across examples when buying products from foreign countries. Here's one from a firm in Taiwan attempting to instruct children on how to install a ramp on a garage for toy cars:

*Before you play with, fix waiting plate by yourself as per below diagram. But after you once fixed it, you can play with as is and no necessary to fix off again.*

Many U.S. firms are guilty of such atrocities when marketing abroad.

The classic language blunders involve standardized brand names that do not translate well. When Coca-Cola first marketed Coke in China in the 1920s, it developed a group of Chinese characters that, when pronounced, sounded like the product name. Unfortunately, the characters actually translated to mean "bite the wax tadpole."

Now, the characters on Chinese Coke bottles translate as "happiness in the mouth."

Several car makers have had similar problems when their brand names crashed into the language barrier. Chevy's Nova translated into Spanish as "no va"—"it doesn't go." GM changed the name to Caribe and sales increased. Ford introduced its Fiera truck only to discover that the name means "ugly old woman" in Spanish. And it introduced its Comet car in Mexico as the Caliente—slang for "streetwalker." Rolls-Royce avoided the name Silver Mist in German markets, where "mist" means "manure." Sunbeam, however, entered the German market with its Mist Stick hair curling iron. As should have been expected, the Germans had little use for a "manure wand."

One well-intentioned firm sold its shampoo in Brazil under the name Evitol. It soon realized it was claiming to sell a "dandruff contraceptive." An American company reportedly had trouble marketing Pet milk in French-speaking areas. It seems that the word "pet" in French means, among other things, "to break wind."

Advertising themes often lose—or gain—something in the translation. The Coors beer slo-gan "get loose with Coors" in Spanish came out as "get the runs with Coors." Coca-Cola's "Coke adds life" theme in Japanese translated into "Coke brings your ancestors back from the dead." And in Germany, Pepsi's "Come Alive with Pepsi" was translated into "Come Out of the Grave with Pepsi." Even when the language is the same, word usage may differ from country to country. Thus, the British ad line for Electrolux vacuum cleaners—"Nothing sucks like an Electrolux"—would capture few customers in the United States.

Such classic boo-boos are soon discovered and corrected, and they may result in little more than embarrassment for the marketer. But countless other more subtle blunders may go undetected and damage product performance in less obvious ways. The multinational company must carefully screen its brand names and advertising messages to guard against those that might damage sales, create an embarrassing image, or offend consumers in specific international markets.

*Sources:* Some of these and many other examples of language blunders are found in David A. Ricks, "Products that Crashed into the Language Barrier," *Business and Society Review,* Spring 1983, pp. 46–50. Also see David W. Helin, "When Slogans Go Wrong," *American Demographics,* February 1992, p. 14.

*Standardized advertising messages: Cross pens uses the same promotion approach in many different countries.*

**Communication adaptation**
A global communication strategy of fully adapting advertising messages to local markets.

Other companies follow a strategy of **communication adaptation,** fully adapting their advertising messages to local markets. The Schwinn Bicycle Company might use a pleasure theme in the United States and a safety theme in Scandinavia. Kellogg ads in the United States promote the taste and nutrition of Kellogg's cereals versus competitors' brands. In France, where consumers drink little milk and eat little for breakfast, Kellogg's ads must convince consumers that cereals are a tasty and healthful breakfast. In India, where many consumers eat heavy, fried breakfasts, Kellogg's advertising convinces buyers to switch to a lighter, more nutritious breakfast diet.[16]

Media also need to be adapted internationally because media availability varies from country to country. TV advertising time is very limited in Europe, for instance, ranging from four hours a day in France to none in Scandinavian countries. Advertisers must buy time months in advance, and they have little control over airtimes. Magazines also vary in effectiveness. For example, magazines are a major medium in Italy and a minor one in Austria. Newspapers are national in the United Kingdom but are only local in Spain.

## PRICE

Companies also face many problems in setting their international prices. For example, how might Black & Decker price its power tools globally? It could set a uniform price all around the world, but this amount would be too high a price in poor countries and not high enough in rich ones. It could charge what consumers in each country would bear, but this strategy ignores differences in the actual costs from country to country. Finally, the company could use a standard markup of its costs everywhere, but this approach might price Black & Decker out of the market in some countries where costs are high.

Regardless of how companies go about pricing their products, their foreign prices will probably be higher than their domestic prices. A Gucci handbag may sell for $60 at home in Italy and $240 in the United States. Why? Gucci faces a *price escalation* problem. It must add the cost of transportation, tariffs, importer margin, wholesaler margin, and retailer margin to its factory price. Depending on these added costs, the product may have to be priced at two to five times the price in another country to make the same profit. For example, a pair of Levi's jeans that sells for $30 in the United States typically fetches $63 in Tokyo and $88 in Paris. A computer that sells for $1,000 in New York may cost £1,000 in the United Kingdom. A Chrysler automobile priced at $10,000 in the United States sells for more than $47,000 in South Korea.[17]

Another problem involves setting a price for goods that a company ships to its foreign subsidiaries. If the company charges a foreign subsidiary too much, it may end up paying higher tariff duties even while paying lower income taxes in that country. If the company charges its subsidiary too little, it can be charged with *dumping*. Dumping occurs when a company either charges less than its costs or less than it charges in its home market. Thus, Harley-Davidson accused Honda and Kawasaki of dumping motorcycles on the U.S. market. The U.S. International Trade Commission agreed and responded with a special five-year tariff on Japanese heavy motorcycles, which started at 45 percent in 1983 and gradually dropped to 10 percent by 1988.[18] The commission also ruled recently that Japan was dumping computer memory chips in the United States and laid stiff duties on future imports. Various governments are always watching for dumping abuses, and they often force companies to set the price charged by other competitors for the same or similar products.

## DISTRIBUTION CHANNELS

**Whole-channel view**
Designing international channels that take into account all the necessary links in distributing the seller's products to final buyers.

The international company must take a **whole-channel view** of the problem of distributing products to final consumers. Figure 16-4 shows the three major links between the seller and the final buyer. The first link, the *seller's headquarters organization*, supervises the channels and is part of the channel itself. The second link, *channels between nations,* moves the products to the borders of the foreign nations. The third link, *channels within nations,* moves the products from their foreign entry point to the final consumers. Some U.S. manufacturers may think that their job is done once the product leaves their hands, but they would do well to pay more attention to its handling within foreign countries.

Channels of distribution within countries vary greatly from nation to nation. First, there are the large differences in the *numbers and types of middlemen* serving each foreign market. For example, a U.S. company marketing in China must operate through a frustrating maze of state-controlled wholesalers and retailers. Chinese distributors often carry competitors' products and frequently refuse to

**FIGURE 16-4**
*Whole-channel concept for international marketing*

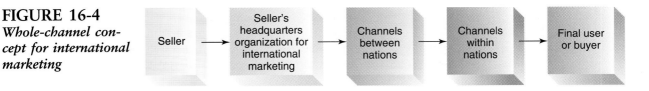

share even basic sales and marketing information with their suppliers. Hustling for sales is an alien concept to Chinese distributors, who are used to selling all that they can obtain. Working with or getting around this system sometimes requires substantial time and investment. When Coke and Pepsi first entered China, for example, customers bicycled up to bottling plants to get their soft drinks. Now, both companies have set up direct-distribution channels, investing heavily in trucks and refrigeration units for retailers.[19]

Another difference lies in the *size and character of retail units* abroad. Whereas large-scale retail chains dominate the U.S. scene, much retailing in other countries is done by many small independent retailers. In India, millions of retailers operate tiny shops or sell in open markets. Their markups are high, but the actual price is lowered through price haggling. Supermarkets could offer lower prices, but supermarkets are difficult to build and open because of many economic and cultural barriers. Incomes are low, and people prefer to shop daily for small amounts rather than weekly for large amounts. They also lack storage and refrigeration to keep food for several days. Packaging is not well developed because it would add too much to the cost. These factors have kept large-scale retailing from spreading rapidly in developing countries.

## ▶ DECIDING ON THE GLOBAL MARKETING ORGANIZATION

Companies manage their international marketing activities in at least three different ways. Most companies first organize an export department, then create an international division, and finally become a global organization.

A firm normally gets into international marketing by simply shipping out its goods. If its international sales expand, the company organizes an *export department* with a sales manager and a few assistants. As sales increase, the export department can then expand to include various marketing services so that it can actively go after business. If the firm moves into joint ventures or direct investment, the export department will no longer be adequate.

Many companies get involved in several international markets and ventures. A company may export to one country, license to another, have a joint ownership venture in a third, and own a subsidiary in a fourth. Sooner or later, it will create an *international division* or subsidiary to handle all its international activity.

International divisions are organized in a variety of ways. The international division's corporate staff consists of marketing, manufacturing, research, finance, planning, and personnel specialists. They plan for and provide services to various operating units, which can be organized in one of three ways. They can be *geographical organizations,* with country managers who are responsible for salespeople, sales branches, distributors, and licensees in their respective countries. Or the operating units can be *world product groups,* each responsible for worldwide sales of different product groups. Finally, operating units can be *international subsidiaries,* each responsible for its own sales and profits.

Several firms have passed beyond the international division stage and become truly *global organizations.* They stop thinking of themselves as national marketers who sell abroad and start thinking of themselves as global marketers. The top corporate management and staff plan worldwide manufacturing facilities, marketing policies, financial flows, and logistical systems. The global operating units report directly to the chief executive or executive committee of the organization, not to the head of an international division. Executives are trained in worldwide operations, not just domestic *or* international. The company recruits management from many countries, buys components and supplies where they cost the least, and invests where the expected returns are greatest.

Moving into the twenty-first century, major companies must become more global if they hope to compete. As foreign companies successfully invade their domestic markets, companies must move more aggressively into foreign markets. They will have to change from companies that treat their international operations as secondary, to companies that view the entire world as a single borderless market.[20]

## SUMMARY

Companies today can no longer afford to pay attention only to their domestic market, no matter how large it is. Many industries are global industries, and those firms that operate globally achieve lower costs and higher brand awareness. At the same time, *global marketing* is risky because of variable exchange rates, unstable governments, protectionist tariffs and trade barriers, and several other factors. Given the potential gains and risks of international marketing, companies need a systematic way to make their international marketing decisions.

As a first step, a company must understand the *global marketing environment,* especially the international trade system. It must assess each foreign market's economic, *political–legal,* and *cultural characteristics.* The company must then decide whether it wants to go abroad, considering the potential risks and benefits. It must decide on the volume of international sales it wants, how many countries it wants to market in, and which specific markets it wants to enter. This decision calls for weighing the probable rate of return on investment against the level of risk.

Next, the company must decide how to enter each chosen market—whether through *exporting, joint venturing,* or *direct investment.* Many companies start as exporters, move to joint ventures, and finally make a direct investment in foreign markets. Companies must also decide how much their products, promotion, price, and channels should be adapted for each foreign market. Finally, the company must develop an effective organization for international marketing. Most firms start with an *export department* and graduate to an *international division.* A few become *global organizations,* with worldwide marketing planned and managed by the top officers of the company. Global organizations view the entire world as a single borderless market.

## KEY TERMS

Adapted marketing mix

Communication adaptation

Contract manufacturing

Countertrade

Direct investment

Economic community

Embargo

Exchange controls

Exporting

Global firm

Joint ownership

Joint venturing

Licensing

Management contracting

Nontariff trade barriers

Product adaptation

Product invention

Quota

Standardized marketing mix

Straight product extension

Tariff

Whole-channel view

## QUESTIONS FOR DISCUSSION

1. With all the problems facing companies that "go global," why are so many companies choosing to expand internationally? What are the advantages of expanding beyond the domestic market?

2. The sale of *alcoholic beverages* in Middle Eastern countries that embrace the Islamic religion is against the law. Yet sales of *nonalcoholic beer* in Saudi Arabia have grown at double-digit rates over the past three years, with brewers expecting annual sales volumes to top 250,000 barrels. This poses a special challenge to marketers who must position their beerlike products as anything but beer. If you were marketing a nonalcoholic beer in Saudi Arabia, what steps would you take to deal with the cultural restrictions on your product?

3. When exporting goods to a foreign country, a marketer may be faced with various trade restrictions. Discuss the effects that these restrictions might have on an exporter's marketing mix:

   ◆ Tariffs.

   ◆ Quotas.

   ◆ Embargoes.

4. The first Honda automobile exported here was described by a U.S. car magazine as "a shopping cart with a motor"; the first Subaru exported to the United States was voted "Worst New Car of the Year." Both companies have become highly successful over the years, however. Discuss the Japanese strategy of long-term commitment to international business objectives. Would the Japanese have left India, as IBM and Coca-Cola did, because of "hassles"?

5. Discuss the steps that an advertising agency could take in entering a foreign market. What types of joint ventures would be worth considering?

6. Which type of international marketing organization would you suggest for the following companies?

   ◆ Cannondale Bicycles, selling three models in the Far East.

   ◆ A small U.S. manufacturer of toys, marketing its products in Europe.

   ◆ Dodge, planning to sell its full line of cars and trucks in Kuwait.

## APPLYING THE CONCEPTS

1. Visit a large electronics and appliance store that sells products such as televisions, stereos, and microwaves. Pick one or two product categories to examine.

   ◆ Make a list of brand names in the category, and classify each name as being either American or foreign. How did you decide whether a brand was American or foreign?

   ◆ Look at where these different brands were manufactured. Are any of the brands that you labelled American actually manufactured abroad, and are any of the brands assumed to be foreign made in the United States? What does this tell you about how much international marketing is being done? Is *global* a better term to describe some of these brands?

2. Entertainment, including movies, television programs, and music recordings, is America's second-largest export category; only aircraft is larger.

   ◆ Go to your college library and find several foreign magazines. Locate pictures, stories, or ads featuring American entertainers. See if you can understand the basic message from the size and layout of the stories. Does American entertainment seem to be interesting or important to people abroad? What, if anything, do you think is appealing to them?

   ◆ India has the largest movie industry in the world, yet few Indian films are ever shown in the United States. Why do you think this is so? Suggest some ways that Indian movie companies might make a bigger impact in America.

# REFERENCES

1. Stephen K. Yoder, "Apple, Loser in Japan Computer Market, Tries to Recoup by Redesigning Its Models," *Wall Street Journal*, June 21, 1985; Neil Gross, "Is It Finally Time for Apple to Blossom in Japan?" *Business Week*, May 28, 1990, pp. 100–1; Andrew Tanzer, "How Apple Stormed Japan," *Forbes*, May 27, 1991, pp. 40–41; Larry Holyoke, "Apple's Man in Japan Steps Up the Mac Attack," *Business Week*, October 31, 1994, pp. 117–18; Kathy Rebello, "Apple's Assault," *Business Week*, June 12, 1995, pp. 98–99; and Kathy Rebello and Peter Burrows, "The Fall of an American Icon," *Business Week*, February 5, 1996, pp. 34–42.

2. See "Top 50 U.S. Industrial Exporters," *Fortune*, August 22, 1994, p. 132; and Edmund Faltermayer, "Competitiveness: How U.S. Companies Stack Up Now," *Fortune*, April 18, 1994, pp. 52–64.

3. "The Unique Japanese," *Fortune*, November 24, 1986, p. 8. For more on nontariff and other barriers, see Philip R. Cateora, *International Marketing*, 8th ed. (Homewood, IL: Irwin, 1993), pp. 44–45; and David Woodruff, "Rougher Trade: The U.S.–Japan Chasm Widens," *Business Week*, July 17, 1995, pp. 30–32.

4. Douglas Harbrecht and Owen Ullmann, "Finally GATT May Fly," *Business Week*, December 29, 1993, pp. 36–37. Also see Cateora, *International Marketing*, pp. 49–51; and Louis S. Richman, "What's Next after GATT's Victory?" *Fortune*, January 10, 1994, pp. 66–70.

5. For more reading on free-trade zones, see Andrew Hilton, "Mythology, Markets, and the Emerging Europe," *Harvard Business Review*, November–December 1992, pp. 50–54; Roberto E. Batres, "Benefiting from NAFTA: New Opportunities in North America," *Prizm*, Arthur D. Little, Inc., Cambridge, MA, First Quarter, 1994, pp. 17–29; Douglas Harbrecht, William C. Symonds, Elisabeth Malkin, and Geri Smith, "What Has NAFTA Wrought? Plenty of Trade," *Business Week*, November 21, 1994; and William C. Symonds, "Meanwhile, to the North, NAFTA Is a Big Smash," *Business Week*, February 27, 1995, p. 66.

6. Bill Saporito, "Where the Global Action Is," *Fortune*, Special Issue on "The Tough New Consumer," Autumn–Winter 1993, pp. 62–65.

7. For these and other examples, see Louis Kraar, "How to Sell to Cashless Buyers," *Fortune*, November 7, 1988, pp. 147–54; Cyndee Miller, "Worldwide Money Crunch Fuels More International Barter," *Marketing News*, March 2, 1992, p. 5; Nathaniel Gilbert, "The Case for Countertrade," *Across the Board*, May 1992, pp. 43–45; and Kwanena Anyane-Ntow and Santhi C. Harvey, "A Countertrade Primer," *Management Accounting (USA)*, April 1995, p. 47.

8. For other examples, see Susan Harte, "When in Rome, You Should Learn to Do What the Romans Do", *The Atlanta Journal-Constitution*, January 22, 1990, pp. D1, D6; Sergey Frank, "Global Negotiating," *Sales & Marketing Management*, May 1992, pp. 64–69; Andrea L. Simpson, "Doing Business in Asia Pacific Requires New Skills," *Marketing News*, August 4, 1994, p. 4; and "The Way We Live," *Advertising Age*, January 16, 1995, p. I3.

9. Louis Kraar, "Pepsi's Pitch to Quench Chinese Thirsts," *Fortune*, March 17, 1986, p. 58. Also see Pete Engardio, "China Fever Strikes Again," *Business Week*, March 29, 1993, pp. 46–47.

10. For a deeper discussion of these and other market entry strategies, see R. Philip Cateora, *International Marketing* (Boston, MA: Irwin, 1993), pp. 325–34; and Avraham Shama, "Entry Strategies of U.S. Firms to the Newly Independent States, Baltic States, and Eastern European Countries," *California Management Review*, March 22, 1995, p. 90.

11. Robert Neff, "In Japan, They're Goofy about Disney," *Business Week*, March 12, 1990, p. 64; and Geri Smith, "NAFTA: A Green Light for Red Tape," *Business Week*, July 25, 1994, p. 48.

12. See George S. Yip, "Global Strategy . . . in a World of Nations?" *Sloan Management Review*, Fall 1989, pp. 29–41; Kamran Kashani, "Beware the Pitfalls of Global Marketing," *Harvard Business Review*, September–October 1989, pp. 91–98; Saeed Saminee and Kendall Roth, "The Influence of Global Marketing Standardization on Performance," *Journal of Marketing*, April 1992, pp. 1–17; David M. Szymanski, Sundar G. Bharadwaj, and Rajan Varadarajan, "Standardization versus Adaptation of International Marketing Strategy: An Empirical Investigation," *Journal of Marketing*, October 1993, pp. 1–17; and Ashish Banerjee, "Global Campaigns Don't Work; Multinationals Do," *Advertising Age*, April 18, 1994.

13. See Patrick Oster and John Rossant, "Call It Worldpool," *Business Week*, November 28, 1994, pp. 98–99; and "In India, Beef-Free Mickie D," *Business Week*, April 7, 1995, p. 52.

14. See Keegan, *Global Marketing Management*, 4th ed. (Englewood Cliffs, NJ: Prentice Hall, 1989), pp. 378–81. Also see Peter G. P. Walters and Brian Toyne, "Product Modification and Standardization in International Markets: Strategic Options and Facilitating Policies," *Columbia Journal of World Business*, Winter 1989, pp. 37–44.

15. For these and other examples, see Andrew Kupfer, "How to Be a Global Manager," *Fortune*, March 14, 1988, pp. 52–58; Maria Shao, "For Levi's: A Flattering Fit Overseas," *Business Week*, November 5, 1990, 76–77; and Joseph Weber, "Campbell: Now It's M-M-Global," *Business Week*, March 15, 1993, pp. 52–53.

16. Mir Maqbool Alam Khan, "Kellogg Reports Brisk Cereal Sales in India," *Advertising Age*, November 14, 1994, p. 60.

17. Dori Jones Yang, "Can Asia's Four Tigers Be Tamed?" *Business Week*, February 15, 1988, p. 47; Shao, "For Levi's: A Flattering Fit," p. 78; and Tim Simpson and Roger Camrass, "Redesigning the Multinational to Compete across Europe," *Prizm*, Arthur D. Little, Inc., Cambridge, MA, First Quarter, 1994, pp. 5–15.

18. See Michael Oneal, "Harley-Davidson: Ready to Hit the Road Again," *Business Week*, July 21, 1986, p. 70.

19. See Maria Shao, "Laying the Foundation for the Great Mall of China," *Business Week*, January 25, 1988, pp. 68–69.

20. See Kenichi Ohmae, "Managing in a Borderless World," *Harvard Business Review*, May–June 1989, pp. 152–61; William J. Holstein, "The Stateless Corporation," *Business Week*, May 14, 1990, pp. 98–105; and John A. Byrne and Kathleen Kerwin, "Borderless Management," *Business Week*, May 23, 1994, pp. 24–26.

# 17

# Marketing and Society: Social Responsibility and Marketing Ethics

Generations of parents have trusted the health and well-being of their babies to Gerber baby foods. Gerber sells more than 1.3 billion jars of baby food each year, holding almost 70 percent of the market. Some years ago, however, the company faced a classic social responsibility situation. Its reputation was threatened when more than 250 customers in 30 states complained about finding glass fragments in Gerber baby food.

The company believed that these complaints were unfounded. Gerber plants are clean and modern and use many filters that would prevent such problems. No injuries from Gerber products were confirmed. Moreover, the Food and Drug Administration had looked at more than 40,000 jars of Gerber baby food without finding a single major problem. Gerber suspected that the glass was planted by the people making the complaints in order to seek publicity or damages. Yet the complaints received widespread media coverage, and many retailers pulled Gerber products from their shelves. The state of Maryland forbade the sales of some Gerber baby foods, and other states considered such bans.

The considerable attention given to the complaints may have resulted from the "Tylenol scares," in which Tylenol capsules deliberately laced with cyanide killed a small number of consumers. At the time, product tampering was a major public issue and consumer concern.

Gerber wanted to act responsibly, but social responsibility issues are rarely clear-cut. Some analysts believed that, to ensure consumer safety, Gerber should quickly recall all its baby food products from store shelves until the problem was resolved. That was how the makers of products such as Tylenol, Contac, and Gatorade had reacted to tampering scares for their products. But Gerber executives did not think that a recall was best either for consumers or for the company. After a similar scare a few years before, the company had recalled some

700,000 jars of baby food and had advertised heavily to reassure consumers. The isolated incident turned out to be the result of normal breakage during shipment. The recall cost Gerber millions of dollars in expenses and lost profits and caused unnecessary alarm and inconvenience to consumers. The company concluded that it had overreacted in its desire to be socially responsible.

The second time, therefore, Gerber decided to do nothing, at least in the short run. It refused to recall any products; in fact, it filed a $150 million suit against the state of Maryland to stop the ban on the sales of Gerber products. It suspended its advertising, monitored sales and consumer confidence, reassured nervous retailers, and waited to see what would happen. This wait-and-see strategy was very risky. If the complaints had turned out to be well-founded and Gerber's failure to act quickly had caused consumer injuries or deaths, Gerber's reputation would have been seriously damaged.

Finally, when research showed that consumer concern was spreading, Gerber aired a few television ads noting its concern about "rumors you may have heard" and assuring buyers that Gerber products "meet the highest standards." The company also mailed letters to about two million new mothers, assuring them of Gerber's quality. In the end, the scare resulted in little long-term consumer alarm or inconvenience, and it caused only a temporary dip in Gerber's market share and reputation.

However, the question lingers: Should Gerber have recalled its products immediately to prevent even the remote chance of consumer injury? Perhaps. But in many matters of social responsibility, the best course of action is often unclear.[1] ■

# C H A P T E R   O B J E C T I V E S

## After reading this chapter, you should be able to:

**1** List and respond to the social criticisms of marketing.

**2** Define *consumerism* and *environmentalism* and explain how they affect marketing strategies.

**3** Describe the principles of socially responsible marketing.

**4** Explain the role of ethics in marketing.

Responsible marketers discover what consumers want and respond with the right products, priced to give good value to buyers and profit to the producer. The *marketing concept* is a philosophy of customer service and mutual gain. Its practice leads the economy by an invisible hand to satisfy the many and changing needs of millions of consumers.

Not all marketers follow the marketing concept, however. In fact, some companies use questionable marketing practices, and some marketing actions that seem innocent in themselves negatively affect society. Consider the sale of cigarettes. If cigarettes were an ordinary product, companies should be free to sell them, and consumers should be free to buy them. But this transaction affects the public interest. First, the smoker may be shortening his or her own life. Second, smoking places a financial, medical, and emotional burden on the smoker's family and on society at large. Third, other people around the smoker may suffer discomfort and harm from second-hand smoke. This example shows that private transactions may involve larger questions of public policy.

This chapter examines the social effects of private marketing practices. We examine several questions: What are the most frequent social criticisms of marketing? What steps have private citizens taken to curb marketing ills? What steps have legislators and government agencies taken to curb marketing ills? What steps have enlightened companies taken to carry out socially responsible and ethical marketing? We examine how marketing affects and is affected by each of these issues.

# ▶ SOCIAL CRITICISMS OF MARKETING

Marketing receives much criticism. Some of this criticism is justified; much is not. Social critics claim that certain marketing practices hurt individual consumers, society as a whole, and other business firms.

## MARKETING'S IMPACT ON INDIVIDUAL CONSUMERS

Consumers have many concerns about how well the American marketing system serves their interests. Surveys usually show that consumers hold mixed or even slightly unfavorable attitudes toward marketing practices.[2] Consumers, consumer advocates, government agencies, and other critics have accused marketing of harming consumers through high prices, deceptive practices, high-pressure selling, shoddy or unsafe products, planned obsolescence, and poor service to disadvantaged consumers.

## HIGH PRICES

Many critics charge that the American marketing system causes prices to be higher than they would be under more "sensible" systems. They point to three factors: *high costs of distribution, high advertising and promotion costs,* and *excessive markups.*

HIGH COSTS OF DISTRIBUTION.   A longstanding charge is that greedy intermediaries mark up prices beyond the value of their services. Critics charge either that there are too many intermediaries or that intermediaries are inefficient and poorly run, that they provide unnecessary or duplicate services, and that they practice poor management and planning. As a result, distribution costs too much, and consumers pay for these excessive costs in the form of higher prices.

How do retailers answer these charges? They argue as follows: First, intermediaries do work that would otherwise have to be done by manufacturers or consumers. Second, markups reflect services that consumers themselves want—more convenience, larger stores and assortment, longer store hours, return privileges, and others. Third, the costs of operating stores keep rising, forcing retailers to raise their prices. Fourth, retail competition is so intense that margins are actually

*Some retailers use high markups, but the higher prices cover services that consumers want.*

quite low. For example, after taxes, supermarket chains are typically left with barely one percent profit on their sales. If some resellers try to charge too much relative to the value they add, other resellers will step in with lower prices. Low-price stores such as Wal-Mart, Home Depot, and other discounters pressure their competitors to operate efficiently and keep their prices down.

HIGH ADVERTISING AND PROMOTION COSTS. Modern marketing is also accused of pushing up prices because of heavy advertising and sales promotion. For example, a dozen tablets of a heavily promoted brand of aspirin sell for the same price as do 100 tablets of less promoted brands. Differentiated products—cosmetics, detergents, toiletries—include promotion and packaging costs that can amount to 40 percent or more of the manufacturer's price to the retailer. Critics charge that much of the packaging and promotion adds only psychological value to the product rather than functional value. Retailers use additional promotion—advertising, displays, and sweepstakes—that add several cents more to retail prices.

Marketers answer these charges in several ways. First, consumers *want* more than the merely functional qualities of products. They also want psychological benefits—they want to feel wealthy, beautiful, or special. Consumers can usually buy functional versions of products at lower prices but are often willing to pay more for products that also provide desired psychological benefits. Second, branding gives buyers confidence. A brand name implies a certain quality, and consumers are willing to pay for well-known brands even if they cost a little more. Third, heavy advertising is needed to inform millions of potential buyers of the merits of a brand. If consumers want to know what is available on the market, they must expect manufacturers to spend large sums of money on advertising. Fourth, heavy advertising and promotion may be necessary for a firm to match competitors' efforts. The business would lose "share of mind" if it did not match competitive spending. At the same time, companies are cost-conscious about promotion and

*A heavily promoted brand of antacid sells for much more than a virtually identical nonbranded or store-branded product. Critics charge that promotion adds only psychological value to the product rather than functional value.*

try to spend their money wisely. Finally, heavy sales promotion is needed from time to time because goods are produced ahead of demand in a mass-production economy. Special incentives have to be offered in order to sell inventories.

EXCESSIVE MARKUPS.   Critics also charge that some companies mark up goods excessively. They point to the drug industry, where a pill costing 5 cents to make may cost the consumer 40 cents to buy. They point to the pricing tactics of funeral homes that prey on the emotions of bereaved relatives and to the high charges for essential auto repairs.

Marketers respond that most businesses try to deal fairly with consumers because they want repeat business. Most consumer abuses are unintentional. When shady marketers do take advantage of consumers, they should be reported to Better Business Bureaus and to state and federal agencies. Marketers also respond that consumers often don't understand the reason for high markups. For example, pharmaceutical markups must cover the costs of purchasing, promoting, and distributing existing medicines, plus the high research and development costs of finding new medicines.

## Deceptive Practices

Marketers are sometimes accused of deceptive practices that lead consumers to believe that they will get more value than they actually do. Deceptive practices fall into three groups: deceptive pricing, promotion, and packaging. *Deceptive pricing* includes practices such as falsely advertising "factory" or "wholesale" prices or offering a large price reduction from a phony high retail list price. *Deceptive promotion* includes practices such as overstating the product's features or performance, luring the customer to the store for a bargain that is out of stock, or running rigged contests. *Deceptive packaging* includes exaggerating package contents through subtle design, not filling the package to the top, using misleading labeling, or misrepresenting size.

Deceptive practices have led to legislation and other consumer-protection actions. In 1938, the Wheeler-Lea Act gave the FTC the power to regulate "unfair or deceptive acts or practices." The FTC has published several guidelines concerning deceptive practices. The toughest problem is defining what is "deceptive." For example, some years ago, Shell Oil advertised that Super Shell gasoline with platformate gave more mileage than did the same gasoline without platformate. Now this was true, but what Shell did not say is that almost *all* gasoline includes platformate. Its defense was that it had never claimed that platformate was found only in Shell gasoline. But even though the message was literally true, the FTC felt that the ad's *intent* was to deceive.

Marketers argue that most companies avoid deceptive practices because such practices harm their business in the long run. If consumers do not get what they expect, they will switch to more reliable products. In addition, consumers are usually wary of deception. Most consumers recognize a marketer's selling intent and are careful when they buy, sometimes to the point of not believing completely true product claims. Theodore Levitt claims that some advertising puffery is bound to occur—and that it may even be desirable: "There is hardly a company that would not go down in ruin if it refused to provide fluff, because nobody will buy pure functionality. . . . Worse, it denies . . . man's honest needs and values. Without distortion, embellishment, and elaboration, life would be drab, dull, anguished, and at its existential worst."[3]

### High-Pressure Selling

Salespeople are sometimes accused of high-pressure selling that persuades people to buy goods that they had no intention of buying. It is often said that encyclopedias, insurance, real estate, cars, and jewelry are *sold,* not *bought.* Salespeople are trained to deliver smooth, canned talks to entice purchase. They sell hard because sales contests promise big prizes to those who sell the most.

Marketers acknowledge that buyers can frequently be talked into buying unwanted or unneeded things, but there are many protections for consumers. Laws require door-to-door salespeople to announce that they are selling a product. Buyers are also protected by a "three-day cooling-off period" in which they can cancel a contract after rethinking it. In addition, consumers can complain to Better Business Bureaus or to state consumer-protection agencies when they feel that undue selling pressure has been applied.

### Shoddy or Unsafe Products

Another criticism is that products lack the quality they should have. One complaint is that many products and services are not made or performed well. Such complaints have been lodged against products and services ranging from home appliances, automobiles, and clothing to home and auto repair services.

A second complaint is that many products deliver little benefit. For example, some consumers are surprised to learn that many of the "healthy" foods being marketed today, ranging from cholesterol-free salad dressings and low-fat frozen dinners to high-fiber bran cereals, may have little nutritional value. In fact, they may even be harmful.

> [Despite] sincere efforts on the part of most marketers to provide healthier products, . . . many promises emblazoned on packages and used as ad slogans continue to confuse nutritionally uninformed consumers and . . . may actually be harmful to that group. . . . [Many con-

sumers] incorrectly assume the product is "safe" and eat greater amounts than are good for them. . . . For example, General Foods USA's new Entenmann's "low-cholesterol, low-calorie" cherry coffee cake . . . may confuse some consumers who shouldn't eat much of it. While each serving is only 90 calories, not everyone realizes that the suggested serving is tiny [one-thirteenth of the small cake]. Although eating half an Entenmann's cake may be better than eating half a dozen Dunkin Donuts, . . . neither should be eaten in great amounts by people on restrictive diets.[4]

A third complaint concerns product safety. Product safety has been a problem for several reasons, including manufacturer indifference, increased production complexity, poorly trained labor, and poor quality control. For years, Consumers Union—the organization that publishes *Consumer Reports*—has reported various hazards in tested products: electrical dangers in appliances, carbon monoxide poisoning from room heaters, injury risks from lawn mowers, and faulty automobile design, among many others. The organization's testing and other activities have helped consumers make better buying decisions and encouraged businesses to eliminate product flaws (see Marketing at Work 17-1).

However, most manufacturers *want* to produce quality goods. The way that a company deals with product quality and safety problems can damage or help its reputation. Companies selling poor-quality or unsafe products risk damaging conflicts with consumer groups and regulators. Moreover, unsafe products can result in product-liability suits and large awards for damages. More fundamentally, consumers who are unhappy with a firm's products may avoid future purchases and talk other consumers into doing the same. Today's marketers know that customer-driven quality results in customer satisfaction, which in turn creates profitable long-term customer relationships.

## Planned Obsolescence

Critics have also charged that some producers follow a program of planned obsolescence, designing their products to become obsolete before they should actually need to be replaced. For example, critics charge that some producers continually change consumer concepts of acceptable styles to encourage more and earlier buying. An obvious example is constantly changing clothing fashions. Other producers are accused of holding back attractive functional features, then introducing them later to make earlier models obsolete. Critics claim that this often occurs in the consumer electronics and computer industries. Still other producers are accused of using materials and components that will break, wear, rust, or rot sooner than they should.

Marketers respond that consumers *like* style changes; they get tired of the old goods and want a new look in fashion or a new design in cars. No one has to buy the new look, and if too few people like it, it will simply fail. Companies frequently withhold new features when they are not fully tested, when they add more cost to the product than consumers are willing to pay, and for other good reasons. But they do so at the risk that a competitor will introduce the new feature first and steal the market. Moreover, companies often put in new materials to lower their costs and prices. They do not design their products to break down because they do not want to lose customers to other brands. Instead, they implement total quality programs to ensure that products will consistently meet or exceed customer expectations. Thus, much of so-called planned obsolescence is

## MARKETING AT WORK 17-1

# WHEN *CONSUMER REPORTS* TALKS, BUYERS LISTEN

For more than 60 years, *Consumer Reports* has given buyers the lowdown on everything from sports cars to luggage to lawn sprinklers. Published by Consumers Union, the nonprofit product-testing organization, the magazine's mission can be summed up by CU's motto: Test, Inform, Protect. With more than five million subscribers and several times that many borrowers, as dog-eared library copies will attest, *Consumer Reports* is one of the nation's most-read magazines. It's also one of the most influential. In 1988, when its car-testers rated Suzuki's topple-prone Samurai as "not acceptable"—meaning don't even take one as a gift—sales plunged 70 percent the following month. Last year, when it raved about Saucony's Jazz 3000 sneaker, sales doubled, leading to nation-wide shortages.

Although nonreaders may view *Consumer Reports* as a deadly dull shopper's guide to major household appliances, the magazine does a lot more than rate cars and refrigerators. In recent issues, it has reviewed mutual funds, prostate surgery,

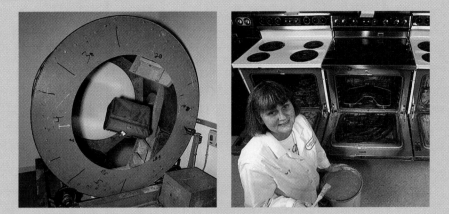

*Consumers Union carries out its testing mission: Suitcases bang into one another inside the huge "Mechanical Gorilla," and a staffer coats the interiors of self-cleaning ovens with a crusty concoction called "Monster Mash."*

home mortgages, retirement communities, and public health policies. In the 1930s, Consumers Union was one of the first organizations to urge a boycott of products imported from Nazi Germany, and it's been calling for nationalized health care since 1937. In the 1950s, it warned the nation that fallout from nuclear tests was contaminating milk supplies. In the 1960s and 1970s, it prodded carmakers to install seat belts, then air bags.

Yet the magazine is rarely harsh or loud. Instead, it's usually understated, and it can even be funny. The very first issue in 1936 noted that Lifebuoy soap was itself so smelly that it simply overwhelmed your B.O. with L.O. And what reader didn't delight to find in a 1990 survey of soap preferences that the most expensive bar, Eau de Gucci at 31 cents per handwashing, wound up dead last in a blind test.

*Consumer Reports* readers clearly appreciate CU and its magazine. It is unlikely that any other magazine in the world could have raised $17 million

actually the normal interaction of competitive and technological forces in a free society—forces that lead to ever-improving goods and services.[5]

### *Poor Service to Disadvantaged Consumers*

Finally, the American marketing system has been accused of serving disadvantaged consumers poorly. Critics claim that the urban poor often have to shop in smaller stores that carry inferior goods and charge higher prices. A recent Consumers

toward a new building simply by asking readers for donations. To avoid even the appearance of bias, CU has a strict no-ads, no-freebies policy. It buys all of its product samples on the open market, and anonymously.

A visit to CU's maze of labs confirms the thoroughness with which CU's testers carry out their mission. A chemist performs a cholesterol extraction test on a small white blob in a beaker—a ground-up piece of turkey enchilada, you are told. Elsewhere, you find the remains of a piston-driven machine called Fingers that added 1 + 1 on pocket calculators hundreds of thousands of times or until the calculators failed, whichever came first. You watch suitcases bang into one another inside a huge contraption—affectionately dubbed the "Mechanical Gorilla"—that looks like an eight-foot-wide clothes dryer, but actually tests durability.

Down the hall in the appliance department, a pair of "food soilers" will soon load 20 dishwashers with identical sets of dirty dishes. A sample dinner plate is marked off with scientific precision into eight wedge-shaped sections, each with different food caked to it—dried spaghetti, spinach, chipped beef,

melted cheese, egg, or something else equally difficult to clean. Next door, self-cleaning ovens are being tested, their interiors coated with a crusty substance—called "Monster Mash" by staffers—that resembles month-old chili sauce. The recipe includes tapioca, cheese, lard, grape jelly, tomato sauce, and cherry pie filling—mixed well and baked for one hour at 425 degrees. If an oven's self-cleaning cycle doesn't render the resulting residue into harmless-looking ash, five million readers will be so informed.

Some of the tests that CU runs are standard tests, but many others are not. Several years ago, in a triumph of low-tech creativity, CU's engineers stretched paper towels across embroidery hoops, moistened the center of each with exactly ten drops of water, then poured lead shot into the middle. The winner held seven pounds of shot; the loser, less than one. Who could argue with that? There is an obvious logic to such tests, and the results are plainly quantifiable.

From the start, Consumers Union has generated controversy. The second issue dismissed the Good Housekeeping

Seal of Approval as nothing more than a fraudulent ploy by publisher William Randolph Hearst to reward loyal advertisers. *Good Housekeeping* responded by accusing CU of prolonging the Depression. To the business community, *Consumer Reports* was at first viewed as a clear threat to the American way of doing business. During its early years, more than 60 advertising-dependent publications, including the *New York Times, Newsweek,* and the *New Yorker,* refused to accept CU's subscription ads.

In 1939, in a move that would seem ludicrous today, Congress's new House Un-American Activities Committee (then known as the Dies Committee) branded CU a subversive organization. And through the years, many manufacturers have filed suit against CU, challenging findings that are unfavorable to their products. However, the controversy has more often helped than hurt subscriptions, and to this day Consumers Union has never lost or settled a libel suit.

*Source:* Adapted from Doug Stewart, "To Buy or Not to Buy, That Is the Question at *Consumer Reports,*" *Smithsonian,* September 1993, pp. 34–43.

Union study compared the food-shopping habits of low-income consumers and the prices they pay relative to middle-income consumers in the same city. The study found that the poor do pay more for inferior goods. The results suggested that the presence of large national chain stores in low-income neighborhoods made a big difference in keeping prices down. However, the study also found evidence of "redlining," a type of economic discrimination in which major chain retailers avoid placing stores in disadvantaged neighborhoods.[6]

Clearly, better marketing systems must be built in low-income areas—one hope is to get large retailers to open outlets in low-income areas. Moreover, low-income people clearly need consumer protection. The FTC has taken action against merchants who advertise false values, sell old merchandise as new, or charge too much for credit. The commission is also trying to make it harder for merchants to win court judgments against low-income people who were manipulated into buying something.

# MARKETING'S IMPACT ON SOCIETY AS A WHOLE

The American marketing system has been accused of adding to several "evils" in American society at large. Advertising has been a special target—so much so that the American Association of Advertising Agencies launched a campaign to defend advertising against what it felt to be common, but untrue, criticisms (see Marketing at Work 17-2).

## *False Wants and Too Much Materialism*

Critics have charged that the marketing system urges too much interest in material possessions. People are judged by what they *own* rather than by who they *are*. To be considered successful, people must own a large home, two cars, and the latest consumer electronics. This drive for wealth and possessions hit new highs in the 1980s, when phrases such as "greed is good" and "shop 'til you drop" seemed to characterize the times. In the 1990s, although many social scientists have noted a reaction against the opulence and waste of the 1980s and a return to more basic values and social commitment, our infatuation with material things continues. For example, when asked in a recent poll what they value most in their lives, subjects listed enjoyable work (86 percent), happy children (84 percent), a good marriage (69 percent), and contributions to society (66 percent). However, when asked what most symbolizes success, 85 percent said money and the things it will buy.[7]

The critics do not view this interest in material things as a natural state of mind but rather as a matter of false wants created by marketing. Businesses hire Madison Avenue advertising agencies to stimulate people's desires for goods, and Madison Avenue uses the mass media to create materialistic models of the good life. People work harder to earn the necessary money to buy these goods. Their purchases increase the output of American industry, and industry in turn uses Madison Avenue to stimulate more desire for industrial output. Thus, marketing is seen as creating false wants that benefit industry more than they benefit consumers.

These criticisms overstate the power of business to create needs, however. People have strong defenses against advertising and other marketing tools. Marketers are most effective when they appeal to existing wants rather than creating new ones. Furthermore, people seek reliable information when making important purchases and often do not rely on a single source such as advertising. Even minor purchases that may be affected by advertising messages lead to repeat purchases only if the product performs as promised. Finally, the high failure rate of new products shows that companies are not able to control demand simply through advertising.

## MARKETING AT WORK 17-2

# ADVERTISING: ANOTHER WORD FOR FREEDOM OF CHOICE

A few years back, the American Association of Advertising Agencies ran a campaign featuring ads such as these to counter common criticisms of advetising. The association is concerned about research findings of negative public attitudes toward advertising. Two-thirds of the public recognize that advertising provides helpful buying information, but a significant portion feels that advertising is exaggerated or misleading. The association believes that its ad campaign increased general advertising credibility and has helped make advertisers' messages more effective. Several media agreed to run the ads as a public service.

*The American Association of Advertising Agencies runs ads to counter common advertising criticisms.*

On a deeper level, our wants and values are influenced not only by marketers, but also by family, peer groups, religion, ethnic background, and education. If Americans are highly materialistic, these values have arisen out of basic socialization processes that go much deeper than any efforts exerted by business and mass media.

### Too Few Social Goods

Business has been accused of overselling private goods at the expense of public goods. As private goods increase, they require more public services that are usually not forthcoming. For example, an increase in automobile ownership (private good) requires more highways, traffic control, parking spaces, and police services (public goods). The overselling of private goods results in "social costs." For cars, the social costs include traffic congestion, air pollution, and deaths and injuries from car accidents.

A way must be found to restore a balance between private and public goods. One option is to make producers bear the full social costs of their operations. For example, the government could require automobile manufacturers to build cars with even more safety features and better pollution-control systems. Automakers would then raise their prices to cover extra costs. If buyers found the price of some cars too high, however, the producers of these cars would fail, and demand would move to those producers that could support the sum of the private and social costs.

### Cultural Pollution

Critics charge the marketing system with creating *cultural pollution*. Our senses are constantly being assaulted by advertising. Commercials interrupt serious programs; pages of ads obscure printed matter; billboards mar beautiful scenery. These interruptions continuously pollute people's minds with messages of materialism, sex, power, or status. Although most people do not find advertising overly annoying (some even think it is the best part of television programming), some critics call for sweeping changes.

*Cultural pollution: People's senses are sometimes assaulted by commercial messages.*

Marketers answer the charges of "commercial noise" with the following arguments. First, they hope that their ads primarily reach the target audience. But because of mass-communication channels, some ads are bound to reach people who have no interest in the product and are therefore bored or annoyed. People who buy magazines addressed to their interests—such as *Vogue* or *Fortune*—rarely complain about the ads because the magazines advertise products of interest. Second, ads make it possible for most television and radio stations to offer free broadcasts, and ads keep down the costs of magazines and newspapers. Many people think that commercials are a small price to pay for these benefits.

### Too Much Political Power

Another criticism is that business wields too much political power. Some senators allegedly support oil, tobacco, auto, and pharmaceutical interests against the public interest. Advertisers are accused of holding too much power over the mass media, limiting their freedom to report independently and objectively. One critic has asked: "How can *Life* . . . and *Reader's Digest* afford to tell the truth about the scandalously low nutritional value of most packaged foods . . . when these magazines are being subsidized by such advertisers as General Foods, Kellogg's, Nabisco, and General Mills? . . . The answer is *they cannot and do not*."[8]

American industries do promote and protect their interests. They have a right to representation in Congress and the mass media, although their influence can go too far. Fortunately, many powerful business interests once thought to be untouchable have been tamed in the public interest. For example, Standard Oil was broken up in 1911, and the meatpacking industry was disciplined in the early 1900s after exposures by novelist Upton Sinclair. Consumer advocate Ralph Nader caused legislation that forced the automobile industry to build more safety features into its cars, and a Surgeon General's report resulted in cigarette companies being required to print health warnings on their packages. More recently, giants such as AT&T, Microsoft, and R. J. Reynolds have felt the impact of regulators seeking to balance the interests of big business against those of the public. Moreover, the influence of any one advertiser on the media is diluted by advertising revenues from many different advertisers. Abuse of business power tends to result in counterforces that check and offset these powerful interests.

## MARKETING'S IMPACT ON OTHER BUSINESSES

Critics also charge that a company's marketing practices can harm other companies and reduce competition. Three problems are involved: acquisitions of competitors, marketing practices that create barriers to entry, and unfair competitive marketing practices.

Critics claim that firms are harmed and competition reduced when companies expand by acquiring competitors rather than by developing their own new products. In the food industry alone during the past decade, R. J. Reynolds acquired Nabisco Brands; Philip Morris bought General Foods and Kraft; Procter & Gamble gobbled up Richardson-Vicks, Noxell, and parts of Revlon; Nestlé absorbed Carnation; and Quaker Oats bought Stokely-Van Camp. These and other large acquisitions in other industries have caused concern that vigorous young competitors will be absorbed and that competition will be reduced.

Acquisition is a complex subject. Acquisitions can sometimes be good for society. The acquiring company may gain economies of scale that lead to lower costs and lower prices. A well-managed company may take over a poorly managed company and improve its efficiency. An industry that was not very competitive might become more competitive after the acquisition. But acquisitions can also be harmful and, therefore, are closely regulated by the government.

Critics have also charged that marketing practices bar new companies from entering an industry. Large marketing companies can use patents and heavy promotion spending and can tie up suppliers or dealers to keep out or drive out competitors. People concerned with antitrust regulation recognize that some barriers are the natural result of the economic advantages of doing business on a large scale. Other barriers could be challenged by existing and new laws. For example, some critics have proposed a progressive tax on advertising spending to reduce the role of selling costs as a major barrier to entry.

Finally, some firms have in fact used unfair competitive marketing practices with the intention of hurting or destroying other firms. They may set their prices below costs, discourage the buying of a competitor's products, or threaten to cut off business with suppliers who sell to competitors. Various laws have been passed to prevent such predatory competition. It is difficult, however, to prove that the intent or action was really predatory. For example, in recent years, Wal-Mart and American Airlines have been accused of predatory pricing—setting prices that could not be profitable in order to drive out smaller or weaker competitors. The question is whether this was unfair practice or healthy competition by a more efficient company against others that are less efficient.[9]

# CITIZEN AND PUBLIC ACTIONS TO REGULATE MARKETING

Because some people view business as the cause of many economic and social ills, grass-roots movements have arisen from time to time to keep business in line. The two major movements have been *consumerism* and *environmentalism*.

## CONSUMERISM

American business firms have been the target of organized consumer movements on three occasions. The first consumer movement took place in the early 1900s. It was fueled by rising prices, Upton Sinclair's writings on conditions in the meat industry, and scandals in the drug industry. The second consumer movement, in the mid-1930s, was sparked by an upturn in consumer prices during the Great Depression and another drug scandal.

The third movement began in the 1960s. Consumers had become better educated, products had become more complex and hazardous, and people were unhappy with American institutions. Ralph Nader forced many issues to public attention, and other well-known writers accused big business of wasteful and unethical practices. President John F. Kennedy declared that consumers had the right to safety and to be informed, to choose, and to be heard. Congress investigated certain industries and proposed consumer-protection legislation. Since then, many consumer groups have been organized, and several consumer laws have been passed. The consumer movement has spread internationally and has become very strong in Europe.[10]

**Consumerism**
An organized movement of citizens and government agencies to improve the rights and power of buyers in relation to sellers.

But what is the consumer movement? **Consumerism** is an organized movement of citizens and government agencies to improve the rights and power of buyers in relation to sellers. Traditional *sellers' rights* include:

◆ The right to introduce any product in any size and style, provided that it is not hazardous to personal health or safety; or, if it is, to include proper warnings and controls.

◆ The right to charge any price for the product, provided that no discrimination exists among similar kinds of buyers.

◆ The right to spend any amount to promote the product, provided that it is not defined as unfair competition.

◆ The right to use any product message, provided that it is not misleading or dishonest in content or execution.

◆ The right to use any buying incentive schemes, provided that they are not unfair or misleading.

Traditional *buyers' rights* include:

◆ The right not to buy a product that is offered for sale.

◆ The right to expect the product to be safe.

◆ The right to expect the product to perform as claimed.

Comparing these rights, many believe that the balance of power lies on the sellers' side. True, the buyer can refuse to buy. But critics feel that the buyer has too little information, education, and protection to make wise decisions when facing sophisticated sellers. Consumer advocates call for the following additional consumer rights:

◆ The right to be well-informed about important aspects of the product.

◆ The right to be protected against questionable products and marketing practices.

◆ The right to influence products and marketing practices in ways that will improve the "quality of life."

Each proposed right has led to more specific proposals by consumerists. The right to be informed includes the right to know the true interest on a loan (truth in lending), the true cost per unit of a brand (unit pricing), the ingredients in a product (ingredient labeling), the nutrition in foods (nutritional labeling), product freshness (open dating), and the true benefits of a product (truth in advertising). Proposals related to consumer protection include strengthening consumer rights in cases of business fraud, requiring greater product safety, and giving more power to regulatory government agencies. Proposals relating to quality of life include controlling the ingredients that go into certain products (detergents) and packaging (soft-drink containers), reducing the level of advertising "noise," and putting consumer representatives on company boards to protect consumer interests.

Consumers not only have the *right* but also the *responsibility* to protect themselves instead of expecting this function to be performed for them. Consumers

*Consumer desire for more information led to putting ingredients, nutrition, and dating information on product labels.*

Nutrition information

Product freshness information   Ingredients

who believe that they got a bad deal have several remedies available, including contacting the company, or the media, and federal, state, or local agencies, as well as taking their cases to small-claims courts.

## ENVIRONMENTALISM

Whereas consumerists deal with how efficiently the marketing system serves consumer wants, environmentalists are concerned with marketing's effects on the environment and with the costs of serving consumer needs and wants. They are alarmed by damage to the ecosystem caused by strip mining, forest depletion, acid rain, loss of the atmosphere's ozone layer, toxic wastes, and litter. They also are distressed by the loss of recreational areas and the increase in health problems caused by bad air, polluted water, and chemically treated food. These issues are the basis for **environmentalism**—an organized movement of concerned citizens, businesses, and government agencies to protect and improve people's living environment.

**Environmentalism**
An organized movement of concerned citizens and government agencies to protect and improve people's living environment.

Environmentalists are not against marketing and consumption; they simply want people and organizations to operate with more care for the environment. The marketing system's goal should not be to maximize consumption, consumer choice, or consumer satisfaction, but rather to maximize life quality. And "life quality" means not only the quantity and quality of consumer goods and services, but also the quality of the environment. Environmentalists want environmental costs to be included in both producer and consumer decision making.

Environmentalism has hit some industries hard. Steel companies and public utilities have had to invest billions of dollars in pollution-control equipment and costlier fuels. The auto industry has had to introduce expensive emission controls in cars. The packaging industry has had to find ways to reduce litter. The gasoline industry has had to create new unleaded gasolines. These industries often resent environmental regulations, especially when they are imposed too rapidly to allow companies to make proper adjustments. Many of these companies claim that they have absorbed large costs that have made them less competitive.

Other companies and industries, however, have found that they can be both "green" *and* competitive. Consider how the Dutch flower industry has responded to its environmental problems:

> Intense cultivation of flowers in small areas was contaminating the soil and groundwater with pesticides, herbicides, and fertilizers. Facing increasingly strict regulation, ... the Dutch understood that the only effective way to address the problem would be to develop a closed-loop system. In advanced Dutch greenhouses, flowers now grow in water and rock wool, not in soil. This lowers the risk of infestation, reducing the need for fertilizers and pesticides, which are delivered in water that circulates and is reused. The ... closed-loop system also reduces variation in growing conditions, thus improving product quality. Handling costs have gone down because the flowers are cultivated on specially designed platforms. ... The net result is not only dramatically lower environmental impact but also lower costs, better product quality, and enhanced global competitiveness.[11]

Thus, marketers' lives have become more complicated. Marketers must check into the ecological properties of their products and packaging. They must raise prices to cover environmental costs, knowing that the product will be harder to sell. Yet environmental issues have become so important in our society that there is no turning back to the time when few managers worried about the effects of product and marketing decisions on environmental quality. Many analysts view the 1990s as the "earth decade," in which protection of the natural environment has become the major issue facing people around the world. Companies have responded with "green marketing"—developing ecologically safer products, recyclable and biodegradable packaging, better pollution controls, and more energy-efficient operations (see Marketing at Work 17-3).

Environmentalism creates some special challenges for global marketers. As international trade barriers come down and global markets expand, environmental issues have an ever-greater impact on international trade. Countries in North America, Western Europe, and other developed regions are developing stringent environmental standards. In the United States, for example, more than two dozen major pieces of environmental legislation have been enacted since 1970, and recent events suggest that more regulation is on the way. A side accord to the North American Free Trade Agreement (NAFTA) set up a commission for resolving environmental matters. And the European Union's Eco-Management and Audit Regulation provides guidelines for environmental self-regulation.[12]

However, environmental policies still vary widely from country to country, and uniform worldwide standards are not expected for another 15 years or more.[13] Although countries such as Denmark, Germany, Japan, and the United States have fully developed environmental policies and high public expectations, major countries such as China, India, Brazil, and Russia are in only the early stages of developing such policies. Moreover, environmental factors that motivate consumers in one country may have no impact on consumers in another. For example, PVC soft-drink bottles cannot be used in Switzerland or Germany. However, they are preferred in France, which has an extensive recycling process for them. Thus, international companies are finding it difficult to develop standard environmental practices that work around the world. Instead, they are creating general policies, and then translating these policies into tailored programs that meet local regulations and expectations.

# MARKETING AT WORK 17-3

## THE NEW ENVIRONMENTALISM AND "GREEN MARKETING"

On Earth Day 1970, a newly emerging environmentalism movement made its first large-scale effort to educate people about the dangers of pollution. This was a tough task: At the time, most folks weren't all that interested in environmental problems. By 1990, however, Earth Day had became a nationwide cause, punctuated by articles in major magazines and newspapers, prime-time television extravaganzas, and countless events. It turned out to be just the start of an entire "Earth Decade" in which environmentalism has become a massive worldwide force.

These days, environmentalism has broad public support. People hear and read daily about a growing list of environmental problems—global warming, acid rain, depletion of the ozone layer, air and water pollution, hazardous waste disposal, the buildup of solid wastes—and they are calling for solutions. The new environmentalism is causing many consumers to rethink what products they buy and from whom. These changing consumer attitudes have sparked a major new marketing thrust—*green marketing*—by companies to develop and market environmentally responsible products. Committed "green" companies pursue not only environmental cleanup but also pollution prevention. True "green" work requires companies

*Corporate environmentalism: Enlightened companies are taking action not because someone is forcing them to, but because it is the right thing to do.*

to practice the three R's of waste management: reducing, reusing, and recycling waste.

McDonald's provides a good example of green marketing. It used to purchase Coca-Cola syrup in plastic bags encased in cardboard, but now the syrup is delivered directly from tank trucks into storage vats at restaurants. The change saves millions of pounds of packaging a year. All napkins, bags, and tray liners in McDonald's restaurants are made from recycled paper, as are its carry-out drink trays and even much of the stationery used at headquarters. For a company the size of McDonald's, even small changes can make a big difference. For example, just making its

drinking straws 20 percent lighter saved the company 1 million pounds of waste per year. Beyond turning its own products green, McDonald's has spent more than $1 billion purchasing recycled materials for building and remodeling its restaurants, and it challenges its suppliers to furnish and use recycled products.

Producers in a wide range of industries are responding to environmental concerns. For example, 3M runs a "Pollution Prevention Pays" program, which has led to substantial reductions in pollution and cost. Dow built a new ethylene plant in Alberta that uses 40 percent less energy and releases 97 percent less wastewater. Herman Miller, a large office furniture manufacturer, set a trend in the furniture industry when it began using tropical woods from sustainably managed sources, altering even its classic furniture lines. It went even further by reusing packaging, recapturing solvents used in staining, and burning fabric scraps and sawdust to produce energy for its manufacturing plant. These moves not only help the environment, they also save Herman Miller $750,000 per year on energy and landfill costs.

Even retailers are jumping onto the "green" bandwagon. For example, Wal-Mart is pressuring its 7,000 suppliers to provide it with more recycled products. In its stores, Wal-Mart runs videos to help educate customers about waste treatment, and the retailer has set up more than 900 recycling drop-off bins in store parking lots around the nation. It's even opening "eco-friendly" stores. In these stores, the air conditioning systems use non-ozone-depleting refrigerant, rainwater is collected from parking lots and rooftops for landscaping, skylights supplement fluorescent lighting that is adjusted by photo sensors, and the road sign is solar-powered.

During the early phase of the new environmentalism, promoting environmentally improved products and actions ballooned into a big business. In fact, environmentalists and regulators became concerned that companies were going overboard with their use of terms like *recyclable,*

*biodegradable,* and *environmentally responsible.* Perhaps of equal concern was that, as more and more marketers used "green" marketing claims, more and more consumers would view them as little more than gimmicks.

Some overeager "green" marketing campaigns were vigorously attacked by environmentalists and lawmakers for making unproven or improper claims. For example, Mobil altered its Hefty trash bags so that they would break down more easily, and then began to market them as "degradable." However, these claims ran afoul of the Environmental Defense Fund and several states' attorneys general when it was learned that the bags only degrade when they are exposed to air and light, whereas most trash bags are buried in landfills. In 1992, the Federal Trade Commission released a set of voluntary guidelines for "green" marketing terms to help guide marketers making environmental claims for their products.

As we close out the century, environmentalism appears to be moving into a more mature phase. Gone are the hastily prepared environmental pitches and products designed to capitalize on, or even exploit, growing public concern. The new environmentalism is now going mainstream—broader, deeper, and more sophisticated. In the words of one analyst:

*Dressing up ads with pictures of eagles and trees will no longer woo an environmentally sophisticated audience. People want to know that companies are incorporating environmental values into their manufacturing processes, products, packaging, and the very fabric of their corporate cultures. They . . . want to know that companies will not compromise the ability of future generations to enjoy the quality of life that we enjoy today. . . . As a result, we're seeing the marriage of performance benefits and environmental benefits . . . one reinforces the other.*

In all, some companies have responded to consumer environmental concerns by doing only what is required to avert new regulations or to keep environmentalists quiet. Others have rushed to make money by catering to the public's mounting concern for the environment. But enlightened companies are taking action not because someone is forcing them to, or to reap short-run profits, but because it is the right thing to do. They believe that environmental farsightedness today will pay off tomorrow—for both the customer and the company.

*Sources:* Quote from Robert Rehak, "Green Marketing Awash in Third Wave," *Advertising Age,* November 22, 1993, p. 22. Also see Joe Schwartz, "Earth Day Today," *American Demographics,* April 1990, pp. 40–41; Eric Wieffering, "Wal-Mart Turns Green in Kansas," *American Demographics,* December 1993, p. 23; David Woodruff, "Herman Miller: How Green Is My Factory," *Business Week,* September 16, 1991, pp. 54–56; Jacquelyn Ottman, "Environmentalism Will Be *the* Trend of the '90s," *Marketing News,* December 7, 1992, p. 13; Peter Stisser, "A Deeper Shade of Green," *American Demographics,* March 1994, pp. 24–29; Jacquelyn Ottman, "When It Comes to Green Marketing, Companies Are Finally Getting It Right," *Brandweek,* April 17, 1995, p. 17; and the special issue on green advertising of *Journal of Advertising,* Summer 1995.

## PUBLIC ACTIONS TO REGULATE MARKETING

Citizen concerns about marketing practices will usually lead to public attention and legislative proposals. New bills will be debated—many will be defeated, others will be modified, and a few will become workable laws.

Many of the laws that affect marketing are listed in Chapter 3. The task is to translate these laws into the language that marketing executives understand as they make decisions about competitive relations, products, price, promotion, and channels of distribution. Figure 17-1 illustrates the major legal issues facing marketing management.

## ▶ BUSINESS ACTIONS TOWARD SOCIALLY RESPONSIBLE MARKETING

At first, many companies opposed consumerism and environmentalism. They thought that the criticisms were either unfair or unimportant. But by now, most companies have grown to accept the new consumer rights, at least in principle. They might oppose certain pieces of legislation as inappropriate ways to solve certain consumer problems, but they recognize the consumer's right to information and protection. Many of these companies have responded positively to consumerism and environmentalism in order to serve consumer needs better.

**FIGURE 17-1**
*Major marketing decision areas that may be called into question under the law*

**Selling decisions**
Bribing?
Stealing trade secrets?
Disparaging customers?
Misrepresenting?
Disclosure of customer rights?
Unfair discrimination?

**Advertising decisions**
False advertising?
Deceptive advertising?
Bait-and-switch advertising?
Promotional allowances and services?

**Channel decisions**
Exclusive dealing?
Exclusive territorial distributorships?
Tying agreements?
Dealer's rights?

**Product decisions**
Product additions and deletions?
Patent protection?
Product quality and safety?
Product warranty?

**Packaging decisions**
Fair packaging and labeling?
Excessive cost?
Scarce resources?
Pollution?

**Price decisions**
Price fixing?
Predatory pricing?
Price discrimination?
Minimum pricing?
Price increases?
Deceptive pricing?

**Competitive relations decisions**
Anticompetitive acquisition?
Barriers to entry?
Predatory competition?

# ENLIGHTENED MARKETING

**Enlightened marketing**
A marketing philosophy holding that a company's marketing should support the best long-run performance of the marketing system.

The philosophy of **enlightened marketing** holds that a company's marketing should support the best long-run performance of the marketing system. Enlightened marketing consists of five principles: *consumer-oriented marketing, innovative marketing, value marketing, sense-of-mission marketing,* and *societal marketing.*

## Consumer-Oriented Marketing

**Consumer-oriented marketing**
A principle of enlightened marketing that holds that a company should view and organize its marketing activities from the consumers' point of view.

**Consumer-oriented marketing** means that the company should view and organize its marketing activities from the consumer's point of view. It should work hard to sense, serve, and satisfy the needs of a defined group of customers. Consider the following example:

> Barat College, a women's college in Lake Forest, Illinois, published a college catalog that openly spelled out Barat College's strong and weak points. Among the weak points it shared with applicants were the following: "An exceptionally talented student musician or mathematician . . . might be advised to look further for a college with top faculty and facilities in that field. . . . The full range of advanced specialized courses offered in a university will be absent. . . . The library collection is average for a small college, but low in comparison with other high-quality institutions."

"Telling it like it is" is intended to build confidence so that applicants really know what they will find at Barat College and to emphasize that Barat College will strive to improve its consumer value as rapidly as time and funds permit.

## Innovative Marketing

**Innovative marketing**
A principle of enlightened marketing requiring that a company seek real product and marketing improvement.

The principle of **innovative marketing** requires that the company continuously seek real product and marketing improvements. The company that overlooks new and better ways to do things will eventually lose customers to another company that has found a better way. An excellent example of an innovative marketer is Procter & Gamble:

> Wisk, a Lever Bros. product, dominated liquid detergents for a generation, and liquids were taking a growing share of the $3.2-billion-a-year detergent market. P&G attempted to topple Wisk with run-of-the-laundry-room liquids called Era and Solo, but couldn't come close. Then it developed a liquid with 12 cleaning agents, twice the norm, and a molecule that traps dirt in the wash water. P&G christened it Liquid Tide and put it in a bottle colored the same fire-bright color as the ubiquitous Tide box. After just 18 months on the market, Liquid Tide was washing as many clothes as Wisk in the U.S., and the two were locked in a fierce battle for the No. 2 position, after powdered Tide, among all detergents.[14]

## Value Marketing

**Value marketing**
A principle of enlightened marketing that holds that a company should put most of its resources into value-building marketing investments.

According to the principle of **value marketing**, the company should put most of its resources into value-building marketing investments. Many things that marketers do—one-shot sales promotions, minor packaging changes, advertising puffery—may raise sales in the short run but will add less *value* than would actual improvements in the product's quality, features, or convenience. Enlightened marketing calls for building long-run consumer loyalty by continually improving the value that consumers receive from the firm's marketing offer.

### Sense-of-Mission Marketing

**Sense-of-mission marketing**
A principle of enlightened marketing that holds that a company should define its mission in broad social terms rather than narrow product terms.

**Sense-of-mission marketing** means that the company should define its mission in broad *social* terms rather than narrow *product* terms. When a company defines a social mission, employees feel better about their work and have a clearer sense of direction. For example, defined in narrow product terms, Johnson & Johnson's mission might be "to sell Band-Aids and baby oil." But the company states its mission more broadly:

> We believe that our first responsibility is to the doctors, nurses, and patients, to mothers and all others who use our products and services. In meeting their needs everything we do must be of high quality. We must constantly strive to reduce our costs in order to maintain reasonable prices. Customers' orders must be serviced promptly and accurately. Our suppliers and distributors must have an opportunity to make a fair profit. We are responsible to our employees, the men and women who work for us throughout the world. Everyone must be considered as an individual. We must respect their dignity and recognize their merit. . . . We are responsible to the communities in which we live and work and to the world community as well. We must be good citizens—support good works and charities and bear our fair share of taxes. We must encourage civic improvements and better health and education. We must maintain in good order the property we are privileged to use, protecting the environment and natural resources.[15]

Reshaping the basic task of selling consumer products into the larger mission of serving the interests of consumers, employees, suppliers, and others in the world community gives a new sense of purpose to Johnson & Johnson employees.

### Societal Marketing

**Social marketing**
The design, implementation, and control of programs seeking to increase the acceptability of a social idea, cause, or practice among a target group.

Following the principle of **societal marketing**, an enlightened company makes marketing decisions by considering consumers' wants and interests, the company's requirements, and society's long-run interests. Such a company is aware that neglecting consumer and societal long-run interests is a disservice to consumers and society. Alert companies view societal problems as opportunities.

A societally oriented marketer wants to design products that are not only pleasing but also beneficial. The difference is shown in Figure 17-2. Products can be classified according to their degree of immediate consumer satisfaction and

**FIGURE 17-2**
*Societal classification of products*

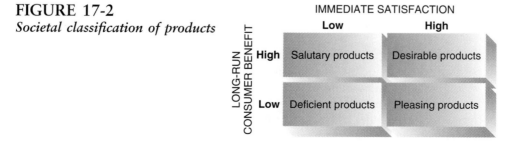

**Deficient products**
Products that have neither immediate appeal nor long-run benefits.

**Pleasing products**
Products that give high immediate satisfaction, but may hurt consumers in the long run.

**Salutary products**
Products that have low appeal but may benefit consumers in the long run.

**Desirable products**
Products that give both high immediate satisfaction and high long-run benefits.

long-run consumer benefit. **Deficient products**, such as bad-tasting and ineffective medicine, have neither immediate appeal nor long-run benefits. **Pleasing products** give high immediate satisfaction but may hurt consumers in the long run. An example is cigarettes. **Salutary products** have low appeal but benefit consumers in the long run. Seat belts and air bags in automobiles are salutary products. **Desirable products** give both high immediate satisfaction and high long-run benefits. A desirable product with immediate satisfaction and long-run benefit would be a tasty *and* nutritious breakfast food.

An example of a desirable product is Archer Daniels Midland's Harvest Burgers:

> Archer Daniels Midland (ADM) is the country's largest agricultural commodities processor. Asked by Mother Teresa to develop a product that would help her feed the world, ADM perfected a soy product which, when mixed with water and cooked, tastes like hamburger. But the soy product costs much less than real meat. Claims an ADM executive, "You can feed 30 times as many people off an acre of land by raising soy alone, than growing soy and feeding it to an animal and then eating the animal." The soy product is also more nutritious—it has 75 percent less fat, 40 percent fewer calories, and less than 30

*Desirable products: Officials in Kiev ordered $100 million worth of ADM's meat-like Harvest Burgers soy product, eliminating the need for an estimated 13 million cows.*

percent of the cholesterol found in a typical hamburger. Thus, the product promises to have enormous economic and nutritional impact. While doing good, it appears that ADM will also do well. It is now selling the meatlike product in Italy, Finland, Hungary, and Russia. In Kiev, where meat shortages are a major problem, officials ordered $100 million worth. They calculate that the purchase would eliminate the need for 13 million cows. Sales are also brisk in U.S. and other consumer markets, where ADM sells the product as Harvest Burgers, aimed at a health-conscious, vegetarian niche.[16]

The challenge posed by pleasing products is that they sell very well, but may end up hurting the consumer. The product opportunity, therefore, is to add long-run benefits without reducing the product's pleasing qualities. For example, Sears developed a phosphate-free laundry detergent that was also very effective. The challenge posed by salutary products is to add some pleasing qualities so that they will become more desirable in consumers' minds. For example, synthetic fats and fat substitutes, such as NutraSweet's Simplesse and P&G's Olestra, promise to improve the appeal of more healthful low-calorie and low-fat foods.

# MARKETING ETHICS

Conscientious marketers face many moral dilemmas. The best course of action is often unclear. Because not all managers have fine moral sensitivity, companies need to develop *corporate marketing ethics policies*—broad guidelines that everyone in the organization must follow. These policies should cover distributor relations, advertising standards, customer service, pricing, product development, and general ethical standards.

The finest guidelines cannot resolve all the difficult ethical situations that the marketer faces. Table 17-1 lists some difficult ethical situations that marketers could face during their careers. If marketers choose immediate sales-producing actions in all these cases, their marketing behavior might well be described as immoral or even amoral. If they refuse to go along with *any* of the actions, they might be ineffective as marketing managers and unhappy because of the constant moral tension. Managers need a set of principles that will help them figure out the moral importance of each situation and decide how far they can go in good conscience.

But *what* principle should guide companies and marketing managers on issues of ethics and social responsibility?[17] One philosophy is that such issues are decided by the free market and legal system. Under this principle, companies and their managers are not responsible for making moral judgments. Companies can in good conscience do whatever the system allows.

A second philosophy puts responsibility not in the system, but in the hands of individual companies and managers. This more enlightened philosophy suggests that a company should have a "social conscience." Companies and managers should apply high standards of ethics and morality when making corporate decisions, regardless of what the system allows. History provides an endless list of examples of company actions that were legal and allowed but were highly irresponsible. Consider the following example:

Prior to the Pure Food and Drug Act, the advertising for a diet pill promised that a person taking this pill could eat virtually anything at

**TABLE 17-1**   *Some Morally Difficult Situations in Marketing*

1. You work for a cigarette company and up to now have not been convinced that cigarettes cause cancer. A report comes across your desk that clearly shows the link between smoking and cancer. What would you do?
2. Your R&D department has changed one of your products slightly. It is not really "new and improved," but you know that putting this statement on the package and in advertising will increase sales. What would you do?
3. You have been asked to add a stripped-down model to your line that could be advertised to pull customers into the store. The product won't be very good, but salespeople will be able to switch buyers up to higher-priced units. You are asked to give the green light for this stripped-down version. What would you do?
4. You are thinking of hiring a product manager who just left a competitor's company. She would be more than happy to tell you all the competitor's plans for the coming year. What would you do?
5. One of your top dealers in an important territory has recently had family troubles, and his sales have slipped. It looks like it will take him awhile to straighten out his family trouble. Meanwhile you are losing many sales. Legally, you can terminate the dealer's franchise and replace him. What would you do?
6. You have a chance to win a big account that will mean a lot to you and your company. The purchasing agent hints that a "gift" would influence the decision. Your assistant recommends sending a fine color television set to the buyer's home. What would you do?
7. You have heard that a competitor has a new product feature that will make a big difference in sales. The competitor will demonstrate the feature in a private dealer meeting at the annual trade show. You can easily send a snooper to this meeting to learn about the new feature. What would you do?
8. You have to choose between three ad campaigns outlined by your agency. The first (a) is a soft-sell, honest information campaign. The second (b) uses sex-loaded emotional appeals and exaggerates the product's benefits. The third (c) involves a noisy, irritating commercial that is sure to gain audience attention. Pretests show that the campaigns are effective in the following order.: c, b, and a. What would you do?
9. You are interviewing a capable female applicant for a job as salesperson. She is better qualified than the men just interviewed. Nevertheless, you know that some of your important customers prefer dealing with men, and you will lose some sales if you hire her. What would you do?
10. You are a sales manager in an encyclopedia company. Your competitor's salespeople are getting into homes by pretending to take a research survey. After they finish the survey, they switch to their sales pitch. This technique seems to be very effective. What would you do?

any time and still lose weight. Too good to be true? Actually the claim was quite true; the product lived up to its billing with frightening efficiency. It seems that the primary active ingredient in this "diet supplement" was tapeworm larvae. These larvae would develop in the intestinal tract and, of course, be well fed; the pill taker would in time, quite literally, starve to death.[18]

Each company and marketing manager must work out a philosophy of socially responsible and ethical behavior. Under the societal marketing concept, each manager must look beyond what is legal and allowed and develop standards based on personal integrity, corporate conscience, and long-run consumer welfare. A clear and responsible philosophy will help the marketing manager deal with the many knotty questions posed by marketing and other human activities.

As with environmentalism, the issue of ethics provides special challenges for international marketers. Business standards and practices vary a great deal from one country to the next. For example, whereas bribes and kickbacks are illegal for U.S. firms, they are standard business practice in many South American countries. The question arises as to whether a company must lower its ethical standards to compete effectively in countries with lower standards. In a recent study, two researchers posed this question to chief executives of large international companies and got a unanimous response: No.[19] For the sake of all of the company's stakeholders—customers, suppliers, employees, shareholders, and the public—it is important to make a commitment to a common set of shared standards worldwide.

For example, John Hancock Mutual Life Insurance Company operates successfully in Southeast Asia, an area that, by Western standards, has widespread questionable business and government practices. Despite warnings from locals that Hancock would have to bend its rules to succeed, Hancock chairman Stephen Brown notes:

> We faced up to this issue early on when we started to deal with Southeast Asia. We told our people that we had the same ethical standards, same procedures, same policies in these countries that we have in the United States, and we do. . . . We just felt that things like payoffs were wrong—and if we had to do business that way, we'd rather not do business. Our employees would not feel good about having different levels of ethics. There may be countries where you have to do that kind of thing. We haven't found that country yet, and if we do, we won't do business there.[20]

Many industrial and professional associations have evolved codes of ethics, and many companies are now adopting their own codes. For example, the American Marketing Association, an international association of marketing managers and scholars, developed the code of ethics shown in Table 17-2. Companies are also developing programs to teach managers about important ethics issues and help them find the proper responses (see Marketing at Work 17-4).

**TABLE 17-2** *American Marketing Association Code of Ethics*

| Members of the American Marketing Association are committed to ethical, professional conduct. They have joined together in subscribing to this Code of Ethics embracing the following topics: | *Responsibilities of the Marketer* Marketers must accept responsibility for the consequences of their activities and make every effort to ensure that their decisions, recommendations, and |
| --- | --- |

actions function to identify, serve, and satisfy all relevant publics: customers, organizations, and society.

*Marketers' professional conduct must be guided by:*
1. The basic rule of professional ethics: not knowingly to do harm.
2. The adherence to all applicable laws and regulations.
3. The accurate representation of their education, training, and experience.
4. The active support, practice, and promotion of this Code of Ethics.

*Honesty and Fairness*
Marketers shall uphold and advance the integrity, honor, and dignity of the marketing profession by:
1. Being honest in serving consumers, clients, employees, suppliers, distributors, and the public.
2. Not knowingly participating in conflict of interest without prior notice to all parties involved.
3. Establishing equitable fee schedules including the payment or receipt of usual, customary, and/or legal compensation for marketing exchanges.

*Rights and Duties of Parties in the Marketing Exchange Process*
Participants in the marketing exchange process should be able to expect that:
1. Products and services offered are safe and fit for their intended uses.
2. Communications about offered products and services are not deceptive.
3. All parties intend to discharge their obligations, financial and otherwise, in good faith.
4. Appropriate internal methods exist for equitable adjustment and/or redress of grievances concerning purchases.

*It is understood that the above would include, but are not limited to, the following responsibilities of the marketer:*
• Disclosure of all substantial risks associated with product or service usage.
• Identification of any product component substitution that might materially change the product or impact on the buyer's purchase decision.
• Identification of extra cost-added features.

*In the area of promotions,*
• Avoidance of false and misleading advertising.
• Rejection of high-pressure manipulations, or misleading sales tactics.

• Avoidance of sales promotions that use deception or manipulation.

*In the area of distribution,*
• Not manipulating the availability of a product for purpose of exploitation.
• Not using coercion in the marketing channel.
• Not exerting undue influence over the reseller's choice to handle a product.

*In the area of pricing,*
• Not engaging in price fixing.
• Not practicing predatory pricing.
• Disclosing the full price associated with any purchase.

*In the area of marketing research,*
• Prohibiting selling or fundraising under the guise of conducting research.
• Maintaining research integrity by avoiding misrepresentation and omission of pertinent research data.
• Treating outside clients and suppliers fairly.

*Organizational Relationships*
Marketers should be aware of how their behavior may influence or impact on the behavior of others in organizational relationships. They should not demand, encourage, or apply coercion to obtain unethical behavior in their relationships with others, such as employees, suppliers, or customers.
1. Apply confidentiality and anonymity in professional relationships with regard to privileged information.
2. Meet their obligations and responsibilities in contracts and mutual agreements in a timely manner.
3. Avoid taking the work of others, in whole, or in part, and representing this work as their own or directly benefitting from it without compensation or consent of the originator or owner.
4. Avoid manipulations to take advantage of situations to maximize personal welfare in a way that unfairly deprives or damages the organization of others.

Any AMA member found to be in violation of any provision of this Code of Ethics may have his or her Association membership suspended or revoked.

## MARKETING AT WORK 17-4

# THE GENERAL DYNAMICS ETHICS PROGRAM

The General Dynamics ethics program is considered the most comprehensive in the industry. And little wonder—it was put together as generals from the Pentagon looked on. The program came about after charges that the company had deliberately overbilled the government on defense contracts.

Now at General Dynamics, a committee of board members reviews its ethics policies, and a corporate ethics director and steering group execute the program. The company has set up hotlines that provide employees with instant advice on job-related ethical issues and has given each employee a wallet card listing a toll-free number to report suspected wrongdoing. Nearly all employees have attended work-

*General Dynamics has developed a model ethics program.*

shops; those for salespeople cover such topics as expense accounts and supplier relations.

The company also has a 20-page code of ethics, which tells employees in detail how to conduct themselves in business. Here are some examples of rules for salespeople:

• If it becomes clear that the company must engage in unethical or

illegal activity to win a contract, it will not pursue that business further.

• To prevent hidden interpretations or understandings, all information provided relative to products and services should be clear and concise.

• Receiving or soliciting gifts, entertainment, or anything else of value is prohibited.

• In countries where common practices indicate acceptance of conduct lower than that to which General Dynamics aspires, salespeople will follow the company's standards.

• Under no circumstances may an employee offer or give anything to customers or their representatives in an effort to influence them.

*Source:* Adapted from "This Industry Leader Means Business," *Sales & Marketing Management,* May 1987, p. 44. Also see Stewart Toy, "The Defense Scandal," *Business Week,* July 1, 1988, pp. 28–30; and Richard A. Baker, "An Evaluation of the Ethics Program at General Dynamics," *Journal of Business Ethics,* Vol. 12, 1993, pp. 165–77.

According to one survey of Fortune 1000 companies, over 40 percent of these companies are holding ethics workshops and seminars, and one-third have set up ethics committees.[21] Further, more than 200 major U.S. companies have appointed high-level ethics officers to champion ethics issues and to help resolve ethics problems and concerns facing employees. For example, in 1991, Nynex created the new position of vice president of ethics, supported by a dozen full-time staff and a million-dollar budget. Since then, the new department has trained some 95,000 Nynex employees. Such training includes sending 22,000 managers to full-day workshops that include case studies on ethical actions in marketing, finance, and other business functions. One workshop deals with the use of improperly obtained competitive data which, managers are instructed, is not permitted.[22]

Many companies have developed innovative ways to educate employees about ethics:

Citicorp has developed an ethics board game, which teams of employees use to solve hypothetical quandaries. General Electric employees can tap into specially designed software on their personal computers to get answers to ethical questions. At Texas Instruments, employees are treated to a weekly column on ethics over an electronic news service. One popular feature: a kind of Dear Abby mailbag, answers provided by the company's ethics officer, . . . that deals with the troublesome issues employees face most often.[23]

Still, written codes and ethics programs do not assure ethical behavior. Ethics and social responsibility require a total corporate commitment. They must be a component of the overall corporate culture. According to David R. Whitman, Chairman of the Board of Whirlpool Corporation, "In the final analysis, 'ethical behavior' must be an integral part of the organization, a way of life that is deeply ingrained in the collective corporate body. . . . In any business enterprise, ethical behavior must be a tradition, a way of conducting one's affairs that is passed from generation to generation of employees at all levels of the organization. It is the responsibility of management, starting at the very top, to both set the example by personal conduct and create an environment that not only encourages and rewards ethical behavior, but which also makes anything less totally unacceptable."[24]

The future holds many challenges and opportunities for marketing managers as they move into the twenty-first century. Technological advances in solar energy, personal computers, interactive television, modern medicine, and new forms of transportation, recreation, and communication provide abundant marketing opportunities. However, forces in the socioeconomic, cultural, and natural environments increase the limits under which marketing can be carried out. Companies that are able to create new values in a socially responsible way will have a world to conquer.

## SUMMARY

A marketing system should sense, serve, and satisfy consumer needs and improve the quality of consumers' lives. In working to meet consumer needs, marketers may take some actions that are not to everyone's liking or benefit. Marketing managers should be aware of the main *criticisms of marketing*.

Marketing's *impact on individual consumer welfare* has been criticized for its high prices, deceptive practices, high-pressure selling, shoddy or unsafe products, planned obsolescence, and poor service to disadvantaged consumers. Marketing's *impact on society* has been criticized for creating false wants and too much materialism, too few social goods, cultural pollution, and too much political power. Critics have also criticized marketing's *impact on other businesses* for harming competitors and reducing competition through acquisitions, practices that create barriers to entry, and unfair competitive marketing practices.

Concerns about the marketing system have led to *citizen-action movements*. *Consumerism* is an organized social movement intended to strengthen the rights and power of consumers relative to sellers. Alert marketers view it as an opportunity to serve consumers better by providing more consumer information, education, and protection. *Environmentalism* is an organized social movement seeking to minimize the harm done to the environment and quality of life by marketing practices. It calls for curbing consumer wants when their satisfaction would create too much environmental cost. Citizen action has led to the passage of many laws to protect consumers in the area of product safety, truth in packaging, truth in lending, and truth in advertising.

Many companies originally opposed these social movements and laws, but most of them now recognize a need for positive consumer information, education, and protection. Some companies have followed a policy of *enlightened marketing* based on the principles of *consumer orientation, innovation, value creation, social mission,* and *societal orientation*. Increasingly, companies are responding to the need to provide company policies and guidelines to help their managers deal with questions of *marketing ethics*.

## KEY TERMS

Consumerism

Consumer-oriented marketing

Deficient products

Desirable products

Enlightened marketing

Environmentalism

Innovative marketing

Pleasing products

Salutary products

Sense-of-mission marketing

Societal marketing

Value marketing

## QUESTIONS FOR DISCUSSION

1. Was Gerber right or wrong not to recall its baby food after customers complained of finding glass fragments in bottles? Without considering what you know about how things turned out, analyze the situation facing Gerber in 1986. What action would you have recommended at the time?

2. Does marketing create barriers to entry or *reduce* them? Describe how a small manufacturer of household cleaning products could use advertising to compete with Procter & Gamble.

3. If you were a marketing manager at Dow Chemical Company, tell which you would prefer: government regulations on acceptable levels of air and water pollution, or a voluntary industry code suggesting target levels of emissions. Why?

4. Should a company's code of marketing ethics apply to subcontractors operating abroad?

5. Compare the marketing concept with the principle of societal marketing. Do you think marketers should adopt the societal marketing concept? Why or why not?

6. If you had the power to change our marketing system in any way feasible, decide what improvements you would make. What improvements could you make as a consumer or entry-level marketing practitioner?

## APPLYING THE CONCEPTS

1. Changes in consumer attitudes, especially the growth of consumerism and environmentalism, have led to more societal marketing—and to more marketing that is *supposedly* good for society, but is actually closer to deception.

   ◆ List three examples of marketing campaigns that you feel are genuine societal marketing. If possible, find examples of advertising or packaging that support these campaigns.

   ◆ Find three examples of deceptive or borderline imitations of societal marketing. How are you able to tell which campaigns are genuine and which are not?

   ◆ What remedies, if any, would you recommend for this problem?

2. Consider contemporary America. As a society, we have many things to be proud of—and many areas where there is more work to be done.

   ◆ Make a list of ten important things that need to be done in America. Your list may include economic issues, education, health care, environment, politics, or any other significant sphere.

   ◆ Pick one issue that is especially important to you from the list above. Using what you have learned from this course, make a list of ways in which marketing principles and tools could be used to help in your issue.

# REFERENCES

1. See Patricia Strnad, "Gerber Ignores Tylenol Textbook," Advertising Age, March 10, 1986, p. 3; Felix Kessler, "Tremors from the Tylenol Scare Hit Food Companies," Fortune, March 31, 1986, pp. 59–62; Judann Dagnoli, "Brief Slump Expected for Sudafed," Advertising Age, March 18, 1991, p. 53; Gerald C. Meyers, "Product Tampering and Public Outcry," Industry Week, August 2, 1993, p. 41; and Laura Zinn, "The Right Moves, Baby," Business Week, July 5, 1993, pp. 30–31.

2. See John F. Gaski and Michael Etzel, "The Index of Consumer Sentiment Toward Marketing," Journal of Marketing, July 1986, pp. 71–81; Faye Rice, "How to Deal with Tougher Customers," Fortune, December 3, 1990, pp. 38–48; Richard W. Pollay and Banwari Mittal, "Here's the Beef: Factors, Determinants, and Segments in Consumer Criticism of Advertising," Journal of Marketing, July 1993, pp. 99–114; and Leah Rickard, "Ex-Soviet States Lead World in Ad Cynicism," Advertising Age, June 5, 1995, p. 3.

3. Excerpts from Theodore Levitt, "The Morality (?) of Advertising," Harvard Business Review, July–August 1970, pp. 84–92. Also see Joel J. Davis, "Ethics in Advertising Decision Making," Journal of Consumer Affairs, December 22, 1994, p. 380.

4. Sandra Pesmen, "How Low Is Low? How Free Is Free?" Advertising Age, May 7, 1990, p. S10.

5. For a thought-provoking short case involving planned obsolescence, see James A. Heely and Roy L. Nersesian, "The Case of Planned Obsolescence," Management Accounting, February 1994, p. 67.

6. See Judith Bell and Bonnie Maria Burlin, "In Urban Areas: Many More Still Pay More for Food," Journal of Public Policy and Marketing, Fall 1993, pp. 268–70; and Alan R. Andreasen, "Revisiting the Disadvantages: Old Lesson and New Problems," Journal of Public Policy and Marketing, Fall 1993, pp. 270–75.

7. See Anne B. Fisher, "A Brewing Revolt Against the Rich," Fortune, December 17, 1990, pp. 89–94; and Norval D. Glenn, "What Does Family Mean?" American Demographics, June 1992, pp. 30–37.

8. From an advertisement for Fact magazine, which does not carry advertisements.

9. Nancy Arnott, "Drugstore Cowboys Shoot It Out," Sales & Marketing Management, August 1994, p. 15; and Glenn Snyder, "Wal-Mart Wins Pricing Case—Or Did It?" Progressive Grocer, February 1995, p. 11.

10. For more details, see Paul N. Bloom and Stephen A. Greyser, "The Maturing of Consumerism," Harvard Business Review, November–December 1981, pp. 130–39; Robert J. Samuelson, "The Aging of Ralph Nader," Newsweek, December 16, 1985, p. 57; and Douglas A. Harbrecht, "The Second Coming of Ralph Nader," Business Week, March 6, 1989, p. 28.

11. Michael E. Porter and Claas van der Linde, "Green and Competitive: Ending the Stalemate," Harvard Business Review, September–October 1995, pp. 120–34.

12. S. Noble Robinson, Ralph Earle III, and Ronald A. N. McLean, "Transnational Corporations and Global Environmental Policy," Prizm, Arthur D. Little, Inc., Cambridge, MA, First Quarter, 1994, pp. 51–63.

13. Ibid., p. 56.

14. Faye Rice, "The King of Suds Reigns Again," Fortune, August 4, 1986, p. 131.

15. Quoted from "Our Credo," Johnson & Johnson, New Brunswick, New Jersey.

16. See Mollie Neal, "Reaping the Rewards of Skillful Marketing . . . While Helping Humanity," Direct Marketing, September 1993, p. 24; and James R. Norman, "With or Without the Ketchup?" Forbes, March 14, 1995, p. 107.

17. For more discussion of basic ethics philosophies, see Carolyn Wiley, "The ABCs of Business Ethics: Definitions, Philosophies, and Implementation," Industrial Management, January 1995, p. 22.

18. Dan R. Dalton and Richard A. Cosier, "The Four Faces of Social Responsibility," Business Horizons, May–June 1982, pp. 19–27.

19. John F. Magee and P. Ranganath Nayak, "Leaders' Perspectives on Business Ethics," Prizm, Arthur D. Little, Inc., Cambridge, MA, First Quarter, 1994, pp. 65-77.

20. Ibid., pp. 71–72.

21. John A. Byrne, "Businesses Are Signing Up for Ethics 101," Business Week, February 15, 1988, pp. 56–57.

22. Mark Hendricks, "Ethics in Action," Management Review, January 1995, pp. 53–55.

23. Kenneth Labich, "The New Crisis in Business Management," Fortune, April 20, 1992, pp. 167–76, here p. 176.

24. From "Ethics as a Practical Matter," a message from David R. Whitman, Chairman of the Board of Whirlpool Corporation, as reprinted in Ricky E. Griffin and Ronald J. Ebert, Business (Englewood Cliffs, NJ: Prentice Hall, 1989), pp. 578–79. For more on marketing ethics, see Lynn Sharp Paine, "Managing for Organizational Integrity," Harvard Business Review, March–April 1994, pp. 106–17.

# Video Case 1
## *Patagonia: Aiming for No Growth*

Patagonia's bright blues, reds, and purples are often spotted on adventurers shooting white-water rapids, climbing mountainsides, whizzing down ski slopes, and occasionally just lying around—anywhere in the world. Patagonia is a study in contrasts—has become a very successful company even though it tries to *discourage* consumption.

Yvon Chouinard, a young Californian, founded Patagonia in 1957 to sell his handmade mountain-climbing equipment. Sales grew slowly until 1972, when he decided to include clothing—rugby shirts and canvas shorts—in his small outdoor-equipment catalog. To move these products, he offered a money-back guarantee, which was feasible only because he sold high-quality, high-priced, and durable products. As sales grew, Chouinard began to design and introduce newer, innovative fabrics, making products such as foamback raingear, pile and bunting outerwear, and polypropylene underwear. Patagonia's strategy has been to compete on innovation rather than costs. The company is known not for low prices but for developing new materials and designs.

The heady eighties were the perfect growth period for Patagonia. Consumers were brand- and not price-conscious—they wanted quality. They had discovered adventure travel and were engaging in outdoor activities in record numbers. Style, individualism, and image were "in." Magazine articles celebrated Chouinard's idea of work—spending six to eight months a year hiking, fishing, climbing, and surfing to "test" his new designs and develop new product ideas. As a "fun hog," he was devoted to any nonmotorized outdoor activity. And as "Patagonia's outside man," he was able to gauge the functionality, comfort, and usefulness of outdoor gear he sold.

Patagonia's concern for the environment contributes significantly to its image. For example, as early as 1972, Chouinard abandoned production of traditional mountain-climbing pitons in favor of chocks that could be inserted into cracks in a rock face, leaving no holes or other damage. Other climbers willingly followed Chouinard's lead by switching to the more environmentally responsible chocks. In 1985, Patagonia began giving away 10 percent of its pretax profits—usually in small amounts of from $1,000 to $3,000—to less well-known environmental groups. Today, it donates one percent of sales or 10 percent of pretax profit, whichever is greater. To date, the company has given away more than $3.5 million, along with free goods that organizations can sell or auction off to raise funds.

In 1991, recession struck, sales stalled, and inventory piled up, eventually causing Patagonia to sell goods below cost. An *INC.* magazine article entitled "Lost in Patagonia" concluded that the firm would not survive. The article claimed that Patagonia lacked "real business managers" who walk the shop floor daily and pay close attention to costs. However, a quick glance around any trail shop will tell you that Patagonia survived. How? First, it maintained close contact with its market through its Guide Line service, which customers can call for help when planning outdoor activities anywhere in the world. Also, each Patagonia catalog features a "Capture a Patagoniac" appeal, soliciting photographs of customers engaging in outdoor activities (and wearing Patagonia clothing, of course). The company uses these pictures in its catalogs, carefully identifying every Patagoniac. Buy from Patagonia, send in your pictures, and *you* might be featured in the next catalog.

Patagonia has also established a no growth policy by dropping 30 percent of its clothing lines and reducing the number of styles it offers (it sells only two styles of ski pants, for example). It no longer buys mailing lists, has reduced the size of catalogs, and limits the number of catalogs it produces to two a year. The company has even reduced its advertising spending, and it sells only to dealers who get preseason orders in first. Patagonia focuses on making multifunctional clothing, such as jackets for skiing, hiking and kayaking. And it is faithful to a basic Patagonia design premise—uncluttered function. Under this premise, it develops totally functional designs that eliminate all unnecessary features, use the least material possible, and last as long as possible.

Patagonia has also adopted an environmental audit to determine the impact of all goods and supplies it uses. This has led them to change dyes and packaging, eliminate the use of formaldehyde, use organic cotton, and work with suppliers to recycle waste by-products. A major accomplishment was the introduction of PCR Synchilla—a fleecelike fabric made with recycled plastic soda bottles. In 1994, production of its pricey PCR Synchilla sweaters, coats, and gloves consumed eight million recycled two-liter bottles.

Through these actions, Patagonia has unleashed a debate about the social responsibilities and obligations of business. Chouinard hopes to decrease consumption in developed countries so that the Earth's inhabitants will not overly tax the planet's resources. But critics contend that his actions will have little effect on consumption levels. Some point out that the key to reducing consumption lies in reducing sales, not the number of styles available in a product category. Other critics contend that consumers turned off by Patagonia's high prices and lack of styles will simply buy a variety of ski pants elsewhere, leaving consumption levels unaffected. Still others claim that Chouinard confuses environmental impact with environmental damage—that use of the Earth's resources should be evaluated on the basis of the tremendous benefits that result. Finally, some people really don't want to reduce their standard of living, and they don't want Chouinard coercing them into doing so. This last argument may be the most telling one—Chouinard may find that changing cultural patterns is no easy task.

## QUESTIONS

1. How does Patagonia exemplify the marketing concept? The societal marketing concept?
2. What type of marketing strategy has Patagonia pursued?
3. How has Patagonia responded to the forces in the macroenvironment?
4. Are the critics right? Or will Patagonia's actions help reduce consumption?

*Sources:* "Can Slower Growth Save the World?" *Business and Society Review,* Spring 1993, pp. 10–20; Fleming Meeks, "The Man Is the Message," *Forbes,* April 17, 1989, pp. 148–152; Edward O. Welles, "Lost in Patagonia," *INC.,* August 1992, pp. 44–57; and numerous company-supplied materials. The author gratefully thanks Ms. Lu Setnicka for her assistance with this case.

# Video Case 2
## *The M/A/R/C Group: Talking to Customers*

The M/A/R/C Group is one of the 10 largest marketing intelligence firms in North America. Its primary philosophy of business is building collaborative partnerships with every client. The M/A/R/C Group chooses to be judged based on the success of their customers and clients. This partnership is fostered through a work team approach, meaning that each client has a team of researchers, a senior partner, an account executive, an analyst, a project manager, and staff experts.

Scott Bailey, a senior vice president at M/A/R/C, describes M/A/R/C's approach as follows: "Talking to customers—that is the real service that we offer our clients. Many marketing managers are too far removed from their market. At M/A/R/C we develop custom-designed research to talk to the client's actual or potential customers—we are the link between the client company and its market.

"There are three ways that we contact customers: telephone, mail, and field suppliers. Through our banks of telephone interviewers, we can select representative and probability samples of users, nonusers, and potential users of the product or brand using random-digit dialing. With computer-assisted interviewing, telephone operators can easily switch from one questionnaire to another as research needs change. If clients prefer, we send mail surveys. They are less expensive but take longer to complete. To talk to consumers in person or to show them products, we can use our field suppliers, who can either do mall intercept surveys or telephone households to identify participants willing to come to a central facility for an interview or test.

"Our research techniques and tools are not the critically distinguishing characteristic of our firm. Instead, it's the customization of each client's research and the all-important contact with our client's customers. We can do a lot of sophisticated computer analyses and graphing. And we have well-known models, such as ASSESSOR for forecasting sales and MACRO EXPLORER for identifying target audiences and developing marketing strategies. But what really matters is the customer contact and the quality of the information collected. Did we contact the right consumers? Did we ask them the right questions?

"Suppose a midsized food-processing firm has developed a nonfat chocolate dessert product but can't decide if they should market it as a thicker-textured pudding-type product or a lighter, fluffier mousse-type product. To help them determine which product version to market, we could use field work—either mall-intercept surveys or interviews in central facilities. Although mall surveys will get results more quickly, mall samples may not be representative. During the day, it might be all housewives. Besides, different socioeconomic groups patronize different shopping centers. Using telephone solicitation to recruit participants for a central-facility interview produces a more representative sample. However, it takes longer and costs more.

"Once the client knows which product version consumers prefer—let's say the mousse product—it could develop several different product concepts. One concept might play off the more cosmopolitan image of mousse as opposed to pudding. Another might emphasize weight control and focus on the light aspect, such as fewer calories. A third concept might be that mousse is perfect when you just want a little dessert—after lunch, perhaps. To determine the most marketable concept, we can describe the concepts over the telephone or mail a written description to consumers. If consumers must see the product, we could use field operators in a mall or central facility.

"Once the company selects a concept, we could use a HUT (Home Use Test) to predict sales or market share. For these tests, we would recruit respondents through a field operation (mall or telephone) and give them samples of the product to use at home. About a week later, through telephone callback interviews, we would find out how they liked the product and the likelihood of their purchasing it and then use these responses to predict the product's market share. At the same time, we would ask detailed questions about pricing or about where consumers shop for such products to help marketing managers with pricing and distribution decisions.

"After the product is introduced, we can track its success by telephoning randomly selected households to determine if consumers are familiar with nonfat dessert products, which ones they use, and why. If the client requires even more information, we can identify users of the product to determine their satisfaction with it.

"For any marketing problem, we can custom design research that provides the right information so that our clients will make the right marketing decisions. That's why we're here."

## Questions

1. Suppose you were responsible for marketing the new nonfat chocolate dessert. What are the pros and cons of the mall intercept or central facility tests to determine which product version to introduce? Which would you use?

2. What are the pros and cons of the different kinds of concept tests? Which would you use?

3. Why would a firm need both a concept test and a HUT?

4. What are the differences in the two types of surveys described in the next-to-last paragraph? Why would identifying users cost more?

*Sources:* M/A/R/C company reports and personal interviews with Scott Bailey of M/A/R/C.

# Video Case 3
# *DHL Worldwide Express*

Michael Douglas as Thomas Sanders in the 1994 movie, *Disclosure:* "Maybe you should send some of the problem disc drives to us to check out."

Malaysian Production Manager: "Sure, I'll send them right away— DHL. You should get them tomorrow."

Although DHL may not be a common household name, it is so well known as an international air express carrier that many businesses—even ones made up for the movies—think in terms of "sending it DHL." DHL began as a small San Francisco firm founded by three entrepreneurs—Adrian *D*alsey, Larry *H*illblom and Robert *L*ynn—to shuttle bills of lading between Hawaii and California. Today, DHL Worldwide Express has become a major international carrier serving businesses around the globe. DHL now has 35,000 employees worldwide, serving 224 countries with 9,700 courier vehicles and 137 aircraft, and connecting 19 major hubs and 1,900 service stations. Ironically, DHL is not as well known in its home country as it is in the rest of the world.

DHL uses a worldwide hub-and-spoke system. Packages, letters, and other documents are collected locally and sent to the nearest service center. From there they are sent to a hub, where they are sorted according to destination and transported to service centers in each country. There they are re-sorted and begin the last leg of their journey to a local destination.

The Brussels hub is a prime example of the system. Each night starting at 10:30 P.M., more than 120,000 documents and packages begin arriving at the hub. As the items are unloaded, workers throw them onto $15 million worth of sorting machines, resembling a crazy amusement-park ride. Dozens of conveyor belts whisk the parcels away. As many as 400 people sort packages and put them on other belts, hurrying to get them loaded on trucks and airplanes by 3:00 A.M.

In another room, more than 50 people frantically read paperwork in dozens of languages so that all the parcels can clear customs. Without them, delivery of packages would be delayed. In-house translators and customs clearance services are among DHL's distinguishing characteristics. Another is that DHL hires its own people to deliver documents and packages abroad, in contrast to most other carriers, which hire local agencies. As a result, customers can be certain that their packages will never leave DHL's hands until they reach their locations.

DHL operates a global information network that enables it to track each item throughout its journey. The backbone of this system is DHLNET—a high-speed data network developed jointly by DHL and IBM. DHL employees enter shipment information when packages enter the system. Each package's airway bill has a unique barcoded number that is scanned into DHL's information network at each stage of its journey. The system provides DHL management with information on routing, delivery times, and volumes. Also, it allows many DHL customers, who are linked to the DHL network through the Electronic Data Interchange (EDI) service, to track their own packages directly. DHL also created a system called EasyShip, which lets customers prepare their own shipping documents and maintain databases of customer addresses in-house. DHL will install an EasyShip computer free of charge in the customer's office or provide software that can be used on the customer's computer system.

In addition to its traditional services, such as overnight mail for documents and parcels, same-day service between locations in the United States and to some foreign countries, and international air freight, DHL has become a provider of logistics services. As corporations downsize and attempt to reduce costs, they have begun to reduce their investment in inventories and warehouses by outsourcing logistics functions. An example is DHL's experience with Japan's Kubota. DHL warehouses spare parts for Kubota computers. When customers call the Kubota service number, they actually reach DHL, which immediately ships needed parts through the DHL system. Another example is Bendon, Ltd., a New Zealand manufacturer of women's lingerie. In the past, it took 10 days for Bendon to ship goods to Australia. However, through its alliance with DHL, Bendon can now accept orders until 1:00 P.M. for next-morning delivery in Australia. By using

DHL's information system, Bendon knows that all its shipments have cleared customs, and it receives delivery reports on all shipments. As a result, Bendon can invoice customers more quickly, improving its cash flow and reducing inventories.

Since the passage of NAFTA, Mexico has become one of the most important non-U.S. markets for air express services. DHL entered Mexico in 1978 and is presently the major carrier there, expediting shipments to 400 Mexican cities. It has in-house customs brokers to provide clearance of goods and to collect all shipping documents for the customer. But competition in Mexico is heating up as hundreds of courier services vie for business there. UPS is making a major push, and the Mexican Postal Service has created Estafeta, Aeroflash, and Mexpost to provide international and domestic services. Some Mexican businesses, unsatisfied with the delivery times and higher prices of private companies, now rely on the Mexican Postal Service. In response, DHL has tried lowering prices by creating special discount tariffs, and it now offers same-day delivery in certain parts of the country.

## QUESTIONS

1. What are the major characteristics of DHL's service? Why would each of these be important to a customer?
2. For buyers of DHL's services, what type of buying situation is each of the following?
   a. delivery of letters
   b. use of the EasyShip computer
   c. use of DHL to warehouse and deliver the buyer's product.
3. What sort of environmental influences affect a buyer's decision to use DHL?

*Sources:* Brian Coleman, "Courier Firms Regroup as Faxes and Factories Alter Delivery Industry," *Wall Street Journal Europe,* May 6, 1993, reprint; Dora Delgado, "Is My Package There Yet?" *Business Mexico,* April 1994, pp. 10–11; John Marcom, "Battle of Zaventem," *Forbes,* April 29, 1991, p. 58; and numerous company-supplied documents. The author gratefully thanks Dean Christon of DHL for his help with this case.

# Video Case 4
# *Rollerblade:*
# *The Asphalt Is Calling*

Legend has it that a Dutchman made the first in-line skates in the 1700s when he nailed wooden spools to strips of wood attached to his shoes. Later, the Victorians of the 1860s tried them. But in-line skates never really took off until two brothers, Brennan and Scott Olson, got the idea to sell them to hockey players during the off-season in the early 1980s. Since then, millions of Americans have answered the call of the asphalt, making in-line skating one of the fastest growing sports in the United States (see Table 1). Who uses them? Just about everyone—kids, hockey players, college students, grandmothers (see Table 2). Why do these folks skate? FUN, FUN, FUN! Of course, many have more pedestrian reasons, such as exercise, hockey, and cross-training; but mostly, it's just for fun.

Rollerblade, Inc., founded by the Olson brothers, is the premier in-line skate company with roughly 50 percent of the market, a position that most would think highly enviable. However, Rollerblade's success in promoting skating has caused it a few major headaches. First, competition has increased as a few dozen other firms have entered the market, making it increasingly difficult for Rollerblade to maintain its market share. Second, some analysts contend that in-line skating is just a fad that will inevitably decline. That could be devastating for a firm like Rollerblade that has only one product. Finally, many Americans use the name Rollerblade when referring to any and all in-line skates, and they refer to in-line skating as rollerblading. To be correct, however, you should say "Rollerblade Skates," and the sport is in-line skating, not rollerblading. If the Rollerblade name becomes generic, the company risks losing its rights to exclusive use of the brand name.

How is Rollerblade responding to these challenges? To distinguish its product from that of the competition, it engages in product design and development. For example, in 1994 Rollerblade introduced a new braking system—the Active Brake Technology (ABT)—that enables skaters greater speed control and stopping power. To reduce dependence on a single product line, the company is adding protective gear—knee and elbow pads, wristguards, and the first helmet designed for in-line skaters.

To protect its brand name, Rollerblade sends information to the media and dealers detailing correct spelling and use of the name. For example, brand names should not be used as verbs—saying or writing "rollerblading" is improper. Rollerblade also asks dealers to avoid using slang terms such as "blader(s)" and "blading."

To counter the predicted decline of in-line skating, Rollerblade is working to attract more skaters through safety campaigns and by offering instruction videos to dealers who give interested skaters free trials and lessons. The company is also the first to introduce television advertising to increase awareness of the sport and to promote the Rollerblade brand.

Between 1992 and 1993, in-line skating did not grow as rapidly as it has in the past. Therefore, Rollerblade has attempted to expand the market by reaching new segments of consumers. Based on consumer information like that in Table 2, Rollerblade is targeting the in-line hockey, youth, and fitness markets. For example, it pitches in-line hockey to ice hockey players in the off-season and to individuals in areas where ice hockey is not well established. And based on a University of Massachusetts study proving that in-line skating is a highly effective, low-impact aerobic workout (it burns 360 calories in 30 minutes for a 150-pound person), the company has developed the "Rollerblade Roll & Tone—An In-Line Skate Workout" brochure for fitness buffs. It contains workouts for beginner, intermediate, and advanced skaters along with tips for beginners on how to get started skating.

TABLE 1  *Growth of In-Line Skating*

|  | 1989 | 1990 | 1991 | 1992 | 1993 |
|---|---|---|---|---|---|
| No. of participants (in thousands) | 3,065 | 4,307 | 6,212 | 9,364 | 12,559 |
| Percentage | — | 40% | 44% | 51% | 34% |

*TABLE 2 Characteristics of Skaters (Numbers in thousands)*

|  |  | 1989 | 1990 | 1991 | 1992 | 1993 |
|---|---|---|---|---|---|---|
| Age | 6–11 | 759 | 1,066 | 2,154 | 3,423 | 4,866 |
|  | 12–17 | 928 | 1,348 | 1,267 | 2,694 | 3,240 |
|  | 18–24 | 598 | 841 | 1,021 | 1,183 | 1,565 |
|  | 25–34 | 409 | 647 | 1,220 | 1,487 | 1,822 |
|  | 35–54 | 285 | 345 | 542 | 495 | 1,001 |
|  | 55+ | 86 | 60 | 80 | 80 | 65 |
| Gender | Male | 1,444 | 2,237 | 3,432 | 5,035 | 6,280 |
|  | Female | 1,621 | 2,070 | 2,780 | 4,329 | 6,279 |
| Income | Under $25,000 | 1,546 | 1,647 | 2,161 | 3,044 | 3,136 |
|  | $25–$50,000 | 1,023 | 1,422 | 2,169 | 3,481 | 4,816 |
|  | Over $50,000 | 496 | 1,238 | 1,882 | 2,839 | 4,607 |
| Geographic location | Northeast | 651 | 831 | 1,469 | 1,720 | 2,889 |
|  | North Central | 849 | 1,275 | 1,435 | 2,646 | 3,963 |
|  | South | 1,048 | 1,458 | 1,749 | 2,306 | 2,899 |

## QUESTIONS

1. What trends can you detect in Tables 1 and 2?
2. Using the information in the tables, evaluate the various age, gender, and income groups as potential consumer targets for Rollerblade. In your opinion, are the exercise, youth, and in-line hockey groups good choices for Rollerblade to target?
3. What stage of the product life cycle is Rollerblade in? Is the company taking the appropriate actions to increase sales in this stage?
4. Evaluate the effectiveness of the actions Rollerblade has taken to protect its brand name and maintain its market position.

*Sources:* David Biemesderfer, "Fast Track," *World Traveler,* Northwest Airlines publication, 1993; Lois Therrien, "Rollerblade Is Skating in Heavier Traffic," *Business Week,* June 24, 1992, pp. 114–115; and numerous materials provided by Rollerblade. The author would like to thank Rollerblade, Inc., for its help with this case.

# Video Case 5
# *Terra Chips:*
# *Eat Your Veggies!*

Consumer, browsing in store: "What are these? Multicolored chips? They are really pretty. Wonder what they're made of—taro, batata . . . What on earth is that? Sweet potatoes from Cuba? Gee, I wonder if they're any good. What's the price? $3.99 for a 6-ounce bag! Could they be worth that . . . ?"

This consumer's pricing question was a major concern of Dana Sinkler and Alex Dzieduszycki when they introduced Terra Chips. Although they knew they had a good product, given the speed with which guests gobbled down the chips at functions catered by the young entrepreneurs, marketing the chips posed many challenges.

Because of the high costs of ingredients, the chips had to be priced higher. If sold in grocery stores, they would not compete well on price with much cheaper chips. Even in higher-priced outlets, placing Terra Chips in snack sections next to other chips might result in consumer price shock. Therefore, Terra Chips were initially sold only as a food-service product. It was almost by a fluke (an order from Saks) that they ended up on retail shelves.

Terra Chips faced other marketing challenges. For example, the product needed packaging and distribution channels that would support its high-price image. Also, Dana and Alex were concerned about whether their new product would appeal to broader markets. Although New Yorkers liked Terra Chips, there were questions of whether they would sell in less cosmopolitan markets.

To deal with these issues, the entrepreneurs hired Keith Bright and Associates of Venice, California, to create a sophisticated silver-and-black package with a colorful picture of the chips on the front. They distributed the chips through upscale outlets such as Saks and Neiman Marcus and eventually sold them through delicatessens, natural food stores, and, finally, a few select grocery chains. After only four short years, Terra Chips are reported to be a $10 million business.

Why have Terra Chips been so successful? The answer can't be advertising— they haven't done any. Instead, Terra Chips created an exciting new category with strong, demonstrated consumer appeal. Although it now has many imitators, Terra really did forge new ground and is now widely recognized throughout the food industry as the "pioneer of the vegetable chip category." In addition to having no additives, Terra Chips are also lower in sodium and fat than regular potato chips, which is probably of more interest to most consumers.

Terra Chips are also beautiful. Sweet potato chips are orange, yucca chips are light colored, and taro chips have thin purple markings. Ruby taro chips come in a beautiful red (with beet juice added), and parsnip chips have a light brown color. A bowl of Terra Chips is extremely eye-catching, making hostesses proud to serve them. Their subtle blend of tastes provides a welcome change from potato chips. The high price creates an image of exclusivity, and the use of "exotic" vegetables has created a cosmopolitan aura.

A gold, ribbon-shaped symbol on the front of each bag informs consumers that Terra Chips were the 1992 and 1993 winners at NASFT's (National Association for the Specialty Food Trade) trade show. In addition, the chips were served backstage at *The Tonight Show,* generating publicity that reinforced the exclusive image. It seems that lots of consumers want to eat the same chips as Jay Leno!

Terra Chips are so popular that Dana and Alex have introduced line extensions: Terra Sweet Potato Chips, Terra Spiced Sweet Potato Chips, and Terra Spiced Taro Chips. The Spiced Sweet Potato Chips are a vibrant orange-red color and have a fiery taste. Seasoned with cumin, cilantro, garlic, and red cayenne, they are the perfect complement to beer. The Spiced Taro Chips, covered with a peppery mix of lemongrass, Thai chilis, lime leaves, and coriander, are the perfect complement for Asian cuisine and seafood, as well as for salads and soups. The extensions are priced lower than mixed Terra Chips, selling for $.99 for a 1.5-ounce bag and $2.99 for a 6-ounce bag.

Even as the chips grow in popularity, Dana and Alex are looking for new ways to increase sales. For example, they plan to sell Terra Chips abroad. However, the chips could suffer image problems in other countries. Although taro may be uncommon in the United States, it is fairly common to consumers in other parts of the world, especially those familiar with Asian foods. Another growth strategy would be to produce private-label chips. However, if consumers recognize private-label chips as Terra Chips, private-label sales could cannibalize sales of the higher-margin Terra Chips.

Another issue is the narrowness of the company's product mix. If veggie chips turn out to be a fad, Dana and Alex understand that Terra Chips will need another product line to sustain sales and profits. For now, however, they are building on their current success while exploring options for the future.

## QUESTIONS

1. Are the Sweet Potato, Spiced Sweet Potato, and Spiced Taro Chips true line extensions?
2. Do you think veggie chips are a fad? Why or why not?
3. In your opinion, would Terra Chips be successful in other countries?
4. Should Dana and Alex make private-label chips? Explain.
5. If you were Dana and Alex, what would your next product be? Why? What other marketing steps would you recommend?

*Sources:* "How to Veg Out and Live Life," *Brandweek,* June 27, 1994; Toddi Gunter, "Chip Mania," *Forbes,* July 19, 1993, pp. 196–198; and numerous company-supplied materials. The author gratefully acknowledges the assistance of Andrew Friedman in the writing of this case.

# Video Case 6
# *Mountain Travel Sobek:*
# *All Over the World*

Would you like to take a trek to Nepal? Raft rivers in Chile? Walk the Great Wall of China? Inspect icebergs and penguins in the Antarctic—up close? If you answered yes, you're not alone. Over seven million Americans engage in adventure travel annually, making it the fastest growing form of travel (30 percent annual growth).

Mountain Travel Sobek (MT-S) is the premier adventure-travel firm, offering trips to seven continents. It was formed in 1991 when the two most venerable firms in adventure travel, Mountain Travel and Sobek Expeditions, joined operations. Mountain Travel, founded by Leo Le Bon, Allen Steck, and Barry Bishop, specialized in trekking and mountain expeditions. It was the first company to offer treks to Everest Base Camp, walking safaris in East Africa, expeditions to Kilimanjaro and Mt. Anyemaquen in China (1981), and the cross-country ski expeditions to the South Pole (1989).

Sobek Expeditions was founded by two river rafters from Bethesda, Maryland—Richard Bangs and John Yost. Their last fling before entering the working world was a rafting trip on the Awash, a little-known and unrun African river. They recruited clients to pay for the trip and, upon successfully completing the adventure, formed Sobek, named for the Egyptian crocodile god who seemed to have guided them through the croc-infested waters of the Awash. Sobek went on to lead the first descents of 35 rivers around the world, including the Bio-Bio (Chile), Bashkaus (USSR), Blue Nile (Ethiopia), and Tatshenshini (Alaska).

During the 1980s, both Mountain Travel and Sobek prospered. Mountain Travel increased its annual departures by 50 percent to 478, and Sobek upped its departures by 70 percent to 415. Annual revenues climbed to more than $7 million for Mountain Travel and to $5 million for Sobek. However, this success disguised deteriorating profitability resulting from the offering of less-profitable trips. With the help of Hap Klopp, former owner of North Face, the companies merged. The new company has improved profitability by combining trekking and rafting trips to the same parts of the world and by eliminating 180 money-losing trips to 100 destinations.

What is an MT-S trip like? If you envision hardship, cold food, and primitive facilities, forget it. Accommodations are actually quite pleasant, with comfortable cabins and spacious tents, and local chefs prepare delicious food. What sets MT-S trips apart is the high-quality amenities, staff who are knowledgeable about local conditions and cultures, and the small size of groups, limited to 15 or fewer. But all this doesn't come cheaply. Trips through the Northeast passage cost more than $10,000, and safaris in Africa can cost more than $4,000. However, not all MT-S trips are this expensive. A trip to the Galapagos may cost less than $2,500, and kayaking in the Sea of Cortez costs only about $1,000.

Who takes these trips? It's mostly men and women aged 30 to 60 years old. However, the average age of adventure travelers is likely to increase in the future. The population of 55-year-old and older Americans will increase from 53 million in 1990 to 75 million by 2010. Older people have higher buying power, greater leisure time, and, lately, a greater inclination to explore. Seniors account for $60 billion of the $293.7 billion travel market, and close to 50 percent of Mountain Travel Sobek's business comes from seniors. In "soft" adventure travel, army jeeps of the past have been replaced by more comfortable land rovers and minivans.

Leo Le Bon claims that the company has changed: "Adventure travel does not lend itself to commercialization; it's most successful when the company is small, specialized, high spirited, hands-on. When corporate America comes to it, it doesn't work." But Richard Weiss, the new president of Mountain Travel Sobek, is more upbeat. While it is true that MT-S offers more easy trips than in the past, the trips still consist of small groups led by enthusiastic guides. Participants can get into the countryside, see wildlife, meet the local population, and experience the feeling of leaving the beaten path.

To appeal to the changing market, MT-S expanded its product offerings by introducing Quick Escapes, short trips to Canada or Baja, and longer ones to destinations such as Morocco, Vietnam, and Bhutan. MT-S has also tried new forms of promotion. One is The Adventure Disc (1993), an interactive Photo CD on which you can hear the calls of wildlife, listen to voices of explorers such as Edmund Hillary, look at hundreds of spectacular photos of the world's wonders, and view shots of MT-S trips. In 1994, the company developed The Traveler, an interactive CD-ROM catalog for the Macintosh and Windows systems produced by Magellan Systems. In addition, MT-S trip information is now available on the Internet. Prospective travelers can examine full tour itineraries, read the company's history, and look at video clips. However, it is not clear whether these promotions reach targeted older consumers or younger, more computer-oriented ones.

Competition is increasing. New adventure firms are entering the industry and some travel agencies now specialize in adventure trips. MT-S's new product offerings and promotional efforts may help distinguish it and give it an edge over competitors. This could be very important if an industry shakeout occurs.

## QUESTIONS

1. Where is Mountain Travel Sobek in its product life cycle? Is the company following appropriate strategies for this stage? What might it do in the future?

2. Do you agree with Mr. Le Bon that adventure travel does not lend itself to commercialization?

3. Evaluate the usefulness of MT-S's CD-ROM and Internet promotions. Why would or wouldn't these be effective means of promotion?

*Sources:* James M. Clash, "Survivalists," *Forbes,* November 22, 1993, pp. 154–156; Jeffery D. Zbar, "More Than a Cool Bus Ride Needed to Sway Seniors," *Advertising Age,* June 27, 1994, pp. 34–37; and numerous company-supplied materials. The author gratefully acknowledges the help of Liz Longstreth in preparing this case.

# Video Case 7
# *Mall of America: The Ultimate Destination for Fun*

Question: Who has . . .
A Wilderness Theater with a variety of wildlife?
Five classrooms, a multipurpose room, and a computer lab?
The site where Harmon Killebrew hit a 520-foot home run?
Forty-five restaurants, nine nightclubs, and 14 theater screens?
Some 4.2 million square feet of enclosed space and 13,000 parking spaces?
The third-largest number of visitors among U.S. tourist attractions?
Answer: Believe it or not . . . *Mall of America!*

When the Mall of America opened near Minneapolis in 1992, skeptics questioned whether it could attract a projected 35 million visitors a year to spend over $600 million. Local retailers worried that the Mall's success would mean their own decline. So, two years later, how has the mammoth mall done?

According to reports, Mall of America has met most of its projections. It attracted more than 35 million visitors in its first 12 months and 60 million within the first 20 months. Weekly visitors vary in number from 600,000 to 900,000 depending on the season, and 30 percent of visitors come from outside a 150-mile radius. Moreover, these results were achieved during the worst retail slump of the last decade.

The Mall's impact on other area retailers, however, was not what they expected. The area's total retail pie seems to have expanded—partly because of an increase in tourists attracted by the Mall. Mall of America actually creates *more* business for other retailers and increases receipts for hotels, restaurants, and other travel-related services. In addition, the Mall has created 12,000 new jobs in Minneapolis, which means additional spendable income.

What can visitors see and do at Mall of America? For shopping, the Mall offers four major anchors: Macy's, Nordstrom, Bloomingdale's, and Sears. It contains several junior anchors such as Oshman's SuperSports USA, Filene's Basement, Service Merchandise, and Linens 'N' Things. It also contains more than 400 specialty shops where visitors can purchase specialized clothing, such as grunge-look merchandise at the Junkyard; gardening supplies at Gardener's Paradise; or anything and everything for a left-handed person at The Leftorium.

For food, customers can choose from 45 restaurants. They can grab a quick bite at a fast-food restaurant such as TacoTime or Dairy Queen. For slower-paced dining, there's the California Cafe and the Twin City Diner. For something different, the Rainforest Cafe features a menu of foods from rainforest countries and a 5,500-gallon fish tank. Or shoppers can stargaze at Planet Hollywood, where they might see Roseanne or Whoopi while sampling California cuisine.

For the family, there's Knott's Camp Snoopy—a seven-acre, indoor theme park with 16 rides, nine restaurants, and entertainments such as panning for gold, visiting the wilderness ranger station, the Peanuts gallery (a cutting-edge video game arcade), and 3D films and musical revues at The Ford Playhouse. The Peanuts Gang—Snoopy, Lucy, and Charlie Brown—are the hosts. For adults, there's America's Original Sports Bar, Knuckleheads Comedy Club, and the Gatlin Brothers Music City with free line-dancing lessons.

Families and singles also like the LEGO Imagination Center with its millions of LEGO blocks to play with and models to look at and buy. Golf Mountain is a state-of-the-art miniature golf course, complete with waterfalls, streams, and trees. At StarBase Omega, an interactive laser game, players are trained in the latest high-tech equipment and transported to StarBase Omega or Planet Previa to fight it out with the Kytefs. The Mall also offers a 14-screen General Cinema Theater showing first-run movies.

Unusual features include the Chapel of Love (the first wedding chapel in an enclosed mall); classrooms from the Metropolitan Learning Alliance (a cooperative effort between local schools and the University of St. Thomas); and a plaque marking the spot of Killebrew's famous home run (Mall sits atop the old site of Metropolitan Stadium).

To attract both customers *and* tourists, the Mall distributes hundreds of brochures, newspaper inserts, and maps in the Minneapolis–St. Paul region; runs joint promotions with local radio stations; runs ads in a local newspaper and commercials on local television; buys billboard space; and works with over 200 tour operators to develop travel packages and with Northwest Airlines to create tie-in packages. It holds major holiday and sales events, attractions at the Events Center, entertainment events in nightclubs, and events to celebrate the addition of new retailers. It has used contests such as the one featured in an insert in *USA Today,* in which the prize was a trip to the Mall. WCCO-AM, a local radio station and the Mall's official information station, relays the latest scoop about what's happening at the Mall to listeners. The Mall's advertising campaign theme is "There's a place for fun in your life."

The good news for Mall of America is that merchant occupancy levels have hovered around 92 percent (right on track). The bad news is that some shoppers have been scared away by rumors of long lines at restaurants, rest-room facilities, and parking lots. To help shoppers deal with the Mall's massive size and find their way around, the Mall provides maps and directories. In addition, it is organized into four "neighborhoods," each of which might be a mini–shopping expedition. To help drivers, exit ramps off freeways guide shoppers into the Mall's parking lots.

Thus, although the size of the Mall of America entices many shoppers, it intimidates others. As an exhilarating shopping, dining, and entertainment experience, the Mall is tops. But the serious question remains: will shoppers use it on an everyday basis?

## QUESTIONS

1. What are Mall of America's target markets? How does it try to serve each one?
2. How does the Mall promote itself to each of its target markets? Why do you think it picked a theme that focuses on fun?
3. Make a list of all the disadvantages consumers face when visiting Mall of America. How does the Mall try to overcome each of those? What else might it do?
4. In your opinion, is the Mall likely to be a long-run success? Why or why not?

*Sources:* William Stern, "Bumpbacks in Minneapolis," *Forbes*, April 11, 1994, pp. 48–49; Eric Wieffering, "What Has the Mall of America Done to Minneapolis?" *American Demographics,* February 1994, pp. 13–16; and numerous materials supplied by the Mall of America. The author gratefully thanks Jayne Lopez for her assistance with this case.

# Video Case 8
# *Ritz-Carlton:*
# *Simply the Best*

When introducing himself to new employees, the president of The Ritz-Carlton Hotel Company says "My name is Horst Schulze. I'm the president, and I'm a very important person around here." After a few seconds he continues, "But so are you. In fact, you are more important to customers than I am. If you don't show up, we are in trouble. If I don't show up, hardly anyone would notice."

These comments reflect Mr. Schulze's attitude that employees are the crucial component in quality service. Therefore, The Ritz-Carlton very carefully selects only those applicants with an appropriate caring attitude. For every new employee at an introductory orientation session, ten others applied, and employees are told that they were not hired, they were selected. Once selected, each employee learns the Ritz-Carlton corporate culture in a two-day orientation, followed by extensive on-the-job training that results in job certification.

Each employee learns The Ritz-Carlton Gold Standards, which include a credo, 20 basics of service, and the three steps of service. The steps include: (1) a warm and sincere greeting; (2) anticipation and compliance with guest needs; and (3) a fond farewell, using the guest's name if possible. Employees may even have to modify their language. They should say "Good morning," or "Good afternoon," not "Hi, how's it going?" When asked to do something, they should respond "Certainly," or "My pleasure." In addition, all employees should learn the 20 Ritz-Carlton basics of quality service, which range from knowledge of one's work area and The Ritz-Carlton Credo to answering the telephone with a smile and wearing immaculate uniforms. At The Ritz-Carlton employees are not servants, they are "ladies and gentlemen serving ladies and gentlemen."

To back up all this training, employees are empowered to handle any customer complaint on the spot and can spend up to $2,000 doing so. And they can demand the immediate assistance of other employees. Twenty minutes later, they should telephone the guest to make sure that the complaint was handled properly. In addition, once employees learn of particular customer wants, such as foam pillows or a desire for a particular newspaper, that information goes into a 240,000 person database so that the customer will automatically get the desired service the next time he or she stays at a Ritz-Carlton.

This attention to quality is not confined to hotel staff. Mr. Schulze and the other senior executives meet weekly to review measures of product and service quality, guest satisfaction, market growth and development, and other business indicators. From top management down, Ritz-Carlton's approach to quality management is characterized by detailed planning. Quality teams at all levels set objectives and devise action plans, and each hotel has a quality leader and work-area teams responsible for problem solving, strategic planning, and setting quality-certification standards for each position.

Each hotel aims to create a two-to-one ratio of internal to external complaints. Internal complaints are made by employees who spot problems in service delivery. By eliminating internal problems, Ritz-Carlton removes the causes of external complaints by customers. Management thinks that solving problems before they arise is cost-effective. Once a problem has occurred, there are additional costs of employee time to fix the problem plus hotel remedies such as complimentary cocktails and a follow-up letter, not to mention the possible cost of losing a customer. Patrick Mene, Vice President of Quality, expresses this as the 1–10–100 rule: "What costs a dollar to fix today will cost $10 to fix tomorrow and $100 to fix downstream."

To ensure that quality standards are maintained, Ritz-Carlton collects daily reports from each of the 720 work areas in each of the 30 hotels it manages. The company tracks measures such as annual guest-room preventive-maintenance cycles, percentage of check-ins with no queuing, time spent to achieve industry-best clean-room appearance, and time to service an occupied room.

Not surprisingly, Ritz-Carlton won the prestigious Malcolm Baldrige National Quality Award in 1992. This moved the firm into very select company—only one service firm had ever won this award. You might think Ritz-Carlton would be satisfied with a customer satisfaction rating of 97 percent, one of the lowest employee turnover rates in the hotel industry (30 percent). But not Ritz-Carlton! Mr. Schulze has set new quality performance standards to be reached by 1996: a 100-percent customer satisfaction rating and a reduction of defects to just four for every million customer encounters.

Eliminating virtually all problems, however, is a costly process that can reduce company profits, and some critics believe that Ritz-Carlton is not sensitive enough to its bottom line. For example, to improve customer satisfaction from 97 percent to 98 percent, some would say, is a marginal improvement that could require a great deal of employee effort and expense for a low dollar return. Besides, how can any firm anticipate all possible problems in order to eliminate complaints? Should it even desire to do so?

## QUESTIONS

1. Why is it important for Ritz-Carlton to insist that employees not think of themselves as servants, but rather as ladies and gentlemen?

2. In what ways does Ritz-Carlton engage in relationship marketing?
3. Is quality at Ritz-Carlton cost-effective? Even if it costs $2,000 an incident?
4. Should Ritz-Carlton attempt to move toward Mr. Schulze's latest goals? Why or why not?

*Sources:* Patricia A. Galagan, "Putting on the Ritz," *Training & Development*, December 1993, pp. 41–45; Charles G. Partlow, "How Ritz-Carlton Applies 'TQM,'" *The Cornell H.R.A. Quarterly*, August 1993; and numerous company-supplied materials. The author would like to thank Stephanie Platt, Manager of Communications, Ritz-Carlton Hotels, for help with this case.

# Video Case 9
# *MTV: Think Globally, Act Locally*

Everyone wants their MTV, and MTV wants to reach everyone. Through its six affiliates and numerous broadcasting arrangements, MTV is seen in over 250 million homes in 64 countries. Its unique blend of video jockeys (VJs), music news, promotions, interviews, concert tour information, specials, and rockumentaries has made MTV an international institution of popular culture and the leading authority on popular music.

At last count, MTV Europe reached more households than MTV U.S. Although it broadcasts in English, MTV Europe has a pan-European tone that appeals to advertisers wishing to reach the entire European market. To tailor its appeal to different European nationalities, MTV Europe broadcasts 40 percent nonanglo videos and tackles local issues such as neo-fascism. Even with this local focus, teenagers in the various countries reached by MTV Europe seem to have more in common with each other than they do with their parents.

MTV Latino originates in Miami and is beamed at Hispanic households in the United States and Mexico, as well as in Central America and South America. MTV Brazil features both Brazilian and international artists in 16 hours of daily programming hosted by Brazilian VJs speaking Portuguese. And MTV's most recent addition is Tierra del Fuego (near the Antarctic). Thus, the vast pan-Latin MTV network now reaches from the northern end of Mexico to the southern tip of South America, offering a diverse mix of North American and Latin music, regional productions, music and entertainment news, artist interviews, and concert coverage. The network helps bridge cultural gaps between nations—people in Chile see Mexican music and vice versa. A case in point is Los Fabulosos Cadillacs, an Argentine alternative music band. Once popular only in Argentina, exposure on MTV boosted sales of the band's records beyond the 400,000 mark throughout Latin America.

Recently, Kodak signed a million-dollar deal with MTV Latino and MTV Brazil to air ads to the pan-Latin audience. To help shape the content of the ads, Kodak's ad agency gave magazines to Latin youths and asked them to clip images that stirred them. The results: They selected images relating to ecology, contamination, AIDS, love, and self-expression. Kodak's campaign is entitled *"Como Tu Quieras con Kodak"* (which, roughly translated, means "As you wish it with

Kodak"). In one ad, an enormous bird flies over frightened spectators protecting themselves from acid rain with black umbrellas. As the bird flies overhead, it leaves behind a glowing Kodak rainbow that brilliantly lights the sky.

MTV Asia reaches 30 countries via satellite. It consists of two networks: a Mandarin-language channel for viewers in Taiwan, Singapore, and China; and an English-language network for South Asia and the Philippines. Both are designed for the 12- to 34-year-old market, and programming is adapted to the musical tastes of this audience. An agreement between MTV and the DD2 Metro Channel (Indian national television) allows the network to broadcast a two-and-a-half-hour block targeted to Indian audiences.

MTV Japan (1992) is customized for Japanese youths. It features music videos from regional bands and international artists and offers programming in both English and Japanese. Also, recently announced is MTV South Africa, making a total of six MTV affiliates in all.

A common thread running through all these MTV affiliates is the use of local VJs, local artists' videos, and programming in local languages. This is the "act locally" side of MTV's operations. On the "think globally" side, MTV sends standardized shows to many parts of the world, including that favorite, Beavis and Butthead. (Can you imagine their dopey laughs and phrases in German, Spanish, and Japanese?) MTV's shows and videos create global fashion trends. For example, the hip-hop look popularized by African-American groups and the grunge look from Seattle have been adopted by teens from Great Britain to Japan. MTV news shows often discuss the same topics around the world. For example, AIDS was covered in Brazil, Europe, India, and even among conservative Asian populations. Finally, MTV advertising is often global in nature. Advertisers include Levi Strauss, Procter & Gamble, Johnson & Johnson, Apple Computers, Nike, Reebok, Pepsi, and Coca-Cola, which has signed an agreement to advertise on all MTV channels around the world. These advertisers fashion ads that mirror the fast-paced, graphic style of MTV shows, with the result that ads around the world are starting to look more alike.

This balancing act of thinking globally and acting locally poses some problems for MTV. On the local side, affiliates would like to have more local programming and music videos that better appeal to their viewers. On the global side, the homogenization of youth is perceived negatively by many parents, elders, and politicians who fear that their countries' youths will lose their national identities and cultural values. These critics are not alone—even Beavis and Butt-head would probably trash global sameness.

## QUESTIONS

1. Why would companies such as Levi Strauss, Coca-Cola, and Apple Computer want to advertise globally on MTV?

2. What kind of marketing mix does MTV use around the globe? Why? What kind of marketing mix is Kodak using in Latin America? What kind of marketing mix is Coca-Cola likely to use around the globe?

3. What effect do you believe "thinking globally" and "acting locally" have on homogenizing the world's youth?

4. Is *Como Tu Quieras con Kodak* a good ad theme for the Latin market?

*Sources:* Matthew Schifrin, "I Can't Even Remember the Old Star's Name," *Forbes,* March 16, 1992, pp. 44–45; Shawn Tully, "Teens—The Most Global Market of All," *Fortune,* May 16, 1994, pp. 90–96; and numerous company-supplied materials. The author gratefully acknowledges the help of Carole Robinson with this case.

# Video Case 10
# *Lands' End: Enticing Customers "Out Our Way"*

"Out our way" is Dodgeville, Wisconsin—a town that could easily be a Hollywood set for an idealized American small town—a place where "the men are good-looking, . . . the women are strong, and the children wear their baseball caps pointed straight ahead." But if you think this is just a sleepy community—maybe an updated northern version of Mayberry—you would be mistaken! "Out our way" is the home of Lands' End—one of the largest specialty apparel catalogers in the U. S.; the company that coined the term "Direct Merchant"; the maker of the nearly indestructible oxford shirts worn by businesspeople, teachers, doctors, accountants, lawyers and other professionals around the globe; sponsor of Garrison Keillor's radio show, *A Prairie Home Companion; and* one of the most consumer-oriented firms in North America.

Lands' End is no small business. It employs 7,000 people—some of whom tend the 1,000 phone lines that are open 24 hours a day for 364 days a year (even in Dodgeville, they take Christmas off) to handle an average of 50,000 calls a day (100,000 during the Christmas season). Some pick and pack tens of thousands of orders a day for delivery two business days later in most of the continental U. S. Some monogram all those shirts, towels, and luggage. Some design and mail two catalogs every year, and some manage and position Lands' End to become the premier global direct merchant.

Not bad for a small catalog company founded in 1963 by a copywriter at Young & Rubicam, Gary Comer, whose dream was to sell sailboat hardware and equipment to yachting enthusiasts!

Why did Lands' End locate in Dodgeville? Initially, the site was chosen because Gary Comer "fell in love with the gently rolling hills and woods and cornfields and being able to see the changing seasons." But he quickly found that "along with all that nature had to offer us, we [at Lands' End] came to know what a remarkable group of people we were joining within the community." The citizens of Dodgeville are hard working (they may milk a cow or two, or finish other farm chores before coming to work); they take pride in what they do and find satisfaction in a job well done. In short, these are just the right kind of people for a company committed to putting the customer first.

As Lands' End has grown, the original sailing equipment catalog has been replaced by a variety of catalogs. Most important is the main catalog which is mailed 13 times a year to 8 million households; and a variety of specialty catalogs—most of which are expansions of the main book's product lines. *Coming Home* carries quality products for the home—primarily the bed and bath; *Lands' End Kids' Catalog* contains comfortable, casual clothing and supplies, such as book bags for children; *Textures* and *Beyond Buttondowns* focus on tailored clothing for women and men, respectively; *The Territory Ahead* features upscale casual clothing for men and women; *Corporate Sales* offers large quantity orders of monogrammable products to teams, clubs, and companies; and *Willis and Geiger,* Lands' End's latest addition, sells apparel targeted to outdoor enthusiasts. In addition to those domestic catalogs, Lands' End publishes an international version of its main catalog for 175 countries, and two foreign language/currency catalogs for the British Isles and Japanese markets. In total, Lands' End mailed around 191 million catalogs in 1994.

To keep up with market trends and the needs and wants of all these consumers is no small task! Therefore Lands' End has a marketing research staff, headed by Doug First, Marketing Research Manager. Doug understands the importance of keeping in touch with customers, because he spent eight years in face-to-face contact with bicyclists—a very demanding group—as manager of a bike shop. Armed with an MBA degree from the University of Wisconsin at Madison, he joined Lands' End seven years ago as a Market Research Analyst.

Doug's group regularly conducts mail and telephone surveys, as well as focus group research. Most of the mail surveys are undertaken to track customer satisfaction or to profile the customer base. A major activity of the marketing research group is the yearly panel survey for which Doug and his staff mail questionnaires to several thousand households selected from the company's mailing lists. Included in the sample are buyers and non-buyers of Lands' End merchandise. While respondents change from one year to the next, the questionnaire is modified only when absolutely necessary. It contains questions that enable Lands' End to profile its customers in terms of education, income, age, and lifestyle activities such as sports and hobbies, and to measure Lands' End's share of mailbox (what percentage of catalogs the household receives that are from Lands' End).

In the past, this research has shown that the typical Lands' End customer is highly educated (nearly 90% have some college education); is likely to live in a metropolitan area; is likely to be employed in a managerial or professional capacity; is probably aged 35–54; has a high income (median income for Lands' End customers is $55,000); and is likely to engage in an active lifestyle through travel or participation in a variety of sports.

A different type of mail survey is a product or wear test. For these "tests," Lands' End sends the product to be tested—possibly a shirt or jacket—to selected customers who are asked to use the product for a specified period of time. For example, a respondent might test the shirt for six weeks and be asked to wash/launder the shirt at least four times. At the end of the test period, the respondent fills out a product evaluation form which enables Lands' End to make decisions about the product.

Telephone surveys at Lands' End are conducted by an in-house staff that uses computer assisted telephone interviewing (CATI) in which an interviewer reads the questionnaire on a computer monitor and enters the answers with the keyboard. Consequently, the information is recorded in a database as it is received and is immediately available for analysis.

Telephone surveys may be done for several reasons. First, they may be regularly recurring studies used to track delivery of catalogs or to find out more about catalog users. Second, they may be ad hoc—that is done for a specific, non-recurring purpose. If Lands' End managers observe a change in sales, that might be investigated by telephone.

Telephone surveys may be undisguised or disguised. If they are undisguised, the interviewer tells the respondent that he/she is calling from Lands' End. In a disguised survey, Lands' End is not identified as the sponsor and respondents are asked general questions about ordering and receiving merchandise from catalogers.

While mail and telephone surveying elicits a lot of information from consumers, sometimes it is necessary to see consumers in action. On those occasions, Doug uses focus groups. For example, if Lands' End wanted to know how people use catalogs, they would gather eight to twelve individuals in a room, give them catalogs and observe the participants' responses through one-way mirrors or by watching videotapes of the sessions. They want answers to questions such as, "Do people look at the cover?" "If so, how long?" "Do they thumb through the catalog page by page or flip it open to different sections?" "Do they look at the top or bottom, right or left side of the page, the pictures or copy first?" "How long do they spend looking at/reading a page?" "Do they read the information about Lands' End inside the cover?" "How do participants use competitors' catalogs?"

Focus groups can also be used to determine how people purchase goods. In these sessions, the moderator might ask respondents to compare several versions of a product (for example, one Lands' End shirt with four other brands of shirts with the labels removed). Participants handle the shirts, discuss which features— colors or buttonholes, for example—they think are important and why. Focus groups can also be used for product comparison tests. Lands' End might ask participants to bring their favorite shirt, jacket or slacks to the session. During the focus group, each participant shows their "favorite" to other participants and explains why it is the favorite. The moderator would also have some Lands' End merchandise with the labels removed to compare to the participants' "favorites."

In August 1994, Brad Gillam, head of the product management team for mesh knit shirts approached Doug. His product team believed that the Lands' End mesh knit shirt was a great shirt that could be made even better, but the team wasn't sure which features customers would like improved. To find out, new research had to be conducted to find out how customers perceived this product *at that time*— what they liked and what they wanted improved. Because mesh knit shirts are such a big seller for Lands' End, the company had to *know* that the consumer wanted *and would buy the redesigned product*. The new mesh knit shirt was to be on the cover as a feature item in one of the main Lands' End catalogs in 1995.

Doug and his staff spent the next four months working on the project. "Because mesh knit shirts are such a big market and this is one of our most important lines—if not the most important—I knew we had to do a top-notch job on this research project," Doug explained in discussing the mesh knit shirt research and re-launch. "We had to get the right information *and* be able to assure the product team that their new shirts would sell."

## QUESTIONS

1. How does Lands' End segment its markets?
2. Why are buyers and non-buyers included in the sample used for the yearly panel survey?
3. Why would Lands' End use disguised and undisguised telephone interviews?
4. Assume that you are Doug First. How would you respond to the mesh knit shirt product manager's request? Explain in detail the type(s) of research techniques that you would use, the type(s) of respondents to be included in the research and the type(s) of information to be obtained.

*Source:* "American Pie," *Gentlemen's Quarterly*, p. 73; Lands' End Publications.

# Company Case 1
## *DoorGuard: Trying to Make a Dent in the Market*

Steven Harris had just purchased the car of his dreams—a shiny red Mustang convertible—and wanted to be sure that it remained dent free. He was particularly concerned about the dents the side panels of his car would inevitably receive in the parking lot at the University of South Carolina where he was a student.

Steven found himself thinking more and more about the problem of preventing side-panel damage. He had always been a tinkerer, and he had fairly well-developed mechanical instincts. Steven remembered one of his professors discussing the success of AutoShades, the cardboard panels used behind auto windshields to keep cars cool. Because the panels could be printed on, companies could use the product as a sales-promotion tool. Steven believed that if he could design a device to protect car doors that also served an advertising function, he too could be successful.

### THE PRODUCT

Steven thought about developing a panel, perhaps made of rubber, that would attach to the outside of the car door. The panel would have to be thin, lightweight, impact resistant, waterproof, and capable of being rolled up for easy storage. It would also have to accept screen printing for advertising purposes. After several false starts, Steven found the right material for the job—a foam panel called Mini-Cell 200 (M200), which was manufactured by a local company.

Having worked his way through the cover-material issue, Steven began experimenting with methods for attaching the panel to a car. He knew that ease of use would be critical to his product's success, as it had been for AutoShades. Steven finally decided to use magnets, which could be easily attached to the foam, making the product easy to use.

Steven also spent an entire afternoon selecting a name for the product. He evaluated several, such as DoorGuard, DDent, DentGuard, AbsorbaDoor, and DoorMate. On pure instinct, he chose DoorGuard.

Steven now had a name, but he realized that he still did not have a complete product. If he used only the magnets to attach the product to a door, what would prevent someone from stealing the panels? After trying several unsuccessful theft-prevention ideas, Steven settled on a cable that attached to the foam panel. After attaching the DoorGuard panel to the door, the user would toss the other end of the cable inside the car, then close and lock the door. Anyone who tried to steal the device would tear the panel, making it useless.

Steven believed he had now developed the perfect product. It absorbed impact from other car doors, resisted theft and water damage, stored easily in the trunk or back seat, and accepted screen printing. Exhibit 1-1 illustrates a DoorGuard panel in use.

**EXHIBIT 1-1**
*Illustration of DoorGuard in Use*

Steven next turned his attention to producing the new product. He approached organizations like Jobs for the Handicapped and Goodwill Industries that might assemble products inexpensively. He eventually found an organization that could do everything needed to assemble and print one set of two panels.

Almost as an afterthought, Steven considered price. Based on a total cost of $14.74 per complete set of two panels, Steven used a 100 percent markup on cost (and a little psychological pricing) to arrive at a suggested retail price of $29.95 per set (see Exhibit 1-2). Now that he had designed, named, and priced the product, Steven considered what market he would attack.

**EXHIBIT 1-2**
*DoorGuard Cost/Price*

| Cost per panel | | |
|---|---:|---:|
| M200 ½″ 1′ × 4′ Panel | $ 2.90 | |
| Cover Material 1½ sq. yds. | 1.12 | |
| Magnets 3′ | .90 | |
| Cable 3′ | .45 | |
| Misc. (screen print, packaging) | .50 | |
| Assembly | 1.50 | |
| Total Cost per Panel | 7.37 | |
| Cost per set of two panels | | $14.74 |
| *Retail price per set** | | $29.95 |

*100 percent markup on cost

## THE MARKET

Steven knew that he should research the market potential but believed that he had little basis for developing a reasonable estimate of DoorGuard's sales potential. Using secondary sources, he found that there were 122.8 million cars in use in the United States. Nearly 80 percent of these cars were at least three years old; 50 percent were at least six years old. Because there were no products comparable to DoorGuard on the market, Steven wasn't certain what portion of the car owners would purchase the new product. AutoShades appeared to be about the only close comparison, but there was a huge cost difference: AutoShades cost from $1.49 to $6.00, whereas DoorGuard would cost nearly $30.00. Many companies gave away sun shades as advertising specialties; few companies would do the same with DoorGuard.

Still, Steven believed that DoorGuard targeted a wide-open market. He knew that last year's new car sales in the United States totaled 9,853,000. Few new-car buyers purchased factory-installed body-protection packages. Steven felt that a person paying $15,000 or more for a car would pay a reasonable price to protect it. This helped to explain the success of AutoShades, which in a single year had sales exceeding $20 million.

If Steven could capture just five percent of the new-car market, he would be selling nearly 500,000 sets. And sales to only five percent of the owners of the 122,800,000 cars on the road would generate sales of more than 6,100,000 DoorGuard sets. With such heady potential in mind, Steven began to think through the details of introducing DoorGuard.

# THE MARKETING APPROACH

Steven considered three different approaches for distributing the product. First, Steven thought that he might interest a national retail chain, such as Sears or Kmart, in carrying the product—both had large auto-supply departments. Two catalog companies also came to mind as potential distributors—Sharper Image and Brookstone. These catalogs reached people who could afford to purchase DoorGuard. Finally, Steven considered selling directly to large companies such as R. J. Reynolds or Anheuser-Busch who could offer the product as an advertising specialty or premium item. Steven wondered which of these distribution avenues would be best, or if he should consider others.

Despite all of this development work, DoorGuard was still just an idea. Steven realized that he had no concrete notion about how to proceed. He knew that DoorGuard could be a great product but now realized how complicated it would be to take the idea to the market.

## QUESTIONS

1. What consumer needs and wants does DoorGuard satisfy?
2. Which of the marketing management philosophies discussed in the text is Steven Harris following?
3. If, as the text indicates, a market is "the set of actual and potential buyers of a product," what market does Steven wish to serve with DoorGuard?
4. What problems does Steven face? Has he forgotten to consider anything?
5. What recommendations would you make to Steven Harris? How can he adopt the marketing concept? What items should he put on his marketing "to-do" list?

*Source:* Adapted from "DoorMate: A New Product Venture" by Thomas H. Stevenson, University of North Carolina at Charlotte. Used with permission of the North American Case Research Association and Professor Stevenson.

# Company Case 2
## *Trap-Ease America: The Big Cheese of Mousetraps*

> If a man [can] . . . make a better mousetrap than his neighbor . . . the world will make a beaten path to his door.

As Martha House, president of Trap-Ease America, contemplated the words of Ralph Waldo Emerson framed on the wall of her Costa Mesa, California office, she wondered whether Emerson knew something that she didn't. She *had* the better mousetrap—Trap-Ease—but the world didn't seem all that excited.

## IF YOU BUILD A BETTER MOUSETRAP, WILL IT SELL?

The Trap-Ease is a clever device that traps mice with simple efficiency. A mouse smells bait inside the trap, and enters a tube through an open end. As it walks up the angled bottom of the trap toward the bait, the mouse is trapped after a hinged door swings closed. The mouse can then be disposed of alive, or it can be left alone for a few hours to suffocate in the trap.

Trap-Ease has many advantages when compared with traditional spring-loaded traps or poisons. Consumers can use it safely and easily with no risk of catching their fingers during loading. It poses no injury or poisoning threat to children or pets. Furthermore, with Trap-Ease, consumers can avoid the unpleasant cleanup mess associated with violent spring-loaded traps. Finally, consumers can reuse the trap or simply throw it away.

These advantages were quickly recognized, with Trap-Ease becoming a "celebrity" product of sorts. It won first place among 300 new products at the annual National Hardware Show. *People* magazine wrote an article about the mousetrap, and numerous talk shows and trade publications featured it. Despite this attention, however, expected demand for the trap never materialized.

## DISAPPOINTING SALES

Martha's initial first-year sales forecast was five million units. However, in its first four months of operation, the company sold only several hundred thousand units. Martha wondered if most new products got off to such a slow start, or if she was doing something wrong. She detected some problems, although none seemed overly serious. For one, there was not enough repeat buying. For another, she had noted that many of the retailers on whom she called used their sample mousetraps as desktop conversation pieces instead of as demonstration devices. Martha wondered if consumers were also buying the traps as novelties rather than as solutions to their mouse problems.

Martha knew that the investor group which had purchased the rights to Trap-Ease from its inventor believed that the company had a "once-in-a-lifetime chance" with its innovative mousetrap. She sensed the group's impatience. She had budgeted approximately $250,000 in administrative and fixed costs for the first year (not including marketing costs). To keep the investors happy, the company needed to sell enough traps to cover those costs and make a reasonable profit.

# TRAP-EASE'S MARKETING PLAN

Martha's early research suggested that women are the best target market for Trap-Ease since they do not like traditional mousetraps. Women want a means of dealing with mouse problems that avoids the unpleasantness and risks associated with standard traps. To reach this target market, Martha decided to distribute Trap-Ease though national grocery, hardware, and drug chains such as Safeway, Kmart, Hechingers, and CB Drug. She sold the traps directly to these retailers, avoiding any wholesalers or other resellers.

The traps sold in packages of two, with a suggested retail price of $2.49. Although this price made the Trap-Ease about five to ten times more expensive than smaller, standard traps, consumers appeared to offer little initial price resistance. The manufacturing cost for the Trap-Ease, including freight and packaging costs, was about 31 cents per unit. The company paid an additional 8.2 cents per unit in royalty fees to the inventor. Martha priced the traps to retailers at 99 cents per unit and estimated that after sales and volume discounts Trap-Ease would realize net revenues from retailers of 75 cents per unit.

To promote the product, Martha budgeted approximately $60,000 for the first year, including $50,000 for travel costs to visit trade shows and retailers, and $10,000 for advertising. Because of the publicity the mousetrap had received, she had spent little of the advertising budget. Still, she had placed advertising in such "home and shelter" magazines as *Good Housekeeping*. Martha was the company's only "salesperson," but she intended to hire more salespeople soon.

# A MARKETING CHALLENGE

In these first few months, Martha had learned that marketing a new product is not an easy task. For example, one national retailer had placed a large order with instructions that the order be delivered between 1:00 and 3:00 P.M. on a specified day. The truck arrived late, and the retailer refused to accept the shipment. To make matters worse, he told Martha that it would be a year before she got another chance. Feeling frustrated, Martha thought about sending the retailer a copy of Emerson's famous quote.

## QUESTIONS

1. Martha and the Trap-Ease America investors feel they face a "once-in-a-lifetime opportunity." What information do they need to evaluate this opportunity? How do you think the group would write its mission statement? How would you write it?

2. Has Martha identified the best target market for Trap-Ease? What other market segments might the firm target?

3. How has the company positioned the Trap-Ease? Do you see any problems with this mix?

4. Describe the current marketing mix for Trap-Ease. Do you see any problems with this mix?
5. Who is Trap-Ease America's competition?
6. How would you change Trap-Ease's marketing strategy? What kinds of control procedures would you establish for this strategy?

# Company Case 3
# *JCPenney: Doing It Right*

For years, many consumers avoided shopping at JCPenney department stores because they considered the merchandise stodgy and cheap. Fortunately, perceptions can change radically and quickly in retailing, with the result that the same consumers are now committed to Penney. What brought them back? Good quality products at reasonable prices. With projected 1994 sales of $20.4 billion and with net income topping $1 billion for the first time in its history, JCPenney is doing things right in the often turbulent U. S. department store industry.

## PENNEY'S HISTORY

Founded in 1902 by James Cash Penney, Penney used a reputation for value to become the dominant ready-to-wear clothes merchant in small town America. During the 1950s and 1960s, Penney opened stores in large suburban shopping malls and broadened its merchandise to include the durable goods that suburbanites needed.

This strategy worked well into the 1970s. However, in the early 1980s, Penney's sales flattened and its profit margins shrank. Worse yet, company research showed that women shop at malls, and they buy apparel, not paint. Penney would have to rethink its merchandise mix.

## A TURNAROUND

When William R. Howell became chairperson of Penney's Board of Directors in 1983, he realized that retailing specialization would be the key to the company's success. Howell launched a multi-year repositioning strategy. First, Penney dropped its major appliance, paint, hardware, lawn and garden, and automotive departments. Next, the company started a $1.5 billion store-modernization program. Finally, in 1988, Penney abandoned home electronics, sporting goods, and photography products. Altogether, Penney discontinued products and services that accounted for $1.5 billion in annual sales.

The new JCPenney focused on apparel and "soft" home furnishings. Penney's core customers—lower- and middle-income families—were exposed to the same media as higher-income, urban families. Although these core customers still wanted to be practical, they also wanted to be in style.

With these changes, Penney moved from a general merchandiser of commodity goods to a chain that offered fashionable, quality merchandise. These changes paid off in 1989 as Penney's net income soared to a record $822 million on sales of $16.1 billion.

Then, the bottom dropped out. In its move toward fashion merchandise, Penney had expanded its selection of higher-priced lines. During the 1990 recession, consumers spent more conservatively, which hammered Penney's earnings. Profits plunged 42 percent in 1990 to $577 million, and they fell again to $528 million in 1991.

Penney's managers decided it was time to refocus on moderately priced merchandise. So they lowered prices and *increased* quality. Penney's expanded quality inspection teams worked with Penney's suppliers to perform more than 60,000 garment inspections every year, checking each garment against stringent quality-control standards.

Then, Penney installed a Direct Broadcast system in 1,100 stores that allowed its buyers to see merchandise by video and place orders via computer. This system slashed the time needed for store buying decisions and improved buyers' ability to shape merchandise mixes to serve particular markets. Penney also adjusted its merchandise mix in 170 stores to serve Hispanic and African-American shoppers. Finally, Penney installed a toll-free, 24-hour, 7-day-a-week customer phone service.

With all this done, Penney's managers realized that they had to do even more to keep the chain from looking like other retailers who had adopted value-pricing strategies. Penney needed a competitive advantage.

# DEVELOPING A COMPETITIVE ADVANTAGE

The competitive advantage came in the form of Penney's own private-label brands. Penney positioned these brands—including Worthington, Hunt Club, St. John's Bay, Jacqueline Ferrar, and Stafford—as national labels that could compete with the likes of Liz Claiborne and the Gap. It challenged the designers and managers for each brand to develop a unique brand identity. Particularly successful are the Worthington and Stafford career-apparel lines and Penney's Arizona jeans. After eight years of development, Stafford is the number one men's suit brand in the country.

Penney now had a competitive advantage—top-quality national brands available at reasonable prices. To promote these brands, Penney initiated in 1995 a "Value Right" national campaign in which hangtags are attached to more than 100 of Penney's best-selling private-label products. These hangtags tell consumers: "If you find a similar item somewhere else and think it is a better value, return this item, and we will refund your money." Previous campaigns showed famous labels, such as Nike and Dockers, alongside Penney's brands. Label closeups told consumers that Penney's products were "pure silk" or "100% cotton." Penney backed up these ads with in-store displays that placed Penney's brands side-by-side with outside brands. Shoppers noticed that the look and quality of Penney's and outside brands were similar, but Penney's brands sold for about 20 percent less.

Thomas D. Hutchens, president of JCPenney merchandising worldwide, explains the strategy: "Today's consumer is insisting upon more than low prices. She is thinking more about quality and fashion, combined with her demand for competitive prices. That's the equation for value."

## WHAT NEXT?

Penney still sees plenty of room for improvement. Since it discontinued hard-line merchandise, each of its more than 1,700 stores averages only $149 in sales per square foot of store space (a traditional way of measuring retail store productivity), which is among the lowest square-foot sales in the industry. Penney's long-range growth is dependent on increasing sales per square foot.

One method is entering international markets. Penney already is ahead of many competitors in international expansion, with its thrust beginning in 1991. Penney moved into foreign markets like Portugal, Japan, and Mexico. Although Mexico represents Penney's biggest effort, with seven U.S.-sized stores being developed, the chain's expansion there has been affected by Mexico's recent political and economic turmoil and by the rapid decline in the value of the Mexican peso.

The question is, can JCPenney lead the way in developing international markets as it has led retailing's turnaround in the United States? And can it do this while continuing to improve its U.S. operations?

### QUESTIONS

1. Which factors in JCPenney's microenvironment have been important in shaping its marketing strategies?
2. Which forces in the macroenvironment have shaped Penney's evolving marketing strategies?
3. What microenvironmental and macroenvironmental factors should JCPenney consider as it enters foreign markets?
4. What recommendations would you make to help JCPenney improve sales in its U.S. stores?

*Sources:* Howard Schlossberg, "Retailers Reassessing Themselves to Stay in Touch with Consumers," *Marketing News,* March 29, 1993, pp. 8–9; Wendy Zellner, "Penney's Rediscovers Its Calling," *Business Week,* April 5, 1993, pp. 51–52; Zina Moukheiber, "Our Competitive Advantage," *Forbes,* April 12, 1993, pp. 59–62; Julie N. Forsyth, "Department Store Industry Restructures for the '90s," *Chain Store Age Executive,* August 1993, pp. 25A–30A; "JCPenney Targets Middle America," *Discount Merchandiser,* August 1993, pp. 106–7; Elaine Underwood, "JCPenney Pitches Ethnics," *Brandweek,* September 13, 1993, p. 10; Bob Ortega, "Penney Pushes Abroad in Unusually Big Way as It Pursues Growth," *The Wall Street Journal,* February 1, 1994, p. 20A1; "JCPenney Reaping the Rewards of Soft Lines Transition," *Discount Store News,* May 15, 1995, p. 45; David Moin, "Penney's to Use Refunds to Tout Its Brand Value," *WWD,* July 13, 1995, p. 2.

# Company Case 4
# *ACT I: Feeling Out the Appliance Controls Market*

Appliance Control Technology (ACT) is part of a specialized industry that designs, manufactures, and sells touch-sensitive digital control panels for home appliances, such as microwave ovens, ranges, and washing machines. Founded by Wallace C. Leyshon, who is also president and CEO, ACT is a company in search of a clearly defined market size.

On the one hand, it is tied to a mature appliance industry that saw growth increase by only five percent annually from 1986 to 1990. Furthermore, the Association of Home Appliance Manufacturers estimates that the number of home appliances per U. S. household rose from 3.3 in 1960 to 4.1 in 1970, to 5.4 in 1982, and to 6.1 in 1987. Industry analysts question whether this level of penetration can increase further.

On the other hand, Leyshon's research predicts that sales of digital control panels for appliances could grow at a whopping 22 percent a year during the early 1990s. Only about 20 percent of American-made appliances now include digital controls. However, one industry analyst notes that, with the success of microwave ovens and videocassette recorders, consumers have become increasingly comfortable with touch-sensitive digital controls. Leyshon believes that increased consumer familiarity has opened the way for manufacturers to include digital control panels in other types of home appliances currently controlled with dials and buttons (electromechanical controls). With a digital control, for example, a standard electric range could offer a wide range of special cooking programs that microwave ovens now provide.

After starting ACT, Leyshon landed a significant contract with a major microwave oven manufacturer. This business provided the financial base ACT needed to survive. However, Leyshon realized that he needed to develop a marketing strategy to attack the appliance controls market. Although there were only a limited number of digital control suppliers and five major manufacturers in the industry, Leyshon could find little readily available marketing research on the appliance controls industry, especially on digital controls.

What he did find was a chart in *Appliance Manufacturer Magazine* from the Association of Home Appliance Manufacturers to show that appliance shipments appeared to be turning down as part of a cyclical business pattern. After bottoming out in 1982 at a level of 24 million units (excluding microwaves), the industry experienced a major turnaround that saw shipments climb to more than 38 million units in 1988 before heading downward again.

When Leyshon discussed this with Gregory Pearl, ACT's director of marketing, both men decided that more in-depth marketing research was needed. Pearl outlined the marketing research process (see Exhibit 4-1) and clarified his thinking about key research issues, including research goals, specific questions for telephone interviews, and interview subjects (see Exhibit 4-2). Finally, he drafted a preliminary version of the questionnaire (see Exhibit 4-3).

Leyshon was pleased with his marketing director's progress. "Okay," he told Pearl, "let's see what you've done. Then we can decide where we go from here."

## QUESTIONS

1. Based on information in the case and in Exhibits 4-2 and 4-3, just what is Leyshon trying to learn through marketing research? What additional trends and information might he want to monitor as a part of his ongoing marketing information system?

2. What sources of marketing intelligence can ACT use to gather information on the industry and its competition?

3. Based on the marketing research process discussed in the text, what is ACT's marketing research objective, and what problem is the company addressing? Evaluate ACT's marketing research process (Exhibit 4-1).

4. What sources of secondary data might ACT use?

5. What decisions has ACT made about its research approach, contact method, and sampling plan?

6. Evaluate ACT's proposed questionnaire (Exhibit 4-3). Does it address the issues raised in Exhibit 4-2? What changes would you recommend?

**EXHIBIT 4-1**
*Steps in ACT marketing research process*

1. Identify and articulate the problem.
2. Identify research goals.
3. Determine the information needed to achieve the research goals.
4. Determine research design.
5. Decide on research sample (i.e., whom to call).
6. Determine content of the individual questions.
7. Construct a questionnaire.
8. Test the questionnaire.
9. Adjust the questionnaire based on the test results.
10. Conduct the interviews.
11. Write up the results of each interview.
12. Write a report.

**EXHIBIT 4-2**
*ACT marketing research design issues*

I. Survey goals
   A. Gain insight into best strategy for approaching the electronic controls market.
      1. Types of appliances
      2. Features
      3. Cost issues
      4. Tactical selling techniques
   B. Determine how ACT can best serve original equipment manufacturers (OEMs).
      1. Research and development
      2. Partnering
      3. Product-development cycle
II. Specific questions to be addressed
   A. What problems do equipment manufacturers and retailers face in making and selling home appliances? How can ACT help solve those problems?
   B. Who are the decision makers in the electronics buying process? Who has the power between the retailer and the equipment manufacturer?
   C. Are there any unidentified issues from ACT's, the manufacturers', or the retailers' perspectives?
   D. How rapidly will manufacturers adopt electronic controls for their appliances, by category of appliances?
   E. How sensitive are manufacturers to the price of electronic controls versus standard electromechanical controls?
   F. What are manufacturers' impressions of suppliers' strengths and weaknesses?
   G. What features and issues other than price drive the use of electronic controls?
   H. How can manufacturers use electronic controls to add value to mid-level appliances?
   I. How can a supplier be a better partner to manufacturers?
   J. What can a supplier do to help speed up manufacturers' product-development efforts?
III. Who should be interviewed?
   A. Manufacturers
      1. Functional areas
         a. Purchasing
         b. Marketing
         c. Engineering
      2. Specific companies
         a. Whirlpool
         b. Frigidaire
         c. General Electric
         d. Maytag
         e. Raytheon
   B. Retailers
      1. Functional areas
         a. Buyers
         b. Store-level management
         c. Floor sales personnel
      2. Specific companies
         a. Sears
         b. Montgomery Ward
         c. Highland
         d. Wal-Mart
   C. Other
      1. Association of Home Appliance Manufacturers
      2. *Appliance Magazine* editor
      3. *Appliance Manufacturer Magazine* editor

**EXHIBIT 4-3**
*Version 1—ACT*
*marketing research*
*questionnaire*

*Introduction*
ACT is conducting a survey of decision makers and industry experts in the electronic appliance controls industry. We would appreciate your help in answering our questions. Your responses will be reported anonymously, if they are reported at all. Your responses will be used to help ACT determine how to serve the appliance industry better.

*Questions*
1.  A. What are your opinions on the level of electronic controls usage, expressed in percentages, in the following appliance categories for 1991 and 1996?

    B. What are your opinions on the average cost per electronic control by appliance category in 1991 and 1996?

| Category | Percent of units using electronic controls in: | | Average cost per control unit in: | |
|---|---|---|---|---|
| | *1991* | *1996* | *1991* | *1996* |
| Dishwashers | ——— | ——— | ——— | ——— |
| Dryers, electric | ——— | ——— | ——— | ——— |
| Dryers, gas | ——— | ——— | ——— | ——— |
| Microwaves | ——— | ——— | ——— | ——— |
| Ranges, electric | ——— | ——— | ——— | ——— |
| Ranges, gas | ——— | ——— | ——— | ——— |
| Refrigerators | ——— | ——— | ——— | ——— |
| Room air conditioners | ——— | ——— | ——— | ——— |
| Washers | ——— | ——— | ——— | ——— |

2.  For each of the following categories, what price must a supplier charge for an electronic control unit such that a manufacturer would be indifferent as to using electronic or electromechanical controls, taking into account the differences in functions and features?

| Category | Price per electronic unit |
|---|---|
| Dishwashers | ——— |
| Dryers, electric | ——— |
| Dryers, gas | ——— |
| Microwaves | ——— |
| Ranges, electric | ——— |
| Ranges, gas | ——— |
| Refrigerators | ——— |
| Room air conditioners | ——— |
| Washers | ——— |

3.  What features, functions, and attributes do electronic controls need to have if they are to be used more often in appliances?

4.  What impact will the upcoming Department of Energy regulations have on the appliance industry?

5.  What can an electronic controls company do to be a better supplier?

# Company Case 5
# Shiseido: Rethinking
# the Future

Successful Japanese companies are suddenly concerned about finding new marketing strategies to suit changing consumer behaviors. In a market known for customer loyalty, Japanese managers are learning quickly that customers have minds of their own and do not necessarily follow expected rules.

Shiseido (She-she-doe), Japan's largest cosmetics company, is learning this lesson from customers like Noriko Shida, a 21-year-old student who is shopping at an upscale store in a chic Tokyo shopping district. As Noriko examines a tube of Shiseido's lipstick, she turns up her nose at the price. "I find good colors at places like this," she sniffs. "Then I go and buy the same product at a discount store." Welcome to the new Japan.

# A UNIQUE MARKETING ARRANGEMENT

For years, retailers agreed to sell *only* Shiseido cosmetics in exchange for Shiseido's commitment to buy back unsold merchandise. With this understanding, Shiseido became both manufacturer and wholesaler and developed a network of 25,000 Japanese retailers. These shops represent about one-half of all cosmetics and pharmaceutical shops in Japan. The system allowed Shiseido to control distribution and develop a pricy image. Shiseido rode this distribution channel and its high prices to annual sales of over 500 billion yen (about $4.8 billion) by 1990.

# ANTITRUST LAWS CLAMP DOWN

Under Japanese antitrust laws, cosmetics manufacturers are not allowed to fix retail prices on items costing more than about $12. That accounts for about 80 percent of cosmetics sold in Japan. However, because of the close relationship that exists between Shiseido and its retailers, most retailers sold Shiseido products at the manufacturer's suggested retail prices.

This cozy relationship changed dramatically in 1995 when Japan's Fair Trade Commission ruled that Shiseido was guilty of retail price fixing and ordered the company to allow retailers to begin discounting its products. Shortly after, Jusco, a major supermarket chain, slashed up to 15 percent off the prices of 800 cosmetics from four manufacturers. In doing so, Jusco challenged Japan's unique cosmetics distribution system that requires cosmetics to be sold with personal counseling. Jusco sells Shiseido products without beauty advisors, believing that it is more important to lower prices than provide costly personal consultations. This challenge will probably take years to settle.

The government's strong position against antitrust violations in the cosmetics industry is the result, in part, of consumer complaints against high prices. U.S. pressure on Japan to open its markets and eliminate antitrust exemptions for all cosmetics have also had an impact. However, widespread cosmetics discounting is not inevitable. With severe competition for market share a fact of business life, many retailers may keep prices high to protect their profit margins.

# SHISEIDO'S MARKETING RESPONSE

Shiseido is responding to these changes by cutting costs and refocusing on lower-priced cosmetics. Robots carry out almost all manufacturing steps at a new automated factory with one-third the employees. It is also looking for more growth overseas. Already, it operates 21 subsidiaries and six factories in 30 countries and expects to increase international sales by 50 percent to 100 billion yen. If it is to reach this goal, Shiseido must do well in the United States. In 1994, the company shifted its U.S. marketing strategy, focusing more on skin-care products and on splashy new print ads. It also renovated sales counters, now located in 820 U.S. department stores, to provide a "new image," with more eye-catching displays.

# WOOING U.S. SHOPPERS

U.S.-based cosmetics companies are discarding sexy models in glamorous locales for scientific-sounding claims, promotional coupons and direct attacks on competitors. Industry executives suggest that these marketing changes reflect increasing consumer savvy and value consciousness.

Although it appears that Tokyo's Noriko Shida may not be much different from shoppers in the United States, it is still questionable whether Japanese cosmetics manufacturers can repeat Japanese successes in the U.S. car and consumer electronics markets. Some analysts argue that the Japanese have a high-tech rather than a high-chic image and that Japanese managers often sneer at image-driven selling, believing that their products perform better than those of their rivals. (Japanese cosmetics companies spend almost 4 percent of their sales on R&D, about double that of American companies.)

A test of Japan's effectiveness in the cosmetics market is how American consumers respond to Shiseido's new line of long-lasting lipsticks. Advertisements focus on the product's specialized lip treatment rather than on glamour. Shiseido's first-year sales goal for the lipstick line is $8 million.

But some observers argue that cosmetics is an image-driven market in which companies have a hard time convincing consumers of product differences. They wonder if American or Japanese companies can succeed with scientific claims and coupons. Can they transform whimsical beauty products into natural, high-tech, essential products? Shiseido's executives are struggling with these questions as they try to understand consumers.

## QUESTIONS

1. How do consumers' cultural, social, personal, and psychological characteristics affect cosmetics shopping behavior, and how do these factors affect the way cosmetics executives see consumers? How are these factors changing?

2. Who is involved in a consumer's decision to purchase cosmetics, and what role does each participant play?

3. What types of buying-decision behavior are involved in purchasing cosmetics?

4. Describe the buying-decision process for cosmetics.

5. What marketing recommendations would you make to Shiseido as it seeks to increase its sales in the U.S. market?

*Sources:* "The Softer Samurai," *The Economist,* May 12, 1990, p. 73; "Facing Up," *The Economist,* July 13, 1991, pp. 71–72; Louise do Rosario, "Make Up and Mend," *Far Eastern Economic Review,* December 19, 1991, pp. 70–71; Emily Thornton, "Japan's Struggle To Be Creative," *Fortune,* April 19, 1993, pp. 129–34; "Fragrance Helps You Live Longer," *The Economist,* October 23, 1993, p. 86; Jennifer Cody, "Shiseido Strives for a Whole New Look," *The Wall Street Journal,* May 27, 1994, p. B5; Suein L. Hwang, "Makeup Ads Downplay Glamour for Value," *The Wall Street Journal,* June 20, 1994, p. B6; Paulette Thomas, "Peddling Youth Gets Some New Wrinkles," *The Wall Street Journal,* October, 24, 1994, p. B1; Joseph T. Lin, "Notes from the Orient," *Cosmetics and Toiletries,* September 1995, p. 19; Cara Kagan, "Shiseido's Look for Lasting Lips," *WWD,* September 8, 1995, p. 7.

# Company Case 6
# *ACT II: Controlling an Industrial Market*

As you recall from Chapter 4, Appliance Control Technology (ACT) designs, manufactures, and markets touch-sensitive digital controls for home appliances such as microwave ovens and washing machines. These controls allow users to direct the operations of appliances without using traditional buttons and dials.

Gregory Pearl, ACT's director of marketing, explains how this technology will transform the way consumers operate many home appliances: "My vision is that someday soon the consumer who owns a midpriced washer will be able to touch a digital keypad once to tell the unit what type of clothes are inside and the washer will do everything else. For example, once the user tells the washer that the load contains delicate fabrics, it will automatically determine the size of the load, add water at the right temperature, and dispense the correct amount of detergent at the right time. That will save consumers time and worry and reduce energy costs."

## DEFINING THE MARKET

Although the home appliance market is considered mature, there is an opportunity for manufacturers of touch-sensitive electronic controls since only 20 percent of home appliances have these controls and most of these are high-end appliances. ACT's goal is to produce digital controls cheaply enough so that manufacturers can offer them in midrange appliances.

There are only five customers for this product: General Electric, Whirlpool, Frigidaire, Maytag, and Raytheon. ACT knows these customers very well and believes that final consumers are ready for touch-sensitive controls on home appliances because they have become used to them on microwave ovens.

ACT has two groups of competitors: the electromechanical control makers and the electronic equipment makers. The electromechanical group is trying to convert to the new technology, but it will be a difficult process for them, since it involves making their own products obsolete. ACT estimates that the controls market in the United States and Europe is about $2 billion a year, with the market equally split between the two areas. Electronic controls account for a little less than 50 percent of the market.

## BECOMING COMPETITIVE

ACT is trying to convince manufacturers to adopt electronic controls for their appliances in a number of ways. First, the company is containing costs by manufacturing products in the United States. Although manufacturing abroad saves labor costs, direct labor is only a small percentage of the product's cost. Going offshore adds shipping costs and fees as well as additional management personnel costs to every product. Moreover, building products in the United States keeps the research and development, engineering, and production staffs together, which facilitates problem solving.

Second, ACT's strategy is to develop standard controls that a manufacturer can use across model lines. Although the touch pad will look different, and the products will have different features, the control unit, microprocessor components, and circuit boards will be basically the same for all units. This enables ACT to make more controls of the same type and at lower costs. ACT passes the savings on to customers and allows the company to be price competitive with manufacturers of standard electromechanical controls.

Third, ACT wants to work with appliance manufacturers at the start of the product development processes to reduce product development lead time instead of coming in late in the process. This approach has already been adopted by the Japanese and Koreans because it avoids unnecessary delays. Gregory Pearl explains: "If Sears decides that it wants to offer a new dryer, it will give the original equipment manufacturer's (OEM) marketing staff suggestions for the new product. The OEM's marketing staff will develop ideas for product features and give those ideas to the engineering staff so that it can develop a preliminary design and give the specifications for the new dryer to its purchasing department. The purchasing department will then send the specifications to suppliers, including control suppliers, who will submit bids to the OEM to supply the parts at certain prices. Negotiations then take place between the suppliers and the OEM on prices and features. By the time all this happens, it has been a long time since Sears said it wanted a new dryer. ACT believes that the process is too complicated and too slow. There's a good chance that by the time Sears's ideas have passed through all these groups, communication problems may have jumbled the message. By jointly developing specifications to meet price and performance objectives, everyone involved in development will have the same information, and the process should go much faster with fewer changes along the way."

## LEARNING MORE ABOUT THE MARKET

Pearl conducted telephone interviews with manufacturers, retailers, and others in the home appliance industry to gain insight into industry practices. He used an open-ended questionnaire (see Company Case 4) as a script for the interviews, and recorded the information from each interview. He prepared a set of exhibits summarizing the results. He explains:

"First, we interviewed 67 people from manufacturers, such as engineers, marketers, and purchasing agents. We also talked to 20 respondents from retailers, such as buyers, and 15 others with industry knowledge. We were interested in determining the respondents' best estimates of the percentage of appliances using electronic controls by type of appliance for 1991 and their projections for 1996. This exhibit summarizes their estimates (see Exhibit 6-1). I also summarized the respondents' key comments on these pages (see Exhibit 6-2). Finally, I developed two tables on market shares and price points that may help (Exhibits 6-3 and 6-4)."

These exhibits contain valuable information that will help ACT shape its marketing strategy.

**EXHIBIT 6-1**
*Estimated electronic controls penetration rates: 1991 and 1996*

| | 1991 (%) | 1996 (%) | 5-Year Change Multiple |
|---|---|---|---|
| Dishwashers | 5 | 10 | 2.0 times |
| Dryers, electric | 5 | 15 | 3.0 times |
| Dryers, gas | 5 | 15 | 3.0 times |
| Microwaves | 90 | 90 | 1.0 times |
| Ranges, electric | 20 | 50 | 2.5 times |
| Ranges, gas | 15 | 40 | 2.7 times |
| Refrigerators | 2 | 5–50 | 2.5–25.0 times |
| Room air conditioners | 10 | 25 | 2.5 times |
| Washers | 5 | 15 | 3.0 times |

*Source:* Appliance Control Technology.

**EXHIBIT 6-2**
*ACT market survey results—selected comments made by survey respondents, grouped by functional area*

**I. Manufacturers: Engineers**

- Suppliers need to tell the story of the electronic system better.
- I feel electronic controls costs are equal to those of electromechanical, or even cheaper if the entire control system is considered.
- An important trend in supplier development . . . is to become involved up front with the manufacturer.
- The issue in electronic controls is not the technology, but the supplier; that is, the technology is reliable.

**II. Manufacturers: Marketing**

- Two to three years in development is too long for any electronics program.
- Why aren't electronic controls in white goods (stoves, washers, dryers, and so on) as reliable as those in microwave ovens?
- Manufacturers perceive that electronic controls costs are not in line with the benefits provided. There needs to be more parity between cost/benefit.
- If electronic controls were at cost parity, they would quickly replace electromechanical controls.

**III. Manufacturers: Purchasing**

- Electronics needs to offer some type of feature to encourage customers to pay a premium.
- Consumers need to be convinced of the reliability.
- Suppliers need to be proactive and innovative.

**IV. Trade Groups, Including Publishers and Editors**

- Electronic controls are the wave of the future.
- Cost is probably the major issue holding back electronics at this time.
- Energy efficiency is now a big problem.

**V. Retailers**

- Price is a major issue.
- Consumers are frightened by the complexity of electronics. For electronics to gain greater acceptance, they need to be simpler.
- If possible, electronics should get down to just one button. Just load the machine, press the button, and let it run.

*Source:* Internal research, Appliance Control Technology.

## EXHIBIT 6-3
*Market shares for major appliances (%)—1990*

|  | ELECTROLUX | GENERAL ELECTRIC | MAYTAG | RAYTHEON | WHIRLPOOL | OTHER |
|---|---|---|---|---|---|---|
| Dishwashers | 19 | 35 | 11 | N/A | 34 | 1 |
| Dryers, electric | 8 | 19 | 15 | 4 | 52 | 2 |
| Dryers, gas | 9 | 13 | 15 | 3 | 55 | 4 |
| Freezers | 32 | N/A | 22 | 6 | 36 | 4 |
| Ranges, electric | 19 | 47 | 11 | 6 | 15 | 2 |
| Ranges, gas | 20 | 34 | 21 | 20 | N/A | 5 |
| Refrigerators | 19 | 36 | 7 | 9 | 27 | 2 |
| Washers | 9 | 15 | 17 | 4 | 52 | 3 |

*Source: Appliance Magazine.*

## EXHIBIT 6-4
*Home appliance industry: key brand names by price point*

| | MANUFACTURER | | | | |
|---|---|---|---|---|---|
| **Price Point** | **Electrolux** | **General Electric** | **Maytag** | **Raytheon** | **Whirlpool** |
| Premium-priced | Frigidaire | Monarch | Jenn-Air<br>Maytag | Amana | KitchenAid<br>Bauknecht |
| Midpriced | Frigidaire<br>Westinghouse | General Electric | Maytag<br>Magic Chef | Caloric<br>Speed Queen | Kenmore<br>Whirlpool |
| Lower-priced | Westinghouse<br>Kelvinator | RCA<br>Hotpoint | Admiral<br>Norge | Caloric | Roper<br>Estate |
| ____ | Gibson | | Signature | | |

*Source: Merrill Lynch.*

## QUESTIONS

1. Outline ACT's current marketing strategy. What decisions does ACT need to make?

2. What is the nature of demand in the home appliance industry? What factors shape that demand?

3. What is the nature of the buying decision process in the home appliance industry? How is ACT trying to change that process?

4. Who is involved in the buying center in a manufacturer's decisions concerning appliance controls?

5. What environmental and organizational factors should ACT consider in developing its strategy for dealing with buying centers?

6. What recommendations would you make to help ACT develop its marketing strategy?

*Source:* Based in part on Tom Richman, "Made in the U.S.A.," in *Anatomy of a Start-Up* (Boston: Goldhirsh Group, Inc., 1991), pp. 241–52. Used with permission. Appliance Control Technology also contributed information for this case.

# Company Case 7
# *Quaker Oats: Dousing the Competition*

Every football fan has cringed while watching two burly football players douse an unsuspecting coach with a large cooler of Gatorade. This dousing is now the ultimate moment following an important win. Although some 40 national and regional brands compete in the sports-drink market, Gatorade has achieved such a dominant position that the brand name has become almost a generic term for the category.

In fact, Gatorade is Quaker Oats's single most important product. For 1994, Gatorade produced about $1.2 billion in sales, about 15 percent of Quaker Oats's sales, and about 17 percent of operating profits. Analysts estimate that Gatorade controls about 81 percent of the sports-drink market, which continues to grow at double-digit rates. It is not surprising, therefore, that many companies are now entering this market. It is also not surprising that Gatorade has sent clear signals that it will fight to defend its market share.

## THE HISTORY OF GATORADE

Gatorade was developed in the 1960s by researchers studying heat exhaustion among University of Florida football players. The researchers devised a drink that prevented the severe dehydration caused by fluid and mineral loss during physical exertion in high temperatures. When the Florida Gators used the drink on the sidelines during the 1966 season, they quickly became known as the "second-half team" because the team consistently outplayed its opponents during the second half. When the team won the Orange Bowl against Georgia Tech, Georgia Tech's coach noted that "We didn't have Gatorade. That made the difference." *Sports Illustrated* reported the remark, and Gatorade was on its way to creating and dominating a new product category—the isotonic beverage or sports drink.

Stokely-Van Camp, which acquired Gatorade in 1967, promoted it not only as a sports drink but also as a health-food product because of its value in replacing electrolytes lost due to colds, flu, diarrhea, and vomiting. During the 1970s, Gatorade realized rapid growth as an increasingly fitness-minded public latched on to the product's benefits. Stokely also developed a strong position for Gatorade in institutional team sales.

Quaker Oats, which purchased Stokely-Van Camp in 1983, saw the opportunity to expand Gatorade's sales by increasing both its distribution and promotion, and it doubled Gatorade's marketing expenditures. Between 1983 and 1990, Gatorade's sales grew at a 28 percent compound annual rate.

## THE PRODUCT AND THE MARKET

When Quaker Oats acquired Gatorade, it found that Stokely had targeted competitive athletes as well as men and teenagers involved in competitive sports. However, Quaker found that Stokely had not positioned the brand well to the general public and that there was no clear message specifying the product's uses.

Quaker decided to develop a narrow, solid positioning for the product based on how southern consumers used it and to market the product in the North. The sports-drink market is highly seasonal and regional, with most sales occurring during the summer months in the southern United States. Consumers in Florida, Texas, and California account for 38 percent of Gatorade's sales.

Quaker Oats also decided to portray Gatorade's users as accomplished, but not necessarily professional, athletes. Advertisements depicted serious athletes who enjoyed sports and Gatorade and who needed supplemental carbohydrates, sodium, and potassium. These athletes reminded target customers of themselves. Gatorade promised to provide rapidly absorbing nutrients that would help the body recover from fluid and mineral loss.

Quaker responded to market changes by introducing Gatorade Light in 1990. This line extension targeted calorie-conscious female athletes. Gatorade Light had less sodium and about one-half the calories of regular Gatorade and came in three flavors. Quaker also introduced Freestyle, a more flavorful drink made with fruit juice. Freestyle targeted people who had more interest in product taste than in rehydration. By 1992, Quaker offered original Gatorade in six flavors selected to appeal to different target groups.

## COMPETITION TRIES TO MAKE GATORADE SWEAT

Competitors did not overlook Gatorade's success and the rapid growth of the sports-drink market. Suntory, a subsidiary of the Japanese beverage giant Suntory, introduced 10-K sports drink in the United States in 1985. 10-K was Gatorade's strongest competitor because Suntory promoted the drink as using salt-free spring water and having a high vitamin C content. Like Gatorade, 10-K focused on grocery store distribution and targeted sports teams. Suntory claimed that 10-K beat Gatorade in taste tests and in repeat purchases.

Coca-Cola, Pepsico, and other companies also dabbled in the market. Coca-Cola introduced Maxx, a powdered sports drink, which never made it out of test markets. In 1989, Pepsi Cola introduced Mountain Dew Sport (MDS), which consumers felt had too much carbonation (Pepsi pulled the product), and subsequently AllSport, a more lightly carbonated drink that came in four flavors. Pepsi distributed AllSport through grocery and convenience stores. In 1990, Coca-Cola reentered the market with PowerAde, a noncarbonated, caffeine-free drink that came in three flavors. Coca-Cola planned to distribute PowerAde only through convenience stores.

By early 1992, Quaker realized that despite Gatorade's rapid growth, new sales were becoming harder to find. Quaker approached Coca-Cola with the idea of teaming up to distribute Gatorade through Coca-Cola's wide network of vending machines and fountains in restaurants and convenience stores. However, the discussions soon broke down.

Coca-Cola continued to challenge Gatorade with PowerAde. Coca-Cola argued that PowerAde had 33 percent more carbohydrates for energy than Gatorade, that it was lighter, that it "went down" easier, and that it quenched thirst without a heavy salt flavor. Coca-Cola would focus on distributing Power-

Ade at "points of sweat," including health and fitness clubs and industrial plant sites. To aid the effort, the firm introduced canned and bottled products. Coca-Cola hoped that this emphasis would also help PowerAde debut on Gatorade's turf, grocery stores. Coca-Cola had 1.5 million points of sale, including one million vending machines, compared with Gatorade's 200,000 points of sale. Coca-Cola also started television and radio advertising and became the official sports drink of the 1996 Olympics.

Pepsi did not stand idly by during all of this. It raised AllSport's 1995 ad budget by 40 percent and hired Shaquille O'Neal and Ken Griffey Jr. as spokespeople. Pepsi's managers claimed that although Gatorade dominated the category, it lacked both taste and the strong distribution system that Pepsi could provide for AllSport. Pepsi had approximately one million points of sale and daily contact with 250,000 retailers that it could use to push AllSport. Like Coca-Cola, Pepsi decided to confront Gatorade in supermarkets, construction sites, and health clubs. As it did with Coke, Pepsi challenged Gatorade with taste tests. It claimed that carbonated AllSport was more drinkable than Gatorade and that AllSport had one-half the sodium, which, according to Pepsi, was all most consumers needed.

After the negotiations with Coca-Cola broke down, Quaker reorganized its operations and formed a separate division to market Gatorade worldwide. It is still pursuing partnerships with other companies to expand distribution to "wherever there's thirst." If Gatorade continues to expand internationally (it is now in 27 countries), it will find competition waiting. In Japan, for example, Coca-Cola already offers a sports drink under the name Aquarius.

## WHAT WILL THE FUTURE BRING?

Quaker Oats realizes just how important this battle is to its corporate health. Gatorade continues to cultivate its sports image by using Michael Jordan and by capitalizing on its multiyear contracts with pro leagues, including the National Football League. Gatorade is also resorting to its time-honored scientific studies to prove that the body absorbs Gatorade faster than water or other soft drinks. This is particularly important as new competitors market themselves as sports drinks, but do not substantiate their claims with solid research findings. Quaker understands that to maintain its dominant position, it must be willing to pursue innovative marketing strategies.

### QUESTIONS

1. What major variables have Quaker Oats and its competitors used to segment the sports-drink market?

2. What type of market coverage strategy did Gatorade use during the early stages of the sports-drink market's life cycle? What coverage strategies are Gatorade and its competitors using now?

3. How have Gatorade and its competitors positioned their sports-drink products?

4. What competitive advantages do Gatorade and its competitors have?

5. Identify new marketing opportunities that Quaker should pursue for Gatorade, including new market segments that it should address. Develop a strategy for addressing one of these opportunities.

6. Quaker Oats's reorganization—forming one division to manage Gatorade worldwide—suggests that the company wants to make Gatorade a global brand, like Coke. Is Gatorade a global brand? What changes should Quaker consider as it markets Gatorade globally?

*Sources:* Michael J. McCarthy and Christina Duff, "Quaker Oats Weighs Linkup With Coke for Distribution of Gatorade Beverage," *The Wall Street Journal,* January 24, 1992, p. A8; Michael J. McCarthy, "Coke Hopes to Make Gatorade Sweat in Battle for U.S. Sports-Drink Market," *The Wall Street Journal,* April 27, 1992, p. B6; Richard Gibson, "Gatorade Unit to Pour It On as Rivalry Rises," *The Wall Street Journal,* April 28, 1992, p. B1; "Gatorade Is Cornerstone to Quaker's Growth," *Advertising Age,* May 18, 1992, p. 12; "Soft Drinks: The Thirst of Champions," *The Economist,* June 6, 1992, p. 83; Richard Gibson, "Coca-Cola and PepsiCo Are Preparing to Give Gatorade a Run for Its Money," *The Wall Street Journal,* September 29, 1992, p. B1. This case also draws from Linda E. Swayne and Peter M. Ginter, "Gatorade Defends Its No. 1 Position," in Linda E. Swayne and Peter M. Ginter, *Cases in Strategic Marketing,* 2nd ed. (Englewood Cliffs, NJ: Prentice Hall, 1993), pp. 1-21. Used with permission; Patricia Sellers, "Can Coke and Pepsi Make Quaker Sweat?" *Fortune,* July 10, 1995, p. 20; Gerry Khermouch, "You Too Can Market a Sports Drink," *Brandweek,* October 30, 1995, p. 38.

# Company Case 8
# *City Year: Running a Nonprofit Like a Business*

City Year represents an innovative initiative to make voluntary national youth service a reality. In 1988, founders Michael Brown and Alan Khazei, both 27-year-old Harvard Law School graduates, became excited about voluntary service and started City Year in Boston. "The idea was to call on young people to meet the challenges facing us and to unite for a real strong public purpose," Brown observes. "The idea behind City Year is to bring young people together from diverse backgrounds—rich, middle class, and poor, from different city neighborhoods as well as from the suburbs—for one year to concentrate on what they have in common and to work for the common good."

Khazei adds that he and Brown also founded City Year "... out of frustration that we have the richest country in the world but also some of the deepest poverty. ... We want City Year to show young people that they can help with these problems and get them excited about service."

## EVERY GOOD IDEA NEEDS A BUSINESS PLAN

Brown and Khazei didn't stop with just an idea. In 1987, working with financial advisors, they developed a business plan that presented the City Year concept, its strategy and objectives, and a projected budget. The plan called for a nine-week pilot program in the summer of 1988. Brown and Khazei designed the summer pilot program to be a miniature version of the planned full-year program. They recruited 50 volunteer young people, deliberately creating a diverse group. They divided the group into five work teams, each headed by a staff member/team leader. Team projects included working with people with AIDS, the homeless, and the elderly.

Brown and Khazei needed about $200,000 to finance the summer project. They turned to corporations for help because they believed that corporations, like individuals, have civic responsibilities. In fact, they believed that corporations would *welcome* the opportunity to help. At the same time, private-sector financing would give City Year the flexibility to try new ideas and to take risks that would not be possible under government financing.

Armed with their vision and a plan, Brown and Khazei set out to find sponsors. They did their homework and paid attention to the budgetary issues they knew were important to corporate managers. They also played up corporate self-interest: Team members would wear T-shirts bearing the corporate sponsor's name as they carried out a summer's worth of good deeds. Thus, Khazei and Brown achieved their $200,000 goal, with most of the support coming from just four sponsors: Bank of Boston, The Equitable, General Cinema, and Bain & Company. Ira Jackson, then Director of External Affairs for the Bank of Boston, later wrote: "They ran City Year like a business. This was the most effective $25,000 in the history of philanthropy at [our] bank."

Following the successful pilot project, the City Year staff recruited 50 volunteers for the 1989–1990 program year. The volunteers, ages 17 to 23, worked from August to June in 10-person teams on a variety of projects. They served as teachers' aides and mentors in the public schools, ran after-school programs, taught violence prevention and HIV/AIDS awareness, rehabilitated public housing, and built parks and playgrounds. City Year's staff overlaid these service projects with an educational curriculum designed to promote critical thinking and teach community-building skills.

During the 10-month service period, City Year pays each volunteer a $125 weekly stipend. At the end of the period, each volunteer receives a $4,725 "Public Service Award" toward educational/vocational training or college loans. Although some people might suggest that these payments violate the spirit of a volunteer program, Brown points out that without the stipends, only young people from wealthier families could participate.

When City Year's recruiter, Kristen Atwood, scoured the city for volunteers, she carried a common message to city and suburban schools: Everybody has something to give to his or her community. Atwood quickly learned that she had to adapt her presentation to the character of the school's population. For example, many city students are interested in jobs, so Atwood stressed that City Year offers jobs that provide good experience for the future. In contrast, suburban students often feel isolated from the "real world." Therefore, Atwood emphasized the idea of service.

## A NEW DIRECTION

Between 1988 and 1992, City Year operated entirely with private funds. However, in 1993, under the Bush administration, City Year first received federal funds as a model for national service. City Year is now part of the AmeriCorps National service network, established by President Bill Clinton. In 1995, AmeriCorp's funding of $7.2 million, combined with nearly $7.4 million from corporate, individual, and other sources, fueled City Year's remarkable growth.

To keep private funds flowing, City Year has initiated a major individual gift campaign as well as a line of apparel and accessories produced and marketed in partnership with the Timberland Company (half the profits go to City Year). Corporate sponsorships have risen 481 percent since 1993, with over 84 percent of companies falling into the repeat-sponsor category. For some companies, these sponsorships involve employee time as well as corporate money. At Keyport Life Insurance, each Friday four employees work with their City Year team at an elementary school on company time.

By 1995–1996, City Year had grown to 670 corps members in seven cities, with an eighth site being planned for the next year. Together, City Year corps members have given close to 2 million hours to turn 230 vacant lots into community gardens, rehabilitate 300 units for affordable housing, serve over 38,000 children, and engage in 45 full-time school partnerships. More than 250 corporations, 25,000 individuals, and the local and federal governments have invested a total of $33 million in City Year.

## LESSONS AND THE FUTURE

Brown and Khazei have learned much in pursuing what they call "public-service entrepreneurship"—applying the skills, methods, and spirit of entrepreneurship to build a thriving nonprofit, public-service institution. As in the business world, they suggest that there are rewarding opportunities in public service for putting untested but highly promising ideas into practice. But this does not mean that success will bring personal wealth. Rather, Khazei and Brown believe that public service requires that we redefine success and focus on the joy of using our skills to the fullest for a worthwhile cause.

What challenges does this successful venture face? Khazei and Brown worry about maintaining and broadening corporate support. They also wonder about further expansion plans. Although they are committed to using lessons learned in private-sector management to continue their success in the nonprofit sector, they realize that the job ahead will be filled with its share of challenges.

### QUESTIONS

1. Who are City Year's customers and what are its products? Who is its competition?
2. Why do you think City Year has achieved so much success?
3. Do private-sector corporations have a social responsibility to support efforts like City Year or other nonprofit activities?
4. How do the nature and characteristics of a service impact on City Year's operations?
5. How has City Year dealt with the issues that shape marketing strategies for service firms?
6. What issues and risks does City Year face as it grows? What recommendations would you make to guide its growth?

*Source*: Based in part on "Not for Profit," in *Anatomy of a Start-Up* (Boston: The Goldhirsch Group, Inc., 1991), pp. 99–109. Used with permission; Rosabeth Moss Kanter, *World Class: Thriving Locally in the Global Economy* (New York: Simon & Schuster, 1995), pp. 194–97; Priscilla Tuan, *Overview of City Year in the National Service Movement*, 1995. Updated in 1996 with the cooperation of City Year.

# Company Case 9
# Polaroid: Taking Vision to the Marketplace

In 1948, Edwin Land, founder of the Polaroid Corporation, introduced the first Polaroid instant camera. By the time Land retired in 1980, he had built Polaroid into a $1.4 billion company. William McCune, Jr., who followed Land as Polaroid's chairman, felt that the company should move away from its dependence on amateur instant photography. McCune led Polaroid's diversification into a variety of high-technology products, but diversification did not pay off.

Consumers, however, were still interested in instant cameras. By 1986, these sales accounted for 55 percent of Polaroid's revenues. To stimulate demand, Polaroid introduced the Spectra camera in 1986, its first major new camera since 1972. The new camera sold well.

Despite this success, Polaroid faced severe competition in the amateur instant photography market. Video camcorders, easy-to-use 35-mm single-lens reflex (SLR) cameras, and one-hour film developing cut deeply into Polaroid's market. Sales of instant cameras fell from a peak of 13 million units in 1978 to 4.5 million in 1990. Polaroid realized that it had to reinvigorate the amateur photography market and expand its base.

## NEW-PRODUCT DEVELOPMENT AT POLAROID

"Skunk works," Polaroid's new product development process, allowed maverick individuals or groups to pursue new-product ideas unofficially and often in secret. These individuals or groups frequently developed these designs with little regard for business strategy. Film and camera development followed parallel paths, a process that invariably resulted in major problems when managers tried to make all the parts work together.

In 1984, a skunk works team from camera engineering began discussing Polaroid's next camera, and a team from film research began to work on possibilities for a new film. The two groups met unofficially to share ideas and soon narrowed the discussions to a film that would fit a smaller camera. They also decided that the new camera should store pictures internally rather than automatically eject them as did other Polaroid cameras.

Unlike some skunk works groups, these two groups sought marketing input. In 1984 and 1985, Polaroid's internal marketing research group learned from focus groups that some customers wanted a smaller camera and its smaller pictures. Polaroid president MacAllister Booth asked his assistant, Roger Clapp, to investigate the idea.

# THE JOSHUA STORY

Enter Joshua. Even as Polaroid was introducing the Spectra camera, Booth, who had just become CEO, realized that Polaroid had to build its next camera. Booth asked Hal Page, Polaroid's vice president for quality, to become program manager. For the first time, Polaroid had a single, high-level program manager responsible for all aspects of new-product development.

Page began a yearlong idea-generation process. Brainstorming sessions began with a training film that featured a cartoon character named Joshua. Joshua is trapped in a box and tries all obvious ways to escape. Finally, in frustration, he gently taps his finger against the box's wall and unexpectedly finds that he has poked a hole in it. He struggles to make the hole bigger and escapes. Joshua sent a message to the hundreds of people who attended Page's brainstorming sessions: To generate truly innovative ideas, employees would have to attack new problems with "out-of-the-box" approaches.

Hal Page also showed the groups a film that dramatically illustrated the value of internal picture storage. The film showed 35-mm automatic camera users at Disney World taking picture after picture, while Polaroid users waited for their camera to develop a single picture then struggled to find a place to store it. Page thought consumers would take more pictures if they did not have to find a place to put each picture as it developed.

Outside marketing consultants who studied the small-camera market for Page concluded that there would be a market for a small camera and that the camera would not cannibalize Polaroid's existing lines. Additional outside studies examined consumer preferences regarding camera size, camera price, and film price.

Polaroid based these studies on the assumption that the new camera would sell for $150. As the studies progressed, however, management concluded that the market at the $150 price would be too small and that it should price the camera around $100. This change required more market studies.

In 1988, Hal Page left Polaroid, and Roger Clapp took over what employees had dubbed the "Joshua Program." Many technical and marketing hurdles remained. Design engineers faced trade-offs between size and other features, such as performance and cost. Clapp stopped the design process and ordered developers to reconsider all trade-offs. As managers reviewed the project, it became apparent that they needed to clarify the lower-priced camera's market potential and conduct new research to get marketing fully behind the program. The last market research hurdle would be an "Assessor Test," conducted by Professor Glenn Urban of MIT's Sloan School of Management.

The Assessor Test involved mock stores at five geographically diverse sites across the country. These stores offered 25 different cameras (both Polaroid and competing models), with prices ranging from inexpensive to expensive. As a part of the interview process, researchers created advertising for the new camera and developed a realistic Joshua camera model. Over a one-month period, 2,400 people—a representative sample of the U.S. population—participated in market interviews and testing at the five stores. The studies convinced Polaroid that there was a market for a small instant camera and it gave Joshua the go-ahead in late 1989.

# VISION TO REALITY

However, with many problems yet unsolved, the camera and film were still in development. Manufacturing had to install a new computer-aided design system (CAD) and a new microcontroller that would make the camera fully automatic. The camera would employ through-the-lens viewing, the same viewing system found in 35-mm cameras. The picture storage compartment would have to hold all ten pictures in a film package. And the camera would have to pass Polaroid's four-foot drop test. Polaroid created a cross-functional steering committee to manage the film-manufacturing process and also concluded that the camera's retail price would be somewhat higher than the $100 target.

By Christmas 1991, the team produced 300 Joshua cameras for nonPolaroid employees to test. This coast-to-coast test represented the earliest time in a product's development that Polaroid had placed cameras with outside users. Polaroid calculated that, by the time it announced the camera, some 15,000 Polaroid and nonPolaroid consumers would have made more than 55,000 images for picture analysis.

# LAUNCHING THE VISION

Polaroid introduced the new camera in Germany in September 1992, followed over the next few months in other European countries and Japan. This sequential introduction would allow the product team to accelerate production gradually. By the time Polaroid brought Joshua into the United States during the summer of 1993, it had a chance to work out production problems and build up the quantities needed for the U.S. market.

Before introduction, the camera needed a name for the marketplace that would make sense in at least 11 languages. The name "Vision" was chosen for the European market to convey the essence of Polaroid's spirit and mission.

For the United States, Polaroid changed the name to "Captiva." Within the first six months, the camera sold between 300,000 and 400,000 units, generating $100 million in U.S. sales, not counting film sales. Demand was so explosive that at times retailers could not keep the camera in stock. Moreover, strong film sales proved that consumers were actually using the camera—a fact that was important to retailers who earned little on camera sales. While margins were low on the camera (retailers typically paid $115 for the camera then sold it for $139), film margins were hefty.

Polaroid is extending the product line with higher-priced and lower-priced versions of the Captiva. To Vicki Thomas, a senior marketing manager for Captiva at the time of the rollout, the camera's success is no surprise. "I didn't have a lot of concerns," she said. "I'd talked to 15,000 people and knew . . . what percentage would reject it and what percentage would accept it."

Polaroid must still decide how to promote the Captiva as its novelty wears off so that it will continue to spur the growth of the amateur instant photography market. It has already used one series of advertisements showing consumers who are intrigued by the camera's film-storage capacity. The campaign's theme is a "Polaroid that isn't a Polaroid." "Where's the picture?" the actors ask.

QUESTIONS

1. Compare Polaroid's traditional new-product development process with the process it followed for Joshua. Would you predict that Joshua (Vision/Captiva) will be more successful than a product developed under the traditional system? Why or why not?

2. As it worked on the Joshua project, did Polaroid do a good job of following the text's eight-step product development process? How could Polaroid improve this process for future products?

3. Whom should Polaroid target with its U.S. promotion campaign for the Captiva, and what promotional ideas would you recommend to Polaroid for developing interest in its new product?

*Sources:* Subrata N. Chakravarty, "The Vindication of Edwin Land," *Forbes,* May 4, 1987, pp. 83–84; Frances Westley and Henry Mintzberg, "Visionary Leadership and Strategic Management," *Strategic Management Journal,* Vol. 10, 1989, pp. 17–32; Jane Poss, "Edwin Land Dead at 81," *Boston Globe,* March 2, 1991, p. 1; Joseph Pereira, "Polaroid Points a Smaller Instant Camera at 35-mm Users," *The Wall Street Journal,* September 11, 1992, p. B1. The majority of this case is adapted from articles in *Viewpoint,* a publication of Polaroid's Internal Communications department, October 1992, especially "The Joshua Story: Polaroid Takes its Vision to the Marketplace." Used with permission of Polaroid Corporation; Gerry Khermouch, "Defying Skeptical Retailers, Polaroid's Captiva Sells Out," *Brandweek,* January 31, 1994, p. 28.

# Company Case 10
# *Silverado Jewelry: A Pricing Paradox*

Silverado Jewelry Store, located in Tempe, Arizona, specializes in handcrafted jewelry made by Native Americans. Sheila Becker, Silverado's owner, is discussing an interesting pricing phenomenon with assistant store manager Mary Meindl.

Several months ago, the store received a selection of mother-of-pearl stone and silver bracelets, earrings, and necklaces. Unlike the blue-green tones in typical turquoise jewelry designs, mother-of-pearl stone is pink with white marbling. In terms of size and style, the selection included a wide range of items. While some were small, round, rather simple designs, others were larger, bolder designs that were quite intricate. In addition, the collection included an assortment of traditionally styled men's studded string ties.

Sheila had purchased the mother-of-pearl selection at a reasonable cost and was quite pleased with the distinctive product assortment. She thought the jewelry would appeal particularly to the general buyer seeking an alternative to the turquoise jewelry usually offered in shops all around Tempe. She priced the new jewelry so that shoppers would receive good value for their money, but also included a markup sufficient to cover the cost of doing business, plus an average profit margin.

After the items had been displayed in the store for about a month, Sheila was disappointed in their sales. She decided to try several merchandising tactics that she had learned as a student at the University of Nevada. For example, realizing that the location of an item in the store will often influence consumer interest, she moved the mother-of-pearl jewelry to a glass display case just to the right of the store entrance.

When sales of the mother-of-pearl merchandise still remained sluggish after the relocation, she decided to talk to store clerks about the jewelry during their weekly meeting. Suggesting that they put more effort into "pushing" this particular line, she provided them with a detailed description of the mother-of-pearl stone and supplied a short, scripted talk that they could memorize and recite for customers.

Unfortunately, this approach also failed. At this point, Sheila was preparing to leave on a buying trip. Frustrated over the sagging sales of the mother-of-pearl jewelry and anxious to reduce current inventory in order to make room for the newer selections that she would be buying, she decided to take drastic action: She would cut the mother-of-pearl prices in half. On her way out of the store, she hastily left a note for Mary Neindl. The note read:

**Silverado Jewelry**

TEMPE, ARIZONA

*Mary —*
*Everything in*
*this case × 2*
*Sheila*

Upon her return, Sheila was pleasantly surprised to find that the entire selection of mother-of-pearl jewelry had been sold. "I really can't understand why," she commented to Mary Meindl, "but that mother-of-pearl stuff just didn't appeal to our customers. I'll have to be more careful the next time I try to increase our variety of stones." Mary responded that although she couldn't quite understand why Sheila wanted to raise the price of slow-moving merchandise, she was surprised at how quickly it had sold at the higher price. Sheila was puzzled. "What higher price?" she asked. "My note said to cut the prices in half." "In *half*?" replied a startled Mary. "I thought your note said, 'Everything in this case *times two*!'" As a result, Mary had *doubled* rather than halved the prices.

## Questions

1. Explain what happened in this situation. Why did the jewelry sell so quickly at twice its normal price?

2. What assumption had Sheila Becker made about the demand curve for the mother-of-pearl jewelry? What did the demand curve for this particular product actually look like?

3. In what type of market is Silverado Jewelry operating (pure competition, monopolistic competition, oligopolistic competition, or pure monopoly)? What leads you to this conclusion?

4. How would the concept of psychological pricing be useful to Sheila Becker? How would you advise her about future pricing decisions?

# Company Case 11
# *Icon Acoustics: Bypassing Tradition*

## THE DREAM

Like most entrepreneurs, Dave Fokos, founder of Icon Acoustics in Billerica, Mass-achusetts, took a long time to develop his dream. Following his graduation from Cornell University where he majored in electrical engineering with a strong inter-est in audio engineering, Dave began working for Conrad-Johnson, a high-end audio-equipment manufacturer, as a speaker designer. Within four years, Dave had designed 13 speaker models and decided to start his own company.

Dave identified a market niche that he felt other speaker firms had over-looked. The niche consisted of "audio-addicts"—people who love to listen to music and appreciate first-rate stereo equipment. These affluent, well-educated cus-tomers are genuinely obsessed with their stereo equipment.

Dave faced one major problem—how to distribute Icon's products. He had learned from experience at Conrad-Johnson that most manufacturers distribute their equipment primarily through stereo dealers. Dave did not hold a high opin-ion of most such dealers; he felt that they too often played hardball with manu-facturers, forcing them to accept thin margins. Furthermore, the dealers concen-trated on only a handful of well-known producers who provided mass-produced models. This kept those firms that offered more customized products from gain-ing access to the market. Perhaps most disturbing, Dave felt that the established dealers often sold not what was best for customers, but whatever they had in inventory that month.

Dave dreamed of offering high-end stereo loudspeakers directly to the audio-obsessed, bypassing the established dealer network. By going directly to the cus-tomers, Dave could avoid the dealer markups and offer top-quality products and service at reasonable prices.

## THE PLAN

At the age of 28, Dave set out to turn his dreams into reality. Some customers who had gotten to know Dave's work became enthusiastic supporters of his dream and invested $189,000 in Icon. With their money and $10,000 of his own, Dave started Icon in a rented facility in an industrial park.

## THE MARKET

Approximately 335 stereo-speaker makers compete for a $3 billion annual U.S. market for audio components. About 100 of these manufacturers sell to the low and midrange segments of the market, which account for 90 percent of the mar-ket's unit volume and about 50 percent of its value. In addition to competing with each other, U.S. manufacturers also compete with Japanese firms that offer products at affordable prices. The remaining 235 or so manufacturers compete for the remaining 10 percent of the market's unit volume and 50 percent of the value—the high end—where Dave hopes to find his customers.

## ICON'S MARKETING STRATEGY

To serve the audio-addicts segment, Dave developed two models: the Lumen and the Parsec. The Lumen stands 18 inches high, weighs 26 pounds, and is designed for stand mounting. The floor-standing Parsec is 47 inches high and weighs 96 pounds. Both models feature custom-made cabinets. Dave can build and ship two pairs of the Lumen speakers or one pair of the Parsec speakers per day by himself. In order to have an adequate parts inventory, he had to spend $50,000 of his capital on the expensive components.

Dave set the price of the Lumen and Parsec at $795 and $1,795 per pair, respectively. He selected these prices to provide a 50 percent gross margin. He believes that traditional retail dealers would sell equivalent speakers at twice those prices. Customers can call Icon on a toll-free 800 number to order speakers or to get advice directly from Dave. Icon pays for shipping and any return freight via Federal Express—round-trip freight for a pair of Parsecs costs $486.

Dave offers to pay for the return freight because a key part of his promotional strategy is a 30-day, in-home, no-obligation trial. In his ads, Dave calls this "the 43,200-Minute, No Pressure Audition." This trial period allows customers to listen to the speakers in their actual listening environment instead of a dealer's showroom.

Dave believes that typical high-end customers may buy speakers for "non-rational" reasons: They want a quality product and good sound, but they also want an image. Thus, Dave has tried to create a unique image through the appearance of his speakers and to reflect that image in all of the company's marketing. He spent over $40,000 on distinctive promotional materials. He also designed a laminated label he places on each speaker. The label reads: "This loudspeaker was handcrafted by [technician's name]. Made in the United States of America by Icon Acoustics, Inc., Billerica, Mass."

To get the word out, Dave concentrates on product reviews in trade magazines and on trade shows. When attendees at one New York show cast ballots to select "the Best Sound at the Show" among 200 brands, Icon's Parsec speakers finished fifteenth. Among the top ten brands, the least expensive was a pair priced at $2,400, and six of the systems were priced from $8,000 to $18,000. A reviewer in an issue of *Stereophile* magazine evaluated Icon's speakers and noted: "The overall sound was robust and dynamic, with a particularly potent low end. Parts and construction quality appeared to be first-rate."

Dave made plans to invest in a slick, four-color display ad in *Stereo Review,* the consumer magazine with the highest circulation (600,000). He also expected another favorable review in *Stereophile* magazine.

## THE REALITY

Reflecting on his experiences during his first year in business, Dave realizes he's learned a lot in jumping all the hurdles that the typical entrepreneur faces. Dave experienced quality problems with the first cabinet supplier. Then, he ran short of a key component after a mix-up with a second supplier. Despite his desire to avoid debt, he had to borrow $50,000 from a bank. Prices for his cabinets and some components had risen, and product returns had been higher than expected (19 percent for the past six months). These price and cost increases put pressure on his margins, forcing Dave to raise his prices (to those quoted earlier). Despite the price increases, his margins remained below his 50 percent target.

Still, Dave feels good about his progress. The price increase does not seem to have affected demand. The few ads and word-of-mouth advertising appear to be working. Dave receives about five phone calls per day, with one in seven calls leading to a sale. Dave also feels the stress of the long hours and the low pay, however. He is not able to pay himself a high salary—just $9,500 this year.

After reviewing his most recent financial projections, Dave believes that year two will be a break-even year—then he'll have it made. He allows his mind to drift to his plans for the introduction of two exciting new speakers—the Micron ($2,495 per pair) and the Millennium ($7,995 per pair). He also wonders if there is a foreign market for his speakers. Should he use his same direct marketing strategy for foreign markets, or should he consider distributors? The dream continues.

## QUESTIONS

1. What functions do traditional stereo dealers perform?
2. Why has Dave Fokos decided to establish a direct channel? What objectives and constraints have shaped his decision?
3. What consumer service needs do Dave's customers have?
4. What problems will Dave face as a result of his channel decisions? What changes would you recommend in Dave's distribution strategy, if any? Will his strategy work in foreign markets?
5. What other changes would you recommend in Dave's marketing strategy?

*Source:* Adapted from "Sound Strategy," *Inc.,* May 1991, pp. 46–56. © 1991 by Goldhirsh Group, Inc. Used with permission. Dave Fokos also provided information to support development of this case.

# Company Case 12
# *Sam's Club: Bulking Up for Competition*

In the early 1980s, Wal-Mart's founder Sam Walton wondered what Sol Price was doing on the West Coast. Price had opened a few very large stores under the name Price Club that offered businesses a narrow line of products, often in bulk sizes, at deep discounts. Walton opened a similar store in Oklahoma City so he could see how the idea worked. He learned the business quickly and well. By the end of fiscal year 1993, Sam's Club was the largest warehouse membership club (WMC) in the United States, with more than 400 stores generating total sales of $14.7 billion, 22 percent of Wal-Mart's revenue.

Despite this success, brutal competition, price deflation, and the economic woes of the early 1990s caused a wrenching shakeout in the WMC industry. For the first time in the $39 billion industry's history, 1993 saw total industry sales decline—by one percent. In addition, the industry experienced a 12 percent membership decline in the same period.

To sustain growth and maintain share, Price Company and Costco Wholesale Clubs, the number two and number three players, merged their 210 clubs to form Price/Costco. However, in 1994 the merger unraveled. Then, the number four player, PACE, a division of Kmart, announced that it would exit the business and sell 99 stores to Sam's. Despite this acquisition, Sam's had 11 straight months of same-store sales that lagged behind prior-year levels.

## WAREHOUSE MEMBERSHIP CLUBS

WMCs buy in quantity and pass lower prices to their customers. Because target customers, mainly small businesses, buy items for resale or for use as operating supplies, the WMCs sell goods in bulk, such as whole cases, or in extra large sizes.

Most warehouse clubs charge customers a membership fee, usually around $25. This fee provides income to the club and accounts for most WMC profits. Membership fees also encourage customers to shop regularly. The typical Sam's Club has an average gross margin of 8.5 percent, while overhead expenses average 9 percent.

From the beginning, the WMCs were operations-driven. They had to keep costs down to attract small-business customers. As a result, the clubs offered no-frills buying, featuring warehouselike buildings the size of several football fields, generally located on the edges of cities. The clubs carry leading brands, but typically feature only 3,000 to 4,000 SKUs (stock keeping units) in comparison to the 70,000 to 80,000 SKUs found in the average discount store. WMCs accept cash only, focus on high inventory turnover, and offer little customer service. Customers have to lug their own large purchases to the checkout line. Many put up with the inconvenience to take advantage of 20 to 40 percent below retail price discounts.

## THE CUSTOMERS

About 70 percent of WMC members are retail (household) members. The 30 percent who are business members account for 65 to 70 percent of WMC sales. In 1992, the Babson College Retailing Research Group surveyed 2,150 WMC customers. The group found that the typical WMC shopper has been a member for 35 months, and one-fourth of all customers shop with someone they know. Shoppers tend to be upscale, with 40 percent having family incomes over $50,000. Frequent shoppers account for most WMC sales.

When the Babson group examined household-customer shopping habits, it found that 92 percent of cardholders buy food for their families and that the average family spends $90 on food per trip. The report estimated that WMCs capture 7 percent of all consumer food dollars. The average family also spends $75 per trip on nonfood products, visits a WMC every three weeks, and travels 13 miles to get there.

On average, business customers spend $103 on food items and $114 on nonfood items. The study found that most small business members buy both food and nonfood items, including office supplies and stationery. Asked for their reactions to the WMC shopping experience, shoppers complained about slow checkout service (many stores lacked scanners), security procedures, package size, crowds, and lack of brand consistency over time.

# SAM'S CHALLENGES

Sam's and the other firms face three problems. First, with Sam's experiencing same-store sales declines of 2.2 percent between 1993 and 1994, growth has slowed dramatically. Sam's must find new ways to stimulate buying.

To attract business customers, Sam's started Club Direct in 1994, which offers business accounts, monthly invoices, fax and phone orders, and delivery. It also shifted the club's merchandise mix by decreasing the average number of food SKUs 15.6 percent between 1993 and 1994 and increasing the average number of non-food SKUs 5.6 percent. (Business customers purchase nonfood products more than food products.) In addition, Sam's representatives are using telemarketing and personal sales calls on individual businesses to recruit them. The chain is also using direct mail to potential customers using SIC codes to shape the promotions. It targets convenience stores with mailings, for example. It also will accept Discover cards, for which it pays only one-half the standard fee. All of its clubs now have scanners.

To attract individual buyers, some WMCs are featuring one-time deals on prestige products like Sony televisions. Sam's also added fresh-food departments and bakeries and launched a private-label credit card to help consumers purchase big-ticket items.

Second, competition is increasing. A few years ago, a WMC might well have been the only WMC in town. No more. Moreover, many supermarkets are installing "power aisles" that feature warehouse-style products. "Category-killer" stores, such as Office Depot, threaten to take away WMCs' business by focusing on price in key categories.

Finally, Sam's and the other WMCs must figure out how to differentiate themselves from each other and from the competition. With every store seemingly trying the same things, each must find ways to stand out.

Although these challenges promise a bumpy road ahead, the industry sales outlook for the next five years is more promising; 5.5 percent growth is projected through 1999 in a tight U.S. market. International expansion may offer WMCs their greatest chance for continued growth. As a result, Sam's and Price/Costco are looking to foreign markets for further expansion. Sam's already has 10 clubs in Mexico, three in Hong Kong, one in Brazil, and plans to open stores in Argentina and Chile.

## QUESTIONS

1. Are warehouse membership clubs retailers or wholesalers?

2. How would you classify WMCs using the categories for classifying retail outlets discussed in the chapter?

3. What retailer/wholesaler marketing decisions have WMCs made? How are those decisions changing?

4. What do you think will happen in the WMC industry during the next five years?

5. What marketing actions should Sam's management take to deal with the challenges the chain faces?

*Sources:* Debra Chanil, "Wholesale Clubs: Romancing America," *Discount Merchandiser,* November 1992, pp. 26–41; and Terry Cotter, Stephen J. Arnold, and Douglas Tigert, "Warehouse Membership Clubs in North America," *Discount Merchandiser,* November 1992, pp. 42–47, used with permission. Also see: Debra Chanil, "Growing Sam's Club," *Discount Merchandiser,* August 1993, pp. 78–80; Dianne M. Pogoda, "The Unsinkable Sam's Club," *WWD,* February 2, 1994; Wendy Zellner, "Why Sam's Wants Businesses to Join the Club," *Business Week,* June 27, 1994, p. 48; "Warehouse Clubs Face Mid-Life Crisis: Industry Shakeout Leaves Two Giants," *Chain Store Age Executive,* August 1994, pp. 26A–28A; Audrey M. Darcy, "Warehouse Clubs: The Rebuilding Begins," *Chain Store Age Executive with Shopping Center Age,* August 1995, p. 29A; Valerie Block, "GE Issues a Private Label Card for Wal-Mart's Warehouse Unit," *American Banker,* September 6, 1995, p. 13.

# Company Case 13
# *Avon: A Promotional Strategy Makeover*

"Ding-dong, Avon calling." With that simple advertising message for over 100 years, Avon Products built a $4.2 billion worldwide beauty-products business, mainly with an army of women selling its products door to door. These "Avon ladies" met with friends and neighbors in their homes, showed products, took and delivered orders, and earned sales commissions. Through direct selling, Avon bypassed the battle for space and attention waged by its competitors on store shelves.

Avon's plan worked well. Most of its up to 500,000-member sales force were homemakers who did not want a full-time job outside the home. They developed client lists of friends and neighbors. Recruiting salespeople was easy, and a good salesperson could develop a loyal core of customers.

## A CHANGING BUSINESS ENVIRONMENT

During the 1970s and 1980s, the environment changed. More women needed to work outside the home with the result that Avon ladies often found no one at home. A mobile U.S. population also made it difficult for salespeople to establish stable client lists. Many Avon ladies also decided to find full-time jobs, and those who were left were sought by other direct marketers. Finally, because of high sales force turnover, many customers who wanted to see a salesperson could not find one.

To deal with these issues, James E. Preston, Avon's new chairman and chief executive, first had to wrestle with the economic downturn of the early 1990s, which depressed door-to-door sales. Preston decided that Avon needed to overhaul its marketing strategy. He cut prices on Avon products, some up to 75 percent, and tried a new compensation program in which sales representatives could earn up to 21 percent in bonuses based on the sales of new representatives they recruited. However, this price cutting and market expansion reduced gross margins and increased costs. Between 1990 and 1991, earnings dropped from $195 million to $135 million as marketing, distribution, and administrative expenses increased from $1.682 billion to $1.746 billion.

## A NEW PROMOTIONAL STRATEGY

Preston turned next to Avon's promotional strategy. Beginning in 1988, Avon had slashed advertising spending, in part to cut costs during three unfriendly takeover attempts. Preston decided that Avon needed to restore the ad budget and pay for it by reducing various sales-promotion activities, especially premiums.

The second step in the revamped promotion strategy was to start selling via a direct-mail catalog. Avon's research revealed that its median customer was 45 years old and had an average household income of under $30,000. Preston believed that catalog sales would attract younger customers with higher household incomes.

Under Avon's plan, salespeople would supply the company with names of

strategy of making burgers according to customer requests instead of serving standardized burgers. Many people still consider this campaign to be Burger King's best ever.

Then Burger King began to flip from one advertising campaign to another, trying to keep its sales growing. In 1982, it introduced the "Battle of the Burgers" campaign, featuring the slogan "Aren't you hungry for Burger King now?" The "Broiling vs. Frying" campaign followed in 1983, driving home the point that Burger King flame-broiled, rather than fried, its burgers. "The Big Switch" theme guided advertising until 1985. All campaigns centered on Burger King's advantages over McDonald's and helped increase market share from 7.6 percent in 1983 to 8.3 percent in 1985.

Then, disaster struck. With its market share peaking at 8.7 percent, Burger King unveiled its now-infamous "Search for Herb" ad campaign. The campaign centered on Herb, an eccentric nerd who was supposedly the only person never to have tasted a Burger King Whopper. Consumers were supposed to search for Herb and earn a chance to win valuable prizes. The campaign flopped. Sales inched up only one percent—far short of 10 percent projections. As consumers focused on Herb, rather than the Whopper, Burger King found its image associated with a "nerdy" personality.

Following "Herb," Burger King's market share began a steady decline. Burger King tried to reverse its slide with its "This Is a Burger King Town" theme in 1986–1987 and then with its "Best Food for Fast Times" message. In 1988, the chain tried the "We Do It Like You'd Do It" campaign, which again focused on flame broiling. However, the campaign never increased sales. In 1989, Burger King launched its "Sometimes You Gotta Break the Rules" campaign to convey the idea that it was "breaking the rules" of the burger industry by flame broiling and individualizing orders.

A more recent campaign, "BK Tee Vee," featured an MTV personality, rapid editing, and a voice-over that shrieked, "I love this place!" The ads targeted teenaged males, but the majority of Burger King's customers—parents and people on the go—found the commercials irritating.

Thus, since the mid-1980s, Burger King has found it hard to persuade consumers that they should prefer its restaurants to those of its competitors. With its long string of lackluster, quick-changing advertising campaigns, Burger King failed to establish a solid image that differentiated it from competitors.

By 1993, Burger King held a 6.1 percent market share, barely ahead of Hardee's 4.4 percent and Wendy's 4.1 percent. It lagged far behind McDonald's, which dominates the industry with a 15.6 percent market share. Moreover, Burger King's sales were growing more slowly than those of its rivals. So, for the fourth time in five years, Burger King sought a new ad agency and a new campaign.

## NOT THE ONLY PROBLEMS

Failed advertising campaigns were only the most visible of Burger King's problems. Burger King also lost its focus on the Whopper by introducing such unrelated products as pizza and tacos. This confused consumers, and many also believed that Burger King served lower-quality food.

In the age of the price-conscious consumer, McDonald's and Wendy's offered lower-priced combo meals. Burger King's higher prices and its refusal to provide discounts contributed to its below-average sales growth. In addition, the dinner-basket program—combo meals along with table service—showed that Burger King was not listening to customers. Fast-food patrons want low prices and quick but high-quality food, not a higher-priced, sit-down meal.

# BACK TO THE BASICS

Management finally locked into a strategy of concentrating on Burger King's core product—flame-broiled, bigger burgers. The company quickly pruned thirty items from the menu. It also launched a new pricing structure featuring $.99, $1.99, and $2.99 value meals that allowed it to compete with McDonald's on price. And the chain's in-store promotional link with Disney's *Lion King, Pocahontas* and *Toy Story* movies exceeded expectations as kids (and their parents) arrived for the moveable action figures that came along with specially priced meals.

Burger King hired a new advertising agency, Ammirati and Puris/Lintas, to communicate a new "back to the basics" advertising message. The campaign, which began in 1995, features Burger King's most competitive advertising in more than a decade with the Whopper going "burger-to-burger" in taste tests against McDonald's Big Mac and Wendy's Single. These taste tests show that consumers favor the Whopper over the competition. In 1995, "it's our customers who speak out," said Paul Clayton, a senior marketing executive at Burger King. "These ads reflect the voice of the people."

These good-news taste tests coincide with a store sales growth of 6.1 percent systemwide in 1994, increased profits of 28 percent, and systemwide sales of $7.5 billion. In addition, in 1994, Burger King witnessed the largest yearly traffic increase—13 percent over the previous year—for any major hamburger restaurant in a decade.

Although Burger King looks better than it did during the "Herb" campaign, it is still facing an uphill battle to win the hearts and stomachs of consumers. While 28 percent of television viewers familiar with Burger King's latest ads liked them, 36 percent said they were ineffective. A mediocre reaction may not be good enough for a company struggling to capture so much lost ground and to pull more customers into its 7,600 restaurants.

## QUESTIONS

1. What are the objectives of Burger King's advertising?
2. Why did Burger King's corporate strategy and past advertising fail to achieve these objectives?
3. What suggestions do you have for Burger King's new advertising campaign?
4. What recommendations would you make regarding future sales promotions for Burger King?

*Sources:* Jeanne Whalen, Gary Levin, and Melanie Wells, "Ammirati's Big Win: It's a $180M Whopper," *Advertising Age,* March 28, 1994, pp. 1, 40–41; Gail DeGorge and Julia Flynn, "Turning Up the Gas at Burger King," *Business Week,* Nov. 15, 1993, pp. 62, 66–67; Kevin Goldman, "Burger King Training Its Sights on McDonald's with Campaign," *The Wall Street Journal,* Sept. 1, 1994, p. B2; Bob Garfield, "BK Finally Catches Fire with Ammirati's Quirky Ads," *Advertising Age,* Sept. 5, 1994; Jeanne Whalen and Gary Levin, "BK Puts Basics on Center Stage in Huge Ad Blitz," *Advertising Age,* Sept. 5, 1994, p. 37; Kevin Goldman, "Burger King Reviews Account . . . Again," *The Wall Street Journal,* Oct. 21, 1993, p. B9; "Consumers Talk Taste: The Whopper Wins! Burger King Launches Most Competitive Ad Campaign in More than a Decade," *Business Wire,* March 9, 1995; "Ad Track: Burger King Ads Get Mediocre Reaction From Consumers," *Business Wire,* July 17, 1995; Ron Ruggless, "Burger King Scores TKO with *Pocahontas* Tie-In," *Nation's Restaurant News,* July 17, 1995, p. 14.

# Company Case 15
# *IBM: Restructuring the Sales Force*

In 1993, IBM's Board of Directors decided the time was right for dramatic action. The once-proud company had seen its sales fall from almost $69 billion in 1990 to $64.5 billion in 1992. In the same period, profits plunged from $5.9 billion to a loss of $4.96 billion. In April 1993, the Board hired Louis V. Gerstner, Jr. to serve as its new Chairman and Chief Executive Officer and to turn the company around.

Just three months into the job, Gerstner announced his first major strategic decision. He identified IBM's sales force as a key source of problems. Observers expected that he would restructure the sales force because it was too large, unwieldy, and slow to meet changing customer needs. Gerstner surprised them by announcing that he would postpone his decision. He argued that immediate, radical reform would pose unacceptable risks to customer loyalty. Therefore, he would try to make IBM's current sales and marketing systems work better.

## GETTING INTO TROUBLE

In his introduction to the 1993 IBM Annual Report, Gerstner wrote that IBM's problems resulted from the company's failure to keep pace with rapid industry change. He also argued that IBM had been too bureaucratic and preoccupied with its own view of the world. He suggested that the company had been too slow to take new products to market and had missed the higher profit margins associated with introducing computers early in a product life cycle.

IBM's customers and industry observers identified IBM's self-centered view of the world as the real problem. They argued that the company had stopped listening to customers. It peddled mainframe computers to customers who wanted midrange systems and personal computers. It pushed products when customers wanted solutions. Moreover, IBM's sales compensation system rewarded mainframe system sales.

Salespeople often insisted that customers buy all their products from IBM and became indignant when a customer used other vendors. They also made "one-size-fits-all" presentations using canned, off-the-shelf marketing programs.

## "ONE FACE TO THE CUSTOMER"

Despite these problems, Gerstner's initial decision not to make strategic changes to the 40,000-person sales force meant that he would continue to carry out changes that former CEO John Akers had begun. Beginning in 1991, Akers had restructured the sales force using a geographic focus. Senior managers acted as account executives for the top IBM clients in their regions. These account executives managed the full breadth of client relationships, including understanding the customer's company and industry, and could call on a pool of regional product specialists and service representatives to satisfy customer needs. The account executives reported to branch managers who reported to "trading area" managers who ultimately reported to regional managers. In foreign countries, a country manager had full control over that country's sales force.

Akers' approach continued IBM's traditional focus on presenting "one face to the customer." The account executive structure allowed the customer to deal with one IBM interface rather than many from each of IBM's product and service areas. Gerstner's reluctance to make changes probably arose after the company's top 200 customers told him they did not want to be confused by 20 different IBM salespeople. However, it was also hard for any IBM salesperson to be familiar with the company's wide range of products and services.

# PURSUING THE IDEAL SALES FORCE

Nevertheless, Gerstner began to tinker with IBM's sales approach. In response to increasing competition, declining sales, and changing corporate buying habits, IBM developed "fighter pilots," sales specialists who tried to push neglected products. Further, Akers had allowed some product lines, like the personal computer and printer divisions, to develop their own sales forces.

Then in May 1994, IBM announced a new salesforce structure. The new plan would have account teams bypass the top branch managers, who previously held sway over their careers, and report directly to the new directors of 14 industry groups. The 14 initial groups included such areas as banking, retail, and insurance and would provide total solutions to customers' business problems. Observers felt that the new system might run into problems in international markets where country heads had held strong, autonomous positions. But Gerstner and his managers had been frustrated by their inability to control the country heads. The new system would shift the salesperson's loyalty to the industry group head. It would also transform account executives from order-takers to business advisers.

IBM indicated it would fill half of the new industry posts with outsiders who had experience in the consulting industry. This was a major change from IBM's traditional policy of promoting from within. IBM also changed the compensation system to base 60 percent of commission on profitability and the remainder on customer satisfaction as measured by customer surveys. Earlier, only six percent of a salesperson's salary above the base salary (the bulk of a person's pay) reflected the profitability of his or her sales.

Observers warned that it would take months or years to implement the changes and that the changes would cause upheavals and power struggles. They also noted that what IBM was trying to do was not new to the computer industry. Digital Equipment Corporation tried the industry-based salesforce idea in 1993 and abandoned it in less than a year. Apparently, DEC felt that the new structure had not helped reverse a sales slide. However, IBM's salesforce changes are not likely to be abandoned, at least not right now, since they coincide with the company's impressive sales gains during 1995.

## QUESTIONS

1. What problems do you see in IBM's objectives, strategy, and structure for its sales force?

2. What objectives would you set for IBM's sales force, and what strategy, structure, and compensation plan would you establish to accomplish your objectives? Identify the tradeoffs involved as you make each of these decisions.

3. Given your recommendations, how would you recruit, train, supervise, motivate, and evaluate IBM's sales force?

*Sources:* Laurie Hays, "IBM's Gerstner Holds Back from Sales Force Shake-Up," *The Wall Street Journal*, July 7, 1993, p. B1. Used with permission of *The Wall Street Journal*. Also see Geoffrey Brewer, "Abort, Retry, Fail?" *Sales and Marketing Management*, October 1993, pp. 80–86; IBM Corporation, 1993 Annual Report; Rob O'Regan, "IBM Sales Force Foes Vertical," *PC Week*, April 25, 1994, p. 3; and Ira Sager, "The Few, The True, The Blue," *Business Week*, May 30, 1994, pp. 124–26.

# Company Case 16
# *Hardee's: Marketing in South Korea*

Despite sometimes strong anti-American sentiments in South Korea, young people there are drawn to the slice—and taste—of Americana that fast-food restaurants represent. South Korean teens and college students find it fashionable to hang out in fast-food restaurants like Hardee's. As a result, American fast-food companies in South Korea target young people, especially girls, who often sit in the restaurants for hours. To accommodate them, South Korean fast-food restaurants are about twice as large as their American counterparts.

## DOING BUSINESS IN SOUTH KOREA

Faced with a saturated U.S. market, one would think that American fast-food chains would flock to South Korea. However, Wendy's has only 13 South Korean outlets, Burger King only 12, McDonald's only four, and Sizzler only two. Why have U.S. fast-food restaurants been so slow to enter South Korea? Although, according to a recent *Wall Street Journal* ranking of 129 countries, South Korea falls into the low-risk category when the political, financial, and economic risks of doing business in a country are analyzed, it is still considered a tough market. Land prices are especially high. A high-traffic site in Seoul, the capital city, can cost $7 million to buy or require a $1 million deposit to rent. Raw material costs are the highest in Asia. Manufacturing wages have gone up an average of 18 percent per year since 1986.

Governmental restrictions, such as high tariffs and limits on certain imports, such as cheese and beef, frustrate fast-food chains. Gaining governmental approval for investment takes time, and foreign firms suspect that the Korean government doesn't really want them there. These factors discourage foreign investment with the result that while the ratio of foreign investment to gross national product is 14.6 to 1 in Singapore, it is only 0.36 to 1 in South Korea.

## ENTER HARDEE'S AND OTHER FAST-FOOD CHAINS

Other factors encourage foreign investors such as Hardee's. These include a rapidly rising standard of living. Disposable income has grown 141 percent since 1986, making South Korea the largest consumer market in Asia after Japan. The average urban household has an annual income of $12,400. One out of ten adults has a college degree, and the number of two-income families is rising. These factors create demand for convenience foods and high-quality products. Overall, however,

Korea's consumer market lags behind that of other Asian countries with about the same level of economic development.

To help break into the South Korean market, Hardee's selected Kim Chang-Hwan as its local franchisee. Mr. Kim converted several stores near student hangouts into Hardee's restaurants. In an "in-your-face" move, the Korean franchise opened its first Hardee's in downtown Seoul, just a few yards from a popular McDonald's. So far store sales have equaled McDonald's. Currently, Hardee's 25 South Korean franchises are under the control of a Franchise Service Coordinator hired by Hardee's.

McDonald's entered the country in 1986 by forming a joint venture with a Korean entrepreneur with plans to open 14 stores by the early 1990s. However, expansion plans were delayed because of the death of McDonald's local partner, and McDonald's is now looking for a new local partner with enough capital to make the franchise work.

In 1995, Sizzler International, another restaurant chain, entered South Korea through a licensing arrangement. With two restaurants in Seoul drawing between 5,000 and 7,000 customers a week, Sizzler's licensing partner plans to open three more Sizzlers over the next 12 months.

## COORS AND PURINA TRY THEIR HANDS

In 1994, Coors Brewing Company announced that it too was moving into South Korea. Through a joint venture with a Korean distiller, Coors hopes to capture about 15 percent of the Korean beer market in its first year. Jinro-Coors Brewing, as the company is known, is the first new brewer in South Korea in half a century and is the first direct investment by a U.S. brewery in a foreign operation. Traditionally, breweries have expanded into foreign markets using contract brewing, licensing, or direct import.

Analysts suggest that U.S. brewers are showing more interest in foreign markets because of slow growth in the United States. While gaining business in the United States means taking it from someone else, the South Korean beer market is growing at 15 percent a year.

Interestingly, Coors is entering South Korea despite Miller Brewing's recent departure. Miller pulled out of the market because of high tariffs and the rising value of Korea's currency.

Like Coors, Ralston Purina also decided to buck conventional wisdom. It constructed a $10 million plant in South Korea to produce its Chex breakfast cereal. But unlike Coors and the fast-food companies, Purina has some advantages. First, it will enter a market that contains no strong local producer. Second, Purina knows the market. It has been operating in South Korea for 25 years, selling feed for livestock and domestic animals.

## MAKING IT EASIER

Despite the efforts of the fast-food companies, Coors, and Purina, the South Korean government is still concerned about the low level of foreign investment. It was so concerned that in 1994 it took out a special advertising supplement in publications such as *U.S. News & World Report* to describe opportunities for foreign investment. According to the supplement and other sources, the government is slowly changing the rules. It has opened 132 out of 224 business sectors to foreign direct investment and now grants automatic approval for projects valued at less than $20 million. It has also streamlined regulations for business start-ups and factory construction. Moreover, foreign companies can now establish wholly owned subsidiaries. The government may also make it easier for foreign companies to bring in additional capital and may offer cheap land to high-tech companies that locate in industrial parks. As a result of these changes, foreign direct investment in South Korea exceeded $1 billion annually between 1992 and 1994.

However, the government has been slow to offer similar benefits to processed food or packaged-goods companies and has been reluctant to allow foreign consumer-products companies to build modern warehouses and distribution networks. Furthermore, the government often holds up products at customs and sponsors anticonsumption campaigns to turn public opinion against imported goods.

As a result of the positive changes and despite the problems, more foreign companies are establishing import offices and sales and distribution channels in South Korea. Managers at Hardee's hope that they can survive the problems and that the fascination with things American will continue. What can they do to keep young Koreans coming back to Hardee's?

## QUESTIONS

1. Based on information in the case, what kinds of trade restrictions does Hardee's face in working within South Korea's trade system?

2. What aspects of South Korea's economic, political–legal, and cultural environments are important for Hardee's to understand?

3. Why have Hardee's and the other companies in the case decided to enter foreign markets and why have they selected South Korea? Do you agree with their decisions?

4. What methods might Hardee's have used to enter the South Korean market, and why did it select the method it used?

5. What decisions has Hardee's made about its marketing program in South Korea? What recommendations would you make about this program?

*Sources:* Adapted from Damon Darlin, "South Koreans Crave American Fast Food," *The Wall Street Journal,* February 22, 1991, p. B1; Marj Charlier, "U.S. Brewers' Foreign Growth Proves Tricky," *The Wall Street Journal,* September 9, 1991, p. B1; Monua Janah, "Rating Risk in the Hot Countries," *The Wall Street Journal,* September 20, 1991, p. R4; and Darlin, "U.S. Firms Take Chances in South Korea," *The Wall Street Journal,* June 15, 1992, p. B1. Used with permission. Also see Robert W. Warne, "Korea: Open for Business (South Korea: Special Advertising Supplement)," *U.S. News & World Report,* June 27, 1994, p. 52; "Fully Automated Brewery for Korea," *Food Engineering International,* October 1994, p. 39; Andrew Horvat, "Reaching Out To Foreign Investment: South Korea Cleans Up Business Rules To Attract Overseas Funds," *The Financial Post,* May 28, 1994, p. S19; "Sizzler Announces Korean Expansion," *Business Wire,* October 19, 1995.

# Company Case 17
## *The Case of Planned Obsolescence*

The president of a major consumer products company with a reputation for quality was concerned about increasing company sales and profits. The company makes a consumer product that requires close manufacturing tolerances for it to work. Any relaxation of these tolerances results in almost immediate product failure and negative "word-of-mouth" advertising. Actions taken to ensure that the product works when it is sold also mean that the product can last for generations.

John, the president of the company, decided to meet with Phil, the production manager, and Henry, the chief financial officer, to discuss a scheme to improve the company's finances.

He began the meeting with the following comment: "Once we make a sale, we make a sale forever. In a sense, our current model competes head-on with a model made half a century ago. Where would Ford be today if everyone still drove around in Tin Lizzies?"

As John distributed sales graphs, he noted, "Our new models don't make our old models obsolete. That's our essential marketing problem. Our sales depend on formation of new families and population growth and very little on replacement. But if we had a seven- or eight-year life to our product line, our sales and profits would look like these." Phil and Henry stared at graphs that depicted actual sales and profits over the last 10 years and predicted sales and profits if the product had a finite eight-year life.

"We have plenty of spare capacity in our plants to accommodate increased sales if we had a seven- or eight-year life expectancy," continued John. "Our fixed costs are not only fixed, but high because of past overinvestment in plant capacity that occurred before we came on the scene. These fixed costs are weighing heavily on our bottom line."

Phil spoke up. "John, we're not going to have another repeat of your fiasco of loosening up the tolerances and having the first product recall in company history?"

"No," answered John. "I want to find a metal alloy that will maintain its technical specifications for at least seven, but not over eight years. After that, normal wear and tear will have reached a point where the manufacturing tolerances are no longer satisfied. Then the product must be replaced."

"John, let me acquaint you with a few technical facts I think you are overlooking in the planned degradation of our product," said Phil.

"Call it market enhancement."

"Market enhancement by product obsolescence and market enhancement by making a superior quality product—there is a difference," answered Phil.

"A big one, Phil," said John. "And what happens when we bring out a new model, which is basically the old model in a new exterior plus an enhancement or two? Nothing. If we can introduce product obsolescence in a manner that our customers will never notice—and I maintain that no one will be disappointed in a product that gracefully dies after seven years of superior service—we can improve profits dramatically. Or we can continue business as usual."

"There is more to corporate life than profits, John," answered Phil. "There is such a thing as consumer satisfaction. Besides, there are technical considerations. Metal wears uniformly with time. For our products to work for seven years and then start to fail, we need to find an alloy that hardly wears for seven years, and erodes like crazy after that. It'll cost a fortune to find such a metal because the various parts are exposed to different wear factors. It would be extremely difficult to have them all timed to fall out of specification on the seventh anniversary of the product. Since we have no parts that are integral with the housing, we will have to redesign the product totally."

"Then we'll have to do it," said John.

"John, slow down." Henry rose from his chair. "We need to think this matter through."

"What is there to think through, Henry? Can't you see the difference between two lines where we quadruple our profits?"

"Okay, let me give you something to think about," answered Henry. "What about the millions we're going to spend on R&D to cheapen our product? Do you think that will affect earnings adversely?"

"Capitalize them, Henry, like you capitalize everything else," snapped John. "Then we'll write off these expenses against earnings a decade away in time."

"I can't capitalize R&D. It will have to be expensed as funds are expended. This will hurt current earnings. If this effort is of a magnitude of expenditure that I think it is, we may even have to cut our dividend." answered Henry.

"Henry, think long term," said John.

"John, what about the impact on the short-term price of the stock as earnings tumble and dividends are cut?"

"Well, I don't plan to own any of the stock myself and I don't think our pension plan ought to own any," responded John. "I'm going to be exercising my options and clearing out. What are you going to do, Henry?"

"I think you've got a problem with insider trading, John. That's what I think."

"Okay, I'm going to do nothing," said John. "What do you think the future value of the stock of this company is going to be when you and I retire? Profits will be four times what they would have been if we do nothing. Sure the shareholders will take a hit, but it's only for the development time to find the right alloy and redesign our product line. Do you think that the shareholders are going to vote against us if we feel that an increase in R&D spending is in their long-term interest?"

"I don't think this will be a small expenditure of funds," said Henry. "Phil do you have any idea what we are talking about in cost and time?"

"Certainly millions, and certainly not less than three years, including bringing out the new model—my guess is somewhere around $10 million and five years of effort, assuming we want to guarantee success."

"But look at profits, look at the value of your pension benefits if we are successful," answered John.

"John, contain yourself," snapped Henry. "Five years to bring the product out, another five or 10 years before the new product line reaches sufficient market share to make replacement meaningful, and then another seven or so years for the time bomb to mature in the form of sales. This is truly one of the longest long-term plans I have seen in my professional life, and for what? I am bothered by spending R&D funds to degrade the longevity of our product. Furthermore, is it ethical to divert shareholder profits for such an expenditure, even to the point of threatening the dividend? Is this the best we can do with the funds entrusted to us by shareholders?"

John paused before answering, "Then Henry, what do you suggest?"

## QUESTIONS

1. What is wrong with John's plan?
2. What would you do if you were in Henry's position? Justify your recommendations.
3. Why is planned obsolescence a dangerous marketing strategy? Explain its dangers in terms of violations of the principles of enlightened marketing.
4. How do you think shareholders would respond to John's plan?

*Source:* James A. Heely, and Roy L. Nersesian, "The Case of Planned Obsolescence," *Management Accounting,* February 1994. Used with permission.

# *1*

# *Marketing Arithmetic*

One aspect of marketing not discussed within the text is marketing arithmetic. The calculation of sales, costs, and certain ratios is important for many marketing decisions. This appendix describes three major areas of marketing arithmetic: the *operating statement, analytic ratios,* and *markups and markdowns.*

## OPERATING STATEMENT

The operating statement and the balance sheet are the two main financial statements used by companies. The **balance sheet** shows the assets, liabilities, and net worth of a company at a given time. The **operating statement** (also called **profit-and-loss statement** or **income statement**) is more important for marketing information. It shows the company sales, cost of goods sold, and expenses during a specified time period. By comparing the operating statement from one time period to the next, the firm can spot favorable or unfavorable trends and take appropriate action.

Table A1-1 shows the 1996 operating statement for Dale Parsons Men's Wear, a specialty store in the Midwest. This statement is for a retailer; the operating statement for a manufacturer would be somewhat different. Specifically, the section on purchases within the "cost of goods sold" area would be replaced by "cost of goods manufactured."

The outline of the operating statement follows a logical series of steps to arrive at the firm's $25,000 net profit figure:

| | |
|---|---|
| Net sales | $300,000 |
| Cost of goods sold | −175,000 |
| Gross margin | $125,000 |
| Expenses | −100,000 |
| Net profit | $ 25,000 |

The first part details the amount that Parsons received for the goods sold during the year. The sales figures consist of three items: *gross sales, returns and allowances,* and *net sales.* **Gross sales** is the total amount charged to customers

**Balance sheet**
A financial statement that shows assets, liabilities, and net worth of a company at a given time.

**Operating statement**
A financial statement that shows company sales, cost of goods sold, and expenses during a given period of time.

**Gross sales**
The total amount that a company charges during a given period of time for merchandise.

during the year for merchandise purchased in Parsons's store. As expected, some customers returned merchandise because of damage or a change of mind. If the customer gets a full refund or full credit on another purchase, we call this a *return*. Or, the customer may decide to keep the item if Parsons will reduce the price. This is called an *allowance*. By subtracting returns and allowances from gross sales, we arrive at net sales—what Parsons earned in revenue from a year of selling merchandise:

| | |
|---|---|
| Gross sales | $325,000 |
| Returns and allowances | −25,000 |
| Net sales | $300,000 |

The second major part of the operating statement calculates the amount of sales revenue Dale Parsons retains after paying the costs of the merchandise. We start with the inventory in the store at the beginning of the year. During the year, Parsons bought $165,000 worth of suits, slacks, shirts, ties, jeans, and other goods. Suppliers gave the store discounts totaling $15,000, so that net purchases were $150,000. Because the store is located away from regular shipping routes, Parsons had to pay an additional $10,000 to get the products delivered, giving the firm a net cost of $160,000. Adding the beginning inventory, the cost of goods available for sale amounted to $220,000. The $45,000 ending inventory of clothes in the store on December 31 is then subtracted to come up with the $175,000 **cost of goods sold**. Here again, we have followed a logical series of steps to figure out the cost of goods sold:

**Cost of goods sold**
The net cost to the company of goods sold.

| | |
|---|---|
| Amount Parsons started with (beginning inventory) | $60,000 |
| Net amount purchased | +150,000 |
| Any added costs to obtain these purchases | + 10,000 |
| Total cost of goods Parsons had available for sale during year | $220,000 |
| Amount Parsons had left over (ending inventory) | −45,000 |
| Cost of goods actually sold | $175,000 |

The difference between what Parsons paid for the merchandise ($175,000) and what he sold it for ($300,000) is called the **gross margin** ($125,000).

In order to show the profit Parsons "cleared" at the end of the year, we must subtract from the gross margin the *expenses* incurred while doing business. *Selling expenses* included two sales employees, local newspaper and radio advertising, and the cost of delivering merchandise to customers after alterations. Selling expenses totaled $50,000 for the year. *Administrative expenses* included the salary for an office manager, office supplies such as stationery and business cards, and miscellaneous expenses including an administrative audit conducted by an outside consultant. Administrative expenses totaled $30,000 in 1996. Finally, the general expenses of rent, utilities, insurance, and depreciation came to $20,000. Total expenses were therefore $100,000 for the year. By subtracting expenses ($100,000) from the gross margin ($125,000), we arrive at the net profit of $25,000 for Parsons during 1996.

**Gross margin**
The difference between net sales and cost of goods sold.

**Operating ratios**
Ratios of selected operating statement items to net sales that allow marketers to assess the firm's performance.

**TABLE A1-1** *Operating Statement: Dale Parsons Men's Wear Year Ending December 31, 1996*

| | | | |
|---|---|---|---|
| Gross sales | | | $325,000 |
| Less: Sales returns and allowances | | | 25,000 |
| Net sales | | | $300,000 |
| Cost of goods sold | | | |
| Beginning inventory, January 1, at cost | | $ 60,000 | |
| Gross purchases | $165,000 | | |
| Less: Purchase discounts | 15,000 | | |
| Net purchases | $150,000 | | |
| Plus: Freight-in | 10,000 | | |
| Net cost of delivered purchases | | $160,000 | |
| Cost of goods available for sale | | $220,000 | |
| Less: Ending inventory, December 31, at cost | | $ 45,000 | |
| Cost of goods sold | | | $175,000 |
| Gross margin | | | $125,000 |
| Expenses | | | |
| Selling expenses | | | |
| Sales, salaries, and commissions | $ 40,000 | | |
| Advertising | 5,000 | | |
| Delivery | 5,000 | | |
| Total selling expenses | | $ 50,000 | |
| Administrative expenses | | | |
| Office salaries | $ 20,000 | | |
| Office supplies | 5,000 | | |
| Miscellaneous (outside consultant) | 5,000 | | |
| Total administrative expenses | | $ 30,000 | |
| General expenses | | | |
| Rent | $ 10,000 | | |
| Heat, light, telephone | 5,000 | | |
| Miscellaneous (insurance, depreciation) | 5,000 | | |
| Total general expenses | | $ 20,000 | |
| Total expenses | | | $100,000 |
| Net profit | | | $ 25,000 |

# ►ANALYTIC RATIOS

The operating statement provides the figures needed to compute some crucial ratios. Typically these ratios are called **operating ratios**—the ratio of selected operating statement items to net sales. They let marketers compare the firm's performance in one year to that in previous years (or with industry standards and competitors in the same year). The most commonly used operating ratios are the *gross margin percentage,* the *net profit percentage,* the *operating expense percentage,* and the *returns and allowances percentage.*

| Ratio | | Formula | Computation From Table A1-1 |
|---|---|---|---|
| Gross margin percentage | = | $\dfrac{\text{gross margin}}{\text{net sales}}$ | $= \dfrac{\$125,000}{\$300,000} = 42\%$ |
| Net profit percentage | = | $\dfrac{\text{net profit}}{\text{net sales}}$ | $= \dfrac{\$\ 25,000}{\$300,000} = 8\%$ |
| Operating expense percentage | = | $\dfrac{\text{total expenses}}{\text{net sales}}$ | $= \dfrac{\$100,000}{\$300,000} = 33\%$ |
| Returns and allowances percentage | = | $\dfrac{\text{returns and allowances}}{\text{net sales}}$ | $= \dfrac{\$\ 25,000}{\$300,000} = 8\%$ |

Another useful ratio is the *stockturn rate* (also called *inventory turnover rate*). The stockturn rate is the number of times an inventory turns over or is sold during a specified time period (often one year). It may be computed on a cost, selling price, or unit basis. Thus the formula can be:

$$\text{Stockturn rate} = \frac{\text{cost of goods sold}}{\text{average inventory at cost}}$$

or

$$\text{Stockturn rate} = \frac{\text{selling price of goods sold}}{\text{average selling price of inventory}}$$

or

$$\text{Stockturn rate} = \frac{\text{sales in units}}{\text{average inventory in units}}$$

We will use the first formula to calculate the stockturn rate for Dale Parsons Men's Wear:

$$\frac{\$175,000}{(\$60,000 + \$45,000)/2} = \frac{\$175,000}{\$52,500} = 3.3$$

That is, Parsons's inventory turned over 3.3 times in 1996. Normally, the higher the stockturn rate, the higher the management efficiency and company profitability.

**Return on investment (ROI)**
A common measure of managerial effectiveness—the ratio of net profit to investment.

**Return on investment (ROI)** is frequently used to measure managerial effectiveness. It uses figures from the firm's operating statement and balance sheet. A commonly used formula for computing ROI is:

$$\text{ROI} = \frac{\text{net profit}}{\text{sales}} \times \frac{\text{sales}}{\text{investment}}$$

You may have two questions about this formula: Why use a two-step process when ROI could be computed simply as net profit divided by investment? And what exactly is "investment"?

To answer these questions, let's look at how each component of the formula can affect the ROI. Suppose Dale Parsons Men's Wear has a total investment of $150,000. Then ROI can be computed as follows:

$$ROI = \frac{\$25,000 \text{ (net profit)}}{\$300,000 \text{ (sales)}} \times \frac{\$300,000 \text{ (sales)}}{\$150,000 \text{ (investment)}}$$

$$8.3\% \qquad \times \qquad 2 \qquad = 16.6\%$$

Now suppose that Parsons had worked to increase his share of market. He could have had the same ROI if his sales doubled while dollar profit and investment stayed the same (accepting a lower profit ratio to get higher turnover and market share):

$$ROI = \frac{\$25,000 \text{ (net profit)}}{\$600,000 \text{ (sales)}} \times \frac{\$600,000 \text{ (sales)}}{\$150,000 \text{ (investment)}}$$

$$4.16\% \qquad \times \qquad 4 \qquad = 16.6\%$$

Parsons might have increased its ROI by increasing net profit through more cost cutting and more efficient marketing:

$$ROI = \frac{\$50,000 \text{ (net profit)}}{\$300,000 \text{ (sales)}} \times \frac{\$300,000 \text{ (sales)}}{\$150,000 \text{ (investment)}}$$

$$16.6\% \qquad \times \qquad 2 \qquad = 33.2\%$$

Another way to increase ROI is to find some way to get the same levels of sales and profits while decreasing investment (perhaps by cutting the size of Parsons's average inventory):

$$ROI = \frac{\$25,000 \text{ (net profit)}}{\$300,000 \text{ (sales)}} \times \frac{\$300,000 \text{ (sales)}}{\$75,000 \text{ (investment)}}$$

$$8.3\% \qquad \times \qquad 4 \qquad = 33.2\%$$

**Markup**
The percentage of the cost or price of a product added to cost in order to arrive at a selling price.

**Markdown**
A percentage reduction from the original selling price.

What is "investment" in the ROI formula? *Investment* is often defined as the total assets of the firm. But many analysts now use other measures of return to assess performance. These measures include *return on net assets (RONA)*, *return on stockholders' equity (ROE)*, or return on *assets managed (ROAM)*. Because investment is measured at a point in time, we usually compute ROI as the average investment between two time periods (say, January 1 and December 31 of the same year). We can also compute ROI as an "internal rate of return" by using discounted cash flow analysis (see any finance textbook for more on this technique). The objective in using any of these measures is to determine how well the company has been using its resources. As inflation, competitive pressures, and cost of capital increase, such measures become increasingly important indicators of marketing and company performance.

# ▶ MARKUPS AND MARKDOWNS

Retailers and wholesalers must understand the concepts of **markups** and **markdowns.** They must make a profit to stay in business, and the markup percentage affects profits. Markups and markdowns are expressed as percentages.

There are two different ways to compute markups—on *cost* or on *selling price:*

$$\text{Markup percentage on cost} = \frac{\text{dollar markup}}{\text{cost}}$$

$$\text{Markup percentage on selling price} = \frac{\text{dollar markup}}{\text{selling price}}$$

Dale Parsons must decide which formula to use. If Parsons bought shirts for $15 and wanted to mark them up $10, his markup percentage on cost would be $10/$15 = 67.7%. If Parsons based markup on selling price, the percentage would be $10/$25 = 40%. In figuring markup percentage, most retailers use the selling price rather than the cost.

Suppose Parsons knew his cost ($12) and desired markup on price (25%) for a man's tie, and wanted to compute the selling price. The formula is:

$$\text{Selling price} = \frac{\text{cost}}{1 - \text{markup}}$$

$$\text{Selling price} = \frac{\$12}{.75} = \$16$$

As a product moves through the channel of distribution, each channel member adds a markup before selling the product to the next member. This "markup chain" is shown for a suit purchased by a Parsons customer for $200:

|  |  | $ Amount | % of Selling Price |
|---|---|---|---|
| Manufacturer | Cost | $108 | 90% |
|  | Markup | 12 | 10 |
|  | Selling price | 120 | 100 |
| Wholesaler | Cost | 120 | 80 |
|  | Markup | 30 | 20 |
|  | Selling price | 150 | 100 |
| Retailer | Cost | 150 | 75 |
|  | Markup | 50 | 25 |
|  | Selling price | 200 | 100 |

The retailer whose markup is 25 percent does not necessarily enjoy more profit than a manufacturer whose markup is 10 percent. Profit also depends on how many items with that profit margin can be sold (stockturn rate), and on operating efficiency (expenses).

Sometimes a retailer wants to convert markups based on selling price to markups based on cost, and vice versa. The formulas are:

$$\text{Markup percentage on selling price} = \frac{\text{markup percentage on cost}}{100\% + \text{markup percentage on selling cost}}$$

$$\text{Markup percentage on cost} = \frac{\text{markup percentage on selling price}}{100\% - \text{markup percentage on selling price}}$$

Suppose Parsons found that his competitor was using a markup of 30 percent based on cost and wanted to know what this would be as a percentage of selling price. The calculation would be:

$$\frac{30\%}{100\% + 30\%} = \frac{30\%}{130\%} = 23\%$$

Because Parsons was using a 25 percent markup on the selling price for suits, he felt that his markup was suitable compared with that of the competitor.

Near the end of the summer Parsons still had an inventory of summer slacks in stock. Therefore, he decided to use a *markdown,* a reduction from the original selling price. Before the summer he had purchased 20 pairs at $10 each, and he had since sold 10 pairs at $20 each. He marked down the other pairs to $15 and sold five pairs. We compute his *markdown ratio* as follows:

$$\text{Markdown percentage} = \frac{\text{dollar markdown}}{\text{total net sales in dollars}}$$

The dollar markdown is $25 (five pairs at $5 each) and total net sales are $275 (10 pairs at $20 + five pairs at $15). The ratio, then, is $25/$275 = 9%.

Larger retailers usually compute markdown ratios for each department rather than for individual items. The ratios provide a measure of relative marketing performance for each department and can be calculated and compared over time. Markdown ratios can also be used to compare the performance of different buyers and salespeople in a store's various departments.

## KEY TERMS

Balance sheet

Cost of goods sold

Gross margin

Gross sales

Markdown

Markup

Operating ratios

Operating statement (or profit-and-loss statement or income statement)

Return on investment (ROI)

# Careers in Marketing

Now that you have completed your first course in marketing, you have a good idea of what the field entails. You may have decided that you want to pursue a marketing career because it offers constant challenge, stimulating problems, the opportunity to work with people, and excellent advancement opportunities. Marketing is a very broad field with a wide variety of tasks involving the analysis, planning, implementation, and control of marketing programs. You will find marketing positions in all types and sizes of institutions. This appendix describes entry-level and higher-level marketing opportunities and lists steps you might take to select a career path and better market yourself.

## DESCRIPTION OF MARKETING JOBS

Almost a third of all Americans are employed in marketing-related positions. Thus, the number of possible marketing careers is enormous. Because of the knowledge of products and consumers you will gain in these jobs, marketing positions provide excellent training for the highest levels in the organization. A recent study by an executive recruiting firm found that more top executives have come out of marketing than any other area.

Marketing salaries vary by company and position. Beginning salaries usually rank only slightly below those for engineering and chemistry, but they equal or exceed those for economics, finance, accounting, general business, and the liberal arts. If you succeed in an entry-level marketing position, you will quickly be promoted to higher levels of responsibility and salary.

Marketing has become an attractive career for some people who have not traditionally considered this field. One trend is the growing number of women entering marketing. Women have historically been employed in the retailing and advertising areas of marketing. But they now have moved into all types of sales and marketing positions. Women now pursue successful sales careers in pharmaceutical companies, publishing companies, banks, consumer products companies, and in an increasing number of industrial selling jobs. Their ranks are also growing in product and brand manager positions.

Another trend is marketing's growing acceptance by nonprofit organizations. Colleges, arts organizations, libraries, and hospitals are increasingly applying marketing to their problems. They are beginning to hire marketing directors and marketing vice-presidents to manage their varied marketing activities.

Here are brief descriptions of some important marketing jobs.

## ADVERTISING

Advertising is an important business activity that requires skill in planning, fact gathering, and creativity. Although compensation for starting advertising positions tends to be lower than that for other marketing fields, opportunities for advancement are usually greater because there is less emphasis on age or length of employment. Typical jobs in advertising agencies include the following positions.

*Copywriters* help find the concepts behind the written words and visual images of advertisements. They dig for facts, read avidly, and borrow ideas. They talk to customers, suppliers, and *anybody* who might give them clues about how to attract the target audience's attention and interest.

*Art directors* constitute the other part of the creative team. They translate copywriters' ideas into dramatic visuals called "layouts." Agency artists develop print layouts, package designs, television layouts (called "storyboards"), corporate logotypes, trademarks, and symbols. They specify style and size of typography, paste the type in place, and arrange all the details of the ad so that it can be reproduced by engravers and printers. A superior art director or copy chief becomes the agency's creative director and oversees all its advertising. The creative director is high in the ad agency's structure.

*Account executives* are liaisons between clients and agencies. They must know a great deal about marketing and its various components. They explain client plans and objectives to agency creative teams and supervise the development of the total advertising plan. Their main task is to keep the client happy with the agency! Because "account work" involves many personal relationships, account executives are usually personable, diplomatic, and sincere.

*Media buyers* select the best media for clients. Media representatives come to the buyer's office armed with statistics to prove that *their* numbers are better, *their* costs per thousand are less, and *their* medium delivers more ripe audiences than competitive media. Media buyers have to evaluate these claims. They must also bargain with the broadcast media for best rates and make deals with the print media for good ad positions.

Large ad agencies have active marketing research departments that provide the market information needed to develop new ad campaigns and assess current campaigns. People interested in marketing research should consider jobs with ad agencies.

## BRAND AND PRODUCT MANAGEMENT

Brand and product managers plan, direct, and control business and marketing efforts for their products. They are concerned with research and development, packaging, manufacturing, sales and distribution, advertising, promotion, market research, and business analysis and forecasting. In consumer goods companies, the newcomer—who usually needs a Masters of Business Administration degree (MBA)—joins a brand team and learns the ropes by doing numerical analyses and watching senior brand people. This person eventually heads the team and later moves on to manage a larger brand. Many industrial goods companies also have product managers. Product management is one of the best training grounds for future corporate officers.

## CUSTOMER AFFAIRS

Some large consumer goods companies have customer affairs people who act as liaisons between customers and firms. They handle complaints, suggestions, and problems concerning the company's products, determine what action to take, and coordinate the activities required to solve the problem. The position requires an empathetic, diplomatic, and capable person who can work with a wide range of people inside and outside the firm.

## INDUSTRIAL MARKETING

People interested in industrial marketing careers can go into sales, service, product design, marketing research, or one of several other positions. They sometimes need a technical background. Most people start in sales and spend time in training and making calls with senior salespeople. If they stay in sales, they may advance to district, regional, and higher sales positions. Or they may go into product management and work closely with customers, suppliers, manufacturing, and sales engineering.

## INTERNATIONAL MARKETING

As U.S. firms increase their international business, they need people who are familiar with foreign languages and cultures and who are willing to travel to or relocate in foreign cities. For such assignments, most companies seek experienced people who have proved themselves in domestic operations. An MBA often helps but is not always required.

## MARKETING MANAGEMENT SCIENCE AND SYSTEMS ANALYSIS

People who have been trained in management science, quantitative methods, and systems analysis can act as consultants to managers who face difficult marketing problems such as demand measurement and forecasting, market structure analysis, and new-product evaluation. Most career opportunities exist in larger marketing-oriented firms, management consulting firms, and public institutions concerned with health, education, or transportation. An MBA or a Master of Science degree is often required.

## MARKETING RESEARCH

Marketing researchers interact with managers to define problems and identify the information needed to resolve them. They design research projects, prepare questionnaires and samples, analyze data, prepare reports, and present their findings and recommendations to management. They must understand statistics, consumer behavior, psychology, and sociology. A master's degree helps. Career opportunities exist with manufacturers, retailers, some wholesalers, trade and industry associations, marketing research firms, advertising agencies, and governmental and private nonprofit agencies.

## NEW-PRODUCT PLANNING

People interested in new-product planning can find opportunities in many types of organizations. They usually need a good background in marketing, marketing research, and sales forecasting; they need organizational skills to motivate and coordinate others; and they may need a technical background. Usually, these people work in other marketing positions before joining the new-product department.

## MARKETING LOGISTICS (PHYSICAL DISTRIBUTION)

Marketing logistics, or physical distribution, is a large and dynamic field, with many career opportunities. Major transportation carriers, manufacturers, wholesalers, and retailers all employ logistics specialists. Coursework in quantitative methods, finance, accounting, and marketing will provide students with the necessary skills for entering the field.

## PUBLIC RELATIONS

Most organizations have a public relations person or staff to anticipate public problems, handle complaints, deal with media, and build the corporate image. People interested in public relations should be able to speak and write clearly and persuasively, and they should have a background in journalism, communications, or the liberal arts. The challenges in this job are highly varied and very people oriented.

## PURCHASING

Purchasing agents are playing a growing role in firms' profitability during periods of rising costs, materials shortages, and increasing product complexity. In retail organizations, working as a "buyer" can be a good route to the top. Purchasing agents in industrial companies play a key role in holding down the costs. A technical background is useful in some purchasing positions, along with a knowledge of credit, finance, and physical distribution.

## RETAILING MANAGEMENT

Retailing provides people with an early opportunity to take on marketing responsibilities. Although retail starting salaries and job assignments have typically been lower than those in manufacturing or advertising, the gap is narrowing. The major routes to top management in retailing are merchandise management and store management. In merchandise management, a person moves from buyer trainee to assistant buyer to buyer to merchandise division manager. In store management, the person moves from management trainee to assistant department (sales) manager to department manager to store (branch) manager. Buyers are primarily concerned with merchandise selection and promotion; department managers are concerned with sales force management and display. Large-scale retailing lets new recruits move in only a few years into the management of a branch or part of a store doing as much as $5 million in sales.

## SALES AND SALES MANAGEMENT

Sales and sales-management opportunities exist in a wide range of profit and nonprofit organizations and in product and service organizations, including financial, insurance, consulting, and government organizations. Individuals must carefully match their backgrounds, interests, technical skills, and academic training with available sales jobs. Training programs vary greatly in form and length, ranging from a few weeks to two years. Career paths lead from salesperson to district, regional, and higher levels of sales management and, in many cases, the top management of the firm.

## OTHER MARKETING CAREERS

There are many other marketing-related jobs in areas such as sales promotion, wholesaling, packaging, pricing, and credit management. Information on these positions can be gathered from sources such as those listed in the following discussion.

# ▶CHOOSING AND GETTING A JOB

To choose and obtain a job, you must apply marketing skills, particularly marketing analysis and planning. Here are eight steps for choosing a career and finding that first job.

## MAKE A SELF-ASSESSMENT

Self-assessment is the most important part of a job search. It involves honestly evaluating your interests, strengths, and weaknesses. What are your career objectives? What kind of organization do you want to work for? What do you do well or not so well? What sets you apart from other job seekers? Do the answers to these questions suggest which careers you should seek or avoid? For help in self-assessment, you might look at the following books, each of which raises many questions you should consider:

1. *What Color Is Your Parachute?*, by Richard Bolles
2. *Three Boxes in Life and How to Get Out of Them*, by Richard Bolles
3. *Guerrilla Tactics in the Job Market*, by Tom Jackson

Also consult the career counseling, testing, and placement services at your school.

## EXAMINE JOB DESCRIPTIONS

Now look at various job descriptions to see what positions best match your interests, desires, and abilities. Descriptions can be found in the *Occupation Outlook Handbook* and the *Dictionary of Occupational Titles* published by the U.S. Department of Labor. These volumes describe the duties of people in various occupations, the specific training and education needed, the availability of jobs in each field, possibilities for advancement, and probable earnings.

## DEVELOP JOB-SEARCH OBJECTIVES

Your initial career shopping list should be broad and flexible. Look for different ways to achieve your objectives. For example, if you want a career in marketing research, consider the public as well as the private sector, and regional as well as national firms. Only after exploring many options should you begin to focus on specific industries and initial jobs. You need to set down a list of basic goals. Your list might say: "a job in a small company, in a large city, in the Sunbelt, doing marketing research, with a consumer products firm."

## EXAMINE THE JOB MARKET AND ASSESS OPPORTUNITIES

You must now look at the market to see what positions are available. For an up-to-date listing of marketing-related job openings, refer to the latest edition of the *College Placement Annual* available at school placement offices. This publication shows current job openings for hundreds of companies seeking college graduates for entry-level positions. It also lists companies seeking experienced or advanced-degree people. At this stage, use the services of your placement office to the fullest extent in order to find openings and set up interviews. Take the time to analyze the industries and companies in which you are interested. Consult business magazines, annual reports, business reference books, faculty members, school career counselors, and fellow students. Try to analyze the future growth and profit potential of the company and industry, chances for advancement, salary levels, entry positions, amount of travel, and other important factors.

## DEVELOP SEARCH STRATEGIES

How will you contact companies in which you are interested? There are several possible ways. One of the best ways is through on-campus interviews. But not all the companies that interest you will visit your school. Another good way is to phone or write the company directly. Finally, you can ask marketing professors or school alumni for contacts and references.

## DEVELOP RÉSUMÉ AND COVER LETTER

Your résumé should persuasively present your abilities, education, background, training, work experience, and personal qualifications—but it should also be brief, usually one page. The goal is to gain a positive response from potential employers.

The cover letter is, in some ways, more difficult to write than the résumé. It must be persuasive, professional, concise, and interesting. Ideally, it should set you apart from the other candidates for the position. Each letter should look and sound original—that is, it should be individually typed and tailored to the specific organization being contacted. It should describe the position you are applying for, arouse interest, describe your qualifications, and tell how you can be contacted. Cover letters should be addressed to an individual rather than a title. You should follow up the letter with a telephone call.

# Obtain Interviews

Here is some advice to follow before, during, and after your interviews.

## Before the Interview

1. Interviewers have extremely diverse styles—the "chitchat," let's-get-to-know-each-other style; the interrogation style of question after question; and the tough-probing "why, why, why" style; and many others. Be ready for anything.
2. Practice being interviewed with a friend and ask for a critique. Or, videotape yourself in a practice interview so that you can critique your own performance.
3. Prepare to ask at least five good questions that are not readily answered in the company literature.
4. Anticipate possible interview questions and prepare good answers ahead of time.
5. Avoid back-to-back interviews—they can be exhausting.
6. Dress conservatively and tastefully for the interview. Be neat and clean.
7. Arrive about ten minutes early to collect your thoughts before the interview. Check your name on the interview schedule, noting the name of the interviewer and the room number.
8. Review the major points you intend to cover.

## During the Interview

1. Give a firm handshake in greeting the interviewer. Introduce yourself using the same form the interviewer uses. Make a good initial impression.
2. Retain your poise. Relax. Smile occasionally. Be enthusiastic throughout the interview.
3. Good eye contact, good posture, and distinct speech are musts. Don't clasp your hands or fiddle with jewelry, hair, or clothing. Sit comfortably in your chair. Do not smoke, even if asked.
4. Have extra copies of your résumé with you.
5. Have your story down pat. Present your selling points. Answer questions directly. Avoid one-word answers, but don't be wordy.
6. Most times, let the interviewer take the initiative, but don't be passive. Find a good opportunity to direct the conversation to things you want the interviewer to hear.
7. To end on a high note, the latter part of the interview is the best time to make your most important point or to ask a pertinent question.
8. Don't be afraid to "close." You might say, "I'm very interested in the position and I have enjoyed this interview."
9. Obtain the interviewer's business card or address and phone number so that you can follow up later.

## *After the Interview*

1. After leaving the interview, record the key points that arose. Be sure to note who is to follow up on the interview and when a decision can be expected.

2. Objectively analyze the interview with regard to the questions asked, the answers given, your overall interview presentation, and the interviewer's response to specific points.

3. Send a thank-you letter mentioning any additional items and your willingness to supply further information.

4. If you do not hear within the time specified, write or call the interviewer to determine your status.

## FOLLOW-UP

If you are successful, you will be invited to visit the organization. The in-company interview will run from a few hours to a whole day. The company will examine your interest, maturity, enthusiasm, assertiveness, logic, and company and functional knowledge. You should ask questions about things that are important to you. Find out about the environment, job role, responsibilities, opportunity, current industrial issues, and the firm's personality. The company wants to find out if you are the right person for the job; just as importantly, you want to find out if it is the right job for you.

# Acknowledgment of Illustration

## CHAPTER 1

1 Courtesy Home Depot; 6 Reprinted with permission of Marriott, International; 7 USTA Nor-Cal; 10 Reprinted with permission of Ford Motor Company; 12 Reprinted with permission of PaineWebber Incorporated; 17 Copyright © Taco Bell Corp.; 20 left © Kees/Sygma; 20 right © Jeffrey Aaronson/Network Aspen; 25 McNeil Consumer Products; 28 © Arthur Meyerson/Reproduced with permission of The Coca-Cola Company; 30 Reprinted with permission of ITT Corporation.

## CHAPTER 2

35 Advertisement courtesy of Levi Strauss & Co.; 39 Xerox Corporation; 45 Reprinted with permission of The Clorox Company; 47 Courtesy of Campbell Soup Company; 51 left Reprinted with permission of The Red Roof Inns, Inc.; 51 right Reprinted with permission of Four Seasons Hotel; 53 © John Livzey; 58 © M. Osterreicher/Black Star; 60 both Photos courtesy of Hewlett-Packard Company; 62 Mark Seliger/Campbell Soup Company.

## CHAPTER 3

69 © Tom Landers/*Boston Globe;* 73 Courtesy of Credit Suisse; 75 Reprinted with permission of Wal-Mart; 78 Reprinted with permission of Toys "R" Us, Inc.; 79 © The Procter & Gamble Company. Reprinted with permission; 80 Photograph by Guzman; reprinted with permission of Houston Herstek Favat; 82 Courtesy of Sears; 85 Reprinted with permission of Chrysler Corporation; 87 © Sally Wiener Grotta/The Stock Market; 94 left © Milan Horacek/The Stock Market; 94 right © Ariel Skelley/The Stock Market; 96 Reprinted with permission of Marriott, Int'l.; 98 Reprinted with permission of Johnson & Johnson.

## CHAPTER 4

103 Courtesy of Black & Decker; 110 Reprinted with permission of Porsche Cars North America, Inc.; 114 © Roger Ressmeyer/Starlight; 116 Courtesy of Information Resources, Inc.; 120 Courtesy of Information Resources, Inc.; 123 Courtesy Focus Suites of Philadelphia/Quirks Marketing Research Review; 124 © Jon Feingersh/Stock Boston; 127 both © Ken Krebs; 130 Courtesy of Roper Starch; 131 © Jane Lewis/Tony Stone Images.

## CHAPTER 5

137 Reprinted with permission of NIKE, Inc., 142 both McDonald's Corporation; 147 © Gabe Palmer/The Stock Market; 149 Fallon McElligott/Lee Apparel Company, Michael Johnson photographer; 152 both McCann-Erickson Worldwide; 158 Reprinted with permission of American Honda Motor Co., Inc.; 159 Reprinted with permission of Pacific Bell Information Services; 164 Courtesy of GE; 168 © Arthur Meyerson/Reproduced with permission of The Coca-Cola Company.

## CHAPTER 6

175 Gulfstream; 180 Reprinted with permission of Intel Corporation; 182 Reprinted with permission of The Dow Chemical Company; 185 Reprinted with permission of Esselte Corporation;

eral Motors;    433 Reprinted with permission of Pepsi-Cola Company;    438 © J&M Studios/Gamma Liaison;    443 Reprinted with permission of Meredith Corporation;    445 © Kathleen Olson;    451 Reprinted with permission of State Farm Insurance Companies;    453 Walt Whitaker, Hallmark Cards, Inc.

## CHAPTER 14

459 Reprinted with permission of The Coca-Cola Company;    464 VISA and the Flag Design are registered trademarks of VISA International. Reprinted with permission;    466 Reprinted with permission of American Standard, Inc.;    467 both Reprinted with permission of TBWA Chiat/Day; 469 VISA and the Flag Design are registered trademarks of VISA International. Reprinted with permission;    472 top left © Patrick Pfister;    472 bottom left © Jodi Buren/Woodfin Camp & Associates;    472 right © George Rose/Gamma Liaison;    480 © Randy Walls/Tony Stone Images; 482 Reprinted with permission of Catalina Marketing Corporation;    484 © Jeff Scheid/Gamma Liaison;    487 © Gamma Liaison;    489 Courtesy 3M Graphics Division.

## CHAPTER 15

495 Courtesy of Eastman Chemical Co.;    499 left © John Henley/The Stock Market;    499 right © Gabe Palmer/The Stock Market;    503 Courtesy

of the DuPont Company;    508 left © Walton Doby;    508 right © Carol Fatta;    512 © Zephyr Pictures;    513 © Rob Nelson/Black Star;    514 Reprinted with permission of American Express; 517 © Lawrence Migdale/Photo Researchers.

## CHAPTER 16

525 © Dennis Budd Gray;    528 top left Courtesy IBM;    528 top right © Caroline Parsons;    528 bottom right © Ted Morrison;    528 bottom right © Greg Davis/The Stock Market;    531 © Wesley Boxce/JB Pictures;    535 © Barbara Alper/Stock Boston;    537 both Prestige & Collections;    540 © Sheila Nardulli/Gamma Liaison;    543 © The Walt Disney Company;    548 all Reprinted with permission of A. T. Cross Co.

## CHAPTER 17

555 © John Livzey;    558 © Laima Druskis/Stock Boston;    559 © Kathleen Olson;    562 both © Enrico Ferorelli;    565 both Reprinted with permission of American Association of Advertising Agencies;    566 © Gilles Bassignac/Gamma Liaison; 570 Courtesy Campbell Soup Co.;    572 left Reprinted with permission of Church & Dwight Co.;    572 right Reprinted with permission of McDonald's Corporation;    574 © Zephyr Pictures    577 Reprinted with permission of Archer Daniels Midland Co.;    582 © Ken Lax.

# Company/Brand Name Index

# Name Index

# Subject Index

# THE WORLD IN 1997

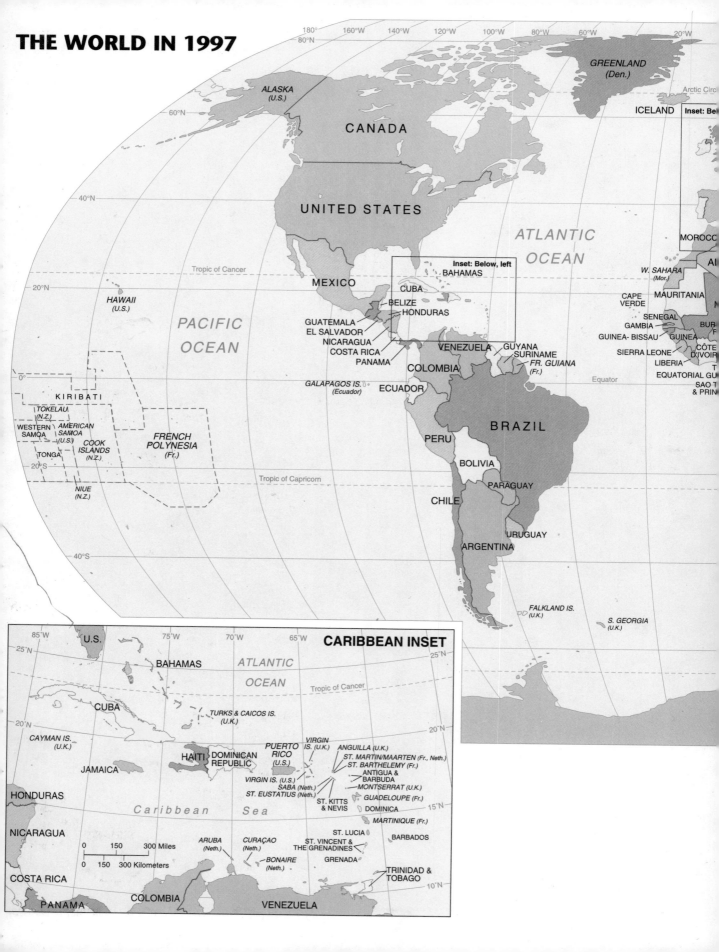

ALASKA (U.S.)

GREENLAND (Den.)

Arctic Circle

ICELAND

Inset: Bel

CANADA

MOROCC

W. SAHARA (Mor.)

Al

UNITED STATES

ATLANTIC OCEAN

60°N

80°N

40°N

180°    160°W    140°W    120°W    100°W    80°W    60°W    20°W

Tropic of Cancer

MEXICO

BAHAMAS

CUBA

BELIZE

HONDURAS

GUATEMALA

EL SALVADOR

NICARAGUA

COSTA RICA

PANAMA

VENEZUELA

GUYANA

SURINAME

FR. GUIANA (Fr.)

COLOMBIA

Inset: Below, left

20°N

CAPE VERDE

MAURITANIA

SENEGAL

GAMBIA

GUINEA-BISSAU

SIERRA LEONE

LIBERIA

GUINEA

CÔTE D'IVOIR

EQUATORIAL GU

SAO T & PRIN

HAWAII (U.S.)

PACIFIC OCEAN

GALAPAGOS IS. (Ecuador)

ECUADOR

Equator

0°

PERU

BRAZIL

KIRIBATI

TOKELAU (N.Z.)

WESTERN SAMOA

AMERICAN SAMOA (U.S.)

COOK ISLANDS (N.Z.)

FRENCH POLYNESIA (Fr.)

TONGA

BOLIVIA

PARAGUAY

20°S

Tropic of Capricorn

NIUE (N.Z.)

CHILE

URUGUAY

ARGENTINA

40°S

FALKLAND IS. (U.K.)

S. GEORGIA (U.K.)

---

## CARIBBEAN INSET

U.S.

BAHAMAS

ATLANTIC OCEAN

Tropic of Cancer

25°N

85°W    75°W    70°W    65°W    25°N

CUBA

TURKS & CAICOS IS. (U.K.)

20°N

20°N

CAYMAN IS. (U.K.)

HAITI

DOMINICAN REPUBLIC

PUERTO RICO (U.S.)

VIRGIN IS. (U.K.)

ANGUILLA (U.K.)

ST. MARTIN/MAARTEN (Fr., Neth.)

ST. BARTHELEMY (Fr.)

ANTIGUA & BARBUDA

MONTSERRAT (U.K.)

JAMAICA

VIRGIN IS. (U.S.)

SABA (Neth.)

ST. EUSTATIUS (Neth.)

ST. KITTS & NEVIS

GUADELOUPE (Fr.)

DOMINICA

HONDURAS

Caribbean Sea

MARTINIQUE (Fr.)

NICARAGUA

15°N

ST. LUCIA

BARBADOS

0    150    300 Miles

0    150    300 Kilometers

ARUBA (Neth.)

CURAÇAO (Neth.)

ST. VINCENT & THE GRENADINES

BONAIRE (Neth.)

GRENADA

TRINIDAD & TOBAGO

COSTA RICA

PANAMA

COLOMBIA

VENEZUELA

10°N